TUESDAY, JANUARY 17, 1893

Iolani Palace - 9. A. M. Sent for Mr S. M. Damon to confer with him on the situation. He told me he had been asked to join a party who called themselves the Executive Council and he had refused but asked what he should do. I told him to go and join the Advisory council which he did and I attribute the leniency of the latter Council to his interposition with them. The Oppositions Proclamations were that I and my Ministers & Marshall should with give up the Government to them which we did at quarter to six P.M. but under protest. Those who kindly assisted us were S. M. Damon, J. O. Carter, Ed Macfarlane, Paul Neuman H. A. Wideman - Two Princes Kawananakoa and Kalaniana ole were present besides S. Parker Min Foreign Affairs Mr. W. H. Cornwell, Minister of Finance, John F. Colburn Minister of Interior and A. P. Peterson, Atty General. Lizzie Pratt came over to sympathise with me Things turned out better than I expected. The Hawaiian flag will not change and so will the Royal Standard. The Opposition Govt will have Armory at Manamana turned into a Barracks - one policeman was shot for doing his duty in trying to prevent a cart loaded ammunition from going through the streets.

# THE DIARIES OF
# *Queen Liliuokalani*
# *of Hawaii*
# 1885–1900

*Edited and Annotated by*

*David W. Forbes*

HUI HĀNAI

HONOLULU

JACKET
*Princess Liliuokalani, circa 1882.*
Menzies Dickson, Hawaii State Archives

*(Detail) Sample of Hawaiian kapa collected on Cook's Third Voyage, from Alexander Shaw's* A Catalogue of the Different Specimens of Cloth, *London, 1787.*
Courtesy Hordern House Rare Books, Sydney

ENDSHEET
*A Panorama of Honolulu from the Reefs.*
(Detail) Robert C. Barnfield, 1886, Mānoa Heritage Center

PAGE I
*Queen Liliuokalani's diary entry for January 17, 1893. The 1893 diary is one of the documents seized in 1895 from Washington Place.*
Hawaii State Archives

FRONTISPIECE [PAGE II]
*Princess Liliuokalani, circa 1882.*
Menzies Dickson, Hawaii State Archives

PAGE VI
*Queen Liliuokalani, eighth monarch of the Hawaiian Islands, circa 1891.*
Hawaii State Archives

PAGE VIII
*Royal Waikiki, 1886. At the left is a portion of the coconut grove at Helumoa, the residence of King Kamehameha V, and later of Princess Bernice Pauahi Bishop (now the site of the Royal Hawaiian Hotel). Just inland of Pauahi's premises was Queen Emma's Waikiki house, formerly that of King Lunalilo (now the site of the International Market Place). The stream, known as Apuakehau, is long gone. Inland to the right of the stream is Ainahau, residence of Princess Likelike and her daughter Princess Kaiulani, deeded to Kaiulani by her godmother Princess Ruth. Queen Liliuokalani's property is further to the right, just outside of the image.*
(Detail) Alfred Mitchell, Bishop Museum Archives

PAGE XXXVIII
*Coconut grove and thatched houses, Waikiki, drawing by Paul Emmert, circa 1853.*
Mānoa Heritage Center

PUBLISHER'S NOTE
The text of the diaries within this edition was selected and prepared for publication by historian David W. Forbes. Hui Hānai thanks the individuals and organizations who assisted him, especially those who provided him access to the diaries of Liliuokalani: Louise Koch Schubert from the collection of her mother, Virginia Dominis Koch; Bishop Museum Archives; and Hawaii State Archives.

Published in 2019 by Hui Hānai
1300-A Hālona Street
Honolulu, Hawai'i 96817

Copyright © 2018 by Lili'uokalani Trust
All Rights Reserved
LIBRARY OF CONGRESS CONTROL NO. 2019940363
ISBN 978-0-9887278-3-0

Distributed by University of Hawai'i Press
www.uhpress.hawaii.edu

Coordinated, designed, and produced by
Barbara Pope Book Design, Honolulu, Hawai'i
Printed in Malaysia by Tien Wah Press, Ltd.

# Contents

FOREWORD  *Trustees, Liliʻuokalani Trust*  VII

Liliuokalani as Diarist  XI
A History of the Diaries  XV
Notes on Editing the Diaries  XXI
Liliuokalani and Her Family  XXIII
The Queen's Residences  XXXV

## The Diaries of Queen Liliuokalani

| | |
|---|---|
| Diary for 1885 | 3 |
| Diary for 1886 | 35 |
| Diary for 1887 | 127 |
| Diary for 1888 | 171 |
| Diaries for 1889 | 211 |
| Heir Apparent, Regent, and Monarch, 1890–91 | 247 |
| Diary for 1892 | 253 |
| End of the Hawaiian Monarchy, 1893 | 311 |
| Diary for 1893 | 315 |
| Diary for 1894 | 405 |
| Counterrevolution of 1895 | 433 |
| Diary for 1895 | 447 |
| Release and Freedom, 1895–96 | 453 |
| A Year of Letters, 1897 | 459 |
| Diary for 1898 | 477 |
| A Summary of 1899 | 509 |
| Diary for 1900 | 513 |
| AFTERWORD | 519 |
| BIBLIOGRAPHY | 523 |
| INDEX | 525 |

# Foreword

Queen Liliuokalani was the last reigning monarch of the Kingdom of Hawaii. On January 17, 1893, a revolutionary action deposed the Queen, which led to her abdication in 1895. Loved and respected by the people of Hawaii, the Queen lived a life of leadership, dedication, and service. In 1909, she created a perpetual charitable trust to care for orphaned and destitute children, with preference given to Hawaiian children. Queen Liliuokalani died in 1917 at the age of 79 at her Washington Place home in Honolulu. In her will, the Queen left the bulk of her estate to the Liliʻuokalani Trust.

Over the years, a succession of dedicated trustees has substantially grown the assets of the Trust, thus ensuring its future viability. These resources assist vulnerable children to help them today and in the future. Through the Trust and its many programs, the courage of the Queen in the face of adversity, loss, and grief has inspired generations of children and their families. Thus, the Queen's legacies of hope, perseverance, and aloha live on. As trustees of the Liliʻuokalani Trust, we, too, are inspired by the Queen, whose example encourages us to be visionary in our outlook, steadfast in the achievement of her Trust's mission, and compassionate in our interactions with others.

In 2013, the Trust published an annotated hardcover edition of *Hawaii's Story by Hawaii's Queen Liliuokalani* as a way of honoring the Queen and presenting her 1898 autobiography to the contemporary reader. In this new volume, *The Diaries of Queen Liliuokalani 1885–1900*, the Queen tells her story in an unfiltered manner through her personal thoughts and reflections on her family, friends, acquaintances, daily events and domestic life, social occasions, state dinners, and political movements and elections. Historian David W. Forbes has helped bring these diaries of the Queen to life with the assistance of Barbara Pope Book Design. His annotations and explanatory passages aid readers in understanding the people and events that had an impact on the Queen's life. The Queen was a central figure in Hawaiian history, and the writings in her diaries are an important addition to the historical records of her time.

*Judge (Ret.) Thomas K. Kaulukukui Jr.*
*Judge (Ret.) Patrick K.S.L. Yim*
*Dr. Claire L. Asam*
Trustees
Liliʻuokalani Trust

# Liliuokalani as Diarist

All the chiefly students who attended the Chief's Children's School in Honolulu between 1839 and 1850 were encouraged to keep journals or diaries as an integral part of their education. The select pupils of this most aristocratic of Hawaiian institutions included Alexander Liholiho, who reigned as Kamehameha IV (January 11, 1855–November 30, 1863); his brother Lot Kapuaiwa, who reigned as Kamehameha V (November 30, 1863–December 11, 1872); William Charles Lunalilo, who reigned as King Lunalilo (January 8, 1873–February 3, 1874); and Liliuokalani's brother David Kalakaua, the last king of Hawaii (February 12, 1874–January 20, 1891). Other members of this select aristocratic circle were Emma Rooke, who became queen consort upon her marriage to Kamehameha IV in 1856, and Bernice Pauahi, a member of the Kamehameha family who married banker Charles Reed Bishop and later founded the Kamehameha Schools.

*Princess Liliuokalani in full court dress and adorned with two Hawaiian royal orders, one on a ribbon sash.*
A. A. Montano, circa 1881, Hawaii State Archives

In the case of most of these children of the alii (chiefs), only fragments of their diaries have survived. Those of Liliuokalani, the last monarch of the Hawaiian Islands, are the single exception. Her diaries, which she kept between 1885 and 1900, contain the private thoughts and actions of her life as heir apparent and monarch of the Hawaiian Islands during one of the most intense, complicated, and politically charged eras in Hawaiian history. These revealing volumes are published here in their entirety for the first time.

The practice of keeping journals and diaries was well established among the Hawaiians when Lydia Kapaakea Paki, as she was then known, was a child. By the time of her birth (September 2, 1838), a wave of foreign traders and merchants, and later a group of American missionaries, had exposed more than three generations of Hawaiians to the idea and importance of keeping written records. After 1820, when arriving missionaries established the beginnings of literacy, the tradition flourished. One of the first diarists who had access to the inner circle of the chiefs was the Reverend Tute Tehuiarii (b. 1781–d. 1858), commonly known in Hawaii as "Kuke." A native of Huahine in the Society Islands, he arrived at Hawaii as a missionary assistant with the Reverend William Ellis in 1823, and became chaplain to Kauikeaouli (Kamehameha III). He kept a journal written in a combination of Hawaiian, Tahitian, and English. Probably the earliest surviving journal of any Hawaiian alii, however, is that of Chiefess Kekauluohi in the early 1840s, when as Kuhina Nui (similar to a co-regent) she recorded various judicial matters and disputes brought before her at Lahaina. Both documents are in the Hawaii State Archives.

Amos Star Cooke, the primary instructor at the Chief's Children's School, accustomed these alii children to a "diary habit." Cooke presided over his own daily journal of massive proportions, which included occasional remarks about the journalistic efforts of his young students, such as the following entries in 1844:

> **January 22, 1844:** This evening some of the boys commenced their journals.
>
> **February 3, 1844:** This afternoon went to bathe as usual, and after our return six of the girls went out with us. All are now writing their journals in the schoolroom.
>
> **August 19, 1844:** This evening the children are seated around me writing their journals.[1]

And write they did. They presented compositions to correct and rewrite, and they kept diaries. While only a few scattered fragments of these juvenile efforts have survived, the alii formed the habit of writing in journals. Later, in 1849 and 1850, when Dr. Gerrit P. Judd made a diplomatic visit to the United States and Europe on behalf of the Hawaiian government, two of the chiefly scholars, Alexander Liholiho and his brother, Lot Kapuaiwa, accompanied him. During their travels, the two "young gentlemen" kept journals. Alexander Liholiho's is with the Hawaiian Historical Society, which published it.[2] Prince Lot's more perfunctory account (in the Bishop Museum Archives) remains unpublished. As useful as this exercise was to the young princes, there is no indication that either of these two future monarchs ever again repeated the performance after their return to the islands.

Emma Rooke (later Queen Emma, wife of Alexander Liholiho, Kamehameha IV) was an intermittent diarist. The volume she kept during her travels through England and parts of Europe in 1865–66 (the original is in the Bishop Museum Archives) reveals an all too common characteristic of diarists: an enthusiastic beginning, with entries then becoming more occasional, trailing off to fewer and fewer remarks, and ultimately concluding with blank pages. Two of her more extensive volumes, for the years 1880 and 1884, survive in the same collection.

---

1. Hawaiian Mission Children's Society Library, Amos Cooke Journal.
2. Alexander Liholiho, *The Journal of Prince Alexander Liholiho*, ed. Jacob Adler (Honolulu: University of Hawaii Press for the Hawaiian Historical Society, 1967).

Of Bernice Pauahi Bishop's journals, only two have survived: an engaging account of a visit to Maui in 1846 (written as a school exercise),[3] and a journal she kept while on a trip to Europe, both also in the Bishop Museum Archives.

With the commencement of his world tour in 1881, King Kalakaua enthusiastically began a journal, and his account of the first stop on that tour (Japan) is of considerable interest. Unfortunately, the tedium of daily record keeping set in, and the king's journalistic efforts ended with his departure from that country.

Although the diaries covered in this work start in 1885, there is an earlier diary for 1878 (in the Bishop Museum Archives), which briefly narrates Liliuokalani's visit to San Francisco (her first trip away from the Hawaiian Islands). Because of the time gap between this year and the next diary she kept, I chose to omit the earlier account. Even within the period covered in this book, there are gaps in the series. The volumes for 1890 and 1891 have not survived. It's not known whether a volume for 1890 existed, but there is evidence of one for 1891, for Liliu refers to it in a letter to her business manager, Joseph Oliver Carter. No diaries remain for 1896, 1897, 1899, or 1900. However, Liliu did originally keep a diary for 1900, for in her 1903 diary (Bishop Museum Archives, not included here), she writes under the date of February 27, "I am busy today copying from my memo book of March 2, 1900." The two surviving fragments of the 1900 diary are included here. The Liliuokalani diaries continue after 1900 with volumes for 1901–03 and 1906; these are not included here.

Collectively, these volumes provide the modern reader with an invaluable record of Liliuokalani's private life, thoughts, and deeds during her rule as Queen of the Hawaiian Islands; her arrest and imprisonment following the unsuccessful counterrevolution of 1895; her abdication; her efforts in Washington, DC, to delay the annexation of her beloved islands to the United States; and her ultimate reconciliation with the changes that had occurred. Though Liliuokalani was never formally crowned queen, she is known and honored throughout the islands and the world as Queen Liliuokalani of Hawaii.

3. Bernice Pauahi Bishop. *A Report of Voyages to and Travels on Hawaii, Maui, and Molokai Undertaken by the Students of the Chief's Children's School in the Summer of 1846* (Honolulu: Bishop Museum Press, 1981).

### Sun. June 10, 1888

After breakfast gave Kilaina —

### Mon. June 11, 1888

Day on Thursday with a grand breakfast 45 sat at the table. The Queen
wore bunting. I pink muslin. Mrs
Parker embroidered ecru muslin. Mrs
Kinnersley white. Mrs Emma Macfarlane
camel's hair mrs. she looked handsome
Florence McLane wore pink cashmere
1 P.M. Boat race. King & myself & party
J.A.C. Mama, Katy, & others went on
board of Pleasure J.A.C. with singers
had good time watching rowers.
Band boys on were on tack of Kaluna
Kakuhua. Beach filled with sea-
pantween on the verandah.
Returned to dinner. 10 P.M. Ball
commences. Full evening dress.
even grandchildren Lili'u in Ralph's
with diamonds. Lettie Parker & Ka—
with diamonds. J.A.C. Minstrels
"Remember kind of rich it"

# A History of the Diaries

Most of the Liliuokalani diaries are written in pocket-size books, published primarily by the Bancroft Company of San Francisco, with printed title pages, leaves of statistics, tables of coinage, and other useful reference materials. These volumes were popular Christmas or New Year's gifts, and it is reasonable to suppose that Liliu's husband, John O. Dominis, gave her many of them. Unfortunately, their small pages forced Liliu to both abbreviate and cram in her penciled remarks—making history so much the poorer. When the Queen had larger-format diaries at hand (for example, those of 1892 and 1893), she expanded more fully on her thoughts, and the diaries for those two years are by far the most important narratives of the entire series.

*Queen Liliuokalani's diary for 1888 encased in a maroon morocco cover, one of the documents seized in 1895 from Washington Place.*
Hawaii State Archives

While historians may regret the gaps in Liliu's commentary on certain crucial political events, the very reason many of the Queen's diaries have survived while others have not lies in the turbulence of 1890s Hawaiian politics. In January 1895, a counterrevolution took place, by which her loyal supporters hoped to restore the deposed Liliuokalani to the throne. When that movement failed, before the Queen's arrest and detention in her former palace, a hurried bonfire at Washington Place resulted in the destruction of records that her enemies could use against her, and it is likely that one or more of her personal diaries may have met this fate. Certainly, the all-important log of visitors disappeared in the flames. In a statement made to the attorney general on January 17, 1895, Washington Place intimate Samuel Nowlein commented: "My men keep a diary of everyone who comes there and how long they stay. Charley Clark kept it. I suppose it is at Washington Place."[1]

William F. Kaae, who had been in the Queen's employ as her private secretary, testified at the time of her trial in February 1895 that staff had also kept a diary or log of all visitors to Washington Place, but that it had been destroyed: "Joe Heleluhe took them in the backyard and they were burned in my presence... I think two days before we were arrested [on January 16, 1895]."[2]

1. Hawaii State Archives, Attorney General Files, Series 506, Box 1.
2. Hawaii State Archives, Attorney General Files, Series 506, Box 1.

The Liliuokalani diaries for 1887, 1888, 1889 (short version), 1893, and 1894 are part of the group of documents known as the "seized papers" that are now held by the Hawaii State Archives. These are among the records seized by order of Republic of Hawaii officials in 1895, after they had taken the Queen into custody with the intent of obtaining evidence that she had prior knowledge of the counterrevolution. They then used this information against her during her trial.

A modern (but highly inaccurate) biography of the Queen[3] states that as she was escorted under arrest from Washington Place to the former Iolani Palace, she saw Hawaii Supreme Court Justice Albert F. Judd approaching her residence to carry out a search of the premises. This is not in fact what happened. The Queen was arrested a little after nine o'clock A.M. on January 16, 1895—and Sanford Ballard Dole, president of the Republic of Hawaii, did not ask A. F. Judd to search the house for evidence until much later in the morning. At the trial of Sam Nowlein, Judd in fact testified that Dole had requested he "make an inspection of the private papers at Washington Place... on the morning of the 16th of January ... just before 12 o'clock noon of that day and I proceeded there with Mr. Brown, the Deputy Marshall.... I found this Diary [meaning the one for 1894] at the desk, the same desk that I know to be Liliuokalani's because I had met her at that very spot on previous occasions; it is in the front room on the Ewa side."[4]

The official list of documents taken from the Queen's safe and her writing desk is carefully headed as follows: "Schedule of papers and documents found in the safe and writing desk of Liliuokalani, by A. F. Judd, between 12 and 4:20 P.M. on Wednesday, January 16, 1895." Judd removed only diaries in which he found comments and information deemed useful as trial evidence. Although he made a second search for incriminating papers and letters at Washington Place, about half of the diaries transcribed here were not seized and remained in the Queen's possession.

Following her trial in 1895, her attorney, Paul Neumann, requested the return of one or more of her diaries to Liliuokalani. The administration refused this request, and the volumes remained housed in several black metal document boxes in the custody of the attorney general. Not until the government turned them over to the territorial archives in 1921 did anyone open the boxes or make their contents available to the public. The government found the diary for 1893 of particular and continuing interest. Immediately upon seizure, the Provisional Government of Hawaii made a typescript transcription—and the minutes of the Executive Council for February 5, 1895, state: "It was voted that after the ex-Queen's diary has been used in Court, to permit the publication of certain extracts therefrom."[5] No such publication occurred.

3. The biography is Helena G. Allen's *The Betrayal of Liliuokalani: Last Queen of Hawaii 1838–1917* (Honolulu: Mutual Publishing, 1982).
4. Hawaii State Archives, Military Commission Proceedings, Series 148, February 6, 1895.
5. Hawaii State Archives, Foreign Office and Executive Files, Series 423, vol. 2.

## A History of the Diaries

After Liliuokalani's death in 1917, Curtis Piehu Iaukea, the manager of her trust, disposed of her personal papers, and it was he who handed over to the Archives of Hawaii, on several occasions between 1920 and 1926, a quantity of Liliu's personal papers. In May 1922, he sent a group of the diaries for 1885, 1886, and 1898, several post-1900 volumes, and some papers to the Bishop Museum Archives. Why and how Iaukea arranged the division of her papers between the two institutions is not known, but he may have been acting under specific instructions from the late Queen.

However, we now know that several diaries went elsewhere. The important 1889 (long version) diary, which somehow escaped Judd's notice in 1895, is now in the private collection of a member of the Dominis family, and through the generosity of its current custodian, its contents appear here in publication for the first time. The Bishop Museum Archives acquired the 1892 journal in 1935 as a gift of Albert F. Judd Jr. There is no record of how Judd (then a Bishop Museum trustee) acquired the volume, but he may well have received it from Curtis Iaukea. It certainly was not part of the group of diaries his father, Albert F. Judd, removed from Washington Place in 1895, for all of these were carefully inventoried upon receipt and retained by the attorney general.

After 1900, Liliuokalani, now known by her own creation as "Liliuokalani of Hawaii" (a title she used on her calling cards), continued to keep diaries. The Bishop Museum Archives has volumes for 1901–03 and 1906, and the Hawaii State Archives, Liliuokalani Collection, has a more complete diary for 1906. This work does not include these later volumes because of their length, and because they postdate the period when she was participating actively in the political destiny of the Hawaiian Islands.

These later diaries record daily events, domestic life, the collection of rents from lessees, and matters concerning the building up of her land-rich but cash-poor estate. Only occasionally does she look back or contemplate past events and what might have been. For reasons unknown, the Queen acquired a fondness for writing in a code in which she substituted numbers for letters. These coded entries appear in her diary, along with comments in both Hawaiian and English. While Roberta Sprague of Honolulu broke the code a number of years ago, the reason for the Queen's coding of some entries and not others is mystifying, for their translation and transcription reveals nothing of a confidential matter.[6] Possibly the use of such a code simply amused her. Typed, unedited copies of these later diaries are available for study in the Hawaii State Archives, Liliuokalani Collection.

---

6. Roberta Sprague's report and notes on how she broke the code are filed with the diary transcriptions in the Bishop Museum Archives, Liliuokalani Collection.

The diaries transcribed in this work are as follows:

**The 1885 Diary** (manuscript in Bishop Museum Archives). Title page: *The Pacific Coast Diary for 1885*. Bound in full gray morocco with title repeated in gilt letters on upper cover. Size 4¾ x 2⅞ inches.

**The 1886 Diary** (manuscript in Bishop Museum Archives). Title page: *The Pacific Coast Diary for 1886*. Bound in full tan morocco with title in gilt on upper cover. Size 4¾ x 2⅞ inches.

**The 1887 Diary** (manuscript in Hawaii State Archives). Printed title: *The Pacific Coast Diary for 1887, Containing Useful Memoranda, and Tables of Reference… Sold by All Booksellers and Stationers on the Pacific Coast.* San Francisco: The Bancroft Company, 1887. Full tan morocco with *The Pacific Coast Diary* in gilt on upper cover. Size 4¾ x 3 inches.

**The 1888 Diary** (manuscript in Hawaii State Archives). Printed title: *The Pacific Coast Diary for 1888, Containing Useful Memoranda, and Tables for Reference… Sold by All Booksellers and Stationers on the Pacific Coast.* 1888. Full tan morocco, enclosed in a removable maroon morocco cover, with a flap covering part of the upper cover and a ribbon to close the same. On the back cover is a white label with "155" printed in red ink. This identifies the diary as one of the seized documents taken from Washington Place in January 1895 following the failed 1895 counterrevolution. Size 4¾ x 3 inches.

**The 1889 Diary** (short version—manuscript in Hawaii State Archives). No printed title. Bound in plain dark maroon morocco, corners rounded, with a white paper label on upper annotated in red ink: "*180.* | L's Diary | *1888.*" It is unpaginated, with ruled lines arranged for use as an account book. Size 6⅝ x 4⅛ overall.

**The 1889 Diary** (full version—manuscript in Honolulu private collection). Title page: *Bancroft's Pacific Coast Diary for 1889, Containing Useful Memoranda, and Tables for Reference. Published Annually*. San Francisco: The Bancroft Company, 1889. Bound in full tan morocco, *The Pacific Coast Diary* in gilt letters on the upper cover. Size 6 x 3½ inches.

**The 1892 Diary** (manuscript in Bishop Museum Archives). Title page: *The Standard Diary—Published Annually for the Trade, 1892*. Limp morocco, with on the cover *Standard Diary 1892* and below that *Her Majesty Liliuokalani* in gilt letters. Size 8¼ x 7 inches.

**The 1893 Diary** (manuscript in Hawaii State Archives). Title page: *The Standard Diary. 1893. Published Annually for the Trade, 1893*. Black imitation morocco covers, with on the upper cover in gilt *Diary | 1893 | Her Majesty the Queen*. On the upper cover of the diary is a white label with "No. 2" in red ink, pasted on at the time of seizure from Washington Place in January 1895. Size 8¼ x 7 inches.

**The 1894 Diary** (manuscript in Hawaii State Archives). Title page: *The Sunset Daily Journal for 1894. Published at San Francisco, Cal. for the Trade*. An attached paper label on the upper cover has the following memorandum: "Exhibit G. [and] Entry under date of December 28 or 29, 1894. 'Signed eleven Commissions.' J. W. Jones, 1st Lieut. Co. D, N.G.H. Recorder. [To the left:] In re Misprision of Treason of Liliuokalani Dominis." Size 8¼ x 7 inches.

**The 1895 Diary** (manuscript in Hawaii State Archives). This diary has been assembled here from two fragments, the first being a memorandum that Liliuokalani kept while a prisoner in Iolani Palace (in the Hawaii State Archives, Liliuokalani Collection). The second fragment consists of dated remarks found on the calling card of a friend (located in the Bishop Museum Archives). The letter from Liliu to Princess Kaiulani, written at Iolani Palace on July 31, 1895, is in the Hawaii State Archives, Cleghorn Collection.

**The 1898 Diary** (manuscript in Bishop Museum Archives). Titled *Excelsior Diary* in gilt on the upper flap of a wallet-form volume. Bound in dark maroon morocco. Size 5 x 3¼ inches.

**The 1900 Diary** (manuscript in Hawaii State Archives). This diary, like that of 1895, has been assembled from two manuscript fragments, both of which are in the Hawaii State Archives. The first is a memorandum in the Queen's hand, transcribed from a now unlocated memorandum book or diary. This largely concerns her association with Dr. Charles Hamilton English of Washington, DC (original in Hawaii State Archives, Liliuokalani Collection). The second fragment consists of a single leaf (of the same or another diary) with a single entry for her birthday (September 2, 1900). This survives in the form of an old photostat in the Hawaii State Archives, Liliuokalani Collection. Another slightly abbreviated version of the same entry in Curtis Iaukea's hand is in the Hawaii State Archives, Iaukea Collection. I have used the version in the Queen's hand in assembling this text.

# Notes on Editing the Diaries

All diaries present problems in preparation for publication, and Liliuokalani's diaries are no exception. Therefore, an explanation of the editorial decisions I employed in preparing these texts will be helpful for the reader. The first decision was to edit as little as possible. At the end of many of these volumes, however, there are memoranda pages and leaves containing miscellaneous accounts. While I have not included the majority of this material here, I have added as bracketed insertions or footnotes any such items that seemed relevant to particular dated entries.

In most of the diaries, entries are in pencil and on tiny pages. Scattered throughout are entries that appear to have been partially or fully rubbed out. Many of these erasures may have occurred because the paper used was identified as "erasable," as I do not see any evidence that Liliu intended to hide facts or obscure the names of individuals with these deletions. When the erased remarks are completely illegible, I have editorially noted the fact, and only occasionally have I tried to fill in missing words or sentences with my best guesses in brackets as to what Liliu wrote.

*Liliuokalani at her Palolo, Oahu, property, 1885. Liliu arranged an excursion to Palolo for the enjoyment of visitors, including Alfred Mitchell, who took this photograph. It was a favored spot, and after a day in the valley (February 1, 1885), she comments in her diary: "Everything so still and quiet... passed the day in planting trees and shrubs... being in the woods I feel supremely happy in the stillness that surrounds me."*
(Detail) Alfred Mitchell, 1885, Bishop Museum Archives

Occasionally the Queen seems to have abandoned a sentence before completing a thought, as if something disrupted her or she was trying to think of the right word and abandoned the effort. With a few exceptions, I have not tried to guess at her thoughts, instead adding a notation in brackets when this occurs, as in [Sentence ends thus]. She also sometimes drew a line through parts of entries; I have included those areas in strike-through text.

Where Liliu has skipped words to save time or space, I have sometimes filled in the obvious omission within brackets. When she has dropped letters at the end of a word (such as "off," which sometimes appears in the diary as "of"), I have silently corrected these lapses of the pen, as well as many misspellings and grammatical errors, for ease of reading. Occasionally I use [sic] or a question mark, [?], to indicate an error or an oddity of thought, unexplained remark, or unknown entity. Where necessary for clarity, I have added apostrophes, commas, and other punctuation marks.

For the most part Liliu wrote her entries in English, though at times she turned to Hawaiian. I have retained Hawaiian-language passages as they occur, and provided an English-language translation in brackets following these sections. Translations of extended passages have been provided by Jason Achiu of the Hawaii State Archives. When Hawaiian words occur in English-language sentences, a translation follows within brackets. In a very few cases, I have silently transposed a word or two in the translations to avoid run-on sentences, a syntax acceptable in the Hawaiian language but awkward in English.

In the style of the day, Liliuokalani frequently used a dash to indicate both a pause and the completion of a sentence. If the dash seemed to indicate a pause, I left the text as written. When a capitalized letter followed the dash, I replaced it with a full stop (a period).

Liliu's diaries often mention individuals only by their first names, sometimes by their informal Hawaiian names, or simply by their initials. Names are sometimes followed by "(k)" or "(w)" indicating kane (male) or wahine (female). Where I am certain of the name, I have provided it in brackets: for instance, [Joe Heleluhe] for "J. H." and [Joe Aea] for "J. A." I have made every attempt to identify persons referred to and have included footnotes for this purpose, but in some cases either it is unclear who the person was or no further information is available.

I have spelled out many abbreviations for the ease of the modern reader—so, for example, "Pd." appears as "paid" and "P.I.R. Co." as "People's Ice and Refrigeration Co." I have also spelled out whole numbers silently for hours of the day through ten, so that "4 P.M." appears as "four P.M."

Footnotes on many of the events only briefly mentioned in the text have been added to explain more fully disasters, political movements and elections, plays at the Opera House, state dinners, and other social occasions. Occasionally, when the Queen says little or nothing about major events that directly affected her world, I have added explanatory text indicated by a double rule with fleuron. This device also indicates my addition of a summary of events when significant time breaks occur between extant diaries.

English-language sources have generally been relied upon rather than Hawaiian-language materials for many of the footnotes, for the reason that Hawaiian-language newspapers of the day generally did not specifically report on events in the way that English-language newspapers did, and many of the occasions and incidents that Liliu mentions in her diaries received no coverage whatsoever in the native press. Whenever I have been able to find a suitable quotation from a Hawaiian-language source, I have included it.

# Liliuokalani and Her Family

Liliuokalani was born Lydia Kamakaeha in a thatched house in Honolulu, September 2, 1838, to Chief Caesar Kapaakea and Chiefess Ane Keohokalole. Keohokalole was the daughter of the famous chief Aikanaka, one of Kamehameha's advisors and strategists, and the great-granddaughter of the great chief Keaweaheulu, another of Kamehameha's councillors.

The site of Liliuokalani's birth was on the slope of Puowaina or Punchbowl Crater, a property of her mother, which is now part of the Queen's Medical Center[1] grounds. She was the sister of David Kalakaua, William Pitt Leleiohoku, and Miriam Likelike Cleghorn. She had other siblings, including Mary and James, both of whom died young, and several whose names have not been preserved. In May 1856, Liliu's father, Kapaakea, told U.S. Commissioner to Hawaii David L. Gregg that "he had had eight children, four of whom were living, David and Lydia being the oldest... and both were good children."[2]

## Lydia Kamakaeha, Our Daughter

According to chiefly traditions, as a baby Lydia Kamakaeha was hanai (the Hawaiian custom of entrusting a child to be raised by nonbirth parents who have close ties to the birth parents) to Chief Abner Paki and Chiefess Laura Konia, the parents of Bernice Pauahi, whom Liliu always regarded as a sister. Although during much of her life people commonly referred to her as Liliu, she bore various names over time. In her youth, Liliu was generally known as Lydia Kapaakea Paki or Lydia Kamakaeha Paki. When she published a piece of sheet music ("He Mele Lahui Hawaii," the second Hawaiian national anthem) in 1867, the cover announced her as Lydia K. Paki (the K. standing either for Kapaakea or Kamakaeha). However, when her parents, Kapaakea and Keohokalole, deeded the land of Hamohamo in Waikiki to her in 1859, she appeared on the document as "Lydia Kamakaeha, our daughter."

She married John Owen Dominis in 1862 as Lydia K. Paki, and afterward she often signed official documents as Lydia K. Dominis. Her brother David Kalakaua acceded to the throne in 1874, and upon the death of the heir apparent (her brother William P. Leleiohoku) on April 10, 1877,

---

1. Queen Emma and King Kamehameha IV founded this institution as the Queen's Hospital in 1859. Its name was changed to the Queen's Medical Center in 1967.
2. David Lawrence Gregg, *The Diaries of David Lawrence Gregg: An American Diplomat in Hawaii, 1853–1858*, ed. Pauline King (Honolulu: Hawaiian Historical Society, 1982), 17.

*Analea Keohokalole and Caesar Kapaakea, the parents of Liliuokalani and her siblings Kalakaua, Leleiohoku, and Likelike.*
Hawaii State Archives

*Lydia Kapaakea Paki, known as Liliuokalani after 1877 when she was named heir apparent to King Kalakaua.*
C. L. Weed, circa 1865, Hawaii State Archives

OPPOSITE
*Royal siblings (clockwise from top left): David Kalakaua, William Pitt Leleiohoku, Miriam Likelike, and Lydia Liliu.*
H. L. Chase, 1874, Hawaii State Archives

Liliu wrote, "At noon... the booming of the cannon was heard, which announced that I was heir apparent to the throne of Hawaii," and added that "from this moment dates my official title of Liliuokalani." The official proclamation of her elevation referred to her as "Her Royal Highness Lydia Kamakaeha Liliuokalani." Many years later, however, when she became an Anglican communicant at Saint Andrew's Cathedral on May 18, 1896, she received a provisional baptism under the name Lydia Kamakaeha. The designation that appeared on her coffin was "Her Majesty, Lydia Kamakaeha Kaolanialii Newewelii Liliuokalani."[3] The Liliuokalani Trust gives her name as Lydia Lili'u Loloku Walania Wewehi Kamaka'eha. In this work, she appears as either Liliu or as Liliuokalani.

## Liliu's Parents and Their Landholdings

In a memo regarding her parents, she recorded that her father, Kapaakea, was born at Ohule, Kuiaha, East Maui, and that her mother, Ane Keohokalole, was born at Kailua, Kona, in 1820, and raised "at Aamaka, Kohala, until she was big, then she was taken to Pololu. It was thought that she was fourteen years of age when she married to Kapaakea."[4] Of their large family, Kalakaua was born in 1836, and Liliuokalani in 1838.

Liliu's mother was once one of the richest chiefs, having inherited vast amounts of land from her father, the great Aikanaka, one of Kamehameha's chief counselors and warriors. As a consequence of the division of lands known as the Great Mahele in the 1840s, Keohokalole relinquished to the land commissioners her claim to 36 properties ranging from small parcels to gigantic land areas on Maui, Hawaii, and Oahu. These included much of Kula, Maui, and vast areas in Kona, Kau, and Kohala. In return for relinquishing these, she received (under Land Commission Award 8452) 41 properties.[5] These included Kealahou, Omaopio, and Pukalani in Kula, Maui (unsurveyed, but having thousands of acres); Honohina, near Hilo (6,000 acres); and in Kona, Hawaii, all of Kaawaloa (2,100 acres), Kealakekua (10,160 acres), and Kealahou (4,071 acres). On the same island, she also held Paauhau (listed as 8,165 acres, but many times larger than that) and Puna (4,919 acres). On Oahu, she owned the land of Kahana (5,050 acres). She probably inherited Malaekahana, also on Oahu (estimated at 3,280 acres), from her husband.

By all accounts, Keohokalole was pleasant, and her husband Kapaakea was handsome. Both were land rich but cash poor, and neither one paid the least attention to the management of their assets, with the result that eventually what should have been a sizable estate to divide among their four surviving children, David Kalakaua, Liliuokalani Dominis, William Pitt Leleiohoku, and Miriam Likelike Cleghorn, had dwindled to very

---

3. This sequence of names is reported in the *Pacific Commercial Advertiser*, November 18, 1917.
4. Hawaii State Archives, Iaukea Collection, Box 1, Folder 6.
5. These lands are listed in Dorothy B. Barrère, *The King's Mahele: The Awardees and Their Lands* (Honolulu: D. B. Barrère, 1994); copy in the Hawaii State Archives.

little. The chiefly couple mortgaged the land of Kahana in 1851, and by 1857 they had sold it to one Ahsing. They sold the Punchbowl property, which ran up the crater from Beretania Street and included the site where Liliu was born, to the Queen's Hospital for $2,000 in 1860. They sold the ahupuaa (land division) of Kealakekua in 1858 to Stephen H. Atkins for $2,000. In Kula, Maui, they disposed of the ahupuaa of Koheo in 1849 and of Aapueo and Makaehu in 1851.

On Hawaii, they mortgaged the land of Paauhau in Hamakua, sold it to one Morrison, recovered it in part through a suit that Kalakaua filed in 1856, and ultimately sold it off to John P. Parker in 1864 for $1,500. It is one of the largest parcels of today's Parker Ranch.

Kapaakea died in Honolulu on November 13, 1866, and Keohokalole died in Hilo on April 6, 1869. Both passed away intestate and deeply in debt, and their heirs had to sell still more lands.

While his parents had let their lands drift away, David Kalakaua paid attention. One of the first things he did upon coming of age in 1856 was to obtain a power of attorney from his parents and act to repossess the land of Paauhau, successfully convincing the court that land fraud had occurred.[6] Kalakaua's firsthand knowledge of the alienation of these lands, and the family's resulting shaky financial standing, to a large part shaped his acquisitiveness when he became monarch and had funds at his disposal. He would die possessed of an impressive real estate portfolio, not a parcel of which he left to his sister Liliu. Liliuokalani was also acutely aware of the importance of acquiring and retaining property, though she would ultimately put the lands she acquired to much better use.

## Liliu's Education and Marriage

Lydia Paki was educated first in the Chief's Children's School. Starting in 1850, she attended its successor institution, the Royal School, on Emma Street after the Chief's Children's School closed. The latter was a day school that she found more congenial, and she lived at Haleakala, the home of Bernice and Charles Reed Bishop on King Street. In early adulthood, she was in a sort of social limbo, finding herself with uncertain matrimonial prospects among a dwindling group of young alii. U.S. Commissioner to Hawaii David L. Gregg recorded in his diary that on May 19, 1856, when Kamehameha IV announced his decision to marry Emma Rooke, Liliu's father Kapaakea condemned the match, claiming that his daughter was more eligible due to her rank, "but declared that if neither the King or any other high chief thought proper to marry her, he would have her married to some good white man, which after all might be much more for her own good."[7]

By Liliu's own account, she was at one time engaged to William Charles Lunalilo—an arrangement that would have been a disaster, for even then

6. Hawaii State Archives, First Circuit Court, Equity 156, *Kalakaua v. Morrison*.
7. Gregg, *Diaries*, 317.

that most handsome and charming of princes was showing signs of the alcoholism that would hasten his end in 1874, when he had been king for only one year. Then, on September 16, 1862, she married John O. Dominis at Haleakala.

Liliu's husband was the son of Captain John Dominis and Mary Jones. Born in Schenectady, New York, in 1831, he arrived in the islands with his mother in 1837. He attended the Royal School, and afterward spent several years gaining experience in both local and San Francisco business houses. He became a naturalized citizen of Hawaii on July 1, 1861, a year prior to his marriage. Dominis became commissioner of Crown lands in 1873 and was reappointed in 1874 when Kalakaua became monarch. He was governor of Maui 1878–86, served as governor of Oahu 1864–86, and was reappointed to that position in 1887–88 and in 1891. He was the chief promoter of the Royal Hawaiian Band in 1870, went with the king to the United States in 1874, and in 1887 accompanied Queen Kapiolani and Liliuokalani to London for the golden jubilee of Queen Victoria. He was the friend and servant of all the sovereigns of the islands, beginning with Kamehameha IV, but, as his obituary remarked, "his retiring disposition and unostentatious manner prevented him from receiving a tithe of the praise that was due to him as a public man."[8]

Dominis was given the title of HRH the Prince Consort upon Liliu's accession to the throne in January 1891. He died at Washington Place on August 27, 1891. Dr. Georges Philippe Trousseau, one of his closest friends, told U.S. Commissioner James H. Blount in 1893: "John Dominis' character was unimpeachable... [but he] was, to use a euphemism, rather irregular as a husband.... He was fond of society, sometimes took more liquor than was good for him, and occasionally (although he never kept a regular mistress) had some love adventures. In this small community, they were reported to his wife, and I can vouch to how she suffered by it."[9]

Mary Jones Dominis, the wife of Captain John Dominis, mother of John O. Dominis, mother-in-law of Liliuokalani, and longtime doyenne of Washington Place, was born August 3, 1803. She arrived at Honolulu on the bark *Jones* on April 23, 1837, and from that time forward made Honolulu her home. From 1846 on, she resided at Washington Place, where she took charge of developing the mansion's grounds, transforming it from a barren and treeless lot into a retreat of great beauty. In a later article on the history of Washington Place, friends remembered Mrs. Dominis as "always carrying [a] watering pot in one hand and a garden trowel in the other."[10]

---

8. *Daily Bulletin*, August 28, 1891.

9. [The Blount Report] U.S. Congress, House of Representatives, *President's Message Relating to the Hawaiian Islands, December 18, 1893*, 53d Cong, 2d Session, Ex. Doc. 47 (Washington, DC: Government Printing Office, 1893), 530.

10. *Pacific Commercial Advertiser*, August 25, 1912.

In 1846, Captain Dominis departed on a voyage to China and was never heard from again. Facing straitened circumstances, the widow Dominis took in boarders. She also appears to have been in ill health. On the occasion of the 50th anniversary of her landing in Honolulu, it was remarked that she was an invalid, "not having left her residence for many years on account of rheumatism."[11] She died at Washington Place on April 25, 1889.

Liliuokalani found living in her mother-in-law's house (for that is what it was) uncongenial, and this induced her to acquire a home of her own, Muolaulani, located at Palama (across the Nuuanu stream from downtown Honolulu).

## The Reign of Kalakaua

The head of Liliuokalani's family was her brother David Kalakaua, who reigned as king of Hawaii 1874–91. Born in Honolulu on November 16, 1836, the son of Chief Kapaakea and Chiefess Keohokalole, his official name (according to his coffin plate) was David Laamea Kamanakapu Mahinulani Naloiaehuokalani Lumialani Kalakaua.[12] Elected by special legislative ballot on February 12, 1874, following the death of King Lunalilo, he was the seventh king of the Hawaiian Islands. He successfully engineered the Reciprocity Treaty of 1875, which went into effect September 9, 1876. That treaty reduced a crippling import tariff levied in the United States against Hawaii-grown sugar and brought great economic prosperity to the islands. He circumnavigated the world in 1880–81, and he was the only Hawaiian monarch to have a coronation, in 1883. Kalakaua was a man of great personal charm, but was beset by political machinations and financial scandals, which clouded his reign. He and his sister Liliuokalani were on friendly terms in public, but had very guarded relations in private, and during his reign she was not one of his inner circle. He died of Bright's disease at the Palace Hotel in San Francisco, January 20, 1891.

King Kalakaua married Kapiolani, a chiefess whom everyone admired. Born in Hilo, Hawaii, December 31, 1834, she was a granddaughter of Kaumualii, the last king of Kauai. In 1852, she married Bennett Namakeha (b. 1798–d. 1860), a court official, and for a period she was governess to the young son of Kamehameha IV and Queen Emma. On December 19, 1863, she married David Kalakaua, and when he became king in 1874, she became queen consort. Of a retiring disposition, she avoided court functions whenever possible, preferring to live in a modest cottage on the makai (seaward) Ewa corner of Punchbowl and Queen Streets (no trace of this residence remains). Her main charitable interests, which gained her the entire community's praise, were the Kapiolani Maternity Home and the Kapiolani Home for Girls.

11. *Pacific Commercial Advertiser*, August 25, 1912.

12. The manuscript memoirs of Curtis P. Iaukea lists these names and adds 12 more, which Iaukea says were "distinctions." Hawaii State Archives, Iaukea Collection, Box 4.

In 1887, she and Liliuokalani made a trip to England and the United States. In later years, when she was in frail health, she retired from public view to Pualeilani, her Waikiki estate, where she died on June 24, 1899.

## Liliu as Heir Apparent, Regent, and Monarch

In 1877, King Kalakaua proclaimed Liliuokalani heir apparent after the death of their brother William P. Leleiohoku. She was regent for about nine months in 1881 while her brother was touring the world, and again from November 1890 to January 1891 while he visited California for the benefit of his health.

The year 1887 was one of triumph for Liliuokalani, but one of political crisis for her brother Kalakaua. It was also a year of family tragedy, when their sister Princess Likelike Cleghorn died at Ainahau, Waikiki, on February 2, 1887. This was the year in which Liliuokalani and Queen Kapiolani made their trip to England to participate in the festivities honoring Queen Victoria's golden jubilee (the 50th year of her reign). En route to England, she and the queen were given all honors in the United States and were entertained in San Francisco, New York, Boston, and Washington, DC. They dined at the White House, visited Mount Vernon, and were received (and reported on enthusiastically) wherever they went. In England, they met a similar reception. At Queen Victoria's golden jubilee ceremony in Westminster Abbey, they had the honor of choice seats among European crowned heads and members of Queen Victoria's immediate family. A political crisis in Hawaii, however, soon dampened the enjoyment of their glorious English experiences.

Kalakaua's profligate lifestyle had left him severely in debt, and as a result he embarked on a highly questionable scheme of raising money through the sale of an opium franchise. This and other matters resulted in a political revolution that forced him to sign a new constitution. The group of Honolulu businessmen who brought on this action presented the monarch with a barely veiled hint that should he refuse to sign the constitution they had written, his removal from office would follow. He agreed to the terms, and the resulting document, the "Bayonet Constitution," severely limited his power. It may have been a bloodless revolution, but, as Curtis Iaukea wrote, "Princess Liliuokalani was furious when she learned that her brother had granted a new constitution and made no attempt to conceal her feelings in the matter."[13] Although she recorded little about the incident in her diary, it set the stage for political actions that would subsequently bring down the monarchy itself in 1893.

On January 29, 1891, following the death of her brother King Kalakaua, she took an oath as queen and monarch. Her husband, John Dominis, died on August 27 during the first year of her reign.

On January 17, 1893, a revolutionary action deposed Liliu, and the

---

13. Hawaii State Archives, Iaukea Collection, Box 1, Memoirs, 222.

insurrectionists formed the Provisional Government of Hawaii, which became the Republic of Hawaii in 1894. In January 1895, following a failed counterrevolution engineered by monarchist sympathizers hoping to restore her to the throne, the government placed her under house arrest (in Iolani Palace) for complicity. She then formally abdicated. A military commission tried her in February 1895, and on the 27th of that month, it found her guilty of "misprision of treason"—that is, of having had knowledge of a treasonous action (the counterrevolution) and having failed to inform government officials. The commission sentenced her to imprisonment for five years, fined her $5,000, and confined her in an upstairs suite of rooms in the former Iolani Palace. On September 7, 1895, the Republic of Hawaii gave her a conditional pardon, and later it fully pardoned her and restored her citizenship.

## Liliu's Inner Circle: Family and Friends

Miriam Likelike, Liliu's younger sister, born in Honolulu on January 13, 1851, was the sibling to whom Liliu was closest. As a child, Likelike was very delicate, and soon after her birth she was sent to Kona, Hawaii, on account of its dry climate, where she remained until the age of six. Returning to Honolulu, she entered the care of the Roman Catholic sisters. She next attended Miss Ogden's school in Makiki, and she finally became a pupil of Miss Bingham at the Kawaiahao Female Seminary. On September 22, 1870, she married Archibald Scott Cleghorn at Washington Place.

When her brother Kalakaua became king in 1874, she was elevated to the title of princess, and briefly served as governess of Hawaii Island (March 29, 1879–September 1880). Contemporaries remembered her as pretty, charming, spoiled, and fond of entertaining officers from visiting naval vessels at Ainahau, her Waikiki residence. She and Archibald S. Cleghorn had a daughter, Victoria Kaiulani. Likelike died at Ainahau on February 2, 1887.

The most important people in Liliuokalani's life after the fall of the monarchy in January 17, 1893, were her niece, the Princess Victoria Kaiulani; her brother-in-law, Archibald S. Cleghorn (Kaiulani's father); and her business agent and most loyal supporter, Joseph Oliver Carter.

Victoria Kaiulani was born at the family residence on Emma Street, October 16, 1875, and christened at Saint Andrew's Cathedral, December 25, 1875, as Victoria Kawekiu Kaiulani Lunalilo Kalaninuiahilapalapa. She bore the name Victoria in honor of Victoria Kamamalu (b. 1838–d. 1866), sister of Kings Kamehameha IV and Kamehameha V, and the name Lunalilo in commemoration of the Hawaiian monarch by that name, who had died a little more than a year before her birth.

In 1889, she was sent to England for her education, and she remained there until 1897. Her aunt, Liliuokalani, designated her crown princess and heir apparent to the throne in January 1891, and from that point forward their political destinies were closely intertwined. In England,

Kaiulani's guardians were former island residents Thomas Rain Walker and Theophilus H. Davies, both of whom did much to press her claim as crown princess after the 1893 overthrow, putting her in the position of competing with her aunt, the ex-Queen. She returned to the islands in 1897, and died at Ainahau, Waikiki, March 6, 1899.

Archibald S. Cleghorn was born in Edinburgh, Scotland, on November 15, 1835. He arrived at Honolulu at age 16 on June 17, 1851, from Auckland, New Zealand, on the brig *Sisters*, with his parents, Thomas (d. September 24, 1853, Honolulu) and Sarah. Cleghorn became a retail merchant, opening stores in Honolulu, Lahaina, and Hilo. He married Likelike Kapaakea, sister of Kalakaua and Liliuokalani, on September 22, 1870, and on October 16, 1875, their daughter Kaiulani was born. There were also three other Cleghorn daughters from an earlier relationship: Helen (d. 1927), wife of James H. Boyd; Annie Pauahi (d. 1897), wife of James Hay Wodehouse; and Rose (d. 1911), wife of James W. (Jimmie) Robertson. In 1887, Cleghorn became collector general of customs, a position he kept until April 15, 1893. He also was a member of the Privy Council until 1891, and governor of Oahu (November 11, 1891–February 28, 1893). An ardent horticulturist, he became president of the Kapiolani Park Association in 1888, was largely responsible for planting trees in the park, and developed his Waikiki property, Ainahau, into a tropical showplace. Archibald Cleghorn died in Honolulu on November 1, 1910.

This introduction has so far identified the various members of Liliuokalani's immediate family who figure frequently in the diaries. However, two persons—who were not of her family but held an important place in the diaries and her life—also need identification here.

Curtis Piehu Iaukea, born December 13, 1855, at Waimea, Hawaii, was the son of Lahapa Nalanipo and J. W. Iaukea. As a young boy, he was the hanai of an uncle, Kaihupaa. Brought to Honolulu, he became a member of the court surrounding Kamehameha III. Then, during the reign of Kamehameha IV, he was chosen as a boy companion to Prince Albert, the young son of that monarch and Queen Emma, and from that date forward he was a loyal courtier. On April 7, 1877, he married Charlotte Kahaloipua Hanks. In 1878, he was named colonel and head of Kalakaua's personal staff. In 1883, he was appointed special envoy to the coronation of Czar Alexander of Russia, and to the courts of Germany, France, Spain, and Serbia, and later that year envoy extraordinary to Japan. In 1887, he accompanied Queen Kapiolani and Princess Liliuokalani to London for Queen Victoria's golden jubilee. In 1891, he was a member of the Privy Council. His governmental positions included collector general of customs (1884–86) and commissioner of Crown lands (1886–87 and 1891).

Following the overthrow, the Provisional Government asked him to remain in government service, which he did after obtaining permission to do so from Liliuokalani. In 1895, he was on the general staff of the Republic of Hawaii, and in 1897, he served as attaché of the Hawaiian

Legation at Queen Victoria's diamond jubilee in London. He was a long-time advisor to Liliuokalani, and in 1909–23 he served as the managing trustee of her trust. He died in Honolulu on March 5, 1940.

Probably the most important person in the Queen's life after 1893, and certainly her most loyal supporter, was Joseph Oliver Carter, who was not a family member. The entire Carter family in fact shared an intimacy with the Queen that no other non-Hawaiian family seems to have had, and for that reason I have included them here as extended members of Liliuokalani's family.

Joseph O. Carter, businessman, agent of the Queen, and loyalist, was born in Honolulu on December 20, 1835. He was the eldest of five sons of Captain Joseph Carter (b. September 15, 1802, Charlestown, Massachusetts–d. August 1, 1850, Honolulu) and Hannah Lord Carter (b. December 25, 1809, Hallowell, Maine–d. January 29, 1898, Honolulu). One of his brothers was Hawaiian diplomat Henry A. P. Carter (b. 1837, Honolulu–d. 1891, New York City), and his nephew George R. Carter would later become governor of the Territory of Hawaii.

Over his long business career, Carter was a "news gatherer" for the *Pacific Commercial Advertiser*, held positions in the post office and the Department of Finance, was consular agent for Japan, and served as a legislator in the House of Representatives during the 1872–73 session. He was also a member of the Privy Council in 1891. In 1893, when he refused to join the ranks of the annexationists because of his loyalty to the deposed Queen, he was discharged from his position as president and manager of C. Brewer & Co., and thereafter many of his former business associates avoided him. Subsequently, Carter became the Queen's business agent and most diligent correspondent, and many of Liliu's letters quoted here (in particular those of 1897) are addressed to him.

On November 28, 1859, he married Mary Elizabeth Ladd (b. June 8, 1840, Honolulu–d. December 15, 1908, Honolulu), one of Liliu's most intimate childhood friends and loyal supporters. The Queen always called Saide, one of the couple's children, "Liliu." Carter remained in charge of the Queen's accounts until 1907. He died in Honolulu, February 27, 1909, having served his monarch faithfully and honorably.

*Paoakalani, 1886. This modest cottage in Waikiki was one of Liliuokalani's favorite residences. It is remembered in the song "Paoakalani," composed by the Queen in the 1870s or 1880s. Following is the opening stanza and its English translation:*

*Anoano liʻulā ka nahele,*
*Ka nohona i Paoakalani,*
*Nihi ana ka leo o ka ʻohe,*
*Kapalili i ka welelau makani.*

*The forest so quiet and calm at twilight*
*At the residence Paoakalani,*
*So soft was the rustle of the bamboo,*
*Quivering at the wind's touch.*

(Detail) Alfred Mitchell, Bishop Museum Archives

# The Queen's Residences

The Queen is so closely associated with Washington Place that many people now assume it was her only residence, but this was not the case. Like many of the alii, Liliuokalani maintained several other residences. These included several cottages at Waikiki, a large house in Palama, a small house in Manoa (she rented this out and probably never occupied it), and a simple country cottage at Waialua, Oahu. Washington Place only became her primary residence following the Wilcox rebellion (1889) and the death of her mother-in-law, Mary Dominis, the same year.

Beginning in 1886 and continuing until 1889, Muolaulani in Palama was the place that Liliuokalani called home. There she had a sense of independence from her diffident and often wandering husband, and from a domineering mother-in-law who made it known that Washington Place was her domain and not her daughter-in-law's. Muolaulani was located on the mauka (toward the mountains) side of King Street (between today's Desha and Pua lanes). Simon Kaai, Princess Ruth Keelikolani's[1] onetime business manager, built and owned the property, and on December 4, 1886, Liliuokalani purchased it at auction through an agent for $8,000. At the time of auction, the property was advertised in the newspapers as having "163 front on King Street, with a dwelling house and commodious outhouses situated thereon. The buildings are capacious and nearly new and in good repair. The main house contains eight large rooms. The grounds are planted with flowering plants and shrubs." Subsequently, on December 20, 1886, Liliuokalani purchased (for $2,000) an adjacent two-acre parcel of taro land from Deborah Mahoe, sole heir at law of the late Paul Kanoa, thereby enlarging the Palama property to about 2½ acres.

On the Muolaulani premises was a cottage that Liliu called "Keala Hale" (sometimes identified as Poikeala Hale), and the name occasionally appears at the end of diary entries, suggesting that the Queen sometimes spent the night there rather than in the main house.

It was in the Muolaulani house that Robert William Wilcox and associates met, assembled a group of Hawaiian followers, and, on July 30, 1889, marched on Iolani Palace in a revolutionary action known as the Wilcox

---

1. Ruth Keanolani Kanahoahoa Keelikolani (b. 1826–d. 1883) was the daughter of Pauahi, one of the wives of Kamehameha II. Her father was Governor Mataio Kekuanaoa and she was the half-sister of Kamehameha IV and of Kamehameha V. She was twice married, had two children, and adopted Leleiohoku, a brother of Kalakaua and Liliuokalani. Ruth was possessed of enormous estates and tracts of land, which she willed to Bernice Pauahi Bishop, and which now support the Kamehameha Schools.

rebellion. Liliu stated publicly (and privately to the king) that she had no knowledge of Wilcox's actions.[2]

After the affair, however, she seems to have lost interest in the place. By 1890, Washington Place had become home, and she had rented Muolaulani out. The terms of one such lease, dated September 27, 1890, to Ernest Hutchinson, required payment of $100 per month, with the lessee charged to "continue to employ Kawehena, now in charge of the premises to keep the garden at $25.00 per month."[3] In May 1896, British Consul Albert George Sidney Hawes (d. 1897) rented it for $65 a month. In 1906, when she was renting Muolaulani to one T. Hayashi for $25 per month, he was also renting the Keala cottage for $10 per month. By 1910, the property had been subdivided into lots suitable for residences and other buildings, and there is now no trace of what must have been a most attractive residence in its heyday.

Hamohamo at Waikiki (then comprising approximately 100 acres) was a much-beloved property that Liliu acquired via her mother's deed on May 13, 1859. It fronted what is now Kalakaua Avenue and ran inland well past today's Ala Wai Canal. Hamohamo included taro patches, rice fields, fishponds, and cocoanut groves, and an interesting map of the property included in the revised edition of Liliuokalani's memoir[4] identifies many of these features.

The Queen's thatched seaside cottage at Hamohamo (on the ocean side of Kalakaua Avenue) was known as Kealohilani. The Liliuokalani Trust in 1928 deeded that portion of Hamohamo, now known as Kuhio Park, to the Territory of Hawaii.

Within the boundaries of Hamohamo were a number of small kuleana (native land claims) owned by other Hawaiians, and for many years, Liliuokalani wisely bought these small landholdings out at every opportunity, thereby gaining a complete title and control of the property. During the late 1880s, she also began leasing out house lots along the Waikiki road (now Kalakaua Avenue).

By 1910, a report of the Liliuokalani estate trustees noted that streets now formed boundaries on three sides of the property (one newly opened street was appropriately named Liliuokalani Avenue), and the trustees formed plans for subdividing it into 27 leasehold lots. Today, Kuhio Avenue divides the property, several large hotels stand on parts of the land, and Hamohamo is perhaps the most valuable asset of the Liliuokalani Trust.

The Waialua, Oahu, cottage, sometimes referred to as Aliiolani Villa, was primarily John Dominis's country house. He assembled the property through four separate purchases between June 1867 and 1874 (the last comprising a little more than four acres at Kawailoa from Princess Ruth).

2. See diary entry for Thursday, August 1, 1889 (236).
3. Hawaii State Archives, Liliuokalani Collection, Liliuokalani Trust Papers, M-397, Box 3.
4. Liliuokalani, *Hawaii's Story by Hawaii's Queen Liliuokalani*, rev. ed. (Honolulu: Liliʻuokalani Trust, 2013). First published 1898 by Lee and Shepard, Boston. The Hamohamo map appears on the endpaper in this book.

The property is located inland from what is today the Kamehameha Highway, between the Anahulu River and the Lokoea fishpond. Lokoea Road runs along one of its boundaries. During Dominis's life, the establishment seems to have been pretty much a bachelor's domain. Liliu's 1892 diary records a long and pleasant stay at this property, and after 1895, she vacationed there on several occasions. After 1900, she rented it out on an occasional basis. Not a trace of the house remains today.

Captain John Dominis, the governor's father, built Washington Place, a two-story columned mansion of coral stone, as the Dominis family residence on property along what is now Beretania Street. Dominis had obtained a leasehold on the property in settlement of a longstanding lawsuit against British Consul Richard Charlton. The Diamond Head half of the original leasehold remained Charlton lease property and was at the time subleased by British Consul General William Miller. The terms of the leasehold to Charlton from the Hawaiian chiefs had been for 299 years, starting on October 5, 1826. On December 12, 1889, when the government agreed to sell at auction the reversionary interest in the Washington Place lot, Governor John O. Dominis bid $250 and thereby obtained a clear title to the property. (The Miller half of the original lease property became part of the Washington Place grounds near the end of century.)

Captain John Dominis laid the foundation for the house about the year 1842, but didn't complete it until the beginning of 1846—he was building and paying incrementally in cash from the profits of several voyages. The architect was island resident Captain Isaac Hart. Captain Dominis departed from Honolulu on a voyage to China on the brig *William Nelson*, August 5, 1846, and he and his ship were lost at sea. U.S. Commissioner Anthony Ten Eyck named the home, in which Mary Dominis continued to live, in honor of U.S. President George Washington.[5] Kamehameha III confirmed this honor on February 22, 1848.

Washington Place did not become Liliuokalani's full-time residence until after the death of her mother-in-law on April 25, 1889. Eventually she was also able to secure the Beretania cottage, the adjoining property on the Diamond Head side of Washington Place, which the family of General William Miller had owned and the McKibbin and Mist families had later occupied. This acquisition doubled the size of her grounds.

Liliuokalani died in the Washington Place mansion on November 11, 1917. In 1919, the Hawaii Territorial Legislature appropriated the sum of $30,000 for its purchase, and, under a condemnation action that forced the estate to sell, then paid $55,000 in full on May 14, 1920, to the Liliuokalani Trust. Since then the mansion has served as the official residence for the governor of Hawaii.

5. Mary Dominis was a great admirer of General George Washington, and was in fact an early member of the Mount Vernon Ladies' Association, the organization that saved the Washington mansion, opened it to the pubic, and still maintains the property. Liliuokalani would visit Mount Vernon twice, once in 1887 and again in 1897.

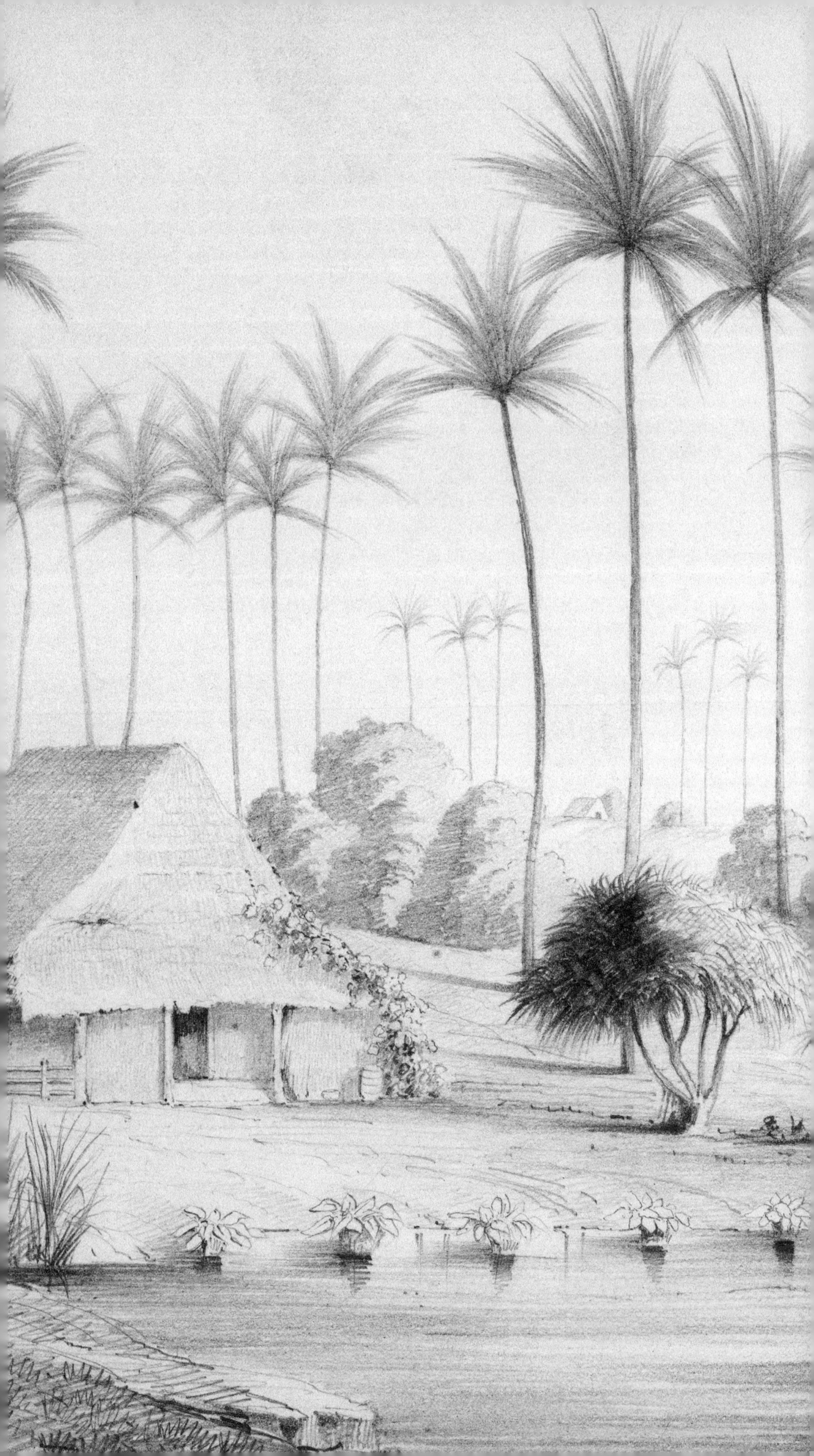

# The Diaries

*As Princess and as Queen, Liliuokalani made excursions throughout the islands. She is shown here at August Unna's residence at Hana Plantation in 1883, where prominent visitors often came to relax and enjoy Unna's hospitality. From left: Unna's brother Oscar; Abraham Fornander, district judge for Maui; John Dominis, the Princess's husband as well as governor of Maui and Oahu; Cecil Brown, Unna's attorney; Miss Sheldon, the Princess's attendant; the Princess; S. W. Kaai, Hana judge (blurred); August Unna, owner of Hana Plantation; D. Toomey, plantation manager; August Unna's wife, Marie, and baby, Else; Matilde Unna, a niece.*
Christian J. Hedemann, Bishop Museum Archives

# 1885

*Tuesday, December 30, 1884.* Left here [Honolulu] for Maui in *Kinau* with only one servant, Joe Heleluhe.[1] Arrived at Maalaea same night 12 P.M. [sic] rested all that day. Next night Dec. 31, went to concert at Masonic Hall [in Wailuku]. Was serenaded but heard not a sound—bright moonlight night.

*Thursday, January 1, 1885.* A grand Sunday school celebration at Wailuku of all Maui and Molokai—Hana school, Lahaina, Kaanapali, and Waihee [schools] were the best. In Bible recitation Makawao was best. In Music Lahainaluna did very well. In the evening a concert was [Sentence ends thus.]

*Friday, January 2.* Weather, good. Made calls on Mrs. Enders, Mr. and Mrs. Grosser, Mrs. Cornwell at Waikapu.[2] Dined at Keapo's nephew's birthday party and drank of water from Kalena.[3] Kukulu i Kahiki [is the] baby's name. Three o'clock was escorted to Kahului by J. W. Kalua[4] and went right on Steamer *Likelike*. Lahainaluna boys also came off, [and also Reverend] Waiamau [the] Kaumakapili Pastor,[5] Judge Kaai,[6] and others bound to Honolulu except Lahainaluna boys.

*Saturday, January 3.* Arrived [Honolulu] seven [A.M.] early—took our folks by surprise. Found John well.

THE DIARY FOR 1885
30 DEC 1884–
8 DEC 1885

Bishop Museum Archives

---

1. Joseph Heleluhe (b. 1855, Kau, Hawaii–d. July 8, 1900, Honolulu) was in the Queen's service from boyhood, and remained a part of her household for life. He was held as a political prisoner in the barracks following the 1895 counterrevolution, but did not later stand trial. He was in charge of Washington Place during the Queen's imprisonment in 1895, and in 1896 he traveled with her to Washington, DC. An obituary in the *Pacific Commercial Advertiser*, July 9, 1900, noted that he was "one of the upper class of Hawaiians and a man in whom the Queen placed implicit confidence. It was due to this that he was made her confidential secretary." He was the husband of Wakeke, whom Liliu frequently mentions in her diaries. Heleluhe was buried in the Kawaiahao cemetery.

2. Lizzie Enders was the widow of Wailuku physician Frank H. Enders. C. E. Grosser was the Anglican clergyman at Wailuku. Adelia Louzada Cornwell (d. 1896) was the wife of King Kalakaua's friend William H. Cornwell, proprietor of the Waikapu sugar plantation.

3. Kalena is a land section in Makawao with a stream of clear mountain water.

4. John W. Kalua (b. March 26, 1848, Pelekunu, Molokai–d. April 10, 1928, Wailuku, Maui) was an attorney in Wailuku, a land agent, a legislative representative from Maui 1880–90, and a Second Circuit Court (Maui) judge 1894–1904. Some of his letters are in the Hawaii State Archives, Liliuokalani Collection.

5. Reverend J. Waiamau (b. 1837–d. September 23, 1901, Honolulu) was the pastor of Kaumakapili Church and many times the chaplain of the Hawaiian Legislature.

6. Samuel Webster Kaai, a school agent, district judge, and agent to acknowledge contracts, resided in Hana, Maui.

*Country school, Maui, 1885. The lyrics for the song "Hawaii Ponoi," by King Kalakaua, are written on the blackboard of this school, which may have also served as a church or Sunday school. On January 1, 1885, Liliu attended a Sunday school celebration in Wailuku that included Bible recitations by students from schools such as the one shown here.*
Eduard Arning, 1885, Hawaiian Historical Society

*Luau, Kawaiahao Seminary, Honolulu, March 7, 1885. On this date in her diary, Liliu noted the grand luau celebrating the first birthday of Samuel H. K. Mahelona. The feast, attended by several hundred, including Kalakaua and Likelike, was held on the grounds of Kawaiahao Seminary, decorated with banners, ferns, maile, ieie, and flowers.*
Eduard Arning, 1885, Hawaiian Historical Society

*Monday, January 19.* Breakfasted with the king. Guests were Prof. and Mrs. Wayland,[7] Mr. and Mrs. Wilder, Col. and Mrs. Judd, and myself.

*Friday, January 23.* Met Mrs. Wayland at the King's Boathouse.

*Monday, January 26.* Breakfasted in the palace with the King. Guests were Mr. and Mrs. Fred Lyman of Hilo and Mrs. Forbes,[8] Col. [Charles H.] Judd, and myself.[9]

*Tuesday, January 27.* Called at Mrs. Forbes but she and Mrs. Lyman were out.

*Saturday, January 31.* Mrs. Kinkead, wife of Gov. of Alaska,[10] and her niece Miss Kibby breakfasted with the king in the Palace. Mrs. K., Miss K., Mr. G. Gray, McFarlane, Col. Judd and Myself—after that the ladies and myself were received [in] private audience by the Queen. At 12 P.M. Mrs. J. Campbell and Miss Kibby, Mrs. Godfrey Brown, John [and] myself visited Mausoleum. One o'clock the two ladies left by *Alameda*. Half past three left for Palolo.

Four o'clock today the Lunalilo Home was open to public inspection—band played there—a bright moonlight—sky very clear.[11] Charlie gave me $200.00. Received a note from J. G. Hoapili.[12]

**Sunday, February 1.** Weather—lovely day [Palolo]. Everything so still and quiet but passed the day in planting trees and shrubs. Is it right? I was taught that it was wrong [to labor on the Sabbath] but some say "the better the day better the deed." I only know that being in the woods I feel supremely happy in the stillness that surrounds me and also feel that of One whom we have been taught to fear were in my presence. A feeling of [Sentence ends thus.]

*Monday, February 2.* Seven o'clock A.M. returned from Palolo—paid our bills and wages, then went to call on Father [Samuel Chenery] Damon. Madame Bouliech there.[13]

---

7. Francis Wayland (b. 1826–d. 1904) was a lawyer, the dean of Yale Law School 1873–1903, and a prominent writer and speaker on sociological topics. The *Daily Bulletin*, January 9, 1885, reported that Professor Wayland and his wife arrived by the *Mariposa* "and will be guests of the Hon. & Mrs. S. G. Wilder."

8. Mrs. Fred Lyman (Isabella) and Mrs. Anderson Forbes (Maria) were daughters of missionary Levi Chamberlain. Lyman was the longtime assistant governor of Hawaii Island.

9. Isabella Lyman writes in her journal: "Monday Jan. 26. Went to breakfast at the Palace at 8½. The governess [sic, governor] & Mrs. Dominis were there besides the King, Mr. Judd, Maria F. [Forbes,] & I. Mr. F. could not go—very sorry—got home near 11." Hawaiian Mission Children's Society Library.

10. Mrs. Kinkead was the wife of John Henry Kinkead (b. 1826–d. 1904), who served as the third state governor of Nevada (1879–83), and then was appointed governor of Alaska by President Chester A. Arthur in 1884. He remained in that office until 1885.

11. "This charitable institution ... a home for aged Hawaiians, is situated to the northeast of the city proper and near the well-known landmark Punch Bowl. The institution was founded and is maintained by the proceeds from the estate of one of the former Hawaiian kings, King Lunalilo, and is named after the donor. The structure is two stories in height, built of Hawaiian stone, the center being surmounted by a high tower from which beautiful views of the surrounding country can be obtained." *Paradise of the Pacific*, May 1893. The Lunalilo Home, which opened in April 1883 just below the present-day Roosevelt High School on Nehoa Street, remained in that location until 1928. The occasion referred to here was the 50th anniversary of Lunalilo's January 31, 1835, birthday.

12. J. G. Hoapili was a district judge who resided in Keauhou. His son David had a stock ranch at Hookena.

13. Madame Bouliech was the wife of George Bouliech, chancellor of the French Legation and a resident of 123 Beretania Street.

Met two officers of French gunboat *Kerguelen*. He came to see [Sentence ends thus.]

*Tuesday, February 3.* Went to Waikiki to see Joe and Paulo[14] fence Wakeke's lot—came home late. Gave Ahi (Pake [Chinese]) $125.00 in advance for building Kaipo's house[15]—and will pay the remaining $125.00 last of the month.

*Wednesday, February 4.* Joe Aea[16] took me in his brake [carriage] to Waikiki as Lucy [a horse] was not able to be used. Kaoliko and Okuu came out to survey Naahuelua's lot. It is not as large as represented to be much to my joy and their chagrin.

*Thursday, February 5.* Weather—fine. My reception day. Early this morning, Joe Aea took me to Waikiki in his brake with *Romeo*. Joe Heleluhe and Paulo put up fence of Kaipo's lot—also gate. Came home one o'clock. Received at three. The Band in attendance. Had a full reception.[17]

*Friday, February 6.* Weather. Very warm. Kaonohiponi's[18] birthday—seven years old today.

Mrs. Unna, Mrs. Wilson, Wakeke, Kaipo and Kawehena, Loe,[19] Mary,

---

14. Possibly Paulo Kahalewai, who appears in the 1885 City Directory as "Capt. Kings Guard."

15. Joseph Kaiponohea Aea (b. June 22, 1882, Waikahalulu, Nuuanu Valley) was the son of Joseph Kapeau Aea (see footnote for February 4, 1885, diary entry, this page) and his first wife, Kahae. "Kaipo," as he was familiarly known, was the Queen's protégé and hanai son. Although he boarded with Mrs. Caroline Bush on Emma Street, he was frequently in and about the Washington Place premises. He was educated at Iolani School and the Kamehameha Schools.

In adulthood, Kaipo worked as the Queen's business agent, leaving her service in December 1909. He was then a stenographer in the office of the city clerk, David Kalauokalani. He was popular and had a brisk social life. Kaipo died at Kealohilani, Liliu's Waikiki beach home, on November 14, 1914, and was buried in the Manoa cemetery.

16. Joseph Kapeau Aea (b. June 28, 1853, Puna, Hawaii–d. January 25, 1911, Pauoa Valley, Honolulu) was long one of Liliuokalani's closest personal retainers, and attended Liliu and John Dominis when they went to England for Queen Victoria's golden jubilee in 1887. In private, he was a well-known violin player with the Royal Hawaiian Band.

After 1896, he and his wife stayed several times with Liliuokalani during her residence in Washington, DC. Aea's first wife was Carrie (or Kahae) Kaheholokalani (or Kaholookalani; b. 1857, Maui–d. March 18, 1929, Honolulu). She divorced him, and then in 1914 married Henry Haole Kamauoha. Aea's second wife, Helen Kanani Aea (b. 1868–d. July 10, 1939), was also an intimate at Washington Place. He had three daughters, Hannah, Mary, and Lydia (Kaloio) and three sons, John Samuel (d. 1919), Joseph Kaiponohea (known as "Kaipo"; see footnote for February 3, 1885, diary entry, this page), and Nihoa, about whom little is known. John was educated in England with Princes David Kawananakoa and Jonah Kuhio, and was given the commemorative name "Kaholopelekane."

17. The reception was at Washington Place "from three to five o'clock." *Pacific Commercial Advertiser*, February 5, 1885.

18. This is Lydia Kaonohiponiponiokalani Aholo, the Queen's hanai daughter.

19. Mrs. Marie Unna was the wife of August Unna (d. April 8, 1885), owner of the Hana Maui Sugar Plantation.

Eveline Malita Townsend Wilson (Kitty) (b. 1849, Honolulu–d. May 21, 1898, Honolulu) was the part-Hawaiian daughter of John S. Townsend and Harriet Blanchard (b. 1831–d. 1911) and wife of Charles B. Wilson. Kitty's grandfather Andrew Blanchard was the captain of the ship *Thaddeus*, on which the first American missionaries came to Hawaii in 1820. Kitty was an intimate friend of the Queen, and was Liliuokalani's companion much of the time during her 1895 imprisonment in Iolani Palace.

Wakeke Ululani (b. 1841, Maui–d. November 21, 1921, Honolulu), the wife of Joseph Heleluhe, was a retainer in Liliuokalani's household. Her parents had been retainers of Kamehameha III and had lived on the palace grounds, and Wakeke served Liliuokalani in the same

Paulo, Joe and I went out. Stackpole drove me out and little Paoakalani had to be footman.[20] Took a drive with Mrs. U[nna] and Mrs. Wilson to my new house [at Palama]. Joe came in and reported this eve of having flogged one Pake [Chinese] severely at Pawaa for stealing firewood—and another lightly for shielding him.

Had a visitor that eve. [The rest is blank.]

*Saturday, February 7.* Weather very warm. Went out to Waikiki with Paulo and Joe and little Kaipo. Very little was done there. Came home and drove out at ½ past four with John to Emma Square, then left him and went to Iwilei for Sophy.[21] She could not come and stay with Mrs. Dominis who is getting weak. Dined with Mr. C. R. Bishop,[22] Mr. and Mrs. W. F. Allen,[23] Mele Allen, Mr. R. W. Meyer,[24] Mr. Faxon,[25] and Kapoli.[26]

---

capacity for many years. Her obituary noted, "Wherever the Queen went, Mrs. Heleluhe was close by, always watchful and helpful in private service." *Pacific Commercial Advertiser*, November 22, 1921. She was the mother of a musician son, James Paoakalani Heleluhe (b. 1880), known as "Prince Jack," and a daughter, Myra (Mrs. George Iona; b. 1879–d. 1935), who was also a part of the Queen's household. Wakeke twice accompanied Liliu to Washington, DC, and after the Queen's death worked in the households of Prince Jonah Kuhio and his widow Princess Elizabeth Kahanu (later Mrs. James F. Woods). The Queen and her contemporaries commonly referred to Wakeke as "Waikeki" or even "Waikiki" (we have standardized the name as Wakeke to avoid confusion).

Kawehena was Liliuokalani's gardener at Muolaulani. Loe (b. 1833, Kohala–d. March 25, 1910, Honolulu) was the wife of Kawehena. Both were retainers of Liliu.

20. Paoakalani, the hanai (adopted) son of Joe Heleluhe, one of Liliu's retainers, sometimes acted as her groom.

21. Sophy or Sophie Sheldon (b. 1851, Honolulu–d. May 23, 1897, Honolulu) was the part-Hawaiian daughter of Henry L. Sheldon, onetime owner of the *Pacific Commercial Advertiser*.

22. Charles Reed Bishop (b. January 25, 1822, Glens Falls, New York–d. June 7, 1915, Berkeley, California) was a banker and philanthropist. Bishop came to the islands in 1846, and from 1849 to 1853 was collector general of customs. On August 17, 1858, he established the Bank of Bishop & Co. in partnership with W. A. Aldrich. On June 5, 1850, he married Bernice Pauahi, daughter of chiefs Abner Paki and Laura Konia.

He was a member of Hawaii's House of Nobles (1859–86) and served on the Privy Council (1859–91). During the reign of King Lunalilo (1873–74), he was minister of foreign affairs. He served for a long time on the board of health, including as its president (1887–91).

Following his wife's death on October 16, 1884, Bishop began withdrawing from island life and politics, ultimately moving to California. He maintained a vital interest in both the Kamehameha Schools and the Bernice Pauahi Bishop Museum. While not a particularly close friend of Liliu, he was always available to offer sound advice. Bishop is buried with his wife in the Royal Mausoleum of Hawaii, Nuuanu Valley.

23. Mrs. Cordelia Church Allen, or Cordie (b. 1837–d. September 22, 1912, Honolulu), a cousin of Charles R. Bishop, came to the islands in 1863 from Caldwell, New York. She met Colonel William F. Allen (son of Judge Elisha H. Allen) in Honolulu, and they married in 1865. For long periods of time, the Allens lived with the Bishops at Haleakala, their King Street home.

24. Rudolph W. Meyer (b. 1826, Hamburg, Germany–d. 1897, Honolulu) arrived in Hawaii in 1848. A surveyor, Molokai rancher, and sugar grower, he would briefly serve Princess Ruth as her business manager.

25. Eben Faxon Bishop (b. 1863, Illinois–d. 1943, Honolulu), a nephew of Charles R. Bishop, came to the islands in 1883, first working as a clerk at C. Brewer & Co. and eventually becoming president of that firm. He was always known as Faxon.

26. Elizabeth (Lizzie) Kapoli was a close relative of Bernice Pauahi Bishop, and an intimate friend of both Liliuokalani and Princess Likelike. Kapoli's position in the Bishop household was of the nature of a relative or retainer rather than that of a servant. She served in the same capacity for Princess Ruth. She married Judge W. P. Kamakau (d. 1873). Lizzie tragically contracted leprosy and was sent to Kalaupapa, where she died July 27, 1891, age 39 years.

At eight eve.—went with John to Mrs. Schmidt's[27] to meet Mr. and Mrs. Unna. Met Mr. and Mrs. Toler.[28] Miss Schmidt [and] several young German ladies and Gents. Band played there for Mrs. U.[29]

Joe came in to say his duties were over. [Entry continues on bottom of next page.]

He spoke of the annoyance caused by Koakanu's claims to Bernice's property and the perjury that they may be committing by the course they were pursuing. Must look into this.

*Sunday, February 8.* Went at seven to Kapalama for flowers and at 11 went to Mr. Eddie Damon's to see Mrs. Damon—gave her the flowers and sympathized with her in her grief.[30]

2:30 went to his funeral at the Bethel, and John and I sat with the family. The King and Mr. [Charles] Judd sat in the pew behind us. Father Damon had many friends and church was full. Mr. Oggel[31] the pastor preached the funeral service. Drove round to see the Japanese at Immigration Depot. Consul [Robert W.] Irwin and family arrived today [on the] *City of Tokio*.[32]

*Monday, February 9.* Waited for Mr. Allen who wanted to see me about Mr. Gilman's message of Aloha.[33]

*City of Tokio* leaves today [and the] *Mariposa* is coming in. Did not find Mrs. Unna at home so had to go to Waikiki without seeing her. She sailed this afternoon in the *Likelike* for Hana. John, Mary, and Mainalulu[34]

---

27. Wilhelmine Schmidt was the wife of Heinrich W. Schmidt (b. 1846, Bremen–d. 1900), a Honolulu merchant. She died in Honolulu on April 2, 1906.

28. William P. Toler (b. 1826, Venezuela–d. 1899, Oakland, California) was the son of an American diplomat. Young Toler, as a midshipman under Commodore John Drake Sloat, was responsible for raising the first American flag over Monterey at the occupation of California in 1846. He was a resident of Honolulu for seven or eight years in the 1880s, building a large residence, later owned by the Frank Hustace family, on Waikiki Beach.

29. "Last Saturday evening by order of HRH the Princess Liliuokalani, the Royal Hawaiian Band serenaded Mr. A. Unna, Consul for Denmark, and Mrs. Unna who are the guests of Mr. H. W. Schmidt, Consul for Sweden and Norway." *Pacific Commercial Advertiser*, February 9, 1885.

30. Reverend Samuel Chenery Damon, editor of *The Friend* and longtime pastor at the Seamen's Bethel Church, had died at Edward Damon's home on February 7, 1885, age 70. Liliu was commiserating with his widow, Julia Mills Damon. Edward Damon (b. 1846–d. 1894) was one of the Damon sons.

31. Reverend Engelbert Christian Oggel (d. November 6, 1910) had been since 1884 Samuel C. Damon's replacement as pastor of the Seamen's Bethel Church. He returned to the United States in the fall of 1887.

32. The SS *City of Tokio* arrived at Honolulu February 8 from Yokohama, with passengers and 948 Japanese immigrants, "the first installment of those expected to come to Hawaii." The *Pacific Commercial Advertiser*, February 9, 1885, enumerated these as: "Farmers, 610 men, 138 women, 58 boys and 37 girls—'servants'; 56 men, 27 women, 11 boys and 11 girls; one man and one female doctors and one girl.—besides this there is an additional doctor... and a little boy child of 18 months, whom nobody owns.... Mr. Irwin is to be congratulated upon having brought to these shores so fine a body of desirable immigrants." On February 10, 1885, the *Pacific Commercial Advertiser* editorialized: "The arrival of the first installment of the Japanese immigrants is the most important event that has happened in Hawaii for many years. It will rank in the future history of this country with even the most exciting events of the past."

33. Gorham D. Gilman (b. 1821–d. October 3, 1909, Newton, Massachusetts), a longtime Lahaina merchant, had returned to Boston. He, Liliu, and Bernice P. Bishop had been friends in both Honolulu and Lahaina, 1845–60.

34. Mainalulu (k) was a retainer living at Washington Place.

went up. Band at Emma Square this evening[35] and Kaipo begs to go. We went in express—came home with Kapoli. My friend called.

*Tuesday, February 10.* Wrote my letter to Emma. Received Charley, Lizzie, Keoluhuna, then came out to Waikiki—had pipe laid. Like[like] came to ask me to her house on Saturday to meet the Schoolchildren of Kawaiahao Seminary,[36] Miss Alexander Principal. May not see my friend till Friday. Went to bed early—Kaipo slept well through the night.

*Wednesday, February 11.* Weather, rainy night. Fine. Went to Waikiki as usual, did not do much—came home dissatisfied. Six P.M., Afook came to tell me one of his horses had been taken to pound by big Joe—told him to come next morning.

*Thursday, February 12.* Weather fine. Rain in night. This is the 11th Anniversary of the King's Accession to the throne and also Firemen's Day, for they turn out on parade today.

Afook has been here and I told him that he ought to pay for his horse to Pound Keeper. He left in disgust. This morning Likelike drove in [and] we went to congratulate His Majesty, but found only the Queen. Went on the grounds to review [the firemen's] parade. Fine turnout.[37]

[At] 12 o'clock, the King received Members of the Grand Order of Kalakaua.[38]

[At] three P.M. We dined with King and Queen and household. Four P.M. Japanese were brought up by Consul Irwin. They wrestled and danced[39]—left at half past five. Passed the day pleasantly.

35. This was the Royal Hawaiian Band, which, according to the 1884–85 City Directory (page 79y), had been established in 1871 (the correct year was in fact 1872) by Professor Henri Berger "and is composed entirely of natives. It is a uniformed body of 30 members, supported by the government, and, besides playing on the occasion of all celebrations, State affairs, receptions, etc., it regales the general public with its melodies twice a week in the pretty Emma square, and frequently gives extra entertainments on moonlight evenings."

Henry (or Henri) Berger (b. 1844, Berlin), a Honolulu resident from June 2, 1872, was the leader of the Royal Hawaiian Band for 42 years. He wrote the music for the Hawaiian anthem "Hawaii Ponoi."

36. "Kawaiahao Female Seminary, located on King Street, opposite the Kawaiahao Church, is a model institution and systematically conducted, partly self-supporting, being assisted by the Government (capitation fees), the Ladies' Benevolent Society, and the missions. It is about 16 years old and doing good work. At present it has 97 pupils, who come from the different islands. All pupils board in the establishment. Terms, $50.00 per year. . . . An institution like this . . . is just what is required to keep young females out of harm's way and refine them." *McKenney's Hawaiian Directory* (San Francisco: L. M. McKenney, 1884), 80c.

37. The fire department parade was a popular annual event. The four volunteer companies commenced their parade from the bell tower at 10:30 A.M. and progressed through the town, stopping before the front gates of the palace, where the king received them. Afterward, there were "entertainments" at each of the firehouses. At Company No. 2 House, there was a catered lunch, and at the No. 4 House, "the boys had some singing, dancing, and guitar playing." *Pacific Commercial Advertiser*, February 13, 1885.

38. "His Majesty the King made the following promotions and appointments to the Royal Order of Kalakaua yesterday. Promoted to the Grand Officers: Their Excellencies W. M. Gibson and C. T. Gulick, and the Hon. H. A. Widemann. To be Knight Commanders: His Ex. E.L.G. Steele of San Francisco, late President of the O.S.S. Co. To be Knight Companions: Dr. G. Trousseau, Col. J. H. Boyd, Major Antone Rosa, and the Hon. L. Aholo." *Pacific Commercial Advertiser*, February 13, 1885.

39. "The Japanese wrestlers gave an exhibition of their skill in the Palace grounds yesterday. His Majesty was much pleased with the friendly contest." *Pacific Commercial Advertiser*, February 13, 1885.

*Friday, February 13.* Went to Waikiki as usual. Aimoku spent the day with me.[40]

It has been a very wet day but we need rain very much. Four P.M. went to Kapalama—found carpenter and painters work almost complete. 7½ I hear the Band at the Hotel. Kaipo groans with pain, perhaps it is rheumatism—but now he sleeps. Telephoned to Vicky Ward[41] [that] I could not come tomorrow. Tomorrow is Konghee day [the Chinese New Year] with the Chinese, and my servants Aho and Amoon are going off.

My friend has arrived.

*Saturday, February 14.* Kalei, Kaonohiponi, and Keala are here waiting and now we start for Likelike's. It is a grand holiday for all children of the Kawaiahao Seminary. Miss Alexander Principal, Miss Malone, Miss Meuther, and Miss Brewer Associates, Mrs. Mahelona and Miss Alice West, Hawaiian teachers. Spent a pleasant day. No Band today.

*Sunday, February 15.* Went [illegible] to services at Kawaiahao. Mr. Parker pastor[42]—Mr. [Henri or Henry] Berger Organist. Three P.M. went to Kamoiliili to Services.

7½ P.M. went to Kawaiahao to hear professor [Francis] Wayland preach.[43] Was very pleased with him. Mrs. Wilder, Mr. C. Brown, Kapoli, and myself in my pew.

*Monday, February 16.* Went to Kapalama. Had one caller. Band at Hotel.

*Tuesday, February 17.* Came out here [to Kapalama] and was disappointed the carpenters did not come out. Planted trees before going home. Had one caller. Band at Skating Rink. Owe J. T. Waterhouse, Fort St.[44] $3.50 for worsted and gold thread.

*Wednesday, February 18.* Spent the day in making calls. Did not have a good night's rest. Went round and paid $3.50 at Waterhouse's [store].

*Thursday, February 19.* Went to Waikiki to help Joe Heleluhe on his place in building a stone wall so as to make more land. Kauehena came also to help. Not much was done. Planted trees at Kaipo's lot.

---

40. John Dominis Aimoku was born January 9, 1883, the son of Mary Purdy Pahau and John O. Dominis. He was taken into the Dominis household as a hanai (adopted) son, but during his early years, he boarded much of the time with Caroline Bush on Emma Street.

Aimoku spent his adult life administering to Liliuokalani, and in letters they addressed each other as "hanai." He lived at Washington Place, was her confidante and an official of her trust, and was acting in that capacity at the time of his death. He changed his name to to John Aimoku Dominis in 1910. On June 19, 1911, Aimoku married Sybil McInerny, the daughter of Honolulu merchant E. A. McInerny. The couple had three children. Aimoku died at Kahala, Oahu, July 7, 1917, several months prior to the death of Liliuokalani in November 1917.

41. Victoria Robinson (b. 1846–d. 1935) was the part-Hawaiian daughter of James Robinson and wife of Curtis P. Ward (d. 1882). The occasion is not recorded.

42. Henry Parker (b. March 2, 1834, Nuuhiva, Marquesas Islands–d. September 7, 1927, Honolulu) was the son of Hawaiian missionaries Benjamin and Mary Parker, who were temporarily stationed in the Marquesas and later lived in Kaneohe, Oahu. Parker was ordained at Kawaiahao on June 28, 1863, and from that date until October 7, 1917, he served continuously as a pastor of that church.

43. According to the *Pacific Commercial Advertiser*, February 17, 1885, Mr. Wayland's lecture on "moral science" was "well attended" and interpreted for the native audience of Kawaiahao by Reverend Henry Parker.

44. Waterhouse & Co., an importer of American, English, and French goods and a general merchandise dealer, maintained two stores, one on Queen Street and another (known as the "No. 10 Store") on the corner of Fort and King Streets.

*Friday, February 20.* Went early to Kapalama, took mats up and went out direct to Waikiki. My old friend came to see me as usual. Planted some more trees.

*Saturday, February 21.* Was busy from early morn. Mr. W. F. [William] Allen brought $800—rents, and brought news that Koakanu's case was lost and that the court had decided for Mrs. Bishop's Will and heirs.[45]

Bought a bedroom Set for Kaipo $40.

I gave the $800.00 to Mr. Wilson.[46]

Mr. Stackpole took Mrs. McGrew, the Dr. [McGrew] and Mr. and Miss Winters and their father up to Palolo to stay till Monday.

*Sunday, February 22.* Stayed at home all day—a showery day.

*Monday, February 23.* Felt rather poorly—had to send for doctor Martin.[47]

Mrs. McGrew and party returned. Curtis Iaukea called to see me about Maule and seemed doubtful about him.[48]

Entertained my friend.

*Tuesday, February 24.* Went to Kapalama to plant roses. Had visitors. Mrs. M. Brown, Mrs. Aldrich, Mr. Mauli, Mr. and Mrs. Kaae called here this eve. Failed to write Hoapili about goats on Keahuolu.[49]

---

45. On December 2, 1884, at a hearing prior to admitting Bernice P. Bishop's will to probate, Pius F. Koakanu objected to the validity of the will and claimed to be a blood relative. The court considered his relationship to the deceased to be too remote under the provisions of the law, and did not admit the claim. Koakanu then appealed. At the appeal proceedings, held January 30, 1885, the court again found Koakanu to be "too far removed," and his claim was denied as of February 18, 1885. (Mrs. Bishop's probate includes a chart detailing Koakanu's lineage. Hawaii State Archives, First Circuit Court, Probate 2425.) Following Koakanu's death on March 2, 1885, the *Pacific Commercial Advertiser* commented on March 5, 1885, that his demise was "caused as his acquaintances report, by remorse and fear."

46. Charles Burnett Wilson was born at sea July 4, 1850, on the British brig *Diana*, en route from Tahiti to the Fanning Islands. He was the son of Charles Burnett Wilson and Terena, "a resident of the Island of Tahiti," and the grandson of Reverend Charles Wilson, an English missionary at Tahiti from 1801. After Charles's father died at sea in 1853, Henry English (on Fannings Island) supported Charles and his brother Richard, their mother having left them in 1855. By 1858, the two boys were in Honolulu under the guardianship of Captain D. Smith. A record of the guardianship is located in the Hawaii State Archives, First Circuit Court, Probate 2339.

On July 19, 1869, he married Liliuokalani's intimate friend Kitty Townsend, who died in 1898. In 1905, he married Mary Ahia (b. 1877, Maui–d. 1947, Honolulu). The diaries mention both women often. A blacksmith by trade, Wilson was both strongly built and strong-willed, and had great influence for some years over Liliuokalani. Many considered him the power behind the throne.

Ultimately, he and Liliu quarreled, and the friendship was broken. His statements about the collapse of the monarchy, given to U.S. Commissioner James H. Blount (in the Blount Report), and further remarks published in the *Honolulu Advertiser*, January 9, 1910, and July 7, 1925, are of great historical value. Wilson died in Honolulu on September 12, 1926. His son was John H. Wilson (b. 1871–d. 1956), a longtime mayor of the city.

47. G. H. Martin, physician and surgeon, "boards [at] Royal Hawaiian Hotel" (1885 City Directory).

48. W. S. Maule was a labor contract agent for Maui and a road supervisor for Maui, Molokai, and Lanai.

49. Liliu inherited Keahuolu, an ahupuaa (land division) in Kona (described in the Hawaii State Archives, Royal Patent 6851, Land Commission Award 8452, as containing 4,071 acres), from her mother Keohokalole. Kalakaua, as estate executor, described it in a July 8, 1869, letter to his sister: "On the mountains the Koa, Kukui, and Ohia abounds in vast quantities. The upper land or inland is arable, and suitable for growing coffee, oranges, taro, potatoes, bananas etc. Bread fruit trees grow wild as well as the Koli oil seed. The lower land is adapted

*Wednesday, February 25.* Felt better and went to Waikiki—told Kaonowai to go to Kahala on Saturday. Gave him fence mauka of Kamaikeaho.[50]

Received Dr. Fitch who came to say Mrs. Parsons would like to call on me.

*Thursday, February 26.* Received at ten A.M., visit from Mrs. Fitch and Mrs. [S. H.] Parsons a friend of hers from Oakland. Mrs. McGrew, Katie, and Tarn came to call this eve.[51] Band at Emma Square.

*Friday, February 27.* Went to Waikiki—was taken ill [and] came home—on my way home [passed] that corner lot, [which] was crowded with people who came to ride the Roller Coaster—felt too ill to stay. Many came in to see me this eve. Regretted not being able to see Tavernier's pictures of Volcano.[52]

My friend was surprised to find me laid up. I told Kapoli I did not need her. Roller coaster first opened today.[53] Many flocked to have a ride. Something new. King and sister went.

*Saturday, February 28.* Am obliged to keep [to] my room. Dr. Martin gave me change of medicine. Dr. Kuehn, Mr. [John A.] Cummins, and Tommy [Cummins] called, as the latter intended sailing by *Alameda* for S.F. with [the two princes] Keliiahonui and Kuhio. These young boys intended to go to San Mateo to be educated.[54]

Charley and Eveline [Kitty Wilson] came in. He gave me $200. Paid out already $115. John gave me this morning a handsome clock—two bronze vases, one kettle—and a young colt by Stanford Cot's sister [a mare?] and Mrs. Holt's stallion.

Judges Kaluhi and Kaulia,[55] Kauahilo, Mrs. Mahelona and [Mrs.] Kawainui—Joe Aea—Kaiulani and Sister [Likelike]—Kahae—Kapoli [visited?].

---

for growing cattle sheep, goats etc. The fishery is very extensive and a fine grove of cocoanut trees of about 200 to 300 grow on the beach. The flat land near the sea beach is composed chiefly of lava, but herbs and shrubbery grows on it." Hawaii State Archives, Interior Department Land. In a 1935 schedule of Liliuokalani Trust landholdings, the parcel is recorded as having 160 acres of coffee lands, 1,000 for grazing purposes, and 2,840 acres of "waste." Hawaii State Archives, Liliuokalani Collection, Liliuokalani Trust Papers.

50. On June 6, 1885, Kaonowai (k) would lease the land, buildings, and fishing rights at Kahala from Liliuokalani at $30 per annum. Bureau of Conveyances, Liber 95, 163.

51. Pauline McGrew (b. 1840–d. 1912) was the wife of Dr. John S. McGrew. Their children were Kate (b. 1873, Honolulu–d. 1963), later the wife of Dr. Charles B. Cooper; and John Tarn McGrew (b. 1876, Honolulu), who spent most of his life in France. Liliuokalani and Pauline McGrew were socially friendly and occasionally corresponded.

52. French artist Jules Tavernier (b. 1844, Paris–d. 1889, Honolulu) arrived at Honolulu late in 1884 and, until his death, specialized in dramatic paintings of the Kilauea volcano. The *Pacific Commercial Advertiser*, February 27, 1885, announced: "This evening there will be a second exhibition of paintings by Mr. Jules Tavernier and Mr. Joseph D. Strong, in the parlors of the Hawaiian Hotel at eight o'clock. The Royal Hawaiian Band will be in attendance." The next day, the newspaper had a long and enthusiastic article about the occasion, and noted that King Kalakaua was one of the notables present.

53. "The Roller Coaster—or as it has been called, the 'coasting roller' was tried yesterday by a committee of the Chamber of Commerce, a delegation from the Hawaiian Agricultural Society... and members of the press, and pronounced a decided success." *Pacific Commercial Advertiser*, February 28, 1885.

54. "By the *Alameda* today the Princes Edward A. Keliiahonui and Jonah K. Kalanianaole, nephews to the King, take their departure for St. Matthew's Hall, California, where they go to finish their education. Their elder brother Prince Kawananakoa is already a pupil at that institution." *Pacific Commercial Advertiser*, February 28, 1885.

55. Two men with the surname Kaulia appear in Liliu's diaries. The one mentioned here was

*Sunday, March 1.* Kapoli came to see me today. Dr. Martin says I must not take another cold on top of this, for if I did it would end seriously with me. A beautiful day. John is *lively* and very generous. Mary called to see me—Manaiki [and] Kaua [came?]—Joe says Kahae is sick. Also Amau's wife is painted up to the eyes.

*Monday, March 2.* Feel much better today hope to be out tomorrow. Gave Manaiki $2.00 for chicken feed. Romeo [a horse] is lost again, went in company with Bobtail. Aimoku is here—Lepeka—John is sickly. Asked Eveline [Wilson] to get one white flannel tihei [kihei or shawl]. Band played this eve at Emma Square.

Target Practice. Capt. Hayley and troops.[56]

Found Romeo at Kalihi with Bobtail. Like[like] came to see me.

*Tuesday, March 3.* Sent Eveline [Wilson] with cards to Mrs. Wayland and Mrs. Japanese Consul Irwin.[57]

Jessie and Kaae—Joe says Kahae is ill. Feel better today and able to walk around. Emma Kapena came to see me.

*Wednesday, March 4.* King came in to see me. [Also] the Queen and Mrs. Swan. $4.50 for calico tihei. King said he had bought house for Wainee. How good he is.[58]

Charlie [Wilson] tells me he has promised to buy Mrs. Bishop's furniture at Kahala.

*Thursday, March 5.* Romeo is lost again. Gave Jessie $2.00, she returned 30 cts. Joe found Romeo at Kalihi—Kainalulu Ahi says one window small. Sent Jessie to Mrs. Small to cut out a dress. She kindly said she would—is going to S.F. by *Mariposa*. The Queen, Mrs. Swan,[59] Lilia,[60] Kapoli, Jessie, and Kaae.[61]

How provoking John is tonight.

---

Asa Kaulia, a district judge for Koolaupoko, Oahu. The second person with this name was J. K. Kaulia, deputy sheriff and tax collector for Hilo. The two men are not always distinguishable in the diary entries.

56. "The artillery practice yesterday afternoon on the beach, beyond Kakaako, was given for the purpose of drill. Brigade-Major Hayley had charge of the exercise, and the guns were handled as in action. The range of the pieces was tested with satisfactory results." *Pacific Commercial Advertiser*, March 3, 1885.

57. Robert W. Irwin was Hawaiian consul general at Tokyo. Mrs. Irwin was a Japanese national.

58. No such property transfer has been found in the Bureau of Conveyances. Kalakaua might have simply purchased a building for Wainee, of whom nothing is known.

59. Mrs. Antoinette F. Swan (b. 1832, Honolulu–d. 1905, Santa Cruz, California) was the part-Hawaiian daughter of early Spanish settler Don Francisco de Paula Marín and wife of Honolulu businessman Lyman Swan. She was an intimate friend of Kalakaua and Queen Kapiolani, who knew her as "Pakeleapine," and there is a photograph of her in the Hawaii State Archives with the king and queen in the garden of Iolani Palace.

60. Lilia (b. August 6, 1854, Lahaina–d. June 13, 1935, Honolulu) was the wife of Luther Aholo (b. 1833), a government official who died at Washington Place on March 16, 1888.

61. Junius Kaae (b. September 17, 1845, Lahaina–d. December 19, 1906, Honolulu) was a government official and legislator. He was educated in Lahaina, and became a sugar boiler for James Campbell. He married (as his third wife) Jessie Kakaihi Lane (the daughter of William C. Lane) on February 3, 1883. He was a noble in the legislature (1882–86) and a member of the Privy Council (1883–91). He served as registrar of conveyances 1886–87, and as an officer in the King's Own. Kaae was involved in the notorious Aki bribery case of 1886, acknowledged as one of the events leading up to and resulting in the "Bayonet Revolution" of 1887. He is sometimes confused with Simon Kaai, but they were not related.

*Friday, March 6.* Kapoli brought me Hoku's [Leleiohoku's] things,[62] also some of [Princess Ruth] Keelikolani's things, which were left me by request of B. P. Bishop. [Mary] Keamalu wants to go to Waialua. I anticipate such pleasure. H. N. Kahulu[63] called, wants to be Judge again for Ewa.

Made bargain with [John W.] Alapai[64] to drag Wakeke's house for $32. Gave Kapoli 50 cts—gave $1.00 for thread and worsted. Gave Aiaumoe $2—for shoes for Aimoku—$3.50 to Wakeke for Kaipo's Shoes and Hat.

King came to see me. Lizzie Victor, Jessie Kaae—Joe.

*Saturday, March 7.* Aimoku, Kaonowai, Mary, and Aikoi have gone by *C. R. Bishop* to Waialua to wait until our party come round. Mr. and Mrs. Daggett.[65] Mr. and Mrs. [C. O.] Berger—Likelike—Kaiulani, John. The people and myself intend sailing Wednesday for a trip round this island.

Mrs. Swan, [John W.] Alapai, Mrs. J. O. Carter, [Mrs.?] Alapai, Kaoaopa, Mr. Bingham[66] came to bargain for Wakeke's house. I charged them $200—but they declined taking any offer. Neumann[67] and John—Lamilami says Mrs. Dominis kept back one dollar for his wages.

Grand Luau at Kawaiahao Seminary—Mahelona's baby birthday—did not go.[68] Band [at] Emma Square.

62. William Pitt Leleiohoku was Liliu's deceased brother. Keelikolani's "things" would have been those Bernice Pauahi Bishop inherited from Princess Ruth.

63. Henry N. Kahulu is listed in the 1884–85 City Directory as "attorney-at-law, district Judge for Ewa, district [and advertised] office No. 5 Bethel Street next Door to the Post-Office, res. Puowaina."

64. John W. Alapai was a road supervisor and later sheriff of Ewa. The 1890–91 City Directory lists him as living at Kapalama Kai.

65. Rollin M. Daggett (b. 1831–d. 1911), a journalist and U.S. congressman, had been appointed U.S. minister to Hawaii July 1, 1881, by President Chester A. Arthur, and held that position until June 1885. During his residence in Hawaii, he became a great friend of King Kalakaua, and collaborated with the king on a book, *The Legends and Myths of Hawaii* (New York: C. L. Webster, 1888).

66. It seems unlikely that Bingham would have been involved in this transaction; Liliu may have made a mistaken entry.

67. Paul Neumann (b. 1839, Prussia–d. July 2, 1901, Honolulu), a lawyer, arrived in Honolulu in the later part of 1883, and established his own law practice soon afterward. He was popular among the royal set; was a member of the Privy Council from December 14, 1883, to March 7, 1891; served as attorney general 1883–86 under Kalakaua; and was reappointed in 1892 by Liliuokalani. He was a member of the House of Nobles 1884–92.

As Liliuokalani's attorney, Neumann was present in the palace on January 17, 1893, when the Queen yielded under protest to the Provisional Government, and he in fact drafted that protest document. He later advised Liliu on the matter of her abdication, witnessed her signature to that instrument, and defended her at her subsequent trial by the Republic of Hawaii in 1895.

Journalist William Bowen, who knew Neumann well, testified before the U.S. Congress: "Paul Neumann is a good-natured man, personally not prejudiced against anybody... that is, individuals; but he disliked the so-called 'Missionary Party' there and the Annexation Party, and he included Mr. [John L.] Stevens among them. Paul Neumann was... always a friend of the Queen, and he was head and shoulders intellectually above any others of her supporters. He was intelligent enough... to see that there were great difficulties in the way of restoration." [The Morgan Report] U.S. Congress, *Hawaiian Islands, Report of the Committee on Foreign Relations, United States Senate, with Accompanying Testimony, and Executive Documents Transmitted to Congress from January 1, 1893, to March 10, 1894*, 52d Congress, 2d Session, vols. I and II (Washington, DC: Government Printing Office, 1894), 674.

68. The luau was in honor of Samuel H. K. Mahelona (b. March 4, 1884), the son of Samuel and Emma Mahelona. *The Friend*, April 1885, extensively covered the event: "The feast given on the spacious back lot at Kawaiahao Seminary a few days ago, in honor of the first anniversary of the birth of the son of Mr. and Mrs. Samuel Mahelona, was in all respects a first-class Hawaiian feast, and the large number of both Hawaiians and haoles present... evidenced their appreciation by the vigor with which they attacked the dainty and sometimes

*Sunday, March 8.* Johnnie [Wilson] and his father [Charles B. Wilson] called [at] seven o'clock on their way to Puuloa. Mr. Wilson says they will [soon] be through painting my house at Kapalama—welcome news. Kitty [Wilson] comes in only for a call. My neighbor comes in for my monthly contribution. I give him $1.00. The King called—[also] Mrs. Coney,[69] Kapoli, John—Mr. and Mrs. Daggett are very kind to call and see me.

*Monday, March 9.* Mrs. Ward called with a rose from Mary Foster.[70]

Sister came also Kaae—Hinau wants me to assist him in his suit against Kamaio.[71]

Wiseman marries tonight[72] and Band is to attend. Kainuuala bought 50 cents' worth of ribbon for Kaipo. Rain tonight. Went home huhu [angry] from here, alright.

*Tuesday, March 10.* Eveline [Wilson] and Kealoha called, the latter came to see if I was going round the island. Sister [Likelike] brought flowers. Heavy showers.

Kaaipulu and [Mary] Keamalu came in town to buy some warm clothing for Kalahiki. Dinner party at Irwin's Consul of Japan. Band attended.[73]

Mr. and Mrs. Daggett called. Mollie had a calf today.

What is there to annoy anyone to say "He mea ike ole ia ia" ["It's a matter not known to her"]—but I have offended someone.

*Wednesday, March 11.* Kailikole came to consult about selling me his land of Palaualelo and I consented to let him place his net house by my bathing house.

Hinau wants to get some money. Charley [Wilson] called but did not say what he had to say. Miss Parker and Mary Green [called]. Kailikole will give me his lot and I am to pay him $450 which was his entire expense.[74]

---

interesting viands. The feast was spread in a large lanai (or tent) not less than seventy-five feet wide and one hundred and fifty feet long … there was seating capacity for several hundred, and they were all there. The lanai was beautifully decorated in true Hawaiian taste with ferns, maile, bunches of ieie, and flowers. A single blue banner with a golden crown indicated where His Majesty the King should sit; and he presided there with royal affability and dignity. The occasion was also graced by the presence of Her Royal Highness Princess Likelike and many of our leading citizens of many nationalities. … Dr. Arning photographed the scene and produced several most admirable pictures."

69. Laura (or Lala) Amoy (or Amoe) Ena (d. February 23, 1929) was the wife of John Harvey Coney, and the sister of John Ena Jr. and Mrs. Levi (Annederia Amoy Ena) Haalelea (d. 1904).

70. Mrs. Curtis P. Ward (Victoria Robinson) and Mary (Robinson) Foster were sisters.

71. The Hinau-Kamaio suit has not been traced, and it may not have come to the courts. In the 1884–85 City Directory, Hinau is listed as a palace employee, residing at 74 Beretania Street. In the 1890 City Directory, he appears as "Hinau Adama Kaeo, coachman, res. Punchbowl."

72. J. E. Wiseman married Mollie Still on March 9 "at the pretty cottage formerly occupied by Mrs. Dudoit." *Pacific Commercial Advertiser*, March 10, 1885.

73. "Mr. R. W. Irwin, His Majesty's Chargé d'Affaires for Japan, entertained at dinner last evening, at his residence on Beretania Street. His Majesty the King, their Excellencies W. M. Gibson, Minister of Foreign Affairs; Paul Neumann, Attorney General; J. M. Kapena, Minister of Finance, and C. T. Gulick, Minister of the Interior; J. Nakamura, Esq., H.I.J.M's Consul to the Hawaiian Islands; Hon. A. S. Cleghorn; Hon. C. H. Judd, His Majesty's Chamberlain; Colonel Claus Spreckels, and W. G. Irwin, Esq. The veranda of the residence was brilliantly lit by rows of colored lanterns, and on the lawn in front of the house the Royal Hawaiian Band, under the leadership of Professor Berger, rendered some choice selections of music during the evening." *Pacific Commercial Advertiser*, March 11, 1885.

74. On April 8, 1885, Puniai (or Kapuniai) Kailikole and his wife Meeau sold a lot in Hamohamo, Waikiki (Apana 2 of Royal Patent 2575, Land Commission Award 2027 in the name of Palaualelo), to Liliu for the agreed price. The deed was recorded on July 21, 1887. Bureau of Conveyances, Liber 108, 82.

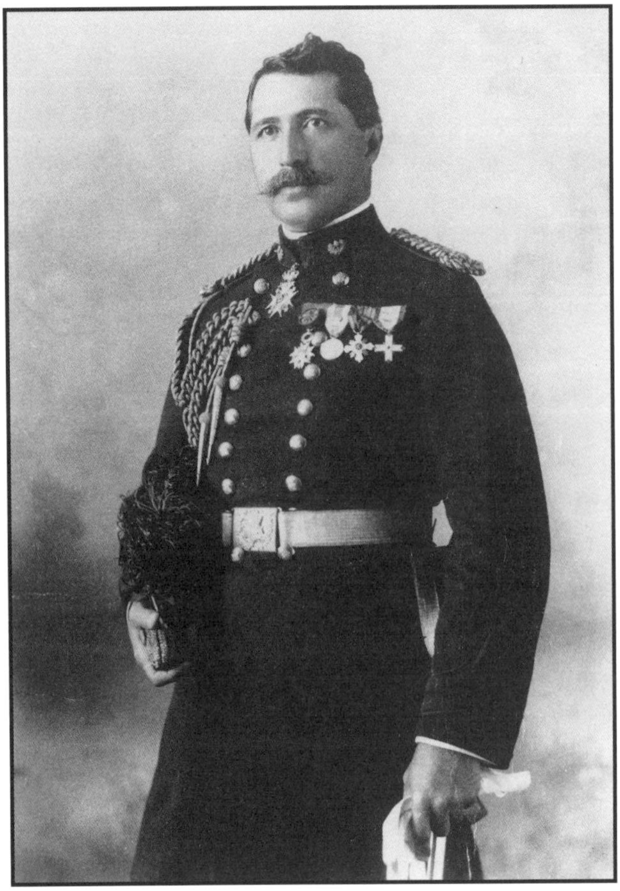

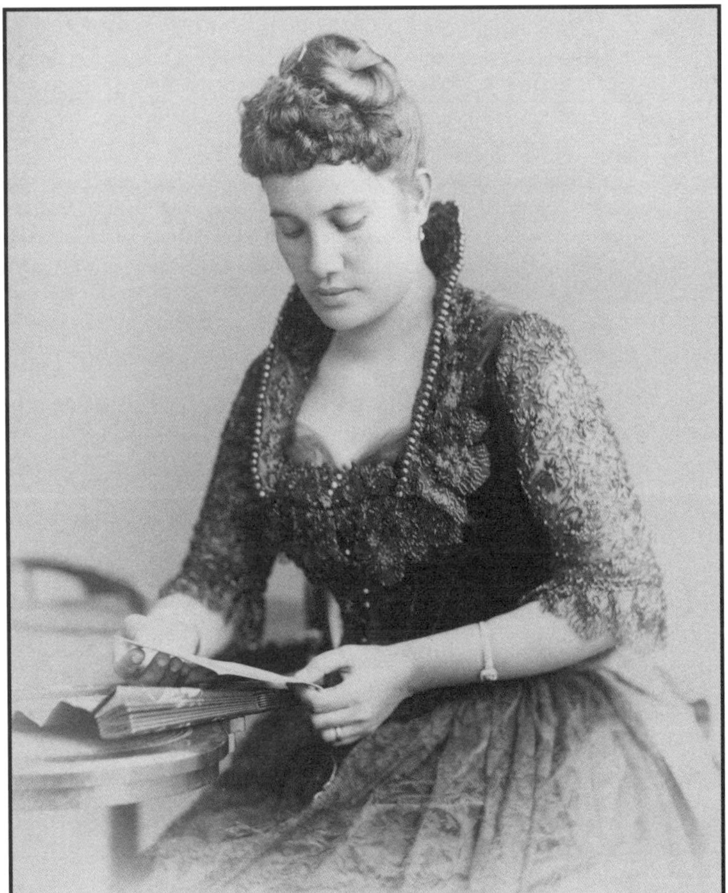

*Mary Lane Ena, Mary Risley Beckley, and Jessie Lane Kaae, friends of Liliu. Jessie and Mary Beckley are frequently mentioned in the diaries.*
Menzies Dickson, Bishop Museum Archives

OPPOSITE
*Curtis Piehu Iaukea and his wife, Charlotte Hanks Iaukea, were palace familiars under the last four Hawaiian monarchs: Lot Kapuaiwa, Lunalilo, Kalakaua, and Liliuokalani. Colonel Iaukea was a loyal court official and an accomplished Hawaiian diplomat. The Queen frequently mentions both Iaukea's in her diaries.*
Hawaii State Archives (Curtis)
Hawaiian Mission Children's Society Library (Charlotte)

Joe is riding Czar.

[In a different hand:] How anxious to make up and yet quick to take offense.

*Thursday, March 12.* Went out [to Palama] for the first time in nearly two weeks, but not till after John had started his trip round the island with Mr. and Mrs. Daggett and Mr. Dayton[75] and Mr. and Mrs. William Holt.[76]

Was pleased to find painters had got through with large house. Mr. Wilson says I must not move in till next week. How slowly everything seems to progress. Sophy and Emma [called]. My friend has called to apologize for his hastiness.

Felt strong and well.

*Friday, March 13.* Gave Kapoli 50 cents for ribbon for Cloud [a horse,] three dollars to Kaaipulu for Kalahiki. Charley came to make arrangements for sand. Telephoned to the Queen. She referred me to Alakema— Frank Hustace is to take the sand out.

*Saturday, March 14.* One dollar to Paulo. 50 cts for pail, 50 cts for cake.

Drove to Waikiki. Was huhu [angry] with Charley's obstinacy in insisting to have his pigpen there. I don't want to have a pig ranch at my place— besides shutting up Joe's place and the only way I see must be through Pupule's. How persistent he can be, but he has been good in many things.

Drove round to band at Emma Square, saw Kahae with Miss Young and she came to my carriage to speak to me. Billy Emerson's 3rd night.[77] [Will] Not be able to go.

*Sunday, March 15.* King called and warned me about new house. [David] Dayton telephoned from Waialua. Governor [Dominis] [is] all right also the party. C. R. Bishop arrived there ten P.M.[78]

Mary Ailau, Kaae, Kaipo went with me to Kapalama. Matting all ready—must move in Wednesday. Two fish to get [for the house dedication]—Manewanewa for gate; Manalo for piko hale.[79]

M. dine [possibly meaning dined at noon]. Must drive in side gate komo mai ma ka welau hope o ka hale a hiki i ka humu o ka hale—Mai poina. [Must drive in side gate enter at the back of the house until reaching the basement of the house—Don't forget.]

King and Queen called.

---

75. David Dayton (b. 1832–d. 1910) was a marshall of the Kingdom of Hawaii and a friend of King Kalakaua.

76. The *Pacific Commercial Advertiser*, March 10, 1885, announced that Governor Dominis and Deputy Marshall David Dayton "will start on a trip around this island to-morrow." On the 11th, the paper noted: "His Excellency Governor Dominis, H.R.H. Princess Liliuokalani, His Excellency the United States Minister Resident and his wife, and Deputy Marshall Dayton, intended to start for a trip around Oahu yesterday, but the rain prevented them." Liliu's diary suggests that in fact she did not accompany the party.

77. Liliu is referring to the troupe known as Emerson's California Minstrels: "The famous Emerson Troupe, the founder of which Billy Emerson, is so well and favorably known here, came down by the *Mariposa* yesterday, and the manager has announced the first of a series of six entertainments to be given commencing Thursday night, at the Music Hall. The troupe is en route for the Colonies." *Pacific Commercial Advertiser*, March 10, 1885.

78. The *C. R. Bishop*, a steamer built in Port Ludlow, Washington, was named on her arrival in Honolulu, September 1880. She became an Inter-Island Steam Navigation Co. ship in 1883, and wrecked at Nawiliwili, Kauai, January 31, 1894.

79. The piko hale is the symbolic umbilical cord of the house.

*Monday, March 16.* Gave Kailikole directions about fish—Wahine aloha, Kaua Kahawaii. [My dear lady friend, Kaua Kahawaii]. Melemai asks for a home. Princess Poomaikelani[80] [and] Archie Cleghorn [called?]. Kapoli brought home Cloud [a horse]. Mr. and Mrs. Allen brought me diamonds—some of Bernice's jewelries, set of earrings, pins, and bracelet.[81]

Kalaiokekoi. Joe H. [Heleluhe] is in Station House—disorderly conduct—bailed [out] at $29. Band at Emma Square—played "Aloha Oe" and encored—good program.

Kaae—Joe—Wakeke and Baby.

*Tuesday, March 17.* Kailikole was unsuccessful about [obtaining] the fish. Funny day—rain and sunshine. Kauikeaouli day.[82]

Band played at palace and came here two o'clock P.M. King's Own Guard went in palace—turned out in their new uniforms, [then] came round here, presented arms, and went back to Armory.[83]

Stackpole, Paulo, and Joe went to Kapalama. Mrs. Townsend returned dress. Joe Aea wants wagon tomorrow. King kindly gave Melemai permission to put a house on his land.

[A later addition:] My friend's kind thoughtfulness.

*Wednesday, March 18.* Keliinohopono [and] Joe went to court—case dismissed. [He was fined] $6 for riding in Cluney's yard on horseback.[84]

Pepe and Kahawaii want me to bid land for them to $1200. Jessie returned. Eveline [Wilson] [came?] with hats. [Charles] Wilson asked me to go to Bernice's [Bernice P. Bishop's residence] to see koa bedstead. John came home at six from Waialua very jolly—said it was so stormy the steamer *C. R. Bishop* could not go in [at] Waialua. So Aiaumoe, Hoomalu, Kaaipulu, Kaaimoku, and Kalahiki could not come up.

80. Princess Poomaikelani was known informally as "Kapo" or "Pooloku." Her full name was Virginia Kalanikuikapooloku Kalaninuiamamao. Born at Piihonua, near Hilo, Hawaii, on April 7, 1841, she was a descendant of Kaumualii, the last independent king of Kauai, and a sister of Queen Kapiolani. She married Hiram Kahanawai, a cousin of King Kalakaua and Liliuokalani, in 1874, and became governess of Hawaii on January 21, 1884, following the death of her sister Princess Kekaulike. Princess Poomaikelani died at Kalihi, Oahu, on October 2, 1895, leaving bequests to Saint Andrew's Cathedral, the Iolani School, Kapiolani Maternity Home, and the Hilo Boarding School. An obituary in the *Daily Bulletin* called her "a Hawaiian woman held in the highest esteem by all."

81. In Curtis P. Iaukea's diary, there is an attached memorandum dated January 17, 1912, which lists this jewelry: "1 coral necklace. 1 coral pin. 1 pr. coral ear rings. 1 Tiger claw necklace. 1 Tiger claw pin. 1 pr.—ear rings. 1 gold bangle inscribed 'A Noire.' 1 gold bangle inscribed 'Homanao Mau.' 1 pr. coral ear rings set in gold. 1 coral pin without pin. 1 crystal necklace." The memo indicates that these were to go to the Bishop Museum. Hawaii State Archives, Iaukea Collection, diary for 1910.

82. Kauikeaouli Day, more familiarly known as the anniversary of Kamehameha III's official birthday, was observed as a public holiday.

83. "The King's Own Volunteers paraded in the afternoon, appearing for the first time in their new uniforms, with white helmets, dark blue coats, and white pantaloons. They left the Armory at two o' clock, numbering 28 rank and file, commanded by First Lieutenant Clark, Captain Nowlein being absent on Maui. Preceded by the Royal band, they visited the Palace, where they paraded before His Majesty, and were complimented by him upon their appearance and drill. After parade a lunch was served, at which were present His Majesty the King, Major R. H. Baker, Adjutant J. T. Baker, and Lieutenants Paulo and Ulukou of the King's Guards (Household troops)." *Pacific Commercial Advertiser*, March 18, 1885.

84. The police court report in the *Pacific Commercial Advertiser*, March 19, 1885, says: "Joe Heleluhe was charged with disorderly conduct on the 14th instant [this month]. Discharged after hearing testimony. He was next accused of heedless driving, and fined $5 with $1 costs." Keliinohopono is not mentioned in the police report.

Mr. and Mrs. [Rollin M.] Daggett, Mr. [David] Dayton, Mr. and Mrs. Holt, Mrs. Emma Beckley, Lily Richards, [and] Sabina [Beckley].

*Thursday, March 19.* Lizzie and Keolaikalani. I heard of Mrs. Fred Macfarlane's remarks about Bernice's dresses that were given [me]. "She might have had jewelry," she said.

Mary came home in a fury—Angry because John preferred to take those folks' luggage in his wagon instead of a small bundle of fish for me—I believe it. It was always so with him. Mr. and Mrs. Daggett [and] Mr. and Mrs. [William] Aldrich called and found John in bed. Glad to get him to sleep instead of being bored to death by his silly maudlin stories. What a life to bear—still I am happy to think that I should have so much forbearance and patience. Patience always has its reward.

*Friday, March 20.* Charlie [Wilson borrowed] $95.00 of A. J. Cartwright. I gave my signature. I told him [Wilson] I had seen Bernice's [Bernice Bishop's] Koa set. Went to Waikiki and bathed at Minnie Aldrich's. Keaumoku came to borrow $5.00, but I gave it to her outright, for she has done many favors for me. Went to see Emerson's Minstrels. What a bosh. Called on Japanese Consul Nakamura and wife, all the Damons, Mr. [Charles R.] Bishop, Mr. and Mrs. Allen.

Have not found my fish yet. How provoking. Gave orders to cart the lumber of W's house and yet nothing done. Am pleased with Kaipo's house but [it is] still not finished. How kind of him to come to see me.

*Saturday, March 21.* Keaumoku brought back the $5.00 she borrowed. Went to the Matinee at two. House full with ladies and children. My Express did not come back for me from [hack driver]. No 290. Went straight to Music Hall from here. Hinano Bower. It rained so much no music at Emma Square this afternoon.

Kailikole [has] no fish—Same report from Kaae and Paulo. A visit of half hour.

I am getting despondent—for one reason or another I cannot move into my house. All alone, alone. Each one attending to their own comfort and *pleasure* and quite forgetful of me. Well, some day they may come in and find me?

*Sunday, March 22.* Sad, sad. Why should I be sad? but my little Kaipo turns his little face to mine and says ue ue [alas, alas]. The dear little thing does not yet know what he has to meet [with] in this world, and yet why should I be sad and brood? Everything around is beautiful and bright.

Kapoli came in to dine with me. King and Queen called and spoke of coming fair. John spent an hour with me, then went out—of course at Jim Smith's.[85]

*Monday, March 23.* Hinau[86] brought box [of] plant Onaona Iapana.[87]

---

85. William James Smith (b. 1839, Papoia, Tahiti–d. 1896, Honolulu) arrived at Honolulu in 1845, attended the Royal School, and for many years was secretary of the board of education and a member of the Privy Council. His residence was across Beretania Street from Washington Place.

86. Hinau, a palace employee, resided at 74 Beretania Street.

87. Onaona Iapana (night-blooming jasmine, *Cestrum nocturnum*) is a plant native to the West Indies.

Manaiki wants chicken feed. Nakookoo is here—and wants to see Spreckels about land.[88] Charlie comes in. I want money—none to give me, [he] finally says he will give me twenty of his own money. Strange I have to borrow from him and by and by will owe [him] like all the other chiefs to their agents—I must get out of this quick and the only way is to ask, after he has paid off furnishing my house, for him to show me his accounts. Eveline [Wilson] brought hat from Sach's[89] and bill at $9 and took Iwaiwa [stems of maidenhair ferns] to trim. She says they have bought a place in Kula[okahua].[90]

Joe came on errand—Did not see him. Why don't Charlie give me at end of each month $250—outright instead of giving me $200 then have me to ask for fifty afterwards to carry me through the month.

*Tuesday, March 24.* Nakookoo is here again to bid me good-bye. Joe and Kahae [Aea] are up to Manoa and do not know he [Nakookoo] is going home. He wishes to be Assessor for some district on Maui but if not there for North Kohala.[91]

Telephoned to Aiaumoe to come home.

*Wednesday, March 25.* Aiaumoe and party are on their way home. Half past three and they have arrived all safe. Give unpleasant accounts of Mary. I begged them to stay till tomorrow.

*Thursday, March 26.* Gave Aiaumoe $5.00 and paid Ahi $105.00. Kaae, Jessie, and I went to Waikiki to look for cocoanuts. Went to Palace with Mr. and Mrs. and Miss Toler and Mrs. Coney—then all drove to Kapalama. Kapoli brought in three of Mrs. [Bernice] Bishop's silk dresses—white and black lace shawls, one dolman, one lace scarf—all of rich material.

*Friday, March 27.* Meant to go to Waikiki but was not well enough. Mr. and Mrs. Kaae. The King and Kaae [called]. Kailikole brought down fish but was not the right one. Jessie and I went to Photo Gallery of J. Williams to see my picture,[92] went to Thrum's[93] and bought book for Kaipo, also

---

88. Claus Spreckels (b. 1808, Lamstedt, Hanover, Germany–d. 1908, San Francisco) was a sugar baron, land owner, and banker. He was an important but controversial figure in island politics in the period 1886-94.

89. N. S. Sachs, 104 Fort Street, promoted "Fancy Goods, Lace Mitts and Gloves, Ladies' and Children's Hosiery.... Special attention is called to the Millinery Department." Running advertisement, *Daily Bulletin*.

90. Kulaokahua was a large stretch of land, formerly known as Kula or "The Plains," running approximately from Alapai Street to Keeaumoku Street. It was being subdivided into large household lots. Liliuokalani purchased the Wilsons' lot on Piikoi Street at Young Street in 1886.

91. The 1884-85 City Directory lists "Hon. J. Nakookoo" as "acting police Judge, res. Railway Ave. Wailuku." He had been a representative in the 1882 legislature.

92. "*PICTURES OF ROYALTY*. Mr. J. J. Williams, photographer, is preparing photographs of their Majesties the King and Queen, their royal Highnesses the Princesses Liliuokalani and Likelike, and her daughter the Princess Victoria. Copies of their pictures will be taken, each bearing the signature of the distinguished sitter, and Mr. Williams intends presenting to the Committee of the Kaumakapili Church Bazaar, to be held in May, all the copies they may want to sell for the benefit of the church fund. On the back of each picture will be printed: Kaumakapili Church Art Studio under the patronage of their Majesties the King and Queen." *Pacific Commercial Advertiser*, March 27, 1885.

93. Thomas G. Thrum, a stationer and bookseller, 106 Fort Street, advertised blank books, writing papers, artists' materials, and "Holiday books and toys in their season."

blocks—spent $1.00. Was visited in the evening. Will go Monday and sit for picture. Went all round to beg for articles for my table at Fair. Dr. Arning[94] came in to call. Gave him some puili [rattles].[95]

Sent Toler, Daggett, Dayton, Smith, Brown, and Pratt some oranges.

*Saturday, March 28.* Had to make use of Wakeke's money for food money. She had $23.50 so I have to make that up, besides that I must give her towards building her house $20 more—and then I must give Kaipo $20 also.

Boat races today—did not go.[96]

Kapoli brought pretty polonaise[97] and rich lace [from Bernice Bishop].

John and I drove out today. Fish is found and Kaae has gone up to place it and tomorrow I must go up and stay.

*Sunday, March 29.* Went to Sunday School celebration at Kawaiahao. Of all the schools that were examined, Waikiki Kai took the palm. Thought Lima[98] deserves great credit for his perseverance with Kakaako. Came right up here [to Palama] and had lunch with our folks. Mr. and Mrs. Kaae, Wakeke, Loe, Kawehena, Aiaumoe, Aimoku, Paulo, Joe H. [Heleluhe], Stackpole, Kaaikuhe, Keamalu, Mainalulu, Kailikole. The King arrived late and dined by himself. Spent a pleasant afternoon, then went home. This is the day I am supposed to take possession of this house. I think that I shall call it Muolaulani.[99]

Mainalulu came home drunk. I am huhu loa [very angry].

*Monday, March 30.* [Weather] damp. This is the day I promised to have my photo taken but did not. I hate to sit for a picture. Sent all my furniture down here. Had many callers. Joe came to see me about many things.

*Tuesday, March 31.* Mrs. McGrew invited me to call and spend next evening with her and also to meet Judge and Miss Rising and Miss Yerington.[100]

Called on Mrs. [W. F.] Allen—made many purchases [of Mrs. Bishop's effects] and still have not all I would like to have. Charlie [Wilson] came for my signature on a note—he sent me $200.00 and that was all.

We met again.

---

94. Dr. Edward Arning had come to the islands November 8, 1883, to study the pathology of leprosy, and on November 19 was appointed a government resident physician at a salary of $150 a month. His Hawaiian passport stamp on June 28, 1886, records his intent to leave by the next departure of the *Australia*. See Hawaii State Archives, Register of Hawaiian Passports. He subsequently departed Honolulu for San Francisco on July 1, 1886.

95. A puili is a rattle made of bamboo and used in dancing hula. Arning was assembling a collection of Hawaiian artifacts, which he took back to Germany.

96. Liliu is referring to a regatta of the Honolulu Yacht and Boat Club, of which a long account appears in the *Pacific Commercial Advertiser*, March 30, 1885.

97. A polonaise is a woman's garment consisting of a waist and full skirt, to be worn over another skirt.

98. David Lima Naone; see first footnote for December 12, 1887, diary entry (167).

99. The name translates as "innumerable royal buds." Muolaulani, Liliu's primary home from 1886 to 1889, was located on the mauka side of King Street past the Nuuanu Stream (between today's Desha and Pua lanes and near the present-day Kaumakapili Church).

100. Judge R. Rising, Miss Edith Rising, and Miss Avery Yerington arrived on the *Alameda* from San Francisco, March 23, 1885. The *Pacific Commercial Advertiser* noted that Rising had long been on the bench of the state of Nevada, and that Miss Yerington was a daughter of H. M. Yerington, president of the Virginia and Truckee Railroad.

The *Evening Bulletin*, April 2, 1885, noted that Judge Rising, Miss Rising, and Miss Yerington had departed on the tug *Alert* bound for Waianae with the king and queen and party.

*Wednesday, April 1.* The King came to see me—said I must go out and catch a certain fish next day for him—Pau-u olena to Kakua[101] for three nights commencing tonight, Laau Ku Kahi [the 18th day of the lunar month]. Jessie and Mary are with me at Hinano Bower.

Today a dividend of $5.00 a share is declared of the Waimanalo Sugar Co. I am one and my share is now $235.00. Went to Mrs. McGrew's and spent the evening. The King was there, Miss Winters, Judge and Miss Rising, Miss Yerington, Mrs. Dickson, and Dr. and Mrs. McGrew. Today I replaced Wakeke's money $23.50.

*Thursday, April 2.* Went to Waikiki about six A.M. with Jessie, Mary, Wakeke, Kaipo, Paulo, Mr. Stackpole to fish. Went to Mr. Bishop's fishing ground. Got lots of Ohua [the young of several kinds of fish]. Got home at half past 12, had lunch, a nap, then dressed for my reception at three. Band played—on account of rain did not have many visitors.

Came home tired and retired early. Telephoned to brother [Kalakaua] and he came about seven with the Queen. I gave him the fish and they went home—then Jessie and I went for Mrs. McGrew and we all went to the Catholic church. Got there at quarter to ten.[102]

*Friday, April 3.* Went down town and made some purchases. It was very rainy. Had one visitor beside the King who called at four o'clock and said the fish I gave him was not the right one—then my friend came.

Joe told [me] that Willie Aldrich wanted my black pair of horses. How could I let him for they are dangerous to drive—and Joe has got to use one to go around this Island with. Manaiki came to tell me that Lamilami went in town and got [Entry ends thus.]

*Saturday, April 4.* Wrote to Charlie for $50. He said he would let me have it on Monday. Minnie Aldrich[103] and Martha Swinton[104] came round to see me and found me making cake. It was a success. John went to Waialua today with Mr. Brown and Dr. Brodie will be back tomorrow.[105]

Kapoli came in to ask me to go to church tomorrow evening at the [Seamen's] Bethel. Gave Alapai $20 (ten belonging to Wakeke)—the other is mine, towards building Kaipo's house. I do not owe Kaipo any more.

*Sunday, April 5.* Kaae spent the day. Mr. and Mrs. Toler came in and made me a present of a carriage robe. Sent Paulo up to Palolo. Kealoha and Kainuuala, Joe and Kahae, and last of all the King and Kahae [came]. I

---

101. Pau-u olena may refer to a young ulua, a species of fish in the jack family (Carangidae). Kakua means "to worship the gods, especially by food offerings; to appeal to the gods." Mary Kawena Pukui and Samuel H. Elbert, *Pukui-Elbert Hawaiian Dictionary* (Honolulu: University of Hawaii Press, 1986).

102. For services on the Thursday holy day before Good Friday, the following day.

103. Minnie or Mary Hale Brown Aldrich (d. 1946, San Francisco) was the part-Hawaiian daughter of J. H. Brown, the granddaughter of early American consul John Coffin Jones, and the wife of William Holt Aldrich (b. 1857–d. 1897). Her husband was the son of William A. Aldrich (b. 1824–d. 1892), an early business partner of Charles R. Bishop. The Aldriches were relatives of the Dominis family and lived at Washington Place for long periods of time.

104. Martha Swinton was the daughter of Henry S. Swinton of Kapalama. Minnie Brown Aldrich was her niece.

105. They made the trip to investigate an outbreak of Glanders, a disease nearly always fatal to horses. The *Pacific Commercial Advertiser*, April 8, 1885, commented: "Dr. Brodie, veterinary surgeon, and Captain J. H. Brown returned yesterday from Waialua, where they had been inspecting horses. Only one horse was found that was suspected of being glandered."

*Koolaupoko, Oahu, 1886. On April 14, 1885, Liliu started on a trip to Kaneohe in the district of Koolaupoko by way of the Pali. The road that linked the Pali road to Kaneohe is shown here. At the Kaneohe home and farm of former Koolaupoko district judge William E. Pii, along this road, Liliu and her large party enjoyed a Hawaiian supper followed by a night of hula and singing.*
Eduard Arning, Hawaiian Historical Society

am not to go around this week, and on Tuesday or Wednesday I must go again and fish at Mokuoeo.[106]

I was not able to go to Church as the King did not leave till late.

*Monday, April 6.* Mary and Mainalulu[107] came home from Waialua—said that John had come back. Nellie Brown brought some cake from Martha. Lizzie Victor and William Holt came on to see me. Sister Like[like] also. Went to Goo Kim's[108] and ordered six yards of white figured lace at 50 cts a yard—then at Waterhouse's No. 10 Store, ten yards [of] pink glacé 10 cents a yd.—five yds of green glacé[109] at same—two collars at $1.00, two tablecloths colored at $2.50 each.

Kauhane and Jessie came in the even[ing]. [Also] My old friend.

*Tuesday, April 7.* Signed a deed of sale for Pau, Kohala bought by Cecil Brown, Attorney of Likelike. He took acknowledgments.[110]

Kauhane [came?] to find out when I would go to Waialua. Joe took Lucy [a horse] to Pawaa.

*Saturday, April 11.* Went to [blank] to have a sea bath at King's cottage by the sea. Mr. and Mrs. Daggett, Princess Poomaikelani—Hon. Kaae, Sophy Sheldon, myself, rowed out from the King's boathouse by the King's Soldiers—spent pleasant day, returned tired. That night most of our party came up here, but I stayed in town because John was not well, although I intended to go to the show.[111]

Stayed till 11½, then came up and went off silently to bed.

*Sunday, April 12.* Rainy. Promised to go to church with Kapoli and Mrs. J. O. Carter. Evening came—the King called and I could not leave. [King] gave me many good advices [as to] what I should do on my trip.

*Monday, April 13.* Mary called to see if we were going round the island. The Queen sent for Kaae's [Entry ends thus.]

*Tuesday, April 14.* Started from Mr. Bishop's to meet Miss Mele Allen and from there start for Koolau.[112]

Arrived at Pii's Kaneohe,[113] at one P.M. Mr. [David] Dayton very kindly attended us to the Pali. Our party consisted of Miss A[llen], Mr. and Mrs.

---

106. A low reef island off Moanalua. Land cards in the Hawaii State Archives show that in 1883, Kalakaua had applied for a 30-year lease of the same.

107. Mainalulu is listed in the 1888–89 City Directory as "messenger, Governor [Dominis] office." He lived at Washington Place.

108. Goo Kim Fui (b. 1826, China–d. May 3, 1908, Honolulu) was proprietor of a large emporium, "Dealer in Dry Goods, China Goods, Clothing, Ladies' Hats, Rice, Kona Coffee etc.," on Nuuanu Street, between Hotel and Beretania Streets. He was also vice consul of China.

109. Glacé is a fabric having a smooth glossy appearance.

110. This was a joint deed dated January 27, 1885, from Kalakaua, Liliuokalani, and John O. Dominis to Princess Likelike for a consideration of $3,000 for the land named Pau, an ili aina (subdivision) located within the boundaries of Pololu ahupuaa (land division) at Kohala, Hawaii. Liliu's mother, Keohokalole, had owned this land. Malcolm Brown, deputy registrar of conveyances, acknowledged the deed on April 7 and recorded it on April 9, 1885. Bureau of Conveyances, Liber 94, 142–43.

111. The show, held at the New Music Hall, was a performance of the San Francisco Dramatic Troupe "composed of the . . . leading artists from the Baldwin Grand Opera House and California Theatres." *Pacific Commercial Advertiser*, April 9, 1885.

112. "H.R.H. the Princess Liliuokalani will start on a trip round the island today, going by way of the Pali, and returning via Waialua." *Pacific Commercial Advertiser*, April 14, 1885.

113. William E. Pii, legislator (1853–54); fence commissioner (1865); marriage license agent (1869); and district judge for Koolaupoko (1877).

*Festive Hawaiian poi supper at Ainahau, the Cleghorn family property in Waikiki. Archibald S. Cleghorn, Princess Likelike, and their daughter Princess Kaiulani initially used the property as their country estate, but it became their primary residence. Cleghorn is shown at left sitting under the large tree. Watered by Apuakehau Stream, Ainahau was in the vicinity of Hamohamo, the much beloved property of Queen Liliuokalani.*
Alfred Mitchell, 1886, Bishop Museum Archives (poi supper)
C. J. Hedemann, Bishop Museum Archives (Ainahau)

Kaae, Mr. and Mrs. W. Holt,[114] Lizzie, Margrete, and Maria Lane,[115] Wakeke, Joe H[eleluhe], Paulo, Kaipo, Mele [Allen], and myself. Started at ten. A nice table was spread and we all did justice to the food. That night hula and singing. I made the policemen sing much to their enjoyment.

---

Queen Dowager Emma, widow of Kamehameha IV, died at 1:50 on the afternoon of April 25, 1885, at Rooke House, her Honolulu residence. She was 49 years of age. The Honolulu *Evening Bulletin* that date commented, "This is one of the sorest bereavements the nation has ever sustained." The queen was laid out in her drawing room at Rooke House, and that evening the Reverend Alexander Mackintosh said a requiem, Their Majesties the King and Queen and other members of the royal family paid a visit, and the court went into mourning until two weeks after the day of the funeral.

---

*Friday, May 8.* Kanikaus [dirges or chants of lamentation] were sung at Luka Hale [Rooke House] by Emma Kapena—Leihulu,[116] Pilipo,[117] Kamaiopili's two daughters,[118] and [blank], John Maipinepine[119] [Sentence ends thus.]

*Saturday, May 9.* Queen Emma's body was taken to Kawaiahao this evening. It was a grand procession—everyone in town turned out to see it.[120]

Strange that she should be taken back to the very church that she and her husband renounced.[121] And many strange things have happened since her death.[122]

---

114. Robert W. Holt (b. 1859–d. 1949) is listed in the 1890 City Directory as "asst. Mgr. of the Hawaiian Commercial Co. res. cor Fort and School Sts." His wife was Annie Harris Holt (b. 1859–d. 1919).

115. Lizzie, Margaret (whose name Liliu spells in a number of ways), and Maria were daughters of William C. Lane (b. 1819–d. December 26, 1895, Kapalama), a rice planter and stock raiser at Makao, Koolauloa, Oahu. Lane had been chamberlain to Kamehameha V, and his sons were both ardent royalists and prominent in political affairs of the 1890s.

116. Alexandrina Leihulu Kapena (b. 1868–d. March 23, 1914, San Francisco) was the daughter of John Makini Kapena and Emma Malo and the granddaughter of Hawaiian historian David Malo. She was married first to Morris Keohokalole in 1887, and later to Henry Clark.

117. Pilipo was one of Queen Emma's servants at Rooke House.

118. Mrs. (Caroline) David K. Kamaiopili (b. 1832–d. May 17, 1900, Kalia, Waikiki). Her daughters were Hannah (Mrs. E. S. Boyd) and Mrs. Ernest Kaai.

119. John Maipinepine Bright (b. 1863, Lahaina–d. April 25, 1943, Honolulu) was a district magistrate and a brother of Mrs. James Campbell.

120. Queen Emma's coffin was removed from her residence, Rooke House, on the corner of Nuuanu and Beretania Streets, on Saturday evening, May 9, via a procession that proceeded down Nuuanu Street, then along King Street to the Kawaiahao Church. Governor Dominis, Liliuokalani, and Princess Likelike were present at Rooke House when the coffin was removed. Observing protocol, the king was not present.

121. Queen Emma, an Anglican, was given a state funeral at Kawaiahao by the specific orders of King Kalakaua, because the Anglican church, a temporary frame building known as the "pro-cathedral," was not large enough.

122. Queen Emma's funeral was scheduled for May 10, but a heavy rainstorm the previous evening so flooded the streets that this became impossible. It was reported on that morning that the water was in some places two feet deep, and the funeral was rescheduled for Sunday, May 17. Another of the "strange happenings" Liliu alludes to was the flood of water in and about her own Palama residence. The *Evening Bulletin*, May 11, 1885, reported, "Out along the Palama Road the country looked like Deutschland with the dykes bursted. The Princess

*Queen Emma, 1866. In 1865, Queen Emma, the widowed consort of King Kamehameha IV (Alexander Liholiho), traveled to England. During her journey back to the islands in 1866, Emma made a brief stop in Washington, DC, where she attended a reception given in her honor at the White House by President Andrew Johnson. She also sat for this portrait by Mathew P. Brady, who had achieved considerable fame for his haunting photographs of the American Civil War.*
Mathew Brady, courtesy of the Library of Congress

*Friday, May 15.* Mrs. Dargie left in *Mariposa* for S.F.[123] We breakfasted at Palace with her, Mr. and Mrs. Frank Brown, and Cecil Brown.[124]

*Saturday, May 16.* D. Malo leased to Choi Pang Sang (Pake [Chinese]) my house lot once owned by Kalama at Manoa, for $130 per Annum. $98 was paid to him.[125]

*Sunday, May 17.* Queen Emma's funeral took place today with all the pomp and ceremony that she could have wished.[126]

Failing in obtaining her wish (the crown of Hawaii), she sought to keep up all the old customs and hulas—calling on people to come to her house to see her court, at which time she would exhibit her kahilis [feather standards] and relics—but today she was carried up to the Mausoleum in all grandeur. The King and I did not go in our carriages but went to the tomb. All the fat women turned out and walked up.[127]

*Monday, May 18.* Hilo came to ask me not to go up to Manoa—brought me $50 from Choi Pang Sang (Pake [Chinese]) for the taro planted by Kihei at Manoa—gave her $25.

*Tuesday, May 19.* Went to the Palace to breakfast with Mr. and Mrs. Daggett.[128] All the Royal family were present. Also Mr. and Mrs. [A. F.] Judd.

---

Liliuokalani's garden [Muolaulani] was like a miniature archipelago, the water flowing deep on all the paths. From the seams of the stone retaining wall on the town side gushed a hundred tiny cascades."

123. Mrs. W. E. Dargie of Oakland was the wife of the *Oakland Tribune*'s editor and proprietor. She had arrived on a visit in early April.

124. Brothers Frank (b. 1841–d. 1902) and Cecil Brown (b. 1850–d. 1917), the sons of Thomas Brown of Kauai, were both in the legislature.

125. The David Malo lease to Choi Pang Sang (or Sung) was for land and a house at Kolowalu, Manoa (Apanas 1 and 2 of Royal Patent 2590, Land Commission Award 1926). The land had seven loi (taro patches) and two loi liilii (small kalo patches); see Bureau of Conveyances, Liber 94, 210. Malo, who was the son of the noted Hawaiian historian David Malo and his wife Hilo, had granted the premises to Liliu in 1881.

126. "The funeral of Her Majesty the late Queen Dowager Emma took place yesterday afternoon [May 17, 1885], with a display of regal pomp and magnificence that has never been equalled on any occasion on these islands. During the past week, while the remains of the royal lady lay in state in Kawaiahao Church, thousands of persons daily visited the building to show their respect for the dead Queen, and each night large numbers assembled to bewail their loss. Last Saturday night the throng of mourners was greater than on any previous one ... and until [midnight] hundreds moved about outside the church to listen to the chants and meles sung by those inside, and many of them joined in the sad refrain.... By noon [on Sunday] Kawaiahao Church was filled in every part with spectators ... the organ gallery [in the front of the church] was occupied by His Majesty the King, the members of the Royal family, the judges of the Supreme Court, His Majesty's Ministers, the Chamberlain and officers of His Majesty's staff, and the few that constituted the choir." *Pacific Commercial Advertiser*, May 18, 1885.

127. "The scene along the line of march in Nuuanu Avenue was very animated. Every available spot where a good view of the procession could be obtained was occupied by spectators, while natives, chiefly women and girls, with very few children indeed, lined the sidewalks, seated themselves upon walls and fences, and patiently awaited the coming of the funeral. These spectators increased in numbers towards the cemetery, and the crowd became quite dense at the summit of the hill on which the mausoleum is built." *Pacific Commercial Advertiser*, May 18, 1885.

128. Rollin M. Daggett had been the U.S. minister to Hawaii since July 1881, and served until June 1885. This was probably an informal farewell.

*Thursday, May 21.* I had a reception today—had a large party come to see my new house [Muolaulani]. Band in attendance. First time Joe has been down since the pummeling he got.

*Saturday, May 23.* Choi Pang Sang paid $32 for Kalama's land at Manoa, which was leased to him by Malo for $130, and this $32 was the remaining amount of the $98 paid to M [Malo] May 16th. Gave Joe $5, which he will refund from his wages.

---

From May 24 to November 1, there are no entries in this diary. A summary of Liliuokalani's activities in that period follows.

On May 29, there was a fair in aid of the building fund for Kaumakapili Church,[129] at which occasion a lavish display of "Hawaiian curios" was on view. It was announced that the king and queen would be present, and that Princesses Likelike and Liliuokalani would both have tables.

On June 16, the Honolulu newspapers reported that Governor Dominis was quite ill at Lahaina. Liliu went to Maui, and returned with her husband a week later. She attended a concert at Kawaiahao Church, at which Miss Annis Montague and Charles Turner sang.

The great summer event was Liliu's excursion in July to Nihoa, or Bird Island, lying to the northwest of Kauai. At first it was planned as a government expedition limited to members of the Survey Department and a few naturalists. Sereno Bishop was the designated surveyor, and the group included Sanford B. Dole, who was a highly respected amateur ornithologist, and J. J. Williams, a photographer. Liliu asked to join the group, and before long a large number of her friends had also signed on, swelling the number of participants to about 200. The *Pacific Commercial Advertiser* gives an account of their departure on the steamer *Iwalani* for Kauai, Nihoa, and Niihau:

> ¶ A very large crowd assembled at the wharf last evening to witness the departure of the excursionists to Nihoa, or Bird Island. The Royal Hawaiian Band was present under the leadership of Professor Berger, and played a variety of musical selections. The most noticeable feature among the tourists was that most of the ladies were robed in calico, while the men wore woolen shirts. Leis of every shade and color were abundant. His Majesty the King, H.R.H. Princess Likelike, and His Excellency J. M. Kapena were among those who came down to see the party off. As the last whistle of the steamer *Iwalani* sounded, three rousing cheers were given, and hats and handkerchiefs waved in the air. H.R.H. Princess Liliuokalani took with her a fine Hawaiian string band to enliven the trip.[130]

---

129. The Kaumakapili Church was originally on Beretania Street at the head of Bethel Street. After a fire destroyed it in January 1900, it was rebuilt in the Palama neighborhood.
130. *Pacific Commercial Advertiser*, July 21, 1885.

A follow-up article tells of the return of the excursionists:

¶ The steamer *Iwalani* returned yesterday bringing the party of excursionists from Bird Island. They had a great number of trophies in the form of feathers and birds, alive and dead. The general sentiment of the party was one of satisfaction at having made the trip, although the crowded state of the little steamer interfered not a little with the personal convenience and comfort of the party.

On the up trip the *Iwalani* touched at several points on Kauai, and H.R.H. Mrs. Dominis and suite landed and were entertained by Mr. Aubrey Robinson at his elegant place.... Niihoa [sic] was made in good time and a landing effected with much difficulty and not a little danger, several of the party having literally to take water. Mr. Jaeger was slightly injured while going ashore, while the boat on which Mr. Williams, photographer, was making a landing, was swamped and his valuable photographic apparatus lost.

The island was explored to some considerable extent, and specimens of its feathered denizens, as above stated, were brought away. Just before leaving, however, it was seen that the dry grass was on fire. The flames soon spread until it became evident that the entire surface would be burned over, thus destroying all the nests and thousands of birds. Doubtless the fire was accidental, caused by the carelessness of some smoker, but it may very well be questioned whether the scientific results of the expedition will compensate for this wholesale destruction.[131]

There was an aftermath to the Nihoa excursion:

¶ *A Luau.* Her Royal Highness Princess Liliuokalani gave a luau, or native feast, at her residence in Washington Place Beretania Street, yesterday afternoon, to those who were with her on the late excursion to Nihoa, or Bird Island. This feast was given in accordance with an ancient Hawaiian custom by which those who have been on a long journey together meet to have a feast, called "hoopau luhi," which may be translated "to drive away the last weariness of the journey." There was a [handsome] native feast, hula dancing, and songs, as well as music by the Royal Hawaiian Band. Their Majesties the King and Queen were present.[132]

On August 4, the *Advertiser* announced Liliu's departure "this day" for Hana on the steamer *C. R. Bishop*.[133] She returned to Honolulu August 9 by the same ship. On August 13, she and the royal family were present at a memorial service for the deceased U.S. President Ulysses S. Grant at the Fort Street Church.

---

131. *Pacific Commercial Advertiser*, July 27, 1885.
132. *Pacific Commercial Advertiser*, July 29, 1885.
133. *Pacific Commercial Advertiser*, August 4, 1885.

September 2 was Liliu's 47th birthday, and the *Advertiser* reported the following:

> ¶ The anniversary of the birth of Her Royal Highness Princess Liliuokalani was kept in a very pleasant manner yesterday. During the day Her Royal Highness... was called upon at her residence, Waikiki, by numerous friends.... The government and engine house flags were flying, and a salute of 19 guns was fired from the shore battery at noon. Her Royal Highness gave a party at that hour to those who accompanied her on the late excursion to Nihoa, or Bird Island. It was a most enjoyable affair.[134]

In October, there was an excursion to the island of Hawaii:

> ¶ H.R.H. Princess Liliuokalani and H.R.H. Princess Poomaikelani, Governess of Hawaii, accompanied by Captain Sam Nowlein and Mrs. J. Kaae, left for Hilo, Hawaii, yesterday by the steamer *Kinau*. They will be gone about two weeks, during which time they will stay at the splendid mansion of the Governess at Hilo. His Majesty the King, His Excellency Governor J. O. Dominis, and Colonel C. P. Iaukea were at the wharf to see the royal and distinguished party off. The *Kinau* flew the royal insignia at her mainmast when she left the wharf.[135]

Liliu and Poomaikelani returned to Honolulu on October 24.

---

[The diary then resumes with two brief entries.]

*Monday, November 2.* Wrote some Letters to Maui to contribute for the King's birthday.

*Tuesday, December 8.* Came very near parting with my dearest friend on account of tattlers—Leave today in *Kinau* [for Hilo].

---

Although the diary ends abruptly at this point, further newspaper articles give an account of the departure for Hilo that Liliu mentions in her final entry for the year, and what occurred during that visit: "Their Majesties the King and Queen and Her Excellency the Governess of Hawaii leave by the *Kinau* this afternoon. The Royal party will land at Lahaina and afterwards visit Wailuku. From there they will proceed to Kailua, Hawaii."[136]

The next day, the *Advertiser* described the scene at the ship's departure:

> ¶ There was a gay scene at the wharf of the Wilder Steamship Company yesterday to witness the departure of the *Kinau* with the Royal party on board. The wharf was crowded with spectators, and the Royal Hawaiian Band... discoursed excellent music. Their Majesties the King and Queen arrived about a quarter before four o'clock, the band playing the national anthem. The Royal Party consisted of Their Maj-

---

134. *Pacific Commercial Advertiser*, September 3, 1885.
135. *Pacific Commercial Advertiser*, October 13, 1885.
136. *Pacific Commercial Advertiser*, December 8, 1885.

esties the King and Queen, Her Royal Highness Princess Liliuokalani, and Her Royal Highness Princess Poomaikelani, Governess of Hawaii; Hons. Samuel Parker, J. A. Cummins, and Col. Chas. H. Judd, His Majesties' Chamberlain. The Royal party went away loaded down with wreaths and leis. As the steamer left her dock the band played "Aloha Oe" and "Hawaii Ponoi." After visiting Lahaina and Wailuku the Royal party will proceed to Kailua, Hawaii. Her Royal Highness Princess Likelike, His Excellency W. M. Gibson, Minister of Foreign Affairs, His Excellency George W. Merrill, United States Minister Resident, Mrs. F. H. Hayselden, Mrs. C. T. Gulick, and Col. C. P. Iaukea were present at the wharf.[137]

The *Advertiser* later reported: "The royal party will go overland to Hilo this week. On the 31st of the month, the anniversary of the birth of Her Majesty the Queen will be appropriately celebrated at the latter place, and it is expected the Royal party will return to Honolulu the first week in January."[138] The *Advertiser* also printed a local account on the reception of the king and queen at Hilo:

¶ Hilo, Hawaii, December 24.
I have just time to say that their Majesties the King and Queen, Her Royal Highness Princess Liliuokalani, and her Royal Highness Princess Poomaikelani... arrived this morning... His Majesty and Sam Parker landed in a double canoe with ten rowers in ancient style. It being rough weather, the Royal ladies preferred trusting themselves to a whaleboat.

On arrival of the canoe in the surf fifty natives testified their loyalty and devotion to His Majesty by rushing onto the surf and picking it up bodily and carrying it to a staging on the beach. The boat containing the ladies was carried in the same way. The King and Queen were received with a salute of twenty-one guns and escorted to the residence of the Governess under a series of arches, each having an appropriate motto in Hawaiian.

The coming week bids fair to be the liveliest Hilo has seen for some time. We hear of luaus, dinners, and receptions without end, and Hilo intends to show their Majesties that it appreciates the kindly interest they have always shown in the advancement of the Hawaiian race. Aloha Ka Moi.[139]

---

137. *Pacific Commercial Advertiser*, December 9, 1885.
138. *Pacific Commercial Advertiser*, December 21, 1885.
139. *Pacific Commercial Advertiser*, December 28, 1885. The closing phrase means "Love to the king."

*Government buildings directly across the street from Iolani Palace, 1889. Government offices and the legislative hall were in Aliiolani Hale, at center with clock tower. Kapuaiwa, an annex building named in honor of Lot Kapuaiwa, Kamehameha V, is at left near Punchbowl Street. The Opera House, at right across from the front gate of the palace grounds, is on the site now occupied by the U.S. Post Office, Custom House, and Court House. The photograph was taken from the rooftop or the front tower windows of Iolani Palace by a member of the visiting Prince and Princess Henri de Bourbon's party.*
Hawaii State Archives

# 1886

*Friday, January 1, 1886.* A beautiful day in Hilo. Went to call on the residents of Hilo with the Queen—distributed money among the King's people.[1]

Called on Mr. and Mrs. Sam Parker,[2] Mr. and Mrs. Graham, Mrs. Hastings,[3] Mrs. Lowrey,[4] who were staying at Mrs. Arnold's.[5]

Had to sail that afternoon on *Kinau* for Honolulu. Bade Queen and Governess of Hawaii good-bye. Met King, Col. [Charles] Judd, and large crowd on the beach and bade good-bye. Those who attended [me] are Sheriff Kaulukou, Mr. Sam Nowlein[6] and daughter [Maili], Miss Sheldon.

THE DIARY FOR 1886

1 JAN–31 DEC

Bishop Museum Archives

1. "The Royal party will celebrate the Queen's birthday Dec. 31st at Hilo, returning to Honolulu the first week in January." *Daily Bulletin*, "Local Diary, Hilo, December 21," January 2, 1886.

"Her Majesty Queen Kapiolani is fifty-one years of age today. The event is being celebrated by the royal family at Hilo, Hawaii. In town [Honolulu] there is a goodly display of flags. The King's Own volunteer military company fired 21 guns at the battery this noon in honor of the anniversary." *Daily Bulletin*, "Local Diary, Hilo, December 31," January 2, 1886.

2. Samuel Parker was a ranch owner and government official under the monarchy. Born at Mana, Hamakua, Hawaii, in 1853, he was the grandson of John Parker, founder of the Parker Ranch. He served as a politician from 1884, and in February 1891 he was appointed premier and minister of foreign affairs in Liliuokalani's cabinet. He and his uncle, J. P. Parker, owned the Parker Ranch, which at the turn of the century comprised about 500,000 acres of land and upwards of 20,000 cattle. In 1906, Sam Parker disposed of his share of the ranch to his niece Thelma Parker (retaining a sheep ranch at Humuula) and the family home at Mana, but eventually these too passed out of his hands. It is said that at Mana he entertained guests (which in the 1860s included Liliu and her husband Dominis on several occasions) with "almost royal splendor." A profligate spender during the Kalakaua era, he would be fighting off several bankruptcy proceedings in the Honolulu courts later as the monarchy fell.

He married twice, first on August 23, 1871, to Harriet Napela of Wailuku, Maui (she died in 1901), and second in San Francisco on January 3, 1902, to Abigail Maipinepine Campbell, the widow of James Campbell and the mother of Princess Abigail Kawananakoa. Parker died at midnight, March 19, 1920, at 66 years.

3. Alice Makee (b. 1859–d. 1913) was the daughter of Captain James Makee of Maui and wife of Frank P. Hastings.

4. Cherilla Lowrey (d. 1918) was the wife of Honolulu merchant Frederick Jewett Lowrey of Lewers and Cooke.

5. The Charles Arnolds were proprietors of a boarding establishment in Hilo.

6. Samuel Nowlein (b. April 3, 1851, Molokai–d. December 6, 1905, Lahaina) was the son of longtime Lahaina entrepreneur Michael J. Nowlein. Sam Nowlein had a long military career. He was captain of the King's Own starting in January 12, 1882. In 1886, he became quartermaster of the Forces; in 1888, major of the Hawaiian Volunteers; and in 1891, major on Governor Dominis's staff. He was a familiar presence in and about Washington Place. He (with Robert Wilcox as his lieutenant) was the prime mover behind the failed 1895 counter-revolution, after which Nowlein turned state's evidence, and he and Liliuokalani did not thereafter speak. Following his and the ex-Queen's trials, he departed Honolulu for Lahaina. His first wife, Lucy, died in Lahaina in 1899. His second wife, whom he married in 1903, was Emma Smithies.

Touched at Laupahoehoe and Mahukona, Kawaihae. Had to leave King's party on account of John's illness.

*Saturday, January 2.* Arrived at Mahukona [and] stayed all day. It was a windy day. Arrived at Lahaina that eve—the old town was illuminated.

*Sunday, January 3.* Arrived at Honolulu at six A.M., found John very low—how thin and emaciated he looks, but surrounded with many kind friends—J. Brown, Capt. Tripp,[7] and Dr. Trousseau[8] and many others. He brightened up when he heard my voice.

*Monday, January 4.* He is just the same, very weak—but we try to make things around him bright and cheerful—scarcely eats.

*Saturday, January 9.* My husband is much better and received their Majesties,[9] Major Hoapili,[10] Ministers Kapena,[11] Sam Maikai.[12]

Early that Morning went to the upper story in Palace to watch the arrival of King and party—line of soldiers under officer Solomon, and Band were in front of steps. The Queen drove up to Palace and came up the steps—the King surprised us from behind.[13]

---

7. Alfred N. Tripp (b. 1840–d. December 28, 1913, Honolulu) was a Massachusetts-born sea captain who arrived in Hawaii on the bark *Aurora* in 1863, and became a more or less permanent resident. He was a friend of both John O. Dominis and Liliuokalani. His obituary says Tripp married into one of the "alii families" but does not further identify his wife. *Pacific Commercial Advertiser*, December 29, 1913.

8. Dr. Georges Philippe Trousseau (b. May 1, 1833, Paris–d. May 4, 1894, Honolulu) was a physician, former sugar plantation owner, and sheep rancher on the island of Hawaii and an ostrich farmer on Oahu. He was a friend of Kalakaua and was the executor of his will. See May 4–7, 1894, diary entries (417–18).

9. The king and queen returned to Honolulu on the *Kinau* from Hilo. The *Pacific Commercial Advertiser* report of dignitaries meeting Their Majesties both at the wharf and at the palace does not mention Dominis, so the meeting may have been private and at Washington Place.

10. Robert Hoapili Baker (b. 1847–d. April 4, 1900, Honolulu) was a descendent of Hawaii and Maui chiefs, and married Emma Mersberg. He was one of the most trusted associates of both Kalakaua and Liliuokalani. His military career was as follows: 1878, lieutenant of the Household Forces; 1884, adjutant, King's Guard; March 1, 1884, appointed major of the Military Forces; and 1889, colonel on the king's staff, a position he held during Liliuokalani's reign. He was also governor of Maui in 1886 and a member of the Privy Council, 1884–91.

11. John Makini Kapena (b. October 2, 1843–d. October 24, 1887, Honolulu) was a long-serving government official. He was a member of the Privy Council, 1863–74; colonel on King Lunalilo's staff, 1873; governor of Maui, 1874–76; member of the House of Nobles, 1876–86; minister of finance, 1876–78 and 1883–85; minister of foreign affairs, 1878–80; postmaster general, 1881–83; special envoy and minister plenipotentiary to Japan, 1882; and collector general of customs, 1886–87. He married Emma Malo in 1863 and was the father of Leihulu, frequently mentioned in Liliu's diaries.

12. Samuel Ikuwa Ulumaheihei Maikai, of a Hawaiian chiefly family, was a military protégé of Kalakaua. In 1885, he was appointed lieutenant, Prince's Own; in 1886, second lieutenant, King's Guard; captain in 1887; and sublieutenant in the Royal Hawaiian Navy, 1887, on the *Kaimiloa* expedition to Samoa. His wife, Annie Lilikalani (whom he married in 1873), was a good friend of Liliuokalani.

13. "Their Majesties the King and Queen being expected to arrive this morning by the steamer *Kinau* arrangements were made for a right royal reception. The royal Guards, headed by the Royal Band, were to escort the royal party from the steamer's wharf to the palace, but through some misadventure the steamer *Likelike* was reported as being the *Kinau*, and, at an early hour this morning, the Royal Guards marched to the beat of a still drum to receive the King and party, who did not arrive. It was deemed best, after the blunder was committed, to receive the party at the palace with a truly civic occasion. As the steamer *Kinau* approached her berth this morning with the royal standard flying from the mainmast, a royal salute of seven-second guns was fired from the battery on honor of the arrival of their Majesties. The Governor's staff—Majors Rosa and Holt and Col. Boyd in uniform were on the wharf when the steamer came in, as also were Hons. W. M. Gibson, J. A. Cummins, A. S. Cleghorn, and others, who accompanied the royal procession to the Palace." *Daily Bulletin*, January 9, 1886.

*Friday, January 22.* Received by *Malulani*[14] a letter from J. G. Hoapili—also a note—on draft for amount of $125.00 and $72.00 in silver from Elena, Super Cargo of *Malulani*—rent for Keahuolu.

*Saturday, January 23.* After all the confinement of attending a sick husband—went to Dr. Brodie[15] about sore eyes. I was touched with caustic. Two hours after, took Kaipo out to drive.

Met Mr. and Mrs. 'so & so' for the first time.

*Sunday, January 24.* Took a drive in afternoon to Waikiki—called at Pupule's to see Hinau and Luhea and found Eveline and Johnnie Wilson.

*Monday, January 25.* Arranged to receive [blank] on consultation on important matters, but she would not permit him to come, on pleas of illness. John is still ill but went out a little while. My old friend spent the evening with me.

*Tuesday, January 26.* The King left on *Malulani* for Kona.[16]

Called on Mrs. Schmidt, Mrs. Loser, Mrs. Canavarro—Mrs. Judd. At seven P.M. went to Mary Ailau's sixth anniversary of their wedding.[17] Myself, the young couple, Mr. and Mrs. Kaae, Miss L. Richards, Harry Auld. Wrote by *Malulani* to J. G. Hoapili[18] [to] acknowledge the receipt of the amount $196—of Keahuolu. Received a note from C.

*Wednesday, January 27.* Answered a note and made arrangements for the evening with him—but earlier went with Jessie to consult the Fortuneteller. She predicted trouble in money matters—which is so through C.B.W. [Charles B. Wilson] but better days are in store. The rest of prediction remains to be seen (Met my new friend—C.) My lucky days are Mondays and Wednesdays—and Months are—April, May, June, Sept., Nov., December. If in 9 or 10 months my wish is not realized do not consult—anymore.

*Thursday, January 28.* Took two hats to Fishel's[19] to trim. Called on Dole[20] with C. B. Wilson, to pay $112.00 the amount due on J. Aea's debt in

---

14. The steamer *W. G. Hall* was also referred to as the *Malulani*.

15. Dr. John Brodie (b. March 7, 1853, Quebec, Canada–d. November 2, 1895, Honolulu), a graduate of McGill University, came to Honolulu about 1877, and practiced medicine in both Hawaii and San Francisco.

16. "The Royal Hawaiian Band was playing on the Inter-Island wharf this afternoon, in honor of the sailing of His Majesty, who left by the steamer *W. G. Hall* [also referred to as the *Malulani*] for Kailua." *Daily Bulletin*, January 26, 1886.

17. Mary Pitman Ailau (b. 1838, Hilo?–d. February 11, 1905, Hilo) was the daughter of the chiefess Kinoole and Benjamin Pitman, a Hilo and Honolulu businessman. Her husband, John K. Ailau (b. 1855–d. January 17, 1894, San Francisco), was a printer and compositor by profession, and a well-known and popular musician of the day.

18. J. G. Hoapili was a district magistrate on Hawaii, residing in Keauhou, Kona.

19. Fishel's (Chas. J. Fishel), located on the corner of Hotel and Fort Streets, was a purveyor of millinery and ladies' cloaks and suits. The name sometimes appears as Fischel.

20. Sanford Ballard Dole (b. April 23, 1844, Honolulu–d. June 9, 1926, Honolulu) was a lawyer, a Supreme Court justice, and the head of both the Provisional Government and the Republic of Hawaii. The son of Reverend Daniel Dole (b. 1808–d. 1878), a missionary and the principal of Punahou School, Sanford studied at Williams College for one year, and then studied law in Boston. He was admitted to the Massachusetts Bar Association in 1868, and returned to the islands in December of that year. On May 19, 1873, he married Anna P. Cate of Castine, Maine. He served in the 1884 legislature and as associate justice of the Supreme Court, 1886 and 1893; president of the Provisional Government, 1893; president of the Republic of Hawaii, 1894–98; and first governor of the Territory of Hawaii, June 14, 1900–November 23, 1903.

mortgaging his Waimanalo [sugar plantation][21] shares towards paying Mr. Parker on Hezekia Aea's account, and received back his Certificates— No. 1029—1030—1032—1033—with notes of release from Dole.

Came home to Muolaulani Hale. How nice to be surrounded with everything luxurious, in one's own home.

*Friday, January 29.* Made arrangement with J. F. Colburn[22] to buy next lot [to Muolaulani] for $2,000 belonging to Kanoa's estate.

*Saturday, January 30.* Went to Govt. building and signed lease of Hamohamo and Kaneloa to Goo Kim.[23]

Turned my affairs over to A. J. Cartwright as C. B. Wilson had resigned.[24]

Rec'd $400.00 of my salary. Went to consult the Queen about Kealahao—no satisfaction. Signed paper at Washington Place giving A. J. Cartwright full Power of Attorney to act for me in all matters. Brought Kaipo up to spend afternoon. Had girls out for the day—drove around to the Band at five—just arrived when Mr. and Mrs. Iaukea passed by very close. Took Kaipo back to Mrs. Bush.[25]

6½ P.M. Went to Hospital to see Kealahao—pretty low. Came home and slept over to Poikeala Hale. T. A. [sic, T. B.] Walker's *trial* today for embezzlement.[26]

21. J. A. Cummins was president and manager of Waimanalo Sugar Co. in the Waimanalo Valley, Koolau. The 7,000-acre plantation had 1,000 acres of sugarcane under cultivation, and the 1884–85 City Directory says it had an "estimated yield for 1884—1,800 tons. Hackfeld & Co. Agents."

22. John F. Colburn (b. September 30, 1859, Honolulu–d. March 16, 1920) was the part-Hawaiian son of John F. Colburn (d. 1861) and Elizabeth Maughan (d. 1889), and a grandson of early Spanish resident Don Francisco de Paula Marín. He was prominent in politics, and was Liliuokalani's minister of the Interior Department at the time of the overthrow. He was subsequently manager of the Kapiolani Estate.

23. This lease, dated January 29, 1886, to Goo Kim Fui (for the consideration of $1,535 at $50 per annum for 15 years), was an extension of an earlier lease of 1884, the lease area including ten loi (irrigated terrace) or kalo patches for the cultivation of rice and taro, adjoining the Kalia stream on the two Waikiki lands. Bureau of Conveyances, Liber 84, 145, and Liber 100, 86.

24. On January 30, Liliu and her husband, J. O. Dominis, being indebted to Cartwright in the sum of $5,000, signed a power of attorney in his favor specifically granting him as their agent, to collect rents and to generally conduct her business. Bureau of Conveyances, Liber 99, 104. The document was canceled October 23, 1888. Cartwright published the following notice in several Honolulu papers beginning February 3, 1886: "Notice. All persons having claims against H.R.H. Liliuokalani will please present them at once (with items and dates) to her agent Alex J. Cartwright."

25. Caroline Paakaiulaula French Poor Bush was a close friend of Liliu. Born in Honolulu in March 3, 1836, the daughter of merchant William French and Lydia Panioikawai Hunt, she first married (in 1856) Henry Francis Poor, and second (in 1873) A. W. Bush. She is now remembered as a friend of the Robert Louis Stevenson family, and that author dedicated a poem to her on the occasion of her birthday in 1889. In the 1880s, Mrs. Bush was living in a house on Emma Street (now part of the Royal School's grounds) and took in boarders (primarily children) to make ends meet. These included both of the Queen's hanai (adopted) children, Kaipo Aea and John Dominis Aimoku. Mrs. Bush died in Honolulu on January 27, 1914.

26. Thomas B. Walker (b. 1848–d. 1932), an island resident starting in 1876, and the husband of Matilda Cummins, a daughter of John A. Cummins, was charged with breaking and entering at the post office, and then removing $2,500 "of the goods, chattels, and moneys of the Hawaiian Government," on January 4, 1886. The trial was scheduled for April 6, 1886, and on April 8 a jury found him not guilty. The *Daily Bulletin* published a full account of the matter in its January 30 and February 1, 1886, issues.

*Sunday, January 31.* Mrs. Dowsett came in early to have a chat in my dressing room turning over some calico—gave her twelve yards. We breakfasted together. Mr. J. W. Robertson[27] called to see if he could write to the King about applying for Mr. Peterson's ~~place~~ office in the Post office. People always come to me to apply for them. I am quite sure I have no more to do with offices than the man in the moon. Drove with Wakeke to Waikiki. Took Kaiulani in, and drove on to the Park. Met Kahuila[28] and Mary Ailau at Hospital gate—they told me Kealahau—Mrs. Molteno and Miss Kenway were all improving.

*Monday, February 1.* Trimmed trees until 11—Curtis Iaukea came in to say he was going to Maui to watch election—in favor of [Luther] Aholo—by Neumann. [Partially erased: "wrote to Aholo not"] to give in—Campbell tries to run to spoil Aholo's votes—Kalua for Opposition, Kia for Govt.—Bosh!

Went to return Oliver's [Oliver Carter's] Hat—bought some whips for Kahili [feather standard] handles $2.25.

A rainy day. 6½ P.M. went to see Dr. Stangenwald[29] but was disappointed—was seized with dizziness. Slept at Hinano Bower. Got letters from Kapoli.

*Tuesday, February 2.* Paid Waikiki Pake [Chinese] $20. Wrote to C. B. Wilson to send by Joe my pictures—[and] new bed, and offered to have Wakeke to go for their certificates of stock and for Aimoku's bank book. Sister called a little while—C. B. Wilson came in and gave me in my keeping, Wakeke's two certificates of Waimanalo stocks, two for Kawehena, and one for Kaipo—besides two shares for Wakeke in Paukaa [plantation] and $50—$20 for Wakeke, $20 for Kawehena and ten for Kaipo, the remaining amount of their dividend of December and January. [Paul] Neumann, the Attorney General, called today to [say] that he had sent Curtis [Iaukea] up to Maui. Joe took his brake to Page to be repaired. Goo Kim and Chulan called to invite me to their Konghee [Chinese New Year] tomorrow. Cartwright called with the bills $5,051.63—imagine my astonishment.

*Wednesday, February 3.* Started for the Palace at nine, went right upstairs and breakfasted with the Queen. At ten the Aha Hoola Lahui met.[30] Ten

---

27. James William Robertson (b. December 1852, Honolulu–d. January 28, 1919, Honolulu) was the son of Supreme Court Justice George M. Robertson (d. 1867). James Robertson married Rosa Cleghorn, the daughter of Archibald S. Cleghorn, in 1876. He was a stationer with H. M. Whitney, and in 1882 he started the *Daily Bulletin* newspaper. On October 1, 1888, King Kalakaua appointed him vice chamberlain, and on March 2, 1891, Queen Liliuokalani appointed him chamberlain. After the 1893 overthrow, he remained in the Queen's service (unpaid) until the formation of the Republic of Hawaii.

28. Elizabeth Kahuila Wilcox (b. March 13, 1857, Nuuanu–d. July 19, 1913, Waikiki) was the wife of William Luther Wilcox. He was the son of Kauai missionaries Abner and Lucy Wilcox, and was a noted judge and court translator.

29. Hugo Stangenwald (b. February 19, 1829, Germany–d. June 1, 1899, Honolulu) arrived in Hawaii in 1853 as a daguerrean artist. He later (in 1858) studied medicine and returned to the islands as a physician. He married Mary Dimond, the daughter of Honolulu merchant Henry Dimond. Following her death in 1865, he married her sister Anne (d. 1914).

30. "Hoola Lahui" (increase the nation) had been an election campaign motto of David

dollars voted for Kealahao. Left them at 11 to attend the opening of a Chinese Club House.[31]

This is also Konghee day and also election day.[32]

Returned to the Palace with Mrs. Dowsett and spent the rest of the day. 8½ P.M. Govt. tickets [their candidates] came ahead. Kekaha, Keau, J. Baker, Lilikalani, for here, Kauahikaua [with "Cecil" written above] for Koolauloa, Amara for Waialua, Kaulia for Koolaupoko, Kauhi for Ewa, and Waianae opposition. Good.[33]

Spent the night at Washington [Place,] gave John the news of the day.

*Thursday, February 4.* A lovely day. A.M. at Washington [Place], from there went to see Kealahao—found her better—came back to Mary Ailau, gave her directions to go to Kamakanoe, and then go to Davies for underclothes for K. Went back to Washington [Place] to wait for Joe's bills. C. B. Wilson came in and tells me those pigs were not his but mine, all the time which I was not aware of before. [He?] gave me a pig. Joe returned the hat. 6½ P.M. went to town. King St. was crowded with Chinese firing crackers. How beautifully the streets are lighted with Chinese lanterns. No doctor—sat with John awhile, then came home.

Kalakaua when he was seeking office in 1874, and soon after, the new monarch and Queen Kapiolani formed the Hooulu and Hoola Lahui Society to aid sick and indigent Hawaiians. Queen Kapiolani was both president and an active participant. This society laid the foundation for the Kapiolani Maternity Home. On December 15, 1891, the minister of the interior granted a charter of incorporation to Queen Dowager Kapiolani, Emma M. Nakuina, Alice Mackintosh, Elizabeth K. Wilcox, and Annie Ulukou, trustees, "under the name of the Kapiolani Home of the Hooulu and Hoola Society, for the purposes of Benevolence and charity and for the general object of providing a Maternity Home where Hawaiian Women can receive proper care and treatment during the period of childbirth." Hawaii State Archives, Flora Jones Collection, manuscript draft. There was also a Hooulu Lahui Society at Kaumakapili Church, but the two groups do not seem to have been connected.

31. "Last evening the celebration of Chinese New Year was begun by the celestial residents with universal spirit. The streets in Chinatown were transformed into beautiful vistas of chromatic light, from thousands of lanterns ranged in mathematical lines from above and below the ever-lasting verandas. A terrific bombardment of fireworks was sustained against the slumbers of all within earshot.... The store on the ground floor of the Benevolent Society's new Club House, King Street, was cheerfully lighted up, and the manager of the firm was there to receive visitors.... The ceremonies connected with the formal opening of the New Chinese Club House commenced at 11 o'clock. The Royal Hawaiian Band had taken a position in front of the building at seven o'clock, and played in their usual effective style, and were relieved a little before 11 by the Reformatory School Band. According to previous announcement and invitation there were present Her Royal Highness the Princess Liliuokalani, His Majesty's Chamberlain Col. Judd [and so on]." *Daily Bulletin*, February 3, 1886.

32. The legislative election of 1886, a contest between the government's National Reform Party and the opposition, the Reform Party, took place at Aliiolani Hale. After the polls closed, "the counting of ballots was completed within a few minutes of seven o'clock, and it was soon known to the multitudes assembled around Aliiolani Hale that the National candidates had won a most emphatic victory. Cheers after cheers were sent up. Orators by the score shouted forth paeans of exultation and victory or apologies for defeat." *Pacific Commercial Advertiser*, February 4, 1886. The final results were announced at ten minutes past eight o'clock— "a signal victory for the government." *Daily Bulletin*, February 4, 1886.

33. The candidates Liliu mentions were Kekaha, the Honorable James Keau, the Honorable John T. Baker, Edward Lilikalani for Honolulu, the Honorable Jesse Amara for Waialua district, Asa Kaulia for Koolaupoko, and A. Kauhi for Ewa, all candidates on the National ticket. Cecil Brown of the opposition defeated Kauahikaua, a National candidate for Koolauloa, by seven votes.

Joe went down according to instructions from me, to collect my bills, and Mr. Wilson told them not to give him my bills but to take them to Cartwright—now this would only delay settlement.

*Friday, February 5.* After breakfast started for Palolo [but] was not successful—turned toward Manoa and found Hilo lying sick. Spoke of the rents—they had used the whole up—came home [and] bought some rheumatic medicine for her. Kuamoo and Kamoehookahi came to complain against [bandmaster Henri or Henry] Berger for saying he would retain $5 of his for not coming to serenade Ahlee on Konghee day.

Louika is in trouble about Hinau's land—can do nothing for her.

Slept at Hinano Bower. P.M. Joe came home from Waikiki—with bags of fish. Sent them around to Kunuiakea[34] and others. Five P.M. Widemann's house is burnt down to the ground.[35]

*Saturday, February 6.* Joe and Willie Aylett called early for advice on borrow[ing] money, $4,000 to buy Mr. Beckley's lot from W. A. [William Aldrich.] Promised to see A. J. Cartwright, was unsuccessful for him but would get it for me.

Had my eyes operated on. Came home to dine, then started out again for Mr. Bishop, while the Band is playing opposite. Saw Willie about the lot, not to give up but to search for some monied man. Hope Joe will take it. Saw Dr. Stangenwald. [He] gave me very little hopes. Slept at Hinano Bower. P.M. Joe went for his brake and brought Romeo [a horse] in. [He] reports Frank and Charlie [horses] to be in a poor condition.

*Sunday, February 7.* At two Kunuiakea and wife and Annie Dowsett dined with me, at four took a drive to Waikiki and brought Aimoku back. After tea went back to Washington [Place] to spend the night. Gave Apo $1 for vegetables. Kahae came in to gas and Joe had to come and take her home.

*Monday, February 8.* Wrote to Curtis. Sent Joe and Paulo to take Piliula and Frank and [horses] out to Waikiki and bring Queen [a horse] back to Pawaa. Send bills to A. J. Cartwright [partially erased: at not come for fear of suspicion.] At nine ½ P.M., [blank] came and went home huhu [angry]—what nonsense. Col. Judd called to consult about garden party. Our folks drunk. Sent Wakeke for Dr. and Mrs. Wight.

---

34. Albert Kukailimoku Kunuiakea (b. June 18, 1851, Honolulu–d. March 10, 1903, Honolulu) was the natural son of Kamehameha III and Jane Lahilahi Kaeo, the daughter of John Young. Although the son of a monarch, he was never in line for the throne, and held his title of prince only by courtesy. He was a cousin of Queen Emma. Albert was in and out of trouble much of his life, and caused problems for Queen Emma's estate. He married Mrs. Mary Poli (d. April 6, 1904) in 1878.

35. "About four o'clock yesterday afternoon the alarm was given for a fire in the residence of Hon. H. A. Widemann on Beretania Street, at Punahou. The first engine to reach the spot was No. 2, but the flames had progressed so far that the saving of the house was impossible. Before the arrival of the brigade the inmates of the house, assisted by neighbors, managed to save most of the parlor furniture and a few prized articles, including pictures of two daughters of Mr. Widemann who died in Germany, a fine oil painting of Kamehameha V, and an upright piano. The house was burned to the ground.... It was supposed the fire originated from children setting off firecrackers in a bedroom.... Mr. and Mrs. Widemann were absent at Waianae and received the news of the disaster by telephone.... The total loss is estimated at $16,000." *Daily Bulletin*, February 6, 1886.

*Tuesday, February 9.* Received a call from Curtis P. Iaukea, came to report himself after his trip to Maui, reports Aholo's success as a member for Lahaina.[36]

Callers came home—busy all morning posting up bills. Two P.M. called for John, took him to Steamer *Kinau*, picked Lu Brickwood[37] up. Drove in with her—offered to have Kaipo stay with them—Lu said she would ask her mother. Slept in Kaipo's bed[room].

*Wednesday, February 10.* Nine A.M. Started for Auction[38] at Queen Emma's, bought Kahilis [royal feather standards]—mats—calabashes—washbasins, came home at two tired—dined and received a call from Annie Hall and Liza Holt. The latter informs me of Jimmie Holt's marriage with Helen Stillman,[39] would like me to come to their dinner [at] four, but I am going to have my reception—[had] a lone cup of tea.

*Thursday, February 11.* Met Mr. Herbert[40]—he would bring my money around of the W. [Waimanalo] Stocks—but I told him my own was all in A. J. Cartwright's hands—[he] said that he would bring those on Saturday. Saw Cartwright—placed bills in his hands. Went to Queen Emma's to see after my purchases—all right. Charlie came in to assure me nothing is wrong about my money. Band is here. Three boys [on the] committee [came] to ask me to be their Treasurer, Willie, Kapua, Kaulelehua—accepted. Time for my reception. Keu ka huhu [So angry]—all right. Mr. Chas Gay[41] called. Invited him to go with us to the Queen's Garden Party.

*Friday, February 12.* Early visit from the Queen. Why should she be in tears—the day of Accession to the throne and yet the King is absent at Kailua. Three P.M. Sophy [Sheldon] and I stopped at Ehlers[42] for gloves—took two pairs—had no money, will pay tomorrow. Took Mr. Gay in [to the Queen's garden party at the palace]. People gaily dressed, flocked in to see the Queen. A pleasant affair.[43]

36. In the final tally of votes, J. W. Kalua, the opposition candidate, received 190 votes, and L. Aholo, the national candidate, received 177 votes. As there were two seats available, both candidates were elected. *Pacific Commercial Advertiser*, February 8, 1886.

37. Louisa Brownscombe Brickwood (b. 1849–d. November 10, 1909, Honolulu) was the daughter of Louisa Ahung Gilman and Arthur P. Brickwood (b. 1807–d. 1883). Known as Lu or Lou, she was an intimate friend of Liliu. She was a schoolteacher at the Royal School on Emma Street, and vice president of the Liliuokalani Educational Society.

38. This was a sale of Queen Emma's "Calabashes, Native Kapas, Leis, Mats and Small Kahilis." The advertisement for the same in the February 8, 1886, *Pacific Commercial Advertiser* noted, "There are over 200 calabashes, made from a variety of island woods such as Kou, Cocoanut, and Koa, and in different styles and sizes. The cocoanut Calabashes upon silver stands, presented to Her late Majesty by members of the Royal Family of Pomare, Queen of the Society Islands, are very interesting as curiosities and also as mementos of two Queens."

39. Helen Anianiku Stillman (b. 1862–d. 1950) married rancher James R. Holt at Saint Andrew's Cathedral on February 10, 1886. She later married John K. Cushingham.

40. Allen Herbert (b. 1821–d. 1921), the Swedish-born proprietor of the Hawaiian Hotel and the Sans Souci resort at Waikiki, was a jovial host, familiarly known as "Papa."

41. Charles Gay (b. 1862, New Zealand–d. 1937, Honolulu) was a member of the Gay and Robinson families, and a rancher on the island of Lanai.

42. B. F. Ehlers, Dry Goods Importers, at 99 Fort Street, in its running advertisement in various newspapers stated that it had "all the latest novelties in fancy goods received by every steamer."

43. "A Royal Party. Yesterday having been the third anniversary of the coronation of Their Majesties the King and Queen, a garden party was given by Her Majesty on the Palace grounds. The party was the great social event of the day and of the season as well. The Queen was attended on the occasion by the Princesses Liliuokalani and Likelike. Besides the high officers of state, foreign ministers, members of the consular corps, judges of the Supreme Court, and

Doomed to another disappointment—J. [John] could not come—may [I] be rewarded yet—well, so I went to the Palace, spent the night and may spend another one yet. I was told J. had gone to Maui. A lovely night—Jessie kept me company.

*Saturday, February 13.* Stole away from the Palace, the Queen still asleep. Went to the hospital. Everyone well—went to see Mother [Dominis], came home.

Breakfasted and sent Wakeke down to pay my Auction bill $183.50 to A. J. Cartwright [and] $3.75 to Ehlers for gloves. Rec'd $50 from Allen Herbert—Waimanalo stocks for my people—Joe A. [Aea] owing me $112, I have detained his money till debt is paid, also Wakeke owed $10. Today her debt is pau [ended]. I keep Kaipo's to add to his bank [account]. Okuu came about Lumahai[44]—Col. Judd [came] about letters from the King. John Holt wants to be Messenger for the House of Legislature, Malo [wants] to be sheriff of Ewa.

Just returned from a drive with Kaipo. Lunalilo Home was opened to the public today. Band plays up there.[45]

Went to [Dr.] Stangenwald—no [word erased]. Went to fortune tellers, from there to Hotel—[continued at top of page] then home—a lovely moonlight night.

*Sunday, February 14.* Aroused by the Queen this morning. Told me she had bought ten more shares of Waimanalo Stock. Annie comes to tell me of *Mariposa* to sail at nine. Received news that John had arrived from Maui sick and hastened up to attend him—a severe cold he took. Mrs. Dr. Wight[46] would like to have her son-in-law appointed Judge for Kohala[47] during Hart's absence.[48]

*City of Peking* arrived off the harbor—too large to come in—over 900 Japanese on board.[49]

---

clergy of the Anglican, Roman Catholic, and other churches, the entrances were thronged with a continuous flow of visitors, from three o'clock until six o'clock. The guests were presented to Her Majesty, who was seated under one of the luxuriant shade trees . . . after which they filed into the Palace and registered their names. The Palace was thrown open to inspection, to the great delight of the guests. . . . Having 'done' the interior of the Palace, the guests amused themselves during the rest of the evening strolling through the grounds. Ice cream, cake, and coffee were served. . . . A noticeable and highly agreeable feature of the whole affair was the perfectly free and easy informality that prevailed. The Royal Hawaiian Band was present and enlivened the occasion with an excellent program of national and other music." *Daily Bulletin*, February 13, 1886.

44. Liliu had been left a life interest in the land of Lumahai on Kauai by Bernice P. Bishop. Okuu's interest in the land is unknown.

45. "By permission of the Hon A. S. Cleghorn, acting Governor, the Royal Hawaiian Band will play at Lunalilo Home on Saturday afternoon, from 3:30 until 5:30 o'clock, in honor of His late Majesty Lunalilo. The home will be thrown open to the general public, who are invited to attend." *Pacific Commercial Advertiser*, February 12, 1886.

46. Mrs. Jane Tompkins (d. 1915) was the wife of Dr. James Wight (b. 1814–d. 1905), physician and sugar planter (from 1850) at Kohala, Hawaii. She was a native of Cape Colony, South Africa. The Wights were in Honolulu for the session of the legislature, of which he was a member.

47. Mrs. Wight's son in law was Remus H. Atkins, a native of Ireland who had married Alice Wight in 1870. It is unclear whether Atkins got the temporary appointment, but he did serve as district magistrate for North Kohala 1894–1920.

48. Charles Frederick Hart (b. 1834, England–d. May 20, 1910, Honolulu), a resident from 1850, was judge of the Second Circuit 1864–68 and 1872–87.

49. "The *City of Peking*, 11½ days from Yokohama, arrived off Waikiki at 9.30 yesterday morning and dropped anchor there. She had on board 938 Japanese immigrants, of whom

Consul [Robert W.] Irwin came back in her.

Accident on the *Mariposa*. Two men killed instantly by steam, three taken to hospital.[50]

*Monday, February 15.* Sat alone watching John. Mary seems to be very distant. Went at four P.M. to Mrs. Dowsett's luau—at six the old folks are supposed to go home and the evening is for the young. A very pleasant affair it was.[51] Came home and was taken sick.

*Tuesday, February 16.* Such a racking headache and pain all over my body—Dr. Martin prescribed. Send for Kaipo [Aea], baby Nihoa [Aea], and Aimoku. The Queen spent the evening with me. All our folks are on the veranda asleep. Loe, Wakeke, Keliiakahai, Paulo, Mary Keamalu, Joe, Mainalulu. Mrs. Wight calls in for a moment.

*Wednesday, February 17.* The doctor came in to see me, says I am in a fair way to recover—fever all gone, but must be careful and not take fresh cold. Band was sent to emigration depot to the Japanese.[52]

[Paul] Neumann and Curtis [Iaukea] came to see us [and] was surprised to find a hospital. John sick in the other room and myself in this. Queen made an early call [at] five in the morning. Sent Joe with $23.00 to pay for the brake.

*Thursday, February 18.* The auction at Hassinger's takes place today—bought Majolica set.[53]

Will go home tomorrow. Jessie [Kaae] and Mahiai[54] came in and spoke of forming a society for women and have a bank of their own—a very good idea.

Instead of idling their time away, the women must be employed in tying feathers for Kahili [feather standards].

*Friday, February 19.* Both John and I are feeling better, and must send the folks home today. The women are still at work tying feathers. Almost all

---

fifty are able seamen, engaged by Mr. Wilder for his Island steamers.... The first debarkation took place about 3:30 P.M., the tug *Pele* bringing the first batch to the immigration barracks. The men were remarkably clean, healthy, strong, and intelligent looking." *Pacific Commercial Advertiser*, February 15, 1886.

50. Shortly after the *Mariposa* arrived (Saturday, February 13, 1886), on her maiden voyage from Sydney and Auckland, there was a boiler explosion, and two men, Richard Carrol and John Whitemarsh, were killed. Two injured men, Eugene Shannon and Tom Hansen, were sent to the Queen's Hospital for treatment.

51. "Yesterday afternoon a grand luau was given at the residence of Hon. J. I. Dowsett [at Palama] in honor of the birthday of his daughter, Miss Mary Dowsett. Her Majesty the Queen, Her Royal Highness the Princess Liliuokalani, Hon. A. S. Cleghorn, and a large number of invited guests were present, and a delightful time was had by all. In the evening a dancing party was held." *Pacific Commercial Advertiser*, February 16, 1886.

52. "There was much delight among the Japanese immigrants at the Immigration Depot yesterday when the Royal Hawaiian Band struck up with the Japanese national anthem, a few minutes past three o'clock. They all crowded around the bandstand and paid the greatest attention.... Bandmaster Berger had prepared a popular program, which lasted until nearly five o'clock." *Pacific Commercial Advertiser*, February 18, 1886.

53. Hassinger's was the residence of Honolulu businessman John A. Hassinger (b. 1837–d. 1902). The auction was advertised as an "important sale of Elegant Household Furniture."

54. Elizabeth Mahiai (b. 1844, Hilo–d. 1914, Honolulu) was the part-Hawaiian daughter of Amoy, a Chinese merchant of Hilo, and the widow of John D. Robinson. She was one of Liliu's closest friends. Her sister Aki, often mentioned in association with Elizabeth, was Lucy Aki Kawahine Puniwai Amoy (1844–1914). Another sister was Kahanuu Meek.

have gone, and there is a sense of loneliness. John and I went out for a drive and stopped at Mr. J. H. Brown's.[55]

Mrs. Kahuila [Wilcox] and Mary Ailau have been here and speak of our Society. Will meet on Tuesday at Mary's house and arrange our rules. Went to take a short drive in Pake's express [Chinese man's hack].

*Saturday, February 20.* A blustering day. A lot of young men gone to Kailua to shoot birds. We met for the first time in two months, t'was their fault. Charlie brought rent of lot in Waikiki $20. I sent him to A. J. Cartwright. Could not go out, but busied myself in trimming roses. An engagement at seven, but [he?] did not come till half past ten. Slept at [Word erased.] Picked the first Gardenia from my row of gardenia plants.

*Sunday, February 21.* Stayed at home on the morning—had no visitors [except?] Mrs. Dowsett and later Mr. A. [Allen] Herbert. He came home from Kalihi hungry, so have to have early dinner. Took a drive to Waikiki at three, saw the two cows and their calfs. They are from good stock. Did not see my husband, though we stopped at Washington Place.

*Monday, February 22.* Waikiki folks came on to tie Kahili feathers. Mary and I breakfast alone. Charlie Wilson brought in bills for my inspection before submitting them to A. J. Cartwright. Many of them I did not approve of. Retired early. Slept in my Huamoena room [a room spread with mats]. This morning met at Mary Ailau's[56] with a party of Hawaiian ladies to form a bank for themselves. Only few members came, so elected few officers—and postponed till Wednesday at ten A.M.[57]

*Tuesday, February 23.* Sent Joe to Waterhouse's [store] to buy some duck canvas for flooring for young people to dance on—and afterwards to meet my niece [Kaiulani] on Thursday.

At one went to the Palace, saw the Queen impatiently awaiting the arrival of the King.[58] Three o'clock he arrives and is received by Band and soldiers—accompanied by John and the Chamberlain. Consul Irwin came in to welcome him home. Left them all in the palace and went to Healani[59] and had lunch and came home to find Sophie [Sheldon] at work at [sewing] machine.

55. John H. Brown (b. 1820, Ipswich, Massachusetts–d. October 23, 1892, Honolulu) was a sea captain, who arrived at Honolulu in 1840, and soon after made a sandalwood-collecting voyage to the South Pacific with Captain John Dominis. Brown was sheriff of Oahu in the 1850s, and later jailer of Oahu Prison. On April 14, 1848, he married Elizabeth Jones, the part-Hawaiian daughter of former U.S. Consul John Coffin Jones. Their daughter Minnie (Aldrich) was a close friend of Liliuokalani.

56. Mary Ailau's residence was on the northwest corner of Nuuanu and Beretania Streets, opposite Queen Emma's residence, Rooke House.

57. At a later date, the *Advertiser* described this organization: "A Woman's savings bank has been organized in this city, to be known as Liliuokalani's savings bank. Fifty will be the maximum limit of membership, and each shareholder must deposit $5 on interest every month in the bank. Mrs. Luther Wilcox is President; Mrs. J. Kaae, Vice President; H.R.H. Princess Liliuokalani, Treasurer; and Mrs. E. M. Beckley, Secretary. It is only for women, and all deposits will be put out at interest." *Pacific Commercial Advertiser*, April 7, 1886.

58. Kalakaua had been on a visit to the island of Hawaii. He returned on the *W. G. Hall* (also referred to as the *Malulani*).

59. Healani was the king's boathouse in Honolulu harbor near the foot of Punchbowl Street, just below Queen Street. It was a two-story frame building on piles, reached by a long plank walk, and was almost exclusively a male domain. The lower room was for boats, and at the time of Kalakaua's death it was inventoried as having a whaleboat, a Samoan canoe, two six-oared racing shells, a six-oared gig, two 14-oar barges, and two long racing boats. Upstairs

*Wednesday, February 24.* Went to Mary Ailau's and met the ladies there. Had our meeting, appointed the officers—named the Society "Liliuokalani Hui [Hoo]Kuonoono" [Liliuokalani Benevolent Society]. Made rules and carried. Adjourned till Tuesday the 2nd of March eight P.M.

Joe drove me down with [my] black span [pair of horses] to Washington Place, we took John in and went to the Japanese Embassy. Met H. M.'s Chamberlain [C. H. Judd], Paul and Mrs. Neumann, Mr. and Mrs. Iaukea, Mrs. [Sarepta] Gulick, Miss Finckler. Slept at Nua Ahua i Puna [an unidentified location].

*Thursday, February 25.* Mrs. Beckley and I went to Thrum's and got ten dollars' worth of Stationery, went to *Saturday Press* office to consult about printing bylaws for "Liliuokalani Hui Hookuonoono."[60]

Made Joe and Paulo put canvas down on dining room for children's dance this eve—Mrs. Hopkins and her two boys,[61] Mrs. Dowsett and six children, Sophy Sheldon, and three [Sentence ends thus.]

*Friday, February 26.* I only remember of going down at 6½ P.M. to Washington Place in an express—spent a few minutes with Mrs. Dominis and Mrs. Wight. Then went to Hinano Bower, stayed half-hour there—then went upstairs to have John commence my Account book with Liliuokalani Hui. Left Kahae and baby at home. O yes! The Waikiki folks went home that day. David Crowningburg[62] called in to ask for something to do. I promised to see Curtis and others, that was how I came to go to town.

*Saturday, February 27.* Went to Govt. House with J. Aea, whilst Joe Heleluhe was collecting my bills. Got money order for my salary, signed it and gave it to A. J. Cartwright. From there went to Waikiki and saw Aiaumoe, left orders about Pake [Chinese], then came home and paid bills and wages—had a dance for the children and retired—tired.

Dreamed of Kahilis [feather standards]. Gave Kauaihilo $5 towards breaking horse in.

*Sunday, February 28.* Sat down after breakfast [and] made out accounts. What an occupation for Sunday—although brought up differently—but I hate to go to church and hear politics and sarcasm preached in pulpit.

At three went to Mr. Wilson's and dined there with Col. J. H. Boyd, Mr. and Mrs. M. [Malcolm] Brown, Mrs. Townsend, Kitty [Wilson], and Johnny [Wilson]. From there went to Washington Place. Lepeka [Rebecca] would like $6—for suit against Mary. Joe Aea agreed to let me have one

---

there was a bedroom and bathroom for the king's use, and a large main room well furnished and equipped for casual entertaining, of which a great deal took place, especially on weekends. Several well-known photographs exist of King Kalakaua entertaining Robert Louis Stevenson in 1889 in the main living room and seaside lanai of the building.

60. Princess Kaiulani's copy of these printed bylaws is in the Hawaii State Archives, Kalanianaole Collection.

61. Abigail Aiwohi was the wife of Charles L. Hopkins (d. 1918), deputy marshall and later Hawaiian interpreter in the courts of law. The two sons were James and Francis Hopkins.

62. David Crowningburg (b. 1839, Maui–d. May 20, 1919, Honolulu) was the part-Hawaiian son of early settler William Crowningburg (b. 1819–d. 1856) of Waikapu, Maui. See second footnote for March 4, 1886, diary entry (48).

share of W. [Waimanalo] stocks to cancel his debt, $112, which I gave to Dole on January 28, 1886. Had a very restless night.

*Monday, March 1.* Went to town—took $10 to Mrs. Bush. When I woke at six, Rebecca came for six dollars, which I gave her, then had my breakfast with Mary. Tried to get all my bills but did not succeed. Went to Mrs. Brickwood's but she was not at home—went to the Queen's and found her not very well. Came home disgusted. Kahae and baby spent the day. John came up to see me a few minutes—would not leave the carriage. The children's dance this eve—and now all have retired. Ordered brooms, mops, pan, etc. Bought from Joe Aea one of his shares of Waimanalo stock for Kaipo No. 1032—and No. 1033—he gave to Kaipo to pay for the $112—paid to Dole to release his W. [Waimanalo] stocks. Kahae came down with Baby. I wonder if she means to stay.

*Tuesday, March 2.* Trimmed trees until 12, then sat down and prepared books for our meeting at three. Met at Mary Ailau's—distributed books amongst members of Liliuokalani Hui [Hookuonoono].[63]

Took their contribution of $5 apiece. Rec'd $100 from 20 members. Sat up to copy in Account book.[64]

Kahae [Aea] said one reason she was so thin was because they were so pilikia [troubled] and besides Joe deserted her half the time. I told her he had not been here for one month. Mary suspects Rebecca for bringing that suit against her. [Word erased.][65]

*Wednesday, March 3.* Went to Wenner's,[66] had my diamond cross fixed for nothing, endorsed a bill for Davis & Wilder, went to Thrum's and paid [above this line she wrote "got receipt"] $10 for Liliuokalani Hui [Hookuonoono]—from there to A. J. Cartwright. He told me that Neumann had been trying to get him to endorse a note on me for $9,000—for Charlie's deficiency,[67] and C. refuses to see it. Threatens to tell the King, John, and everybody else. Placed in his (Cartwright's) hands in presence of C. Wilson and Joe Heleluhe the sum of $100—on deposit from the Hui. Promises to let me have notebook tomorrow. Went up to Washing-

---

63. The Liliuokalani Hui Hookuonoono (the Liliuokalani Savings Society) was a savings society for Hawaiian women, organized on this date at the home of Mary Pitman Ailau. The society's account book for 1886–87 has attached to its inside front cover a printed copy of its constitution, and the first entry (March 2, 1886) has a list of members. According to Liliu's diary, the Hui formally disbanded on February 3, 1888, and distributed its assets among the members. Hawaii State Archives, Liliuokalani Collection, Box 13, Account Book for Liliuokalani Hui Hookuonoono.

A Hilo branch of this society, organized in association with Isabella Lyman, survived until the early 20th century.

64. The account book records 15 members: E. M. Beckley, Mrs. L. Wilcox, Pehikulani Auld, Mrs. Kamakanoe, Mrs. Emma Hoapili, Mrs. Elizabeth Mahiai Robinson, Mrs. J. Kaae, Mrs. Kealoha Hugo, Mrs. Kahae Aea, Miss Leihulu Kapena, Miss Maili Nowlein, Miss E. Kahoalii, Miss L. Nakanealoha, Miss Lily Richards, and Miss Carrie Wilcox.

65. No reference to this suit has been found in the Hawaii State Archives Indexes.

66. Wenner & Co., Manufacturing Jewelers, Fort Street, advertised itself as "Diamond setters, engravers and Dealers jewelry of all kinds. Shell and Kukui jewelry made to order."

67. See March 6 and 23, 1886, diary entries (48–49, 54) for a discussion of Charles Wilson's "deficiency."

ton [Place] and found a present of a book from Sinclair.[68] Sent Joe to buy butter 50 cents, ink, 50 cents bread. I ordered two gallons of Ice Cream of Hart for next day.[69]

*Thursday, March 4.* After breakfast drove to A. J. Cartwright to get my book for monies deposited with him of $100 for Liliuokalani Hui [Hookuonoono], then went to Wenner's for my watch, promise to pay soon. Then to Mrs. Brickwood's to see Mrs. Lyman—then drove to the King. Saw letter from [John] Bush saying he would like assistance in money to pay his taxes.[70] The idea that he should come back and plead distress to the King after saying all that he did against Govt.

King says John Richardson would never get recognition from him, Kepoikai [was] dishonest at Spreckels [bank, and] Crowningburg could not have his civil rights returned until after five years.[71] Came home, made bouquets. Had reception—Kaiulani and several young friends came and had their dance, while grown people called on me. Guests went home—band went home. Sat to tea, then came to Washington Place, spent night.

*Friday, March 5.* Joe Heleluhe came for me at seven. I left John sound asleep. Had my breakfast, then went and asked A. J. Cartwright what he would give for money deposited day before. He said five percent. Had to be satisfied. Went to Wenner's, paid $4.50 for repairing watch, and drove up to Emma Kapena's—found her breakfasting with Liwai Kauai and Kamaka Hart. Then went on to Mary Carter's. Met sister [Likelike] there. Brought home some plants, coming home by School St., and stopped at David Crowningburg's—then came home, went right to gardening.

At three P.M. Neumann came to see me about Charlie's affair. Told Neumann that A. J. Cartwright, after examining my accounts and after paying his $5,000, found that I was in his debt $12,000—[and he] refuses to pay any more towards Wilson's debt. A. J. Cartwright Jr. brought a bill in at the time and left. Neumann says A. J. Cartwright was right. Laid down [plant] slips. Slept in Sister's room.

*Saturday, March 6.* Must send Joe for Bookcase. Gave Joe $20 for clothing, Aiaumoe $5 for Pupule. This day seems like a Sunday. Busy all morn-

---

68. This was probably one of Francis Sinclair's privately printed books of poetry rather than his wife Isabella Sinclair's *Indigenous Flowers of the Hawaiian Islands* (London: Sampson Low, Marston, Searle, and Rivington, 1885).

69. Elite Ice Cream Parlors (Hart Bros. proprietors) was at 75 Hotel Street, and it also offered for sale "island and foreign curios." 1884–85 City Directory.

70. John E. Bush (b. February 15, 1842, Honolulu–d. June 28, 1906, Honolulu) was a newspaperman and politician. In his early years, Bush learned printing and was in the employ of the *Hawaiian Gazette*. He was a close associate of Robert Wilcox and played an active role in the politics of the late 1880s and 1890s. He was governor of Kauai, 1877–80; served on the Privy Council, 1878–91; and was a member of the House of Nobles, 1880–86. During the 1880s, he served briefly as minister of the interior, 1880; minister of foreign affairs (ad interim), 1880; president of the board of health, 1880; minister of finance, 1882–83; and minister of the interior (again), 1882–83. On December 23, 1886, he was appointed "Envoy Extraordinary to Samoa and Tonga, also High Commissioner to the Sovereign Chiefs & Peoples of Polynesia," but Kalakaua ordered him to return to Honolulu in June 1887. During 1890–92, he was in the House of Representatives. He was not related to Liliu's friend Mrs. Caroline Bush. The letter Liliu refers to has not been found.

71. David Crowningburg, once a partner in a Makawao, Maui, ranch (Brewer & Co.), had been tried and convicted in Wailuku in June 1883 on the charge of having sold ranch cattle and kept the $6,000 proceedings. On December 18, 1891, Liliuokalani and her Privy Council granted Crowningburg a full pardon and restoration of his civil rights.

ing with Gardening. Mahoe and [blank] called. Charlie [Wilson] and Wundenburg[72] came at one to arrange about C's [Charlie's] predicament as A. J. Cartwright refuses to pay the remaining $4,000. Promised I would consider the matter over. Four P.M. went with Mr. and Mrs. Lyman[73] and children to Band, then drove out to Kulaokahua and came home. Met brother [Kalakaua] who had been here.

*Sunday, March 7.* While breaking fast, Mr. Bush and J. Kawainui came in to see me—I was surprised. Spoke of ordinary things, then when going home Bush went over to next lot and pounded a boy for abusing a valuable colt. Went to consult John about my letter to A. J. Cartwright about Wilson's $4,000, to let another party advance it. Drove John down to steamer *G. W. Elder* [from San Francisco]. Took him to Palace, then we came home. Afternoon waited for Brother [Kalakaua], but he did not come. Kaulukou[74] and another man called, then John came. When he went, [I] changed dress, then retired, but at noon I spent [Sentence ends thus.]

*Monday, March 8.* At 7½ A.M. sent Joe Heleluhe with letter to A. J. Cartwright requesting him to let other party advance money of $4,000 to C. B. Wilson, and for security let them have the Salary.[75]

At same time went up to Palace and found Brother in his room getting ready to receive Sam Parker and other gentlemen to breakfast, while band played.[76] Came downstairs—Capt. Hayley was pacing floor. Went on to see Queen at Healani [the boathouse]. Drove home, breakfasted, and went out gardening.

3½ P.M. Mr. A. J. Cartwright calls and agrees to my proposal.[77] Five P.M. C. B. Wilson came and I gave him my answer. Annie Dowsett and John came little later. At seven I went with John to Hotel.[78] After band [concert,] Joe Aea came for me and drove me home. Kahae and baby hid from Joe—how funny!

---

72. Frederick W. Wundenburg (b. January 23, 1850, Hanalei, Kauai–d. January 10, 1908, Honolulu) was the son of Godfrey Wundenberg. He was a clerk with T. H. Davies & Co., and then served as postmaster general in Honolulu, October 15, 1886–May 2, 1891. He was a monarchist, and on February 12, 1895, after confinement on a charge of complicity in the recent insurrection against the Hawaiian government, Wundenberg accepted clemency, agreeing to leave the country by the SS *Australia* on February 23, 1895. He returned later.

73. Rufus A. Lyman (b. 1842, Hilo–d. 1910) was the son of missionary David B. Lyman. In 1866, he married Rebecca Brickwood, a part-Hawaiian ward of Lot Kapuaiwa (Kamehameha V). Rufus was a close friend of that monarch, and an advisor and right-hand man to Princess Ruth Keelikolani, longtime governess of Hawaii.

74. John Lot Kaulukou (b. 1841, Keauhou, Kona–d. June 6, 1917, Honolulu) was a longtime government employee who served in the House of Representatives, 1880–86; on the Privy Council, 1883; as a member of the board of education, 1884; postmaster general, April–July 1886; marshall of the kingdom, July 31, 1886–February 8, 1888; attorney general, October 6–23, 1886; and senator, 1889.

75. On March 8, 1886, Liliuokalani and her husband signed a lease for land at Waikiki Waena [central Waikiki] to Tai Kie et al. The acknowledgment was signed on March 9. Bureau of Conveyances, Liber 100, 53.

76. "His Majesty the King gave a breakfast at Iolani Palace yesterday morning, at which the following invited guests were present: Captain Medorun Crawford, Major A. S. Bender, Hon. J. L. Kaulukou, Mr. Julius H. Smith, and Major A. B. Hayley. The Royal Hawaiian Band was stationed on the Palace grounds and played a choice selection of music." *Pacific Commercial Advertiser*, March 9, 1886.

77. The proposal would have been about extricating Wilson from his financial troubles.

78. They attended a concert by the Royal Hawaiian Military Band, which commenced with the "King Kalakaua March" and concluded with "Hawaii Ponoi."

*Tuesday, March 9.* Went to look for John at Govt. building—drove with him to Palace—told the King I would come up with him to Hawaii. Left him there, went to Washington [Place] for John's valise—from there went to Palace with Curtis [Iaukea], sent for John who was at Privy Council. John and I signed our lease with Pakes [Chinese]. Went to Govt. [building] to take Acknowledgements.[79]

Went home at 1½ P.M. Dined with Kahae—said Joe had not been home since she hid from him night before. Quarter to three, drove in haste to steamer *Malulani.*

Wharf was crowded. Band and everyone else on board except King. He arrives and then Curtis [Iaukea] and [Major] Hayley. John and Archie bid good-bye. Brother [Kalakaua] kindly gives up his berth to me and sends Joe to guard my door with others from curious eyes of passengers. Arrive at Kawaihae eight A.M. S. P. [Sam Parker] leaves [the steamer] at Kailua at one. Send for Kapoli to come on boat.

*Wednesday, March 10.* Many passengers come on board for Hookena.[80]

Arrived at this place [Hookena, Hawaii] four P.M. Amongst passengers is Hoopii—who would like to lease Haumea's Kuleanas [native land claims] again for $20. I told him [I] would think the matter over.[81]

Nothing of importance transpired during the day. Band plays for our supper, retires and [we spend] a quiet night.[82]

Kapoli and Jessie wait on me. Good night.

*Thursday, March 11.* After breakfast Brother [Kalakaua] and I ride over to Kealia. Keawehawaii has charge of the land—he tried to find out whether I intend to retain him or not; or whether I would put someone else there or not. He is a scamp. He told me there was no pia[83] and yet I saw them in his house. The loulu and hala [leaves][84] he sells for his own benefit to pay his lease. They wash and bathe in the pond. Must tell them not to do it again. At ten A.M., met [D. H.] Nahinu alone in parlor and I made mention of H. [Hezekia] Aea's debt of $238—that Kamaki would have to resume it, also $15—owing to me by H. Aea. He said that he would consider it over with his daughter. I told him that would be best, then after that we would all consult together. I told Kaleimoana to ask Kahalekou (k) and Hana (w) to lease my lots on Keauhou for $40.

---

79. This lease dated January 29, 1886, to Goo Kim Fui (for the consideration of $1,535 at $50 per annum for 15 years) was an extension of an earlier lease of 1884, the lease area including ten loi or kalo patches for the cultivation of rice and taro adjoining the Kalia stream on the two Waikiki lands. Board of Conveyances, Liber 84, 145, and Liber 100, 86.

80. "The steamer *W. G. Hall* [also referred to as the *Malulani*], with his Majesty the King and H.R.H. Princess Liliuokalani on board, arrived at Hookena, Hawaii, on Wednesday afternoon at four o'clock. At the different landings between Honolulu and that place, the Royal Hawaiian Band played a number of selections on the upper deck of the steamer. The natives flocked in large numbers along the shore. The Royal party was received by Hon. D. H. Nahinu, member-elect for south Kona, and conducted to his residence." *Pacific Commercial Advertiser*, March 15, 1886.

81. There is no record of any such lease.

82. An article noted that on March 11 "the band gave a concert at the residence of Hon. Mr. Nahinu, at which all Hookena assembled . . . and the band was enthusiastically applauded." And later: "On Thursday evening the band gave a moonlight concert on the beach at Hookena. It was a glorious night and the concert was largely attended. The native songs by the band boys took immensely, and were loudly redemanded." *Pacific Commercial Advertiser*, March 15, 1886.

83. Pia is Polynesian arrowroot, *Tacca leontopetaloides*.

84. Loulu is the native fan palm, *Pritchardia*; hala is the screw pine, *Pandanus tectorius*.

*Friday, March 12.* Went to see the school with the King. Lopaka [Robert K. Amalu] is teacher and teaches in English. Very well conducted.[85]

While there sent Joe with note to Keawehawaii for some loulu and pia. Came home at 12. At four, steamer *Kinau* arrived with 100 passengers for this place. Lei lehuas[86] [sent] by George Beckley from the Princess Poomaikelani.

*Saturday, March 13.* After breakfast we all went to church to see Celebration of Sunday School on this island. At 12 King made a speech and took the hearts of the people by storm. Many of them shed tears.[87]

He left soon after, but the congregation was dismissed to go and take their lunch, but he had told them he would leave me behind to stay till the examination was over. He went over to Kailua in his boat, stopping at Keauhou for lunch.

The examination passed off well—told them I would offer a prize for October next when the schools would meet at Hilo for the best class. Exercises were closed at half past five. Rain came on as soon as we arrived home. It was a blessing to these parts. C.W.P. Kaeo[88]—came for a wonder but I heard he was one of the strongest oppositionists. Bought by money.

*Sunday, March 14.* Had family worship with Nahinu after breakfast. Was not able to attend morning service on account [of] diarrhea. Went at four P.M. to church. It was crowded. Took up contributions for the maintenance of the Hilo [Boarding] School. $10,000, the amount wanted.[89]

$25.70 was taken there and placed in A. O. Forbes' [hand,] he being one of the Board of Trustees. Slips of con. [contribution] papers were distributed around, one given to me for the Nihoas. Came home and sat mauka with folks. Kaeo dined with us today. [Reverend] Forbes came in and spent the evening. Had no ideas that [D. H.] Nahinu was such a man as I have since found him to be. Am sorry to be obliged to broach the subject of debt to him again tomorrow—after all his kindness to me.

85. "On Friday morning His Majesty and the Princess visited the school and were highly pleased. About one hundred and twenty-five children were in attendance. A graduate from Lahainaluna is the teacher, assisted by his wife, a former pupil at St. Andrew's Priory." *Pacific Commercial Advertiser*, March 15, 1886.

86. Lehua is the flower of the native ohia tree (*Metrosideros* spp.).

87. "The Sunday School festival at Hookena, Hawaii, last Saturday, was largely attended and carried through successfully. The presence of His Majesty the King, the Princess Liliuokalani and the Royal Hawaiian Band added much to the success of the festival … at eight o'clock the band played in front of the residence of Hon. D. H. Nahinu, where the Royal party was staying. In the meantime the Native church was rapidly filled. As it only holds about three hundred, a large lanai was erected to further accommodate the people, and this was also crowded. It is estimated that over eight hundred people were present. At ten o'clock His Majesty and the Princess arrived at the church, the band playing the National Anthem. As they entered the building the entire audience stood up.

"The exercises started with prayer by the Rev. A. O. Forbes. This was followed by singing and recitation by the different schools from the Kohala district.… After this came the chorus 'Home Maikai.' His Majesty delivered a brief address, which was listened to with the closest attention, and then a recess was taken.

"At ten o'clock the exercises were resumed.… A novel feature at the festival was ice cream, sold by an enterprising native from Honolulu, but the people did not take to it. Bandmaster Berger and the Rev. Mr. Forbes were the only two white men at the festival." *Pacific Commercial Advertiser*, March 17, 1886.

88. Charles W. P. Kaeo (b. 1854–d. 1908), later known as the blind preacher of Kona, is listed as C.P.Y. Kaeo, magistrate of South Kona, resident of Hookena, in the 1884–85 City Directory.

89. Liliu is referring to the Lyman Memorial Fund for the Hilo Boarding School. See second footnote for December 16, 1886, diary entry (124).

*Monday, March 15.* Rose early but did not breakfast until ten—while band played—Kaimiola (w) brought some ao loulu [finely woven mats of loulu], says Keawehawaii was sick. Told her to go back and have mats made and not to wash [and bathe] in pond, but clean it and run fish in it. Bought $4.58 worth of pia, to be a member of the Hookena Hui. Will send up $10 for my share this year. Signed a paper to contribute $100 for Hilo [Boarding] School. 12½ P.M. met Nahinu and his daughter and consulted about Hezekia's [Hezekia Aea's] debt. Wife says she was willing to pay half, which would be $159. I told them I would go back and see A. J. Cartwright.

Steamer is coming round the point. All is ready. We are on board but many more boatloads to come. Now we weigh anchor and leave for Keauhou. Arrive there at four—and at Kaawaloa at five, at six stop for the King at Kailua. It is eight, and passengers for Mahukona leave us. Joe went off to see Mr. Smithies[90] and bring off bottle of rum. It is so nice for sea.

*Tuesday, March 16.* Tuesday morning, stop at Maalaea [Maui]. At noon pass Lahaina and arrive here at five P.M. Precise. Drive up to Palace with the King. Greet the Queen and Likelike, then drive up to see John. But was disappointed. Came home [to Muolaulani], found Kahae and baby waiting for me. At dark they left and I had a lone supper. Sitting alone on veranda [in] bright moonlight with my thoughts.

*Wednesday, March 17.* Anniversary of Kauikeaouli, his birthday. All companies turn out to practice at target at Auwaiolimu with two bands.[91]

Wakeke and I go to see Kaipo. Took bouquets to Mrs. Allen and Mrs. Bishop. Went to Like's [Likelike's] and got slips [of plants], then came home to dine. Mr. and Mrs. R. A. Lyman join me, then Mrs. McGrew and Mr. Gay call. After they had gone, Mrs. Dowsett came in and we all went to drive. It rained so we had to come home. There was a luau for gents at J. A. Cummins'. The King and others attended, band was there—Joe came home late. Wakeke and I were sitting up. A lovely night.

*Thursday, March 18.* Rose late. An adventurer came to sell jelly. Sent Joe to buy some. No such person as Rohen [person unknown]. Planted roses all the morning. Drove down at three to see John and Mr. Bickerton.[92] He advises me to send for Joe. Accept the half offered by Hezekia's wife,[93] then make Joe ship H. A. Sent J. H. [Joe Heleluhe] for J. A. [Joe Aea], after

---

90. John S. Smithies (b. 1832, Newfoundland–d. 1902) resided in Hawaii for 50 years. He was port surveyor of Mahukona, and for a time was the proprietor of the Tourists' Retreat, offering guides to the volcano from Honuapo, Kau.

91. The birthday of Kamehameha III (Kauikeaouli) was observed as a public holiday: "The King's Own and Mamalahoa Guards met at the armory in the morning and marched to the Palace. Later on the former company marched to the back of Punchbowl for target practice. They were joined in the afternoon by the Honolulu Rifles, Prince's Own, and Mamalahoa Guards. His Majesty the King, accompanied by Col. Judd, was present in the afternoon and witnessed the shooting. After the shooting was over the different companies marched to town, headed by the Royal Hawaiian Band. The Reformatory School Band was also present." *Pacific Commercial Advertiser*, March 18, 1886.

92. Richard Frederick Bickerton (b. 1844, London–d. December 10, 1895, Honolulu) was a lawyer and later first associate judge of the Hawaiian Supreme Court.

93. On June 30, 1886, Kaehuwahanui and her husband, Huaka Kuihelani, would mortgage their property (a house lot on King Street and two parcels in Wailuku) to the Liliuokalani Hui Hookuonoono, for the consideration of $4,046.39. Bureau of Conveyances, Liber 103, 9–10. Hawaiians of the period seldom used their personal names, so it is not surprising that Liliuokalani has identified Huaka Kuihelani as Hezekia, perhaps thinking of Reverend Hezekia Aea, who died in 1872. There was also a son, Gus Hezekia Aea.

giving him directions sent him home, but he said he was staying in town in Mr. Stanley's old cottage—had a room there.[94]

Mr. and Mrs. and the Misses Feer call[95] and then Mr. Bishop—was so glad to see him. After tea went to town with Mainalulu, then took a drive with John round the square, from there went to Music Hall to Ventriloquist.[96]

Then took him home and came back [two words illegible] in a drenching rain.

*Friday, March 19.* Did some gardening in the morning. Afternoon had callers—Mr. and Mrs. Mitchell, Mrs. Allen, and Mrs. Severance, Miss Mitchell.[97]

Two strangers from Sweden called with Mr. and Mrs. Schmidt.

After tea went up to Washington Place to take John out to drive. Went to see the Prince's Own and the Queen's Own drill—got tired went back to Washington Place, but after I went to bed, John went out again.

*Saturday, March 20.* Seven o'clock Joe came to take me home, but as I passed Stanley's house I saw J [word crossed out, possibly Joe Aea] staying there peep out. Hurried back to meet Annie. At one drove down to meet Kaiulani and Miss Gardinier[98] and take them to the Matinee. [Saw] the ventriloquist, Millis,[99] then drove round town to band. Left them at Washington Place. Then came home. Spent evening at home and slept in sister's room.

*Sunday, March 21.* Went to church at Kawaiahao—from there went with Wakeke and Joe to Waikiki. Went in the afternoon to Waikiki Church, then came home, supped, and went to Kawaiahao again. Just while at supper, [John] Kapena and Kia[100] called, and after they left, John came—but I told him that I would sleep at Washington Place, so he went home.

---

94. Referring to Stanley's old cottage: R. H. Stanley (d. 1875), a New York–born attorney, had arrived in 1858, and was for a time attorney general under King Kalakaua (1874–75). His cottage was on the Macfarlane family premises on Hotel Street.

95. This was the family of F. Feer, French commissioner.

96. The *Pacific Commercial Advertiser*, March 18, 1886, announced performances of Fred W. Millis, "the Monarch ventriloquist and Humorist," at the Hawaiian Opera House. Then the paper reported: "A very large audience greeted . . . the ventriloquist at the Hawaiian Opera House last evening on the occasion of his second appearance in this city. Her Royal Highness Princess Liliuokalani and His Excellency Governor J. O. Dominis occupied seats in the Royal box." Millis opened with a "ventriloquial sketch" and the second part of the program "consisted of feats of ventriloquism interspersed with songs and witty sayings, which kept the audience convulsed with laughter from beginning to end." *Pacific Commercial Advertiser*, March 19, 1886.

97. Mr. and Mrs. Alfred Mitchell were of New London, Connecticut. Mrs. Annie Mitchell was a granddaughter of New Yorker Charles Tiffany and one of the heirs to his vast fortune. Their daughter Alfreda would marry Hiram Bingham III in 1904. The Mitchells would be in the islands again in 1891 and 1892.

98. Miss Gertrude Gardinier arrived at Honolulu in April 1885, and was Princess Kaiulani's governess until she married Albert W. Heydtmann at Saint Andrew's Cathedral, May 10, 1887. She later lived on the U.S. East Coast.

99. The Opera House was "crowded in every part with children and adults who went away highly pleased. . . . Their Royal Highnesses the Princesses Liliuokalani and Likelike and the little Princess Kaiulani occupied seats in the Royal box." *Pacific Commercial Advertiser*, March 22, 1886.

100. Mrs. Elizabeth Kahele Nahaolelua (generally known as Lizzie Kia, or E. Kahele Kia) was the wife of Kia Nahaolelua (d. June 13, 1901), son of longtime Maui governor Paul Nahaolelua (d. 1875). She became a close friend of Liliu, and would live for periods of time with her children in one of the cottages at Washington Place.

Wakeke and I went to church at Kawaiahao and passed Joe and his fiancé, but left before service was over. Millie Kinney[101] spoke—very interesting. Sent Wakeke home, and slept at Washington Place.

*Monday, March 22.* Joe came for me but I had sent for Kaae and wished him to make up with Jesse—said he would. Arranged with him who should be elected for offices at Legislature, J. Waiamau, [F. J.] Testa, [Samuel] Nowlein, Keaha, Joe. Came home, wrote letters to all members [of the Legislature] on Hawaii, then went to see John off [to Maui]. Just in time. Jessie went with me and we brought Kaae home with us—supped and sent them home, and drove with Wakeke to the Hotel. It was full—band played well—Curtis [Iaukea] passed us—drove to Washington Place and waited for Joe and both came home. Band was ordered to Palace—Gents' entertainment there. Was not pau [finished] till four A.M. This morning John gave up my diamonds and key of escritoire. Slept at Keala Hale.

*Tuesday, March 23.* Went in garden, planted slips. Jessie and Kaae came and breakfasted with me and Portuguese girl came and wanted to stay with Kahae and tend baby. Told her to come back tomorrow. Jessie Kaae and I sat and wrote more letters to send to Maui and other parts. Went to dine with the King, and Curtis came and joined us. It was jolly. Curtis came to report he was Governor for the time and offered services.[102]

While dining, he told me he wished me to read Minister of the Interior's report on C. B. Wilson affair.[103]

Charlie [Wilson] came in to attach my water pipe [to] Government water. Gives good force. Took a nap. Jessie went home after tea. Wakeke and I sat on veranda until Telephone rang. [Illegible] was coming home. Slept in Sister's room.

*Wednesday, March 24.* After breakfast Kaae came up to help me finish my letters. 12 P.M. he went home, but while here Mr. and Mrs. Whitney[104]

---

101. Miss Mary C. Kinney was a teacher in the Fort Street School. In 1893, she became Mrs. Phillip H. Dodge.

102. The records of the governor of Oahu show no such temporary appointment. Curtis Iaukea was subsequently governor October 4, 1886–August 5, 1887.

103. This was an investigation into financial irregularities in the city's Water Works Department, then in charge of Charles B. Wilson. On October 7, 1885, Minister of the Interior Charles T. Gulick had requested that J. S. Walker, auditor general, "make at your earliest convenience a thorough examination of the condition of affairs in the Office of Superintendent of waterworks in this city." On November 4, 1885, Walker informed Gulick that matters were far worse than suspected: he had found more than 400 delinquent water accounts, and when he asked to see the books, he "was informed that they did not keep books." Only the stubs of receipts were located, and he reported that "lately, however, they have given that up, taking for granted that the cash on hand was the correct sum to report to the department." In his January 13, 1886, account to the king, Gulick summarized the irregularities and totaled delinquencies at $13,292.85. After Wilson and an assistant admitted a deficiency "for which he could not account," totaling $11,278.75, on January 14, 1886, Wilson was ordered to pay the sum owed to the Interior Department.

In the report, there is an "on account" receipt from A. J. Cartwright dated February 17, 1886, for $5,000, and promissory notes (in the amount of $1,000 each) from Wilson due to be paid June 30, 1886; November 30, 1886; April 30, 1887; September 30, 1887; and a final payment of $569 due December 30, 1887. Wilson was able to secure funds to bail himself out of trouble by conveying his house and lot at Young and Piikoi Streets to Liliuokalani (February 11, 1886), but surprisingly he kept his position. The records of the case are found in the Interior Department files in a thick bound volume. Interior Department (subject file), Box 57.

104. Henry Martyn Whitney (b. 1824, Waimea, Kauai–d. 1904, Honolulu) was the first Honolulu postmaster.

came to see me, and also to tell me that he had some idea of making some changes in their department to advance Manaku[105] to Peterson's office[106] as chief Clerk but to lessen the salary $2,400 and wished me to see the King and let him know. Three P.M. sent for Kahae and baby. They came and we spent the night down here. Slept in "Nua Lehua." Today Kaheu hired another Pake [Chinese] boy. Money gave out—and must live on Wakeke's money left to her when I went to Hookena. Kahae asked me for some money—told her I had none.

*Thursday, March 25.* Found some slips, went gardening till 12—got ready to go [to] Mary Carter's lunch to meet Mrs. Mills of Oakland. She wished to see Willie Aldrich.[107]

Had a very pleasant time but it was showery when came home. Sat with Kahae and baby, then went gardening again, but was soon told baby had gone, so we supped, then she went home. There is to be a dance at the Hotel this eve but I cannot go, because no one to go with. Was waked up in the middle of the night and found someone had entered my room. I thought it was a burglar—perhaps Wakeke.

*Friday, March 26.* Half past eight A.M. went to town to see Mrs. Dominis. Half past nine went out to Waikiki, took saltwater bath, then went up to Paoakalani. Was tired and slept great portion of the day. Did little planting and came home at half past six. Mr. [Samuel G.] Wilder had a dancing party at his house—no invite. Slept in "Nua Lehua." Came home half past one.

*Saturday, March 27.* Wakeke went after the children in Kawaiahao Seminary to come out [to] spend the day. Made six calls in morning, then came home to dinner four P.M. Made three calls, then went round to the band—from there to Mr. [C. R.] Bishop's. [He] showed me improvements he had made in Keoua Hale.[108]

As I left the thought struck me how strange that I should have come to see them so often of late oiai ua hala koʻu kuleana e hiki aku ai ia wahi aka nona ke kumu i alohaʻi. [As I left the thought struck me how strange that I should have come to see them so often of late as my reason for going to that place is gone, for she (Bernice Pauahi Bishop) was the object of my affection.] Slept in "Nua Lehua."

*Sunday, March 28.* After breakfast went to Palace to see the King—he had just risen. Kissed the Queen, then delivered message to the King from Mr. Whitney. The King said he had no objections to Manaku's [post office] promotion and would like to see him advanced in position. From there went to Kawaiahao quarterly celebration. Exercises were good today. Came home, dined, and went to call on Mrs. Ward [and] Mrs. Beckley, and to

---

105. David Manaku (b. 1854–d. 1890, Honolulu) is listed in the 1884 City Directory as a postal delivery clerk, and in 1888 as assistant postmaster.

106. J. B. Peterson was assistant postmaster general.

107. Mrs. Susan L. Mills (b. 1825–d. 1912) was the wife of Dr. Cyrus T. Mills. The couple had earlier been at Punahou School, he as president and she as matron (both as teachers), 1860–64. She is best remembered for having established Mills Seminary (now Mills College) in Oakland, California. William Holt Aldrich (b. 1857–d. 1897), a cousin of J. O. Dominis, had been one of her pupils at Punahou.

108. Keoua Hale on Emma Street had been completed three years earlier for Princess Ruth Keelikolani. Bernice Bishop had inherited it from Ruth.

warn C. B. Wilson not to make any alterations in the men who had charge of Water & Co. [sic] Came home, supped, and now waiting for my friend [following phrase written above line] who did not come.

The King said that Mr. Whitney only had a right to appoint his subordinates. Was told that the Band was going to Hilo to attend Kapo's [Princess Poomaikelani's or Kapooloku's] birthday.

*Monday, March 29.* Drove down to Washington Place and took John to Palace to breakfast with their Majesties—Judge Ogden [Hoffman], Mr. and Mrs. Spreckels,[109] Mr. and Mrs. Neumann, Mr. and Mrs. Irwin, John, and myself.[110] After breakfast send all around for Joe—he was not to be found. Seven P.M. went after John and went up to [Mrs.] Mill's reception at Punahou with Willie and Minnie Aldrich—very pleasant affair.[111]

Left John at Washington Place and came up home. Joe came back after band—he had been sick since Saturday. He at five, made wreaths of all the pretty flowers: Tuberose, Gardenia, honeysuckle, heliotrope for next day.

*Tuesday, March 30.* Stayed at home all morning planting—half past two went to Palace to see the King—half past three went to wharf to see the King off. Took a turn to Kulaokahua, then came home. Joe left us and started right out to Waikiki for grass. P. came in and spent evening. It was blowing and raining when [he?] went home. Wakeke was there—Jessie was with me when the King went away. King went to Hilo with Band.

*Wednesday, March 31.* Downtown in the morning—and in the afternoon had a meeting [with] Kahuila [Wilcox], Mrs. Beckley, Mary Ailau, and myself to consult about having to admit 30 new members to our Hui [Liliuokalani Hookuonoono]—also to change our day of meeting to first of month. All parted to meet at Mary Ailau's next day.

Drew $400 from A. J. Cartwright, paid servants—discharged Apo [my] cook—to little Pake [Chinese] boy—if he comes here, I will send him to Keonelua. Kahae must have some money, for she has not sent her Pake [Chinese] boy down for his money.

---

109. Claus Spreckels (b. 1828, near Hanover, Germany–d. December 26, 1908, San Francisco) was a sugar magnate, power broker, and banker. Spreckels came to America in 1846 and achieved great prosperity. He first established a large sugar refinery in California. He then became interested in Hawaii in 1876, following the passage of the 1875 Reciprocity Treaty with the United States, and cultivated the friendship of King Kalakaua. Several years later he purchased from Princess Ruth her claim against the government for the Crown lands of Wailuku, and established the Hawaiian Commercial and Sugar Company on Maui.

In 1885, he established a bank, Spreckels and Co., that was a major lender to the Hawaiian government, and for a time he became the power behind the throne. In 1886, he had a falling out with the king and promptly left the islands—not returning for some years.

110. The breakfast party was in honor of Ogden Hoffman, longtime judge of the U.S. District Court of California. Hoffman arrived on the *Mariposa* for the benefit of his health, March 21, 1886. An announcement of his arrival stated: "As an admiralty lawyer he has no equal in the United States and no superior in Great Britain. Judge Hoffman is known among his associates as a genial companion, and brilliant conversationalist, and a ripe and accomplished scholar." *Pacific Commercial Advertiser*, March 22, 1886. The Iolani Palace guestbook, held in the Hawaii State Archives, lists the guests as Miss Leonora Irwin, Ogden Hoffman, Liliuokalani, and Mr. and Mrs. W. G. Irwin.

111. The reception at Punahou was to honor former teacher Mrs. Susan L. Mills. *The Friend*, April 1886, remarked that the assemblage of former pupils of Mr. and Mrs. Mills at the Punahou reception was a "gathering of the tribes."

*Thursday, April 1.* While at breakfast Mrs. Bush telephoned to come up immediately—Kaipo was very ill. He had spasm from eating mangoes. Dr. McKibbin called in and gave directions and he got better—left them a few minutes to attend a meeting [of the Hui]—took in 19 new members.[112]

Went right up to Carrie Bush's spent the rest of the day, and then left Wakeke to sleep up there.[113] Slept at Washington Place, for I felt worried about Kaipo.

*Friday, April 2.* This morning came home to breakfast. Went to Mary Ailau's to meet the Hui [Hookuonoono] and take contributions—from 17 new members took $170.50—receiving $10.50 from each—$10 going for Hui and .50 to Mrs. Beckley for expenses—$100 from old members making $270, which I took right away to A. J. Cartwright and deposited with him for Liliuokalani Hui [Hookuonoono]. At one P.M. Wakeke drove me up to Punahou to see closing exercises of that term and hear Oliver's [Oliver Carter's] composition. Had to leave at three to see Dr. Brodie about my eyes. Came home in a shower—4½ P.M. received Mrs. Mills, Mrs. Sam Damon, Mother Damon.[114]

*Saturday, April 3.* At ten went to Mary Ailau's to wait for members of Hui. Kahuila [Wilcox], Mary Pahau, Mary Stillman came and those were all. Mary Stillman gave me her ten and half [dollars]. Kahuila brought $10.50 for Kapo, a member who had never been proposed. Kept the money. At four P.M. went to see Kaipo who did not seem to be very strong—spent the eve there. At eight that evening went with the Queen, John, Mrs. Swan to Music Hall.[115]

Found Archie, Kaiulani, and Miss Gardinier. All went home pleased. Rec'd letters from Hilo.

*Sunday, April 4.* Went to Bethel, heard Mr. Oggel at 11 A.M. Came home and dined at three. Went to Kamoiliili Sunday School, came home had tea, and went to hear Wm. Noble at Kawaiahao—same old story—"Temperance."[116]

Took Annie Dowsett home, came back.

*Monday, April 5.* Kaaiaumoe came down and gave me $10.50 for Kainuuala and ten [dollars] more for the next two months for Liliuokalani Hui —$10.50 for Kalahiki and $5 more for the next month for Hui, $10.50 for Meeau for Hui. Had meeting for proposing new names of ten new members. Only nine members paid, and I took $90 [of] that amount to A. J.

---

112. The 19 new members are listed in the Hui Liliuokalani Hookuonoono account book under April 1, 1886. Hawaii State Archives, Liliuokalani Collection, Box 13.

113. This was at Mrs. Bush's residence at 40 Emma Street.

114. Julia Sherman Mills (b. 1818, Torringford, Connecticut–d. June 19, 1890, Cheyenne, Wyoming) was the widow of Reverend Samuel Chenery Damon (d. February 7, 1885). The Damons arrived at Honolulu on October 19, 1842. He was the longtime pastor of the Seamen's Bethel Church, and from 1843 the editor of *The Friend*.

115. The occasion was another performance by Fred W. Millis, the ventriloquist.

116. William H. Noble, announced in advertisements as "the famous Gospel Temperance lecturer of London" (b. 1842), arrived on the *Mariposa* on March 21 for, according to *The Friend*, March 1886, "two weeks of solid work in the interest of God and Humanity and the drink curse in our midst." He was honored with a reception at the YMCA, and spoke at the Fort Street and Kawaiahao Churches.

*Queen Kapiolani wearing her coronation gown, 1883. She is seated on the king's dining room chair, over which a red-and-yellow feather cape associated with Keopuolani, wife of Kamehameha I, is draped. A second feather cape drapes the table on which her crown is displayed on a cushion.*

*Princess Liliuokalani noted in her diary on April 30, 1886, that King Kalakaua, accompanied by Queen Kapiolani, opened the legislature. The queen wore her coronation gown, "a robe of Royal maroon velvet trimmed with real ermine. The front, which was of white satin, was embroidered in gold with fern and taro leaves" (*Hawaiian Gazette, *May 4, 1886).*
Hawaii State Archives

*King Kalakaua's landau in front of the Hawaiian Hotel on the corner of Hotel and Richards Streets. The king's top-hatted driver sits atop a hammercloth, the fringed cloth that covers the coach box of a royal carriage.*
Hawaii State Archives, circa 1886

Cartwright. He had gone to Auction Sale [of Corporation Stocks] and I gave the money to Bruce Cartwright. Came home, dined, then went down again to see John off [for Hilo]—vessel full, Miss Gove [?] and the [blank] came to see Sam Parker and that tall man off. It was funny to see her take her hat off to bow to people and so S. Parker did the same. Good-bye.

C. [Charlie Wilson] said he could not come by, arranged for next day. Mary Carter invited me for Picnic on Thursday [at] Palolo.

[At top of page:] *Daily Honolulu Press* was brought [out] for first time.[117]

*Tuesday, April 6.* Was gardening all morning—and received by *Malulani* letters and three loulu hats from J. K. Kauanoe. One letter from Kaehuwahanui[118] with Hawaiian Postal Money Order—Wailuku—No. 25207—for the amount of $11.25—signed W. A. McKay.[119]

Went to call on Mr. Unna and Mathilda but met her on the way—promised to take her out to Likelike's next day.

*Wednesday, April 7.* Sophie spent the morning with me, then at three P.M. called round for Mrs. Unna and Mathilda to go to Mrs. Cleghorn's. The Japanese were all there. Consul Irwin took me to table—Taro Ando[120] sat opposite us. Came home tired. Kalu paid A. J. Cartwright $50—[for] fishing right.

*Thursday, April 8.* Sophie [Sheldon] breakfasted with me, then we all started for Palolo. Found Mrs. Herbert waiting. Put her in Hanakeoki [a carriage?] with our folks—Left Mrs. Lewers[121] and girls waiting at Mrs. Dillingham's[122] for rest of party. We went on. Had lovely day with the Mitchells, Kaiulani, Mary Carter, Oliver, Liliu [Carter], Kate Lewers. Came home at four—arrived home [at] six. Changed [and] went to Minister Ando's reception. Almost everyone there.[123]

Came home half past ten, could not sleep on account [of] coffee.

*Friday, April 9.* At nine Joe drove me to Palace to wait for Mrs. Mills, Mrs. Unna and niece, Mary Carter, Nellie Fuller, Mary Foster, and some strangers. After going all over, we bade them good-bye, then sent to Malcolm

---

117. The meaning of this statement is unclear. The *Daily Honolulu Press* was issued from September 1, 1885, to the end of June 1886.

118. Kaehuwahanui (d. June 28, 1908, Honolulu) was the wife of the Honorable Huaka Kuihelani of Maui (b. ca. 1806–d. Feb. 21, 1892), member of the House of Nobles under Kalakaua.

119. William A. McKay was postmaster of Wailuku, Maui.

120. Japanese Consul Taro Ando arrived in Honolulu in February 1886, bearing the title "His Imperial Japanese Majesty's Diplomatic Agent and Consul General" and replacing then-consul Jiro Nakamura. Ando's official audience with King Kalakaua took place on February 24, 1886. Ando remained in Honolulu until October 1889.

121. Catherine (Mrs. Robert) Lewers (b. 1843, Honolulu–d. December 31, 1924, Honolulu) was the sister of J. O. Carter.

122. Emma Smith was the wife of Benjamin F. Dillingham (b. 1844–d. 1918), capitalist and founder of the Oahu Railway and Land Co. in 1888. The Dillinghams lived where the Central Union Church now stands (at Punahou and Beretania Streets), about midway from town to Palolo Valley.

123. "On Thursday evening an elegant party was given at the Japanese Consulate, Nuuanu Valley, by Mr. and Mrs. Taro Ando. The decorations in the interior of the house were very fine, and the front of the building was illuminated with Japanese lanterns. The evening was spent in social conversation, and refreshments were served in the most bountiful manner." *Pacific Commercial Advertiser*, April 10, 1886.

Brown to come over and take Kapukini's acknowledgement of her signature making over her land on Wailuku and giving me power to lease it until her indebtedness to the estate of Leleiohoku was paid.[124]

The amount was $150—but interest amounted to something. Must ask A. J. Cartwright.

Went to see *Zealandia* off—then came home. Mrs. Dowsett and Annie came over for a little while before tea.

*Saturday, April 10.* Nine years ago since my brother Hoku [Leleiohoku] died. Spent morning in sewing curtains for windows. [Two words illegible.] At two, sat with Mary Carter and Mrs. Turton at Music Hall to hear F. Millis.[125]

From there visited Queen, then brought home plants. Set them out immediately—had tea—sat down to finish my curtain, then my Memo.

Heard of Ned Dowsett's arrival by *Likelike* deranged. Some said he was in love with Angela Widdefield—others said something else—would not believe it.

*Sunday, April 11.* Went at half past five A.M. to the new battery[126] to wait the arrival of *Kinau*. ½ past six came on sight, ¼ to seven reached the wharf, after salute drove round to wharf—was crowded and lined with soldiers. After King's carriage passed with [his] Aides Iaukea, Boyd, Holt, we drove next, took shortcut, got to Palace first and received the King, my husband, and others. Troops came marching in front of Palace while King and Queen, John and myself, Kapena and wife, [John L.] Kaulukou and wife, Kahea [Beckley] and wife, Iaukea, Boyd, Holt, and Hayley, Berger, and others present. Came home, breakfasted, in garden till 11— took nap till one, dined at three, went to Waikiki. Nearly lost my cow. [Continues at bottom of previous page:] Visited Annie Turton on my way home. She was staying at Neumann's. Came home in a shower.

[Added to top of page:] Kapukini left for Salt Lake with five Mormon elders, and took Hoapili.[127]

*Monday, April 12.* Went to Govt. building and got papers from M. [Malcolm] Brown which Kapukini made,[128] empowering me to use her land at Wailuku till her debts to Leleiohoku's estates were paid. Took it and left it at A. J. Cartwright's. Three P.M. went to the doctor about my eye. Five P.M.

---

124. Kapukini's April 9, 1886, power of attorney to Liliu and J.O. Dominis was acknowledged before Malcolm Brown, deputy registrar of conveyances, the same day. Bureau of Conveyances, Liber 99, 156. There is not now any record of her indebtedness to the Leleiohoku estate.

125. Fred Millis advertised: "Positively last night ... Last and farewell appearance" for Saturday night and a "Grand Matinee" in the afternoon for ladies and children, "Children under 12 years, 25 cents; over and adults, 50 cents."

126. This was a shore battery used primarily for saluting purposes. In this case, the Royal Household troops fired the salute.

127. The *Pacific Commercial Advertiser*, April 11, 1886, records the departure of the Mormon elders (but not by name) on the *Alameda*. The account mentions Kapukini, "a native woman," and says that they were accompanied by "a native boy," presumably Hoapili. The Register of Hawaiian Passports (Hawaii State Archives) identifies the Mormon elders as Alonzo A. Brim, Isaac Fox, George Cluff, John R. Trilby, and Van Ransler Miller. Neither Kapukini nor Hoapili was issued a separate passport.

128. This was a power of attorney to Liliu dated April 9, 1886. Bureau of Conveyances, Liber 99, 156.

C. [Charles Wilson?] telephoned he could not come. Seven P.M. while having my tea John came in—he must have had something on his mind. I went to town with him and left word with Wakeke to come down with buggy. Went after Mary [and] all three went to Washington Place. Could learn nothing from John. Mary and I went to Square, then came home with Joe. Had bleeding of the nose badly.

*Tuesday, April 13.* Got telephone [call] from the King to come up and see him on matters. [Henry M.] Whitney to be dismissed, [John L.] Kaulukou to take his place—Whitney [had] sent for stamped envelopes amounting to over $100.00—interfered with politics [and] election. Desha[129] opened Hayselden's letter that was to be sent to the other islands and gave it to Kawainui to be published.[130]

Everett is going out. John is going to be detained here. Fornander is going out—[as he] voted for Govt. but helped opposition.[131]

12½ P.M. went to lunch at Bethel,[132] came home, dined, then went over to see Annie after writing two letters, to Governor of Hawaii and another to Kaehuwahanui.

Feeling unwell, sent Wakeke for Kaipo. He stayed the night with me.

*Wednesday, April 14.* Breakfasted with Kaipo, went out to pick flowers for Bethel lunches.

Kamahiai [Mrs. Elizabeth Mahiai Robinson] came in. She cut Kaipo's hair. Charley [Wilson] came and brought note from Kunane [Kalakaua] to sign. [Henry] Whitney came to tell me he was pau [finished]. I was so sorry for him.

Joe took Kaipo and Mahiai home. I expect J. A. [Joe Aea] to come and make over papers of Waimanalo Stocks to Kaipo. 12 ? J. A. is going to Waikiki to take cows to Manoa, will not come here till tomorrow.

Spent the rest of the day in making out my report for Liliuokalani Hui. Went to town to see John about sending [in his] resignation of Governorship of Maui, and [to] take King's appointment as Generalissimo of all islands with salary of $12,000—two years. Did not say anything. Went

129. George Langhern Desha was a registry clerk at the post office.

130. Joseph U. Kawainui was then editor of the *Kuokoa* newspaper. The Hayselden letter has not been traced.

131. This appears to have been a "purge list" advanced by Kalakaua and Walter Murray Gibson. The persons Liliu mentions are Henry Martyn Whitney, the first Honolulu postmaster (served 1850–56 and February 1883–April 15, 1886), a member of the Privy Council, and a legislator; George Langhern Desha, a post office clerk; Thomas W. Everett (b. 1825–d. 1895), a longtime civil servant, sheriff of Maui, and governor of that island; and Abraham Fornander (b. 1812, Sweden–d. 1887), a Hawaiian historian and longtime judge on Maui, whose judgeship concluded on December 27, 1886.

132. The Bethel Church announced a ladies' lunch "this day, Tuesday from 11 A.M. to two P.M. at the Bethel vestry, King Street." The bill of fare was "Chicken Pie, cold meats. Mashed Potatoes. Chicken and Potato Salads. Pies. Ice Cream, Cake. Coffee and Tea. Plus Homemade Bread and Butter," and as a footnote the announcement added: "Donations of fern and flowers and palm leaves gratefully received." *Pacific Commercial Advertiser*, April 13, 1886.

"The basement of the church presented a glowing appearance. Twenty-two tables, decorated with flowers and tastefully spread, were served by a like number of beautiful ladies, who hovered about like fairies, dispensing their graceful attentions." *Daily Honolulu Press*, April 14, 1886.

to bed at Washington Place. Manaku came to see what his fate should be.[133] King came today, four P.M.

*Thursday, April 15.* Breakfasted alone. Joe Aea brought me $30—from Hilo for [taro] patches of Paniani in Manoa and will send $10 more, as it was the amount leased to Pake [Chinese]—this must go to Cartwright.

12 P.M. went to Bethel lunches with Annie Turton, came home, had dinner at three. Went to Dr. Brodie, came home rested. 5½ P.M. Jessie and Kaae came to return my dresses. John came at seven. I drove in town with him to meet Annie Turton. Kaae and wife came in town on my buggy. 7½ A. [Annie] and I went to Band. Lovely night. After drove A. and left her with Mr. and Mrs. Neumann. Came home with Joe. The Chinaman who paid for Paniani's land in Manoa is called Maoni—Insian [sic] is his Pake [Chinese] name. [Several words erased.][134]

*Friday, April 16.* Rose at six, slammed my door to rouse the folks. After breakfast William Auld came in.[135]

I told him to run for Sergeant at Arms for Legislature. Went to see Annie [Dowsett], was glad to see her out and better.

Wrote to Father Damien to see that Kumuhonua has possession of the house. Wrote to Makaike scolding him for selling the house.[136]

Stay at home. Seven P.M. Lovely night. Went to the gate and saw Mr. Dowsett stand at corner 20 minutes. Carriage drove up with Annie and they drove up to Asylum. Ned [Dowsett] brought home very low. [Word erased, then a scrolling flourish.]

---

133. David Manaku was appointed assistant postmaster.

134. In her 1901 diary (available at the Bishop Museum Archives but not included in this work), Liliu notes on July 22 that the land was named Hamamakawaha, and had been deeded to her by "Paniani of Apiki's kuleana [native land claim]."

135. William Auld (b. August 7, 1842, Honolulu–d. March 10, 1902, Honolulu), a lifelong resident of Palama, was a carpenter and a wheelwright, and had a butcher shop on Nuuanu Street. He was long in government service, served in the Hawaiian military, and at the overthrow of the monarchy was superintendent of the insane asylum. In 1893, he retired to private life but remained a firm supporter of the royalist cause—and an intimate friend and advisor to Liliuokalani. His wife was Mary Adams, the daughter of Captain Alexander Adams.

136. Liliu's letter to Damien is as follows: "[Honolulu,] April 16, 1886. Dear Sir. I received your letter some weeks ago informing me of the actions of Makaike and of his selling the house to other parties. I have been waiting for Kumuhonua's brother who was on the other islands before I did anything in this matter. Now he has returned and gives the whole matter in my hands. I wish to ask you to see that Kumuhonua has her right. If the question was to be raised she has the entire right to the whole house because it was built by her brother's money, but in the first place he built it for Poka, his wife's aunt, but after her death, not wishing to be entirely regardless of her husband, he suggested that Makaike and Kumuhonua should have the house and it ended in her separating from there, which I was sorry to have her do, and now he has gone and sold it.

"I would advise you to take possession of the whole house for Kumuhonua, and empower you to act for her in that matter. I will write also to Makaike, which I enclose in this letter for you to read before delivery to him. You can consult Mr. Meyers on this matter if you choose, but as I said at first you had best put her in possession of the whole house. [*signed*] Liliuokalani"

A postscript followed: "Makaike will have to return the money to whoever he sold the house to. Kolohe maoli [very unprincipled]." Project Damiaan Vandaag, Damien collection Leuven, nr. 50.1. In the same folder is another letter (nr. 50.2) from Liliuokalani to Damien dated August 27, 1888, dealing with the effects of Kumuhonua, who was recently deceased.

*Saturday, April 17.* Made bouquets for vases. Annie T. [Turton] telephoned [she] could not go to Queen's. Harry ill. 2½ P.M. went to Dr. Brodie's about eyes. Four P.M. went to take John to drive. Spoke [to John] at Emma Square of the King's wish to make him Commander in Chief of all the islands, and he said he wished to keep Oahu. After band [concert] left him at his gate and came home. Slept in N. [She may mean Nua Lehua.]

*Sunday, April 18.* Joe came for his brake, and hearing we were all going to Waikiki, went for his wife and child. Brought it back and said they could not go. We started at ten. 12 P.M. bathed in sea with Aimoku and all the women, Eveline and Johnnie [Wilson] came in. 2½ P.M. dined. Four P.M. Charley [Wilson] came back from the Park in a hurry—fire in town. Took Eveline home. 5½ came in town—several houses on fire. Streets crowded. Ladies out, sister and I are there. 6½ P.M. had to go round by School Street to get back here [Muolaulani]. Had tea, then went down again to Hooliliamanu bridge [Palama] to watch the fire. Streets crowded with people.

Nine P.M. heard of Emma Kapena's death from excitement at Kunuiakea's—Mary Bairo [?] had her handkerchief round her neck.[137]

11 [P.M.] Heard the report [about Emma Kapena] again, 'tis true. Went up. Stayed till one A.M., came home in Curtis' express [with] Wakeke, Emma Beckley.

---

The fire that Liliu mentions here is generally known as the Chinatown fire of April 18, 1886, and was the first of two such disasters (the second would occur early in 1900). It began shortly before four P.M. in a two-story wooden building (housing a Chinese lottery room over a restaurant), at the corner of Hotel and Smith Streets. The blaze rapidly expanded in both directions along Hotel Street—the most heavily populated portion of the city—making a clean sweep until it reached King and Nuuanu Streets. Frequent explosions were heard due to the illegal storage of gunpowder, kerosene, and other combustibles, housed in nonconforming buildings. The fire destroyed Smith Street and went up Maunakea Street almost to Beretania, then advanced to the Nuuanu River and Smith's Bridge.

The conflagration also advanced toward the harbor and the ironworks. The old police station burned, as did Chinese Engine Co. No. 5. On Nuuanu, Wing Wo Tai's new brick building went, as well as the Anchor Saloon and the Seamen's Bethel Church on the corner of Bethel and King Streets. Immediately below the Bethel, firefighters dynamited the old seamen's

---

137. "We regret to announce the death of Mrs. J. M. Kapena, wife of His Excellency the Minister of Finance, which took place last evening at the residence of Mr. Albert Kunuiakea, Palama. The deceased was calling there with her husband, and hearing the fire bells ring, asked the latter to go with her to the fire. In rising from a chair she burst a blood vessel and fell back dead. The body was removed to the family residence, Nuuanu Valley, shortly after six o'clock. Her death was not unexpected to those who knew her intimately. The deceased lady, who was of high rank, was a daughter of David Malo, the Hawaiian historian, and about forty-two years of age." *Pacific Commercial Advertiser*, April 19, 1886. Emma Malo, known for her singing, was born on Maui on August 6, 1846, and married John M. Kapena in 1863.

home to save the threatened post office at Merchant and Bethel. The burned area was in a roughly oval shape, and the destroyed blocks comprised about 60 acres.

People removed much of the portable property beyond the Nuuanu River to Palama, and churches became sanctuaries for the homeless. The closely packed buildings and narrow lanes and streets made access by firefighters all but impossible, and the balconies overhead turned into fire-traps. The water mains proved completely inadequate, and the immense throngs of people attempting to save what property they could blocked the narrow streets. Cinders spread out as far as Thomas Square and up Nuuanu Valley. Of the several thousand left homeless, about 350 were Hawaiians.

The fire was described as "the greatest pecuniary calamity that has befallen Honolulu," and the damage was estimated to be in excess of a million dollars.[138] Immediately after the event, an investigative report to the king urged that the authorities widen and straighten streets in the area, and that they pay more attention to requiring that buildings meet fire codes.

---

*Monday, April 19.* Nine A.M. Awa (Pake [Chinese]) brought me $10 to make up the $40, which was the amount that Paniani's lot in Manoa was leased for, done by Hilo with Mooni (Pake).

Went at 11 A.M. [to Emma Kapena's.] She was laid out in her coronation dress. Stayed till four P.M., came home, was too tired to go up again. Strange so few came. David Maluaikoo led sad Leihulu [Kapena] to coffin to take last look. Apo came to clean house. Slept [at] Nua Lehua. Left four lau niu [cocoanut leaf] fans for Batty[139]—will bring home more by and by—go on to get breakfast for poor [burned-out] people. Most people have sought their friends. Many gone to immigration depot.

*Tuesday, April 20.* Sent flowers up to Emma's. Annie Turton came on to have breakfast with me—told me lots about Lahaina. Poor breakfast—sent her up with Joe—went down to Washington Place for John at three P.M. Went over to English church to funeral [of Emma Kapena]. King and Purvis,[140] Sister, John and I, and many of her friends—poor Emma.[141]

Sorry I did not call on the Nihoas. Took John home. Strung wreath of Gardenias and Tuberose for [double scrolling flourish] and made bouquet, no one came. Sat up till one—a lovely night.

People still at the ruins.

---

138. *Pacific Commercial Advertiser*, April 1, 1886.

139. Bathsheba Allen (b. 1849, Honolulu–d. February 11, 1914, Honolulu) was the part-Hawaiian daughter of James Robinson and wife of Honolulu merchant Samuel Clesson Allen. She was the sister of Mrs. Victoria Ward.

140. Edward W. Purvis (b. 1857–d. 1888) was an acting chamberlain in 1882, and a colonel on King Kalakaua's staff, 1884–86.

141. Emma Kapena's funeral took place at Saint Andrew's Cathedral. The *Advertiser* noted the presence of the royal family and government officials: "The Government offices were closed at noon, out of respect to the deceased lady, and the Government flags, as well as those on board HBMS *Satellite* and *Heroine*, were flying at half-mast." *Pacific Commercial Advertiser*, April 21, 1886.

*Wednesday, April 21.* Rose at six. Went in garden at nine A.M. Went to Washington Place, moved all my old duds up to Wakeke's two rooms, and gave my old house up to Mrs. Dominis' two Pakes [Chinese]. I hated to, but John would have it so—so I must yield. Tore down the lau niu [cocoanut leaf thatching] so as to leave open the whole lanai. Dined at home. Slept at Washington Place for the first time for nearly a whole year.

People still turning over the debris [of the fire] for what they could find.

*Thursday, April 22.* After breakfast Joe came for me [to go] down to Waikiki. Horses are thin—must bring them up. Went down to bathing place—full of leaves—many ferns dead. Miss Joe—find him reading my Memorandum by the taro patch. Aimoku brings me two Papaya. Nice dinner, plenty fish. Half past six came home, brought beautiful rose—as large as a small saucer. Magnificent! Put several slips out—slept at Nua Lehua.

*Friday, April 23.* Seven A.M. Took my large rose to Annie Dowsett. [She] says the doctor says he [Ned Dowsett] will get well. After breakfast went to Batty's [Bathsheba Allen's]. Left four fans—went to Kaipo [and] left his coat—went to Rebecca's, then to Govt. House to see John about making calls. Must give Willie $2 for brackets. Four P.M. went with John to call on Mr. and Mrs. [Taro] Ando—they were out. Went next to Mr. and Mrs. Nakayama[142]—found them in, went to Mrs. Neumann's, found her and Annie [Turton?] and her husband in. A. had a dose of W [a blank line follows] in bed.

*Saturday, April 24.* Went after Kaipo, [then] went to Kawaiahao Church yard to Emma's [Emma Kapena's] grave and left a bouquet. Went to Kamoiliili about Pake [Chinese] patches—came home. Hilo brought me lease of Paniani lot. Mary [Bairo?] had been here. Said she had nothing to do with J.M.K. [John M. Kapena]. Four P.M. Kaipo, Joe, and I went to Makiki baseball [field]—Band there. Hawaii against Benedicts. Hawaii beat Benedicts.[143]

[Line of text erased.] Took Kaipo home. Wanted to pay Willie [Bush?] for box—would not take it. Slept at Nua Lehua—came home late.

*Sunday, April 25.* In garden all day—made bouquets for Emma's [Emma Kapena's] grave. Planted violets by Poikeala. 11 A.M. went to Kawaiahao [and] left flowers on E's grave. Found Kahae in my pew with Mrs. Townsend.[144] Met Kahawaii after Church, spoke about giving my Kula [pasture land at] Kaauwaeloa [in Palolo] to Wong Kin—must come tomorrow. Sophie tomorrow.

142. Kakichiro Nakayama was appointed as a staff member in the Japanese consular office in 1885.

143. This was a baseball competition. "Notwithstanding the presence of a foreign steamship, just arrived, in port, a large number of residents assembled at the Makiki recreation grounds on Saturday afternoon, to see the match between the Benedict and the Hawaii Baseball Clubs. Professor Berger had the Royal Hawaiian Band stationed in front of his house, adjoining the grounds, presenting players and spectators with a delightful program. The match was a closely contested one, the fortunes of the day shifting markedly twice, finally leaving the Hawaii [team] three behind in the score, which was Benedict 22, Hawaii 19." *Daily Bulletin*, April 26, 1886. (Liliu could have left the game when the Hawaii team was ahead, hence the incorrect score tally in her diary.)

144. Mrs. Townsend was Harriet Blanchard Townsend (b. 1831, Honolulu–d. 1911, Honolulu), the part-Hawaiian daughter of Andrew Blanchard, captain of the bark *Thaddeus*, on which the first American Protestant missionaries came to the islands in 1820. She was the mother of Liliu's intimate friend Kitty Townsend Wilson.

*Wednesday, April 28.* At three P.M. was warned of Sister's illness. Met Kunane [Kalakaua] out here—came out with John at five P.M. Went back to town to dress for dinner party. Got [to] Mrs. Neumann's at six. King, Mr. and Mrs. Gulick, Mr. Gibson, Mr. Spreckels, Miss Fowkler, [?] John and I, our host and hostess.[145]

Woke at six from Poikeala [Hale], saw Kalana with fish—said the King had told him to run for chaplain of Legislature. While talking with him, a Mynah bird lit on my lap. I took it as a good omen. After breakfast drove out for Kalihi—met Governor Kanoa[146] who made me happy by saying I could have the next lot [adjacent to Muolaulani]. Mahiai returned my silk Kihei [shawl].

After dinner party went to Likelike's, took Jimmie Boyd—found the King and Curtis there. Sat up till four A.M. [At] six A.M. King, Curtis, Jimmie went home.

*Thursday, April 29.* Ainahau. Stay[ed] till four P.M., then went home. Went to concert with John, the King, Mr. Judd. He [?] saw me and hid behind those in front. Slept at Nua Lehua.

Six P.M. Had meeting of Committee to decide on what steps to take to assist those burnt out by fire—[Reverend] Waiamau, [Henry] Waterhouse, Achi,[147] myself. Was asked to see Ministers and find out what measures the Govt. has taken—and let them know. All right.

*Friday, April 30.* Went at seven A.M. to see Gibson—[he] gave satisfactory answer. On my way home [to Muolaulani] Kealiiakahai met Joe on Fort St., said he would come up with hats from Kona. Said he would come up after seven.

11 A.M. got ready to go to opening [of] Legislature. Sophie [Sheldon] accompanied me. Arrived in time—the building full of ladies and gold lace [officers from] HMS *Satellite*, *Triumph*, and *Heroine*, King and Queen surrounded with Kahilis [royal feather standards], Aides, and Governor [of] Oahu.[148] Ceremony short—Queen dressed in her Coronation dress

---

145. According to the *Advertiser*, the guests also included Princess Likelike and A. S. Cleghorn, but there was no mention of a Miss Fowkler. The account also said: "The Royal Hawaiian Band was stationed on the grounds and played a choice selection of music." *Pacific Commercial Advertiser*, April 30, 1886.

146. Paul Puhiula Kalakaua Kanoa (b. June 10, 1832–d. March 18, 1895, Honolulu) was the governor of Kauai, January 1881–July 1886. He was the hanai (adopted) son of Paul Kanoa (d. 1885), the former governor of Kauai, who held the same office 1846–77. His sister was Deborah Mahoe.

147. William Charles Achi (b. 1858, Kohala–d. 1928, Honolulu), a Hawaiian-Chinese lawyer, was a great-grandson of Puou, one of the warriors of Kamehameha I. He studied at Hilo Boarding School and Oahu College (Punahou), read law under W. R. Castle, and was admitted to the bar February 1887. He was an authority on land titles. Achi was one of the promoters of the lottery scheme of 1892–93, and remained prominent in politics after annexation in 1898. His son by the same name was a judge on Kauai.

148. In its account of the opening of the legislature, the *Hawaiian Gazette* reported: "At noon sharp the boom of cannon and the performance of the National air by the band gave notice of the approach of his Majesty and suite to the building, and shortly after preceded by six kahili [feather standard] bearers, their Majesties entered, accompanied by H.R.H. Princess Liliuokalani, Hon. J. O. Dominis, Hon. A. S. Cleghorn, the Cabinet, the Chief Justice and members of the Supreme Court, His Majesty's Chamberlain and Vice Chamberlain, Col. Iaukea, Col. Boyd, Col. Macfarlane, Major B. Hayley, Major Rosa, and Major Holt.

"Their Majesties and Princess Liliuokalani ascended the platform, upon which chairs had been placed, and seated themselves. The members of the Cabinet took their seats on the hall facing those occupied by their Majesties, behind them were placed the members of

and I wore mine.[149] Short speech and all is over. None of the wives of the members of the Bench attended.

*Saturday, May 1.* Aiaumoe gave me $10 for Meeau [Mrs. Kailikole] toward her share of Liliuokalani Hui [Hookuonoono]. Paid $5 today and five remains—also for [Miss] Kalahiki's next month [dues of] Liliuokalani Hui [Hookuonoono]. Rec'd from A. J. Cartwright $400 salary, $50 [for] Waimanalo stocks. Gave Wakeke $10 [and] Loe $10, kept Kaipo's $25 and Joe's $5—till he asks for it. Went at ten to Mary Ailau's. Received $270 from members of Hui—$25 more to come in. Paid for Mary Pahau.[150] Must get it back from John. Busy all day—4:30 P.M. went to Emma Square [and] from there drove to see sister. Found her better so came home. Took milk from Dowsett [a cow] today.

*Sunday, May 2.* Broke the Sabbath, may I be forgiven. Ten A.M. went to Ainahau to see sister—a little better. After lunch took nap. [Drs.] Trousseau [and] McKibbin woke me about Sister. Pronounced her case [as a] miscarriage, too bad. Came home at six and went to church—Kawaiahao was full. Mr. Bray of *Morning Star* addressed congregation.[151] Slept in Nua Lehua.

*Monday, May 3.* Planted violets. S. Kaai came to see me. Aiau came with note from Joe—to pay him $8.00—telephoned—wrote a note to come for me at Mr. Bishop's. Breakfasted in the Palace with King—Mr. and Mrs. and Miss [Alfreda] Mitchell and cousin, Col. and Mrs. [Charles H. Judd] and Miss [Pauahi] Judd, John and I.[152] After that went with John to Govt. House.

Accepted Deborah and her Husband [James] Mahoe's lease for next lot. Ordered $ [blank] worth of timber to fence from Allen Robinson. Sent Joe to pay $178.38 worth of bills.

Slept at [scrolling ornament] Hale. Sent Wakeke to tell all the members of Liliuokalani Hui [Hookuonoono] to meet at Mary Ailau's next day.

---

the House of Nobles, and still further back seats of the Representatives. On the right of the platform chairs had been placed for the ladies of the Court and attendants, those present being Mrs. C. T. Gulick, Mrs. Paul Neumann, Miss Sophie Sheldon, Mrs. Samuel Parker, Mrs. James Kaai, and Mrs. E. K. Lilikalani." *Hawaiian Gazette*, May 4, 1886.

149. The queen was attired in "a robe of Royal maroon velvet trimmed with real ermine. The front, which was of white satin, was embroidered in gold with fern and taro leaves. Ornaments, Diamonds. Her Royal Highness Princess Liliuokalani . . . was attired in a satin dress embroidered in front with gold embroidery, and having a court train of gold brocade. Ornaments, diamonds." *Hawaiian Gazette*, May 4, 1886.

150. Mary Purdy Pahau (b. June 12, 1831, Waimea, Hawaii–d. December 5, 1923, Honolulu) was the daughter of pioneer Waimea rancher Harry Purdy, and from about three years of age she was also the hanai (adopted) daughter of Captain William Backle (b. 1773, Virginia–d. 1866, Honolulu), who had once commanded a vessel for Kamehameha I. Mary Purdy was the wife of Hiram Kolomoku Pahau (d. December 16, 1880) and the mother of John Dominis Aimoku. In 1918, during a dispute over the late Queen's will, Mary testified, "I came to know Lydia Kamakaeha (Liliuokalani) and [we] attended the Royal School together. . . . This acquaintance lasted up to the time of the Queen's death. . . . I was her aikane, her friend." Hawaii State Archives, Liliuokalani Collection, M-397, Liliuokalani Trust Papers, Box 2, Folder 17.

151. Isaiah Bray (b. 1844, Massachusetts–d. 1915, Honolulu) was captain of the missionary packet *Morning Star* (the fourth vessel by that name), maintained by the Hawaiian Board of Missions to supply its stations in Micronesia. Bray had just returned from his second voyage, and his remarks delivered at Kawaiahao Church were an account of that trip.

152. In its note on the breakfast, the *Pacific Commercial Advertiser*, May 5, 1886, said that Mr. Tiffany accompanied the Mitchells.

*Tuesday, May 4.* Cleaned the room but was taken ill with pain in back of neck and top of head. Sent word down to members that I would not be there. Sent for officers of Liliuokalani Hui [Hookuonoono]. Did some business and borrowed $200 from Hui. Note endorsed by President and Secretary [of the Hui]. Gov. [of] Hawaii [Princess Poomaikelani] comes in. Mrs. Kuihelani and Mary, Jessie, Linohu, Emma B., David came in. King came in, Leihulu and Mrs. Kapena[153]—Mary Stillman, Miss Brickwood all sent their dues today.

*Wednesday, May 5.* Went in Palace, met Members of Hooulu Lahui. Proposed that some of the money in the Bank belonging to the Society be given towards assisting the people burnt out by the fire. The King called in by the Queen, gave opinion that it was not right. My request was refused. Proposed by the Queen that entertainment should be given and carried. Five P.M. went out to Sister's and slept out there.

*Thursday, May 6.* Joe came for me at Sister's [and] we drove to Judge McCully's to get his opinion about next lot.[154] McCully says only Debora [Kanoa] could sell it. Charley Wilson wants papers of denization for Norrie—[I] said I would see Gibson. Went to Palace to arrange about aiding those burnt out. Arranged all committees for Saturday. King returned and did not like it. Postponed till Friday week a drill [and] Sat week concert. Came home, found a note from Joe to send for baby Nihoa.[155] Wakeke brought me home from Palace and we went right up. Wakeke went for baby and brought him home. Told Manuela to make me some frames. Went to Palace with John to a ball given for Admiral Seymour.[156]

C. asked why I had forgotten him. Slept in Nua Lehua.

*Friday, May 7.* Baby [Nihoa] cried good deal yesterday and Joe came to see about him. Agreed to send for Kahae to stay here till after baby's birthday. Wakeke and I sent evergreens to YMCA. Seven P.M. We went for Mary Carter and all went to see Kalei and other young ladies recite.[157]

On our way up met Kahae coming down to baby. Asked her if she was going to stay with baby—she said she would stay till after baby's birthday. The entertainment was splendid. Everybody there delighted to see me. Promised to give one doz. fans to Mrs. [C. M.] Hyde. Came home. Slept in Nua Lehua Hale.

153. Liliu must mean John Kapena's mother, as his wife (Emma Kapena), Leihulu's mother, had died at Kapalama on April 18, 1886.

154. This refers to a lot next to Liliuokalani's Muolaulani premises, not a lot adjacent to McCully's premises below Punahou Street.

155. Nihoa was a son of the Aeas.

156. "On Thursday last [May 6], His Majesty gave a ball to welcome Admiral Sir Michael Culme Seymour and the Captains and officers of HMSs *Triumph*, *Heroine*, and *Satellite*. The affair was a very brilliant one and was a thorough success. The Palace was illuminated with many colored lights and the grounds were lit up with torches.... The affair was of an unofficial character, the King entertaining as a private gentleman. There was of course the state quadrille, but the lack of state formality only added an extra charm. Dancing was kept up with great spirit.... The uniforms of the naval officers and the gay dresses of the many young ladies set off by the more somber but perhaps more artistic dresses of the elder ladies made a very pretty and animated scene." *Hawaiian Gazette*, May 11, 1886.

157. This was a benefit entertainment held by the Gleaners Society. The *Advertiser* reported: "The programme consisted of addresses, reading of a poem, music and the representation of different countries in national costume. It was most creditably rendered by the young ladies of the society. The entertainment was for the benefit of the Kawaiahao Female Seminary, and quite a handsome sum will be netted." *Pacific Commercial Advertiser*, May 8, 1886.

*Saturday, May 8.* Mr. Oggel came round with subscription paper to ask me to subscribe for Bethel [Church].[158] Sent him to A. J. Cartwright. Mr. Frank Austin brought list for people burnt out by fire. He asked me to use my influence to get him position of engrosser [a copyist] to the house of Legislature. [Henry M.] Whitney brought his book of Photographs, which he intends to send to Mr. Borel in Switzerland.[159]

Three P.M. took Mrs. Dowsett and John out to Cricket Match between Honolulu and Man of wars men.[160]

Band out there. Rainy afternoon. Left John, came home, seven P.M. went with John to concert at Music Hall.[161]

Came home in a heavy shower.

*Sunday, May 9.* Rose early. After breakfast sat and read papers. S. Kaai came in.[162] Wanted to know about what the King's plans were. Did not know. Stayed at home all day. Paulo gave notice of his intention to leave. [I] Said he might. Sent for a Pake [Chinese].

*Monday, May 10.* Aiu came, said he would stay, and [I] was glad to have him. Paulo thought I would ask him to stay but I wouldn't. He cried bitterly but he has been too naughty. He took his traps after I paid him $23.00, went for an express, then went to Waikiki. Went to see Sister. Came home, slept on Nua Lehua. [John W.] Kalua came in, and we spoke

---

158. The fire of April 18, 1886, destroyed the Bethel Church. Reverend Engelbert Christian Oggel, who had replaced Samuel Chenery Damon as pastor of that church, was probably soliciting subscribers for a new edifice. When this plan was not realized, the Bethel congregation consolidated with the Fort Street Church, becoming Central Union Church.

159. The album was of great interest and the subject of a report in the *Advertiser*: "It will be in the recollection of many of our readers that M. Eugene Borel, Director of the Universal Postal Union, Berne, Switzerland, represented this kingdom at the recent international Postal Congress at Lisbon, for which he received the thanks of this Government.... It was therefore deemed advisable to send M. Borel some token of official recognition which he could accept, and the Hon H. M. Whitney while Postmaster General thought that an album containing portraits of the Royal Family and pictures of Hawaiian scenery, etc., would be an agreeable gift. Accordingly about two months ago he set about preparing one, and by Wells Fargo & Co.'s express yesterday one of the handsomest albums ever produced in the Kingdom was forwarded by the Post office authorities.... There are eight pages of portraits, twenty-eight of views, and five of ferns and mosses. Among the portraits are the King and Queen, Princess Liliuokalani, Princess Likelike, Princess Kaiulani, and Governor Dominis. The views [are] of the Palace, Government building, Hotel, the Queen's Hospital, and other points of interest. A picture of Hilo Bay is likewise effective. Mr. F. L. Clarke has mounted thirty-five specimens [of] ferns and mosses, and one page of silversword, furnishing the name of each. Mr. Whitney mounted them himself." *Pacific Commercial Advertiser*, May 10, 1886.

160. "The cricket match on Saturday at the Makiki baseball grounds between a team picked from HMS *Triumph*, *Satellite*, and *Heroine* and the Honolulu Cricket Club resulted in a decided and well-earned victory for the visitors.... His Majesty the King, H.R.H. Princess Liliuokalani, His Excellency Governor Dominis, and a large concourse of spectators, among whom were a large proportion of the fair sex, watched the game with interest. The result of this match shows that the Honolulu C.C. cannot expect to compete with any team composed of real cricketers unless they devote some little time to practice between matches." *Pacific Commercial Advertiser*, May 10, 1886.

161. The concert at the Opera House was a farewell performance by the "Campobello troupe"—the program included selections from Donizetti (the duet "Cheti Cheti"), two selections from Rossini, a prelude and fugue by Bach, and Mozart's Sonata no. 7.

162. S. W. Kaai was a legislator in the 1880, 1886, and 1898 sessions. Note: This is not Simon Kaai (d. 1884), a longtime politician and government official, and the previous owner of Liliu's Muolaulani residence.

of Charlie Wilson's case, and he said I should see the King [as to] what his opinion might be.

*Tuesday, May 11.* Went to Palace. King said we might do as we pleased. Got news by telephone from the Queen that no more ice cream party—everything sent home—don't know the reason. Four P.M. the King came personally to tell me that the Subscription party was pau [canceled]. He told me more of Charley [Wilson]—what shall I say.

*Wednesday, May 12.* Eight A.M. while at breakfast Joe came to tell me about Waikiki and Aho.

Must go down and see. Stayed till 1½ P.M. He [Joe] seemed in mortal dread. Got home in time for dinner.

*Thursday, May 13.* Went to Palace at 12 P.M. Mrs. Neumann, Mrs. Gulick, the Queen, and Pooloku [Poomaikelani]. [It was] Kealiiahonui's birthday.[163] Hanohano maoli [truly magnificent or glorious]. All the ministers and Legislative Assembly and their ladies. After dinner Admiral came in, then the King and all the Gents went on board the *Triumph*, Seymour.[164]

I came home and after tea went to YMCA with Mary Carter to an entertainment given by P. C. Jones[165] to sailors on board the *Triumph*. Spent a pleasant evening.

*Friday, May 14.* Went to see Sister [Likelike], she was asleep—came to see Sam Damon, he was improving—had been very sick, blood poisoning. He told me he had $500 in hand, which belonged to the people to assist burnt out people. Came home to dinner, went to Mary Carter's for Society book. Went to Cordie Allen's about forming a society. Went to see [John] Kapena—very ill—out of his head, speech thick. Went to Miss Alexander's and got their society book. Came home, had tea, went up and met Mrs. Allen and Faxon Bishop at YMCA. The house was full. Horatio G. Parker—recited[166]—was introduced though didn't want to. Sat up till two writing plans for next day. Invitations sent out [added at top of page] yesterday and day before.

*Saturday, May 15.* Went at ten to Kawaiahao. Ladies responded to my call. Told them my object in calling them, to form a society to educate young Hawaiians. All were willing—divided into two. First division to be under

---

163. "Yesterday being the anniversary of the birth of Prince Edward Keliiahonui, who is attending school at San Mateo, California, Her Royal Highness the Princess Poomaikelani, Governess of Hawaii, gave a grand luau at the Palace in honor of the occasion.... A most elegant spread, à la Hawaiian, was laid out in the basement story of the Palace, to which all did ample justice." *Pacific Commercial Advertiser*, May 14, 1886.

164. Captain Sir Michael Culme-Seymour, baronet, hosted a party on board the HBMS *Triumph* for the ministers and members of the legislature. The party "was attended by a large number of our society people both old and young." *Pacific Commercial Advertiser*, May 14, 1886.

165. Peter Cushman Jones (b. December 10, 1837, Boston–d. April 23, 1922, Honolulu) was a Honolulu resident from 1857. He served as Liliuokalani's minister of finance 1892–January 13, 1893, and the Provisional Government reappointed him January 17–March 15, 1893. He was a partner with the firm of C. Brewer & Co., 1871–99; founded what became the Hawaiian Trust Co.; and was one of the organizers of the Bank of Hawaii.

166. Horatio Parker's program at the YMCA hall was well attended. It was reported that "the versatile reader pleased his hearers with some fine bits of humor" and "the scene from Hamlet was given with full understanding of the text and in a quiet manner, in keeping with the ... melancholy Dane." *Pacific Commercial Advertiser*, May 15, 1886.

sister [Likelike], the other under me. Adjourned at one, till three P.M. third Thursday.[167]

Came home, [then] went down to King's boathouse to a luau for Admiral Seymour and Representatives[168]—left them at four P.M. Went to Washington Place to Nihoa. Subscriptions for burnt out [persons] $30 was received. Came home tired. Slept in Nua Lehua. It must be that K. is still huhu [angry] with me, what shall I do? Kawehena dead drunk. Expected to sleep [two words erased] but something went wrong [word erased] sick—bosh.

*Sunday, May 16.* Sent for Kaipo and Aimoku one P.M. Sent them with Wakeke to bathe in sea. Dined at two. Four P.M., was laying off under the trees with Kahae, baby, and Wakeke [when] John drove in with Capt. Hayley, Sir Robert Musgrave, Capt. Rose, [blank] Boyd, and [blank]. Five P.M. Took Aimoku back to Waikiki. Went and saw Sister, brought Kaipo home to Mrs. Bush. Lovely night. "Thou art so near and yet so far."[169]

Mary Beckley[170] came to tell me to come to their house and dine—tomorrow [is her son] Henry's birthday.[171]

*Monday, May 17.* Busy all morning—12 P.M. went to Mary Beckley's dinner. [Samuel G.] Wilder and son, Mrs. Parker,[172] Mrs. J. Ena,[173] Mrs. Buchanan,[174] myself, Mr. and Mrs. Iaukea.

167. This diary entry records the formation of the Liliuokalani Hui Hoonaauao (aka Hui Hoonaauao Liliuokalani or Liliuokalani Educational Society), of which Liliuokalani writes: "In the year 1886, I organized an educational society, the intention of which was to interest the Hawaiian ladies in the proper training of young girls of their own race, whose parents would be unable to give them advantages by which they would be prepared for their duties in life." See *Hawaii's Story*, 139–40. The main purpose of the organization was to grant scholarships to Hawaiian and part-Hawaiian students. Two maheles (divisions) were established, the first at Kawaiahao Church, with Princess Likelike as president, and the second at Kaumakapili Church, under Liliuokalani. Liliu was treasurer. Records of the Hui for 1886–87 are in the Hawaii State Archives, Liliuokalani Collection, Liliuokalani Trust Papers, M-397, Box 2.

The Liliuokalani Collection has a small record book for the second division, which records the first meeting of that division at Kaumakapili Church on May 18, 1886. There is also a later constitution (circa 1890) of the same, which includes a drawing of the society's badge.

In a January 15, 1912, memorandum (Hawaii State Archives, Liliuokalani Collection, Liliuokalani Trust Papers), Curtis P. Iaukea says that after the overthrow of the monarchy "the society ceased to have any active existence... The society was formally disbanded in February 1912, and all remaining assets were transferred to the Queen." In her diaries, Liliuokalani refers to this organization variously by its Hawaiian and English-language titles.

168. She refers to the members of the House of Representatives who were then in session.

169. This was a popular song of the day, composed by Alexander Reichardt (b. 1825–d. 1888), the first line of which is: "I know an eye so softly bright, that glistens like a star of night."

170. Mary Camille Risley (b. 1855, Waimea, Hawaii–d. 1950, Honolulu) was an intimate friend of Liliu and was often present at both Washington Place and Muolaulani. She married George C. Beckley in 1873.

171. Henry P. Beckley (b. May 17, 1876, Waimea, Hawaii–d. February 13, 1955, Honolulu) was later a Red Cross worker in Siberia and an aide to Hawaii Governor Wallace R. Farrington.

172. Harriet Panana Napela Parker (b. 1849), the only daughter of Napela, was the adopted daughter of Huaka Kuihelani (b. 1804–d. 1892), of a chiefly family related to Mrs. Napela. Liliuokalani's friend and confidante John Richardson of Wailuku was Harriet's brother. Harriet married Samuel Parker at Wailuku, Maui, August 23, 1871, and died in New York City, July 5, 1901.

173. Mary Lane (b. 1859–d. 1890) was the wife of John Ena Jr.

174. Emma Fitzsimmons was the wife of W. R. Buchanan.

Came home and at four P.M. went to meet Nihoas at Washington Place. None came, but brought plants home. Arranged with Aiaumoe to take baby away on Sat. Told Joe about it and he was glad.

*Tuesday, May 18.* Wrote all the morning a new Constitution for our Educational Society. Three P.M. went to Kaumakapili [Church] to meet members of Hui Hoonaauao Liliuokalani [Liliuokalani Educational Society]. They contributed $35.80. There was a good deal of feeling of hookae [discontent] because they wanted to belong to the First Division.

*Wednesday, May 19.* Stayed at home. Nakanealoha[175] came to get some flowers. Four P.M. Jessie [Kaae] came to say that her husband did not want her to be a member any longer of the Hui Hoonaauao because it was beneath her kulana [rank or position]. After tea we sat in Kaipo's room with baby. He [Joe Aea?] came home tight and wanted to talk. Went back and had a row with his wife, she was at fault he said, she got a Kahuna [sorcerer] and tried to Anaana us [curse by means of prayer and incantation]—she was ashamed of that.

*Thursday, May 20.* 10½ A.M. took Joe and went out to Waikiki. Told Aho to clean up the yard and other places. Dined there, came home at five P.M. Left Joe at Washington Place to get bundles. Came home and went to see Mr. Anderson at Music Hall[176] with Mary Carter and John. Found Haaheo[177] in box. Crowded. Came home and rested in Nua Lehua.

*Friday, May 21.* Went to breakfast but she [Kahae?] would not speak to me, funny? It ended in her scolding me. Told her she was foul mouthed. She came in to tea with the intention of scolding but Annie D. [Dowsett] came.

*Saturday, May 22.* Aiaumoe did not come till one P.M. [At] two, the King came and went home. Wanted to know if I could take medicine again. Called for Kahae to come and in Wakeke's presence told her that in 10 days she was to pay up $782.00 and the interest on it, the sum she owed me for Joe's land at Waikahalulu, [or?] I would send Kaipo back to her and deprive him of money, then left her. Aiaumoe took Nihoa [Aea] away to Waikiki.

Went to Music Hall with Liliu [Sadie Carter] and Cushman Carter.[178] After performance went to see Kaipo. Left him and came home. Kini came to know if they had any money for the church. Told him would send him word next day. Meheula scolded her [Kahae] for her imprudence to me.

175. Elizabeth (Lizzie) Nakanealoha (b. 1848–d. August 15, 1929, Honolulu), the wife of John Mana, was one of the Queen's closest friends. In her will, the Queen left Mrs. Mana a life interest in a lot on Ohua Street, Waikiki.

176. Professor Anderson, who advertised himself as "Great Wizard of the North, Cosmopolitan Monarch of Magicians, Philosopher Scientist, and Traveler"—announced four performances between May 20 and 27. The *Pacific Commercial Advertiser*, May 19, 1886, promised: "Professor Anderson's reputation as a magician is worldwide and needs no comment, [and] Madame Louise Maude Anderson will appear in her marvelous clairvoyance."

177. Mary Haaheo (b. April 24, 1874, Honolulu–d. March 8, 1933, Honolulu) was the daughter of Major David Leleo Kinimaka, a cousin of King Kalakaua and Liliuokalani. She was raised as a child in the king's household, and was later the wife of Dr. Robert Atcherley.

178. Henry Cushman Carter (b. June 27, 1880, Honolulu–d. July 3, 1918, Sierra Madre, California) was the son of J. O. and Mary Carter.

*Sunday, May 23.* After breakfast went to Waikiki to Kaipo's cottage. Spent the day there. Came home late in the evening. He brought the brake home and stayed a little while, for I wanted to see him about our affairs, a very sad one. Sent list of items how money was spent by C.B.W. [Wilson] for church. To meet me next eve, at Washington Place. Came home. John had been here to ask me to go to church with him, and for me to come up—nine P.M. I slept in Washington Place.

*Monday, May 24.* Sent note to Joe to come up here. It is Queen Victoria's Birthday and very quiet—only the Band played at Wodehouse's.[179]

Told him [John] I was not prepared to be his wife but I would let him know this eve. Went to Hotel, then went to Washington Place. My friend came—I told him to come next day. Slept [at] Washington Place. Curtis came up to my carriage while [I was] sitting with Annie Turton—told me Pua was going by the *Australia*. Mary Carter and Mrs. Oggel came to invite me to come up next eve to a reception for Mr. and Mrs. Locke Richardson and I accepted. Lepeka placed in my hands $12.50 for the people burnt out by fire.

*Tuesday, May 25.* Joe came for me seven A.M. Mary told me about his coming. As soon as she was gone, Breakfasted and sat down to work. 12 P.M. Joe and Kahae came to mihi [apologize] and she did so in presence of Wakeke and Loe, and her husband, saying she was sorry for all the bad words she had said about me and promised on the future never to say anything bad about me. Eight P.M. John and I went to Mrs. Oggel's reception and enjoyed it much. Slept at Washington Place.

*Wednesday, May 26.* Had company all day. Two P.M. Charlie brought in Report of President of Board of Health with my report in it.[180]

Mr. and Mrs. Ando called. Four P.M. Wakeke and I went to call on Mrs. T. H. Davies, Mrs. C. N. Spencer of Kau,[181] Mrs. [Paul] Neumann, Mrs. Iaukea, Mrs. Beckley, Mrs. T. R. Walker.[182]

Came home and John came right in and wanted me to come downtown and I did. Oh, called on Mrs. Banning[183] also and Mr. and Mrs. Pfluger.[184]

---

179. Major James Hay Wodehouse (d. Abingdon, England, July 13, 1911) was British consul and later British commissioner in Hawaii 1867–97. His residence was on Emma Square.

180. *Report of Her Majesty Queen Kapiolani's Visit to Molokai, by H.R.H. Princess Liliuokalani, July 1884* was published as *Appendix to the Report on Leprosy of the President of the Board of Health to the Legislative Assembly of 1886* (Honolulu, 1886), iii-xvii. This report includes Queen Kapiolani's address to the residents of Kalaupapa and their responses, followed by Liliu's critical examination of all aspects of life at the colony, and thoughtful suggestions for needed improvements. Liliu concludes: "I cannot help stating that ... the condition of things are [sic] much better than that at my former visit in 1881."

181. Annie E. Brown, daughter of Captain Brown, married rancher Charles N. Spencer of Kau, Hawaii, on January 23, 1862.

182. Mary Matilda Burd was the wife (from 1878) of Thomas Rain Walker (d. 1908, England), who arrived at Honolulu in 1868 and eventually became a partner in Theo. H. Davies Ltd. The Walkers were close friends of the Cleghorns, and later in England they saw much of Princess Kaiulani. Mrs. Walker died in England in 1908.

183. Clarissa Hannah Armstrong Banning (b. 1840–d. 1904) was the daughter of Richard Armstrong. Her husband, Frederick Banning, was head of the firm of Hoffschlaeger Co., Honolulu (he died August 8, 1886, San Francisco). Mrs. Banning was a schoolmate of Liliu at the Royal School.

184. William Pfluger was the operator of a merry-go-round carousel on Queen Street. For several years in the 1880s, the Pflugers rented Queen Emma's Nuuanu house, Hanaiakamalama.

Passed Joe and Kahae [Aea] on the way to the Hotel. Leihulu came in this morning and returned the list of Kapena's lands[185] to me [and] at same time told me of David Laika's imprudence to her in her father's presence and the latter never said a word.

*Thursday, May 27.* Sophy [Sheldon] placed in my hands $40.00 she had collected for people burnt by fire and Kainuuala [had collected] $2.25 for the same purpose. Sophy stayed awhile and told me of Leihulu's hiding herself at Governor Kanoa's on account of ill usage at home.

Annie Turton came in and dined, and Kapena and Mr. Abel, son of Consul Abel, came in my back door—did not stay long. Sophy, Annie, Wakeke, and I went to a fair given by Mrs. [C. M.] Hyde's "Lima Kokua," a Society formed for educating young girls. They realized $400.00.[186]

Drove down to Waikiki and left Annie at Mrs. Frank Brown's and came out here [to] Muolaulani. Slept in Nua Lehua.

*Friday, May 28.* After breakfast spent [morning] in garden. At 11 Mrs. Pashard and son, and Miss Austin came to see me. Went away delighted. Went down to Mary Beckley's to see her report. All right. At noon today there is a luau in barracks and target shooting.[187]

100 years ago La Pérouse came to Lahaina.[188]

Stopped at Frank Damon's[189] to see if we could have the Chinese Y.M.C.A. He said he would try to get it for us—in meantime, went to Mrs. Dominis and she said we might meet at Washington Place. Sat up till 11 writing, was started [startled?] by steps. A drunken man slept here till four A.M.

*Saturday, May 29.* Went to town, got home in time for dinner. Then drove up to Mary Carter's. Found Mother Dickson, 87 years old,[190] waiting for the [Memorial Day] procession and [as] they passed by, she stood erect in front of us and no one took notice of her. She had presented the G.A.R.

---

185. John M. Kapena (who was still alive at this point but would die on October 22, 1887) had considerable property, but would go bankrupt as of April 15, 1887. Lands under his control included two large parcels (195 acres at Kaamola on Molokai, and 32 acres at Ukumehame on Maui), which had been David Malo's and were supposed to go to Malo's granddaughter, Leihulu Kapena. However, these properties were under mortgage and were sold in settling Kapena's estate. Leihulu subsequently sought their return in court, but was unsuccessful, and all she got at the end was $282.23. Hawaii State Archives, First Circuit Court, Probate 2525.

186. The fair was held at the YMCA for the benefit of Kawaiahao Seminary. "Various articles of beauty and utility were disposed of at good prices [and] the sale of refreshments increased the amount." *The Friend*, June 1887. The name of the society translates as "helping hand."

187. "The Royal Household Guards will have a luau on Friday at 12 o'clock noon. After the Luau they will participate in artillery shooting at Kakaako. Ships, boats, and canoes are warned against passing the line of shooting during practice." *Pacific Commercial Advertiser*, May 27, 1886.

188. French explorer Jean-François de Galaup, Comte de La Pérouse (b. 1741, Albi, France–d. 1788), arrived off Makena, Maui, on May 29 and departed from the islands on May 30, 1786. For an account of his travels, see *Voyage de La Pérouse Autour du Monde* (Paris: L'Imprimerie de la République, 1797).

189. Francis Williams Damon (b. 1852–d. 1915), the son of Reverend Samuel C. Damon, was superintendent of the Chinese mission and resided on Chaplain Lane.

190. Mrs. Sarah Dickson (b. 1798, Boston–d. July 26, 1888, Honolulu) was the wife of Captain Joshua Dickson. She lived for many years in Cincinnati, Ohio, before coming to Honolulu in 1867. Her obituary noted that she was "one of the many intensely patriotic females who gave an impress to the early history of the American Republic, and seemed to inspire their countrymen with noble purposes." *Pacific Commercial Advertiser*, July 27, 1886.

Co. with $150 [for] Decoration Day.[191] Band and procession went by, drove round and found the engines at work, so had to go round by School St.—just in front was procession coming back.

That evening met at Washington Place, and went down to Waikiki, but didn't go home till morning. Saw Jim Brown's carriage out there. Who could have been in it?

*Sunday, May 30.* Came home [in] broad daylight. Did not go to church, but Annie Turton came over this morning and sat awhile. Am huhu [angry] with Wakeke—she knows that I am going to dress, but she goes off and dresses herself and gets in the carriage while I am mending shoes and dresses, instead of waiting on me first. Joe also is cross because I tell him to leave black horse until he came after him [sic].

Eveline comes over to Kaipo's house. While dining Joe and Kahae comes over from town. She is still cross. All come home 6½ P.M. They stay till my express came for me, then went home, although trying to pick a quarrel.

*Monday, May 31.* Received $450—from A. J. Cartwright, paid $220 toward Ahahui [club] Liliuokalani Hookuonoono. Aiaumoe tells me that for the three doz. fans Meeau made for me, and three pillows, I owe her $5.25. Today have paid Kainuuala and Kalahiki's last $5. Out [illegible] Kahaloipua and Minnie Widemann[192] came to return my call.

Wrote all evening until eight, then went up to Kaipo's.[193] He had gone to sleep. Went back to Washington Place disappointed. Gave C. Bush $10. Band played on board *Australia* till 11.[194]

*Tuesday, June 1.* Met the Hui Hookuonoono ladies. They contributed $240. 12 P.M. came home, dined at one, and bought some leis for Annie [Turton]. Told Wakeke to cook some dry fish and take poi[195] also on board *Australia* for Annie. She [Wakeke] said she was ashamed. I may be ashamed some day when she can't get her money. Three P.M. met ladies of Hui Hoonaauao at Washington Place—they contributed $24—left in a hurry as everyone had friends going in Steamer. Mrs. Curtis [Iaukea] is gone and other Kamaainas.[196]

Came up, had tea, slept in Hinano Bower. T. [Tamar?] saw Alice Brown at wharf.

Hinau and Poole died today.[197]

---

191. May 29 was observed as Memorial Day by "Geo. W. DeLong Post no. 45 (of California) of the GAR (Grand Army of the Republic)" and all "honorably discharged" soldiers, sailors, marines, and members of the GAR. On this occasion, the company assembled in town and marched up to Nuuanu Cemetery, where they held a memorial service for their fallen comrades. The procession included the Royal Hawaiian Band, the Prince's Own, the King's Own, the Mamalahoa Guards, and the Honolulu Rifles.

192. Wilhelmine (Minnie) Widemann (b. 1862–d. 1929) was the daughter of Judge Herman Adam Widemann (b. 1822, Hanover, Germany–d. 1899, Honolulu) and (from 1888) the wife of John McKibbin Dowsett. Kahaloipua was the wife of Curtis Iaukea.

193. Kaipo Aea was living at Mrs. Caroline Bush's house on Emma Street.

194. A reception was held on the *Australia* of the Oceanic Steamship Co. The king and Governor Dominis are listed as having attended; Liliu is not mentioned.

195. Poi is taro cooked, pounded, and mixed with water.

196. This was the maiden outward-bound voyage of the *Australia*. The *Daily Bulletin*, June 3, 1886, noted that her departure was a "gala occasion" and that "his Majesty was on the wharf as was [sic] also other notables." A kamaaina is one born of a place.

197. The Honolulu City Directory lists Hinau as a palace employee, residing at 74 Beretania Street. Poole is not identified.

*Wednesday, June 2.* Bought books for Mary, Tamar,[198] and myself at Oat's[199] $4.50. Wrote all morning. Mrs. Ivers and Mrs. Ben Holliday, and Miss Irwin[200] came to invite me to come to the boat house on Sat. 12 P.M. Started to pay bills, was too late. Met the officers of Aha Hookuonoono, borrowed $100 at ten percent—found my mistake. Must meet again tomorrow.

*Thursday, June 3.* $34.60 belongs to 2nd Division [of the Aha Hookuonoono] [and] $20.70 to 1st Div.

Great preparations. Ten A.M. took $110.60 to Mr. [Francis W.] Damon—for burnt out people. $55.30 to A. J. Cartwright for Hui Hoonaauao, $45.00 for Hui H[ookuonoono] Liliuokalani. Borrowed $200 of Hui H[ookuonoono] Liliuokalani. Note endorsed by officers. The Band Boys brought and placed in my keeping $200.00 as their Puuku Nui [chief treasurer]. D. Naone, Vikoli, Pua, Aylett. Three P.M. had a reception for Liliu, her mother Mary, Oliver.[201]

Annie Dowsett dined with me. Lots of people called. After five Band went home. Mary Carter and I went to meeting of Women's Board of Missions. Speeches made, singing and prayers, came home tired.

*Friday, June 4.* Sunday School celebration at Kaumakapili [Church]. Would like to meet committee of Hui Hoonaauao. Must buy my present for best class. Stayed at Kaumakapili till exercises were over at two. Kamoiliili [Sunday School] was the best. Maemae [Sunday School] next. Concert at Kaumakapili. Went with Poomaikelani, Kanoa, Iaukea, Jessie, and Kaae to the concert. The Church was half full. Performance pretty good. Came home from the Palace, found my friend waiting for me. [Scrolling ornament.]

Took Band boys' money to A. J. C. [Cartwright] $200.

*Saturday, June 5.* Am engaged in the evening to John to go to theatre. Busy all the Morning. Wakeke begins to ride a high horse also and wants to leave me. I accept, but tell her that I would not pay for Kalei's schooling, which opens her eyes and [she] is glad to apologize. Kawehena and Loe[202] would like their money and to go also. I wonder what it would be like to be left all alone.

One P.M. went to Palace—everybody gone except Kapo [Princess Poomaikelani]. I think they are all huhu [angry]. We go to King's boathouse. Had pleasant time down there. Came home, left Kaipo at Palace—everyone had returned [and] looked thunders at K. [Kapo?] Went to theatre with John[203]—it was stupid, came home. Spent two hours in Like's [Likelike's] room—slept [at] Nua Lehua.

---

198. This is probably a reference to Tamar Makaiki (d. June 4, 1899), who married Reverend Moses Kuaea in 1870. When Kuaea died May 5, 1884, his estate included a half-acre lot at Waikahalulu, Nuuanu, under mortgage to Liliu, which she purchased at auction for $1,390. Hawaii State Archives, First Circuit Court, Probate 2234.

199. J. M. Oat & Co., news dealer and stationer, was located at 25 Merchant Street.

200. Mrs. Ben Holliday would marry William G. Irwin on November 9, 1886. Mrs. Ivers was her sister and Miss Irwin was W. G. Irwin's sister. They were all residents of San Francisco.

201. This was a party honoring three members of the J. O. Carter family, all with June birthdays: Mary E. Ladd, the wife of J. O. Carter (b. June 8, 1840); Liliu (or Sarah) Mitchell Carter (b. June 1, 1872), later wife of Winfred Howard Babbitt; and J. O. Carter's son Joseph Oliver Carter, generally known as Oliver (b. June 12, 1868).

202. Kawehena is in the 1884–85 City Directory as a retainer of Liliuokalani, at Washington Place. In the 1888 City Directory, he appears as her gardener, residing at King and Liliha (near or on the Muolaulani premises). Loe was his wife.

203. At the Opera House were Harry Emmet and Arthur Branscombe, advertised as "the

*Sunday, June 6.* Perhaps will go to Waikiki. Oh!—no—must go to Kawaiahao and did go. It was full. Came home with Mary and dined. Telephone rang for me to come out [to Waikiki]. Stayed out [at] Waikiki all afternoon and slept out there.

*Monday, June 7.* Had nothing to eat since yesterday. Could not enjoy my breakfast. Misses Alexander and Malone [call?]. See about girls at school. Mrs. and Miss Spreckels call. Iaukea tells me Aiaumoe went to him for liquor, shall he give it to him. Must advertise Kaipo's house. Am to have a meeting at four o'clock of Committee of Relief Fund. Brown to meet Iaukea here tomorrow.

Kanoa's Mother is to be buried this Afternoon.[204]

No concert tonight but tomorrow night. Gave Mr. Damon $426.50 [for the] fire relief fund. Will he come? Received $5.00 from Mrs. C. Hiram. Went for John and drove to P. C. Jones' party. 8½ P.M. Mr. Louisson's house is burnt down.[205]

It is also election night of Fire Department.[206]

Locke Richardson gave readings at P.C.I. [North Pacific Missionary Institute]. John lost cloak.

*Tuesday, June 8.* Made arrangements to meet Locke Richardson here today at ten. He came with his wife [and] with Mrs. [blank]. At three had meeting of Officers of Hui Liliuokalani Hookuonoono, because Mrs. Kuihelani wanted to borrow money to pay off her indebtedness to Wilder & Co. $1046.37/100. Decided to wait until tomorrow when Mrs. Beckley is to report about the case—to meet at Washington Place at four P.M.

Kahae came early this morning, for what I did not know—looking slouchy, and said she wanted a cocoanut and did take it. I think, though, that she came for a different purpose. Jessie and Annie Dowsett stayed till ¼ to eight. I [He?] came according to promise and stayed till ten, then went to Steamer *Zealandia*. A lovely moonlight night.

*Wednesday, June 9.* While breakfasting with S. Kaai, John came in and expressed a wish to go to Waikiki to stay until after the 12th. I was glad at the proposal and sent messages to have the house cleaned up. Kaakaole proposes to have me take charge of her affairs and keep money for her.

Great Comedians in their world-renowned drawing room entertainment 'Bonbons' [promising] Glorious songs, Screaming [Comedies] and 'Uproarious fun.'" The *Pacific Commercial Advertiser*, June 7, 1886, noted that "H.R.H. the Princess Liliuokalani and His Excellency Governor Dominis were present in the Royal box, and Colonel and Mrs. Spreckels and Miss Spreckels occupied the opposite box."

204. "Mrs. [Kahanaauwai] Kanoa, widow of the late Hon. P. Kanoa, died at her Palama residence yesterday. The funeral will take place this afternoon at four o'clock." *Daily Bulletin*, June 7, 1886.

205. Morris Louisson was a partner in the firm of M. S. Grinbaum & Co., merchants, 39 Queen Street. His residence was at the corner of School and Fort Streets.

206. The annual election of officers for the Honolulu Fire Department was a festive event. The *Pacific Commercial Advertiser*, June 8, 1886, noted that the building of Engine Co. No. 2 was illuminated with three large lanterns, emblazoned with the names of candidates Wilson, Asch, and Hustace, and that the Royal Hawaiian Band was stationed outside the building. The polls opened at seven P.M. The fire at the Louisson residence interrupted the election, but after a tally of the votes, Charles B. Wilson was elected chief engineer, Julius Asch assistant engineer, and Frank Hustace second assistant engineer.

Pehikulani [Auld][207] gave me $5 for Hui Hookuonoono. Met at Washington Place with officers of Hui Hookuonoono and Mr. and Mrs. Kuihelani. Mrs. Beckley reported the results—will meet again on Sat. Morn. Ten A.M. Arranged to have whist party here on Tuesday after our sewing Society Hoonaauao.

*Thursday, June 10.* Must go [written above line: send] after my bonnets at Fishels at noon. Must send a note to Sophy [Sheldon] to tell her to go out with us to a concert at Music Hall, then go right out to Waikiki with us that night. Must send Mary Purdy with the folks this afternoon and Mainalulu. Sophy came over and went with us to Concert,[208] then we all went to Waikiki. John is unusually attentive.

*Friday, June 11.* Will go to the races at the Park.[209]

Went out and had to sit on the Lunamakaainana's [House of Representatives] stand. Kaiulani and I. John has been very attentive—but I mention it because it is so unusual and am happy to have him so. John Cummins wins all the races. The Queen and Poomaikelani and I in the Club House. Races? my heart is not in the races. Returned at five P.M. from the races.

Had supper out on the grass. Eight P.M., he came to see me and was rather in a fault finding mood. However, he became good natured and slept up here [partially erased: John is...lovesick] what a change. Woke [illegible] and went home.

*Saturday, June 12.* This morn must meet Hui at Washington Place ten A.M. Must be here surely at six P.M., for I expect a visitor. Had a telephone from Mrs. [Henri or Henry] Berger about the Band and saying John could not be found.

Went to town and found him at Hotel. Went with him and made all arrangements about band, then left him and went to meeting at Washington Place. Agree to see Wilder about assuming Kuihelani's debts. He was willing to let Hui Liliuokalani Hookuonoono [reimburse him] at $1,000 1st July, and then $200 every month until debt is paid, which will take five months. Kuihelani paying us 10 percent from the day we pay Wilder. Placed in Sam Damon's hands $36 for relief fund. He said [he] was willing to send Esther to stay in school vacation time. Mrs. Holokahiki[210] said she had not notified Hui Hoonaauao. Took Kaipo, Willie, Lola, and Carrie to drive. Came home tired.

207. Mrs. Catherine Pehikulani Auld (b. 1842, Molokai–d. October 7, 1900, Honolulu) married first James Lawrence Lewis, a cooper (d. April 6, 1875), and then James Auld, a printer who was owner of the *Pacific Commercial Advertiser* in partnership with J. H. Black.

208. This concert at the Opera House was advertised in the newspapers as a "Grand farewell concert by the talented young trio Lula, Pauline, and Else Joran, the favorite buffo baritone Signor Luigi Lencioni, and first appearance of Mlle. Leonora Aldini, prima donna soprano." A review commented: "It is long since lovers of music in Honolulu had an evening of so much exquisite enjoyment." *Pacific Commercial Advertiser*, June 11, 1886.

209. The annual Kamehameha Day races at Kapiolani Park commenced at 11 A.M. There were in all eight races scheduled, and one of the favored horses was J. A. Cummins's Queen Kapiolani.

210. This was Annie, the wife of W. L. Holokahiki (d. February 4, 1889), an attorney at law at 5 Bethel St. and resident of 38 School Street near the bridge. 1884 City Directory.

*Sunday, June 13.* Must go and hear Locke Richardson read the Bible at the Lyceum this eve with John and Annie D. [Dowsett]. Spent morning watering plants. Two P.M. dined with Mrs. Dominis. Went to Waikiki four P.M., brought home papers. Went to church with Annie and John at the Lyceum. Heard Locke Richardson. Slept at Washington Place.

*Monday, June 14.* Nakookoo came to see me about Kapukini's land at Wailuku—told me about Kahae singing at [one line erased] fire like any street girl and other things. Kuihelani and wife came, and [I] dismissed them, saying I would send them word when ready. Kaakaole complains about water at Wailuakio [Palama?]. Will meet Mary and Joe at Bishops' this eve. Rec'd letter from Kakina about Daniela at Lumahai [Kauai] saying they were Kamaainas [acquainted]. Sent letter to Alee of Chulan & Co.[211] to say that I would act right by natives. Met Damon, Achi, [and] Waiamau decided to have W. find out first the real necessities of the people and report at next meeting. Sam Damon says my grain and hay has arrived.

*Tuesday, June 15.* Went [and] bought leis $1.00. Went for Jessie and bought maile plants[212] $1.00 on the way. Had paina Kapu [private luncheon]. Two P.M. came to our Hui Hoonaauao meeting at engine No. 1. They contributed $11.10—that day came home and went to town again to meet Doctor. John sat with me till eight. He came home and we went to Waikiki. Told me all particulars. Aiaumoe forgot to shut the whole house—funny. A lovely night.

Heard of the fight. She saw my carriage and was furious—went with Joe to C. [Commercial] Hotel.[213] [She] Raised a row about Joe's drinking [and] made use of my name, for which he pounded her—every right. She was under liquor and haul.[214] He is too good for her, a wife who would drive him from home with constant scolding.

*Wednesday, June 16.* Came home and met Mehau on the way. Tamar and Mrs. Holokahiki came here to arrange their [account] books—could not get it right. Told them to leave it and I would arrange all myself. Four P.M., they went home. After tea drove down and met Mary [Carter] at Washington Place and we drove to Govt. Place to see drill—it was splendid.[215]

Mary left me in good hands [and I] slept at Paoakalani. [Partially erased passage reads: John is kind and attentive.] Says mother is sick. Rec'd $1.10 from Mrs. C. Hiram.[216]

---

211. Chulan & Co. was a general importer at 21 Nuuanu Street, and proprietor of a rice mill on Queen Street. Alee or Ah Lee was a partner in the firm, and in 1888 served as Chinese consul.

212. The maile is a native twining shrub, *Alyxia olivaeformis*.

213. The Commercial Hotel on the corner of Beretania and Nuuanu Streets included a saloon and billiard parlor.

214. "Haul" or "haul in" refers to an individual being taken into police custody.

215. This was a moonlight drill on Palace Square by the King's Guards and volunteer companies under the command of Major J. H. Boyd.

216. L. Kainana was the wife from 1879 of Charles Hiram, King Kalakaua's coachman, who also for a time operated a carriage-for-hire operation at No. 98 Nuuanu Street "below the Commercial Hotel." In 1890, Hiram would be "fatally shot" by Lui, a South Sea Islander. *Pacific Commercial Advertiser*, May 10, 1890.

*Thursday, June 17.* Mrs. Holokahiki told me she has met Mrs. Hamauku[217] [and] was told she gave $25. She also told me of Joe beating Kahae Monday night for going in Commercial Saloon and [of having] told barkeeper not to give him drink and other reasons. Told me Tamar would soon bring money from Mrs. Hamauku. Tamar came and brought $1.50 for Mrs. H., dined with me, and went home. Annie was here all morning, as was Kunane [Kalakaua] who said he was coming tomorrow early to give apu Popolo.[218]

Four P.M. went for Mary Carter with Annie and all went to Sewing Society at Mrs. Damon's.[219]

Stayed till ten P.M. Heard Mr. Locke Richardson read. Came home tired. Slept in Sister's room—was cross and out of sorts. Heard Kahae was at M. [Minnie] Brown's. Recd. $1.45 from Tamar for Mrs. Hamauku. Saw akualele [fireball].

*Friday, June 18.* Received of Mrs. A. Rosa[220] $68.55 for Fire Relief Fund. Ke [?] went home and Kunane [Kalakaua] came with Kaae, so I took my popolo apu. It was so hohono [acrid smelling]. After he had gone John came to see if I would receive Mrs. Abell and daughter, said I would at 11 tomorrow. C. B. Wilson came and reported about Gulick's report [as minister of the interior] to the Legislature—also a plan of Colonization to borrow one Million from Govt. and buy up all Ewa and Waialua land and sell them by shares.[221]

Said I would see Brother [Kalakaua] about it. Charlie would like to carry out his railroad scheme.[222]

Leihulu [Kapena] would like to know what to do about her future. Will write to Mahoe to see Kaleikini. Lucy invites me for tomorrow [to] Maili's [Miss Mailiokalani Nowlein's] birthday.[223]

217. Hamauku is listed in the 1888 City Directory as "waiter, Iolani Palace, res. servants Bldg." Mrs. Hamauku (presumably the man's mother) is listed as a widow.
218. This is a medicinal tonic (apu) made from popolo berries (black nightshade, *Solanum americanum*).
219. This was the 34th annual meeting of the Stranger's Friend Society, established to aid sick and destitute travelers. Activities included sewing. The *Advertiser* noted Liliu's presence and said of the event: "During the evening a choice literary and musical program was given. Professor Locke Richardson delighted everyone with his excellent reading.... Refreshments of a very palatable nature were served." *Pacific Commercial Advertiser*, June 18, 1886.
220. Mrs. Johanna Ladd (d. 1891) was the wife of Major Antone Rosa.
221. The "colonization," or, as it was more familiarly known, the "great colonization land scheme," was a grand plan to purchase and consolidate four Oahu ranches: Kahuku and Honouliuli (owned by James Campbell) and Kawailoa and Waimea (owned by John H. Paty). The price offered for Campbell's holdings was $600,000 and included most of his lands in the Ewa district. Benjamin F. Dillingham via his prospectus offered to form a corporation and sell shares in the "Hawaiian Colonization Land and Trust Co.," which would control the properties. The project fell flat. See Paul T. Yardley, *Millstones and Milestones: The Career of B. F. Dillingham* (Honolulu: University Press of Hawaii, 1981), 100–105.
222. William R. Austin of London secured a franchise from the 1886 legislature to build and operate a street railway in Honolulu, backed by Skinner & Co., London. This was probably the "scheme" Liliu refers to here.
223. Elizabeth Kololou Mailiokalani Nowlein was the daughter of Samuel Nowlein. In 1887, the Hawaiian government sent her to Italy, where she studied art in Florence for one

King and Kaae came over—so I took my apu [a tonic drink]. He came late and did not stay long.

*Saturday, June 19.* Ten A.M. John brought Mr. and Miss Abell—had a very pleasant visit from them.[224]

Many visitors. Kunane [Kalakaua] was here. The children came out. Told Kunane about Dillingham's [colonizing] plan. [He] said [he] would not grant it. Had visitors all day.

Five P.M. Went to Mrs. Nowlein's luau. All sorts of people. Sam Parker took me to table—King took Maili—16 years old today. Stayed till after dinner. [Then] came right home. A very showery night. Those people sat up very late making all sort of noises. Likelike came to bid me good-bye.

*Sunday, June 20.* My last apu [tonic drink] is to be this morn. Ke kuu molohai [I am so drowsy]. Stayed at home all day, but John came to see me.

*Monday, June 21.* Expected to see or hear some news from Joe but did not—so I telephoned for Carrie [Bush] to bring Kaipo anyway next day. Asked Mrs. McGrew to come. Went to Breakfast at Palace with Mr. and Miss Abell and Mr. Abell.[225]

Mary Carter asked me to go to exercises tonight, so I asked Annie D. [Dowsett] to go with me. We went and it was a rainy night—suddenly in the midst of the exercises of the Jug breaking concert there was a cry of fire. It was Ryan's boathouse and Mr. Laine's Grain house burnt to ground.[226]

Had Ice cream, then took Mary home, then came home. Slept in Nua Lehua.

*Tuesday, June 22.* Kaipo's birthday, will be four years old today. Asked no one but Carrie [Bush] and the children, and Mrs. McGrew. Sophy and Kuahine [sister] came in also. Only killed a pig but he was well and hearty. How it pains me to think that for all my kindness to Kaipo and her children that I should receive abuse in return? And yet it seems hard to give Kaipo up. Well, time may work changes yet. I cannot sleep here, I must go in town. John was glad I had come.

*Wednesday, June 23.* Kahawaii gave me two dollars for [the] two Nihoas, Pepe and Wainu. Gave Sophy [Sheldon] $5.50 to get some trimming for Mrs. Dowsett's bonnet. John sent message for me to come in town to hear the band this eve.

Had a visit from Governor Kanoa. Told me the next lot [to Muolaulani] was going to be leased to Pake [Chinese]. Well, I will have to let it go at

---

year. She married George E. Smithies in 1892. He died in Honolulu on December 12, 1919; she died on May 18, 1918.

224. Mr. A. G. Abell and family arrived on the *Mariposa* from San Francisco on June 12. He was former island resident Alexander Gurdon Abell (b. 1819–d. 1890), a U.S. consul 1845–46, and later a California merchant.

225. The Iolani Palace guestbook (Hawaii State Archives) lists the breakfast guests as Alexander Abell, Madeline C. Abell, Walter S. Abell, Liliuokalani, J. O. Dominis, and C. H. Judd.

226. Henry B. Ryan's boat-building premises were at 196 Queen Street. Laine and Co., importer of hay, grain, and feed, maintained a warehouse adjacent to Ryan's lot.

$440—too much. Mr. Francis Gay came, would like to have the upper flat on Kalalau.[227]

Dressed and went down to meet John. Went to band at Hotel,[228] then slept at Washington Place.

*Thursday, June 24.* Came home [to Muolaulani] this morning. King and [Junius] Kaae [were] first visitors. Kapena and Kaukau next—came to see [me] about horse impounded. Mrs. Sargent and Mrs. [James W.] Merrill, Mrs. Wight, and Miss May. Went with Mrs. Dowsett for John and went to Mrs. Dickson's to hear Locke Richardson.[229]

Had a real nice time [and] came home with Annie [Dowsett]. She had on her new bonnet I made for her. When I came home, sent Joe back to unharness, but heard some strange sound in Keala Hale. It seems Joe had gone there to stay.

*Friday, June 25.* Half past nine went with Mary [Carter] to Punahou College. Stayed till half past 12, [then] came down to Punahou Preparatory examination. The Legislature came out to Punahou [and] had some fun with them. Did not leave examination till after five.[230]

Came home, dined, and went to Sam Parker's party with John—came home at half past 12. Slept at Washington Place.

*Saturday, June 26.* Went to town with Mary Carter, bought a picture as a prize for Sunday school tomorrow. It will also be [Henry] Cushman Carter's birthday, so got him a mug at West & Dows also.[231]

Took Mary home and came here and telephoned to brother [Kalakaua] who came out and gave me an Apu [a tonic drink]—it was a big one. Hope it will be all right.

7¼ A.M. Drove out to Dillingham's to return his papers on colonization.[232]

---

227. Francis Gay (b. 1858, New Zealand–d. 1928) became a resident of Kauai in 1864, and was one of the founders of the sugar estate Gay & Robinson on Kauai. Kalalau is a large land area on Kauai, including a valley. Nothing came of this matter.

228. "Last evening a concert was given at the Hawaiian Hotel by the Royal Hawaiian Band, complimentary to Mr. A. G. Abell and his daughter Miss Abell. The front of the hotel was tastefully illuminated with colored lanterns. On the veranda were noticed Her Royal Highness the Princess Liliuokalani, His Excellency Governor Dominis, His Excellency Geo. W. Merrill, United States Minister Resident, and Mrs. Merrill, together with a number of our leading citizens. Mr. Abell, who is here for the benefit of his health, is the Grand Secretary of the Grand Lodge of California, Free and Accepted Masons." *Pacific Commercial Advertiser*, June 24, 1886.

229. Richardson recited passages from Shakespeare's comedy "As You Like It." The reading "was attended by a large and appreciative audience." *Pacific Commercial Advertiser*, June 25, 1886.

230. "The exercises at Oahu College commence at 9:15 this morning and will be in the Bishop Hall of Science. The graduating exercises will be held in the Fort Street Church at 7:30 in the evening." *Pacific Commercial Advertiser*, June 25, 1886. On June 26, the *Advertiser* noted: "The closing exercises of the Punahou Preparatory School were held yesterday and were very satisfactory to the large audience present." Punahou Preparatory was on a lot adjacent to Washington Place.

231. $11.50 is added above the entry—probably for both items purchased.

232. Benjamin F. Dillingham's "colonization scheme" is summarized in a footnote following the June 18, 1886, diary entry (81).

William Achi arranged with me to meet week from yesterday with committees of Fire Relief Fund. Joe Aea has a warrant served on him for beating Kahae last Sunday.[233] She is laid up. I had to write to Dayton to release him till Monday.

Leihulu [Kapena] came to see me. I really would like to see her independent of her father. Cannot go to Mrs. Nowlein's luau. Slept in Keala Hale.

*Sunday, June 27.* Sunday morn went to Kawaiahao [Sunday] School celebration. All schools did well but Kakaako [School] did best, and so my prize as first prize was awarded to them.[234]

Came home with Mrs. Haalelea and Kapoli. She had a dream and King interpreted it, and so I told her to kill a pig and send it to him tomorrow. Kapoli and I spent the day. Mr. and Mrs. Herbert came over and sat with me awhile. Lots to do tomorrow. Slept in Poikeala [Hale].

*Monday, June 28.* Many visitors—Mrs. Banning. Wrote my [account] books out. Went to Mary Beckley's and left her book with her. Meant to go to Hotel to [Locke Richardson's] reading, but John sent note saying it was postponed. Locke Richardson was sick.[235]

So in evening went to Jessie's to tell her of our meeting tomorrow. Slept at Washington Place.

Joe's trial came off this morning. Kahae told all, beginning from Emma Square. He said he beat her because she was neglectful of his clothes. Postponed till next day. She sought him at Kapena's place and [he] threatened to beat her again if she did not go in. He sent her off to Manoa. She begged to go back to him. He is drinking awfully.[236]

*Tuesday, June 29.* Mr. Dillingham came about his colonization scheme. Mr. Francis Gay has got ahead of him. ~~Went to Mrs. Beckleys & gave her report book of Society Hoonaauao.~~ Went to Washington Place about Kaehuwahanui's mortgage. Will go this eve to Ball at Mr. Pfluger's for Dr. Arning.[237]

---

233. See June 28, 1886, diary entry (this page) for an account of the trial.

234. The quarterly exhibition of Sunday schools was held at Kawaiahao Church. The *Pacific Commercial Advertiser*, June 29, 1886, reported: "The building was crowded in every part with the parents and friends of the pupils. Her Royal Highness Princess Liliuokalani was present. Mr. Berger presided at the organ, and with the assistance of several members of the band discoursed selections of music at intervals. The first prize, a neatly-framed picture, 'Christ the Way of Life,' presented by the Princess Liliuokalani, was awarded to the Kakaako Sunday School. The Manoa Sunday School took the second prize."

235. The announced performance, according to the *Pacific Commercial Advertiser*, June 28, 1886, was to be Richardson's recital of Shakespeare's *Othello* in the "great drawing room of the Royal Hawaiian Hotel."

236. "Police Court. Before Police Justice Bickerton. Tuesday June 19th. Joe Aea, for assault and battery on Kahae, was ordered to file a bond in the sum of $25 to keep the peace towards the complainant for six months." *Pacific Commercial Advertiser*, June 30, 1886.

237. This was a farewell reception for German physician Dr. Edward Arning, given by J. W. Pfluger at his residence. The *Hawaiian Gazette*, July 6, 1886, noted: "Last Tuesday evening Dr. Arning and Messrs J. F. Hackfield, J. W. Pfluger, and Muller entertained at their residence. No pains were spared to make the party a delightful one, and success crowned the efforts of the hosts. The exterior of the house was brilliantly illuminated with Chinese lanterns, and all the trees in the garden bore their share of flashing and twinkling lights. The guests were received by Mrs. C. H. Judd and Mrs. H. Glade.... Besides the drawing room, a spacious temporary ballroom had been made of the makai veranda.... About 11 a supper was served, after which dancing was again resumed.... During the evening His Majesty conferred the Order of Kapiolani upon Dr. Arning."

After 11, left the Ball. Slept at Washington Place. He came home drunk, said he would not see me again for a week, all right. As you like it—Oh! Joe paid $25 to [the courts] keep peace for six months.

*Wednesday, June 30.* Slept at Washington Place. Rec'd from A. J. Cartwright $450—$220 goes to Hui. Returned to Kawehena his Waimanalo Stocks No. 1013 and No. 1034. Paid $20, owe him $18. Kawehena $10, owe $19. Joe $40, owe $10. Paid Hart $4.25. Paid Sam Damon $94.91 for grain. Kept $10 from all my servants—must pay them all next month. Four P.M. went to make calls—met Sam Damon. He offered to send Hay at a little over $32 for two tons—called on Mrs. Ivers, Miss Irwin, Mrs. Holliday, Mrs. Allen, and Mr. Bishop. Met Mr. Dole there—I am going to await his arrival.

---

On June 30, 1886, by request of the king, all the members of the cabinet tendered their resignations, and the king set about appointing a new government, with Walter M. Gibson as its head. Gibson became premier and minister of the interior, in place of Charles T. Gulick; Robert J. Creighton, minister of foreign affairs (June 30–October 13, 1886), in place of Walter M. Gibson; the Honorable Paul Puhiula Kanoa, minister of finance (June 30, 1886–October 13, 1887), replacing John M. Kapena; and John T. Dare, attorney general (July 1–October 13, 1886), replacing Paul Neumann. The *Pacific Commercial Advertiser* (which was under Gibson's ownership at that time), July 1, 1886, announced in an editorial: "The new administration will have the benefit of the ripened judgement of His Excellency, Mr. Gibson in its deliberations. Governor Kanoa is a gentleman of great influence among his countrymen... while the two other members of the Cabinet, Messrs. Creighton and Dare, in addition to some knowledge of Hawaiian Affairs, bring considerable experience from other fields."

---

*Thursday, July 1.* Nine A.M. Met at Mary Ailau's for taking in contributions to Hui Hookuonoono. Rec'd. $240. Went to steamer so see the Bannings off [and] Mrs. Hayley, Mrs. Ivers, Mrs. Holiday left. Came home and waited for Kaiulani to dine with me—did not come.

Band is here [for] My reception but I am so tired. Well, must make an effort.

Five P.M. Hear the Ministers appointed [are] Gibson—Minister [of the] Interior, Creighton, [Minister of] Foreign Affairs, Dare, Attorney General, Kanoa, Minister of Finance.

L. Kauai[238] wants to know who was to be Governor of Kauai—did not know.[239]

Went to Washington Place with Mr. and Mrs. and Miss Mary Carter, to an entertainment given by Mrs. D. [Mary Dominis] to her friend.[240]

238. L. Kauai was a legislator and judge of the Waimea District of Kauai.
239. Anna Lanihau succeeded Paul Kanoa as governor of Kauai on July 31, 1886, and held the office until 1888.
240. A. S. Cleghorn, in a letter to Likelike on July 2, 1886, reported on the entertainment: "Mr. Richardson gave [his] reading at Washington Place last evening—and Miss Gardinier,

Took them home and came home, slept in Nua Lehua. Paid six [dollars] to [Mary] Keamalu. Paid W. [William] F. Allen $50 rent [for] Pawaa.

*Friday, July 2.* Borrowed $150 from Hui Hookuonoono. Paid $20 to J. Polapola $12½ to Pamalo. King came at 12 P.M., had tea and took nap. He told me about Charley's deficit to Government. Must bring [a relief] bill in Legislature. Sent for [Representative] Kalua and Charley [Wilson]. Kalua said he would bring it in. King told me about Leihulu [Kapena]. He was going to put [John] Kapena on pension [of] $5,000 two years—will have $200 a month, $50 is to go to Leihulu. Kahinu came here today to ask about pig for Nihoa's birthday—told her to keep it for mine. She told me lots of Kahae—nothing new but to mihi [apologize] to her—and to Joe, but he told her to mihi to me his Akua [divine one]. She is not inclined.

*Saturday, July 3.* Paid Antone Lopez $5.80. Carrie Bush $10, Keamalu $1. Wakeke killed a pig and mihi [apologized] for her sins to me. I went down with Joe at 4½ P.M. to Washington Place to meet John, but he came to meet me on horseback, and told me to go to Emma Square. [Said] he would meet me there, and he came after band was over. Met John at gate [of] Washington Place and went right out to Waikiki. Met Capt. Hayley and C. O. Berger, Sam [Parker], and Billy Cornwell. Mary was surprised to see us together once more.

Lizzie Jordan[241] came to borrow $25 of our Hui. Promised to meet Hui on Monday. Eight P.M. telephoned to Archie [Cleghorn] and he came over to Hamohamo, stayed till ten, went home. Lots of fireworks.

*Sunday, July 4.* Kapoli arrives with Joe and Sophie comes after. Spend a very quiet day—do not even go to bathe in sea. Eight P.M. Fireworks and all retire at ten.[242]

*Monday, July 5.* Woke five A.M. Must hurry down as a painter is coming to the house. John feels loath to come home and leave Waikiki, but I can't help it. Ten A.M. Went with John to Skating Rink to hear exercises of the 4th—very good.[243]

Lots of people—came home at two, dined, and went down again for John, then went and called on Mr. and Mrs. Merrill.[244]

---

Kaiulani, and I went—The King was there, and all the best Society People. Kaiulani went at three o'clock to her Aunt's and came to the reading with her and sat between me and the King. We were home by ½ to ten." Hawaii State Archives, Cleghorn Collection.

241. Mrs. Elizabeth "Lizzie" Jordan (d. July 9, 1891, Honolulu, age 31) was a dressmaker and the proprietor of the Hawaiian Bazaar, a curio store at 127 Fort Street.

242. "A grand display of Fireworks will take place at eight o'clock P.M., from a barge anchored off the wharves at the foot of Fort Street. It is intended to have a creditable display of Fireworks, and it is hoped that the place will give a good view to the juvenile community of Honolulu. All are invited to be present." *Daily Bulletin*, July 2, 1886.

243. As the fourth of July fell on Sunday, patriotic exercises were held the following day. An advertisement in the *Pacific Commercial Advertiser*, July 5, 1886, informed the public: "The literary exercises will take place in the Central Park Skating Rink, on the corner of Punchbowl and Beretania Streets, from ten to 12 o'clock A.M." The program included music by the Royal Hawaiian Band, a prayer by Reverend C. M. Hyde, an address by the American consul, a reading of the Declaration of Independence, and patriotic songs.

244. George W. Merrill (b. June 26, 1837, Turner, Maine–d. January 10, 1914, San Francisco) was a lawyer and diplomat, a graduate of Bowdoin College, and a Civil War veteran. Merrill moved to Nevada in 1863, where he was a district attorney, representative in the legislature, and in 1883 secretary to the governor. On April 2, 1885, he was appointed U.S. minister resident to the Hawaiian Islands, where he served until his recall on September 23, 1889. He then lived in San Francisco.

Took him home and came home only to find Deborah [Mahoe] here waiting my arrival. [She] offered the land to me, I proposed to buy it out and out, she said yes.[245] Took a nap—woke up, dressed, and went to dance—Fourth of July. Went to Washington Place and slept there—botheration. John Padekin[246] ma [and company] were drunk—no chance to sleep.

*Tuesday, July 6.* Came home at seven—found Deborah [Mahoe] waiting for me. Still offered me her land. Nine A.M. signed a paper requesting W.S.S. [Wilder Steamship] Co. to accept $200 from Liliuokalani Hui Hookuonoono every month until Kuihelani's debts are paid and we assume their debt. Told Cartwright about Deborah's offer of land and also to [Paul P.] Kanoa. The latter sent me to John Colburn but met John and Deborah. John proposed to lease [Deborah's land]. Went to Mary Beckley's to consult about Hui Hoonaauao. Must go to meeting three P.M. Aiaumoe paid to me $30, rent of Kahala—he wanted to give me $15 towards Kainuuala's share [in] Hui Hookuonoono for next three months.

The Hui Hoonaauao met and contributed $8.25. Went home and went in garden. Telephone—said yes—was a calm still night and so warm, so slept on veranda. We spoke of celebrating my birthday of pig mohai [sacrifice] and mihi [apology or repentance].

*Wednesday, July 7.* Received of Mr. W. F. Allen, $75 for Kaakaole next January, the same amount every six months for [the water of] Wailuakio[247] for her lifetime. Drew from A .J. Cartwright [from] Hui Hookuonoono $685.00, leaves $130 in Cartwright's hands for Hui. Paid A. J. Cartwright $50 rent of Pawaa. Ten Sian [unknown name] lot $13.70 for Hui Hoonaauao 2nd Division. Place in Mr. Damon's hands $83.80, [for] Fire Fund and list to W. Achi. The $685—and the $315 I had in hand of Hui Hookuonoono, made the amount $1,000. [It] was placed by me in Mrs. E. Beckley's hands to give to Antone Rosa[248] to pay to Wilder Steam Ship Co. for Kuihelani's indebtedness. We met in Minister [of] Finance Office when money was given to E. Beckley.

Ten A.M. went to Mrs. Haalelea and left her book as Treasurer for Hui Hoonaauao, also our Account with A. J. Cartwright. Came to Washington Place to take up matting. Dillingham comes to see me at five P.M. Mrs. Wight [gave] $4 for Hui Hoonaauao, gave them to Mrs. Haalelea. John Colburn and I agreed to lease next [door] premises $200 a year. Sent for Deborah to tell her.[249]

245. The land offered was adjacent to Muolaulani. See third footnote for July 7, 1886, diary entry (this page).

246. John Padekin is listed in the City Directory as "No. 59 Driver Baggage Express with Ashley & Hebbard." The firm advertised as "expressmen and draymen, American Express Co. 81 King St." in 1885. In the 1888 City Directory, he is listed as "John Padigan, driver Sander's Baggage Express Co. res. Beretania St."

247. Wailuakio was probably a spring or other water source in Palama. See June 14, 1886, diary entry (80).

248. Antone Rosa (b. 1855, Molokai–d. September 12, 1898, Honolulu) was a lawyer, and served as attorney general (1886–87) under Kalakaua. He was acting governor of Oahu in 1887 and became acting adjutant general of the military forces; assistant secretary to the king; a legislator, 1890; and a member of the Privy Council, 1887–91.

249. This was a lease of land (signed this date) from Deborah Mahoe, "heir of Paul Kanoa, deceased and her husband S. K. Mahoe." Bureau of Conveyances. The property was on the Ewa side of Muolaulani, having a frontage of 115 feet on King Street and a depth of 517 feet. The terms were for 20 years at an annual rental of $200. It was acknowledged July 7 by Deborah

*Joseph Kaipo Aea (at left) and John Dominis Aimoku, the hanai (adopted) sons of Liliuokalani, circa 1890. Kaipo was born at Waikahalulu (one of the Queen's properties in Nuuanu) in 1882. Aimoku, the son of the Queen's husband John O. Dominis, was born in Honolulu in 1883.*
Virginia Dominis Koch Collection

*Makaloa mat, one of three in Likelike's collection (present whereabouts of the mat are unknown), in the garden at Ainahau, 1885. Liliuokalani and her sister Likelike were enthusiastic collectors of Hawaiian artifacts, and both were interested in disseminating them for study by others. Dr. Eduard Arning, a German scientist studying leprosy in Hawaii, took the photograph and recorded in his notes that the intricate design was adapted from Hawaiian kapa patterns. A woven inscription indicates that the mat was created as a gift for a Kaniula Kuula. In arranging the mat for this photograph, Arning pinned it to a clothesline in the garden. The young men holding the mat are part of the Cleghorn household staff.*

*In early 1889, Liliu's diaries record the forwarding of a collection of Hawaiian shells and other "curios" for exhibition at that year's Paris Exposition as well as her (unfulfilled) interest in attending.*
Eduard Arning, Hawaiian Historical Society

*Thursday, July 8.* Must go to Kakaako to open meeting house. Must go with John to readings at Tom May's.[250]

Went to Kakaako. King was there—took up $102.05. King sent $20—making $122.05. John and I signed lease of next door lot from Deborah. I contributed $2.75 toward Puaikalani Church.[251]

*Friday, July 9.* To Cordie Allen to lunch at 12. Met Mrs. Dickson, Mrs. Glade, Mrs. Jones, Mrs. Merrill, Miss Abell, Mrs. Freeborn. While dining, [the] *Malulani* came in sight. My Sister [Likelike] and the Governess [Poomaikelani] on board. Left there at three. Put lace curtains up [in] Keala Hale—how nice it looks. Four P.M. John came up to say we should not go to Spreckels'—but band would go.[252]

Kapoli and I went to drive and we waited for him [John Dominis], but got tired and had to take her home. As soon as I got back to Washington Place he came home—slept in Keala Hale. Telephoned to [Curtis P.] Iaukea to come next day. I wished to see him on matters of importance to himself. [Iaukea] Must not accept Ministry.[253]

*Saturday, July 10.* Went to town to John, then went to Palace and saw the King. Asked him if he would accept [it] if the opposition party would offer to pay Spreckels to free government from indebtedness to him. King said he would.[254]

Gave up going to make calls with John, have to do it myself. Went at three [and] called on Mrs. Jones, Mrs. Oggel, Mrs. Wight, and I then went to call on Mrs. May[255] [and] Mrs. Sam Parker, [then] went to band. Came home, had tea, and received Iaukea. Promised him I would see King and use my influence not to have him removed from Customs House.[256]

One A.M. house on fire at Pauoa but was too sleepy to get up.[257]

and S. K. Mahoe, and recorded on July 8. On December 26, 1886, Liliu would purchase the property for $2,200. The two parcels were in the ili ainas (subdivisions) of Kapaha and Keoneula and included three loi (taro patches).

250. Tom May (d. Bournemouth, England, May 27, 1910) arrived in Hawaii in 1868, and joined his Uncle Henry May in the firm of May and Co., later becoming its head. His obituary stated that he had "interests in sugar plantations." *Pacific Commercial Advertiser*, May 29, 1910. May returned to England about 1905.

251. Probably a branch chapel of Kawaiahao Church.

252. The occasion was a surprise party at the Spreckels mansion on Punahou Street, on the occasion of Colonel Spreckels's 58th birthday. The *Pacific Commercial Advertiser*, July 10, 1886, called it "one of the pleasantest affairs of the season." Dominis's decision not to attend may have been for political reasons.

253. He didn't.

254. This refers to the Hawaiian government's attempt to free itself from the increasingly dictatorial Claus Spreckels. According to Jacob Adler, his biographer, "By the beginning of 1886 Spreckels was the chief creditor of the kingdom and held $700,000 of the total public debt of $1,300,000. Kalakaua, tiring of Spreckels' dictation, sought a loan in London to pay him off. Kalakaua also felt that creditors at so great a distance would not trouble themselves about the internal affairs of the kingdom." Jacob Adler, *Claus Spreckels: The Sugar King in Hawaii* (Honolulu: University of Hawaii Press, 1966), 182–83.

255. Julia A. May was the wife of Thomas May (d. England 1910), the head of Henry May & Co. The May residence was on Kinau Street.

256. Curtis Iaukea was collector general of customs September 20, 1884–September 30, 1886, then became chamberlain of the royal household.

257. The *Daily Bulletin*, July 12, 1886, reported that the fire consumed a house occupied by Hawaiians (not named) and that the cause was suspected to have been "from the smouldering ends of firecrackers."

Charlie came over and I told him of the meeting with Brother [Kalakaua]. Said he would see if they would back [word missing]. And so if this matter is accomplished, I will have been a mediator between Opposition and the King—I hope so.

*Sunday, July 11.* Morn. J. W. Kalua calls in and is in a very odd mood. Did give him advice about being regardless [reckless?] in the way he spoke. I think he felt my rebuke. Mentioned about the transfer of [the government] debt to Bishop & Co., from Spreckels.[258]

Kaai came in, tells me of same matter as Kalua.

D. Naone, Keliaa Koahou, Lima, Frank Kapu came to consult about tea party. Five P.M. [John L.] Kaulukou calls and still on same subject, but I mention about my indemnity bill, said he would assist. He wants me to speak for him with Brother [Kalakaua] for being Marshall for the Kingdom.[259]

After tea went down to Washington Place, slept there. Went first to see Kaipo [rest of line and a half erased] if I have to part with him. I fear it will have to end so.

*Monday, July 12.* Must receive Mrs. Pfluger and her friends from Australia. At 12 P.M. Came home, King and Queen had been here. Lizzie Rogers came over to bid good-bye and pay her dues for Hui Hoonaauao 60 cts for rest of year.

Mary Ailau came about my Kahilis [feather standards], for a Kumu [staff of a kahili]. She and Kahuila [Wilcox] would like to haku [assemble] one for me. She told me that the foreign community were fierce against Kunane [Kalakaua] and would like to set him aside and place me on the throne. Why, it is the first I've heard of it since Annie Turton told of it, and I was astounded. I hope it will not end in that.

*Tuesday, July 13.* Must meet ladies' first division Hui Hoonaauao to consult on next month's tea party. Met at three, decided to give it here. Sister was at meeting. Mrs. [C. O.] Berger and I presided. Asked of Members to all come. Saw Joe [Aea] and mentioned to him about deeding lot No. 4 at Waikahalulu to me.[260] He was quite agitated and said that would just bring things to a crisis. He would beat her [his wife] and go to prison. That would not be right, but she acts so ugly about what seems most reasonable to other people.

*Wednesday, July 14.* Must meet ladies of [the Hui Hoonaauao] second [division] to consult on [blank]. Went to Legislature with Mrs. Dowsett. $10,000 asked [in the Legislature] for bones of Chiefs.[261]

---

258. This was an idea that government officials were advancing—to transfer government obligations from the Spreckels Bank and thereby rid themselves of the increasingly dictatorial policies of Claus Spreckels.

259. John L. Kaulukou was appointed marshall on August 2, 1886.

260. See July 17, 1886, diary entry (93) for a further discussion of this deed.

261. This was one of Kalakaua's pet projects. In the legislature, Representative Kaulukou "gave notice of a joint resolution, appropriating $10,000 for the relief of the Board of Genealogy of Hawaiian chiefs, entered that day by Rep. Kaulukou, which caused considerable comment. One representative pointed out some $20,000 had already been appropriated during the past four years. Rep. Dole said that while the object was a good one, a voluminous report had already been issued, and 'It discussed Darwin's theory of descent of man, but what

Our indemnity bill mentioned [in the legislature], hope it will pass. Had the dyspepsia bad—had to go to Dr. Martin and got relief right away. Saw John Colburn about path, must widen. Deborah wants to be Governess of Kauai. Promised to let her know.[262]

$20.00 was contributed today toward tea party [of the] 2nd Division Hui Hoonaauao. To be a drill tonight and tomorrow night. The King gave notice at the drill that all were to go to Kaumakapili to tea party tomorrow night. Sam Damon very kindly allowed three feet of fence in Bishop's lot near mine put back to widen street next to this lot [at Palama] that Debora [Mahoe] leased me for 20 years.

*Thursday, July 15.* Steamer sails today. Gave $7 to Kaaunoa of Hui Hoonaauao [funds] to make Ice Cream. He said he would work for us for $5.00. King sends word to postpone our [tea] party till Monday. Am suffering with dyspepsia. Was better at seven P.M. and went to Emma Square to [hear] band, and at nine went on front of Palace with Wakeke to see drill.[263]

Came home—Alarm of Fire—small house on esplanade. Slept uneasily—Wakeke lomi-ing [massaging] me in Nua Lehua. Wong Kim paid me $400—rent of Palolo for two years.[264]

*Friday, July 16.* Went to Govt. building [to] see Charlie [Wilson] about taxes. Wong Kin's cattle were taken up by P. Milton.[265]

John and Kalua tried to persuade me to go up to Kalawao with Legislature.[266]

Got business with Brother [Kalakaua]. Told him what was expected [if] he should accept monies from people [who are] foreign residents to make a new cabinet. He told me the present one was not by Spreckel's—[He] Would not be obliged to borrow from residents as since Gibson's entrance as Minister [of] Interior [June 30, 1886,] $60,000 has been returned to Govt. Treasury.

Good news. It was late when my friend came bringing good news and joy to me. Everything seems brighter now to me. [Two words erased] came town and told me Lydia [two words erased] disease took suddenly the day [line and a half erased] went up to Kalawao.

---

has that to do with Hawaiian Chiefs.'... Rep. Kaulukou remarked that 'Dole was opposed as usual, for preserving the remains of Hawaiian chiefs.'" *Daily Bulletin*, July 14, 1886.

262. The appointee was Anna Lanihau, not Deborah Kanoa. See second footnote for July 1, 1886, diary entry (85).

263. This was the second of two elaborate battalion drills of the Honolulu Militia (the first having taken place on the previous evening). The companies formed at the armory and proceeded to the square in front of the palace. The *Daily Bulletin*, July 16, 1886, noted: "The band played during the drill and ... a large concourse of people, chiefly natives" witnessed the event.

264. Liliuokalani held the land of Kaauweloa in Palolo under lease from the government. The transaction mentioned here would have been a sublet.

265. Philip Milton (b. 1834, Chile–d. 1890, Honolulu) leased land at Kaauweloa in Palolo from Liliuokalani and others, on which he ran cattle and raised grapes. The lease from Liliuokalani was for 24½ acres for ten years at an annual rent of $30.

266. An investigative legislative committee departed Honolulu for Kalawao, Molokai, on the *Likelike*, the evening of July 16. The *Daily Bulletin* and the *Pacific Commercial Advertiser* published full reports of the tour on July 19, 1886. Liliuokalani did not go with the group.

*Saturday, July 17.* There is to be a tea party at Kakaako to contribute for church. Cakes sent in by Mrs. [J. O.] Carter, Mrs. Haalelea, Mrs. Rosa, Mrs. Beckley, Mrs. Wilson. Six P.M. after Band [concert], Mrs. Wight and I went to Kakaako and saw *Likelike* return from Kalawao. Commenced to serve Ice Cream at six. People flowed in, lots of money. King, Kaulukou, Kanoa, Mrs. Wilder, and lots of respectable people came. Mr. Wolters, Joe's friend.[267] They raised $180.00.[268]

Went from there to Waikiki. Gave Kahuila [Wilcox] $6 of Hui Hoonaauao [funds]. Monsarrat[269] took deed to Waikahalulu. Joe Aea signed, but Kahae flew into a rage and refused.[270]

*Sunday, July 18.* Early came home from Waikiki, ran into a meat cart—no harm done to carriage but Czar [a horse] was cut—he should not have shied—did not get over fright, so overslept till nine. J. Holt came with Milikoa [a horse]. After breakfast went to ride. Went to Wilson and to John's, then to Carrie Bush to come over on Wednesday with children. Came home passing by Kaumakapili [Church]. Saw people contributing [to the?] King inside, [illegible] had no money. Three P.M. took Mrs. Wight to [illegible,] said she would send some limes down. Seven P.M. slept in town.

*Monday, July 19.* Wrote to [George] Jackson to let me have another boy from Reformatory school.[271]

Mrs. C. Clark took 1 doz eggs—$1.00. Rebecca gave $1.00 for Hui. Sent Wakeke and Tamar to collect money from Hui. Curtis says he'll come. Gave Keliaa $10 from Mrs. J. Wight toward Kakaako Church. Had promise of $5 from Mrs. Hopper for this same church—sent by Oliver Carter. Joe had to get a new boy from Reformatory school in Sam's place. Daniel is his name.[272]

267. William Wolters was a salesman with H. Hackfeld & Co. and resided on Beretania Street. 1884 City Directory.

268. "A tea party was given last Saturday evening in the new church at Kakaako. The party was held under the auspices of H.R.H. Princess Liliuokalani, for benefit of the church fund. Among those present were His Majesty the King, His Excellency Mr. Kanoa, Minister of Finance; Hon. Samuel Parker, members of the Legislature ... Mrs. J. O. Carter and others. The amount of the receipts was $176." *Pacific Commercial Advertiser*, July 20, 1886.

269. This is either Marcus Douglas Monsarrat (b. 1857, Honolulu–d. 1922, Honolulu), a well-known surveyor, or his brother James Melville Monsarrat (b. 1854–d. 1943), an attorney and notary public. They were sons of Marcus C. and Elizabeth Jane Dowsett Monsarrat.

270. On July 17, 1886, Joseph Aea conveyed title to Liliuokalani of a lot at Waikahalulu (in Nuuanu), which he had purchased in 1882 from Mr. and Mrs. Kuaea. Bureau of Conveyances, Liber 108, 122. By Hawaiian law, property deeds required that both parties of a marriage had to agree and sign separately, and the index of conveyances shows that Kahae did not sign away her dower rights to the property until April 29, 1890.

271. George Edward Gresley Jackson (d. 1907, San Francisco) came to the Hawaiian Islands in 1878, and in 1880 was employed by the government to make a series of maps of harbors (originals in Hawaii State Archives). On April 20, 1887, he was made commander of the Royal Hawaiian Navy, and put in charge of the *Kaimiloa* on a diplomatic expedition to Samoa. As of March 1886, Jackson was in charge of the Boys' Reform School at Palama, which hired out boys for day labor.

272. "Daniela," age 14, found guilty of "malicious mischief," was committed to the Boys' Reform School for his minority on January 20, 1886. Sam, known as "Kamuela," had been bound out by indenture as of February 8, 1880, to Liliuokalani as "a general servant" at $2 monthly wages for three years (and $30 at the completion of his indenture). He was ten years of age at the time. Hawaii State Archives, Series 296, Box 2.

*Tuesday, July 20.* The ladies of the 2d Division [Hui Hoonaauao] meet today to have our monthly meeting and tea party. Leihulu paid $10 for month of August [for] two shares of hers. Hui Hoonaauao contributed $7.00. Kahuila [Wilcox] and Carrie [Bush] gave 25 cts towards Hui. Today Wakeke [went] with Mrs. Hopper's[273] five dollars to Keliaa.

*Wednesday, July 21.* Kahuila [Wilcox] sent for one Doz. eggs. Saw Monsarrat and told him not to stir that matter up about Waikahalulu land that Kahae borrowed 782 dollars for in 1882. I told him I intended it [the land] for baby Nihoa [Aea] but since she has not signed her name I cannot will him any land. Monsarrat said that he never sent anyone up to Kahae to get her to come down to sign her name. There must be some storytelling somewhere. Kalaikuo paid $1.20 as member of Hui Hoonaauao. Nihoa is one year old today. Killed a pig—a hookupu [ceremonial offering]. Sent them back to Waikiki, went out afterwards with Jim. Grand Ice Cream party by Hui Naauao [Liliuokalani Hui Hoonaauao]. Lit up by electric lights—tents look pretty, so [do] the girls. Got $225.72. Kunane [Kalakaua] and his soldiers came to drill and have Ice cream.[274]

*Thursday, July 22.* We ought to give Kakaako $2.70 for eggs. Received from Jennie Clark[275] $8.50 from caps and returned $2.25 to her and 10 cts tea and 25 cts from Mrs. Keau. Went in the evening with Mary Carter to Exhibition of the Royal School at 7½ P.M. At Y.M.C.A. [Alexander] Mackintosh, Principal, conferred a prize on S. Kekumano. Kalakiela acted [the role of] Mrs. Caudle—curtain lecture—well.[276]

273. Mrs. Hopper was the wife of James Hopper, proprietor of the Honolulu Steam Rice and Planing-Mill and the Pacific Brass Works, Fort Street.

274. The *Pacific Commercial Advertiser*'s July 22, 1886, article focused more on the novelty of the electric light display than on the drill: "An exhibition of Electric lights was given for the first time in Honolulu at Palace Square last night. Five lamps had been placed in position under the direction of Mr. C. O. Berger, as follows: One at the Palace, one at the Government building, one on Richards street in front of the Palace gate, and two on King Street.... Shortly after seven o'clock last night the electricity was turned on and as soon as darkness increased the vicinity of Palace Square was flooded with a soft but brilliant light, which turned the night into day. The exhibition was well advertised, and by 7:30 o'clock the streets leading to Palace Square were filled with moving people. By eight an immense crowd had gathered. Before nine o'clock the Royal Hawaiian Band commenced playing and the military companies soon marched into the Square.... The Battalion drill took place under the command of His Majesty the King... After the drill, the companies stacked arms and adjourned to the Government building grounds, where a tea party was given, under the auspices of the Society for the Education of Hawaiian Children, organized by Her Royal Highness the Princess Liliuokalani and Her Royal Highness the Princess Likelike."

275. Jane (Jennie) Kahakuwaiaoao Keakahiwalani Buckle was born at Hale Ola, the family home in Honolulu, August 21, 1859. She was the daughter of William Wahinepio Kahakuhaakoi Buckle and Malina Kuluehu Kaneiakama. Her father, of a chiefly family, served on the Privy Council under Kalakaua and was governor of the Oahu Prison. Jennie married Charles Henry Clark (d. 1938, Honolulu) in 1879. She was an intimate friend of Liliuokalani, and when the ex-Queen was imprisoned in 1895, Jennie accompanied her to Iolani Palace and for a time lived with her there as a lady companion. Jennie died in Honolulu on April 6, 1948.

276. The *Advertiser* had a long account of the exercises, which commenced at 7:30 P.M. with an opening chorus titled "Footsteps on the Stairs." "This was followed by a recitation by S. L. Kekumano entitled 'Despair.' He delivered it remarkably well, and at the conclusion received hearty applause. Next came Kelekoma Haui, who gave a recitation entitled 'Clerical Wit.'... George Rosa... appeared with 'A Scene from Pickwick.'... The next performance was the gem of the evening. It was a character piece, delivered by J. L. Kalakiela, entitled 'Mr. Caudle Has Been to Greenwich Fair.' The piece put the audience in a roar, and called forth enthusiastic applause.... Perhaps it could not have been done better by a professional....

Kahae was there and it suited her to a T. Had a meeting of the Hui at three P.M. at Mary Ailau's. Sent Committee [consisting of] Mrs. Cummins, Mrs. Owen Holt, [and] Mrs. Wilcox to thank the King for his assistance night before. Many complaints, but it is best to make up. Asked committee to send in their bills. Told Aiaumoe to see if her mouth would not be silenced forever about saying things about me ... would see.

*Friday, July 23.* Went with Wakeke to Kahehuna [to the] Royal School Examination—very good, what I saw of it.[277]

Bought riding dress and sent it to Mrs. Townsend to make up—she was at Carrie Bush's.

*Saturday, July 24.* Went with Mrs. McGrew to Mrs. Collins' and rode in an elevator.[278]

Came home to my money counting. Four P.M. Mrs. McGrew came to take me to drive in her Phaeton, went to Emma Square. Had tea, went and left my carriage at Washington Place, [then] went to Jessie's. Found them at Supper, so they gave me some Poi Ka-i o Ewa [an excellent, fragrant poi from Ewa] and lawalu Oopu [oopu fish wrapped in ti leaves and broiled]. Went upstairs, John was not there, so waited for Joe. Went to Waikiki but Aiaumoe had not commenced. He had postponed till next week.

*Sunday, July 25.* Woke up at 9½ A.M. Breakfasted at ten, spent the day in cleaning up my room. Went down to Hookumukalani after dinner at four. Strung hala leis, went back and had tea. Slept till three A.M., came home. I had a dream about Kahilis [royal feather standards], one in particular took my attention. Black above Kumu pauku yellow—small black pauku on top dotted with red—saw a middle-aged woman pa-u mao—Ahu ula lower part pauku waena yellow—round the neck red, lauoho piipii ua o ka hina. [Black above, basic section yellow—small black section on top dotted with red—saw a middle-aged woman—green skirt—feather cape lower part red, middle section yellow—round the neck red, curly hair gray with age.]

*Monday, July 26.* Breakfasted at the Palace. Went to Eveline's [Eveline Wilson's] to try [on my] riding dress. Went to see Mrs. J. Campbell[279] about joining Hui Hoonaauao Society 1st Division—she was out. Went to Carrie's, then came home. King telephoned me he would come next morning. Slept at Washington Place. Gave Jessie $13.50 of Hui Hoonaauao to pay for Ice $3.50, express $1. David white cotton 9 + 1 short.

---

The Principal ... stated that the first prize in written examination for the past year was awarded to S. L. Kekumano and he was proclaimed Captain of the school for the ensuing year. The principal then announced that H.R.H. Princess Liliuokalani had kindly consented to put the medal on the fortunate recipient's coat." *Pacific Commercial Advertiser*, July 23, 1886.

*Mrs. Caudle's Curtain Lectures* by Douglas Jerrold (London: The Punch Office, 1846) was a popular and humorous text of the day.

277. This was the 46th annual examination of the Royal School, held on the morning of July 23. The *Pacific Commercial Advertiser*, July 24, 1886, noted that besides Liliu, guests included Princess Likelike and Kaiulani. The Royal School stands on the land named Kahehuna.

278. Mrs. Collins (wife of Douglas Collins) is listed in the 1884 City Directory as a "Ladies' Nurse" residing at 21 School Street. The elevator was in Mrs. Lack's building on Fort Street, and it connected a gun shop with a ladies' fancy goods department above.

279. Abigail Maipinepine was the wife of Hawaii capitalist James Campbell (b. 1826, Londonderry, Ireland–d. 1900, Honolulu). Mrs. Campbell was a staunch supporter of the Queen.

*Tuesday, July 27.* King came with Kaae, we went to see where the houses should be placed. Told me there would be another electric light [display] soon, we ought to give another tea party on that night. After he left, went out over to Annie Dowsett's and told her about [it]. She made all plans right away. Was in next yard all day. Four P.M. Jessie came over about silk holoku [dress], must finish before I go to Hilo. Went together to Washington Place. Found Committee [from] Kakaako [Church] waiting for me to consult about money. Proposed to put in bank, they proposed to lend it out, so I gave in. Slept at Washington Place.

*Wednesday, July 28.* Joe came for me at seven, said the King was waiting for me, so hurried home. Took some more apu [a tonic drink] 8 times today. Six P.M. Annie D[owsett] has been [here and] gives word to Members about Tea party here on Tuesday. How good of her. Have a bad cold. Waiting, oh? watching. [Scrolling flourish, then a line and a half erased.] How restless ever changing where I could find rest and peace. Is this [word erased] or is it imagination. Slept well.

*Thursday, July 29.* Seven A.M. Kunane [Kalakaua] has arrived with Kaae—two Apu more—no impression. They went home. Kakina[280] arrives with chickens and Awa[281] from Lumahai [Kauai]—tells me people are all right. Kaakaole drew $2.00—leaves $73 of her money. Father Sylvester[282] invites me for tomorrow's examination of St. Louis College. Want to tell Joe not to go to Waikiki.

*Friday, July 30.* Two P.M. Arrived at St. Louis [College] in time for examination—King had already arrived, the house crowded, Mrs. McGrew attended me on this occasion. Was going home, but was asked to help deliver the prize.[283]

I cast my eyes around and sure enough she was there with veil over her eyes. At five came home. Slept at Keala Hale.

*Saturday, July 31.* Kaua placed in my hands $120—to pay Mr. Castle for her indebtedness. Slept at Paoakalani.

*Monday, August 2.* Paid today the sum of $165.00 to [blank line]. Hui Hookuonoono met at Mary Ailau's. Had no report to give so took contributions. [The Hui] voted $100 loan to Mary Ailau, and for security she left three lei hulus [feather leis]—and I borrowed $115—both at the rate of 10 percent. Placed $200 of Hui $ in Mrs. E. Beckley's hand to pay into Wilder's hands for Mrs. Kuihelani's debts and keep receipt.

---

280. John Kakina (b. 1838, Kona, Hawaii–d. January 19, 1904, Hanalei, Kauai) was a Lahainaluna School graduate, a legislator in 1874 and 1880, and a district magistrate of Hanalei, 1898–1904. He was a tenant on Liliuokalani's Lumahai, Kauai, land and was an awa planter.

281. The shrub awa (*Piper methysticum*), also known as kava, is used ceremonially and medicinally.

282. Father Sylvester was the principal of Saint Louis College.

283. The *Advertiser* noted that the closing exercises at Saint Louis College "were attended by an immense crowd" estimated at 2,000 persons, and that guests included the king, Liliu, Likelike, A. S. Cleghorn, and other prominent government officials. "The prizes were distributed from the stage by Their Royal Highnesses, the Princess Liliuokalani and Likelike, Hon. A. S. Cleghorn, and the Bishop of Olba. They consisted of beautifully bound books and chromos." *Pacific Commercial Advertiser*, July 31, 1886.

Went at one P.M. with Wakeke to a luau at Mrs. McGuire's. Had nice time. Went to band, then slept at Washington Place.

*Tuesday, August 3.* Stayed at home almost all day getting ready for first division Hui Hoonaauao. Three P.M., it met here.[284]

Gave back Kaua's money to her to pay to Castle, $120.00 [to] buy land in Palolo.

*Thursday, August 5.* Had a reception—many called. Mary Cook came to keep me company and help receive.

*Saturday, August 7.* Spent the day in [blank]. Slept at Paoakalani.

*Sunday, August 8.* Spent the day in sleeping and eating. Four P.M. watered plants in my bathing place—the whole has been neglected for a long time and Joe had to attend to it. Stayed till Monday morning. Aiaumoe had a great deal to say about so and so. Let her do what she pleased. "O ka waha kou e kole." ["A gabbling mouth will talk."]

*Monday, August 9.* Returned early to Kapalama [and] packed. The King came at 12 to see me. At 3½ P.M. went to Palace to bid Queen and Poomaikelani good bye. The latter could not come [with me to Hilo?] on account [of] two large abscesses. King could not leave Legislature, so I had to come alone. Band all aboard. Mary [Beckley?] and daughter came, latter not asked. Mrs. Kuihelani said she was going but I had no idea I was to pay her passage.[285]

Ten P.M. reached Lahaina. Arrived Mahukona, six A.M. Joe and Kaehuwahanui went ashore two hours. All police came to see me and brought pigs and poi, also Kohala Sunday Schools—C. Stillman[286] never even came off, because he said the train was going to start and he would be left behind. Nonsense.

*Tuesday, August 10.* Reached Hilo, nine P.M. Smooth passage. Hilo wharf full of people. Went to Governess Poomaikelani's house accompanied by torches. Band was sent to Court House. Had many contributions next day. Received police, then dismissed them. The Queen's room was assigned to me. How musty.

284. "H.R.H. Princess Liliuokalani and her associates in the education of indigent Hawaiians met at the residence of the titled lady on the afternoon of the 3rd inst. [this month] and transacted business connected with the object of the society. After the business was ended the ladies present prepared to assist in receiving guests invited, and for whom refreshments had been amply supplied. Mrs. Charles B. Wilson and Col. James Boyd received the guests invited, on arrival, and presented them to the royal hostess. A season of song preceded the performance of instrumental music, and at intervals the busy hum of conversation and ripple of laughter showed that all present were engaged in the agreeable occupation of enjoyment.... The reception hours were from six to 9.30 P.M." *Hawaiian Gazette*, August 10, 1886.

285. "Her Royal Highness the Princess Liliuokalani, Her Royal Highness Princess Likelike, and her Royal Highness Princess Poomaikelani, Governess of Hawaii, with a large number of attendants, also Prof. H. Berger, left by the steamer *Kinau* yesterday afternoon to attend the Sunday School convention of the Island of Hawaii, which will be held at Haili Church, commencing next Sunday. As the *Kinau* left the wharf the Royal insignia was displayed at the mainmast, and as the vessel passed out through the channel, a Royal salute of 21 guns was fired from the shore battery by the Household Guards." *Pacific Commercial Advertiser*, August 10, 1886.

286. Charles K. Stillman (b. 1864–d. 1925) was a port surveyor of Mahukona, Kapaau.

*Loi kalo (taro patches) at Onomea Bay, just north of Hilo.
In August 1886, Liliu visited Hilo and received hookupu (gifts),
including poi, from the people of the district of Hilo.*
Alfred Mitchell, 1892, Bishop Museum Archives

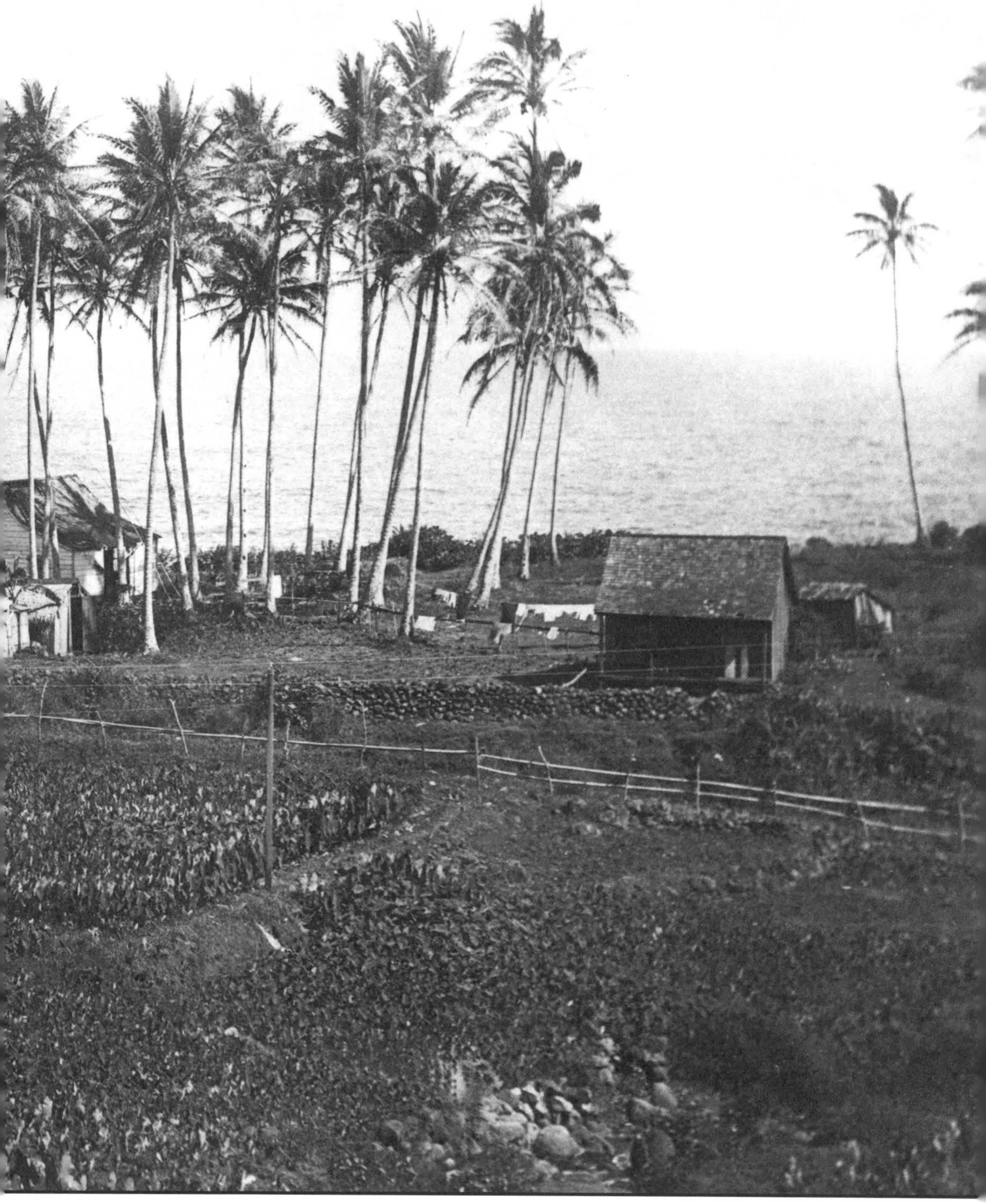

*Wednesday, August 11.* Nice weather. 8½ A.M. had breakfast and band played—Mary Ailau, Mrs. Kuihelani, Mrs. [Kapoli] Kamakau, and myself. Mrs. Hapai usually breakfasted or took meals together. Bought two dresses and one muumuu for Mary and daughter for they came unprepared. Mrs. Hapai got them. Four P.M. had a reception of Hilo ladies and gentlemen. Band played at Court House. Everything in my room seems musty and damp.

*Thursday, August 12.* Rained some, made arrangements for Concert to raise funds for Sunday School Convention. One P.M. Owed Mary Ailau for eight pieces of Muslin at $3 a piece and one for $2.75—three ie [baskets] at $2 apiece—five handkerchiefs $1.50 a piece. Rather unpleasant. A grand concert at 7½ P.M. Assisted by Band. Mrs. Kamakau, P. Puuohau, and J. Heleluhe and others.

Slept in next, or rather, my old room.

Concert pretty good—Mr. and Mrs. Hapai and Mr. [Fred] Lyman accompanied me, also G. C. Beckley. [Continues below:] Only $50.00 and certainly there were over 300 people there.

*Friday, August 13.* Breakfasted and band played, then sat down to write Brother [Kalakaua] and Poomaikelani, then went to ride with my party and Moanauli,[287] Pilipo,[288] Frank Austin. Had a nice ride. Came home, received Mary Beckley and Lizzie Doiron,[289] they went to Honolulu on steamer. Dined—napped—dressed and supped, then went to a reception at Wainaku,[290] came home at 11—sat up till 12 Midnight. Slept again in my old room. That old bed with spring mattress which stands so high—I have to make a spring to get into it.

Rec'd hookupu [tributes] from people of Piihonua—pigs—poi—bananas—sugar cane—pears, and sent some down [to Honolulu].

*Saturday, August 14.* Breakfasted in a hurry—no band. Ten A.M. went with Mr. and Mrs. Lyman, Mr. and Mrs. Hapai,[291] and our party to Sunday School Celebration. Exercises pretty good with assistance of band—left at four P.M.[292]

287. John W. Moanauli (b. Kohala, Hawaii–d. January 21, 1913, Honolulu) was the son of Kainapau (first cousin of High Chief Naihe), and served as a representative in the legislature 1878–1911.

288. This was probably J. W. Pilipo, who was appointed third lieutenant, Leleiohoku Guard Cavalry, in 1883.

289. Elizabeth Doiron (d. 1898) was the part-Hawaiian daughter of French-born Alfred Doiron (b. 1814–d. 1901).

290. "Mr. and Mrs. John A. Scott gave a delightful reception to their friends...at their new mansion [at Wainaku] on the 13th inst. [this month.] Her Royal Highness Princess Liliuokalani was present and brought with her the Royal Hawaiian band. The number present was probably larger than any reception given in many years in the district of Hilo. The rain did not seem to deter anyone." *Pacific Commercial Advertiser*, August 23, 1886.

291. G.W.A. Hapai (b. 1840–d. 1908, Hilo) was a police magistrate and longtime Hilo judge. His son Henry was also a well-known Hilo judge.

292. Isabella Lyman notes in her diary: "August 14. Great S.S. Celebration day. We went over about ten o'clock with Mrs. Dominis—the natives had a lunch under the big Lanai near the Church. Fred & I ate lunch there with Mrs. Dominis & went back & stayed till near four o'clock. Mrs. D. very tired & headache. I rode home in the carriage with her & came & got ice for her." Hawaiian Mission Children's Society Library, Isabella Lyman Diary.

In the evening we all went to concert given for band boys—realized $109. Gave $20 for repairs [to] Haili Church—$5 to [Henri or Henry] Berger—$5 for programs, $ rest for Boys. Slept in my old room. Kalapana [Sunday school] took the prize—a silver pitcher and goblet. Kauila was teacher of the class.[293]

*Sunday, August 15.* Went to church in morning, listened to six pastors— then stood up and made a speech—the church was full [but] only three band boys present. Said that "he leo kai kau ia mai ma luna ou a oia ka'u i hii mai la a waiho i mua o lakou o ia ke aloha o ka Moi. A he wahi ukana i hooili ia mai o ia he Aloha o Ke Lii Kiaaina a no'u iho ma na hoike ana o na makua me na keiki ua hoopiha ia ko'u naau i ka mahalo a e hoi ana au a hoike aku i keia mau mea i ka Moi. Piha ia na mea a pau i ke aloha." [Said that "a message was placed upon me which I have brought to present to them and it is concerning the king's love. And a small package was sent, which was the greetings from the governor. For myself, by the expressions of the parents and children, my heart was filled with admiration. And I will go back and report these things to the (king). Everyone was filled with love."]

7½ P.M. Union meeting [of] foreigners and natives—very nice. Ua pau ka ona i ka hoi ana mai, a o kahi Joe kai ona. [Upon coming back, the drunkenness was over; Joe was the one drunk.]

*Monday, August 16.* Rainy morning and Mrs. Hannah Evans[294] came over to see us, but while having lunch at one Mrs. L. Severance[295] came for me in wagon and took me to Ohele, where we got into boats and rowed to Cocoanut Island. While the gentlemen and ladies bathed, others wandered over the island and others prepared tea. We had a splendid time and enjoyed ourselves much—7½ P.M. returned and the band was playing at the Court House. Friends bade me goodnight and others came home.

*Wednesday, August 18.* Placed $20.00 in Mr. Lyman's hands for repairs of Haili Church—part of proceeds of concert of [August 12.][296]

*Friday, August 20.* Laid [off] at Mahukona all day till four P.M., [when] we left for Honolulu. While at M. [Mahukona] almost everyone went on

---

293. In its account of the Sunday school celebration, *The Friend*, September 1886, noted Liliu's presence and said: "The Princess had provided a prize of a beautiful silver flacon and cup for the school which should be adjudged to have excelled. The prize was neatly inscribed on the outside in Hawaiian: 'No ke Kula Sabati i lanakila. Na Liliuokalani, Hilo, Aug. 14, 1886.'" The prize was awarded to the Kalapana school.

294. Hana Kaniau Evans (b. Lahaina–d. 1932, Honolulu) was the granddaughter of Maui chief Kaniau, and wife of Thomas E. Evans. She was a close friend of both Queen Emma and Queen Liliuokalani.

295. Mrs. Lucinda Clarke Severance (b. 1843–d. 1921) was the wife of Luther Severance (b. 1836–d. 1917), sheriff of Hawaii, postmaster, customs collector for Hilo, and son of Honorable Luther Severance (1800–1855), former U.S. consul in Honolulu.

296. Isabella Lyman says in her journal: "August 18. Gave a lunch to Mrs. Dominis at one o'clock. Mrs. Severance & Mrs. Ailau, & her three ladies in attendance besides our ladies. She had Mr. Berger & the Band come & we had a place fixed for them under the Norfolk pine & got a lunch for them. The party did not break up till after four o'clock.

"August 19. Went to say good-bye to Mrs. Dominis ma [and company]. Got a box of plants for her." Hawaiian Mission Children's Society Library, Isabella Lyman Journal.

shore. Clara wrote me [to] invite to come up—had headache—did not go. Mrs. Laura Wight[297] [sent me a] verbal invite through George Beckley. How strange, and I had been there so often before. Got to Makena [Maui], then to Maalaea—Nakookoo sent $105—lease of Kapuiki's land by G. Beckley—and he took the whole for my passage. It was fearful rate, well, pau pilikia [troubles are finished].

*Saturday, August 21.* Arrived [Honolulu] at six A.M. King at the wharf while salute was fired [and] band boys sang—all came home. Governess Poomaikelani, Mr. and Mrs. [Paul P.] Kanoa came home with me. Many came all day. Ten P.M. Joe came home drunk—he had to be sent to bed. [He] had been with Pilipo and that set and he seldom gets drunk. Kaaiaumoe told of Aimoku's illness but is better. [Scrolling ornament.]

*Sunday, August 22.* Rose at eight, came to breakfast. When through, John came to see me about going to Palace next morn—prepared lunch in pail—John went home. Stayed all day in [word erased] writing and amusing myself and had lunch. Heard Kaai's voice but he went home. [At] two dined, then returned to [illegible] how pleasant to have a place of seclusion to go to when one feels tired and never be disturbed. Six P.M. Mary Ulili and Mrs. Kuihelani came to see me and Mrs. Dowsett supped with me. [Then a line and a half is erased.]

*Monday, August 23.* Breakfasted in Palace to meet Mr. Armstrong, a rich Englishman.[298] Wrote to Mrs. [Isabella] Lyman and others. Went to Steamer *Kinau*, then came home and Mr. and Mrs. Kuihelani accompanied me home. Sat and planted a few flowers. Annie came in—in a nice mood. 7½ P.M. went to see Kaipo—saw him to bed, then went to band [and] from there slept at Washington Place. Kahaunaele came to see why dress was given her—[I told her I] gave dresses to all [at] Waikiki and here.

*Tuesday, August 24.* Spent the morning in arranging Mrs. Holokahiki's report for Hui Hoonaauao. Poor Leihulu—things turned out differently and everything was left to Kapena by Kaleikini.[299] Advised her to see Mr. Bickerton.[300]

---

297. Laura Wight (b. October 17, 1861, Honolulu–d. 1954, Honolulu) was the daughter of Samuel G. Wilder and the granddaughter of Dr. and Mrs. G. P. Judd. She was the wife of Charles L. Wight, manager of the Mahukona railway.

298. Henry R. Armstrong of London was the nephew of Sir Alexander Matheson of the commercial house of Matheson & Co. (later Jardine, Matheson) of London and Hong Kong. Of this breakfast, the *Pacific Commercial Advertiser*, August 24, 1886, reported: "On Monday morning His Majesty the King gave a breakfast at Iolani Palace in honor of Mr. H. R. Armstrong. Besides the Royal host and his guest there were also present: Her Majesty the Queen, H.R.H. Liliuokalani, His Excellency Governor J. O. Dominis, Hon. Col. George W. Macfarlane, Hon. Samuel Parker, Major A. B. Hayley, and Hon. Col. C. H. Judd, His Majesty's Chamberlain." Later in December 1886, Armstrong would be appointed Hawaiian consul in London.

299. Mrs. Martha Kaleikini Kapena was the widow of Jonah Kapena (and both were parents of John Makini Kapena, Leihulu's father). "Everything" probably refers to lands including parcels once owned by David Malo, Leihulu's grandfather. More precise information on these holdings or how Leihulu lost any legal claim to them has not been determined.

300. In 1889, Leihulu, by then Mrs. Morris Keohokalole, sought redress in the courts for return of her lands, citing fraudulent deeds. She was not successful.

Went at three P.M. to meet Hui Hoonaauao. Contributed $6.30 from Hui. Arranged to take one of Maria [or Mary] Beckley's children and to send committee to inquire about other children of Mikaaole and Kaopa and report next month, to meet on September 6th. Seven P.M. went up to Kaae's and sent him to invite Company Prince's Own. Came to Washington Place and got homesick, so came home to Nua Lehua. Wrote and went to bed.

*Wednesday, August 25.* Charley Wilson came in after breakfast, then I went out with Kaonohiponi to Eveline's [Eveline Wilson's] and we all went to Waikiki to pluck geese feathers. Went on and had lunch with Mary Beckley, and came home and bought $2.10 worth of books [notebooks] for Hui Hookuonoono of Hilo. Came home tired, walked about the garden. Mrs. Hayselden and Edith Turton[301] called, and Mrs. Wight and Mrs. Mary Hadley Cook.[302] She asked me if she could stay with me. I wish I could keep her here. Wakeke took her home. Mrs. Hayselden made me a present of a fine mat of Lau hala. Mary Cook wanted to stay with me.

*Thursday, August 26.* Mr. Bickerton was first visitor [to Liliu's monthly reception, this time held at Waikiki], to advise that Cartwright is to take charge of Leihulu's [Leihulu Kapena's] affairs. He said he would—send for Leihulu and [if] she was willing, to A. J. Cartwright [and] says he was going to try and annul Kaleikini's deed to J.M.K. [John M. Kapena]. Mary Beckley and Lizzie Doiron came at my request, and I asked if her sister would take care of another baby (Nihoa) for me. A. J. Cartwright wants to know about lands in Manoa. What shall I say, must see about it. [John?] Telephoned to me that he hardly thought he would come, but I told him I would not be here, but after the band at Hotel, I was going to stay at Washington Place.

*Saturday, August 28.* Stayed and breakfasted, but afterwards went to Palace to see Queen for umekes [calabashes] and met Curtis [Iaukea] there. King told me about not being able to confer order on Mr. Berger. At one P.M. King, Curtis, and C. H. Judd came and lunched with me before going over to Reformatory School.[303]

Curtis [Iaukea] told me C.H.J. [Charles Hastings Judd] was going to be removed [from office] and he [Iaukea] installed as Chamberlain.[304]

301. Talula Hayselden (b. 1849, Georgia–d. May 16, 1903, Honolulu) was the daughter of Walter M. Gibson and was co-owner of the island of Lanai with her husband, Frederick Hayselden. Edith Turton (b. 1868–d. 1892, Honolulu) was a relative of the Lahaina Turtons.

302. Mrs. Mary Duncan Hadley Cook (b. May 21, 1839, Honolulu–d. December 23, 1918, Honolulu) was the wife of Thomas E. Cook, a founder of the Hana plantation. She first married (in 1854) James C. Hadley (d. 1862). She was a niece of Liliu's close friend, Louisa Brickwood, and a cousin of Emma Buchanan.

303. This was to a luau at the Boys' Reform School, which the king and a full cast of prominent government officials attended.

304. Charles Hastings Judd (b. September 3, 1835, Honolulu–d. April 18, 1890, Kualoa, Oahu) was a son of Dr. Gerrit P. Judd and a close friend from childhood of King Kalakaua. In 1873 (under King Lunalilo), he was major of the Honolulu Cavalry and colonel on the king's staff, and he was reappointed in 1874 when Kalakaua came to the throne. He was a member of the House of Nobles, 1879–86. On July 6, 1878, he became Kalakaua's chamber-

They went over [to the luau] and Mrs. McGrew and I went to take a drive. Came home, had tea, and waited for ten to strike. There was a grand time over to Nowlein's—boys singing half drunk and all the time [I] sat in Keala Hale [the last two words partly erased and replaced with a scrolling flourish]. H. R. Armstrong, the monied man from England, left at eight P.M. for San Francisco.

*Sunday, August 29.* Spent today in quiet seclusion and meditation, looking over pictures and foreign papers. Two P.M. Curtis came but did not see him. At five again he came with Kanoa and told me that he was to take charge [as chamberlain of the household] next day—would see me again next day. Spent night in Keala Hale. It seems as if I was far from care and [illegible] happy. [The last sentence is partially erased and concludes with a scrolling flourish.]

*Monday, August 30.* Went to Nua Lehua and slept again till 8½ A.M. After breakfast sat and wrote letters all day—but while eating, [John M.] Kapena came in, then S. W. Kaai and T. [?] Kalama, then Kaiulani and Miss Gardinier, then [J. A.] Kaukau. Finally all went home. At one had lunch and Kunane [Kalakaua] came and sat down to lunch. He enjoyed his meal very much, then told me he had dismissed C.H.J. [Charles H. Judd]. The latter took it hard.

Kapena told me after the King left, that he would like to take Curtis's place. I told him to go and try, and he got it.[305]

Went to band and [then] slept at Hinano Bower. Hattie Hiram, Mr. Kana, Lizzie Victor, and L. Kahelemauna came and wanted to know what they should [do] about their present. Said whatever they saw best.

---

A letter written by Edward W. Purvis, Charles H. Judd's assistant, reveals the machinations behind Judd's unexpected dismissal from his position as chamberlain and Purvis's subsequent resignation:

> ¶ October 2, 1886. I suppose Theo [Purvis] has told you that I resigned all my appointments the day after my chief [C. H. Judd] was turned out in such a scandalous manner. You know of course that Gibson has been trying for this ever since he came into office. As far as I can learn there was great pressure brought to bear on the King. Suddenly, the Cabinet at a critical moment (the negotiation of a loan) brought to bear on the King. He was to go, or they resigned. The King is much to blame for the manner in which the affair was done. Up till seven o'clock that day Judd was with him, and as friendly as ever. At 12 J. went home to lunch, at 12:30 Curtis Iaukea drove out to Judd's house with a letter from Gibson dismissing J. and his new commission (C. I.'s). J. refused

lain and private secretary. Until he was abruptly forced out of office, he was one of the king's most intimate friends. Walter M. Gibson seems to have engineered his dismissal. See Edward Purvis letter following August 30, 1886, diary entry, this page.

305. John M. Kapena's appointment as collector general of customs was announced on September 4, 1886.

to take dismission from Gibson and returned to town to tender his resignation to the King himself. At two P.M. Curtis, accompanied by Hassenger came to the office, demanded the keys of the safe, and forbade the removal of papers. This made my chief mad. He told Curtis that he should keep the keys as long as he chose, and should use his own discretion as to the removal of papers. Curtis then backed down.

Meantime, no reason had been given for the dismissal, Gibson's letter merely saying "for good and sufficient reasons." Rex was in hiding somewhere and not to be found. About six P.M. we heard he was at the boathouse, so J. immediately went there. He told Rex that he did not recognize Gibson's letter, that he came to resign to him, and would like to know what reason or reasons he had for dismissing him. Rex said that the Cabinet had made an issue, and that he (J.) had been accused on good authority of writing and giving hints to opposition papers, more especially of certain squibs signed "Zip" in the *Gazette*. From that day to this Judd has not seen Rex.

The fact of Judd and Rex having been such friends since boys, and the many kindnesses done to Rex before he became King made his action of allowing Gibson to strike the blow, especially dastardly. There must have been large money promises made by Gibson.[306]

*Tuesday, August 31.* Pigs, presents from people, poi, one Champagne box from Aholo, one sofa pillow from Likelike, $450 from A. J. Cartwright, and $57 for himself and wife as H. [honorary] members of 1st Division of Hui Hoonaauao. Mrs. McGrew brought $1.00 for Hui Hoonaauao. She was glad C.H.J. [Judd] was put out—champagne, Gin, beer—two cases each. Sheriff of Ewa [Liwai K. Halualani] discharged today. Kahilis [feather standards] came home today. Mrs. Allen has erysipelas. [Scrolling flourish.] Gave Aiaumoe $28—for himself and Nihoa.

*Wednesday, September 1.* Gave Aiaumoe $20 and $8 for Nihoa. Gave Wakeke $10. W. [Waimanalo] stock, also Kawehena. Aiaumoe gave me $5 for Kalahiki, $5 for Kailikole. Paid back to Hui $115.00 [with] interest, which [equals] $126.50, $5 for Kahae, for Kainuuala, for myself.

Men putting up tents—King taking great interest in preparations. Tents are put up, chairs sent, everything lively. Six P.M. Members of Hui Nihoa[307] came and brought large kahilis [royal feather standards] and their presents for my birthday—with speeches they presented a large marble clock and cut glass ware—beautiful. I made a speech in return, and they all wept. All spent the evening here, and the King and Curtis also. They went home at nine P.M. I retired. Mary slept in my room as I expected to be woke up at four A.M.

306. A copy of this letter is in the Hawaii State Archives, Edward W. Purvis Collection.
307. The Hui Nihoa was an informal and short-lived association of friends who had gone with Liliu in July 1885 to Nihoa Island. It is quite likely that they collected some of the feathers used in fabricating the kahilis (royal feather standards) from that island.

September 2, 1886, was Liliuokalani's 48th birthday. The *Hawaiian Gazette* announced on August 17, 1886: "The Princess will be 'at home' at two o'clock on the afternoon of that day, at her Muolaulani Residence, Palama, to the members of the following societies: The first and second divisions of Liliuokalani Educational Society, Hookuonoono Society, and Nihoa Society. Members of those societies will please regard this as an intimation that Her Royal Highness will be pleased to receive them on that day at the hour and place above mentioned."

Both the *Pacific Commercial Advertiser*, September 3, 1886, and the *Hawaiian Gazette*, September 7, 1886, published long accounts of Liliuokalani's birthday celebration at Muolaulani.

---

*Thursday, September 2.* Gave Joe $50, Kawehena 10 W. [Waimanalo] Stock. Four A.M. was woken up by Kahaunaele e kahea ana i kuu inoa [calling my name], then Wakeke ma [and group], then Pupule ma, then Mao ma. Presently Joe came in to wish me well, then others. At 6½ the marshall Kaulukou and police—speeches, and I answered. Hookupu [a gift offering] $80. King came and others, ten callers. 11 [A.M.]—Hui Hoonaauao 1st Division [came] with presents set of silver teaspoons, forks ½ doz. each—C.P.I. [Curtis P. Iaukea] Screen—vase L. Hart—Set salt spoons Mrs. Hayselden, Silver ladle [from] Gibson—Silver card case, Fred Hayselden, E. Turton, Sugar tongs—Banner [from] Mather—S[ugar] tongs, Nellie Everett—Fish fork and spoon, Sam Parker.

12 P.M. King and Queen arrive. He made a short address, then conferred Grand Cross order of Kapiolani [on me]. I knelt to receive Cordon from King, and Queen pinned on the Star, then I rose to kiss their hands, and they my forehead. Guests wept—we adjourned—then came back to parlor. Received the 2nd Division of the Hui Hoonaauao and their presents [an] Ice pitcher and two goblets and ice bowls [of] silver. Hui Hookuonoono presented [a] Silver coffee and tea set. Then went to see Prince's Own drill, and they presented me with Silver teaspoons. Liliu [Carter] gave me one doz. jelly glasses—Lola Bush Japanese scarf. P. O. [from the post office employees?] $40, King and Queen $50 each, J. D. Strong, picture.[308] Poomaikelani $40.

Dined at two, eight tables spread and everyone full. After dinner there was hula till night. All went home except King, Princess Poomaikelani, and others. Curtis went home and left J. Boyd. [John] Bush was fawning around King for office and begged [me] to make him my head man. Not much [chance]—a man that would go over to opposition, then come back, is not worth notice.

---

308. The *Pacific Commercial Advertiser*, September 3, 1886, noted that Joe Strong's gift painting depicted "the cultivation of the taro plant. It is a gem."

*Friday, September 3.* Was taking a nap when Laiki woke me up and said Nihoas were coming up to dine with me. Some of them came. Stayed till seven P.M. and all went. Came over here—slept, cleaned house—fearfully dirty. Rained several times.

*Saturday, September 4.* Still cleaning up and put my presents away. Good people of Hamohamo went home. Gave Pupule $6—Keamalu $1. Went to band with Mrs. Wight. Came home, had tea, and went back to Washington Place. Oliver Stillman was married to Miss Molteno.[309]

Stopped at Kaipo's [at Mrs. Bush's] and gave Mrs. Bush $12.00. [Line and a half of entry erased.] Mother [Dominis] with John. It seems not—stayed to Skating Rink [one line of entry erased] to her house he stayed short time and went home he saw [one line of text erased].

*Sunday, September 5.* Gave Aiu $18—and Mary Ailau $47 for muslins. Went to drive and saw a man whose name was Sam Kaino, breaking pickets from Branch Hospital [fence]. Reprimanded him and guard. The latter said he was inside and could not see what was going on outside. Went to Kawaiahao, saw Kahae. She left before service was over. Stayed at home [line erased].

*Monday, September 6.* Must meet Hui Hoonaauao 2nd division, at three P.M. Read report. Went to King's boathouse to bathe. Paid Thrum $2.10, bought cards for Hilo children. 50 cts bought brush and comb for [Several words erased.] Paid milk $5. Hollister $40—[illegible] $18.00.

*Tuesday, September 7.* Must meet Hui Hoonaauao 1st Division [to] consult about girls to educate. Contributed $443.00—gave account book to Mrs. Haalelea. The 1st Division has $155—altogether. Gave $12.10 for Afook. Paid Miss Malone $59 for Kalei ma [and associates] tuition. Paid Mrs. E. [Emma] Beckley $200 to give Wilder & Co. toward Mrs. Kuihelani's [debt].

*Wednesday, September 8.* Mrs. Beckley called and left me receipt from Wilder & Co., for $200 towards Mrs. Kuihelani's aie [debt]. Miss Malone wanted me to try and get them [Kawaiahao Seminary] a carriage. Went to Waikiki to see Nihoa. He was better. Went to see Archie [Cleghorn,] he was better. Went to see John [Dominis,] he was better—said he would be out tomorrow. Came home. [Several words erased.]

*Thursday, September 9.* Spent the morning in planting and dined. Joe left me at Engine Co. No. 1, and went and paid Waterhouse $122. Allen & Robinson $1.38, [and] Wiseman for Portuguese plowman Garcia $30. Had meeting [of] Hui Hoonaauao [Division] 2. Will educate Kinoole Beckley, [and Abbie] Paiaina's girl, [at] boarding—[also] one of Hoopii's daughters, and one girl at Waikahalulu for day scholar. Must tell Joe about pig and about baby Nihoa.

Lizzie Doiron gave 10 cts. for Hui. "And my love watch keeping."

309. Oliver Stillman and Miss Molteno were married at the Roman Catholic Church by the Bishop of Olba, September 4, 1886. At the reception held afterward at the Stillman residence on School Street, King Kalakaua was present, but Liliuokalani was not.

Regulated my books. Rain! how it pours in Keala Hale. Have to pay $5 deficit. Came home, oh, how angry—well, tears are of no use.

Hanakeola [Mrs. Kinimaka] and Makanoe are committees to report on girl at Waikahalulu. Who could that have been that came in and went out again. [Line and a half erased.]

*Friday, September 10.* Trimming trees all morning. [R. W.] Aylett, [David] Naone, Kapua, and Vikoli, officers of the Hui Puali Puhi Ohe [Officers of the Formation of Players of Wind Instruments—that is, the Band Association] came. Placed $300 in my hands to invest in A. J. Cartwright's Savings bank[310] and receipts from R. W. Aylett for the same.

Gave Tamar and Jennie Clark [for] three dresses for Paiaina's girl, 18 yds of white cotton and $7.55 belonging to Hui [Hoonaauao] to clothes. Hoopii is not in need. [She has a] House lot at $12 a month, lands in Mr. Castle's care, and a man to support her. Anna has her child. Paid Pake [Chinese] for bread 80 cts. Joe came and told me he had already done what I told him—to kill a pig, a mohai [a sacrifice] [illegible] up [at] his house. Kaae wanted to know when we were going down. Decided not to go round the island till the last week of this month. Paid six dollars and 25 cts, and 75 cts for his work, and discharged him. [Two words erased.]

*Saturday, September 11.* Went and breakfasted at Washington Place while band played. John is better today. Went to Palace with Mrs. Wight and forgot all about Mrs. Beckley and Jennie Clark and Mrs. Kuala till I got up to Lizzie Victor's.[311]

Sister, Kapooloku, Mrs. Beckley, Mrs. Fernandez,[312] and Mrs. Whiting sat down. I was so provoked with myself for going—now I have to give up the King's [invitation?]. Sent Joe to pay to Mr. Cartwright $300 for the Band boys. Had a new cook today, Ahoi[313] and his wife. Spoke to Queen about reminding [John L.] Kaulukou to enforce the law about children being out after dark.[314]

Went to Waikiki and took my food to last till Monday [at] Paoakalani. Gave $7.15 to Jennie Clark to get what they could for Paiaina's girl. How good she and Tamar are to do my bidding.

*Sunday, September 12.* Woke up at ten A.M. and breakfasted on cold meat. Joe made tea, so that was all right. Spent the day in cleaning out bathing place. Was cross all day.

---

310. A small account book for this organization shows deposits for June 3, September 10, and December 11, 1886, totaling $1,000, and interest of $4.00. Hawaii State Archives, Liliuokalani Collection, Box 5, Document 314.

311. Elizabeth Kalanimea Victor, the wife of Keawe (Joseph?) Victor, had a house lot and several taro patches in Pauoa Valley.

312. Minerva (Davis) Fernandez (b. 1858, Hana, Maui–d. 1936, Honolulu) was the wife of Abraham Fernandez (b. 1857, Lahaina–d. 1915, Honolulu), a Honolulu businessman involved in politics.

313. Ahoi or Ah Hoi, a Chinese cook at Muolaulani, is listed in the 1884–85 City Directory.

314. No such law appears in the Published Compiled Laws of 1884 or the Session Laws of 1884 or 1886. Perhaps Liliu is referring to a police regulation.

*Monday, September 13.* Received Japanese Captain of the *Tsukuba*. Mary Carter was present when he and Mr. Ando came.[315] We agreed to give a picnic for them. But we have been so busy. The ladies of the 2nd Division of the [Liliuokalani] Educational Society were here all day to help and sew clothes for Paiaina's daughter. Finished three dresses, three shirts, three pants, eight chemises, six sheets, eight pillowcases, two mosquito netting, in fact fitted her out completely [for school]. Dine with them, then sent them home. Kapoli stayed [and] we went to see the drill but it was so showery the soldiers were dismissed, so took Kapoli home and I slept at Washington Place. Got permission of Kawehena to have his house moved down for me. Nihoa was taken to Mary Beckley's today this morning; she asked for [illegible] for I was going to give it to Hannah as she has written me to take care of it, but Mary asked for it.

*Tuesday, September 14.* Stayed at Washington Place to work with the men who came from Waikiki. Five P.M. John came home mad. A warrant had been served on him and I by Dole, because Sam Parker and John Paty would not pay our note of $6,000. 7½ P.M. John and I went up to Mr. and Mrs. Ando's reception. William Holt[316] came while I was dressing. (I wonder what he wanted). King and Queen, Mr. and Mrs. Cleghorn, John and I, and other noted people [were at the reception].[317]

He brought me home. [Two words erased.] Paiaina's girl and Kinoole Hammond[318] were placed at school by 2nd Division Hui Hoonaauao [and] L. Lucy Woolsey by 1st Division H.H. Liliuokalani. One child of Hoopii [placed] by 2d Division [in a] Day School. Paliuli Deverill did not enter school.

*Wednesday, September 15.* Went to Washington Place with people to drag Kawehena's house. Got it on rollers, then dragged it halfway. All went home to come back next day. How good of them to come to my call. [Two words erased.] John told me about Sam Parker's failure. Princess Poomaikelani spent the day with me and she told her plans for the King's birthday. It is a grand affair, but I fear it will be too large to undertake. She would like to make every Society take a part. That is right, but would they all want to give a calabash? 1st Division H.H. [Hui Hoonaauao] had to buy mattress for Lucy Woolsey. Saw Mary Carter about having a picnic on Saturday, but was told King was going on board.

*Thursday, September 16.* Went to Washington Place. Pooloku [Poomaikelani] and officers of Hui H[ookuonoono] Liliuokalani 2nd Division met to consult on what to give the King on his birthday. Decided on Ipu laau

---

315. This was Captain Y. Fukushima, of HIJM training frigate *Tsukuba*, and Taro Ando, the Japanese diplomatic agent and consul general in Honolulu. The king had previously received them at the palace. Liliu's reception took place at Palama.

316. William Holt was the overseer at Waimanalo Sugar Co.

317. Japanese Consul Taro Ando gave this reception in honor of the captain and officers of HIJM frigate *Tsukuba*. The *Pacific Commercial Advertiser*, September 15, 1886, noted that it was "one of the most successful society events of the season."

318. This was possibly a child of Eugene Hammond, a hack driver for James Dodd.

[calabash] and to call the aid of Kapena, Bush, Kanoa, Iaukea, Aholo, Kaulukou to consult on matter of hookupu [tributes] [for the] King's birthday. Was surprised I had not called on the Ministers.

Keala Hale.

*Friday, September 17.* Kapena, Bush, Iaukea, Kanoa, Holt met here to consult Governess of Hawaii [Poomaikelani] and I about [the celebration for the King]. Concluded to print notices in paper about birthday.[319] Spent the day at Washington Place.

*Saturday, September 18.* Had a meeting at Kawaiahao with all my societies. Told them all to bring as presents to the king some wooden calabashes on his birthday. Some had umekes [calabashes] and those who hadn't are each to contribute—to come to Washington Place. Aukau $3.00—Mrs. [Emma] Mahelona $3.50, Mrs. Napoleon[320] and Pamahoa [and] Lepeka $3.50 each, and Kanalulu, Kamiki, Mary Naone each gave $3.00.

*Sunday, September 19.* Telephoned to Jessie to send messages all round to Hui Hookuonoono [members] to go to contribute at Kaumakapili. King, Queen, Likelike, Kaiulani, Pooloku, and myself were there. All the Hui [Hoonaauao] except 1st Division. Kalua on the platform to call the apanas [divisions]. Expected Joe at three P.M. Did not come till six P.M. Lizzie Doiron came to tell me of Cecilia's [Cecilia Arnold's?] arrival and more about the baby. They insisted on it that she should have it but under their eye. So she took it that day but he [?] did not like it.

*Monday, September 20.* Went to Palace. King had guests, so I went to see Pooloku [Poomaikelani] at Healani [boathouse]. Made out notices how to order Judges and Sheriffs, while band played. Went to Washington Place, sent for J. Holt so I gave him directions what to do about those Circulars.[321]

*Tuesday, September 21.* Kailikole gave me $3.50 for Meeau's umeke [calabash], Jessie, Naone, and Annie Naone each gave me $3.50 toward umeke. I went to Mary Beckley's to see how Nihoa was. He had not come down but would on Thursday. Hannah Evans was there. Spent the rest of the day there. [Scrolling flourish.]

*Wednesday, September 22.* [Scrolling ornament.] he would not come again till Saturday and I thought all the time it was Thursday.

*Thursday, September 23.* Went to see John, found him at Govt. building. Saw Mrs. McGrew, took her to Washington Place to lunch. Agreed to go to King's boathouse on Monday. Got a Memorandum from J. W. Kalua showing what Members of Legislature went against our bill. Came home to tea and went out again with intention to go to P. C. Jones's to a reception given to H.A.P. Carter. Had to stay [at Washington Place] as Mrs.

---

319. The *Hawaiian Gazette*, September 21, 1886, ran the following notice: "Hons. P. P. Kanoa, L. Aholo, John A. Cummings, John E. Bush, and John L. Kaulukou have issued a call to all Hawaiian subjects and friends of the Hawaiian nation, to join with them in a loyal and loving celebration of the fiftieth birthday of His Majesty the King, on the 16th day of November next."

320. Mrs. Pamahoa Napoleon (b. 1830–d. 1894) was the mother of Mrs. Emma Mahelona, Mrs. E. P. Low, Mrs. J.H.S. Keleo, and Mrs. J. U. Kawainui. "Pamahoa" probably refers to one of Mrs. Napoleon's daughters.

321. The circulars may have been similar to the notice published in the *Hawaiian Gazette*. See footnote for September 17, 1886, diary entry, this page. Liliu's accounts at the end of the diary show a payment of a dollar to the *Daily Bulletin* for advertising for the First Division.

Dominis was not so well. Could hear the band distinctly. Kaaipulu gave birth to a girl [at] five P.M. Kamakaihona [Incomplete; perhaps it is the child's name.]

*Friday, September 24.* Came home 7½ A.M., had a lone breakfast, saw Charlie talk to men who are working on pipes. He came in at 11 A.M. Told him about our bill and its failure.[322] We were quite excited about it. Must make one effort and wrote to brother.[323]

*Saturday, September 25.* Received J. A. Cummins, J. E. Bush, J. M. Kapena, Aholo, Kaulukou. I spoke first of Charley's [indemnity] Bill. They concluded to pass it to ease my mind. Aiaumoe gave me five dollars to Kainuuala for umeke [calabash] [for] H.H.L. [Hui Hoonaauao Liliuokalani]. Wainee gave me $6 for her umeke. Hui Nihoa—Gave W. six dollars to Jessie [Kaae]. A. J. Cartwright came to relieve my mind on Summons.[324]

Kapo came [at] four P.M. Went to Kaipo's 5½ P.M. Came home, Jessie [Kaae] was waiting here for me. 7½ P.M., King and [Paul] Neumann came in. Went to see Nihoa at Kapiolani Park, and felt so sorry for him. [Scrolling ornament.]

*Sunday, September 26.* Went to Waikiki with Joe. The place was in sad neglect. [No] Salt fish so [we] had to kill a chicken [and] had just enough poi to last a day—[At] Paoakalani. Had nice bath in my bathing place.

*Monday, September 27.* Went to see Mary [Beckley] about Nihoa and also sent one fine mat and Mosquito net by Aiaumoe. Went to see Panana [Harriet Parker] and baby,[325] [then to] Luau at L. [Lizzie] Victor's—did not go. Went round to Emma Square with Mrs. Wight after John had come for me to come down town. He was quite jolly and insisted on going around to see Mahiai [Robinson], Aki, and Kahaunui and take them to the Square. They ran away from him. So had to go after Martha. Slept at Washington Place. Went to see if Mrs. Brickwood would take Nihoa.

*Tuesday, September 28.* Gave $5 to Jessie for Kainuuala's umeke [calabash]. Consulted Kalua about Keamalu's affairs. Told me to telephone for those folks and I did so. It seems Luhau went $200—bond for Polani's property in 1873 and never settled it, but just took possession. Keamalu would be lucky to get that property. [Two words erased.] Went twice today to see if Mrs. Brickwood would take Nihoa. She was not at home.

322. Liliuokalani sponsored this bill to provide relief for Charles Wilson over financial discrepancies in the water board. It entered the legislature but did not pass.

323. Liliuokalani's letter to the king is as follows: "Sept. 24, 1886. Brother, The line is tossed to you, and from you there is life. I've heard that the bill sponsored by Charles Wilson and I, has died. And its death was due to those of the government's party, not the opposition as was assumed. Nahale, Kaukau, Kaunamano, Nahinu, Palohau, Amara, G. Richardson were of the government's party, and A. Kaulia the opposition. They are the reason this bill has failed.... Therefore I rightly make a request of you, Brother. You have a powerful voice and if you were to speak to them, they would not deny your voice.... One of them has said that they would not have acted thus if you had said something.... I do not wish to burden you, if you are able to instruct the members of the Legislature to resurrect [the bill] and pass it in Charles' favor, then I will be most happy. Your loving sister, Sister." Hawaii State Archives, Liliuokalani Collection, Box 18, Seized Document No. 22. Translated from the Hawaiian by Jason Achiu.

324. See September 14, 1886, diary entry (109).

325. James Kekooalii Parker (b. September 20, 1886, Honolulu–d. February 6, 1963, Waianae, Oahu) was the youngest of nine children born to Samuel and Harriet Napela Parker.

*Wednesday, September 29.* Mary Ward is to be married tonight. Got one set of silver spoons, forks, and teaspoons for John to give tonight. Mr. Hustace is the happy man. Saw the wedding cake made by Mrs. Swan. Very handsome.[326]

Owe Wenner [a jeweler] $22, for fish knife and spoon, $5.00 for two hatpins, $16 for card case for Liliu Carter to present to Irene Ii, who is to marry C. A. Brown tomorrow night.

Col. J. H. Boyd returned this morn from Ocean Island. Reports the men in distress had just left the island a few days before. Left three dogs on the island and they built a tin house, some tanks, planted trees, and took formal possession of the island.

Hinano Bower. A nice wedding [of Frank Hustace and Mary Ward, with] lots of presents—lots of friends.

Consulted J.W.K. [Kalua] on Keamalu—two men arrive from Waialua for Ehukai [?] tell their evidence.[327]

---

On September 13, 1886, the steamer *James Makee* arrived at Honolulu from Kauai with the chief officer and six crew of the British ship *Dunnottar Castle*, which had wrecked at Ocean Island on July 15. The rescued sailors had left Ocean Island in a longboat and, after a 52-day voyage, had landed at Kalihi Wai, Kauai. They informed authorities that they had left their captain and 22 men on the island. A government rescue effort chartered the SS *Waialeale*, which departed for Ocean Island on September 14. Upon arrival there, they found a bottle containing information that the *Birnham Wood* had rescued the 29 persons and taken them to Valparaiso.

As the Hawaiian government had not formally annexed Ocean Island as part of the Hawaiian Islands, King Kalakaua had requested that the rescue group (headed by Colonel James H. Boyd) take formal possession of the island. This they did by erecting a small house or shed and water tanks, planting several trees, and raising the Hawaiian flag. Ocean Island (or Moku Papapa) thereby became a recognized part of the Hawaiian group.

The *Waialeale* returned to Honolulu on September 29, and the Honolulu newspapers printed full accounts of the expedition the next day. An elaborate manuscript map of the island with several watercolor vignettes by artist Joe Strong, a member of the expedition, is in the Hawaii State Archives.

---

326. "On Wednesday evening Mr. Frank Hustace and Miss Mary Ward were united in marriage by the Rev. H. H. Parker. The ceremony took place at the residence of Mrs. Ward.... The house was brilliantly illuminated with colored lights, and the Royal Hawaiian Band provided excellent music. The bridesmaids were the Misses Ward, sisters to the bride, and the groomsmen were Messrs. Charles Hustace and J. F. Morgan. After the ceremony the newly married couple held a reception, and a ball closed the celebration. Their Majesties the King and Queen and their staff, Princesses Liliuokalani and Likelike, His Excellency Governor Dominis, and Hon. A. S. Cleghorn were among the guests." *Hawaiian Gazette*, October 5, 1886.

327. This may have been in preparation for the case of *Keamalu v. Luhau* (a bill for partition of land), which would come before the Supreme Court of Hawaii in 1888. Hawaii State Archives, First Circuit Court, Equity 627.

*Thursday, September 30.* Irene Ii is to be married tonight.[328]

Went with Jessie Kaae to Mr. Cartwright—he gave me $400, my allowance of salary, and told me that W. [Waimanalo] Shares had been reduced 2½ per cent. Paid Joe $50. Loe and Kawehena $40, Ahoi $18.75, Kaluna $3 for screws. Saw Emma Beckley—compared notes of our Hui Hookuonoono. She thanked me for having her salary raised.[329]

John not so well today.

Kawehena's house all finished except painting inside. Must stay at home and finish report. Band is playing at A. F. Judd's. Irene [Ii] is married—Mr. Judd was so emphatic in saying he wished we had asked him for Irene's place. [At] Nua Lehua. All alone am sad and dreary, in the Hazel Dell.[330]

*Friday, October 1.* Kalahiki $5 for [Hui] Hookuonoono, $5 for umeke [calabash]. Kainuuala $5 for umeke, $1.50 for Meeau's umeke. Joe gave me $5 for Meeau Hui Hookuonoono—Loe and Kawehena gave me $5 each for umeke. I gave one [dollar?] lulu [donation] toward Kaiulani funds to buy Mrs. Kavanaugh's seat in Hui Hookuonoono, who resigned today and withdrew her $40 and 1.5 interest. [Received from?] M. [Maluhi] Reis $5 for umeke. Mary Beckley took $200 to Wilder & Co. $400 contributed by H. Hui. Borrowed of Hui Hookuonoono $240. J. [Jessie] Kaae brought me $5 for herself and $5 for Maria Lane [for] H. Hookuonoono and 50 cts each for being late. Five P.M.

*Saturday, October 2.* Went to Washington Place, stayed till 5½ P.M. to see the men finish their work. Gave each $1. They gave up the fishing right of Hamohamo, Kalu ma [and his people]. No band [concert] today—they were at Wharf. Went to Waikiki.

*Sunday, October 3.* Woke at eight. Breakfasted on Aku and Kumu [two species of fish]. Slept all day and had bath. It was cold so did not stay long. Day soon went by and night came on. [At] Paoakalani.

*Monday, October 4.* Keala Hale [with scrolling flourish above]. Joe gave me $1 for Kaiulani. Ana gave me 50 cents for her umeke [calabash]. Kamiki Aea 50 cts. Umeke. Kanalulu 50 cts. Mrs. and Miss Nowlein gave me each $1 for Kaiulani.

Hui Hoonaauao Liliuokalani met today. $4.50 was contributed. Gave two dollars toward paying for A. Paiaina's shoes [and] 30 cts for something else. Called L.H.H. [Liliuokalani Hui Hoonaauao] to meet next day and

328. On Thursday evening, "Mr. C. A. Brown was married to Miss Irene Ii, ward of the Hon. Chief Justice, A. F. Judd. The ceremony was performed by and at the house of the Rev. Dr. Hyde.... The reception was afterwards held at *Rosenheim*, on Nuuanu Avenue, the residence of the bride's guardian.... The Royal Hawaiian band was stationed in a marquee erected on the lawn, and pealed forth a jubilant wedding march on the arrival of the newly wedded pair... and soon the Hawaiian national [anthem] announced the arrival of H.M. the King, the Royal princesses, and their respective staffs." *Hawaiian Gazette*, October 5, 1886.

329. Emma Kaili Metcalf Beckley (b. 1867, Waialua, Oahu–d. 1929, Honolulu), the daughter of Theophilus Metcalf and his chiefly wife Kailikapuolono, first married Fred K. Beckley, and second, in 1887, married Reverend Moses Keaka Nakuina (b. 1867–d. 1911). She was librarian and curator of the Hawaiian Government Museum (under the Department of Foreign Affairs).

330. "The Hazel Dell" by G. Friedrich Wurtzel was a popular minstrel song of the day.

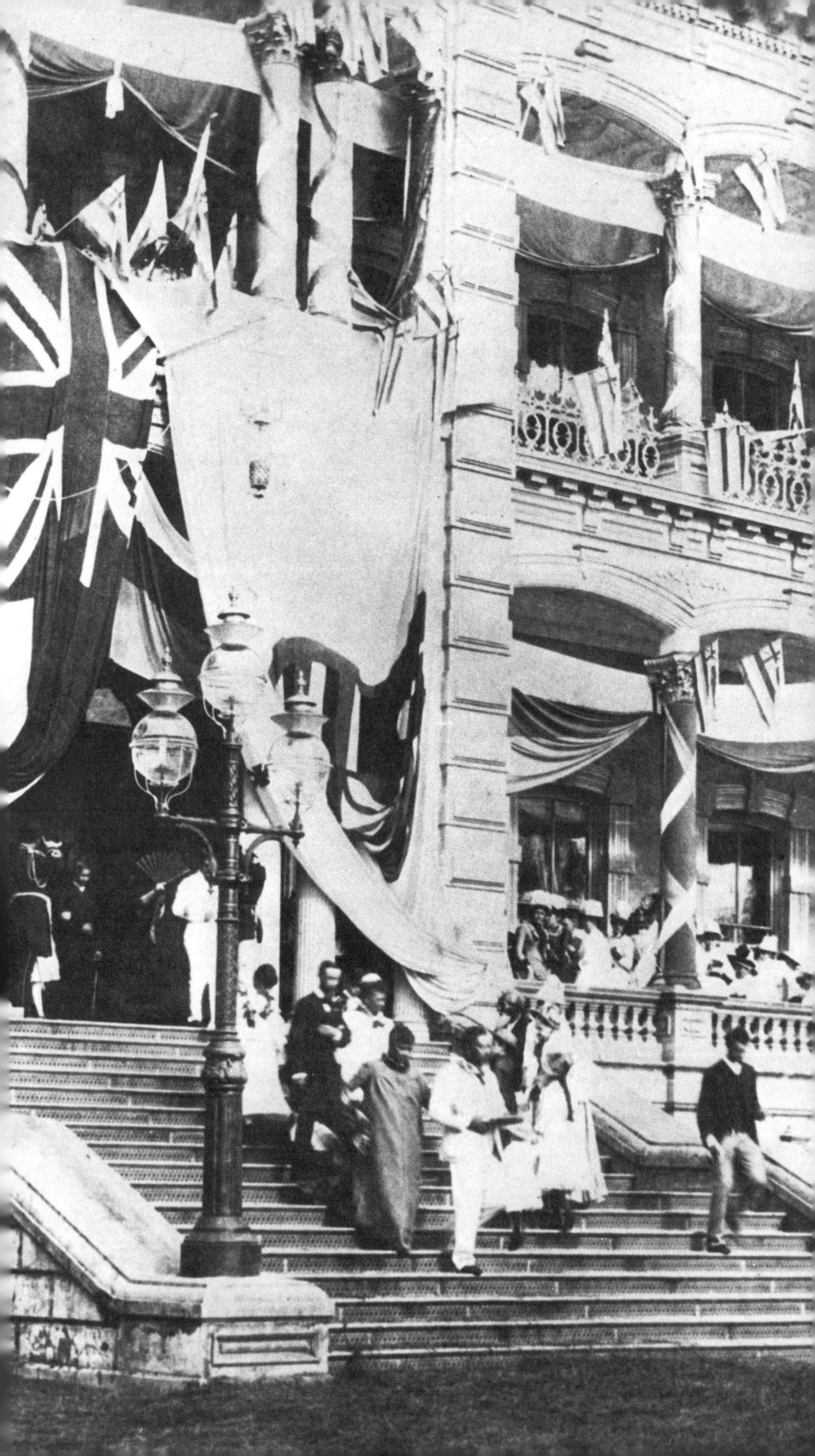

*A party on the enclosed lanai at Ainahau in celebration of Princess Kaiulani's eleventh birthday on October 16, 1886. The presence of the two kahili (feather standards), held by attendants on either side of the princess, signifies her royal rank as heiress presumptive to the throne of Hawaii.*
Alfred Mitchell, 1886, Bishop Museum Archives

OPPOSITE
*King Kalakaua and Crown Princess Liliuokalani lead the procession to the front garden of Iolani Palace during the king's golden jubilee celebrating his fiftieth birthday on November 16, 1886. The royal consorts, Queen Kapiolani and John O. Dominis, follow. In her November 15 diary entry, Liliu describes a ceremonial procession and presentation of gifts to the king at the palace on that day. At midnight, a 21-gun salute from the battery at Punchbowl signaled the start of jubilee festivities.*
(Detail) J. J. Williams, Hawaii State Archives

consult about how to contribute on Kaiulani's birth for next day at Mary Ailau's. Aholo came to ask for Mr. [Tom] Evans[331] to be [appointed] Deputy Sheriff for Makawao. Went to see King, he told me John was pau [finished] being Governor of both Islands. Gave up my trip and telephoned all around the island. John [was] made Commander in Chief, a new office, Curtis [Iaukea] Governor of Oahu, R. H. Baker Governor of Maui.

*Tuesday, October 5.* Loe gave $1. Kainuuala $7. I went down to meeting at Mary Ailau's. Gave Loe $1. Kalei $1. Kainuuala $1. Kahae $1 to Emma Beckley. Lizzie Victor brought Becky Brewster's money of L.H.H. [Liliuokalani Hui Hoonaauao] $5.53.

D. [David] Malo sent me two puaas [pigs] and poi. Went back to Washington Place to console John, who was loath to give up [the office of] Governor [of] Oahu. Slept there. He did not sleep, as he thought that Governor was higher in rank than Lt. General.[332]

*Wednesday, October 6.* Woke up early. John had not slept all night—so I walked to Palace, no King—walked to Boathouse, found him there, and saw Poepoe[333] and pig Mohai [sacrifice]. Spoke to King about John's worrying and he told me to go back and tell him not to worry, but just do as he was told. That pacified him [John], and I came home to a late breakfast. Moon shone so bright. Came over [several words erased, possibly: to Keala Hale] till got tired, then went to Nua Lehua. Keamalu told me Poepoe had charged $20 more, so I told them to give him up and take Kalua. Poepoe decided to take the case. Postponed because Kinney asked for Luhau. Saw Keamalu with case [of] oil not ordered by me.

*Thursday, October 7.* [Two-line entry erased.]

*Friday, October 8.* [One-line entry erased.]

*Saturday, October 9.* Woke at 4½ A.M. huhu [angry]. Planted ferns and roses. Went to Jessie's, then came to Washington Place. Gave to Jessie Kaae for Kalahiki, Kailikole, Loe, Kawehena, and Nihoa, and M. [Maluhi] Reis $30 for Umekes [calabashes] of L. H. Hookuonoono at $5 each.

Stayed at Washington Place and took nap till the band at Emma Square woke me at 4½ P.M. Came home—had tea and went to town again to McGuire's.[334]

At 6½ P.M. Kunane [Kalakaua] came in to tell me of C. B. Wilson again. Minister [of] Interior Gibson has found that he [Wilson] had drawn full amount for that new reservoir, and paid the men far less than the amount drawn. Gibson found out from receipts. Charley will have to resign [from the waterworks]—so I must submit.

From Mrs. McGuire's, stopped at Washington Place—came home

---

331. Thomas E. Evans (b. Canada) was a deputy sheriff, postmaster, and school agent at Lahaina, and the husband of Liliu's close friend, Hannah Kaniau.

332. John O. Dominis remained governor of Oahu until August 23, 1888, and was reappointed March 2, 1891, serving until his death on August 27, 1891.

333. Joseph Mokuohai Poepoe (b. 1852, Kohala–d. 1913, Honolulu) was an attorney at law and newspaper editor, and resided on School Street.

334. The James W. McGuire residence was on Beretania Street near Makiki Street.

[and] slept at Hinano Bower.[335] How cosy. Came home [to Muolaulani]. Three P.M. Dr. McWayne [came], had consultation. I must go to his office tomorrow.[336]

*Sunday, October 10.* Came home and breakfasted. Went to Bethel [church] to hear Mr. Oggel preach, text—"Honor thy Father and thy Mother." 3½ P.M. to Dr. McWayne's. Examination . . . almost a complete closing of the mouth of the womb. This was the cause of all my complaints ever since stoppage. [Several lines erased.]

*Monday, October 11.* After breakfast went to Waikiki and took Jessie. Paina Kapu [private meal]—Jessie Joe, Aiaumoe, Keanu, and I. Three P.M. came to Engine Co. No. 1. Few members were waiting. Umeke [calabashes] came and [were] distributed—most were cracked, but twelve remained. Something must be done. Members of second division [of Hui Hoonaauao] took theirs, left 12. Came home and had tea, then drove to Washington Place and waited till Joe came for me. Mrs. Wight waited, sat with me. Slept soundly.

Gave to Mrs. Haalelea $41.50 for umeke [calabashes] for members 2nd Division H.H.L. [Hui Hoonaauao Liliuokalani.]

*Tuesday, October 12.* Went to Mrs. C. O. Berger's,[337] and found Mrs. Fred Macfarlane there. Spoke of Umeke and concluded to ask Herrick to stop the holes up so water could stay—he said he would.[338]

Mary Ailau went to Kauai and left in my charge $36 belonging to Members of Liliuokalani H. [Hui] Hookuonoono. Kaaiaumoe left $1 for Kalahiki and $1 for Meeau, for Kaiulani.

Drove to Kauluwela and told Pepe that Kahawaii ought to have her half in the lot, but Pepe's husband says he ought to have ⅓ because he paid two thirds of the money for the lot. Kahawaii says she is willing to give up her share on the house.[339]

Dined alone. Queen goes to Kauai with Minister [Paul] Kanoa.[340]

335. This was a cottage adjacent to Washington Place.
336. Dr. Albert McWayne (b. 1856, Geneva, Illinois–d. November 18, 1899, Honolulu) married Lucy Robinson, the part-Hawaiian daughter of James Robinson.
337. Martha Widemann was the part-Hawaiian wife of German-born businessman Charles Otto Berger (d. 1895, age 47) and the sister of Emilie Macfarlane.
338. William E. Herrick (d. 1893) was a wood and ivory turner at Bethel Street near King Street.
339. This seems to have been a dispute over a small parcel of land at Kauluwela that Pepe and her husband E. W. Makawalu had received from Mrs. Kahawaii, which was afterward mortgaged to Henry Dimond for $150 according to the Bureau of Conveyances, Liber 117, 46. A frosty tone is suggested, as the June 24, 1889, conveyance is "to Mrs. Pepe from Mrs. Kahawaii." No personal names appear on the document, and their agent, S. M. Kaaukai, signs it in their place.
340. "Her Majesty the Queen, accompanied by Mrs. P. P. Kanoa, Mrs. L. Ululani, and Mrs. E. L. Kauai, leave by the *Iwalani* this afternoon for Kauai, to be absent two weeks." *Pacific Commercial Advertiser*, October 12, 1886. The following day, the paper reported: "A few minutes before the sailing of the steamer, Their Majesties the King and Queen drove down to the wharf, and were received by His Excellency Governor C. P. Iaukea, His Majesty's Chamberlain. His Excellency Paul P. Kanoa Minister of Finance, Brigade Major A. B. Hayley, and an immense throng of loyal Hawaiians were present at the wharf to witness the departure of the steamer."

*Wednesday, October 13.* [Entry erased.]

*Saturday, October 16.* Six A.M. Arranged flowers all morning for Bernice's [Bernice Pauahi's] grave—second anniversary of her death. Pricked my fingers with thorns of roses. What lovely flowers. As she loved them in life we will deck her grave in death. Hurried home to take Mrs. [James] Wight to Waikiki—she wouldn't come, Huhu [angry]. Legislature [session] over—very few present—what does it predict? Queen at Kauai—sister and I not present—few foreign representatives—no ladies present. Could just manage to get a quorum.[341]

The King's remarks were brief, and the whole ceremony lasted only fifteen minutes.

Went to Kaiulani's 11th birthday—Liliuokalani Hui Hookuonoono contributed $48—Mary Pahau and Pokini did not contribute. Lots of money and lots of friends. Came home at four P.M.[342] Went to Waikiki at 7½ P.M. My hand begins to trouble me.

*Sunday, October 17.* Spent day at Paoakalani. Can scarcely touch anything, my hands pain me so.

*Monday, October 18.* Returned home to get ready for trip—Maria King sent $1.20 for entrance fee [for] Mahele [Division] 2nd Hui Hoonaauao. Must propose her name next meeting. [I] leave for Wailuku by *Likelike* and John leaves for Lahaina in *Kinau*.

*Wednesday, October 20.* One P.M. Wailuku women 7½ P.M. halawai [meeting].

*Thursday, October 21.* One P.M. Wahine [women] 7½ Waihee church.

*Friday, October 22.* Ma Paia one P.M. Wahine 7½ halawai me ka lehulehu [At Paia one P.M. women, 7½ met with the people].

*Saturday, October 23.* Came back to Wailuku.

---

341. On the conclusion of the legislature (October 16, 1886), the *Pacific Commercial Advertiser*, October 18, 1886, commented somewhat ingeniously on what had been an irresponsible session: "It is premature to review the work of the Session as a whole, but it may be said generally that much of it was thorough. Owing to the peculiar constitution of parties, and to the paramount influence of the Crown, the Legislature often presented disappointing features, but despite these drawbacks it is doubtful whether other legislative assemblies, more favorably circumstanced, have not at times exhibited as much mental aberration and moral obliquity."

342. "A dazzling assemblage of the royalty, nobility, and gentry of the Kingdom was witness on Saturday afternoon at the elegant residence of H.R.H. the Princess Likelike and the Hon. A. S. Cleghorn, at Waikiki to celebrate the eleventh anniversary of the natal day of their daughter H.R.H. The Princess Kaiulani.... The well-kept grounds looked their very best. Never did the avenue of palm trees present a grander aspect, nor the superbly laid flower beds a more varied one.... The sumptuous reception room was no less pleasing to the eye. Here the numerous guests were received ... [and] conveyed to the apartment where the little Princess ... awaited her friends and well-wishers, guarded on either side by a pair of kahilis [feather standards], the emblems of her rank.... His Majesty the King arrived shortly after two o'clock, attended by his Chamberlain, the band meanwhile playing the national anthem." The reporter noted the many gifts tendered to the princess, including "$1 each from all the members of the Liliuokalani Educational Society." *Pacific Commercial Advertiser*, October 18, 1886.

Liliuokalani also made a Lahaina stop, of which the *Pacific Commercial Advertiser* carried a long account:

> ¶ On Friday evening H.R.H. Princess Liliuokalani arrived from Maalaea, per Likelike and was welcomed on landing by a large concourse of people, the national anthem being sung by some thirty of our best voices, and the chorus taken up by our whole throng, the effect being most inspiring. The royal party were then escorted to the carriages awaiting them and were driven through two lines of torches to the residence of the Commander-in-Chief of our Forces, His Excellency John O. Dominis. The grounds there were beautifully illuminated, and a large concourse of people soon filled the place. After a short rest Her Royal Highness and suite, His Excellency Governor Baker and lady, several Government officials, and two or three foreigners sat down to a ... repast "à la Hawaiian," during which time our best musical talent had arranged themselves on either side of the walk leading from the entrance to the house, and there during the whole evening poured forth in rich strains, our sweet Hawaiian melodies. Several guitars and a violin were used for accompaniments. This pleasant public demonstration of the aloha for the heir apparent was brought to a close about one A.M. During the day (Saturday) the Princess received many callers, and in her quiet way made everyone feel perfectly at home. This afternoon about four o'clock a grand luau was given in honor of our Royal guest on the Court House square, of which most of our foreigners and many Hawaiians availed themselves. The spread was excellent, and not a little is due to Governor Baker and his courteous manner in making the affair most sociable. About six o'clock the Royal Party, the Governor, and suite returned to the house, and the evening has been characterized by singing, dancing, and general merriment. The *Kinau*'s whistle was the signal for bringing to a close the varied social two days' pleasure and the party was escorted to the wharf through a perfect blaze of torches, when was sung our anthem, and sung too, with heart as well as to voice, and so ends the visit of our Royal lady.[343]

*Sunday, October 24.* In Wailuku.

*Monday, October 25.* Makawao, spend the night at Kamaole. Kaakaole $2.

*Tuesday, October 26.* Ulupalakua, stay one day.

*Wednesday, October 27.* At Makena hold a meeting.

*Thursday, October 28.* Go to Wailuku.

[Liliuokalani returned to Honolulu on the *Kinau*, October 30.]

---

343. *Pacific Commercial Advertiser*, October 25, 1886.

*Monday, November 1.* Met the Members of Liliuokalani Hui Hookuonoono at Mary Ailau's. They contributed $509. $200 sent to pay Wilder & Co. Mary Ailau borrowed $100. I borrowed $204—Hanakeola borrowed $10—lent Mary Pahau $5.00. Paid Kawehena $20, Loe $20, Joe $45—Awai $20, Aiaumoe $21. Hui Hookuonoono for Kahae and myself [and] S. Kalei. The Liliuokalani Hui Hookuonoono and Hui Nihoa met at Engine House No. 1—to take calabashes. They went home well satisfied. Good meeting.

Took $10 to Kaipo, from there went to band, then slept at Hinano Bower. [Two lines erased.]

*Tuesday, November 2.* $5.95 contributed today by H.H.L. [Hui Hoonaauao Liliuokalani]. Went up to Mary Ailau's, then from there to Carrie Bush's for flowers, and on to Mrs. Carter's. Some nice bouquets, all to take to Bernice. Two years ago she was taken up there [to the Royal Mausoleum] and placed among the dead. Whose turn will it be next? Cordie [Allen] soon came up, and we went through the same sad duty. Sophy [Sheldon] and I drove home to [see baby] Nihoa. He was asleep. Mrs. McGuire took us over to Mrs. Wilson to see her Kahilis [feather standards]. They are beautiful. Three P.M. met 1st and 2nd Divisions of H. H. Liliuokalani. After contributions of dues—appointed Mrs. Goo Kim and [Mrs.] Hopkins to see Puuohau's family—and [the] report was to take Koi in [as a scholarship recipient in] Mrs. Deverill's girls' place.[344] Appointed all to meet at Washington Place nine A.M. 16 November.

*Wednesday, November 3.* Went to Washington Place. Ellen Cleghorn[345] gave me for Kaiulani's dues of Liliuokalani Hui Hookuonoono $46.50 and I filled out passbook and gave to Helen [Boyd] in return. Took the three remaining calabashes to Mrs. Fred Macfarlane—did not see her but left them with Patty Berger.[346] Spent $21.24 for dresses for Nakapuahi and others. Gave Kaakaole $2.00 and Kapule [a] bottle of Gin and sent her off in the express.

*Thursday, November 4.* Stayed at home all day. John came up with Mr. Brown and wanted $70 for Mattress and pillows—the idea—and yet I do his washing at $10 a month besides making [him a] present of $300 a year.

How it rains—yet the band came. Mr. and Mrs. Aholo and Mr. Creighton were the only ones that came.[347]

Arranged for a dance for the [Cabinet] Ministers on Monday. Told Mr. McAllister to hire an express and come down and [several words erased] for me, which he did.[348]

---

344. Maria Puuohau is listed in the 1888 City Directory as a domestic with Liliuokalani at Muolaulani. Koi is possibly Annie Puuohau, who is listed in the 1888 City Directory as a pupil at Kawaiahao Seminary.

345. Ellen Cleghorn, a niece of Archibald S. Cleghorn, was visiting from New Zealand.

346. Mrs. Frederick Macfarlane (Amelia or Emilie, b. 1858, Lihue, Kauai–d. 1947, Honolulu) was a part-Hawaiian daughter of Judge Herman A. Widemann. Patty Berger was her sister.

347. Mr. Robert J. Creighton (b. 1835, Derry, Ireland–d. 1893, San Francisco) was a lawyer and, in 1888, minister of foreign affairs. The occasion was Liliu's monthly reception at Palama. The *Pacific Commercial Advertiser*, November 5, 1886, (not having read the Queen's diary) reported: "In spite of the unpleasant weather yesterday, Her Royal Highness the Princess Liliuokalani held her regular monthly reception, which was well attended."

348. William B. McAllister is listed as "dentist, cor. Fort and Hotel (upstairs)" in the 1885 City Directory.

*Saturday, November 6.* Promised to go to Charley Booth's birthday—but forgot that I had previous engagements at Eveline's with Mrs. McGuire, so must fulfill it. Telephoned to Carrie Bush to come here with all the children, and had a good time. How it rains. 10½ yes, he is coming home.

*Sunday, November 7.* Paid $2.50 for Carrie Bush's express [hack hire] with the children yesterday.

*Monday, November 8.* Must get Rebecca a blue dress—and give her some gourd seeds. Must go to Kaumakapili at three P.M. to meet members of Hooulu Lahui. Rec'd from Mooni $100 for land in Manoa. D. Malo has already taken $27. Gave Kaakaole $2.

*Tuesday, November 9.* Pooloku [Princess Poomaikelani] came up to see about poles for banners. Must see Lucas. Mrs. S. [Sam] Nowlein gave me $2.20 for herself and Poomaikelani for the rest of the year Mahele [Division] 2, Hui Hoonaauao Liliuokalani.

*Wednesday, November 10.* Went to see Kunane [Kalakaua] about the procession on the 15th. Three P.M. went to Hui Hooulu Lahui [meeting], collected $7.70 and must give it to J. Waiamau. For a wonder Kahae actually came up and bowed to me with the rest of the Members of the Hui.

*Monday, November 15.* Busy all morning. Gave Kaakaole $2.

Five P.M. All the Nihoas collected at Washington Place—procession was formed and went to Palace with the present to the King. We were received by Their Majesties with kindness, the present being placed in the midst and the Nihoas stood in a circle. After the speech the Queen retired, and we had Ice cream and coffee—while the Kawaihaus sang to entertain us. 8½ we bade the King good night and all went home.[349]

---

King Kalakaua's golden jubilee birthday commenced "at midnight...by a Royal Salute of 21 guns from the battery on the summit of Punchbowl Hill from whence a row of bonfires simultaneously shot their flames into the heavens. Rockets were also fired off at intervals, and the mountain was brilliantly illuminated, casting a ruddy glare over the mauka side of the city. The bells rang out a merry peal from the several churches, conveying the alohas of each religious body to the Sovereign."[350] As Liliu's diary indicates, the celebration had already begun with a procession to the palace, and a hookupu or ceremonial presentation of gifts. The festivities continued for several days and included a luau and a ball.

---

349. Although the main events surrounding King Kalakaua's jubilee took place on his birthday, November 16, ceremonies began the day before. The *Advertiser* reported the presentation of the Nihoas: "At six last evening the Nihoa Society called at the Palace in a body to present their respects to His Majesty, whom they presented with a very handsome present in the shape of a calabash of native wood, silver mounted with a shield bearing the dates 1836 and 1886. Dependent from the shield is a pair of rare feathers. Before leaving the members of the society rendered several native songs." *Pacific Commercial Advertiser*, November 16, 1886.

350. Reporting on the festivities continued in the *Pacific Commercial Advertiser*, November 17, 1886.

*Wednesday, December 1.* Meeau gave me $5 for Hui Hookuonoono. Aiaumoe gave me $10, five for Kalahiki and five for Kainuuala of Kalahiki's money. Wakeke paid to me $10 she borrowed of me last month, five for umeke [calabash], and five for Hui Hookuonoono. Louisa Brickwood gave me $5 for Liliuokalani Hui Hookuonoono. Mrs. Kanoa gave me 50 cts for Miriam Koko, a new member. Joe commenced to take care of my house. Paid Loe and Kawehena $40, Joe $50, Aiaumoe $20. Returned to Liliuokalani Hui Hookuonoono $220.40. Collected from Hui $245. Received $5 from Hanakeola [Mrs. Kinimaka], made $470.40 in adding my amount returned. Gave Mrs. Emma Beckley to take to Wilder & Co. $200—leaving $270. Hanakeola borrowed $50 to be returned on February and March 1887, paying $25 each month.

*Thursday, December 2.* Had my reception today. Had only four visitors.

*Friday, December 3.* Gave Joe $2 to take to Kaakaole. Had a meeting of the 1st Division of H. H. Liliuokalani. Contributions over $10. Nominated Mrs. Hill Vice President in [lieu of] Mrs. C. O. Berger resigned, [and] Miss Ladd in [lieu of] Mrs. Fred Macfarlane—Miss Lou Brickwood Assistant Treasurer. Decided to take Kohoni and educate her at Kawaiahao Seminary. Thanked the Society for [Entry ends thus.][351]

*Saturday, December 4.* One P.M. went to a fair at English Sisters' [school]. Spent $12 on lunching [with] friends and buying dresses for babies.[352]

Went to the Palace in the evening—stayed till 11—then got tired of the Hula and singing[353] and went home. Could not find Joe. He has been neglectful since the Jubilee.

---

[351]. "The Liliuokalani Society, First Division, met on Friday afternoon at Engine Company No. 1's rooms, on King Street, the Princess Liliuokalani presiding. There was a small gathering. Mrs. W. Hill was elected Vice President, Miss Brickwood Treasurer, and Miss Ladd a Directoress, and other vacancies were filled. The Princess expressed her approbation of the Society, and thanked the members for so ably seconding efforts in its behalf." *Hawaiian Gazette*, December 7, 1886.

[352]. This was a fancy fair held at Saint Andrew's Priory in aid of the building fund for Saint Andrew's Cathedral. The *Pacific Commercial Advertiser*, December 4, 1886, reported that in the schoolroom, the Hawaiian table had been in the charge of Mrs. Mackintosh, Louisa Brickwood, Stella Keomailani, and Kapoli Kamakau.

[353]. The evenings of hula and chanting at the palace during King Kalakaua's birthday festivities were the subject of disapproving remarks in the press. The *Hawaiian Gazette*, December 7, 1886, made two separate comments: "A select hula party was given at the palace Saturday evening. All haoles who had strayed inside were gently led to the gate and passed out. Not even malihinis were excepted." It continued: "Hulas and weird music in the region of Richards Street [in the bungalow] seemed to be in 'high' favor during the past week in the evenings, to the intense disgust of many who were in close proximity thereto."

The *Pacific Commercial Advertiser*, December 7, 1886, was more condemnatory in its editorial: "The hula has become a social ulcer which must be healed if decent people are either to live here or to visit this country. It entraps the young and unwary; it waylays the old; and it coins money for men who pursue their disreputable calling under license of the authorities.... The hula may have powerful protectors, but it must go. Its days are numbered. The public have had a surfeit of it. There is a limit to all things, and that limit has been reached.... At the same time innocent amusement should be provided for the native people. They should be taught dancing and other innocent enjoyments, and so fit them to the level of educated for-

*Sunday, December 5.* Did not go to church. John and Mary came in an express and took Aimoku and I out to Sam Parker's [at Waikiki] to see John and Hanai[354]—from there went to Hamohamo—fearfully neglected. Came home, then drove over to Mrs. Dowsett's. Glad to have him [John?] go home. No fun in going with [partially erased] drunken people.

*Monday, December 6.* Spent the morning at the Palace arranging presents and taking list of the presents—dined at three, went to town at seven P.M. Took three dresses for Jessie to make. Went to Eveline's, asked C. B. Wilson about Pepe's $100. He told me to go to Cartwright and foreclose. Came back to Washington Place and waited for Joe. He came for me at 10½ and we came home. Sent $1,000 worth of bills to A. J. Cartwright. He said he would pay them off in a week, but I must not get in debt any more. A good advice and I must follow it. Promised to send Kimoteo [Timoteo] of Waialua $10—towards Sunday School.[355]

*Tuesday, December 7.* Spent morning in copying list of things presented to the King on his 50th birthday—sent it up to Curtis [Iaukea] by Joe.[356] Took nap after dinner, was good for nothing rest of the day. A lovely night—bright moonlight. Retired at ten.

*Wednesday, December 8.* Am very lazy today.

*Thursday, December 9.* Went up to Palace and disposed of things here and there. Saw Poomaikelani.

*Saturday, December 11.* Received officers of Hui Puali Puhi Ohe [Band Association]. They brought me $500.00—signed two receipts. Asked if they had anything to say. They answered no, but it seems they were dissatisfied with Willie. Kaipo spent the day with me. King came over to see J. Spencer about house.[357] Went to reform band [Reformatory School Band], then went to Emma Square and took Kaipo home. Same evening went downtown, paid N. Sachs $1.25,[358] Wolfe $1. Bought some groceries.

*Monday, December 13.* Went and took band boys' money to A. J. Cartwright, he kept the [account] book. He told me to see Aholo and ask him to pay him [Cartwright] Charley's indemnity bill.[359]

---

eigners instead of permitting them to remain … dragging foreigners down to the level of lasciviousness, barbarism, and utterly demoralizing the rising generation of Hawaiian youth."

354. John P. Parker (b. November 25, 1827, Kohala, Hawaii–d. November 22, 1891, Honolulu) was a son of John Parker, founder of the Parker Ranch on the island of Hawaii. He married Hanai at Waimea in 1845, and the couple lived variously at Mana, the ranch headquarters in Hamakua, and Puuopelu in Waimea. Liliuokalani and her husband were guests of the Parkers on various occasions during the 1860s.

355. Reverend E. S. Timoteo was the pastor of the Waialua (Protestant) Church, and resided in Kapalama Uka.

356. A copy of this list is in the Hawaii State Archives, Liliuokalani Collection.

357. John Spencer was a carpenter listed in the 1890 City Directory as living at Kapalama.

358. N. S. Sachs, the popular millinery house, was located at 104 Fort Street.

359. In the Interior Department files labeled "Investigation of Honolulu Water Works Case of March 1886" (concerning Charles Wilson and departmental cash shortages), there is a February 17, 1886, receipt from Cartwright in the amount of $5,000, and promissory

Eight P.M. went to Hui Hooulu Lahui [meeting]. Saw Mrs. Aholo and asked her to tell Aholo to come down. Decided to have meeting next Monday at Kaumakapili to contribute and send a present to the Queen. Went with Kapoli to see her place[360] and arrange about building her a house, as I do not think in conversing with Cordie [Allen] that Mr. Bishop wants her to live there again. Consulted with Cordie about Bernice's Birthday, Sunday. Went at seven P.M. to see Mrs. Dominis—sleeps all the time.

*Tuesday, December 14.* Aholo came—asked him if the Govt. could pay Charley's indemnity bill—he said he would see. Sent Joe up to get Kahili [feather standard] handles—over twenty were returned from Mausoleum. Keha'a came and made arrangements about Christmas day [and?] about S. [Sunday] School. Tamar gave me $1 for H.H.L. towards present for Queen. Told her to propose to Annie Kaholokahiki[361] to resign from Hui as officer.

*Wednesday, December 15.* Was very good all day. Spent the morning in calling—had to send for Mr. Boyd to invite young friends. Band serenaded Mrs. Dominis. Six P.M. went to dine with the Allens, expecting Mr. Bishop to return. Stayed till 8½, then came home.

*Thursday, December 16.* Busy all morning arranging flowers. Had young folks here to dance—to meet the young princes, Kawananakoa, Keliiahonui, Kuhio. Had a very pleasant time. Mr. Burt of Hilo[362] wanted to know about the Lyman Memorial.[363] Told him I had promised to give $100.00. Lizzie Doiron came and said that she was going to look for a house to hire for herself—could not stay with Mary, so I told her to take one of those rooms at Washington Place for the present.

*Saturday, December 18.* Gave Kaakaole $2.00. Went for Kaipo, took him to [Entry ends thus.]

*Sunday, December 19.* This [is] Bernice's birthday—and we went to her casket and decked it with flowers. As usual Mrs. J. O. Carter and Mrs. Alfred Bush [Caroline Poor Bush] besides Mrs. [Cordie] Allen and myself made bouquets, wreaths, and arranged flowers in different shapes,

---

notes to the government for $1,000 each due on June 30 and November 30, 1886, and September 30, 1887, and a balance payment of $569 due December 30, 1887.

360. Lizzie Kapoli Kamakau held a lease for land in Nuuanu from Charles R. Bishop, but at the time of her death in 1891, the only property listed in her probate was a small parcel of taro land near Liliha Street. Hawaii State Archives, First Circuit Court, Probate 2748.

361. Annie was the wife of David Kaholokahiki, listed as "Servant of C. I. Hiram, King's stables" in the 1888 City Directory.

362. Arthur W. Burt was the principal of the Hilo Boarding School. He arrived in Hilo in May 1886 from Cincinnati, Ohio.

363. In 1882, a printed appeal was distributed to the patrons and friends of the Hilo Boarding School, with the idea of securing an endowment of $10,000, to be known as the "Lyman Memorial Fund of Hilo Boarding School." The income of the fund was intended to provide teachers' salaries. In 1886, it was announced that $5,000 toward this object had been received—as well as an additional $2,000 in pledges. See "Jubilee Notes, Hilo Boarding School, June 1886." The latter printed circular is sometimes found bound in with *The Friend.* See the Hawaii Mission Children's Society Library file of that periodical.

and all very pretty. From there went to Kaumakapili Sunday School. Contributions taken for children's Newspaper.

*Monday, December 20.* Decided to give a concert[364] on Saturday, three P.M.

Delivered into Mr. Geo. Castle's[365] hand the list of Subscribers towards Lyman Memorial and $150—for Queen, Kapo [Kapooloku or Princess Poomaikelani], Kawananakoa, Keliiahonui, Kalanianaole—and the King shared my $100—and Curtis [Iaukea] returned to me $50. Three P.M. went to Hooulu Lahui [meeting]—received $18.50.

*Wednesday, December 22.* $2.00 from Ikuwa for tickets.

*Thursday, December 23.* $48.00 from Kahae for tickets $7.50.

*Friday, December 24.* From Leihulu [Kapena] $9.50.

*Saturday, December 25.* Received from [Kaumakapili] concert $64.50 at the gate—$118 from committee.[366]

*Sunday, December 26.* $3 from Kahae.

*Monday, December 27.* $12.00 from Lizzie Doiron. Gave Kaakaole $2.00. Bought a silver mug at E. O. Hall for $24.50—have to pay $5 for the marking—[$]418.50 + $5 + $5—from me making $298 altogether. Hanakeola $12.00—through Tamar.

*Tuesday, December 28.* Received from Tamar $1.50 for Mrs. Ada Smith's ticket, but they borrowed it again. Tamar, Mary Alapai, Naai [Entry ends thus.]

*Wednesday, December 29.* Received from Jessie $11.00 for tickets. Mary Alapai and Naai returned theirs they borrowed yesterday, making [column of figures] altogether $218.50.

*Friday, December 31.* The Queen's birthday. 8½ A.M. Went with Hui Hooulu Lahui to Palace—King, Queen, Mr. and Mrs. J. A. Cummins, Kaulukou, Malia, [and] Kahai were on the front steps. Our present was a Silver cup. At 11 A.M. the Queen received everybody. The same evening a dancing party was given to see old year out and New Year in. Danced with Capt. Goni. [At] 12—everybody wishing Happy New Year.

---

364. "A musical entertainment, under the leadership of H.R.H. Princess Liliuokalani, will be given at Kaumakapili Church Saturday evening December 25th at 7:30 P.M. The proceeds of this entertainment will be for the benefit of the Second Division of the Liliuokalani Educational Association. We bespeak a large attendance." *Pacific Commercial Advertiser*, December 23, 1886.

365. George P. Castle (d. 1932) was a philanthropist and business executive, and the son of missionary Samuel N. Castle.

366. While Liliu is nonspecific on the nature of the entertainment, the *Hawaiian Gazette*, December 28, 1886, says: "On Christmas night, a musical entertainment was given in aid of the Second Division of the Liliuokalani Educational Society, which was well attended and the results, pecuniarily, must have been gratifying to the recipients. The entertainment was under the leadership of the Princess Liliuokalani, and reflected great credit on all concerned."

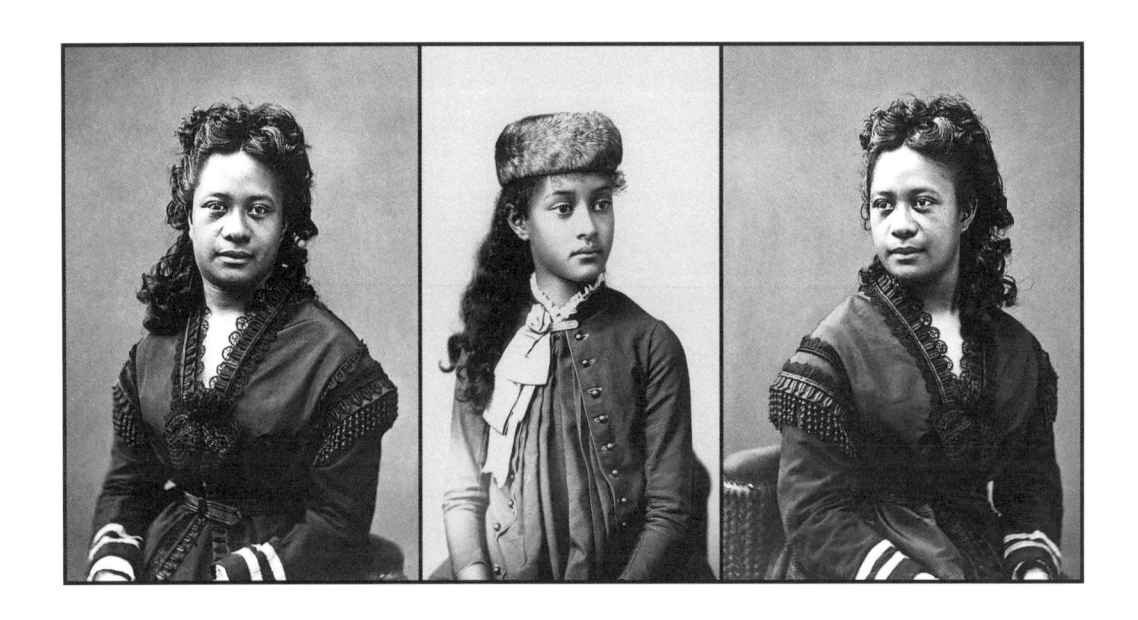

*Princess Likelike (left and right) and her daughter, Princess Kaiulani (center). In a letter dated July 20, 1884, Likelike wrote to Kaiulani (who was preparing to return to Honolulu from Hawaii Island by the steamer* Kinau*): "My darling... I am sending you a Peacock cap—it's to be worn at the back of the head, tie the strings in front, wear it when you land here. It is your old lei on a new cap, I hope you will be pleased with it" (Hawaii State Archives).*
A. A. Montano, circa 1881, Hawaii State Archives (Likelike)
J. J. Williams, circa 1884, Hawaii State Archives (Kaiulani)

# 1887

*Saturday, January 1, 1887.* Tamar gave Joe 75 cts for H.H. Liliuokalani Hoonaauao. Went to Washington Place [and] from there started for the Palace. Kunane [Kalakaua] was ill, so I had to take his seat at dinner. Capt. [Luis A.] Goni of Chilean Corvette [the *Pilcomayo*] waited on me, and my husband on the Queen.

Many guests at the Palace. [James M.] Monsarrat told me Kahae had said she would come to his office on Monday and sign deed for Lot No. 4 [at] Waikahalulu. Hula in the evening. Wakeke and all came home [at] 12½ midnight.

Keala [Hale].

Last night [at] midnight Lizzie Pratt and I made up after 13 years. Everybody in the room rejoiced. She made up with four different parties. [Major] Hayley had something to do with it but [also] Kunane [Kalakaua].[1]

*Sunday, January 2.* Went to Kawaiahao to see Hattie Kawainui's baby christened. I named the baby Lydia Kealiiakahai.[2]

From there went to the Palace. Kunane [Kalakaua] was better. Stayed at home and looked over my account book. Keala [Hale].

*Monday, January 3.* Met Liliuokalani Hui Hookuonoono. They contributed only $200.00 today—and I paid back $220.40 of last month with interest. Thought [Though?] Emma Beckley said I should give $247.90, which I did not willingly—and Mary paid back her $100 with interest. Mary's, mine, and contribution amounts to $557.90. $150 of that was taken to Wilder & Co., Mary Ailau again borrows $100, I borrow $200—leaving $107.90. Wakeke borrowed $5—of me, Kalei, and Kahae.

Three P.M. went to D. Aikanaka Dowsett's Luau.[3] King and Queen and Mrs. Wodehouse [there]—lots of people—nice time.

Keala [Hale].

*Tuesday, January 4.* Will meet Directors [of] First Division of [Liliuokalani] Educational Society nine A.M. [and at] three P.M. the whole society. They did not meet on account of its being so rainy. Paid Loe $40, Joe $45, Ahoi $18, Nakapuahi $7. Took $13 to Nihoa and $12 to Kaipo.

THE DIARY FOR 1887
1 JAN 1887–
4 JAN 1888

Hawaii State Archives

1. The long estrangement may have been the result of friction following King Kalakaua's election early in 1874, Mrs. Pratt being a staunch ally of Queen Emma, Kalakaua's political foe.

2. Hattie Kawainui was the wife of Joseph U. Kawainui (b. 1843, Hana, Maui–d. October 23, 1895, Honolulu), the liberal-minded editor and publisher of *Ko Hawaii Pae Aina* (1878–82), who subsequently assumed the editorship of the *Kuokoa*. He had a masterful command of both Hawaiian and English and was a favorite of King Kalakaua. He was a representative in the 1887–88 legislature.

3. David Aikanaka Dowsett (b. Nov. 2, 1875, Honolulu–d. Nov. 1924) was the son of James Isaac Dowsett, Liliuokalani's neighbor at Palama.

*Princess Likelike, standing at right on a garden path at Ainahau, 1885, almost submerged amidst the foliage of palms, bananas, and lilies. When Princess Likelike and her husband, Archibald Cleghorn, moved to Ainahau in Waikiki in the mid 1870s, the property was shaded by hau trees and coconut palms and probably not much else. Cleghorn proceeded to vigorously landscape the grounds, and in ten years the tropical profusion shown in this photograph was the result.*
Eduard Arning, Hawaiian Historical Society

50 cents to Lola [Bush]—Lydia [Aholo] and Kaipo. Gave Carrie Bush $7.00 for Willie Bush—Joe.

*Wednesday, January 5.* At eight P.M. Hooulu Lahui Society of Kaumakapili [and] Hooulu Lahui [met] at Palace. Queen [Kapiolani] Pres. Grace [Kahoalii][4] Secretary—Annie Dowsett Treasurer, Sally Trip—Annie Maikai—Mrs. Swan—H. Lilikalani—Kulaa. $34.45 contributed. I paid dues $2.70. King gave $1,000 to this Hui. The Queen gave [$]369.95 [Liliu then adds this up to $1,404.40]. Jessie Kaae and Maria Lane each paid $5 with 50 cents fine. They both paid 50 cents towards Mary Ailau.

Bought Diary for J. Aea of 1887. Went to meet Hooulu Lahui at Kaumakapili. Members contributed $2.95. Put it in Alapai's hands to give to [Reverend] Waiamau. Decided that they would give Luau to raise funds.

6½ P.M. Joe and I drove to Washington Place where he left me, and John and I went to Installation of Officers of Oceanic Lodge.[5]

Stayed to one dance. Jennie Clark and M. A. [Mary Ann] Lemon[6] took me to Washington Place to wait for Joe to take me back [to Muolaulani].

*Thursday, January 6.* My reception at three P.M.[7] Paid 50 cents sugar—$1 tea. $2 Dress [for] Paaluhi. $4 Aimoku [for a] Kihei [shawl]. $2 M. Beckley and L. Doiron, $2 calico one $2.25. Diary [for] Joe H., $26 poi man. It has been fearfully rainy day.[8]

11 A.M. went to see Poomaikelani [who is] sick—there I heard Queen was sick also. Three P.M. the band was on hand—only seven [at reception]. Annie Dowsett, Annie and Mary Buckle, Jennie Clark, Kanalulu, Mr. Webb,[9] Mrs. Jackson—she was bossy. Spent [for] oranges 25 [cents], limes 25 [cents]—soap 25 [cents]. There is to be a dance tonight at Dora Dowsett's.[10]

*Friday, January 7.* 2nd Division Liliuokalani Educational Society at three P.M. We will meet at Engine House No. 1. Was busy all morning mending dresses, then dined at two, and started for meeting. Sent two dollars for Kaakaole. Only six members came to meeting. While there Katie Harvey[11]

---

4. Grace Kamaikui Wahineikaili Kahoalii (b. Waianae, Oahu–d. 1916, Honolulu) was a chiefess cousin of Queen Emma, and one of the beneficiaries named in her will.

5. More exactly, this was the Lodge Le Progres de l'Oceanie (a Masonic order) on King Street.

6. Mary Ann (Wond) Lemon (b. 1844, Waialua, Oahu–d. November 13, 1919, Honolulu) was the daughter of Mary Luluhia Kamalu and William Wond and wife of James Silas Lemon.

7. "Her Royal Highness the Princess Liliuokalani will hold her regular monthly reception this afternoon from three to five o'clock at her residence, Palama. The Royal Hawaiian Band will be in attendance." *Pacific Commercial Advertiser*, January 6, 1887.

8. "The cessation of the storm yesterday rendered unnecessary the calling for tenders for a mud scow to carry passengers between Fort Street and the Government buildings, along the line of Merchant Street, that has been in contemplation." *Pacific Commercial Advertiser*, January 8, 1887.

9. J. S. Webb was an employee in the Foreign Office.

10. Dora Dowsett (b. 1865, Honolulu–d. 1939, Maui) was the daughter of Samuel Henry and Mary McKibbin Dowsett, and later was Mrs. Randal Von Tempsky of Maui. The Dowsetts and McKibbins lived at the "old Miller Premises" at 79 Beretania Street, adjacent to and now a part of the Washington Place grounds.

11. Katie Harvey was the part-Hawaiian daughter of Michael Harvey of Kalihi Valley and wife (1895) of Edward Hanapi.

came in to tell me that Kahalewai Cummins[12] and her grandchild had been thrown from wagon. Dismissed meeting and went out there. Neither were hurt. Came back to Washington Place. Mother [Dominis] was not very well nor was John. A pelting rain came on as we came home. Telephone message [from John?] that he would not be back to close up and for Nakapuahi to do it.

*Saturday, January 8.* Rain, rain, rain. Annie came here and told me she thought that committee would not agree to an entertainment, [and] since they had money, why not use it until it is done. 4½ A.M. Was woke from deep sleep—I dreamt that I stood on a lava bank and it was D. Kaukelehua that assisted me, then he spread a white tapa on the next bank and climbed himself. Then told me to climb up—which with some trouble I did. They say that some good fortune is coming to me—my friend confessed that. Well so and so.

*Sunday, January 9.* After breakfast, went to see the Queen, but found her quite well—from there went to see John who was sick in bed. Mother [Dominis] is failing. She gave me a chandelier. Stayed till 5½ P.M., came home. [Scrolling "L."]

A rainy night. We had some differences, he was wrong. I told him to bring a pig and confess to me, and ask my forgiveness. He did not want to at first, but afterwards he did. I forgave. [He] was gone all day, came home tipsy—has lice.

*Monday, January 10.* Went to town to see John and stopped at Cordie Allen's to see if Willie [Allen] has improved in health and took her some pieces of silk. She showed me her handsome silk quilt. Three P.M. went to Hooulu Lahui Society. They decided to give a Luau and that tickets should be sold by members. It will come off 22nd of this month. The same evening went to Music Hall to see some Amateurs perform.[13] $3.00 was contributed for Luau—and $2.40 for monthly dues. Band at Music Hall.

*Tuesday, January 11.* Mrs. S. [Samuel] Nowlein brought in her dues of this month for Liliuokalani Hui Hookuonoono—$3.00 and 50 fine and so with Maili Nowlein $5.00 and 50 cents fine. Wrote to J. W. Kalua to carry on Keamalu's case.[14] I hear his appointment is postponed on account of Scandal.[15]

Band at Hart and Love wedding[16]—Hinano Bower.

Three P.M. went to meeting, found no one. Went on to Kapoo [Kapooloku] to see if she would not make up with her Sister [Queen Kapiolani] and King. She said yes at first—so I was happy to think that I could do

---

12. Kahalewai Cummins (b. 1830, Hawaii–d. September 10, 1902, Honolulu) was the wife of John Adams Cummins. They lived at Pawaa.

13. Liliu means the Hawaiian Opera House, where on January 10 there was an "Amateur Dramatic Performance of J. Palgrave Simpson's three-act comedy 'A Scrap of Paper.'" *Pacific Commercial Advertiser*, January 10, 1887.

14. Keamalu's case was an ejectment suit between Keamalu (k) and Luhau (k) over land at Kauluwela, which the former had inherited from Polani. The case would come to court in January 1888. Hawaii State Archives, First Circuit Court, Law 2568.

15. The "scandal" is nowhere explained.

16. This was the marriage of Edmund W. Hart, an operator of the Hawaiian Bell Telephone Co., and Annie K. Love (the daughter of James Love) at Saint Andrew's Cathedral.

some good. Lively girls Mary, Lizzie Keo, Becky, Kamaka, Noe, Kaina, Hattie, Helii, and Keliimana. Telephoned to Napelakapu and Kunane [Kalakaua] that we would come next day. "Hoolale a ka Ukiu." ["Incited by the cold Ukiu wind."]

*Wednesday, January 12.* Went home at seven A.M. Ahoi [the cook] did not seem right. After breakfast went to meet Poomaikelani and she would not make up, so had to go and tell the Queen that she need not expect her sister—she asked why—I said "Marie." Three P.M. met Hui Hoonaauao Liliuokalani. $3.90 was contributed and 50 cents was given to Tamar to pay for book for Puhi—[and] 25 cents for two weeks' tuition.

Poor Piikoi is dead—and as we are at meeting, he is being carried to his last resting place.[17] Hinano Bower. Band at Morgan and Love wedding.[18]

*Thursday, January 13.* Sister [Likelike] is 36 years old today—and is not strong. Went out at 12 [P.M.] Too early—no one came till three—fearfully hungry—dined and came home. Joe had some tickets ready. I gave 50 of $1.50—and 25 cts to Kanalulu. Waiting—retired. [Scrolling "L."]

*Friday, January 14.* Mrs. Aholo took 50 $ tickets and disposed of them all before 12. Sent 108 to Kahoe, 50 to others—making 200 [tickets] altogether. Hope the luau will be a success—tomorrow will print some more.

Named Johnnie's Company of fire laddies. Came to enquire after Abbie Paiaina.[19] Miss Alexander[20] reports improvement in her eye. Mrs. and Miss Brodie—Not at home.[21] Called on Fannie Benson,[22] is improving.

He told me he was only going to town, then would come back, 9½ not returned—John came, though, at 7½, had lots to sew for Waialua.

Joe pd. $4.03 advertisement for 2nd Div[ision] Hui Hoonaauao Liliuokalani.

*Saturday, January 15.* Keawehawaii paid $200 to A. J. Cartwright [for] rent of Kealia [Hawaii] and gave me $18 from lot at Kealia for Loulu [leaves] and grass. One suit for Kaipo $8, dress for Nihoa one for $3.50— one for $2.00—stockings .25; $1.00 to nurse, 50 cts to Freddy, 25 cts candy.

Wind and rain. How good.

*Sunday, January 16.* Lolii [relaxed] after breakfast till two P.M. Dined, then drove round after the girls—Kainuuala, Jessie, Sophy, Leihulu—but it rained, so had to come right home.

---

17. "Death of a Band Boy. On Tuesday afternoon William Piikoi, a son of Mr. William Wond by his first wife, Lydia Piikoi, died of galloping consumption. The deceased was a member of the Royal Hawaiian Band for two years, playing the cornet. His poor health compelled him to give it up. The funeral took place yesterday afternoon from the Roman Catholic Cathedral, and was largely attended. The King's Own, of which the deceased was a member, turned out and took part in the funeral procession.... Piikoi was about 23 years of age." *Pacific Commercial Advertiser*, January 13, 1887. Lydia Piikoi was Liliuokalani's cousin.

18. James F. Morgan (b. 1861–d. 1912), a Honolulu businessman, married Maggie Love on January 12, 1887.

19. Abbie was the daughter of Reverend Paiaina, pastor of Kamoiliili Church.

20. Mary Elizabeth Alexander was an instructor at Kawaiahao Seminary, and afterward at Maunaolu Seminary on Maui.

21. Mrs. and Miss Brodie were the wife and daughter of Dr. John Brodie, who resided at 81 Beretania Street.

22. Fannie was the wife of Henry Benson, of Benson and Smith retail druggists.

His Excellency Walter Murray Gibson's birthday—63 years old but he looks all of 78. Poor Gibson, why should they put all the blame on him only?[23]

Wind and rain.

*Monday, January 17.* Gave Wakeke $4 of 2nd Division Hui Hoonaauao towards buying two woolen blankets for Abbie P. and Violet Beckley, and she borrowed of me $2.00 for Kailipanio's blanket. Went to Jessie's at nine A.M. [and] began to work with girls on Waialua things. Three P.M. met members of Hooulu Lahui Society of Kaumakapili [to] consult on matters.

Dance at W. M. Gibson's.[24]

Mrs. Hayselden—kokoke hanau apopo paha [almost giving birth, tomorrow perhaps]—Hinano Bower. I was harsh to John, and so he went to bed huhu [angry]. Poina wau i ka ninau ia Kahae no kana mau tickets. [I forgot to question Kahae regarding his tickets.]

Wind and rain.

*Tuesday, January 18.* Went upstairs to ask John's forgiveness for my harsh words, and he actually kissed me—although he provoked me to say what I did in praise of Mr. Gibson whom everybody hates—sometimes without cause, but he [Gibson] bore it for the King.

Bought Child's Bible for $8.00.

Windy weather.

*Thursday, January 20.* Received from Mrs. J. T. Baker[25] $5 of her share of Liliuokalani Hui Hookuonoono and she owes 50 cents for delay—it was left by Mrs. Emma Beckley here. Went to Waikiki to paina kapu [a private meal]—Lilia Aholo gave me $49.00 that she got for selling tickets.

Keala [Hale].

*Friday, January 21.* Mrs. Aholo gave me three dollars from tickets she sold. Luka Panui returned to me 50 cts for only one ticket that she sold. I gave to Alapai to pay for pig $2.50. Went to Cartwright's office, he said he would foreclose mortgage on [land at] Kaneakua $100—belongs to Kahawaii and Pepe[26]—must get rent of two lands at Manoa. Afterwards went to Kaumakapili to make preparations for luau tomorrow. Gave Alapai

---

23. Gibson (who was actually 65), though still the premier, was reaching the end of his political reign in Hawaii. He had made many enemies among the opposition factions, and the "debacle of Gibson's Samoan adventure [the *Kaimiloa* voyage in the summer of 1887] sharpened the determination of his political enemies to get rid of the man and his pernicious influence on Kalakaua." Jacob Adler and Robert M. Kamins, *The Fantastic Life of Walter Murray Gibson: Hawaii's Minister of Everything* (Honolulu: University of Hawaii Press, 1986), 178–79.

24. Gibson's birthday falling on a Sunday, a celebration was held on Monday the 17th. "In the evening there was an informal reception and dance, which took place in the large lanai adjoining the residence.... During the reception the Royal Hawaiian Band...played a choice selection of music.... Invited guests...included His Majesty the King, Her Royal Highness, Princess Liliuokalani, [and] Lieutenant General the Hon. J. O. Dominis.... At nine o'clock dancing commenced...until 11 o'clock, when an elegant supper was served in the dining-room." *Pacific Commercial Advertiser*, January 18, 1887.

25. This was Chiefess Ululani, the wife of John Tamatoa Baker of Hilo (b. 1852, Wailupe, Oahu–d. 1921, Pauoa, Oahu). She served as governor of Hawaii Island, 1886–88.

26. Kahawaii and Pepe were sisters.

$7.50 for Potatoes and $18.00 for pigs—all from Mrs. Aholo's money. Mrs. W. A. Achi[27] brought $32.50.

*Saturday, January 22.* Kahanu gave me $2—I owe .50. gave Ahoi $1—Joe $2—tea, coffee, sugar, butter. Joe $2—he returned $1.50 [to?] Mrs. Aholo. Wakeke 25 cts. laulau $1. Coffee—Kapoli $10.35. Sophy tea $9.05. Foraths [?] $4.00 $1.50 door. Gave to Kaakaole $2.00. Received from Luau[28] at Kaumakapili $238.15. [A struck-out memorandum for this date appears at the end of the diary: Emma Beckley about Wilder's & Kuihelani Mortgage—No satisfaction.]

*Monday, January 24.* Sally gave 50 cts for Hui [Hooulu] Lahui. Kahae sent by Joe Aea $35.75. Kahele gave .50 for Hui [Hooulu] Lahui.

Ten A.M. met J. W. Kalua here about being Sheriff of Maui. Told him he could not have it if he kept on drinking. I think he will try to do right. Told him to be kind to his wife [and] when we hear good reports we will give him an office.[29]

Maule is here to thank the King and I for [appointment] office [of] Road supervisor in chief [for] Maui.[30]

Sally called and dined with Kahoupokapu 2–3 P.M. Met Hui Hooulu Lahui and thanked them for their help. Told of receipts of luau. Sally told me today of Annie Dowsett's conduct at meeting of Hooulu Lahui Society at Palace, where she was making signs behind my back to Queen.

*Tuesday, January 25.* Lepeka gave 50 cents [to] H. L. [Hui Lahui.] I paid $1, for three knives and $7 to furnace [?] to Hui Lahui—making $8.00. Kaakaole 50 cts—Mrs. Allen's and C. R. Bishop's birthday.

*Wednesday, January 26.* Alapai was off and on paying bills—paying $3 to Donnelly—$2 to Kukula, $50.50 to Waterhouse.

*Thursday, January 27.* 4½ A.M. woke up—okaikai kou hoa 'omaua pu me ke Kiowai [both of us are bad-tempered, me and Kiowai].

[At] seven—the folks from Waikiki came down to work. Kanakaole told me sister was very sick. Gave Joe $5 belonging to Hui Hooulu Lahui to pay to [*Hawaiian*] *Gazette* for printing [luau] tickets. This leaves $207 for Hui Hooulu Lahui. Mrs. Aholo will have to return $10 and Kahae $2.50.

Spent the whole day with Sister [Likelike]—how ill she is—she thinks this bursting of the lava flow in Kau is for her—a piece of superstition—but we are all so. Sent for King and Queen. Kapo [Kapooloku] is here with me. She and I are to sleep here.

---

27. Isabella Alapai, wife (from 1883) of attorney William Charles Achi (b. 1858–d. 1928).

28. "This afternoon at two o'clock there will be a grand luau at the Kaumakapili Church under the patronage and direction of H.R.H. Princess Liliuokalani. The proceeds will be devoted to the work of the Hoola Lahui and Hooulu Lahui Societies. It promises to be a very successful affair. The Royal Hawaiian Band will be in attendance." *Pacific Commercial Advertiser*, January 22, 1887.

29. John W. Kalua received no such appointment.

30. Attorney W. S. Maule was commissioned in January 1887 as "road supervisor in Chief of the Islands of Maui, Molokai, and Lanai" in place of George E. Richardson, who had been appointed circuit judge of Maui.

11 o'clock. One A.M., three [A.M.] [here] and yet my thoughts are at home. Emma found my book at Mary Ailau's.

*Friday, January 28.* She [sister Likelike] is better and in less pain, but [I] must stay with her today. Five P.M. Joe came for me—nothing of importance took place except that [blank] [is] in good spirits. Alapai brought some nice fish—why are all these presents. The *W. G. Hall* took many passengers to Kau to see the Volcano.³¹

*Saturday, January 29.* My husband came home last night—we meet at Leleo's—tells me he has been sick—I am on my way to Like's [Likelike's] 9½ P.M. Kapoli comes out for me, a dream—all nonsense—and so have to fuss etc., etc. Back again [at Muolaulani]. Nua Lehua.

**Tuesday, February 1.** Liliuokalani Hui Hookuonoono three P.M. Hui Hookuonoono. I ka la 10 o keia Mahina e hookaa mai ai i Hanakeola $27.50 no kona aie i ka 1st Dec. '86 [Liliuokalani Benevolent Society three P.M. Benevolent Society. On the 10th of this month, pay Hanakeola $27.50 for her loan of the 1st Dec. '86] from contributions of Liliuokalani Hui Hookuonoono $609.90.

*Wednesday, February 2.* Likelike died at five P.M. at Ainahau.³² All her family were present. [At] 7½ P.M. Archie told me to put away all of Sister's Jewelry and nice things. Tonight she will be taken to town to the Palace.³³

*Friday, February 4.* 2nd Division [Rest of entry is blank.]

*Monday, February 14.* ~~Kapiolani gave me $10 for Hooulu Lahui, Hanakeola gave me $27.50 for L.H. Hookuonoono.~~

───────────

The *Pacific Commercial Advertiser* announced the order and protocols to be observed for Princess Likelike's funeral:

> ¶ The funeral of Her late Royal Highness Princess Likelike will take place on Sunday [February 27] from Iolani Palace. At 9:30 o'clock in the morning there will be a service in the throne room, for which quite a number of verbal invitations have been issued. At one o'clock the

---

31. The lead article of the *Pacific Commercial Advertiser*, January 26, 1887, headlined "Great Eruption. Mauna Loa Again Breaks Forth. A Flow of Lava from One to Three Miles in Width," informed readers: "The steamer *W. G. Hall* [also referred to as the *Malulani*] arrived yesterday afternoon from Hawaii bringing the most sensational news about the great eruption of Mauna Loa. The news spread like wildfire through the town." The article concluded: "The Steamer *Wm. G. Hall* leaves for the Volcano at ten o'clock Friday morning and there is no doubt she will carry a number of passengers who are anxious to see the great eruption."

32. "The death of Her Royal Highness Princess Likelike at 4:45 last evening was not altogether unexpected, although when the announcement was made it took most people by surprise. This lady, though in somewhat delicate health for several months past, did not appear to be [seriously] ill, and it was thought that . . . a change of air and scene would speedily restore her to her usual health and spirits. Unfortunately a change for the worse took place a few days ago. . . . The King and Queen, Princess Liliuokalani, and other members of her family were unremitting in their attention. . . . His Majesty the King had left the sick chamber a few minutes before the death of his sister, but Her Royal Highness Princess Liliuokalani and her husband, Hon. A. S. Cleghorn, were present, together with the medical attendants and many of her personal retainers." *Pacific Commercial Advertiser*, February 3, 1887.

33. Likelike lay in state in the throne room. On the morning of February 3, the Anglican Bishop of Honolulu and Reverend Alexander Mackintosh held a requiem service, and the public was admitted to pay its respects between 10:30 A.M. and 2:30 P.M.

funeral services will commence in the throne room and will be conducted by the Bishop of Honolulu and the Revs. Alexander Mackintosh and George Wallace. At this service there will only be present the Royal family, His Majesty's Ministers, members of the Privy Council, House of Nobles and Legislature, the Diplomatic and Consular corps, and the Supreme Court Justices. The music will be sung by thirteen members of the St. Andrew's Cathedral (second congregation) and by the Kawaihau Club, the latter taking their position on either side of the body as Kahili [feather standard] bearers. The procession will form at one o'clock precisely.[34]

---

*Sunday, February 27.* Sad day in Iolani Palace. [At] nine A.M. The Throne room was filled with Archie's friends, there were morning services held, and the King, Archie, Kaiulani, Poomaikelani, and myself by the remains of my dear sister Like, and all to satisfy Archie. It seems like making a publicity of our grief. One P.M. services again, and her remains were placed in the hearse with all the pomp that is due her rank, and then taken up to her last resting place. Kawaihaus stood around her and sang during service and at the Mausoleum. All return to Palace. Stayed till eight P.M. Went to Hinano Bower and slept.

*Monday, February 28.* Went back to Palace and breakfasted [and] sent our baggage home. Four P.M. took Archie and Kaiulani out to Ainahau, then returned to Palace. After supper all the clubs came in to sing. Kawaihau's, Iolani's, Queen's, Healani's, and Ohuokalani's. Eveline and I left at ten—the rest were shut up till next morn.

*Tuesday, March 1.* Rec'd from A. J. Cartwright $400, through Joe Heleluhe. Went to bid King and Queen good-bye—did not see him—but saw the latter. Had lunch with our folks, then sent them home to Waikiki. Five P.M. came home and slept in Nua Lehua. Wakeke lomied [massaged] me to sleep.

*Wednesday, March 2.* Ten A.M. went up to Mausoleum with Archie, Sophy, [and] [J. H.] Boyd, [and] took some flowers up. Had a call from Mr. and Mrs. W. F. Allen and Sally Tripp. She told me that John Colburn was going to be in Custom House, and they would be removed from Kawa [the prison]. Marcus [Colburn to] take their place.[35] There was skating. [Sentence ends abruptly thus.]

*Thursday, March 3.* Rec'd $850.00 from W. F. Allen for Kaakaole. Sent her $2.00 from last lot of money. She has $15 more of that lot. Sent receipt to W. F. Allen.

*Tuesday, March 8.* Mrs. E. M. Beckley placed in my hand five dollars for Lewai Baker and two dollars' fine for last two months. One for E. Hoapili and $81.10. The remainder of the amount paid to Wilder & Co., which was in Liliuokalani Hui Hookuonoono $150—towards payment of Mrs. Kuihelani's Mortgage.

34. *Pacific Commercial Advertiser*, February 26, 1887.
35. Marcus Colburn (b. 1858–d. 1901, Palama, Oahu) was in the draying business. These appointments were not made.

*Queen Kapiolani wearing the blue-velvet and peacock-feather gown that she wore at Queen Victoria's Jubilee in London in 1887 and at the opening of the Hawaiian legislature in 1888. The gown is preserved (in part) in the Bishop Museum.*
Walery, Photographer to the Queen, London, Hawaii State Archives

*King David Kalakaua, eighth monarch of the Hawaiian Islands. Kalakaua was fond of displaying (and wore elegantly) the royal orders and decorations of his own creation and those awarded to him by European and Asian rulers and heads of state.*
Hawaii State Archives

*Monday, March 14.* Mrs. Kuihelani paid me for Liliuokalani Hui Hookuonoono $108.31, interest on Wilder's note and $30.00 on the principle, which is $2,068.89.

*Thursday, March 17.* Rainy. Met at Mary Ailau's with members of Liliuokalani Hui Hookuonoono. Emma [Beckley] and I read our reports. Gave 14 members their share $63.50 each and they left the Hui. I told them to go to E. M. Beckley on Saturday morning at ten and she would give them 14 cents due them. Grace gave notice she and Hanakeola would leave this month. Most of the members were present. A meeting was appointed to consult about the rest of the money, for tomorrow. Mary Ailau, Hanakeola, and I had paid Hui $182.28 over and above what should be right and Hui voted it should be returned to me. I did take it back. That night I told him [John?] I intended to will all to my people after John, the King, and Kaiulani have passed on.

*Friday, March 18.* Met at Mary Ailau's today. Hui decided to go on with our contributions. Was appointed President, Kamakanoe Vice Pres., Mrs. Aholo Secretary, Mrs. Alapai, Assistant Secretary.

*Saturday, March 19.* Sent for Kaipo—how he has improved. Mrs. Maikai[36] came, what object had she? Time will tell. After dinner sent Kaipo home with Wakeke as he had to go for shoes. Joe took me to Chief Justice Judd to consult on Like's will. He said he would respect the wish of the dead— that means he would oblige Archie to give bond for all that he used of her [Likelike's] property during her [Kaiulani's] minority.[37]

*Sunday, March 20.* Went to Kawaiahao—from there Wakeke, Aimoku, and I went out to Hamohamo—how neglected it looked. Went next to Ainahau, dined and spent the afternoon, and came home just before Joe, who had been to Manoa.

*Monday, March 21.* Joe asked me to return what he had signed over to me of lot he bought of Kuaea—in fact, the money was borrowed of me by Kahae in 1882. The amount was $782 and little over in the month of August, I think. She said when she got the money she would return it. She must have asked him yesterday when she heard it was my intention to will my property to all my people, to whom I had assigned lots, after John, the King, and Kaiulani were dead. Mary Ailau [and] Kaehuwahanui were here. The latter gave me for Liliuokalani Hui Hookuonoono $50 toward payment of principle which was $2,068.95. [In margin above entry:] Today the water was brought from Wailuakio.

---

36. Annie K. Lilikalani was the wife (from 1873) of Samuel I. U. Maikai.

37. By the terms of her will, Princess Likelike had first bequeathed all jewelry, furniture, and personal effects to her daughter Kaiulani, and then set up a trust with A. J. Cartwright as trustee, for the support first of Kaiulani, then of her husband A. S. Cleghorn. Following this, should Kaiulani die without children, Likelike directed that the whole of her estate be paid over to her brother and sister (Kalakaua and Liliuokalani). Likelike was possessed of considerable property in Honolulu, Waikiki, and on the island of Hawaii, and Liliu's concern may have been to make sure Cleghorn's three other daughters, who were not her sister's children, did not end up inheriting Likelike's property. Hawaii State Archives, First Circuit Court, Probate 2512.

*Tuesday, March 22.* Mr. and Mrs. Canavarro[38] [and] Mrs. Gay called. I went to call on Mrs. and Miss McIntyre, Mr. and Mrs. Walker—to condole with them.[39] [They] Were quite calm.

*Wednesday, March 23.* Today intend to go for ferns at Nuuanu valley.

*Friday, March 25.* Like's will was read and had to be put off, because it required three weeks' notice in papers before anything could be done.

*Saturday, March 26.* Had a pig killed for all those who went up for plants. Heard that [blank] was Hapai [pregnant].

*Monday, March 28.* Mrs. Kuaea took $22.50 of Hui Hoonaauao [funds] to pay for tuition of Emma Kawao, and Louisa Harrison [as] day scholars. Mrs. Kuihelani paid me $50.00 towards Liliuokalani Hui Hookuonoono.

Must see Cartwright about Will,[40] band boys' money, Kahae's debt. Kaakaole $2.00.

*Wednesday, March 30.* Sent for A. J. Cartwright about my affairs and Like's will. He spoke of my debts and Kahae's. He will see [James?] Monsarrat again about it. John was here also. Came with Mrs. Davies and daughter and two Misses, and Mr. Schaefer[41] and Mr. French.

Sent Joe to draw band boys' money. He brought drafts on Bishop & Co., one for $800.00, the other for $200.00.

*Thursday, March 31.* Received from Rebecca Kahaawinaaupo $130.00—sent it to A. J. Cartwright to deposit. Received from A. J. Cartwright $400, my monthly allowance. ~~Signed Endorsed notes on Bishop & Co. for $1,029.41 for band.~~

*Friday, April 1.* Met at Mary Ailau's as usual to contribute towards Liliuokalani Hui Hookuonoono. $175.00 was contributed.

9½ A.M. endorsed notes on Bishop & Co. for band boys. Mary Ailau paid to Liliuokalani Hui Hookuonoono $50.00 but [she] still owes $50.33. Emma Beckley placed $6.50, the remainder of monies contributed by Hui for expenses. The Hui has now been reduced to thirty members.

*Saturday, April 2.* Met at Mary Ailau's for Liliuokalani Hui Hookuonoono for this month. $85.00 was contributed, I contributed $10 for Kaiulani

38. Mr. and Mrs. Antonio de Souza Canavarro. Antonio (b. 1849, Oporto, Portugal–d. April 22, 1914, Honolulu) arrived in Hawaii as consul for Portugal in 1882, and remained consul general after the fall of the monarchy. She, an Englishwoman (according to his obituary), "became a convert to Theosophism, leaving for India years ago, where, it is believed, she still resides." *Pacific Commercial Advertiser*, April 22, 1914.

39. These were the wife, two daughters, and son-in-law of Hugh McIntyre (b. Scotland–d. March 9, 1887, San Francisco, at age 73). An island resident since 1846, McIntyre was proprietor of H. E. McIntyre & Bro., grocers, provisions, and feed suppliers, located at the corner of King and Fort Streets. He was the father of three sons and two daughters. Son Hugh E. McIntyre (b. Tahiti 1844–d. Honolulu 1912) was president of Henry May & Co. A daughter was Mrs. J. S. Walker. McIntyre was interred at the Nuuanu cemetery March 20, 1887.

40. See second footnote for March 19, 1887, diary entry (138).

41. Frederick August Schaefer (b. 1836, Bremen, Germany–d. March 11, 1920, Honolulu) arrived in Hawaii in November 1857, became a prominent merchant and sugar broker (F. A. Schaefer & Co.), and in 1879 married Elizabeth Robertson, the daughter of Supreme Court Justice George M. Robertson and the sister of James W. Robertson, Liliuokalani's chamberlain. Schaefer very agreeably maintained a strict policy of never participating in the politics of the islands. He was a particularly close friend of the Cleghorns.

but now am sorry I did so, for I fear I will have no show for getting it. Placed $260 in A. J. Cartwright's [custody] for Hui Liliuokalani Hookuonoono.

*Sunday, April 3.* Stayed at home in the morning. Three P.M. John and I went to Mrs. Severance's funeral.[42] From there went to see Hookaea[43] at Hamohamo. Came over to see Kaiulani and Archie—they were not at home.

Early this morning at six got a note from Kunane [Kalakaua] saying he would like to have me go to England with the Queen. I was so astounded I could not answer for some time. Only a week to prepare. John has had consent given him to go also with the Queen—and he is delighted. He says I must take a man with me but I would rather make use of the money myself. What would go to the servant would be so much less enjoyment for us.

*Monday, April 4.* Must surely make my will. Bright moonlight night. Indeed, all my thoughts are for going without any feeling of regret for home.

Three P.M. Had meeting of 2d Division Hui Hoonaauao. Told them to try and learn to conduct the meetings themselves, [and] to appoint Princess Poomaikelani President. They did not know of my going, not even Wakeke.

*Tuesday, April 5.* Mrs. Kuihelani paid for Liliuokalani Hui Hookuonoono $58.00.

*Wednesday, April 6.* Three P.M. Met first Division of Liliuokalani Hui Hoonaauao.

*Thursday, April 7.* Rec'd from Hanakeola the sum of $25.00 amount borrowed [from] Liliuokalani Hui Hookuonoono.

*Friday, April 8.* Sent to [Remainder of sentence is blank.]

*Saturday, April 9.* Sent to A. J. Cartwright $186.50 [Liliu wrote $202.50 above this amount] belonging to 2d Division [Hui] Hoonaauao. Gave Joe message to return to Kahawaii and Pepe their money. $120.00. Also Hui Hooulu Lahui had $164.40. Is a busy day, reminding Wakeke and Joe of many things. Met Mr. M. [Marcus] Monsarrat and asked [him] how could [I] fence my part of Joe's lot in Waikahaluu. He said I would have to go to Commissioners. [I] asked him to attend to it. [He] said he would.

*Monday, April 11.* Mrs. Dominis had a fall and John didn't know anything about it.

*Tuesday, April 12.* We leave today in *Australia*. All my folks, even to [Luther] Aholo—[Antone] Rosa, [John Lot] Kaulukou witnessed my will today—in favor of John, after that of my brother or niece—after them to be divided among my people.[44] Had Kaipo and Aimoku besides others breakfast with me [at Muolaulani]. That is over—Kiss good-bye—am so glad to go. Went to Kawaiahao [Seminary] to bid children good-bye—went to Palace [and] to Mrs. Dominis, then to Steamer *Australia*. Capt. Houdlette.

---

42. Mrs. Anna H. Severance (d. April 2, 1887, Honolulu, age 85 years) was the widow of the Honorable Luther Severance, former U.S. consul in Hawaii.

43. Hookaea was a servant at Hamohamo.

44. No copy of this will has survived.

Wharf full: never saw it like that before. Steamer full also.[45] I took Joe Aea and John took Charlie Kaiaiki.[46]

Went early to my berth. Am seasick. Had luck for Dr. Martin was on board.

---

Liliu gives another, more poetic account (in Hawaiian) of her departure:

> ¶ Upon the coming of a little ray of light of the dawn of this Tuesday morning, the 12th of April, there was seen the preparations by some persons who were readying their bags and suitcases preparatory to boarding the Steamship *Australia*.
>
> After the morning repast, I went to bid farewell to the members of the household, who showed me the warmth of their love by their grief-stricken farewells, though it has been many years that we have lived together, and they are faithful members of the household.
>
> At ten o'clock, I left the charming home [Muolaulani] adorned with beautiful flowers from Japan,[47] and [flowers] from several other places, and from faraway Philadelphia also; but the best of all to my mind are the cherished leaves of my ancestors; that is, the maile, ginger, palapalai fern, lehua, ieie fern [sic], and other plants that were brought here from the mountains to decorate my beautiful home.[48]
>
> I bade good-bye to all of those things, and went on to see the girls and teachers of the Kawaiahao Boarding School for girls. I was there

---

45. "ROYAL DEPARTURE. Never before has such an assemblage been seen at the departure of a steamer from this port.... The majority were native Hawaiians... who were dressed in holiday attire and wore leis of fragrant flowers. The departure of Her Majesty the Queen and H.R.H. Princess Liliuokalani and suite for San Francisco was the main reason for such a crowd.... A few minutes after 11 o'clock, the volunteer military companies and a platoon of police arrived at the wharf.... At the head of the gangway on either side were a Hawaiian and American flag. The Royal Hawaiian band was stationed on the wharf.... At half-past 11 o'clock the strains of the national anthem, 'Hawaii Ponoi,' and the presenting of arms by the troops, announced the arrival of the royal party. H.R.H. Princess Liliuokalani was the first to ascend the gangway. The Princess was covered with leis and was cheered to the echo as she boarded the steamer. Marshall Kaulukou then cleared the gangway and Her Majesty the Queen, leaning on the arm of the King, went on board. From all sides came cheers and 'alohas' which the Queen acknowledged in a very gracious manner. Lieutenant General Dominis had to go through considerable handshaking before he was able to board the vessel, and this ordeal was continued on board. The deck of the vessel was literally swarmed with people and locomotion was difficult. Nearly all the passengers, some hundred and fifty, wore leis.... Punctually at noon the lines were cast off and the noble ship with her valuable cargo... swung out into the stream. The Royal standard was flying at the foremast.... When outside the channel the pilot... left the vessel on charge of Capt. Houdlette.... The Queen could be seen standing by the back rail on the center of the steamer waving her handkerchief." *Pacific Commercial Advertiser*, April 13, 1887.

46. Charlie Kaiaiki was a servant of J. O. Dominis. He traveled to England under Dominis's passport.

47. This was the onaona Iapana or night-blooming jasmine, *Cestrum nocturnum*.

48. These native plants would have been gathered from wild populations at higher elevations. Palapalai (*Microlepia setosa*) is a native fern; lehua is the blossom of the ohia tree (*Metrosideros* spp.); and ieie (*Freycinetia arborea*) is a woody climber used in basket weaving and religious ceremonies.

only a few minutes, then entered the Palace Grounds to see the High Chiefesses, the young Princess Kaiulani, the Princess Poomaikelani, and the Hon. A. S. Cleghorn. Then I entered upon the shrubbery of Washington Place, and lovingly embraced Mother [Dominis], and then went to the wharf.

The wharf was filled with people. Never was there seen a time like this before—the Nobility, the Prominent People, the wealthy, the people who are not customarily seen at that place, the soldiers, the Buglers, standing erect, all of them with signs of affection upon their faces.

The deck was crowded with friends aboard the Ship; The King, and a multitude of friends. I saw Sam Parker, and Billy Cornwell, and certain other persons.

Then the steamship *J. A. Cummins* moved; upon it was the Royal Hawaiian Band, captivating us with the sounds of music from their horns, as if clutching at my heart to turn back; but that cannot be.

The current is carrying us along. The three (3) ships [the *Australia*, the *Cummins*, and the *Eleu*, the latter a tugboat] sailed along together until they were near the Lighthouse, then the guns of the Battery began firing a Farewell Salute. They continued to sail together until they sailed beyond the people, and were well beyond Puu o Manoa [Rocky Point]. Then the *Eleu* turned about, to return to the Town, and after a little while, the *John A. Cummins* followed, all the while bidding us farewell in voices of affection.

Most of the people sat on deck; but later, little by little, they disappeared into the cabins.[49]

---

*Wednesday, April 13.* So seasick—kept to my berth, only going to my meals. Charley [Kaiaiki] is so good for he is not sick, but Joe has hardly been near me on account of seasickness. Charley, Jimmie McGuire,[50] [and] Joe Aea had one st[ate]room. Hookano[51] stayed with the Queen's stateroom—Curtis [Iaukea] and [James H.] Boyd had one, and John and I had ours—it was so small and close. Nice weather. Dr. Martin advised me to go on deck, so I did and felt better.

*Thursday, April 14.* The we[ather] [Entry ends abruptly thus.]

[The two following diary entries appear in a separate memorandum.][52]

*Friday, April 15.* Nothing of importance was seen today; the ocean is as calm as usual; however, it is beginning to get colder; we are nearing Cali-

---

49. Hawaii State Archives, Liliuokalani Collection, Box 1, Folder 3. Original in Hawaiian, translation by Jack Matthews.

50. James W. L. McGuire (b. 1862, Kainaliu, Kona–d. 1941, Honolulu) was an overseer at the palace. He kept a journal of the trip to England, a typescript copy of which is in the Hawaii State Archives. James W. L. McGuire, *A Short Description of Queen Kapiolani's Voyage to England to Attend the Jubilee Celebration of Queen Victoria of England in the Year 1887* (typescript, Hawaii State Archives, Library Collection, 1957). He published the journal in Hawaiian as *He Moolelo Pokole no ka Huakai a ka Moiwahine Kapiolani a me ke Kamaliiwahine Liliuokalani a ka Iubile o ka Moiwahine Victoria a Beretania Nui* (Honolulu: Collegiate Press, 1938).

51. Hookano (also spelled Hookanu) (w) was a palace servant.

52. Hawaii State Archives, Liliuokalani Collection, Box 1, Folder 3.

fornia, perhaps. The illness that prostrated the passengers is subsiding somewhat, and a few of them are now appearing over here and over there.'

*Wednesday, April 20.* Noon. One of the passengers, in the forward part of the Ship, has died. She is the mother of the Manager of the Sugar Plantation at Heeia. Mrs. Downer [Downey] is her name.[53] She boarded the ship, due to a quiet compulsion that her health would improve; however, she died, leaving a grandchild, without parents, who was left in custody of the Chief Steward, and who will be returning upon this Steamship.

---

Liliuokalani's diary does not record their arrival at San Francisco, but from the journal of James McGuire[54] we learn that the royal party arrived at San Francisco on April 20 to an enthusiastic reception. They were met by the Hawaiian consul, and taken to the Palace Hotel on Market Street. During their stay, they visited places of interest including the fire department and the U.S. Mint. On the 25th, Queen Kapiolani held a public reception. She also visited Saint Matthew's Hall, a military school in San Mateo, to see her three nephews. Additional excursions included inspections of the Opera House and the San Francisco Art Association. The Bohemian Club held a luncheon. On April 27, the party departed for Washington, DC, on a specially prepared private railway car.

---

*Friday, April 29.* We arrived at Salt Lake [at] 11. Met the Elders [of the Mormon church] and [other] officials. Kapiolani ma [and associated company] [met] seven wahine 15 kane [seven women and 15 men; entry ends thus.]

*Saturday, April 30.* Nani ka mauna me na muliwai Giness [The mountain and the rivers of Genesis are beautiful] and [Entry ends thus.]

**Tuesday, May 3.** Arrived at Washington eight [P.M.] [H.A.P.] Carter, [General] Gilman, Gen. Taylor of Army, Lieut. Rogers of Navy met us at depot. Took us to Arlington house.[55]

*Thursday, May 5.* Breakfasted alone—thought that everyone had gone out. Ten A.M. went to the Arsenal to see the drill on the banks of the Potomac. Queen and party inspected ranks. Drum Major nice. [To] Gen. Gibson's house. One P.M. Queen and party received at Hawaiian Legation, Diplomatic Corp. [At] 2½ was presented by Gen. Pike[56] and 20 Masons at Arlington House. Went to races. Gen. Sheridan[57] bet for me and won $4.00 on Omaha. Called for few minutes at Mr. Brown's residence [and] met his Mother-in-law Mrs. Commodore Phelps.

*Friday, May 6.* Ten A.M. went to Mount Vernon on the "Dispatch" from the Navy yard. Boat [was] named *Kapiolani*. All eminent men were there:

---

53. Mrs. Downey's son Terence was assistant overseer of the Heeia Agricultural Company at Heeia, Oahu.
54. McGuire, 3.
55. This would have been a Washington, DC, hotel rather than the Lee mansion at Arlington, Virginia.
56. Albert Pike (b. 1809–d. 1891) was a lawyer, soldier, author, and scholar of Masonic ritual.
57. Michael Vincent Sheridan (b. 1840–d. 1918) was a Civil War general.

Endicott and Baird [Bayard]. Sherman waited on Queen. Mr. Evarts on myself.[58] Went up the Potomac. Mr. and Mrs. Carter and Belle[59] went with us. The forts fired salute as we went past. Fort Washington saluted with whistle but [at] Mount Vernon, all hats off [and the] Queen's flag was lowered. Capt. Cowles was captain. Was shown Mrs. Washington's bed she died on [and] his study [and the] banquet hall. Party of ladies had charge—Mrs. Lawton, President [of the Mount Vernon Ladies' Association]. Returned four P.M.

At 7½ went to President's Dinner. Wore black velvet. Sat on President Cleveland's left.[60] C. J. Waite[61] attended on me to table. After dinner went home, band serenaded us. Went to bed. John sick.

*Saturday, May 7.* Queen went to State department—I did not go. Stayed to pack up. 2½ P.M. Left Washington on train. Miss Emma Jones gave me a cup [of] Chestnut [wood from a tree] planted by George Washington. Miss Julia Phillus [?] [gave] a lock of his hair to Queen. John [is] better.

Mrs. May Bradley brought [her] baby, and she and husband came to depot. Gave Lottie Carter and Belle [Carter,] also Mrs. B.—lei pupu Niihau [Niihau shell leis]. Rodgers and Tabor and Brown accompanied us to depot.

*Sunday, May 8.* [Boston.] Woke early and breakfasted. Queen could not go, feet sore—so went to Park Street Church[62] with Mr. and Mrs. Gilman.[63]

---

58. William Crowninshield Endicott was secretary of war; Thomas F. Bayard was secretary of state; John T. Sherman, a former secretary of the treasury, was at that time president of the U.S. Senate (he later served as secretary of state); William M. Evarts, a former secretary of state, was then a U.S. Senator from New York.

59. Belle, or Isobel Carter (b. 1863–d. 1941), was the daughter of H.A.P. Carter. She was later Mrs. Crehore.

60. While Liliu is surprisingly undescriptive in her record of this event, a full account appeared in the *New York Times*, May 7, 1887: "The White House was a blaze of splendor this evening for the ceremonial dinner to Queen Kapiolani given by President Cleveland. The entire lower floor was thrown open for the entertainment. The East room was decorated with tropical foliage [and] the suite of drawing rooms on the west were tastefully decorated.... The table was laid for 34 persons.... At each cover was a beautiful bouquet, a bunch of La France roses tied with heliotrope satin for the ladies, and a Bon Silène rosebud and two large pansies for each gentleman. There were seven wine glasses at each cover and a goblet for Apollinaris water, and there were stands of strawberries and confections upon the table.... At eight o'clock Prof. [John Phillips] Sousa swung his baton and the Marine Band played the 'Presidential Polonaise.' The first strains brought the couples in the following order: The President and Queen Kapiolani, the Chief Justice and the Princess Liliuokalani, Secretary Bayard and Mrs. Carter, Lieut. Gen. Dominis and Mrs. Waite.... Mrs. Cleveland wore her wedding dress. The Queen wore a Court dress of Hawaii, a full flowing robe of white with a yoke and a straight front that was covered with silken embroidery of leaves and wild roses and yellow peahen feathers in natural colors.... She wore a broad crimson sash across her breast.... The Princess Liliuokalani wore high-neck dress of black silk, train of black velvet.... The gentlemen of Her Majesty's party wore plain black evening dress coats, and two of them wore royal orders."

61. Liliu means Morrison Remick Waite (b. 1816–d. 1888), chief justice of the U.S. Supreme Court.

62. The Park Street Church in Boston was the congregation where the various companies of American missionaries heard their final instructions from the American Board of Commissioners for Foreign Missions before departing for the Hawaiian Islands.

63. Gorham Gilman, who during his long residence on Maui was a friend of Liliu in her

Joe sat in Choir and Charley with congregation. Joe sang with them. Mayor [Hugh] O'Brien and wife called, [also] William Lee.[64] Four P.M. went with Mr. and Mrs. Gilman and Mr. Bond[65] and Queen to Trinity Church. Drove round by Boston Common—lots of people. After dinner went with Mr. and Mrs. Beckley, Mrs. Wall, Mr. Bond to Music Hall to hear A. [Arthur] Sullivan's last production. Whole choir applauded when I entered. I rose and they applauded again. It was grand. Shepard[66] came, Snelling[67] and son also. After concert Ben Pitman and wife came.[68]

---

In Liliuokalani's autograph book,[69] the following appears under the entry for Boston, May 13, 1887:

> *The citizens of Boston have been delighted with your visit*
> *and will long remember the pleasure it has given them.*
> *Our relations for over half a century have been very intimate*
> *and long may they continue.*
>
> Hugh O'Brien
> Mayor of Boston

---

*Monday, May 16.* [New York City]—Went to [Metropolitan] Museum with Queen, Carter, John, and Mary Beckley in Central Park. What beautiful drives—handsome turnouts, ladies drest up to suit—Grooms in liveries—Must get suits for mine.

*Tuesday, May 17.* Do not feel well and have to stay at home. John and Joe stayed up with me. All the rest have gone to take a trip to Governor's Island.

Wrote to Mme. Noel & Robillard of Paris[70] to make me two court dresses, one corset, two pr. gloves [and] headdress to match, two pr. black shoes, all for $500.00—two other dresses for outdoors, for $75 each, and a fan, Mantilla, two bonnets, two [pair] gloves for $50.00—making $700.00 altogether.—The idea—The Queen is going to have her dress made here—train too short, only one yard.

---

youth, did much to make Liliu's and Kapiolani's Boston visit pleasant. In later years, however, he became a proponent of annexation, and the friendship ceased.

64. William Lee, a cousin of John O. Dominis, was a partner in Lee and Shepard, the publisher of the Queen's memoir, *Hawaii's Story by Hawaii's Queen Liliuokalani*, in 1898.

65. Lawrence Bond, former island resident and vice Hawaiian consul in Boston, 1884–93, published an account of the Hawaiian royals in Boston in the *New York Times*, June 11, 1887.

66. Charles A. B. Shepard was William Lee's partner in the publishing house of Lee and Shepard, Boston.

67. N. Greenwood Snelling was a relative of John O. Dominis. His first name is not known.

68. Benjamin F. Keolakalani Pitman (b. 1851–d. 1918, Boston) was the part-Hawaiian son of Hilo merchant Benjamin Pitman and the chiefess Kinoole. He was the brother of the Queen's close friend, Mary Pitman Ailau.

69. Hawaii State Archives, Kahn Collection.

70. In the address portion of the diary, Liliu lists her as E. Robillard-Noel, 161 rue Saint-Honoré, Paris.

*Wednesday, May 18.* Am not any better. It is colder here than any other place we have been to. Must write to Alice Lee. Nothing more. Amuse myself in looking outside of window.

*Thursday, May 19.* Still alone. Had a call from Mrs. J. B. Williams. Could not drive with her on account of illness.[71] She sent Dr. Loomis. He gave me some medicines. Joe sat up and watched, all [the others] went to theater. Dr. said my cold is called Bronchitis and a touch of Asthma.[72]

*Friday, May 20.* New York. Fifth Avenue. Victoria Hotel. Still at home all alone. Queen and all have gone to take pictures, to see Vanderbilt's house, [and] to Mrs. J. B. Williams' lunch.[73] Wrote to Kunane [Kalakaua] and Wakeke. Piehu [Iaukea] went out on his own hook, and came home with Fred Allen.[74] Doctor [Loomis] called again, says I am better but must not let the wind blow on me. Williams family each sent bouquet.

[The royal party departed New York for England on May 25, 1887, on the steamship *City of Rome*.]

*Thursday, June 2.* Arrived in Liverpool and the walls [wharves?] were lined with people—on the tender and Aft. [of the] *City of Rome*. Went to North Western Hotel—[On the] Wharf was guard of Honor with 100 Soldiers brought by train. Mr. Armstrong, Janion, Davies, Staley,[75] Hoffnung[76] came and met us on board. Synge and Mayor of Liverpool—the whole party escorted by mounted police to Hotel. Dined [with] Mr. Synge, Armstrong, Davies, Janion, and Hoffnung.[77]

*Friday, June 3.* Breakfasted in side room with John and Queen. Lunched at 12 N. [noon] at Town hall given by Mayor. Met Lord Derby and went to table with him—Queen and Mayor. From there went to Museum—then to Organ recital by Mr. Best, Queen's organist. Went home—Queen and party [and] Mr. and Mrs. Armstrong went to see [Wilson] Barret in

---

71. Mrs. Florence Williams on May 21, 1887, signed Liliu's autograph book with the sentiment "In memory of pleasant days, and old times. With love. Florence M. Williams." Hawaii State Archives, Kahn Collection. In the address section of Liliu's 1888 diary, she appears as Mrs. James B. Williams, 63 E. 54th St., Stamford, Connecticut.

72. Under addresses in the 1888 diary, Dr. Loomis is at 34th Street West next to Fifth Avenue.

73. James McGuire, who was one of the Hawaiian party, wrote in his journal: "At ten o.c. Her Majesty got ready to go have some photos taken at one of the best houses in New York. After she was through she got ready to go to visit Vanderbilt mansion which is on Fifth Ave, and a most magnificent mansion.... Her Majesty was very much pleased with her visit." McGuire, 20.

74. Frederick Allen was the son of Judge Elisha H. Allen of Honolulu.

75. Thomas Nettleship Staley (d. May 4, 1905, Cheshire, New Brighton, England) was the first Anglican bishop in Honolulu.

76. Abraham Hoffnung was a London businessman (of the firm Hoffnung & Co., later Skinner & Co.) who had done much business in the islands. The two crowns used in King Kalakaua's coronation were ordered through his firm. Hoffnung became a naturalized Hawaiian by act of the legislature in 1886, and was then appointed "His Majesty's chargé d'affaires at the court of Saint James."

77. Robert F. Synge was a Foreign Office official. W. R. Armstrong was the Hawaiian consul in London. Harold Janion, the son of former Honolulu businessman Robert C. Janion, was the Hawaiian consul in Liverpool. Theophilus H. Davies was the well-known head of a Honolulu business house.

*Hamlet*. I stayed [home] on account of cold. Saw Mrs. A. B. Hayley with Mr. Armstrong's younger brother go to a room.[78] Geo. Macfarlane[79] and servant stayed there also—*Mrs. Janion and daughters came often to see us.*[80]

*Saturday, June 4.* Started in train at ten A.M., arrived at Norwich at three P.M. Met at depot by Mr. [William J.] Steward and taken to his Rackheath Hall. Met Mrs. Steward, Miss Gange, [and] Mr. and Mrs. Stanley.

*Sunday, June 5.* Walked in the grounds [of Rackheath Hall], went to Norwich to services. Met Mayor Bullard and wife at door of Cathedral.

*Monday, June 6.* Visited three cathedrals, then went to Guild Hall and lunched—returned from there to Mr. Taylor's. Was entertained handsomely—had band—came back to Rackheath Hall. A dress dinner—low neck and short sleeves.

*Tuesday, June 7.* Arrived in London three [sic] P.M.

---

From Liliu's notation on her arrival in London on June 7 until her entry on Monday, June 20 (in which she mistakenly records the departure time from Liverpool as the time of arrival in London), her diary is blank. However, James W. L. McGuire, who was accompanying the royal party to England, records the following in his journal, commencing with the departure of Queen Kapiolani and Princess Liliu from Liverpool:

> ¶ Tuesday 7 (June)... We had breakfast at 9 o'clock, after which the Queen [Kapiolani] and Liliu went out for a short drive and back as we were to leave here [Rackheath Hall] today for London... by the 2 o'clock train. At 12 o'clock the Queen planted a tree that was brought for her so as [sic] Mr. and Mrs. Steward may always remember her visit. A very handsome silver spade was made for that purpose which

---

78. Maude Hayley was the wife of Englishman Major Andrew Burrill Hayley, who had been in service to King Kalakaua as equerry, master of the horses, and organizer of the mounted police on Maui and Oahu. Mrs. Hayley, who was a "Gaiety Girl" on the London stage prior to her marriage, had appeared in amateur dramatics in Honolulu. Her affair with Captain Owen Richard Armstrong would result in a scandalous divorce the following year. See *London Times*, April 21, 1888. Captain Armstrong's elder brother, Henry R. Armstrong, was the Hawaiian consul in London.

79. George W. Macfarlane (b. 1849, Honolulu–d. February 19, 1921, New York City), a close friend of King Kalakaua, served under him as chamberlain and was present with the king when he died at the Palace Hotel in San Francisco on January 20, 1891. After the overthrow of the monarchy, Macfarlane attempted to aid Liliuokalani in regaining revenues from the Crown lands, and she frequently mentions him in her diaries. In 1896 he married Julia Albu, an English concert singer, and in his later years he lived in New York and London.

His obituary said: "Colonel MacFarlane was of a breezy reminiscent type, a fine conversationalist, the trend of whose talk invariably was inclusive of names of people prominent in many capitals of the world... of diplomats, generals, admirals, people of the stage, while kings and queens and princes and princesses were his boon companions." *Honolulu Advertiser*, February 22, 1921.

Liliu's diaries also occasionally mention his brothers Fred and Edward (Ned).

80. Mrs. Domatilla Rodriguez Vida Janion was the widow of Robert C. Janion, a Honolulu merchant active in the 1840s and 1850s. The comment about Mrs. Janion is italicized because it is obviously a later addition to the diary.

the Queen made it a present to the Lady of the house. After having a light lunch we started for the depot and got there just in time. After bidding our friends good bye we started off on our journey.... We arrived at London at 7 o'clock. At the Depot there were great crowds of people. There were carriages there awaiting to take us to the... Alexandra Hotel.... We got to the Hotel in a few minutes and were shown to our rooms. This is not a large Hotel but is more of a family Hotel.... At 8 o'clock we had our dinner, after which we spent the evening at home.[81]

Young McGuire then provides a summary account of what the Hawaiian royals did during the following week. On the 8th, he says the Queen received company in the morning and did not go out at all. On the 9th, he notes, "The Queen and Liliu received company this afternoon and also spent the day at home." On the 10th he writes: "At 4 o'clock the Queen, Liliu, Gen. Dominis, Mr. Hoffnung [and] Curtis went for a drive in Hyde Park and got home at 6.30... at 7 o'clock had dinner, after which Their Majesties got ready to go to the opera at Her Majesties Theatre. At 8 o'clock they took carriages and drove there."

On the 11th, the Hawaiian visitors all went to the Albert Hall to hear Madame Adelina Patti at a matinee performance, and on the 12th, they went to church. There was a dinner and reception at the Hoffnung residence on the 13th, and on Tuesday, the 14th, Queen Kapiolani visited a medical college "where ladies are taught to be Doctoresses," and then went to an organ exhibition. (This was the same organ that would later be sent to Honolulu for Kaumakapili Church.) On the 16th, their Majesties went to an agricultural hall, and on the 17th, they witnessed a military drill at the royal barracks, followed by an evening at the Lyceum Theatre.

On the 18th, McGuire notes that "we breakfasted at 8 o'clock, after which we got ready to go out, as the Queen and Liliu were going to have some photographs taken. At 10 o'clock we got into carriages and drove to Regent St. at Walery's [studio] and spent a few hours there."

James McGuire says nothing about any shopping expeditions made by either Liliuokalani or her husband. However, a memorandum dated June 8, 1887, at the end of Liliu's diary shows that she made the following purchases:

Diamond Pendant $660.
Marguerite $180.
Necklace $800.
Butterfly $420.
By Mr. Hoffnung. Not pd.

---

*Monday, June 20.* Queen Victoria arrived from Scotland at 11 A.M., with Princess Beatrice of Battenberg.[82] 1½ P.M. the Queen [Kapiolani] and myself, accompanied by Gov. [Dominis], Iaukea, and Mr. R. Synge, went

81. McGuire, 28–29.
82. Princess Beatrice (b. 1857–d. 1944), daughter of Queen Victoria and wife of Prince Henry of Battenberg (b. 1850–d. 1896).

to Buckingham Palace to call on the Queen. [We] were met at the door by Earl [of] Latham, Queen's chamberlain, and Sir [Henry] Ponsonby took us in to visitors' room.[83]

Siamese, Japanese, and Persian Princes came in same room. Two ladies in waiting to Victoria came in. We were soon called in to meet her. [Robert F.] Synge[84] went with [us] as far as the door, and in a small room we found her with the Prince and Princess Henry of Battenberg and Duke of Connaught.[85] She [Queen Victoria] kissed the Queen [Kapiolani] and shook hands with me. Iaukea stood behind their seat—only a few words passed between them [and] a few to me. We [then] left.

---

Curtis Iaukea is more expansive about this event in his memoirs:

> ¶ On Monday, June 20th, the day before the Jubilee ceremony Queen Victoria received her Majesty Queen Kapiolani and the Princess Liliuokalani at a private audience on behalf of Hawaii and its royal family [and] they offered felicitations to their Royal Hostess. This reception at this time and while the city was filled with members and representatives of royal families from all over the world was indeed a signal honor.... Lord Salisbury received us [and] Lord Latham and the Honorable Secretary Ponsonby appeared to conduct us to the audience chamber. Queen Kapiolani entered attended by myself, to be followed by Princess Liliuokalani attended by the Honorable R. F. Synge.... In the audience chamber a sofa was placed at the farther end and on either side of it, a chair had been placed. The room was absolutely bare of other furniture. Queen Victoria was seated on the sofa. His Royal Highness the Duke of Connaught stood by a window and the Prince and Princess Henry of Battenberg stood near him. Our Royal hostess greeted Queen Kapiolani cordially, kissing her on each cheek as she welcomed her. The two Queens were seated on the sofa, the Princess Liliuokalani occupied one of the chairs whilst I interpreted the conversation.... Queen Victoria recalled with pleasure King Kalakaua's visit, and the two Queens discussed matters of mutual interest. The audience was indeed a success.[86]

---

*Tuesday, June 21.* A grand day. At ten John and Boyd left for Westminster Abbey—11. Queen, Curtis, Synge, and I went in [Queen] Victoria's carriage—two Grooms [and] two footmen in red liveries, amidst of a dense crowd from top of balustrade five stories high. Our carriage was escorted

---

83. Edward Bootle-Wilbraham (b. 1837–d. 1898), first earl of Latham, was lord chamberlain 1886–95. Sir Henry Ponsonby (b. 1825–d. 1895) was private secretary to Queen Victoria 1870–95.

84. Sir Robert Follet Synge (b. 1853–d. 1920) was a long-time Foreign Office official in London and son of William Webb Follet Synge, who had been British Commissioner in Hawaii in 1862–65.

85. Prince Arthur, Duke of Connaught (b. 1850–d. 1942), was a son of Queen Victoria and later governor of Canada.

86. Hawaii State Archives, Iaukea Collection, Box 1, manuscript memoirs, 206–8.

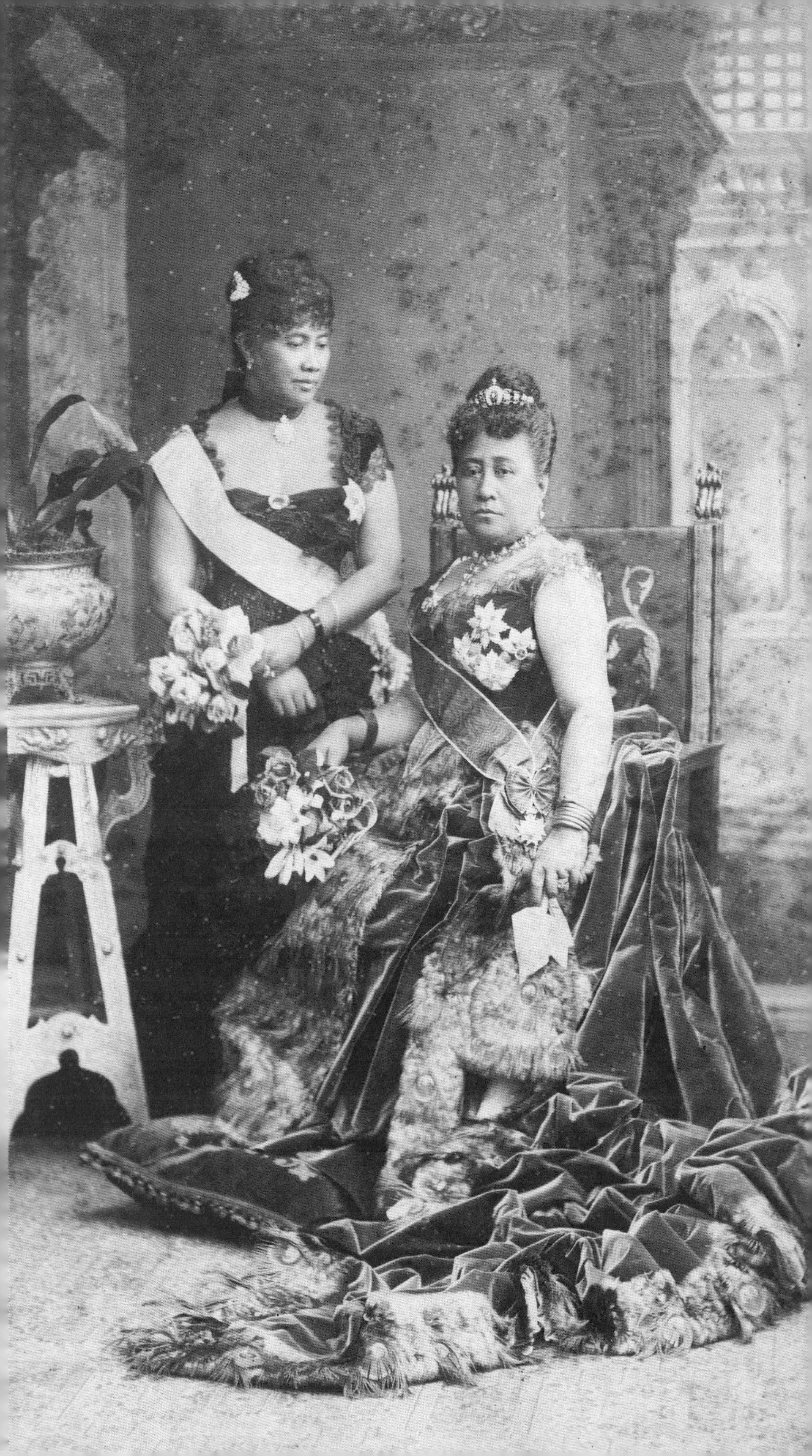

*John Owen Dominis as a boy, 1847. The American painter Joel Blakeslee Knapp painted an oil-on-canvas portrait of Dominis that hung in the drawing room of Washington Place. This photographic reproduction by J. J. Williams (circa 1886) was a gift from Liliuokalani to Mary Carter.*
Hawaii State Archives

RIGHT
*Governor John Owen Dominis, 1887.*
Walery, Photographer to the Queen, London, Virginia Dominis Koch Collection

OPPOSITE
*Princess Liliuokalani (left) and Queen Kapiolani, accompanied by John Owen Dominis, attended the fiftieth anniversary of Queen Victoria's accession to the throne on June 21, 1887, in London. While there, Liliuokalani purchased a butterfly brooch and wore the elegant piece made of diamonds, rubies, and gold in her hair, as seen in this photograph. A memorandum dated June 8, 1887, at the end of Liliu's diary lists the purchase of the brooch.*
Walery, Photographer to the Queen, London, Bishop Museum Archives

by the Queen's Life Guards. Streets lined all the way with Navy and Army—Millions of people. Queen and I had [our] places [in Westminster Abbey] with Queens and Kings of Europe. I sat by Grand Duchess of Mecklenberg, cousin to the Queen, and [in] front of Prince Albert Victor. The Queen curtsied to us.

---

James McGuire describes the departure of Queen Kapiolani and Princess Liliuokalani from the Hotel for Westminster Abbey as follows:

> ¶ At 10 o'clock Gen. Dominis and J. Boyd got into their carriages and were driven to the Abbey and at 10:30 the royal party [parties] that were staying at the Alexandra Hotel got into their carriages as follows: The first carriage contained Mirza Hissam Sultan of Persia and Suite. The second carriage contained the Prince Varoprakar of Siam and Suite. The third the Prince Komatsu of Japan and Suite and the fourth contained Queen Kapiolani, Liliuokalani. Col. Iaukea and Mr. Synge. The first three carriages were not so grand as the carriage that was sent for the Queen... the grooms men were dressed in a very handsome suit of scarlet plush and gold trimmings... the Queen's carriage was a covered carriage trimmed with scarlet velvet and gold chord draped very handsomely and the driver wore a scarlet suit of velvet and gold trimmings, knee britches and a three cornered hat and powdered wigs and so were the foot men.... It was the finest state carriage I ever saw. Then there were about 60 life guards on fine black horses... dressed in scarlet jackets and white pantaloons with a steel helmet... and each man had a drawn sword. As the Queen entered the carriage they saluted her and as the party started for the church the life-guards rode in front and back and on the sides of the Queen's carriage. It was a grand sight... There was a tremendous crowd at the Hotel door to see the Queen and such cheering as I shall never forget.[87]

---

Curtis P. Iaukea describes the assembly at the abbey and the aftermath in greater detail in his memoirs:

> ¶ On the left of Queen Kapiolani was seated the Queen of the Belgians and just behind us the Grand Duchess of Mecklenberg-Strelitz, cousin to Queen Victoria. Seated quite near us were their Majesties, the King of Denmark, the King of Belgium, the King of Saxony, the King of Hellenes. Their Royal Highness the Crown Prince of Austria-Hungary, the Crown Prince of Greece, the Infanta Don Antonia of Spain, the Crown Prince of Sweden and Norway, the Princess Victoria of Prussia, the Duke of Edinburgh, His Imperial Highness and Grand Duke Serge of Russia, and many more.... After the ceremony we attended

87. McGuire, 34.

a luncheon at Buckingham Palace where the Prince of Wales attended Queen Kapiolani and the Duke of Edinburgh escorted the Princess Liliuokalani. The luncheon table ran the entire length of the huge banquet hall and at it were seated the kings and queens attending the ceremony. After the luncheon the guests were permitted to view the gifts that had been sent to the Queen from all over the world. Among them we noticed Hawaii's gift of a monogram worked out in royal yellow feathers encased in a frame studded with diamonds.[88]

---

*Friday, June 24.* Visited the tower of London with Mr. and Mrs. [Henry R.] Armstrong,[89] Mr. and Mrs. Stanley,[90] Miss Stanley, and John. Mr. Farrer the Warder took us around [and] showed us the dungeon, the wells, the rack, Prince's grave, and all. The Crown Jewels and the Mace.

*Sunday, June 26.* Took the train at 10½ A.M. John, Mr. and Mrs. Armstrong, Mrs. Stanley, Mrs. [Paul] Neumann, [James] Boyd, Nowlein, and I took train going past by Palace through pretty country, stopping at a Station. There met Skinner[91] and two rich gentlemen stopping at an inn.

*Monday, June 27.* Visited the tower with the Queen [Kapiolani] and Mr. Synge and Curtis Iaukea.[92]

*Tuesday, June 28.* Dine up. Dyspepsia, did not go to [Entry ends thus.][93]

*Wednesday, June 29.* Stayed at home all morning. At four P.M. o ka mau no o Synge o ka pulale—ua paa no kuu lole o ka hala no ia o ke kaa. Kau wau ma ke kaa elua me Keoni and Boyd. I hiki aku ka hana, e noho wale ana no na Lii e hoka ai—o ka mea o ka miki mua ana. [At four P.M. Synge, as usual, in a rush. My dress was finally ready, but the carriage had left—so I boarded the second carriage with John and Boyd. When we got to the event, the royals were waiting in near frustration—the outcome of arriving early.][94]

88. Hawaii State Archives, Iaukea Collection, Box 1, manuscript memoirs, 208–10.

89. Henry R. Armstrong, Hawaiian consul in London, partner in Skinner & Co. of London, and nephew of Sir Alexander Matheson of Jardine, Matheson & Co. of London and Hong Kong.

90. Edward Henry Stanley, 15th Earl of Derby (b. 1826–d. 1893), member of the House of Lords, was colonial secretary (1882–85).

91. Skinner was the head of Skinner & Co. at numbers 3 and 4, Great Winchester Street, London Wall. The firm was the successor to Hoffnung & Co, with whom the Hawaiian government had done extensive business, including ordering the two crowns for the 1883 coronation.

92. James McGuire records that they visited the Tower of London only on the 24th, and that on the 27th they visited the "American Exhibition." McGuire, 37–39.

93. James McGuire records in his journal that on this date Their Majesties attended an evening ball "at the Guild Hall where some 5,000 people were present . . . and spent a most enjoyable evening." McGuire, 39.

94. Here Liliu is surprisingly vague. In her memoir, she says that on the afternoon of June 29, "The final entertainment given to the party of royal visitors from all quarters of the globe, was a garden party tendered by Her Majesty Queen Victoria, and [at] which she herself and all her good and beautiful children were present." *Hawaii's Story*, 204–6.

In *Hawaii's Story*, Liliuokalani says that upon their return to the hotel from Queen Victoria's Garden Party at Buckingham Palace, which took place on June 29, "we received news which changed at once the current of our thoughts. This was the revolutionary movement, inaugurated by those of foreign blood, or American birth, in the Hawaiian Islands during our absence." Liliu is here referring to the July 1887 movement by Honolulu businessmen to curtail King Kalakaua's extravagances, and to force him to sign a new constitution that severely limited his authority as monarch, an action that infuriated Liliuokalani. Chronologically, however, the garden party took place on June 29, the revolution in Honolulu took place in early July, and she and her party did not learn of that event until they reached New York on July 11, 1887.

James McGuire reports that the royal party departed London for Liverpool on Saturday, July 2, "mid the cheers of the people who had gathered... to get a last look at Queen Kapiolani." They arrived at Liverpool in the afternoon, and by five o'clock "we started on our way out." On Sunday, he relates, they were off the coast of Ireland—and there they made a short stop at the port of Queenstown.[95]

*Sunday, July 3.* A very quiet Sunday at sea, the only thing that attracted some attention was the arrival on board of some Irish women with some articles for sale. Arrived at Queenstown, Ireland, at 11 A.M. A tug came off with passengers, then returned with John, Boyd, Joe A., and Charley Kaiaiki, and other passengers. A middie [midshipman] was sent ashore to bring Admiral Carpenter's compliments. On his return a salute was fired. When tug returned, [it] brought John and others off with Admiral [Carpenter] and wife to visit Queen.

*Monday, July 4.* On the SS *Servia*, Cunard line, passed a quiet day.... A young lady who came in the care of Capt. McKay sent to ask if they could make speeches—he sent answer "they don't have such things on board."

*Thursday, July 7.* John is sad today and so am I. Is there trouble or sorrow at home[?]

The SS *Servia* arrived off New York on the morning of July 11, 1887, and the *New York Times*, in its coverage of the arriving Hawaiians, noted that Queen Kapiolani was found on the deck "enjoying the bracing breeze and gazing admiringly at the beautiful aspect of the great Bay in the morning sunlight.... [However,] Her Majesty's reverie was suddenly broken by Gen. [actually, Colonel] Iaukea, the royal chamberlain, who had a copy of the *Times* [the issue of July 11, 1887] in his hand containing an account of the supposed revolt and overthrow of the Cabinet in Hawaii.

95. McGuire, 40.

The General's translation of this article was the first intimation Her Majesty received of the troubles at home." The reporter then obtained statements about the political situation from as many of the party as he could, and concluded with this: "The royal party leave this evening for San Francisco by special car over the New York Central [line]. A brief halt will be made at Niagara Falls, and another at Chicago after which the journey will be a continuous one to the Pacific coast."[96]

The royal party departed San Francisco on the *Australia* for Honolulu at two P.M. on July 19, 1887.

---

*Saturday, July 23.* Lovely day. Nothing but knitting to do—but as fast as my needles fly my thoughts seem to fly even faster. A nap after breakfast. Joe wakes me up to go to luncheon—that is over. Then comes dinner. I retire.

*Sunday, July 24.* Bright day at sea. My heart is sad, tho'—for affairs at home seem dark. My poor brother!

*Monday, July 25.* We are nearing home. What lovely weather.

---

On July 26, 1887, the *Australia* arrived off Waikiki. Governor Cleghorn and staff met the queen and princess, and Liliuokalani, General Dominis, Curtis P. Iaukea, and Colonel J. H. Boyd boarded the tug *Eleu* and headed to the harbor to meet a royal salute. The USS *Adams* and HBMS *Conquest* were dressed and a salute was fired. The Royal Hawaiian Band played "Hawaii Ponoi" and the crowd gave three cheers. The king welcomed the royal party at the front entrance to the palace.

---

*Tuesday, August 2.* Meeau sent me $5.00 for her dues—Hui Hookuonoono.

*Wednesday, August 31.* Drew my allowance from A. J. Cartwright for this month, $400.00, also $60 [for] Kaipo's shares Waimanalo stocks.

*Thursday, September 1.* Bought one share from Joe Aea, the last one he had for Kaipo—for $150. Paid $120—at first, [and a] few days after paid him $30.00.

*Monday, September 5.* Hui Hookuonoono Division 2 met at Hale Akala [the palace bungalow], contributed $10.00—placed in Poomaikelani's hands.

*Thursday, September 22.* Went up Nuuanu valley for ferns—while there, received news of Keliiahonui's death.[97] Came home but did not go up [to the palace] till next day.

---

96. *New York Times*, July 12, 1887.

97. Prince Edward Abel Keliiahonui, born May 13, 1860, at Kaalaa, Honolulu, was 18 years old at the time of his death. His father was David Kahalepouli Piikoi and his mother, Princess Kekaulike, was a sister of Queen Kapiolani. His brothers were Princes Jonah Kuhio Kalanianaole and David Kawananakoa.

The *Advertiser* announced: "At three o'clock yesterday afternoon His Highness...breathed his last at Iolani palace. For some time he has been prosecuting his studies at St. Matthew's

*Friday, September 23.* Went to Palace.

*Sunday, September 25.* Keliiahonui was buried from Iolani Palace [at] two P.M. Services short—but quite grand one for him.[98] King told me that efforts were being made to "cede Pearl River to U.S."—He would resist it.[99]

*Monday, September 26.* Gave Tamar Meekapu $15.00 from Hui Hoonaauao Mahele [Liliuokalani Educational Association, Division] 2nd to payment of expenses of Puhi. Sent Aholo [and] Nahinu copies of *Elele*.[100]

*Today—a day of importance in H[awaiian] History. King signed a lease of Pearl river to U[nited] States for eight years to get R [Reciprocity] Treaty. It should not have been done.*[101]

*Tuesday, September 27.* After paying for Puhi's expenses Hui Hoonaauao, Division 2, Tamar returned $3.00.

Hall, San Mateo, California, and about two weeks ago was taken ill. The resident physician at St. Matthew's, Dr. Baldwin, thought it best for the young Prince to be sent to his native land, and consequently he arrived on the *Australia* Tuesday, but in such a weak condition that he had to be carried from the vessel to a carriage. Arriving at the Palace, medical aid was summoned, and it was found he was suffering from an attack of typhoid fever. At one o'clock yesterday afternoon Drs. Robt. McKibbin and Trousseau . . . said it was impossible for the young man to live more than a couple of hours. . . . He died at three o'clock." *Pacific Commercial Advertiser*, September 22, 1887.

98. The prince lay in state in the bungalow rather than in the palace, but the actual funeral service took place in the throne room. He was buried in the royal mausoleum.

99. "The cession of Pearl River, a matter that agitated the minds of the people of this community in 1873, seems to be coming to the front again, and doubtless will become a very strong factor on the politics of this country in the coming session of the Legislature, to meet in May next. At the present time we shall have little to say on the subject. Setting the political side of the question to one side, many will look with favor on a measure that would be likely to serve the interests of either party or persons for the time being, leaving the future to care for itself." *Pacific Commercial Advertiser*, September 30, 1887.

100. *Ka Nupepa Elele* was a weekly Hawaiian-language newspaper. There is no record of what issues Liliu distributed or why.

101. Liliuokalani's comment beginning with "Today" is italicized because it is in a slightly different hand from other entries on the page. The lease document referred to is a supplementary convention to the Reciprocity Treaty of 1875. The treaty eliminated U.S. tariffs imposed on sugar imported from Hawaii and resulted in significant benefits to American planter interests in Hawaii. The document signed by Kalakaua on October 20, 1887, under pressure from his cabinet, granted the United States exclusive access to Pearl Harbor and was key to the U.S. agreement to extend the Reciprocity Treaty past its 1886 expiration. The section that Liliu would have found objectionable is Article II: "His Majesty the King of the Hawaiian Islands grants to the Government of the United States the exclusive right to enter the harbor of Pearl River in the island of Oahu, and to establish and maintain there a coaling and repair station for the use of vessels of the United States, and to that end the United States may improve the entrance to said harbor and do all other things needful to the purpose aforesaid."

Before negotiations on the supplementary convention to the treaty concluded, Godfrey Brown, Hawaiian minister of finance, in a letter to H.A.P. Carter, the Hawaiian envoy in Washington, DC, made the Hawaiian government's position clear: "Honolulu, September 27, 1887. I have the honor to inform Your Excellency that at a Cabinet Council held at the Palace yesterday afternoon, His Majesty the King agreed to the Senate amendment to the Treaty on the condition that . . . Hawaiian Sovereignty and Jurisdiction are not impaired, that the Hawaiian Government is not bound to furnish land for any purpose, and that the privilege to be granted is coterminous with the treaty, is accepted by Mr. Baird [secretary of state]. If these explanations of our understanding are accepted, Your Excellency will please prepare and execute the necessary documents, and send the treaty here for ratification at your earliest convenience." Hawaii State Archives, Foreign Office and Executive Files, Treaties.

Although signed on October 20, the action did not become official (through a public proclamation) until November 29, 1887.

*Thursday, September 29.* Spent morning ~~at home~~. Afternoon went to Waikiki with Annie Turton and all our folks—Charley and Kitty [Wilson], Alice and Mal. [Malcolm Brown], Jimmy [McGuire] and George [Macfarlane] and all people went fishing—such fun. Bright moonlight night, caught lots of fish. Capt. Kempf of *Adams* came over with [Antone] Rosa and Jimmie Robertson.

*Friday, September 30.* Drew on A. J. Cartwright $400 for my monthly allowances. Did not draw Kaipo's shares of Waimanalo Stocks this month.

**Saturday, October 1.** Rec'd letter from Skinner & Co—Successors to A. Hoffnung & Co. London, by Steamer *Germanic* informing me my carriage will be here Middle of December, and one box with two dresses from Mrs. Armstrong, and one case of stuffed birds from Mr. Taylor. Cost of carriage £251.9.9. Cost of collection £6.12.1—making a total of £258.1.10—draft to be presented at sight to Bishop & Co.[102]

Do not draw Kaipo's W. [Waimanalo] Stocks this month, which amounts to $30.00 at 5½ pr. ct. [from] six shares.

*Monday, October 3.* Rec'd from Mrs. Jennie Clark $107.40 H. Mc. [sic]—taken from Post office.

*Tuesday, October 4.* Mary returned books of Hui Hoonaauao 1st Division of Sec[retary].

*Wednesday, October 5.* Hui Hoonaauao Mokuna [Division] 2. $3.00 contributed at meeting at Engine House No 1. $1.25 given to Mrs. Meekapu towards payment to Puhi's tuition, leaving $1.75, which I add to $107.40 given me by Mrs. Jennie Clark last Monday.

---

On October 8, 1887, Robert William Wilcox, the budding Hawaiian revolutionary and politician, and his Italian bride, Gina Sobrero, arrived in Honolulu, and from that date until his death in 1903 Wilcox and Liliuokalani had intertwined political relationships and played pivotal roles in each others' lives.

Wilcox, the son of American sea captain William Slocum Wilcox and Kalua Makoleokalani, was born February 15, 1855, at Kahulu, Honuaula, near Ulupalakua, Maui. He received a high school education on Maui at the Haleakala Boys' Boarding School in Makawao, where one of his classmates was Lorrin Andrews Thurston, who became one of his chief adversaries in future years. In early adulthood, Wilcox taught school at Honuaula, Maui (1875–80). Then the Hawaiian government sent him on scholarship to Italy, where he enrolled in the Turin Military Academy and then the Royal Application School for Artillery and Engineer Officers. Robert Napunako Boyd, who would join him in the 1889 revolution, was a fellow student.

In 1890, Wilcox was a representative in the legislature, and he was elected again in 1892 as leader of the Liberal Party. His loyalties shifted from time to time, depending upon the circumstances. In his testimony

---

102. The decimal points in these figures separate pounds, shillings, and pence.

before the legislature on June 10, 1890, Wilcox summarized his activities following his return to the islands from Italy:

> ¶ When the present Ministry came into power, I was sent for [to return to Hawaii], but did not receive a very cordial reception from the Minister of Foreign Affairs, and I could see that native Hawaiians did not stand much of a chance of getting government positions, as strangers were preferred. I was badly treated by the Government, looked upon as a vagabond.... I applied to His Majesty and he proposed to make me major of the household troops, but the ministers objected. Mrs. Dominis [Liliuokalani] tried to get me in as Governor in place of her husband, but again the ministers objected. I applied at the Survey Department without success.
>
> I then applied to Thurston. He gave me very little satisfaction, and finally advised me to return to Italy.... Finally he offered me a position in the Survey Department. I think to drag a chain at a salary which would not keep a cat alive.... I... went to California where I obtained a place at three times the salary which I had been offered here.
>
> I returned in about a year. The elections were approaching, and I thought there was a chance for me on raising up my downtrodden countrymen. Mrs. Dominis received me kindly, and I opened an office in my line of business as surveyor and tried to get some work, but the Reform Party did everything they could to prevent me. Finally myself and some others who felt that native Hawaiians were not properly treated, organized. The society was started with peaceful intentions at first and meetings were held over [at] Nowlein's. Charlie Wilson was present. We had a declaration of intentions "Hawaii for the Hawaiians."[103]

Wilcox was the principal participant in three serious Hawaiian revolutionary actions. On July 30, 1889, he headed an insurrection with the intention of restoring the constitution of 1864 and of placing Liliuokalani on the throne in the stead of her brother Kalakaua. After the rebellion's failure, the government charged him with treason, but a jury of his countrymen did not convict him. In 1892, the government again committed him for treason, and again the jury discharged him. In January 1895, he was one of the leaders in the rebellion against the Republic of Hawaii, seeking the restoration of Liliuokalani to the throne. The coup failed and resulted in her abdication almost immediately afterward. Put on trial after his capture, Wilcox proudly admitted his guilt.

Wilcox first married on June 15, 1887, in Turin, Italy. His bride was "Lady Maria Carolina Isabella Luigia Sobrero, aged 23 years, daughter of the late Colonel Barone Lorenzo Sobrero, and Donna Vitorias of the Princes Colonna."[104] Wilcox and wife came to the islands in 1887, arriving on the *San Pablo* on October 8, 1887, and for a period lived in the Queen's Palama residence. The Wilcox marriage was not a happy one, and she returned to Italy and obtained a divorce. On August 20, 1896, Wilcox married Mrs. Theresa Owana Kaohelelani Laanui Cartwright.

---

103. *Pacific Commercial Advertiser*, June 12, 1890.
104. The marriage certificate is in the Hawaii State Archives, Foreign Office and Executive Files, Box 65.

He was a charismatic speaker, and while Liliu was often wary of his actions and motives, his almost universal popularity among her subjects forced her to deal with him. She did not much care for either of his wives.

In 1900, Robert W. Wilcox was elected Hawaii's first delegate to the U.S. Congress under the Home Rule Party, and he served in Washington, DC, until 1902, when Prince Jonah Kuhio Kalanianaole defeated him. He died in Honolulu on October 23, 1903.

---

*Tuesday, October 11.* Paid to J. Aea $30.00 the remaining amount of W. [Waimanalo] Stocks sold to Kaipo Aea for $150.00. Spent morning planting at Keala [Hale].

Kaakaole $2.

*Friday, October 14.* Came from Waikiki to [Keala] Hale—plant ferns. Back to Waikiki and slept.

*Saturday, October 15.* Went to town to make calls—was told John had returned from Waialua and was very sick. Stayed to nurse him.

Went to consult Dr. Martin about [John's] rheumatism in the heart. Was relieved.

*Sunday, October 16.* After breakfast, went to Waikiki to luu kai [bathe in the sea] and did not feel well enough to go up in the [Palolo?] valley.

*Tuesday, October 18.* Lent $2 to Kaakaole.

*Tuesday, October 25.* Wrote to A. J. Cartwright to give Joe $350.00 to pay K. [Kapuniai] Kailikole for his land at Waikiki.

*Wednesday, October 26.* Came to town—gave Kawehena two dollars to take to Kaakaole.

*Thursday, October 27.* I sent order on Bishop & Co. to pay Kailikole $850.00 for Kalea's Kuleana [native land claim] at Waikiki.[105]

*Friday, October 28.* Came to town on business. Did not do much, did more gossiping with Annie Turton. A party was given at Armory by four ladies—Mrs. Boardman[106] and others [and] Edith [Turton] went. Mrs. Dowsett came over and spent eve. Keala [Hale].

*Saturday, October 29.* Mary Ailau paid $55.00, the rest of the amount borrowed on Jan. 30th, which was $100.00. In April she paid $50.33—but I will make up the rest for her—and [I] returned her three feather leis. Woke up early, found no one up.

*Monday, October 31.* Drew from A. J. Cartwright $400.00, my monthly allowance. Signed paper for freight for Set [of] harness from England and package [of] liveries. £85.15 S. charges $30.89.

**Tuesday, November 1.** Paid wages. Will not draw Kaipo's W. [Waimanalo] stocks this month, which will amount to $30.00 at 5 percent for six shares.

---

105. This was a purchase from Puniai Kailikole and Meeau, his wife, of a kuleana located within the boundaries of Hamohamo at Waikiki, previously owned by Kelea. See footnote for March 11, 1885, diary entry (15). The transaction was executed April 8, 1885, but not recorded until July 21, 1887. Bureau of Conveyances, Liber 108, 82. The discrepancy between the latter date and this later diary note is unexplained.

106. Mrs. Boardman was the wife of George E. Boardman, deputy collector of customs. The *Pacific Commercial Advertiser*, October 29, 1887, identified the event as a "dancing party."

At noon on November 3, 1887, the king opened an "Extraordinary Session" of the legislature at Aliiolani Hale. Liliuokalani was among those present, and it is surprising that she makes no mention of the event in her diaries. It was not, however, a happy gathering, as British Consul James Hay Wodehouse informed the Foreign Office in London on November 9:

> ¶ It was...with the greatest difficulty that His Majesty was induced to attend the ceremony, nor is it to [be] wondered at, that He should have been reluctant to undergo such a public humiliation, and to swallow so bitter a pill as the Speech which His Ministers had prepared for Him, for he was compelled not only to pass judgment on the favourite measures of the last Session, such as the "Opium Bill," the "Act to Organize the Military Forces of the Kingdom," the circumstances connected with the "Negotiation of the Loan in London," and the "Appropriation Bill of 1886," but to declare [publicly] what he had the greatest aversion to, that He took great pleasure in informing His Parliament that the Treaty of Reciprocity with the U.S. had been [definitely] extended for seven years...with the addition of a clause granting to National Vessels of the U.S. the exclusive privilege of entering Pearl River Harbour, and establishing there a coaling and repair Station. Whereas it is well known to me that it required the strongest pressure by the whole Cabinet to induce him to consent to the measure.[107]

*Friday, November 4.* Went to Waikiki—luau by myself. Ten A.M. Telephone from King. Wants to consult about Ministers in case Brown, Thurston,[108] and Green and Ashford[109] went out. I think he will have Wilder.[110]

---

107. Hawaii State Archives, Series 375, Copies of British Documents.

108. Lorrin Andrews Thurston (b. July 31, 1858, Honolulu–d. May 11, 1931, Honolulu) was a lawyer, government official, and revolutionary. Thurston first served in the legislature in 1886, drafted the 1887 Bayonet Constitution that Kalakaua was forced to sign, served as acting attorney general in 1889, and in 1892 was elected to the House of Nobles. In 1893, immediately prior to the fall of the monarchy, it was Thurston who convinced Sanford Dole to assume the leadership of the Provisional Government. Thurston was a member of the Advisory Council and a special commissioner and later envoy to Washington for the Provisional Government. The Queen singled out Thurston as her chief enemy. For more on Thurston's role in Hawaiian politics, see his *Memoirs of the Hawaiian Revolution*, ed. Andrew Farrell (Honolulu: Advertiser, 1936).

109. Clarence Wilder Ashford (b. February 24, 1857, Port Hope, Ontario, Canada–d. July 2, 1921, Honolulu) was King Kalakaua's attorney general (July 1, 1887–June 14, 1890), served as a captain in the Honolulu Rifles in 1887, served in the House of Representatives in 1892, and was a judge in the First Circuit Court 1914–19. He and his brother Volney (both practicing lawyers) were participants in the tangle of island politics between 1887 and 1895.

110. She is referring to the ministers who assumed office following the enactment of the Bayonet Constitution: Godfrey Brown was minister of foreign affairs (July 1–December 28, 1887); Lorrin A. Thurston was minister of the interior (July 1, 1887–June 14, 1890); William Lowthian Green was minister of finance (July 1–December 28, 1887); Clarence W. Ashford

*Saturday, November 5.* Sent Kaakaole $2.00 [illegible]. Sent for Lou [Louisa] Brickwood and she came to dine with us. After that she went round to members to collect money—raised $27.00. Stayed down here that night.

*Sunday, November 6.* Went back [at] six A.M. without [John] Paoakalani to Waikiki. Stayed there all day planting—should have gone to church.

*Monday, November 7.* Annie Turton and Edith [Turton] left for Lahaina. Miss them much.

Joe [Heleluhe] commenced [assembling] white Kahilis [feather standards]. Paid Mellis $4.00 for *P.C. Advertiser* and *Daily Gazette*. Stopped to see John about going next night to Mausoleum. Stopped to ask C. B. Wilson to go up next day to write [down] names of [on the?] coffins [at the Royal Mausoleum] next day. Got out to Waikiki late. Slept well.

Today John, Charley, and others advised me not to sign paper of crown lands away.[111]

*Wednesday, November 9.* Came to town and went to Palace. King told me he had appointed Curtis as one of his Commissioners for Crown Lands.[112] Went to wedding [of] Swanzy to Julie Judd at 11.[113] [At] 12 went to Mausoleum to take Kahilis [feather standards] out. Joe Aea, Joe Heleluhe, [John] Mana, Kalukou, and [John] Paoakalani. Lucy objected but had to give in.[114] Seven P.M. Bernice and [her] relations were put into her new vault to be sealed up. [Hale] Naua took them over by torchlight. Finished taking 22 bodies at 2½ Thursday morn.[115]

---

was attorney general (July 1, 1887–June 14, 1890). Samuel G. Wilder, who had served as minister of the interior (1878–80), was not appointed to any cabinet position at this time.

111. This is a reference to a proposal by the king's trustees to secure the settlement of his debts from revenues of the Crown lands. See diary entry for November 20, 1887 (163).

112. Curtis Iaukea held the position of commissioner for Crown lands starting in August 30, 1886, and was reappointed August 4, 1887, and again (by Liliuokalani) March 3, 1891. Here perhaps Liliu meant that Iaukea had been appointed a commissioner for the king's personal estate.

113. The marriage of Francis Mills Swanzy of T. H. Davies & Co. to Julia Judd, the daughter of Colonel Charles Hastings Judd, took place at Saint Andrew's Cathedral. The *Pacific Commercial Advertiser*, November 10, 1887, reported that it was "one of the most brilliant social events that has taken place in this city in a long time." The attendees included the king, Princess Liliuokalani and Governor Dominis, Princess Kaiulani and her father, A. S. Cleghorn, and members of the consular corps.

114. Lucy Peabody (b. 1840–d. 1928) was a cousin of the late Queen Emma, and had been her closest friend and confidante. The objection may have been over moving kahilis (royal feather standards) that were once Queen Emma's.

115. The *Pacific Commercial Advertiser*, November 12, 1887, reported: "The removal of twenty coffins, containing the remains of deceased royal personages, from the royal mausoleum ... to the vault constructed in accordance with the provisions of the will of the late Hon. Mrs. Bernice Pauahi Bishop, was carried into effect with fitting solemnity between the hours of 7:30 on Wednesday evening and 2 o'clock on Thursday morning in the presence of H.R.H. Princess Liliuokalani, H.R.H. Princess Poomaikelani, His Excellency Governor Dominis, Hon. A. S. Cleghorn, in addition to the bearers. The historic episode occupied more than six hours in its performance.... The following are the names of those whose remains were deposited in the new vault:"

*Thursday, November 10.* Reached Waikiki 2¼ A.M. Slept till 7½.

*Friday, November 11.* Paid Joe $10.00. It should have been paid him before when he cleaned house with Johnnie. Said he would get a pig for next day to receive Mrs. Kia. Finished one Kahili [feather standard].

*Saturday, November 12.* Paina [feast] at 12 at Waikiki—spent morning in decorating my house Kealohilani. How nicely everything is growing.

1½ P.M. went to Manoa and gave Hilo one patch in Nanauki's kuleana [native land claim] and house lot to take care [of] for me and to sustain her, although I have willed it to Kaipo. But—I don't know—sometimes they are ungrateful.

Went back to Waikiki so that Joe and Wakeke could go to Kawaiahao Seminary. All alone until Mrs. F. Gay came in to see me about Kamakahala [?]—but in truth it was about W [?] to be Minister of Cabinet.

*Sunday, November 13.* Did not feel well, nevertheless went through different houses. Heard Ahoi [the cook] scold Paaluhi. What an end—to be wandering and not know it. Quiet day—yet passed quickly.

*Monday, November 14.* Came down from Waikiki to Muolaulani. Busy all day writing. Slept at Washington Place. John and I discoursed on the weakness of everyone: The King, the Court, the City [?] wants to get rid of the Rifles and yet do not dare to. How laughable.

Breakfasted with the King, Queen, and two princes. King had plans for borrowing money but [I] am sorry for him—fear it will never be realized.[116] Concert Emma Square, but went to Hinano Bower and sat up with John. Mother [Dominis] is failing.

*Tuesday, November 15.* Placed in Mrs. Jennie Clark's hand the sum of $107.00 drawn from Post Office; also $1.75 remaining of contributions of meeting amounting to $3.00. $1.25 given there [?] to Tamar [Meekapu] to pay for one scholar's tuition.

Joe has not quite finished his Kahili [feather standard]—will wait till Thursday. [Scrolling "L."]

*Wednesday, November 16.* Woke up early four A.M. Paoakalani [a horse] harnessed up—we drove by Kaipo's—no one up. Waited at Washington Place, only few came, so went to Hookupu [tribute or ceremonial offering]—King was well on his 51[st] birthday.[117] May he live many more.

[The newspaper report on the entombment of the Kamehameha family line in the newly completed vault included the list below.]

| | |
|---|---|
| Kaahumanu I | William Pitt Leleiohoku |
| Kamamalu I | Keaweaweula |
| David Kamehameha | John William Pitt Kinau |
| Kaahumanu II (Kinau) | Queen Kalama |
| Kekuanaoa | Queen Emma |
| Kamehameha V | Prince of Hawaii |
| Kamehameha IV | Paki and Konia |
| Victoria Kamamalu | Ruth Keelikolani |
| Moses Kekuaiwa | Hon. Mrs. Bernice P. Bishop |
| Keola Paki Bishop | |

116. See November 20, 1887, diary entry (163).

117. The *Pacific Commercial Advertiser*, November 16, 1887, announced the king's birthday

Met children going to hookupu. Must have got 1,000 or more—came to Muolaulani [and] dressed—but how it pours. Must go to races[118] so start off in rain. Met my husband at wharf—lots of people—3½ P.M. races are over. Pours again. Nua Lehua.

*Thursday, November 17.* Still it rains till we are flooded from water in new lot flowing into this [the Muolaulani premises] and makes both a large pond.[119] Having kahilis [feather standards] made.

*Friday, November 18.* More kahilis—Our folks are still here hard at work anxious to return to Waikiki. [Scrolling "L."]

*Saturday, November 19.* No luau [for Hale] Naua [Society] on account of rain.

*Sunday, November 20.* For a moment, bright sunshine. Had a long visit from the King. [He] Showed me letters from Griffin & Co., of London. [He] wants to borrow million to pay his debts, $298,000.68, and asks me to sign off Crown Lands. Told him [I] had advice not to do so. [He] came again in evening for same purpose. How sorry I am for him, for he appears to be anxious to make up for the past.[120]

---

and continued: "At eight o'clock this morning the Royal Hawaiian Band and the Royal School Cadets will pay their respects to the King at Iolani Palace. The chief event in the celebration of the day will be the regatta to be held on the harbor.... The Legislature adjourned yesterday until Thursday morning out of respect to His Majesty's birthday. We congratulate His Majesty on the auspicious event and trust he may live to enjoy many happy returns of the day." Nothing about the hookupu (ceremonial exchange of gifts) appeared in the press.

118. The races included a regatta under the auspices of the Hawaiian Rowing and Yachting Association, "of which His Majesty is at once the President and liberal patron." *Pacific Commercial Advertiser*, November 17, 1887. The same day this newspaper reported, "The Inter Island Steamship Co. with their usual desire to accommodate, placed their wharf at the disposal of the Regatta Committee.... A portion of the wharf was reserved for use by members of the royal family, and during the day H.R.H. Princess Liliuokalani [and] His Excellency Governor Dominis... occupied seats there."

119. The *Daily Bulletin*, November 17, 1887, commented: "The heavy rains of yesterday, last night, and today have turned the valleys [into] rivers and the streets and yards into lakes and ponds."

120. Curtis Iaukea says the following about the king's financial affairs: "On resuming the Chamberlainship, after I had returned from the Jubilee of Queen Victoria, I found the King's household and financial affairs in somewhat a chaotic state. Pressure was being brought to bear upon the King to cause immediate restitution to be made of the sum of $71,000 to Aki, a sum far beyond his ability to pay as I knew to my sorrow when trying to borrow money of the bank and Mr. Damon, prior to leaving for the Jubilee.

"The Cabinet headed by L. A. Thurston had advised such restitution to be made so as to avoid further publicity in the matter, the King having admitted receiving the money.... and assumed all responsibility in the matter.... Early in November the Cabinet submitted a method of liquidating the King's present outstanding liabilities, including the $71,000.... This was after I had submitted a full statement of the King's debts amounting to $81,000 exclusive of the Aki claim. The Cabinet ministers were so dumbfounded at this state of affairs that they recommended all claims be paid pro rata, and not the Aki claim as previously insisted on.

"In order to secure funds to meet this obligation the King executed a deed of trust covering property and other sources of income, to a group of trustees, S. M. Damon, J. O. Carter, and myself.... The trustees were empowered to lease, sell, or otherwise raise funds on the assets... which virtually amounted to control of the King's entire estate. A unique situation indeed for a King.... We did, finally, manage to clear off the debts against the King and things went smoothly for a short while." Hawaii State Archives, Iaukea Collection, manuscript memoirs, 225–28.

For first time in a whole year John was attentive—Washington Place. Went to Fort St. Church[121] with Mary Carter.

*Monday, November 21.* Went to Jessie's, sat awhile, then went to Palace. Breakfasted with King, Queen, Kaiulani, and two Princes.

Sorted feathers for Joe. Evening with John to Wilder's reception.[122]

Slept there [at Washington Place.]

*Tuesday, November 22.* Went to John Ena's[123] to see him about shares in Inter Island Steam Navigation Co. John wants to invest $300.00 for Aimoku, and I would like to draw out Kaipo, John, Lilia [Aholo], and Hana Aea from [?] and place with theirs.

Gave Joe H. $2.00 for Kaakaole, [and] $1 for gin [?] for her—making three. Waited for Joe A[ea]. Jessie Kaae came. After she left, went to Washington Place and slept.

*Friday, November 25.* Band [at] Thomas Square. Was telephoned by Wilson about rumors King was receiving Austin secretly.[124] Told him yes, but openly—about borrowing millions. Told him I was aware of it and saw no harm if he could raise money to pay off his creditors here.

*Saturday, November 26.* Went to Palace to [Hale] Naua luau—officers all invited and Commissioners and wives came. Very pleasant till five—Company went home—then all was lively [Two illegible words follow.][125]

*Sunday, November 27.* All day at home.

*Monday, November 28.* Went to Washington Place—had luau for people.[126] Went to drive with Mary Carter, Eveline, Alice Brown, Kaipo, and Aimoku.

*Tuesday, November 29.* Went to see Mr. [C. R.] Bishop about Kahilis [feather standards]. He did not care for them unless valuable. He spoke about Kauikeaouli and Liholiho [Kamehameha III and Kamehameha II] not being put in vault with Bernice and that he still was waiting to have them put in. Must see King tomorrow.

*Wednesday, November 30.* Rec'd $400 from A. J. Cartwright. Joe draws Wakeke's $5.00 for two shares W [Waimanalo] stocks. It has gone down

---

121. The Fort Street Church (Congregational), located on the Ewa corner of Fort and Beretania Streets, was established in 1856 to serve the English-speaking community. It would subsequently merge with the Seaman's Bethel Church and become the Central Union Church.

122. "An 'event of the season' was the reception given by Mr. and Mrs. S. G. Wilder to Mr. and Mrs. G. P. Wilder at Eskbank last evening. Mr. and Mrs. Wilder arrived by the last steamer from the Coast, where they were recently married. Miss Lillian Kimball, now Mrs. Wilder, is a graduate of Mills College. . . . A large number of friends of the family, including members of the royal family . . . assembled." *Daily Bulletin*, November 22, 1887.

123. John Ena Jr. (b. 1843, Hilo–d. 1906), a Chinese-Hawaiian capitalist, was employed by J. R. Foster & Co. (later the Inter-Island Steam Navigation Co.), first as a bookkeeper. In 1883, when the business incorporated, he became its business manager and secretary of the Inter-Island Steam Navigation Co.

124. For more about Frank Austin, see footnote for October 13, 1888, diary entry (203).

125. The Hale Naua Society was founded September 24, 1886. See *Hawaii's Story*, 141.

126. The occasion (not reported in the press) was probably in honor of Hawaiian Independence Day.

to 2½ per cent. Will not draw Kaipo's [dividends] till obliged to, so his six shares will amount to $15.00 this month.

Saw the King about bodies of two Kings—well, he may settle it with Mr. Bishop as he could, but my sympathy is with the latter.

**Thursday, December 1.** Did not have reception because [I] had to go to Mrs. Campbell's ball at Waikiki.[127]

Ten A.M. had meeting of Hui Hookuonoono, received [blank] Mrs. Alapai, and Kamakanoe took [it] to A. J. Cartwright. Did not draw Kaipo's six shares, Waimanalo stocks, $15.00 at 2½ per cent.

*Saturday, December 3.* Rain.

*Sunday, December 4.* Joe gave luau—invited three members [of the Legislature?]—subject [discussed?] Min. Govs. bill—Police bill. Military bill.[128]

*Monday, December 5.* [At top of page above date:] Vote of Censure to Ministers in house.[129] He halawai mahele 2 hola ten—hooholo e hana ia he Aha mele i ka po 24 o keia mahina—hooholo ia e hana ia he Ahaaina hulahula ma ka armory i ka po la elua o Jan. Hookupu a ka Hui 9.00 no ka ice cream. Haawi ia mai ma kuu lima 29.00 no ka Hui e hoihoi i ka Panako. Lend ia e au 20.—ia Jennie Clark 20. no ke kuai ana i na lole tableau. [A meeting (of the) 2nd Division, ten o'clock—Resolved that a concert be held on the evening of the 24th of this month. Resolved that a ball be held at the Armory on the evening of Jan. 2. The Society will contribute $9.00 for ice cream. In my hand is $29.00 for the Society to return to the Bank. I lent $20 and Jennie Clark lent $20 to buy tableau costumes.]

---

127. "The reception and dance at the residence of Hon. James and Mrs. Campbell last evening was a most brilliant affair. There was a large number of invited guests present." *Pacific Commercial Advertiser*, December 2, 1887.

128. The titles of the bills are from the headings of each, as printed in the Session Laws of 1887. The governor's bill was "An Act to Abolish the Office of Governor." The police bill was "An Act to Provide For and Regulate the Internal Police of the Kingdom." The military bill was "An Act to Provide For the Organization, Regulation, and Discipline of the Military Forces of the Kingdom."

The governor's bill resulted in a complete deadlock between the king and his ministers and the legislature, owing, as British Minister James Hay Wodehouse wrote, "to the claim made by His Majesty, that he has, under the Constitution, an absolute veto, whereas they claim that the veto to be effective must be countersigned by a Minister.... The excitement was kept up... by angry articles in the so-called Government organ, the 'Daily Gazette' and which were responded to by equally menacing language... in the native newspaper." Hawaii State Archives, Series 375, Copies of British Documents, Wodehouse to the Foreign Office, December 20, 1887. The matter was referred to the Supreme Court for a decision.

129. On December 5, Representative Cecil Brown introduced a resolution of censure of His Majesty's government for "violating the spirit, intent, and meaning of article 20 of the [new] Constitution," in that they had given D. H. Hitchcock, "an elective member of this Assembly, an office of emolument or salary... that of Crown prosecutor... for the Third Judicial Circuit... now being held at Waimea, Hawaii." *Pacific Commercial Advertiser*, December 6, 1887.

Article 20 of the constitution of 1887 (on the division of powers between the executive, judicial, and legislative powers of government) states specifically that "no Executive or Judicial officer... shall be eligible to election to the Legislature... or to hold the same position of an elective member of the same."

Gave Keamalu $7.00—$5.00 to give his brother at Koolau. He goes over to get him to give up or pay his share [of] expenses in case Keamalu wins Polani lands. Charlie telephones that 17 shares at $95 a share are to be had.

[The entry continues at the head of the next page:] Haawi ia Jennie Clark $14, no ka Tableau mai ka M. 2. [Jennie Clark gave me $14 for the tableau from the second division (of the Liliuokalani Hui Hoonaauao)].

*Tuesday, December 6.* Met Luna hoohana [manager] of 2d Division [of the Liliuokalani Hui Hoonaauao] at Hale Akala [the bungalow] and with President hooholo ia e hoohana ia $475.00 i loko o ka Hui Ice Co. Elima noho $95.00 no ka noho. Koe $31.00 ma ka waihona a 100. ma kuu lima no ia hui. Kuka koke me na luna o ka Hui Hookuonoono. Ae ia e hookomo $570.00 ma ka Ice Co. ua lawe ia mai (a koe aku ia A. J. Cart[wright] $805.00) ma ka $95.00 no ka noho 6 noho no ka hui.—3 noho no Kamakanoe $285—i loaa ma iau, 3 noho no Kaipo ma $285.00—huina pau $1,615—ua waiho ia keia puu kala ma ka lima o Charley Wilson apopo loaa mai na shares 150—no ka M. 2. 185 no ke H. K. i lawa ai ka Kaipo i hoi 2 koke aku no. [Met the manager of (the) 2nd Division (of the Liliuokalani Educational Society) at Hale Akala (the bungalow) and with the President. It was decided that $475.00 would be invested in the (People's)Ice Company. Five shares at $95.00 per share. That leaves $31.00 in the account, and $100 in my hand for that Society. Had a quick discussion with the officers of the Hui Hookuonoono. It was agreed to invest $570.00 in the Ice Co. which was withdrawn (leaving $805.00 with A. J. Cartwright). At $95.00 per share, six shares are for the Hui—three shares for Kamakanoe, $285.00 which I have received, and three shares for Kaipo and the others $285.00, for a total of $1,615—this sum was left in the hands of Charley Wilson and tomorrow we will receive the shares. $150. from the 2nd Division and $185. from the Hui Hookuonoono to cover Kaipo's share which should be reimbursed soon.]

*Wednesday, December 7.* Met committee at Washington Place, distributed $200 and $200.50 [worth of] tickets among them to sell. Rec'd $20 from Kamakanoe. One P.M. Kamakanoe, Beke, Kaai, Jennie Clark came up to arrange for tableau. Kapoli told me [Mr.] Bishop would like me to fix kahili[s] [feather standards] up. Will meet at Stella's [Stella Keomailani Crockett's] house to rehearse. Rec'd my certificated for stocks, 17 shares in Ice Co., from C. B. Wilson.

*Saturday, December 10.* Waited for members, none came—Kealawa told [me] that I must malama i ke Kanawai. Poakolu pau. [Kealawa told me that I must uphold the law. Wednesday done.]

*Sunday, December 11.* Went to Washington Place. Could do nothing with John, he was fuzzy. Went to C. B. Wilson's. Met lot of young men planning to get up a company—told Wilson not to do anything but to remain calm and quiet because I hear from Wakeke the King had said I was a Kipi [a rebel.]

*Monday, December 12.* Mr. and Mrs. Wilson came to stay with me. She is very nice and so is he. Women came to sew dresses for tableau. Done very well—She drove me to band.

It is an excitable day at Legislative Hall. King vetoed Gov[ernor's] bill [and] Military bill—[but?] could not get a majority [to sustain him?]—King *had* to ask *me* (after all he said) to help him. So [I] sent Joe and Kawehena to Lima.[130] He voted with King. House sent committee to asking [sic] King to change his veto. No.[131] My own room is cold. Wilcoxes have my other room. Keamalu brought in case today.

*Tuesday, December 13.* Wrote to S. Kaai to mortgage lands to me for $1,000—in case he was liable.[132] Wrote to D. H. Nahinu to take charge of lot [at] Kealia [Kona, Hawaii Island]. Wrote to Judge [J. G.] Hoapili to rent house at Keauhou—to sell the coffee and send me money.

Visit from Rand. He is awful—too polite.[133]

To Leihulu's to rehearse.

*Friday, December 16.* [Under this date Liliu has mistakenly entered the following:] December 25—1886—At concert—rec'd $241.25.

April 11th sent to A. J. Cartwright, $202.50—paid $48.75 to tuition this year. [A memorandum in cash accounts at the end of this diary shows that Liliu had paid $20 each for tuition of Abigail and Violet Beckley, and small sums for several other children through the Liliuokalani Hui Hoonaauao.]

*Tuesday, December 20.* Young James Dowsett[134] came today and told me that they wanted me to be Queen, because they said they could not do

---

130. David Lima Naone (b. 1854–d. 1900) was a legislator, 1887–88. His obituary remembered him as "one of the foremost Hawaiians in Honolulu in church and public affairs." *Pacific Commercial Advertiser*, December 29, 1900.

131. On December 9, 1887, the king informed the president of the legislative assembly that he was returning without signature the "Act to Abolish the Office of Governor" and gave his reasons for so doing. The legislature moved that it "consider whether these bills should become law or the veto be sustained." The subsequent debates and speeches on the matter were reported in detail, particularly in the *Pacific Commercial Advertiser*. At stake was first, the question of the king's veto power under the new constitution of 1887, and second, the perimeters of the balance of power between the legislative and executive branches of government. After intense debates, the legislature sent the matter to the Supreme Court for a decision.

132. The liability is nowhere explained, and there is no record of any such mortgage.

133. Possibly Reverend F. E. Rand, a missionary in Micronesia, who was in Honolulu on several occasions in the 1880s.

134. James Isaac Dowsett Jr. (b. 1858–d. 1895), the son of J. I. Dowsett Sr., was a member of the legislature during the 1887–88 session. An account from Volney V. Ashford includes this statement: "The King, after the revolution [of 1887,] became very stiff and surly when he saw that he could [not?] run things to suit himself, and the Reform League began to see that they would have to use some means to hold him down. It was at that time that these parties met in a place not far from the present Government building and finally made plans by which James Dowsett was deputized to call on Liliuokalani, then heir to the throne, to see if she would accept the throne if her brother abdicated. That was said to be Ashford's scheme. Dowsett came back with the answer that Liliuokalani was favorably inclined towards the idea and that she would send somebody to consult with the plotters. That 'somebody' came on the very evening, but everybody was disgusted on discovering who he was." *Pacific Commercial Advertiser*, March 29, 1900.

anything since the King vetoed Military—Gov. [and] police bills. [I] told him if it was particularly necessary if the King abdicate[s] I would—if The King was doing wrong—I would, but not till then. In the evening I went and told the King.

Told C_____ of it and went to [the tableau] rehearsal at Leihulu's. Slept at Washington Place.

*Wednesday, December 21.* Still getting ready for Tableau.[135]

*Thursday, December 22.* Evening went to the Wedding of Marie, one of the scholars of Kawaiahao Seminary. Mr. W. R. Castle waited on me to my seat. Kaiulani and Helen [Cleghorn] were there. During the evening Castle asked to see me next day—I acquiesced—at ten A.M. came home—went to Keala [Hale] [for] Tapas [quilts]—took it home.

*Friday, December 23.* Ten A.M. Mr. Castle came according to promise. He wanted to know if I would take the throne, or go to the King and influence him to sign bills. [I] said he could explain it better than I—for me, I could not sit on a throne where violence was used to my brother.[136] Very good rehearsal—and very tired.

*Saturday, December 24.* Busy at Kaumakapili [Church] decorating,[137] two P.M. received a Christmas present of $100.00 from H. W. Schmidt for 2d Division Liliuokalani Education[al] Society [and] $10.00 from Theodore Cramp for same.[138] Made $114.00 at door, $211 after from tickets, $335.00,

---

135. The tableau was being planned as part of the December 24 entertainment at Kaumakapili Church in aid of the Second Division of the Liliuokalani Educational Society.

136. Liliuokalani provides an account of an exchange with Castle in *Hawaii's Story*, 218–21. Lorrin Thurston, in his memoirs, says that he never knew of "any negotiations between W. R. Castle and Liliuokalani," and that upon reading such a statement in her book, he asked Castle for a clarification. According to Thurston, Castle then provided the following written statement: "It had been repeatedly asserted to me that Liliuokalani was scheming to force her brother to abdicate in her favor. This came to me from so many sources, that I decided to hear from her own mouth what her intentions were. I accordingly waited upon the lady, and stated to her that I was informed that she thought Kalakaua should abdicate in her favor, and further I was informed that if he did so abdicate, she would accept the position of sovereign. I thereupon asked her if she had been correctly quoted, and if she would, in fact, accept the position if it were offered to her. To my inquiries, she gave me a positive statement that she thought her brother should abdicate, and that if he did, she would accept the position as sovereign." Hawaii State Archives, Thurston Papers, manuscript of memoirs, 561–63. A slightly edited version appears in Thurston's published *Memoirs*, 178–79. The document provided by Castle to Thurston has not been located.

137. The decorating was in preparation for a concert to be held on December 24 by the Second Division of the Liliuokalani Educational Society. The *Daily Bulletin*, December 23, 1887, commented: "The concert to be given at Kaumakapili Church tomorrow evening promises to be a great success. The program has been published and is a full and attractive one. The money derivable from this concert will be applied to a most worthy object, namely the education of Hawaiian girls on the English tongue. As already stated in the *Bulletin* there are several pupils at Kawaiahao school and two day pupils at Miss Corney's school, maintained by the Liliuokalani Educational Society. The intention of Princess Liliuokalani and the lady members of this society is to raise a fund, the interest of which will be devoted to educational work."

The concert program, published in another column of the *Daily Bulletin*, lists two tableaus, "Othello and Desdemona" and "Sculpture," in part one, and two tableaus, "Le Gynecée" and "Gems and Jewels," in the second part.

138. Heinrich W. Schmidt (b. 1846, Bremen, Germany–d. 1910, Honolulu) was a Honolulu merchant. In a letter, he said: "Your Royal Highness will kindly excuse my absence from

making $435.00. $19 from Isabella [Achi]—makes $454.00 and some more to be returned.

*Sunday, December 25.* Went to Kaumakapili Sunday School Celebration.
*Monday, December 26.* Went to Palace, told King of plans, and also told him of $1,000 [needed] for Mrs. [Gina] Wilcox. He said he hadn't the money [and] that I should try to get something for Wilcox to do. Told her of it. She is nearly heartbroken—wished she had not married him.[139]

*Tuesday, December 27.* Rec'd $28.75 from Kaehuwahanui and $4.50 from Carrie Wilcox.

**Wednesday, January 4, 1888.** Lulu a ka Hui Hoonaauao [proceeds for the Hui Hoonaauao] $5.45—hui me $418.00.

[This list appears below:]
    Poomaikelani's tickets   37.58
    & Hui   5.45
    418.00
    455.95   [total]

[The diary ends thus.]

---

the Concert tonight on account of the Christmas festivals [in] my family circle. At the same time I am anxious to contribute my share towards the grand object of the Liliuokalani Society and therefore enclose herein a bank note for $100 for the education of a Hawaiian girl. Mrs. Schmidt considers this her best Christmas present and joins me in the best wishes for the Society and its Members." Hawaii State Archives, Liliuokalani Collection, Box 5, December 24, 1887.

The *Pacific Commercial Advertiser*, December 26, 1887, mentioned Theodore Cramp's arrival December 24 from San Francisco on the *Alameda*, and identified him as "of the ship-building firm of William Cramp & Son, Philadelphia."

139. Gina Wilcox made her dissatisfaction with her husband, the islands, and Liliuokalani abundantly clear in the memoir she issued under the pseudonym of "Mantea." She obtained a papal divorce in 1895 on the grounds that Wilcox was not a Catholic when they married, and she obtained a civil divorce in 1900. She died in Rome on March 27, 1916. Gina Sobrero, *An Italian Baroness in Hawaii: The Travel Diary of Gina Sobrero, Bride of Robert Wilcox, 1887*, trans. Edgar C. Knowlton (Honolulu: Hawaiian Historical Society, 1991), 191.

*Elizabeth Kapoli Kamakau, one of Liliu's closest friends and often mentioned in her letters and diaries. They had known each other always, went to school together, and were both talented musicians and composers of Hawaiian songs. Kapoli lived for long periods of time in the Charles R. Bishop household, as well as in that of Princess Ruth Keelikolani. Her continual presence in both households suggests that Kapoli had a family relationship with Pauahi and Keelikolani rather than simply the status of a trusted retainer.*
Menzies Dickson, circa 1882, Hawaii State Archives

# 1888

*Sunday, January 1, 1888.* Went to Kawaiahao [Church] to begin a new year in wiping away all feeling of animosity of the past year away, towards [blank], maybe he will leave politics aside hereafter. Went to see Aholo and Mrs. Dominis—[then] to Kaiulani and Archie—not [at home?]

*Monday, January 2.* Made great preparations for Ball 2nd Division [of the Liliuokalani Educational Society]. Told John to bring Capt. Wiseman.[1] Ten A.M. King had reception.[2]

All the opposition [party] were there except Dole, Jones, Castle, Austin, Thurston, Rice, Waterhouse, Young.[3] Came home rested, in evening went down to Armory. It was decorated very prettily.[4] Everyone dressed well, and gents in dress coats and gloves. Sir William Wiseman, Capt. of HBMS [*Caroline*], came on to the ball as well as many officers of USS *Vandalia* and *Mohican*. Mr. A. Herbert attended me.

*Tuesday, January 3.* Had a meeting of 2d Division Liliu Educational Society. Contributed $5.45. After meeting went over to [see] Poomaikelani—to count monies rec'd from concert. $502.25—from Concert [of] Dec. 24, 1887. Expenses $85.28, leaves $418.97—$321.50 Poomaikelani's tickets—$6.45 from Joe and Hui—make $455.95. Joe [brought?] $45.00 from Waimanalo Stocks for Kaipo at 7½. [Entry at foot of page:] Keala 7.

*Wednesday, January 4.* Jennie Clark took from me to A. J. Cartwright $415.95 being original amount—$40.00 was taken out to pay Violet and Marie Puuohau's Tuition. This $415.95 belongs to 2d Division Liliuokalani Educational Society.

THE DIARY FOR 1888
1 JAN 1888–
5 JAN 1889

Hawaii State Archives

---

1. Sir William Wiseman was a captain in the Royal Navy and a ninth baronet (b. 1845–d. 1893). Wiseman had arrived on HBMS *Caroline* December 23, 1887, from San Francisco, and during the ship's visit of almost five months, he and the Cleghorns became great friends.

2. The next day, the *Pacific Commercial Advertiser* reviewed the occasion: "Yesterday their Majesties the King and Queen held a New Year's reception at Iolani Palace, between the hours of 11 A.M. and one P.M. The reception took place in the throne room and was largely attended.... Those present in the throne room in attendance were H.R.H. Princess Liliuokalani, H.R.H. Princess Kaiulani, His Excellency Governor Dominis, and Hon A. S. Cleghorn. Among those who paid their respects were the Chief Justice, members of the Diplomatic and Consular Corps, Justice of the Supreme Court, members of the Legislature and Privy Council, and a large number of our prominent citizens."

3. The Opposition Party members were Sanford Dole, Peter C. Jones, William R. Castle, Jonathan Austin, Lorrin Thurston, William H. Rice, Henry Waterhouse, and Alexander Young. The word "except" would appear to be a mistake—she probably meant "including," since the *Advertiser* report specifically said that many of the men she mentions were in fact attendees.

4. "The interior of the building was tastefully decorated and a large number of people were present.... A string band played for dancing." *Pacific Commercial Advertiser*, January 3, 1888.

Wakeke had to take Kalei from me, and I had to take Keala away and place her in Miss Corney's school.[5]

Mrs. Wilcox went to consult Mr. Schaefer about tickets to raise money on her earrings.[6] Mrs. Damon came to see me about supporting one or two of John Sheldon's children. Joe, Wakeke, and Kuaiwa and Kimekona[7] return to Waikiki to stay till house for nets is finished.

[Below entry:] 7½ Keala was tipsy and cross.

*Thursday, January 5.* Schaefer called to arrange to raise $500.00 to pay Mrs. [Robert] Wilcox's way to Italy.

Received $17.00 for 17 shares of PIR Co. [People's Ice and Refrigeration Co.] at $1.00 a month. Miss Alexander came to offer [money] from Atherton[8] to educate Keala. Five of these shares are for 2d Div. Liliuokalani Education[al] Society. Jennie came in to see about monies that Poomaikelani gave. I told her. Jennie Clark tells me Poomaikelani has $1.00 for Hui 2d. M [Mokuna, Division]—added to $5.00 of PIR Co. makes $6.00.

Mr. and Mrs. Wilcox came in my buggy. I start on brake and Prince behaves badly and it is an escape for me. John came for me and takes me to Washington Place.

*Friday, January 6.* Took Mrs. Wilcox's subscription paper back to Schaefer and told him to go to A. J. Cartwright for $20.00 for me. Went to see Sophie [Sheldon] and children.

Three P.M. Went to Engine House No. 1. to meet 1st Division [Liliuokalani Hui Hoonaauao]. Only Leihulu [Kapena], Annie and Mary Buckle, Mrs. Kaulukou, and myself. The last contributed $3.50—the others 50 cts each, took it to Lou [Louisa Brickwood]. She was sick and on the sofa with Archie [Cleghorn] by her side. Came home after tea, sat up till ten o'clock to figure up my accounts. Mr. and Mrs. [Robert] Wilcox out. John came, I was out.

*Saturday, January 7.* Joe left certificates for Kamakanoe [for] three shares in P.I.R. [People's Ice and Refrigeration] Co. No. 231—I pass it over to her with $3.00 and still hold one for Kaipo and Bros. No. 232 in the same Co., for three shares—and $8.00—one for Liliuokalani Hui Hookuonoono for six shares No. 233—in same Co., and six dollars and one for L. H. Hoonaauao for five shares and $5.00 [certificate] No. 234 in same Co.

Drove Mrs. Wilcox to Waikiki—and Mr. Wilcox has $81.50 in my safe.

*Sunday, January 8.* Stayed at home all day.

---

5. Miss Sarah Frances Corney (d. April 12, 1903, Honolulu, age 77) had been a resident for 66 years, and was long the principal of the Pohukaina School at 43 Punchbowl Street.

6. Gina Wilcox says in her memoir: "I arrived at the Italian Consul's [Schaefer's] with my jewels, and I begged him to hold them in exchange for a sum that might permit my husband and me to leave this hateful country as soon as possible." The reason she gives for leaving was that "the government have decreed the death of my husband." This was not so. Wilcox was unemployed and broke. *An Italian Baroness in Hawaii*, 122.

7. Kuaiwa is listed as "Hostler, HRH. Princess Liliuokalani, res. King above Liliha Streets" in the 1888 City Directory. Kimekona appears in the same directory as a seaman with the Inter-Island Steam Navigation Co.

8. Joseph Ballard Atherton (b. 1837, Boston–d. April 7, 1903, Honolulu) was of the firm Castle & Cooke.

*Monday, January 9.* Gave Kamakanoe her certificate for three shares in P.I.R. [People's Ice and Refrigeration] Co. This is Aimoku's birthday, five years old. John sent a pig.

Keamalu went to Court but his case did not come off. Went to town but could not find Mariane. Kamakanoe told many things about Kapo and money. R. [Robert] Boyd seems to think it would be well to have revolution. I disabuse his mind on that matter.[9]

John came for me to see about nurse [for his mother]. After tea Joe and I drive to band [concert], then went to Washington Place. How cold. Carrie Wilcox gave me six dollars for Mrs. [Robert] Wilcox. Spoke about dance—said they might have my stables. Bought napkins and took them to Prissilla [sic] to sew.[10]

*Tuesday, January 10.* Went to Mrs. Allen's to see about lunch and went to Kaipo's. Joe took me to Mary Ailau's—bought $10 of songbooks.[11] Saw Archie at English Club, [he] told me Kaiulani was sick. Keala [Hale].

Met three members of 1st Division [Liliuokalani Hui Hoonaauao]. No meeting.

John Kalama's case came off today, decided in his favor.[12]

*Wednesday, January 11.* John brought news of [his] Aunt Lee's death. We went together for Mariane—will get lunch for us tomorrow.

Mrs. Wilcox gave me two tickets for Mrs. Allen, Nos. 98 and 100. He [Mr. Robert Wilcox] applied to Mr. Bishop as clerk in bank—did not get it. David Crowningburg came to borrow money—poor fellow.

*Thursday, January 12.* Am busy all day getting ready for my lunch at two for Mrs. Wilcox. Mr. Cochelet,[13] Mr. Schaefer,[14] Mrs. and Miss Canavarro,[15] Mr. and Mrs. Bouliech,[16] Father Sylvester,[17] my two [boys], and

9. Robert Napunako Boyd (b. Sept. 3, 1864–d. September 9, 1914, Honolulu), the brother of James H. Boyd, was at this point an unemployed and frustrated job seeker, who would the next year act on his revolutionary ideas. In his testimony during the trial of Albert Loomens, another follower of the July 30, 1889, Wilcox Revolution, Boyd gave the following reasons for joining that movement: "I was sent to be educated in Italy where I got my diploma; and when [I] came back I was simply a street vagabond. I applied to the government for position and they offered me a very inferior one. I did not want to hurt the King but to put the Ministers out of office." *Pacific Commercial Advertiser*, October 11, 1889.

10. Possibly this was Priscilla Hinu Puuohau.

11. This is *Ka Buke o na Leo Mele Hawaii* [*The Book of Hawaiian Songs for the Good and Happiness of Hawaiian Homes*] (Honolulu: *Pacific Commercial Advertiser*, 1888), first advertised in the *Hawaiian Gazette*, January 7, 1888, with the comment: "The compilers are Keakaokalani and J. M. Bright, members of the Hawaiian Glee Club—the opening song is 'Hawaii Ponoi.'"

12. In October 1887, Judge John Kalama of Makawao was charged with embezzlement, specifically that he had accepted $51.00 from one Akao of Kula for a retail store license, which he had apparently overlooked or forgotten about. A trial took place at Lahaina on December 30, 1887. Kalama pled not guilty. The court granted a change of venue to Honolulu, with a trial before a Hawaiian jury. On January 10, 1888, the jury returned a verdict of not guilty. Hawaii State Archives, First Circuit Court, Criminal 1217.

13. Adrien Laurent Cochelet was consul and commissaire of France, residing at 96 Hotel Street. He departed from Hawaii on March 10, 1888.

14. Frederick August Schaefer (b. 1836–d. 1920) was consul of Italy.

15. Antonio de Souza Canavarro was commissioner and consul of Portugal.

16. George Bouliech was chancellor of the French Legation (he departed from Hawaii on March 10, 1888).

17. Father Sylvester was the principal of Saint Louis College.

John and I. Dr. McGrew did not come. Very pleasant affair—Band played. 7½ P.M. Eveline [Wilson] helped me today. All went to meet Capt. W. Wiseman Bart, of HBMS *Caroline*. Met Mirlees and Miss Watson.[18] Came home tired [illegible].

*Friday, January 13.* Ten A.M. Mary Ailau brought me 13 copies of Keaka's Song Book. Paid her $10.00—Gave Kaakaole $2.00.

Sent Carrie Bush $12.50 for herself [and] $20.00 to get clothes for Kaipo. Kuaiwa went for her and Kaipo and Aimoku to take to store to buy clothes. The *Min*[19] arrived today [from London] with my carriage and box. Monday [it] will be opened.[20] Mr. and Mrs. Wilcox—gone to Mrs. Bouliech.

*Saturday, January 14.* Parties came to me and asked if I would consent to take the throne. I gave them the same answer as I gave to the [Hawaiian] League, that is, "I would take it when he abdicates" not otherwise.

Gave Joe Aea $3.00 one for John, $1 for Lydia, $1 for Hana, from Ice Co.

*Sunday, January 15.* Had to stay at home on account of politics. I am glad to see how the people are beginning to show some interest in the state of affairs of the present day. This party is the "Hawaiian League,"[21] very reasonable requests they make, but [I] will not do anything until he [Kalakaua] abdicates of his own accord.

*Monday, January 16.* W. [Wilson] comes in to consult W. [Wilcox] on matters of importance. I advise them to use only respectful words and no threats, but to explain the situation to him [Kalakaua] how everything and the state of the Country might be changed should he abdicate, if only for a year. Then he should take the reins again, and reign peaceably the rest of his life. W. and W. went to the King, and after explanations, he told them he would think it over.[22] I waited at Hinano Bower. Can [Entry ends abruptly thus.]

18. A mistake. Liliu actually met Scottish visitors Mr. and Mrs. Renny Watson and Miss Mirrlees. See footnote for January 18, 1888, diary entry (175).

19. The British bark *Min* had also arrived with "the large new organ for Kaumakapili Church... packed in eleven large cases," which both the queen and Princess Liliuokalani had heard played in London the previous year. "The advent of such a large and powerful organ marks a new era in the musical history of the Hawaiian Islands," commented the *Pacific Commercial Advertiser*, January 14, 1888.

20. The arrival of Liliu's new carriage, which the press did not take note of, was probably the vehicle that she later referred to in her diaries as "my state carriage."

21. Businessmen frustrated by the king's policies (particularly his veto power regarding legislative matters) formed the Hawaiian League late in 1886, and it gained power and numbers in 1887. The league was largely responsible for forcing reforms and a new constitution on Kalakaua in June of that year. A notebook listing 405 members of the league (and a draft of its constitution) is in the Hawaii State Archives, Lorrin Thurston Papers. The memoirs of Lorrin A. Thurston and of Sanford B. Dole are essential documents for an understanding of this organization.

22. According to his memoirs, Lorrin Thurston (who was then minister of the interior) obtained a written statement from Charles B. Wilson on his (Wilson's) and Wilcox's evening interview with the king in the garret tower room of Iolani Palace: "We found the King alone. He asked us what we wanted; we told him that we were a committee representing those who thought the interests of the community required that he abdicate and that his sister Liliuo-

*Tuesday, January 17.* Came home. W. [Wilson] told me the result of their proposition to the King—he said [we should?] wait a while—I said yes. Then wait.

*Wednesday, January 18.* All is peace. Breakfasted at the Palace given for Mr. and Mrs. [Renny] Watson and Miss Mirrlees of Scotland.[23] Nahinu of Kona brought $16.50.

King told me, "Supposing I should sell the country, what then?"

*Thursday, January 19.* This morning telephoned for A. J. Cartwright. He came at one—gave him my list of accounts of moneys belonging to Liliuokalani Hui Hookuonoono—it amounted to $3, $343.95, and $1,390.40, the money contributed in 1887. He instructed me to get the mortgage so as to cancel it from the Hui.

*Saturday, January 21.* There was a Luau at Kanoa's at five P.M. There were speeches made at Armory by Wilcox before the people [and] he ended by getting them to appoint committee of five to ask King's opinion on state of Government.[24] They went—no King to receive them, he was at [Kanoa's] Luau. King said to Kanoa that I was Kipi [rebellious], [and] that when he said to me he was going to sell country, I looked displeased—so what he said on Wednesday was a threat. I don't care what he does but I fear that Million [dollar loan] will burn his fingers.

John went to Waialua with Miles. Hinano Bower, Mary Cook went to help Miss Davis nurse Mother [Dominis].[25]

---

kalani be made queen. He demanded our reasons; we gave them. He argued with us and continued the argument until nearly 11 o'clock. Finally we told him that the question was no longer open to argument, that we wished him to abdicate voluntarily; if he did not do so, we should be obliged to remove him by force. He replied: 'Well, gentlemen, if that is your decision, I do not agree with you, and you will have to do what you think best.' Our committee withdrew." Hawaii State Archives, Thurston Collection, manuscript of memoirs, 181–83.

23. Mirrlees Watson Co. was a Glasgow manufacturer of sugar mills and other machinery. The *Hawaiian Gazette*, January 24, 1888, in commenting on the palace breakfast, noted: "During His Majesty's visit to Europe in 1881, he made a special visit to Scotland, where he enjoyed the generous hospitality of Mr. Watson and Mr. Mirrlees in Glasgow and the Highlands. One of the great features of the visit was a trip to Loch Lomond, Scotland's most beautiful lake."

24. "Robert W. Wilcox addressed a crowd of natives on Saturday from the steps of the Armory. From what he said there is evidently trouble ahead. A committee of five was appointed to wait on the King in regard to the present situation, to report at another meeting to be held today." *Pacific Commercial Advertiser*, January 23, 1888. The *Hawaiian Gazette*, January 24, 1888, had a more expansive notice: "An impromptu mass meeting of natives took place Saturday evening, in the vacant lot between the Brewer and the Pacific Navigation Co.'s buildings. Mr. Robert Wilcox mounted the old armory steps and harangued the crowd, dwelling mostly on wrongs he had sustained at the hands of the Government on declining to make a place for him in the public service after expending large sums of the public money in educating him abroad.... After this gentleman had expended all the eloquence at his disposal ... he gave away to the illustrious J. M. Poepoe."

25. Miss Mary Jane Davis (b. 1841, Eastcombe, Gloucestershire, England–d. January 11, 1930, Honolulu) became a member of the Washington Place household as nurse for Mary Dominis in 1888 and remained in the household until Liliu's death in 1917. Miss Davis was a sister of the Reverend Samuel H. Davis (b. 1838–d. 1926), for many years pastor of Christ Church at Kealakekua, Hawaii.

*Sunday, January 22.* Stayed home till four P.M. Went to see Kaiulani. She was well. Rec'd a letter from Kapoli telling me that she had been reported to Board of Health and perhaps will be sent to Kalawao.[26] Poor Lizzie—sat thinking of her all evening and writing Music.

*Monday, January 23.* Wilcox and committee went up to get answer from King—he refused to receive them till Chamberlain came back from trip round the island with Sir William Wiseman. Saw Antone Rosa about Puu's mortgage, [and] also Kuihelani's. Puu's Mortgage was $200.00 at 12 pct. for five years since '84. Saw Charlie [Wilson], asked me to come up. Eight P.M. I went. Talked over events. Heard that [the Hawaiian] League is only waiting to press me to accept the throne. Strange I should hear something about it every day. Came back to Washington Place. John came home from Waialua. Mother [Dominis] no change.

*Tuesday, January 24.* After breakfast J. Waiamau came to tell me of meeting tomorrow afternoon three P.M.—after that, he told me the people were very much against the King's weakness, and would I take the throne if he abdicates. I said I would. They said they would call a meeting to see the King. This is another party [to address the subject] yet without knowing one of the other.

*Thursday, January 26.* Paina Kapu [private meal] at Keala [Hale].

*Friday, January 27.* Drew from A. J. Cartwright $713.00 of Hui Hoonaauao 2d [Division]. Invested $665.00 in Ice Co. stocks, which makes seven shares at $95.00 a share—took one for me, three for Aimoku, making 11 shares altogether. Went to drive with Mary Carter.

*Saturday, January 28.* Received certificates in PIR Co.[27] one for me No. 241—three shares for J. Aimoku. No. 240—seven shares for Hui Liliuokalani Hoonaauao No. 242. These were given me today by J. Ena.

Today I returned to A. J. Cartwright two Ice Stock certificates No. 242—with seven shares—No. 234 holding five shares—and $50.00 besides. 3½ P.M. went to call on Mrs. Campbell with Mary Carter and Liliu [Carter].

*Sunday, January 29.* Told Wakeke to give notice of Meeting of H[ooulu] Lahui at ten Thursday the 2d of February, three P.M. First Div. [to meet] the same day. Drove in my carriage to Archie's [Archie Cleghorn's] where John was. Sir William Wiseman, Mr. Schaeffer, Lou Brickwood, Bonny Monsarrat, Mr. Giffard[28] were [also] there. John got in and we came home. It is a very easy carriage, My State Carriage, on horses.

---

26. Elizabeth (Lizzie) Kapoli Kamakau was not admitted to the Kakaako holding station until March 1, 1888. She was then sent to Kalaupapa. See diary entry for May 1, 1888 (184). She died at Kalaupapa on July 27, 1891, age 39.

27. People's Ice and Refrigeration Co. (John M. Sass was president and manager, Peter M. Sass was vice president, and John Ena Jr. was treasurer and secretary) incorporated on February 7, 1885. The company, which initially offered ice for purchase at one cent per pound, merged with the Union Ice Co. in 1890, and eventually was sold to the Hawaiian Electric Co. and dissolved in March 1902.

28. Walter M. Giffard (b. 1856, Island of Jersey–d. July 1, 1929, Honolulu) and his part-Hawaiian wife (Martha Brickwood, sister of Louisa) were close friends of the Cleghorn family.

*Monday, January 30.* Stayed at home, not feeling well. 7½ P.M. went to C.R.B. [C. R. Bishop's residence.] Cordie [Allen] was suffering with sore eye. Told W. F. Allen [we] wanted $60 for Kaakaole.

Told Bishop what the King had said about Kauikeaouli and Liholiho [Kings Kamehameha III and Kamehameha II]. Bishop said he wanted inscriptions of plates of those [coffins] placed in Bernice's vault. I said [I] would get it from [Charles] Wilson.

Was in a feverish state. Slept at Washington Place. Mrs. Dominis is pretty well out of mind.

This month Liliuokalani Hui Hoonaauao will draw $12.00 of Ice Stocks left in A. J. Cartwright's hands.

*Tuesday, January 31.* Must get money from A. J. Cartwright. Did not do it. Mr. and Mrs. Kuihelani, Mrs. Emma Nakuina, [and] A. Rosa met to consult about transferring Mortgage from Liliuokalani Hui Hookuonoono to me—but did not do much. Then Huaka Kuihelani wanted to know the amount as he might give it to Sam Parker to pay it up. Kaehuwahanui [Mrs. Kuihelani] is not willing. Rosa said he would take papers of transfer out and give them to A. J. Cartwright. So there is another delay of I don't know how long.

Kunane [Kalakaua] went to Kona [on the *Kinau*] to find Kamehameha's bones and bring them to [the Royal] Mausoleum.

Saw Kapoli and tried to persuade her to make up her mind to go to Kalawao.

[Allen] Herbert said he would send pair [of] horses for me.

---

King Kalakaua's search for ancestral remains for the mausoleum resulted in his obtaining in Kona the bones (in braided caskets) of the chiefs Umi and Liloa (son and father), and another bundle in kapa (bark cloth) said to contain the bones of Kamehameha I. These were placed in the Royal Mausoleum of Hawaii in Nuuanu, subject to the ownership of Prince Jonah Kuhio Kalanianaole. In 1918, Kalanianaole suggested to Governor Lucius Eugene Pinkham that the remains be removed to the Bishop Museum based on their "great historical value, and I know of no better place than the Museum from which may be learned all of the historical value which may be taught by them."[29] The bones were removed from the mausoleum on March 15, 1918. In one of the bundles examined at the museum was found a gold signet ring and a letter of Kalakaua, dated February 8, 1888. The translated text of the letter is as follows:

> ¶ This ring was placed with the bones of Kamehameha I on the night of Kane, in the month of Hilina (of the Naua calculation), which is the 8th day of February, A D 1888. As a means of remembering the day, his bones were deposited in this Royal Mausoleum, at Kawananakoa, in the city of Honolulu, Island of Oahu, of the Hawaiian Islands.

29. Hawaii State Archives, Governor's Files, Letter from Kalanianaole to Governor Lucius E. Pinkham, Washington, DC, January 15, 1918. Translator unknown.

Which were discovered at the secret cave of Kahiku-o-ka-Moku by Kapalu Kamalama, and from him to the King, on the 5th day of February, Sunday, on the Ahupuaa [land division] of Kaloko, in the Ili Aina [subdivision] of Kiikii, in North Kona, Island of Hawaii, and Nahale, Kahoo Palapala, the witnesses.

[These] Were placed on board the ship *Malulani* on the evening of the 6th, arriving at Honolulu, at Iolani Hale, at four o'clock of the afternoon of the 7th, where same were kept for the time being, and on the night aforementioned, were placed on the Mausoleum, in the presence of witnesses, Her Royal Highness Princess Poomaikelani, Major J. K. Kahalewai, Kauai, and Wahinekona. Done on this 8th day of February, AD 1888. (signed) Kalakaua.

In 1994, persons active in the repatriation of Native Hawaiian remains removed the bones from Bishop Museum to an undisclosed location.

---

*Wednesday, February 1.* Drew $400.00 [added above: and $135] from A. J. Cartwright, my monthly allowance, and Kaipo's dues of Waimanalo Stocks since Sept. to Jan. 31, which amounted to $135—the whole amounting to $535.00. Bought a book for Mr. Wilson to write his inscriptions of plates on coffins at Mausoleum—cost $1.75.

Had message from Archie reminding me of the anniversary of Sister's death tomorrow. He thought it bad taste to have my reception [that day]. If he were only true to her memory, for I hear he had proposed to Lou [Louisa Brickwood].[30]

7½ P.M. went to Wilson's—spent evening there.

*Thursday, February 2.* The anniversary of Like's death. Did not have reception. Kaiulani and others took flowers to her grave.

*Friday, February 3.* Liliuokalani Hui Hoonaauao contributed $6.20.

Received. $3,343.96 from A. J. Cartwright, at ten A.M., at Muolaulani. Took the whole amount to pay members of Hui Kuonoono at Mary Ailau's. All [Hui members] met there for Hui Hoonaauao. Poomaikelani present. Contributed $5.45—after that, the other Hui [members] were paid off: 35 members at $66.87—15 at $3.87—28 at various contributions, some $50.00 one $40, four at $45.00, three at $35.00, eight at $25.00, two at $20, and today they were discharged and Hui broken up today for good.

This afternoon went to Kaumakapili—no meeting. Appoint [meeting] for Monday ten A.M. Slept at Washington Place. Mrs. Dominis seems very bright.

*Saturday, February 4.* Went and sat with [Luther] Aholo—talked politics, he seemed inclined to blame Wilcox, but when I explained all, he said King should abdicate.

Mrs. Dominis not so well. Took piece of grass cloth from her drawer to Mrs. Townsend to make shroud. Went to Mary Ailau to luau given by Hui Kuonoono—a farewell to me [from the members].

---

30. If he did so, nothing came of it.

Received $190.00 from Kahuila [Wilcox,] $190 from Makanoe, $380 from three Buckles,[31] $95 from Meeau and Kalahiki each, $190 [from] [Lizzie] Nakanealoha, $95—from Kaipo, and $95 [from] myself to buy shares in Ice Co. stocks, making 14 shares—Kaipo [Aea] has $40.00 and I borrow $55, from [name erased] to fill in another share for him. He has money in W. S. [Waimanalo stocks] so he can pay it back next month.

*Sunday, February 5.* Was naughty all day—counted money instead of going to church. May I be forgiven.

*Monday, February 6.* I will put in Mr. Ena's hands by Joe H[eleluhe] $1,425: $145 in gold $400, in silver, $880 paper—sent $93.37 to Archie for Kaiulani's H.K. [Hui Kuonoono], $111.37 to Geo. Smithies, M. [Mary?] Stillman's share in Hui Kuonoono, $5.00 to Emma Nakuina—so these parties are all paid. Gave to Aiaumoe $37.74, the amount left of Meeau and Kalahiki's money. The amount of $1,425.00 is to buy 15 shares in Ice Co., two to Kahuila [Wilcox], two [for] Kamakanoe, two [for] Kaipo, four [for] Buckles, two to Makaihona and Kalahiki, two [for] [Lizzie] Nakanealoha, one to me.

Breakfasted in Palace. Asked Queen to hunt up papers of transfer of lots on Hamohamo—said she would. [She] told me Annie Dowsett tried to get Hui Hooulu Lahui to buy $3,500.00 of stuff belonging to Major [the entry continues on the previous page] Hill, Tahiti Lemonade man.[32] Society could not "see it" unless she endorsed the amount.

John came for me to go up with him—was overjoyed at decision in favor of King's veto.[33]

Band [at] Emma Square—Hinano Bower. Heard of her [person unknown] illness, thin, very thin—E mihi mua iau [She should first apologize to me]. Kahuila [Wilcox] ma [and associates] came and went without

31. These were probably the children of William Wahinepio K. Buckle (d. 1884, Honolulu). Buckle was part Hawaiian and came from a chiefly family. He was a member of the Privy Council at the time of his death.

32. This was Major F. J. Hills, who with one "Nuu Vahine" was proprietor of the Tahiti Lemonade Works at "Sunny South" and of a depot on Hotel Street. In December 1887, Hill sold the lemonade business to John E. Brown for $3,000. When Brown took over in January 1888, he discovered a deficient inventory. Instead of 800 dozen bottles (valued at $600), only 300 dozen could be found, and additionally the essences used in the bottling process were inferior and valueless. Brown took Hill to court in April 1889, but Hill seems to have skipped town for Los Angeles. Hawaii State Archives, First Circuit Court, Law 2779.

33. This was a Supreme Court decision regarding the case of *Everett v. Baker*. A seemingly minor matter, in fact the case directly challenged the king's veto powers under the 1887 constitution. Thomas Everett, the plaintiff and sheriff of Maui, by virtue of the Governor's Duties Act passed by the last legislature, sought to secure the transfer of certain records pertaining to the office of Governor Robert Hoapili Baker of that island. The king had returned that act with a message setting forth reasons why he refused to sign it, and the question now before the court was whether the king's refusal required the assent of the cabinet or was an individual right of the monarch. The justices paid specific attention to article 48 of the 1887 constitution, which they acknowledged "was the intention of its framers to curtail the King's power on government," and in summation decided that the "Act to provide for the discharge heretofore performed by the Governors of the different Islands" had not become law, as the king had disapproved it in the manner provided for by the constitution. The decision thus upheld the king's veto power. Those present in the court when the decision was announced and read included Dominis, C. R. Bishop, and Curtis Iaukea. The court decision was printed in full in the *Pacific Commercial Advertiser*, February 8, 1889.

their certificates. Poomaikelani told me Mokihana stole $5—belonging to Hui Hoonaauao.

*Tuesday, February 7.* Rec'd one certificate in Ice Co. for me, No. 245 (two shares)—one for Kaipo Aea [Joe Kaiponohea Aea], No. 247—two for Kamakaihona and Kalahiki, No. 248. Gave Kahuila [Wilcox] certificates for two shares, Kamakanoe the same, [Lizzie] Nakanealoha two—three Buckle girls, four shares in Ice Stocks—Rec'd amount for 12 shares and $86.00 for Kuonoono, which I must send to A. J. Cartwright. He must have drawn or ought to draw $12.00 for 12 shares in Ice Stocks for Hui Hoonaauao Liliuokalani.

*Wednesday, February 8.* Ten A.M. met Hui Hooulu Lahui and heard their report [concerning] One old woman at Kalaepohaku, two old men at Kawa and one woman—will send round again to see them.[34]

Three P.M. had meeting at Engine [Company] No. 1, only nine members. Postponed till next Tuesday. Made five calls. Spent night here—too dark to go out.

*Thursday, February 9.* Kaehuwahanui [Mrs. Kuihelani] placed $20.00 in Silver and [$]20 in gold for Hoopii to invest for them—and the former left $95 to buy shares in Ice Co. [Reverend J.] Waiamau wants me to give a Concert for benefit of Kaumakapili church.

Mary Beckley had a dream—King said he would come here. Mrs. Iaukea invites me to bring ladies in waiting to Palace Monday next [at] two P.M.

Kunane [Kalakaua] came to see me; he brought me money from Keahuolu. Aloha ino—hele a kuawehi [What a pity—things have taken a dark turn].[35] Told me to tell Wilcox to explain matters with Austin Minister [of] Foreign Affairs.[36] He wanted me to arrange matters with Queen about kuleanas [native land claims] in Hamohamo. He wanted to lease Keahuolu at $200 a year, for 10 years. I gave my consent.[37]

*Friday, February 10.* King went to Kailua [Kona] with Iolani Club.[38] Will not be back for three weeks. Signed bond Bishop & Co. for Amt. of $341.97 supposed amt. invested [in] 1874—for Emma Watson ($45.00) for John, Carrie, Hannah Aea—($45.00) each, and Kaipo Aea $75.00 since 1882—and Kulamanu in 1886—$27.00.

*Saturday, February 11.* Gave .50 to Joe to post letters—$6.00 to pay back to Ice Co. with list of shares that I hold for me, Kaipo, John Aea, and sisters Makaihona and Kalahiki and $2.00 for Wild Fruit Cure[39] and Alcohol.

*Alameda* arrived [at] seven this morn.—will leave at ten tonight. Mr. and Mrs. [Robert] Wilcox will go in her to San Francisco. Telephoned to order express for them, 7½ P.M. They bade me good-bye. Perhaps I may see them again.

---

34. Kalaepohaku is a land within the Kapalama district. Kawa is a land (and a fishpond) located on the mouth (Ewa side) of the Nuuanu River.

35. The "dark turn" evidently refers to Kalakaua's financial difficulties.

36. Jonathan Austin (b. 1829, Saratoga, New York–d. December 2, 1892, Waikiki), resident of Hawaii from 1877, served as minister of foreign affairs December 28, 1887–June 17, 1890.

37. There is no record in the Bureau of Conveyances that Kalakaua actually did lease Keahuolu from Liliu, and when she did lease it later, it was for a much greater amount.

38. The Iolanis were a group of musicians.

39. This was a patent medicine.

*Sunday, February 12.* I miss Mr. and Mrs. Wilcox at breakfast, and all through the day. 11 A.M. went to church, contributed 25 cts. Came home and spent the day in wandering through the rooms. [Reverend J.] Waiamau came in. Four P.M. went to Washington Place—John is sick.

*Monday, February 13.* Gookim's[40] $3.50 debt—went to [J. T.] Waterhouse's, bought yd. of blue cashmere—McInerny's,[41] 2 hats, $16.00, 2 black suits [for] men $50.00 debt.

Four P.M. went on [my] state carriage to Palace to Queen's tea party. Kitty [Wilson], Alice Brown,[42] and Minnie Aldrich in my large carriage. Two turnouts looked well. At five we drove down to Waikiki. Queen came in with two Princes in State Carriage—Mr. and Mrs. Iaukea arrive in their new carriage, just as we were leaving. Kaiulani—stopped at Washington Place and came home. Had tea, went to concert [at] Kaumakapili. Good singing—pretty good house. Heard of Mr. Steward's death in England.[43]

*Thursday, February 16.* Busy all day. Breakfasted at Palace given to Theo [Theophilus] H. Davies, HBVC [Her British Majesty's Vice Consul] England, and nephew Mr. Jackson—John and I, Kaiulani and Archie, two Princes, Mr. and Mrs. Iaukea.[44]

Went home, found Eveline [Wilson] at work with flowers. Had Mrs. [Mary] Carter also to help.

7½ P.M. [Muolaulani.] Guests came in. Reception was for Theo Davies and nephew—Queen, Mr. and Mrs. Iaukea, [Mr.] Bishop, and many of most prominent citizens, Cookes, Waterhouses, also many Hawaiian friends. It was a brilliant affair.[45] [Afterward] Muolaulani was stripped of all flowers, for it seemed to me as if my house was like a grave, as if death were present.

*Friday, February 17.* The servants stayed up to clear up and put things in place, then quiet once more reigned [at] Muolaulani.

*Saturday, February 18.* Joe paid $36.00 [for] Ice cream, $5.50 [for] ladies' fingers, $2.00 candies, $3.00 cake—to Hart.

*Monday, February 20.* Went around to A. J. Cartwright to see if $156.00 could not be drawn from the whole Amount, and a separate book be held for 1st Div. Liliuokalani Education[al] Society. A. J. Cartwright says we had better not as all monies were put in stocks and cannot be separated. He told me that the Liliuokalani Ed. Society had no more money in his

---

40. Goo Kim's was a dry goods and clothing store on Nuuanu Street.

41. M. McInerny, men's clothing and ladies' and gents' shoes, occupied the corner of Merchant and Fort Streets.

42. Alice Brown (b. 1871, Honolulu–d. 1943, Honolulu) was the wife of William L. Peterson. Her obituary said she was a "descendant of a royal Hawaiian family." *Pacific Commercial Advertiser*, October 22, 1943.

43. William J. Steward was the owner of Rackheath Hall near Liverpool, where Liliu and Queen Kapiolani had been entertained en route to London to attend Queen Victoria's golden jubilee in 1887.

44. On February 14, 1888, Liliu, Queen Kapiolani, and Princess Kaiulani had attended an afternoon garden party at the Davies' residence in Nuuanu Valley. The *Pacific Commercial Advertiser*, February 15, 1888, reported it as "a most brilliant affair."

45. According to the *Hawaiian Gazette*, February 21, 1888, "The mansion and grounds were brightly illuminated, the Royal Band furnished music, and a distinguished company enjoyed the pleasures of the occasion."

hands except $50.00—but I told him Liliuokalani Education[al] Society 2d Division has 12 shares in Ice stocks at $95.00 a share, that would make it then, $1,180.00 belonging to the Society, but the showing of our passbook is different—strange. That day I saw by his book [that the] Hooulu Lahui Society of Kaumakapili has $173.80 in his hands.

Slept at Washington Place. Mother [Dominis] is much better. I think she tries to slide down on purpose.

*Tuesday, February 21.* Want Keala[46] to get ready. Puuane, Naili, and Kapahi came to see about mortgage, which I want to buy—amount was $200.00.[47] They told me Hooku's son was named Kemohe—he lives at Pukuilua in Hana, Maui, near Puuiki.

[At bottom of page:] Muolaulani.

*Wednesday, February 22.* Making preparations to go to Waialua by *Kaala* tomorrow. $1.50 to Ahoi for fish for Steamer. Must leave Joe Heleluhe to take care of my new horses. Drove out to Hamohamo after some clothes. Plants all doing well. Will take Sam, Mainalulu, Ahoi, Kawelo, Keala.

Hoohana [to manage].

[At bottom of page:] Keala [Hale].

*Thursday, February 23.* Left Honolulu by Steamer *Kaala*[48] [for Waialua] with Princess Kaiulani, Rose Robertson and children, Helen Cleghorn,[49] and servants. Before we left, Kaulukou came in and told me, he had advice from Supreme [Court] bench, if [Asa] Kaulia brought suit for his amount $41.00, which Legislature deprived him of, he would gain his suit. If so, we would all recover our own salary on [the matter?] being unconstitutional.[50]

Gave Joe $20 to buy clothes for people. Left $10.00 with J. A. [Joe Aea]. John came down with us—Asked A. J. Cartwright if he could pay for hay.

*Friday, February 24.* After breakfast all went to Mrs. Gay's[51] except myself and Kawelo and few servants. Amused myself sewing. John went back to town by Steamer *Kaala*. [At] five Kaiulani and party came back, all so joyous and happy.

**Thursday, March 1.** Took *C. R. Bishop* and all returned to town. Arrived in a shower of rain. Prevailed on Archie to let Kaiulani stay here with me, for a week.

*Saturday, March 3.* Paid Carrie Bush $25.00 for February and March— towards Kaipo's board.

*Monday, March 5.* Rec'd $15. Kaipo Aea's W [Waimanalo] Stocks, also $2.00 for his two shares Ice Stocks, $3.00 for J. Aimoku's two shares Ice

---

46. Keala (w) was a servant of Liliu at Muolaulani.

47. There is no record of this mortgage in the Bureau of Conveyances. The property was probably a kuleana (native land claim) within the boundaries of Hamohamo, at Waikiki.

48. The steamer *Kaala* was built in San Francisco in 1887 for Herman A. Widemann. The Inter-Island Steam Navigation Co. acquired the boat in 1889, and it wrecked in January 1898.

49. Rose Robertson (from 1876 the wife of James W. Robertson) and Helen Cleghorn (later in the year to become the wife of James H. Boyd) were daughters of Archibald S. Cleghorn and half-sisters of Princess Kaiulani.

50. Nothing regarding this matter has been found.

51. Mrs. James Gay (Mary Ellen Richardson of Maui); her husband was the proprietor of the Mokuleia Ranch.

stocks for Kalahiki and Kamakaihona stocks $3.00 Kaipo and Bros. shares Ice stocks, $2.00 for myself—Ice Stocks. Invested $93 for Mrs. Kuihelani and have two left for her.

*Thursday, March 8.* Went out collecting money for 1st Div. Educational Society—got $3.00 from Mrs. Hill, $3 from Mrs. Coney, Lizzie and Mrs. Haalelea, $5 from Mrs. Iaukea. Planted ferns.

*Friday, March 9.* Did not sleep all night and went back to Muolaulani— sad and yet why should I be. Must pack quickly as we must be on board *J. A. Cummins* at five A.M. [for Waimanalo].

*Saturday, March 17.* J. A. Cummins' birthday, a lot of young men came over. Horse racing at noon. Four P.M. Luau. 7½ P.M. Tableaux and dancing.[52]

**Saturday, April 7.** Joe went and drew $36 belonging to Liliuokalani Hui Hoonaauao, in Ice Co. amount for last three months, which should have been drawn by A. J. Cartwright every month. ~~Must send it to him soon.~~

*Sunday, April 8.* Went to Waikiki with Jennie Clark and people [and] had bathing in the sea—luau at one—hoonoho akua [to be possessed by a spirit?] today. Was sorry to see her [Jennie] in that condition.

*Monday, April 9.* Rec'd from A. J. Cartwright amount of $341.97 cents, the supposed amount belonging to J. K. Aea—John, Lydia [Aholo], and Hannah Aea—Emma Watson[53] and Kulamanu in Bishop's Bank and whose books thro. A. J. Cartwright were supposed to be lost. Gave Carrie Bush $12.50 for Kaipo's board. Mr. and Mrs. Jas. [James] Campbell sailed today for Europe.

*Tuesday, April 10.* Went to Pawaa with the people, weeding. At 11 A.M. went to Bertha von Holt's wedding—to F. W. Glade. Splendid and grand wedding, beautiful presents.[54] They went to Kauai—band played her off.

11 years ago since Hoku died.[55]

*Friday, April 27.* Returned to town with intention of going to reception given by Honolulu Ladies to officers of ships in Port.[56]

---

52. John A. Cummins celebrated his 53rd birthday at Waimanalo on March 17 "in the most successful manner. A large party went from Honolulu including their royal highnesses the Princesses Liliuokalani, Kaiulani, and Poomaikelani. Several horse races took place in the morning, followed by a most sumptuous luau, to which all did ample justice. The health of the worthy host was drunk, amid much enthusiasm.... Mr. Gonsalves the photographer was there with his camera and took several views of the plantation, groups of the guests, and the interior of the house.... In the evening there was a grand entertainment given by the Na Lani Ehiku Minstrels." *Pacific Commercial Advertiser*, March 20, 1888.

53. Emma Watson was later Mrs. Abraham Opunui.

54. "One of the most popular and brilliant weddings that has ever been solemnized [at Saint Andrew's Cathedral] was that of yesterday when Mr. Frederick William Glade of Kekaha, Kauai, was married to Miss Bertha Louise von Holt of this city." The *Advertiser* lavishly described the flowers, the ceremony, the costumes, the reception, and the presents, which it noted as "very numerous, rare, and costly." *Pacific Commercial Advertiser*, April 11, 1888.

55. Hoku, Liliuokalani's brother William Pitt Leleiohoku, had died April 10, 1877, in Honolulu, age 22 years.

56. This was a reception given to Rear Admiral Lewis A. Kimberly and officers of the USS *Vandalia* and the USS *Adams* on Friday evening, April 27, 1888, at the Hawaiian Hotel. The *Pacific Commercial Advertiser*, April 29, 1888, called the event "one of the most brilliant and successful affairs ever given in Honolulu." Attendees included the king and staff, Prince David Kawananakoa, General Dominis, and members of the diplomatic corps. Liliuokalani appears not to have attended.

*Saturday, April 28.* Gave to Wakeke $15.00 of the amount received from Ice Stocks last 7th inst. [this month] (which amount was $36.00) of Liliuokalani Hui Hoonaauao—to pay for tuition of one girl. [Blank space follows.] Violet not being charged for having been absent a good deal. Paid $15 for Lydia Aholo.

*Monday, April 30.* Went to Berger's Auction. Bought ferns.[57] 12 P.M. went to wedding reception of Mina Widemann and J. Dowsett.[58] Finished the day by going out to Kehaulani.

Sent Mamo [feathers], Ee,[59] and red Kahili [feather standard] with tortoiseshell handle back to Mr. Bishop. Band at E. Sq. [Emma Square] did not go.

**Tuesday, May 1.** Went to Kakaako to bid Kapoli good-bye.[60] Went to lunch with Cordie Allen. Dined with Jennie Clark.

Three P.M. went to Annual Meeting of 1st Division of Liliuokalani Educational Society. Offices appointed—I am President, Lou [Louisa Brickwood], Vice President, Mrs. Brown, Secretary, Mrs. W. E. Foster, Treasurer, Alice B. [Brown], Joanna,[61] Eveline [Wilson], Mrs. Hill, Annie Buckle, Directoresses.

I paid $13.75 to Lou Brickwood, the amount received from dues unpaid from members for last year. Mr. J. H. Brown was admitted member to our Society.

*Wednesday, May 2.* Received Sir William at one P.M. Dined at two, [at] three P.M. went to Hooulu Lahui Society. Contributed $3.00, passed it to Mary Alapai to keep till required. Came home and got ready for King's ball—brilliant affair.[62] Met. W. Irving Bishop, the mind reader. Came home at four A.M. with Jimmie Boyd.

*Thursday, May 3.* 10:30 A.M. King and Iaukea left for Kailua on HBMS *Caroline*, Sir William Wiseman, Capt.[63]

57. This was an auction sale of household furniture at the residence of bandmaster Henry Berger opposite the Makiki recreation grounds. The *Pacific Commercial Advertiser*, April 30, 1888, announced, "A free bus will leave the corner of Beretania and Fort Street at 9:30 o'clock A.M. to convey intending purchasers to the sale."

58. John McKibbin Dowsett married Wilhelmine (the daughter of H. A. Widemann) at Saint Andrew's Cathedral on the morning of April 30. "At the residence of the bride's parents, Hotel Street, the newly married couple held a reception from noon to three o'clock.... Their Majesties the King and Queen, H.R.H. Princess Liliuokalani, H.R.H. Princess Kaiulani, His Excellency Governor Dominis, Hon. A. S. Cleghorn, and a large number of our leading residents attended the reception." *Pacific Commercial Advertiser*, May 1, 1888.

59. Ee are the "yellow underwing feathers of the oo bird." *Pukui-Elbert Hawaiian Dictionary*.

60. Mrs. Elizabeth (Lizzie) Kapoli Kamakau, one of Liliu's closest friends, now had a confirmed case of leprosy (the Kakaako receiving infirmary was holding her), and she was about to be sent to Kalaupapa. See footnote for January 22, 1888, diary entry (176).

61. Joanna (d. 1891) was the widow of W. N. Ladd and at this time the wife of Antone Rosa.

62. The king's ball was held in honor of Captain Sir William Wiseman of HBMS *Caroline*. The *Pacific Commercial Advertiser*, May 3, 1888, noted that Queen Kapiolani was dressed in "a magnificent robe of black velvet trimmed with costly mamo leis," the same that she had worn at Queen Victoria's golden jubilee in London.

63. The *Pacific Commercial Advertiser*, May 4, 1888, said: "Yesterday morning at 10:30 o'clock HBMS *Caroline* left the harbor with His Majesty the King on board, for Kailua, Hawaii.... When His Majesty got on board the *Caroline* the Hawaiian Flag was run up to the mainmast, and salutes were fired from the *Vandalia*, *Caroline*, *Razboynik*, *Tssukuba*, and the shore battery. In all 105 guns were fired."

*Friday, May 4.* Bought horse for Kaipo $60.00.

*Tuesday, May 8. Australia* sailed 12 P.M. Haunani and Farley[64] left in her besides [Captain] Kempff.

*Tuesday, May 15.* Spent day in [over]seeing women decorate Armory. Went with Mr. and Mrs. H. W. Schmidt and Bella Weight[65] to the Ball of 2nd Division Liliuokalani Educational Society [at the Armory]. Very pleasant affair. Got $145.40. W. Irving Bishop and Minnie Aldrich came in. Went home to Washington Place. W. I. Bishop offered to give an entertainment to assist the 2nd Division.

    Rec'd from Ball [for] Liliuokalani Hui Hoonaauao M. [Mokuna, Division] 2nd. $145.40. [Then follows a list of names and amounts totaling $217.50.]

*Wednesday, May 16.* Came back to Muolaulani. Watered my ferns. Four P.M. John came for me [and] we went in [Nuuanu] valley as far as electric [power]house.

*Thursday, May 17.* Paid bills of expenses of Ball of 2d Division—Amounted to $37.40. Makanoe sent me by Joe $2.00 for tickets. [At the foot of the page:] Keala [Hale].

*Friday, May 18.* Keala [and?] Poomaikelani gave me $5.00 for tickets $1.00 for lemonade. $1.00 for herself, making $7.00 in all.

*Saturday, May 19.* Went to see Mr. Jake Brown about W. I. Bishop's entertainment. Met at John's office. Went home with John [to Washington Place] and sent for Kaipo and Aimoku. All went to drive, and carriage broke. Had to send them home. Came back [to Muolaulani] after tea and went to Kaumakapili rehearsal.

*Sunday, May 20.* Woke up, saw my blinds had been opened—was much surprised.

*Tuesday, May 22.* King and Queen arrived from Hawaii—John went down to meet them.

*Wednesday, May 23.* Went to tell the Queen about that blind man who needed assistance. Jennie Clark with me. Met Mrs. Wilcox there and she gave Jennie $93 she had collected from tickets for ball. Inquired for the King—was out. [Below:] Mr. Saffrey [is] the Blind man.

*Thursday, May 24.* Called Makanoe and Jennie Clark—gave them $6.00 to purchase some things for the Hui Hoonaauao Children. Went to Waikiki with Jennie and Milaina,[66] Mahiai [Robinson], Aki and John came out that night. Took Kaipo and Aimoku out with us.

---

    "The *Caroline* reaches Kailua to-morrow at noon, and in the afternoon the King will give a luau in honor of Sir William Wiseman and the Officers. On Saturday the *Caroline* will leave Kailua for Esquimalt, British Columbia."

    64. Haunani Judd (b. 1865–d. 1935), the daughter of Charles H. Judd, had married Arthur Christopher Farley in March 1882, and afterward lived in the United States. The Farleys had been on a home visit.

    65. Isabella May Weight (b. 1871) was Mrs. Schmidt's younger sister.

    66. This was Mrs. Milaina (Melinda) Ahia (b. 1840, Lahaina–d. Honolulu, February 18, 1897). Her father, Kale, had been a cook in the household of Reverend Dwight Baldwin of Lahaina, and she was named Melinda in honor of Baldwin's sister. She married first the Reverend James Hunnewell Moku about 1860 (d. 1869), and second, Abraham Ahia. Her

12 P.M. Had meeting of 1st Division [Hui Hoonaauao] Directresses. Mentioned about making Mrs. Hill Treasurer—about refunding to 2d Division $44.00 to fill two shares. Write notes to ladies who have never paid—to accept Mrs. Hobron as member. Accepted.

*Friday, May 25.* Made preparations for kolau [sic—possibly hukilau]. Nine P.M. All started. Makanoe, H. Kawainui, Hanakeola, Mary Purdy, Lilia Aholo and sons. Caught lot of fish. All went home at 12.

*Saturday, May 26.* Took a drive to Piolani [Kapiolani] Park with Mahiai [Robinson] ma [and party]. She had never seen the long bridge and park.[67] Got caught in shower. Sent Kaipo and Aimoku home. John did not come home on acct. [of] heavy rain, but he went on board HBMS *Cormorant* Capt. Nicolls' Ball.[68]

*Sunday, May 27.* John only came home this morn. All the girls went up to Paoakalani. Came back [at] three—dined quickly and came to town to make preparations for opening of Legislature.

*Monday, May 28.* Breakfasted in Palace. There seems to be some hitch about Proroguing [the Legislature]. The King would like to have it done at the Palace and told Green so.[69] He never told the assembly but the Ministers kept to themselves and would not come to the Palace—so King sent to ask the Chancellor [Albert F.] Judd to Prorogue it for him. He did it by Commission. Joe was busy all day making preparations for tomorrow.[70]

*Tuesday, May 29.* Dressed in black satin with silver spangles. Diamond Spray in hair, Diamond Star on throat ribbon, pearl and silver necklace, Kalakaua order and cordon, diamond solitaire in each shoe buckle complete my dress for opening of Legislature. Drove in State Carriage after John, then to Government Building. Joe [Heleluhe] and Kuaiwa [were dressed] in full livery [of] blue and silver. King opened in person. Queen wore peacock dress. Kaiulani in pink satin, and looked sweet. Mrs. Judd looked sweet. Mrs. Iaukea [in] black with yellow plumes—Eveline [Wilson] [in] white with red plumes. A grand affair.

*Wednesday, May 30.* Went up at three [to mausoleum] with Mary Carter and Jennie and Annie Buckle to see decorated tomb—then came back to

---

obituary in *The Friend*, March 1897, said: "For many years she has been connected with the household of Liliuokalani with whom she was much attached."

67. The "long bridge" ran from the Diamond Head side of Liliuokalani's Hamohamo property along the shore almost to the entrance of Kapiolani Park.

68. This was a reception on board the HBMS *Cormorant* in honor of Queen Victoria's birthday. The *Hawaiian Gazette*, May 29, 1888, observed: "There was a goodly number of guests from shore present, who were entertained chiefly with a variety performance by the crew. Capt. Nicolls did all in his power to enhance the pleasure of the event, presiding at the piano himself.... The party broke up at a late hour, singing 'God Save the Queen.'" The *Cormorant* had arrived at Honolulu from South America April 15, 1888.

69. William Lowthian Green was minister of finance, 1887–89.

70. This was the first opening of the legislature under the new constitution of 1887. Despite Liliu's comments about the king wishing that it take place at the palace, the session commenced at noon on May 29, in the legislative hall of Aliiolani Hale, and the king did read his speech. See May 29, 1888, diary entry, this page.

Campbell's tomb[71]—stayed till five, came home tired. Went to bed at 8½ P.M. Was woken by a noise on veranda—it was a man—prowling round the premises. It was 12½ past.

Today wrote to A. J. Cartwright to give Joe $281.00 to pay for mortgage of Naili and Puu. Paid whole over to A. Rosa and [it] only needs recording.[72]

*Thursday, May 31.* Sent Joe with order to Cartwright for $400.00. Gave Society $7.00 more toward payment of expenses of mortgage.

*Friday, June 1.* Had a meeting at ten A.M. 2d Division [Hui Hoonaauao]. Rec'd $6.00 from Poomaikelani $14.25 from H. Kawainui, dues of past months, and $7.00 cont [contribution]. $27.70. Joe gave Mrs. Kawainui's statement of how the 2d Division stands [which] will appear in papers tomorrow.[73] Had a meeting of 1st Division [Hui Hoonaauao]. Three P.M. Mentioned of accepting Mrs. Hobron as Honorary Member. Spoke of paying to 2d Division $34—so as to claim two shares in Ice stocks—accepted and paid. Paid back $4.95 what had been due 1st [Division] Dues from Ice Stocks past four months. Next month will meet at Washington Place. Gave W. C. Lane $10.00 for two shares in Koolau Hui.[74] Today 2nd Division has $265.00 in my keeping and so Keala ma [Keala and party].

*Monday, June 4.* Nine A.M. Went to Kawaiahao Seminary to see children of Liliuokalani Hui Hoonaauao [scholarships] go through their examination. Did very well.[75] Got home at two. Dined and rested. Five P.M. Hattie Kawainui brought bills for girls' tuition, gave her $45 [which] leaves $220.00. Seven P.M. went to Kawaiahao again to a wedding of one of the girls—Sarah Maalea to Albert Trask.[76] From there went to lecture by Dickinson on the Alhambra.[77]

[Returned to] Washington Place, all tired out, and found John was laid up with rheumatism. Had to stay in Hinano Bower.

71. She meant the Campbell family tomb in the Oahu cemetery, located on the right side of Nuuanu Avenue below the Royal Mausoleum.

72. This deed, dated May 22, 1888, from Naili and his wife Puu, concerns property at Punaluu, Oahu, and Hamohamo, Waikiki.

73. The report has not been found in any of the English- or Hawaiian-language newspapers of the time.

74. William C. Lane was the proprietor of the Makao rice plantation and stock ranch (300 acres under cultivation) in the Koolauloa District. Nothing is now known of the Koolau Hui (the term means a collective organization of that district).

75. "The closing exercises of the Kawaiahao Seminary took place as announced yesterday, occupying from nine until past 12. There was a very large gathering of friends.... Mrs. Dominis was present among others and remained the entire morning, expressing a great deal of approval of the general proficiency as well as the marks of progress of the scholars." *Pacific Commercial Advertiser*, June 5, 1888.

76. In its notice of the marriage, the *Pacific Commercial Advertiser*, June 5, 1888, said that Mrs. A. F. Judd played the *Lohengrin* wedding march, and that the guests included Princess Liliuokalani and Kaiulani.

77. This was Sidney Dickinson, an art lecturer from Boston. "Professor Dickinson's lecture at the Hawaiian Opera House, this evening, on the Alhambra and Moorish occupancy of Spain, will treat one of the most romantic chapters of history." *Pacific Commercial Advertiser*, June 4, 1888.

*Tuesday, June 5.* Reached home [Muolaulani] six A.M. Packed until 9½, went on board *Malulani*. 11½ vessel left wharf on arrival of King and Queen and band boys. Wharf full of spectators. Off for Kailua.[78]

*Saturday, June 9.* [Kona.] Went to ride with Jessie, Melaina [Ahia], and others. Before starting sent Ahoi to see what the matter was with Joe. Found him very sick—brought home two large pineapples. Sam Paia had skittish horse. Rode all round Keahuolu and lunched with Mrs. C. Clark, Hoapili, and Kanehoa. Five o'clock reached the beach—Steamer *J. A. Cummins* arrived with J. A. Cummins and family and Mr. Dodd.[79]

The steamer came in style—beautiful. Mrs. Kynnersley[80] went up with me. That evening all spent the evening in pavilion—band played. Mrs. S. Parker, Mrs. H. Macfarlane.

*Sunday, June 10.* [Kailua.] After breakfast gave Milaina 50 cts.

*Monday, June 11.* Began the day [at Hulihee] with a grand breakfast— 45 sat at table. The Queen wore bunting. I, pink muslin, Mrs. Parker embroidered ecru muslin, Mrs. Kynnersley white. Mrs. Emma Macfarlane, garnet cashmeres—she looked handsome. Governess Ululani [Baker] wore pink cashmere.

One P.M. boat race. King and myself and party, J. A. Cummins, Maria [Puuohau], Katy, and others went on board of steamer *J. A. Cummins* with singers, had a good time watching rowers. Band boys on veranda of Kamakahonu.[81] Beach filled with people and Queen on the veranda. Returned to dinner. Ten P.M. Ball commences. Full evening dress. Queen [in] green holoku, I [in] silk in black and white with diamonds. Hattie Parker [in] black with diamonds. *J.A.C.* [the *John A. Cummins*] [at] Nine o'clock [was] illuminated [and] fired off rockets.

*Tuesday, June 12.* Went to Hookena.[82]

*Sunday, June 17.* Arrived [at Honolulu] from Kailua by *Kinau*.

*Monday, June 18.* Gave Mrs. Kawainui $2.50 to payment of two girls at Pohukaina [School].[83]

*Friday, June 22.* Milaina Ahia gave me $100.00 to keep for her.

---

78. "Leaving by the steamer *W. G. Hall* [also referred to as the *Malulani*] this morning are their Majesties the King and Queen, Princess Liliuokalani, Princes Kawananakoa and Kealiiahonui.... The royal party are destined for the King's country seat at Kailua, Hawaii, where they will remain until after the races and sports with which the local populace will celebrate the eleventh of June." *Pacific Commercial Advertiser*, June 5, 1888.

The *Daily Bulletin*, June 6, 1888, noted, "Princess Liliuokalani arrived half an hour before the departure of the steamer and boarded without ceremony."

79. James Dodd (b. 1848, Belfast, Ireland–d. January 21, 1900, Honolulu) was the popular proprietor of the Pantheon Saloon and Livery Stable.

80. Mrs. Kynnersley was the wife of a Kohala sugar plantation proprietor.

81. Liliu was referring to a two-story frame house located at Kamakahonu, in Kailua, Kona.

82. On this excursion, the royal party visited the Captain Cook Monument at Kaawaloa and had their picture taken. A copy of this photograph is in the Hawaii State Archives.

83. Pohukaina School was a public school located on a lot between Punchbowl and Likelike Streets, opposite the gates of Iolani Palace. The main building of the Hawaii State Library now occupies the site.

*Saturday, June 23.* Busy all day. Ten A.M. went to Mrs. Allen's to hear Mrs. Williams relate the history [of] Maria Theresa.[84] Came home.

*Tuesday, June 26.* Went at 3½ P.M. to Mrs. Hobron's reception.[85] Went with Mary Carter. Wore black velvet and Diamonds.

*Wednesday, June 27.* Rec'd. from W. Irving Bishop by J. A. Cummins for Liliuokalani Hui Hoonaauao $81.30. Ten A.M. went to Waikiki with folks to get cocoanut leaves for hats. Hurried to our readings at Mrs. Allen's but was belated. Band at Hotel. Divided Mr. B's [Washington Irving Bishop's] money between 1st and 2nd Divisions of Liliuokalani Educational Society, each having $40.65. Took $5.50 from 1st [Division] to pay for bed for Maria Puuohau.[86]

*Thursday, June 28.* Came home at 7½ P.M. from Washington Place. Two P.M. went to Waikiki to a picnic at Hobron's place.[87]

Had a pleasant time—it was [Henry] Cushman Carter's birthday.

Eight P.M. went to the reception at A. F. Judd's given to Mr. and Mrs. Van Slyke.[88] Wore a blue satin and lace, pearls, and silver ornaments.

*Saturday, June 30.* I have $3.00 more for Milaina.

Rec'd $400 from A. J. Cartwright. Paid out Levey's bill $98.83[89]—Iron Foundry $83.92[90]—$5.00 for saddle. $10 for same, $13 for poi.

[At bottom of page:] Keala [Hale].

**Sunday, July 1.** Stayed home in morning watering plants. Afternoon drove out to meet Lou [Louisa Brickwood] at Ainahau. Found Archie, Kaiulani, Helen [Boyd], Nellie and Mabel [Robertson] at home [with] Mr. Moses of *Mohican* and two other officers [who] came on her.[91] Jennie Clark went with me. Returned at six. Came home with Romeo [a horse], wagon broken and hurt all over. Served right.

[At bottom of page:] Keala [Hale].

*Monday, July 2.* Met ladies of Liliuokalani Educational Society 1st Division. Only vice president Lou [Louisa Brickwood], Secretary [Mrs.] Brown, and

---

84. Maria Theresa (b. 1717–d. 1780) was the queen of Hungary and Bohemia, archduchess of Austria, and mother of Marie Antoinette, queen of France.

85. Frances E. (Grey) Hobron (b. 1825, Connecticut–d. March 5, 1906, Honolulu) was the wife of Captain Thomas H. Hobron. A resident since 1852, Captain Hobron established the Grove Ranch at Makawao, Maui, as well as the Kahului Railroad, and promoted interisland navigation.

86. Maria Puuohau (later Mrs. George H. Piltz) is listed in the 1888 City Directory as a domestic for Liliu, residing at King and Liliha (at Muolaulani).

87. This was the Waikiki residence of the Thomas Hobron family, in the vicinity of what is now Hobron Lane.

88. Lucius Van Slyke (d. 1929) of the University of Michigan came to the islands in 1885 as a teacher of natural sciences at Oahu College; the Hawaiian government also employed him part-time. In July 1888, he returned to Michigan, so this was probably a farewell reception.

89. Louis J. Levey was an auctioneer and general commission merchant, Fort and Queen Streets.

90. Theophilus H. Davies was president of the Honolulu Iron Works, located at Queen Street below Nuuanu and Maunakea Streets.

91. The USS *Mohican* (Captain Davis) arrived at Honolulu from Samoa on July 1, 1888, and departed for San Francisco on July 8. She had made previous visits to Honolulu.

ABOVE

*Kaawaloa, Hawaii, June 12, 1888. A royal party including the king, queen, and Princess Liliuokalani visited Kailua, Kona, to participate in celebrations commemorating Kamehameha I. During their stay, members of the party visited Kealakekua Bay and the Captain Cook monument at Kaawaloa. In this photograph, Liliu is standing between Kalakaua (in white suit) and John Cummins (in dark suit with beard).*

*John Adams Kuakini Cummins was the son of high chiefess Kaumakaokane Papaliaiaina (cousin of Kamehameha I) and Thomas Jefferson Cummins Jr.*
Hawaii State Archives

OPPOSITE FROM TOP

*A party of royals and friends celebrated the fifty-third birthday of John Cummins at Waimanalo on March 17, 1888. The royals arrived from Honolulu by steamer for a day of horse races, luau, tableaux, and dancing. Seated in the front row (from left) are Princess Kaiulani, Princess Liliuokalani, and Princess Poomaikelani (in dark dress).*
J. A. Gonsalves, 1888, Hawaii State Archives

*John Cummins (in dark suit), founder of Waimanalo Sugar Co., most likely at his Waimanalo country home, Mauna Loke, 1890. His daughter Matilda is in the white muumuu.*
W. Richardson, Bishop Museum Archives

*Waimanalo Sugar Co. plantation and mill consisted of 7,000 acres, about 1,000 of which were planted in sugar. According to the 1884–85 Honolulu Directory, the plantation's estimated crop for that year was 1,800 tons. In the Queen's diaries there are several references to the purchase of Waimanalo Sugar Co. shares for herself, her dependents, and the ladies of her savings society.*
Alfred Mitchell, 1886, Bishop Museum Archives

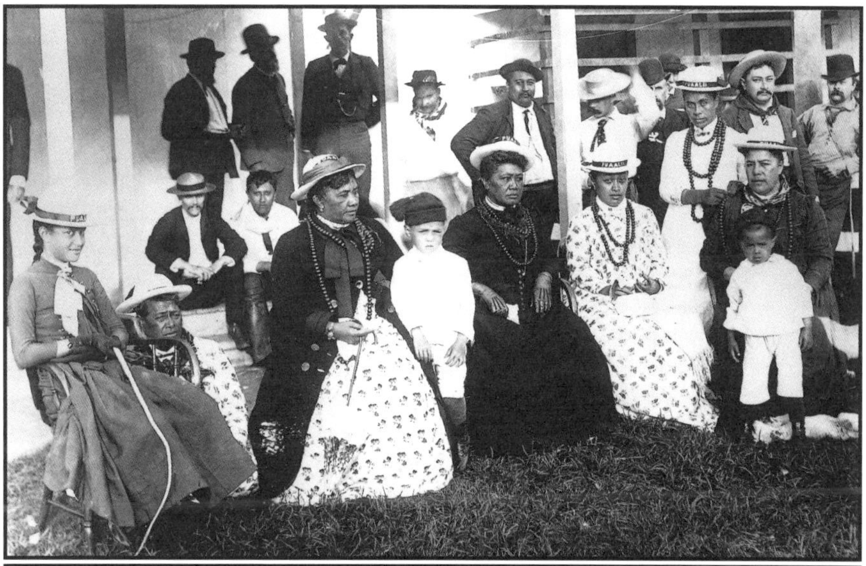

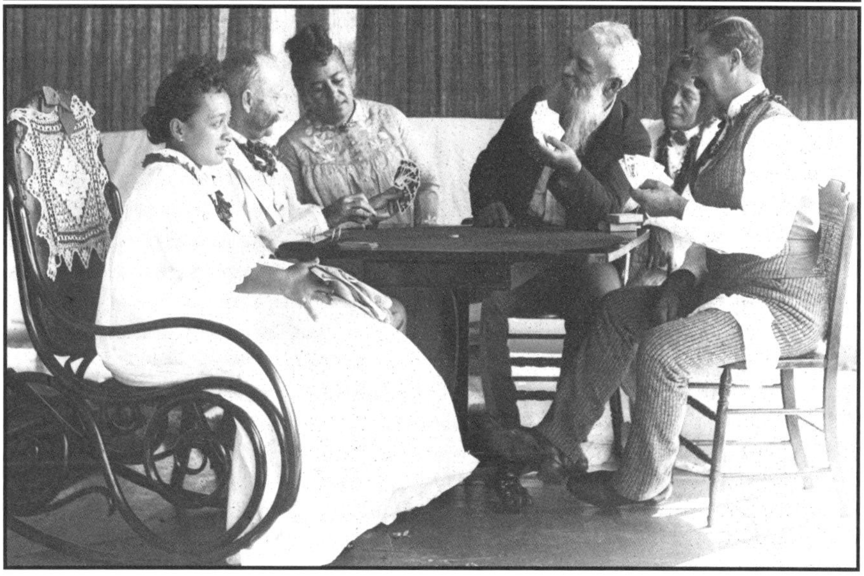

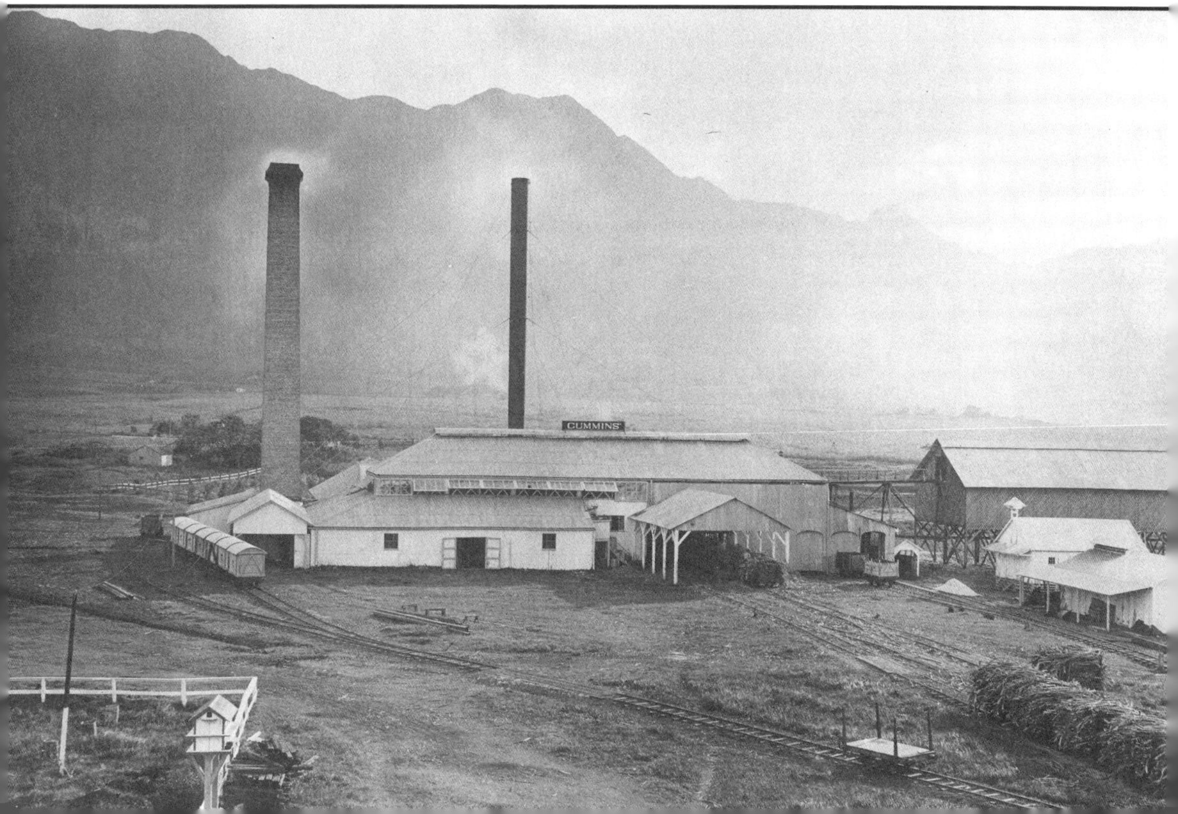
CUMMINS'

I met. Meeting was half over when Mary and Annie Buckle, Mrs. M. Brown, and Mrs. C[harles] Hopkins came to Washington Place. Amount [of] $40.00 and over was raised by circular being sent to Members. After expenses paid, $85.00 left of W.I.B. [Washington Irving Bishop] money added to the other, amounted to over $70.00.

8½ P.M. went over to evening party at Mrs. Dowsett's given for Annie and Lizzie recently returned from California.[92]

John went home and left me here [at Muolaulani]. Folks have raised Carriage house on to next lot. The people begin to move Kawehena's house on to next lot.

*Tuesday, July 3.* Ten A.M. Charlie came in, brought patterns. Mary Cooke came to see me but [I] was engaged. Went to meeting 2d Division [of the Liliuokalani Educational Society], only nine members present. $7.60 dues was contributed, also $42.00 from Mrs. Holokahiki from tickets of Ball. [Two words erased.]

Kawehena's house is moved to place, also the carriage house.

*Wednesday, July 4.* 11 A.M. John came to see if I was going to [the Fourth of July] oration, [I] said not, but would go to Mrs. Merrill's reception.[93]

At three went for John and went round. It was very crowded—from there went to see Mother Dickson. He [John] being in regimentals, it pleased her very much. Took him home, then came home. 7½ dressed for Ball at Honolulu Rifles Armory. A brilliant affair from the highest to maids and dressmakers attended and cooks—but all had good time. The way-up people wouldn't dance.

*Thursday, July 5.* 12 P.M. Maria King died so quietly, no wailing.[94]

Breakfasted [with] K. [the King]—stayed there till two P.M., came [home] and dressed for reception—a very good one. Went back, had dinner, came in to tea, then returned and stayed [at Mrs. King's] till morning and came home. Had no band on account of death of neighbor [Mrs. King].

[At bottom of page:] Keala [Hale].

*Friday, July 6.* Six A.M. went over to Mrs. King's—no flowers, so sent over several bouquets and Kieles [gardenias] and Magnolias.

---

92. The two Dowsett daughters had returned to Honolulu on the *Alameda* on June 10, 1888. The *Evening Bulletin* reported on July 3, 1888: "The residence of Hon. J. I. Dowsett and Mrs. Dowsett, at Palama, was a scene of beauty, gaiety, mirth, and happiness last night.... Within was a teeming profusion [of] beautiful flowers, [and] disposed about the main building, along the walks and among the trees and shrubbery, were Chinese and Japanese lanterns ... creating a picture of fairy-like enchantment.... Every member of the Dowsett family, which is a big beginning for any party, was there. Miss Dowsett had recently returned from a visit to California, and Miss Annie and Miss Elizabeth are at home on vacation from school."

93. This was a Fourth of July reception at the U.S. Legation, and the hostess was the wife of U.S. Minister George W. Merrill. The king and Colonel Curtis Iaukea also attended.

94. Maria King (b. 1841–d. 1888) was the part-Hawaiian widow of Captain Thomas King (d. 1863) and the mother of Sarah (Mrs. Jacob Brown). The King homestead at Kapalama was adjacent to Muolaulani, Liliuokalani's residence.

Three P.M. Went as agreed on to Washington Place with Miss Annie Buckle to Meeting of 1st Division [of the Liliuokalani Educational Society]. Only three, so came home. Antone Rosa came in today to ask for allowance of Wailuakio water for Deborah Kanoa's [kalo] patch. I told him we will think it over. Joe brought home $21.00 from share of Ice Stocks—Six he gave to A. J. Cartwright for [Hui] [Hoo]kuonoono.

[At bottom of page:] Keala [Hale].

*Saturday, July 7.* Busy all morning. Four P.M. went to Band. Eight P.M. went to entertainment given by officers of HBMS *Cormorant* and Ethel Wodehouse and Mabel Rhodes[95]—for benefit of British Benevolent Society.[96] Dressed in blue satin [and] cape point lace, dress ornaments, diamonds, and pearls. Why not dress richly, it is our duty to the public to look nice. King, Princess Kaiulani and father, myself [with] Mrs. Aldrich, and Mr. G. W. Macfarlane in attendance.[97]

At ten A.M. went to Mrs. W. F. Allen's to hear Mrs. Florence Williams discourse on Eloise.[98]

[At bottom of page:] Keala [Hale].

*Sunday, July 8.* Stayed at home all day washing Maile bushes. I think this is a good way of spending Sunday. Five P.M. went over to look at improvements in next premises.

*Monday, July 9.* Breakfasted with King at Palace to meet W. Irving Bishop, the mind reader. Mr. J. A. Cummins, Princess Poomaikelani, [and] Curtis Iaukea, and W. I. Bishop was presented with a decoration of the Order of Kapiolani. He was pleased and surprised. Band over, came home.[99]

Heard today [that] the Order [of Kapiolani] was not of the Queen but founded from our great-grand Aunt Kapiolani who ignored Pele, and accepted the God of Heaven.[100]

95. Ethel Wodehouse was the daughter of British Commissioner James Hay Wodehouse. Mabel Sidney Rhodes, the daughter of Henry Rhodes (b. Victoria, BC–d. 1937, Ayrshire, Scotland), would marry Dr. Dugald Campbell on July 8, 1890.

96. The British Benevolent Society was established in 1860. In 1888, British Commissioner James H. Wodehouse was president, and A. S. Cleghorn was secretary and treasurer.

97. The *Daily Bulletin* reported on July 9, 1888: "There were [sic] lots of amusement at the Opera House on Saturday night when the officers of HBMS *Cormorant* and a number of Honolulu ladies and gentlemen combined to give an entertainment in aid . . . of the British Benevolent Society, and hearty laughter shook the audience all over. . . . The royal box was occupied by the King, Princess Liliuokalani, and Princess Kaiulani."

98. "Eloise" (correctly spelled Héloïse) (b. 1101–d. 1164) is remembered for her celebrated love affair and correspondence with French theologian Pierre Abélard (b. 1079–d. 1142).

99. "According to custom," noted the *Daily Bulletin*, July 10, 1888, "the Royal Hawaiian band played within the Palace enclosure during breakfast hour on Monday morning. Princess Liliuokalani, Princess Poomaikelani, Hon. J. Cummins, Col. Iaukea, and Mr. W. I. Bishop breakfasted, by invitation with the King." The king conferred on Bishop the insignia of "Grand Officer of the Order of Kapiolani" in the blue room prior to the meal.

100. This was the chiefess Kapiolani (b. Hilo–d. May 5, 1841, Honolulu), whose "defiance of Pele" took place at Kilauea crater in December 1824, when she said the following: "Jehovah is my God. He kindled these fires. I fear not Pele." This often reprinted action and statement went far in missionary efforts to Christianize the islands, and was the subject of a poem by Alfred Tennyson.

Heard also that all the Huis were to be called together to consult about raising funds to build a house where we could hold our meetings in future.

$25 from W. F. Allen for Kaakaole. Antone Rosa came to consult me on Luhau's case. I want him to act with Hatch in this case.[101]

*Tuesday, July 10.* Kanakahou[102] commenced on the arch of my bath. I will name it Puuohulu [esteemed hill or mound].

Nothing of note happened today. Four P.M. Received G. W. Macfarlane, Miss Amy Crocker, and two other ladies who giggled.[103]

Grotto.

*Wednesday, July 11.* Kalei and I went to Mr. Cartwright's for Kaipo's money shares of Waimanalo. He gave me $15.00. When we came home, Joe [said he] had been to Cartwright for the same and gave me $15.00—I must return it to A. J. Cartwright.

*Thursday, July 12.* Paina K. [Kapu] Kieaki me ke Kane Hope me na ohua—Pau. [Private meal with Kieaki and the Assistant Man and the retainers—Completed.]

*Friday, July 13.* Muolaulani.

Washington Place, got some shells.

*Saturday, July 14.* Sat. P.M. went to drive with John out to Park. Paid Mamala $10.00, Kanakahou $15, Kaakaole two dollars, [and] [David] Crowningburg $20.00. How happy it made him. He brought two kukui necklaces to sell but what I gave him was beyond expectation—he [said he] would go straight to market for his family was starving.

*Sunday, July 15.* Spent the day at Aiea with Dr. McGrew, the King, two Princes, Miss Amy Crocker, Mrs. Bender, Mrs. Couch, Mr. Gillis [sic, Gilling], W. I. Bishop—John and Tom Cummins, G. W. Macfarlane and Ned [Macfarlane], John and I. Nice day.[104] My object [was] to enjoy and also to take the chance to see all along the beach—on account of future prospects—[following] the Treaty of Puuloa.[105]

*Monday, July 16.* Breakfasted in Palace with King with intention to ask Queen to permit me to hold Mortgage on Pualeilani but brother [Kalakaua] told me not to mention it till by and by. Went to see Mr. Cartwright

---

101. Luhau's case was a petition for a division of land. Luhau (k) and Keamalu (w) were joint tenants of a parcel of land at Kauluwela, in Honolulu, containing 1.25 acres, that was divided by School Street, with each portion having several cottages. On August 1, 1888, Keamalu petitioned the court for a partition of the same. Francis March Hatch was Luhau's attorney. Hawaii State Archives, First Circuit Court, Equity 627.

102. Kanakahou, a laborer, resided at 115 School Street.

103. Amy Crocker (b. 1863–d. 1941) was the rich, adventurous, and many times married daughter of Judge E. B. Crocker of Sacramento. In 1936, she published a memoir aptly titled *And I'd Do It Again* (New York: Coward-McCann, 1936).

104. The McGrews had a summer house (a simple cottage with a large lanai) and a cement swimming pool at Aiea, on a point overlooking Pearl Harbor. Named Kapuniakaia, it remained a family property until the beginning of the Second World War, when it became a part of the Pearl Harbor naval base.

105. Liliu was referring to Pearl Harbor—specifically to the interests in the same acquired by the United States via the Reciprocity Treaty of 1875, which King Kalakaua had extended in 1887. See footnotes and diary entries for September 25 and 26, 1887 (156).

about water for next premises. Returned to him $15.00 he gave to Joe on the 11th inst. [the month] for Kaipo's W. [Waimanalo] shares. Received Miss Eliza Brewer and Lottie Carter.[106]

*Tuesday, July 17.* Hona came to take care of my horses.

*Wednesday, July 18.* Sent $5.00 to Lou B[rickwood], $3.00 from Mrs. Wight and $2.00 from Ice Co. She sent back $3.00 by Wakeke—ought to have been $2.75.

*Thursday, July 19.* Mr. Cartwright came over to see me about improvements on [my Palama] place [Muolaulani], and perhaps I may have next lot.

*Friday, July 20.* Nihoa's birthday.

*Saturday, July 21.* Ten A.M. Drove with Wakeke by School St. to our reading at Mr. Bishop's. Had an accident with harness above Waikahalulu Bridge. Got out and unharnessed quickly, sent horse over by W. Walked across bridge, met Joe Aea. Took his carriage and drove over. Lecture nearly over. Mrs. F. Williams mentioned about my Society.

Two P.M. Went to Nihoa's birthday with Nellie Smith, Mrs. Atkinson, Mrs. Smith, Mrs. Fayerweather, Mrs. Foster, Liliu [Carter], Miss Wight, Leihulu, and others.[107] Four P.M. brought Mrs. Smith out here with John. Came home ten P.M. Went to Puuohulu.[108]

Lovely night. John came in.

*Sunday, July 22.* Went after John and went out with folks to Waikiki. Found my house and things saturated with honey. Joe broke roof open and took out honey—bucketsful. Bathed, dined—took a nap and came home. John came in evening to tell me Capt. McNair of *Omaha* and wife were coming next day.[109]

*Monday, July 23.* Met Mahiai [Robinson] and Aki [her sister].

—had dream and stuff. Alapai didn't say what he wanted.

Nihoas came to surprise me. Kahae and Nihoa came over. Kahuila [Wilcox], Leihulu [Kapena], and others. Letter from Sophie [Sheldon]—Macfie [had] been stabbed by wife [over] his baby with mistress at Anahola.[110]

---

106. Miss Brewer was probably a visitor from California. Lottie or Charlotte Carter was a daughter of J. O. Carter.

107. Nellie Smith was Nellie Richardson, the wife of George Smith, proprietor of Benson and Smith, druggists, Honolulu. Mrs. Atkinson was the wife of Alatau T. Atkinson (d. 1906), longtime superintendent of public instruction. The second Mrs. Smith is unidentified. Mrs. Fayerweather was Mary Kolimoalani Kekahimoku Beckley, the wife of Abraham Henry Fayerweather, and the granddaughter of Captain George Beckley. Mrs. Foster was Mary E. Robinson (b. 1844–d. 1930), the wife of Thomas R. Foster, and later the donor to the city of Honolulu of her home and grounds, now Foster Botanical Garden on Nuuanu Avenue. Miss Wight was probably the daughter of Dr. James Wight of Kohala. Liliu frequently mentions Leihulu, the daughter of John M. Kapena, in her diaries.

108. Unidentified location, possibly a cottage near Muolaulani—but not the land named Puuohulu in the ahupuaa of Lualualei on the western coast of Oahu.

109. The USS *Omaha* (Captain McNair) arrived in Honolulu from Mexico on July 14, 1888, and departed from Honolulu on August 18.

110. Probably Robert A. Macfie, junior vice president and manager of the Kilauea Sugar Co. in Kilauea, Kauai. The incident was not reported elsewhere.

Capt. and Mrs. McNair called—found us covered with leis. Jessie and Kaae stayed till 9½ and went home. I sat on veranda and enjoyed the moon. ½ to 11. Puuohulu.

*Tuesday, July 24.* Aki comes in again and prays. How good she is. Alapai wants to borrow $200.00 of me. I sent him with note on A. J. Cartwright for Hooulu Liliuokalani, Kaumakapili [Division] money which amount is $173.80 with interest. Did not see him return.

*Wednesday, July 25.* Nine A.M. went to Pohukaina [School] examination. Stayed till 12. Sallie, Keola, Keliiakahai, Kahalione, Louisa Kanae, Mary Ulili of 2nd Division [Liliuokalani Hui Hoonaauao] did very well.

Alapai borrowed today $200.00—to be returned in six months at 10%, $173.30 belong to Hui Hawaii Lahui of Kaumakapili, $26.20 belongs to me, and [Alapai?] places five carts and four horses with harness for sale.

*Thursday, July 26.* Home all morning. 7½ P.M. John and I went to Concert at Hotel.[111] 9½ Came home. Was told of many [persons] being taken to Kalawao, Lydia[112] among one.

*Friday, July 27.* M. [noon] Went to Royal School. Did not go in, there were so many people. Stopped at Carrie Bush's to see the boys. Found them placed at side table. Three P.M. went to St. Louis College, King, Queen, Archie. Very nice.[113] Sat out on veranda till ten P.M. ulana ie [wove baskets] till 11 and retired.

*Saturday, July 28.* Lou [Brickwood] and Kitty Brown came to bid farewell. They told me they were on their way to deposit money of 1st Division Liliuokalani Educational Society amounting to $145.00 in Mr. W. J. Smith's hands of Educational Department. Heard also of S. G. Wilder's death at seven A.M. A good man gone.[114]

All alone, I'm sad and dreary. I paid to Lou [Brickwood] .25 of 2d Division [Liliuokalani Educational Society].

*Sunday, July 29.* 11 A.M. John and I went up to Mrs. Wilder's and to see the

---

111. This was a "complimentary concert" for Captain McNair and officers of the USS *Omaha*, at the Hawaiian Hotel. The *Pacific Commercial Advertiser*, July 27, 1888, reported: "The building and grounds were never more superbly illuminated with electric lights and colored lanterns. Princess Liliuokalani, Gov. Dominis, U.S. Minister Merrill, British Commissioner Wodehouse, officers of the warships, and a great throng of citizen and stranger ladies and gentlemen were present. A very pleasant dance in the parlors followed."

112. This was Liliu's namesake, Lydia Nathaniel, the daughter of Thomas Nathaniel (or Nakanaela), who was a member of King Kalakaua's singing club. She was sent to Kalaupapa, Molokai, on November 13, 1888, and died there February 11, 1892.

113. She is referring to the closing exercises at Saint Louis College. The *Pacific Commercial Advertiser*, July 28, 1893, noted the presence of various members of the royal family and said there was an "immense audience."

114. Samuel Gardner Wilder died on July 28, 1888. Born in Leominster, Massachusetts, in 1831, he grew up in Illinois and came to the islands in 1857. In 1858, he married Elizabeth Judd. He went into the sugar business first in Makawao, then with his father-in-law, Dr. Gerrit P. Judd, at Kualoa, Oahu. Wilder had extensive interests in the lumber trade, founded the Wilder Steamship Co., constructed a railroad on the island of Hawaii (Kohala in 1881), and improved a similar operation at Kahului, Maui, which he had acquired in 1884. He was a political ally of King Kalakaua, actively campaigned for his election in 1874, was a noble in the legislature 1874–88, served as minister of the interior 1878–80, and was president of the legislature until shortly before his death.

children. Came home at four P.M. Spent afternoon with Mother Dominis while John went to [Wilder's] funeral. Came home with pain in my right side. Poultice [of] mustard—felt better.

*Monday, July 30.* Stayed at home. Mr. Cartwright made offer [for me] of next lot $3,500.00. [They] will give him answer next week. Kuihelani paid interest on mortgage. $2,068.89=$308.80.

*Tuesday, July 31.* Gave Kaakaole $2.00. Lou [Brickwood] and Kitty Brown went by *Australia* today.[115] Wharf was full. Rec'd $400.00 from A. J. Cartwright. Paid off all servants except Aiaumoe and Hana.

King came to see if I would speak to Archie about Kaiulani—[said she] must have a good home. Slept [at] Washington Place, John sick and mother [Dominis] sick.

**Wednesday, August 1.** Went to [Dr.] Brodie's for more medicine. One P.M. attended a Memorial at Legislative Hall. Good remarks were made by [Representatives] Paehaole and Willie Kinney. Was attended by Minnie Aldrich. Wilder's family were there and [also the] Dicksons.[116]

Keala [Hale].

*Thursday, August 2.* Did not find Mrs. Smith. Went to Alice Hastings—Mrs. Kitchen sick—tumor.[117]

Saw John and Mrs. Dominis. Did not find Panana [a horse]—went to Mary Beckley. Heard of David's engagement to Eva.[118]

*Friday, August 3.* Mrs. Dominis 85 years [old] today. Breakfast at Washington Place. Mary [Carter?] came in to break fast with me. John is sick. Had to hurry home [to Muolaulani] on account of painters—getting along well.

2d Division [Liliuokalani Hui Hoonaauao] meeting at ten at Engine House—decided to meet at Washington Place in future. Contributed $6.05 and $1.20 rec'd from Kamiki for last year's dues.

*Saturday, August 4.* Mrs. Clark and Mrs. Kawainui came. I gave the latter $6.00 back of Hui M. [money and] $2 to pay the two boys at Engine House.

*Sunday, August 5.* Lovely day.

*Monday, August 6.* Joe gave me $25 of PIR Co., for us and party. Bought two more shares of PIR Co. at 97.00 a share—for 2d Div. Liliuokalani Hui Hoonaauao.

115. Catherine (Kitty) Fornander (d. 1905), the wife of Captain John H. Brown, and Louisa Brickwood returned to Honolulu from San Francisco on the *Australia* September 18, 1888.

116. The Wilder memorial service began in the legislative hall at one P.M. Liliu and Princess Kaiulani were seated on the platform to the right and left, respectively, of the president of the legislature. A resolution was offered and moved, and officials offered condolatory remarks. The *Pacific Commercial Advertiser*, August 2, 1888, reported that the Honorable A. P. Paehaole remarked: "This man was a strong supporter of Hawaii, and it was a great calamity to a nation to lose such a citizen as S. G. Wilder.... He has been a father to this nation. His administration of the various offices he filled ... was marked by a decided and permanent benefit to the nation."

117. Alice Makee Hastings (b. 1859–d. 1913) was the daughter of Captain James Makee of Maui, wife of Frank Hastings, and sister of Julia Kitchen.

118. Prince David Kawananakoa (d. 1908) did not marry Eva Parker. He instead married Abigail Campbell in San Francisco on January 6, 1902.

*Monday, August 13.* Joe brought me $25.00 from Ice stocks—bought two more shares at $97.00—for 2d Division Liliuokalani Education[al] Society.

*Wednesday, August 15.* Mr. Cartwright gave me my account books to study over, for he tells me I am indebted to him $3,000.

*Thursday, August 16.* Rec'd Certificates of two shares in Ice stock, belonging to 2d Division Education[al] Society. Sent $2—to Kaakaole.

*Thursday, August 30.* Returned Mr. Cartwright's account books.

*Friday, August 31.* Drew from A. J. Cartwright, $600—$400 my monthly allowance [and] $200 to pay off the painters who painted my house. Made Joe present of $20.00 besides his wages. Rec'd $30 from A. J. Cartwright for Kaipo six shares Waimanalo stocks.

**Saturday, September 1.** Stayed at home all day. Mahiai [Robinson], Aki, and Kahanuu [Meek] brought me present of two Kahili [feather standards], one Royal Standard. Jessie and Jennie put up curtains all day.

Iaukea sent me picture. Jennie Clark gave me a tea set of cups and saucers, Kalanienoho a box of handkerchiefs, Henry H. Carter ½ doz coffee spoons, Mrs. Dominis tea strainer [and] salt spoons ½ doz.

[At bottom of page:] Keala dancing hulahula.

[Under a section at the end of the diary titled "Letters," Liliu added the following on this date: "R. A. Macfie invites (me) to make a visit" (to Kauai) "answd. 11th."]

*Sunday, September 2.* Stayed at home all day. Mahiai stayed with me and helped fix furniture. Today is my jubilee—50 years old, yet feel young. King and David [Kawananakoa] had breakfast with me.

*Monday, September 3.* Heard John was sick and sent Mahiai and Kainuuala to see. They told me he was sick. Ten A.M. he made his appearance.

King, David [Kawananakoa], Archie, and Kaiulani breakfasted with me. Band played. Liliuokalani Educational Society 2d Division contributed wooden calabash. [Hale] Naua Society contributed $36.00, friends gave $37.00. I presented silk flag to Royal School Cadets. Reception was over at five P.M. Some friends came on at six after supper—hulahula. Tired.[119]

---

119. "ROYAL JUBILEE RECEPTION. The fiftieth anniversary of H.R.H. Princess Liliuokalani . . . fell upon Sunday 2nd inst. [this month.] Throughout the night native lady retainers of Her Royal Highness chanted meles in her honor at the Palama residence. A reception was held at the same place from 12 P.M. to three P.M. on Monday, to which a general invitation had been issued through the press. This was a fine social success, about two hundred callers registering their names besides many who overlook that formality. Neatly engrossed addresses were presented by the Liliuokalani Educational Society, the Naua Society, and the Royal School Cadets, to each of which the Princess responded with a brief acknowledgment. Among the many gifts were the following: a beautiful kou wood calabash, inlaid with koa decorations, on a Koa and Kou stand, engraved artistically in relief with an appropriate inscription, from the Second Division of the Liliuokalani Educational Society . . . half a dozen silver teaspoons, in satin-lined casket, from Mr. Henry C. Carter of New York. A unique pair of kahilis [feather standards] made of bamboo, in imitation of fuchsias with crowning pieces of magnolia, from Hawaiian ladies. . . . The Royal School Cadets appeared with their address, 75 strong and wearing their white and red uniforms under the command of Q.M.G., L. Nahora Hipa, military instructor to the schools. They were presented by Her Royal Highness with a beautiful flag and they gave the military salute in coming and going . . .

*Wednesday, September 5*. Had meeting of H.H.L. Mokuna elua [Hui Hoonaauao Liliuokalani, Division 2] at Washington Place. Contributed $2.10. Decided to meet at Muolaulani next day to sew some clothes for scholars, and to alter Constitution and Articles. They adjourned. Great excitement of Chinese on account of bill before Legislature.[120]

*Thursday, September 6*. Pehikulani [Auld], Kahae, A[nnie] Holokahiki, Kealoha H[ugo,] H[attie] Kawainiu, Wakeke, Jennie Clark [met]—to sew for Kuahine Sheldon. Decide to meet at Washington Place on Tuesday next to alter Article of Constitution.[121]

*Friday, September 7*. Waihoikaia[122] asked to leave me. I discharged him and Sam Paia.

*Saturday, September 8*. Joe drew $14.00 for 2d Division this month.

*Monday, September 10*. Gave Sophy Sheldon $4.53 to get Kuahine Sheldon a [mosquito] netting. Mahiai and Aki went home. John went to Waialua—I went to Band [concert], then slept at Hinano Bower.

*Tuesday, September 11*. Stayed for Meeting L.H.H. [Liliuokalani Hui Hoonaauao] Committee—nothing done. Came home [and] wrote letters.

*Monday, September 17*. Keamalu[123] borrowed $98.00 and I gave him $1.00 belonging to Kamakaihona's Ice stock, to buy something for her birthday. Gave Milaina [Ahia] $1.50 of her money. She has $107.00 left.

*Tuesday, September 18*. [Entry drawn from memorandum at end of diary:] The Liliuokalani Hui Hoonaauao had $1,240.59 in A. J. Cartwright's hands. $459.00 was invested in Ice Stocks on [blank] of Dec. 1887. $715.59 was invested in same P.I.R. [People's Ice and Refrigeration] Co. $50.00 still remains with Hui. From Dec. 1887, until this day, the Society has drawn $108.00 interest.

---

and otherwise gave three cheers for the Princess before marching away.... Princess Liliuokalani was dressed in cream-colored satin with silk trimmings and was generally congratulated upon her hale and hearty appearance." *Pacific Commercial Advertiser*, September 4, 1888.

120. On June 19, 1888, Representative W. A. Kinney introduced bill 57 in the legislature, a proposed amendment of article 47 of the 1887 constitution (stating that "the Legislature has full power and authority to amend the Constitution"). Kinney's proposed bill in its final form stated: "The Legislature may restrict or prohibit the admission of Chinese, or any body or class thereof, into this Kingdom; may name and limit the occupation or employment in which Chinese, or any body or class thereof, may lawfully engage in this Kingdom, the estate, and interest on land they may acquire or acquiring hold, and the number of years they may lawfully reside in this Kingdom.... The Legislature may provide for the enforcement of the provisions of this amendment and laws enacted thereunder in any manner it may deem proper." Original and amendments filed in the Hawaii State Archives, Series 222, Box 89-3.

The *Pacific Commercial Advertiser*, September 5, 1886, announced: "The Chinese amendment will come up today... for final action." It also noted: "The outcome of the largely attended mass meeting of Chinese at the theater a few evenings ago was the appointment of a large committee of influential and well-known Chinese, who have submitted a memorial to the President of the House upon the proposed amendment." The memorial is also printed in that issue. When the Chinese amendment did come up that afternoon, the Chinese community was present in force. The bill lost by a vote of 25 to 17.

121. Liliu is referring to the constitution of the Hui, not that of the Kingdom.
122. Waihoikaia was a servant at Muolaulani.
123. Keamalu was a painter living at Hamohamo, Waikiki.

*Monday, September 24.* Keamalu borrowed .75 [for an] express .75. Paid for Keala and Keliiakahai's tuition $2.50 for last quarter $1.75 for Keala's books. Keamalu borrowed $1.00 to go home with to Waikiki.

Gave back to Kaua her papers of her lands and list of indebtedness to Castle and others. She afterwards came back with Kip Yam—of Man Yick Wai loi [?].

*Tuesday, September 25.* Gave Joe a set of books [in which] to copy all my bills and to keep my accounts. Keamalu came again to town. I wonder what he is trying to do. Rebecca left Washington Place and took all her things away—because John shot pigeons.

*Wednesday, September 26.* Rebecca left Washington Place because John shot pigeons.[124]

Charlie Wilson told me that he had arranged with Bishop & Co. to let me have $12,000.00—at 7½ percent, to pay every 6 months until 3 years expires—will arrange about papers. John is willing.

[Certificate] No. 284 P.I.R. [People's Ice and Refrigeration] Co.

*Thursday, September 27.* Gave Kaakaole $2. John came to tell me he wanted someone to stay with his mother—[I] said I would see to it. Sophy [Sheldon] wanted to take Kuahine [Sheldon] from school on Saturday. Yes. Joe came down to put down new matting in his house. After tea Wakeke and I went for Milaina, she said she would come next day. Went for Mary Cook to spend night [with Mrs. Dominis]. Yes.

We slept at Washington Place. Found Mary Pahau already there. Milaina will go and stay with Mrs. Dominis in Rebecca's place.

*Friday, September 28.* Woke up early—went round to see the deserted rooms—all clean. Breakfasted, then came home. Milaina wants Mary Mahoe to come and stay with her—Yes. Naholowaa[125] was told this morning to move her house away from where it stands. Telephoned to Mary Cook to go and sleep again at Washington Place.

*Saturday, September 29.* Melaina and Mary [Mahoe] met me at Washington Place. They will take Rebecca's rooms. Paid her $7.50, and will give her more by and by. Told Ahoi and Aona[126] that they must save some money so when I go away they will buy their own food. Yes. Told Aona I would not buy him rice but would pay him $18.00. He wanted 50 cts more. Raised Kuaiwa's [salary] to $10.[127] The [certificate] number of the shares in Ice stock bought for 1st Division [of Hui Liliuokalani Hoonaauao] is 284—entitled to two shares. Bought of Wenner a gold bar for watch chain $4.00.

P. R. Isenberg called—first time since he was a boy.[128]

---

124. This entry repeats information in the entry of the previous day.

125. This was Mrs. Keahimakani Naholowaa (d. 1894), who is listed in the 1890 City Directory as residing in Manoa. She had other Honolulu properties, including "the Blue Gate," a somewhat dubious tavern. No record has been found of the building in question.

126. Ahoi appears as "Ah Hoi" in the directories as cook for Liliu at Muolaulani; Aona is there listed as a government messenger, residing at Kapalama.

127. Kuaiwa was Liliu's hostler at Muolaulani.

128. Daniel Paul Rice Isenberg (b. 1866, Kauai–d. April 13, 1919, Honolulu), was the son of Paul and Maria Rice Isenberg. He was a stockholder in the Lihue Plantation on Kauai, and in Honolulu he maintained the Waialae Ranch.

*Sunday, September 30.* Sent two homestead papers. One of Becky Kaai, one for Debora Mahoe's next [door] lot; [also] Deed of Kamookahi Naholowai's deed. Kamookahi Naa Haleaa—Palolo. Man Y [Yick] Wai [land at] Pahupahuapuaa. Leased to Taiku Aseu.

*Monday, October 1.* The Queen and John have gone to Waialua. Jennie and I went to see them off and came home. Had Jennie Clark, Mary Buckle's two children, and Kaipo and Aimoku to dine with me. Puaa o Kaiu [a pig from Kaiu?]. 2:30 P.M. drove up to Washington Place with Mary [Carter?] to meeting [of] First Division [of Hui Liliuokalani Hoonaauao]—no one came except Lou Brickwood. She told me Mrs. John Brown was going to resign [from] being Secretary, so decided to continue to work if she was willing—she said yes—and would take Louisa Hoopii in place of Lucy Woolsey who has been taken by Father Clement [as a] day scholar in Catholic school. Gave Lou [Louisa Brickwood] a certificate of Share in Ice Stock to keep for first Division [Certificate] No. 284. [At top of page:] Wrote to A. J. Cartwright for papers of this place—sent.

*Tuesday, October 2.* Borrowed Milaina's money $110.69 to pay Lam Yip, at 8%.[129] Gave J. Aea $23.00. Keamalu tells me Hatch[130] wants $50.00 for himself for Court. Summed up Keamalu's debt $537.00.

*Wednesday, October 3.* ~~Borrowed $50 of L.H. Naauao to pay Mr. Hatch for Keamalu's land case seeing that Charley is so slow about managing~~ money matters with S. M. Damon. Creditors coming every day. Keamalu borrowed $8.00 to buy Gin,[131] one for fish. Keamalu went to Aki's uncle ~~and asked him to sue Kahanukai~~ [?] to sue $1,000.00 ~~damage for taking his wife which he will do with assistance~~ of W. Achi who is his lawyer, instead of suing—W. Achi puts him off.[132]

Ten A.M. Met members of 2d Division [of Liliuokalani Educational Society]. No contributions. Three P.M. Met Hui Lahui—no contributions—gave notice [of] next [meeting] at third November. [Scrolling "L" at bottom of page.]

*Thursday, October 4.* Breakfasted with Charley [at] Hamohamo—wanted all papers, would come in, so took some more papers, deeds, Leases.

*Friday, October 5.* Charley told me Mr. Hatch was examining my papers to see if they were correct—before Damon would close arrangements with me for fear of mistake like Bush's case.[133] Mr. Cartwright called to ask if I had got through examining papers—told him not.

*Saturday, October 6.* Sent to J. Waiamau a report of Hooulu Lahui Society with a note for him to send [it] to print, and for him to make Statement on coming November third [meeting]—at Kaumakapili.

Informed A. J. Cartwright that I wanted to manage my affairs. He said he would [hand them over] and that I owed him $10,000, and yet his acknowledged notes are $9,227.77—how funny.

---

129. Lam Yip was a tailor at 19 Nuuanu Street.

130. Francis March Hatch (b. 1852, New Hampshire–d. 1923, Honolulu) was a prominent lawyer and later judge of the supreme court, active in the movement for annexation and a signer of the annexation treaty.

131. Unknown what "gin" is in this context—not alcohol.

132. No record has been found of this threatened divorce.

133. No such law case has been identified.

*Sunday, October 7.* Did not go to Church, left that for Wakeke and Joe. Four P.M. Drove out to Waikiki [and] told Charlie all about it. Six P.M. Supped and went to Kaumakapili. Dry Sermon. Sereno B. [Bishop] [on] Children when they call, parents hear and come, so God hears those who call on him. I wonder if he thought of God when he chased some children the day he surveyed Keamalu's land, and said some very ungodly words and nearly gave up surveying. [Liliu adds at the foot of the facing page:] He let "his angry passions rise"—[Two erased words follow.]

*Monday, October 8.* Breakfasted with the King, Queen sick. Poomaikelani came—pau huhu [her anger is ended]. 1½ P.M. A. J. Cartwright brought his accounts—mercy! $10,120.64 [in debt]—fearful—Must examine into it. All my papers returned: Leases [and] deeds—vouchers from 1883— 40 Waimanalo Stocks of mine, six for Kaipo—six Ice Stocks of [Hui Liliuokalani] [Hoo]kuonoono—and 12 of Liliuokalani Hui Hoonaauao 2d Division.

Gave Kahai his deed between Kapukini and me: $150.00 is paid and pau pilikia [trouble ended]. Keamalu and Kaaipulu deeded their land of Luhau to me. Had to pay $5.50 for Acknowledgements. Gave H. [Hattie] Kawainui $3.75 to pay for Louisa Hoopii and Mary Ulili of 2d Division [of Hui Liliuokalani Hoonaauao], and Alice Kanaluhi of mine.

[At top of page:] Gave Mrs. Lyman $24.00 of my dues of Hilo Hookuonoono.[134] Gave $12 of it to Hana Makana.

*Tuesday, October 9.* Received [Remainder blank.] Returned to John Dominis $27.00 of Aimoku's with book of shares in Ice Co.

*Thursday, October 11.* Paid $3.50 for Stationery and $5 for Iron bed, [and] $3 for mattress for Louisa Hoopii of 1st Division in Lucy Woolsey's [place]. John, Pratt, and Miles[135] started for round the Island by way of Pali. Had Kaipo and Aimoku here all day.

[A script L, then:] At the grotto.

*Friday, October 12.* Gave Kaakaole $2. Went to Alice Brown's to sing and found Hanna Palmer there.[136] Came home—Cartwright asked me to let him furnish [illegible] with money from Mary Beckley at 7 [percent]— there was policy in it to place me under their thumbs. Telephone [call] from A. [Asa] Kaulia [that] John Kaelele would sell his portion for $20. John and party gone to Punaluu. Mary Carter lunched with me.

*Saturday, October 13.* Went out early to [Charles] Wilson, heard that all had been mortgaged to Bishop & Co.—don't like it. Waited for Alice and Hana [Palmer]—[did] not come.

    134. This was a savings society for Hawaiian women, established in Hilo in 1886 by Liliuokalani and Mrs. Isabella Lyman.

    135. J. W. Pratt was superintendent of the Mutual Telephone Co. E. R. Miles was manager of the Hawaiian Hotel Carriage Co., General Livery, Feed, and Sale Stable—opposite the Royal Hawaiian Hotel.

    136. Hanna (or Hannah) Smithies (b. 1856–d. 1938, Honolulu) was the daughter of John Smithies and (from 1883) the wife of John A. Palmer.

Stayed three hours at grotto, till four P.M. Seven P.M. Went to see Mr. [C. R.] Bishop and Mrs. [Cordie] Allen. He told me it was impossible to get money from England—Experts from England would buy plantations from owners and not from Frank Austin. I told him what [Austin's] intention was—[He said the] Scheme would not pass but they would pay Austin for [his] trouble.[137]

*Sunday, October 14.* Stayed at home till four P.M., went round for Mrs. Haalelea and drove her out to see Kaiulani. Found her croqueting with Capt. Graham of USS *Alert*,[138] Hay Wodehouse, Mr. Giffard, Annie Cleghorn, and Tommy Cummins. Met her governess for first time, was pleased with her.[139]

*Monday, October 15.* Breakfasted with King. Told him of what I heard. Told me he is glad they did not ignore the [Austin] scheme entirely and that they should be willing to deal with English capitalists, is better than to send experts back without any agreements being made, for if negotiations are still kept open with England it shows we are still worthy of recognizance.

*Tuesday, October 16.* Spent the morning in making fern wreaths and flowers for Bernice's grave. Four years today since she died. And one wreath for Kapili [Likelike].

Two P.M. went to Kaiulani's reception with John. Was received by Prince David. The King was there and many others. Grand reception, Officers and everybody.[140] Came home to supper and went out to Mrs. Molly Brown's to a rehearsal. Lovely night. King came over with Prince David, had some music [and] came home at 12.

*Wednesday, October 17.* Aki and Lizzie [Elizabeth Mahiai Robinson] came and brought my hats home. I bought Annie Buckle's share in Ice Stocks at $95 for Kaipo. [At bottom of page:] Thomas Sq.

*Thursday, October 18.* Signed papers Mortgaging most of my lands to Bishop & Co. for $12,000.00. Chas. Wilson took it to them—noon Fred

---

137. Frank H. Austin had been working on a scheme to buy up and consolidate sugar plantations on Hawaii Island, with financing to come from London investors. Yardley, 108–10.

138. The USS *Alert* (Captain J. D. Graham) had arrived in Honolulu on September 15. Graham was previously in the islands in 1874 as an officer on board the USS *Benicia* and was in that capacity when King Kalakaua made his first tour to America in November of the same year. Graham was an old acquaintance of Colonel Charles H. Judd and John O. Dominis.

139. Miss F. Riesburg arrived in Honolulu on the *Mariposa*, from Auckland, New Zealand, on August 25, 1888. Her length of employment as Kaiulani's governess was less than a year.

140. Kaiulani's reception in honor of her 13th birthday was held at Ainahau from two to six P.M. The *Pacific Commercial Advertiser*, October 17, 1888, reported that it had been agreeable in every respect: "His Majesty the King was present from the opening at two o'clock, and H.R.H. Princess Liliuokalani ... arrived a little later.... Princess Kaiulani received the callers at the corner of the large lanai in rear of the main residence, resting between presentations upon a comfortable divan.... Mrs. Reisberg [sic, Miss Riesburg], her governess, attended upon her while Mrs. James H. Boyd gracefully assisted in the honors of the occasion.... The setting and decoration of the reception room were superb. Luxurious furniture, rich and stately kahilis [royal feather standards], works of art, screens, Japanese umbrellas, palms, flowers, and foliage were arranged with taste and effectiveness."

Macfarlane[141] took my Acknowledgement. Gave $50 to Kaai for Oo's[142] and $6 for her passage to Kona. Rec'd $20 from Joe for fish of Waikiki. [At bottom of page:] Emma Sq.

*Friday, October 19.* Received deed of Sale from Asa Kaulia of J. Kaelele to me his portion of Polani (w) Estate by I. Keau, and Joe took it and had it recorded. Paid Asa Kaulia $26.00 by Keau for deed and expenses. Sent by C. [Charles] Wilson draft on Bishop's Bank to F. M. [Francis March] Hatch for drawing [up] deeds and Mortgages $114.00.[143]

Paid $31.50 to Lizzie Jordan for trimming hats.

[At bottom of page:] Hotel.

*Saturday, October 20.* Sent Joe with draft on Bishop & Co. for $1,387.04 to pay bills with—also a note to C. Bolte, treasurer of Waimanalo Sugar Co., for Dividends of 40 shares for me, six for Kaipo, two for Wakeke. Telephoned to Willie, he said a baby had arrived last night so [he] must not go to the minstrel show.[144]

Rec'd $200.00 forty shares, $30 of Kaipo six shares to.

*Sunday, October 21.* Went to Kawaiahao [Church] ten A.M. After church went to Amoe's [to Laura Amoe's or Amoy Coney's] and had nice lunch. At two P.M. went to Waikiki, found Curtis [Iaukea] and Pua [Charlotte H. Iaukea] and babies [and] Henry Bertelmann[145] at Paoakalani. Had consultation with Charlie [Wilson]. Decided to write to A. J. Cartwright to send his bill. Came home tired. Wore my new bonnet from Luukia.

*Monday, October 22.* Received bill from A. J. Cartwright, $10,120.64. Signed for him a draft on Bishop & Co. for that amount. Paid $18.00 for aquarium—folly—when trying to save, [and] $1 for paddy, .25 for cart.

*Tuesday, October 23.* Sent a draft to A. J. Cartwright on Bishop's Bank for amount $10,120.64 and received a receipt in return. He advertised in papers of giving up my affairs.[146]

Signed papers of release from A. J. Cartwright and Acknowledgment by C. H. Gulick, acknowledged.

---

141. Frederick Washington Macfarlane (b. 1853–d. 1929) was a brother of Liliu's close friends Ned and George Macfarlane. He was at that time a cashier for Bishop & Co.

142. The Hawaii Oo [*Moho nobilis*]. Liliu was attempting to obtain several pairs of Oo from Hawaii Island and transport them to Kauai. In her autobiography, she wrote about these birds, "They are true Hawaiians; flowers are necessary for their very life." *Hawaii's Story*, 229.

143. This was a deed dated Oct. 12, 1888, from John Kaelele to Liliu for a lot at Kauluwela. Bureau of Conveyances, Liber 113, 306.

144. The minstrel show was an evening performance at the Opera House by the Honolulu Amateur Minstrel Company. "Every reservable seat had been secured before the opening of the doors [and] a good many persons had to stand throughout the evening." *Daily Bulletin*, October 22, 1888. The newly born baby has not been identified.

145. Henry C. Bertelmann (b. 1859, Koloa, Kauai–d. 1921, Honolulu) served with the rank of colonel on the staffs of King Kalakaua and later Queen Liliuokalani.

146. Cartwright's advertisement read: "Notice. The conditions of the power of attorney authorizing [me as] an agent for H.R.H. Liliuokalani, having been fulfilled, said power has this day been revoked and cancelled. ALEX J. CARTWRIGHT. Honolulu, Oct. 23, 1888." *Daily Bulletin*, October 23, 1888.

*Wednesday, October 24.* Gave Joe $20 to pay for surveying land in Manoa. Told him to look after a patch. Charles Wilson brought my account book with bank. 7½ p.m. went to rehearsal at Mrs. Brown's.

*Thursday, October 25.* Kaakaole $2.00. Went to Waikiki to Kaipo's house with Mahiai. Same day commenced repairs on my cottage.

**Friday, November 2.** Fourth anniversary of Bernice's death.[147] Went to Waikiki. Paina K [paina kapu, a private party], Mr. and Mrs. Clark, Wakeke, Mahiai, Eveline, J. H. [Heleluhe] [danced?] Hula Pele—strange thing.

*Monday, November 5.* Ten [?] a.m., compared notes with J. Waiamau of Hooulu Lahui Society [of] Kaumakapili. Eight a.m. Breakfast with King at Palace. Ten a.m. called on Mrs. and Miss Bishop.[148]

2.30 p.m. Received Mrs. Allen, Mrs. and Miss Bishop. Joe received $55.00 from Kahuakai—left word to pay $30.00 to Government for Kaauweloa [a parcel of land in Palolo].

*Tuesday, November 6.* Gave Joe $30—for what? Started for Kahala—Makanoe, J[ennie] Clark, H[attie] Kawainui, Mary Alapai, Maria Aiu, Wakeke, Naholowai, Charley Clark, Mary Aiu, [and] Esekela. Jennie found a ring. Inscription inside "Frank Auerback"—Aug. 28, 1867.[149] Virtu Tunxit mon non e separabit—outside, masonic emblem [a triangle with an eye in the center].

*Thursday, November 8.* Still at Kahala—nothing particular happened today. 5:30 p.m., Charlie Wilson came over,[150] shot four plovers for my breakfast. Stayed till 11 p.m.—[then he] went back to Hamohamo.

*Friday, November 9.* Charlie Clark, Joe Heleluhe, and two boys came over from Honolulu, brought papers. People went to fish, caught lots. Four p.m. whole party returned to Honolulu.

Seven p.m. went out to Alice Brown's—no one at home—returned to Washington Place. John had gone to dine at Palace with King for *Brooklyn* and *Alert* officers.[151]

11½ p.m. was woken by serenaders. Wiliokai[152] ma me [and company, with] Capt. Graham of *Alert* and Lieut. Doning [or Dening?] of *Brooklyn* and Sam Parker.

147. Bernice P. Bishop died at Kaakopua, her Emma Street residence, on October 16, 1884. Her funeral took place at that residence on Sunday, November 2, 1884.

148. The Bishops are not identified more specifically.

149. Frank B. Auerback (b. 1861–d. 1902) was an island resident from 1884. The ring was probably his father's.

150. As of November 11, 1885, Wilson and S. M. Damon held a five-year sublease from Liliu (to commence January 1, 1886) of the "Kahala flats" at Waialae for $40 annually.

151. "Friday evening His Majesty the King gave a dinner at Iolani Palace in honor of Capt. Wilson of the USS *Brooklyn*, Capt. Graham of the USS *Alert*, and officers of the two ships. In all sixteen sat down to dinner. The Palace was brilliantly illuminated . . . and the Royal Hawaiian Band played appropriate selections during the dinner." *Daily Bulletin*, November 10, 1888. The *Brooklyn*, described as a "noble old battle ship of Mississippi campaign renown," had arrived on October 15 from Nagasaki. The *Alert* had been in port since September 15, 1888.

152. Wiliokai (Kaina or Cain David Wiliokai) would be one of Liliu's guards at Washington Place in 1894. Wiliokai's father was Kawehena.

*Saturday, November 10.* Gave Kaakaole $2.

*Monday, November 12.* Rec'd $34.00 from Ice [Company] Shares. Breakfasted with Kunane [Kalakaua].

*Tuesday, November 13.* The King went to Wailuku in *Kinau* at four P.M.[153] Ten A.M. I went and asked him to return Waiomao and Pualeilani to me. [He replied?] Aloha ole [without affection] and puts me off to the Queen.
   Rain.

*Thursday, November 15.* Heavy rain all day.

*Friday, November 16.* Cleared up. Gave a dinner to Hooulu Lahui [Society] of Kaumakapili. Very few came. Ninito and Mr. Sumner[154] came with Nancy's daughter[155]—Mary Carter and [son] Cushman—Jennie Clark, Mr. and Mrs. Alapai, Maria Aiu, Maria Apo, [and] Esther.

*Monday, November 19.* A grand ball given to Admiral Heneage of HBMS frigate *Swiftsure*, by the King at the palace. Mary Carter and Oliver and Mary [Ailau?] went with me. The Queen wore peacock and velvet dress. Mrs. Neumann's was next-best dress.[156]

*Tuesday, November 20.* Two P.M. went with Mary Carter and [her son] Cushman to Music Hall to see the Silbons perform.[157]

*Wednesday, November 21.* Received from Hattie Kawainui and Jennie Clark $15.50 dues from members of Liliuokalani Hui Hoonaauao Division 2. Had a meeting at three P.M. of Members to consider about having tables at coming fair since the Queen said we were to send our Articles to her table.[158] Went upstairs [at Washington Place] to see John, found him very sick.

---

153. The *Daily Bulletin*, November 9, 1888, announced: "His Majesty the King leaves for Waikapu, Maui, next Tuesday, and will be the guest of Major W. H. Cornwell. On the 16th there will be a series of horse races at Waikapu, to celebrate His Majesty's birthday."

154. Ninito (b. 1838, Tahiti–d. July 21, 1898, Honolulu) was a member of the Tahitian royal family who had been betrothed to Moses (brother of Kings Kamehameha IV and V), but Moses died of the measles in 1848 shortly before her arrival. She later married John K. Sumner, son of Captain William Sumner. Her burial from the Catholic Church on Fort Street was the equivalent of a royal funeral.

155. Nancy Sumner Ellis (d. 1895, Honolulu) had a daughter, Victoria Sumner Ellis (b. 1875–d. 1921), who was later the wife of Eugene D. Buffandeau.

156. The *Pacific Commercial Advertiser*, November 20, 1888, noted: "A grand ball was given by His Majesty at Iolani Palace last night, in honor of Rear-Admiral Algernon C. F. Heneage of Her Britannic Majesty's Navy. The palace was splendidly decorated and illuminated for the occasion, its numerous ... electric lights turning night into more than the brightness of day.... The King appeared in plain evening dress with white waistcoat, adorned with a royal sash.... The queen was attired in her magnificent peacock robe and train." The account did not describe Mrs. Neumann's dress.

157. The event was at the Opera House. The performers were the Silbon Pantomime Company, whose advertisement in the *Pacific Commercial Advertiser*, November 19, 1888, announced that they would "introduce for this night only their Beautiful Roman studio Act of Living Models of Marble Gems." The matinee was at 2:30, "prices adults 50 cents, children half price."

158. This was in preparation for a grand bazaar for the benefit of Queen Kapiolani's favorite charity. The *Pacific Commercial Advertiser*, November 23, 1888, announced: "The Secretary of the 'Ahahui Hooulu and Hoola Lahui Society' [Grace Kahalewai] has issued circulars to the friends of the society, soliciting the contribution of articles and also loans to the exhi-

*Thursday, November 22.* The Makaainana's political meeting came off this evening. Very orderly. J. E. Bush, President, T. K. Nathaniel, Secretary, F. Metcalf, Corresponding Secretary. (No good.) [It] should have been: D. Pua, President. W. H. Cummins, Vice President, J. M. Poepoe, Secretary, [and] S. Kaeo, Corresponding Secretary.[159] [Below entry:] Washington Place.

*Friday, November 23.* So rainy [I] did not go back to Washington Place and John still sick. Gave Kaakaole $2.00. She has only $5.00 more in my possession.

*Saturday, November 24.* Had Ninito [Sumner] with me all day. *Alameda* [is] expected with the Baseball tourists—not a sign [of the vessel]. John is still ill and [I] may sleep here tonight—Washington Place.

*Sunday, November 25. Alameda* has arrived. Baseball tourists on board. No game can be played.[160] Lou [Louisa Brickwood] and I take a drive in my state carriage and stop at Washington Place to dine. Tonight the King gives a dinner to the tourists,[161] must not go.

*Monday, November 26.* Slept at Washington Place and came home [to Muolaulani] and breakfasted. *Alameda* left at ten last night.

Gave $12.50 to pay for grain, and Kainuuala's $31.00 for buying lumber for Aiaumoe's house[162]—to Joe Heleluhe. Paid Aona $15.00 and discharged him. Gave Joe $23.00 to give his Mother as she did not go home to Manoa for fear of Chinaman. Mr. Allen Herbert[163] has returned.

*Tuesday, November 27.* Puttered around the grotto. [He?] said all would be right by and by—but how expensive.

---

bition of any Hawaiian relics, implements, articles of manufacture, or curios that they may possess, which will add to the attraction of the occasion. The articles loaned . . . will be receipted for and insured and great care will be taken to return them. . . . The fair will be held at the Armory of the Honolulu Rifles on December 23rd."

159. The *Daily Bulletin*, November 23, 1888, in its reportage on the meeting of the Hawaiian political association Makaainana (meaning "common people") at the Honolulu Rifles armory, said: "Messrs D. Lyons, Bush, Kaulukou, and others addressed the meeting. A platform was adopted, one of the planks being as follows: 'That all officers of the Hawaiian Government who are under the present constitution appointed to office by His Majesty the King and His Majesty's Ministers should be elected by the people, and that the Constitution should be amended so as to have all Government officers chosen by popular election.'"

160. The arrival of a world-touring American baseball company had been widely publicized in the press, and elaborate plans were made for entertaining them on their projected arrival en route to Japan on Saturday, November 24. The *Alameda*, however, did not arrive until the next day, which meant that due to Hawaii's Sunday laws the players could not give the public the anticipated baseball exhibition.

161. The dinner was a luau, which took place on the grounds of Queen Kapiolani's private retreat, on the corner of Queen and Punchbowl Streets. The *Pacific Commercial Advertiser*, November 26, 1888, noted: "A large throng of natives and foreigners aided the guests of the evening in doing justice to a sumptuous national feast." The baseball team left at ten that evening for Japan. Liliu's remark "I must not go" suggests that the occasion was planned for gents only.

162. Aiaumoe (k) lived on the Queen's Hamohamo property.

163. Allen Herbert (b. about 1821, Sweden–d. July 3, 1921, Honolulu) was the popular proprietor of the Hawaiian Hotel.

*Wednesday, November 28.* Too bad—After all the trouble of sending blocks and screws and lumber out, Keamalu declares that no one shall move the house away from his premises. Hanakeola's [Hanakeola Kinimaka's] house is burnt and she off to baseball ground.[164] Charley Brickwood buried today.[165]

*Thursday, November 29.* Received $60.00 from J. Heleluhe [for] rent of Keauhou, Waikiki. Children are out [of school] for Thanksgiving day.[166] Went to see the boys at Carrie's [Carrie Bush's]—Kaipo feverish—bought for them 25 cents of potato and 25 cents of Apples.

*Friday, November 30.* Drew $416.00 [salary] from Govt., paid out to servants $152. Started two Subscription papers for Hanakeola among Hui Hoonaauao Liliuokalani Division 2, and others in town.

**Saturday, December 1.** Hattie and Jennie Clark returned $53.00—Makanoe $26—for Hanakeola. Had usual Hui Hoonaauao 2nd Division meeting—nothing done. Kealoha Hugo gave .25. Decided to give $17.00 towards buying clothes for Hanakeola and children and they got them on Monday. Jennie gave me $1.20 cents from Kamaka Stillman[167] for Hui Hoonaauao 2d Div.

*Sunday, December 2.* Stayed at home all day.

*Monday, December 3.* Makanoe, Wakeke, Jennie Clark, and Hattie Kawainui got Hana's [Hanakeola's] clothes—she said all she wants was a house [and] what is left of money is to go for paying workmen. She gives up her lot to me till $200 of lumber is paid. Had meeting of Hui Hooulu Lahui at Kaumakapili, they gave $5.00 towards Hanakeola's [aid].

*Tuesday, December 4.* Joe Aea $15.00—[he has] gone to Maui with Knights [of] Pythias and full band.[168] Took a drive with Ninito [Sumner] and Kapilikea.[169]

---

164. "House Burned. About 10:30 yesterday morning fire broke out in the house of Mrs. D. Leleo Kinimaka, widow of a former Major commanding the King's Guard. The house is a two-story one on the Ewa side of the Kawaiahao Girl's seminary, and the fire started in a small bedroom on the upper floor. Messrs. John Nott and John Dower saw the flames early, and went to work saving the contents.... The lower story was saved with only a slight external scorching of the walls, but the upper one was reduced to ruins. As far as could be learned there was no insurance. A four-year-old son of Mrs. Kinimaka started the fire with matches, having run away from his sisters, who were playing croquet on adjoining premises, a few moments previous to doing the mischief. The mother was at the Makiki recreation grounds watching a baseball game, and was terribly surprised at the condition of her domicile when she returned after the fire." *Pacific Commercial Advertiser*, November 29, 1888.

165. Charles Brickwood, a printer and the eldest son of Arthur P. Brickwood, died November 28, 1888, age 36, at Moanalua.

166. This was an observance of the U.S. holiday, not the annual November holiday celebrating Hawaiian independence and commemorating the November 28, 1843, recognition of Hawaii by Great Britain and France as an independent nation.

167. Kamaka Stillman (b. January 10, 1823, Kohala, Hawaii–d. Honolulu, July 25, 1924), the wife of Henry Stillman, was a descendant of Hawaiian chiefs including Chiefess Kahaopulani, her grandmother, who secretly reared the infant Kamehameha I.

168. The Knights of Pythias were off to Maui on a "pilgrimage" on the *Likelike* (December 4) for the express purpose of instituting a lodge. The *Pacific Commercial Advertiser*, December 8, 1888, reported on the excursion, the inauguration of the building, and other festivities. Joe Aea was a member of the Royal Hawaiian Band.

169. Kapilikea was John K. Sumner's Hawaiian name.

*Friday, December 7.* Stayed at Washington Place all day with Kaipo and Aimoku, sent them home with marbles.

*Sunday, December 9.* Knights of Pythias party return M [noon] today.

*Monday, December 10.* Gave Hattie Kawainui $61.00 to pay for three girls' tuition of Hui Hoonaauao Liliuokalani Mokuna [Division] 2. Sat with her and husband and watched my Oo birds. Makane brought $3.00 for Hanakeola.

*Tuesday, December 11.* 17 years ago since Kamehameha V died. Most of my [Oo] birds died today. They would have been at Pupukaniao[170] today if the *Mikahala* had not been detained, and [I] hope a few will live to get to Kauai tomorrow. Too bad. Francis Gay will be disappointed. Heard Kahae was very sick.

*Saturday, December 15.* Rec'd. from Waimanalo Stock $300.00 dividend and $45.00 for Kaipo.

*Monday, December 31.* The Queen's birthday. Went in state carriage to reception. Many ladies present. Wore black velvet and diamonds. Queen wore Peacock dress and diamonds.[171] Went back to Waikiki.

**Saturday, January 5, 1889.** Paid to Mrs. [Caroline] Bush $12.50 cts for Kaipo. No more money for Kaakaole.

170. Pupukaniao is an area on Kauai.
171. "Her Majesty held a state reception for ladies at Iolani Palace from 11 A.M. till two P.M. It was very largely attended by both native and foreign ladies. The Queen received in the Throne room, dressed in her beautiful court dress of peacock feathers, which she wore at Queen Victoria's court during the Jubilee. Her Majesty was attended by Lady-in-waiting Mrs. James W. Robertson. There were present Princess Liliuokalani, attended by Mrs. W. H. Aldrich, and Princess Kaiulani, attended by Misses Riesburg and Cleghorn. Major J. D. Holt and Adjutant Levi I. Kaiama were in attendance upon the royal party. Mr. J. W. Robertson, acting Chamberlain to the King, ushered visitors into the presence of the Queen.... The blue drawing room was very beautifully decorated, there being a superb display of ferns, flowers, etc., arranged by the deft hands of Mrs. Robertson and Mrs. James W. McGuire." *Pacific Commercial Advertiser*, January 1, 1889.

*Healani, the king's boathouse, a two-story framed building on piles in harbor shallows at Honuakaha. Situated below Queen Street (about where Halekauwila Street now crosses), it was approached from land by a plank boardwalk from the foot of Punchbowl Street. The lower floor was for various sea vessels, and the upstairs included a bedroom, bathroom, and large main room. The boathouse was maintained largely as a bachelor's domain where Kalakaua frequently entertained friends and sometimes visiting dignitaries.*

*In her diary Liliu notes her various visits to the boathouse— to meet with the king, with Kapiolani, and with Poomaikelani, and to attend luau. The structure is long gone, and much of the shallow part of the harbor was subsequently dredged and filled in for city expansion.*
Hawaii State Archives

# 1889

There are two diaries for the year 1889: a short version in the Hawaii State Archives, and a full account of the year, which is in a private collection. The Hawaii State Archives diary, which runs only to February 8, 1889, is in the Liliuokalani Collection filed with "Seized Documents"—that is, one of the mass of papers, diaries, and documents removed from Washington Place following the Queen's arrest in 1895. It was catalogued until recently as 1888 because Liliuokalani mistakenly gave the January 1 entry the date of the year that had just concluded, and continued to make her entries with the error. The longer diary for 1889 follows the short version.

*Tuesday, January 1, 1889.* Wakeke, Joe, Jennie Clark, [and] Hattie Kawainui went to town to open Hanakeola's house. John and Mainalulu went in my buggy and left me and Kaipo and Aimoku and all the Kawaiahao girls. Saw Czar and Mana [horses] in express, and other women in it. Joe lent the horses for a livelihood—hard up.

Annie Dowsett came back from San Francisco few days before the Queen's fair [held on December 23, 1888]. So thin. Gave a Statement of Hooulu Lahui Society—a very poor one—$6,000.00 in different banks and Govt. bonds. Only spent $57.00 in one year and a half. Milaina has $119.50 in my possession.

[The dates for Wednesday, January 2, to Tuesday, January 8, 1889, are penciled in but no entries follow.]

*Wednesday, January 9.* Surprised to find Kalei still out here. We all went to Washington Place. On our way left [my] Watch at Mr. Eckart's to repair.[1]

*Thursday, January 10.* Took back from J. [Joe] Heleluhe $105.00 of 2d Division Liliuokalani Hui Hoonaauao. Napunawai head man of Kealia [Kauai] brought [me] $200.00—placed in bank.

*Friday, January 11.* [D. H.] Nahinu came in at 15 minutes to eight A.M. and brought me only $4.50, having spent $20.00 on repairing loko [fishponds] at Kealia [Kona]. Gave 50 cts to buy this book, 50 cts for fish, $18.00 to J. Aea—[and] $3.50 to J. Aea for copying Kamaliikane's lease from Land Office. Told Joe to write to Kamaliikane[2] for 1 bag of coffee to send to Paris Exhibition. Told J. [Joe] Heleluhe to find out [about] the Kuleana [native land claim] the Queen had in Hamohamo. Found it was

THE DIARY FOR 1889 [SHORT VERSION]
1 JAN–8 FEB

Hawaii State Archives

---

1. Max Eckart was a jeweler and watchmaker, located at Bethel near King Street.
2. Kamaliikane (k) is listed in the 1890 City Directory as a laborer at Keauhou, Kona.

*A luau at the king's boathouse in honor of Abraham Hoffnung (Hawaiian Kingdom Charge d'Affaires in London) and his wife, 1888. Kalakaua, Mrs. Hoffnung, and Kapiolani are seated at the far end of the table, flanked by hand-held kahili. Formal entertainments at the boathouse were rare but lively affairs, and within its confines relative informality was the rule of the day. On this occasion, guests relax on the floor, the fern-clad table is bountiful with food and champagne, a violinist provides music, and waiters stand by.*
Hawaii State Archives

[from] Pupuka's daughter Malie married [to] Kelekona, who sold it to the Queen. Royal Patent 4631, Kuleana 10677. Sent J. Heleluhe to tell Chulan[3] that he was backwards in his rents. Told J. Heleluhe about giving Govt. [a] portion of lot near bathhouse at Waikiki. Lizzie Victor came to see me to apologize. Jennie Clark [and I?] spent afternoon croqueting.

*Saturday, January 12.* Found out today I have paid Kainuuala twice, once on the 26th of November, and on the 8th of this month. Signed leases of Keahuolu to Kunane [Kalakaua]. Received $200.00 of Waimanalo Stocks and $80.00 for Kaipo of same at 5 per. ct. Paid [for] *Pae Aina* and *Makaainana* [newspapers] $18.00. Gave $2.00 to Aiaumoe. Joe Heleluhe told me he had gone to A. J. Cartwright to see if Chulan & Co. had been correct in his payment. He showed Joe his cashbook of last payment—correct.

*Sunday, January 13.* Mainaulu telephoned that John was very sick, so drove up to C. [Charles] Wilson's. He told me to send Joe up to his office next day [and] he would give him Memorandum.

*Monday, January 14.* Miss Pepoon[4] sent through Wakeke $3.00 for 1st Division [Hui Hoonaauao].

*Tuesday, January 15.* John sent for Aimoku and Kaipo to spend the day. Mrs. D. did not see my likeness. Lou Brickwood paid me $1.50 for envelopes of 1st Division. I paid Lou $2.00 of Ice Stocks of 1st Division. She showed me Louisa Hoopii's bed had been paid on Dec. 15. She paid $8.00 so I had to pay her $4.00 stocks—we made it even by my taking $4.00.

*Wednesday, January 16.*—J. M. Monsarrat took our acknowledgement of lease of Keahuolu with King. Kaipo and Aimoku are here. Gave C. Wilson names of Songs to get Copyrights. Gave Paoakalani 35 cts to buy a book. Received from Mary Alapai $30.00 from pig—gave her $10.00—gave to Joe Heleluhe Lease of Keahuolu, he passed them over to J. M. Monsarrat to record.[5]

Went to meeting at three P.M. at Louisa Brickwood's of [Hui Hoonaauao] Committee to put another scholar in Kawaiahao Seminary, decided on Lokai's daughter—decided to leave Lily Auld's girl till the Annual meeting. Paid Lou $43.00 for Miss [Helen A.] Pepoon for 1st Division.

*Thursday, January 17.* [No entry follows.]

*Friday, January 18.* Joe H. told me he had sent notes twice to C. B. Wilson—no notice taken. I told him to go personally to him. Joe gave me lease of Keahuolu with Kunane [Kalakaua]. Joe returned $210.00 of Aimoku's and $105.00 of Kaipo's money. People's Ice and Refrigeration Co. wouldn't take it.

Joe H. gave me $5.00 returned by Mr. Parke of Mr. M. Hewitt who went into bankruptcy soon after I bought the *Young Ladies' Journal*.[6]

---

3. Chulan was leasing land at Hamohamo, Waikiki, to cultivate rice.

4. Miss Helen A. Pepoon (b. 1865) arrived in Honolulu on September 1, 1888, and remained until June 1891. She was the principal of the Kawaiahao Seminary, and had formerly been the principal of the Fox Lake Seminary, Wisconsin.

5. I have not located this transaction in the Bureau of Conveyances.

6. News dealer and stationer Alexander M. Hewitt declared bankruptcy on January 8, 1889. Schedule B (disbursements) in the proceedings includes the following: "Jan 1, 1889.

Went to call on Mrs. and Dora Dowsett, found Miss McBryde[7] there. Went up to Mrs. Bush's with slates and a primer for Kaipo and Aimoku and two pairs [of] sleeve buttons. Called on Mr. and Mrs. James Campbell, left John at Washington Place, drove out to see Queen and Poomaikelani. Queen told me she will not give any money to Kaumakapili church till she had good Security for it.[8]

Met Sam Parker out there—Eight P.M. Mr. [John F.] Bowler said [Rev. C. M.] Hyde[9] and others did not want the church [used] for only political purposes. Told him that I would let him know tomorrow. Bowler told me G. Herman and perhaps Widemann would help if Queen did not.

*Saturday, January 19.* Small bag flour, ess [essence of?] lemon, Ham, tin [of] lard, $1 of coffee. 1: chocolate, 2 pounds fresh, 25 cts. Potato, 25 cts Macaroni. 1 pound crushed sugar. = $9.22 at H. McIntyre's [grocery store].

Sent for [Reverend J.] Waiamau. He told me his plan was to give out shares $10,000.00 [worth of] shares and for each to pay in four years—very good plan.[10] Told Waiamau what [John] Bowler had said. He was glad.

Went to [hear] Band and went to return Aimoku's $210.00. John took it upstairs [but he] did not like so much silver [coinage in the house?].

*Sunday, January 20.* Waiamau tells me that the King told him the Queen would not pay the [Kaumakapili] church debts off. Gave Joe Heleluhe $3.50 to pay [for an] Account book. Sam Parker was the means. [?] Ahoi paid my grocery bill $9.22 to H. McIntyre.

Found lease of Kamaliikane inside Hui Hoonaauao Account book. Joe brought back my watch—gave him $3.00 to pay repairs. Wrote out Constitution for new Society, Limahana.[11]

Kaiaiki wanted to buy house at Keauhou—let him know by and by. John Bowler telephoned that he and Widemann would take Mortgage on Kaumakapili Church.

---

Paid to J. Heleluhe for subscription to *Young Ladies' Journal* for Mrs. Dominis, not filled as charged. $5.00." Hawaii State Archives, First Circuit Court, Law 2741.

7. This was a daughter of Judge Duncan McBryde (b. 1802–d. 1858) of Wahiawa, Kauai.

8. In putting up their new edifice on Beretania Street, the trustees of Kaumakapili Church had run up large debts. *The Friend*, December 1888, reported: "Kaumakapili Church, whose new building has cost $57,000, is troubled with creditors' claims for some $7.000 still unpaid. The trustees have sent in an application to the Hawaiian Board, asking that arrangements may be made to mortgage the property, to satisfy these oppressing claims." The major creditor, John F. Bowler, was owed some $5,000. Bowler (b. 1825, Massachusetts–d. 1925, Honolulu), a Honolulu builder, had brought an action before the courts to settle an unpaid debt for work on the assembly room of Kaumakapili Church.

The *Pacific Commercial Advertiser*, January 24, 1889, said that the trustees had decided to mortgage the property to the Lunalilo estate for $6,000 to pay the debt, and P. C. Jones had offered to endorse a note for $1,000. *The Friend*, February 1889, noted that "satisfactory results" had been attained by P. C. Jones, H. Waterhouse, and W. O. Smith acting as a "special committee," and the claim was acknowledged as paid in full on April 26, 1889. Hawaii State Archives, First Circuit Court, Law 2803.

9. Charles M. Hyde (b. 1832, New York City–d. 1899, Honolulu) was an American Board missionary who arrived at Honolulu in 1877 to head the North Pacific Missionary Institute. He worked with Hawaiian churches and with the Hawaiian Board of Missions, and was a trustee of the Kamehameha School. His wife, Mary (b. 1840, Brimfield, Massachusetts–d. 1917, Ware, Massachusetts), was a hard-working minister's wife, and founded the Lima Kokua (Helping Hand) Society at Kawaiahao Church.

10. See second footnote for January 18, 1889, diary entry (this page).

11. This was a sewing society.

Hattie and Mrs. S. Kaai called this afternoon, want a large potato. Charlie Wilson will see Mins. [the government ministers] about my going to Paris[12]—and about Mortgage on [Kaumakapili] church.

*Monday, January 21.* [Three-line entry erased.]

*Tuesday, January 22.* Gave Kaakaole $2.00. Started a new [sewing] society for Hawaiian ladies, [named it] Limahana.

Gave Milaina an Account book showing she had $119.50 in my possession.

*Wednesday, January 23.* King came over at ten A.M. Met Alapai[13] and told them to stand firm. Went at six A.M. to get advice from [Antone] Rosa. He told me he represented Widemann and Trustees of Kaumakapili [Church] ought to accept their offer to pay off creditors of Church $7,000.00. Hard to get trustees together.

Queen telephoned that Annie Dowsett was up there trying to straighten out accounts of Hooulu Lahui Society. Ninito [Sumner] came to ask me to go to Catholic School on Friday.

[The dates for Wednesday, January 24, to Wednesday, January 30, 1889, are penciled in but no entries follow.]

*Thursday, January 31.* Rec'd. Mon. D. Anglaide—French commissioner [who called] with Mr. [Antonio de Souza] Canavarro, then Edward Clifford—who shewed me drawing he took of Kaiulani—very good—wanted to take mine.[14] I gave him one of my pictures. He sent me prescription of medicine for leprosy.[15]

Received some others—forgot who—but John was there.

[The dates for Friday, February 1, to Tuesday, February 5, 1889, are penciled in but no entries follow.]

**Wednesday, February 6.** Joe [Heleluhe] told me today he would like to put up a shanty at corner of Kaipo lane. I said he might. He expects to make lots of money.[16]

Hassinger[17] and C. [Charles] Wilson came in to see about articles for Paris Exhibition.[18]

12. Liliu had evidently hoped to attend the Paris Exposition Universelle to be held that year. Nothing came of the idea.

13. John W. Alapai was a trustee of Kaumakapili Church. The *Pacific Commercial Advertiser*, March 17, 1893, disparagingly called him "the heathen old deacon of Kaumakapili...[and] one of the leaders of the Hui Kalaiaina [who] figured conspicuously in a tall hat and dark coat on the memorable 14th of January" (the day when the attempt to enact a new constitution took place).

14. Englishman Edward Clifford arrived in Honolulu on the *Australia* December 1, 1888, with the express purpose of visiting Father Damien at Kalawao, Molokai. An artist, he painted a portrait of Damien that hangs in the Chapel of the Church Army, London, England. Another of his portraits (this one of Charles Reed Bishop) is in the Bishop Museum collection. The whereabouts of his drawing of Kaiulani is unknown, and there is no record that he completed a portrait of Liliu.

15. Clifford advocated gurjum balsam (tree) oil as a possible cure for leprosy.

16. Joe Heleluhe was planning to open a milkshake business. See full version of this section of Liliu's diary for February 9–10, 1889 (222).

17. John A. Hassinger (b. 1837, Philadelphia–d. 1902, Honolulu) was chief clerk in the Interior Department.

18. Both the Hawaiian government and King Kalakaua were interested in promoting Hawaii by exhibiting at the Paris Exposition Universelle, scheduled to open on May 5, 1889,

*Thursday, February 7.* John came in and did not want to invest in railway. Sent for Charlie [to ask] if it would be safe for me to invest in Oahu Railway—told me he'd find out.[19]

My friend[20] tells me I will be successful in any enterprise—lots of money—must not go away.[21] [She says the] King must not go—two deaths in the family—will not be successful in his project—a flaw in the papers. One man (G.W.M.) [George W. Macfarlane] faithful to him, the other (Austin) not and will fail. Mother [Dominis] will die soon—and one lady sick. To be careful of Poi enterprise—there will be seven officers, when eighth man comes in there will be a failure—must not get him. If the King has plenty of money, he will stay in that house, if not—he will never enter it again if he goes away—[she says] I am going far away by and by—but am going soon on short trips.

Went to Concert at Music Hall. Very few [attended]—good music.[22]

Met King in box. Told him [I] will go see him tomorrow.

Six P.M. Annie Dowsett came. Tells me she [is] going to California.

[At top of page above the entry:] Joe asked to lease Pawaa—I said yes $300.00 a year—will come in Saturday for papers.

*Friday, February 8.* According to promise I went to the Palace [and] told the King my errand—[he] did not seem to like it. Queen sick with boils, wonder if it is cancer—eating tea with butter the very worst thing.

---

and run to October 31, 1889. The exhibition solicited a wide variety of exhibits, and eventually Hawaii sent 53 cases of goods to Paris. Kalakaua also expressed an interest in attending (as did Liliuokalani), but, due to political developments at home, neither of them was able to do so. The king and queen, Princess Poomaikelani, and Liliu all loaned items. A long list of these shows that Liliu sent 40 packages of shells. In addition, she loaned two Niihau mats, a pair of slippers fashioned of pumpkin vines, a framed bouquet of shells, kukui nut leis, a model of a grass house, and several calabashes. Hawaii State Archives, Foreign Office and Executive Files, Box 36.

19. This was the commencement of what became the Oahu Railway and Land Co., founded by Honolulu businessman Benjamin F. Dillingham. His prospectus for the same, in a long letter dated January 19, 1889, appeared in the *Daily Bulletin* and was issued as a broadside prospectus titled "Oahu Steam Railroad." Copy in Hawaii State Archives, Dole Collection.

Regarding the proposed enterprise, Dillingham stated: "It is about three and a half years since I ventured to try to interest the people of this country in a scheme to unlock its wastelands, by bringing certain large and valuable tracts on this island within easy reach of this city, by means of a railway fifteen to twenty miles in length." The prospectus then laid out details of the proposed rail line, its costs, and its potential earnings, including freight and passenger revenues, and then solicited investors to subscribe for bonds: "Are there not 1,500 people in this country who will risk $100 each in an enterprise like this?" Liliu eventually acquired a small amount of stock in the company.

20. "My friend" refers to Gertrude Wolf, a German-born fortune-teller who came to Honolulu in the late 1880s under unknown circumstances. She appears to have adroitly obtained information on the palace politics of the time, which she cleverly "foretold" to the Queen, thereby gaining considerable influence with the latter. Miscellaneous accounts and occasional references in the Queen's diaries show that she was also in Liliu's employ for several years. On April 4, 1894, she married Charles D. Chase, a real estate agent. She died May 24, 1896, age 38 years, in Honolulu.

21. Wolf was referring to a proposed trip to the forthcoming Exposition Universelle in Paris.

22. This was to hear Enrico Campobello of Her Majesty's Theatre, London, and his company at the Hawaiian Opera House. The *Pacific Commercial Advertiser*, February 8, 1889, reported: "In the presence of His Majesty, Princess Liliuokalani, Hon. John O. Dominis . . . the artists who form the Campobello Company made their first appearance last evening. It is to be regretted that so few of our musical friends thought proper to encourage by their presence this excellent combination."

Met Hui Limahana at Washington Place. Paid for five pillowcases 50 cts. began two Kapa apana [a quilt with appliqued patterns] for J [Jennie] Clark—bought one—had got $2.00 [for] sewing hat—$3.50 was made today. To meet on Monday a luau for Kala paid .50 for pig. Joe Heleluhe told me lots of people still at Waikiki.

[The dates for Saturday, February 9, to Tuesday, February 26, 1889, are penciled in but no entries follow. The notebook is thereafter blank.]

THE DIARY FOR 1889 [FULL VERSION] 1 JAN 1889– 1 JAN 1890

Honolulu Private Collection

*Tuesday, January 1, 1889.* At Waikiki. John went to town—Wakeke, Jennie C[lark], Hattie Kawainui, J. Heleluhe went to housewarming [for] Hanakeola's house. Band came out to serenade. Kaipo and Aimoku are with me, and girls from Kawaiahao Seminary, C[harles] Clark, and children. Luau and croquet on the afternoon. Races at Kapiolani Park.

*Wednesday, January 2.* Moved in town—Jennie Clark, Hattie Kawainui, and Lydia Aholo help cleaning house—Curtains look pretty—tired, retire at 11.

*Thursday, January 3.* Went to Mrs. Cordie Allen for advice how to start meeting. Went ten A.M. to Washington Place to meet 2nd Division—nothing to do. Four P.M. had meeting 1st Division of Liliuokalani Ed. Society—30 members present—$82.00 contributed by members. E. K. Wilder says she is not a member. Mrs. Lewers [?] and daughter join.

*Friday, January 4.* John came boozy. Woke by humbug, [?] will come tomorrow, Aki and Kahanuu [Meek]—Joe told me he had [Entry ends thus.]

*Saturday, January 5.* Mahiai [Robinson] went home. Croquet till two. Four P.M. went to Helen Boyd, took Secretary's book to her. Went to see Annie Cleghorn—She and Kaiulani out. Paid Mrs. Bush 12.50 for Kaipo, gave her [for] Willie, Lola, Aimoku 10 cts each, [and for] Austin [Strong] .05 [5 cts].[23] Sent Mary pig for Aimoku.

*Sunday, January 6.* Stayed at home all day, not feeling well.

*Monday, January 7.* Rec'd $26.00 by Joe for Ice Stocks. Called meeting [of] officers 2d Division [Liliuokalani] Education[al] Society about investing in Ice Stocks at $105.00 a share, all consented. Gave to Joe Heleluhe $105.00 for Kaipo—$105.00 for 2d Division Liliuokalani Educational Society. $210.00 for Aimoku to buy share in Ice Stocks.

Spent afternoon croqueting. Charles and Jennie Clark spent evening with me. Went to Mary Alapai's to see her and Maria Aiu. Called on King and Queen. They had called a meeting to raise more money to help Hanakeola's hale papaa [burned house].

*Tuesday, January 8.* Paid to Kainuuala her $312.00 drawn from Bishop's Bank to pay Willie's burial expenses. [Double "L" follows.] The whole day was spent reading—read King's lease of Keahuolu—did not like it.[24]

23. Willie and Lola were children of Mrs. Caroline Bush. Aimoku was Liliu's hanai (adopted child), and Austin Strong was the son of California artist Joe Strong and his wife Isobel.

24. This lease to the king may never have been effected, for no record of such a transaction has been found in the Bureau of Conveyances.

*Wednesday, January 9.* Aimoku's birthday. Rec'd from W. F. Allen $37.80 for Kaakaole. Luau at Washington Place. Carrie Bush, her two children, Aimoku and Kaipo, myself. Told Miss Malone to tell her scholars not to peep over fence again.[25]

Croquet rest of day. Took my watch to Eckart's to mend.

*Thursday, January 10.* Took back from Joe Heleluhe $25.00 of 2d. Div. of Hui Hoonaauao Liliuokalani. Napunawai told me not to trust Kauanoe.

[Script "L" inserted.] Went to Thomas Square—met C. [Charles] Wilson, he wanted me to [convey to] the Government, few feet on makai side of road near [my] bathhouse. I said yes. He told me Chulan was in arrears of rent.

*Saturday, January 12.* Stayed at home with Jennie Clark [all] afternoon playing Croquet till seven P.M. [Script "L."] Was told John was sick.

*Sunday, January 13.* Washington Place. Came here to attend John's sickness. [Mr. Frank S.] Pratt came in—said the Government could not give any more bonds—refused Hooulu Lahui Society money—had to place [the money] in Postal bank. Lily Auld wanted 1st Division [of the Educational Society] to take [young] Lily Auld to educate. Gave me Niihau shell necklace.

*Monday, January 14.* Breakfasted in Palace—puaa, lei ilima, halii nahele [roast pig with ilima leis spread out on greenery]. King, Queen, Poomaikelani, Kawananakoa, Kuhio, Lidia P., Beke Colburn, me. Mrs. Dowsett and committee of Hooulu Lahui [Society] came in [to] settle accounts of [the December] fair—looking black. Sent for Waiamau. They were fasting. Rain. Lovely night. [From memorandum on back blank leaf:] Jan. 14. Answered note from Frank Gelina [Green?] asking for forgiveness for using foul language at me.[26]

*Tuesday, January 15.* I told [Reverend] Waiamau to borrow Hui Lahui money to pay off Kaumakapili debts [of] $3,500.08—hope he will get it. Kaipo and Aimoku here.

*Wednesday, January 16.* Had meeting [of Liliuokalani Educational Society] 1st Division at Lou's [Louisa Brickwood's], will take Kaaumoau [as a] scholar. Gave her $3.00 from Miss Pepoon for 1st Division. She paid me $1.50 for envelopes.

*Thursday, January 17.* Waiamau told me he hoped to get money from the Queen. Gave Joe $10.00 to buy bed for Kalahiki. Wrote to San Francisco to find out about Copyright [of music]. Thurston says it costs $5 and $1 for Acknowledgement.

---

25. Miss N. J. Malone (d. 1926, Pasadena, California) was the principal of the Punahou Preparatory School, located adjacent to Washington Place on the present Saint Andrew's Cathedral grounds.

26. Liliu's January 14, 1889, letter, says: "Dear Frank, I was very glad to find on reading your note that you were sorry for what you said the other day, and [I] forgive you with all my heart. I hope that you will also keep your promise and if you do you will never be sorry—and try and remember that motto that 'you must think twice before you speak.'... Your friend Liliuokalani." Hawaii State Archives, Liliuokalani Collection, Box 7, retained draft.

*Friday, January 18.* Joe gave me [returned to me?] lease of Keahuolu with Kunane [Kalakaua] $220.00.

*Saturday, January 19.* Stayed at home till Mary Kamiki brought some fish, gave her .50 for fish. Four P.M. went to drive. Took back to John Dominis $210.00 of Aimoku.

*Sunday, January 20.* Jimmie and Helen Boyd spent the day with me. Somebody was huhu [angry] this morning.

*Monday, January 21.* Gave Joe $3.88 for account books, Ahoi $7.22 to pay H. McIntyre, $3.00 to pay for my watch. Charles Kaiaiki wants to buy house at Keauhou.[27]

*Tuesday, January 22.* Went to Washington Place. Started a sewing Society. Came home, dined, [and] Croqueted. Seven P.M. [Reverend] Waiamau tells me again no money and [P. C.] Jones and party will take [the Kaumakapili Church] mortgage up—too bad. John Bowler has been playing double game all round.

Mr. Finley arrived—wife will come by and by.[28]

*Wednesday, January 23.* King came here—met Alapai, told him to work and stand firm, not to give in to opposition party. Rec'd news of J. Nakookoo's death.[29]

Young Hee writes he has paid Keohoka's lease rent. Will answer these.[30]

*Thursday, January 24.* Gave J. H. $100.00 of Waimanalo stocks to pay C. R. Bishop's bank. [Reverend] Waiamau and [J. W.] Alapai says Kaumakapili Church is mortgaged to Lunalilo Estate. Charles Wilson says it is for the best. He says it would cost $550.00 to [go to] Paris and back. Cut roots of orange tree and forgot [Allen] Herbert—Mahiai came back.

*Friday, January 25.* Went after Ninito [Sumner] and went to Catholic school to see girls exercise. Very nice. Took her home, drove and left black feathers for Lepeka to make leis. Left poetry [?] with D. Nape's wife.[31]

Found vines all cut down at Washington Place. [Scrolling "L."] Bad cough.

*Saturday, January 26.* Started for Waikiki at 11 A.M. with Mahiai [Robinson], bathed in sea, had lunch on manini[32] and lipoa[33] on beach, came home, dined at four. Saw Kaae, Kaiue, Kahonuu [?], Ake, Keliilani out there.

*Sunday, January 27.* Waiamau told me there would be a contribution at K [Kaumakapili]. King should be there to explain all. Sent Joe with $100.00.

27. Kaiaiki had accompanied John O. Dominis to England in 1887 as his manservant.

28. James Finlay is listed in the 1890 City Directory as "fireman, Oahu Railway and Land Co." The Finlays lived at the corner of King and Palama Streets. Mrs. Finlay and children arrived at Honolulu on February 6, 1889.

29. J. K. Nakookoo, a member of the House of Representatives during the session of 1882, lived at Kohala, Hawaii.

30. In the address section at the end of the diary, Liliu noted: "Young Hee Wailuku, has leased Kapeiki's land [Wailuku?]." Young Hee, listed in the 1890 City Directory as "butcher and stock raiser, Wailuku," also had a large ranch in the district of Kula, Maui.

31. David Nape was a musician with the Royal Hawaiian Band.

32. The manini is the convict tang, *Acanthurus triostegus*.

33. Lipoa describes two species of seaweed, *Dictyopteris plagiogramma* or *D. australis*.

King did not go—went for Jessie [and] took her out to Waikiki [on] Pain's tram[car]. He came out in tramcar. Came home in the evening.[34]

*Monday, January 28.* Did not breakfast at the palace but at Kalaaukala—only the royal family. King said he heard I was going to Paris—Ministers told him so.

*Tuesday, January 29.* Drove over to C. Wilson to tell him we could not go to Paris,[35] then to John to go to Opera.[36]

*Wednesday, January 30.* Mrs. J. Carter spent forenoon here—a surprise—found [me] cleaning shells.

John called to know if we were going to reception. Eight P.M. went to Mrs. Afong's reception—everybody there almost.[37]

*Thursday, January 31.* Signed draft $416.00 my monthly allowance. Went four P.M. [to] Lunalilo Home.[38]

Mr. and Mrs. Deverill are to leave.[39]

Learned today Charles Hopkins and Kua are to be put out.[40]

Went to see Rosa [Rose] Makee[41] in *Patience*. Lt. Pears, Lt. St. John, Alice Hastings principal parts. Capital.[42]

---

34. Tramcars (streetcars) commenced passenger service from town to Waikiki on January 26. The *Pacific Commercial Advertiser*, January 28, 1889, noted that the cars were "crowded all day yesterday," and that on January 29, King Kalakaua stepped into one of the cars in front of Iolani Palace and rode out to Waikiki.

35. Liliuokalani had entertained the idea of traveling to France to see the great Paris Exposition Universelle of that year.

36. The opera was Gilbert and Sullivan's *Patience*, advertised in the *Pacific Commercial Advertiser* as "complete with Full Chorus and Orchestra," at the Opera House. The following day, the *Pacific Commercial Advertiser*, January 30, 1889, reported that the performance had been an "unqualified success" and continued: "There sat in the royal proscenium box Her Majesty the Queen, their Royal Highnesses Princess Liliuokalani and Princess Poomaikelani, and Hon. John O. Dominis, while the opposite box was occupied by Her Royal Highness Princess Kaiulani, attended by Miss Riesberg (her governess), Misses Cleghorn and Widemann, and Capt. Acland and Lieut. Kingsmill, R.N." Liliu attended several performances.

37. "Last evening Mr. and Mrs. C. Afong held a reception at their residence, Nuuanu Valley, in celebration of the Chinese New Year. The front of the house was most beautifully decorated with different colored lanterns, and what with the electric light and the illumination of the tastefully laid-out grounds the scene was a very charming one. The Royal Hawaiian band occupied a position on the grounds and added much to the pleasure of the evening.... The invited guests ... were warmly welcomed by Mr. and Mrs. Afong and their charming daughters. Among those present were ... His Majesty the King, attended by Mr. J. W. Robertson ... H.R.H. Princess Liliuokalani, H. H. Prince David Kawananakoa, Hon. J. O. Dominis, [and] Hon. A. S. Cleghorn.... Refreshments of a most substantial nature were served in abundance in the dining room [and] the elegant billiard room was visited by a number of the guests." *Daily Bulletin*, January 31, 1889.

38. This was for a public reception honoring the late King Lunalilo's birthday. The *Pacific Commercial Advertiser*, February 1, 1889, reported it as "probably the finest celebration of the day ever had." Visitors included the king and queen, Liliuokalani and Dominis, Princess Kaiulani and her father Mr. Cleghorn, and prominent citizens of the town. The building was decorated with flags, banners, and bouquets of flowers, and the Royal Hawaiian Band played "Hawaii Ponoi" on the king's arrival.

39. Mr. and Mrs. W.E.H. Deverill were in charge of the Lunalilo Home.

40. Charles Hopkins was deputy marshall. In 1890–91 he would serve as marshall of the kingdom. Josiah Kua is listed in the 1888–89 City Directory as "2nd clerk, Marshall's Office."

41. Rose Makee (later Mrs. E. D. Tenney) and Alice Makee Hastings were the daughters of Captain James Makee of Rose Ranch at Ulupalakua, Maui.

42. For remarks on the performance of *Patience*, see footnote for February 2, 1889, diary entry (221).

*Friday, February 1.* Spent morning in wrapping shells to be sent to Paris Exhibition. Four P.M. went with Poomaikelani and 30 women to ride on tramcar.[43]

Gave band boys letter to Mana to fish in sea.[44]

We arrive at Waikiki and they leave. Caught plenty fish—sat right down and supped and watched hulas—went to bed.

*Saturday, February 2.* Came home this morn, tried croquet. Four P.M. Rested for tonight. *Patience* again. Took seats in middle of house with Kunane [Kalakaua] and Kawananakoa, nice performance.[45] Money spent—lots for nothing.

*Sunday, February 3.* Cross today. Spent morning in sorting out curios for Paris exhibition.

One P.M. Went out to a luau given by Henry Poor for Mr. and Mrs. Robert L. Stevenson. King and myself went. King was presented with a golden pearl by Stevenson.[46]

*Monday, February 4.* Paoakalani. Nine 30, went to Mrs. Allen's—she spoke of [sponsoring] one girl for Education[al] Society. Told her if Govt. would pay half, we [would] pay half.

Ten A.M. L. H. [Liliuokalani Hui] Hoonaauao—$1.50 contributed. [At] 11. Limahana wahine [women's sewing society]—six sheets, 7 pillowcases made. Paid 1.00.

---

43. The *Daily Bulletin*, February 2, 1889, noted: "H.R.H. Princess Liliuokalani went to Waikiki on the tramcars yesterday afternoon, returning this morning. The car on which she rode was decorated with evergreens and flags."

44. Mana is listed in the 1888–89 City Directory as "Fisherman, Waikiki." He was probably in charge of several fishing grounds owned by Liliu. He is not to be confused with John Mana, who was a close friend of the Queen.

45. "The third and final performance of 'Patience' at the Opera House by our Amateur Dramatic Company on Saturday night was witnessed by another full house.... Miss Rose Makee was about as perfect as she could be." Another article of the same date noted: "After the performance of *Patience* at the Hawaiian Opera House ... the whole of the performers went over to Iolani Palace in response to an invitation from His Majesty the King and partook of an elegant supper laid out in the dining hall. The performers were all in their stage costumes and they thoroughly enjoyed and appreciated His Majesty's hospitality." *Daily Bulletin*, February 4, 1889.

46. "LUAU AT WAIKIKI. Sunday afternoon a luau in Hawaiian fashion was given by Mr. Henry F. Poor at Manuia, Kapiolani Park, in honor of Mr. and Mrs. R. L. Stevenson and party. The guests, having spent several months among the islands of the South Seas, were prepared to relish native cookery, and though, owing to the delicate health of Mr. Stevenson, his party was necessarily limited, it was none the less enjoyable.

"The feast was purely Hawaiian, there being no foreign dish upon the table. Aside from pig, fish and fowls, roasted underground, were many strange [to foreigners] edibles: pu-pu, opihi, two kinds of opae, koelepalau, and kulolo, taro and sweet potato poi, besides others, all beautifully arranged upon a bed of fern leaves.

"The party consisted of His Majesty the King, H.R.H. Liliuokalani, Mr. J. W. Robertson, Mr. and Mrs. R. L. Stevenson, Mr. Lloyd Osbourne, Capt. Otis, Mr. A. W. Richardson, Mrs. Brown, Miss Brickwood, Miss White, Miss Fitzsimmons, Mr. Henry Poor, Mr. and Mrs. Strong, Miss Julia Hunt, and Mrs. C. F. Bush.

"After the feast Mrs. Stevenson presented His Majesty with a rare golden pearl brought from the Low Archipelago, while Mr. Stevenson read ... [his poem] 'The Silver Ship, My King.'" *Daily Bulletin*, February 4, 1889.

Among the well-known and frequently published photographs taken of the event by Arthur Richardson, one memorializes Liliu and Robert Louis Stevenson conversing.

Eight P.M. went to [Hale] Naua meeting at Palace—Ball afterward—came home [at] two.[47] [Above the entry is "12 P.M.," then scrolling "S's."]

*Tuesday, February 5.* Charles Wilson came to examine articles [for the Paris Exposition Universelle]. [John A.] Hassinger will come tomorrow. Cummins and Clark came to see me about poi enterprise. [Alan] Herbert wants to take me on a trip.

*Wednesday, February 6.* Charlie [Wilson] and Hassinger came and approved of articles to go to Paris.[48] Mrs. Finley came.[49]

*Friday, February 8.* Spent day at Washington Place. Ten A.M. went to tell King not to go away, he told me about Helen's dream—something [is] going to happen to our family. Mrs. Finley tells me the same—a woman—who will it be?

Sewing Society [Limahana wahine] met, paid 50 cts for 5 pillowcases. Joe brought me $200.00 of Waimanalo stocks. 30 for Kaipo. [Scrolling "S's."]

*Saturday, February 9.* After breakfast Mary Cook came to have me pay for her boy's schooling $35.90—give it to James [?] at her K. School. Mrs. [Annie] Holokahiki wanted to borrow $100.00—none to lend her. Melemai wanted money, is hard up, no work—had none to give him. Joe Aea wanted [to] lease Pawaa—gave him $5.00, hard up too—lots of poor people. Joe H. is erecting milkshake shanty at Waikiki.

*Sunday, February 10.* Stayed at Washington Place all morning—drove out at eight P.M. with Minnie Aldrich and Helen [Aldrich] to the Park. Stopped at Joe's Hut and had milkshake. Went back with Jennie Clark. Joe had made $19.00. Kahae and Nihoa came in, sat a few minutes.

*Monday, February 11.* Sewing Society at Washington Place—only made .50 for sewing a hat for Makanoe. Had paina wehe i ka hua olelo no Pele. [Had gathering to compile a list of words relative to Pele.] Naha dined with us. John bought tickets for Music Hall—India Rubber men. Donaldson Brothers. John and I sat in box.[50]

---

47. "The annual meeting and fete of the Hale Naua Society were held at Iolani Palace last night. Proceedings of the evening opened by the members of the society, of which His Majesty the King is the founder and head, marching in procession with regalia into the Throne Room, round the sides of which the guests were seated. The retiring Secretary, Mrs. Ulukou, and Treasurer, Mrs. Kahalewai, read their respective reports for the past year. Hon. Antone Rosa delivered the annual lecture, his theme being 'the Antiquity of this Part of the Universe.'

"His Majesty formed the Hale Naua Society—in plain English, 'The House of Wisdom' on the model of the Psychical Society of London, only on somewhat broader lines. The London association devotes itself almost exclusively to researches in spiritual phenomena, while the Hawaiian seeks to establish amiable relations between the material and spiritual economies of nature.... After business and intellectual exercises, dancing began and was gaily sustained until about 11 o'clock, when a sumptuous dinner was served in the state dining room. Afterward dancing was resumed with zest and maintained until after midnight.... The whole event constituted a grand entertainment." Among those attending the event were Mrs. Thomas Stevenson and Mrs. Robert Louis Stevenson. *Pacific Commercial Advertiser*, February 5, 1889.

48. In a column on exhibits to be sent to the Paris exposition, the *Pacific Commercial Advertiser*, February 8, 1889, noted: "Princess Liliuokalani has contributed a superb collection of rich Hawaiian relics and curiosities."

49. Mrs. Finley [or Finlay] told futures by reading cards.

50. Performing at the Opera House, per their advertisement in the *Pacific Commercial*

Fire down at Nolte's—He 2 Pake [There were two Chinese] one haole [Caucasian] burnt.[51]

*Tuesday, February 12.* Went to Palace—[anniversary of] Coronation day. Spoke to Queen about going to San Francisco for change. She said she'd like to know how. She would like to see Hooulu Lahui house[52] built before she does. [Among miscellaneous memoranda at the end of the diary is the following:] Feb. 12. Answered R. W. Wilcox's letter telling him only way to do was to wait for coming session of Legislature, and everything will be all right. Wrote to M. Gray & Co. [San Francisco] inquiring about prices for binding music.

*Wednesday, February 13.* Po io Hua [thirteenth night of the new moon].

Naha, William and Mary Auld told me Mrs. Finley had been cautioned by Judge Foster[53] never to practice fortune-telling. Asked James Boyd[54] about license for [selling] meat and salmon—[he says] one [is] $20 and $2 for stamp, the other $20 and $2 for stamp. Spent morn. [Scrolling "S's."] Luau for Hui to start it. Paid Puhu $30.00 for Kaneloa.

*Thursday, February 14.* Akua [fourteenth night of the new moon].

Spent morn. [Scrolling "S's."] Four P.M. Jennie Clark, Wakeke, and I went out to Waikiki, stopping at J. Boyd's for information. Had tea—same party to fish—enough for them. I started to explain to Hui—most are willing—25 members.

*Friday, February 15.* Hoku [night of the full moon]. Slept at Waikiki. Had a meeting [at] four P.M. All consented to join. Tomorrow contribute [sic].

From February 9 to this day, J. H. [Joe Heleluhe] has made over $50.00.[55]

Lent Kaakaole $2.00.

*Saturday, February 16.* Four P.M. Drove out to Kaipo's cottage. P.M. met people of Waikiki. Chose officers of Hui Imi Pomaikai o Waikiki [Waikiki Improvement Association].[56] $79.00 contributed. 10:30 P.M. Came home. Tramcar full.[57]

---

*Advertiser*, February 9, 1889, were "Wilson & Cameron's Specialty Company of American & European Artists." The acts included the Donaldson brothers, announced as "The wonder of the 19th Century in their great act 'Les Hommes Elastiques.'" The company was first advertised for February 9 and their final performance was on February 11.

51. The fire occurred after a gasoline tank caught fire at the Beaver Lunch Saloon, in the Campbell block on lower Fort Street. Nolte, the proprietor, and several of his employees were injured.

52. Possibly meaning a health care facility.

53. William E. Foster was a police station judge.

54. James H. Boyd (d. 1915) was a clerk in the government land office. He was married to Helen Cleghorn, Princess Kaiulani's half-sister.

55. That money came from his Waikiki milkshake stand.

56. Nothing has been found on this informal group.

57. "Flocking to Waikiki. The streets were alive with vehicles of every sort on Saturday afternoon—the weather being perfectly charming—and among the equipments were noticed some fine spans, evidently recent importation. The cars also were crowded throughout the day, especially those bound to Waikiki, which seemed to be the destination of the crowds, seeking a stroll in the park and cocoanut groves. It is a fact, though it will scarcely be believed, that there are families who have lived in Honolulu for years, and have never till now been able to visit with their children this charming place, on account of the expense. It was a pretty sight to see, on Saturday afternoon, a train of three cars crowded full with happy children, in

*Sunday, February 17.* Stayed at Washington Place. John sick.

*Monday, February 18.* Monday Sewing Society made $8.00. Seven P.M. went out to Waikiki—read and passed Constitution [of the Hui Imi Pomaika o Waikiki]. Contributed $68.00 by members of H. I. Pomaikai.

*Tuesday, February 19.* Kawananakoa's birthday, 21 yrs. Meeting of the Hooulu Lahui Society. Officers of last year nominated over again. King said Society ought to put up building for Lepers.

Ball in the evening—I was matron. Very pleasant ball.[58]

*Wednesday, February 20.* Still at Washington Place. Sewing Society made $3.00. Rec'd $49.00 for Hui Imi Pomaikai—in safe. They have $180.00 to start business. Went to Waikiki at six P.M. to meeting. Appointed Kahi Secretary in place of Puuohau. Kaipo and Aimoku stayed—Aimoku sick.

*Thursday, February 21.* Washington Place. Cutting trees down. Called on Mrs. Elisha Allen—she is charming.[59]

*Monday, February 25.* Two P.M. Took in ten new members for Waikiki market.

*Tuesday, February 26.* Took off large limb of India Rubber tree. Pd. J. H. [Joe Heleluhe] $4.50 for Nihoa's share in Waikiki market. Kaipo and Aimoku went home this afternoon.

*Thursday, February 28.* Mary Kamiki gave me only $4.00 for Keliimahiai's share in H.I.P. [Hui Imi Pomaikai o Waikiki].

**Friday, March 1.** Rebecca gave me $13.50 for her and two Johns.

*Tuesday, March 5.* Kahae went to Maui for her health.

*Wednesday, March 6.* Rec'd $26.00 of Ice Co.'s stocks—three [for] Kaipo, one for Kuihelani, 14 [for] Hui [Hoo]Naauao, two [for] Kalahiki—three [for] Kaipo and Bro, three [for] Aimoku.

*Saturday, March 9.* Waikiki Market was opened and $16.00 realized. Slept at Kaipo Hale.

*Sunday, March 10.* $10.00 realized from Market.

*Monday, March 11.* Only $5.00 from Market.

*Tuesday, March 12.* Only $4.00 from Market.

holiday attire and decked with wreaths, returning from the beach, where they had been to enjoy a picnic." *Pacific Commercial Advertiser*, February 18, 1889.

58. "A BRILLIANT AFFAIR. The twenty-first anniversary of the birth of H.H. Prince David Kawananakoa was celebrated yesterday evening at Iolani Palace by a grand ball. The decorations in the grand hallway, blue room, and dining hall were extremely handsome and effective. Here and there about the hallway stood immense potted palms and ferns of the choicest kind and beautiful bouquets of flowers were resting in the alcoves on either side. The blue room looked very pretty, as also did the dining hall. Numerous bouquets of flowers occupied prominent positions in the Throne room where the dancing took place. The latter room was brilliantly illumined with the electric light crystal chandeliers. Mrs. Jas. W. Robertson, wife of the Vice Chamberlain, supervised the decorations, assisted by Mrs. Geo. E. Boardman and James McGuire." *Daily Bulletin*, February 20, 1889.

59. Elisha H. Allen (b. 1836–d. 1906), Hawaiian consul general at New York, and his wife, Julia Herrick, arrived on the *Alameda*, February 18, for a long visit. Allen was the son of the Hawaiian judge and diplomat by the same name and had lived in the islands as a young man.

*Thursday, March 14.* Kicked by a horse.

*Friday, March 15.* Miss Davis paid .15 for two pounds meat.

*Saturday, March 16.* John Cummins races at Kapiolani Park[60]—returned to [Sentence ends thus.]

*Tuesday, March 19.* Gave Joe $18.00 to pay off bill of Hui for meat to Waller.[61]

*Wednesday, March 20.*—Gave Kaakaole $2.00—and Limapuupua to make two hats. Cut India rubber tree down. Miss Davis paid me 15 cts [for] 2 pieces [of] steak.

*Thursday, March 21.*—Kahala leased to Iaukea.[62] Aiaumoe placed $50.00 in my keeping—$4.50 to pay Kalahiki.

*Friday, March 22.*—Joe borrowed $20.00 to pay [back] on Sunday.

*Sunday, March 24.*—Joe did not pay me $20.00 he borrowed of me.

*Monday, March 25.*—Gave Kaakaole $2.00. Pd. Limapuu[pua] $1.00 for two Ii.[63] Bought red dresses for bathing, ordered another lei.

*Tuesday, March 26.*—Gave J. [Joe] Aea $10.00—Met at Washington Place to make up dresses—signed off one note to Bishop & Co. of $1,173.87.[64]

Went to funeral of J. Campbell's baby.[65]

Pd. $10.00 to Kinilau for ferns—$16.75 to [James] McGuire.

*Wednesday, March 27.*—Met again to sew bathing dresses.

*Thursday, March 28.*—John came to tell me Mary had gone on to Waialua. Paid Kaakaole $2.00 again this week. Received $200.00 again this month of Waimanalo stocks.

*Friday, March 29.*—John, John Paty, Isenberg, Sam Parker, Capt. Ross went to Waialua, will return Monday.[66] Four P.M. went to Waikiki stayed till night. Came home.

---

60. The Honorable John A. Cummins had issued several hundred invitations to a barbecue and horse races at the Kapiolani Park track for Saturday, in celebration of his 54th birthday. There were bicycle races, as well as more than 12 horse races, and ample prizes were awarded. See *Pacific Commercial Advertiser*, March 18, 1889.

61. Gilbert J. Waller was the proprietor of the Metropolitan Meat Co. at King and Bethel Streets.

62. Liliuokalani had inherited a lifetime title to the ahupuaa (land division) of Kahala from Bernice P. Bishop, on conditions that allowed her to make short-term sublets, which were generally for between three and ten years. Hawaii State Archives, Liliuokalani Collection, Trust Records. Curtis Iaukea probably had such a lease on a beachfront lot.

63. Liliu may be referring to lei made from feathers of the apapane bird (Hawaiian honeycreeper, *Himatione sanguinea*).

64. The bills payable section at the end of the diary identifies this as a payment "on note of Mortgage for $1717.00" (the numbers are inconsistent).

65. James Campbell, the only son of capitalist James Campbell, died March 23, 1889, age three years and six months. The funeral took place at Kawaiahao Church.

66. "A GAY PARTY. Last Friday a party of gentlemen, consisting of Hon. J. O. Dominis, Major Sam Parker, Major Seward, Capt. [John] Ross, Messrs. J. H. Paty, W. M. Giffard, Paul Isenberg Jr., C. H. Eldridge, and E. R. Miles, left town in a four-in-hand team for Waialua. Arriving there in good order they put up at the Dominis and Paty homesteads. The time was spent in shooting plover, turkeys, etc., Sam Parker making sad havoc among the birds. The party returned to town on Tuesday, after having had a real good time." *Daily Bulletin*, April 3, 1889.

*Saturday, March 30.* Went to Waikiki with the women and bathed with their red dresses. [Word erased.] After bath had lunch in Joe's dining room. Kalei and teachers and schoolmates came down to bathe also.

**Wednesday, April 3.** Appointed officers of Liliuokalani Hui Hoonaauao, Hattie Kawainui, Vice President, Lilia Aholo, Secretary, I, Treasurer. Went on with our Hui Huinahema [Sewing Society], but left them at two P.M. to attend reception at Punahou.[67]

Had tea and then felt burning in my left hand—on the back.

*Thursday, April 4.* J. A. Cummins and Tom [Cummins] came to call and asked if he could do something for me, said [I] wanted single and double harness and pair of horses. Invited to supper—went and had a good time. Ninito [Sumner] and King and all their folks. "Aohe kanaka aia i Mana." ["There are no people in Mana."] Only at night that pain.

*Saturday, April 6.* Pd. Mrs. Bush $13.00 for Kaipo.

*Monday, April 8.* Breakfasted in Palace[68]—asked King to give Pualeilani to me.[69]

*Sunday, April 14.* Walked on beach with Mary Kamiki—saw men employed in putting up posts of Roller coaster at Long Branch.[70]

*Monday, April 15.* Employed Kalua to protest against Gribble's putting up Roller coaster.[71]

*Tuesday, April 16.* Feel that burning again in the palm of my left hand. Lilia Aholo's case came off today—court approved but not discharged.[72]

---

67. The occasion was an "at home" of the Oahu College ladies. The *Pacific Commercial Advertiser*, April 4, 1889, reported it as "in all respects a brilliant occasion."

68. "His Majesty entertained Mr. Robert Louis Stevenson at breakfast this morning. There were present: His Majesty the King, H.R.H. Princess Liliuokalani, H.H. Prince Kawananakoa, Mr. Robert Louis Stevenson, Mrs. Thos. Stevenson, Mrs. Robert Louis Stevenson, Mr. Lloyd Osborne, Mr. and Mrs. J. D. Strong, Mrs. A. W. Bush, Mr. H. F. Poor, and Mr. Jas. [James] W. Robertson, Vice-Chamberlain." *Daily Bulletin*, April 8, 1889.

69. Pualeilani, the estate at Waikiki, owned by King Kalakaua, was located inland from the Waikiki road (now Kalakaua Avenue) and on the Honolulu side of Liliuokalani's Waikiki property, Hamohamo.

At the time of this entry, the property was under a mortgage, so perhaps Liliuokalani had hoped to secure the same by a title transfer. See first footnote for February 23, 1892, diary entry (277). This did not occur, and after the king's death in 1891, it became Queen Kapiolani's main residence. Later Prince Kuhio had a home on the grounds. The property was sold by the Kapiolani estate in 1913 and subdivided.

70. The roller coaster would open at Waikiki Beach in June. The *Pacific Commercial Advertiser*, May 22, 1889, noted: "Our reporter visited Long Branch, Waikiki, yesterday and saw the working of the toboggan slide [into the ocean] at that place.... The platform of the arrangement is reached by a flight of stairs and the chute or slide is twenty inches wide. This narrow width gives a great momentum to the toboggan as it slides over the rollers for about 200 feet until the water is reached.... To a young person, either male or female, this pastime cannot be otherwise than delightful and it gives an excitement which ordinary bathing lacks." The article noted that there were "47 dressing rooms for gentlemen" and 18 "boudoirs for ladies," that a bathing platform and a trapeze would be added, and that a restaurant was promised. Each toboggan ride was to cost five cents.

71. Theodore Graham Gribble was manager of the Hawaiian Tramways Co. It is not known why Liliu opposed the operation, and no written protest over the roller coaster has been found.

72. Lilia Aholo (b. 1854–d. 1935) was the widow of Luther Aholo, a former minister of the interior who had died at Washington Place, March 16, 1888. Lilia Aholo had been married

*Thursday, April 18.* Paid Joe for Market, $3.00 for this week.

*Friday, April 19.* Friday. Wilcox surveyed boundary and could not find stake.[73] While under Hau trees, Hilo and Kahae came home from John Ena's—jolly from wine.[74]

*Saturday, April 20.* Wilcox did not succeed in finding starting point of boundary of Hamohamo. Heard of [blank] being on a drunk. Minnie [Aldrich] and babies were with me. J. H. Boyd brought memo of Pualeilani and mortgage, $5,000.00—four years since 1887, to H. A. Widemann.

*Sunday, April 21.* Stayed at Muolaulani all day. Wilcox did not go out [to Waikiki]. No one came.

*Monday, April 22.* Pd. Kalu $3.50 for this week's market—$1.50 for Kulolo and jerk beef.

*Friday, April 26.* Mrs. Dominis died 20 minutes of nine peaceably.[75]

*Friday, May 3.* Paid J. Dominis $9.00 for three months' dues of Ice Stocks for Aimoku.

---

On May 6, 1889, the British consul, Major James Hay Wodehouse, had an interview with King Kalakaua regarding the rumor of his projected departure to visit England and France, and also queried the king about his knowledge of the Hawaiian League's formation.

> ¶ I asked His Majesty if he thought it was prudent to absent himself from His Kingdom at the present time when there were rumours afloat, which possibly had reached him, that a new League was being formed for the purpose of bringing about his abdication or deposition. He said he was aware that some time ago there was a project for His

---

three times, and she had four children ranging in age from eight to 30. There was no will and no cash, but there were several pieces of real estate. Liliuokalani bore some of the funeral expenses, and had the Aholos' young daughter, Lydia, move in with her. On February 26, 1889, Mrs. Aholo petitioned the court for the allowance of accounts and final distribution. The court accepted her accounts on April 15, but because there was property on Maui and Molokai, a guardianship of the two minor heirs continued for several years. Hawaii State Archives, First Circuit Court, Probate 2559.

73. Robert W. Wilcox had just commenced his surveying business. The *Pacific Commercial Advertiser*, April 26, 1889, noted: "Mr. R. W. Wilcox, who was a Hawaiian government pupil, studying engineering in Italy, has hung out a sign as 'civil engineer and surveyor,' on the Damon block, corner of King and Bethel Streets."

74. In 1889, John Ena Jr. was secretary of, and a major stockholder in, the Inter-Island Steam Navigation Co. His town residence was at 138 Beretania Street, but he also had a home at Waikiki in the vicinity of what is now John Ena Road.

75. "A conspicuous and venerable figure passes out of sight in the death of Mrs. Mary Dominis which occurred at Washington Place at half past eight o'clock on Thursday morning. She was born on August 3d, 1803, so that she was in her 86th year at death. Mrs. Dominis arrived in the islands from New York on April 23rd, 1837, in the bark *Jones*, commanded by her husband, Capt. J. O. Dominis, after a voyage of 150 days. Since eleven years later her life has been clouded with a great sorrow, her husband having about that time sailed for China in the brig *Nelson*, never to be heard of again. Mrs. Dominis had been confined to her house for many years prior to her death with the infirmities of age. For years the anniversary of her birth has been a social event of moment, the Royal Hawaiian Band invariably playing a serenade in her honor at Washington Place." *Pacific Commercial Advertiser*, April 26, 1889.

abdication... but he had not heard of this new one, and He added that He did not believe that His sister would listen to it.... The King then said, if you can satisfy me that I should incur a risk in leaving my Kingdom, I will not go.[76]

---

*Wednesday, May 8.* Recd. $34.00 of Ice Stocks—gave $8 to Joe, sent two to Louisa Brickwood—kept $12 for 2nd Div. [of Liliuokalani Hui Hoonaauao.]

*Saturday, May 18.* Liliuokalani Hui Hoonaauao met—19 members. $10.10 cts contributed.

*Tuesday, May 21.* Ball tonight for officers of *Cormorant*.[77]

*Wednesday, May 22. Cormorant* sails today—Band played her off.

**Monday, June 3.** Went to Hilo with John.[78]

*Saturday, June 22.* Kaipo's birthday. 12 P.M. Luau on veranda. John sick. King came in—Jennie [Clark] and children came in. Two P.M., went to Moanalua [to] lunch by S. M. Damon to H.A.P. Carter.[79] Concert [held] for lights of Kaumakapili Church.[80]

*Monday, June 24.* Got $184.25 from Concert.

*Wednesday, June 26.* Dinner party at Sam Parker's. [Guests were] Queen, Chief Justice [Albert F. Judd] and wife, Mr. and Mrs. H.A.P. Carter.

*Friday, June 28.* 7.50 Band at Hotel—Meeting of Hawaiian Amateur Musical Society. Committee of five appointed for Tuesday.[81]

76. Hawaii State Archives, Series 375, Copies of British Documents, Wodehouse to Foreign Office—London, Lord Rosebury.

77. The *Pacific Commercial Advertiser* in announcing the departure of the *Cormorant* on May 22, 1889, said that she had been in Hawaiian waters for six or seven months. The May 23, 1889, issue of the *Advertiser* noted that the "Reception and Ball" was "of the usual success." Liliuokalani's presence was not noted.

78. Liliu and Dominis departed on the *Kinau* on May 31, and returned to Honolulu on the same vessel on June 8. In her diary, Bella Lyman wrote the following of Liliuokalani's 1889 presence in Hilo: "June 3. Fred [Lyman] went with Liliuokalani ma [and company] to see the new road.... June 4. Made a jelly cake for Mrs. Dominis, Lu [Lou Severance] also made a cake & we went with the Hooulu Lahui [Society] to call on her & carried it.... June 5. Very busy. All the women came. Mrs. Hapai came with HRH Liliuokalani ma. A shower hindered some near noon. Had the feast on the Lanai & after it the meeting of the Society & Mrs. Dominis gave us a talk." Hawaiian Mission Children's Society Library, Isabella Lyman Journal.

79. "Last Saturday afternoon the Hon. S. M. Damon and Mrs. Damon gave a luau at their country residence, Keawamaile, Moanalua, in honor of Mrs. H.A.P. Carter. The lanai where the luau was held was decorated in a very pretty manner with flowers and maile, the work of the native girls who reside in Moanalua, as a compliment to Mrs. Carter. There were two tables, one spread à la Hawaiian, the other à la European. Both were loaded down with good things.... After the luau, coffee and fruit were handed around to the guests who were mostly seated on the banks of the fishpond.... The Hawaiian Quintette Club gave some most delightful vocal and instrumental music. Among those present... were: H.R.H. Princess Liliuokalani, attended by Mrs. C. F. Bush, His Honor the Chief Justice and Mrs. Judd, [and] His Ex. H.A.P. Carter." *Daily Bulletin*, June 24, 1889.

80. This event was advertised on multiple days in the *Pacific Commercial Advertiser* (for an example, see the June 21, 1889, edition) as a "Grand Concert... in Aid of Kaumakapili Church, Under the Patronage of H.R.H. Princess Liliuokalani. At Kaumakapili Church. Commencing at 7:30 P.M. Sharp. Tickets One Dollar."

81. "A meeting of the Amateur Musical Society will be held this evening at 7:30 at the Y.M.C.A. for the purpose of re-organizing and election of offices. Everyone interested in vocal music should make a point of attending." *Daily Bulletin*, June 28, 1889.

*Saturday, June 29.* Nellie Everett[82] and I bought Japanese dresses.

*Sunday, June 30.* Went to Kaumakapili Sunday School—dined at two.

Eight P.M. went to Palama—saw my silver fishes were gone—[saw] Aikanaka [David Dowsett] sneaking around the garden.

Took the tram partway [from Washington Place?]—left word [I] could not go to Muolaulani tomorrow.

**Monday, July 1.** Woke early, went out to Waikiki, moved Kaipo's furniture up to Joe's room at Paoakalani—leased Kaipo's hale [house] to Merry-go-round [people]. Told Kaleipua I would go to Kauai next week. Went to boathouse—watched the *Likelike* go out.

*Tuesday, July 9.* Left by *Waialeale* for Hanalei [Kauai]—[with] Joe, Jennie Clark, Aiaumoe, Ahoi, Kuaiwa. Had pleasant passage down.[83]

*Wednesday, July 10.* Arrived at Kilauea [Kauai] six A.M., left at 11—arrived at Hanalei three P.M. Kanoa, Milaina [Ahia], and [John] Kakina awaiting us at the beach.[84]

*Thursday, July 11.* Went to Lumahai—dined at [the house of] Chulan's luna [overseer or manager].[85] After listening to people went round to see the land—Kakina has not been fair to me—he has sold all the Awa without our leave, leased houses, and done other tricky things. Stayed overnight at Mr. Geo. Titcomb's.[86]

*Saturday, July 13.* Left Hanalei—10—lunched at Mr. Koelling's[87]—left there at 12½ P.M., arrived at Kilauea 1½ P.M., lunched with Mr. and Mrs. Macfie[88]—3½ P.M. left there and arrived at Niumalu ¼ to nine P.M.[89]

*Sunday, July 14.* Stayed quietly all day. Hannah and Lou Titcomb, Henry Sheldon, and Tom Cummins called to see me.[90] Hoau i ke kio wai Puamile—hua. [Swam in the small pool Puamile—frothy.]

*Monday, July 15.* Spent the day making hats.

*Tuesday, July 16.* Left Niumalu for Waimea—arrived at four P.M. Bathed in Wailuila. Saw Kaenaku dance.[91]

---

82. Ellen Richardson Everett (b. 1834–d. 1890), of Waikapu, Maui, was the part-Hawaiian wife of Thomas W. Everett, a longtime government official on Maui.

83. "Princess Liliuokalani went by the *Waialeale* yesterday to make the circuit of Kauai, and will visit at Kalalau." *Pacific Commercial Advertiser*, July 10, 1889.

84. "The Princess Liliuokalani visited Hanalei by the *Waialeale*. She went down to attend to some land matters. She was received by the Hon. Paul Kanoa and a number of friends." *Pacific Commercial Advertiser*, July 16, 1889.

85. Chu Lan & Co., rice planter, was the lessee of the valley lands of Princeville Plantation Co., Hanalei, Kauai.

86. George Titcomb, the son of Kauai resident Charles Titcomb (d. 1883), is listed in directories of the period as a "stock raiser."

87. Charles Koelling was the manager and proprietor of Princeville Plantation Co.

88. Robert Macfie, a Scotsman, was vice president and manager of the Kilauea Sugar Co. His family owned the plantation.

89. Liliuokalani would have stayed with Paul P. Kanoa, former governor of Kauai, at Niumalu near Nawiliwili Bay.

90. Henry Sheldon was a blacksmith at the Makee Mill at Kealia. Tom Cummins may be a mistaken identification—she probably meant James H. Cummins, an overseer at Kapaa.

91. There are two Kaenakus of record. One of this name was married in 1854 to "Kauai," presumably Judge Kauai, with whom the Queen stayed. In 1877, another Kaenaku (a daughter?) married John T. Unea of Lawai, Koloa.

*Mokuaikaua Church and Hulihee Palace from the beach at Kamakahonu, Kailua, Kona, 1889. On October 9, 1889, Prince Henri de Bourbon, Count of Bardi, his wife, and their traveling companions arrived in Honolulu from Yokohama on the City of Peking. They traveled to Kailua, Kona, where King Kalakaua entertained them at Hulihee Palace and then accompanied them to Punaluu. Hulihee Palace is the large white two-story structure on the far shore.*

OPPOSITE
*Punaluu Hotel, Kau, Hawaii, 1889. While on Hawaii Island, the king and his guests may have spent a night at this hotel built and operated by entrepreneur Peter Lee. These photographs of Kona and Kau are part of an album of Hawaiian scenes and views assembled for a member of the traveling party.*
Hawaii State Archives

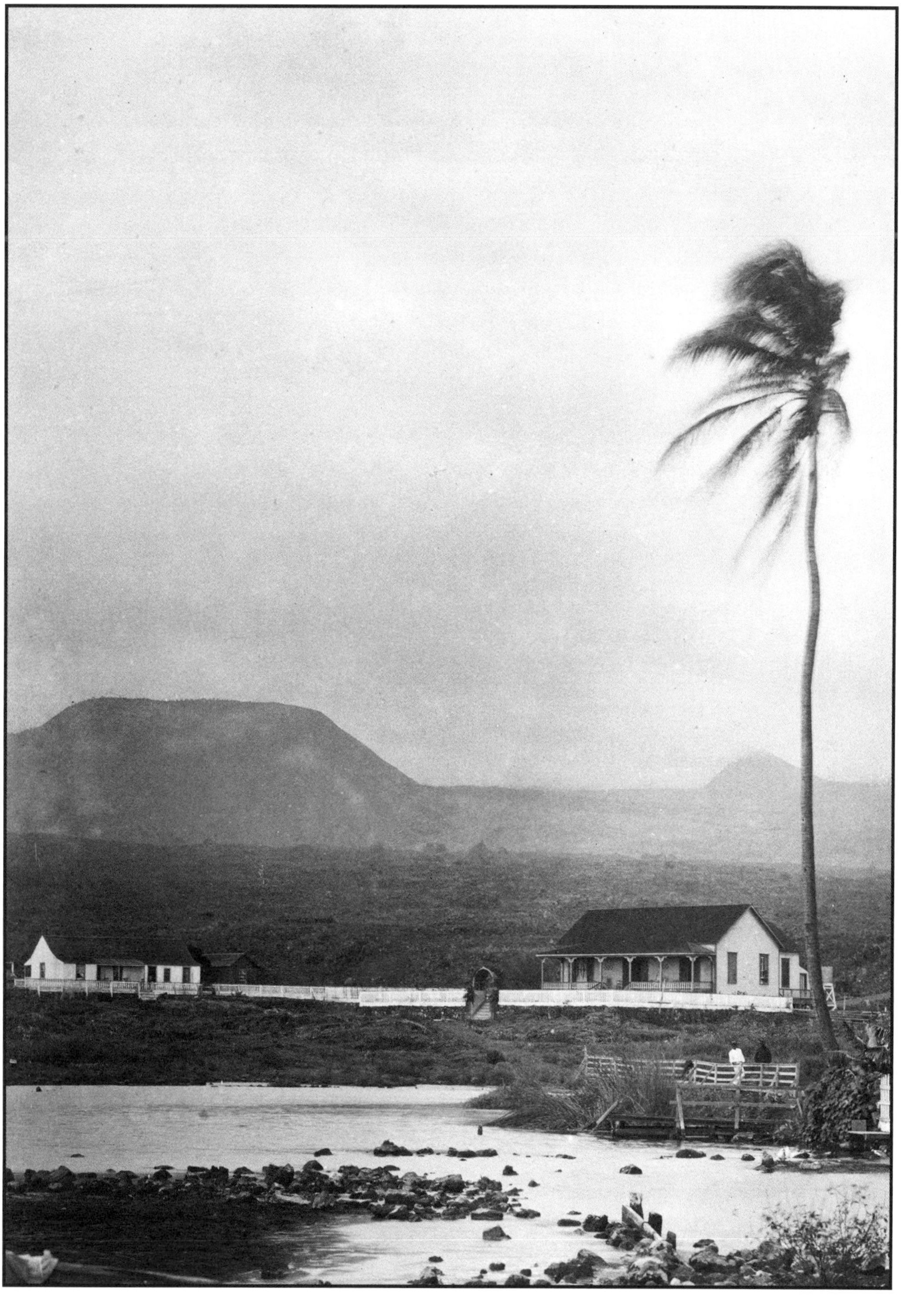

*Wednesday, July 17.* Took a drive to Nohili—saw the Wailiula o Mana [Mirage of Mana].[92] Received a letter from Miss Davis saying John was sick and is little better. Great improvement made in Mana—sugar plantations.[93]

*Thursday, July 18.* Went by invitation of Francis Gay on board of *Waialeale* to see the Ahi o Kamaile [firebrands of the Kamaile cliff].[94] Milaina [Ahia], Kaehuwahanui, and Aiaumoe [and] Kuaiwa went on board of Steamer *Akamai*,[95] met Lily Auld, Mr. and Mrs. G. Titcomb at Nualolo—arrived back at Waimea.

*Friday, July 19.* This morning—Stayed at home at Liwai Kauai's house [at Waimea] and braided hats.[96]

*Saturday, July 20.* Left Waimea for Niumalu—stopped to say good-bye to the Gays—Saw Mother Sinclair, Mrs. Robinson, Mrs. Gay—Mrs. Aubrey Robinson, Miss Gay,[97] Mr. Brigham.[98] Arrived at Niumalu six P.M.—after lunching at Koloa.

92. "This wonderful optical illusion [the mirage] will occasionally greet the traveller about three miles beyond Waimea. The bare sandy tract that stretches along the road seems to have been transformed into a lake of water, where the forms of cattle can be seen reflected as they appear to feed upon submerged vegetation, and the trunks of trees seem to rise from the water." Henry M. Whitney, *The Tourists' Guide Through the Hawaiian Islands* (Honolulu: Henry M. Whitney, 1890), 104.

93. "Mana Plantation (H. P. Faye & Co.) 1,000 acres, 250 acres under cane, estimated yield 1,000 tons, men employed 50, 6 miles R.R. post office Kekaha." 1888 City Directory.

94. Liliu is referring to a special display of fireworks, unique to the north shore of Kauai, whereby logs of papala (*Charpentiera obovata*), a small native tree with light, inflammable wood, were "on dark nights... lighted and thrown from cliffs on the north shore of Kauai into the wind, which tossed them about or let them float gently downward." Marie C. Neal, *In Gardens of Hawaii* (Honolulu: Bishop Museum Press, 1948), 284–85.

95. The new Hawaiian steamer *Akamai* (Captain William Lawrence) advertised in the *Pacific Commercial Advertiser*, July 15, 1889, that she would "sail for Koloa, Eleele, Hanapepe, and Waimea, Kauai, at five P.M."

96. Edward Levi Kauai, the judge of the Waimea district and a legislator (1886), was appointed commissioner of private ways and water rights for Waimea, 1887, and marriage license agent, 1876–86.

97. Liliu refers to the family of Mrs. Elizabeth Sinclair (b. 1800, Glasgow, Scotland–d. 1892, Makaweli, Kauai), who arrived from New Zealand in 1863 and purchased the island of Niihau from Kamehameha V on January 23, 1864. The purchase was in the name of her sons James and Francis, but it was Mrs. Sinclair who was in command of their sheep ranch. Her obituary said she was "possessed of an active business mind which enabled her to be the ruling spirit and manager of her large property." *Hawaiian Gazette*, October 15, 1892.

The family members Liliu mentions were: Helen (Mrs. Charles B. Robinson) and Jean (Mrs. Thomas Gay), Mrs. Sinclair's daughters, and Alice, wife of Mrs. Sinclair's grandson, Aubrey Robinson. Miss Eliza Gay was the daughter of Captain Thomas Gay. Ida von Holt's memoir contains a family photo taken at Makaweli House in 1893. Ida Elizabeth Knudsen von Holt, *Stories of Long Ago: Niihau, Kauai, Oahu* (Honolulu: Daughters of Hawaii, 1985, 93).

98. William T. Brigham (b. 1841, Boston–d. 1926, Honolulu), the director of the Bernice Pauahi Bishop Museum (from 1888), was on a visit. The *Pacific Commercial Advertiser*, July 16, 1889, reported: "Professor Brigham arrived in Kauai by the *Waialeale*. He landed at Kilauea and spent the day driving about to see the sights of that picturesque spot, among other places viewing the celebrated Kukui Grove near Maulua Gulch. He drove over to Hanalei where he rejoined the *Waialeale* and proceeded to Waimea. In the vicinity of the latter he will remain some three weeks and will be the guest of Mrs. Sinclair."

*Sunday, July 21.* [Honolulu] Arrived at five A.M. [on the *Waialeale*]. Drove with Jennie up to house. John still asleep. Drove up to Muolaulani. Sent Jennie Clark to wake [Robert] Wilcox up. Found him with Kaiue and Kauhaeahu. Picked a bouquet for Capt. Campbell and drove home.[99]

[Robert] Wilcox came down, told me he would take care of house at Palama. I said no—I was coming out next day with people to clean house. Wrote to him to move away from there to Kawehena's house.

*Monday, July 22.* Went to Muolaulani with people, saw [Robert] Wilcox move his traps to Kawehena's house. Did not finish.

*Tuesday, July 23.* Went again with people to Muolaulani.

*Wednesday, July 24.* Finished cleaning up.

*Sunday, July 28.* Went up to Muolaulani ten A.M. While wandering around the garden, [Robert] Wilcox and Mahaulu[100] came and stood a moment—latter went away. Kaaha[101] came—saw us sitting under Banyan, stopped a moment, [then] went on. Kauhaeahu came also—nothing of importance said—stood up, went home.

*Monday, July 29.* Went to Muolaulani—was alone till two P.M. He [Wilcox] came and said "e hana aku ana wau." ["I'm going off to work."] Told him to desist—that he was a revolutionist and would do more harm than good for the Govt. Told him also to go and tell the King about it before he did anything. [He] said he was afraid the King would say no. Told him he would find himself hanging some day.

---

On July 30, 1889, Honolulu was convulsed by what has generally been known ever since as the Wilcox Rebellion. It was the most serious riot that had occurred in the city to date, and it involved both Kalakaua and Liliuokalani. Early in the morning of that day, a party of about 250 armed Hawaiians led by Robert William Wilcox, Robert Napunako Boyd, and a newly arrived Belgian named Albert Loomens assembled at Liliuokalani's Palama house (where some of them had planned the action) and marched to town. They arrived at the mauka gate of the palace at four A.M., and demanded and gained entrance to the grounds. They learned that the king was not in residence, and they also found themselves opposed by the government forces. Captain Robert Waipa Parker refused their demand that he surrender the palace. He was under strict orders from the king not to do so, and he successfully defended the building with

---

99. Charles J. Campbell is listed in the 1890 City Directory as "master steamer *Mikahala*, Inter Island Steam Navigation Co. Res. Palama."

100. Archibald Scott Mahaulu (d. 1916, Honolulu) was a clerk in the chamberlain's office, and resided at Palama and King Streets. He became involved in the July 30, 1889, Wilcox rebellion but was not ultimately prosecuted. Eventually he became a judge at Waialua, Oahu.

101. Hiram Kaaha was foreman of the bindery department for the Press Publishing Co. He would be caught up in the July 30, 1889, rebellion and charged by the government with conspiracy but not ultimately prosecuted.

about a dozen soldiers of the King's Guard. Volunteer forces (the Honolulu Rifles) also positioned themselves in the Opera House on King Street, in the tower of Kawaiahao Church, and in residences along Richards Street. Firing began and continued for some time, resulting in casualties. By 11 A.M. the insurrectionists had retreated into a building. The *Pacific Commercial Advertiser* in its July 31, 1893, account reported:

> ¶ [They had] taken shelter on the bungalow situated on the Palace grounds, and the fire of the rifles slackened to only an occasional shot as rioters came within their range.... By noon... the surrender of the rioters was only a question of a few hours. Yet it was apparent that stronger measures had to be taken to drive them from the bungalow where they were safe from the rifle shots.... About noon four deserters from the rioters climbed up and leaped over the Palace walls, one of whom had been seriously wounded in the hand by a rifle ball.... About thirty rioters surrendered to Lieut. Parker at one P.M. and were disarmed and kept in confinement in the basement of the Palace, until removed to the Station House at a later hour.... For some hours the Government Building had been held by a detachment of the rioters, but about 12 [P.M.] these were dislodged by the volunteers.
>
> Early in the afternoon it was planned to make a closer attack upon the rebels' stronghold ... but it was not until 5.30 P.M. that active operations in this direction actually begun. A corps of volunteers took up a position in the Coney premises [mauka at Diamond Head corner of Richards and Hotel Streets] and from there Dynamite bombs were thrown at the doomed building. While this bombardment lasted the sharpshooters from the Opera House kept up a steady and furious fusillade, until finally, after an hour's bombardment the rioters rushed from the building waving a white sheet upon a pole and shouting "peace" "surrender" etc.
>
> The gates were thrown open, and a force of volunteers entered and took the whole of the rioters prisoners. The firing ceased about seven P.M. and Wilcox was marched to the Station House at 7:15 P.M.—his comrade prisoners arriving at the lock-up a few minutes later.

The notion that Wilcox was trying to restore Hawaiian rights and the powers of the king, which the Bayonet Constitution of 1887 had significantly weakened, is inaccurate, as the testimony during the subsequent conspiracy trials of both Wilcox and Boyd revealed. Another widespread rumor is closer to the truth: that Wilcox intended to secure the person of the king, compel him to abdicate in favor of his sister Liliuokalani, the heir apparent, and also demand both a new constitution and a new cabinet. Palace insider Curtis Iaukea has this to say about the Wilcox rebellion:

> ¶ Among Wilcox's followers the King had a close friend the Hon. J. H. Kaunamano, a Representative from Hamakua, Hawaii. He was among

the inner circle of the Wilcox group and kept the King informed of the plans of the plotters which were... in the interests of restoring to the King much of his lost power.

In late July we learned that the day had been set for the coup. The King made preparations for defense of the Palace or grounds as the plan was to simply have the rebels walk in and take over. About midnight I was sitting in the Chamberlain's office in the basement of the Palace when the King came downstairs. We discussed the situation and were about to take our departure when the sentry knocked on the door saying that someone wished to speak with His Majesty. The correct password had been given but the sentry seemed dubious that a caller should wish to speak to the King at such an hour. It was Kaunamano, greatly agitated. He informed the King that he had just discovered that the plotters would shortly march on the Palace, seize it, and if possible the King himself, and, that instead of following through with the original plan they were going to place the Princess Liliuokalani upon the throne. This was startling and alarming news coming at almost the last moment. The King showed remarkable composure, quietly gave orders to guard the Palace and the grounds and calling for his carriage, together we drove through the quiet streets to the boathouse where His Majesty retired for the night and I drove home, with the caution not to divulge what had happened during the night to anyone.

In the morning we knew that the Wilcox rebellion was a failure. The leader and some of his followers marched on the Palace as previously arranged but to their dismay they found the Household Guards under Captain Parker were not taking sides with them as they expected. Wilcox and a few of his leading lieutenants found shelter in the King's bungalow.... Later in the morning they were driven from this refuge by a bomb thrown by young [James] Hay Wodehouse who was with the government forces.[102]

---

*Tuesday, July 30.* Seven A.M. Heard Wilcox was in the palace with 200 men, H[onolulu] Rifles getting ready. 8½ firing began—[Samuel] Damon tried but could not see Wilcox.[103]

102. Hawaii State Archives, Iaukea Collection, Memoirs, typescript, 237–38.
103. "A Cabinet council was held early in the forenoon [of July 30, 1889]... to demand the surrender of Wilcox; and his Excellency S. M. Damon was appointed to carry out the demand.... At ten A.M. Mr. Damon... proceeded to the King Street entrance of the Palace grounds, but not before several shots had been exchanged between the Honolulu Rifles and the rioters within. Mr. Damon was subsequently refused admission, and at this time the rioters had turned the field pieces upon the sharpshooters who had found a lodgment on the Opera House opposite to and commanding a range of the grounds. Mr. Damon, who was attended by Lieutenant Kamana, had to escape between the two fires which had now become heavy." *Pacific Commercial Advertiser*, July 31, 1889.

Kaaha, with King's carriage, went to Honuakaha[104] for King—He refused to enter carriage. Firing all day, all desert except A. [Archibald Scott] Mahaulu and J. Kauhane.[105]

8½ P.M. Wilcox gave himself up. 15 men killed—H. [Henry] Waterhouse shot Kike, S. [Sanford] B. Dole shot one, J. Dowsett and Ned [Dowsett] shot one. R. Boyd [Entry stops abruptly.][106]

Ministers wanted W. A. [William Aldrich] to come out with Riflemen—he refused—Ministers promised [clemency?] and money and everything—when he got it [he said] he would.

*Wednesday, July 31. Malulani* took Poomaikelani and Luther Aholo and Hattie Hiram.[107] Many arrests. Much sympathy with Wilcox amongst people and they knelt to him. [He stated] It was not his intention to spill blood—but since they were shot at they had to begin. Robt. Parker[108] kept Palace, Kahalewai[109] kept Barracks.

*Thursday, August 1.* Went at seven A.M. to Boat House to see King. Assured him that I had nothing to do in this insurrection. Wilcox was headstrong [and] would not wait till Legislature.[110]

104. Honuakaha was the location of the king's boathouse at the foot of Punchbowl Street.

105. James Kauhane (d. 1894, age 37) was a son of Reverend James Kauhane, a longtime member of the House of Representatives.

106. On the matter of the casualties, the *Pacific Commercial Advertiser*, August 2, 1889, reported: "The five men killed in Tuesday's riot were named as follows: Lioka, Poni, Sam Tucker, Pelulua, and Kawaiwai. Another died of his wounds the following day... named Keki.... The wounded victims are: George Markham, wounded in left shoulder; Robert Boyd, wounded in leg and on head above left ear, and Kamai shot through right thigh and through right hand... Walu shot in right hand and Thomas Hopa shot through right thigh, the bone of which is broken. The names of the three wounded men, who were removed to Oahu Prison, are: Keawe, Makolo, and Kuaumoua [Kuaumoana]."

107. The *Pacific Commercial Advertiser*, August 1, 1889, said it was the steamer *Mikahala* that departed for Maui and Hawaii, with Princess Poomaikelani and Luther Aholo on board. Hattie Hiram was not listed, but she may have gone as an unlisted deck passenger.

108. Robert Parker (b. May 15, 1856, North Kohala, Hawaii–d. June 6, 1937, Honolulu), also known as Robert Parker Waipa, was a cousin of Samuel Parker and a grandson of John Parker, founder of the Parker Ranch. Robert Parker moved to Honolulu in 1881 and became a lieutenant in the household guards. C. B. Wilson later put him in charge of the police station. In August 1891, he was made a captain and ultimately a senior captain.

"Capt. Parker was in command of a detail of royal troops when Robert W. Wilcox and his revolutionists captured Iolani Palace with the intention of forcing King Kalakaua to abdicate in favor of his sister the Late Queen Liliuokalani. The royal troops held out in the upper floor of the palace. Early in the evening Wilcox surrendered and he and his rebels were captured." *Pacific Commercial Advertiser*, May 15, 1937.

109. John P. Kahalewai was an adjutant in 1886, and a major in the King's Guard in 1887. "It is reported that Captain Kahalewai of the King's Guard was arrested yesterday; charged with, in some way, giving assistance to the rioters." He was not ultimately prosecuted. *Pacific Commercial Advertiser*, August 2, 1889.

110. An important report on the rumor of Liliu's participation in the revolt appeared in the press: "The name of H.R.H. Princess Liliuokalani was freely made use of in the streets yesterday in connection with the revolution, and in view of this fact a *Bulletin* reporter called on the Princess at her residence, Washington Place, this morning, and in the presence of her husband, Hon. John O. Dominis, asked the following question: 'Reports being around that you were implicated with Wilcox in his designs, and that he had secret meetings at your Palama residence which you attended, will you say whether or not such is the case?'

In the aftermath of the failed rebellion, there was both sobering reflection and a period of assessment. The town suffered noticeable physical damage:

> ¶ The Queen's Bungalow suffered most; and it is terribly shattered by the dynamite bombs, especially in the roof and second story. The furniture, of this portion of the building some of which was rare and valuable, was utterly ruined; and the whole structure was most definitely shaken and riddled with shot. The Opera House is very much damaged.... Grapnel shells burst in the upper portions of the structure tearing and slashing everything in their way. One grapnel shell passed through the front door and flew over the auditory to the King's box, behind which it exploded with destructive effect. Four of the front windows had several panes of glass smashed.... The injuries to the Palace and Government buildings are comparatively light.[111]

On August 12, Robert W. Wilcox and Albert Loomens were brought before the Police Court and charged with treason. The *Advertiser* later reported:

> ¶ The political situation remains very much as reported a month ago, the insurrection of Wilcox and his followers having been completely suppressed. The arrests have been quite numerous... confined almost wholly to native Hawaiians and half breed. The only foreigners implicated have been one Belgian and one Chinese. Sixty-two persons have been bound over for trial at the October term of the Supreme Court. Taken as a whole the position of the Government is stronger today than before the insurrection.[112]

Lowering the six-foot-high wall of the Iolani palace grounds was an immediate order of business. The *Pacific Commercial Advertiser*, August 10, 1889, reported:

> ¶ The Palace wall is now in process of modification; and will, when temporarily fixed, be three feet six inches all around.... The Palace is the most imposing building in Honolulu; and it was a big mistake to ever have planned its seclusion from public view by a high stone wall similar to what surrounds prisons.... In the large city of London...

---

"The Princess replied that she knew nothing whatever of Wilcox's intentions until the Ministers informed her after her return from Hilo in June; that after being so informed she at once told Wilcox she did not approve of his designs if such was his intention, and told him he should desist without further delay; that she had never been present at any of his meetings.

"The Princess also stated in conversation that Wilcox had been living at her Palama residence, but after her return from Kauai a couple of weeks ago, she ordered him away from the house and he took up his quarters in the servants' cottages in rear. The Princess also said that when Wilcox was in San Francisco she received a letter from him. In reply she wrote that if he had any designs he need not return, but if he only intended to come just before the election and run as a representative that would be all right." *Daily Bulletin*, July 31, 1889.

111. *Pacific Commercial Advertiser*, August 1, 1889.
112. *Pacific Commercial Advertiser*, August 24, 1889.

Buckingham Palace... has a neat iron railing in front, and the fine facade... is visible from the street.... The enclosure, now thrown open to public view, ought to be improved by the setting out of choice trees and shrubs that, in time, should make the Palace grounds the most beautiful in the city.

The unstated but obvious concern of the government was to prevent further revolutionary occurrences.

---

*Sunday, September 1.* Went to Kaumakapili and contributed $5.00 towards Waiamau's salary—Kapali of Micronesia[113] preached and H[enry] Waterhouse sat in pulpit. Very few attended.

*Monday, September 2.* [I am] Fifty-one years today and John sick. Had luau to a few—reception of Queen.[114]

Three P.M. First Div. Liliuokalani Education[al] Society [meeting].

*Tuesday, September 3.* 2nd Div. Liliuokalani Education[al] Society meet at ten to 12 P.M. Then Sewing Society met till one P.M.

*Wednesday, September 4.* Went to Palace—to Hooulu Lahui Society. Asked that reports be published, that no money be expended for building purposes—meeting not satisfactory. Had prayer meeting in Palace. Spoke of having prayers said all over the Islands—agreed to send word to King first.

Hinano Bower. Strange dream, four horses on way—drawn through water.

*Thursday, September 5.* Strange visitor [three words erased] He aha kou manao—he aloha no wau [i] kuu aina hanau—e paa iho i na pe [pepa?] Lohe he pepa inoa ke hoouna e ia ana i Amelika e hoomau ia ko makou Kuokoa. E paa ana—i ko lakou wahi a ke kau. [Strange visitor (erasure) What do I think—I love my dear birthland—(I will) Hold fast to the documents. I hear a petition is being sent to America that our independence should be maintained. (They) will hold fast—to their place until summer.] [Then a scrolling ornament.]

*Friday, September 6.* Called on Mrs. Allen, Mrs. Gussie and Charley Carter,[115] Mrs. McGrew. Hunted up papers of S. K. Paaluhi, Hamakua Hawaii. Told Kalua I preferred $200.00 in money [rather] than in land.

---

113. David Kapali (d. January 1909, Honolulu) and his wife, Tamara Kealakai Kapali, both missionaries with the Hawaiian Evangelical Association, were stationed in Micronesia beginning in 1865. They returned to Honolulu in 1880.

114. The *Evening Bulletin*, September 2, 1889, in its notice of Liliu's birthday, said, "The Royal Hawaiian Band serenaded the Princess at her residence, Washington Place this morning." On September 3, the *Bulletin* reported: "Her Majesty the Queen called on Princess Liliuokalani yesterday to congratulate her on her 51st birthday. The Queen was attended by Princes Kawananakoa and Kalanianaole and Mr. J. W. Robertson, Acting Chamberlain, and Mrs. Robertson."

115. "Gussie" or Sybil A. Carter (b. March 16, 1843, Honolulu–d. September 1, 1904, Honolulu) was the daughter of Dr. G. P. Judd and wife (married 1862) of H.A.P. Carter. Her son, Charley or Charles Lunt Carter, would be killed at Waikiki at the start of the January

*Saturday, September 7.* My visitor came again—must have personal interview.

*Sunday, September 8.* Went to hear Rev. Bicknell[116] preach at Kaumakapili. Rice[117] and H. Waterhouse[118] were in my pew. Good sermon, gave $1.00.

Two P.M. went to Palolo [to] look at land near Kaua. Went to Waikiki—[had a] Milkshake.

Eight P.M. Consulted [a fortune-telling] friend, a lady—[who] told me to take care and not interfere. [That the] King would suffer death in fane [sic]—woman dying [would] leave me property—Succeed in suit of Toboggan—Light-haired man will try to cheat me about sale of land. A change for me—Money! Money! Money!

*Monday, September 9.* John went to Waialua.

*Tuesday, September 10.* 7.30 P.M. W. A. [?] came with ASMOLLIE [?]—Tried to influence me to [illegible]—did not succeed.

*Monday, September 16.* Went to Eveline's [Eveline Wilson's], she told me Ashford ought to be made to give up guns and [that] Marshall Soper[119] is an old woman. Had a meeting. Charlie [Wilson] scolded [me] for selling my stocks today of Waimanalo—very angry.

*Tuesday, September 17.* Rec'd. $400.00 today from [Paul] Isenberg for my sorrel span [pair of horses]. Rec'd $8,050 from stocks—$200 paid to Morgan[120]—left $7,850.00—2 stocks of P.I.R. belonging to Kaipo and Bros. $170 of same belonging to Kaipo and $900.00 of W[aimanalo] Stocks belongs to Kaipo—making $1,325 belonging to Kaipo ma [and associates].

*Wednesday, September 18.* Joe Heleluhe took $7,800 to Bishop's Bank on my account—he and Kahawai paid $400.00 to W. R. Castle to pay for three Kuleanas [native land claims] at Palolo—$200.00 having been previously paid belonging to Mahoe, Kelikana, Kalakuaole. Went to Palolo and stayed at Kahawailoa. L. [Lilia] Aholo paid to me $7.78 dues of Members of the

---

1895 counterrevolution. Another son, George R. Carter, would be a governor of the Territory of Hawaii (1903–07).

116. Reverend James Bicknell (b. 1829, Tahiti–d. 1892, Honolulu) was the son of an English missionary to Tahiti, and a longtime resident of Hawaii, where he served parishes on the island of Hawaii.

117. William Hyde Rice (b. July 23, 1846, Punahou School, Oahu–d. June 15, 1924, Lihue, Kauai) was a legislator, a Kauai landowner, and the governor of Kauai (February 8, 1892–February 28, 1893, when the Provisional Government abolished the office).

118. Henry Waterhouse (b. 1845, Tasmania–d. 1904, Honolulu) was the son of Honolulu merchant John Thomas Waterhouse. He was a representative in the 1874 legislature, and a noble during the 1883–88 sessions. He was also a member of the Advisory Council of the Provisional Government of Hawaii, 1893–94, and a senator under the Republic of Hawaii, 1895–98. Henry Waterhouse was an active member of the Hawaiian Board of Missions.

119. John H. Soper (b. 1846, Plymouth, England–d. July 27, 1944, Honolulu) was marshall of the Kingdom September 30, 1884–July 31, 1886, and February 8, 1888–July 1, 1890. He became a prominent military officer during the time of the Provisional Government and the Republic of Hawaii.

120. James F. Morgan (b. 1861, New York–d. 1912, San Jose, California) was an auctioneer and businessman. The payment would have been Morgan's commission for arranging the sale.

Hui Hoonaauao 2nd Division. Mentioned that I'd [?] like to lease Waikiki lots and in Palama to C. L.

*Friday, September 20.* Charley Clark and Mr. [James F.] Morgan met me at Muolaulani. Told Morgan I wanted $35,000 for Muolaulani, then returned to Palolo. John Cummins returned from San Francisco. Made mention again about selling lots at Waikiki.

*Saturday, September 21.* Moved over to Kaleohano's house and killed a puaa luau [luau pig].

*Monday, September 23.* Recd. $15.00 from Aiaumoe [for] rent of Kahala. Joe Heleluhe came to see me about black horses.

*Tuesday, September 24.* Palolo. Went to town to Palama—bade Hattie Akeo good-bye—gave her $15.00 towards my share of Hui Hookuonoono in Hilo to give Mrs. F. [Fred] S. Lyman and Keala. Eight P.M. Went with Archie [Cleghorn] to Dr. Trousseau's reception to his sister. Queen was there. When she entered everyone left the room except for Mr. [Charles] Bishop, Mrs. [Ellen Harvey] McCully, Mrs. [Richard] Bickerton, Kahalewai [Cummins], Mrs. [Herman] Widemann, [entry continues at top of next page] Koa, Kuhio, and myself. What does it mean?[121]

[At] Hinano Bower.

*Wednesday, September 25.* Archie told me last night that Sir William Wiseman wanted me to go in Palace and beg the King not to sign documents of Protectorate gotten up by A. [Albert] F. Judd.[122]

*Thursday, September 26.* Charlie Clark said as soon as possible he would come out with Morgan and stake off the lots at Waikiki.[123]

*Sunday, September 29.* Mr. [James] Morgan and Charlie came out to Waikiki and I showed him what portions and lots I wanted to have sold. Mr. Morgan told me other portions would not do but [he] would some day with Charlie stake off lots.

---

121. "A Pleasant Reception. Last evening Madame Morrisseau and Capt. J. Morrisseau held a reception at the residence of Dr. Georges Trousseau who is the doctor's sister. Madame Morrisseau . . . has with her son been visiting the islands the last two months, and intends shortly to return home. The reception was an exceedingly pleasant affair, the Hawaiian Quintette Club furnishing vocal and instrumental music. Refreshments were served. Among those present were Her Majesty the Queen, attended by Mr. J. W. Robertson, Acting Chamberlain, and Mrs. Robertson, H.R.H. Princess Liliuokalani, Hon. A. S. Cleghorn, Their highnesses Kawananakoa and Kalanianaole." *Evening Bulletin*, September 25, 1889.

122. The idea of a protectorate seems to have been a product of the Honolulu rumor mill. The *Pacific Commercial Advertiser*, September 27, 1889, in its "Island News Summary," commented, "A rumor has started among the natives on the 25th that the Ministry had made a treaty annexing the islands to the United States, and that Mr. Carter was to be the bearer of the document to Washington. No such treaty has been drafted or proposed, nor would it under any circumstances be entertained by the Government."

John E. Bush called a "mass meeting" protest at the Chinese Theater on September 26, at which the participants passed a resolution: "Whereas Grave rumors are current that a proposition has been submitted to your Majesty containing clauses almost amounting to a protectorate by the United States Government, which rumors have seriously alarmed all loyal subjects of Hawaii." *Pacific Commercial Advertiser*, September 27, 1889. A committee subsequently did meet the king at the palace, and they later submitted a resolution to the cabinet.

123. The surveyed lots were the part of the Hamohamo premises that fronted the Waikiki road (now Kalakaua Avenue). See footnote for October 16, 1889, diary entry (242).

*Thursday, October 3.* Charlie Clark told me that lots had been measured and would soon be advertised. I told him those who bought lots mauka could have the privilege of 50 ft. on beach, but [I] would like to get $100.00 for each lot.

*Saturday, October 5.* Some dancers came over to hula but [I] would not hookupu [make a tribute or ceremonial offering]. I have no money to throw away on hulas.

*Sunday, October 6.* Harry and Lily Auld are spending the day, also C[harles] Clark. Hanna Holt[124] and Amoe are also here.[125]

*Friday, October 11.* C. [Charles] B. Wilson came to caution me to be careful what I said—don't know what will be in six months. Wilcox gave evidence [in court] for Loomens.[126]

[Wilcox] Said King encouraged him by sending him messages through [Robert] Hoapili Baker—reversed times and told him when to come out—to begin right away with his men—he obeyed. 30 July [he] sent for King—he would not come back to Palace—and he wondered and sent message to King—he sent message—pela iho [that's all]—and never came—he found then that he had been betrayed. Wilcox['s] motive [was] to have new ministers and new Constitution and support the King.[127] John still sick—went to drive.

*Sunday, October 13.* Morn. John went out to drive, we met at dinner. Three P.M. Jennie [Clark] and I went to Palolo, stayed till five, [then] came home.

*Monday, October 14.* Good deal [of] excitement and talk about Wilcox's statement in court. C.R.B. [Charles R. Bishop] came to caution me—be careful and not accept any offer to throne and to be careful what I say—that they will sustain Kunane [Kalakaua] on the throne—Good. Antone Rosa says be cautious and not talk, to tell King when asked not to go in Court and stand on witness stand. Others tell me a party is going to put Kaiulani on throne by disqualifying me—and have a Council of Regency and Archie.

John and Joe Heleluhe went and entered $7,800.00 to my account, barring $1,352.47 cents, which will be paid in January, 1890. All my papers have been returned by Bishop & Co. Received Kaiulani's picture today.

124. Hanakaulani Holt (b. 1843–d. 1904) was the wife of Owen J. Holt.

125. Clarissa Amoe Coney (d. 1911) was the wife of Julian Monsarrat, longtime manager of Kapapala Ranch, Kau, Hawaii.

126. Robert Wilcox's testimony was at the first of the rebels' trials—that of Albert Loomens, which commenced on October 7, 1889. Loomens, a Belgian artilleryman, arrived in Hawaii May 1889. He became an associate of Wilcox in the revolutionary schemes of July 1889, for which Loomens (not Wilcox) was convicted and sentenced to death on the charge of treason. Loomens's sentence was commuted to one year and banishment, terms that he accepted.

127. Wilcox's statements under oath received full coverage in the *Pacific Commercial Advertiser*, October 12, 1889. As to the matter of Wilcox's motives, Robert N. Boyd, who was wounded in the rebellion, was called as a witness for the prosecution, and testified that Wilcox had proposed forming a secret society "to give back to the King the rights that had been taken away from him and overthrow the ministry." But then, in his testimony on October 9, Boyd stated more ominously: "I have lost all confidence in Wilcox.... Wilcox thought he could accomplish his object of becoming dictator and then place the King in his rights afterwards. He told me he thought the King was weak and he would proclaim himself dictator and place the town under martial law." *Pacific Commercial Advertiser*, October 10, 1889.

*Wednesday, October 16.* Kaiulani is 14 years old today. Began to advertise sale of lots at Waikiki.[128]

*Wednesday, October 23.* Sent by J. Heleluhe, $352.00 to bank to pay my debts of $1,352.47, leaving $1,000 to pay some other day.[129]

*Friday, October 25.* Prince and Princess de Bourbon, Count Zileri, Count Luchessi, Baron Heydebrandt, Baroness Hertlinger sailed away in *Australia*. Kawananakoa, Kuhio, and Jimmie McGuire sailed also for England.[130]

---

On October 25, 1889, the Belgian Albert Loomens, who had been convicted by a jury of the crime of treason against the Hawaiian government, received his sentence of death from the chief justice of the supreme court. However, on the following day, the Privy Council, having received a petition for clemency from 1,746 persons (mostly Native Hawaiians), commuted the sentence to one year of imprisonment, followed by banishment. The sentence went into effect as of November 21, 1889.

---

*Monday, October 28.* Sent by Joe [Heleluhe] to S. M. Damon or bank towards my debt of $1.352—$100.00—leaves $900.00 more to pay.

*Tuesday, October 29.* Rec'd from C[harles] Clark $1,989.50 but $700.00 was pledged [?] by him, $994.50 belonged to Liliuokalani Hui Hoonaauao Division 2nd. $248.63—to Aimoku, $82.87 cts to Kaipo, and only $673.00 remained to me of Ice Stocks sold yesterday to Wilder & Co.

*Wednesday, October 30.* Recd. [Rest of entry blank.]

*Thursday, October 31.* Sent by Joe today $500.00 to pay in bank towards

---

128. During October and November 1889, auctioneer J. F. Morgan advertised in the *Hawaiian Gazette* an "Auction Sale of Desirable Building Lots," these being part of Liliuokalani's Hamohamo property at Waikiki. The nine lots, on the inland side of Kalakaua Avenue "adjoining the bridge," were each to be sold for a 20-year leasehold, and the advertisement also announced: "Parties purchasing any of those lots will receive gratis a 20-year lease of 50 feet of land on the Beach for erection of bathhouses and bathing facilities."

129. In an account book recording transactions of the Liliuokalani Hui Hoonaauao, there appears the following cancellation of the People's Ice and Refrigeration Co. stocks: "October 23, 1889—Sold at $85.00 a share to Wilder & Co. [and] This day sold all shares amounting to 12 in all in P.I.R. Co. belonging to L.H. Hoonaauao M2 [Mokuna 2, Second Division] at $85.00 a share at a loss of $146.00." Hawaii State Archives, Liliuokalani Collection, Liliuokalani Trust Papers, M-397.

130. "Among the sixty-five cabin passengers leaving today by the SS *Australia* for the coast are Count and Countess de Bardi, who are known in their native country, Austria, as Prince and Princess de Bourbon. These royal tourists came to the Hawaiian Islands by the SS *City of Peking* on the 9th inst. [this month] and during their short sojourn of two weeks amongst us have made a very favorable impression.... Baroness Hertling, Baron Heydebrandt, and Count Lucchesi and Zileri form part of the suite." *Pacific Commercial Advertiser*, October 25, 1889. Princes Kawananakoa and Kuhio were also passengers on the *Australia*. Curiously, Liliu does not record her attendance at the grand ball, held at the palace on Wednesday the 24th in honor of the titled Austrians and their suite.

paying off my indebtedness of $1,352, leaving $300.47 to pay Bishop & Co.[131]

**Saturday, November 2.** Sent by Joe Heleluhe to pay in bank $200.00 for paying off debt of $1.352.47, leaving $200.00 more. When that is over, I must pay A[llen] & Robinsons $1,000.00—then Kaipo's. Paid Mrs. Bush $25.00 today.

**Wednesday, December 4.** John and J. Robertson returned from Waialua and left [Mr.] Toler, Mrs. Booth and daughter, Miss Moore, Willie and Minnie Aldrich at Makaha.

**Thursday, December 5.** Started to put lanai round my [Waikiki] bathing house.

**Saturday, December 7.** Finished lanai round my bathing house—enjoyed my bath.

**Sunday, December 8.** Luau'ed on mats at bath house. Sea bath with Jennie Clark, Mary Ailau.

**Saturday, December 14.** Received news of corruption of police department—Policemen disobey Soper's orders.[132]

**Sunday, December 15.** Heard of smuggling done by officers of Custom House—everyone implicated—ministers aware of it but dare not do anything for most of officers are Rifle men—eight cases of guns and ammunition brought by *Discovery*.[133]

**Monday, December 16.** Had a meeting of the Hooulu Society in this house ten A.M. Pres.—Sec.—Treas.—Mr. and Mrs. Alapai, Mrs. Maria Aiu, Maria Lokai, and Wakeke present. Reported $200 in my hands [and] $32 of contributions in J. Waiamau's name. News of open corruption in Customs House or Finance Department.[134] Pili.

**Tuesday, December 17.** [Reverend] J. Waiamau borrowed $50.00 of Hooulu Lahui Society of Kaumakapili at 10 percent, to be paid six months from today. Pili.

---

131. In the memorandum under this date at the end of the diary is the following list:
   *Amount of money belonging to Kaipo Aea in my care $1,231.48*
   *For John Hannah & Lydia Aea $248.61*
   *Milaina Ahia $114.00*
   *Aiaumoe $57.00*
   *Mrs. Kuluhau 1 Ice Stock $95.00*
   *___ gold of Hoopii $20.00*
   *Kalahiki 4 Ice Stock $190.00*
   *L. H. Hoonaauao Mahele 2 $994.00*

132. There is no specific mention of this matter in records of the sheriff or marshall. However, an oblique note in the *Hawaiian Gazette*, December 17, 1889, says: "The Marshall's order, for the captain on duty to remain in the Station house is very often disregarded."

133. The American bark *Discovery* (Captain McNeil) arrived at Honolulu December 10, 12 days out from San Francisco. Nowhere does the press mention the eight cases of guns.

134. The *Pacific Commercial Advertiser*, December 13, 1889, commented only: "Rumors are current affecting the standing of several officials in regard to illicit opium transactions." The *Hawaiian Gazette* on December 17, 1889, printed an almost identical notice.

*Wednesday, December 18.* Paina malu [quiet meal] [at] Muolaulani. Jessie, Sophy, Wakeke, Joe, Mary, [and] Milaina. J. Cummins invited me to come to Mett's wedding to Miss Meyerberg [sic, Mersberg] tomorrow.[135]

Went to Musicale at Palace, eight P.M., only Hotel people there—Professor Sauvlet[136] and others perform—Very Pleasant.

*Thursday, December 19.* Founders' Day of Kamehameha School, Bernice's birthday. John and I went out to exercises. Put up box of plants for Mrs. L. A. Booth. Miss Mayerberg [sic, Mersberg] marries tonight but [only] John has gone. Walter Waiamau and Maria Needham marries this eve.[137] Rheumatism prevents me from going to either.[138]

[Liliuokalani and Jennie Clark departed Honolulu for Lahaina, Maui, on the *W. G. Hall*, December 24. Liliu would remain there until January 4, 1890.]

*Monday, December 30.* [Lahaina.] Mrs. Fred Horner and Mrs. Decoto.[139] Mrs. Tom Hayselden[140] called to see [me], also Miss Dickenson.[141] Band Concert at Court House Square.

---

135. "Yesterday evening Mr. Carl Mett, accountant in Messrs. Bishop & Co's Bank, and Miss Ida Mersberg were united in marriage [at Kawaiahao Church]." *Evening Bulletin*, December 20, 1889. It was noted that at the large public reception held after the ceremony, guests included the king, and the Royal Hawaiian Band played on the grounds of the house.

136. During the month of December, Professor G. Sauvlet advertised in the *Pacific Commercial Advertiser* for "piano, violin, and singing Lessons" at his residence at 195 Nuuanu Avenue, "or will visit pupils at their residence." Sauvlet and his wife remained in Honolulu until November 1890.

137. "The Kawaiahao Young Ladies' Institute was brilliantly lighted up last evening.... The occasion was the marriage of the oldest son of Rev. Mr. Waiamau, pastor of Kaumakapili Church, to the niece of Mr. Needham, Superintendent of the Reformatory School. The large audience Hall and adjoining room were packed with a large assemblage of gentlemen and ladies. Rev. Dr. Beckwith performed the ceremony.... The groom has been employed on Mr. Waterhouse's Queen Street store for several years, while the bride has been connected for some years with the Makawao and Kawaiahao seminaries." *Pacific Commercial Advertiser*, December 20, 1889.

138. Under Friday, December 20, in the section "Bills receivable for December," Liliu lists the following:

*Chulan $600.00*
*Keawe hawaii $200.00*
*Kamaliikane $70.00*
*Kalakaua $200.00*
*Milton $30.00*
*Akaiko $120.00*
*Tien Lian $50.00*
*Damon $40.00*
*Gookim $820.95*
*[Total] $2,130.95.*

139. Mrs. Horner was the wife of W. Y. Horner (d. 1898, Lahaina), a resident of Maui since 1879 and manager of Pioneer Mill Co., Lahaina. Their daughter Sarah in 1889 married W. L. Decoto, head overseer for Olowalu Sugar Co., and subsequently for Pioneer Mill Co.

140. This was the wife of Thomas J. Hayselden (d. 1891, Lahaina), who advertised in 1890 "groceries, provisions, dry and fancy goods, hay and feed, and drug store, Lahaina."

141. Miss Dickenson was a daughter of longtime judge and schoolteacher Henry Dickenson (d. 1876).

*Tuesday, December 31.* Went out shopping—bought coat and J. [John] presented it [as a] New Years' present to T. Evans $15.00.

Had a reception at Court House. Capt. and Officers of *Mohican* were present. Mr. and Mrs. Evans, the Honorable Richardson[142] and Mr. and Mrs. Kepoikai,[143] Miss Daniels,[144] Mrs. Pikao, the Baldwins.[145] It was a grand ball for Lahaina.

12 P.M. [sic] Happy New Year.—This morning went up to Aholo, heard from old woman and Kaioholokai that Aholo was using some Crown lands.[146]

[In the miscellaneous memoranda at the end of the 1889 diary there is the following:]

*Wednesday, January 1, 1890.* [Lahaina.] General Sunday School celebration. Officers of *Mohican* were present. I attended with Mrs. Everett, Jennie Clark, Milaina. Band boys headed the procession. Luau at 12—poor fare. Stayed till five P.M. Concert in the evening. Pretty Good.

Recd. $68.15 cts at concert. Gave to W. Aylett[147] $35.00 for band boys, returned the rest to Pali.[148]

[Liliuokalani returned to Honolulu on the morning of January 4, 1890.]

---

142. George E. Richardson (b. 1850–d. 1892) was a representative in the legislature, 1882–86; a member of the Privy Council, 1886–91; and from 1887, judge of the Second Circuit Court (Maui).

143. A. Noa Kepoikai (b. 1861, Wailuku–d. May 9, 1911, Wailuku) was a legislator and circuit court judge.

144. Nancy Daniels (d. 1923, Honolulu) was the daughter of Wailuku merchant W. H. Daniels. She would marry K.R.G. Wallace in 1891.

145. David Dwight Baldwin (b. 1831, Honolulu–d. June 16, 1912, Honolulu), a teacher at Lahainaluna, was married to Lois Gregory Morris.

146. The inference is that Aholo was using certain Crown lands on Maui for his own purposes. No record of this matter has been found.

147. Remigius William Aylett (b. 1856–d. 1922) was part Hawaiian and was one of the earliest members of the Royal Hawaiian Band.

148. Reverend Adamu Pali was the longtime pastor of the Lahaina Protestant church.

*King Kalakaua lying in state in Iolani Palace's throne room, 1891. On the morning of January 29, 1891, the* Charleston *appeared off Diamond Head with flags at half-mast and telegraphed a message to shore that Kalakaua was dead. Celebratory arches intended to honor the king's return were hastily draped in mourning and Liliuokalani became the monarch of the Hawaiian Islands. In this photograph, Queen Kapiolani rests her head against the king's casket, which is adorned with his crown, sword and scepter, and a royal feather cape associated with Kamehameha I. Kahili (feather standards) mark the presence of the alii, confirm his authority, and guard his remains. The feather pau (skirt) of Nahienaena, the daughter of Kamehameha I, covers the bier. On February 15, 1891, the king was interred at the Royal Mausoleum.*
Bishop Museum Archives

# Heir Apparent, Regent, and Monarch
## 1890–91

For the years 1890 and 1891, no Liliuokalani diaries survive, although there is evidence from the Queen's letters that she kept a diary for at least one of these years, 1890. The loss is unfortunate, for during these two years, Liliuokalani, the crown princess and heir apparent, assumed the duties of regent when her brother Kalakaua traveled to California in November 1890, and then succeeded him as the eighth monarch of the Hawaiian Islands after his death in January 1891. This section will provide a summary of her activities during this period.

The year 1890 commenced with a New Year's Eve celebration of the birthday of Queen Kapiolani at Iolani Palace. Then the country (and Liliuokalani) focused on the forthcoming elections of candidates from the National Reform Party, which they supported, against the Reform Party, which they opposed. According to an editorial in the conservative newspaper *The Friend*, the Reform Party's platform was one "of gratifying testimony to the restless control which Reform principles have gained here" (a direct reference to the Bayonet Revolution of 1887 and the Bayonet Constitution), while the National Reform Party "belongs to the Wilcox side and ... should this National Reform Party obtain a majority in the next Legislature, there is no doubt that Wilcox and Bush would at once make strenuous efforts to overturn the new Constitution and restore the King's lawless power."[1] Following the February 5 election, *The Friend* decried the lack of secret ballots and commented, "We are certain that there was a strong Wilcox terrorism among the natives in Honolulu.... What we want is the Australian ballot."[2] A majority elected the National Reform ticket, which carried Oahu with two exceptions: Cecil Brown beat John E. Bush by 13 votes, and Robert Wilcox won over William C. Achi.[3]

The election over, the established social order prevailed for some months until the legislature opened in May.

On April 7, Liliuokalani gave an informal reception to "strangers" (or important visitors) in the Palace Blue Room. On April 9, a special performance of Gilbert and Sullivan's *Mikado* was held at the opera house

---

1. *The Friend*, February 1890.
2. An Australian ballot was one printed at public expense, on which all nominated candidates appeared, and then distributed only at the polling place and marked in secret. This form of ballot was first used in the Hawaiian Islands in the February 2, 1892, election. See *The Friend*, March 1892.
3. *The Friend*, March 1890.

before a large audience, with the king, Princess Liliuokalani, her husband John O. Dominis, and Archibald S. Cleghorn in the royal box. On May 6, Liliuokalani and Dominis were also present at a Grand Musicale in the palace, an occasion announced as the first of a series. The performers were stationed in the blue room, and chairs for the audience were set up in the dining room. Feather capes were displayed in the throne room for the admiration of guests.

The 1890 legislature opened at noon on May 21 in Aliiolani Hale, with an impressive assemblage of royals and government officials, and a perfunctory speech by the king. Liliuokalani, attended by Mrs. Aldrich, was present and seated on the dais.

A week later (May 28), Liliuokalani and Queen Kapiolani were present at the formation of the Hospital Flower Society, which took place at the YMCA. She, the queen, and Princess Poomaikelani graciously offered to pay for growing flowers in a plot on the hospital grounds.

On May 29, the USS flagship *Charleston* arrived from San Francisco. It would be that ship that would take King Kalakaua to San Francisco late in 1890, and would return his body to the Hawaiian Islands on January 29, 1891.

June 11 found the king, queen, and Liliu out at Kapiolani Park observing the races, with the Jockey Club entertaining them "in fine style."[4]

The Kapiolani Maternity Home, on the corner of Beretania and Makiki Streets (formerly Princess Kekaulike's residence), opened on June 14, 1890. This facility, which had begun under the mantle of the Hooulu Lahui Society, Queen Kapiolani's favorite charity, offered modern facilities, nursing care, and medical supervision for Hawaiian women. The king, queen, and Liliuokalani attended the opening and were given special tours through the new operation.

On July 19, Liliuokalani was present at the state ball honoring French Admiral de Prémesnil and officers of the ship *Dubordieu*, which was followed by an elegant supper in the grand dining hall.

Liliuokalani's diaries (of other years) include frequent mention of her attendance at the theater, and she was present on July 30, 1890, when Frances Hodgson Burnett's *Little Lord Fauntleroy* played for the first time in Honolulu. The press described the event as "a splendid performance."[5] Liliu and Dominis were among those in the royal box, and Liliu so enjoyed the play that she saw two performances of it.

But legislative matters and the tangled politics of the day dominated the news. On June 13, following a want of confidence vote in the legislature, the entire cabinet sent in resignations to the king, and on the 17th a new cabinet formed, comprising J. A. Cummins, minister of foreign affairs; Godfrey Brown, minister of finance; Charles N. Spencer, minister

---

4. *Pacific Commercial Advertiser*, June 12, 1890.
5. *Pacific Commercial Advertiser*, July 31, 1890.

of the interior; and Arthur P. Peterson, attorney general. The editor of *The Friend* declared this was "rather a compromise Cabinet, politically satisfactory to none, not strong, nor likely to command much support."[6] Liliuokalani was of the same opinion and would successfully force this cabinet to resign when she assumed the throne early the next year.

The main topic of political agitation was the effects of the constitution of 1887, known as the "Bayonet Constitution" from the manner in which its supporters forced it upon the king. The Hawaiian population deeply disliked it because of a restrictive voting clause, which disenfranchised many Native Hawaiian voters.

The conservative newspaper *The Friend* editorialized: "The only occurrence of any apparent importance during the month with respect to politics has been the presentation to the King of a petition by a Committee of Hawaiians, asking for a convention of the People...to prepare a new constitution and declaring that the present one has robbed them of their right."[7] Eighty prominent Hawaiians presented this petition urging reform measures to the king on August 14. The king, queen, Liliu, and Governor Dominis were on the dais of the throne room when the group presented the document to the king.

The *Pacific Commercial Advertiser* reported that the king received it "with much state and formality" and answered the petitioners: "I commend the propriety with which you have presented the wishes of the peoples, using your constitutional right to present their petition for the redress of grievances. I shall submit the matter to the Legislature and request that body to take the steps required to carry out the desires of my people."[8] This he did, and members of the House of Representatives entered the matter into their session as Bill 125: An Act to Convene Delegates to Frame a Constitution for the Hawaiian Kingdom. A house committee, after considering the matter, offered unanimous support of such amendments.

In the House of Representatives, there occurred on September 9 what the *Advertiser* characterized as "incendiary talk" by Robert W. Wilcox, who had just taken his seat after the government's failed attempt to convict him of treason: "Rep. R. W. Wilcox is on the warpath and if his opponents...vote against his measures, he is going to blow up buildings, kill, make the streets of Honolulu sticky with blood. All this he told the House yesterday, would come to pass if the Hawaiians did not get their rights.... Rep. Bush seconded Rep. Wilcox nobly. He denounced the missionaries for importing firearms; told how they were conspiring to overthrow the government, and set up a republic.... He did not offer any particular

---

6. *The Friend*, July 1890.
7. *The Friend*, September 1890.
8. The *Pacific Commercial Advertiser*, August 15, 1890, has an account of the procession of the petitioners to the palace, their reception by the king and government officials in the throne room, and transcriptions of both the petition and the king's response.

verification of these charges, but wound up with a dark hint at the coming end of the world."[9]

Wilcox's speechifying continued that evening at a mass meeting called for that purpose.

The legislature closed on Friday, November 14, and the king's 54th birthday celebration took place on the 15th with a traditional hookupu (ceremonial offering) early in the morning, a reception for Native Hawaiian societies and government officials, a regatta in the harbor, and a torchlight procession through town organized by the Fire Laddies. When the latter arrived at the palace, an address was publicly read, followed by three hearty cheers. This would be King Kalakaua's last public function in Hawaii.

On November 21, 1890, the Foreign Office officially announced the king's intent to visit California for the sake of his health. On the morning of November 25, he bade farewell to the queen and others of the royal family at Iolani Palace, and, as prearranged, issued a proclamation through the Foreign Office appointing "our beloved subject and sister, Her Royal Highness the Princess Liliuokalani, as Regent of our Kingdom ... during our absence."[10] At one P.M., King Kalakaua departed for San Francisco on the USS *Charleston*, and Liliuokalani became regent for the second time.[11]

In California, King Kalakaua was feted, and he toured the southern part of the state. The month of December found the monarch ailing but still engaged, and staying at the Coronado Hotel in San Diego. But he returned to San Francisco a very sick man, and on January 20, 1891, he died of Bright's disease (a type of kidney inflammation) in his suite in the Palace Hotel. The U.S. Navy immediately put the USS *Charleston* at the service of the Hawaiian government, and the ship returned the king's body to the islands with all honors. On the morning of January 29, the *Charleston* appeared off Diamond Head with flags at half-mast, and telegraphed a message to shore that Kalakaua was dead. The celebratory arches intended to honor the king's return were hastily draped in mourning, and Liliuokalani the regent became the monarch of the Hawaiian Islands. The justices of the Supreme Court swore her into office that day.

The court went into full mourning until two weeks after the king's funeral on February 15, 1891, and remained in half-mourning for an additional two months. Tributes from around the world arrived from friends of the king and heads of state. Queen Victoria and U.S. President Grover Cleveland sent touching letters of condolence.

But affairs of state would brook no delay, and Liliuokalani right from the start made her desires known. The government expected that as a constitutional monarch, she would agree to have the late king's cabinet

---

9. *Pacific Commercial Advertiser*, September 10, 1990.
10. This proclamation is in the Hawaii State Archives, Foreign Office and Executive Files, 68—oversize.
11. Liliu had first been regent during King Kalakaua's world tour, January 20–October 29, 1881.

continue in office, but she refused to accept this, making it very clear that she intended to select her own ministerial advisors. She sought an opinion from the Hawaiian Supreme Court, which upheld her decision.

In April, Kaiulani, still in England for her education (where she had been since 1889), was proclaimed heir apparent to the throne.

In May, the new Queen and John O. Dominis, now elevated by proclamation to His Royal Highness, made a tour along the Kona coast of Hawaii Island, and then continued to Maui and Molokai, returning to Honolulu on June 6.

Then, on the afternoon of August 27, 1891, while the Queen and friends were planning an early September birthday celebration at Washington Place, Dr. Georges Trousseau, who was then attending to an ailing Dominis, summoned her abruptly with the words: "Madame, your husband is dying, your presence is required."[12] John O. Dominis died that day, and for the second time in a year, Liliuokalani was plunged into mourning, this time over the loss of a husband she relied on greatly for his sound advice on political matters. His funeral took place on September 6.

In October, the *Advertiser* reported: "Her Majesty the Queen, since the funeral of His Royal Highness the Prince Consort, has been living quietly in Honolulu, and may be occasionally seen in her carriage or making her frequent morning rides on horseback. Notwithstanding the mischievous reports to the contrary… Her Majesty enjoys excellent health."[13]

On October 20, Liliuokalani, accompanied by Prince Kawananakoa and James W. Robertson, paid a visit to the studio of artist William Cogswell, where she examined government-sponsored portrait commissions of herself and of the late King Kalakaua, and a three-quarter-length likeness of her late husband. She expressed herself "as being well pleased with the artist's work."[14]

In November, the *Advertiser* reported: "Her Majesty has begun to take breakfast again in Iolani Palace, and to celebrate this auspicious event Mr. Berger's string orchestra took up their positions on the Palace veranda and gave a very pretty concert during the meal, singing several of the newly revived native songs."[15]

12. *Daily Bulletin*, August 28, 1891.
13. *Pacific Commercial Advertiser*, October 17, 1891.
14. *Pacific Commercial Advertiser*, October 21, 1891.
15. *Pacific Commercial Advertiser*, November 10, 1891.

*A visit with Irene Ii Brown in Waipio, Oahu, 1892. The Queen spent the 1892 New Year holiday with family and friends at her home in Waialua on Oahu. On January 5, she recorded her departure and describes that en route to Honolulu she and her companions "arrived at Mrs. Irene Ii Brown's place [Waipio] where a nice supper was laid out."*

*This photograph, set before a grass house on the property, was probably taken following the lunch. The Queen (in dark dress) is seated center. Irene Ii Brown is standing directly behind her, between Prince David Kawananakoa (on the left) and Prince Jonah Kuhio Kalanianaole (on the right). Colonel Sam Parker (on the left) and the Honorable John Adams Cummins (on the right) are lounging at the feet of the Queen. Rebecca Kahalewai Cummins, wife of John, is seated third from the right.*

Hawaii State Archives

# 1892

*Friday, January 1, 1892.* At Waialua with Mrs. C. B. Wilson, Mrs. Jennie Clark, Hon. J. Richardson, Major J. W. Robertson. One P.M. We went to services at Waialua Church, the occasion being that of presenting a large clock to the Church or Trustees, and also of three dozen hymnbooks.[1]

After the exercises were over, we were escorted by the Hui Hololio a Kalanianaole [Kalanianaole Horse Riding Association] as far as Kalaikini's place,[2] where the Hui went on and went through maneuvers on horseback. Their uniform was white holoku and red pau [white dresses and red skirts or aprons]. Leihulu[3] is with us. We were escorted home by the party. Had a very pleasant [time]. It was my Chamberlain [James W. Robertson] who presented the clock today, and it was his first speech. My poor John—Everything around reminds me of him for he loved to come here [and] this beautiful lanai was built by him to receive me on my tour around the Island, but he never lived to see it. Devotional exercises are part of the program of the day.

*Saturday, January 2.* Waialua. Prince Kalanianaole and Archie Mahaulu and Morris Keohokalole[4] arrived today, also Marshall C. [Charles] B. Wilson and Col. [Curtis] Iaukea, so also [added to] the above are Mrs. C. B. Wilson, Mrs. Jennie Clark, Mrs. Morris Keohokalole, J. W. Robertson my Chamberlain, Col. J. [John] Richardson, and myself, eleven in all who sit down to our meals. People of Waialua are very kind, besides contributing chickens and turkeys they sent large pig, two cows, and a pig every day. How it rains—and it is so cold.

THE DIARY FOR 1892
1 JAN–31 AUG
Bishop Museum Archives

---

1. On the presentation of the clock to the Waialua Protestant Church, the *Daily Bulletin*, January 6, 1892, reported: "Her Majesty the Queen returned from her New Year's trip to Waialua by yesterday afternoon's train from Manana. The Queen and party greatly enjoyed their short stay at Waialua. There was no function given at the place except the presentation of a clock to Liliuokalani church by the Queen after whom the new church was called at dedication. Major J. W. Robertson, Chamberlain, made the presentation to the trustees at a service held on New Year's day, making a brief speech in so doing. Judge S. H. Kamakee, trustee, responded. It is a fine New York clock with a dial two feet in diameter, the hours being marked with the twelve letters of the Queen's name—L-I-L-I-U-O-K-A-L-A-N-I, instead of the usual Roman numerals. The clock is a calendar one, showing, besides days of the week and dates of the month, the moon's phases, the weeks of the year, and the year itself.... Hon. J. Richardson gave an address in connection with the presentation ceremony."
2. Kalaikini was a taro planter at Kahuku, Oahu.
3. Leihulu Kapena was now Mrs. Morris Keohokalole.
4. Morris Kahai Keohokalole (b. 1865, Wailuku, Maui–d. January 10, 1932, Honolulu) was a clerk in the Interior Department. He married Leihulu Kapena on November 5, 1887.

*Liliu's home in Waialua was on the banks of the Anahulu River near Loko Ea fishpond (her home is to the right of the view shown at top). On January 1, 1892, she presented a clock to the Liliuokalani Protestant Church (shown above), a wood structure newly built and named in her honor. It replaced the 1840 adobe congregational church, Ka Ahahui Kahu Malama Waiwai o ka Ekalesia o Kawailoa ma Waialua. The hours on the clock are marked by the letters of her name, L-I-L-I-U-O-K-A-L-A-N-I.*
Theodore Severin, Hawaii State Archives (Anahulu)
Hawaiian Mission Children's Society Library (church)

*Sunday, January 3.* Waialua. After devotions comes breakfast—at 11 we all go to church except Mr. Wilson. It was so nice to hear the congregation sing. Kept in my room for the rest of the day until time for devotions at five P.M. It is very cold, the wind blowing from the north. Leihulu and her husband [Morris Keohokalole] went over to Laie to see some friends and came home late. Early tomorrow morning Morris will return to town.

*Monday, January 4.* Waialua. Soon after breakfast Mr. Wilson, Mr. Iaukea, Prince Kalanianaole, and A. Mahaulu went out shooting. Eveline, Jennie, Leihulu, and I stayed at home and amused ourselves in different ways. We had the new side curtains put on of Puaiwa Hale and made it very comfortable. Mr. Richardson and Rev. Timoteo, with the help of Mrs. L. K. Mahoe and Mrs. Kamakee, helped to get them into position.

The gentlemen returned at six P.M. loaded with plovers and ducks—over 60 birds between Mr. W. [Wilson] and Curtis, and the prince [Kalanianaole] had shot 12—the result was a late supper.

*Tuesday, January 5.* Waialua. An early breakfast and a pleasant start for town. Besides the Jackson's team[5] there was Mr. Wilson with Iaukea, Mr. White's bus with Mr. Robertson, Mrs. Clark and Mary Kamiki, our faithful maid who took such good care of my husband until his death, Kihikihi and his load,[6] the boys with Waiolu and Uwila—five wagons and six outriders. I had almost forgotten to mention the Prince and Mahaulu's buggy making six in all.

Arrived at Mrs. Irene Ii Brown's place [Waipio] where a nice supper was laid out. Soon after lunch Gov. Cleghorn and Prince Kawananakoa arrived. At four we all left by the train for town, and arrived at depot at five P.M., where the Minister Parker and Mr. Widemann were awaiting us. Quite a crowd assembled and drove home with Gov. Cleghorn and the two Princes.

*Wednesday, January 6.* Washington Place. Ten A.M. Eveline and I drove up to Mrs. S. B. Dole's to hear Mrs. Florence Williams lecture on the life of Madame Guion. The room was filled with ladies of best class, and Mary Carter joined us that morning. It was enjoyable.[7]

---

5. Wallace Jackson was a popular African-American hosteler who had come to Hawaii from Kentucky at King Kalakaua's bidding. In the 1890 City Directory, he is listed as "Proprietor Enterprise Carriage Co. 60 King st. and stable Punchbowl nr. Pauoa Road."

6. Possibly J.W.S. Kihikihi, a maker of poi at No. 19 Beretania Street, who advertised in the 1884–85 City Directory: "My Poi is made from none but the Best Taro, and sold at Lowest Living rates."

7. Mrs. Florence Williams (who had given a popular series of lectures on famous women in 1888) announced a course of six lectures, on Madame Guyon, Madame de Staël, and George Sand, and three lectures on George Eliot's works, at Mrs. Dole's house. The *Pacific Commercial Advertiser*, January 7, 1892, called it a "Literary Treat" and acknowledged the presence of the Queen, Mrs. J. O. Carter, and Mrs. Wilson. "Those who heard Mrs. Williams on her previous visits needed no other incentive to listen to her again . . . and the consequence was that the parlors were filled with a large and appreciative audience, some being compelled to find seats on the veranda." Madame Guyon (Jeanne-Marie Bouvier de la Motte-Guyon, b. 1648–d. 1717) was a French spiritual writer whose ideas were often at odds with Catholic orthodoxy. Madame de Staël (Anne Louise Germaine de Staël-Holstein, b. 1766–d. 1817) was a French author, traveler, and philosopher. George Sand was the pen name of writer Amantine-Lucile-Aurore Dupin; George Eliot was the pen name of Mary Ann Evans.

I had to hasten home on account of Minister Parker who was to come at 12 to lunch. Found H.R.H. Prince Kawananakoa, Mrs. Minnie Aldrich, Mrs. Irene Brown, Mr. J. Richardson, and all sat down to lunch. I paid Mrs. Allen three dollars for Mrs. C. B. Wilson, and did not pay my own towards lecture at Mrs. S. B. Dole's.

Four P.M. Had a Cabinet Meeting. Ministers [Samuel] Parker, Spencer,[8] and Whiting[9]—Upon [the subject of] giving luau on the 29th of this month—my Accession to the Throne—they decided on having [appropriating] $1,300 for the luau [and] $1,500.00 for the dinner party which is to take place on the 24th of February, and on the 17th of March will be the Ball. All these are State entertainments, the latter of which will cost $2,000.00.

*Friday, January 8.* Washington Place. Mr. C. P. Iaukea brought some money from the Crown Lands to the amount of One thousand Nine hundred and ninety five ($1,995.00). Had a meeting of Liliuokalani Educational Society M2 [Mokuna 2, the Second Division] and decided to have Silver badges [made] for each member as it only costs $1.25 each—that it would be a lasting Memorial of their Membership for this Society.

Mr. J. W. Robertson told me that Mr. John Ena had told him that they the Stockholders of the Volcano House would like to have me assist them, and they would be willing to let me have some shares in it. He also told me that one share was $25.00. So I told J. W. Robertson that I had already given the amount of One Thousand to Mr. Wilson this very morning towards that object, so that we were aware that I am to receive 40 shares in the Volcano Stock Co.[10]

Mary Alapai wanted to borrow Three Hundred dollars to pay off the interest of a Mortgage on her property which was $1,000.00. I mentioned it to Joe Heleluhe—he'd see about it.

*Saturday, January 9.* This is Aimoku's birthday and he is nine years old today, and I have invested $500.00 for him in the Postal Savings Bank. The number of his passbook is 6.929. I have also put some money to the amount of Five hundred dollars in the same bank for Joseph Kaipo Aea,

---

8. Charles Nicholas Spencer (d. March 6, 1893, Honolulu) was minister of the interior June 17, 1890–September 12, 1892, and commissioner of Crown lands 1892. He was long a resident of Naalehu, Hawaii Island—but he was not related to the large Spencer family then residing at Waimea, Hawaii.

9. William Austin Whiting (d. January 18, 1908, Honolulu), a native of Charlestown, Massachusetts, and a graduate of Harvard Law School, arrived in the islands in 1881. Liliuokalani appointed him attorney general on February 25, 1890, and he remained in office until November 11, 1892. In 1893, he became judge of the First Circuit Court, and he was later a Supreme Court justice. In 1895, he had the unenviable duty of presiding over ex-Queen Liliuokalani's trial.

10. In 1890, Lorrin A. Thurston obtained a lease from the Bishop Estate of the land on which the Volcano House stood, and formed the Volcano Stock Company in order to put up a more modern hotel for tourists. The new building, with greatly improved accommodations, opened in May 1891, and the company then began to offer $50 all-inclusive tours to the hostelry from Honolulu, "which covers all expenses including steamer ticket, reserved stateroom, meals, board and lodging at Hilo or Kau, transportation to and from the volcano ... and board, steam sulphur baths and guide into the crater, and four nights' accommodation at the Volcano House." This was a running advertisement in the *Pacific Commercial Advertiser.*

and the number of his Passbook is 6.930. Through Joe Heleluhe I paid the Govt. $1,461 for that land at Palolo called Kaauweloa.[11] The party who invested the above amount for the boys is Mr. J. W. Robertson.

*Sunday, January 10.* Washington Place. After breakfast went to the mauka yard to see how the Cow was getting along—she gives only 3½ quarts in the morning and 2½ in the evening, and yet they say she ought to yield more. Lima Naone comes for his contribution 1.50 cts for monthly contribution for foreign lands. 11 A.M. went to Kawaiahao and contributed again $1.00 towards furnishing the church with Hymnbooks. Already six doz. books had been contributed by me, and enough money was raised to pay for eight doz. more books. Returned by Mrs. Haalelea's and found Mrs. Graham very ill and just out of danger—so young and lovely.[12] 11 P.M. went to Palace to Prayer Meeting—after that drove to Waikiki, then home.

*Monday, January 11.* Iolani Palace. 7.30 A.M. Came here to breakfast while band played. Only the Marshall and Mrs. Wilson. Soon Mary Carter comes in, and at ten we all take a drive to Mrs. W. F. Allen's—"not at home" says Hana Kamaiopili[13]—so we drive around awhile and return. Shall stay here till after Election Day, the fifth of February. Minister [Samuel] Parker thinks we ought to give Japanese decorations to S. M. Damon and W. G. Irwin, so letters go to Japan to that effect.

*Tuesday, January 12.* Iolani Palace. Mr. Robertson asked if Minister Parker has spoken to me about having [Wallace] Jackson for head groom. I said he had but I could not take him just yet—until the Legislature met, as I would like a Cook, a Butler, and a Groom all at $75.00 a month, so it was proposed to wait.

*Wednesday, January 13.* This is the fifth anniversary of Like's death and Archie has called with carnations in buttonhole. He has been very active in trying to work the old leases of Crown Lands in such a way that they might be broken. He has consulted lawyers, judges, and others, thinking I suppose of the time when his daughter should come on the throne, but

11. On October 25, 1889, Liliu applied to the minister of the interior for "that certain piece or parcel of Land situated at Palolo, Oahu, and known by the name of Kaauweloa. And I hereby offer the sum of Two hundred and fifty dollars for the same. Said premises said to contain an area of 38.33 acres." A penciled note below added, "This land is leased to the applicant for 10 years from May 15, 1882—Lease 317." According to the attached government survey report, the land was "Kula and Taro land"—with a value of "Not less than $1500, probably much more," and because it was rented at $100 per year, "the offer is entirely too low." Hawaii State Archives, Interior Department of Land.

On October 20, 1891, Joe Heleluhe wrote to the minister of the interior: "On behalf of Her Majesty Liliuokalani, I make application that the 38-33/100 Acres of... Kaauwaeloa, Palolo, Island of Oahu, be sold for $400.00. Her Majesty now holds a lease of this land. It is agreed to cancel this lease if it is agreed to sell this land absolutely at auction." Hawaii State Archives, Interior Department of Land. An annotation on the verso says: "Recommends that this land be divided into two lots, each having an area of 18 acres and to put it up for sale at an upset price of $500 each [parcel]."

12. Mrs. Graham was Eleanor Kaikilani Coney, Mrs. Haalelea's niece. See January 30, 1892, diary entry (267–68).

13. Hannah Kapualeilani Kamaiopili (b. 1869, Lahaina–d. 1925, Honolulu) was the daughter of Maui judge David K. Kamaiopili. On October 19, 1892, she would marry Edward S. Boyd of Honolulu.

why doesn't he wait until I am gone.[14] I do not think it a wise thing to do, as they tried to take the Crown Lands away from the King last session, and it is risky to stir the question up again—I shall mention it to him.[15]

Ten A.M. Went with Eveline and Jennie Clark to Mrs. Florence Williams' lecture at Mrs. S. B. Dole's. The subject was Madame de Stael. Many of the principal ladies of the town were there and the gathering very pleasant. Next meeting to be at Keoua Hale on [Entry ends thus.][16]

Hastened home with Irene to meet Minister Parker who brought two rich gentlemen from Chicago, Mr. Fleming and Mr. forgot his name— Lunch with Prince David, Mr. Parker, Jennie, Eveline, Irene Ii. Four P.M. Major Robertson brought Lieut. [not named] and his wife and Mrs. Robertson. It has been a lovely day and now at seven it is storming outside— lightning and thunder. Joe Aea told me that Kuhi was willing to let me have part of his patches in Manoa 16 loi for $1,600.00 and I to stand expenses and mortgage of $90.00.

*Thursday, January 14.* Nine A.M. Mr. Henry T. Waterhouse called to inform me of Kuhi's Mortgage to H. Dimond being only $90.00 with [a] few dollars interest. Perhaps 5.00 or 7.00 is willing to transfer to me. Saw notice of Mary Alapai's debts in *Advertiser* and sent for her.[17] She tells me their debt is $7,500.00—I offer her $8,500.00 for the whole of her place, at same time will permit her and her husband to stay on the place during their lifetime, [she said] she'd consult her husband.[18]

Drove out with my new bays and took Mary Carter home. Wrote to

---

14. Curtis P. Iaukea was then the Crown lands commissioner, and Liliuokalani most likely learned about the matter from him. Nothing about this matter has been found in the records of the Crown lands commission or in Cleghorn's personal papers.

15. Liliuokalani must be referring to continuing discussions on the settlement of the late King Kalakaua's debts. As late as November 19, 1892, the *Pacific Commercial Advertiser* reported: "A discussion arose in the House yesterday which brought up the question of the title to the Crown Lands. In 1890 the Legislature passed an act for the relief of the King. It provided for the issue of $110,000 in bonds, the proceeds to be applied to the payment of the royal debts. The act required the Crown Land Commissioners, with the consent of His Majesty, to execute an agreement to pay into the Hawaiian Treasury the sum of $20,000 yearly until the amount of the bonds should have been paid." The question that arose was whether the agreement was in force following the death of the king, and thus involved determining the nature of the domain known as the Crown lands. The matter was referred to the judiciary committee. The 1892 legislature did not pass any bill regarding the Crown lands.

16. "Mrs. Florence Williams gave her second lecture on Wednesday forenoon at Mrs. Sanford Dole's. Her Majesty was present and even a larger number of ladies than were at the first lecture." *Pacific Commercial Advertiser*, January 15, 1892. The next lecture was scheduled for Wednesday the 20th at Keoua Hale, Mrs. C. R. Bishop's home on Emma Street.

17. "ALAPAI ESTATE. Notice is hereby given that Mele Alapai and John Alapai, her husband, having conveyed all their Real Estate, excepting their homestead in Palama, to the undersigned in trust, they no longer have control over the same; and that all rents due the estate must be paid to me; and that I will not be responsible for any debts or obligations contracted by either of said parties. Chas. T. Gulick, Trustee. Honolulu, Jan. 13, 1892." *Pacific Commercial Advertiser*, January 14, 1892. The trust deed is recorded in the Bureau of Conveyances without specifics.

18. Nothing seems to have come of this proposition.

Kaiulani[19] and also to Nini Wilson. Bought a dozen [bars of] toilet soap and perfumery over $25.00 worth.

*Friday, January 15.* Iolani Palace. Archie told me Mr. Widemann was willing to transfer Pualeilani to me, the Mortgage on it being $10,000.00, and as the Queen Dowager [Kapiolani] is likely to have another attack of paralysis, the Doctor says, he [Widemann] is willing to let me hold the Mortgage or buy the place. I told Archie not to stir up any question about the Crown lands as we are just as likely to lose it as Mr. Widemann is a prominent party to turn them over and [their] becoming government lands. Princes Kawananakoa and Kalanianaole and Mr. Parker came in to lunch, also Irene Ii [Brown], Minnie Aldrich, Mollie Sheldon, and Ailene Aldrich. Parker would like the Kamehameha Order conferred on him and I offered to decorate him on Accession Day. I ordered 108 badges for the Liliuokalani Educational Society 2nd Division—54—for the Members and 54—for the scholars they are to educate.

Minister Parker went over to stables to inspect and will call tenders to make plans for stables, while two Princes and I play croquet. Parker also wanted to see Joe about luau. *Monowai* not arrived yet.

*Saturday, January 16.* Iolani Palace. Archie saw Mr. Bishop about giving Mr. [Sam] Parker…Grand cross of the Order of Kamehameha—they called a meeting [at] two, and decided that they should not give it. Although Parker did not ask it, I thought the services he had rendered me and the Nation during this, the first year of my reign, was such that made him worthy of high recognition. Made a sketch and submitted it to Minister Parker of a new decoration to be called the Order of the burning torch of Liliuokalani. Nothing transpired.[20]

At noon Prince David lunched with Kitty [Wilson] and I—Kitty and I drove out the bay horses. They are strong and fine-looking horses. Of the plans for the Reception of the 29th Mr. R. [Robertson] thought that Governor Cleghorn ought to stand with me on the dais after I told him not to take the other chair away, he thought Mr. C. as father of Kaiulani

---

19. The text of Liliuokalani's January 14, 1892, letter to Kaiulani is as follows: "Your father was here yesterday morning and reminded me that it was your mother's birthday and that he had taken some flowers to the Mausoleum. Time has flown by so rapidly that I could scarcely realize that it is five years since she died.

"I called on Annie Wodehouse at Aina Hau and everything seems to look so lovely—just the same as when you were here. Annie is looking so well and handsome and the baby healthy and strong. Hay had just gone to town and Mr. and Mrs. Schaefer were there with their children….

"Your father is talking of raising your house at Aina Hau. I daresay it will be a grand house when raised, but I told him you ought to come to the Palace and stay, of course Aina Hau will be very nice for a country residence…. We still look forward to the time we may have you back to us…. Your aunt, Liliuokalani." Hawaii State Archives, Cleghorn Collection.

20. This sketch depicts the Hawaiian crown above crossed kapu (taboo) sticks and a flaming torch with Liliuokalani's name in script below. Original in Hawaii State Archives, Liliuokalani Collection, M-93, Box 3, Document No. 119.

is entitled to it—but I know he is not. No one is unless I marry—but I don't think that will ever be.

*Sunday, January 17.* Iolani Palace—Rained all last night thundered and lightninged—Is still raining. Lunched at 12 P.M., then slept on my chair in the Blue room—how long I did not know, but was woke up by singing in the Hall. Keamalu conducted services and his brother assisted. Luhana, Kiliwehi, Keala, Julia, Kaauwai were all that was present. Five P.M. Raining still and very damp.

*Monday, January 18.* Iolani Palace. A bright morning after a night of heavy rains. The band playing for breakfast. Mr. Parker called in about Kamehameha Order, saying that if Mr. Harris as 1st Associate Justice, and R. C. Wyllie as Foreign Minister had the Grand Cross—why should he not be entitled to it. Mr. C. R. Bishop called at ten A.M. We spoke of the [Royal] Orders. He said, as Chancellor of the Order, he did not think that Mr. Parker ought to expect the Grand Cross as it was only given to the Royal family and to those who have been in service a long time—and that Mr. Wyllie had been in service 22 years when the Order was given to him, and that he [had] assisted in getting up the Order with Kamehameha fifth. I told Mr. Bishop that it was not Mr. Parker's fault but my own wish, as I felt that Mr. Parker had rendered very valuable services since my reign, although it is hardly a year, still through his quiet management with parties outside the Government it has been able to exist—else the Government would have been bankrupt and many other stipulations and actions which have been for the benefit of the people and the nation, and I thought worthy of recognition of the highest order. I conferred on him (S. Parker) the Chancellorship of all the Orders except Kamehameha—The Royal Order of Kalakaua and the Royal Order of Kapiolani and the Star of Oceania. In the By-Laws of the Kamehameha Order it says The King *has* a *right* to confer any order on anyone he likes, and if it has been withheld by Mr. C. R. Bishop, I do not insist on having it, because I respect his age, [and] secondly, on account of my connections in his wife's family.

*Wednesday, January 20.* Iolani Palace. Received petition from Hilo from prominent residents to pardon Watson who was implicated in the murder of Goto, the Japanese on Hawaii.[21]

Rec'd from Iaukea Agent [of] Crown Lands—Two thousand six hundred—$120—in paper, five in Silver, the rest in gold—three being in doubloons. Joe Heleluhe called for $175.00 to pay for land at Waialua bid in by Sam [Samuel] K. Mahoe—and for the above sum paid to S. K. Mahoe, he will Mortgage the land to me for the term of two years. In case he does not pay it at time specified, he will deed it to me.[22]

---

21. W. D. Watson and three accomplices, W. C. Blabon, J. R. Mills, and Thomas Steele, had been convicted of manslaughter in Hilo on May 14, 1890, for the murder of Katsu Goto, a Honokaa storekeeper, on the morning of October 29, 1889. Watson had received a sentence of four years' hard labor, and Blabon five. A special committee (including Supreme Court Justices Richard Bickerton and Sanford B. Dole) addressed Watson's petition to the Queen for executive clemency in a long report dated June 3, 1892, to the Privy Council, which did not recommend clemency. Hawaii State Archives, Series 203.

22. No record of this transaction has been found in the Bureau of Conveyances.

I signed a Commission for Sam Parker decorating him with the Knight Grand Cross of Kapiolani.

Mr. John Ena called at nine A.M. to ask me for money to assist them in their Campaign—to run for Noble.[23] I am not at all sanguine [as] to his being elected—and also to help *Holomua* [a newspaper] to merge into one paper with *Elele Poakolu*[24]—which Mr. Walker says requires $1,500.00. I promise him One hundred on both affairs. They say I must for the good of the Public. But I think I hadn't ought to give any for the campaign because I would just be in politics or assisting it, which I should not do. One year ago today, my dear Brother [Kalakaua] died in San Francisco. Eveline, Jennie, Irene, Minnie, Jessie, Lucy Nowlein, Makanoe, Lilia Aholo, Miss Davis, John Baker all go up to decorate [the Mausoleum]. Kaniu also—Prince David and Prince Jonah came up also. Lunched & spent afternoon at the lower house, came home five P.M. We placed a bouquet on my dear husband's casket.

*Thursday, January 21.* Iolani Palace—I made a mistake and all that has been written on the opposite page [Liliu is referring to the text indicated above by the two dotted rules] only transpired today. In addition I would write I received from Mr. C. B. Wilson, my Certificates of 40 shares in Volcano House Co. at twenty-five dollars a share. I also received information from C. B. Wilson that the old Reform Party are working in a new Rifle Company—they now have fifty Members—C. A. Brown, Albert Lucas, M. C. Stocker, J. Rothwell, F. Wundenberg, C. Widemann—are Members of which all are working under Government. F. S. Dodge, T. S. Douglas, J. J. Egan, J. H. Fisher, Geo. Lucas, Jack Lucas, C. W. Macfarlane, Bob More, N. Peterson, A. R. Rowat, J. L. Torbert, L. G. Torbert, J. H. Wodehouse, W. E. Wall, M. Colburn & Geo. Wilson, A. G. Ashley, Geo. Dillingham. C. B. Wilson says I must throw away Seven Thousand dollars to secure proper evidence in regard to these parties—I call this blood money and [it] must be looked into. Two thousand five hundred I deposited in my safe this evening, I kept the rest for food money.

I told Sam Parker he had better accept what Mr. Bishop offered the other day, and that was the Knight Commander of Kamehameha 1st Order. It is only one step more to the first. We will think it over. Went to Concert given by boys of Kamehameha School.[25]

*Friday, January 22.* Iolani Palace. I was mistaken in what I wrote yesterday about those young men forming a new Rifle Co., but I have been told

23. John Ena Jr. was elected a noble in the 1892 legislature.

24. Liliu has identified this newspaper inaccurately. *Ka Nupepa Poakolu* was published between 1882 and 1885, and was succeeded by *Ka Elele Poaono*, and then by *Ka Nupepa Elele*, a strong supporter of the National Reform Party, which was published weekly between December 12, 1885, and April 16, 1892, in Hawaiian and English. In the final issue, the editors announced that a daily, *Ka Lei Alii o Hawaii*, was to succeed it; no issues of the latter are known to have survived. The *Elele* did not merge with the *Holomua*. See Esther K. Mookini, *The Hawaiian Newspapers* (Honolulu: Topgallant, 1974).

25. The *Pacific Commercial Advertiser*, January 22, 1892, reported: "The concert of the Kamehameha Glee Club [at the Opera House] last night was attended by a fair audience, though not as good a one as the occasion deserved.... The different selections were all well received, and some of them, especially the comic songs, brought down the house."

*Boys from the Kauai Industrial School, Malumalu, Kauai.*
Alfred Mitchell, 1892, Bishop Museum Archives

OPPOSITE

*Kalapaki, the William Hyde Rice home on Nawiliwili Bay, Kauai. Six months after becoming queen, Liliuokalani made a tour of the islands in 1891, arriving on Kauai on July 8. She was a guest of William Hyde Rice and his family at Hale Nani, their home in Lihue.*

*Liliuokalani visited the industrial school at Malumalu, as well as Wailua Falls, Kealia, Hanalei, Waimea, Koloa, and even the neighboring island of Niihau. Princes Jonah Kuhio Kalanianaole and David Kawananakoa, both born in Koloa, were among the entourage that accompanied her.*

*Rice held a farewell luau for the Queen at Kalapaki attended by hundreds. As a tribute to the Queen, Rice sent for drinking water from the legendary spring at Kipukai.*
Alfred Mitchell, 1892, Bishop Museum Archives

*Getting water from the spring.*
Alfred Mitchell, 1892, Bishop Museum Archives

BELOW

*Peter Malina, cowboy at Kipukai, a ranch owned by William Hyde Rice.*
Alfred Mitchell, 1892, Bishop Museum Archives

since that they are to protect the throne and my person should any disturbance arise. Mrs. Hayselden called to see me before leaving for Lahaina. Charlie would like the $7,000.00 to help—he did not say. Harry Swinton wanted to see me about taking up his brother Charlie's debts and places that lot between [Tom] May's and [Lot] Kaulukou's on Beretania Street at my disposal. The amount wanted was $3,500.00. Went up to Minnie Aldrich's and made all arrangements for Joe Heleluhe and Harry S. [?] Attorney for Charlie to meet at 11 A.M. next day at S. M. Damon's. Drove out to Wakeke's with Irene [Ii Brown], Eveline, and Jennie Clark.

*Saturday, January 23.* Iolani Palace. Sent for Aimoku and Kaipo. While croqueting with them Miss Smith and her brother Jared came in to thank me for my assistance to their school. At two P.M. walked over to Music Hall to see the "Great Wizard of the North" perform.[26] Very good. From there went to Keoua Hale to see Mr. C. R. Bishop, but found Capt. and Mrs. Kautz[27] and sat down with Jennie Clark and had tea with them.

Spent a few minutes, then went over to the band. At 11 A.M. According to agreement Joe Heleluhe came down to meet Mr. Swinton, but saw Mr. Damon and was told [he] must pay in to Mr. D. $120.00 first, which he did from my own hands.

Last night there was a stormy meeting of the Liberal Party at Waikiki Church. They began to be personal. Mainalulu said they did not want to hear personal remarks. Wilcox says "shut up"—someone outside says, "I slap your mouth"—Wilcox [responded]—"if you come in here I throw you out of the window"—confusion and everyone goes home. C. W. Ashford says of J. H. [Joe Heleluhe] that he is like a fat dog chained with a fat billet—While speaking, Billy Cummins interprets—Frank Archer says, "you do not interpret right"—"you better come and interpret then" says Billy—and some [more] confusion.[28]

*Sunday, January 24.* Iolani Palace. Heard there was exciting meeting at the Rifle Armory at Manamana—Mr. Dillingham by the Native Sons of Hawaii made speeches inside to a large audience of most of the best citizens of this city.[29]

26. The *Daily Bulletin*, January 20, 1892, announced a matinee performance by Professor Anderson: "The latest Parisian sensation, Haunted Pavilion! The most wonderful act on this great earth. Prof. Anderson will in full view of the audience, vanish instantaneously into space.... Grand Matinee for Ladies and Children. Prices children 25c. Adults, 50c. Doors open at two; performance at 2:30." In its review of the matinee performance, the *Bulletin* on January 25 included the tantalizing notice that at the next performance Anderson "would exhibit the unparalleled feat of severing a woman's head from her body."

27. Albert Kautz (b. 1839, Georgetown, Ohio–d. 1907), a naval officer, was stopping at Honolulu on the USS *Pensacola*. Kautz entered the navy as a midshipman in 1854, saw Civil War service, and became a commander in 1865, a captain in 1885, and a rear admiral in 1898, in charge of the Pacific Squadron. He was at Samoa March–April 1899 during the island's second civil war.

28. This meeting at Waikiki received some press coverage. The *Pacific Commercial Advertiser*, January 23, 1892, had a long report headlined: "The Political Pot. It boiled over at Waikiki last night.... Wilcox Thinks the People Must Be Fools at Waikiki—Ashford Denounces Heleluhe as a Fat Dog with a Collar and a Chain." Frank Archer's comments were directed at W. H. Cummings, who was then interpreting remarks of the Honorable A. Marques.

29. This meeting at the armory was on January 23. Benjamin F. Dillingham was a candidate on the Sons of Hawaii Party ticket for representative from the third district. He had

Mr. C. W. Ashford and the Liberal Party [were] out in the street in front of the building both abusing each other and striving for the coming Legislature.[30] Kaleipua and Debora came in, brought lei hala. 10:30 A.M. Willie Rice calls in and [then] went to church. Eveline and I went to Kawaiahao—Parker preached—"The voice of the people is the voice of God." After church drove up Liliha street, Judd, Nuuanu, Pauoa, by Mormon Church and home.[31]

Two P.M. Prayer meeting on the lower Hall [basement of the Palace]— Mr. Fernandez always makes his prayer in English and from the Episcopal Prayer Book, and I think he puts in a few words of his own.[32]

Four P.M. Drove up to Manoa behind Czar and Prince, my black span [pair of horses]. The Kapili house [nowhere explained] is almost finished—Kiliwehi is with me, Eveline [Wilson] being poorly. I think in two weeks everything will be complete.

*Wednesday, January 27.* Iolani Palace. Cartloads of pigs, chickens, turkey, cattle, all arrive from different Islands of the group contributing towards the grand luau that is to take place on my Accession day.

*Thursday, January 28.* Iolani Palace. Men, women, and children from Waikiki are here to help get ready for the Luau. People and carpenters are active decorating the large lanai in front of the Palace, but on the right of the path, cart and cartloads of greens from Waimanalo, to decorate and for imus [underground ovens], come in.

I signed three Commissions conferring for Mr. Robertson, Mr. Richardson the K. [Knight] Commander of the Royal Order of Kalakaua, K. [Knight] Companion of Kapiolani and [blank]. Mr. Parker, the Chamberlain [James Robertson] and I looked over the list who are to sit at the table—I arrange the Prince Kawananakoa on my right and Cupid [Prince Kuhio] next with Mrs. Sam Parker, Gov. Cleghorn on my left with Mrs. Stevens.[33] Mr. R. [Robertson] took the list to Archie and he felt hurt. It seems that they had already made out a list for him to be on my left, on the dais—and on my right at the table. That would be a great

---

already made a similar speech (reported in the *Bulletin*, January 21, 1892), denouncing the opposition candidate, Ashford, as "the destroyer of Hawaii's opportunity" at the Portuguese Benevolent Society hall.

30. After reporting the Dillingham speech, the *Pacific Commercial Advertiser* noted: "After C. W. Ashford left the armory on Saturday evening . . . he walked across the street with a number of his followers and took a position on the steps of a store on the corner of Punchbowl and Beretania Streets. The small gathering grew larger every moment to hear the loud harangue of the speaker. No doubt it was one of the most vituperative speeches ever made in the presence of a public gathering in this city." The paper reported that Ashford's remarks had included such statements as claims that Dillingham and Thurston were "pious frauds who are members of fourteen churches, and at present are in contact with boodlers and opium smugglers" and members of "that missionary and blackleg gang across the street," meaning those assembled in the Armory. *Pacific Commercial Advertiser*, January 25, 1892.

31. The Mormon church was at 87 Punchbowl Street.

32. Abraham Fernandez (b. 1857, Lahaina–d. 1915, Honolulu) was a Honolulu merchant and the husband of Minerva Davis Fernandez. He was a prominent Mormon, although Liliu's reference to his use of the English prayer book at services would indicate he was fairly liberal as to his religious beliefs.

33. Mrs. Mary Lowell Stevens was the wife of John L. Stevens (b. 1820–d. 1895), the U.S. minister to Hawaii.

mistake, which the public would not accept. I should be alone—until Kaiulani arrives.

The reception room [that is, the throne room]—The Princes, the Chancellor, the Ministers, the judges of Supreme Court, the Queen's Staff behind the Princes, then Kahili [royal feather standard] bearers. On the left Governor Cleghorn, Mrs. Judd—the Ministers' wives and wives of Judges of Supreme Court—Mrs. R. [Robertson], the ladies of the Staff—behind Gov. C., the ladies in waiting and behind them Kahili bearers—below the Judges' wives—Privy Councillors of State and their wives—[at the] foot of the room Capt. Kautz and officers—below, Judges of S.C. [Supreme Court, and the] Diplomatic Corp. I think this arrangement would be satisfactory to all parties.

This has been a disagreeable day. Still showery and yet we must go to the Concert.[34] Prince David, Archie, Eveline, and Mr. Robertson occupy the Royal Pew. Col. Iaukea sings very nicely—so does Miss Kulamanu Ward sing very sweetly.

Ten o'clock and Mrs. [Samuel] Parker and Mrs. W. H. Rice [and] Mrs. Robertson are still decorating and the Hui Hololio [Riding Society] still talking in the basement.

*Friday, January 29.* Iolani Palace. Promptly at five A.M. the sentry woke Mahoe up and she woke me. I dressed myself in a hurry and went down to the hall and managed to raise one candlestick, and the light from that was hardly sufficient to see anything at the further end of the hall, while I could hear the steady tread of the Orderly as he paced to and fro. At six. It is still dark and the girls are busy finishing up the decorations with flowers left the night before. Half past—and Mr. J. A. Cummins arrives with his family with their hookupu [tribute or ceremonial offering]. Capt. and Mrs. Kautz of the *Pensacola* and others, besides the Princes Kawananakoa and Kalanianaole. The latter's riding society arrived and went through some maneuvering. Their uniform was white and red—very pretty—then my [riding] society in blue and gold. Hundreds are on the veranda to witness the hookupu and performance—Marshall Wilson and police march up with leis to hookupu—very pretty sight, and as they march in, the Royal Guards, already in line, salute as they come in—then the Guards and all disperse to return at 11. That hour soon arrives and all officials in full uniform arrive. Below the dais on the right are the two princes, on the left Gov. Cleghorn. The Chancellor and Minister below the Princes—the wives of the Ministers below the Governor on the left—

---

34. The concert, held at Kaumakapili Church on January 28, 1892, celebrated the first anniversary of Liliuokalani's ascension to the throne. The *Pacific Commercial Advertiser*, January 27, 1892, noted, "Her Majesty the Queen will honor the concert with her presence." The program published in the same article lists organ selections by Taylor, a "Concert Fantasia" sung by Miss Kulamanu Ward, a "quartette" by Curtis Iaukea, the Queen's composition "Aloha Oe" to be sung by the Kawaiahao Seminary Chorus, and "Hawaii Ponoi" sung by the Kawaiahao Church Choir. Tickets were priced at 25 cents.

Ladies in waiting behind Gov., Staff behind Princes. [At] 1:30 P.M. the public arrive—One hour a constant stream, then the luau. A magnificent affair, and everyone on the ground had something to eat. Presented Charlie Wilson [with the] "Knight Commander Order of Kalakaua"—tears came in his eyes. R. W. Wilcox and party came to reception and luau. All the nice people are here today. [Entry continued on top margin:] Archie did not like being placed on my left. He is only Governor, and cannot come before the chancellor even if his daughter is here. She can be on my right but that does not give him the right to be there.

One year ago my brother's body was brought home on the *Charleston* and this is the first year of my reign. It has been a sad year to me.

*Saturday, January 30.* Iolani Palace. Went down after breakfast to the lanai where over a thousand had feasted yesterday and now the ohuas [servants] from Waikiki and from the Hale ohuas [servants' house] were busy washing dishes.

Thousands of plates, bowls, umekes [calabashes], large platters for puaa [pig], tiny saucers for kukui [relish], alamihi [crab], and all sorts of native delicacies. Many have assured me that they had a good time, but some are discontented because they did not get what they considered their *proper positions* at the table, but it was utterly impossible for the ushers to place anyone against so many people who simply came and took their seats—[the ushers being] Messrs. E. Stiles, Palmer Woods, Carl Widemann, Maurice [Morris] Keohokalole, George Smithies, and other clerks from the Government building.[35]

This is the last day for entering a protest to the Government about the Waikiki roads and Joe Heleluhe has gone to enter one as the present line laid out cuts right through my bathhouses at Waikiki.[36]

---

35. The *Pacific Commercial Advertiser*, January 30, 1892, noted that the luau was held "in the large pavilion erected in the Palace grounds several months ago.... Within were twenty tables, each seating twenty guests or more, besides a long semicircular table at the end towards the Morning, where the 'nabobs' were to be ensconced. In all about five hundred guests sat down at the 'first table' [at half past three].... Prayer was offered by Bishop Willis, after which the large company were able with a clear conscience to give their undivided attention to the solids and dainties with which the tables were literally piled.... A neighboring smaller pavilion was provided for the plebs who all succeeded to the larger building as soon as abandoned by the first set of occupants.

"Before, during, and after the luau, the lawns were covered with strolling groups [and] ... the indefatigable Mr. Berger and his boys were planted in the stand west of the pavilion where they played at intervals."

36. On January 30, 1892, Joseph Heleluhe submitted two claims for compensation for widening of the Waikiki road (now Kalakaua Avenue); the first claim was for the inland portion of Hamohamo having a street frontage of 604 feet, as the proposed road widening would take 3,936 square feet from the property (for which he put in a claim of $2,000); the second claim was for the makai portion with 695 feet of running frontage (which would take away 10,600 feet of property), for which he asked $10,600 in compensation. In both claims, he asked that all fences be moved to the new road line at government expense. Hawaii State Archives, Interior Department, Subject: Roads, Waikiki—Box 51. (The file examined does not show what compensation was actually provided.)

Mrs. John Graham[37] was just able to come out after a long illness. She tells me she will leave on the *Australia* of Tuesday—I think this trip will cure her of homesickness for Hawaii, for although she may have enjoyed herself to a certain extent here, it has not been what she expected, and now she is homesick for her own home and longs to be with her husband who is so devoted to her.

*Sunday, January 31.* Iolani Palace. Did not go out but Capt. Nowlein invited us to his house, their moopuna's [grandchild's] birthday at seven P.M., and [I] accepted. Mr. Parker and Mr. Richardson called [and] laid out plans for State dinner. Signed a letter to Queen Victoria and to the Prince and Princess of Wales on account of death of Prince Victor Duke [of] Clarence and Avondale.[38] [Parker and Richardson] Lunched with us and they [then] went home. Two P.M. Prayer meeting—quite full—Carrie Bush and Mrs. Townsend and Mr. A. Fernandez also present.

Four P.M. drove out to Waikiki. Heard that Mr. Cummins, John Ena, and others has asked him (Joe Heleluhe) to go to Kamoiliili to make speeches. I was surprised because John Cummins had said they would not support Joe because they put Frank Archer up against [him][39]—but Frank is not so well known although he belongs to the Native Sons of Hawaii. Frank Archer is a good Christian and steady young man and a hard worker, and although not rich, maintains his family as a hardworking mechanic. Joe Heleluhe is an enterprising young man who has lived under my employ commencing as a groom, and ending in being my private secretary and Agent to all my lands—at a salary of only fifty dollars. In the latter capacity he has been brought into contact with people of all classes, from the best financial men of the country, to the commonest Pake [Chinese] tiller of the soil—which gives him an insight into human character, and also a little knowledge of diplomacy. He is the choice of the Mechanics' Union and Hui Kalaiaina [Society] for the 1st Ward.

*Monday, February 1.* Iolani Palace. As usual the stringed [sic] Band played—I don't like it—for they are not perfect yet with their violins, and such discordant sounds are brought forth, which is trying to the nerves. Only Mr. and Mrs. Wilson and I sit down to table. After breakfast Mrs. Lidia Davis came in to tell me her father Mr. M. Davis[40] would like to

---

37. Eleanor Kaikilani Coney (b. 1867, Honolulu–d. 1943, Lihue, Kauai) was the daughter of John Harvey Coney and Laura (Lala) Amoy Ena Coney. On December 17, 1885, she married John L. Graham. In 1895, she became the wife of the well-known Dutch artist Hubert Vos. Her daughter Anna Graham married the American millionaire Jay Gould II.

38. Albert Victor Christian Edward, created duke of Clarence and Avondale and earl of Athlone (b. 1864, Frogmore, Windsor, England–d. January 14, 1892, Sandringham House, England), was the grandson of Queen Victoria, son of the Prince of Wales (later Edward VII), and brother of King George V of England. A poem by Liliuokalani in memory of the prince is in the Hawaii State Archives, Liliuokalani Collection, Box 2.

39. Frank Archer (b. 1857, Hanalei, Kauai–d. 1931, Hoolehua, Molokai) was a carpenter and housebuilder. During the territorial years, he was a member of the House of Representatives, 1911–21 and 1929.

40. Moss Davis (d. 1895, Honolulu) was the proprietor of the New York Bazaar, a dry goods and clothing business at 17 Nuuanu Street. Davis and family lived at Waikiki on a lot at Hamohamo that they leased from Liliuokalani.

lease the grounds around their house from me but she did not know for how much. I told her I would consult J. Heleluhe as I did not want to do anything without his knowledge for fear he would do something that would clash against my arrangements or I against his. She will soon be confined in March and would like the house to be in proper position on Kapiolani's lot from Pupuka's Kuleana [land claim] before that time. That lot is just large enough for the house to stand on without room for a garden or pleasure ground according to the decision given in court.

Mrs. [Emma] Nakuina wanted to borrow money $3,000.00 to save her property at Kalihi comprising 22 acres of taro land. I don't see how I could help her, for I have so many places to spend my money—one of those being the promise to buy lands for the support of My Educational Society (Second Division). The officers of that Society met to consult about six vacancies at Kawaiahao Seminary and decided that Kamakanoe, Mary Alapai, Kahae, Milaina, Mary Aki, and H. Kawainui shall be the Members to send their daughters to be educated by the Dominis fund,[41] and these proceedings to be submitted to the general meeting.

*Tuesday, February 2*. Iolani Palace. After breakfast, received Mrs. Florence Williams, who presented me with a book of Scriptures and prayer for every day in the year. I told her I would read it very often and that I was doing so now. She told me how very careful I ought to be and not to cede Pearl Harbor—I told her that she has been reading Bush's paper[42] and there was no truth in my signing away any portion of that place— I had signed a Treaty purely Commercial in its nature, and one that would not cede any portion of Hawaii. She seemed relieved.

Mrs. Gay wants something for her husband to do. Went to bid Goodbye to Mrs. Graham and sent her off in my carriage. Paid Mr. Connally $600.00 for my new bay span [pair] of horses. Called to see Mrs. Evans— poor woman—she was packing to go up to meet her husband at Wailuku[43]— heard here that where she was staying is offered for sale at $3,000.00 by Dr. McGrew. Rec'd John's and Likelike's photo from Friedlander.[44] They are excellent likenesses and life size. Gave my consent to Minister [Sam] Parker that Mr. Hastings should be secretary under him of all the [Royal] Orders—he says Mr. H. would arrange everything in a systematic way.[45]

Poor Jennie [Clark]! I am sorry she is married to such a man.

*Wednesday, February 3*. Iolani Palace. This morning it is rather showery and all are interested in the election of today. Everything has been quiet and orderly. Had lunch with Princes Kawananakoa and Kalanianaole—

41. Perhaps a fund set up by Liliuokalani in memory of her late husband.
42. This was the newspaper *Ka Leo o Ka Lahui*, which included some reportage in English.
43. Thomas E. Evans had just moved from Lahaina to Wailuku and commenced a new career. The 1892–93 City Directory lists him as "sugar boiler, Wailuku Sugar Co."
44. Friedlander was a photographic retouch artist in San Francisco, popular for those wishing to have photographs worked up to full-size crayon drawings suitable for framing.
45. Frank P. Hastings (b. Portland, Maine–d. 1897, Washington, DC) was on the foreign office staff. He was the husband of Alice Makee. She was the daughter of Captain James Makee, proprietor of the Ulupalakua Plantation and Ranch on Maui. Hastings served as Sam Parker's secretary in keeping records of the distribution of royal orders, until the fall of the monarchy.

Jennie Clark, Eveline. Puaa [pig], and raw fish, lei ilima twined with maile—ladies wore white dresses for the occasion—in other words, it was a small luau.

Four P.M. was woken by Minister Parker who told me everything was ready in case of a riot as those who called themselves the Liberal Party had said if they did not get elected, they would make a disturbance and try to unseat me from the throne by force of arms. They are 300 strong and mostly composed of men who have no interest or money in the country, common day laborers who wander the streets without object and mostly live from hand to mouth—in fact, the roughs. They have been trying to buy up some ammunition but through the energy of Marshall Wilson these have been taken up by the government.[46] Wilcox and Bush are at the head of this party—two soreheads who are huhu [angry] because I did not make them Ministers at the commencement of my reign. Although they call themselves liberal, it is really only from personal motives that they are striving. The better portion or class of people offer their services to protect the throne and city property. Will they fire the town?

Seven P.M. the Liberal party are all in as representatives for this island excepting one. Those in are Bush for Koolau—Wilcox Waialua, Pipikane 2nd District, Ashford 3rd district, S. K. Aki 4th district, S. K. Pua 5th District—A. Kahi Independent, W. C. Wilder—Independent 1st District.

12 midnight—All is peace.[47]

*Thursday, February 4.* Iolani Palace—Nobles nominated yesterday are J. A. Cummins, six years.—J.M.S. Williams, six years.—Paul Neumann, six years.—John Ena, six years. Arthur P. Peterson, six years. So far the nominations have been even and on Saturday we will learn of the results of the elections on the other islands. Joe Heleluhe did not get nominated for the 1st district.

Went up to the garret, third story of this Palace for the first time. There are very nice rooms and a Hall. The room at the mauka end of the hall is filled with valuable curiosities collected by King Kalakaua and are given to the Hale Naua.[48]

---

46. The *Pacific Commercial Advertiser* informed the public on February 3, 1892, that Wilson had ordered all saloons to be closed on that day "and remain so until seven o' clock this evening." In another notice, the *Advertiser* noted: "It is reported that the Marshall took possession of all the ammunition, etc., in the hands of private firms and carried it off to the Police Station."

47. The threat of an election night disturbance was overblown and no incident occurred. On February 4, the *Pacific Commercial Advertiser* noted, "The election passed off very quietly yesterday. The nearest approach to excitement were efforts of a few Hawaiian orators in the vicinity of the Chinese Engine House." The "It Is Reported" column made a tongue-in-cheek comment that "another young Hawaiian who was educated abroad at this country's expense [meaning R. W. Wilcox] was manufacturing dynamite bombs yesterday to throw at the haoles, if the Liberals were defeated."

48. The Queen's cousin Mrs. Mary Haaheo Atcherley, in an August 28, 1928, letter to the *Honolulu Star-Bulletin*, said of the rooms: "As a young girl I have had the responsibilities of entering the sacred refuge of the Hale Naua properties...one hour before each monthly meeting was held. The refuge was a hall which opened from the winding stairway leading up to the flag attic from the same entrance to the King's library...[where] I have handled the royal robes belonging to the order, the calabashes, mats, tapas, round stones, [and] idols of stones."

Ten A.M. went to call on Mrs. Ward, and from there went with her, Eveline, and Jennie to Mrs. F. Williams' lecture.[49]

Came home, found Kawananakoa and for a wonder, Irene [Ii] drove in with Mrs. Hyde. I thought I. [Irene] was never going to come here again. 1:30 P.M. Had a meeting of the Liliuokalani Education[al] Society 2nd Division in which they decided to send children of the following named members—Makanoe, Milaina Ahia, Alapai, Kahae, Mary Aki, and H. Kawainui.

Four P.M. went to Mrs. Allen's to call on Bernice Walbridge.[50] Came right home. Mrs. Allen told me that there was to be a meeting of the Portuguese Benevolent Society next day and [she] would like to have me go.

*Friday, February 5.* Iolani Palace. 12 P.M. Princes Kawananakoa and Kalanianaole Mrs. Minnie Aldrich and Irene Brown came in to lunch. Gave $50.00 to Kalanianaole for Fire Co. No. 4—for luau also one puaa [pig], a large one, and one barrel of poi. Had nice time singing.[51]

Two P.M. went with Eveline Wilson to Mrs. Canavarro's to a meeting.[52] Appointed officers for the year for the Portuguese Benevolent Society —there was only one Portuguese there, it was Mrs. Soares.[53]

*Saturday, February 6.* Iolani Palace. Signed Commissions for J. Mott Smith, [as] Envoy and Minister Plenipotentiary,[54] and one for H. A. Widemann to be one of the Commissioners for Crown Lands[55]—and a letter to [U.S.] Secretary Blaine accrediting J. M. Smith as Hawaiian Minister to the U.S.

---

49. Mrs. Florence Williams's talk was on the subject of the English novelist George Eliot and her works.

50. Bernice Parke Walbridge (d. 1929) was the daughter of longtime Honolulu resident Marshall William C. Parke and wife of Russell D. Walbridge (b. 1850, New York–d. 1899, Honolulu), the manager of the Wailuku Sugar Co.

51. The volunteer fire companies were gearing up for their annual parade through Honolulu on February 6, 1892. The *Pacific Commercial Advertiser*, February 8, 1892, reported that the popular event had included a stop at the palace to pay respects to the Queen. "When the parade reached the palace grounds a big crowd of people were present at the Square and saw the different companies march in line before the Queen who was standing at the entrance to the Palace." Her Majesty was presented with a complimentary letter, and when the different companies withdrew, "they halted in front of the Palace steps and gave three more cheers for Her Majesty."

52. Mrs. Miranda Bates Canavarro, the wife of Antonio de Souza Canavarro, consul of Portugal, resided at 128 Beretania near Alapai Street.

53. Mrs. Rachel Fernandes Soares (b. 1862, Springfield, Illinois–d. November 2, 1895, Honolulu) was the wife of Reverend Antonio Soares (b. Urzelina, Saint Jorge, Azores Island–d. March 19, 1930). He had arrived at the islands in 1890, was ordained at Central Union Church on June 14, 1891, and was for many years the pastor of the Portuguese Protestant Church in Honolulu.

54. Dr. John Mott Smith (b. 1824–d. August 10, 1895, Honolulu) arrived in 1850 as a dentist, became prosperous in business, married Ellen Dominis Paty, and was a close friend of Liliuokalani and the Cleghorns. In the Queen's January 28, 1892, letter to President Benjamin Harrison, she says of Mott Smith: "He is well informed of the relative interests of the two countries and of our sincere desire to cultivate to the fullest extent the friendship which has so long existed between Our two countries." Copy in Hawaii State Archives, Foreign Office and Executive Files, Hawaiian Officials Abroad. Mott Smith resigned from his position as minister of finance to accept the diplomatic position.

55. Widemann had served previously as Crown lands commissioner in 1874 and 1891.

*Sunday, February 7.* Iolani Palace. [Rest of entry blank.]

*Monday, February 8.* Iolani Palace. Had a cabinet meeting in regard to appointment of Governors for other islands. Agreed upon Willie H. Rice for Kauai and John T. Baker for Hawaii[56] and could not decide on anyone for Maui just yet. Gave Mr. Rice his Commission in presence of Princes Kawananakoa and Kalanianaole, Minister Parker, Minister Widemann, Hon. Paul Isenberg,[57] and Hon Col. J. Richardson,[58] then all sat down to lunch [with] also Mrs. Mary Carter, Mrs. C. B. Wilson, Mrs. J. Clark.

The band played here as usual. Mr. C. A. Brown called and said he was in trouble and asked if I would excuse Irene from coming here anymore. I am afraid that he is troubled with the green-eyed monster.[59] It is a very disagreeable complaint to have. It should have been the duty of the Chamberlain to usher in the abovenamed parties, but he was not here, and is seldom in the office before ten in the morning, and often out in the afternoon.

A lovely moonlight night—went round to Band at Emma Square with Eveline, Jennie Clark in Mr. Quinn's Express[60]—then drove round to see Carrie Bush—then left Jennie at her gate [Liliha near King Street] and drove home to Palace.

*Tuesday, February 9.* Iolani Palace. Left Palace at 10:30 A.M. for Waikiki. Off and on are showers. Eveline, Jennie, and Lucy Nowlein came down with me, but before we started, had conversation with C. B. Wilson. Told him I thought Capt. Nowlein is just the man for Governor for Maui, and he coincided with me. But who shall I put in his place—the Prince Kalanianaole, he said.[61]

I thought it a good plan. So started to Waikiki. One P.M. Mr. Sam Parker found us at [my] Waikiki bathhouse, and told me of reception for next day at 11 A.M. for Capt. and officers of the English gunboat *Pheasant*—then they went home while we sat down to lunch. Had lots of good things, pig, chicken, turkey puolos [steamed bundles], raw & cooked squid, loli [sea cucumber], limu [seaweed], papai [crab], and ended with cake.

---

56. John Tamatoa Baker (b. 1852, Wailupe, Oahu–d. 1921, Pauoa, Oahu) was governor of Hawaii Island February 8, 1892–January 1893. His wife, the chiefess Ululani, had held the same office 1886–89.

57. Paul Isenberg (b. 1837, Dransfeld near Hanover, Germany–d. 1903, Bremen, Germany) came to the islands from Bremen in October 1858 and married first at Lihue in 1861 to Maria Rice (d. 1867) and then at Bremen in 1869 to Beta Glade. Instrumental in developing the Lihue Plantation into a financial success, he also served as a noble in the legislature, 1874–90.

58. John Richardson (b. 1863, Waikapu, Maui–d. 1917, Honolulu) was a representative in the 1884 legislature and a noble during the 1887–88 session. He was a member of the Privy Council in 1891, and on December 29 that year was appointed colonel on the Queen's staff.

59. "The green-eyed monster" is envy or jealousy.

60. James Carrol Quinn (d. May 24, 1915) was a partner with Manuel Reis in the United Carriage Co. and livery stable, which had its office on King near Fort Street.

61. Samuel Nowlein did not get the appointment. Thomas W. Everett became governor of Maui, serving from May 17, 1892, to 1893 when the office was abolished. Charles B. Wilson was appointed marshall of the kingdom on March 4, 1891, and remained in that office until January 23, 1893. Prince Kalanianaole did not replace him.

*Wednesday, February 10.* Iolani Palace. Abraham Fernandez came to consult me in regard to appointment of Road supervisor in place of Major Hebbard.[62] They promised to put a native in that position but they [sentence ends thus]. Would like a decoration also as he had heard that others were to be decorated, but I told him that it was a mistake. That Parker was arranging to get all Royal Orders in some shape as no accounts or records had been kept by other Chancellors and Orders will not be conferred in future as promiscuously as they used to be. Mr. Parker would like papers of Denization given Mr. R. Brenham. Whiting and Widemann are opposed to it, Parker and Spencer in favor. It rests for me to decide—I gave my consent as his wife is a Hawaiian lady.[63]

*Friday, February 12.* Iolani Palace. This day was my Brother's [Kalakaua's] accession day and during his lifetime was observed with pomp and ceremony—how sad!

Signed papers of denization for Mr. R. Brenham—so that it might be eligible for him to practice before our Courts.

Read a letter from Minister J. Mott Smith to Minister Parker saying that President Harrison of the United States had declined to sign the Treaty prepared by himself and Secretary Blaine as he had been advised by some members of [among] the Senators who discouraged as to its acceptance by the Senate as one objection being that the Republican party is committed to a protective policy—which is controverted by this Treaty, it being really a Free Trade measure. Again the President has been interviewed by California Citizens who have assured him that fruit grown in that State will be injured and that free refined sugars will ruin refiners of San Francisco and will throw all sugar trade into hands of the Islanders—Too bad.[64]

12 P.M. went to Muolaulani to a luau given by the Liliuokalani Hui Hololio [Liliuokalani Riding Society] to me—I attended it with Prince Kawananakoa and my Chamberlain Mr. Robertson, Mrs. Wilson and Mrs. Jennie Clark, and Mrs. Nancy Eldridge, and many others. 2:30 P.M. We went back to the Palace and [at] four P.M. the Hui turned out in red paus [riding skirts]—They looked very prettily.[65]

*Sunday, February 14.* Waikiki Seaside residence. Did not sleep well at all—Dreamt that a dead man wanted to strangle me—so when I went to

62. Abraham Fernandez did not get the position. Major Henry F. Hebbard (a member of the Honolulu Rifles) had been Oahu road supervisor since July 15, 1887.

63. San Francisco lawyer Robert B. Brenham married Annie Kahawalu Dowsett in 1890. His application to Parker for "Letters Patent" in order to practice law in the islands is dated February 8, 1892. Hawaii State Archives, Denization Records.

64. Liliuokalani has here summarized a letter from Dr. John Mott Smith, her Washington, DC, representative charged with negotiating modifications to the Reciprocity Treaty of 1875 with the U.S. government. The letter referred to here, dated Washington, DC, January 30, 1892, arrived at the Foreign Office in Honolulu on February 11, 1892. Hawaii State Archives, Foreign Office and Executive Files 62, Treaties.

65. The *Pacific Commercial Advertiser*, February 13, 1892, noted: "The late King's coronation day was observed by Her Majesty yesterday. A luau was given at Palama in the morning and in the afternoon Her Majesty received the different riding societies at the Palace."

bathe in the sea a strange fear came over me that a Shark might take hold of me, so hastened out of the water after a few dips.

*Monday, February 15.* Waikiki Seaside Residence. Mr. David Crowningburg came here to pawn his ring. He had pawned it three times and always won it back. I refused to take it, but told him [I] would advance him the money, but he declined to take it unless I took the diamond ring. It was worth $150—but [he] would let me have it for $100.00. I had only $75.00 which I gave him and [said I] would give him the rest tomorrow, so he left the ring with me. I also gave him $10.00 present to get some tools by which he could earn a livelihood by making ivory necklaces.

*Tuesday, February 16.* Seaside Residence. Was obliged to go to town. Mr. David Crowningburg called, and I gave him the remaining amount which was $25.00. He mentioned that he would like the appointment of under Road Supervisor and told me he had been promised it.

After my duties were over at the Palace I came back—Minister C. [Charles] N. Spencer called to inform me of his intention to go to Kalawao [Molokai] the next day and Mr. David Dayton, President of the Board of Health, intended to go with him—and if I had any message to send. I sent my Aloha to the Lepers. That was all I could do—but I did want him to see about the Lepers—if they still needed a bathing house. I thought they did as they had asked for one when I went there a year ago—and they had estimated the cost at $600.00—I hoped he could give his attention to it. They would try and be back on Sunday.

Mrs. A. F. Judd and daughter [Agnes Elizabeth] returned today by the *Australia*. The latter seemed in good health after her severe illness in Wellesley College. She sent me a basket of nice candies.

*Wednesday, February 17.* Seaside Residence. Ten A.M. went up to Mrs. Hobron's to Mrs. Florence Williams' lecture on the French Revolution. They did not commence till quarter to 11. The room was soon filled and it seemed so close that I soon fell asleep. I was so ashamed, but I could not help myself. I used to wonder at Kamehameha V's going to sleep, also my brother Kalakaua when they went to entertainments—how they could go off to sleep—but now I can understand. After a hard day's work of thinking and excitement, naturally when in a room where everything is still a sense of drowsiness comes over one which is difficult to overcome. After reading was over, we drove Mrs. J. O. Carter and left her at Hotel—went to [Washington] Place, and from there came out [here]. Found Miss Davis waiting for us. Gave directions about sending me some wool for lamp mat. Joe Heleluhe called on Mr. W. O. Smith and was paid $267.50, the amount that was borrowed of me by J. Kaae one year ago which was $250.00—interest amounting to $17.50.

*Thursday, February 18.* Seaside residence. Mrs. Irene Brown and Mrs. Minnie Aldrich came out to spend the day. We bathed in the sea and had a good time. Little Harry and Mary Clark came out also. Nothing particular transpired during the day. Joe Aea came up to talk business in regard to putting up houses on his lot out here—That he knew of a man who was willing to lend money by building houses and he could let the rent go for payment. Wrote to Miss Davis to deliver my note to Achoy discharging him.

*Friday, February 19.* Hale Mauliola. Seven A.M. Col. Iaukea called to see me in regard to payment of lands bought last Saturday February 13—of Kalakaua's estate and amounted to $12,000.00.[66] I asked him to make such arrangements as he could out of receipts of Crown lands, and also from amounts of John's Estate of which Mr. W. F. Allen is Administrator, and for which I signed a note for $2,400.00. I signed also a note of Bishop & Co.—giving receipts of Crown Lands for four months, for the sum of $8,600.00—all giving my Bonds and Stocks for security for that time until note is paid. Had conversation with Mr. Widemann in regard to list of invitations for State dinner. When Mr. Robertson came up, we decided that the Chief of the staff might have a seat at the table, but not the rest of the staff. They and the ladies in waiting shall have a table in the corner room [at] which they [may eat] at the same time with the others. Mr. Widemann also mentioned that Gov. Cleghorn being father of the Heir Apparent ought to be first on my right—that if I did not put him on my right Cleghorn would withdraw, and so would his daughter. I explained—or rather he went on to say, that the Princes were mere boys and that they had not the standing in the community, and it would be doing them an injury to push them forward by placing them above Archie. I told Mr. Widemann, Minister of Finance—that I placed them there because they were to be regent in case of my death before Kaiulani arrived at age, and they would act with the Ministers and Chancellor of the Kingdom as a Council of Regency. For that reason I want them to be worthy of their position by making them acquainted with Government work, and to begin at the lowest round of the ladder. But above all, to respect themselves. Mr. Widemann had nothing more to say. I also explained to him that as Mr. Cleghorn was only Governor I could not place him over My Ministers. Therefore as Governor and Commander in Chief, he must be content to be near my person on my left. Kaiulani shall be on my right on all occasions, but that was no reason why he should be there. So I told my Chamberlain Mr. Robertson about it, and also [said] that Mr. Cleghorn ought to be willing to give in to my arrangements. So at the coming State Dinner Kawananakoa shall be next to me and take the opposite side of

---

66. The auction of 37 parcels of land from King Kalakaua's estate took place February 13 in the salesroom of James F. Morgan. In its report of the business, the *Pacific Commercial Advertiser*, February 15, 1892, said: "Her Majesty [Liliuokalani] purchased 22½ acres situated at Pawaa, Punahou, Oahu. The price paid was $7,000.00 [and] Her Majesty [also] purchased 455 acres situated at Kalihi, Oahu, for $4,600." The Kalihi land was known as Kamanaiki (Royal Patent Grant 3424). In 1923, the Liliuokalani Trust sold the mauka portion of this parcel (337.47 acres) to the Territory of Hawaii to become a forest reservation.

the table, and Kalanianaole must come in with me. Koa [Kawananakoa] will have to take Mrs. Parker, and Archie, Mrs. Judd.

Talked with Mr. R. [James W. Robertson] about the coming Children's Fancy Ball in costume on Monday. Cunning little Royal cards had been issued to the little ones, and they are so pleased.

Jessie is here putting up curtains for the windows of this house—my seaside residence.

*Sunday, February 21.* Seaside cottage. Iaukea and his wife came out to spend the day. She came first with her children, and he, being great churchgoer, went to church first. When Iaukea arrived, we spoke of Mr. Bishop's notes and Mr. Widemann's mortgage of Pualeilani of $10,000.00—but Mr. Widemann begged not to foreclose the Mortgage if I wished to return it to him.

*Monday, February 22.* Iolani Palace. Sent for Minister Widemann and consulted him in regard to appointment of Governors of Maui and the salaries of Governors all over the Islands. I had not quite got through when he left. I wanted to say that if they had some duties given to them it might be worthwhile to give the Governor of Oahu a salary of $3,400 a year, and those of the other islands $2,000.00 a year—that if Piehu [Iaukea] could get salary sufficient to maintain him he would be Governor of Maui.[67]

Bishop Olba remains still unconscious.

Mr. W. said let the Tax Assessors remain as they are but let them turn the money over to the Governors—I told him to consult his colleagues. Minister Parker returned from Hawaii today on the little English gunboat *Pheasant*, Capt. Blair.[68]

Iaukea gave me the deeds of the lands [I] purchased from Kunane's [Kalakaua's] estate, Iwilei, Mananaiki, and Pawaa, the whole amounting to $12,600.00. Iaukea took them to be recorded.

As I write, the bells are tolling from the Catholic Church, which announces the death of the Bishop of Olba.[69]

Joe gave me $485.00 the interest of [D. H.] Nahinu's mortgage on his property in Kona.

There was held [at the Palace] a nice fancy ball for the children of prominent citizens, started by Mr. and Mrs. [F. A.] Schaefer.[70] The prin-

67. This did not happen.

68. "HBMS *Pheasant* returned from her cruise to Kawaihae today, and anchored in the naval row. While outside the harbor, the gunboat engaged in some sharp gun practice." *Daily Bulletin*, February 22, 1892.

69. The Right Reverend Hermann Koeckemann, bishop of Olba, died February 22 at the Catholic Mission. Born in 1828, Osberen, Westphalia, Germany, Father Herman arrived in Honolulu on November 11, 1854. He was consecrated as bishop of Olba in San Francisco, August 28, 1881. The *Daily Bulletin*, February 23, 1892, reported that Governor Cleghorn called at the Catholic Mission and "on behalf of the Queen tendered the services of the Royal Hawaiian Band for the funeral."

70. A children's fancy ball had been held at Rosebank, the Schaefer residence in Nuuanu Valley. The Queen, learning of its success, asked to have the event repeated in Iolani Palace. The *Pacific Commercial Advertiser*, February 17, 1892, reported: "Her Majesty the Queen has invited the children who participated in the fancy dress party at Mr. and Mrs. Schaefer's to the Palace on Monday evening at 7:30 o'clock. The Queen was much interested in the accounts given of

cipal families were W. G. Irwin, Schaefers and their connections, the Kings and Sopers—the Woods, the Monsarrats, the Cartwrights and the Widemanns and Bergers and MacFarlanes, the Neumanns, T. R. Walker, J. S. Walker, and [George] Smith of Benson and Smith. The Minuet was danced by Miss Schaefer and [Bessie] Laurence, the Spanish dance by Gardie MacFarlane and Miss Schmidt.[71]

*Tuesday, February 23.* Iolani Palace. Iaukea was told yesterday that he should consider himself Chief of the Staff. He gave me a package of papers of Mortgage of Pualeilani. It is at present held in Antone Rosa's name for the King and mortgaged to Widemann.[72]

Made arrangements for Minister Parker for salary for Governors. He said they ought all to have $3,000. I doubt they will get it—He told me he will have to go to Maui with his wife and family on account of the death of Kuihelani.[73] How sad.

Eveline [Wilson] moved to the bungalow last night.

*Wednesday, February 24.* Iolani Palace. Nine A.M. Archie called to read Kaiulani's letters to me in [which] she asked for decorations for Lady Wiseman and Mrs. Macfie.[74] She [Kaiulani] was well but Mr. T. H. Davies did not want her to go to Brighton. Mr. D. did not think her [well enough?].

---

the party and the description published in the *Advertiser* and her kind intention to entertain the children at the palace is the result. Parents and guardians are of course invited with them."

71. "The children's fancy dress ball which took place at the Palace last night was one of the most delightful which eyes ever looked on in this little Kingdom. The ball was a repetition, with additions and embellishments, of that described in the *Advertiser* last week Monday. The original intention had been to confine invitations to parents or other relatives of children taking part in the masquerade, but curiosity to see this unique and charming spectacle was so general that the lines were broken through and so many invitations issued that a large and fashionable audience was present.

"The Palace was bright with electric lights, the large hall, throne, reception, and dining rooms tastefully decorated with flowers, when the carriages began to file into the west gate in a long line. It was pretty to see the little costumed creatures come dancing up the stairs accompanied by their mamas, who for the nonce were thrown into the shade. Before eight o'clock everyone was there."

The *Advertiser* then printed a complete list of the young attendees and their costumes, identifying, for example, Irmgard (Gardie) Macfarlane as a "Spanish Dancing Girl," Miss Minnie Schmidt as a "Tyrolean Girl," and Else Schaefer and Bessie Lawrence as "Ladies of the Court of Louis XIV."

"At eight o'clock the makai door [of the throne room] was opened, and through it came the children marching two by two and arranged according to the height, the smallest leading off. . . . Each child was presented to Her Majesty by the Chamberlain, Major J. H. Robertson, by name. All of the children bowed, except Else Schaefer and Bessie May, who made pretty, old-fashioned curtsies. . . . Never surely have any Honolulu children passed prouder hours than those . . . before Hawaii's Queen last night." *Pacific Commercial Advertiser*, February 23, 1892.

72. A June 21, 1892, schedule of King Kalakaua's debts lists two notes to H. A. Widemann dating from April 30, 1880, and May 1, 1888, totaling $9,400, with the following notation: "These notes were signed by A. Rosa and secured by property at Waikiki, the title of which was in Mr. Rosa['s name.] He has now conveyed the property to Kapiolani and the administrator has paid the notes." Hawaii State Archives, First Circuit Court, Probate 2720.

73. The Honorable Huaka Kuihelani (b. 1802?–d. February 21, 1892, Wailuku) was a chief; a member of the House of Representatives, 1855–73; a member of the House of Nobles, 1873–86; a member of the Privy Council, 1883 under Kalakaua; and a longtime judge at Wailuku. He was the husband of Kaehuwahanui, and the uncle and stepfather of Mrs. Samuel Parker.

74. These letters have not been found, and the decorations were not awarded.

*Friday, February 26.* Washington Place. W. D. Alexander called at the Palace this morning to consult me in regard to having a room in the Government house for preserving books, pamphlets, and papers that are lying in a heap in that building and [says that] with a proper person to sort out and arrange them nicely it would be worthwhile, as many of those are historical since the time that the Government was in those premises opposite the Engine Co. No. 2.[75] He suggested Mr. H. [Hoes] the Chaplain of the *Pensacola* might be asked to take that position with a small salary to do the work as he showed an aptitude in that direction. So I propose to write a letter to Mr. W. D. Alexander that he might ask Mr. Stevens American Commissioner to give Mr. H. leave of absence.[76]

*Sunday, March 6.* Washington Place. Did not go to church today—Minister Parker called and objected to postponing the ball—for many reasons. I said I would leave it to the Ministers since it was to be a state affair. He called again this evening to say the Ministers had met and decided to have it take place on the 17th inst [this month]. He will give a dinner on the 19th and the three Ministers will give a ball when the other admirals arrive.

---

The postponed ball mentioned in the Queen's March 6 entry took place on the evening of Thursday, March 17, 1892, and was the subject of a lengthy report the following day.

> ¶ Yesterday evening Her Majesty Queen Liliuokalani gave a State Ball at Iolani Palace, the first since her accession to the Throne. It was an exceedingly brilliant event, the attendance being unusually large.... Half past eight o'clock was the hour mentioned on the handsome invitation...but long before that time the invited guests began to arrive. The carriages containing the guests entered the Palace grounds by the Richard street gate, and drew up at the steps facing that street. Over the steps was a tent-like covering. Here the guests were conducted down the flight of steps by members of Her Majesty's staff and conducted to the dressing rooms, gentlemen going to the right in the

---

75. The old Government House was located on the Ewa corner of Hotel and Union Streets (the Engine Co. was on the Diamond Head side of Union Street). The government had moved the archives from that location to its new building in about 1874, and they had been largely inaccessible since that time.

76. Reverend Roswell R. Hoes, a naval chaplain and the founder of what became the Hawaiian Historical Society, arrived in Hawaii in September 1891 aboard the USS *Pensacola*. He soon after met W. D. Alexander, who suggested that he compile a Hawaiian bibliography including the titles of all books, pamphlets, and other government-printed material. Hoes commenced the project, and in the process examined the contents of crates stored in the basement of the government building, which he found in disarray and deteriorating. See David W. Forbes, *Hawaiian National Bibliography 1780–1900*, vol. 4 (Honolulu: University of Hawaii Press in association with Hordern House, Sydney, 2003), 439.

On February 27, 1892, the Queen, through James W. Robertson, addressed a letter to W. D. Alexander in support of the project and forwarded a second one to U.S. Minister John L. Stevens on the same date. The leave of absence, however, did not take place.

Chamberlain's office, the ladies to the left on the other side of the hallway, where a large room was specially fitted up for their accommodation.... Arriving on the main floor the invited guests entered the throne room, where Her Majesty held an informal reception, standing just in front of the dais. It was a charming sight in the throne room, for it was most beautifully decorated, the electric light chandeliers were producing an effect that was highly picturesque.... On the dais stood a number of magnificent kahilis [royal feather standards], and also a tabu stick. The mirrors were banked with choice flowers at the foot, while pretty vines hung from the top. The grand hallway was an object of admiration from all. On either side were banked all kinds of potted plants. In the alcoves stood handsome bouquets, their perfume being most fragrant. At the head of the stairway was the first letter of the word *aloha*, made of evergreen wreaths, and on the steps on either side stood potted plants.

Dancing was carried on in the throne room and also the dining room, which was tastefully decorated. The Royal Hawaiian Orchestra was stationed at the mauka end of the hall and played for dancing. On a raised platform to the left of the back veranda was the band of the U.S. Flagship *San Francisco*, which played between dances. [The account then lists the order of 14 types of dances, commencing with "Lancers" and ending with a "galop."]

When dancing was going on, the scene was very brilliant, many of the ladies were wearing very elegant costumes. The grounds were illuminated with hundreds of colored lanterns, so arranged as to produce a fine effect on approaching the Palace.

An elegant supper was served in the lanai in front of the Palace shortly after 11 o'clock. The interior of this building was elaborately decorated with flags and streamers, and lit up by electric light. There was an abundant supply of choice edibles.... The arrangements of the ball were in the able hands of Major Jas. [James] W. Robertson, Her Majesty's Chamberlain.... There was not a drawback of any kind, and those present voted it the finest ball ever given in Honolulu.[77]

The article concludes with a four-column list of the attendees.

---

On March 7, 1892, English poet and essayist Sir Edwin Arnold (b. 1832– d. 1904), best known for his epic poem *The Light of Asia* (1879), made a one-day stop in Honolulu en route to Japan. In Honolulu, he was met by William G. Irwin and escorted through the town. He visited Mr. and Mrs. Samuel Parker, and it is probably through Parker's assistance that he was granted a private audience with Queen Liliuokalani, at 4:20 that day at Washington Place. Arnold's account of his visit (published in *Paradise of the Pacific*, June 1892) is as follows:

77. *Pacific Commercial Advertiser*, March 18, 1892.

¶ I was a little laughed at by my American companions for feeling somewhat shy of entering the presence of her Majesty in my pea-jacket and ship-board attire. But deshabile is the custom of the islands and the "Hon. Sam [Parker]" first Minister of the Crown, was himself wearing a shooting-jacket and straw hat; while the father of the Heir Apparent [A. S. Cleghorn] also accompanying us, was resplendent in a red tie and white waist-coat....

As for Her Majesty, she is "every inch a queen," and bears with noble grace and lofty gentleness the lonely honours of her rank. When we passed from the ante-room of her palace [Washington Place] guarded by a Hawaiian soldier in white uniform, and filled with objects of ancient island royalty and portraits of island potentates departed, we found in a pretty inner apartment, seated, and attended upon by two ladies-in-waiting, the good, enlightened, sweet-faced, and kind-hearted Liliuokalani. The Queen rose, with all the simplicity of a lady welcoming friends, to receive us, and shook hands cordially with each of our party, as each was presented.... Dressed in complete mourning, she wore a black robe of silk crepe, cut loose below the bosom after the native fashion and she carried a black lace-edged handkerchief, but no ornaments, except a magnificent diamond ring. Her countenance distinctly handsome; and of the most decided Hawaiian type, has the color of coffee, and is surmounted by thick black hair, growing luxuriantly, touched here and there with silvery flecks.

At first sight the Queen's wise eye and heart commands your true respect and loyalty. Her voice has the soft musical intonation heard in the speeches of all her countrymen, and I have seldom listened to English more perfect or more graceful than that spoken by Her Majesty. She did me the honor to place me in a chair by her side and to enter upon an animated conversation. A blue lotus-blossom expand[ing] in a silver cup upon the table gave occasion for us to talk of the flowers and trees and fruits of the Archipelago.... Her Majesty was pleased to describe to us her visit to England at the time of Queen Victoria's Jubilee [in 1887], with the splendid memories of which her heart and mind were full. She recounted to me, with charming enthusiasm, how she sat near our Queen in West-Minster Abbey, and what the Queen said to her, and how kind and great-hearted the English Sovereign was, and about the German Crown Prince, how soldierly and grand he looked, and our late departed Prince, the Duke of Clarence, how courteous and agreeable he showed himself to her. It was delightful to sit in the milk-warm air... and thus listen to the low, pleasant tones of this dark Island Queen, so gentle in her bereavement, so stately and truly royal in her womanly simplicity.... I shall always preserve the flowers which she gave me, and the memory of her gracious and kindly "aloha" at parting.

*Saturday, March 19.* Healani Hale. Made my first official visit today on board—of the *San Francisco*. Minister Parker and Mrs. P., Minister Spencer and Mrs. S., Minister Widemann and Mrs. W., Attorney General Whiting, Major Robertson and Mrs. R., Mrs. Wilson and Jennie Clark. I had almost forgotten to mention Governor Cleghorn and Prince Kawananakoa. The staff [attending me] are Cols. Iaukea, Holt, Bertelmann, J. Richardson, Boyd. Admiral Brown received us and took us all over the ship. I got on board better than I thought I would, but was pretty tired when we got home.[78]

*Monday, April 11.* Hale Kealohilani [Waikiki]. Spent the morning in arranging our furniture and making things look more presentable. 11 A.M. Minister Parker came out with Col. Richardson and brought the Proclamation out for me to sign. It stated that the Legislature was to open on the 28th of May. Nothing as yet has been done about the Governor of Maui.

This morning while Col. Boyd was here, several matters came up in regard to the Interior Department. He was confident that he could undertake to run the office if Mr. Hassinger was to be promoted. Questioned him in regard to clerks under him—was satisfied with his explanations. We heard that it was Mr. Thrum who wrote that article in *The Friend* this month against the late King my brother[79]—that he spends most of his time writing for his Annual instead of attending to his duties in his office [as registrar of the Bureau of Conveyances].[80]

The funeral of the late Associate Justice L. McCully takes place this afternoon 1½ P.M. My Chamberlain Mr. Robertson said no notice had been sent him in regard to the funeral, so I told him to ask H.R.H. Prince

---

78. "Her Majesty Queen Liliuokalani, accompanied by about fifteen members of the court and cabinet in full court dress, paid an official visit on board the U.S. Cruiser *San Francisco*, Flagship of the Pacific Squadron, last Saturday afternoon.... A large concourse of citizens... witnessed the embarkation, which was made promptly at 1:07 P.M.... As soon as the royal party arrived, Her Majesty, accompanied by her immediate household staff, was received by Flag Lieutenant George L. Dyer, aide-de-camp to Admiral Brown, and escorted to the boats, which immediately cast loose and proceeded to the Flagship, where Her Majesty was received by Admiral Brown.

"As Her Majesty stepped over the gangway and upon the ship's deck, a national salute of twenty-one guns was fired and the Hawaiian Royal Standard was hoisted at the main.... During the visit Her Majesty expressed in the warmest terms her admiration of the cruiser and pleasure at the welcome accorded her." *Pacific Commercial Advertiser*, March 21, 1892.

79. The offending article, titled "The Crown Lands," appeared in *The Friend*, April 1892, and included the following comment: "It has long been felt that the public interest required that the Sovereign's life interest in these extensive lands should be commuted for a stipend, and the lands sold for homesteads to actual settlers. It now appears that the late King defrauded both his successors and the nation by leasing a large proportion of these lands on thirty-year leases at low rates. He undoubtedly received therefore large sums in hand, to relieve his pressing necessities. The worst of it is, that these leases are good in law."

80. Liliu was referring to *Thrum's Hawaiian Almanac and Annual*, begun by Thomas G. Thrum in 1875, in which for more than 50 years he published a wide variety of articles on historical subjects.

Kawananakoa to go in the State carriage, and he to accompany the Prince to the Church, and from there home.[81]

*Saturday, April 30.* Iolani Palace. Had a few [people] come in to sing and try my new piano.[82] Ladies who came are Mrs. Admiral Brown, Mrs. Lt. Dyer, Mr. and Mrs. McDonald, Mrs. W. F. Allen, Mrs. and Miss Dora Dowsett, Mrs. Molly Brown, Mrs. Mott Smith, Mrs. J. O. Carter, Master Hugh Brown, Miss May Cummins, Miss Annie Holmes, Miss S. V. Patch—Col. Iaukea.

*Monday, May 2.* Iolani Palace. Four P.M. Called on Mr. and Mrs. Mitchell of New York.[83] Promised to come and hear Miss Frieda Mitchell play the next evening.[84] Minister Parker called and said we might get Mr. Everett to accept the Governorship of Maui for the present until we could get a pension for him and a good salary for Governors, say $3,000.00 a year, then he is to resign and a new appointment to be made for Maui.[85] Have not appointed anyone yet for Circuit Judge of Maui, because Attorney General Whiting protests against [A. Noa] Kepoikai. They want Mr. C. Hopkins to go up—but I have other plans for him.

*Tuesday, May 3.* Iolani Palace. [Rest of entry blank.]

*Thursday, May 19.* Iolani Palace. Wilcox—V. V. Ashford, Bipikane, and many others [and] Lot Lane are arrested for Treason—Marshall Wilson with the consent of Judge Dole had to act, as the Cabinet was so indifferent to all the excitement being made by these parties having secret meetings

---

81. Judge Lawrence McCully died Sunday, April 10, 1892, at his Pawaa, Oahu, residence. Born in New York City on May 28, 1831, he graduated from Yale in 1852, and came to Hawaii in December 1854. He read law and was admitted to the bar in 1859. He was deputy attorney general, and Kalakaua later appointed him as second associate justice of the Supreme Court. The *Daily Bulletin*, April 11, 1892, remarked that McCully was "one of the ablest and most upright Justices it has had since organization." McCully received what amounted to a state funeral.

82. "A ROYAL PIANO. Her Majesty the Queen was presented with a handsome and valuable piano yesterday. The presentation took place in the throne room of the Palace, and was made by Messrs. John Phillips, J. H. Soper, and J. F. Hackfeld, the committee appointed for that purpose. The following description of the piano is taken from a New York journal:

"'There is now on exhibition in the warerooms of Messrs. J. and C. Fischer, 110 Fifth Avenue, a rare specimen of one of the firm's grand pianos made to order for Queen Liliuokalani of Hawaii. It is made of a native wood sent here for that purpose . . . and the veneers having been sawed here. The wood is called Koa. . . . Worked out and fitted and finished as it has been by Messrs. Fischer, it is a marvellously beautiful wood adapted for the case of a grand piano.

"'On the front and inner side of the fall board the royal coat of arms and insignia are artistically painted with effect, and the piano will prove an adornment to the Royal Palace at Honolulu.'" *Pacific Commercial Advertiser*, April 23, 1892.

83. This was Mr. and Mrs. Alfred Mitchell. Mrs. Mitchell was an heir to Charles Tiffany's fortune (Tiffany & Co.), as he was her grandfather. Under "Kauai Notes," the *Pacific Commercial Advertiser*, May 2, 1892, reported that Mr. and Mrs. Alfred Mitchell and family, of New York, had been among the party at Governor Rice's, honoring Paul Isenberg, on the 29th of April: "Mr. and Mrs. Mitchell and family who have been visiting Kauai for the past three months, doing up the whole island pretty thoroughly, leave today [April 30] for Honolulu, San Francisco, and thence to their home [in] New York City." The Mitchells departed for San Francisco on the *Mariposa* on May 5.

84. Alfreda, one of the Mitchell daughters, would later marry Hiram Bingham III.

85. Thomas W. Everett would become governor of Maui on May 17, 1892, and served until the Provisional Government abolished the position in January 1893.

and ordering guns and pistols. Wilson informed W. R. Castle secretly of this matter [and] what should he do but go and inform Ashford of it and when the arrests were made all the guns had disappeared. What does this all mean? It looks as if the Missionary party are really at the bottom of all these disturbances and the Ashfords and R. W. Wilcox are their tools.

---

Liliuokalani's diary entry for May 19 concerns a threatened revolutionary movement against her government, which Marshall Charles B. Wilson nipped in the bud. Of this movement, Sanford B. Dole wrote:

> ¶ Not long after the advancement [accession] of Liliuokalani, Robert Wilcox, supposed to have been in sympathy with her in the uprising of 1889, ... was engaged with others in a movement to enlist support of the Hawaiians in a revolution to supplant the Queen and establish a republic, of which Wilcox was not slow in announcing himself as a candidate for president. Public meetings were held, and the plans and the hopes of revolutionists were publicly discussed. The government, mindful of Wilcox's former attempt, eventually arrested him and over a dozen of his associates on the charge of treason.[86]

The arrest Dole mentions took place on the morning of May 19. On the complaint of Marshall Charles B. Wilson, Dole, as a justice of the Supreme Court, signed warrants of arrest for V. V. Ashford and others accused by C. B. Wilson of the crime of treason. The court issued warrants for Robert W. Wilcox, Lot Lane, George Markham, Kaimimoku, Kahahawai (k), J. W. Bipikane, John Brown, Manuel Ross Jr., George W. Maxwell, Robert Palau, Alexander Smith, Kaahiwaina (k), S. K. Kila (k), Paloka (k), Manuel Espinda, Jim Crow (or Kino Kolo), and D. (or P.?) Keliikuewa (k). The specific charge was as follows:

> ¶ In contravention to the laws and in opposition to the authority of the Queen's government ... did unlawfully, falsely, maliciously, and traitorously, imagine, plot, attempt, and intend to raise and levy war, insurrection, and rebellion against the Queen's Government, and to dethrone and destroy Her Majesty the Queen in order to fulfill and bring into effect the said traitorous compassings, imaginations, and intentions of them ... and did with divers other persons also owing allegiance to the said Kingdom, unlawfully, maliciously, an[d] traitorously assemble and gather together on the 10th day of April 1892 and on divers days thereafter up to and including the 16th day of May 1892 in Honolulu ... and then and there [did] so plot and attempt ... contrary to the duty of allegiance.[87]

Alfred S. Hartwell and William R. Castle, counsel for the defendants, demurred to the charge "as being insufficient and objectionable for uncer-

---

86. Sanford Dole, *Memoirs of the Hawaiian Revolution*, ed. Andrew Farrell (Honolulu: Advertiser, 1936), 67–68.
87. Hawaii State Archives, First Circuit Court, Criminal 1652.

tainty" and claimed that "no overt act has been charged." Justice Sanford B. Dole reasoned, "I am of the opinion that plotting to dethrone and destroy the Queen is an overt act itself," and overruled the demur on May 20, 1892.[88] Many of those initially arrested were discharged, but the court committed Robert Wilcox, Lot Lane, Robert Palau, John Brown, H. K. Kaohiwaena, and Paul Keliikuewa for trial on June 9.

On June 9, 1892, Judge Dole discharged Ashford and Markham, but committed Wilcox and several others for trial. At their trial, evidence showed that rather than committing the act, those charged had only rather carelessly planned the act, and ultimately, on June 25, 1892, the court discharged all the conspirators without finding them guilty.

---

*Saturday, May 21.* Iolani Palace. Four P.M. Miss Julia Smith[89] of Kauai came to see me about giving another concert for the Kauai Industrial School.[90] After all arrangements were made, she told me that Mr. Hartwell told her to come and tell me not to have any fears, that he would make such arrangements as to get them [Ashford and Wilcox] out of harm's way or where they can do no harm. I thanked her and told her I had no fears about them.

*Wednesday, May 25.* Iolani Palace—Three P.M. Miss Julia Smith again called to reassure me in regard to the case of Treason. Mr. Hartwell sent her to tell me that everything will be all right in the end, that Wilcox and Ashford would both go to prison. I thanked her and said I watched the case with great interest. When she withdrew I wondered what she meant—and what did Mr. Hartwell mean by sending me such a message—and yet, all Mr. Hartwell's pleadings were in favor of the prisoners, saying their actions were not treasonable.

---

On May 28, the legislature opened. It was Liliuokalani's first legislative session as monarch. It was the longest and most combative session under the monarchy, and it was also to be the last session under that form of government. The *Advertiser* provided the public with a long account of the event:

> ¶ A large audience of residents and visiting tourists gathered at Aliiolani Hale to witness the interesting ceremonies connected with the biennial opening of the Hawaiian Legislature, which occurred on Saturday the 28th day of May, at noon. The household Guards were

---

88. Hawaii State Archives, First Circuit Court, Criminal 1652.
89. Anna Juliette Smith (b. 1857–d. 1900) was later the wife of J. K. Farley. Judge A. S. Hartwell was her brother-in-law.
90. Kauai Industrial School, founded at Koloa by Reverend J. W. Smith and his family, opened in October 1889 under the charge of Robert W. Andrews, with 19 boys "who are to have the benefit of manual training and industrial drill as well as elementary English and mathematical studies." The school was undercapitalized, and closed after 1897.

drawn up in battle array in front of the building and the [Royal] Hawaiian Band faced them on the other side of the driveway. The band played and the troops presented arms as the various local and foreign dignitaries drove up.

Within the Legislative Hall seats for members of the Privy Council of State and their wives were reserved against the eastern wall of the building while the two front rows were occupied by the Diplomatic and Consular Corps.... On the opposite or western side of the room were seated members of the Cabine[t] and Her Majesty's staff with their ladies, Judges of the Supreme Court and their wives, the Anglican Bishop and wife, Governor Everett of Maui, and Governor Rice of Kauai.... In the middle also fronting the throne were placed seats fo[r] the Nobles and Representatives of the Legislature....

Promptly at noon Her Majesty entered the Chamber, escorted by Chief Justice and Chancellor Judd and accompanied by His Excellency A. S. Cleghorn, Governor of Oahu, Princes Kawananakoa and Kalanianaole, Major Robertson, Her Majesty's Chamberlain, members of the royal staff, and ladies in waiting. The members of the Cabinet preceded the royal party. Prayer having been offered by the Rev. H. H. Parker, Her Majesty read the Royal Address, first in Hawaiian and afterwards in English, the audience remaining standing. Nothing could be heard of the address, as the noise from the halls and corridors drowned every other sound. The scene presented at the reading was delightful to the eye, flowers, kahilis [feather standards], rich dresses, and feather cloaks presenting a brilliant piece of color.[91]

---

*Saturday, June 4.* Iolani Palace. Heard from the little lady [Miss Wolf] that Mollie Sheldon was in the family way and she thinks by Mr. W. but she was surrounded by four young men besides—five or six months gone.

*Friday, June 10.* Iolani Palace. Had news of V. V. Ashford's release and they say they could make no case of it. It looks very suspicious. Reports say that Hartwell and Dole had agreed to let the man off.[92]

*Saturday, June 11.* Iolani Palace. Went to races [at Kapiolani Park]. Sat at the Club House a half hour, then went to our stand which was once the Widemann stand. Saw Mollie [Sheldon] across the track and noticed she looked rather large but if I hadn't known it, wouldn't have noticed anything. She looked very nicely. It is very dull out here.[93]

---

91. *Pacific Commercial Advertiser*, May 30, 1892.

92. The main intent of the government at this point was to get Ashford out of the country. In a letter of December 14, 1892, referencing the May 1892 incident, Lorrin Thurston noted that "the flight from the country of the most active fomenter of the trouble, V. V. Ashford, disconcerted and disheartened the others who had worked with him." Thurston, *Memoirs*, 235. See also last two footnotes for June 11, 1892, diary entry (285–86).

93. The *Pacific Commercial Advertiser*, June 13, 1892, said only, "Her Majesty attended the races on Saturday for a short while."

2:30 P.M. left for Punahou. Very nice to see Sunday School children enjoy themselves.[94] On my arrival heard from Chief Justice Judd that V. V. Ashford had left last evening by one of the Wilder's steamers.[95] Heard afterward that V. V. [Ashford] was paid $25,000.00 to leave the country for fear he would expose the Annexation party.[96]

---

In the following diary entry for June 18, 1892, Liliuokalani gives a rambling account of the life of Captain John Dominis, almost certainly derived from Fraulein Gertrude Wolf's fortune-telling cards and services as a medium, rather than from any specific records, and the reader should approach them with skepticism. The paragraph about Captain Dominis's arrival in Hawaii, and his 1846 departure, however, is most likely a summary of the Queen's knowledge of her husband's family history. The top of the page has been cut off, obliterating the date and one and a half lines, and the text continues uninterrupted on the page for Sunday, June 19.

---

*Saturday, June 18.* ... about Capt. John Dominis. She [Fraulein Wolf] says that by writing to the Consul at Wien or Vienna, satisfactory information may be received in about 15 weeks or 15 months—Three letters will be without satisfaction but the 4th will bring news from an elderly gentleman. [She says] Capt. Dominis was born in the year 1803—of parents of high standing and birth. His mother was born in 1776 or 1778 and was a lady of rank—of middle height, rather stout, and usually wore a stern expression on her face. She may have been an Austrian lady. Her name, I think,

---

94. "One of the most pleasant and enjoyable picnics of the year was that given by the Central Union Sunday School on the 11th of June at Punahou. There was a large attendance of the pupils and their parents and others. The teachers and the older members of the church did their utmost to please the little ones and they succeeded in their efforts admirably.... At 12:30 o'clock, the real picnic commenced.... The refreshments were so prepared as to suit the varied tastes of the different nationalities of all ages represented there. Cakes of all descriptions were plentiful. Coffee, watermelons, soda water, etc. were supplied to all.... Her Majesty the Queen arrived during the afternoon and remained at the picnic for several hours." *Pacific Commercial Advertiser*, June 13, 1892.

95. In an article titled "Where Is Ashford?," the *Pacific Commercial Advertiser*, June 13, 1892, said: "The common talk around town yesterday was to the effect that the vessel [the steamer *Hawaii*] was chartered to carry V. V. Ashford away from the scene of his late trouble.... Hon. C. W. Ashford was questioned yesterday about his brother's whereabouts, but he returned evasive answers.... Ashford has not been seen since Friday, and it is almost certain that he has packed up and left our sunny shores."

In a second article in the same issue titled "Six Dismissed," the *Advertiser* published the June 10 decision of Supreme Court Judge Dole, dismissing Ashford and a number of others, and committing Robert Wilcox, Lot Lane, and four others for trial, "on the charge of treason by a plotting or attempt to dethrone or destroy the Queen."

96. The Queen is here referring to the Annexation Club, which a group of Honolulu businessmen formed in 1892. They were apprehensive that the Queen might try to subvert the 1887 constitution, and convinced that ultimately a union with the United States was the best means of securing a stable government. It was with this idea that Lorrin Thurston in fact went to Washington, DC, on March 29, 1892, returning June 4, to sound out the U.S. government on the idea. Thurston summarizes the matter in the manuscript of his memoirs. Hawaii State Archives, Thurston Papers, Box 1, 825–50. There is no record of the alleged payment to Ashford.

was Leopold or Leopoldina Dominisi del Galo or nearly like it or perhaps it was the family name. Her husband was an Italian of higher rank than she and was born in 1771. He was also middle height and had a fine military bearing and supposed to be the son of a Duke for she saw a Ducal crown—with a bright gem in the centre. Three sons and a daughter were born to them. He died by the sword on fighting a duel and so did one of his sons who had very light hair and fair complexion. There were left two brothers and they quarreled and one of them left for foreign parts. He landed in America, went under an assumed name calling himself Capt. John Dominis and married a Miss Mary Jones of Boston, a lady of large circle of well-to-do relations. They must have been married in the year 1830 or 1831 for their first child was born in 1832, and afterwards two girls were born—and grew up to the ages of 12 and 13, then died. Captain Dominis brought his family out to these islands in 1836 and left them out here while he went back and forth between China and this port, being Master Mariner never fail[ed] to go as Commander. He built a handsome [house] for his wife and son but left the islands just before it was completed, on the 15th of August 1846, he left Honolulu for China on the Brig *William Nelson*. The passengers on this voyage were George Brown Esq., U.S. Commissioner, and his son George. Nothing has been heard from him since. During his lifetime he only once made reference to who he was or mentioned his family connections. It was to his wife and son (when the latter was very young), he said that he was born in Trieste and that he came of a family of high standing and respectability, he also spoke casually of a Marquis, but did not mention any names. She says Capt. Dominis' sister is still living and very old. That he met with foul play and was strangled in his bed by a person who had delicate white hands like that of a lady and wore a brilliant ring on the 3rd finger of the left hand. He wore a white flannel shirt and the neck was left open and after strangling, the body was thrown overboard, but when she tried to find out more, Capt. D's spirit shook his finger and he made signs of quarter to 12 at night—then did not wish for her to seek any more, shook his hand of disapproval, and disappeared with the hands around his neck.

*Monday, June 20.* Iolani Palace. Sent for Mr. Neumann and gave into his possession statements from Henry Poor telling all about himself and his incarceration by certain parties.[97]

97. This document is an 11-page missive from Henry Poor to the Queen in which he discusses his detainment and treatment in jail on a charge of shortages in the post office. Hawaii State Archives, Liliuokalani Collection, Seized Document No. 33. The *Pacific Commercial Advertiser*, June 6, 1892, reported the following about the matter: "Henry Poor, an ex-Post Office official and at present discharging the duties of secretary of the Road Board, is in trouble. On Saturday morning he was arrested on a charge of embezzling Government property. The supposed crime is said to have been committed while Poor had charge of the Postal Savings Bank. It is alleged that he drew money from the bank belonging to other people, by signing their names to checks, and that his crime has just been discovered. The amount of bail has been placed at $25,000." The specific transactions that got Poor into trouble are listed in an article about his trial in the *Pacific Commercial Advertiser*, September 6, 1892.

Poor's letter is of considerable importance because it also includes summaries of several jailhouse discussions he had with Robert W. Wilcox regarding the actions that resulted in Wilcox being charged with treason.

*Tuesday, June 21.* Iolani Palace. Sent today by Steamer *Australia* a description of my husband's father and his family connections as given me by a medium, with a view to find out what family he belongs to. His mother being an Austrian, and his father an Italian, and both of high birth. I sent a copy of Capt. John Dominis' picture, and one of John when he was fourteen, and another one taken 1885, another 1887. She [the medium] tells me I may receive 1, 2, 3 letters but the fourth will be the one to find out the truth. It may be true and I hope that my wish may be realized and the truth be revealed. How strange all these things are that are told me. There will be a marriage for so-and-so in five weeks.

Governor and Mrs. Rice[98] and baby came to see me this morning, also Miss [Julia] Smith again of Koloa.

*Monday, June 27.* Iolani Palace. Had to go to Kamehameha School to see examination of scholars.[99] Took Mrs. Cordie Allen home at 12 and came home with Mary Carter and Kitty [Wilson]. Mr. [H. P.] Baldwin called—had quite a long conversation about legislative matters. He asked if there was anything he could do in the House.[100] I mentioned (1) for $5, or $7,000.00 for Kaiulani's traveling expenses—(2) to support the Military Bill at $66,000.00, said he would.

*Tuesday, June 28.* Iolani Palace. Received a call from Governor and Mrs. Rice at eight A.M.—they return to Kauai today. 10:30 A.M. Went with Mary Carter, Kitty Wilson, and Jennie Clark to Kamehameha Preparatory School examination—same evening went to Kamehameha Hall to evening exercises of older scholars—with Governor Cleghorn and Princes Kawananakoa and Kalanianaole.[101] Archie got very angry when I told him I had no power—after some remarks he made.

*Wednesday, June 29.* Iolani Palace. [Entry ends thus.]

*Thursday, June 30.* Iolani Palace. Had reception of Capt. Rooke and officers of HBMS Ship *Champion* at 12 P.M.[102] Mr. Sam Parker called at four P.M.

---

98. Mary Waterhouse Rice (d. June 28, 1933) was the daughter of Honolulu merchant John T. Waterhouse and wife of William Hyde Rice. The baby was Charles Atwood Rice, who became a well-known Kauai businessman and politician in the 20th century.

99. "The public exercises of the Kamehameha School were held at Bishop Hall yesterday. There was a large attendance . . . [and] Her Majesty the Queen, attended by the ladies in waiting, was present during the whole of the exercises." *Pacific Commercial Advertiser*, June 28, 1892.

100. Henry Perrine Baldwin (b. August 29, 1842, Lahaina–d. July 8, 1911, Makawao, Maui) was a pioneer sugar planter and the son of a Lahaina missionary, Reverend Dwight Baldwin. H. P. Baldwin served as a member of the House of Nobles (1887–92) and as a senator (1895–1904). Liliuokalani had been his guest at Makawao during her October 1891 visit to Maui.

101. "The annual exhibition of the Kamehameha School was held at Bishop Hall last evening. . . . At about half past seven, her Majesty entered the hall, accompanied by Governor Cleghorn, the young Princes [Kuhio and Kawananakoa], and ladies in waiting, and shortly thereafter the exercises were opened with prayer by Dr. Hyde, followed by the singing of the full school chorus. . . . All the work showed the results of faithful study and preparation. . . . The debate on the merits of the quarrel which led to Captain Cook's death was well sustained on both sides. . . . The singing both of the school chorus and the glee club was of a high character. . . . Everyone who was present at the exhibition last night must have gone away feeling that the Kamehameha schools are an institution of saving power for the Hawaiian race." *Pacific Commercial Advertiser*, June 29, 1892.

102. HBMS *Champion* (Captain Eustace Rooke) arrived at Honolulu June 27 from Esquimalt, BC, and anchored in Naval Row. The *Champion*, which had anchored at Honolulu about

Showed him how weak my position was under this new Constitution which made [him?] very angry.

Signed bills (1st) Appropriating money for band, flags, and salutes—(2nd) for $18,000.00 for Volcano Road—(3rd) To provide a Police Justice for Hana, Maui—(4th) to provide a Police Justice for Waimea, Kauai.[103]

*Friday, July 1.* Iolani Palace. 8:30 A.M. Had conversation with J_____ about what I told him in regard to M_____ and many other things that took place—it was all very true. Strange—the little lady [Miss Wolf] could not give her attention to my German lesson. Her thoughts were all given to Mr. Tripp and Mr. R. W. Wilcox and what they had done with the guns that W. [Wilcox?] had sent for. Kitty tells me there will be a change for her and Charlie [Wilson].

Signed paper of Denization for H. E. Cooper.[104]

11 A.M. Went to Kiawe grove by Helumoa to a luau given by Members of Hui Manawalea [Relief Society] of Kaumakapili—Mary Carter, Eveline, and Jenny attended me. Mrs. [Emma] Dillingham, [Miss] Hartwell, Miss Smith, Mary Green, Mrs. Day, Mrs. Severance, Mrs. Oscar White, Miss Austin were there. Had nice time.

*Saturday, July 2.* Iolani Palace. Was visited by W. O. Smith[105] to know if I had any suggestions to make for lepers, as they [the legislative committee] leave at six P.M. for Kalawao [Molokai]. Told him the boys at Kalawao needed a bathhouse that would cost $600.00. He mentioned about vaccination to be more cautious—of Kalalau to let it remain as it is—to let present Board of Health remain, all of which we agreed upon.[106] Iaukea

---

two years previously, "will remain in port about 10 days to coal, when she will leave for a cruise around the islands, departing about the end of July for the South Seas." *Pacific Commercial Advertiser*, June 28, 1892. On July 25, 1892, the *Champion* again returned to Honolulu, having in the meantime annexed Johnson's Island to Great Britain.

103. These bills are published in the 1892 Session Laws as Bills 7, 8, and 6, respectively.

104. Henry E. Cooper (b. 1857–d. 1929), a California and Hawaii businessman, resided in Honolulu from 1891. Active in island politics, he was the chairman of the Committee of Safety, which overthrew the monarchy. He was also a judge of the First Circuit Court, and a government official under the Republic of Hawaii, serving variously as minister of the interior, attorney general, minister of finance, and, in 1896, minister of foreign affairs. Hawaii State Archives, Henry E. Cooper Collection.

105. William O. Smith was a lawyer and government official (b. August 4, 1848, Koloa, Kauai–d. April 13, 1929, Honolulu). The son of missionaries James William and Millicent Knapp Smith, he was admitted to the bar in 1875. Smith was a member of the House of Representatives for Maui (1878–84) and a member of the House of Nobles (1887–88).

Smith was one of the principal participants in the 1893 overthrow. He was a member of the Executive Council of the Provisional Government (January 17, 1893–May 22, 1895), and also held the position of attorney general, an office he retained until March 20, 1899. Smith's private papers in the Hawaii State Archives include an account of his participation in the January 1893 overthrow. At the suggestion of Curtis P. Iaukea, Liliuokalani later appointed Smith a trustee of her estate, a position he served with distinction.

106. W. O. Smith was a member of the legislative committee appointed to examine conditions at Kalaupapa. The *Pacific Commercial Advertiser*, July 5, 1892, had a long report on the committee's July 2 visit and said that Smith and "about twelve others" paid a visit to the Bishop Home for girls, where they received a list of grievances, which, Smith responded, would receive "the careful attention of the committee." On July 7, the *Advertiser* published a resume of Smith's Molokai remarks: "We have come as a committee sent by the Legislature to investigate your condition, and find out your actual wants.... Before coming here I called on your Queen,

tells me to be cautious in my choice of Ministers, that I did not owe Mr. Bishop anymore. [Also] that today I may draw $350.00 on Hawaiian Construction Co., but have received nothing yet.

*Sunday, July 3.* Iolani Palace. Went to morning services at Kaumakapili. Contributed $1.00—good singing. Mr. Wray Taylor at the organ. Very tedious sermon from J. Waiamau. By the bye—promised Waiamau that I would pay $300.00 for putting up electric lights of Kaumakapili Church.[107]

1:30 P.M. Drove up to Manoa, stayed there a few minutes, then went down to Waikiki. The moment we reached [there] I went off to sleep and slept till five P.M. Woke up—cut some melon with Kitty Wilson and Wakeke.

*Monday, July 4.* Iolani Palace. Ten A.M. No band this morning. Went alone to Boat House as K. had to consult Miss W. [Wolf], Mr. Iaukea, Mr. M. Brown, Eveline, Jenny Clark, Prince Cupid [Prince Kuhio], Julia Hunt, Lala, Kaipo and Aimoku, all the schoolgirls, Mr. S. Parker, and Mr. Herbert.

*Thursday, July 7.* Iolani Palace seven A.M. No German [lesson] how strange and what strange doings are going on. Well, must wait for want of confidence [in the legislature,] where is the delay?[108] Mr. Samuel Parker will finally let out that vote will never come until he gave the word—but I heard from others that they were waiting for Claus Spreckels—to come down and make the Cabinet—but perhaps we may have something to say about it.

Great preparations for the evening. After requests made for invitations from certain parties, I at last consent to send invitations to Dr. Anderson, Mr. Harold, and Mr. Whaley to the ball.[109] At 8:30 the Ball was opened— the Members of the Legislature coming first in a body to pay their respects,

who desired me to give you her aloha. Her Majesty the Queen wished us to as much as lies in our power... promote your welfare and lighten your burdens."

107. The Queen acted as promised. The *Pacific Commercial Advertiser*, July 18, 1892, reported: "During the past week there have been placed in position in Kaumakapili Church three crystal electric light chandeliers. The centre one is of a most handsome design, and has forty lights. The other two at either end of the church hang lower into the church than the centre one, and have each twelve lights, making a total of sixty-four lights. These chandeliers were selected by Her Majesty the Queen, and it is through her generosity that they have been placed in position. They will look grand when lit up."

108. The *Pacific Commercial Advertiser*, July 21, 1892, noted: "The resolution of want of confidence comes up today.... It emanated from Representative Wilcox, who has just taken his seat after what he probably regards as persecution by the Government [his detention on a charge of treason], and thus has the earmarks of retaliation. The introducer frankly stated that he wants a seat in the Cabinet, and no doubt would consider the adopting of the resolution as entitling him to that position."

In a column on the legislative proceedings, discussing the no-confidence resolution, Wilcox "claimed that it was right and proper that a Hawaiian should introduce a such a resolution [and] held that if the Queen were to appoint a Cabinet exclusively of native Hawaiians, Her Majesty would receive the support of all reasonable members of the House." *Pacific Commercial Advertiser*, July 21, 1892. After a lengthy session, members laid the resolution on the table.

109. Captain William Whaley (of the yacht *Halcyon*) was known to be an opium smuggler. A report in the *Pacific Commercial Advertiser*, July 7, 1892 (reprinting the same article from the *San Francisco Examiner* of June 23, 1892), described a previous visit by Whaley to the islands: "As he found the climate agreed with him and Queen Liliuokalani's court most attractive, and as he had plenty of money, he proceeded to enjoy himself." An index card on Whaley in the Hawaii State Archives has an annotation by archivist A. P. Taylor: "*Halcyon* brought opium from China, landed it on Lanai, and Whaley came to Honolulu on a steamer. Whaley cut quite a figure in Honolulu with his Champagne dinners and entertainments."

then the public. It was a brilliant affair. The Minuet was danced for the first time this evening.[110]

1:30 I retired to my room. [At] two—Miss W. [Wolf] brought her cards. She told me at ten next morning, a gentleman will call on me with a bundle of papers where it would bring lots of money across the waters. She says I must have the House accept it—it would bring $1,000,000. She saw the image of a man in another country with bundle of paper in his hands—is not very tall—not very stout, but had gray hair and beard—gets into a small boat—gets into a larger boat—but misses the larger vessel. His name is C. S.—Claus Spreckels.

*Friday, July 8.* [Top left corner of page is missing] come on Tuesday then what she [Miss Wolf] says is true. She saw fourteen men—they were R.E.F.O.M. what does that mean?—I told her.[111] They want to appoint three men in the new cabinet, T. S., Y. A.—A.—Alexander? [she asks], I say yes—[the others are] Thurston, Smith, and Alexander Young. Oh, she says, don't appoint them, they want to snatch the crown from your head. You ought to appoint S. P., C. S., J. E., or S. D. and A. P.[112]—they will make a good Cabinet—but you are going to appoint and the house will reject you [and] send down again and they refuse, but I must be firm, after that everything will be alright—but when C. S. [Claus Spreckels] does get here he will spend $25,000—among the members. [She says] I am going to marry, how can that be and to whom? 3:30 A.M. I retire and Miss Wolf goes home.

Iolani Palace. Woke at eight. Miss Wolf came at nine—till ten. When she felt that the man [Thomas E. Evans] was in the house, I sent her home. 10:25. Sure enough—the man came up with bundles of papers—and spoke of lottery—how strange she should have told me. Told him to send me a copy—he went home. S. P. [Samuel Parker] came four P.M., saw T.E.E.'s card[113]—asked if he had spoken of lottery—had to tell him a white one—and found he knew all about it, just as Miss W. had said. I wonder how all will end.

*Saturday, July 9.* Iolani Palace. Instead of reading out German, we [Liliu and Miss Wolf] read cards, and was surprised when Miss W. [Wolf] told me that Mr. Sam Parker and Mr. Neumann knew about lottery papers

---

110. The ball was held at Iolani Palace in honor of the nobles and representatives of the legislative assembly. There were 14 dances, commencing with a "Lancers" and concluding with a "Galop," including a minuet, "which was a most delightful innovation." Refreshments were served on the mauka veranda during the evening, "and shortly after 11:30 o'clock an elegant supper was served in the dining hall." *Pacific Commercial Advertiser*, July 8, 1892.

111. Liliuokalani presumably told Miss Wolf that the initials stood for "Reform," meaning the Reform Party.

112. That is, Sam Parker, Claus Spreckels, John Emmeluth, Sam Damon, and A. P. Peterson.

113. The mysterious "T.E.E." was Thomas E. Evans, the husband of Liliu's friend Hannah Kaniau. Evans was a spokesman for the consortium attempting to introduce a lottery in the islands. He left the islands for his prospective Chicago investors immediately following the passage of the opium bill by the legislature, just before the overthrow in January 1893, and in California he learned both of that action and of the immediate nullification of the bill by the new Provisional Government. He was ruined financially, and never returned to the islands. Several of his letters to the Queen, contained in Hawaii State Archives, Liliuokalani Collection, discuss the matter.

and would be the means of bringing the measure before the House—that Mr. T.E.E. would not like anything done before he saw me, as he mentioned secrecy to her—that he would be with me at ten, and will tell me things important. [She says] that there were two wills, one broken and the other still sealed, that she will be the means of getting it for me—but the Queen will not live long.[114] [And] that Mr. Claus Spreckels will not be here on Tuesday.

Sure enough he [Evans] did come at ten. Spoke of Sam's [Samuel Parker's] seeming favorable to the lottery as he would place it as a source of revenue to the Government, but he also said that Peterson was a friend of mine. That along [about] November, annexationists are going to induce the natives to vote for the President of the United States. Paha [perhaps] they will try for here—that is their dodge. The little woman [Miss Wolf] tells me not to consult Mr. Wilson on the matter of lottery or anything, as he had no influence in the house. He has only three members in the house. She [?] must not go to the Queen [Kapiolani] for three or four days.

*Sunday, July 10.* Iolani Palace. Went to Kawaiahao—Kapu preaches on Nebuchadnezzar—very tedious and left before it was over.[115] 12 P.M. lunched with Eveline—she told me that Capt. Nowlein had said he was sorry he gave those cannons without consulting me[116] but he had only obeyed the orders of Minister Parker. Capt. Nowlein thinks Wilson ought to be Minister that the Cabinet might be strong. Told her [Eveline] it was too late. I preferred he should remain as Marshall until after the Crisis—as surely there will be one in a few days.[117]

Had W. [Wilson] gone home when I wanted him [to]—everything would have been all right, but when I asked him to go home, he said he would resign—[then] the scandal came out about Mollie, now I can't make him Minister. She confessed it was her doing at the request of Miss W. [Wolf?][118]

*Monday, July 11.* Iolani Palace. [Top of page is torn off, deleting date and one line of text] till after she has told Queen Dowager. I sent for Minister Spencer—told him my hopes on regard to Military Bill for $66,000.00, and Police at $125,000.00, also mentioned that if country was poor why send band to Chicago, or why should Hawaii be represented there?[119]

---

114. Exactly whose will she refers to here cannot be determined. She may be referring to Kalakaua's estate, in which case the queen mentioned is Queen Kapiolani.

115. Reverend W. B. Kapu (b. 1833–d. 1896, Honolulu) was the longtime pastor of the Waioli Church in Hanalei, Kauai. Nebuchadnezzar was the king of Babylon, 562 BC.

116. This probably refers to the fact that following the July 1889 insurrection, the cabinet ministers ordered all military arms and equipment to be removed from the palace grounds (including several cannon) and stored at the marshall's office. Nowlein was captain of the King's Own in 1892.

117. The reference to a forthcoming crisis is over Liliu's intent to retain Wilson as marshall of the kingdom, in opposition to the desire of her cabinet to have him removed from office.

118. There is now no record of such a scandal.

119. The 1890 Appropriation Bill granted the King's Own $62,000, and gave an additional $2,500 in aid to volunteer military companies. The 1892 Appropriation Bill allowed the Queen's Own $50,000 and separated the pay of police into several accounts. Salaries for the Oahu police came to $90,000, and salaries of police for the island of Hawaii totaled $38,597.00. The 1890 Appropriation Bill, under the line item "Band, Flags, and Statues," listed $50,000,

Best not to pass that $40,000.00 and he agreed with me. I pointed out to him the subsidies given to the Steamship line[120]—of thousands paid for Immigration by Govt.[121] what part is the Govt. to receive—what indeed?

[I?] Proposed that all properties should be taxed at one percent, of outgoing properties [exports?] which means sugars and other staples—That all lands should be taxed to the fullest extent [and] that these Assessors are not doing exactly the right thing.[122] Last of all [we] must fight against R. W. Wilcox's resolution to Annex Hawaii to U.S.[123]

*Friday, July 15.* Washington Place. Moved up [stairs?] to have a rest and to search for papers belonging to my husband.

*Sunday, July 17.* Washington Place. After breakfast went to Kawaiahao services, then lunched and sorted out D. C. Waterman's papers,[124] finally slept till five.

but did not specify anything for a Chicago trip. However, in the 1892 Appropriation Bill, in the list under "Foreign Affairs," there appeared the sum of $12,000.00 for "Expense of sending the Band to Chicago, and providing literature for distribution at the World's Columbian Exposition." (The Exposition dedication ceremonies were held in October 1892.)

120. Under "Miscellaneous," the 1890 Appropriation Bill included a "Subsidy to Steamer, between Honolulu, Molokai, Lahaina, and Lanai . . . $5,200.00," and under the Finance Department, a "Subsidy to the Oceanic Steamship Company . . . $48,000." The 1892 bill retained only the Inter-Island Steam Navigation Co. subsidy.

121. In the 1890 Appropriation Bill under "Miscellaneous," the sum of $60,000 appeared as "Aid to Immigration." In the 1892 Appropriation Bill, salaries for bureau employees and incidentals totaled $11,700—but the bill listed an additional $10,000 for "encouragement of Immigration."

122. The "Act Relating to Internal Taxes," passed by the 1892 legislature, stated in Section 11: "All real property within this Kingdom and all personal property within this Kingdom, subject to the exemption and exceptions hereinafter set forth . . . shall be subject to an annual tax of one percent upon the value of the same." The same act provided for more-stringent control of tax assessors.

123. Perhaps more as an annoyance to the government than anything else, R. W. Wilcox, on July 9, presented a resolution in the legislature that included the following statement:

"Whereas the United States Government has taken no action toward occupying or improving Pearl Harbor and whereas we believe that the geographical position and natural advantages of Pearl Harbor render it so valuable to any great nation as a coaling and naval station that we may reasonably expect to obtain in exchange for its concessions and privileges as important and beneficial as those we enjoyed for some years under the Reciprocity Treaty . . . and whereas the disastrous financial depression due to our changed standing in the markets of the United States make it imperative that some immediate action be taken to secure relief . . . resolved that a committee of five members of this House be appointed to visit Washington and ascertain the disposition of the United States Government in regard to Pearl Harbor . . . and also to negotiate for the cession of Pearl Harbor for adequate compensation and in general to use their best efforts to obtain closer relations with that country." *Pacific Commercial Advertiser*, July 11, 1892.

Then, at a mass meeting held at the armory on July 12, Wilcox stated: "The purpose of the resolution, if carried, is to find out what America intends to give us in return if we were to cede Puuloa. . . . I say if Puuloa is given to America, that would give us independence forever. . . . If we give away Puuloa to America, we will fear no longer about annexation, for America would then be satisfied. America does not want another inch of our land." *Pacific Commercial Advertiser*, July 13, 1892.

Wilcox's arguments failed to impress his audience, and Representative Joseph K. Nawahi worked hard to nullify the former's arguments.

124. Daniel C. Waterman (b. 1802, New Bedford, Massachusetts), a factoring agent in Honolulu, died at sea on the *Moses Taylor* on June 18, 1871. John O. Dominis was co-executor of Waterman's estate, and the business papers Liliu refers to (largely letters received from

*Saturday, July 23.* Washington Place. Asked Fraulein [Wolf] to come over and help me find those papers I wanted, and [we] went down cellar—could not find it [and] asked her to strain all efforts. She told me she could see a yellow paper written as a confession to his son. In the left corner it read thus "Confession," in the right corner is "May 7, 1837." The letter began—"to my son John Owen. The last word from your father before departing is you must be devoted to your Mother and respect her. Leopold del Galo Dominisi." Here the strain was too great and the medium could see no more. John discovered this paper 28 years ago—latterly he wanted to show it to me and one day we had a quarrel so he made up his mind never to disclose to me who he was, and before he died, hid the paper so I shouldn't find it. [At bottom right corner of page:] Cottage XXX

*Sunday, July 24.* [At bottom right corner of page:] XXX

*Monday, July 25.* [At bottom right corner of page:] XXX

*Tuesday, July 26.* Washington Place. Met the cabinet this morning and they impressed on me the necessity of ~~dismissing~~ accepting Mr. Whiting's resignation, saying that Whiting had said to Minister Spencer "that he would not go into the house again."—so I decided with them to appoint Mr. Widemann, and for Creighton to do the work. 12 p.m. met Mr. Whiting and he returned his portfolio.[125] The place will remain open for a while. [At bottom right corner of page:] XXX

*Wednesday, July 27.* Washington Place. Had conversation with Minister Parker about Attorney General [position] and [we] could not agree—so nothing was done. One p.m. went to Examination with Eveline and Jennie [Clark], stayed till four.[126]

Mrs. Vida was waiting for me to ask if I would do something for her Henry—He had to be sent away from here for getting into all sorts of mischief. Her fond mother's heart must bleed for him.[127]

Mrs. H.A.P. Carter called with Miss Carrol, head nurse of Queen's Hospital. Mr. Knudsen also called,[128] then Mr. Parker came. [At bottom right corner of page:] XXX

---

San Francisco, New Bedford, and Howland Island, ca. 1862–65) are now held in the Bishop Museum Archives, Liliuokalani Collection. The Hawaii State Archives contains an additional collection of Waterman papers.

125. The cabinet minutes for this meeting have not been located. The *Pacific Commercial Advertiser*, July 28, 1892, reported: "It was generally understood yesterday that the Queen had accepted the Attorney General's [Whiting's] resignation, and had temporarily appointed Minister Widemann to fill the position." Charles Creighton (the son of Robert J. Creighton) is listed in the 1892–93 City Directory as "deputy attorney general."

126. The "examination" was part of the closing exercises at Saint Andrew's Priory School. The following day the *Pacific Commercial Advertiser* noted that among the honored guests present were the Queen, Governor Archibald Scott Cleghorn, and Major James Hay Wodehouse.

127. Mrs. Vida was the widow of Daniel Vida (b. 1835, Santiago, Chile–d. 1890, Honolulu), a Honolulu resident since 1850, where his father was a merchant and for many years consul for Chile. Daniel was variously in the cattle and sugar businesses. There is no record detailing Henry's "mischief" or the circumstances of his being "sent away."

128. Valdemar Knudsen (b. 1820, Sweden–d. 1898, Waiawa, Kauai) was resident in Hawaii from 1851 as a rancher and cane grower. He represented Kauai in the legislature in 1862–90.

*Thursday, July 28.* Washington Place—11:15 A.M. After long discussion with Minister Parker, decided to sign for Mr. H. A. Widemann a Commission as Attorney General pro tem. Asked Mr. P. if it was particularly necessary and for what reason—as I thought the whole Cabinet ought to meet when any measures are brought forward—he said I was right. Consulted W. [Wilson?] about Ministry, told me the above course was right, until the right time.

She [Miss Wolf] told me that Mr. E. [Evans] was coming with that paper, that he was going to tell me that Mr. Parker was going to work against it, which was all true. I told E.—to go to Kamauoha, explain it all to him, and ask Marsden to approve the proposition.[129] I had no doubt he would succeed—but to go cautiously.

Sent two Kuina Kapa [bedcovers] up to William Auld. Heard from N. [Nowlein] that when I signed Widemann's Commission, Wilson will be dismissed—told him to tell their party one of the stipulations was that he should not be dismissed—nor should any changes in any department be made. These were special stipulations [I] made before I consented to appoint Widemann.

Medium says, a paper will be brought in on a Monday in fourteen days [or] two weeks or 30 days—Mr. E. [Evans] is coming in [at] 11 or 12 today and will talk about a dark man who is against the H. L. Co. [Hawaiian Lottery Company.]

*Friday, July 29.* Washington Place. [Miss Wolf says] There is a Constitution being framed by three parties—in fact there are three. This one or one of those "will be signed but it will take two years before it goes into effect—And Mr. P.—will go around with a paper or petition for my good. Must not discharge Joe [Marsden?] yet, for he [would] do me some harm."

Received a list from Marshall Wilson of those who are supposed to be in Opium smuggling: H. Macfarlane (not known), C. E. Williams, Lewis Bros., C. Gertz, M. Adler, G. C. Beckley or S. G. Wilder, V. V. Ashford (left the kingdom), W. Larsen (not known), Hyman bros., T. Evans, F. Turrill, J. Good, C. Lucas (not known), Mr. [Albert] Barnes of Wailuku, [A. T.] Hopke, Wailuku, Goo of Wailuku, C. Dwight, S. Dwight, H. de Fries, [W. C.] Peacock (not known), P. [Paul] Neumann (not known), W. Whaley, Camerinos, J. W. Holt, W. Holt. [He] left out Chinese.

*Saturday, July 30.* Washington Place. Revelations of a medium. Met girl with a queue at Mrs. M's[130]—her neighbors told her about a piece of land her husband owned [that] they spent all they had to a native lawyer to try

---

129. Joseph Marsden (b. 1850–d. 1909, Berkeley, California) came to the islands in the 1870s, first living on the island of Hawaii. In 1890–92, he was a noble in the legislature. In 1891, he went on a mission to India and Java on behalf of the Planters' Labor and Supply Co. He was commissioner of agriculture in 1893. He was responsible for the introduction of the mongoose to the islands in an attempt to control rats in the cane fields, an action that earned him the nickname of "Mongoose Joe." In January 1893, the Provisional Government would send him to Washington as one of the commissioners advancing annexation.

130. The August 7, 1892, entry suggests that M.'s surname is most likely Mana.

to recover it. Advised her to send for A. [Arthur] Peterson and she would surely recover her land. How could she have known all the above facts, if she were not gifted with the power of second sight. She was told she was full of love—that there were two large men she loved—one she has most interest for is [blank] has seen her three times though forbidden last week, still thinks of her and she indifferent. She confessed all true but not till she had tried to hide the truth and she had met him three times in nine days. She wanted to know if he would desert her entirely, she said yes when she is in her coffin. There was a lawyer coming to her—it all came to pass.

*Sunday, July 31.* Washington Place. Seven A.M. The Medium told me all she knew or had to [blank] to tell me. It was all true. But she told of a ring for me and they were startled—will it ever be? It remains to be seen.

Instead of going to Church went to Waikiki to rest, bathed in the Sea, and had a nap. Woke up and waited for [blank] to make confessions but none came for he was loath to confess. They say confession is good for the soul.

*Monday, August 1.* Washington Place. 11 A.M. Went in Onipaa [here Liliu means her carriage] to Kealohilani [at Waikiki]—had a nap till lunch was ready at two. Two princes were there, Eveline and Jenny, Iaukea and the Members of the Hui Hololio Liliuokalani [Liliuokalani Riding Society], P. P. Kanoa and wife, and others. Stayed till five P.M., [then] drove home. Received copy of a Constitution from Mr. [blank]—was not pleased with it—but there are many being framed in town. Retired at nine—expected to hear confessions today but none was made.

*Tuesday, August 2.* Washington Place. Had Cabinet meeting in regard to the dismissal of the Police on the recommendation of Committee in Ways and Means, and acted upon by H. A. Widemann Attorney General Ad Interim. I said no dismissal ought to take place until the recommendation becomes a law—and there it stands until Thursday.

10:30 A.M. went to Muolaulani—Met. J. N., S. N.—W. W. [Joseph Nawahi, Sam Nowlein, William White] and set to work on important measures.[131] Worked until two P.M. Had lunch with Eveline [Wilson], then took a nap while the gentlemen went to the L [legislature]. 4:30 P.M. Met again and discussed on the questions of the morning—our work is completed and only waits for the Proroguing of the Legislature. Five P.M. they went home and Kitty [Eveline Wilson] and I came home—Milaina was there with me. Paid Miss Davis $170.00 for household expenses. Was told another constitution was being framed.

---

131. "Important measures" is an oblique reference to the formation of the new constitution, which Liliu would attempt to enact in January 1893. Joseph K. Nawahi (b. 1854, Hilo–d. September 14, 1896, San Francisco) was a politician, lawyer, and newspaper editor. He was a longtime legislator (House of Representatives, 1872–92), popular with his constituents, and he served very briefly as minister of foreign affairs (November 1–8, 1892). His wife, Emma Aima Nawahi (b. 1849–d. December 28, 1935, Hilo), continued as the editor of *Ke Aloha Aina* (1896–99) following her husband's death. She was a friend of Liliu, and the Hawaii State Archives, Liliuokalani Collection, contains a large file of her letters, written to the ex-Queen during the 1896–98 period.

*Wednesday, August 3.* Iolani Palace. Spent all day with my societies—Liliuokalani Hui Hoonaauao M. 2 [Mokuna, Division 2] from ten till 11—the Hui Hololio [Riding Society] till 12—the Hui Hookuonoono Kawaluonalani[132] from one till three, bought $23.00 worth of tickets for concert. Told Piehu [Iaukea] I would pay for the first year's rent of his lot at the beach bought of Queen Dowager. He has already paid $77.50 each for our lots.[133]

The Medium again—Why does she tell me these things.

*Friday, August 5.* Washington Place. Strange revealings of a Medium. Miss W. [Wolf says] That Captain Dominis's rank was more than that of a Marquis on the Mother's side. She might have been the daughter of a Duke or Duchess and were a very rich family. Capt. Dominisi was the second son. A quarrel sprung up between him and his elder brother, which made him throw up his right to the property and leave the country. The younger brother watched the quarrel with a glad heart because he knew that he would come next to all that property. After a space of some years the eldest brother died and two years after the eldest brother's death, the youngest brother confessed on his dying bed and made a bequest that they should search for his brother (Capt. D.) willing all the property to him—but as the search was in vain, the papers were returned to a Registry of government building or big building burnt, the house was burnt as were also the papers. This youngest brother left a wife and two sons and one daughter. As no one claimed that immense property, the wife and children made their claims and held possession of it. The sons spent a good deal of the property in horse races and gambling which disheartened their sister and compelled her to enter a Catholic nunnery of Convent and took the veil. These children are cousins to John O. Dominisi. The eldest son of Capt. D.'s younger brother is yet alive, and is the one who holds the property. His sister [the entry continues on the page for Saturday, August 6] who took the veil became an Abbess and her name was Sister Sophie or Soprita de Sdlg-Abbtisin [sic]. He has no idea of relinquishing any of the property. I will receive three letters from Europe but none of any importance, but the fourth will finally reveal his relationship and their rank to My John or rather what Capt. Dominisi was.[134]

*Sunday, August 7.* Washington Place. The M [Medium, Miss Wolf] was invited by the girl with a queue to go up to Pauoa with Helene to a luau—her niece's husband Mr. Mana will come for her in a brake at noon. The occasion was the [illegible] birthday of Mrs. Spencer, sister in law of J. S.[135]

---

132. The term "Kawaluonalani" refers to Liliu as the eighth sovereign. "Hookuonoono" means "to prosper." Nothing is now known of this hui, or society.

133. No record of this land transaction has been located in the Bureau of Conveyances.

134. This long account on the ancestry of the Dominis family is derived from the imagination of Liliu's medium, Miss Wolf, whose revelations on John Dominis and his family cannot be believed or taken seriously. For a more plausible account, see a paper by Dr. Ante Kovacevic, "On the Descent of John Dominis," *Hawaiian Journal of History* vol. 10 (1976): 3–24.

135. J. S. is probably John Manukanikaoneanea Spencer (b. 1858–d. 1926) of Palama, the half-brother of Samuel K. Pua and onetime sheriff of Hawaii Island. Mana is John Mana, who in 1882 married Hattie Kanoa of Kaneohe. The Manas were close friends of Liliuokalani. Helene has not been identified.

Mr. E. and others were there. Queue [girl] told her she was going to Manoa to stay, her husband was already there—will stay two weeks. We went to Waikiki with Eveline, Mr. and Mrs. Iaukea, Jennie Clark and children, Piehu Liilii, and Lorna.[136]

*Monday, August 8.* Washington Place. Carrie Bush came to see me about McWayne and Smith[137] and I consented.

*Tuesday, August 9.* Washington Place. I keia ahiahi i oki poepoe ia ai o Kaipo—Inoino maoli ka Kauka McWayne oki ana. Ua huki kana i ka foreskin a loihi a laila oki pahupu [a l]aila humuhumu hou—Me ka upa ka hana ana o laua o Geo. [George] Smith. [Washington Place, this evening Kaipo was circumcised. Dr. McWayne did a truly horrible job of cutting. He pulled the foreskin until it was extended, then completely severed it, then stitched it. He and Geo. Smith did it with scissors.]

*Wednesday, August 10.* Washington Place. *Australia* arrived and brought Mr. C. R. Bishop—also a letter was received from Mr. Von Schonberger acknowledging the receipt of Mr. Robertson's letter in regard to Capt. Dominisi. He has sent enquiries to the registry office and will send word again.

*Thursday, August 11.* Washington Place. Will have to tell Ka inside of ten days and after that will try a chance to catch her—Must not strike them but tell him if he will do right by him, [?] he will fully do him justice. It seems she will catch so he must try first.

*Saturday, August 13.* Washington Place. Queue girl came to the Medium, told [sic] had come in to have a good time. Mr. and Mrs. Mana called on her. She told him she was without work but not to be desperate—by and by will be brighter days. Queue girl stayed to take care of children. Would go back Monday. The Hui Noeau sang *The Crusader* at Kawaiahao. Miss Nolte sang unusually well, and so did Leihulu. The latter sprained her ankle so had to sit down while singing her solo. The whole went off very well considering it is a very difficult music, and it is to be wonder'd at that the Hawaiians could sing such music—this is their first conquest.[138]

*Monday, August 15.* Washington Place. Gave a breakfast to Mr. and Mrs. Spreckels, Hon. C. R. Bishop, Mr. and Mrs. Parker, Mr. and Mrs. Allen. Mr. and Mrs. [William G.] Irwin, Mr. and Mrs. Damon, Gov. Cleghorn, Hon. W. [William] H. Cornwell, Robertson, and myself.

---

136. The two latter were Curtis Iaukea's son and daughter.

137. Albert McWayne (b. 1856, Geneva, Illinois–d. November 18, 1899, Honolulu), a physician at 34 Alakea Street, was the husband of Lucy Robinson, the daughter of Honolulu merchant James Robinson. George W. Smith was a druggist in the firm of Benson and Smith, 113 Fort Street.

138. According to an advertisement in the *Pacific Commercial Advertiser*, August 13, 1892: "The Hui Mele Hawaii Noeau will repeat the concert of the 'Crusader' at Kawaiahao Church... on Saturday Evening, August 13, [1892,] at eight o'clock." Like the first concert held on July 30, this was to benefit Kawaiahao Church. "The cantata will be given in Hawaiian under the management of Mrs. Haalelea, with appropriate Tableaux, Costuming, etc. Solos by the well-known Amateurs Miss F. Nolte, Mrs. Leihulu Keohokalole, Mr. Robert Kapua, assisted by an efficient chorus orchestra under the direction of Prof. H. Berger with the help of D. K. Naone and D. L. Naone."

[Medium says] 15 days from today or 15th of next month, the danger of losing [?] success will be over—six days after will have my success.

*Tuesday, August 16.* Washington Place. Medium [says] Inside five or six months, [I] will have a present of $150,000 or $50,000—and every year after signing of the paper and as long as their lease lasts, will receive 10 or $15,000 for pocket money from the head of the H. L. Co. [Hawaiian Lottery Company.] F.H.H. is coming across the waters about the Cabinet but not to listen to him—I believe her predictions for all she has told me has proved true. She says Widemann will leave.

12 [P.]M—will give a reception to Admiral Parrayon of the Flagship *Dubordieu*.[139]

Heard from Milaina that K__ was searching for her husband.

Mr. and Mrs. Spreckels called. I thought he had something important to say—but all he did say was how much money he had made—that he made the [Sugar] Trust come to his terms, that [with] others in S.F. he put his foot on the [Sugar] Refiner's neck and meant to keep it there, and he had also his foot on the necks of the people here and meant to keep it there. We'll see about that.

Mrs. P. Lewis, her daughter and daughter-in-law called.

Mr. A. P. Peterson called to say that if he knew that after the Ministers being put out he may come in again, he may be one again, he would give his consent but not otherwise. I gave him my assurance I would appoint him again, so he consented to take the Attorney Generalship.[140]

*Wednesday, August 17.* Washington Place. Mr. Parker came in, our conversation was upon increase of revenue. He said Claus Spreckels had offered $800,000.00 to the Government and proposed to close up the Postal Savings Bank.[141] I did not agree with him and said if we could possibly do without borrowing from either banks to do so, and he coincided with my views. I also told him that I did not think the depositors would draw their money out, but they only said it to scare the government. We are to consult this afternoon about taxes on property in case monies are drawn from the Postal Savings Bank, and to authorize Minister of Finance to levy taxes at ½ per cent on all properties above $5,000.00. And also to tax all properties that leave the country at ½ or 1%.

My medium told me yesterday I would hear more about the lottery

---

139. This was an official audience at the palace in honor of Rear Admiral E. M. Parrayon, commander in chief of the French navy in the Pacific. Captain K. Besson was the captain of the FFS *Dubordieu*. The *Evening Bulletin* reported that the Queen was attended by Prince Kawananakoa, the Honorable A. S. Cleghorn, and other government officials, and that her ladies of the court were Mrs. Parker, Mrs. Spencer, Mrs. Widemann, Mrs. Bickerton, Mrs. Wilson, and Mrs. Clark.

140. Arthur P. Peterson served as attorney general June 17, 1890–February 25, 1891. He would not be reappointed to the office until January 12, 1893.

141. The Postal Savings Bank, established under a Hawaiian statute of 1884, opened July 1, 1886. The bank paid depositors interest at the rate of 4½ percent "on deposits of $5.00 and multiples thereof" and advertised in the 1892 City Directory that "Married women, and also minors over 7 years of age, may deposit in their own name, [and] Depositors are secured by government bonds held in trust by the postmaster general." It remained in operation until after annexation in 1898.

[and] that Mr. E. [T. E. Evans] is coming soon to tell me of a W.H.C.—who is he? I told her it was W. H. Cornwell.[142] Sure enough, E. [Evans] says C. [Cornwell] was opposed to him [and] that he should be head of the [lottery] enterprise here. It all came true. [Medium says I] Will get sad news across the waters in six months.

Mr. and Mrs. Spreckels left in *Australia*—we are all glad that he is gone, but [he] will be back in January. Sent my music by mail all corrected.[143]

*Thursday, August 18.* Washington Place—Did not see any of the Ministers.

*Friday, August 19.* Washington Place. After breakfast drove down to Palama—found the carpenters still at work at Muolaulani. Went to Waikiki. Joe's house is almost finished—went on to Mrs. [Caroline] Bush's and found Kaipo not quite cured. Hasten'd home on account of Ball this evening at the Palace. Rested all the afternoon.

*Saturday, August 20.* Washington Place. Gave a grand ball to Admiral Parrayon of the French flagship *Dubordieu*, Admiral Brown and son and officers were all present—all the officers were present.[144] So much has been said about Mr. Whaley and his being a smuggler[145] that I was loath to invite him, but I have since heard that so many of our supposed respectable residents are also involved in smuggling that I felt if I invited them, I might as well invite him against public opinion—Am I right? *Bin ich recht*? Slept at the Palace. Hastened home because I wanted the Medium to read Kahae's cards.

142. William H. Cornwell (b. 1842, Brooklyn, New York–d. November 18, 1903, Waikapu, Maui) was a financier, a poker-playing friend of King Kalakaua, and the proprietor of the Waikapu Sugar Plantation. He served in the House of Nobles 1890–92, was a major on the Queen's staff, and was twice minister of finance between November 1, 1892, and January 17, 1893. He married Blanche Macfarlane in 1870. He appears in the 1887 political pamphlet titled "The Gynberg Ballads" under the pseudonym "de Horsey Cornbin" in the Hawaii State Archives, Kahn Collection. The pamphlet is an illustrated satirical piece presenting a barely disguised summary of politics in and around Kalakaua's court.

143. This was most likely a collection of the Queen's compositions, sent off for publication in San Francisco by Roesch & Co. A bound collection of 11 songs, including "Aloha Oe," "Hooheno," and "The Queen's Jubilee," with a presentation inscription from the Queen to Colonel Curtis P. Iaukea, Iolani Palace, October 24, 1892, is in the Hawaii State Archives, Kahn Collection.

144. "Yesterday evening Iolani Palace was one brilliant blaze of light, the occasion being a grand ball given by Her Majesty Queen Liliuokalani in honor [of] Rear Admiral E. M. Parrayon and Captain F. Besson and officers of the French Flagship *Dubordieu*, now visiting this port. The interior of the handsome building was decorated and illuminated with wonderful effect. The Throne Room with its handsome furniture, crystal electric light chandeliers, and floral decorations presented a most charming and attractive appearance.... Shortly after 8:30 o'clock... Her Majesty received Admiral Brown and officers of the *San Francisco*, and then the other invited guests.... Dancing commenced shortly after nine o'clock." *Pacific Commercial Advertiser*, August 20, 1892.

145. William A. Whaley, owner of the yacht *Halcyon*, had been the subject of considerable interest to Honolulu customs house authorities. An article on the occasion of that vessel having just left Port Townsend, Washington, for the Pacific, identified the *Halcyon* as the "famous smuggling schooner," and said she then had on board 2,590 pounds of opium and 60 Chinese. *Pacific Commercial Advertiser*, September 9, 1892. In 1895, Whaley, George Lycurgus, and D. G. Camarainos were involved in an opium-smuggling operation, whereby the *Halcyon* brought opium from China and landed it on Lanai, while Whaley came to Honolulu on a steamer. For a long account of Whaley and his yacht, see the *Pacific Commercial Advertiser*, January 4, 1927.

*Sunday, August 21.* Washington Place. Six P.M. Just returned from Mr. Parkers at Herberts', Waikiki.[146]

Astonished Mr. Parker by telling him that I had appointed Mr. A. P. Peterson my Attorney General.[147] He said he would tell his colleagues about it. I came home—Mr. P. called on Mr. Widemann and sent for Minister Spencer. After conference they concluded to send and ask Mr. P. Neumann if he would accept being Attorney General. He said he would.[148]

*Monday, August 22.* Washington Place. While at breakfast Mr. Neumann called. I asked him to walk in and have a cup of coffee—he declined but said he wanted to see Mr. Wilson, so thinking it was something about the police, Mr. W. went out. He soon found out that the Ministers had asked him (Neumann) to be A.G. but I said to Mr. W. [Wilson]—I had already appointed Mr. Peterson. Mr. N. [Neumann] was so annoyed that he went downtown and told Mr. P. [Peterson] that he was not wanted by the Ministers and he knew that the Queen did not want him—[and asked?] if Mr. Peterson wouldn't join him in getting up a vote of want of confidence and he agreed. Tonight there is to be a meeting to that effect—but the subject of the meeting will be Horner's bill.[149]

Nine P.M. Went out in an express with Eveline and Capt. Nowlein—Manuel Reis as driver[150]—to see Mr. Sam Parker at the park—told him about the meeting. He said he had no fears—he was confident they [the Cabinet] would not be put out.

---

146. Allen Herbert's beachfront property at Kapiolani Park, Waikiki, had a main house and three cottages adapted for family use, which he let out. In September 1892, it became an annex of the Royal Hawaiian Hotel in Honolulu. It then continued as the Hotel Park Annex, advertising that "the main building will be reserved for the guests of the Hotel, but it may be rented for Picnics, Bathing Parties, Dinners, and Dances."

147. Arthur P. Peterson was attorney general under King Kalakaua June 12, 1890–February 25, 1891. Although the proposed August 1892 appointment did not happen, he would hold the office January 12–17, 1893. Peterson was later held in confinement for complicity in the counterrevolution of 1895, and on February 13, 1895, he agreed to leave the country to avoid prosecution and not to return, and he sailed for San Francisco on or about the last of February.

148. Under King Kalakaua, Paul Neumann had been attorney general (December 14, 1883–June 30, 1886), and under Liliuokalani, he would again hold that office (August 29–30, 1892, and September 12–October 17, 1892).

149. "The banking bill, titled 'The Hawaiian Bank Act,' was introduced on June 24 [1892] by John M. Horner, noble from the island of Hawaii, and was referred to a special committee. It called for the establishment, in the post office at Honolulu, of a bureau to be known as the 'Bank of Hawaii' authorized to circulate money 'made of gold, silver, or paper, or of either or all of them.' It was in fact a fiat money proposition, and was dubbed 'the rag money bill' by one of the Honolulu newspapers, which said it was 'fraught with the most disastrous consequences to the poor first and then to the capitalists.'" *Daily Bulletin*, August 19, 1892. "On August 22, after three days' debate, a motion to indefinitely postpone the bill was defeated, mainly by votes of native Hawaiians, and it was referred to a new committee. Three of the ministers voted with the majority in favor of the bill and this fact may have contributed to the downfall of the cabinet eight days later." Ralph S. Kuykendall, *The Hawaiian Kingdom*, vol. 3, 1874–93 (Honolulu: University of Hawaii Press, 1967), 543. When the bill came up for action in August, the *Pacific Commercial Advertiser*, August 23, 1892, termed the bill "the Horner monstrosity."

150. Manuel Gildos Reis (b. 1850, Oporto, Portugal–d. 1939, Honolulu) married Eugenia Maluhi Keohookalani (b. 1865, Hulihee, Kona–d. April 19, 1942, Honolulu) of a chiefly Kona family.

*Tuesday, August 23.* Iolani Palace. Had a stormy discussion with Minister [Parker?] about the situation. He said if I persisted in having Peterson in the Cabinet, [H. P.] Baldwin and the Reform party will not loan us money. I said I was not afraid, I had Mr. Spreckels' assurance and Mr. Damon's, that we could have money whenever the Government needed it.

---

Although the Queen records nothing in her diary about an August 23 excursion "with lady friends" to the Pearl Harbor area, the *Advertiser* does take note of this interesting event:

> ¶ Yesterday morning when the 5:45 train pulled out of the depot for Ewa, one coach contained Her Majesty the Queen and her suite with a number of lady friends, who were the guests of Mrs. Dr. McGrew, and all were bound for the McGrew's seaside home to spend the day.
>
> It is almost three years since Her Majesty, who was then the Princess Liliuokalani, paid a similar visit, and at that time she observed an old Hawaiian custom—that of planting a tree or shrub of some kind. It was a ginger plant, and yesterday leis and wreaths were made from the very same flower and presented to Her Majesty.
>
> The entire party spent a pleasant day, which was enlivened at intervals by songs and music rendered by some bright native girls, protégés of Her Majesty, and returned to town by the five o'clock train.
>
> Mrs. McGrew proved to be a most charming hostess, as ever, and her guests were Her Majesty the Queen and suite, Mrs. H. W. Severance, Mrs. Samuel Parker, Mrs. Parke, Mrs. Haalelea, Mrs. S. Allen, the Misses Waterhouse, Mrs. J. S. Walker, and Mrs. J. O. Carter.[151]

---

*Wednesday, August 24.* Iolani Palace. [Medium says] 12 days from today everything will be all right.

I am set on having Mr. P. [Peterson] for Attorney General but the Cabinet do not seem to like [it] on account of Mrs. P.[152]

*Thursday, August 25.* Iolani Palace. Had conversation with Minister [of the Interior] Spencer on account of financial state of the country. He tells me that something is being done in the House about it, but I fear not in a way to my satisfaction or what is right and *just*. [Illegible word, then "One" with "w" possibly meaning Wolf written over it] tells me that queue girl is still there in the valley—and that Mrs. M. [Mana] is going to stay with her. Will she stay as his [?] Ohua [servant], I wonder? Heard that H. will not live long.

*Friday, August 26.* Iolani Palace—let Miss W. [Wolf] know my intention in regard to K.—since her stay up there [sic] she must see him at five P.M. Made arrangements also about going to her house, or rather about furniture for the new house. I had conversation again with Mr. Parker about

---

151. *Pacific Commercial Advertiser*, August 24, 1892.
152. This reference to Mrs. Peterson is nowhere explained.

[appointment of the] Attorney General. Told him my mind had not changed—he said that I must suffer the consequences, for we could not [get] any loan from either banks. I said we must make a trial.

Received at three P.M. Sir George Dibbs, Premier of New South Wales, and Lord Villiers, son of Governor Villiers of Australia.[153]

Received my new dress by the *Mariposa*—will it be my wedding dress? Everything complete—parasol, fan, shoes, stockings—also a picture of Lord Gough.[154]

*Saturday, August 27.* Washington Place. Mr. Parker and Mr. [C. N.] Spencer both came in regard to Peterson for Attorney General. They could not be in accord with him, and they left me unchanged in my opinion, for I felt that Mr. Peterson would do what is right—but unfortunately he has no one to back him while Neumann has Spreckels & Co., and Bishop & Co. It is so cruel to have them come with their business to me on this day when I want my own thoughts to myself—as it is the Anniversary of my husband's death—but to bring state affairs before me and of such complicated nature.

10.30 A.M. Took our flowers and emblems up to decorate his [J. O. Dominis's] casket, remained two hours and came home.

Four P.M. Was told there was bicycle race.[155] Went to drive to Park and saw Kaipo and Aimoku. On my way home saw Jim on cars—Frau [Fraulein Wolf]—came in distress and said he had not been to her—[She] Knew he thought everything would be disclosed and it was—he was told of it and went home huhu [angry], nothing brought success. In regard to Cabinet [she says?] everything was dark, had better wait till Monday morning. He had seen her three times that week—Mr. E. [Evans] will call at 10:30 tomorrow [with] what he proposes to accept. He will say that I should say to them, [that] I would not nominate Mr. N. [Neumann] until you all vote for this H. L. [Hawaiian Lottery] Bill and they will promise too. Jim got angry and started to go home—I called—he did not come back, perhaps he did not hear.

*Sunday, August 28.* Washington Place. Did not feel well enough to go to Church so stayed at home. 10:30 A.M. Mr. E. [Evans] did call as she said, and he did suggest all that she predicted he would. He had been working very hard. Told him to come in tomorrow morning.

Four P.M. Drove up to Manoa, stayed at [blank] till near six, drove up to the end of the valley, and met Mr. and Mrs. Iaukea with a large party of ladies and gentlemen going home. Soon after came home. Fraulein [Wolf] says he will soon come home and in ten days everything will be all right as before—as he will insist on her going home.

153. Both men were on board the *Mariposa* bound from San Francisco to Australia and made a brief stop in Honolulu. The reception would have been of an unofficial nature.

154. Sir Hugh Gough (b. 1779–d. 1869) was an English field marshall, said by the *Dictionary of National Biography* "to have commanded more general actions than any British officer of the century, the Duke of Wellington excepted." There is no record of who sent the picture to Liliu, his or her reason for doing so, or the present whereabouts of the same.

155. The bicycle race was announced in the *Pacific Commercial Advertiser*, August 27, 1892, "to take place this afternoon at 3:30 o'clock over the King Street course."

Mrs. C. A. Brown so kindly sent me a bouquet for John's casket—but Wilikoki [Wilcox] is down town and will not be able to send it.

*Monday, August 29.* Washington Place. Ten A.M. Mr. Parker and Mr. Spencer both came in. I told them I would only accept Mr. Neumann as Attorney General on certain conditions—and they consented. The H. L. [Hawaiian Lottery] Bill will be brought in by Mr. W. White.[156]

Mr. E. [Evans] came in all worn out. I told him not to trouble himself anymore, that it will end right. 11:30 A.M. Had audience of Capt. Wiltse and officers of the USS *Boston*—nice set of men.[157]

One P.M. went to Wm. Auld's 50th birthday.[158] After the luau there was a hula, but I felt no interest in it. Capt. Wiltse and I were engaged in conversation, and at four P.M. had to hasten home to my duties—listened to the band [at Emma Square] a while and came home.

*Tuesday, August 30.* Iolani Palace. Drove after breakfast back to Palace. Heard S. K. Pua[159] brought in a resolution to have Marshall Wilson dismissed from office.[160] Attorney General Neumann said to table it, which caused a commotion. W. C. Wilder immediately brought in a vote of want of Confidence. It took up the whole afternoon and this night—and ended in a dismissal of the Ministry.[161] She [Miss Wolf] met him and told [him]

---

156. William White (b. 1859, Lahaina–d. 1925, Honolulu) was a part-Hawaiian descendant of early Maui settler John White. He was in the legislature as a representative from Lahaina (1890–92), and was the prime mover in pushing the lottery bill through during the final days of the 1892–93 session. White was also a highly visible political agitator in the days immediately prior to the January 17, 1893, overthrow.

157. Captain Gilbert C. Wiltse (b. 1838, New York–d. April 26, 1893, New York) of the U.S. cruiser *Boston* arrived at Honolulu on August 24, 1892, and anchored in Naval Row. It was Wiltse who made the fateful decision on January 17, 1893, to land American troops from the *Boston*, along with revolving cannon, two Gatling guns and ammunition, a company of artillery, two companies of blue jackets, and one company of heavily armed marines. One of the officers was Lieutenant Lucien Young, who would later write *The Boston at Hawaii* (Washington, DC: Gibson Bros., 1898).

158. "William Auld, the keeper of the Insane Asylum, was 50 years of age yesterday, and the event was celebrated by a grand luau given on the grounds at the Asylum. Her Majesty was present, as were a number of prominent officials and citizens." *Pacific Commercial Advertiser*, August 30, 1892.

159. Samuel K. Pua (b. Oct. 27, 1867–d. August 6, 1932), the son of David and Mary Nahakuelua Pua, was a legislator, House of Representatives, in 1892, and eventually became sheriff of Hawaii County.

160. Pua's resolution stated: "Whereas the present Marshall of the Kingdom, C. B. Wilson, has allowed gambling, opium dealing, and other forms of law-breaking to flourish unchecked, and the Police Department under his administration has shown much more disposition to affiliate with criminals than to enforce the laws of this Kingdom, notwithstanding the large sum of money squandered for detectives; and whereas the answers given by him to various questions propounded to the late Attorney General by members of this Legislature have been vague, evasive, and wholly unsatisfactory; and whereas the Marshall is commonly reported to exercise a pernicious illegitimate and occult influence at the Court of Her Majesty the Queen, which tends to bring Her Majesty's Government into contempt and disrepute. Now. Therefore, be it Resolved that it is the sentiment of this Legislature that the said C. B. Wilson is utterly unfit to occupy any position of profit or trust under this Government, and that Her Majesty's ministers are hereby requested to remove him immediately from the office of Marshall of the Kingdom." *Pacific Commercial Advertiser*, August 31, 1892.

161. On the afternoon of August 30, Representative W. C. Wilder introduced a resolution

everything about queue girl and how much his friend thought of him by fitting every measures [sic] for these things and he promised to do right by her. She won her wager. Here in the Palace was woken up at 11 and told that I had no Ministers.

[Although Liliuokalani had been greatly in support of the proposed lottery bill, curiously, on August 30, when the legislature reintroduced that long-dormant bill, so frequently mentioned in her diary, the Queen made no note of that action.]

*Wednesday, August 31.* Iolani Palace. J. Kauhi, J. Kaunamano,[162] Nahinu[163] called, and asked to nominate Parker [as minister of finance][164] over again and if not, to nominate anyone from the House. Will think the matter over. The Cabinet resigned this morning. Asked them to retain their portfolios until I formed a Cabinet. 12 P.M. Received Major Wodehouse and he presented his credentials from the Queen [Victoria] appointing him Minister Resident.[165]

D. W. Pua came at 11 A.M. Hoped I would retain Minister Parker. One P.M., A. P. Peterson called [and] after explaining the situation, I asked about appointing a new Cabinet. He proposed [Dr. Georges] Trousseau, Finance, Gulick, Interior,[166] [John] Ena, F. A. [foreign affairs], [Paul] Neumann [attorney general], a cabinet that would be favorable to the H. L.

---

of want of confidence, charging the cabinet with "lack of ability to cope with the economic crises or to carry out the laws for the development and advancement of the country." Kuykendall, 551. The resolution was taken up, and at the conclusion of the debate, the measure was adopted by a vote of 31 to 10, and the ministers then promptly resigned. Kuykendall, 552, provides an interesting analysis of that vote.

The *Pacific Commercial Advertiser*, August 31, 1892, editorialized: "The Cabinet were removed primarily because they were weak and vacillating at a time when weakness and vacillating meant ruin. They were afraid to have principles and afraid to stand by any which they may have had. The House has done right in removing them, and the only criticism . . . is that it was not taken two months ago."

162. J. H. Kaunamano (b. ca. 1830–d. May 3, 1902, Honolulu) of Hamakua, Hawaii, was a road supervisor, coroner and tax assessor, legislator in the House of Representatives (1864–92), and member of the Privy Council (1884–91). He was a close ally of King Kalakaua, and was the king's secret informant on Robert Wilcox's real motives for the 1889 rebellion.

163. D. H. Nahinu (b. 1828, Hookena, Kona–d. September 13, 1893, Hookena) was a Lahainaluna graduate, district judge schoolteacher, postmaster and tax assessor, and deputy sheriff for South Kona. He served in the legislature, House of Representatives (1864–86), and as a member of the Privy Council (1886–91).

164. Parker would be reappointed to the position on October 17, 1892.

165. "The promotion of Major James Hay Wodehouse to the rank of Minister Resident [from that of British commissioner] is a well-merited appreciation by Queen Victoria and her Government of his long service as British representative in Honolulu where he had resided continuously for more than a quarter of a century. . . and during his long service he has not only enjoyed the fullest confidence of his own sovereign but also of the four Hawaiian sovereigns to whom he has been accredited. . . . If any official ever deserved a generous pension from his Government, it is Major Wodehouse." *Pacific Commercial Advertiser*, September 3, 1892.

166. Charles T. Gulick (b. 1841–d. November 7, 1897, Honolulu) arrived at the islands in 1850. He was from boyhood a friend of Kalakaua, and served as his minister of the interior in 1883, and minister of finance (acting) in 1886. He strongly supported Liliuokalani during her reign, and after the overthrow he was involved in politics leading up to the counterrevolution of 1895. He married Mrs. Sarepta Thompson, also an ardent royalist and a friend of Liliuokalani, in 1876.

[Hawaiian Lottery] Bill. Kamauoha, Pua, and Koahou came in to say they wanted Hawaiians in Cabinet—made no promises.

Five P.M. Gov. Rice[167] called saying he was sent by certain parties to say they did not want Mr. Parker or Mr. Neumann returned in the coming Cabinet—said I would think it over. [He also said] that Parker showed race feeling and Neumann for tabling resolution and also that N. had offered to pay $30,000—(not true) to Marsden if he brought in the H. L. [Hawaiian Lottery] Bill. M. [Marsden] declined. Rice also asked if I would receive the Committee appointed to form a Cabinet. I said at ten tomorrow.[168]

Strange the Fraulein would say Marshall W. [Wilson] must resign and [in] 10 weeks [he] would get a better appointment in the lottery business. Mehrtens will be Marshall. Queue wants to see Fraulein [Wolf] and ask if she could see Jim. F. [Fraulein] wants to discourage her. Will know tomorrow.

[There are no further entries in this diary.]

## September to December 1892: A Summary of Events

September 2 was the Queen's birthday. The government offices were closed and the day was celebrated with a regatta in the harbor, a yacht at Pearl Harbor, and a luau at the palace. In the morning between six and eight A.M. at the palace, the Queen received hookupu (tribute or ceremonial offering) from her subjects. At 11 there was an official reception of officers and diplomatic representatives, and a grand luau took place in the afternoon in a pavilion on the grounds. At the regatta in the harbor, a crew of "Native Boat Boys" defeated a crew from the USS *Boston* in a series of boat races. These festivities concluded, the tangle of island politics resumed its fractious course. In his history of Hawaii, R. S. Kuykendall says: "The feature of the 1892 Legislative session that gave it a unique character was the long and bitter struggle for control of the cabinet.... During the session, seven resolutions of want of confidence were introduced; four of them [were] adopted, forcing the resignation of four cabinets.... A factor of great important influence was the circumstance that no one of the three parties (Reform, National Reform, Liberal) had a majority of the Legislature."[169]

The cabinet in place when the 1892 legislative session commenced (May 28, 1892) was largely that which the Queen had appointed in Feb-

---

167. William Hyde Rice, governor of Kauai, had been in the 1890 legislature but was not a member of the 1892 session.

168. There is no record of the proceedings of this meeting. The *Pacific Commercial Advertiser*, September 1, 1892, noted that the town topics were both the ousted cabinet and "figuring who were to be the new advisors of the Queen.... In the afternoon at the request of Her Majesty, the Privy Council met at the Palace, but nothing is known of their deliberations. Street talk had it that the Honorables W. C. Wilder, S. M. Damon, and J. Ena had been sent for by Her Majesty during the day regarding the formation of the new ministerial body.

"The Queen has requested the officials to remain in office until their successors are appointed, which event is not likely to occur until next Monday."

169. Kuykendall, 548–49.

ruary 1891 soon after she became monarch. On August 30, 1892, the legislature voted that cabinet out of office, and on September 12, the Queen appointed a new government composed of Edward C. Macfarlane, minister of finance; Samuel Parker, minister of foreign affairs; Charles T. Gulick, minister of the interior, and Paul Neumann, attorney general. Before the new cabinet even assumed power, the *Pacific Commercial Advertiser* commented: "The position assumed by the advisors of the Queen is like that of despotic Russia and Turkey, maintaining the exploded doctrines of former centuries."[170] The *Advertiser*'s comments appear to have been not directed at the monarch but at the backstage machinations of Macfarlane and Charles B. Wilson, the latter a principal advisor to Her Majesty, and a man whose influence many on the community feared. Cleghorn, in his letter to Kaiulani on September 13, 1892, on the matter of the new cabinet, observed: "You will see Parker and Neumann are from the old cabinet. The House adjourned yesterday morning till tomorrow at ten o'clock and I hear they are going to remove the new Cabinet as they do not want any of the old one.... I think your Aunt [Liliuokalani] should have selected better men."[171] While removal did not immediately occur, this cabinet managed to survive only one month.

On Saturday afternoon, October 15, 1892, Liliu gave a luau at Palama in honor of Kaiulani's birthday, but the flattering press reportage that usually publicized such occasions was absent.

On October 17, the legislature ousted the cabinet by a want of confidence resolution (the vote being 31 to 15). The following morning the editor of the *Pacific Commercial Advertiser* commented, "A Big Majority Cuts off their Official Heads," and government operations again ceased, awaiting the formation of still another cabinet or government. But public attention was temporarily diverted from that dissolution when Robert Wilcox became the subject of an attempted assassination. The affair took place at dusk on October 17 at King and Alakea Streets, directly in front of the office of Wilcox's newspaper *The Liberal*, when politician James W. Gibbs, a member of the Mechanics Union, accosted Wilcox. The *Advertiser* reported that Gibbs had "applied a vile epithet" to Wilcox, and then brandished a gun. Wilcox "grappled with Gibbs," who fired his pistol—but the shot missed its intended target. Liquor was involved. The *Advertiser* called the matter "an exciting time on King Street."[172]

The great community preoccupation was watching actions of the legislature—specifically the progress of two pieces of legislation, the opium bill and the lottery bill. The smuggling of opium into port had become a major concern, and the opium bill was an attempt to control the business by means of licensing its sale. The lottery bill, which the Queen's supporters had introduced, was of more serious public interest. Backed by a gambling syndicate from abroad, it faced widespread opposition by

170. *Pacific Commercial Advertiser*, September 12, 1892.
171. Hawaii State Archives, Cleghorn Collection.
172. *Pacific Commercial Advertiser*, October 18, 1892.

civic and business leaders and was the subject of editorials and letters urging its defeat.[173]

On September 24, after the ladies of Honolulu had presented the Queen with their petition of opposition, Mrs. Elizabeth Hall (one of the presenters) informed the same newspaper that "Her Majesty said substantially, that she realized the seriousness of the subject, and would give our petition due consideration; that she should make no promises, but would lay the matter before her Cabinet and consult with them."[174] "The lottery snake has been wounded, but it is not by any means dead," reported the *Advertiser* on September 26.[175] Then, on October 13, that bill came up for its first reading.

As of November 1, the Queen's proposed cabinet replacement was William H. Cornwell, minister of finance; Joseph Nawahi, minister of foreign affairs; Charles T. Gulick, minister of the interior; and Charles Creighton, attorney general. These candidates, however, never took up their portfolios. They were presented to the legislature at 10 A.M., and by noon the vote was against them 26 to 13, and the predictable comment from the *Pacific Commercial Advertiser* the next morning was: "Another 'Back Stair' ministry has come and gone." Liliuokalani then had to assemble still another slate of cabinet officials for legislative approval, and again A. S. Cleghorn commented on the matter to his daughter: "Your Aunt has not been wise in appointing her Cabinet.... Things are very unsettled at present.... I hope the Queen will not drop into the bad lot your uncle [King Kalakaua] got around him. Let us hope for the best."[176]

On November 7, Cleghorn again wrote Kaiulani: "We have not a Cabinet yet, she [the Queen] has named a good one...and I think when they take office all will go well."[177] Cleghorn here refers to what became known as the "Wilcox government" because the Queen had asked sugar planter George N. Wilcox, the Kauai-born son of a missionary, to aid her in forming it. This cabinet, which was publicly announced on November 9, consisted of George N. Wilcox, minister of the interior; Mark P. Robinson, minister of foreign affairs; Peter C. Jones (husband of the daughter of a missionary), and Cecil Brown, attorney general. Regarding the new appointees, the *Pacific Commercial Advertiser* agreed with Governor Cleghorn's assessment: "The Cabinet is certainly a strong one.... The Legislature can now devote itself without interference to the serious business of the session.... The Cabinet [crisis] is ended, and a strong ministry has taken its seat."[178] The *Advertiser* also noted that "the message from Her Majesty...was received with applause." Again writing to his daughter Princess Kaiulani, Cleghorn commented: "The new cabinet are going

---

173. See in particular the *Pacific Commercial Advertiser*, September 23, 1892.
174. *Pacific Commercial Advertiser*, September 24, 1892.
175. *Pacific Commercial Advertiser*, September 26, 1892.
176. Hawaii State Archives, Cleghorn Collection, November 2, 1892.
177. Hawaii State Archives, Cleghorn Collection, November 7, 1892.
178. *Pacific Commercial Advertiser*, November 9, 1892.

on very well and I hope they will not be removed.... Anyone who wishes to remove the present cabinet have not the good of the cabinet at heart."[179]

This replacement cabinet would remain in office until the legislature voted it out on January 12, 1893. When this happened, the *Advertiser* commented, "The change of ministry will not however lead to any political disturbance or unrest. It is believed that a new one will be appointed speedily... the Legislature will adjourn at once, and the work of government... may move on unimpeded...." [180]

The Queen's ultimate replacement candidates for government (announced from Iolani Palace on Friday, January 13, 1893) were: Samuel Parker, minister of foreign affairs; John F. Colburn, minister of the interior; W. H. Cornwell, minister of finance; A. P. Peterson, attorney general. This slate was presented to the legislature at 2:25 on the afternoon of January 13, the 170th day of the session, and approved by that body. It was then announced that the Queen had signed bills licensing the distilling of liquors and the bill to amend the judiciary act, and at 2:55 in the afternoon the house adjourned. What then occurred in the afternoon was the Queen's attempt to replace the existing constitution with one of her own, without going through the process specifically provided in the existing constitution. Although her ministers convinced the Queen to delay in order to avoid a crisis, her attempt to force a new constitution on January 13, 1893, precipitated the revolution that immediately followed.

Early in November 1892, when a reporter for the *San Francisco Chronicle* interviewed him, Paul Neumann was asked: "Then there is nothing serious in the friction between the Legislature and the Queen?" He replied: "Nothing whatever, at least nothing that portends violence or revolt."[181] As the history of the next three months proves, he couldn't have been more wrong.

When on December 31, 1892, Cleghorn wrote Kaiulani a New Year's letter, he commented: "The Queen is well and we are all very anxious for the Legislature to adjourn. I was in hopes it would be over by the end of the year, but it now looks as if it would not adjourn till the 15th of January. It will be the longest in Hawaiian history."[182] As it turned out, it was also the last legislative session under the monarchy.

    179. Hawaii State Archives, Cleghorn Collection, November 17, 1892.
    180. *Pacific Commercial Advertiser*, January 14, 1893.
    181. The interview was reprinted in the *Pacific Commercial Advertiser*, November 21, 1892.
    182. Hawaii State Archives, Cleghorn Collection, December 31, 1892.

*January 14, 1893. The Queen in her carriage about to return to Iolani Palace after proroguing the legislature in Aliiolani Hale. White kahili (feather standards) and puloulou (kapu sticks), symbols of chiefly rank, flank the vehicle. Members of the Royal Hawaiian Band in white uniforms are at the left.*
(Detail) Christian J. Hedemann, Bishop Museum Archives

# End of the Hawaiian Monarchy, 1893

January 1893 found the legislature still in session, but finally winding up its business. The three areas of greatest discussion and dissension in the legislative hall had been the constitutional convention, opium, and lottery bills. The legislature killed the first of these early in the session—a bill calling for a constitutional convention, which the late King Kalakaua had proposed in 1890, to draft a new constitution to replace the 1887 version.

The lottery bill was thought to be essentially dead, but on January 10, when several opponents of the bill were absent, Representative William White managed to railroad the bill through. The legislature then passed both the opium licensing bill and the lottery bill, despite intense public campaigning against them. The Queen's cabinet took the position that both were needed for revenue, and advised Her Majesty that as the legislature had passed them, she had to sign both bills into law. This she did in spite of the controversy surrounding them, and historians have cited the two measures as among the reasons the monarchy fell.

The Queen's cabinet, known as the Wilcox government, fell by a want of confidence vote in the legislature on January 12, just two days before the legislature was to conclude, and the next morning the Queen hurriedly appointed a new cabinet consisting of Samuel Parker, minister of foreign affairs; John H. Colburn, minister of the interior; W. H. Cornwell, minister of finance; and Arthur P. Peterson, attorney general. But as events transpired, they would assume their offices only briefly.

The great crisis that ended the monarchy came in response to an attempt by the Queen to proclaim a new constitution because of the failure of the legislature to approve a constitutional convention. She wanted to replace the one forced upon Kalakaua in 1887, one which, according to the Queen, a majority of the kingdom's registered voters opposed. In doing so, she hoped to enable Native Hawaiian subjects to gain more control of Hawaii's political and economic direction. Many in the business community feared that this new constitution plus continued political unrest would adversely affect their investments and political power.

On the morning of January 14, 1893, the Queen informed her ministers of her plan to proclaim the new constitution, a draft of which they already had for review. The Queen was determined on her course, and after proroguing the legislative session, she returned to the palace and, in the blue room, demanded that her ministers sign or consent to the proposed constitution. She had planned to present the new constitution at a cere-

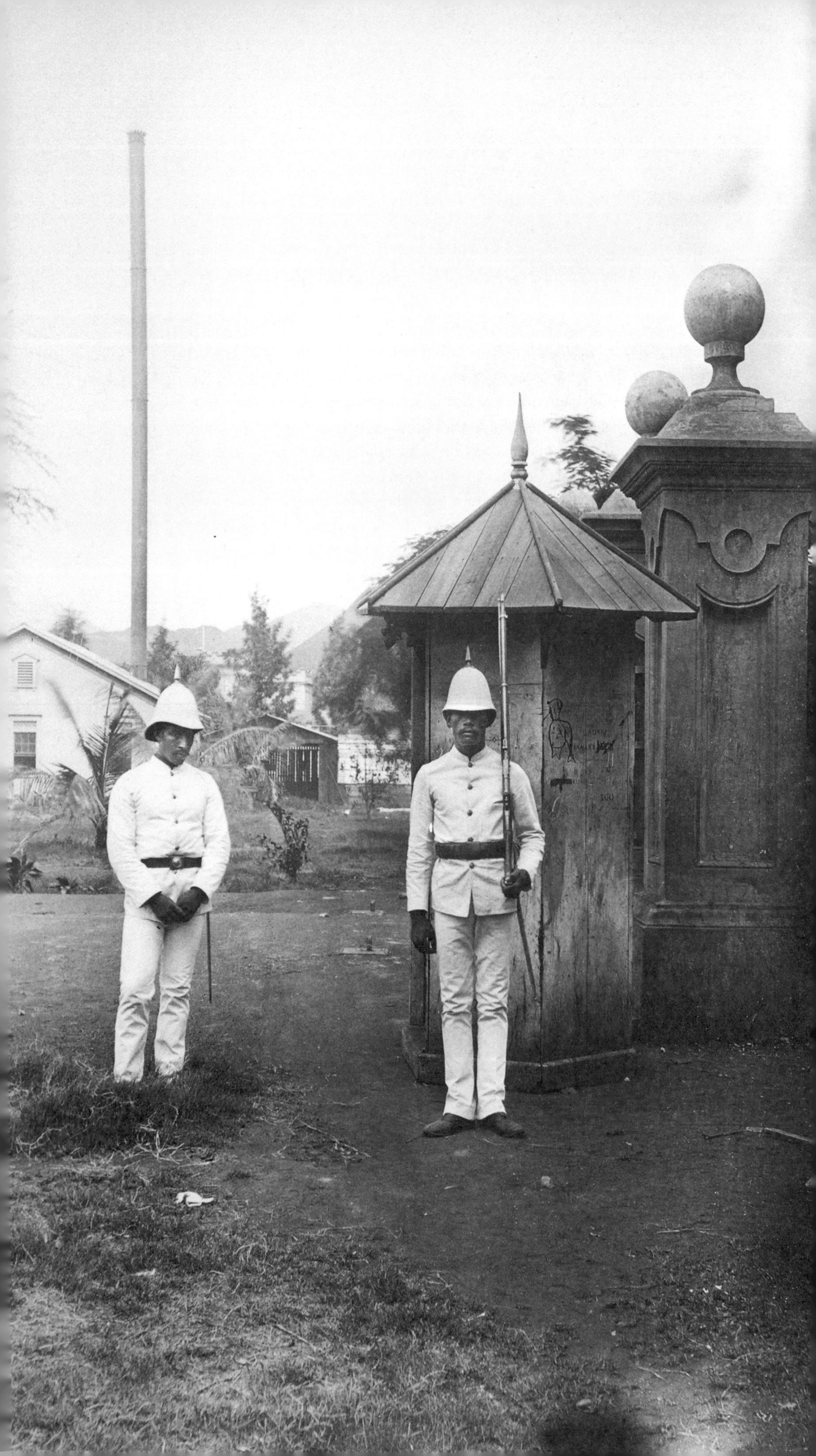

mony in the throne room, where legislators, members of the supreme court, and other dignitaries had assembled at her invitation. Her cabinet members, whom she had expected would support her attempt, were now firmly against the action, pointing out that by the terms of her oath of office it was an illegal act and could lead to an uprising. When the Queen would not budge, several of her ministers went across the street to Aliiolani Hale to discuss matters with the leading lawyers in town (including her political opponents Lorrin Thurston and William O. Smith), and with members of the diplomatic corps. The lawyers considered the Queen's actions to be outside the bounds of the current constitution, which provided a means for making changes through the legislative process. They advised that the Queen's actions would ring the death knell of the monarchy. The diplomatic corps urged the ministers to inform Her Majesty that she must abandon the idea.

The several ministers returned to the blue room and, after a stormy session, the cabinet was able to convince the Queen to temporarily postpone her plan. The Queen proceeded to the throne room and told her guests that she had intended to promulgate a new constitution, but yielded to her ministers. She then addressed her subjects who were gathered on the palace grounds, asked them to depart peacefully, and stated that she would make an attempt to enact a new constitution at a later time. It was at this point that Lorrin Thurston, W. O. Smith, and others decided that the Queen was "in revolution" and had to be removed from office. They formed a committee of safety and took steps to create and declare a provisional government. And, with the support of American military personnel stationed in Honolulu Harbor to protect the life and property of American residents, that is precisely what happened three days later, on January 17, 1893.

*Two members of the Royal Guard stand inside the Likelike Street gate of Iolani Palace beside a hexagonal guardhouse, circa 1889. The palace's electric plant (the industrial-looking building with a tall smokestack) is in the background. Hale Koa, also known as Iolani Barracks, is the light-colored coral-block structure in the distance. The barracks housed the Royal Guard, whose responsibility it was to guard the sovereign and the treasury. Following the overthrow of the Hawaiian monarchy on January 17, 1893, the Royal Guard was disbanded.*
Hawaii State Archives

*Prior to 1889, Iolani Palace was secluded from public view by a high coral-block wall. The wall was lowered in 1889 following the Wilcox Rebellion, and for the first time the public had an unobstructed view of the palace grounds. Here a group of neatly dressed schoolchildren have assembled by the Likelike gate. Their school is visible in the background (now the site of the Hawaii State Library).*

Hawaii State Archives, circa 1890

# 1893

*Wednesday, January 11, 1893.* Iolani Palace. This has been a day of excitement about the Lottery Bill. The Legislative Hall is full of people, foreign and natives, and Diplomatic corps all interested in the Bill, for or against. Four P.M. The Bill has passed its 3rd reading.[1]

*Friday, January 13.* Am told by Iaukea that Mr. Giffard has my shares on Hawaiian Agricultural Co. stocks—195—shares in all and he will hold them till my $2,500 for Cogswell pictures are paid.[2]

*Tuesday, January 17.* Iolani Palace. Nine A.M. Sent for Mr. S. M. Damon[3] to confer with him on the situation. He told me he had been asked to

THE DIARY FOR 1893
11 JAN–31 DEC

Hawaii State Archives

---

1. The lottery bill, titled "An Act Granting a Franchise to Establish and Maintain a Lottery," thereby granted to D. H. Cross of Chicago, W. B. Davenport of St. Louis, John Phillips, J. J. Williams, Samuel Nowlein, and William C. Achi of Honolulu a monopoly to establish and maintain a lottery for the term of twenty-five years, paying to the Hawaiian Government $500,000 each year in quarterly installments in advance, the proceeds to provide a subsidy for an ocean cable between Honolulu and "a port on the North American continent," the construction of railroads on Oahu and Hawaii (Hamakua to Hilo), for Honolulu harbor improvements, the "encouragement of industries," and for Pearl Harbor. *Laws of Her Majesty Liliuokalani . . . Passed by the Legislative Assembly at Its Session 1892* (Honolulu: 1893), 334–41. Many influential business houses, churches, and the missionary faction greatly opposed the bill. Nevertheless, the Queen signed it on January 13, 1893. The lottery bill was promptly canceled by Act No. 6 of the Executive and Advisory Councils of the Provisional Government on January 25, 1893.

2. I have moved this entry here from the memoranda section at the end of the diary. In the Hawaii State Archives, Iaukea Collection, M-70, Box 4-7, there is a letter dated October 20, 1892, from William Cogswell to Iaukea, asking him to thank Her Majesty "for the interest she has taken in the portraits" (of King Kalakaua and of Liliuokalani). Cogswell noted further: "I have somewhat regretted letting them go at 3,000."

With this is a receipt for the same, dated October 19, 1892:

"To full length portrait of His Late Majesty Kalakaua

"Including frame 1500.

"To full length portrait of

"Herself—with frame 1500.

"Received payment—W. Cogswell"

3. Samuel Mills Damon (b. March 13, 1845, Honolulu–d. July 1, 1924, Honolulu) was a banker, business executive, horticulturist, and philanthropist, and the son of Seamen's Bethel chaplain Reverend Samuel Chenery Damon. He joined Charles R. Bishop in the banking business in 1870, was admitted as a partner of the Bank of Bishop & Co. in 1881, and as of June 1, 1895, became sole proprietor. In 1884, on the death of Bernice P. Bishop, Damon inherited the ahupuaa (land division) of Moanalua, a vast property west of Honolulu, which he developed into a spectacular garden modeled after an English park, a portion of which remains and is open to the public.

During Liliuokalani's reign, Damon served as minister of finance 1889–90, and in that capacity he held the same portfolio 1893–1900. He served on the Advisory Council of the Republic of Hawaii, and was minister of the interior 1899–1900. He retired from public life in 1900. He was well liked in the business community and was always a staunch friend of the Queen, a friendship that she acknowledges here and in her 1895 diary.

join a party who called themselves the Executive Council and he had refused but asked what he should do. I told him to go and join the Advisory Council, which he did, and I attribute the leniency of the latter Council to his interposition with them. The Oppositions Proclamations were that I and my Ministers and Marshall should give up the Government to them, which we did at quarter to six P.M., but under protest.

Those who kindly assisted us were S. M. Damon, J. O. Carter, Ed Macfarlane, Paul Neumann, H. A. Widemann. Two Princes Kawananakoa and Kalanianaole were present besides Sam Parker, Minister Foreign Affairs, Mr. W. H. Cornwell, Minister of Finance, John F. Colburn, Minister of Interior, and A. P. Peterson, Attorney General.

Lizzie Pratt came over to sympathize with me. Things turned out better than I expected. The Hawaiian Flag will not change and so for now [nor] will the Royal Standard. The opposition Govt. will have Armory at Manamana turned into a Barracks. One policeman was shot for doing his duty in trying to prevent a cart loaded [with] ammunition from going through the streets.[4]

---

J. O. Carter, in a letter to James H. Blount dated May 3, 1893, includes a summary of what took place in first the government building and then the blue room of Iolani Palace on the afternoon of January 17, 1893:

> ¶ There was a deal of excitement [at the government building] and earnest discussion going on among groups of persons, and while standing among them I overheard among other things that Minister Stevens had recognized the new government.... I asked what was required of me and was told that a committee was to be sent to the palace to inform Her Majesty the Queen that she was deposed and to assist her in making any protest she desired to make, and that I was to be of the committee. I joined the party headed by Mr. Damon, and proceeded to the palace, where in the blue room, was Her Majesty, one or both of the young princes, the Hon. H. A. Widemann, and Paul Neumann,

---

4. The Hawaiian was a policeman named Leialoha, and this was the only shot fired at the end of the monarchy. "At two o'clock on the afternoon of January 17, 1893 (the day that the monarchy fell), Captain Good of the volunteer military was at the E. O. Hall hardware store obtaining arms and munitions to take to the Drill shed, loaded a wagon, and drove off. At the nearby intersection of Fort and King Streets a Hawaiian police officer, Leialoha, seized the horse's bridle and demanded that Good go to the police station. A wordy altercation ensued. Finally, Good drew a revolver and shot Leialoha. Immediately the shot was heard—it was something like the shot at Concord that 'was heard around the world,' the city leaped into action. The police officers watching the committee of safety rushed to the corner. The Committee... left the office by a back door and walked to Aliiolani Hale, the Government building, the seat of the monarchial government. They entered the office of the Interior Department... asked for the surrender of the office, which was promptly given. Henry E. Cooper [then] went to the front entrance and there read a proclamation... proclaiming the cessation of the royal government." Hawaii State Archives, A. P. Taylor Collection, Box 2, Folder 1, unpublished paper.

Her Majesty's ministers, E. C. Macfarlane, and others. Mr. Damon informed Her Majesty of the establishment of a Provisional Government, and of her being deposed, and that she might prepare a protest if she wished to. An awkward pause followed, which I broke by addressing Her Majesty, expressing sympathy, and advised her that any demonstration on the part of her forces would precipitate a conflict with the forces of the United States; that it was desirable that such a conflict be avoided; that her case would be considered at Washington, and a peaceful submission to force on her part would greatly help her case; that the persons in command of her forces at the barracks and the police station should be ordered to surrender. The Hon. H. A. Widemann then addressed Her Majesty, fully endorsing my advice.... The Hon. Paul Neumann was requested to prepare the protest for Her Majesty's signature, and I was also requested to assist in preparing the document. While the protest was in course of preparation word was sent to Marshall Wilson to disband the force at the station and surrender the building, arms, and ammunition. After the protest had been signed by Her Majesty and the ministers, word was brought that Marshall Wilson refused to give up the station house except upon the written command of Her Majesty. The order was prepared, signed by the Queen, and sent to the marshall. The protest was [then] placed in the hands of President [Sanford] Dole.[5]

The Queen's protest document (below), signed by Liliuokalani, is also signed by her cabinet ministers, Samuel Parker, William H. Cornwell, John F. Colburn, and A. P. Peterson, and is addressed to Sanford B. Dole "and others composing the Provisional Government of the Hawaiian Islands." It is endorsed as follows: "Received by the hands of the late cabinet this 17th day of January, 1893. Sanford B. Dole, Chairman of Executive Council of Provisional Government."[6]

¶ January 17, 1893

I, Liliuokalani, by the Grace of God and under the constitution of the Hawaiian Kingdom, Queen, do hereby solemnly protest against any and all acts done against myself and the constitutional Government of the Hawaiian Kingdom by certain persons claiming to have established a Provisional Government of and for this Kingdom. That I yield to the superior force of the United States of America, whose minister plenipotentiary, his Excellency John L. Stevens, has caused the United States troops to be landed at Honolulu and declared that he would support the said Provisional Government.

*The Queen's Protest Document Refusing to Acknowledge the Provisional Government's Authority and Yielding to the Authority of the Government of the United States, January 1893*

---

5. This document was published in the Blount Report, 56–57.
6. A typescript of the protest is filed in Hawaii State Archives, "Proceedings of the Executive and Advisory Council: Provisional Government, January 17, 1893–April 18, 1893," Series 425, vol. 1.

Now to avoid any collision of armed forces, and perhaps the loss of life, I do under this protest and impelled by said forces, yield my authority until such time as the Government of the United States shall, upon the facts being presented to it, undo the action of its representative and reinstate me in the authority which I claim as the constitutional sovereign of the Hawaiian Islands.

Done this 17th day of January A.D., 1893.

[*signed*] Liliuokalani.

The new political order established as of January 17, 1893, was the Provisional Government, so called because at first the new government expected that a treaty for the annexation of Hawaii to the United States would almost immediately follow. This did not happen. The Provisional Government remained in place until July 4, 1894, when the Republic of Hawaii was proclaimed. Throughout Liliuokalani's 1893–94 diaries, she commonly refers to the new government as the P.G. These initials also identify a person loyal to or sympathetic to that government. It was a term of derision among the royalists.

---

*Wednesday, January 18.* Iolani Palace. I mean to go to ride and then return to Washington Place to stay.[7]

*Friday, January 20.* Washington Place. Went to the Mausoleum and went to Waikiki to bathe. Returned from there at one P.M. and found a note, brought me by C. A. Brown from the Provisional Govt. telling me not to fly the Royal Standard anymore. I sent the note to Mr. Paul Neumann and he told me to follow instructions, which I did.[8]

*Tuesday, January 31.* Washington Place. Sent for Kaipo Aea's and Aimoku's passbooks on the Postal Savings Bank Nos. 6929 and 6930, and asked Capt. Nowlein to draw the amount. Walter Hill[9] would not give it [to] him till the books were countersigned by Robertson, so he gave me his own money and kept the books. I passed this amount, which was $1,000.00 with the $1,200 drawn from Bishop's Bank on Saturday, all to Mr. Neumann as his pay. I also signed a Mortgage on this place [Washington Place], Hamohamo, [and] all lands left me by Bernice Bishop, to Mr. S. Damon

---

7. Palace intimate Curtis Iaukea writes of what occurred this day: "Mr. Dole on assuming the Government ... sent for me and made a request of me to remain in office and continue in the administration of the Crown Lands, of which I was then and had been for many years past Commissioner and Land Agent....

"Girding up my loins, I called on the Queen, informed her of what had taken place, stressing the point that my duty was to royalty first and not to those of her enemies. Much to my relief, she responded by saying, 'Stay where you are and keep an eye on the Crown Lands revenues. They are mine and I'm going to be restored to the throne when the United States Government is fully informed of the wrongful manner [in which] the overthrow of the monarchy was accomplished.'... After expressing my deep sympathy with her... I bid her aloha, and as I took her hand to kiss it with eyes filled with tears, I felt a slight tremor that for the moment inspired the feeling that the worst had come and all was at an end." Hawaii State Archives, Iaukea Collection, Box 2, manuscript draft of his memoirs.

8. This note has not been located.

9. Walter Hill (d. April 22, 1895, Australia), postmaster general, May 2, 1891–April 1, 1893.

for the sum of $10,000. I borrowed of him for [the use of] My Commissioners—Kawananakoa and Neumann, and also for $7,000.00 I owed him before, making $17,000 altogether.[10]

I signed a power of Attorney according to him [Neumann] all the power and right to transact all matters between the President of the United States, and Myself and for the Hawaiian people.[11]

*Friday, February 3.* Washington Place. Nothing of importance transpired in regard to myself. 11.30 A.M., Mr. C. W. Ashford came to call. In our conversation he remarked the throne would never be restored to me, and my Commissioners to Washington—Prince David and Neumann would never meet with success.[12]

He thought it would startle me, but I showed him only a look of unconcern. He next asked what the Government were doing for me. I said, "showed me consideration by sending [to] me whenever they thought necessary to inform me of what is going to transpire." "I see you still have a guard of honor." Yes, Capt. Nowlein and 16 men—"and all the difference."

---

10. This mortgage dated January 30, 1893, was recorded in the Bureau of Conveyances, Liber 139, 347–48, and was re-registered with slight alterations on April 22, 1893, in Liber 139, 421.

11. Liliu's power of attorney to Paul Neumann says in part: "I, Liliuokalani ... have made, constituted, and appointed ... Paul Neumann Esquire, my true lawful and sufficient attorney for me and in my name, place, and stead, to negotiate, arrange, and agree with the United States of America and the President, the Secretary of the Department of State thereof, and with any other (if any) representative or official ... for such official or other consideration, benefit, and advantage as in the opinion of my said attorney shall may or can be obtained from the United States of America as well for myself and family as for the said Kaiulani in consideration of existing conditions and circumstances. And if no official consideration for myself or said Kaiulani shall in the opinion of my said attorney be obtainable from the United States of America, then and thereupon and in such case to arrange and agree upon such pecuniary considerations benefits and advantages as can or may be secured for myself and family and for said Kaiulani from the United States of America, and whether the same shall be in the form of payment at one time of a sum of money to myself or of distinct sums of money to myself and said Kaiulani or in payments of stated sums of money annually or oftener for a fixed term of years or a fixed period or periods of time."

The document was acknowledged before Albert F. Judd, chief justice of the Supreme Court, on January 31, and thus became a public document. It is reproduced in the Blount Report, 400–401. An unsigned draft of the same is in the Hawaii State Archives, Liliuokalani Collection, Box 18, Seized Documents.

The full text was first published in Hawaii (after the power of attorney had been canceled) in the *Pacific Commercial Advertiser*, June 10, 1893. See second footnote for June 10, 1893, diary entry (357).

12. Clarence W. Ashford, who had been Kalakaua's attorney general (July 1, 1887–June 14, 1890), was in 1893 the editor of the English-language pages of the Hawaiian newspaper *The Liberal*, owned by Robert W. Wilcox. At this date, that paper was rather surprisingly outspoken in its support of annexation. While none of the articles are signed, there is little doubt that Ashford wrote most of the English text. In the February 1 issue, he said under the heading "A Lost Opportunity": "The late Queen and her advisors must be infatuated. How else shall we account for their perverseness in defying the laws of fate, and seeking to turn back the Car of Progress. It is too late in the 19th Century to rationally hope for the restoration of the monarchical forms which have been overthrown by the people.... We rejoin that a monarchy which could not protect itself against a small minority of the people does not deserve to exist, much less to be regalvanized into life."

Responding to Ashford's remarks, the February 2, 1893, issue of the *Daily Hawaii Holomua* (in which the Queen had a financial interest) commented, "Evidently Mr. Ashford does not consider the monarchy one of 'the deadest things alive' though he tries at least very hard to persuade himself and others that it is dead, and buried and beyond resurrection."

Two P.M. Salute by the USS *Boston,* of 21 guns for President Dole and Ministers on going on board and return.[13] Wrote a long letter to J. T. Baker by *Kinau* about questions given him.[14]

*Saturday, February 4.* Washington Place. [Entry ends thus.]

*Sunday, February 5.* Washington Place. It is a gloomy day and it rains, rains, rains.[15] Do not feel like going to Church—perhaps never more. I never saw a more unchristian like set as these Missionaries, and so uncharitable as to abuse me in the manner they do from the pulpit.[16] Is it Godly—No. It makes me feel as if I would not like to do anything more for Churches—etc., etc.

*Monday, February 6.* Washington Place. Ten A.M. Mary Carter called with Mr. and Mrs. Hecker and their young boy of twelve. He is a builder of R. R. Cars—is here to rest. Will soon go to the Volcano.[17]

Went out for the first time today.

---

13. "Hons. S. B. Dole, Minister of Foreign Affairs and President of the Provisional Government, J. A. King, Minister of the Interior, P. C. Jones, Minister of Finance, and W. O. Smith, Attorney General, paid an official visit to the U.S. cruiser *Boston* at 2:15 o'clock this afternoon. The Hawaiian flag floated from the steam launch on which the Ministers were conveyed to the cruiser. When President Dole and his colleagues mounted the steps the Hawaiian flag was run up to the masthead of the *Boston* and a salute of twenty-one guns belched from the ship's sides on recognition. When the Ministers left another salute of twenty-one guns was given. A large crowd flocked to the boat landing, wondering what all the firing was for." *Evening Bulletin*, February 3, 1893.

14. While the letters of Liliu to J. T. Baker have not survived, George H. Williams, sheriff of Hawaii, refers to one of these in a letter of April 12, 1893, to Marshall E. G. Hitchcock in Honolulu: "There is no doubt about the fact, that the so-called 'Hui Aloha Aina' or a part of them, are getting ready for some coup. There were 3 letters received by the Hui; one from Nawahi to Kekua, one from J. S. Cummins to J. T. Baker, and one from the widow Dominis to J. T. Baker. The abovenamed gentlemen read as much as was fit for me to hear from the first two letters at their meeting on Monday last, the 10th, the last letter was not produced at that meeting, but Mrs. Baker told Mrs. B. Brown that the ex-Queen told them to 'get ready for the time to come' [or] 'E hoomaukaukau no ka wa e hiki mai ana' and as Capt. Brown explains to me, it means to rescue the ex-Queen when a suitable time arrives.... The entire contents of the letter of Mrs. Dominis are only known to the Executive Council of the H.A.A. [Hui Aloha Aina] which consists of: Henry West, Keawehano, Kaeha, Kekoa, Kauhane (Puueo), Honuakau, and J. T. Baker." Hawaii State Archives, Series 363, Box 3.

15. The *Pacific Commercial Advertiser*, February 4, 1893, commented: "The rainstorm which has been wetting Honolulu down very steadily for thirty-six hours is one of the biggest for several years.... A good many yards have been flooded.... At Palama around Robello's lane, everything was under water, while the Waikiki residents are in fear of being drowned out entirely.... The taro patches and fishponds are under water, and the fish... are swimming around at their own sweet will. Kapiolani Park is flooded."

16. On Sunday, January 22, 1893, for instance, one week after the overthrow, Reverend Thomas L. Gulick delivered a sermon in Central Union Church, across the street from Washington Place, on the subject of Esther and Ahasuerus. His remarks, when published in the *Advertiser*, bore the heading "Evils of Monarchy" and were pointedly directed at the deposed Queen: "A beautiful woman raised out of obscurity and suddenly made the queen of a mighty realm is very liable to become proud and tyrannical; but such was not the case with Esther. She was not of the number of those, who, when they have attained to high position, forget their former benefactors, and think themselves too wise or too great to receive counsel from the humble." *Pacific Commercial Advertiser*, February 1, 1893.

17. Franz Joseph Hecker (b. 1846–d. 1927) was a capitalist, the organizer of the Peninsular Car Co., and the president of its successor, the Michigan-Peninsular Car Co. (in Detroit). The Heckers had arrived at Honolulu on the *Australia*, January 25, 1893.

*Tuesday, February 7.* Washington Place. Jennie McGuire and her mother were here. Jennie came to fit my dress. I was told of many things of those who I thought were my best friends.

*Wednesday, February 8.* Washington Place. It is just a week ago today since the Commissioners, Prince David [Kawananakoa] and Hon. Paul Neumann went on the *Australia* for San Francisco and then on for Washington. It has rained ever since they left, and this after[noon] is the first time it has cleared up. Went to Paoakalani—came home at two.

Drove by the Palace and would not look at the American flag over the Government building.[18] Time may wear off the feeling of injury by and by—but my dear flag—the Hawaiian flag—that a strange flag should wave over it—may heaven look down on those Missionaries and punish them for their deeds.

*Thursday, February 9.* Washington Place. Vice President Sam Damon called this morning and I congratulated him on his being appointed V.P. of the Provisional Government.[19] He told me it was decided by the Advisory and Executive Council that I should continue to receive my salary which is $1,250.00. Further he could not say for fear of losing the whole.[20] He said he was anxious about the *Claudine* as it is fully time for us to hear of or from her, or from those who went to Washington in her—Lorrin

---

18. The American flag was first raised over Aliiolani Hale (the government building) on February 1, 1893, at which time U.S. Minister John L. Stevens issued the following proclamation: "At the request of the Provisional Government of the Hawaiian Islands, I hereby, in the name of the United States of America, assume protection of the Hawaiian Islands for the protection of life and property, and occupation of public buildings and Hawaiian soil, so far as may be necessary for the purpose specified, but not interfering with the administration of public affairs by the Provisional Government. This action is taken pending, and subject to, negotiations at Washington." *Pacific Commercial Advertiser*, February 1, 1893. The article continued: "The raising of the flag does not, of course, indicate a cession to the United States. The Hawaiian flag still floats in the yard, the Palace, Barracks, Police Station, Custom House, etc., remain in the hands of the Government."

19. "In accordance with Act 11 now in effect, Mr. S. M. Damon, was, this day, unanimously chosen Vice President of the Provisional Government of the Hawaiian Islands. James B. Castle, Secretary of the Executive and Advisory Councils. Honolulu, Feb. 4, 1893." This notice was first published in the *Pacific Commercial Advertiser*, February 10, 1893.

The *Daily Hawaii Holomua*, February 7, 1893, in announcing the appointment commented: "A wiser selection could not have been made and the Advisory Council deserves credit for this display of good sense. If there is one foreigner... who has the confidence of the Hawaiians, it is Mr. Damon."

20. The Queen's salary was continued until March. On March 20, 1893, a report to President Dole by Alexander Young and E. Suhr says: "There is now no reigning Queen of the Hawaiian Islands and any portion of the appropriation voted by the last Legislature as the Queen's salary, paid to the now ex-Queen, is unwarranted by law. And we believe a grave mistake has been made by the Provisional Government in paying from the Appropriation for the Queen's salary already made to the Ex-Queen through her Chamberlain or otherwise. Besides, we fear that the gravity of the mistake has been intensified by evidence that the Ex-Queen, whose pecuniary needs were sought to be met by said payments, has been devoting large sums of money for the purpose of frustrating the main aim and object of the Provisional Government. We therefore recommend that no further payments be made to the Ex-Queen out of the appropriation... and that no payments from the Treasury of any nature whatever be made to the Ex-Queen until suitable provision has been made by the Provisional Government for such purposes." Hawaii State Archives, Foreign Office and Executive Files, Executive and Advisory Councils, Miscellaneous Reports.

Thurston, W. R. Castle, W. C. Wilder. [A long blank space follows.] The household expenses will be the same.

After Mr. Damon went home, Mr. Parker told me that he heard that Mr. Damon said that if the throne should be restored to me he would leave the country a ruined man, on account of the Amount borrowed by the Provisional Govt. of him, and of course they have no legal Authority to run the country into debt, and who is to stand all this, will it be Mr. C. R. Bishop?

11 A.M. went to Paoakalani, and spent two hours—it was delightful.

*Friday, February 10.* Washington Place. This has been a day of great excitement on the arrival of the *Mariposa*,[21] as news was received of the arrival of Thurston and other Commissioners in 8½ days by the *Claudine*, and that they had already been in Washington three days when the *Mariposa* sailed.[22] The best news received was that the President had received my Autograph letter and had decided to wait until our Commissioners arrived,[23] so that their Mission had to wait all that time much to their chagrin. Five reporters came down in the *Mariposa*.[24] I would not see any of them.

*Saturday, February 11.* Washington Place. Went to Hamohamo at ten A.M. Made Kuaiwa clean my house and I helped him in decorating it so as to look presentable, as it had not been inhabited for a long time.

*Sunday, February 12.* Washington Place. After breakfast, [it] being a lovely day, Kuaiwa drove me out to Paoakalani, where I spent a quiet day. All alone with only my kahus [advisors], Kaaipulu, Milaina, Hana, Aiaumoe, and Haalou. Arranged my room prettily—then had my lunch, upstairs, then afterwards joined the folks downstairs. Took a nap at four P.M. went downstairs—how lovely! Too lovely to come home but had to.

I forgot about Mr. Hayselden who called to see me about ten A.M.

*Monday, February 13.* Washington Place. Three women came in all dressed

---

21. By the arrival of the *Mariposa*, Honolulu residents learned of American opinions regarding the proposed matter of annexing the islands to the United States: "The indications of a strong current in favor of annexing Hawaii are unmistakable. State Legislatures have passed resolutions in its favor, Chambers of Commerce have endorsed it, Senators and Representatives have declared themselves for the measure; mass meetings even have been held.... Such a general outburst of feeling was not anticipated here, and it certainly justifies the belief that all the ends of the late political movement will be achieved." *Pacific Commercial Advertiser*, February 11, 1893.

22. The *Pacific Commercial Advertiser*, February 11, 1893, reprinted a San Francisco notice of January 30: "The Hawaiian Commissioners left for Washington at five P.M. yesterday well pleased with the reception accorded them in San Francisco and in full confidence in the ultimate success of their mission."

23. The *Daily Hawaii Holomua*, February 14, 1893, announced: "The Queen's protest and autograph letter were presented to President Harrison by Senator Felton of California who wired to Mr. Spreckels on San Francisco the assurance of the President that no steps would be taken before Her Majesty's envoy was heard."

24. The *Daily Bulletin*, February 10, 1893, said: "The Bulletin office has been visited by Mr. C. E. Washburn of the San Francisco bureau of the Associated press, Mr. W. S. Smith of the *Chronicle*, and Miss A. E. Knapp of the *Call*, who have come here to write up the situation." The same paper noted that Edmund Mitchell of the *Melbourne Age* was also in town.

in white with yellow handkerchiefs on their necks and red bands on their hats—defying the remarks of Emerson about Kahunas [sorcerers], but I wish they would not come here.[25]

Cornwell and Parker only [just] heard of the Power of Attorney [to Neumann] and seemed quite worried about it.

*Tuesday, February 14.* Washington Place. Told Messrs. Cornwell and Parker not to be worried about that power of Attorney—that we could write by next opportunity and tell Mr. Neumann not to make use of the latter part of that. I also told them Joe [Heleluhe?] had already come to some understanding [with Neumann?] that it should not be used until all other arrangements had failed. But they would not be satisfied. I told Mr. Parker that very document had been in his hands on the day it was made out—he only glanced it over and put it down. It laid on my table a whole week and he did not touch it—but now the people downtown were worrying them and now they are frightened about it. I told them not to do anything until we heard from the Commissioners, and not to be frightened about these folks.

*Wednesday, February 15.* Washington Place. Maria Kaiapulua came to tell me all about what Emma Nakuina had told her the day before. She warned me in regard to her. I told her Emma had subjected me to a lot of questionings worthy of a lawyer. Maria brought me four cocoanuts

25. Liliu's reference to Joseph Swift Emerson and "kahunas" was the outcome of his having attended a church meeting of a Native Hawaiian group, the Society for the Suppression of Idolatry, on Monday evening, February 5, 1893. The following account of the same appeared in the *Daily Bulletin*, February 7, 1893, under the headline "Devotions Disturbed. Disruption of a Prayer Meeting With Political Dynamite. A Visitor Miscalculates Hawaiian Feelings on Affairs":

"The members of the little native church at Kapuuloko near the Fish market held their regular prayer meeting yesterday evening. As is usual at these meetings a subject was proposed for discussion among members. The subject was, 'Whether it is right to worship two Gods?' Argument was going along peaceably when Mr. Jos. Emerson entered the church and after listening a little while, asked to be allowed to take part in the discussion. Mr. E. was given permission and spoke for some time, finally bringing in the name of the dethroned Queen and reflecting on her career. Among other remarks he is said to have referred to stories that the Queen was in the habit of consulting kahunas regarding her chances for restoration to the throne.

"Some of the congregation arose in a body and demanded that Mr. E. close his mouth or he would be summarily removed. S. Kaloa, a native preacher, then addressed the meeting, saying that 'a committee of church members had had communication and meetings with Her Majesty during a year past, and she had told them emphatically she did not believe in kahunas. Now here came a foreigner and told them that she was harboring them. Who would they believe, this man or their committee who has been in constant communication with the Queen?'

"Mr. E. asked all who were in favor of the Queen returning to the throne to stand up. All stood up with the exception of five, one a clerk in the office of the Board of Missions.

"Kaloa then interfered and asked who dethroned the Queen, was it her people? Another, did Mr. E. consider that the members of the Council [of the Provisional Government] where not a single Hawaiian was present, represent the people? The argument became hot and finally Mr. Emerson retired and Kaloa held the fort.

"A committee from the Church has an advertisement in a native paper calling on all members to pray to God for the restoration of the Queen."

The article then continued with an interview with Emerson, which gave his side of the story.

said to be from the old tree at Pokai at Waianae—and some sticks of Ko Manulele [and] Eleele.[26]

*Thursday, February 16.* Washington Place. John Sheldon, editor of the *Holomua*'s case, was to come off today. The Advisory and Executive Councils wanted to try the case themselves but Mr. Dole would not permit [it] as Mr. Hatch had said it was not the proper course to take [so] it was finally turned over to Judge Frear. The case postponed till tomorrow.[27] John Ena came. [Under this date in her cash account, Liliu recorded: "Paid to J. Alapai—funeral expense of son. $20.00."]

*Friday, February 17.* Washington Place. 9.30 A.M. Wrote to Claus Spreckels and Co., to give my stocks in the Hawaiian Agricultural Co. to Sam Parker and he will try and dispose of them for me. 11.10 A.M. John Ena came to inform me of my interest in the *Holomua*, that I ought to do away with it. It has shown a spirit of antagonism towards the present Government and if I am to encourage such a spirit, the Provisional Government will withdraw from me all recognition in the way of providing for my allowance which they are now studying over, or by withdrawing the guard of honor, etc, etc. I told Mr. Ena that I did not read the papers, that I consider myself entirely removed from politics and was living in complete retirement.

*Saturday, February 18.* Washington Place. Mr. Parker came in [and] we spoke about selling those stocks so low but considered afterwards that it would be best after all so I might be free from Mr. [Spreckels?]. They were going down to Waikiki with Mr. Canavarro to entertain the five reporters.

*Monday, February 20.* Washington Place. Mr. Nawahi came in in great trouble about his Insurance and I gave him $140.00. He said he would try and refund it soon—mercy only knows how. I am trying to stint myself to pay off what I owe. 11 A.M. I asked Minister Parker what he had done with my Hawaiian Agricultural shares. He said he had sold them through Mr. Chas. T. Gulick to Ed. Jones[28]—100 shares had [each] been sold for $95.00 (Oh! What a sacrifice).

He said he paid Mr. Giffard $3,000 and now he had the rest in his hands amounting to $6,954.30. I told him I only owed Mr. Giffard $2,500.00.

---

26. Two varieties of Hawaiian sugarcane, *Saccharum* spp.

27. On January 30, 1893, the Executive Council of the Provisional Government enacted "An Act Concerning Seditious Offenses," which stated: "Everyone commits a misdemeanor who publishes verbally [or] otherwise any words or any document with a seditious intention." Following this enactment, John Sheldon, editor of the *Holomua*, was arrested February 15, 1893, for publishing a "contemptuous article" about the Provisional Government. President Dole had earlier summoned him for an interview in which Dole informed him: "We do not think it proper for you to instill in the minds of the people that the Queen is still a Sovereign.... She has surrendered her authority and has referred her matter to the United States... and we expect the newspapers, if they wish to continue, to recognize the situation and to criticize us fairly.... We will not tolerate any incitement to disorder." Hawaii State Archives, Foreign Office and Executive Files, 1893, Miscellaneous Documents.

The government had no particular interest in prosecuting Sheldon, who was in fact a "dummy" editor of the newspaper. They were after the actual editor, an Englishman named G. Carson Kenyon, alias "Friday," and Edmund Norrie, "a hanger-on of Sam Parker's," who assisted "Friday" in writing the English page of the newspaper. See *Pacific Commercial Advertiser*, February 16, 1893. The matter went to the Supreme Court and both the *Daily Bulletin* and the *Advertiser* reported the procedure in full. On the matter of Liliu's suspected financial interest in the *Daily Hawaii Holomua*, see first footnote for March 31, 1893, diary entry (335).

28. Edwin A. Jones (d. 1898), son of C. Brewer & Co. executive Peter Cushman Jones.

He then told me, he wanted to keep the rest of the money for his own debts as everyone was pressing him. I told him I could not spare it as I was deeply indebted also, and needed the money myself. He must return the rest. There were 95 shares remaining not sold. You must return them. He was very angry.

*Saturday, February 25.* Washington Place. Received a letter from S. B. Dole, President of the Provisional Government, stating that they had heard from reliable sources that there were people who came in here in the Midnight and for that reason they, the P.G., had seen fit to withdraw my guards at the end of the month.[29]

*Sunday, February 26.* Washington Place. Went out to Waikiki and spent the morning in removing all the furniture from Hookumukalani [Hale]. After lunch walked down to see Kalu who is very sick, and met Eveline [Wilson] at Pupule's gate. They will come down to Kealohilani[30] later. The sky looked lowering, still I had my bath and returned at 5.30 P.M.

*Monday, February 27.* Washington Place. Spent the day at Waikiki with the people while they weeded a large lot. Lucy Nowlein, their little hanai [adopted child] Kaiu, [and] Mrs. Hopkins are new ones that came in. Four P.M. Minister Parker and Mr. English came over. The latter read to me a letter (supposed to have come from me) which is very nicely written, but as Mr. Neumann has asked me to stay in complete retirement I rather hesitate. It is Mr. Chamberlayne the editor of the [*San Francisco*] *Examiner*[31] who thinks I ought not to remain silent while the other *party were saying untrue things about me.*[32]

*Tuesday, February 28.* Washington Place. Mr. Robertson told me that he had had conversation with Judge Dole, President of the Provisional Government, about their withdrawing my guards and the latter told him it was because the guard at McKibbin's corner had seen an English sailor come from here and went up to him and tried to snatch his gun and

---

29. The Provisional Government had notified Liliuokalani verbally that they would provide her with a guard of 16 men and one officer for Washington Place. Hawaii State Archives, J. W. Robertson to the Executive Council, January 19, 1893. However, on February 25, 1893, Dole notified Liliu by letter: "Reliable information has been received that numbers of persons unconnected with your household have been freely admitted within the premises at Washington Place at unreasonable hours of the night—Under these circumstances the Government find that the guard . . . is of little use and had better be removed. . . . This will be done at the end of this month." Hawaii State Archives, Liliuokalani Collection, Box 19, Seized Documents.

Dole derived his "reliable information" from a February 18 report from by J. H. Soper, commander of the National Guard of Hawaii, which includes the following statement: "During the night of the 15th inst. [this month] until the next morning, squads of British redcoats, and blue jackets, were seen going in and out of Washington Place, one squad alone being estimated by Lieut. Coyne, at twenty men, and as nearly as we can estimate, fully thirty-five of these men must have passed in and out, at different times during the course of the night. [The report concludes:] There seems to [be] concurrent testimony enough to justify the belief—that the guard allowed Mrs. Dominis is thoroughly disaffected towards the Government, I would therefore recommend that they be disbanded without delay." Hawaii State Archives, Foreign Office and Executive Files, 1893, Military Reports.

30. Kealohilani was Liliu's Waikiki beach cottage.

31. Mr. S. S. Chamberlain arrived at Honolulu February 10 as special correspondent of the *San Francisco Examiner*. He was in town for about two weeks.

32. The conclusion of this sentence has been italicized because in Liliu's 1893 diary, she writes almost all entries in ink, but on the page where this appears, she writes this passage in pencil with a different slant to the letters, indicating that it was a later addition.

failing to do so ran up the lane and the guard shot at him. He said he saw the sailor go into McKibbin's yard.[33] That guard told a falsehood—what does this sailor know of this locality so recently arrived. Minister Parker started to say something about Mr. Wodehouse the English Minister Resident when the women came in. Alapai tells me the people are indignant at the withdrawing of my guards.

*Wednesday, March 1.* Washington Place. Wrote to Hon. Paul Neumann and Prince David. To the former about Mr. Ashford's coming to propose that I should accept offers of money from the P.G. as maintes [?] and then there would be no more trouble as I need not expect ever to go back to the throne again—that it would be the easiest way to settle matters and then send for Neumann to come back—the old snake!—about his trying to start a new society called a Civil Rights League—and that I had told all my friends not to join. This affair is simply gotten up by him not for any patriotism, but this will end in their all being arrested, that it would injure our cause at Washington. I also wrote that the most popular wish here is for Commissioners to be sent down here and to have an election—whether for Monarchy or Annexation, and was sure that it would be for the former. [In Liliu's cash account for this date, she recorded "from Provisional Government $1,250." This was her monthly salary—the last she would receive.]

*Sunday, March 5.* Washington Place. Left this morning for Paoakalani and although it is Sunday, I am afraid that it has not been as sacredly kept as it ought. The matting was put down, bedding moved in, new curtains hung. Capt. Nowlein and Mr. Fernandez came out. Received from him a pearl knife and a measure. Told Mr. Fernandez not to join any league or Association until after we learn from Washington. [On this date, Liliu's cash account memorandum shows: "Lent to J. Nawahi $400."]

*Monday, March 6.* Washington Place. Spent the day at Waikiki. Capt. and Mrs. Nowlein and Mr. and Mrs. Charlie Hopkins were there, also lots of soldiers who have no work. Gave them aaho [purlins or rafters for a thatched house] to cut from date trees—they did quite a lot. Hopkins helped me to make mauu brooms.[34] I gave mine to him as a memento of the day tied with Kawaihau [a singing society] ribbon. No News—on our way home met lots of carriages going out to Mr. Herbert's at the Park [to an entertainment] given by Mr. and Mrs. Smith to the Honolulu people who have entertained them.[35] Sent McGuire down to boathouse to take my sideboard down to Paoakalani—It was put in Hookumukalani [Hale].

*Tuesday, March 7.* Washington Place. Told Capt. Nowlein what I heard last eve, from C.B.W. [Charles B. Wilson] what two men said while working on Pauahi Bishop's grave—that they heard that Capt. Good had said that when they rec'd news in my favor he would be the one to take my

---

33. Soper's report to President Dole also discussed this incident. See footnote for February 25, 1893, diary entry (325). The McKibbin property (the old Miller residence) adjoined Washington Place on the Ewa side. McKibbin's corner was on Beretania Street at Miller Street.

34. *Mauu* is a general term for sedge or straw.

35. "Mr. J. P. Smith, a tourist, entertained a party of friends last evening at a supper. The affair took place at Herbert's Waikiki premises. The band was in attendance." *Pacific Commercial Advertiser*, March 7, 1893. The Smiths left Honolulu for San Francisco on the *Alameda* on March 9.

life. I also told J. Nawahi and Mr. Parker of it. J. Nawahi borrowed of me $450.00 to pay off Mortgage to Mr. Scott of Wainaku. The Mortgage was assigned to me. The money I loaned belonged to the Hui Hololio [a horse riding association]. *One hundred—and the rest was mine.*[36]

*Thursday, March 9.* Washington Place. Went to Waikiki with Capt. and Mrs. Nowlein and baby Keoma. The soldiers and Kaiu spent morning in cutting bamboos while pake [Chinese] Carpenter was enlarging my lattice fence. I busied myself all day in arranging my room in Hookumukalani [Hale]. It is all ready excepting the Mosquito net—but with all that a sense of loneliness comes over me.

*Friday, March 10.* Washington Place. Heard of the arrival of the *Monowai* early this morn. Mr. W. C. Wilder and C. M. Cooke returned by her. They were greeted by their Missionary friends and they hadn't much to say nor did they have any joyous ways to show that they had had success—they simply said soup.[37]

We on our part had news from E. C. MacFarlane that [Annexation] Treaty would be put off till next session [of Congress] in December—that Cleveland would advise Commissioners to be sent out here[38]—which is just what the people want, and to have an election would be fair to all and satisfactory to the people—whether for a Monarchy or Annexation.

*Saturday, March 11.* Washington Place. Mr. Parker came in to talk about matters in politics. He found me cross and with $12,000 worth of bills in my hands. I had just sent Joe Heleluhe to pay a bill for $50.00 to Donnel and to Club Stables $70.00 for boarding my new horses.

Sam told me everything about commissioners in America will be all right but I did not feel satisfied with his actions about my money. He asked if I would consent to meet Mr. G. W. Macfarlane. I said I would—he went over and Mr. M. soon came over. After reading his brother Ned's letter he left. I was pleased to hear about Ned's efforts in helping our cause. Now on their arrival at Washington, Neumann sent him and the Prince David to New York to present my Autograph letter to Pres. elect

---

36. The italicized sentence is a later addition in pencil.

37. "The *Monowai* brings little that is new in regard to the negotiations at Washington. No action had been taken by the Senate prior to the sailing of the steamer on March 3rd, so that the question is left to the Cleveland administration to settle." In another article, the *Advertiser* noted, "Paul Neumann is working very hard with Senators and Representatives, trying to get a delay in the ratification of the [annexation] treaty. He has stated that annexation is inevitable, and he only wants to get as much as he can for the ex-queen." *Pacific Commercial Advertiser*, March 11, 1893.

38. Liliu received this information via a letter from George Macfarlane: "March 10th, 1893, 9:30 A.M. Your Majesty. I have the honor to transmit to you at my brother's request the following very satisfactory Telegram which my brother [Ned] dispatched at the last minute from Washington....

"'G. W. Macfarlane, Honolulu. Inform Queen, Senate refuses action Treaty—Everything our way, and arranged Cleveland Inaugural address tomorrow, will favor Commissioners being sent to Honolulu. Thurston is disgusted. Princess was here, and made good impression, returned to England 22nd. Will return on through steamer. E. C. Macfarlane.'

"I congratulate Your Majesty, on the good news and the fact that my brother's Telegram of last week has been confirmed today, which showed that they were working to defer action on the Treaty, to carry it over to the Cleveland Administration—he has also carried his other point, to have a Commission sent out here from Washington, by the President.... Your Majesty's most obedt. Servt, G. W. Macfarlane." Hawaii State Archives, Liliuokalani Collection, Box 18, Seized Documents.

Cleveland accompanied by a Précis of our situation. On their arrival at N.Y., they met Mr. Brien, President Cleveland's secretary, and through him, sent them to the President at Lakewood.[39] President on receiving the Précis immediately ordered the Précis to be published in the [*New York*] *World*—which shows an inclination to recognize our cause. Neumann also found that Foster had suppressed publishing our Précis.

[Ned] Macfarlane on hearing of Kaiulani's intention to come to the U.S. was going to tell Mr. Davies not to be forward and officious, for fear the Americans would feel jealous, and our cause injured.[40] Ned said [they] will work to send Commissioners out.

Mr. Francis Gay called and after greetings spoke politics. Said he had asked Dole what they would do if Commissioners came out from U.S. [and] was answered—they would not recognize them, also that if the C's [Commissioners] were to favor election and succeed, they would send protest to England—which would be absurd.

*Sunday, March 12.* Washington Place. 6.30 A.M. Kahuakai after saying prayers for us went home and I was left alone in the Library and Mrs. Hattie Kawainui and her sister from Hana came to see me. I could not make up my mind to see her, after all that her husband said about me in the *Nupepa Kuokoa*.[41]

Spent the rest of the day in the house reading foreign news. Sent Miss Wolf early this morning with some Spanish hens' eggs and told her to give them to Mr. H. Congdon—to use as he pleased.[42] My turkeys doing well, also my Spanish hens, my white turkey, also Hawaiian geese.

---

39. The Grover Clevelands were then living in Lakewood, New Jersey.

40. The *Pacific Commercial Advertiser*, March 11, 1893, reprinted a New York newspaper notice that appeared on Kaiulani's arrival at that city: "New York, March 1. Princess Kaiulani, niece of the deposed Queen Liliuokalani of Hawaii, arrived here today on the steamer *Teutonic*. With her were Theophilus H. Davies and Mrs. Davies, the English guardians of the Princess, Miss Davies and Miss Wartoff, the companions of the Princess. E. C. Macfarlane, ex-Minister of Finance . . . and Dr. Mott-Smith, present Hawaiian Minister to this country, went down the bay on the revenue cutter *Chandler* to meet the young Princess. She had come to the United States, she said, more for the purpose of learning and observing . . . than to make a petition for her crown."

Another article dated New York, March 2, 1893, and also reprinted in the *Advertiser* on March 11, said: "The coming to America of Theophilus H. Davies with the Princess Kaiulani is regarded by Paul Neumann, E. C. Macfarlane, and others as a most unfortunate thing for the anti-annexation movement, and they have not hesitated to express themselves regarding it. Neumann . . . said that the step was a most unwise one. Macfarlane said that he did not know any good reason for the presence of Kaiulani here, and that her coming was an unfortunate thing for his side of the case. . . . Dr. [Mott] Smith, the Hawaiian Minister, [said] the Princess has no business here, the Queen has not abdicated the Hawaiian throne and she can have no official weight."

41. The offending article appeared in the February 11, 1893, issue of the *Nupepa Kuokoa*, under the heading "Huakai Kuai Ia Hawaii" ("Trip to Sell Hawaii"):

"The news about town is that Mr. Paul Neumann was given full authority to sell and convey the Hawaiian Islands to the United States. By what power does the deposed Queen have [the right] to send a representative to sell the land?

"The government is for all the people, not just a single person. Neumann's trip is not in the interest of the people, but is a trip that will destroy the Hawaiian people. We challenge all opposition newspapers to deny the truth of this news.

"Behold this betrayal of the Hawaiian people, and consider that it was not so long ago that the native people of the land were ill treated by that ancient system of government." Translation by Jason Achiu.

42. Henry Congdon (proprietor of Henry Congdon & Co.) sold wholesale wines and liquors at 88 Fort Street, and resided at the Hawaiian Hotel.

*Monday, March 13.* Washington Place. Went out to Waikiki with the intention of working at Paoakalani but found Alapai had not sent any earth so went to Kealohilani. Mrs. Nowlein and the Capt. with ten soldiers started to work on the stone wall. I spent my time in writing out list of my songs that I composed. They were a hundred in all—still there must be some more. Left Waikiki at five P.M. Spent evening on the back veranda listening to Portuguese band of the Provisional Government.

*Tuesday, March 14.* Washington Place. Gave to Captain Nowlein $1,000.00 to pay my bills with. I am $11,000 less in debt to the people. Had word sent to me that I must be careful of myself and not go out in the streets as I have been doing, as she had heard that I might be shot.[43]

*Wednesday, March 15.* Washington Place. Mrs. Nowlein made me a present of a delaine dress.[44] Gave Jessie Kaae $2.50. I heard again [the admonition] to take care of myself for fear I would be shot. The P.G. are preparing for a contest if the news were to come of my restoration. Gave the key of the [Hale] Naua closet at the Palace[45] to Capt. Nowlein. Told Mr. Robertson to bring my music away from the Hawaiian News Co.[46] Robertson told me that my basket from England had arrived. Heard that [Paul Puhiula Kalakua] Kanoa had a stroke of Apoplexy.

Heard also that Minister of Finance P. C. Jones has resigned[47]—one reason was the Executive Council wanted George Smithies' position[48]— another is he did not approve of all these firearms that have been imported by Willie Hall's firm and came by *Monowai*.[49]

Heard from Mr. Parker that Mr. Dole went to Mr. W. G. Irwin[50] to try to borrow some money. This shows that money is scarce and Mr. Damon would not lend any more. I heard there is only $16,000 more in the treasury. Mr. T. C. Porter will take Minister Jones' place.[51]

*Thursday, March 16.* Washington Place. Mr. Damon called and offered to do something for me. I thanked him and told him [that] from my salary I was trying to pay my debts. I inquired after Mr. P. C. Jones' health and was told he was threatened with apoplexy. After he left, heard that W. G.

43. This was a street rumor, frequently retold (with little real evidence to support the threat) through much of 1893.

44. A dress made of lightweight wool or a wool-cotton blend.

45. The Hale Naua closet was upstairs in one of the attic rooms of the palace. See first footnote for February 4, 1892, diary entry (270).

46. The proprietor of the Hawaiian News Co. on Merchant Street was Provisional Government official John H. Soper. Liliu's dislike of Soper would have led her to remove her music sheets.

47. Peter Cushman Jones, who had been Liliuokalani's minister of finance 1892–January 13, 1893, was reappointed by the Provisional Government and served January 17–March 15, 1893. His letter of resignation to Dole, dated March 12, says simply, "I find it impossible to continue and perform the duties of the Office owing to my state of health." Hawaii State Archives, Foreign Office and Executive Files, 1893, Executive and Advisory Councils.

48. George E. Smithies (b. 1864–d. 1919) was an assistant clerk in the Interior Department, and the husband of Maili Nowlein, from a prominent royalist family of Lahaina.

49. William W. Hall's firm was the mercantile house E. O. Hall and Son Ltd., at Fort and King Streets, of which he was head. Peter Cushman's wife was Hall's sister.

50. William G. Irwin was the president and manager of Wm. G. Irwin & Co., a major sugar factor and commission merchant, of which Claus Spreckels was vice president. Irwin was also a principal in Spreckels and Co., bankers, at Fort near Queen Streets.

51. Theodore C. Porter (d. 1898, California) was an accountant. He was the minister of finance March 15–May 29, 1893, and at the same time was a member of the Executive and Advisory Councils of the Provisional Government. P. C. Jones was the minister of finance.

Irwin would probably ask Mr. W. O. Smith to step out. Wrote by USS *Alliance* to Mr. Neumann and the Prince David. My Kahilis [royal feather standards] were sent back [from the Palace] tonight, 12 in all, amongst them were 'Kaolohaka' and 'Keaka'.[52]

*Friday, March 17.* Washington Place. My Japanese whatnot and two mattresses and two mosquito nets and Kahili handles were brought from the palace, also two Ihe [spears], given me by Emma Kanoa. I sent them to Muolaulani. Gave W. Aylett $50.00 and paid Pierre Jones for translating.[53]

Early this morning the old Royal Hawaiian Band came to serenade me. I felt so sad for them yet admired them for their patriotism. The streets were full of people and they shed tears for me and for the band. Allowed [Sentence ends abruptly.]

*Saturday, March 18.* Washington Place. Hattie Hiram and Lizzie Doiron came to tell [ask] me what I thought of their going around to collect names for their new association The Hui Aloha Aina.[54] I told them it would be better for them to wait till our Commissioners returned from Washington. Rev. Kekahuna[55] came in and I asked him to send us more pili [grass] for my house—said he would send it. [Name erased] came in after they left and said he found [name erased] arranging [name erased] clothes, when she saw him she did not know what to do. I told them they ought to get a divorce since they could not live together in peace and each to marry the one of their choice. He said he thought so too, and retire to country life. He said [K—, then rest erased] would not eat with [two erased words] was present and they could do without each other, they better marry.

Mrs. J.C.A. Cummins came in—told me about Capt. Wiltse and Lt. Young.[56] They are fearful of being Court martialed on his return. Hear tonight of Herring shooting D. L. Huntsman for going after his wife.[57]

---

52. A receipt dated March 16, 1893, and signed by D. W. Kanoelehua says, "Received from Jas. W. Robertson, twelve Kahilis [royal feather standards] for Her Majesty Liliuokalani." Hawaii State Archives, Foreign Office and Executive Files, Executive and Advisory Councils, Miscellaneous Documents. The document does not individually name the kahili.

53. Pierre Jones (b. 1841–d. 1915), an English-born and Europe-educated teacher and bookkeeper, was a resident of Hawaii from the 1860s. He was fluent in French.

54. The Hui Hawaii Aloha Aina (Hawaiian Patriotic League) formed on March 4, 1893. John A. Cummins was appointed honorary president, Joseph Nawahi, acting president, and J. H. Kaunamano and J. W. Bipikane, vice presidents. The introduction to the group's constitution said: "Whereas vital changes in our country have taken place, which may affect its independence and the civil rights of its subjects and citizens, thereby rendering indispensable a compact and zealous union between all men who love the country, irrespective of party or creed—Therefore, Resolved that we, the patriotic, peaceful, and loyal subjects and citizens of Hawaii Nei, for the purpose of peaceably guarding our civil rights, do hereby form ourselves into a league under the following constitution." *Pacific Commercial Advertiser*, March 14, 1893. Membership was open to all Native Hawaiians over 20 years, and foreigners were allowed to join as honorary members.

55. Reverend J. Kekahuna appears in the 1893 City Directory as "preacher, Waianae."

56. This report probably has to do with the following incident. The *Hawaiian Star*, April 14, 1893, reprinting an article from the *Bulletin*, noted: "Captain G. C. Wiltse, who was relieved of the command of the cruiser *Boston* in Honolulu harbor by Captain B. F. Day, has been ordered to Washington to report his reasons for his action in landing an armed force in Hawaii."

57. August Herring shot Dow Lee Huntsman Saturday night at the Herring residence on Liliha Street. At the time of his death, Huntsman (who was rooming in the Herring house) was a reporter for the *Liberal*, a newspaper owned by Robert Wilcox. The paper reported that the "case remains in doubt notwithstanding a number of rumors." Kalakaua had sent Herring, who was part Hawaiian, to Italy in 1887–88 to study sculpture.

Huntsman had no good word for anyone or for me. It is a punishment? I think [so] for I have never harmed him.

*Monday, March 20.* Washington Place. Kaunamano asked my opinion in regard to Hui Aloha Aina.[58] I told him not to encourage it now, and to remain perfectly passive till we heard from our Commissioners to Washington. That it would be injurious to our cause. Mr. S. Parker said Mr. Irwin has his reasons for appointing T. C. Porter.[59] I told him that was all right and if Mr. Irwin was only wise he would be Dictator today until Mr. Neumann returned. The P.G. has given out that there would be a meeting tonight at the Music Hall. Irwin will object. I am told by Capt. Nowlein the object the P.G. had for seeking the [Hale] Naua curios was to search for Kihapu, and Maui's Makau [Hook]. No one will know where 'Kihapu' is taken. Or where Maui's 'Makau' is.[60]

I have told Mr. Robertson to tell Hopp[61] to take my piano[62] up to Muolaulani and for McGuire[63] to take my husband's writing table and my lanai [?] up there also. Frank will move up to my stable at Muolaulani today. D. L. Huntsman is buried by the rebel company of which he [was in] Company.[64] R. W. Wilcox and V. V. Ashford went in the 2nd carriage.

*Wednesday, March 22.* Washington Place. 9.30 A.M. Steamer *Australia* arrived. Joe Marsden of the P.G. Commissioners had to come back. He had nothing to stay for as Mr. L. A. Thurston and W. R. Castle would stay to watch the result of their Treaty at Washington—so two of their Commissioners had to come back with their heads hanging down. J. E. Bush also returned. [In her cash account for this date, Liliu records: "Pd. to Bishop & Co. by P. Neumann $212.89. Int. on note of $17,000."]

*Thursday, March 23.* Washington Place. Mr. J. A. Cummins called to say that his friend General Schofield will be here soon as one of the U.S. Commissioners—that he would do all he could for our cause.[65]

---

58. "The Hui Hawaii Aloha Aina held their second public meeting the evening of this day at Arion Hall," noted the *Pacific Commercial Advertiser*, March 21, 1893. The *Advertiser* coverage included a transcription of members' remarks, but nothing from J. K. Kaunamano. At this meeting, it was also announced that an organizational meeting of Hawaiian Patriotic Women would be held on March 23.

59. Theodore C. Porter was a teller at Spreckels & Co. bank, at which Irwin was manager.

60. On March 31, 1893, W. F. Allen made a report to the Executive and Advisory Councils on which items remaining in the palace were the property of the late King Kalakaua. With respect to the "Books and Curios claimed by the Hale Naua Society," he stated: "Nothing has been delivered, but all is in the possession and keeping of the Government, and I find it impossible to decide what curios came from the Government Museum till the return from Molokai of Mrs. Emma Nakuina, the former custodian of the Museum, whose evidence I require." Hawaii State Archives, Foreign Office and Executive Files, Executive and Advisory Councils, 1893, Miscellaneous Documents. Kihapu (the famous conch shell of Waipio) and Makau (Manaiakalani, the great fishhook associated with the demigod Maui) are both at the Bishop Museum.

61. John Hopp was of Hopp & Co., a manufacturer and dealer in furniture, located on King near Bethel Street.

62. The koa wood piano presented to the Queen had been in the Iolani Palace throne room. A receipt for the removal of the same "from James W. Robertson custodian of Iolani Palace," dated March 30, 1893, and signed J. Hopp & Co., is in the Hawaii State Archives, Foreign Office and Executive Files, Box 40, Miscellaneous Documents.

63. James W. McGuire was proprietor of a baggage and express business at 84 King Street.

64. The Huntsman funeral took place at the Queen's Hospital on March 21. The *Pacific Commercial Advertiser*, March 22, 1893, said: "Company A of the National Guard turned out almost to a man to pay their last respects to their murdered comrade."

65. John McAllister Schofield (b. Sept. 29, 1831–d. March 4, 1906, Florida), a soldier, was

Mary C. [Carter] also came and warned me to be careful in what I said—that they had rec'd a telegram from Neumann saying [American] Commissioners will come down and that [Annexation] Treaty had been withheld by President Cleveland. I told her when they arrived I would send message through Mr. Macfarlane. She told me also that they had made him [her husband, J. O. Carter] suffer through their friendship for me—how hateful. Mr. J. M. Monsarrat brought and delivered to me all the papers connected with the Mortgages which he had handed to me by Mary A. and James T. Leach, and I made over to my husband. First on the list is [to] J. M. Monsarrat $1,500, and 2nd Kamohoalii, $225, 3d to J.W.L. Lapauila $300. 4th to James A. Akina $300. Qau Wa $150, Manuel Perry $750, Ellen P. Clark $400, Kealoha $200, C. K. Ayau $800, accompanied by their notes.[66]

Messrs. Parker and Cornwell came in to say the latter was going up to Maui [but] would be back next week. Mr. Cummins told me Parker had lots of money—where did he get it? It may be he embezzled my money—will find out. Archie told me he will lose his place[67] because he was a royalist. He read me letters from Ned Macfarlane.[68] John E. Bush was to have Mass meeting but the Provisional Government suppressed it.[69]

Recd from J. H. $100 rent of Akaiko. Paid $50 for part of Pawaa—he took $9. To pay Kosila.

*Friday, March 24.* Washington Place. Misses Nawahi, Hiram, Webb, Kaae, Meekapu came in this morning and told me of the society they were about to start.[70] Wanted to know my opinion. I told them they might go about it

prominent in the U.S. Civil War, during which he became brigadier general, served as secretary of war 1868–69, and in 1870 took command of the Pacific Division. He visited Hawaii in 1873 on the *Benicia*. Schofield promoted the interests of the United States in acquiring Pearl Harbor. He retired from active service in 1895. Schofield did not come to the islands as a U.S. commissioner, as suggested here.

66. On June 23, 1891, James T. Leach and his wife, Mary, transferred a group of nine mortgages held by various parties, 1887–90, to John O. Dominis. Bureau of Conveyances, Liber 131, 209. Leach appears in the City Directory of 1893 as "engineer steamer Mikahala, res. 137 Fort St."

67. Archibald S. Cleghorn held the position of collector general of customs until April 18, 1893. The rumor of his pending removal was generally known. On March 23, Robert W. Wilcox wrote to Porter, the new minister of finance: "I am told that Mr. Cleghorn is to be asked to resign from the position of the Collector General of Customs; Therefore, I respectfully ask of you the appointment to the said position." Hawaii State Archives, Minister of Finance Correspondence.

68. These letters have not been found.

69. The *Pacific Commercial Advertiser*, March 23, 1893, reported that J. E. Bush would "address the natives at 7:30 o'clock this evening at Palace Square." Despite the Queen's remark about its having been "suppressed," the meeting proceeded on schedule. The following day, the same newspaper noted: "About a thousand people gathered at Palace Square last night to hear Mr. Bush give impressions derived from his recent visit to America." Bush's self-aggrandizing remarks about Americans, the annexation commissioners, and "land grabbers" included the bizarre statement that "I have declared myself an annexationist providing you consent to it but finding you oppose, I have nothing more to do."

70. The society, a women's auxiliary to the Hawaiian Patriotic League, had its formational meeting at Arion Hall on March 27, 1893, when about 160 persons signed up. Mrs. F. W. Macfarlane, the president elect, made an address giving a brief outline of the organization formed "chiefly to act as a committee of welcome to the members of the United States Commission when they arrive" (meaning U.S. Commissioner James H. Blount). Mrs. Macfarlane was appointed president, and the honorary presidents were Mrs. T. R. Foster, Mrs. F. S. Pratt, Mrs. J. A. Cummins, Mrs. S. C. Allen, and Mrs. C. A. Brown. There were also an enormous number of vice presidents, as well as members appointed to executive and financial committees.

now since we know now that Commissioners are to be sent out here to investigate. Charles Wilson wanted to know about the *Holomua*. I told him bills ought to be sent out and we would all pay up. He wanted to know about our Genealogy. I gave it to him. He said he would come again.

*Saturday, March 25.* Washington Place. Wiliokai came to say he was notified by J. C. King of the Provisional Government that he must leave the Mausoleum and to deliver up the keys to Maria Beckley Kahea.[71] Although I was astonished, it is better for her to be there than to have another person. Hattie Hiram and Jessie Kaae are full of patriotism and want more directions about Hui Aloha Aina. All the principal Hawaiian Ladies will join. Mr. Cummins and Major Seward[72] wanted the magazine they lent me. Mr. C. said he would come again to let me know something.

Capt. Nowlein told me the posts and Oa [rafters] of my hale [house] had arrived. Joe Aea came about his wife—she never went home but she always had a new dress. Where did they come from? I told him I gave her some money now and then as she was helping around the house—he thought she got money from Lehua.

---

On March 29, 1893, U.S. commissioner James H. Blount arrived at Honolulu. He had been commissioned by U.S. President Grover Cleveland to investigate the political situation in Hawaii, specifically what part the United States had played in the overthrow of the Hawaiian monarchy on January 17, 1893. He collected considerable evidence during his investigation, and the Queen's diary frequently mentions both Blount and his report, so he merits a biographical note.

James H. Blount was a U.S. congressman and special commissioner (b. September 12, 1837, Georgia–d. March 8, 1903, Macon, Georgia). Blount fought on the Confederate side during the Civil War, but afterward worked valiantly for a restored Union. He served as a representative in the U.S. Congress from 1872 until March 4, 1893, when he resigned voluntarily. In April 1893, U.S. President Grover Cleveland designated him a special commissioner to investigate the political situation in Hawaii—specifically the part that the United States, under the orders of Commissioner John L. Stevens and Captain Wiltse of the USS *Boston*, had played in the downfall of the Hawaiian monarchy on January 17, 1893. Blount and his wife arrived at Honolulu on March 29, 1893, and remained until August 8, 1893.

---

71. On March 24, 1893, Kaina or Cain David Wiliokai, the keeper of the Royal Mausoleum, was informed by the Interior Department that Mrs. Maria Beckley Kahea had been appointed keeper of the grounds and the Royal Mausoleum in his place, and he was directed to deliver the keys of the mausoleum, grounds, and keeper's house to the latter. See Hawaii State Archives, index card. In the 1894–95 City Directory, he is listed as "Mgr. Hawaiian Quintette r. 14 Richards St."

Maria Beckley Kahea (d. 1909) was the sister of Fred K. Beckley (b. 1845–d. 1881), who had been governor of Kauai under Kalakaua.

72. Major W. T. Seward (d. December 5, 1907, Washington, DC), a native of Guilford, Connecticut, had served in the American Civil War (hence his title). He would be heavily involved in the 1895 counterrevolution, specifically in the business of smuggling guns into Hawaii and landing them at John Cummins's sugar plantation in Waimanalo. He was tried and sentenced to 35 years' imprisonment and a $120,000 fine "for procuring arms and munitions for the Wilcox rebels." President Dole pardoned him on condition that he leave the islands, which he did.

Working under specific instructions from President Cleveland, Blount conducted interviews (mainly with Hawaiian loyalists) and compiled massive documentation on events leading up to Lililuokalani's overthrow. The U.S. House of Representatives published all of this on December 18, 1893, in what is known as the Blount Report.

---

*Wednesday, March 29.* 9.30 The *Rush* is reported inside the harbor and only one Commissioner on board—Honl. J. H. Blount of Georgia and his wife.[73]

11 A.M. J. W. Robertson went on board, sent in his card, and was received by him [Blount] in the forward Cabin. He gave the Queen's Compliments, then afterwards offered the carriage to drive up or anytime that he would wish. Mr. B. thanked [him] and declined very politely, but said he would drive up in his own carriage, but would call on the Queen someday.

~~Two p.m.~~ Mr. R. [Robertson] saw McGrew, Hartwell, Scott, Hastings, H. Castle, Stevens, and Severance, and Lt. Fox of Admiral Skerritt's staff.[74] This is a day of excitement and the town is decked with American flags and the girls went down to decorate the Commissioner [Blount] and lady. A committee of the Hui Aloha Aina called on them and offered the Hawaiian National Band for the evening. Ministers Parker and Peterson called at seven P.M.

Mr. Blount asked if the majority of the people were annexationists— he [Parker] said not. [Blount asked] If it is true that it was the U.S. that was the means of the situation of Hawaii—he [Parker] said yes, that it [was] Stevens' doing. How was it that the Queen promulgated the Constitution—had she done wrong—he [Parker] said she had not because at the advice of her Ministers she yielded and did not do any wrong.

[John Lot] Kaulukou and others called to see him. He [Blount] was pleased to hear so many Hawaiians speak English so well.

*Friday, March 31.* Washington Place. Mr. Robertson called this morning and told me the Provisional Government had notified him verbally that after today he was to receive no more salary—but that he would make a protest. Jessie Kaae told me she was going over with Jamie Miles to Koolau to take signatures for [those joining the] Hui Aloha Aina.

---

73. James H. Blount, his wife, and his private secretary, Ellis Mills, arrived on the U.S. Revenue steamer *Richard Rush* (Captain Hooper) on March 29. The *Pacific Commercial Advertiser*, March 30, 1893, editorialized: "The arrival by the *Rush* of ex-congressman James H. Blount, who has been sent as a special Commissioner to inquire into the situation, will occasion no solicitude to the friends of good and progressive government on these islands. If Mr. Cleveland has sent Mr. Blount here after the full information which had already been laid before the State Department at Washington, it can only be because he is determined to act on an enterprise of such pith and moment only after the fullest survey of the field. The friends of annexation are not afraid of the investigation." While it deemed Blount's arrival a "gala day," the *Advertiser* commented that he "was not disposed to be communicative yesterday."

74. Liliu is referring to Dr. John S. McGrew; Judge Alfred S. Hartwell; educator M. M. Scott; Frank Hastings of the American consulate; Henry N. Castle, editor of the *Pacific Commercial Advertiser*; and Henry W. Severance, U.S. consul; all were island residents. John L. Stevens was the U.S. commissioner 1892–93. Lieutenant Fox was on the *Rush*.

9.30 Mr. Sam Damon called and told me that the Provisional Government had decided not to let me draw any salary in future because I still encouraged the *Holomua*. I told him that from the day John Ena told me to give up the *Holomua* I had done so and also told J. Heleluhe to give up the paper—he said he would do so but that they ought to pay up what they owed him.[75]

Damon asked me if I send articles or had anything to do with the paper's [comments] against Mr. Stevens or the Provisional Government. I said no. Then he told me he had three times interceded for me but to no purpose and that he would tell them I had no interest in the paper. I sent Joe to tell him he had none also. Damon explained of how my affidavit had got into Stevens' hands.[76]

Dole was at Stevens' place and Damon took it to show to Dole and Stevens took possession of it, but it was mean of Stevens to publish it. I sent for Mr. Peterson and he came at 12.30. I showed [him] C. B. Wilson's diary,[77] he said it would be hurtful to our cause if it were given to Mr. Blount, as his statement.

*Saturday, April 1.* Washington Place. At 11 the Hawaiian flag will be raised while the Stars and Stripes will be hauled down over the Government building.[78] Nine A.M. Mr. J. O. Carter called and I asked his advice as to what we should do when the flag is raised. He said keep perfectly quiet and not to cheer for it would be aggravating to the Americans. I immediately sent Nawahi to tell the people to be quiet which they did, and [they] behaved very well. Their feelings of joy were suppressed while the men all took their hats off while tears of joy streamed down the cheeks of men as well as women.[79]

---

75. The columns of the *Daily Hawaii Holomua* (particularly its English-language page) continued to annoy the Provisional Government. The *Pacific Commercial Advertiser*, in its March 30, 1893, editorial, termed the paper a "mongrel sheet . . . edited by a brace of anonymous rascals who dare not avow their identity in print." By this the newspaper meant G. Carson Kenyon and Edmund Norrie, not John Sheldon, the publicly identified editor.

The *Pacific Commercial Advertiser*, February 16, 1893, detailed Liliuokalani's financial interest in the *Holomua*: "As to the ownership of the paper the public will be surprised to know that it was sold to and is nominally owned by Joe Heleluhe, the coachman of the ex-Queen. When Wilson was marshall, he opened the preliminary negotiations with Mr. Waller, the then owner, and then the matter was turned over to Mr. Kenyon, who completed the arrangements for the sale. The paper was then turned over to Heleluhe. The foregoing group of names will naturally suggest that the real owner of the sheet is the ex-Queen and that is considered by those who know to be the case."

76. She probably means her power of attorney.

77. Charles B. Wilson's diary has not survived. It was probably burned with other documents following the aborted January 1895 counterrevolution.

78. One of Commissioner James H. Blount's first actions was to order the removal of the American flag flying atop the government building and the restoration of the Hawaiian flag on April 1. John L. Stevens had virtually established a temporary American protectorate by raising the U.S. flag. At the same time the *Hawaiian Star* announced: "Commissioner Blount does not lower the colors with a view to restore the monarchy but to put the Provisional Government on an independent basis of its own, so that he, as a representative of a power not responsible for local administration, may negotiate with it. Neither does the withdrawal of the naval arm mean that the royalists will be permitted to revolt. If the peace is disturbed the American forces will land again." *Hawaiian Star*, April 1, 1893.

79. The Hawaiian newspaper *Ka Leo o Ka Lahui*, April 1, 1893, had this to say: "Hawaii's

The Royal Hawaiian Band at Emma Square, circa 1889. The band was founded in 1836 during the reign of Kamehameha III. In her diaries, Liliuokalani frequently mentions attending their concerts. In 1893, the Provisional Government required band members to sign an oath of loyalty swearing that they would not support the Queen or her government. All but two band members refused to sign and were discharged. They asked Ellen Wright Prendergast, Liliu's close friend, to express their sentiments, including their loyalty to the Queen. The result was the song "Kaulana Na Pua," a political protest also known as "Mele Aloha Aina" or "Ai Pohaku."
Hawaii State Archives

OPPOSITE
"Mele Aloha Aina" was published in 1895 by Hawaiian loyalist F. J. Testa as the opening song in Buke Mele Lahui (Book of National Songs), a collection of over 100 political and patriotic Hawaiian songs. The fifth and final stanza from page two of Buke Mele Lahui is included here with its English translation.
Hawaiian Historical Society

336

# BUKE MELE LAHUI.

## MELE ALOHA AINA.
[AI-POHAKU.]

Kaulana na pua o Hawaii,
Kupaa mahope o ka aina,
Hiki mai ka elele a ka lokoino,
Palapala alunu me ka pakaha.

Pane mai Hawaii-Nui-o-Keawe,
Kokua na Hono-o-Piilani,
Kakoo mai Kauai-o-Mano,
Pau pu me ke one Kakuhihewa.

Aole e kau e ka pulima,
Maluna o ka pepa a ka enemi,
Aole makou a e minamina,
I ka puu dala a ke Aupuni.

Ua lawa makou i ka pohaku,
I ka ai kamahao o ka aina,
Hoohuiaina kuai hewa,
I ka pono kivila o ke kanaka.

Mahope makou o Liliulani,
A kau hou Ia i ke Kalaunu,
Hainaia mai ana ka puana,
Na pua i aloha i ka aina.

*We back Liliu[oka]lani*
*She will be crowned again.*
*Tell the story*
*Of the people who love their land.*

English translation from *Na Mele o Hawai'i Nei*
by Samuel H. Elbert and Noelani Mahoe,
(Honolulu: University of Hawaii Press, 1970)

I went up to Hinano Bower and slept all day and did [a] little writing. This is a day of anxiety to me. I am more tired from thinking than from actual work. Five A.M. at Family worship read from Psalms 20 Ch. 1.v.[80] [and] hymn 322 in native hymnbook.[81] After prayers told Kahuakai to bear the good news and asked them to notify the Kaumakapili members to pray and give thanks for our flag.

*Sunday, April 2.* Washington Place. Spent a quiet day at home—writing. Joe Aea stood watch while Capt. Nowlein went home to rest—nothing of importance transpired. Heard that the P.G. were enlisting more men.

*Monday, April 3.* Washington Place. Mr. Parker called in and told me that he had been breakfasting with Mr. Blount. He had asked him where the Queen's Constitution was. Mr. Parker had said that I destroyed it after the company dispersed. Mr. Blount wanted to hear more from Mr. Parker—and he told him he would have to ask the questions.[82] W. H. Cornwell told him he would have to give his testimony in the best way he could.

Joseph Nawahi called at 2.30 P.M. and told us that the Army of the Provisional Government had been called to congregate at the barracks—to appear in full uniforms—and it is feared that they meant business but with whom will they fight? He also told me that Saturday while the P.G. were in Council, Mr. Blount stepped in and without sitting down asked them "whether any of the American people had been killed or hurt—they said not—whether any property had been injured—they said not." He turned round and went out without saying a word. They thought him very queer. Mr. Blount told Mr. Parker he would call on me after everything is settled.

---

Beloved Flag Flies Again. With hearts filled with awe and tears flowing to the ground . . . was the huge assembly gathered at Aliiolani Hale this past Saturday morning to confirm the news . . . about the American flag being pulled down and the beloved flag of Hawaii being raised again. . . . At exactly 11, the sound of a trumpet resounded, and at that point the striped flag of America was seen coming down as the beloved flag of Hawaii rose like an angel ascending to Paradise. . . . As for the assembly of people . . . when they saw it gently rising upward, like a billow-dancing Kaupu bird [an albatross], no tears were restrained. . . . Great was the affection, as was the excitement."

80. Psalms 20:1, "Jehovah answer thee in the day of trouble."

81. The hymnal referred to is *Ka Buke Himeni Hawaii* (New York: Ko Amerika Ahahui Teraka, 1885); hymn 322 is "Ke Hea Nei Iesu" ("Our Heavenly Father Calls").

82. Blount's interview with Parker on April 6, 1893, was the date on which Parker provided the former with a detailed account of the Queen's attempt to present a new constitution in the blue room. "She said, 'I sent for you gentlemen; I was requested by my people to promulgate a new constitution. I want you gentlemen to sign it or consent to it.' They all looked to me. I said, 'Your Majesty, we have not read the constitution, but before we read it, you must know it is a revolutionary act. It cannot be done.' She said: 'Read it; see what it is.' On that point we said, after we had read it, 'We advise you to give it up—not to think any more about it.' By that time she had got pretty well excited, and some of my colleagues said: 'If you insist upon it, we will resign.'" Parker then said he had a private conversation with the Queen about the document. "I told her I would not and my colleagues would not agree to it. There were a good many words passed between us. She said: 'Why don't you resign.' I said I would not resign unless it was according to law." Blount Report, 437–45.

*Diary for 1893*

Passed over to Joe Memo of Mortgages of Mary Leach by J. M. Monsarrat, and Kapiolani's lease of Kealohilani, Waikiki—also notes of same and Mortgages of the above, ten in all—gave them all to J. Heleluhe. Mary Carter asked me why I sold my shares—Mr. Carter would have given me more for them, he would have managed to raise money for me and still I would hold my shares. I simply said yes, yet I thought of Mr. Parker and his actions. Is it embezzling? But I must have patience for these trying times.

Lively has two kittens.

W. F. Reynolds wants 250 copies of "Aloha Oe" and "[He] Mele Lahui Hawaii."[83]

Heard of J. H. Boyd, George Smithies, Tripp's dismissal by the P.G.[84]

*Tuesday, April 4.* Washington Place. Heard from Mr. Robertson of one of the crowns being stolen last Saturday night.[85] Over 300 soldiers were in the Palace basement that night—some of Mr. Robertson's decorations were taken.

Christine went this morning to Amelia Macfarlane's and asked her what the heading of the Hui Aloha Aina list would be.[86] A. Macfarlane told her they would not put it on till the last—that it was to be for the Civil Rights of the people and for our independence. Is it not then to restore our Queen to her throne? Why, that will be left to the Commissioner—

---

83. W. F. Reynolds (d. 1909) was the proprietor of the Golden Rule Bazaar at 83 Fort Street, which advertised sewing machines, school stationery and exercise books, "the cheapest line of Guitars and Mandolins," and "sheets of music received by every steamer."

84. Boyd and Smithies were assistant clerks in the Interior Department; Captain Alfred N. Tripp was the jailer of Oahu Prison.

85. On April 5, 1893, the *Pacific Commercial Advertiser* announced: "Plundered! Kalakaua's Crown is Left Without Ornaments." The robbery had been discovered on Monday morning (April 3) when James Robertson, Liliuokalani's former chamberlain, was in the process of turning over the property of his office to the new government. Originally, the crowns of Kalakaua and Kapiolani had been housed in a handsome box, and kept in a vault at Bishop & Co.'s bank (George Macfarlane said they were in the custody of the Spreckels Bank until about 1890, when Kalakaua asked for their return). In the palace, they were kept in a locked trunk in the chamberlain's office. When Robertson turned them over to the new government, he found the lock broken. The box containing the Kalakaua crown had been opened—all that was found was the velvet cap. Later some of the filigree of the crown was discovered in a small closet in the chamberlain's office. On June 14, one George Ryan, a 25-year-old discharged palace security guard who had a criminal record and several aliases, was arrested for the theft of the crown jewels, said theft having taken place on the first or second of April. He had pried out the jewels, sold a few of the stones, and sent others to friends in Missouri. The *Pacific Commercial Advertiser*, June 26, 1893, reported that Ryan had served time in Oregon and was supposed to have also been in Oahu Prison in 1887 under the name of "Jack McVeigh." On August 22, George Ryan (now identified as "alias Preston Horner") was convicted of larceny in the second degree, and sentenced to three years' imprisonment and a fine of $200.

A record of Ryan's trial appears in the Hawaii State Archives, First Circuit Court, Criminal 1828. For a full account, see Albert P. Taylor, "The Loot of the Coral Throne," *Paradise of the Pacific*, December 1925, 43–51. Several drafts of archivist Taylor's narrative are also in the Hawaii State Archives, A. P. Taylor Collection, Box 1, Folders 12 and 19.

86. Amelia or Emilie Macfarlane (b. 1858, Lihue, Kauai–d. 1947, Honolulu) was the wife of Frederick W. Macfarlane and the part-Hawaiian daughter of Judge Herman Widemann. The matter of the "heading" for the Hui's petition to Blount was to cause great dissension among the ranks. See last footnote for April 17, 1893, diary entry (343).

if he thinks she is not wrong he will restore her, if she is, he will not restore her. Christine says they will not do anything.

*Wednesday, April 5.* Washington Place. Slept at Mrs. Nowlein's [on King Street]—report was out that there might be an assault on me. More investigations are going on. 12 P.M. Mr. Parker was to go again to Mr. Blount's. Wrote a long letter to Mr. Neumann and told him all that was transpiring. Rec'd $190.00 of dividends of Pahala. Sent an order to Pacific Music Co. [in San Francisco] to send down 150 copies of "Aloha Oe" and 150 of "He Mele Lahui Hawaii."[87]

*Thursday, April 6.* Washington Place. Jessie Kaae and Jennie Harvey came in to report their success.[88]

*Friday, April 7.* Washington Place. *Alameda* outside. Send Robertson in State Carriage for the Prince David, Paul Neumann, and [Ned] Macfarlane—all drive up here. People crowded down to wharf. Blount was there and saw all. Crowd followed carriage up here accompanied by Hui Kalaiaina. Three P.M. A luau given to the Prince by the people, Neumann, [Samuel] Parker, Macfarlane, [William H.] Cornwell—[and] others [Joseph] Nawahi, [John A.] Cummins, [John E.] Bush, [William Shaw] Bowen, [Prince] Kalanianaole, [John L.] Kaulukou.[89]

*Saturday, April 8.* Washington Place. Keaha and his friend came in my room while I was asleep and woke me up with their meles. Was not quite rested—should not have been woken up—saw two ahui hala [clusters of pandanus fruit] brought by them. Was startled by seeing them commence to pound each other in my presence. Asked Joe Aea what all this meant, and left the room. He and Milaina told those two to go home. Kaipo and Aimoku were here and [I] sent by the latter twenty dollars to Mrs. Bush.

*Sunday, April 9.* Washington Place. Mr. and Mrs. Nordhoff called at 11 A.M.[90] He asked me about having so many Cabinets in so short a time. I told him it shows the influence the Reform Party had in the House. The National Reform [Party] joined in with the reform [party] to ask me to

---

87. In a memorandum at the end of this diary, Liliu recorded: "Pacific Music Co. 206 Post St. San Francisco Cal. Prices of Sheet Music in S.F. 7 a sheet, 25 books cloth bound at $1.50 a book—1 Book in Plush $15.00."

88. Jessie Kaae and Jenny Harvey had been soliciting members for the political association Hui Aloha Aina. See first footnote for March 18, 1893, diary entry and first two footnotes for March 20, 1893, diary entry (330–31).

89. The *Hawaiian Star*, April 8, 1893, noted, "John [A.] Cummins, Prince David, Capt. Morse, and several ladies had a private banquet at the Hawaiian Hotel last evening." The account added, "The return of Prince David and Messrs. Neumann and Macfarlane was celebrated by a luau at [Queen] Kapiolani's house at Waikiki."

The same newspaper, on April 10, reported that at that luau, E. C. Macfarlane had made a "loud proclamation" that "Blount had orders to restore the Queen ... to the natives and others assembled [and that] the royalists were greatly elated, and ... this morning, the natives were circulating the rumor that the Queen was to be restored." Macfarlane later denied having made these remarks.

90. Charles Nordhoff (b. 1830, Westphalia, Prussia–d. July 14, 1901, San Francisco, California) was a journalist for Harper & Bro. (publisher of weekly and monthly journals), 1857–61; the *New York Evening Post*, 1861–72; then the *New York Herald*, 1874–90. Afterward he continued to forward news articles to that newspaper. He was the author of a number of books. The *Hawaiian Star* devoted much space in its columns to declaring Nordhoff's articles on Hawaiian affairs distorted and inaccurate.

yield to their request to nominate one of their number to form a Cabinet. As I was aware that that was my own right by the Constitution, I paid no heed to their request but made my own Cabinet. And they were angry at what they considered my obstinacy. Mr. Nordhoff said that was outrageous, certainly it was. He said, Have you any friends amongst the P.G.? I said yes—Mr. Dole and Mr. Damon. [He] was glad to hear it. [He asked] Is it not true that the U.S. Minister sought to make trouble? I think so. It began with my reign. Mr. Stevens made a speech which was overbearing in its purport, October 1892.[91] He called and I asked Parker and Neumann to stay. He came with H. L. Severance—sat down in his chair, threw his left leg over the arm, leaned back and poured forth his complaint against my Government—[and] read International laws on the right of a U.S. Minister. I stood up and said, "I would leave that matter to my Ministers." I forgot to tell him what Mr. Severance said to me the day after at a Central Union Church social when Severance [said] he was astonished to hear Mr. Stevens speak—He was not aware of what he (Mr. Stevens) was going to say.

Heard of the withdrawal of the Police who watches here.

*Monday, April 10.* Washington Place. Jessie and Jennie were here and told me that C.W.A. [Ashford] met a person last eve who asked him if he thought the Queen was going to be restored, he said "Yes." "What, and have things returned as before?" "Yes, why." "Well the United States must restore everything as before or there would be a blot on her name."

The question Senator Blount asked the Provisional Government has not been answered yet and that is: "Has the Queen's overthrow been done by the U.S. or her people?" Paul Neumann wants to impress on me two things, the love of my people, and their future welfare—that their rights be restored and maintained. Told me he had personal intercourse with Cleveland, and was promised justice. Must ask Spreckels not to support Provisional Government—must dismiss Cabinet. Tomorrow 10.30 [to] receive Mini[sters] and Dr. Bowen. [At] 11 Major Wodehouse and Bowen.[92]

91. John L. Stevens made his remarks in October 1892 following public disapproval over his inaction in sending out the USS *Boston* in search of a missing boat from the wreck of the American ship *W. A. Campbell*, on which were six or seven men, a woman, and a child. Charles B. Wilson said to U.S. Commissioner James H. Blount that following censure from the Honolulu press, "Minister Stevens took such exception to those articles that he forthwith visited the minister of Foreign Affairs, and stated that he wished a personal interview with Her Majesty.... On the appointed day and hour, Minister Stevens, accompanied by Consul-General H. W. Severance, arrived at the Palace. He was ushered into the Queen's presence.... He was asked politely to take a seat, and did so, flinging one leg over the arm of the chair, and in this uncouth position before a lady he most heatedly announced to the Queen, and to her amazement, that he was not there as plain Mr. Stevens but as envoy extraordinary and minister plenipotentiary of the United States of America. Then drawing himself up to an erect posture, [he] proceeded in a very ungentlemanly tone to inform the Queen that it was of the President of the United States of America addressing the queen of Hawaii. He then went on to say that he was not to be insulted by any newspapers of her realm, and said he referred to several articles which had been published in the 'Bulletin,' copies of which he had brought with him to place before Her Majesty. He expected an apology from the Queen, and also that she give him redress for the insult he had received.... At the conclusion of this most insane and unheard-of proceeding.... Her Majesty properly referred him to her ministers." Blount Report, 552–75.

92. William Shaw Bowen (b. 1847–d. 1907, East Greenwich, Rhode Island) was an assistant surgeon in the U.S. Navy, a newspaper correspondent, and, at the time of his visit to the

Told Neumann [I] will be guided by him in all matters. Robertson says Wodehouse and Canavarro think I ought not to publish Queen Victoria's letter[93]—didn't intend to. Heard that in two weeks everything will be settled then, he (Blount) is going to enjoy a good time. Fraulein [Wolf] says between the 21st and 25[th] I will be restored to the throne.

*Thursday, April 13.* Washington Place. Heard this afternoon four P.M. from [blank] and she heard from Mr. Osmer[94] who is married to a native, that they have all (the soldiers of the Provisional Government) been called in to the Palace and the Govt. building as well as the barracks—to watch as they heard that my friends were going to try to restore me to the throne tonight. I never had any idea of doing such a thing—would not do so until told by the U.S. Commissioner to do so. Later I heard that the P.G.s had [Rest of sentence blank, followed by a line, then:] Miss Pope [Rest is blank.]

*Sunday, April 16.* Washington Place. Sent word to Mrs. James Campbell to accept the Presidency of the Hui Aloha Aina a na Ladies. She told Milaina that she would. Mr. C. [Campbell] told Milaina that he heard the Queen was to be restored on Friday—by Senator Blount. This story corresponds with the story told me by Kaulukou, who gave Mr. Cecil Brown as his authority. C. B. [Cecil Brown] would not dare to deceive Mr. Campbell if it were not true.

*Monday, April 17.* Washington Place. Sam Parker borrowed 25 shares of my Hawaiian Agricultural Stocks to pay some of his debts as W. R. Castle and others are suing him.[95] We cannot afford to let him appear before Court at this time while Commissioner Blount is here. Paid A. S. Cleghorn $100.00 through J. W. Robertson.[96] [Liliu's cash account for this date says: "To A. S. Cleghorn $100, Sam Parker $2,500.00, Miss Davis $12 = $2,600.00."]

Nine A.M. The Committee of the Ladies' Patriotic League [Hui Aloha Aina o na Wahine] met at the Arion Hall and from there presented their Memorial asking Mr. Blount that the Queen should be restored to the

---

islands, editor and proprietor of the *New York World*. Bowen arrived on April 7 and remained until April 26. The policy of his newspaper had been opposition to annexation, but in testimony before Congress in 1894 (Morgan Report, vol. 1, 666–74), Bowen stated, "I had not been in the islands over twenty four hours before my personal sympathies tended toward the side of annexation." Nevertheless, while in Honolulu, he ingratiated himself among the royalists by suggesting that he had a close friendship with President Grover Cleveland.

93. The letter, dated March 8, 1893, says only: "We have received and referred to Our advisors the Letter which you addressed to Us of the revolt which had taken place in Your Kingdom. We wish you a happy issue from Your present difficulties, and We take this opportunity of renewing to Your Majesty the assurance of Our highest consideration and regard. And so We recommend You to the Protection of the Almighty.... Your good friend, [*signed*] Victoria R.I." Hawaii State Archives, Liliuokalani Collection, Box 18, Seized Documents.

94. J. Osmer was a turnkey at the station house in 1894.

95. This was probably a threatened action, settled privately, and not recorded in court documents.

96. Parker's debt was of long standing. In a memorandum at the end of this diary, Liliu writes: "Mr. Parker's notes of indebtedness to me. Nov. 1st 1892. Promised to Pay thirty days after date, the sum of $2,500.00 [and] May 7, 1893. $2,500.00 at 7 percent."

Throne.[97] They were led by Mrs. James Campbell and received cordially by the American Commissioners—and when they returned and reported to the Society [of] 300 present they were cheered, much to the dismay of the other party, and Mrs. Fred Macfarlane and her party had to resign. Mrs. F. Macfarlane, Kaaniau Pratt, Martha Giffard, Treasurer, Grace Kahalewai, Sec., Mrs. Foster, Mrs. Ward, and two others.[98]

*Tuesday, April 18.* Washington Place. John Parker and Tutsey Dowsett were married yesterday at her father's house. He is only 18 years and she is 20.[99]

Mr. Claus Spreckels and family arrived by the *Australia*.[100] He expressed himself as being happy that Sam Parker was in sympathy with the Queen.[101] There is good deal of meaning in such expressions in our favor. Mr. Irwin seemed quite crestfallen.[102]

*Wednesday, April 19.* Washington Place. Up to this hour, nine A.M. Sam Parker has not given me any notes for those shares [of stock] he has taken of mine. He disposed of 100 shares last month, where I do not know—and now day before yesterday he borrowed 25 shares again and has not given me any notes. I must insist on his giving me notes. Mr. E. C. Macfarlane

---

97. This document, addressed to Blount, pleaded "that Hawaii may be granted the preservation of its independent autonomy and the restoration of its legitimate native monarchy under our Queen Liliuokalani in whom we have full confidence." Morgan Report, vol. 2, 1299–1300.

98. The prelude to this presentation by the Ladies' League was stormy and contentious. Following a dispute over the form of their proposed "memorial" to U.S. Commissioner Blount, Mrs. F. W. MacFarlane, Mrs. Mary Foster, Mrs. Elizabeth Pratt, and Mrs. Giffard (the treasurer) resigned, and immediately thereafter Mrs. James Campbell assumed the president's office. "The retiring officers it is said have been suspected by the victorious wing of the Ladies' League in conspiring to put ex-Queen Dowager Kapiolani on the throne. When as president Mrs. F. W. Macfarlane drew her memorial, a rumor was quickly transported throughout the leading native members of the League that certain haole lawyers were working silently among the members of the League for a petition to put Kapiolani on the throne. When the half-white and full blooded native women got word of this report they made up their minds to be on the alert when the memorial came up for its first vote. When it did come up a week ago a number of native women soon raised an objection because Liliuokalani's name was omitted. Explanations from the officers were of no avail as the suspicion was overwhelming. Although Mrs. Macfarlane and a number of the most influential ladies of the League have resigned, the association will be continued under Mrs. Campbell, and strife is promised to be at an end, at least for the present." The article then prints the text of both their address and the memorial to Blount. *Pacific Commercial Advertiser*, April 18, 1893.

99. John P. Parker, the son of Samuel Parker, married Elizabeth Jane Dowsett at the Dowsett residence in Palama, April 17, 1893. He was 18, and would die in Honolulu on May 8, 1894, age 19 years. They had one child, Thelma (b. March 1894), who became the heir to the great Parker Ranch.

100. Mr. and Mrs. Spreckels were accompanied by their daughter Emma and son Rudolph.

101. The English-language page of the *Holomua*, April 19, 1893, has a highly flattering article about Spreckels and his concern for the Native Hawaiians: "We know that Claus Spreckels has come here to set things right, and to give another proof of his consideration and respect for the Hawaiian people, in such a manner as will benefit both them and him, and the Hawaiians can with patience and confidence allow their national life to rest on the hands of a man like Commissioner Blount, while leaving their domestic affairs to the care of Claus Spreckels."

102. William G. Irwin, Spreckels's partner in the Spreckels Bank, when interviewed by the *Hawaiian Star*, May 26, 1893, diplomatically stated: "When Mr. Spreckels is here . . . I leave all the politics to him and I attend to business, and if anyone wants to talk or ask about politics I send them to him." The *Hawaiian Star*, June 7, 1893, published a letter of Irwin in which he said: "I would say that I fully agree with Col. Spreckels in his opinion that annexation pure and simple . . . would prove a disaster instead of a boon to these islands."

has just called to tell me that he and J. O. Carter had heard from Mr. Nordhoff, who heard from Dr. Bowen, that he and President Dole had called on me or were going to do so, to offer to pension me off.[103]

I told him that as yet they had not called on me but they may yet, that I was not aware of it. He was astonished. Macfarlane further says that Nordhoff told him that Mr. Blount had told him this proposition of Dole's was neither from him or [from] the President of the U.S. I told him if such was Dole's proposition, I would say I would take it under advisement. I told him also I would leave matters entirely to the decision given by Mr. Cleveland. Must not tell S. P. [Sam Parker].

Paid Kwong Sing $132.00[104] for all jobs done by him. [Liliu's cash account gives the figure as $182.00.] He assured me Joe Heleluhe paid for his own lumber.

2.10 P.M. Mr. Nordhoff has just called to say that he heard from good authority that Mr. Dole was coming to ask me to abdicate, and would impress on me that it was the wish of President Cleveland or Mr. Blount.[105] Mr. Nordhoff says neither has given any statement to that effect. I assured him I would be on the watch. I judge that Nordhoff and Bowen are here for certain purposes and will act with Blount. Nordhoff assures me Blount has supreme power—though not plainly expressed, means as much—*and I think he will (I mean Mr. Blount), reinstate.*[106]

*Thursday, April 20.* Washington Place. Mr. Cummins simply came to see me [on] his usual calls. M. Kahai [and] her niece Annie Holmes are going to the World's Fair—will go by the *Australia*.

Sam Parker told me Mr. Claus Spreckels was coming to see me at 12 P.M. He came sharp at the hour.[107]

---

103. In Blount's letter of April 26, 1893, to Secretary of State Walter Q. Gresham, Blount remarked: "On Sunday, the 16th instant [this month], I was out walking and met [Dr. Bowen] on the street riding in a buggy. He left the buggy in the hands of his friend Mr. Sewall, and joined me in a walk of some length. Before it was concluded he said to me that he and Paul Neumann were arranging a meeting between President Dole and the Queen, the object being to pay her a sum of money in consideration of her formal abdication of the throne and lending her influence to the Provisional Government with a view to annexation to the United States . . . to which I made no response." Morgan Report, vol. 1, 668. Later, while testifying before the U.S. Congress, Bowen said: "One day while dining with Paul Neumann I said: 'I think it would be a good thing if the Queen could be persuaded by the Provisional Government; it would make matters harmonious.' . . . Neumann agreed with me . . . but he said it could not be done. . . . There were several conferences. Mr. Dole said he would not make any propositions himself and asked me what I thought the pension ought to be. . . . I said I thought the Queen ought to get a very handsome pension out of the crown lands. . . . The result was that Mr. Dole told Mr. Neumann that if the Queen would make such a proposition to him it would receive respectful attention." Morgan Report, vol. 1, 671.

104. The 1892–93 City Directory lists "Kwong Sin Chong & Co., contractors and builders, King near Maunakea Street."

105. No such event occurred.

106. The italicized section is a later addition in pencil.

107. "*Ka Leo* states that Col. Claus Spreckels paid a visit to the ex-Queen at Washington Place yesterday morning. They conversed for nearly half an hour." *Pacific Commercial Advertiser*, April 21, 1893.

After explaining our situation I asked him to help us. That help was to be in the shape of not loaning the Provisional Government any money and they would naturally collapse. Must ask Mr. Neumann to return the Power of Attorney I gave him, as it will not be needed any further. He will give me all help he could but he must not play second fiddle. He would see and confer with Mr. Blount and let me know. He said it would be well to give to Hawaiians capable of positions in the Govt. I told him I was sure that President Cleveland would, after receiving Blount's statement, decide in our favor—for it was by force of American arms that placed us in this situation and now America for its own honor's sake must place us where we were before. How to get us back? By the assistance of the U.S.

Paul Neumann called 4.30, said he might go to San Francisco—but it all depended on what turns up with Blount. Did Spreckels call? Yes. What did he say, that [he] would help us? Yes—that's right.—No truth in the report that he [Neumann] was going to Japan—he must wait to see how things might develop by Saturday. C. B. Wilson wants to get a copy of Dole's letter about stopping me from flying royal standard. Neumann wants papers belonging to land at Palama—to Washington Place and Hamohamo.

*Friday, April 21.* Washington Place. Joe brought me papers and deeds of Palama, of Washington Place, of Hamohamo, Waikiki. I sent him with these to place personally in Mr. Neumann's hands. C. T. Ai[108] wrote a note and came in person to tell me of a clairvoyant. He is a boy of 12 years of age—entire stranger here—[he came here?] from eight to 12:30 P.M. [I was?] told that on the 15th of June everything would be restored—that Mr. Blount has full power to transact and restore—that J. Nawahi and Mr. Cummins may be in a Cabinet, also Mr. Parker but not Mr. Bush never Mr. Wilcox. He says he had to go thousands of miles beyond Tahiti on account of tidal wave. They released him.

11 A.M. Mr. and Mrs. McCarthy called—very pleasant people. Heard that Mr. Blount told [asked] Hui Kalaiaina if it was true that I had said if they brought their constitution, I would support them with a guard of soldiers to protect them. No truth.[109]

[John E.] Bush and [Joseph] Nawahi called on me and told me the Stars and Stripes would be raised on Monday.

*Saturday, April 22.* Washington Place. Heard from Sam Parker [that] Mr. Spreckels went to see Mr. Blount yesterday morning and met them afterwards at his [Spreckels's] bank. Blount told Spreckels that he [Spreckels] was father to the Lottery bill and all other vices and he had denied it. Yet in other matters they had agreed. Here Mr. Parker explained that he had worked it [the lottery bill] through because Hawaii was in need of funds— so Spreckels was satisfied. I asked Sam to give me notes of the money he had borrowed of me.

108. C. Thomas Ai, "clerk with V. V. Ashford. res. Palama," 1894–95 City Directory.
109. Blount's record of his meeting with the Hui Kalaiaina on April 21, 1893, affirms Liliuokalani's denial of this rumor. Blount Report, 445–46.

What conflicting stories are told about Mr. Blount's authority, some say the American flag will be raised again, others say not. Paul Neumann says if the Provisional Government was to make offers for me to Compromise, I must accept, but I must not forget what Mr. Nordhoff said, [and] that was when the P.G. made any such proposition, to send word to him and he would inform Mr. Blount. Mr. Parker has been sounding me and I think Mr. Spreckels sent him—Mr. Neumann says his going [to San Francisco] depends on me. I told him I would let him know by Monday.

Kawananakoa has been here. I signed a Mortgage to Bishop & Co. and S. M. Damon [on] the premises [of] Kapalama and Hamohamo and Kealia and Lumahai, for $17,000 I borrowed on 30 of January 1893—but paid interest of three months which was $212.39. I also signed a note for four thousand on Bishop & Co. for what I do not know. My head was so muddled with State and other matters that if this has to be added to the $17,000—well, I would go frantic. Actually Willie Rice came and called when he had been signing [against?] Annexation, Mr. Wilson was here—told him what I thought, [that] in case there was a restoration they must resign when everything is settled. He said yes—he said [he] asked if anyone was to come to propose to compromise not to consent. I told him I could judge what my answer would be when they came. [In her cash account for this date, Liliu records: "Pd. to Bishop & Co. by P. Neumann $212.39 Int. on note of $17,000."]

*Sunday, April 23.* Washington Place. [No entry follows.]

*Monday, April 24.* Washington Place. Nine A.M. Sam Parker came and yet seemed to be beating about the bush. Mr. Neumann left with me a receipt for two notes of $3,500 each on Bishop & Company. He said he would go on Wednesday to San Francisco and perhaps on to Japan. In case he did not go on to Japan, Mrs. Neumann would send his letters on to him. I said since there was nothing to be done until U.S. gave a reply, perhaps he had ought to return the Commission I gave him—he said he would. Met Mr. Blount at 12 P.M. Asked if it was true that he and Cleveland were supposed to have joined with the P.G. in asking me to abdicate—I said not. No one had asked me to abdicate, though messages had been sent to me to find out. I had reserved my answer to myself. He told me he had no authority to act in anything. [He] Would like to know the names of those who wanted annexation and yet signed the petition for lottery. Send for Willie Aldrich and he would give me a list. Mr. Blount said he had withdrawn the troops and raised the Hawaiian flag—but whatever we did for ourselves he had nothing to do with. Mr. and Miss Spreckels called. Told Mr. Blount that many more petitions will come in from all parts. Sent Mr. Robertson over to assure Mr. Blount that as there are stories going around that I had abdicated—to say there was no truth in it and not to believe any stories. That I had placed everything in the hands of the U.S. and with my people, am waiting patiently for her decision.

"Malie" says the 14th to 20 of June will be the time to return [and that] There are eight men of the P.G.s who are watching to shoot me. I must do penance, for 50 days.

*Tuesday, April 25.* Washington Place. Mr. P. Neumann returned his Power of Attorney and also Commission as Envoy Extraordinary and Minister Plenipotentiary to the President of the U.S. of America.[110] Besides giving me a note for $1,600 on Bishop & Co, the latter of which I do not understand. I am so sorry as I am sure he has been faithful to me—but there has been so much maneuvering and wire pulling with Mr. Spreckels. I understand the P.G.s have been trying to turn Mr. Spreckels over to keep me from being on the throne.[111] J. R. [Jimmie Robertson] says I must keep to myself that I had Mr. Neumann's C. [Commission] and never to give it up—I must try and remember it. Sam Parker tried to get from me whether I had Mr. N.'s Commission—I kept my own secret—as Mr. Spreckels had told me to, and also Neumann. Sam Parker also gave me a receipt for $10,000.00 at 9 perct.—to term of six months. He still owes me and must give me a note for $4,500.00 tomorrow. Our or my—ohuas [servants] have all been sent away from Haimoeipo[112] and most of them have gone to the boathouse. Malie wants to see me tomorrow eve at six P.M. in the cottage.

Gave Willie Aldrich my genealogy—he said he would give it to Mr. Neumann and it was approved by the latter. W. [Willie] also tells me C. B. Wilson is having a statement made for Mr. Blount but in it he makes complaint of me and lauds himself up—and also my Genealogy.[113] [In her cash account for this date, Liliu records: "Rec'd from S. Parker a note $10,000."]

*Wednesday, April 26.* Washington Place. Mr. S. Parker came in I asked him

---

110. These documents (subsequently cancelled) are in the Hawaii State Archives, Liliuokalani Collection.

111. The *Hawaiian Star*, April 20, 1893, said: "Claus Spreckels called on President Dole at the Foreign Office yesterday and held a long consultation with him regarding the political situation here. Mr. Spreckels assured the President that his position would be one of support to the Provisional Government. He was of the opinion that the Hawaiian Islands could not return to the monarchical form of government.... Mr. Spreckels visited President Dole again this morning."

The next day, an editorial in the *Star* said: "Mr. Spreckels admits that the monarchy is dead but he is not ready to commit himself to annexation." A lengthy article in the same issue noted the following: "This proof of his discernment was given a day after his arrival and Mr. Spreckels had not concealed from anyone, least of all from Mrs. Jno. O. Dominis upon whom he made an early call. The ex-Queen was quite importunate on the subject of a return to the throne but she got no comfort from the Sugar King. He told her in explicit terms that royal institutions here had come to a decisive end."

112. Haimoeipo was the name of the lot where the palace servants were housed. It is now the site of the state capitol building.

113. Wilson's statement, "Facts in relation to the revolution of 1893, and the causes which led up to it," dated May 15, 1893, appears in the Blount Report, 552–75. The document does not discuss the Queen's genealogy.

to go and see Mr. Neumann off—he said he would. Hannah Evans [and] Jennie Clark drove down to decorate Mr. Neumann with leis.[114]

Dr. Bowen called to see me before going on board the *Australia*—he told me of the scandalous article written by the *Advertiser* [and] of its untruth.[115] I told him that was usually the case with that paper, [and] what it said about Mr. Blount was untrue.[116]

Dr. Bowen says Mr. Blount said he was pleased with his visit to me. Dr. also said Mr. Dole said he had to fight hard to prevent the Council of the Provisional Government from preventing [sic, taking] my liberty. When they do I will ask for protection.

P. Kaaua[117] and his wife Naai have made over to me $8.00 each for $16.00 they borrowed of their shares in Hui Hawaii Kawaluonalani. Receipt for $100.00 from F. M. English[118] for last Nov. and Dec. Another receipt from Bishop & Co. for $212.39 but $16.00 returned [?]—by Paul Neumann.

Another thing Dr. Bowen said was, if he could do anything for me. I said I would like the American people to assist in seeing that justice is done to my people. [He asked] Have you anything to ask for yourself? There is no doubt should you or these Islands get annexed to U.S., you would be generously provided for. I said that was not what I wished: "What is good for my people is all I asked for." He admired the nobility of my sentiment and fully appreciated it.

---

114. "Paul Neumann will leave for San Francisco today for the purpose of seeing his first grandson. The little fellow was born on Easter Sunday. Mr. Neumann expects to return on the *Australia* with Mrs. Neumann. He will then take a trip to Japan on business of a private nature." *Pacific Commercial Advertiser*, April 26, 1893.

115. The following editorial comment had appeared in the *Pacific Commercial Advertiser* that morning: "Dr. Bowen, the amiable and genial editor of the *New York World*, leaves somewhat unexpectedly, on the *Australia* this morning. He has talked with all sorts and conditions of men while here, and has made good use of his excellent opportunities to get an insight into the meaning of the situation.

"Dr. Bowen speaks guardedly, as becomes an experienced journalist and a man of the world; but it is obvious that those who have represented him as a rank royalist have misrepresented him altogether. The *World* is not committed to any anti-annexation policy. It is simply opposed to the concluding [of] a treaty before full investigation."

116. Liliu's reference to Blount is now unclear, but probably she was referring to an Associated Press report (unlocated but later reprinted in the *Pacific Commercial Advertiser*, April 30, 1893), "His method of speaking is rather slow and deliberative ... but as he goes on he becomes more animated, and his sentences contain a rude and pure eloquence.

"It is known that he first suggested to President Cleveland the plan of sending someone to investigate the condition of the islands, and it is believed that he was selected because his temperament is that of a judge rather than an advocate."

117. Paulo Kaaua is listed in the 1892–93 City Directory as "drayman Hustace & Robertson. res Kukuluaeo."

118. The payment was for secretarial costs. The *Hawaiian Star*, April 11, 1893, reported that the Queen's "appeal to the American People," published in the March 9, 1893, *San Francisco Examiner*, had been written by F. M. English. English, who had been in the islands since 1890, is listed in the 1892–93 City Directory as "Law student, Merchant opp. Post Office. res. Emma Square." The date of his departure from Honolulu is unknown, but the *Hawaiian Star*, July 10, 1893, printed a letter from him dated Denver, Colorado, June 21, 1893, which he signed as "Late Secretary to Her Majesty Queen Liliuokalani."

The *Hawaiian Star*, December 13, 1893, in refuting an article by English on the Hawaiian revolution published in a Denver newspaper, said that he was "a British hater of everything American ... long and perhaps is yet a paid controversialist on the ex-Queen's side."

*Thursday, April 27.* Washington Place. Nothing of note transpired. At 11 A.M. Mr. Wetmore and Mr. [W. W.] Naughton, reporters of the *Examiner,* called. They were well pleased with their visit—had no idea I spoke English so well and thought I would have to call the aid of an interpreter. Thought me a superior woman. Heard from "Malie" that the Provisional Government had split and [was] in trouble.

Ikuwa came in and wanted [me] to give ear to his petition—that I should consent to have his Kahuna [sorcerer] come and kala me.[119] I knew that he was sent by Kamaka, Cecil Brown's Kahuna, so I knew this must be a catch. I told him the Bible is my guide and [I] only receive instructions from there.

*Friday, April 28.* Washington Place. Sam Parker told me he had been calling on Spreckels the night before. Spreckels had told him the Chamber of Commerce had met yesterday and he had asked them a question. They were not in favor, ⅔ against and Joe Carter was one of those for his request. The result was he told them he would have nothing to do with them.[120]

Sam Parker offered to him a power of Attorney to administer the Government, Spreckels said he did not want it. I admonished Sam—it was not for him to offer—happily he [Spreckels] did not accept.

I sent Mr. Robertson to ask Mr. Blount if [it would be] convenient to call round at 7.30 P.M.

*Saturday, April 29.* Washington Place. Sent for Kaipo and Aimoku. Read an article in the *San Francisco Chronicle* written by Walter G. Smith, a man that had been kicked out from San Francisco for some heinous offense, and [who is] now accepted by these Missionary elements who are as bad as he—who tries to injure my character, but I feel myself above such imputations and all my friends who know my habits know what is true.[121]

---

119. Kala is "prayer to free one from any evil influence." *Pukui-Elbert Hawaiian Dictionary.*

120. The Chamber of Commerce's minute book for 1883–94 (Hawaii State Archives, Chamber of Commerce Collection) records no such meeting.

121. On the typescript copy of this diary made by the Provisional Government in 1895, there is at this point a later annotation by territorial archivist Robert C. Lydecker, referring the reader to the minutes of the sixth meeting of the Archives Commission, November 8, 1907, and filed with executive documents of October 25, 1907, "as to Mr. Smith's character." In the minutes of the commission, there appears the following:

"Mr. Walter G. Smith appeared before the board and stated that it having come to his knowledge that there were certain statements in the diary of Ex-Queen Liliuokalani detrimental to his character, and not wishing the statements contained therein handed down to posterity uncontradicted, requested that the Board afford him such relief as was consistent with its duty, and if possible expunge the statements complained of. He also laid before the Board testimony as to his character, signed by John P. Young editor of the *San Francisco Chronicle.*

"The Chair stated that the Board was desirous of affording Mr. Smith all the relief possible, but that it had no right or authority to expunge anything from any document in the Archives. After some discussion Commissioner [George R.] Carter moved that the testimony... be received and filed in the Archives, and that the Librarian make a marginal note referring to it." Hawaii State Archives, Minutes of the Board of Commissioners of Public Archives. The testimonial letter referred to was from John P. Young, managing editor, *San Francisco Chronicle,* dated October 25, 1907, saying that Walter Gifford Smith, a "staff correspondent of the *San Francisco Chronicle* ... was chosen to represent us because of his character and efficiency, and that he was regarded by the *Chronicle* and its management as the most capable man that could be sent to represent the paper." Hawaii State Archives, Papers of Governor Frear, filed under the heading "San Francisco Chronicle."

Malulani. Paina kapu [private meal]—At Hinano Bower. Prince David dropped in and lunched with me, Kaipo and Aimoku, Lauae Kapuni.

*Tuesday, May 2.* Washington Place. Mr. Sam Parker tells me Mr. Spreckels is going to Maui and he would have to go up too—but that he needed money—and perhaps it would be a good chance for him to speak about his own affairs. So he asked me to loan him one of my other certificates, so I gave him one with 25 shares of Pahala stocks and he gave me a note for $2,500.00 and said that when Mr. Spreckels settled his affairs he would see I was paid in full.

*Monday, May 8.* Washington Place. Parker tells me Mr. Spreckels told him to tell me to continue to remain in peace and quietness and all will end well.

*Tuesday, May 9.* Washington Place. Sent for Mr. C. R. Bishop at eight A.M. Had conversation with him in regard to the situation. He was not pleased, but I forgot that I had been abused falsely by the rebels, and perhaps he believed them to be true. I forgot also that they had not even hesitated to vilify my character—else I would have tried to disabuse his mind in regard to that, but time was short and he had to go at nine A.M. And we said good-bye—and [I] still felt as if there was a chasm between us. I am sorry—but time only could erase such a breach.[122]

Sent Capt. Nowlein to Mr. Damon to say if my house was to be searched for arms I would rather have him do it. Mr. D. said no one would do it. I authorized Mr. Damon through Capt. Nowlein to pay the Insurance on this house, which is $200.00, to C. O. Berger as agent of [Mutual Life] Insurance Co.

Rec'd a letter from Pacific Music Co. saying they had sent 80 copies of "Aloha Oe" and 24 of "He Mele," but none has been received.

*Wednesday, May 17 [sic, May 10].*[123] Washington Place. How stupid of me for not looking at the dates—and am a week ahead—Mr. Parker brought news that Mr. Blount had been appointed in Mr. Stevens' place, the latter has been told to turn over the Legation to Mr. Blount—How mortifying—there is a meaning to all this and it is interpreted in this way—that Mr. Blount will restore everything as he found it and then go home in June.

*Thursday, May 11.* Washington Place. Nothing new except arrival of the *Belgic* from San Francisco and brought Commissioner C. L. Carter[124] of the Annexation party back, and instead of his landing at the wharf, was landed at Dr. Trousseau's boathouse—and he sneaked home—but there were some people at Kakaako who recognized him and called after him "there goes the Commissioner for Negro Immigrants."[125]

---

122. Bishop departed Honolulu for San Francisco on the *Oceanic* on May 9, 1893, and from this date on he apparently made San Francisco his primary residence.

123. With respect to the entry for May 10, which is incorrectly written as May 17, Liliu seems to have written in the date and "Washington Place," then realized her misplacement of the entry, which she then corrects. The page for the May 10 entry is blank.

124. Charles Lunt Carter (b. 1865, Honolulu–d. January 7, 1895, Waikiki), the son of H.A.P. Carter, was killed at Diamond Head during the January 1895 counterrevolution.

125. "Charles L. Carter, one of the [annexation] treaty commissioners of 1893, had busied himself, while the treaty was in abeyance, in trying to induce American Negroes to come

Mr. Blount met Lt. Jerome Feary[126] and asked how he could get round to the Marine Railway—so Feary led him around. He asked, "Where do you live"? "At the Queen's Boat House"—"who lives in it?" "Several families who were sent away from the long building[127] sold by the P.G." "Where are you going"? "To the Queen's."—"Then you had better go." "I will see you over first, Mr. Blount," says Frank, "it would make us all happy to see our Queen go back on the throne"—"Patience," said he—"and everything will be all right." This is very encouraging.

*Friday, May 12.* Washington Place. Was not able to find anything of importance in my Memorandum book of the year 1891. Mr. Blount asked Mr. Parker what we were doing, meaning the people. He knew there was a memorial being got ready but [asked] why are they so long about it. He was aware of the untruthfulness of the statements of the other party. Mr. Egan told Mr. McIntyre that during the other revolution it was the *Adams* that furnished them with ammunition and this time it is the *Boston*.

*Monday, May 22.* Washington Place. Mr. Parker brought news that Mr. Claus Spreckels was taking a memorial around amongst the principal firms in town to take their signatures expressing their opinions against Annexation or any form of Government that would be injurious to the interests of Commerce and Agriculture. Had a heavy cold—declined to see Mrs. McCully[128]—I suppose she has heard of brighter prospects for us—She declined to bow one day.

*Tuesday, May 23.* Washington Place. Joe Heleluhe brought $146.25 rent of Kamanaiki, Kalihi [from] Antone & Barrate,[129] and $9.33½ cts of 5 months' Ice [Company] dividends.

*Wednesday, May 24.* Washington Place. Rec'd news from P. Neumann by his daughter Anita—in which he says that he had heard that on his arrival in San Francisco a new Commission was going to be formed and to be headed by Sam Damon, he wanted me to ascertain if there was any truth in the statement. I wrote immediately to Mr. J. O. Carter—No answer.

Mrs. Blount returned from Volcano—she was well received by the people & rec'd. two lei hulus [feather leis]. Joe went out to Waikiki [and] was caught by K—with K—. Mr. Parker brought news that Mr. Blount had said Mr. John L. Stevens, American Minister to Hawaii, went back

---

to the islands. But President Dole ended this idea forthwith by ordering Carter to cease his activity because it had too many dangerous possibilities involving the color line." William A. Russ Jr., "Hawaiian Labor and Immigration Problems before Annexation," *Journal of Modern History* 15, no. 3 (September 1943): 207–22.

126. Jerome Feary was the part-Hawaiian son of Louis Jerome Feary (who arrived in Hawaii in 1850). He may be the same person listed in the 1892–93 City Directory as "F. W. Feary, 1st Lieutenant, King's Guard, Barracks."

127. The long building had housed Iolani Palace employees and was located adjacent to the barracks on Palace Walk (now Hotel Street).

128. Mrs. Ellen Harvey McCully (b. 1831, New York) was the widow of Supreme Court Justice Lawrence McCully (d. 1892).

129. M. A. Barrete (or Barete) and Richard Anton (or Antone) had held a lease of Kamanaiki in Kalihi from King Kalakaua and renegotiated the same when Liliuokalani purchased the property from Kalakaua's estate. They relinquished their lease as of August 2, 1904. Hawaii State Archives, Liliuokalani Collection, Box 1, Document 38.

to the U.S. on the steamer *Australia* with a history which had never been paralleled before in Hawaii for placing our Country in such a position before and with such a weak Cabinet [that] his actions in supporting a few men to rebel proved successful.

May he be made to suffer as much as the many pangs he has caused amongst my people. He took back with him the remains of his daughter.[130] Her death I consider a judgment from heaven.

*Thursday, May 25.* Washington Place. Mr. C. T. Gulick called and left his report[131] for me to read. C. B. Wilson called and told me he thought some statement ought to be made by my Cabinet—I think so too, but there is a member in the Cabinet who I am sure is working strongly and in sympathy with the present Government—however, I will try. Three P.M. Mr. Parker called. I told him to notify the other Ministers, Colburn, and Peterson, to be here tomorrow at ten A.M. Their statements as a Cabinet must go to prove that this present Government is simply there and the Authority given them simply to bide the time when the U.S. will restore us our former Government. To prove that a party of few had bound themselves together to take the Govt. in their own hands, and with the assistance of the U.S. Troops their plans were made successful. We beg of the new Minister Commissioner Mr. Blount to restore us what had been wrested from us and replace the Queen as well as our Government as before.

*Friday, May 26.* Washington Place. Ten A.M. The Ministers met, Parker, Colburn, and Peterson—Cornwell will be down [from Maui] on Sunday. The subject before the Cabinet is that they should make a statement as a Cabinet of the situation. Mr. Colburn states that the civil rights organization was going to call a mass meeting to protest against the new treaty sent by the Provisional Government.[132]

*Saturday, May 27.* Washington Place. Nothing has yet taken place except that the P.G.s are getting frightened and are carrying pistols.

*Sunday, May 28.* Washington Place. Heard from Minister C. [?] that Mr. Spreckels said plainly there is nothing for him to do now but help restore me to the throne [and] that it would be well for me to appoint a new Cabinet—proclaim new Constitution—proclaim Martial law, etc., etc. Mr. Spreckels will call on me tomorrow M [morning]. That he wants a

---

130. John L. Stevens's daughter, Grace, drowned in a boating accident at Kukaiau Landing on the Hamakua coast of Hawaii Island on January 30, 1893. In the Queen's autobiography, Liliuokalani writes, "His own daughter went as a messenger to the largest one of the islands of my kingdom to secure names for a petition for the annexation of the Hawaiian Islands to the American Union, and by an accident lost her life, with the roll containing the few names she had secured." *Hawaii's Story*, 286.

131. An interview between Blount and Charles T. Gulick dated May 13, 1893, and Gulick's statement, titled "A Footnote to Hawaiian History, May 8, 1893," appear in the Blount Report, 276–78 and 279–303, respectively. Gulick's lengthy prepared statement to Blount is the document that Liliu refers to here. An additional statement by Gulick (dated May 12, 1893) on the actions of U.S. Minister John L. Stevens and Captain Gilbert C. Wiltse on January 17, 1893, also appears in the Blount Report, 351–53.

132. On May 31, 1893, the Queen's ministers (Samuel Parker, W. H. Cornwell, John F. Colburn, and A. P. Peterson) addressed a long letter to Commissioner Blount regarding the events of January 13–17, 1893. It was signed "Liliuokalani R." The text appears in the Blount Report, 81–83, and also in the Morgan Report, vol. 2, 1355–57.

*Diary for 1893* 353

new Constitution immediately on the return of power, appoint my Ministers, do away with Judd and others, and proclaim Martial law.[133]

*Monday, May 29.* Washington Place. Mr. Parker came and broke fast with me, informed me that Mr. Spreckels would be here at noon—that he would draw the $95,000 they [the Provisional Government] owe him[134]—that he would be the means of putting me back on the throne—that he [Spreckels] was going to make Mr. Irwin sign the Anti-Annexation list [and] he would make Mr. Hatch withdraw from the Provisional Government [so?] it lessens their strength. Mr. P. tells me of Mr. Gay's death[135] and also [that of] J. S. Walker.[136]

Mr. Cummins says he has a new Constitution made by Marques, Bush, Rickard,[137] and himself. Henry C. Carter called to pay his respects.

J. W. Robertson tells me of news by yesterday [yesterday's mail arrival] that it was heard in Washington that a new treaty would be sent but no recognition will be given except through Mr. Blount, [and] on that [news] there will be no mass meeting this eve. Mr. Marques came in and left his Constitution with me. Mr. Claus Spreckels called at quarter to 12 P.M.—and told me all that Mr. Parker has stated, and proposes to have Mr.

---

133. In a letter of Albert Willis to U.S. Secretary of State Walter Q. Gresham, December 9, 1893, the latter was informed that on December 5, C. B. Wilson had left with him a document that was in fact a detailed "proposed course of Procedure" upon receiving news of the Queen's restoration to power. These included the appointment of a commander in chief and staff, the proclamation of martial law, the registration of "all loyal citizens," the surrender of "all arms and ammunition in private hands," the "reappointment of all officials," and the "arrest of all persons implicated or concerned in the late overthrow." Morgan Report, vol. 2, 105–6.

134. "It suited Col. Claus Spreckels a few weeks since to make a sudden call upon the Government for the payment of overdue notes to the amount of $95,000. Payment of these notes had been tendered last February, but the holder had preferred to let them run on. As the sudden demand was made at the time of year when receipts are least, there was danger of embarrassment to the Treasury. A number of earnest friends of the government came promptly to their help, and the whole amount was speedily paid, and Col. Spreckels' apparently hostile attack frustrated.

"This debt was incurred by the Queen's government last fall, in order to meet the drain upon the Postal Savings Bank, caused by the alarm created by the Queen's Cabinet fiascos at that time." *The Friend*, July 1893.

The *Hawaiian Star*, June 1, 1893, announced: "At 11 o'clock this morning Minister of Finance [S. M.] Damon walked into Claus Spreckels & Co's Bank and handed over to cashier Spalding forty-five thousand dollars as part payment of the Spreckels loan of $95,000 which was demanded by the bank last week. The wealthy gentlemen who have assumed the Spreckels obligation have perfect faith in the stability of the government."

135. James Gay (b. 1841, New Zealand–d. May 28, 1893, Waialua, Oahu) arrived in Hawaii in 1863. He was part of the extended family of Sinclairs and Gays, best known for their ownership of the island of Niihau. At the time of Gay's death, he was engaged in raising horses on his large stock ranch.

136. John Smith Walker (b. 1826, Aberdeen, Scotland–d. May 29, 1893, Honolulu) arrived in Hawaii in November 1854, and became a prosperous shipping and sugar magnate, and a public servant. He was minister of finance under King Kalakaua 1874–76 and 1880, and an auditor general 1886–87. He was a member of the Privy Council and president of the legislature in 1886, 1890, and 1892. He had been seriously ill and unable to attend to business for several months prior to his death. His obituary says he was "a man of pleasing manners, agreeable disposition and generous nature, for whom everybody had a good word." *Pacific Commercial Advertiser*, May 30, 1893.

137. William Henry Rickard (b. 1846, Cornwall, England–d. 1899, Honokaa) arrived in Hawaii in 1867, and began as a stock raiser in Honokaa, Hawaii. He was a representative in the 1890 legislature. Rickard was later part owner and manager of the Honokaa Sugar Co.

Antone Rosa as Attorney General when I go back [on the throne]. I asked him to help me make a Cabinet, he said he would. He will stay until everything is settled. Says when he draws money from them they will fall to pieces—they will not require guns—he and Blount will do everything. They must suffer those missionaries for overthrowing my government, and their property *must* pay for all. Robertson said the U.S. will make a treaty showing we must recognize the right of America above all other nations. Mr. Spreckels says Mr. Wilson must be Marshall.

*Friday, June 2.* Washington Place. Today the Provisional Government turned Iolani Palace into Govt. offices.[138]

*Saturday, June 3.* Washington Place. Mr. Cornwell tells me that the Community is indignant that the Provisional Government should attempt to make use of the palace for their offices.[139] Mr. J. O. Carter told Cornwell and Parker that H. M. Whitney had said that it was Mr. Blount that told them to do so. Mr. Parker asked Mr. Blount if it was true, he said no, and that if Parker wanted a written statement he would give one. Mr. Parker said no, he did not want one. Mr. Cornwell says the report downtown is [that] on Monday they will proclaim a Republic. We will see what Mr. Spreckels says.

*Monday, June 5.* Washington Place. 9.30 A.M. Major Wodehouse called to say he had heard that a Republic was to be proclaimed today by the Provisional Government, but that it was not true[140]—he had hoisted his flag but not in recognition of a Republic—it could not be [recognized] except by the voice of the people. He wanted to know what I thought of it, that I should not have any fears. I told him that my subjects had told me not to lay myself open to be shot at as Capt. Good had openly said that he would be the one to shoot me. Mr. Hall had said that the streets would flow with blood if I was to be reinstated. He [Wodehouse] said I must find proofs as to what Good said. He said, "I am nearby and my Colleague also, should you need assistance send to us and we will attend to it." "Have you anyone near and how many?" I said 20 or 25. I told him whatever form of Govt. they may proclaim, we would wait till we heard from U.S.

Major Seward told me Mr. Bush had sent him to warn me about laying himself [sic, myself] open to be shot at. I thanked him. Wodehouse

---

138. "At an Executive and Advisory Councils meeting this date, it was 'Resolved: The offices of the Executive Council shall be in Iolani palace, which shall hereafter be the seat of government and shall be known as the executive building. Meetings of the Advisory and Executive Councils shall be held in the executive building. Aliiolani hale shall hereafter be known as the courthouse.'" *Pacific Commercial Advertiser*, June 3, 1893.

139. On June 2, 1893, the offices of "the Interior, Foreign Affairs, Finance, and Attorney General's departments moved from Aliiolani Hale to the Palace. The Blue room [was assigned] to the Minister of Finance; the Tower room adjoining to the Auditor-General; the dining room to the Interior Department; the throne room to the Council Chamber; the library for the Foreign Affairs Department; and the bedroom mauka for President Dole's private room and the room makai the Library for the Attorney-General.... The furniture, tapestries, and carpets have all been removed and stored in the bungalow or in the unoccupied rooms upstairs." *Hawaiian Star*, June 2, 1893.

140. "On Saturday there was a rumor current that a Republic would be proclaimed today. President Dole was seen regarding the rumor and he stated that there was no foundation for it. In fact all he knew about the rumor was what he had heard on the streets." *Pacific Commercial Advertiser*, June 5, 1893.

said he and Blount would act together. Mr. Spreckels and Mr. Blount had conference of two hours. Today the P.G.s take formal possession of the Iolani Palace—and have called the building the Capitol.[141]

*Tuesday, June 6.* Washington Place. Mr. Parker says Mr. Spreckels will demand $150,000 of the Reciprocity Sugar Co. Bill White says he is going back to Lahaina by the *Malulani*. He [William White] told Mr. Blount the Lottery Bill was his—he proposed it because he thought it was good for the Government—so he watched his chance and railroaded it through the House. He told Mr. Blount that it was he who worked for the overthrow of the Wilcox and Brown cabinet for the express purpose of passing the Lottery [bill]—Bribery? He had heard there was, but none of it went into his pocket. He had told Cecil Brown he would upset his Cabinet. Mr. Spreckels had said they should pay up before the first of July.

Mr. Robertson told me last Friday night, Mr. Oleson,[142] Damon, and Dole were closeted together until 12 midnight—if so was it they who sent the Provisional Government Soldiers 40 in number to occupy Mr. Wall's house all night.[143]

I told Nawahi to retain a clause in my new Constitution that the appointment of Nobles should be mine.[144]

*Wednesday, June 7.* Washington Place. Mr. Parker told me Mr. Dole had asked him to call on him. Parker asked if he [Dole] was not afraid to be seen talking to a royalist. Had been told if he signed annexation he would be worth a Million. Mrs. Kia [Nahaolelua] called with tears in her eyes and told me, Mrs. Ward had rushed in and told her that her dear friend's husband had told her that the P.G. were going to deport me today—16 men with masks and guns would carry me off, if not today, tonight.[145]

---

141. "This morning at ten o'clock the government will take formal possession of the executive building. . . . At the hour mentioned President Dole and the members of the Executive Council will walk over from the courtroom and with a simple ceremony possession will be taken of the new executive quarters. Commencing today the entrances to the executive building will be thrown open, and the public can enjoy a walk in the pleasant grounds." *Pacific Commercial Advertiser*, June 5, 1893.

142. Reverend William Brewster Oleson (b. 1851, Portland, Maine–d. 1915) came to the islands in 1878 and became principal first of the Hilo Boarding School and then, in 1886, of the Kamehameha School for Boys. He resigned in July 1893 and left for the United States. In later years, he returned to the islands, and at the time of his death he was secretary of the Hawaiian Board of Missions.

143. The *Hawaiian Star*, June 1, 1893, noted the "occupation" by Company B of the National Guard at the Wall premises. Walter Eugene Wall (b. 1867–d. 1944) was a Honolulu resident from 1880 and a longtime government surveyor. The Wall home was on Beretania and Miller Streets, opposite Washington Place.

144. Liliu was intent on retaining article 57 of the proposed constitution of January 1893, which stated: "The Queen appoints the nobles, who shall hold their appointments during life." This would have been an increase in the power of the monarch from that assigned by the 1887 constitution (article 58), which specified a public election for the nobles for specific periods of time. The constitutions of 1864 and 1887 are included in the Blount Report, 338–51. The draft of the proposed January 14, 1893, constitution appears in the Morgan Report, vol. 2, 1855–64.

145. The *Hawaiian Star*, June 9, 1893, reprinted an article from the *Bulletin*: "Owing to a rumor set afloat from the annexation camp yesterday, that an attempt would be made to deport Queen Liliuokalani by the steamer *City of Peking* if that vessel came last night, some of the Queen's friends kept watch at Washington Place."

Mr. Parker ~~Mr. C. Hopkins~~ was sent for and he went and told Mr. Wodehouse. I told Mrs. Kia [Nahaolelua] also to tell Major Wodehouse. This eve Parker, Hopkins, Wilson came in. During the evening two men were seen by Major Wodehouse climbing over the fence of the Punahou Preparatory School. Our people were all stationed along the fence all round this yard. They came near to my Cottage where Joe Aea and Willie Ahia were stationed when Joe swore at them and spoilt all. He might have waited till they jumped over. They tried [to get] over the [Priory] Sisters' yard, [and] at McKibbin's and Mrs. Dowsett's.

*Thursday, June 8.* Washington Place. 12 P.M. Mr. Spreckels came to reassure me on regard to my danger—that they would (the P.G.) not dare to harm me. He asked if I was in need of money not to hesitate to let him know—I thanked him. J. G. Hoapili called, I would not see him. Today there is a meeting of the Missionaries of all the islands—Kauhane spoke on politics.[146]

*Friday, June 9.* Washington Place. Mrs. Hattie Akao[147] came in with Mahiai [Robinson]. She said she knew her son did not carry a gun nor has he and his sister signed the Annexation list—nor had she or her husband signed either side—they as the saying goes [are] on the fence. Mr. Parker called on Mr. Dole informally but Mr. Spreckels had cautioned him to be careful how he answered. Parker thought it was their intention to make a compromise but this event of these spies of Wednesday night has spoilt their plan; Mr. Spreckels [says] this [shows] they begin to feel shaky. Mr. Dole said they knew nothing about the affair the other night, that he would like an affidavit from our side. Mr. Parker said on account of their spies and action by the sanction of the Marshall [E. G. Hitchcock], the Royalists considered my life in danger and with the actions of many men in the next yard of the P.G. and also the articles of the *Star* to deport me,[148] they had placed the matter in the hands of the Diplomatic [Corps].

---

146. Reverend James Kauhane (b. 1838–d. 1907, Honolulu), son of chiefess Alapai, was a district judge of Kau and a veteran pastor of the native church in that district. He served as a member of the House of Representatives (1862–88) and of the House of Nobles (1890–92). The occasion was part of the annual meeting of the Hawaiian Evangelical Association, of which *The Friend*, July 1893, said, "The moderator chosen was Rev. J. Kauhane, who was vice president of the late Legislature, and a leading Annexationist." None of the main Honolulu newspapers reported Kauhane's remarks.

147. Mrs. Akao [possibly Akau?] had a son, Arthur Akau, listed in the 1892–93 City Directory as "Private, King's Guard, Barracks."

148. The *Hawaiian Star*, an aggressively pro-annexation paper, had suggested the idea of banishment as early as April. The following remark appeared in the April 13, 1893, issue : "If the plotting Queen and her clan of intriguers were banished by the first steamer, there would be peace now and annexation soon." Then an editorial on May 8 said, "It is pretty generally admitted now that it was a mistake not to have shipped the ex-Queen abroad when she was denied of her throne.... That was one of the errors of a hurried time which, if it had been avoided, would have left the annexation cause in much better shape than it now is.... Its [banishment's] severity might, of course, be modified by some provision for the expenses of travel abroad, but this is a matter of detail. The main thing is to have the disturbing influence of the royal pretender [the Queen] out of the way when the time comes to tranquilize the country."

Lorrin Thurston, in a confidential letter to Dole (Washington, DC, June 13, 1893), said: "It seems to me that the deportation of the Queen will go a long way towards decentralizing the opposition. As long as she remains there she forms a rallying center around which all malcontents will gather, and would be especially dangerous on the contingency of any outbreak occurring." Hawaii State Archives, Series 404, Box 53.

Mr. Dole said it was not with their knowledge—while they conversed, Smith, King, and Damon came in—Parker came away. The Diplomats are all of one mind. Mr. Parker brought a protest which is intended to be presented to the Marshall asking if he was aware of the actions [of] these spies—he gave a verbal answer, that he sent them to reconnoiter. Mr. J. W. Robertson was offered Molly Brown's place. Molly had embezzled $1,600.00.[149] I told him they would make him sign annexation—he'd better wait a little.

The two spies were Wagner and Gibbs.[150]

*Saturday, June 10.* Washington Place. Paina [feast] in Hinano Bower. Mrs. Kia [Nahaolelua] told me she had heard from the same source, and these ladies had asked not to have their names mentioned—that Mr. Gibbs and [Mr.] Wagner had both been paid $5,000.00 to take my life—and that the *Morning Star* was still laying off and on outside.[151] [Mrs. Kia also said?] My haole friends drove them away by following them and chased them far away from here and they never came back.

Today was distributed a copy of my Power of Attorney to Mr. Neumann.[152] When it was first made out by Mr. Hartwell and brought to me, I had asked Mr. Neumann if that was the usual course taken on occasions like that, he said Yes, in the presence of Mr. A. F. Judd and was immediately acknowledged by him. It is the object of the Provisional Government to make me hated by my people.

*Sunday, June 11.* Washington Place. 11 A.M. the Kamehameha schoolboys [and] Kawaiahao [Seminary] Girls are in the Central Union Church.[153]

---

149. This is nowhere explained. Molly was probably a man's nickname.

150. Charles Wagner may at that time have been a customs house employee. In the 1896 City Directory, Howard F. Gibbs is listed as a police officer, and Charles Wagner appears as a private in the National Guard. They were working occasionally as informants (spies) for the Provisional Government.

151. There is no evidence that any such assassination was planned. In fact, the *Pacific Commercial Advertiser* reported the following in its June 10, 1893, issue: "The unreliable mouthings of the *Bulletin* and *Holomua* for the past two days regarding the rumors of the deportation and assassination of the ex-queen caused an *Advertiser* reporter to call on the Provisional Government yesterday to investigate these royalist charges. In reply... the attorney general said: 'There is not the slightest truth or foundation for the reports that the ex-Queen is to be deported. The fact is, we prefer to have her here exactly where she is, and I believe President Dole has so expressed himself before when the newspaper reporters have asked the same question.... As to these rumors [of assassination,] the government heard them with indignation. At first we considered both the rumors you mention as not worthy of notice, but learning afterwards they were believed by Liliuokalani and her friends, President Dole sent for Mr. Samuel Parker. Mr. Parker met the Cabinet this morning [meaning yesterday] at ten o'clock. President Dole called his attention to the rumors and asked him as to the facts. Mr. Parker stated that both rumors regarding deportation and assassination had come to them in such a way that they had believed them to be true. President Dole assured Mr. Parker that the rumors were entirely without foundation and that if Liliuokalani's life was in danger she was entitled to the same protection as any other citizen.'"

152. The Provisional Government first printed and distributed a Hawaiian-language translation of the Queen's power of attorney to Paul Neumann (signed on January 31, 1893, and canceled as of April 25) among the Hawaiian-speaking community as a means of discrediting the Queen in the eyes of her subjects. The *Pacific Commercial Advertiser*, June 10, 1893, published the English version under the heading "Pau! The Ex-Queen Non-Suits Her Own Case." The same document appeared in the June 9 issue of the *Hawaiian Star*.

153. This would have occurred as part of the annual meeting of the Hawaiian Evangelical Association.

Mr. and Mrs. Blount and Mr. and Mrs. Nordhoff returned from Spreckelsville [Maui] where they had a large concourse of people to greet them. They [the people] asked in their speeches to have me restored, and wanted to know when. He [Blount] answered that he would not tell but would wait for instructions.

*Monday, June 12.* Washington Place. Heard today that the reason that Mr. Ashford was [not?] permitted to come back[154] was because Mr. Dole did not dare to decide otherwise, else his wickedness would be exposed. Mr. Dole with four others were called upon to shoot the King in 1887. Mr. [Volney] Ashford was one of the five—they drew lots and it fell to Mr. Dole—He had not the heart to do the deed so the King was not shot.[155]

12 P.M. The members of the Hui [Liliuokalani] Hololio met here and had prayer meeting. 2.30 P.M. a nice luau.

Mrs. Spreckels and Miss Emma [Spreckels] called on their return from the luau at Kalihi, which was a very dull affair.[156]

Mr. Dole called early this morning on Mr. Blount and said that the Queen's party were making trouble—and Mr. Blount said he has heard all about it and knew that it was the P.G. spies that were making trouble. Mr. Blount told Mr. Parker that our people must not do anything or take notice of the P.G. spies.

*Tuesday, June 13.* Washington Place. Mrs. Kia told me she heard that the Marshall had resigned—because he did not approve of any underhanded work. So with Mr. Klemme. My worst enemies are Morgan [A long blank space follows.]

Mr. Spreckels says Miss Emma Spreckels [his only daughter] is a strong Royalist.

154. Liliuokalani said she learned of Volney Vaillancourt Ashford's June 11, 1892, departure while at a Sunday school festival at Punahou School: "While engaged in conversation . . . Mr. Albert F. Judd, the Chief justice, approached me, and inquired if I could descry a vessel which was making her way slowly out of the port. . . . Then he went on to volunteer the information that on board that craft was Colonel Ashford, who . . . was secretly taking his departure." *Hawaii's Story*, 236. It would appear that the Queen's government had utilized an easy method of ridding itself of Ashford without a public trial. Ashford's troubles are discussed in the May 19, 1892, diary entry (282–84).

155. Volney Vaillancourt Ashford (b. New Hope, Ontario, Canada–d. 1900, San Francisco), the brother of Clarence W. Ashford, was the more radical of the two brothers. In his account of the Hawaiian League, Lorrin A. Thurston remarks: "During the development of the organization, in the first half of 1887, many problems arose. One of the most important was how to precipitate the issue [of reforms] with Kalakaua. . . . V. V. Ashford became one of the knottiest problems in the formative stage of the league. Although a vigorous member, he was . . . the evil genius of his brother Clarence, an able man and kindly disposed. . . . He was devoid of principle, ruthless toward others, as evidenced by his proposal that the King be shot in cold blood. . . . A strong conservative wing of the league was convinced that less radical measures than the overthrow of the monarchy were required . . . [and] among the leaders of the conservatives were Sanford B. Dole and P. C. Jones. . . . Radical policies advocated by V. V. Ashford drove them to resign from the committee and the league." Thurston, *Memoirs*, 137–38. There is no evidence that Dole was involved in the way the Queen's informant suggests he was.

156. The luau, under the sponsorship of the "Masonic ladies," was held at Mr. Allen Herbert's premises in Kalihi. The *Pacific Commercial Advertiser*, June 9, 1893, announced that the feast would commence at noon and that "during the afternoon, dancing will take place furnished by the Hawaiian Band."

I placed in Mr. Robertson's hands one of those Memorials, protesting against the actions of the party who called themselves Committee of Safety. Mr. Robertson took it to Mr. Nordhoff.

Mr. Cornwell and Parker called. The former told me that while on Maui he received a letter from Honolulu giving a full statement of all that transpired on Wednesday night last [June 7], and Mr. Blount was made acquainted with the particulars. Early yesterday Mr. Dole went to see him (Mr. B.). The latter asked why such people were prowling around the Queen's [premises]—Dole said he thought they were conspiring. It was very fortunate Mr. Blount had already heard.

*Wednesday, June 14.* Washington Place. The steamer *Australia* arrived bringing Mr. Neumann and the news that Mr. Thurston had presented his credentials on the sixth of this month to President Cleveland and had not been recognized. Mr. Thurston went to Chicago.[157]

Mr. Maertens' boy of seven years fell from a mango tree—his skull is said to be cracked.[158]

Mr. Parker wanted to borrow some more stocks.

*Thursday, June 15.* Washington Place. Last night the Provisional Government Soldiers carried guns in the street while they stood guard.

Everything all quiet. Eight boys of the Kamehameha School graduated today.[159]

This afternoon the Cabinet of the P.G. sent word to Mr. Blount they would like to see him, he sent word back that if they wished to see him they could find him any hour of the day at his office. They went over to him—the reason is not known—it is supposed it was to ask Mr. Blount if he would recognize Kaiulani or Queen Kapiolani as Queen.

---

157. Thurston in his "Dispatch No. 1" from Washington on June 13, 1893, informed Dole: "After presenting my credentials to Mr. Gresham on the 6th, I informed him I was extremely desirous of forwarding to you . . . a telegram indicating if possible what the policy of the administration concerning annexation was to be, stating that the present conditions were causing a heavy strain on the Provisional Government. . . . He replied that he was extremely busy that day, and made an appointment with me for ten o'clock the next morning. I was unable to see him, however, by reason of his being occupied with other business until nearly noon, at which time I had an interview with him for about twenty minutes. . . . He replied, 'You can tell them that your credentials as Minister will be received and that you will be presented to the President in due course.' . . . He made no reply, however, to my question as to whether the United States government proposed to take any action concerning the Islands. . . . 'I am unable to tell you what the President is going to do in the matter for the very good reason that I do not know, and I do not think the President knows himself.' . . . Upon Friday the 9th of June, by previous appointment, I met Mr. Gresham at the State Department and he accompanied me to the White House where I was presented to President Cleveland." Hawaii State Archives, Foreign Office and Executive Files, Series 404, Hawaiian Officials Abroad.

158. The *Pacific Commercial Advertiser*, June 15, 1893, reported that Willie Maertens, the son of William Maertens of Hoffschlaeger & Co., had fallen 25 feet from a mango tree at Punahou Preparatory School (adjacent to the Washington Place premises), and that he was in serious condition.

159. According to the *Daily Bulletin*, June 16, 1893, there were actually 14 graduates: David Ai, Robert Baker, Henry Blake, Isaac Harbottle, James Harbottle, Mathew Hoonani, Kaili Kanehe, Noah Kauhane, Moses Kauwe, Solomon Mahelona, Samuel Mahuka, William Meheula, Abraham Pihi, and John Wahinemaikai.

*Friday, June 16.* Washington Place. Mr. Parker told me Mr. Spreckels was going to give a dinner party only to Anti-Annexationists—48 in number.[160] He [Parker] wanted me to sign or endorse some checks for the Amount of $4,500. I declined. He is in great pilikia [distress],[161] so am I.

*Saturday, June 17.* Washington Place. Mr. Magoon[162] came this morning but I would not receive him. Mr. Nawahi says he saw Mr. S. M. Damon in Mr. Maroon's office, trying to mortgage all his lands—He has succeeded partially to Mortgage some to J. Phillips, the painter[163]—Does he mean to skip too? Mr. Cecil Brown has gone to Hilo or Hawaii. Mr. W. F. Allen is better. Mr. Nawahi has gone to take down the receipts of Crown lands— so as to see how much has been spent by the Provisional Government.

*Monday, June 19.* Washington Place. 9.30 A.M. Mr. Charles Nordhoff and his daughter Elsie S. Nordhoff called. Only captain Nowlein was present. Mr. Nordhoff told me he had taken in our situation from the first since his arrival and could arrive at only [one] conclusion, that the Queen should be restored. The people wished it. They loved their sovereign—and the whole has principally been a filibustering act. Nothing should be done but to restore the Queen. Mr. Spreckels was inclined to favor a Republic—but they had a talk and now he favors restoration.

[Nordhoff said] He never was in a place [before] where the people had no hesitation to tell lies and stick to it. He hadn't had a very pleasant visit here on that account. He was going on the *Australia* and would be back very soon (Will it be with a restoration?). He was positive it will be very soon—but we must continue to remain quiet. This has been the principal thing in our favor. Spoke well of Mr. J. O. Carter and his family. [I] Thanked Mr. Nordhoff for the good he had done for my people by writing such favorable articles for our side and stating the whole truth. He said his daughter was a true Royalist.

*Tuesday, June 20.* Washington Place. Mr. Parker called and we nearly had a quarrel about the Constitution. He will soon come back with Adolph Spreckels. Sure enough, they did come with Rudolph Spreckels and Mr. Carter [sic], manager of Spreckelsville [Plantation].[164] It was a pleasant

---

160. The elaborate dinner "with a French menu" took place at the Hawaiian Hotel on June 20, 1893, and was in honor of the arrival in town of Spreckels's son Adolph. The guest list (published in the *Hawaiian Star*, June 20, 1893) shows that many of the guests were in fact royalists. "The party separated about midnight, after an hour spend in discussing fragrant Havanas, Champagne, etc."

161. Samuel Parker was facing bankruptcy. Following a meeting of his creditors at the chamber of commerce on July 23, 1893, the *Hawaiian Star* reported on July 24, 1893: "It would appear that Mr. Parker is hopelessly bankrupt, there being about $14,000 interest overdue on the first mortgage and about $10,000 on the second. The unsecured debts will probably run up to $60,000 or $70,000." A committee comprising P. C. Jones, Godfrey Brown, W. C. Wilder, Herman Focke, and H. A. Widemann was appointed to look into the matter.

On July 29, the *Hawaiian Star* noted: "Parker's affairs are in a hopeless condition, and the more they are examined into the worse they appear." Eventually, however, Parker resolved his tangled finances privately.

162. Probably John Magoon (b. 1830–d. 1905) who appears in the 1892–93 City Directory as "Capitalist. Old Capital Building. 199 Queen Street."

163. No such record has been found in the Bureau of Conveyances.

164. Liliuokalani may have been referring to Hugh Center, listed as the Spreckelsville Plantation manager in the 1892 City Directory.

visit, they all went mauka to have a look at my Pear [avocado] tree. It was loaded with fruit.

The Ladies of the Hawaiian Patriotic League presented a gold-headed Kauwila[165] cane to Mr. Nordhoff and [to] Miss Nordhoff a Kukui[166] pin. The Memorial to Mr. Nordhoff was very prettily worded and tears filled his eyes while he read it and blessed the two ladies who presented it. We have won his sympathy for their loyalty to their Sovereign—and because we have done no wrong.[167]

*Wednesday, June 21.* Washington Place. [Entry ends thus.]

*Monday, June 26.* Washington Place. Delivered my statement to Mr. C. T. Gulick for him to correct[168]—he is sick and weak from the grippe. I understand from Capt. Nowlein that Mr. Blount expects his successor on the *Alameda*.

The President, Secretary, and Treasurer [of the Provisional Government?] drew from the Postal Savings Bank the amount of $1112.61—with interest from Jan. 3—which is $17.19.

*Tuesday, June 27.* Washington Place. Mr. Gulick has seen Mr. [J. O.] Carter and found that my manuscript would require more study. I am afraid he will not have it ready by Thursday. Today the Directors of the Hui Hookuonoono Kawaluonalani met to make some changes in the Constitution.

*Wednesday, June 28.* Washington Place. Queen Dowager Kapiolani and Princess Poomaikelani have just called to see me. They told me P. P. Kanoa was better since he went to stay with Kahuila Wilcox. Kahuila has a Kahuna [sorcerer].

*Belgic* came in this morning, must write to Kaiulani. 12 P.M. had to send my letter to Kaiulani through Mr. T. R. Walker—as the P.G. have always opened my letters—no matter who I write to my letters will always be intercepted. If they have read the contents of my letters, in one they will have found that I have directed her not to consent or act or accept any other advice but mine in regard to our situation. The other letter [to Kaiulani] was about receiving Prince M. Hamed Ah Kahn Nawab of Rampur, India.[169]

165. The cane was made of the wood of the kauwila or kauila tree (either *Alphitonia ponderosa* or *Colubrina oppositifolia*).

166. This would have been a pin made of a gold-mounted, polished nut from the kukui tree, also known as the candlenut tree (*Aleurites moluccana*).

167. Charles Nordhoff of the *New York Herald* was presented with an embossed gold-headed cane by the Hawaiian Women's Patriotic League, and an elaborate testimonial of appreciation by the Hawaiian Patriotic League, the latter saying in part: "Your letters to the *Herald* have been a fearless and truthful expose of the great injustice that has been committed against the Hawaiian Queen and People, and all your statements have touched upon the unpleasant truth so close as to have caused the parties exposed to wince." *Daily Bulletin*, June 21, 1893.

168. See July 14, 1893, diary entry (364).

169. In her letter to Kaiulani of June 1, 1893, referring to "Hamed ah Kahn, the Nawab of Kampur," Liliuokalani writes: "I hope you will receive him kindly and show him what attentions you can and politeness when he comes to see you. I am quite pleased with his looks and manners.... His color is that of our own race so there sprung a feeling of sympathy right away and I felt acquainted right away." Hawaii State Archives, Cleghorn Papers.

The prince had just made a brief stop in Honolulu. According to the *Pacific Commercial Advertiser*, May 30, 1893: "An Indian Prince, the Rajah of Rampur, with five servants and a party of seven in attendance ... arrived on the steamer *Gaelic* yesterday.... The Prince is a

Hanakeola was buried today [at] two P.M. She died yesterday.[170] [In her cash account for July 3, Liliu records paying "To Hanakeola's casket $50."]

*Thursday, June 29.* Washington Place. Mr. Rudolph Spreckels called and will leave at 12 P.M. The P.G. spoke disparagingly about his father and Rudolph wanted to shoot the man who spoke disparagingly.

---

Two entries in the Queen's diaries (June 30 and July 13, 1893) discuss one of the most famous and tragic incidents of the 1890s in Hawaii: the pursuit of a community of individuals diagnosed with leprosy who had isolated themselves with their families in remote Kalalau Valley on Kauai. The most famous of these individuals is Kaluaikoolau, or Koolau. Under the terms of an act of the legislature of 1865, he was subject to removal to Kalaupapa, Molokai. The Provisional Government and the board of health continued to follow that policy, which Kamehameha V had enacted into law. In Kalalau Valley, there were estimated to be about 28 residents with leprosy. After issuance of a general order for their removal, Louis H. Stoltz, deputy sheriff for Waimea, Kauai, and several other people met with the group. Some surrendered, while others—including Koolau, who was told his family could not accompany him to Kalaupapa—resisted and fled into the interior of the valley.

In June 1893, Stoltz returned with a dozen armed policemen with the objective of taking Koolau prisoner. On Monday, June 26, they began to scour the valley. On Tuesday, Koolau shot and killed Stoltz.[171] The shooting triggered prompt action in Honolulu. President Dole proclaimed martial law in the districts of Waimea and Hanalei "and a squad of soldiers and a field gun were dispatched to Kauai. Including the Kauai police, the entire expedition comprised some eighty men."[172] On July 6, during the course of the siege, the fugitives killed two military men—Private John Anderson and Private John B. McCabe, a Civil War veteran—and another soldier, John Husberg, fell and died when his rifle accidently discharged. Captain King reported: "In this awful wilderness Koolau controls the situation and it is suicide to attempt to capture him."[173]

Koolau, who was with his wife and child, escaped apprehension. He died in 1896, having lived in Kalalau as a fugitive for almost three and a half years. His wife, Piilani, published a memoir in Hawaiian in 1906, which has been translated into English and reissued in recent years.[174]

---

bright, fine-looking young gentleman of about twenty, was educated in England, and the subjects in his dominion's number it is said eleven millions." The *Gaelic* departed for San Francisco on the 30th.

170. "Mrs. Hanakeola Leleo Kinimaka died yesterday at her home on King Street near the Kawaiahao Seminary. She was the widow of the late Brevet Captain David Leleo Kinimaka of the old household guards and leaves a son and two daughters—she was well known among the natives." *Pacific Commercial Advertiser*, June 28, 1893.

171. Anwei Skinsnes Law, *Kalaupapa: A Collective Memory* (Honolulu: University of Hawaii Press, 2012), 230–34.

172. Aubrey P. Janion, *The Olowalu Massacre and Other Hawaiian Tales* (Honolulu: Island Heritage, 1977), 99. Janion, a Maui author wrote a sympathetic account of Koolau and Piilani.

173. Janion, 102.

174. Piilani Kaluaikoolau, *The True Story of Kaluaikoolau: As Told by His Wife, Piilani*, trans. Frances N. Frazier (Honolulu: Kauai Historical Society, 2001).

*Friday, June 30.* Washington Place. The Hui Hookuonoono Kawaluonalani met and contributed $66.00.

The *Waialeale* left for Kauai yesterday at five P.M. with Prince Kunuiakea on board and 25 soldiers of the Provisional Government. They went down with the intention under Deputy Sheriff Deverill's charge and one brass piece, a cannon, to take prisoner those men who shot Mr. Stoltz, Deputy Sheriff of Kauai. Mr. Stoltz was only doing his duty in obeying the orders from the P.G. to arrest all the lepers in Kalalau and take them to Kalawao.

The *Alameda* arrived with the news that Judge Sneed[175] need not come down until everything was settled by Mr. Blount. He wants Mr. Blount to finish everything up himself after commencing his investigations of our situation.

**Monday, July 3.** Washington Place. [Entry ends thus.] [On this date in the cash account section of the diary, Liliu records this receipt: "From J. Heleluhe—rent of Hamohamo $820. 75."]

*Wednesday, July 12.* Washington Place. Told Hannah Evans to give our congratulations to Minnie Aldrich and to warn her not to be foolish with her money.[176]

Mr. Parker came and asked if Mr. Neumann and I had had conversation about his [Neumann's] open letter to Mr. Dole of yesterday's *Bulletin*.[177] I told him I knew nothing about it, nor had I seen Neumann. Mr. E. Macfarlane wanted to know also. They seem to think that this letter must be a side play of Neumann's for a consideration—but I do not think so. I wonder why they distrust him. Macfarlane says that Mr. Blount says this will be the last batch of letters that he will send [to Washington] and he would like my Constitution. I placed it in Macfarlane's hands for him to give to Mr. Blount. I told Macfarlane also to ask Mr. J. O. Carter to finish my statement as soon as possible.

*Thursday, July 13.* Washington Place. The *Australia* has just arrived, no news as yet has been received from Washington. *Iwalani* has returned from Kauai, bringing back the bodies of the three men[178] that were shot

---

175. The *Hawaiian Star*, June 26, 1893, picking up a notice from Washington, DC, stated: "June 14th. It is reported here tonight that President Cleveland has decided to appoint a successor to Mr. Blount at Honolulu.... Rumor has it that judge [J.L.T.] Sneed of Memphis is the man selected for the post... considered one of the ablest lawyers of the Tennessee bar... [and] one of the best constitutional lawyers in the country." The appointment did not take place.

176. Minnie stood to inherit from the estate of her father-in-law, William H. Aldrich, who died in San Francisco on March 3, 1892. He was once a partner in the Bank of Bishop & Co.

177. Paul Neumann's communication, "An Open Letter to the Hon. S. B. Dole, President of the Provisional Government," published in the *Daily Bulletin*, July 11, 1893, says: "Do you, do your colleagues, does the Council, and do your partisans believe that a government established under the circumstances under which this Government was created—a government existing without, I will not say against, the consent of the Hawaiian people, can be permanently maintained. This, you know, is not probable, it is not possible.... It is not necessary to advance the proposition that annexation is entirely impossible; it is undeniably impossible without an expression of the will of the Hawaiian people. The United States would not, without such an expression, annex this country in any form or under any conditions.... The American nation are not filibusters, and that instead of attempting to gain annexation by legitimate efforts at the Islands, you tried by foreign and unlawful assistance to knock Mr. Stevens' ripe pear off the Hawaiian Tree. It was a misdirected blow. The United States did not spread the bag to receive the pear, it is hanging there yet."

178. The three soldiers were John Husberg, John Anderson, and Civil War veteran John B. McCabe. Their funerals were held on Sunday the 16th.

at by Koolau. Koolau has not been caught. Most of the lepers at Wainiha crossed the mountains and joined Koolau. The Provisional Government Troops have been returned with all their ammunitions and guns. Kahuwila Wilcox tried to start our H[ui] A[loha] Aina members to get up contributions for the lepers. But I told them not to do anything.

*Friday, July 14.* Washington Place. E. C. Macfarlane sent to see if my Statement [to Blount] was correct. I told him I was satisfied and signed it, though it is more as a diary as I had given my formal statement through Mr. Neumann to President Cleveland.[179] I have made an appeal to the American people—and now they say I am right and ought to be restored—and lastly this statement I have given is more like a diary. When Mr. Nowlein received my copy I sent also the letter John Colburn wrote me[180]—with a request it should be returned to me. Macfarlane said he would.

*Saturday, July 15.* Washington Place. Spent the morning in putting up a bar to protect my ferns. Mrs. Nowlein came and brought me a present of a pretty muslin dress ready made.

Mr. and Mrs. [Claus] Spreckels called at four P.M. He said he was going to Washington next Wednesday by the *Australia*. He will say to the President that it is his wish that the Queen should be restored to her throne, and the Country to be restored to its former state, [as] a Government under a Monarchy and myself at the head. He wanted that a new constitution should be promulgated [and] that I should appoint the Nobles. He wanted that my Ministers would be composed of such representative men as could be found—hoped that I would not encourage the establishment of any other enterprise such as the lottery, etc. Now in regard to my interfering in enterprises that would be beneficial to the Mechanics and laborers provided they do not interfere with the Sugar industry, I do not see why I should prevent the working classes from having or making money for themselves. To watch for Mr. Spreckels' interest if it keeps within the pale of the law is all that he ought to expect and not more than the law provides for. I said nothing. I never like to make promises, and I do not think he ought [to] say who I should appoint for Ministers. I will appoint such men who would act with me and not study the interest of any individual or firm.

Joe Aea came to say to me, he wanted Kahae to go down to Kane's office[181] that they should sign papers of separation. She wants to but there was a drawback about the children.

---

179. The Queen's very long statement to Blount appears in the Blount Report, 390–403, and is reprinted in the Morgan Report, vol. 2, 1664–77. Her statement or letter to President Cleveland, dated January 31, 1893, is in the Morgan Report, vol. 2, 1675–76.
180. This letter has not been located.
181. Samuel Kapoi Kane (b. 1858, Waimanalo–d. 1903, Honolulu) was an attorney at law. His obituary identifies him as a "well-known lawyer." *Pacific Commercial Advertiser*, December 6, 1903.

*Wednesday, July 19.* Washington Place. Mr. and Mrs. and Miss [Emma] Spreckels left by the *Australia* for San Francisco today.[182] Mr. Spreckels will go right on to Washington to see if he could do something for our situation. While making a speech on the steamer wharf to the people who flocked down to see them off, Mr. A. F. Judd's two sons who are on their way to Harvard College[183] hooted and stamped and made all the noise they could, helped by Mr. C. M. Cooke and Mr. Hosmer and another teacher of Punahou. How little and how small. Mr. H. C. Carter of New York and Mr. and Mrs. J. T. Burke of Denver, Colorado, went well decorated by the people.[184]

*Thursday, July 20.* Washington Place. Began to dig a well and will put up a windmill.

*Saturday, July 22.* Washington Place. Kahakuakoi's moopuna [grandchild] died today and I gave her $50.00. Alapai's moopuna also died [and] he borrowed on his share in the Hui Hookuonoono Kawaluonalani 9.00. [Liliu's cash account under this date shows "Kahaoni's coffin $5." This may refer to either of the two moopuna.]

*Wednesday, July 26.* Washington Place. Wrote a long letter to Ninito [Sumner] telling her about our situation, that I am living in confinement waiting the decision of the U.S. For this reason it would not be well for Arii paea [chief or royalty] Kealatane Ariimanihinihi[185] and Kamakahuila to come now and make me a visit—but to wait till everything was settled, then when they come everything would be in peace [and] then they would enjoy their visit. I sent them pictures of Washington Place by Mr. Joedicke. [?] [In her cash account for this date, Liliu records a payment: "For windmill at Washington Place—$161.25."]

*Saturday, August 5.* Washington Place. Mr. J. O. Carter called and asked me if I would receive Mr. Blount sometime today—and that Mr. Blount would send George Harrison a half hour before time to notify me. I said I would receive him and he went back to deliver the message. After he left I felt a heavy pain come over me as if I was going to have the grippe.

182. In an article on Spreckels's departure, the *Hawaiian Star*, July 19, 1893, reported: "Ex-King Claus was the cynosure of all eyes. He paraded the deck absolutely embowered in leis and wreaths, his head rising amid the expanse of roses and posies like a pumpkin in a big flower patch.... Miss Spreckels was also radiant with leis, having about a hundred of them on, and she made herself agreeable to her friends by waving a small silk Hawaiian flag.... Among the throng about the ex-king was John Cummins, Major Seward, Editor Kenyon, Sam Parker, Antone Rosa, Charley Wilson, Mr. Fernandez, A. S. Cleghorn, Prince David, [and] J. E. Bush."

183. The two Judd sons, Albert F. Judd Jr. and James R. Judd, were both bound for Yale College.

184. The Burkes were tourists from Denver, who arrived in early June and "engaged quarters at the San Souci." *Hawaiian Star*, June 7, 1893.

185. Alexandra Kealatane Ariimanihinihi (b. 1866–d. 1918) was the daughter of Alexander Salomon (b. 1820–d. 1866), a well-known Tahitian businessman, and his chiefly wife, Ariioehau (b. 1821–d. 1897). Alexandra, who married Norman Brander (b. 1864–d. 1930), was a sister-in-law of Pomare V (b. 1839–d. 1891), the last king of Tahiti. The letter has not survived.

Sent for Dr. Trousseau and asked him to give me something to relieve me as I wanted to meet Mr. Blount today, which he did.

Four P.M. George came. [At] 4.30 precisely Mr. B. came. He said he had come to let me know that he was going to leave for the U.S. on Tuesday next unless some special news was to arrive that day which would require him to stay. He asked if on his going I thought there would be any danger of a disturbance—I told him I thought not. I could from time to time—have notices [put] in the paper for the people to keep the peace, until we receive news from U.S. He told me Mr. Dole has assured him that no harm would come to me. Mr. B. says I must have faith that they will keep their word. He says—I am leader of the people, I must lead them in the right. When he left here—he [said he] wanted no demonstration, no presents, nor any notice from the people. He wished I would select such men as J. O. Carter and E. C. Macfarlane to help me in the administration of the Government. When I told him that the P.G.s had threatened to take my life—should news be received of my restoration, what ought I to do? He said, "isn't Admiral Skerrett[186] here—and also the British and other Commissioners?"

*Monday, August 7.* Washington Place. Told Miss [Lucy] Peabody what Mr. Blount said about presents, [that] he could not accept any presents as he is an official employed by the American Government.[187]

*Tuesday, August 15.* Washington Place. Cleghorn came and asked why I did not make arrangements for E. C. Macfarlane to go to the U.S. as such had been the instructions from Mr. Blount. I told Mr. C. I was not aware Mr. B. had said so—we then made arrangements for his trip. I asked Gov. Cleghorn to borrow of W. G. Irwin $1,000.00, and he said he had no authority to do so—so I will have to borrow money from some other person.

It seems Mr. Irwin has received letters from Mr. Spreckels informing him that he had transferred all his stocks here to his sons.[188] When Mr. Irwin realizes the change it will be a very great change. He will find he could not easily hoodwink J.D.S. [John D. Spreckels] as easily as Claus Spreckels. I asked Sam Parker to write over and tell Mr. Spreckels about it.

---

186. Rear Admiral J. S. Skerrett, in command of the Pacific Station, arrived at Honolulu on the USS *Mohican* on February 10, 1893. He had previously been in Honolulu in 1874 in command of the USS *Portsmouth*, and he assisted in putting down the riot at the time of King Kalakaua's election. His correspondence from Honolulu with the secretary of the navy, February 27–November 16, 1893, is in the Morgan Report, vol. 2, 2208–19.

187. The *Hawaiian Star*, August 7, 1893, published news of the pending departure: "As is usual with him [Blount] the Minister has said little about his intention to leave us, and the news only came out when Mrs. Blount declined a dinner invitation, saying that her husband and herself intended to take passage for California on the *Gaelic* tomorrow night." The *Gaelic* departed for San Francisco with the Blounts as scheduled.

188. This report also appeared in the *Hawaiian Star*, August 18, 1893, via an interview with "a prominent employee of Claus Spreckels." When a *Star* reporter asked, "Do the transfers include everything the Sugar King has here?" the answer was "Everything! Real estate, stocks, credits, and the like. The family residence and other real estate will go to his daughter Emma and his sons get the rest." The paper then printed a copy of Spreckels's July 14, 1893, deed to his daughter. That document as printed does not include the Punahou Street residence.

*Wednesday, August 16.* Washington Place. Mr. Parker calls and tells me that he did not write to Mr. Spreckels to inform him, but it seems that Irwin had already written himself explaining all about it. So I was glad to excuse Sam about it. I do not feel like borrowing ever again from him after this, though Irwin is sorry. Our friend sends words to me to beware how I open my letters—there might be explosives in it. He saw W. O. Smith and two others try it in one of the rooms in the Palace.[189]

Last night a man went in the P.P. [Punahou Preparatory] School house at twilight and came out at four A.M. He wore a long cloak. No electric lights [here?] tonight and yet they [are on?] all around town.

Ask Mr. Robertson to see if he could get some Commissions and seals ready—100 are wanted.

*Thursday, August 17.* Washington Place. Nothing of importance. Last night there was a spy in the Punahou Preparatory School yard.[190] He wore a long cloak—and a dog followed him—He was there all night. No electric light tonight. Mr. Robertson says none [no commissions] to be had but will have some printed.

*Saturday, August 19.* Washington Place. Drove out to Waikiki with Capt. Nowlein—and the others are to follow. Stopped outside of Joe Heleluhe's—he is very sick—did not see him. Joe Aea came out, though, and kissed my hand, as well as the rest of the Waikiki folks. They were so glad to see me down there. They are my faithful Kahu [attendants].

Drove up to Paoakalani—as green as ever. Mrs. Nowlein soon came out with our food. Although I had a cold it seemed to do it good to have a change. The well was being dug but only four feet deep. Joe and Kahae [Aea] went down [to the lawyers]—did not get divorced. Came home in afternoon, in an express with Capt. Nowlein, and Charlie Warren[191] seated in front.

Kahele told me lots of stuff coming from a person in the employ of the P.G.s—wanted to know what they are to do—warned me to be careful in opening my letters—that they would put some kind of combustible substance in my letters.

Heard today that the Government asked Admiral Skerrett to help them.

*Sunday, August 20.* Washington Place. As I expected, watches were set by the P.G.s in the streets—carriages stopped and questioned as well as foot passengers. Today the P.G.s started a report that the Royalists were going to start a war against them so they asked of Admiral Skerrett to send some men on shore to protect them.[192] The Admiral said they were

---

189. There is no evidence of any such experiment.

190. The Punahou Preparatory School was adjacent to Washington Place on the Ewa side, and is now part of the grounds of Saint Andrew's Cathedral.

191. Charles Warren (b. 1867, Waihee, Maui–d. March 10, 1946, Olaa, Hawaii) was a personal servant to King Kalakaua and served in the palace under Liliuokalani. The 1892 City Directory lists him as "quartermaster King's Guard, barracks." He was a mounted policeman during the republic, and then went to Hilo at the turn of the century.

192. In a follow-up to an earlier notice in the *Hawaiian Star*, that paper reported on August 21, 1893, that Admiral Skerrett had ordered a battalion of the fleet "to hold itself in readiness,

the Government and ought to be able to take care of themselves—When required he would land his men to protect American interests—so they were hoka [thwarted]. I have no doubt that the guards were stationed in the streets because I went out.

*Monday, August 21.* Washington Place. It is reported that Mr. S. B. Dole, the President of the P.G.s, is demented. That he is not responsible for anything he says. Last Saturday there was a meeting held at his house to consult on his business and he could not answer intelligibly. He took into Council a certificate from his physician saying he was not well and required rest.[193] He is to go to Kohala to rest at Puuhue ranch for two weeks (if he does not go to Frisco for good) and come back. Many P.G.s have gone. The Emersons (O. P. and J.)—Hatch is Vice President.[194]

*Tuesday, August 22.* Washington Place. Cold still hangs on.

*Wednesday, August 23.* Washington Place. [Entry ends thus.]

*Thursday, August 31.* Washington Place. Had a meeting of Hui Hookuono-ono Kawaluonalani. Thirteen members present. $34.00 contributed. Distributed little Hawaiian flag-*badges to the soldiers*[195] *and to my ohuas* [servants].

*Monday, September 18.* Washington Place. The arrival of the Steamer *China* has caused a good deal of commotion today in town by the news received—that Mr. [Albert S.] Willis of Kentucky has been appointed U.S. Commissioner to Hawaii, and Mr. Ellis Mills, U.S. Consul General.[196] It does not please the P.G.s. The news also of four new vessels of war coming to protect the islands is not pleasing to them also. They think there ought to be no plebiscite—and they are right, but I think they ought simply to

---

under command of Lieut. Lucien Young, to come ashore in Honolulu to protect American property. The Admiral acted on his own responsibility. He got the facts of a contemplated uprising from the Executive building but was not requested to intervene. The authorities simply told him because he is the senior American representative here and had a right to know."

Pursuing the investigation further, the *Star* reporter unearthed two stories. One was that the royalists had been arranging to gather at Diamond Head and receive arms and ammunition, shipped in a schooner from the coast. The second story was that "another plot to overturn the government by the use of dynamite had been discovered and exposed."

193. Dole, in an August 19, 1893, letter to the Executive Council, writes: "Finding myself unable to attend to public business because of ill health, I desire to be temporarily relieved from the demands of official work and suggest that the vice President be called upon to assume my official authority for the time being. I enclose a physician's certificate in relation to my state of health." On October 19, 1893, Dole resumed his duties. Hawaii State Archives, Foreign Office and Executive Files, Executive and Advisory Councils.

194. On August 17, 1893, Francis M. Hatch was appointed vice president, replacing W. C. Wilder, who was to be away for several months.

195. By "soldiers" Liliu means those assigned to guard her. The italicized section was written in a different hand at a later date.

196. W. O. Smith, in a letter of this date to S. B. Dole, repeats this information and continues: "All quiet here. The Royalists are jubilant about today's news.... One thing is quite certain, that is, that the U.S. propose to do something. It is rather refreshing to think of the U.S. compelling us to settle the matter by popular vote. Sam Parker said to Wray Taylor today, 'Damn you fellows—we've got you now. It will be settled by votes—You fellows have got to get out and we will put the Queen back.' But we won't worry too soon." Hawaii State Archives, Dole Papers, in U-117.

turn everything back as they found it—however, we will wait the arrival of those two persons—and those ships of war if the newspapers speak true.

*Tuesday, September 19.* Washington Place. Seven P.M. Our friend through Kahele sent me information in regard to his leaving his employer. He left on the day of the arrival of the *Philadelphia*, just as he had informed us on the night of the tenth that he would leave very soon. Now last night Kahele said that his employer was not pleased when he told him [W. O.] Smith—that he would leave—why, said he? Because I have a better place offered to me. He is now at the hotel awaiting the arrival of Mr. E. [Ellis] Mills. This unknown person says I need not have any more fears that anyone would harm me—that he will be Mr. Mills' secretary—that when the Commissioner (Mr. Willis) arrives, he will restore me to the throne. I suspect he must have been placed by Mr. Blount as secretary to Mr. Smith for a purpose. He in that position must have learnt all the plans of the P.G. and must surely have sent his statements to Mr. Blount.

*Wednesday, September 20.* Washington Place. Have been warned twice today to take care of myself. First by C. W. [Charles Wilson], second by Mrs. G. [Gulick]. The former proposed that I should move to Waikiki or to Muolaulani where the P.G.s could not get at me as easily as here—their party owning the Central Union Church[197] and the Punahou Preparatory School—could easily shoot at me from there—and what would prevent them from shutting off the travelling [street traffic] and shutting me in. I told him to speak to Major Wodehouse about it. He went on to say he had no fears about these days but when the Commissioner Minister Willis arrived then would be the time of danger, for Mr. Emmeluth[198] and Henry Waterhouse said to Mr. Logan[199] and to Mr. W. that I would not live to get on the throne.

Mrs. G. [Gulick] says I must not lay myself open to the P.G.s for they would shoot me at sight. I have such confidence in what Mr. Blount said when he went away, that I have no fears.

*Thursday, September 21.* Washington Place. Mr. Parker tells me that Mr. Widemann told him the [monarchical] Cabinet ought to resign now—he said he thought not—that they ought to be the ones to put everything to rights—then after that they should resign. I told them I would notify them when I thought it was the proper time. Charley [Wilson] called again at three P.M. to say he had been to see Major Wodehouse and told him, that he and his friends had fears for my life—that he wanted to know what sort of protection he (Wodehouse) could give. Wodehouse said he could receive me in his house but he could not vouch for the P.G.s not shooting or firing into his house. Wodehouse would advise me to go to Waikiki.

197. Central Union Church was then directly across from Washington Place.
198. John Emmeluth (b. 1853–d. 1910, Honolulu) was the proprietor of a hardware store at Nuuanu and Merchant Streets. He served on the Advisory Council of the Provisional Government, January 16, 1893–May 2, 1895.
199. Daniel Logan (d. January 1925, Canada, age 72 years) was the manager of the Bulletin Publishing Co. and the editor of the *Daily* and *Weekly Bulletin*.

*Friday, September 22.* Washington Place. Sent for Sam Parker with the intention of telling him about the fears my friends had for my life—but decided afterwards not to when I thought that he is a good friend of Mr. W. G. Irwin's—and would be likely to tell him—so I turned the subject on [to] something else. We talked about Mr. Irwin's anxiety on not hearing from Claus Spreckels nor from John D. [Spreckels].

*Saturday, September 23.* Washington Place. Major Wodehouse came to say that he would advise me to go to Waikiki or some place out of town on Monday morning. He has seen many cases of liquor going to the Palace for the P.G. soldiers [who] might get drunk, and rush over here and get into a fight, and no one knows what may happen to me. He would not advise me to go to his house. Perhaps if I applied to Admiral Skerrett, he might be able to protect me, but he thought Skerrett hardly had the power that Blount had. I told Wodehouse I thought I would be safe in my own house, where I could be near my friends.

Last evening Kahele came over to report from our old unknown friend—When Mrs. W. told him she was not sure whether he said there would be an election or not—he was quite annoyed and reproved her for inattention. He told her it was all newspaper talk about elections—they would simply restore me, that was all. He told her he would scarcely have time after this to meet her hereafter for all his time will be taken up to write up his books. He may before Mr. Mills comes.

*Thursday, September 28.* Washington Place. Heard this eve from C. B. Wilson that there was really a party who had formed themselves into [a group?] and made a vow that should they hear news of my restoration—they would take my life—they are part of the Annexationists—Gunn, Egan, Ables, Stratmeyer, Henry Waterhouse, Emmeluth, Atherton, and others, [also] Wagner [and] Klemme.[200] Wilson warns me not to open myself to be shot at. Their party are getting reckless.

After he left I sent for Mr. Robertson and gave him my instructions that as soon as the Steamer *Alameda* arrived to watch and see if any news of importance was to arrive on our favor, that he should visit the Admiral [Skerrett] and ask to give me protection. I thought Jimmie [Robertson] rather doubted the propriety of acting as I directed. Next day everyone expected good news. *Robertson on finding out there was nothing of importance to communicate to me, did not go to the Admiral.*[201]

*Friday, September 29.* Washington Place. The *Alameda* has arrived and no news—not a line. I inquired how Dr. Wood, Mr. C. M. Cooke, and sympathizers of Annexation looked? They told me a hangdog expression—alright, then we will be satisfied. Eveline [Wilson] is here. Mr. J. E. Bush and his little girl are here. He had no news.

---

200. There is no evidence that such a group ever formed.
201. The italicized sentence is a later addition.

*Sunday, October 1.* Washington Place. Major Wodehouse, Mrs. and Miss Scarth of Canada called—very nice people.[202]

7.30 P.M. Mr. Hayselden[203] called—I told him I wanted him to assist me in the administration of the Government when the Restoration takes place—as Marshall. He said he would be faithful to me and Country. He would have time as I did not expect to hear anything till Saturday the 7th on the arrival of Mr. Ed Macfarlane by the *Australia*.

*Monday, October 2.* Washington Place. Willie Aldrich placed $40.00 in my hands, rent of their house [at] Waikiki.

Received a beautiful handkerchief, from Paymaster [blank] of the *Philadelphia*.

*Tuesday, October 3.* Washington Place. Educational Society met at ten A.M. Twelve members present. Nothing of importance was brought forward. I mentioned that on account of the political situation I wanted to bring away all our children of the society, but that Willie Castle had chosen to detain them so I considered that from the 9th of September we are not responsible for this last month. Contribution was taken with the result [of] $1.50. Minnie [Aldrich] called to say how pleased she was with their house at Waikiki.

*Wednesday, October 4.* Washington Place. 7.30 P.M. Kahele called to say she had heard from our informant that she had met Mr. without-a-name at the esplanade—he had only little to say—as there were many people around watching the *Miowera* as she laid on her side at Puuiki reef.[204] He told her he had received letters by the *Alameda* from Blount, Mills, and Spreckels. Here I am inclined to doubt—Mr. S. very seldom writes. What they wrote is not to be told because Mrs. War[d's?] daughter was nearby, but he said Commissioner Willis and E. G. Mills would soon be here—then everything will be all right. Her daughter was not pleased because she spoke to him, a stranger.

*Thursday, October 5.* Washington Place. Nothing of importance transpired.

*Friday, October 6.* Washington Place. Paina [meal] in Hinano Bower.

*Saturday, October 7.* The *Australia* has arrived and Mr. E. C. Macfarlane is on board. Mr. Robertson has seen him and has just come on to say Mr. Mac[farlane] had no news to bring, as everything in Washington seems to be very quiet, but that he would call in a day or two to pay his respects.

202. The Scarths were the wife and daughter of William Bain Scarth (b. 1837–d. 1902), a Scottish-born timber merchant, ship owner, and political figure in Ontario and Manitoba, Canada. He was in the Canadian House of Commons 1887–91.

203. Fred H. Hayselden (b. 1850, Brighton, England–d. 1924, Honolulu) was the proprietor of the Lanai stock ranch and a resident of Lahaina. He married Talula, the daughter of Walter M. Gibson.

204. The *Miowera* (part of the Canadian-Australian steamship line), while en route from Sydney to Vancouver, BC, went aground at the entrance to Honolulu Harbor on the evening of October 2. The *Pacific Commercial Advertiser*, January 6, 1894, reported her as off for San Francisco after being stuck on the reef for 40 days and lying in the harbor for two months.

While the *Australia* was off Waialae she blew a whistle to Mr. P. Isenberg[205]—it was immediately telephoned to town and all over the city—Mr. W. F. Allen was seen to tremble. He was seized with nervousness and was enquiring excitedly the cause of the whistle blown—was the American minister on Board? and is Consul General Mills with him? Why should he fear—does he feel that the end is coming near?

Mr. Parker called to say he had seen Mr. M. and what little he had learnt he had given to Mr. Norrie[206] for the *Holomua*.

Mr. C. T. G. [Charles T. Gulick] called at ten A.M. to ask if I had authorized Emma de Fries[207] to borrow of him the Amount of interest due to note to Damon on $10,000.00—that it was $156.00. I told him it was a fraud. I have already given Damon $700.00 through J. Heleluhe. Mr. A. Herbert [Entry ends thus.]

*Sunday, October 8.* Washington Place. Many sick people in the servant's quarters—Milaina, typhoid, Hopekaa, la grippe—Kauhane, la grippe, Nahaleha indigestion.

Lahela, Hakau, Piipii, Alapai, Kailaa, and [blank]—have called in to join [us] in family worship and every one of them prayed.

*Monday, October 9.* Washington Place. Mrs. C.T.G. [Gulick] called to find out if I had heard any news from Mr. Blount or the States—not a word. She explained about E[mma] de Fries. Mary Carter and daughter came in to bid me good-bye as she (the latter) was going by the *Australia* to San Francisco.

*Tuesday, October 10.* Washington Place. Spent the morning in the garden and could not see Major Wodehouse. He wanted to know if I would receive a reporter from Australia. I declined. Louis Morningstar[208] wanted to see the Queen—but could not. He expressed much disappointment.

---

205. Daniel Paul Rice Isenberg (b. 1866, Lihue, Kauai–d. 1919, Honolulu) was the proprietor of the Waialae Breeding Ranch.

206. Edmund Norrie (b. 1859, Denmark–d. 1939, Honolulu) worked at the *Holomua*. In a statement made to the Danish Consul July 8, 1895, in preparation for a claim against the Republic of Hawaii, Norrie stated that at the time of the 1895 counterrevolution, "I was employed by the Holomua Publishing Co. as editor in chief of the *Hawaii Holomua*. ... Under the instruction of my employers I had advocated a policy favoring the restoration to Her Throne of Queen Liliuokalani, they holding that she had been deposed unjustly and wrongfully and that the best interests of the country would be advanced under a Monarchical Form of Government." Hawaii State Archives, Attorney General Files, Series 506, Box 14.

207. Emma Kanoa de Fries (b. January 20, 1856, Kusaie Island, Micronesia–d. 1923) was the daughter of Reverend Kanoa, a Hawaiian missionary to Micronesia and a descendant of Maui and Hawaii island chiefs. Her husband was Henry Howard Kauauanuiamahi de Fries. At the end of the century, Mrs. de Fries engaged in one of the endless genealogical disputes that were published in the Hawaiian newspapers, advancing her children to the ranks of princes and princesses. In 1901, she attempted to claim former Crown lands. *Pacific Commercial Advertiser*, October 23, 1901.

208. Louis Morningstar, who bore the title of "the boy globetrotter," arrived at Honolulu September 29, on the SS *Alameda*, and that day walked into the offices of the *Hawaiian Star* with letters of introduction from the *San Francisco Chronicle*. He was then judged to be about 13 years of age and by his own account had been born in Germany and had lived in Saint Petersburg,

Eight P.M. Mr. E. C. Macfarlane called to pay his respects. He arrived in San Francisco and went on to see Mr. Nordhoff in Coronado. Spent one night with him and daughter—went back and saw Spreckels. Told J. D. [Spreckels] that he was going to New York and Chicago, then back. He [Macfarlane] reached Washington 10th September. Mr. Blount called on him and spent two hours—was told not to let anyone know that he had seen him except Mr. J. O. Carter. [Blount] asked how everything was in Hawaii [and] was told everything was in peace and quiet. He was glad to hear it—he was much afraid that disturbance would arise, but it was wonderful what power the Queen had over her people—and it was the best thing for us. It has been the main chance of our success. He said, within five or six weeks from now Mr. Willis and Mr. Mills will be there, and Mr. Willis will have his instructions. They will first call on you and Mr. Carter. He must not be seen or known to have called on Mr. M. [Macfarlane], that next day he should call on Mr. Gresham and say nothing about him—he would advise M [Macfarlane] not to stay long in Washington—for himself [Blount] he would leave immediately as his steps were being dogged and he must go back to Georgia. He was annoyed the P.G.s should mention his wife's name. [Entry continues onto the page for October 11.] Mr. Macfarlane met Secretary [of State] Gresham. Was immediately ushered into his presence—while all the others had to wait. From one to five their interview lasted. Mr. Macfarlane was allowed to say all he had to say without interruption. Found Mr. Gresham a man of great shrewdness and broad mind [and] great intelligence. He found that Mr. Gresham seemed to take great interest in our cause—asked about the Queen and her capability—again about taking an election whether there would be an equal voting—Mac. Said no, it would simply end in the Queen and no other—and why no other? Because we would have no other. "How strange you should have such a love for her." Mr. Macfarlane impressed on him that Mr. Stevens had conspired against us. He left with encouraging words. Mr. Macfarlane met W. D. Alexander.[209]

He [Alexander] had not yet met the President or Gresham—couldn't get access to him.[210] He was tired of waiting and wants to come home. He knows no one, [Frank] Hastings is not there nor is Thurston. Macfarlane met Mr. Mills and dined with him and Mr. Larens and another gentleman and left next morning the 11th.

Russia; New York City; parts of Texas; and San Francisco. The *Star* engaged him to write an account of his pending visit to the volcano, duly published in the October 7, 1893, issue.

209. William D. Alexander, who had been sent to Washington, DC, by the Provisional Government to assist in negotiating a treaty of annexation, commented in a letter to Dole (September 13, 1893): "Mr. E. C. Macfarlane was here two days this week, but, I think, not for any political object, except to find out, if possible from Willis, what Cleveland intends to do with us. 'His Saccharinity' Claus Spreckels has not arrived here yet from Chicago." Hawaii State Archives, Series 404, Box 53.

210. The reference is unclear, for Alexander in a letter to Dole of September 13, 1893 (in a postscript dated the 14th), says: "I had an interview with Secretary Gresham this noon." Hawaii State Archives, Series 404, Box 53.

*Leialoha, an unarmed policeman, was injured by the only shot fired at the end of the monarchy.* "At two o'clock on the afternoon of January 17, 1893 [the day that the monarchy fell], Captain Good of the volunteer military [under the auspices of the organizers of the uprising] was at the E. O. Hall hardware store obtaining arms and munitions to take to the Drill shed, loaded a wagon, and drove off. At the nearby intersection of Fort and King Streets a Hawaiian police officer, Leialoha, seized the horse's bridle and demanded that Good go to the police station. A wordy altercation ensued. Finally, Good drew a revolver and shot Leialoha." *The Queen noted the incident in her diary. The policeman recovered from his injury.*
San Francisco Examiner, March 1, 1893, Hawaii State Archives

*On March 29, 1893, James H. Blount arrived in Honolulu from Washington, DC, commissioned by President Grover Cleveland to document the events leading up to Liliuokalani's removal from the throne. One of his first actions was to order the removal of the American flag flying atop the government building and the restoration of the Hawaiian flag while he investigated what part the United States had played in the overthrow and the circumstances of the revolution. Loyalists affirmed their allegiance to the monarchy and Hawaiian autonomy in numerous ways, including creating quilted renditions of their beloved flag. This quilt, made in 1896, belonged to Mark P. Robinson, who served as Liliuokalani's minister of foreign affairs.*

Hawaiian Mission Children's Society Library

He is going back to meet the Gilligs[211] at the Hawaiian Hotel. The Hawaiian National Band is playing tonight.

*Wednesday, October 11.* Washington Place. Had a call from Louis Morningstar. He kissed my hand on his entrance and gave me an account of his travels—will go round the world touching at Japan, China, Africa, back to Germany to see his mother, then will reside in New York and send all his earnings to his mother—gave me his photo. He was pleased when I presented him a bouquet.[212]

Mrs. Evans came in, had a great deal to say about Willie and Minnie [Aldrich] and the Fergusons who are hard up for money and would borrow of them.

Mrs. Kahele came in and told me that that person who has been reporting had another message, that was, he had received letters from Blount, Mills, and Spreckels—that Mr. Mills and Mr. Willis would be detained and had written for Capt. Nowlein [that he?] should raise an army now to get ready for the restoration. Shall she tell the Captain—I said No, I would tell him myself. The Captain could not act until I told [him]. Here I felt there was a catch—and that this man is a fraud—as if we would be foolish enough to make such a mistake. The P.G.s would be after us and then there would be a commencement of a row.

*Thursday, October 12.* Washington Place. [Louis] Morningstar went right over to the editor of the *Hawaiian Star* and told him to put his article in his newspaper but he expected to be paid. So W. G. Smith of the [*Hawaiian*] *Star* promised him two dollars for his article about his visit to the Queen. So he related all that transpired—that he kissed the Queen's hand on his entrance—she gave him a bouquet which he said he would take back to his mother—and she asked him to write in her visitor's book and what he wrote and that he enjoyed his visit. The *Star* man promised to order a new suit of clothes for him.

Old Mahoe Nahaleha died this morning from constipation. He had been a whole month without movement.

*Friday, October 13.* Washington Place. Great was Morningstar's horror when he read *Star* last evening and found in his article the word ex-Queen—so he went to the editor and reprimanded him and told him

---

211. The Gilligs arrived in Honolulu on October 7, 1893. Harry Gillig (b. 1859–d. 1909), son of a Virginia City, Nevada, silver mining millionaire, was married in 1890 to Amy Crocker, the daughter of Judge E. B. Crocker of Sacramento, California. The Gilligs had previously visited Hawaii March–May 1890, at which time they saw much of King Kalakaua.

212. Morningstar's account of his visit to Washington Place appeared in the *Hawaiian Star*, October 11, 1893: "I never had a nicer time in all my life. I went to the place where the Queen lives, and gave my card to her captain [Samuel Nowlein]... but the Queen did not wait for it. She was sitting in a chair all by herself, and she called out, 'How do you do, Louis Morningstar?' Her hand was held out and I kissed it as they do to queens at home and told her I was very well indeed. She said she had read all about me in the papers and told me I was a brave boy.... The Queen said that she would give me one of her pictures before I went."

that if he did not change it he would never write any more articles for his newspaper.[213]

This evening Captain Nowlein came to me and told me that Mr. J. F. Fowler had told him that Mr. W. W. Hall was going to serve an execution on me soon—for the amount of $572.00 which I owe him. I told him I could do nothing nor pay any money, I had none. My friends would help me, but to say nothing.[214]

*Saturday, October 14.* Washington Place. Mr. Robertson has just come in to tell me he had had conversation with Mr. Magoon in regard to my account with E. O. Hall and Son. That he would see me first but not to act any further until he heard from him, and to keep this matter quiet. What was his surprise to find I already knew about it and many others.

Louis Morningstar wants my picture and wants to show me his new suit of clothes.

*Sunday, October 15.* Washington Place. Stay at home. Four P.M. Prayer meeting with our people.

*Monday, October 16.* Washington Place. Today is Kaiulani's birthday— today she has arrived at her age of maturity which is eighteen—and is by the laws of the country—eligible to the throne or to assume office as Regent during my absence, or as Queen at my death.

Preparations are being made for a luau by the Liliuokalani Educational Society M2 [Mokuna 2, Second Division].[215]

*Tuesday, October 17.* Washington Place. The *Oceanic* has arrived bringing the American Consul General E. G. Mills.[216] The people are so glad to see him back. The P.G. party have no news from him and our party has bright looks in return, it gives us encouragement.

---

213. The *Star* had referred to Liliuokalani as the ex-Queen only in comments about the Morningstar interview, not altering the young man's narrative where he referred to her as the Queen.

214. On October 13, 1893, E. O. Hall and Son Ltd. brought a complaint before the courts against Liliuokalani Dominis for "the sum of five hundred and eleven [and] 72/100 Dollars for goods, wares, and merchandise" charged between January 2, 1892, and January 12, 1893. The four-page inventory of goods charged included such items as a sink plug, hatchets, a scrub brush, two lawn sprinklers, piping, tooth powder, paints, a wheelbarrow, and an electrical bell. A copy of the summons was served on Liliu on October 17 and the matter appears to have been settled privately. Hawaii State Archives, First Circuit Court, Law 3359.

215. "The Hookupu [ceremonial offering] and luau given at Mrs. Dominis' in honor of Miss Cleghorn's [Princess Kaiulani's] eighteenth birthday is in progress as the *Star* goes to press. The ex-royal band is playing on the grounds, about 150 schoolchildren are congregated in front of the fence or on the steps of the Central Union Church, a few adherents of ex-Royalty are on watch in front of the building [Washington Place] to keep out the *Star* reporters. The luau is laid out in the rear of the building." *Hawaiian Star*, October 16, 1893.

216. The *Hawaiian Star* continued to suggest that Mills was English. However, it did print a notice from Sanford B. Dole, minister of foreign affairs, that Mills "has presented to this Department the commission from the President of the United States of America, appointing him to be Consul-General of the United States of America at Honolulu, which Commission is found to be in due form, therefore he . . . is acknowledged by the Provisional Government of the Hawaiian Islands." *Hawaiian Star*, October 20, 1893.

The news of Minister Willis being detained was that he and party were snowbound on the summit of the Rocky Mountains. He will be here by next steamer on the 26th.

Mrs. Kahele [Nahaolelua] called again to tell me that that man who was our friend sent a message that I ought to write to all the other islands sending for all the important people by this steamer to come down, because after this week all the steamers are to be stopped—to write also to the other islands to fire all the plantations—that these messages were sent him by Mr. Spreckels—what a story. Now I see that he must be a tool of W. O. Smith. Mr. Spreckels would not send me such a message for he has an interest in all the other plantations.

*Monday, October 23.* Washington Place. Rec'd a note from E. C. Macfarlane asking me to send him a list of such lands left out of Mr. Damon's Mortgage, also of my stocks. Nothing of importance has turned up—so spent the afternoon in turning over my valuable papers.

*Tuesday, October 24.* Washington Place. Two days more, then the *Mariposa* will arrive. I hope the American Minister Willis and family is on board—and then will we receive the Message from the U.S. as to what mine and Hawaii's future shall be. I must keep up my courage for it would never do to fail at the last moment.

Sent Joe Heleluhe down to E. C. Macfarlane who will examine the list with J. O. Carter and H. A. Widemann of my stocks and unencumbered lands—they are: Taro land in Paalaa, Waialua $1,000; Lot in Waiakea $200; 25 shares in Mutual telephone worth $250; 2 Haw[aiian] Ramie [Co.] $200; 1 Kapiolani Park [share] $50; 45 shares Haw[aiian] Agrl. Co. $4,500; Oahu R[ailway] & Land Co. [shares] $5,000 bonds; Hawaiian Construction Co. [shares] $12,000; Volcano [House] Co. 40 shares at $25—$1,000. Mr. Widemann will advance money to pay Damon's Mortgage off—then I will be free from these people. I am sure I have more property than my debts which are only $19,000, and my Palama residence will cover the whole.

10.30 A.M. The sailors and Marines of the USS *Philadelphia* landed, marched up Richard St. and stopped in front of Major Wodehouse's house and went through some exercises, then marched down Beretania St. [and] Alakea St. back to their vessel. Several thought there would be a restoration. [However,] Coming events [have] cast their shadows before. Mr. Cornwell called—he is going right up this afternoon to Waikapu with [Francis M.] Hatch and two or three others.

*Wednesday, October 25.* Washington Place. My friends H. A. Widemann, E. C. Macfarlane, and J. O. Carter Jr. are helping to pay my liabilities which of course I could have been able to pay had I been permitted by the P.G. to retain my salary—but of course it is their object to humiliate me in the eyes of the world. So these kind friends have come forward to help me and Joe [Heleluhe] has placed in their hands papers and Royal Patents of lands to be mortgaged to them and they want my shares of Pahala also.

*Thursday, October 26.* Washington Place. No steamer today—everything quiet as usual.

*Friday, October 27.* Washington Place. Early this morning the *Mariposa* arrived but no Minister Willis. What can be the matter? And what the delay? No one can say.[217]

I have placed in Joe Heleluhe's hands my stocks of Pahala plantation Nos. 164 and 165—of 20 shares in one and 25 in the other, to be given in E. C. Macfarlane's hand to go also as security for $30,000.00 with some of my lands.[218]

*Monday, October 30.* Washington Place. Mr. Widemann [Entry ends thus.]

*Tuesday, October 31.* Washington Place. The Kawaluonalani Society met at 11 A.M. and contributed sixty-five dollars. Mrs. and Miss Scarth called with Major Wodehouse. They were on their way home to Canada since she had received news of her husband's appointment as Lord Lieutenant of Canada.[219]

Three P.M. Mr. Widemann brought in a slip of paper [with] the amount he had paid out for me which was $30 and with $224 more to pay off school bills.[220] Gave me good advice in future.

**Wednesday, November 1.** Washington Place. Heard from Hana [Hannah Evans] that Wm. Aldrich had given Henry Poor a pounding in the streets. The latter threatened to shoot Willie, for calling him a son of a B.

*Thursday, November 2.* Washington Place. Jennie Clark came over and took two banners—the Riding Society and the Educational [Society] over to Lucy Peabody's to show Mrs. James Campbell. 7.30 P.M. Kahele came in to tell me Mrs. Ward had brought a message from that man who kept

217. A notice in the *Hawaiian Star*, October 27, 1893, says that Willis was expected on the *Australia* on November 4.

218. On October 27, 1893, Liliuokalani executed a mortgage to H. A. Widemann "for and in consideration of the sum of Thirty-two Thousand dollars, lawful money of the Hawaiian Islands" that conveyed to him the following lands; Kamanaiki in Kalihi, Oahu (purchased from King Kalakaua's estate in 1892); 22-45/100 acres at Pawaa, Oahu; land at Kaauwaeloa in Palolo; Hamohamo in Waikiki; the Washington Place premises; the ahupuaa (land division) of Honohina, on Hawaii; the ahupuaa of Keahuolu, at Kona, Hawaii; lands that were a portion of the ili (land divisions within an ahupuaa) of Kapahaha and Keoneula, Oahu; the property known as Muolaulani in Palama, Oahu; the ahupuaa of Haleaha, Koolauloa, Oahu; and 45 shares of stock in the Hawaiian Agricultural Company.

In return she acknowledged payment in "gold coin of the U.S." and signed three promissory notes (two for 10,000 and one for 12,000), payable with interest at the rate of 8 percent. She signed the document in the presence of E. C. Macfarlane and Charles T. Gulick, and Thomas G. Thrum, registrar of the Bureau of Conveyances, recorded it October 31, 1893, at 9:35 A.M. Bureau of Conveyances, Liber 145, 278.

219. Mrs. Scarth and her daughter departed Honolulu for Vancouver on the *Warrimoo* on October 31, 1893. William Bain Scarth was a leading (but unsuccessful) contender for the position of lieutenant governor during 1893–94.

220. In the Hawaii State Archives, Liliuokalani Collection, Box 2, Folder 18, are two slips of paper tabulating the costs of schooling to be paid by the Liliuokalani Educational Society. The list for January–June 1893 shows that 20 girls were on scholarship at Kawaiahao Seminary, at a cost of $500.

his name so secretly—that last night a meeting took place and all the members of the P.G.s were present, so were also Admiral Skerrett and Mr. Mills, and that he was secretary of the meeting. Mr. Dole got up and said he was ready to return Queen Liliuokalani on the throne and hoped all the others were of the same opinion. Smith and Emmeluth stood strongly against it and finally they won.[221] He told Mrs. W. [Ward] that now he is with Mr. Mills as clerk and was independent of the P.G.s.

I told Kahele I was more convinced than ever that he was a fraud and spy because the Admiral [Skerrett] and Consul General [Mills] would never enter any local political meeting—for they would be immediately recalled—in the second place Mr. Boyd does all Mr. Mill's writing and no other—so we must not believe any more that came from her, but to keep up the ruse. Fraulein [Wolf] tells me that she is engaged to Mr. C. [Charles D. Chase.] Shall she marry him? Certainly, says I.

*Saturday, November 4.* Washington Place. The *Australia* has arrived bringing the U.S. Commissioner A. S. Willis[222] and wife and son, T. H. Davies, W. C. Wilder and wife, Mr. and Mrs. [C. M.] Hyde, and several others. As soon as the plank was set, Mr. E. Mills and J. Boyd went on board and soon they came down with the Commissioner and family on another plank, so as to avoid the line of soldiers and police which the P.G.s had placed in line to do him honor [and which] of course he could not accept—but they were not at all abashed, nor disheartened, but immediately went to the American Legation and made a call, but both the Minister and Mrs. Willis were tired and would not see them.

Mr. T. H. Davies called on me and showed me some of Kaiulani's pictures which are very nice. He wanted to go into a[nother] room which we did [so] that he might read me something. It was a proclamation [from Kaiulani] to the People showing them that now she has arrived at her Majority (18 years) she wished to show her love for them and asked their love in return, that she would be loyal to them, her subjects—and so on.

Well, I think it presumptuous on his part—and said he had better postpone the publication till after the settlement of our situation, which will surely take place in a few days—What cheek![223]

---

221. No hint of this business appears in the minutes of the Executive Council. On October 31, Dole informed the council only that "Admiral Skerrett will call at 11 A.M. tomorrow, to bid an official good-bye." Hawaii State Archives, Foreign Office and Executive Files, Minutes of the Executive Council.

222. Albert Shelby Willis (b. January 22, 1843, Shelbyville, Kentucky–d. January 6, 1897, Honolulu) was a lawyer, congressman, and diplomat. In September 1893, President Grover Cleveland appointed Willis envoy extraordinary and minister plenipotentiary to Hawaii, to investigate the circumstances of the overthrow of Queen Liliuokalani. Willis remained at his post for about three years, and died in Honolulu of pneumonia, January 6, 1897.

The *Daily Bulletin*, November 4, 1893, said: "Hon. Albert S. Willis, United States Envoy Extraordinary and Minister Plenipotentiary, with Mrs. Willis and their son, has taken Snow Cottage, Hawaiian Hotel Grounds, where Mr. Blount had the United States Legation. An American flag is flying from the staff in front of the house."

223. Although Liliu was increasingly wary of Theophilus Davies's support of Princess

Mr. Marques is anxious to know beforehand who are to be [the] Ministers for fear they might not agree. I told him I did not see why they should not. If they were doubtful they could be easily made to resign. He was fearful Mr. Bush might make trouble. I told him there was a remedy for all such actions—that Mr. C. T. Gulick should be Minister to Hawaii— there is plenty of time for that. Mr. Marques left [and] Mr. Macfarlane came and brought me encouraging news. It would take place in a few days—one day next week. Asked Capt. Nowlein to take two positions at once but have not yet told him what they are.

*Monday, November 13.* Washington Place. At 11 A.M. Mr. E. Mills called to pay his compliments—wished that he might soon be excused but stated that for certain reasons of their own, he would ask if I would waive ceremony and call at the American Legation and that as soon as possible—[and asked] if my chamberlain would come with me. Told him we would be over at 11.30. Wired for Mr. Robertson, told him to come over in an express, and we would be at the Legation [at] 11.30. Manuel Reis drove us down.

On arrival the Minister of the U.S. [Willis] received me in the parlor and Mr. R. [Robertson] withdrew with Consul General Mills. Minister Willis began by saying that Grover Cleveland, President of the United States, sends kind greetings to you. He wished me to express to you his deepest sympathy for you, and regretted very much that through the wrong actions of the U.S. Minister to Hawaii [John L. Stevens] I should have been made to suffer and also my People. (I bowed.)

The request he makes is that should there be restoration, that you would show great magnanimity of spirit and of justice to those who have been the means of placing your country in this situation by granting to them their lives, their property, and all that belonged to them. [He continued:] I wish also to say that if you have anything to say, let it be open, and from the heart without hesitancy: that all that is spoken between us must be sacred for two or three days at least. [The text then jumps back to the page for November 12.] Mrs. Willis is in the next room, and no one will enter to disturb us. (I suspect she must be taking down our conversation behind the curtain in writing.) Mr. Mills is in the room opposite us with Mr. R[obertson] and will not hear us. I said that in regard to his remarks about granting those people P.G.s their lives or amnesty, I would have to consult my Cabinet. Minister Willis said I need not consult them but what would I do or my own decision be? I told him

---

Kaiulani in the event that the monarchy should be reinstated, Davies always supported Hawaiian independence. In an interview published in the *Hawaiian Star*, November 4, 1893, he made the following statement: "I believe that the Hawaiian race should settle their own difficulties without outside interference. I think the whole matter can and will be settled by the vote of the Hawaiians, but I have no means of knowing when that vote will be taken.... I would let every native Hawaiian or foreigner have a vote as well as naturalized citizens. I don't believe in serving under two flags.... As to the form of government resulting from such a vote it would undoubtedly be a limited monarchy, such as now exists in England."

that our laws read that those who are guilty of treason shall suffer the penalty of death, and their property confiscated to the Government. If any amnesty was to be made, it was that they should leave the country forever—for if they were permitted to remain, they would commit the same offense over again, seeing that they had once caused a revolution in 1887 and this was a second offense, and the next I feared would be more serious than this for our country and our people.

He said that if such was my decision, that he would write to President Cleveland and inform him of the fact and await further instructions. He expected to hear in about a month's time from today [November 13].

It is a long time to wait but we must have patience. Did I apprehend any danger to my life? Yes, I do. How and in what way? By the spies that still continue to creep or prowl about in the next yard and onto the schoolhouse at dead of night, equipped with loaded revolvers and belts full [of] cartridges—[The text then jumps back to the page for November 11.] Officers in the employ of the P.G.s as head lunas [supervisors] over prisoners or Road supervisors are all provided with revolvers—and also special police—and where at one time I felt free to go to anywhere with freedom—now I could not. It has been more than a month since I have been out of my premises. He said he would send word to the P.G.s—that they must have no more parade or display of arms—or have any more unnecessary specials and spies. He would invite me if I thought necessary to stay at the Legation [or] on the *Philadelphia*. I thanked him and said [I] would prefer to stay at my own residence and to continue with my guards to watch me—but if I found myself in danger—might I call on him for protection. He said it would be rather awkward to have me go on board or if I had their marines to watch me on shore, as it would be outside of their usual course, but if danger required, he hoped I would notify him and he would see what protection would be accorded to me—and offered me the privilege of coming to the Legation. I thanked him again—[He asked] Have you any soldiers? I have 16. Have they no arms? No. They were taken away from us but we have only one revolver and that the officer has—but never had used it—but in case they came in our yard, they will use it. That is all I will say at present on the former subject.

I would ask if you know of any men in whom you had confidence as men of honor and integrity and to name four—I mentioned J. O. Carter, E. C. Macfarlane, [the text then jumps back to the page for November 10] Joseph Nawahi, and John Richardson. He said I am glad to hear you speak in that way of Mr. Carter or have that feeling for him—for I have the same. After inquiring of these men, he said he would see them before three days—Nawahi has been to more than five Sessions and Richardson to two. Once more strict injunctions of secrecy, and I left.

There was great comment [about town?] on the actions of the American Minister in my calling first—that he ought to have done so—but such course as etiquette is set aside where diplomacy is required. Mr.

Mills went down town and was besieged by the young men in town but he simply answered—Did the Queen say anything? No, said they—"I *knew she* wouldn't," was his answer with a smile.

Five P.M. Mr. S. Parker called on Minister Willis this afternoon and returned very cross to think I should have been the first to call, instead of his calling first. I said nothing. He said Mr. Willis had asked if he could name 12 representative men, which he did. Also [asked] about the Constitution. Why was not the old constitution a good one? Because it was promulgated at the point of a bayonet—if another Constitution had been promulgated it would take four years before it could take effect. Minister Willis said it could take effect in less time—either in ten days or ten hours. He went home and left me with plenty of food for thought.

---

In Willis's report to U.S. Secretary of State Gresham, November 16, 1893, he reports the Queen's remarks of November 13, 1893, as follows:

> ¶ After a formal greeting, the Queen was informed that the President of the United States had important communications to make to her and she was asked whether she was willing to receive them alone and in confidence, assuring her that this was for her own interest and safety, She answered in the affirmative.
>
> I then made known to her the President's sincere regret that, through the unauthorized intervention of the United States, she had been obliged to surrender her sovereignty, and his hope that, with her consent and cooperation, the wrong done to her and to her people might be redressed. To this, she bowed her acknowledgements.
>
> I then said to her, "The President expects and believes that when reinstated you will show forgiveness and magnanimity; that you will wish to be Queen of all the people, both native and foreign born; that you will make haste to secure their love and loyalty and to establish peace, friendship, and good government." To this she made no reply. After waiting a moment, I continued: "The President not only tenders you his sympathy but wishes to help you. Before fully making known to you his purposes, I desire to know whether you are willing to answer certain questions which it is my duty to ask?" She answered, "I am willing." I then asked her, "Should you be restored to the throne, would you grant full amnesty as to life and property to all those persons who have been or are now in the Provisional Government, or who have been instrumental in the overthrow of your government." She hesitated a moment and then slowly and calmly answered, "There are certain laws of my Government by which I shall abide. My decision would be, as the law directs, that such persons should be beheaded and their property confiscated to the Government." I then said, repeating very distinctly her words, "It is your feeling that these people shall be

beheaded and their property confiscated to the Government." She replied, "It is." I then said to her, "Do you fully understand the meaning of every word which I have said to you, and of every word which you have said to me, and if so, do you still have the same opinion?" Her answer was, "I have understood and mean all I have said, but I might leave the decision of this to my ministers." To this I replied, "Suppose it is necessary to make a decision before you appointed any ministers, and that you were asked to issue a royal proclamation of general amnesty would you do it?" She answered, "I have no legal right to do that, and I would not do it." Pausing a moment, she continued, "These people were the cause of the revolution and constitution of 1887. There will never be any peace while they are here. They must be sent out of the country, or punished, and their property confiscated." I then said, "I have no further communication to make to you now, and will have none until I hear from my Government, which will probably be three or four weeks."

Willis concludes this report with the statement that he was forwarding a cypher telegram: "Views of the first party so extreme as to require further instructions."[224]

---

*Tuesday, November 14.* Washington Place. Eight A.M. Kaunamano wanted items for his paper *Aloha Aina*. Told him to publish—Hoomanawanui—Manaolana—Malama i ka Maluhia. [Be patient—Be hopeful—Keep the peace.] Mr. Parker and Mr. Richardson breakfasted with me and afterward went to see Mr. Willis.

Mr. Robertson called to say that Major Wodehouse wanted to know how it was that I had called on Minister Willis. Mr. Robertson ventured on his own account to say that Mr. Mills had called here to ask me to call on Mr. Willis. I told Mr. R[obertson] that I had not told him so, or anyone so—that after Mills called—I had simply asked him to call an express, and that I wanted him to go with me to call on the U.S. Minister—Mr. Robertson reported all this to Mr. Wodehouse. I asked of Wodehouse that this fact may not go further. Mr. R. [Robertson] further said that Mr. Wodehouse [said] I ought to ask protection of the U.S. Minister—he had done his part—but did not know the result. I told Mr. Robertson to thank Mr. Wodehouse and tell him I had no doubt everything would be all right. What was my surprise, Mr. R. [Richardson] returned with a message from Minister Willis saying that he would see that I would be protect[ed] whenever I would say the word—I had to tell Mr. R. [Richardson] that all that had been settled by us yesterday, although I had not told him. Minister Willis was going on board at 11 and on his return will await my answer. I told [him] to assure Mr. Willis that it was on account

---

224. This document was published in the Morgan Report, vol. 2, 2086–89. The stenographic notes of this interview are in the National Archives, Washington, DC, filed with U.S. Consular (Honolulu) Records.

of the anxiety of my subjects that had brought him over but [that] the Queen would wait and watch.

*Wednesday, November 15.* Washington Place. There seems to be great commotion on the part of the P.G.s. Hacks with armed men driving about— What's up? All imaginary fears—they think (the P.G.s) that we will do something—perhaps be restored. How foolish of them.

*Monday, November 20.* Washington Place. Wrote out my German lessons for the first time last night and this morning my little teacher [Miss Wolf] was quite pleased to see that I had made some progress.[225]

1.30 P.M. Mr. Parker and Mr. Richardson called and had lunch—when over, Mr. Parker left and I told Mr. R. [of] some plans, which would be of advantage to officials on Maui.

Seven P.M. Mr. Hayselden called and pressed me to ask of Minister Willis' aid by sending someone to protect me, as it was considered by my friends that my life was in danger from seeing the number of men with arms that surround my place—they only mean harm and might finally make a break [and] assault us and we are not protected—for we are without arms—and they are armed to the teeth. On his departure I told the Captain [Nowlein?] to wire for Mr. Robertson and he soon arrived. Told him I felt I ought to ask of the U.S. Minister for protection—That armed men were prowling around our vicinity and I considered their presence dangerous. Mr. Robertson went and soon returned saying Minister Willis would see that I did get some protection. [Willis said?] send him some names of those policemen and he will ask that they be sent to guard me. He also said that on Thursday news will be received of importance to us—that he himself had not given any opinion to any on the opposite side, or even encouragement.

*Tuesday, November 21.* Washington Place. Mr. Richardson and Hayselden returned by the *Hall* to Maui. At ten A.M. Sent six names of Hawaiian policemen to Mr. Willis by Mr. Robertson. One P.M. Robertson said Minister Willis had seen Mr. Damon, had told him that he would like to have six policemen whose names were on the list to be sent to stand guard on the Queen's place and to keep all spies away from Miller's lane, and in the [preparatory] school premises next to us. This will not be mentioned.

One P.M. Two policemen are here—their instructions are to watch everyone who comes in and goes out.[226]

---

225. A notebook of these exercises is in the Hawaii State Archives, Liliuokalani Collection.

226. The armed men patrolling the streets were the subject of a disapproving letter in the *Daily Bulletin*, November 22, 1893: "I would like to enquire what is the reason of the extraordinary display of military force made every night in the streets of Honolulu since the arrival of Minister Willis. The state of things here, previous to his arrival, was exactly what it is now, and yet the saviours of the country (!!) did not deem it necessary to have armed men parading the streets every night.... Now, how much is all this tomfoolery going to cost the poor taxpayers? We understand that every night there are 200 extra men and spies under arms patrolling through the streets or stationed on certain thoroughfares. Two hundred men at five dollars a night makes seven thousand dollars a week.... more than the cost of running the monarchy."

*Thursday, November 23.* Washington Place. 9.30 A.M. Mr. Cleghorn called to ask whether he hadn't ought to put an article in the *Bulletin* saying, it had been authorized to say, there was no truth in the statement published in the *Star* last evening—I told him to do so.[227]

10.15 A.M. Major Wodehouse came in on the [same] question. I told him, I had told Mr. Robertson not to trouble Minister Willis, as I had heard he had said the *Star* was not a truthful paper—and Mr. Willis would not believe I had said anything about him or my situation, since he knew [that] what was said [in that interview was] contrary to facts.

11.30 Mr. Nawahi and Wilcox called. Nawahi said he heard that last Wednesday Minister Willis went on board with Mr. Mills of the *Philadelphia*—and afterwards President Dole, Mr. Damon, Smith, and King met them. They did not stay ten minutes on board but while there Mr. Willis notified them that his Government's instructions to him were to restore the Queen to the throne.[228]

---

227. The *Hawaiian Star*, November 22, 1893, published an interview with an unidentified "eminent Royalist leader" who informed them that "Her Majesty says that in her interview with U.S. Minister Willis, she declared that she would not permit herself to be restored to the throne unless she could be assured of the armed protection of the United States Government. She is well aware that she is not strong enough to hold her own and that, without the aid of a foreign power, her tenure of authority would be brief." On the matter of Princess Kaiulani as a possible successor, the "Eminent Royalist" continued: "It is possible . . . that out of deference to the bitter feeling here in the American community, the United States may choose, in restoring the monarchy, to finally compromise on the heir apparent. In that event the Queen, who desires to mount the throne first, would abdicate in return for a large subsidy. An arrangement of this kind is being pressed by Mr. Davies."

Cleghorn's (unsigned) notice of refutation appeared in the *Daily Bulletin*, November 23, 1893: "We are authorized to contradict in the most emphatic sense the statement made in yesterday's *Star* regarding utterances of the Queen on the question of restoration. There is not a word of truth, we are assured on the best authority, in the whole statement."

228. In a letter from Washington, DC, November 10, 1893, W. D. Alexander informed Dole: "I have just learned that a letter of Gresham addressed to Cleveland is to appear in the papers tomorrow morning which is Royalist in the extreme, [and] strongly recommends the restoration of the ex-Queen to her throne. It is quite lengthy, and is a piece of special pleading, in the style of Paul Neumann. . . . It will be telegraphed all over the country in the morning. . . . Probably it is published to justify Willis' instructions, which will come to light later here. . . . It would seem that Gresham does not want us to form a permanent government. If there is to be a protectorate, he wishes it to be a protectorate of a Monarchy." Hawaii State Archives, Series 404, Box 53.

In his letter of November 14, 1893, to Dole, Lorrin Thurston said: "I called on Mr. Gresham this morning at ten o'clock, [and said] 'a statement has been published purporting to be a letter from you to the President recommending the restoration of the Queen . . . and desire to ask you if it is a correct statement.' He replied, 'Yes, of course it is true.' I said, 'I wish then to ask further whether it is the intention of the United States Government to carry out the policy therein indicated by force; or, in other words, whether, if the Provisional Government declines to accede to the request of the United States Government to vacate in favor of the Queen, United States troops will be used to enforce the request.' He replied, 'I am not at liberty at present and have not the time to answer that question.'"

Continuing on the possibility of U.S. intervention, Thurston informed Gresham: "'If you attempt to restore the Queen by force, there will be no thought of fighting with your troops. There will be no thought on the part of the Provisional Government of firing on the American Flag or shooting at troops wearing your uniform; but the Queen will be restored in no other way, and unless you are prepared to maintain a force on shore or hold her in position, she will be overthrown as soon as your troops leave.'" Hawaii State Archives, Series 404, Box 53.

Nothing more was said by him but the P.G.s said they would make a resistance. It seems too strange to be true—and seems very impolitic on Willis' part to make such a statement. I am told he speaks very freely on subjects he should not and [is] reticent when information is wanted. Mr. Wodehouse said Mr. Willis should not have received the American League. I believe Willis never spoke to them.[229]

*Saturday, November 25.* Washington Place. The [monarchical] Cabinet had a meeting at Mr. Peterson's. Tried to come to some plans about what course they should take, but could arrive at no conclusion—postponed till tomorrow.[230]

*Sunday, November 26.* Washington Place. Three P.M. Ministers Parker and Cornwell called and said they had been up to a meeting at Mr. Peterson's. They had decided to let me know that they would go and ask of Minister Willis what his intention was and what were his future plans in regard to our situation that they might make some decided plans.[231] I told them not to. I knew already everything and when it was time, the right time, I would let them all know.

What about forming plans about Commander in chief to control the Volunteers or Army? I told them I was Commander in Chief and would say the word when the proper time came. Mr. Parker then said, "but I

229. The American League meeting (of "three gentlemen") took place on November 13, and the "memorial" it presented appears in the Morgan Report, vol. 2, 1242–43. The *Star*, November 17, 1893, published Willis's response to the memorial: "I have my instructions which I cannot divulge . . . but this much I can say: That the policy of United States is already formulated regarding these islands, and that nothing which can be said or done either here or there can avail anything now . . . while performing my duties or carrying out the United States' policy, I shall have no need of aid from you or other resident Americans. I wish to state positively that any outside interference will not be tolerated by the United States."

230. This meeting was precipitated by the publication of a November 10, 1893, letter from Secretary of State Gresham to the U.S. president, on U.S. policy toward the Hawaiian Islands, which concluded: "Should not the great wrong done to a feeble but independent state, by an abuse of the authority of the United States, be undone by restoring the legitimate Government? . . . Our government was the first to recognize the independence of the Islands, and it should be the last to acquire sovereignty of them by force and fraud." See the *Hawaiian Star*, November 24, 1893.

231. In response to the publication of the Gresham letter, Honolulu annexationist supporters called for a mass meeting at the Drill Shed for the evening of November 25, to consider the situation, and (as the *Daily Bulletin* of that date noted) "to impress Minister Willis with the strength of the annexation movement." On November 27, the *Hawaiian Star* published both the speeches given at that rally and their resolution, "That we support to the best of our ability the Provisional Government in resisting any attack made upon it which may be contrary to the usage of nations."

The *Hawaiian Star*, November 29, 1893, reported, "A gentleman who does much charitable work among the natives and is on intimate terms with some of their leaders, called at the *Star* office today and told them [that] 'a native just from Washington Place said to me this morning that Minister Willis had told the Queen she would go back in a few days.' As soon as the *Arawa* has left the port Minister Willis will issue his ultimatum to the Provisional Government, notifying them to surrender possession of the Government buildings, Palace, Barracks, and Station House, as he has been notified by the President of the United States to restore Liliuokalani. A certain reasonable time will be given the Provisional Government, say thirty-six hours to make necessary arrangements, at the expiration of which, if his demands have not been complied with, the United States forces will be landed [to] restore her by force. This restoration is to be on Saturday next."

will go to the American Minister and find out." I told him if he did "it was not with my consent." Our conversation ended. Mr. Cornwell was just as nice about it as could be—he is a little gentleman.

*Monday, November 27.* Washington Place. Mr. Parker was not satisfied with my suggestion yesterday, but on pretext of going to the American Legation he went over and did try to get something out of the Minister, but did not get any word worth keeping—but it is very annoying. The worst of it is he told Minister Willis I sent him. [In her cash account for December 1, Liliu records the receipt "Rent of Spreckels & Co. for Honohina—$500.00."]

*Monday, December 4.* Washington Place. Told Mr. Richardson he had better tell Mr. Parker to resign when I told him to. He as one of the Cabinet had committed a great crime—of treason—in fact they all had—turned against me and followed Mr. Thurston the Agitator's instructions—and allowed themselves to be guided by him until the overthrow of my throne. Mr. Richardson thought I ought to aʻo kuu kanaka i ike ia i ka hewa ana i hana ai. [Mr. Richardson thought I ought to advise my people so they know of the wrongs he has done.]

I told him I would do so. He has a great failing and that is of repeating everything I told him or anything he heard—so the downtown folks are very wary of him and will not say anything in his presence. Gave him a good talking-to in John's [John Richardson's] presence—on what [was in] Mr. Thurston's letter—where Thurston admitted that it was the Cabinet who went to him after I had told them of my intention to promulgate a new Constitution, and it was Colburn who asked T [Thurston] that they must support the Cabinet "Against the Queen"—(what a confession) or they would resign. Mr. Parker had nothing to say.[232]

*Tuesday, December 5.* Washington Place. Richardson, Hayselden, [and William] White all went back to Maui about some cases in law.[233]

*Monday, December 11.* Washington Place. Capt. Nowlein handed me $90.00 of Pahala plantation dividends from J. O. Carter.

7.30 P.M. Mr. Robertson told me he called on Mr. Willis at four P.M. and delivered my message, and that was that should Mr. Parker or any other of the Ministers call on him not to consider their words as coming from me—that if I had any message to send it would be through him (Mr. R.). Mr. W. thanked him, [and said] he would do so. Robertson said that a spy had come in the yard [and] our folks had given chase as far as the fence and let him go. Willis said why not have caught him?—because he was beyond our limit, and perhaps he would have shot our man and caused a conflict with the government people and we wish to avoid that. He said it would give him good reason to act.

---

232. Liliu is referring to Thurston's letter or statement in answer to Blount's report. The *Pacific Commercial Advertiser* published the letter on December 4, 1893. Under the date of April 15, 1893, John F. Colburn had also supplied Blount with an account of his actions. See the Blount Report, 30–35, and the Morgan Report, vol. 2, 1304–9.

233. The December session of the Second Circuit Court opened at Lahaina on December 6, 1893.

My statement to Mr. Blount was given in the *Star* today.[234] Mr. Cornwell, it seems, was quite angry, I heard, with me—but he had best say nothing. They have all got themselves into trouble according to John Colburn's statement last Friday in the *Bulletin*, and in many things [it] accords well with Mr. Thurston's letter printed at Washington last Month and received here December 4th.

---

The *Pacific Commercial Advertiser*, on December 4, 1893, published the Thurston letter—actually a very long report, dated Washington, DC, November 21, 1893, formulated in reply to Blount's report. Thurston's account gave a lengthy resume of the events of January 13–17, 1893, and answered what he called "personal attacks upon me and those associated with me in the Provisional Government." The remarks also concerned Colburn, the Queen's minister of the interior, and the "stormy interview" the cabinet had had with the Queen over their refusal to sign her proposed constitution. Colburn's letter of response, which appeared in the *Bulletin* on December 6, 1893, is of such importance that I include it here to clarify the matter of his conduct and that of Lorrin Thurston:

> ¶ Honolulu, December 5, 1893
> Editor, *Bulletin*.
>
> L. A. Thurston ... has seen fit to reply at length to Commissioner Blount's report and drag all that he could about my conduct, and what I did and didn't say to him on the few days prior to the events long to be remembered, January 17, 1893. Therefore I take this occasion, with your indulgence, to relate what I did and said during those memorable days. I will also mention some things Mr. Thurston said and did on the same dates.
>
> Thurston says that on the 14th of January, at ten o'clock, I went to him greatly excited and told him of the Queen's intentions to promulgate a constitution and asked his advice, but fails to say what advice he gave me. The facts are as follows: A little after nine o'clock on the morning of January 14, 1893, after my colleagues and myself had returned from the palace, I learned that it was the Queen's intention to promulgate a constitution after the prorogation of the Legislature. I immediately called my colleagues together and we discussed the matter, and we all concluded we would not agree to any such proposition. Mr. Parker went over to the Queen to inform her that if our information was correct she should abandon the idea then and there, as we would not consent to it. After Mr. Parker left us, I came out of the Government

*Colburn's Letter of Response to Thurston's Reply to Blount's Report, December 5, 1893*

---

234. This statement appeared in the *Hawaiian Star*, December 11, 1893. It came from the State Department in Washington, DC, which had released the same on November 25 as part of disclosures accompanying the Blount Report, and was received in Honolulu on the morning of December 11. The statement that Liliuokalani provided Blount is printed in the Blount Report, 390–403, and the Morgan Report, vol. 2, 1664–77. The *Hawaiian Star* printed an abbreviated version. Not surprisingly, in the December 12 issue, the editor commented: "The ex-Queen's statement to Mr. Blount will go into political literature beside her power of attorney to Neumann as a complete giveaway."

building and went direct to Mr. A. S. Hartwell's office, told Mr. Hartwell what I had heard and the discussion the Cabinet had had in regard to the matter, the position we had taken, and further said to him, if the Queen insists upon promulgating a constitution, I would resign at once, as I did not take a seat on the Cabinet pledged to any such policy. I asked him to write me out a resignation, so that I could have it ready should I need it.

Mr. Hartwell, who has always been a friend of mine and occasional advisor, and who one hour before that called upon the Cabinet in the private office of the Minister of Interior and congratulated us upon our appointment, said: "Have you any objections to my asking Mr. Thurston to come over and talk with us?" I replied that I did not, whereupon he went to the telephone and rang up Thurston and asked him to come over at once. In a short time Thurston appeared and I narrated my story over again. When I finished, Thurston tipped his hat on the back of his head, rubbed his forehead, and said, "I don't know what to do about this matter."

I spoke up and said: "I am not going to be party to any new constitution, even though I may be opposed to you and your friends in regard to the ousting of the Brown-Wilcox cabinet. I propose to place myself right in the eyes of the business community and consequently I will resign rather than give my consent to it." He looked at me and said:

"Colburn, you have a tremendous responsibility on your shoulders, and don't you resign or think of it under any consideration, because if you do the Queen will appoint another Minister at once, and they would not hesitate to countersign and acquiesce in promulgation of the same, and before we know it the people of this country would have a constitution shoved down their throats." While we were talking W. O. Smith accidently dropped in the office. Thurston went on and said, "Go to the Queen at once and advise her to give up the idea."

I replied that we had sent Mr. Parker there, but as yet had not heard from him. Thurston said, "You go and tell her." I replied I could not see her at that particular time, as she was dressing preparatory to closing the Legislature. He spoke up and said:

"What difference does that make? Go and see her now even if you have to see her naked." I refused; whereupon he asked if Peterson was solid with my views, and I said yes. He then asked if I would go for Peterson and bring him here at once. I went after Mr. Peterson. Upon meeting him in his office I told him about my conversation with Hartwell, Thurston, and Smith, and informed him that they would like to see him with me. We immediately repaired to Hartwell's office when the same old story was gone through and the discussion was ended by Thurston asking Peterson if he would give his consent to have him (Thurston) start out and see what support he could get to back the Cabinet in the stand they would take against the promulgation of the new constitution and not resign.

We retired and prepared for the Legislature, which was to close in half an hour from that time. Upon our leaving the palace I went direct to Thurston's office to inform him of what had taken place, he having become by change of circumstances a co-worker with us for the common good of all. I did not find him there, but later did see him standing in the hallway of the Government Building. I invited him to Mr. Peterson's office, and there we discussed that subject together with a large number of businesspeople, whom I invited there for that purpose; it was there that Thurston submitted to Peterson for his approval his plan of opposing the Queen by force, and declaring the throne vacant; the US forces in the meantime being landed to virtually do the work. We remained at the Government Building until the Queen sent for us.

Upon going to the palace, W. O. Smith came riding up in a hurry and stopped me opposite the Kamehameha Statue. He said: "Don't be afraid, Colburn, the troops of the *Boston* are already to land; the munitions of war are all in the boats, and they can be ashore in a very short notice." I replied that the three of us that had retired from the palace were returning there and I expected the Queen would abandon her project. He said, "Let us know if you want the troops and you can get them, as the public well knows." The Queen did abandon her project.

Later in the afternoon I met Thurston again and told him I thought the trouble was all over. He replied, "Not much, she proposes to spring this Constitution some day, and we can't believe otherwise." However, I walked down with him to his office. While there Messrs. Wundenberg and J. B. Castle came in. We discussed what had transpired during the day.

Thurston asked if I would take a proposition into consideration. I did not know what he meant, and left him, saying I was too tired to entertain any proposition. After I left him I stopped in at W. O. Smith's office, where there was a large throng of people gathered, and as I walked in they called upon me to relate what had happened during the day, and what I thought would be the Queen's actions later. I repeated to them what I had told Thurston. When I got through talking, Mr. Hartwell handed me a piece of yellow paper. I saw at once it was Thurston's handwriting and it was a request to J. L. Stevens, American Minister, and Capt. Wiltse of the *Boston* to land troops to assist in dethroning the Queen. While I was reading it Thurston came in and said, "You sign that document, Colburn, and get your colleagues to sign it, and place it in the hands of someone you can trust, say Mr. Hartwell, for it may happen the Queen will cause you to be imprisoned, so as to carry on her work of promulgating the new Constitution." I replied I would have to consult with my colleagues before I could or would sign any document of that nature. However, I kept possession of it until Peterson came into the same place a few minutes later, and I handed the document to him. That document is at present in the archives of the United States at Washington.

Sunday morning, little before six o'clock, Thurston called at my house and asked me to accompany him to Peterson's house, which I did. On arriving there Thurston said he had something of a confidential nature to tell us, and if we were opposed to it to treat it as such. He went on to say that a number of gentlemen had met at his house the night before, and they had decided to dethrone the queen, had appointed a Committee of Safety, naming them, and they had sent him to us to ask if we would not take the initiative, i.e. to have us declare the throne vacant and establish a Provisional Government. The committee desired us to sign the request to Stevens and Wiltse that was handed to us the evening before, and to change some of the words to suit this occasion. Peterson then asked what element wanted the Queen dethroned, and for what reason. Thurston replied that it was the business community, and that it was her intention to promulgate a constitution at some future date. We told him that we would never allow [her] to do so. He replied, that they could not trust her, and the suspense was equal to sleeping on a smouldering volcano; it meant that they had to sleep with their rifles all the time, and they would not and could not stand it. He went on and said:

"We want you to do this work without saying a word to either of your colleagues, Parker and Cornwell, because the former is a treacherous liar, and Cornwell does just what Parker tells him to do; they are not to be trusted and we want nothing to [do] with them." I asked him if Judges Judd and Dole were present at the meeting and he declined to answer. Mr. Peterson then informed him that if this was a movement of the business community he desired to consult with some of the business gentlemen and get their views, and would give his answer as early as possible. Thurston agreed and departed. Later in the same day he called again at my house, but did not see me. I have not seen him from that day to this. Peterson and I consulted with our colleagues and six responsible businessmen of this city. Acting on their suggestions, the cabinet issued a proclamation, which was also signed by the Queen, assuring the public that no further attempt would be made to promulgate a new constitution. Thurston was furnished with an answer to this dethroning proposition. Peterson and I would not be traitors to the Queen and the constitution we had taken oath to support.

I deny having any conversation with Thurston upon what the Queen had said to Peterson, as the words that Thurston used were never spoken in the Blue room. I never told Thurston that Kaluna had said he wanted the blood of five white men if he could establish a new Constitution, as I knew nothing about a new Constitution till Saturday morning.

Thurston has the weakness to say things when he thinks it will fit the occasion best, and the man who has openly said what he said on the platform of a mass meeting, "that he would sleep with the devil if he could gain the point," is illustrative of his character and principle.

*Diary for 1893* 393

When Thurston wanted to convert me into an annexationist, he wrote me a very friendly letter from Washington, dated March 16, 1891, in which he states: "I give you credit for acting as you saw best in the interest of Hawaii." At present Thurston cannot see annexation staring the country in the light he and his party would like to have it, and he has probably seen my full and complete statement as furnished to Mr. Blount, therefore he has no further use for me, for the present, and wants to make the American public believe that the overthrow of the constitutional Government was caused by what I did (not) say or do.

John F. Colburn

---

*Friday, December 15.* Washington Place. Five minutes of 12 P.M. Consul General [Ellis] Mills called and said "if I could call on Minister Willis tomorrow, he would be glad to see me at whatever hour I would choose to name, but let it be early." I said if nine A.M. would do—he said yes—and would like to have Mr. Carter present to testify on both sides. Would like to have me notify Mr. Carter—and all this must be secret. I said I would.

One thirty P.M. Mr. J. O. Carter came on Mr. Robertson's notification to him from me and I asked him to meet me at Minister Willis's at nine A.M. tomorrow. I have no idea of what will transpire. He said perhaps I am watched but I do not care. I said I thought he was [watched] and told him to look at the windows of the Central Union Church opposite, where there are spies. He said he would go right over. Carter said the P.G.s are very angry because they can find out nothing from Willis. He went on to say that it was not very nice to see soldiers going about with guns in the streets.

Seven P.M. Told Mr. Robertson I had to meet Mr. Carter at Minister Willis' next morning at nine. We must plan some way to be near so as to be there promptly and run no risk. He suggested that I should go to Mr. George MacFarlane's cottage for the night and go right over from there. He and Capt. Nowlein immediately arranged that I should go through the Sisters' yard[235] with Mr. Charles Clark and C[harles] Warren and meet the Capt. at the Sisters' front gate. Milaina started at 11 P.M. for the Hawaiian Hotel, and Mr. Robertson went over to George M[acfarlane's]. Quarter after 11, Warren, Clark, and I went through the Sisters' yard and Sister Albertina opened the gate for me. I shook hands with her, passed through the gate, [the entry continues on the page for December 16] got into the Captain's carriage, and was driven to the Hotel premises. Met Mr. Robertson and Mr. Macfarlane and followed him [George Macfarlane] in[to] his cottage [on the hotel premises]. Found Milaina waiting. Went to bed and [James W.] Robertson and [Sam] Nowlein sat up watching all night. At nine sharp, I walked in the Legation of the American Minister,

---

235. That is, they went through the adjacent Saint Andrew's Priory School grounds to Emma Square.

found Mr. J. O. Carter there. [I] Had a conference with the American Minister and all that transpired on the 13th of November was read over and found that everything was correct. Willis asked if I still adhered to what I said at a former meeting. I said I did—[Willis continued] "that [even] after the President had asked for clemency for these offenders?" I said yes. I feared the lives of myself and people would be endangered— and that if any clemency were shown it must be in the sparing of their lives—but they must not be permitted to stay—they and their children— for I felt that if they remained they would still continue to be a disturbing element. Minister Willis then said that Mr. Mills would have his [Mr. Willis's] statement ready by Monday and that he would bring it up here, for Mr. Carter and I to read over—and to consider.[236] [I] Left there and went over to Macfarlane's with Mr. Carter. He [Carter] said that capital punishment is not thought of in these days all over the world and that some clemency might be exercised, that "Vengeance is mine saith the Lord" is what ought to be. I said yes—that it would not be their lives, but that they must be banished. He left and I had my breakfast.

At two-thirty Jim Quinn drove round and Milaina and I drove home. But there is great excitement round town to find I was not at the house [Washington Place]. Mr. W. O. Smith went and asked Minister Willis where I was—Whether there or on the *Philadelphia*. He said he did not know—I was not there and [he] did not think I was on the *Philadelphia*. Came home, lunched with the Captain [Nowlein] and Chamberlain [Robertson].[237]

*Monday, December 18.* Washington Place. Palau, Damien, Kahaleaahu, Keawehawaii, Kapoino, Kauahi, Brown, Kailikane, Kaieha, Kahimalani, Beni Paakai, Elenike, Pa, Puakalehua, Mokuahi, Daniela Keahiaa, S. Haluapo, Kealakai, Laiaha, Nahoolewa have all been dismissed from the police for not consenting to carry guns for the P.G.s.

Ten A.M. Mr. Willis came almost immediately after Mr. Carter so that we scarcely had a chance to converse and perhaps would have been able to agree on what course to take—so when Minister Willis arrived and when we were asked the same questions as on the Saturday previous—I still held on to the same answer as that of Saturday—and when we were asked to sign I did so—and Mr. Willis and Mills left.[238] I had almost forgotten to say that after we had signed the previous statement, Minister Willis read over to me the advice from the President Cleveland saying

236. In the Queen's second interview with Willis, he asked her "whether the views expressed [in the first interview] have been in any respect modified since that conversation?" to which the Queen replied, "They have not." But she then continued that this did not include the death penalty, only banishment. A full transcription of this second interview with Liliuokalani (signed by both the Queen and J. O. Carter) appears in the Morgan Report, vol. 2, 2108–11.

237. The *Hawaiian Star*, December 18, 1893, reported (erroneously): "Late this afternoon a rumor that seemed authentic went about to the effect that Minister Willis was at work with the ex-queen upon the text of a new Constitution and that there were points of dispute about it yet to be settled."

238. Albert Willis's visit to Washington Place was for the purpose of having Liliuokalani and J. O. Carter sign and verify the transcription of her December 16, 1893, interview, attesting that the same was "full and correct in every particular."

that he was very much surprised that I should have hesitated to acquiesce at his request, to say once more that he would wish me to grant those people *full pardon* [and] that if I did not consent—he would not have anything more to do with us.[239]

They all left and I was left to my thoughts—it was a great struggle. After reading a few passages in the Bible, an idea crossed my mind and I immediately adopted it. I sent Capt. Nowlein to Mr. Carter to say I would like to confer with him ten minutes before four (the hour set for the last reading). At 3.30 a note was brought by Mr. Cornwell from Mr. Carter saying Mr. Mills would not be ready until six. I immediately penned him (Carter) a note saying, I would be ready but I would wish him to come earlier—that I might tell him that after long consideration I had concluded it was best for me [the entry continues on the page for December 19] to accede to the request of the President and also to accept his [J. O. Carter's] good advice.

Here I must mention that I did this fully conscious that I have yielded in this, and to all the annoyances attending the freedom of those irresponsible people who have threatened my life, who have deprived me of my salary, and my people of their rights. There was another thing I forgot to mention, it is that "My Government after the restoration is to assume all the debts and responsibilities that they (P.G.) have incurred"—so that after all the racket the P.G.s have kicked up, "I must forgive them wholly" and [in] every way. Well, I *do not call this justice*—still I have no choice but I must make the best of it, only when everything is restored it will keep the government pretty wide awake and use [sic] stratagem.

Mr. Mills and Carter came at 6.30. I told Mr. Carter that we could not afford to lose a friend in the U.S. (in the presence of Mr. M.) that after long consideration etc., etc.—so Mr. Mills went home and I said to Mr. Carter I wished him to say to Mr. Willis I would ask of him to permit me to withdraw what I had stated in our previous interview, and that I would do all the President asked. At nine P.M. I signed a paper to President Cleveland saying I would forget and forgive—and so Mr. Carter went away happy. He said we had no choice and I find his ideas alike mine. It is the request of a strong man over a small child. How will my people feel? They must abide by my decision, and our future will be a bright one.

---

239. The telegram from Secretary of State Walter Q. Gresham to Willis, dated December 3, 1893 (which is the document read to Liliu), says in part: "Should the queen refuse to assent to the written conditions, you will at once inform her that the President will cease interposition in her behalf."

In his December 18, 1893, message to the Senate and House of Representatives, forwarding to them the Blount Report, President Grover Cleveland said: "I instructed Minister Willis to advise the Queen and her supporters of my desire to aid in the restoration of the status existing before the lawless landing of the United States forces at Honolulu on the 16th of January last, if such restoration could be effected upon terms providing for clemency.... In short, they require that the past should be buried, and that the restored government should reassume its authority as if its continuity had not been interrupted. These conditions have not proved acceptable to the Queen, and though she has been informed that they will be insisted upon, and that, unless acceded to, the efforts of the President to aid in the restoration of her Government will cease, I have not thus far learned that she is willing to yield them her acquiescence." Morgan Report, vol. 2, 1266. The letters to Minister Willis from the secretary of state appear in the same document on 1271–73.

[Here the Queen has added a draft of her letter to Minister Willis, on which she has indicated the time as "Ten P.M."]

¶ To His Excellency Albert S. Willis. Envoy Extraordinary and Minister Plenipotentiary, U.S.A.

Sir: Since I had the interview with you this morning I have given the most careful and conscientious thought as to my duty and I now of my own free will give you my conclusions.

I must not feel vengeful to any of my people. If I am restored by the United States I must forget myself and remember my dear people and my country. I must forgive and forget the past, permitting no proscription or punishment of anyone, but trusting that all will hereafter work together in peace and friendship for the good and for the glory of our beautiful and once happy land.

Asking you to bear to the President and to the Government he represents, a message of gratitude from [me] and from my people, and promising with God's grace, to prove worthy of the confidence and friendship of your people, I am, with assurances of respect

Liliuokalani<br>Washington Place<br>Honolulu Dec. 18th 1893

[Liliu has annotated the letter as follows:] The above is a letter written to Min. [Minister] Willis on the 19th. [The] wording by Mr. Carter and taken and delivered by him.[240]

---

On December 19, 1893, Albert S. Willis, U.S. envoy extraordinary and minister plenipotentiary, called on President Dole and his cabinet at the Foreign Office in Honolulu, and on behalf of U.S. President Grover Cleveland delivered a memorandum "on the Hawaiian question," expressing President Cleveland's decision that Liliuokalani should be promptly restored. This communication is followed by President Dole's written response to Cleveland's demands.

*Memorandum expressing U.S. President Grover Cleveland's decision that Liliuokalani should be promptly restored, December 19, 1893*

¶ [Albert S. Willis to Sanford B. Dole]
Honolulu, December 19, 1893.

Mr. President and Gentlemen: The President of the United States has very much regretted the delay in the consideration of the Hawaiian question, but it has been unavoidable....

The President deemed it his duty to withdraw from the Senate the treaty of annexation which had been signed by the Secretary of State and the agents of your Government and to dispatch a trusted repre-

---

240. This is one of two letters Liliu addressed to Willis on this date. The other letter is the more formal version, which Willis read to the officials of the Provisional Government. Both letters were subsequently published in the Morgan Report, vol. 2, 2112–16.

sentative [James H. Blount] to Hawaii to impartially investigate the causes of your revolution and ascertain and report the true situation in these islands....

Upon the facts embodied in Mr. Blount's reports the President has arrived at certain conclusions and determined upon a certain course of action with which it becomes my duty to acquaint you:

The Provisional Government was not established by the Hawaiian people or with their consent or acquiescence, nor has it since existed with their consent.

The Queen refused to surrender her powers to the Provisional Government until convinced that the Minister of the United States had recognized it as the de facto authority and would support and defend it with the military force of the United States and that resistance would precipitate a bloody conflict with that force.

She was advised and assured by her ministers and leaders of the movement for the overthrow of her government that if she surrendered under protest her case would afterwards be fairly considered by the President of the United States.

The Queen finally yielded to the armed forces of the United States then quartered in Honolulu, relying on the good faith and honor of the President when informed of what had occurred to undo the action of the Ministers and reinstate her and the authority which she claimed as the constitutional sovereign of the Hawaiian Islands.

After a patient examination of Mr. Blount's reports, the President is satisfied that the movement against the Queen, if not instigated was encouraged and supported by the representatives of this government at Honolulu; that he promised in advance to aid her enemies in an effort to overthrow the Hawaiian Government and set up by force a new government in its place, and that he kept this promise by causing a detachment of troops to be landed from the "Boston" on the 16th of January 1893 and by recognizing the Provisional Government the next day when it was too feeble to defend itself and the constitutional government was able to successfully maintain its authority against any threatening force other than that of the United States already landed.

The President has therefore determined that he will not send back to the Senate for its action thereon the treaty which he withdrew from that body on further consideration on the 9th day of March last.

In view of these conclusions I was instructed by the President to take advantage of an early opportunity to inform the Queen of this determination and of his views, as to the responsibility of our government. The President, however, felt that we by our original interference had increased responsibilities to the whole Hawaiian community, and that it would not be just to put one party at the mercy of the other. I was therefore instructed at the same time to inform the Queen that she would pursue a magnanimous course by granting full amnesty to all who participated in the movement against her, including persons who are or who have been officially or otherwise connected with the Provisional Government, depriving them of no right or privilege which they enjoyed before the revolution of last January, and that all obligations created by the Provisional Government in the course of administration should be assumed.

In obedience to the command of the President I have secured the Queen's agreement to this course and I now deliver a writing signed by her and duly attested, a copy of which I will leave with you I will read now that writing....

> ¶ I Liliuokalani, in recognition of the high sense of justice which has actuated the President of the United States, and desiring to put aside all feelings of personal hatred or revenge and to do what is best for all the people of these islands, both native and foreign born, do hereby and herein solemnly declare and pledge myself that if reinstated as the constitutional sovereign of the Hawaiian Islands, that I will immediately proclaim and declare unconditionally and with out reservation to every person who directly or indirectly participated in the revolution of January 17th 1893 a full pardon and amnesty for their offenses with restoration of all rights, privileges and immunities under the constitution and the laws which have been made in pursuance thereof and that I will forbid and prevent the adoption of any measures of prescription or punishment for what has been done in the past by those setting up or supporting the Provisional Government.
>
> I further solemnly agree to accept the restoration under the constitution existing at the time of said revolution and that I will abide by and fully execute that constitution with all the guarantees as to person and property therein contained.
>
> I further solemnly pledge myself and my government if restored to assume all the obligations created by the Provisional Government in the proper course of administration, including all expenditures for military or police service; it being my purpose if restored to assume the government precisely as it existed on the day when it was unlawfully overthrown.
>
> Witness my hand this 18th of December 1893
> Liliuokalani
> *Attest:* J. O. Carter

It becomes my further duty to advise you Sir, the Executive of the Provisional Government, and your Ministers of the President's determination of the question which your action and that of the Queen devolved upon him, and that you are expected to promptly relinquish to her, her constitutional authority. And now, Mr. President and Gentlemen of the Provisional Government, with deep and solemn sense of the gravity of the situation and with the earnest hope that your answer will be inspired by the high patriotism which forgets a self interest and I the name and authority of the United States of America, I submit to you the question: Are you willing to abide by the decision of the President?

[To this President Dole responded:] The Government will take the matter under consideration and answer you as soon as they are ready....
[Mr. Willis then said:] Yes Sir. Gentlemen, good day.[241]

Following is Dole's December 23 written response to Willis.[242]

¶ [Sanford B. Dole to Albert S. Willis]
Department of Foreign Affairs
Honolulu, December 23, 1893

Sir: Your Excellency's communication of December 19, announcing the conclusion which the President of the United States of America had finally arrived at respecting the application of this government for a treaty of political union with that country, and referring also to the domestic concerns of these islands, has had the consideration of the Government....

While we accept the decision of the President of the United States declining further to consider the annexation proposition as the final conclusion of the present administration, we do not feel inclined to regard it [as] the last word of the American Government upon this subject....

The additional portion of your communication referring to our domestic affairs with a view of interfering therein, is a new departure in the relations of the two governments....

We do not recognize the right of the President of the United States to interfere in our domestic affairs. Such right could be conferred upon him by the act of this Government, and by that alone, or it could be acquired by conquest. This I understand to be the American doctrine, conspicuously announced from time to time by the authorization of your Government....

Upon what, then, Mr. Minister, does the President of the United States base his right of interference?...

If your contention that President Cleveland believes that this government and the ex-Queen have submitted their respective claims to the sovereignty of this country, to the adjudication of the United States is correct, then, may I ask, when and where has the President held his court of arbitration? This Government has had no notice of the siting of such a tribunal and no opportunity of presenting evidence of its claims. If Mr. Blount's investigations were a part of the proceedings of such a court this government did not know it and was never

---

241. "Stenographic Report of Interview of His Ex. A. S. Willis Dec. 19, 1893." Hawaii State Archives, Foreign Office and Executive Files, Box 41, "Overthrow, Sundry Documents on the." The transcription of Liliu's communication to Willis appears in the Morgan Report, vol. 2, 2115. Willis says in his covering letter (dated December 20, 1893) that he received the Queen's letter "this morning at 9:30 o'clock."

242. This letter has been widely published. The original is in the National Archives, Washington, DC. A transcription (from which this has been taken) was published in Ethel M. Damon's *Sanford B. Dole and His Hawaii* (Palo Alto, California: Pacific Books, 1957), 274–88.

informed of it; indeed... we never knew until the publication of Secretary Gresham's letter to the President Cleveland a few weeks ago, that the American Executive had a policy of interference under contemplation....

I am able to assure your excellency that by no action of this Government, on the 17th day of January last or since that time, has the authority devolved upon the President of the United States to interfere in the internal affairs of this country through any conscious act or expression of this Government with such an intention.... My position, is briefly, this: if the American forces illegally assisted the revolutionists in the establishment of the Provisional Government that government is not responsible for their wrong doing. It was purely a private matter for discipline between the United States Government and its own officers. There is, I submit, no precedent in international law for the theory that such action of the American troops has conferred upon the United States authority over the internal affairs of this government. Should it be true, as you have suggested, that the American Government made itself responsible to the Queen, who, it is alleged lost her throne through such action, that is not a matter for me to discuss, except to submit that if such is the case, it is a matter for the American Government and her to settle between them. This Government a recognized sovereign power, equal in authority with the United States Government and enjoying diplomatic relations with it, can not be destroyed by it for the sake of discharging its obligations to the Queen....

No man can correctly say that the Queen owed her downfall to the interference of American forces.... If the American forces had been absent the Revolution would have taken place, for sufficient causes, for it had nothing to do with their presence....

I am instructed to inform you, Mr. Minister, that the Provisional Government of these Islands, respectfully and unhesitatingly declines to entertain the proposition of the President of the United States that it should surrender its authority to the ex-Queen.... Your Excellency's obedient servant,

Sanford B. Dole
Minister of Foreign Affairs

---

*Wednesday, December 20.* Washington Place. Heard that Minister Willis has sent for the President and Cabinet and had long conference with them—nothing has been heard from that meeting.

Heard my Cabinet had an indignation meeting this morning, and high language was heard. In the afternoon Mr. Cornwell and Parker were allowed to come in. Parker had felt indignant that he was kept out. I told him he ought to respect orders, and obey them and come another time. Told them also the American Commissioner was working for the restoration. When he succeeds, he will notify us and I will send for them.[243]

243. The *Hawaiian Star*, December 26, 1893, reported: "It is well known that there is a split in the Royalist camp over the fact that Mrs. Dominis has of late entirely ignored the

*Thursday, December 21.* Washington Place. Read articles in the *Holomua* against myself, showing enemies have been permitted to insert incendiary articles in as we thought [it] the only friendly paper for our cause. I asked Mr. Robertson to find out who did it, or wrote it.[244]

Nawahi came in [at] four P.M. and seemed pained to think that nothing of any kind was heard in regard to our position. I told him the American Commissioner was trying to get them (P.G.) to yield, but they are still holding on. He will give them time to consider and be as patient with them as long as he possibly could. Am told Cecil Brown speaks very bitterly against me—Why? Ich kann nicht sagen. [I cannot say.] [On this date in her cash accounts, Liliu recorded payment to "Miss Wolfe Christmas boxes for girls $11.40." and "For Kiliwehi & Kailinaoa's clothes $12.50."]

*Sunday, December 24.* Washington Place. The *Corwin* sailed at four A.M. Minister Willis and Consul General Mills wired to the *Philadelphia* to send off a boat for them and they were conveyed to the *Corwin* at two A.M. and at four A.M., they left and went on board the *Philadelphia* till broad daylight. It gave cause for considerable excitement round town. The President of the P.G.s [Dole] was seen to call at Minister Willis' at six P.M. and it was supposed that he took their final answer—and so the *Corwin* has gone with my answer to Mr. Willis and also [that] of the Provisional Government.

*Monday, December 25.* Washington Place. The story is out that the answer of the Provisional Government to the proposition given by Mr. Willis to accept the offer of the Queen for complete amnesty was refused. That they would not yield up the Government to the Queen even if she promised amnesty.[245] The story of my promise to grant amnesty has given the royalists chance to find fault with me. They have gone so far as to write a memorial to me, but they will be ashamed of themselves by and by.[246]

so-called members of her late Cabinet and instead has relied on the counsels of Joe Carter. Among those who have felt quite hurt . . . is W. H. Cornwell. . . . The story is going the rounds that Billy Cornwell was so worked up over the matter that he called on Mrs. Dominis to remonstrate with her about it. She received him very courteously and kindly and some time was spent in conversation, but whenever Cornwell commenced to discuss the political situation she turned the conversation in other channels. At last Billy gave it up in disgust and prepared to leave. As he was going Mrs. Dominis asked him if he would deliver a note for her. He said he would be only too happy. When he got outside he found it was addressed to Joe Carter, and immediately the atmosphere in the vicinity grew blue and sulfurous."

244. An article in the *Hawaiian Star*, December 23, 1893, gave a very different slant to the policy of the *Holomua*: "For several months, the *Holomua*, known as the private newspaper of the claimant to the throne, has been filled with seditious language. That journal has uniformly assailed the title and the personnel of the Provisional Government, has libeled its members, tried to break down its credit, and has prophesied its overthrow. It is now engaged in making the assertion that the Government will soon be destroyed." The editor of the *Star* then suggested that the *Holomua* newspaper should be charged under the Sedition Act.

245. See section preceding December 20, 1893, diary entry (396–400).

246. The main thrust of the memorial from the Hui Aloha Aina to the Queen seems to be that they had not been consulted in the matter. The document, dated December 25, 1893, and signed by Joseph Nawahi, J. A. Cummins, J. W. Bipikane, J. E. Bush, A. Marques, W. H. Rickard, John Ross, and W. S. Seward, states that the Hui "feel that it is an imperious duty incumbent upon them to respectfully represent to Your Majesty that the members . . . are at present laboring under serious apprehensions and fears, lest through ill-advised and hasty concessions the future of the Kingdom may be jeopardized at the very moment when the impending restoration of Your Majesty would otherwise fill the hearts of your people with

[On December 27 under cash accounts, Liliu recorded payment to "Mary Pitman for Naua spear $15 (and) Ahuula liilii (a small feather cape) $30. = $45.00." (and) "Mary Pitman for herself $20 for hulu pue $6. = 26.00."]

*Thursday, December 28.* Washington Place. [Entry ends thus.]

*Friday, December 29.* Washington Place. Mrs. Gulick called and we talked over the situation. Forgotten what was mostly said, but [we] dwelt on the President's message. She tells me of the wonder felt by everybody and if its result would be favorable. Mr. Richardson [said] about the same.

Mr. Robertson and Captain Nowlein came in and said that a man jumped over the wall by the front gate and was led up to the Capt. and taken and put out by our watchman.

*Saturday, December 30.* Washington Place. Mr. Parker and Richardson came in, and the former told me that he intended going to San Francisco and would take Richardson with him. He had met the Patriotic [Society] Members [the Hui Aloha Aina] and they had told them it would be a good thing for them to go to Washington to represent our side. Mr. Neumann also thought the same. I told them I would think the matter over. After thinking the matter over, I could not help feeling that he would not be the proper person, since through their resistance, it has partly been the cause of our situation. Having been one of the Members of the Cabinet—the Congressmen would see and think of him as having been one of those who opposed the Queen, it would injure our cause and end unfavorably. Mr. Colburn had once written an article and it was published say[ing?] that the U.S. ought to do us justice,[247] if not then we would turn to another nation—which was not right for a Minister to utter such words—but Mr. Parker had once told Blount that he did not wish to be Minister under me[248]—and since the U.S. intends to restore me—his presence there would be harmful.

---

rejoicing." The apprehensions arose from their learning of Liliu's secret meeting with U.S. Minister Willis, and the committee further suggested that her agreements might "be a violation of all constitutional principles, and would not be binding upon your restored cabinet, nor on any other that may follow." Hawaii State Archives, Attorney General Files, Series 506, Box 1, Folder 16.

247. The "Colburn article" Liliu probably refers to had appeared in the *San Francisco Call*, and was reprinted in the *Hawaiian Star*, May 15, 1893: "Ex-Minister Colburn of Hawaii has declared in favor of the restoration of the Queen. He does not think the deposed Queen had a fair deal. He now says: 'If the United States believes in fair play it will reinstate our Queen and let the rebels suffer what they deserve.' The rebels are supposed to be the present Provisional cabinet. It is presumed that Mr. Colburn would be satisfied with the execution of the ringleaders and the banishment of subordinates. If this can be done the Queen will be restored to what Mr. Colburn considers her rights."

248. When interviewed by Blount on April 6, 1893, regarding the reinstatement of the Queen, Parker actually said: "I would not accept the same position I had before the revolution unless there was a protectorate. If she said: 'I want you to be in the same position you held before this revolution took place—minister of foreign affairs,' I would say, 'No, unless you have it under a protectorate.' It is of no use looking to England, Japan, France, or Germany. All our benefits are derived from the United States." See the Blount Report, 437–45, and the Morgan Report, vol. 1, 711–19.

Eveline [Wilson] told me there was a meeting at Punahou. Many P.G.s were present. Someone asked for the keys of the Punahou Preparatory School for them to go into at night to watch our side. It was granted. Prof. Hosmer[249] said if there was one that had any murderous intention against Mr. Wilson, should they ever cast eyes on Mrs. Wilson that thought would be immediately dispelled. Has he a soft spot in his heart?

*Sunday, December 31.* Washington Place. 7.30 P.M. Services over the way [at Central Union Church] and as the Congregation sang praise to God their spies were lurking under the Waikiki corner to the number of eight men—what are they doing there? Capt. Good and the man at the Government nursery were in the Punahou P[reparatory] school premises— Ten men in Miller's lane—nearly 30 over to the entrance of the Episcopal Church—all armed with pistols, some with guns. Capt. Nowlein is quite nervous and wishes that Mr. Robertson was here. I sent Capt. [Nowlein] over to talk the matter over—they consulted Capt. Rooke of the *Champion* and they agree that Wodehouse should go to Minister Willis and tell him that he ought to tell the P.G.s to disarm these people who are surrounding this place—if they did not do so the English and Japanese would land—to keep the peace. Minister Willis said he would send for Damon and tell him to disarm men. Capt. Rooke sent word for me to have no fears. Minister Wodehouse said Minister Willis was doing all in his power.

Ten P.M. Those men have dispersed.

12 Midnight. Woke up by the sound of bell and bombs—the Hawaiian National Band playing "Hawaii Ponoi"—and firecrackers. Bells ringing the old year out and the New Year in—all that transpired in 1893 is of the past, and we commence anew with the New Year. Thankful to our Creator for all we have enjoyed during the past and hoping for all that is good for the future. That our Nation may be restored by President Cleveland and Congress is my earnest prayer and of My people, to our just Rights.

249. Frank Alvan Hosmer (d. 1918) was the president of Oahu College starting in 1890.

*Iolani Palace and grounds. The grounds on the Diamond Head (or southeast) side of the palace were originally designed with circular plots of grass surrounded by gravel paths and planted with unusual botanical specimens. While this formal garden arrangement is long gone, a few of the palms shown here are still growing. From January 16 to September 7, 1895, during her incarceration by the Republic of Hawaii, the Queen was restricted to a bedroom suite on the southeast corner of the second floor and its adjacent tower room and lanai.*
Severin-Bolster, circa 1890, Hawaii State Archives

# 1894

*Monday, January 1, 1894.* Captain Nowlein's fears were not allayed. Parker and Richardson—tell of news from Capt. Rooke at Cummins' luau that there was danger to me about these spies. Not satisfied with the assurances of the P.G.s. Last night Willis called at Damon's and talked over the danger to me—came away with promise of D. [Damon] for my safety. Rec'd letter from W. O. Smith ten A.M. saying he'd send more men to guard me if wanted. Sent it to J. O. Carter. He took it to Minister Willis and explained the danger of these men being my guards as they are irresponsible and once threatened my life. My own people would satisfy me best. Carter and Theo. H. Davies called. Mr. Robertson showed me his statement about Parker, offer'd his place to Carter—he declines and proposes [William H.] Rickard. Says A.P.P. [A. P. Peterson]. His interview with Marshall Hitchcock explaining the uselessness of the P.G. police as they permitted a man on Thursday night or morning two A.M. to climb my fence without interfering—they were all there and saw it. He told Willis I could not feel safe till I had Hawaiian police. Minister W. [Willis] asked Damon if there were not six good Hawaiian policemen who could be sent to guard the Queen—he said there were. Damon censured Robertson for not coming to him instead of troubling Willis all the time. R[obertson] said to W[illis] the Queen does not feel safe with these men so near her and would like to come to the Legation, but feared she would be placing you in an awkward light, so will try to bear [it] but would like native police. Willis thanked me for having thought of him. Would send native police. Nawahi wants [to see the] Blaine Treaty with [H.A.P.] Carter 1889.

*Tuesday, January 2.* Peterson would only give up to Neumann. Parker says Hatch is going to San Francisco to influence Spreckels for Republic—that Damon said I made a mistake not to accept Cleveland's offer, so I have lost our case, he [Parker?] said he thought not.

*Wednesday, January 3.* Jennie Clark says the Restoration Cottagers are going to fast so will I fast also? Said yes. [Reverend] Timoteo[1] said prayers with me 8:30 A.M. Had one German [lesson] with Fraulein. [She] told me Ch [Chase? name erased] said that A [name erased] had asked me if those things said about my attempts were true. He said no. How do you know? I have a chance to know from the best authority. I may not tell. Well, I will not press you. He had respect for his silence and said no more. Miss

THE DIARY
FOR 1894
1 JAN–29 DEC

Hawaii State Archives

---

1. Reverend E. S. Timoteo was the pastor of the Waialua Church.

Davis went to picnic with Sisters Albertina and Beatrice[2] at Mrs. Grace's [at] Hanaiakamalama.[3] Went upstairs, spent three hours in fasting, meditation, and prayers. At one I broke fast. [At] Two Mr. Parker and Richardson came in [and] had lunch. Said Hatch and Thurston were going in the *China* for San Francisco. Richardson said A. F. Judd would resign as soon as restoration took place. That Whiting signed Annexation Treaty.[4]

*Thursday, January 4.* The Hoonaauao L[iliuokalani] M2 [Mokuna 2 or Second Division] met today—nothing done—contributed [blank] $5.25. Prince Kalanianaole called, told me of Missionary girls and boys at Waialua [who] made tour of island, stopped at Pelelo's and used my paddock. Cheek. Mary Aki gave me her bill $25. Kaiu copied a draft of Treaty made by Blaine and [H.A.P.] Carter during 1889—Cabinet of Thurston, Damon, Austin, Ashford. Sent a copy to J. E. Bush. Robertson said [he] had called on Min[ister] Willis, took him copy of the above and of Thurston's Cabinet [statement?]—saying they would not have Annexation.

Willis was surprised no native police had been sent [to me]. Two days ago they [the P.G.s] promised they would. He declared they [the Provisional Government] would not dare to harm me under the circumstances and he wants to see me out. Damon says so would he. Robertson called on Wodehouse and told him all. [Entry continues above and on margin:] He thought it would be best not to trouble Willis any more as he had heard him say that he was tired and wishes Congress would settle the question. He would not notice the unkind things said of him or Cleveland. Wodehouse did not like to see me go for a drive just yet. Sent Nawahi copy of Blaine Treaty.

*Friday, January 5.* W. Aylett borrowed $65.00 to pay for some instruments for the Hawaiian Band. Sent J. Aea to see Minnie Aldrich about his cottage.[5]

Fraulein [Wolf] wanted to know about Capt. Good. Capt. Nowlein saw Good at the next yard. He was there half the night and was near when Wodehouse said that Willis would see that all was right last Sunday night at our gate. Hoonaulu's brother came to see me. He returns to Victoria by tomorrow's *Australia*. Joe took some eggs from my Brahmas for his hens to hatch. Heard that P—is very anxious to get appointed Commissioner for Hawaii to Washington. Will not do it—it will be like snubbing Willis. Parker came few minutes—said I ought to appoint Minister to Washington and Consul to S.F. Told him this isn't the time. John R[ichardson] does not seem to have any settled purpose so after all must do my best.

---

2. Anglican Sisters Albertina (b. 1840, England–d. 1930, Honolulu) and Beatrice (d. 1921, Honolulu) had both come to Hawaii in 1867 under the auspices of Miss Sellon, founder of the order of the Society of the Most Holy Trinity in England. They were in charge of the Saint Andrew's Priory School.

3. The John Grace family was renting Hanaiakamalama, the late Queen Emma's Nuuanu Valley home.

4. William Austin Whiting had served as Liliuokalani's attorney general February 25, 1891–July 27, 1892.

5. Minnie Aldrich was renting Joe Aea's Waikiki cottage for $40.00 per month.

*Saturday, January 6.* Eveline spent the day. Fraulein [Wolf] told me that Capt. Good told him [Nowlein?] they heard I was going to hoist the Royal Standard so they came to prevent [it]. He said he didn't think I would do such a foolish act. It would spoil my cause.

Heard from Eveline [that] Bowie [?] [and] Bowler and others are watching the P.G. [men] in streets—that it was really the purpose of Capt. Good, Kidwell, and Rhodes to seize my person that night, take me to the Palace, and keep me as State Prisoner—through Willings [?] Mr. Parker and Peterson went to San Francisco on the *Australia*, to see if Mr. Spreckels would not help him [Parker] out [financially] and if he failed would borrow from Hibernian bank. Planted ten Mulang[6] trees.

*Monday, January 8.* Promised one Mulang [tree] to Archie. Rec'd Mr. and Mrs. [Japanese Consul], they presented me a very handsome table cover. Mr. and Mrs. Kaili called. Mr. Robertson and Capt. Nowlein came in. Paid Miss Davis $150.00—all I owed her—also the Imperial Insurance Co., Bruce Cartwright agent $50.00 for Palama residence. Kaniu spent the night here. Said Alapaki [Albert F. Judd] told her when the restoration took place he would resign. Sent copies of Dole's letters to Robertson. One about dismissing my guards, the other about sending a Commission on *Claudine*, it was a refusal.

*Tuesday, January 9.* Mr. W. H. Cornwell and John Richardson returned to Maui yesterday. I told them that should we receive news at an early day I would tell my Chamberlain to inform them immediately.

Sent Archie's plant [the Mulang tree] to his place [on] Emma Square. Was sorry to hear that F. H. Hayselden promised to support the P.G. Saw a letter from W[illiam] White that people at Maui are registering to support P.G. Paid Miss Wolf $50. Owe her $200 more.

*Thursday, January 11.* Mr. F. S. Pratt died four P.M.[7] Sent Wakeke and Joe H. [Heleluhe], Milaina, Keamalu.

*Monday, January 15.* Mr. F. S. Pratt was buried from the English Cathedral yesterday, Mr. Mackintosh officiated. Mr. Nawahi came—told him to tell his party to hold together and their strength is in their silence—that I did not decorate him and W[illiam] White for any other reason but their patriotism and firmness in their principles. Told Mary Carter to tell her husband [I] would like him to be one of my Cabinet but left to his option to accept here or Washington. Today also I had conferred with Mr. Willis [?] about cabinet. If he accepts W.—I will have Macfarlane here and vice versa. If he accepts I will have [the] salary raised.

*Tuesday, January 16.* Yesterday the P.G. sent an invitation to the Diplomatic Corps and to the Admirals [?] to join them in the recognition of the

---

6. The Mulang tree (*Michelia champaca*), part of the magnolia family, is a large evergreen with intensely fragrant flowers.

7. Frank S. Pratt (b. 1829, Boston), a resident since 1850, had been the longtime registrar of public accounts, and more recently the Hawaiian consul general at San Francisco. In 1864, he married Elizabeth Kekaaniau (b. 1834–d. 1928), the chiefess daughter of Laanui and Owana.

Anniversary of their revolution or Accession tomorrow. They all declined, which made Mr. Dole feel very bad.[8]

Mr. Hayselden called before going back to Maui.

*Wednesday, January 17.* One year ago I signed away under protest my right to the throne. The P.G. opened the day with Horribles—parade and reception, illumination at night.[9]

*Thursday, January 18.* 4:30 P.M. Mr. J. O. Carter called, we spoke of a Cabinet [position] and he declined but proposed Mr. E. C. Macfarlane, also of Mr. Hind[10] and Mr. Mark Robinson.[11] I told him I thought there ought to be a native. He said Mark was a good one. I told him he would not be recognized by the people.[12] I offered [a post in] Washington, he declined.

7:30 P.M. I sent for Mr. Wodehouse—told him what [had] passed between Carter and myself—he sustained Carter's opinion, but I told him Hind and Robinson owed the P.G. and therefore [would] be their tools only.

*Friday, January 19.* This A.M.—eight—wrote a note (privately) to Mr. Wodehouse to explain more fully my opinion of R. Hind and M. Robinson. They were Annexationists, members of Reform Party, and the Reform [Party] today are the P.G.s who are in power today. At Mr. Carter's suggestion I will appoint two men whom I know he will approve of, [the first Liliu does not identify] other will be Mr. Neumann.

*Saturday, January 20.* Had conversation with Mr. P. Neumann.

---

8. In its coverage of the Provisional Government reception held in the council chamber (formerly the throne room of the palace), the *Daily Bulletin*, January 17, 1894, commented: "No official callers outside of the P.G. military officers appeared. Messrs. Glade and Schmidt, consuls for Germany and Sweden and Norway respectively, were the only representatives of the diplomatic [and] consular bodies who attended but they are well-known partisans of the annexation movement and were there only in their private capacity. . . . A few officers of the American warships were present in civilian clothes. . . . It was noted that there was no display of bunting on the warships in port."

9. The *Daily Bulletin*, January 17, 1894, reported: "The celebration of the first anniversary of the P.G. began at sunrise this morning with a national salute from the field battery. This was followed at 6:30 o'clock with the antiques and horribles parade. A number of broken-down animals driven to rickety vehicles paraded the streets, several going their own way. After a drive about the town the participants put up and, sad to relate, the prizes of $10, $7.50, $5, [and] $2.50 were all won by royalists."

The "illumination" took place at the palace in the evening. Joseph B. Atherton, J. B. Castle, Alfred S. Hartwell, Professor Hosmer of Punahou School, Henry Waterhouse, William O. Smith, and A.G.M. Robertson made speeches.

10. Robert Robson Hind, proprietor of the Hawi Mill and Plantation Co. on the island of Hawaii, served as a noble in the legislature of 1890–92. His son John Hind's memoir says that Robert Hind was a royalist and "retired to San Francisco in 1893 when Queen Liliuokalani was dethroned." John Hind, *John Hind of Hawi (1858–1933): His Memoirs*, ed. Robert Renton Hind (Manaoag, Philippines: Carmelo and Bauermann, 1951).

11. Mark P. Robinson (born 1852, Honolulu–d. April 2, 1915, Honolulu) was the part-Hawaiian son of Englishman James Robinson, who founded a ship chandlery business in Honolulu in 1822, amassing a considerable fortune. Mark Robinson was for some time (prior to 1882) member of a lumber importing firm, Allen and Robinson, and an investor in other businesses. He was a representative in the 1887 and 1888 legislative sessions.

12. This was a puzzling comment, for Robinson was well respected about town.

*Saturday, January 27.* Poor Jack Ailau's body was brought back on the *Australia* accompanied by Mary his wife. He died on the 17th and at the same hour that a year ago I signed away under protest the control of the Nation to the P.G.s. Before Jack's death he mentioned it to his wife.

*Monday, January 29.* John Keakaolani Ailau's funeral took place yesterday. Last night the Kawaihaus sat up and sang dirges—and songs they used to sing together with the deceased under all the other chiefs.

Friends sent in flowery emblems all so beautiful—from rich and lowly—and all vied together in showing their respect to him. He was loved and respected by those who knew him. I wrote a letter to his mother to soothe her. Wrote a long letter to Kaiulani. Told her that it is the wish of the people she married one of the Princes David or Jonah—that Kalakaua had arranged she should marry the Japanese Emperor's nephew. I am pleased with it.[13]

*Tuesday, January 30.* Mary Ailau came in to see me, poor Mary. Mr. Cornwell called 11 A.M., spoke about Mr. Wilson's draft of procedure in case of restoration. Told him [I] did not approve of [it]. Had he (W.) asked me my opinion, would have told him it was a matter for the Cabinet and Privy Council—not citizens. Told Cornwell to call on Minister Willis casually and tell him, and hoped he would take no notice of Wilson's statement.[14]

**Saturday, February 10.** Rec'd from Capt. Nowlein a copy of Blount's report—must return it on Monday. Parker was here—learn't nothing [from] me so he went to Mr. Wodehouse.

*Monday, February 12.* Paid Nihoa $39.40 and [Hui Hookuonoono] Kawaluonalani tuition $22.75—Major Seward told me at Mr. Cummins', John Colburn had said, if there should be a new Cabinet, there would be another revolution. That the Ashfords would help him—that Mr. Wilson's plans were drawn up with the help of J. Colburn and the Ashfords—that he and J. Walker had fixed Mother Dominis' tombstone. How good. [Above the entry in the top margin she writes:] Yesterday was the birthday of heir apparent of Japan. No notification was given to the P.G.

---

13. Liliuokalani's January 29, 1894, letter to Kaiulani is as follows: "My dear Kaiulani,... You have asked me a direct question and I must be candid with you—in regard to Prince David I had not thought of mentioning to you about your future until the proper moment arrived, but as you already mention it—it is best you should know. It is the wish of the people that you should marry one or the other of the Princes, that we may have more Aliis. There are no other Aliis who they (the people) look up to except Prince David and his brother, who would be eligible to the throne or worthy of it, and so they turn to these two Aliis to make the throne permanent, according to the constitution. To you, then, depends the hope of the nation, and unfortunately we cannot always do as we like.... When your Uncle the late King was living he made arrangements that you should be united to one of the Japanese Princes. He is the nephew of the Emperor of Japan. It seems that the young Prince was here on the *Naniwa*, on his first trip last year, but our position was such that he could not present himself, so I have not seen him.... I shall be very glad if such an alliance could be consummated between you two." Hawaii State Archives, Cleghorn Collection.

14. Wilson's draft of procedure is discussed in footnote for May 28, 1893, diary entry (353).

ABOVE
*Joseph O. Carter and Mary Ladd Carter. Joseph Carter acted as the Queen's advisor, agent, and loyal supporter. He was a member of the Privy Council in 1891. Mary Carter was one of Liliu's most intimate childhood friends and loyal supporters. Both Carters are frequently mentioned in the Queen's diaries.*
Hawaii State Archives

*Sanford B. Dole, president of the newly proclaimed Republic of Hawaii, and his wife, Anna, at their residence on Emma Street, July 9, 1894. On December 4, 1896, Liliuokalani paid an early morning courtesy call to the Doles at their home prior to her departure that day for Boston and Washington, DC. It was an extraordinary gesture on the Queen's part, and the Doles were respectful, welcoming, and gracious.*
Hawaiian Mission Children's Society Library

*Judge Herman A. Widemann and Kaumana "Mary" Kapoli Widemann (seated center), their children, and their grandchildren, 1886. Widemann was a German-born capitalist who served in the Queen's government and was both a close friend and a financial advisor. He, his Kauai-born wife, and their entire family were ardent royalists.*

*Upon learning of Widemann's death, the Queen wrote in a March 4, 1899, letter to her brother-in-law Archibald Cleghorn: "So Mr. H. A. Widemann has passed away. One of Hawaii's best Kamaainas [long-standing residents]. It is a pleasure to know that he has provided for his wife and family and not left them in need—and they are such a large family to provide for" (Hawaii State Archives).*

J. J. Williams, Hawaii State Archives

*Tuesday, February 13.* Mr. J. O. Carter took away some of my old Oahu R. & L. Co.[15] bonds and gave me four new ones, Nos. 172-183-186-253, he told me to keep Nos. 23-24-25 of the old new ones [a blank space follows] and 3500—the new $1,500.00—he told me to collect $525.00 of the old Bonds.

Heard today that that child of Lillian Lyman was by Eddie, Sam Damon's son. The very picture of the Damons. Rufus Lyman doesn't hesitate to speak of it. Mr. Sam Damon paid her passage and expenses over [to San Francisco] to get rid of the child and have it over there—on its delivery she could not be so inhuman and brought the child back.[16]

While sitting on the veranda with Eveline the P.G. soldiers went by. There was P.G. Mass meeting at the iron shed. Lot of Portuguese nominated [a blank space] as Minister Foreign Affairs.[17]

*Wednesday, February 14.* Joe Heleluhe called at office of O.R.L. Co. and received instead of $425.00 only $350.00, [they said] that they would notify us when to call for the rest—which is $75.00. A very rainy day, laid out some violets. Nawahi tells me their letters in Hilo have been trifled with.

*Wednesday, February 21.* Signed for contributing toward English church $100.00 but paid only $20.00 today, the rest some future day. [The cash account at the end of the diary does not show any additional amount contributed.]

*Monday, February 26.* Hannah Evans called, then Mr. Parker and Cornwell called. I told them of what I had heard Minister Colburn had been doing—that he had called yesterday on the P.G.—had met them in W. O. Smith's office. Asked Parker and Cornwell to try and find out what he was there for.

*Tuesday, February 27.* Mr. C. A. and Rudolph Spreckels, Messrs. Parker and Cornwell, and Bond[18] brother-in-law of Gus called—then came Mrs. and Miss Neumann and Mrs. C. [Charles] N. Spencer and Mrs. Bowler.

*Wednesday, February 28.* Parker came in to say he had not seen J. F. Colburn as the latter had made explanations in the *Holomua* of Monday about his visit to Mr. Kinney's office—purely private matter.[19]

Kitty Long has been summoned to appear in Cartwright against Cartwright case. Kinney advises Colburn to send her away.[20]

---

15. This was the Oahu Railway and Land Co.

16. Lillian Louisa Lyman (b. 1866, Hilo–d. 1894, Hilo) was the daughter of Rufus Lyman and Rebecca Hualani Brickwood Lyman. There is no record of the child mentioned by Liliu.

17. The American League took over the meeting of the Annexation Club, and nominated D. B. Smith for the Advisory Council as successor to F. M. Hatch, who resigned. That appointment never occurred. Hatch, who had served as vice president of the Provisional Government August 17, 1893–January 4, 1894, then served as minister of foreign affairs December 15, 1894–November 6, 1895.

18. The *Pacific Commercial Advertiser*, February 26, 1894, identifies W. E. Bond as "a well-known journalist of San Francisco."

19. Colburn's "explanations" in the *Holomua* have not been found, but the next sentence of this diary entry seems to explain his visit as personal, not political.

20. Kitty Long, actually Catherine or Caterina A. Long (b. April 16, 1875–d. January 8, 1949, Honolulu, as Mrs. Benjamin H. Wright), was the daughter of an Italian-born merchant in Honolulu, Charles Apiani Long (Long being his assumed name). Charles Long died in Honolulu, September 8, 1880, and on December 4, 1880, his widow, Julia, married John F. Colburn. The Cartwright case may have been related to Theresa Owana's pending divorce from Alexander J. Cartwright Jr.

*Thursday, March 1.* Hannah Evans came. I gave her $15.00. [She] Asked if she might keep accounts for Fernandez, [in the] *Holomua* office. I said no—they had nothing to pay her with.

*Friday, March 2.* Sent J. Heleluhe to O. R. & Land Co. for the remaining amt. due to me of Bonds and received $175.00.

[From Liliu's cash accounts for Saturday, March 10: "From sale of Nahinu Mortgage to Pake, and $1,100.00 to be Pd. in 3 mos.—Rec'd. $530.00."]

[From Liliu's cash accounts for Tuesday, March 20: "To Auhea for Ualapue (Molokai) Rent—$100.00."[21]]

*Saturday, March 24.* The *Australia* arrived and no news by her of our situation. Mr. W. D. Alexander the Missionary Historian who has proved himself a liar has returned by her.[22] His word in future will not be believed, as his statements at Washington have been proved otherwise than the truth.

*Monday, March 26.* Kainana brought some fish from the Queen Dowager [Kapiolani] and has told me I could have ¼ of an acre for the rest of the term of her lease at one dollar a year.

*Friday, March 30.* Sent Kainana to ask Queen Dowager to lend me her Kuauhau [genealogy] books. Q.D. said I must "uku" [pay] her. I was willing. Spoke to Kawananakoa about the Fair.[23] He seemed to look at it only as a Charitable affair—while Mr. Campbell set his foot down and would have nothing to do with it, as well as the others who have withdrawn.

*Saturday, March 31.* Mary Carter and husband leave today for San Francisco by the *Australia* on account of his health. Was told by Mr. Parker that a move was going to be made by the Royalists to call a mass meeting to prevent people from voting at coming election of the P.G.—that he had said to Mr. Damon that the U.S. would restore the Queen. Damon said he admired our persistence. Kainana sent word by Auhea that she will be here Monday with Genealogical books by different historians.[24]

Luau at Maternity Home $20. [From Liliu's cash accounts for this date: "To Leis, 3.50. David Malo's Funeral expenses $30."]

*Monday, April 2.* Five P.M. Kainana came and said she will be here tomorrow and bring [genealogy] books. Mr. [D. H.] Nahinu and son and his wife came to consult about their lands and mortgages. I've told them the only thing they could do now is to wait till the auction day and bid on it.[25]

21. Auhea (b. 1839–d. May 16, 1899, Honolulu) was a chiefess and first cousin of the late King Lunalilo, and was known as Auhea the Second or Kekauluohi. She first married Jesse Crowningburg (divorced in 1866); second, Kaiapeelua in 1877 (divorced in 1881); and third, Lokana of Molokai. She attempted to bring a suit against the Lunalilo estate for property, an action in which Liliuokalani supported her. Liliu interested Clarence W. Ashford in taking up the case on a contingency basis, but nothing came of the matter. Because of her family connection, Auhea was buried within the enclosure of King Lunalilo's tomb at Kawaiahao Church.

22. Liliu's assertion that Alexander was a liar is not explained.

23. She didn't identify this, but it was probably a Honolulu church fair.

24. Liliuokalani and the chiefess Auhea the Second were assembling genealogical information detailing their relationships to Charles Kanaina and to King Lunalilo (Auhea being a cousin of Lunalilo's), with the idea of pressing a claim for a portion of that estate. In the Liliuokalani Collection, Box 1, Document 11, is a three-page manuscript in Liliuokalani's hand detailing that relationship. There is also a contemporary 19-page typescript detailing the relationships of Kanaina and King Lunalilo with Auhea.

25. No record of either the mortgage or a pending auction of property has been found in the *Pacific Commercial Advertiser*.

*Tuesday, April 3.* Had full meeting of the Hui Hoonaauao Liliuokalani Division 2. Contributed $7.10. Appointed officers for coming year. Henry Poor's house at Waikiki burnt down.[26]

Liliu Carter called to see me, this morning Piliaoao [a horse] was taken to Puahala and Lehua [a horse] [to] Manoa. Waiola and Waianu must be sent to pasture.

*Wednesday, April 4.* Mr. Parker said Sam Damon has told him twice that if the President [U.S. President Cleveland's demands] were to be sustained by the Senate, they (the P.G.s) would yield right away but not before. Fujii[27] said he would insist on the Japanese receiving franchise. P[arker] says the Chinese could not be permitted the same privileges because there is no treaty with China. There ought to be mass meetings, he says. I do not think so. Miss Wolf is to be married to C. D. Chase. [From Liliu's cash accounts for this date: "Made Miss Wolf (a) present of $50—wedding (gift)."]

*Thursday, April 5.* Manu came to see me and was quite overcome on account of [his] love for my brother. Wrote to Mr. [Charles T.] Gulick asking him to write by *Monowai* to Mr. J. O. Carter and tell him what Mr. Parker told about Senate. Told Mr. R. W. Wilcox the same to write to Moreno all about what Damon said to Parker. Told Nawahi to stick to their principles—if they thought it best not to yield to those who are agitating a Mass meeting to do so. Mr. Wilcox tells me that it has been decided at a meeting at Widemann's [that] there should be a mass meeting to have resolutions made and read to them (people) protesting against the Constitutional Convention of the P.G.—then to present it to American Commissioner Willis and send copies to Foreign Representative.

*Friday, April 6.* Mr. J. E. Bush called—told me at the meeting at Widemann's, Norrie said Damon had told them to call a Mass meeting—Widemann at first refused, afterwards yielded—On Damon's suggesting this, the people ought to be cautious and keep away.

*Saturday, April 7.* This [is] Princess Poomaikelani's birthday. Sent Joe to pay bills. $411.80 to T. H. Davies—*Holomua* $4.14. Ice Co, $4.20, McIntyre $80.50.

*Monday, April 9.* The Hui Hawaii Aloha Aina have issued circulars to all members not to go [tonight] to the Mass meeting. Mr. Parker said that they have asked Tim Murray[28] to have their league at Palace Square to help keep the peace. Mr. Widemann and Campbell and all those white members who got the meeting up will not speak but will make the native do it for them as cats'-paws. Ashford is the starter, the Agitator.

---

26. Henry Poor's house, known as Manuia Lanai, was on a beachfront lot fronting Kapiolani Park. It was the setting for a famous 1889 luau given by his mother Mrs. Caroline Bush, in honor of Mr. and Mrs. Robert Louis Stevenson.

27. Saburo Fujii, a diplomatic agent and the Japanese consul general, worked and resided at Nuuanu near Beretania Street.

28. Timothy Bartholomew Murray (d. February 1902), a blacksmith and wagon maker, was at 44 King Street near Maunakea.

*Diary for 1894* 415

The policy of the H.H.A.A. [Hui Hawaii Aloha Aina] is to keep quiet and not do anything since President Cleveland is doing everything for us so all we have to do is to keep quiet. If the haoles wish to get up a meeting let them do it, not us. The [*Ka*] *Leo* [newspaper] has succeeded in quieting the people. The Civil Rights league seems to be afraid that the Hawaiians will vote for the Constitutional Convention and register— that is the cause for the meeting, but the people are on their guard and will obey the [*Ka*] *Leo o Ka Lahui*. What matters it if they do get up their Constitution and establish a Republic, when the U.S. is ready, she will undo all that her minister has done. It is strange that Mr. E. C. Macfarlane should not see the sense of this point since he was the one who Blount told to come home and keep quiet and tell the people to keep so.

They tell me the square was full of all sorts of people but few Hawaiians, who went only to see and not join. Mr. Wilcox said Mr. Emmeluth will be one of the speakers. Neumann heard of it and said he would go home and not come to the meeting—he kept his word.

Rosa's speech is not very clear—Kaulukou's also is a repetition. Ashford's is the clearest—but they had a P.G. for an interpreter, W. L. Wilcox. There is the cloven hoof.[29]

---

The mass meeting to which the Queen refers took place on the evening of April 9, 1894. The *Pacific Commercial Advertiser* reported the following:

> ¶ Palace Square was crowded last evening at the royalist mass meeting, there being about 2,000 people present, about one-third of the number that turned out at the last meeting that was held there. A large number were Chinamen and supporters of the Provisional Government who had come from curiosity.... On the platform were C. W. Ashford, J. L. Kaulukou, J. F. Bowler, L. J. Levey, John Phillips, F. H. Redward, Antone Rosa, C. B. Wilson, T. A. Lloyd, and J. K. Kahookano. C. W. Ashford opened the meeting saying that Kaulukou had been appointed chairman, and L. J. Levey, secretary for the evening.[30]

Lot Kaulukou gave a long address, saying: "We have been called together... to consider our rights, personal and otherwise."[31] J. H. Kahookano remarked, "The annexationists propose to call a Constitutional Convention, and to that end they are calling upon all to register, above all, they want the Hawaiians to register. But we all know that this Constitutional convention is

29. William Luther Wilcox (b. July 8, 1850, Waioli, Kauai–d. July 13, 1901, Honolulu), the son of Kauai missionaries Abner and Lucy Wilcox, was a jurist and a highly respected court translator. He was married to Elizabeth Kahuila (b. 1857–d. 1913), one of Liliu's close friends. It is not certain why Liliu here chose to refer to Wilcox as "the cloven hoof," a common reference to Satan.

30. *Pacific Commercial Advertiser*, April 10, 1894. A copy of this article is in the Hawaii State Archives, Attorney General Files, Series 506-2-10, as part of a deposition for E. G. Hitchcock "on the matter of claim of C. W. Ashford."

31. *Pacific Commercial Advertiser*, April 10, 1894.

only a blind, as their ultimate aim is annexation.... The Provisional Government supporters are railroading this scheme in order to hurt our cause at Washington."[32] John Phillips, C. W. Ashford, and Antone Rosa made additional remarks.

The meeting concluded with a resolution of opposition to the scheme "until a definite and final reply to said protest of the Constitutional government of Hawaii shall have been received from the government of the United States."[33]

---

*Thursday, April 19.* The San Francisco steamer arrived and Admiral Walker and staff came in her.

*Saturday, April 21.* Admiral Walker took charge of the *Philadelphia* and Admiral Irwin retired. The latter came to Mrs. Chase's to stay. I sent him a Kihei and a woolen blanket to use. He was pleased with the kihei, which was thrown over him by Mrs. Chase when he took his naps every day, and the care shown by Mr. and Mrs. Chase was appreciated. He said he'd take the kihei with him when he went home—and I gave my permission and he seemed more pleased when he found I had sent it for his comfort.

*Sunday morn [April 22].* The admiral was so pleased when on his waking [Entry ends thus.]

*Monday, April 23.* Mrs. Fernandez called to tell me A. P. Peterson went to call on them and seemed to be very excited and had taken strong drink. He told them, Sam Parker, Charles Wilson, Prince David, Edmund Norrie, and many others of their clique were very angry with me for interfering in politics, and Macfarlane was with them. That they would try and work for David to get him on the throne. I said all right, let them do it.

Eveline has just told me Charlie Wilson [her husband] wants to know what I thought if he accepted the Marshall ship under the P.G. I said he must not. Mrs. Finley says if a paper comes to sign it. Gulick showed me a letter from J.O.C.[34] in which he says he will watch events but as the President Cleveland has always won on all his measures, he certainly will in this.

*Tuesday, April 24.* Kitty [Rest of the entry is blank.]

*Wednesday, April 25.* Signed a mortgage to J. A. Akina and told J. Heleluhe to bring money back.[35] He was paid $300.00 and [I] have not seen it yet. He came home drunk and would have lost all his money but by chance he had some in his pocket, but the rest he has to replace. Bill Cummins and other P.G. fellows were the ones who got him drunk.

*Friday, April 27.* 1:30 P.M. Admiral John Irwin and Staff and Lt. Adams and Lt. Parmenter and wife called. Enjoyed their visit. At three, Consul of the French Vizzavona[36] called—at 3:15 two Mormon missionaries called.

---

32. *Pacific Commercial Advertiser*, April 10, 1894.
33. *Pacific Commercial Advertiser*, April 10, 1894.
34. Not located.
35. This mortgage is not in the Bureau of Conveyances.
36. Antone Vizzavona was the acting French consul starting in December 1891, and from

Mrs. Wilson and Mrs. Evans were present and Capt. S. Nowlein did the duties of Chamberlain. [From Liliu's cash accounts for this date: "Paid H. A. Widemann interest of my Mortgage for 6 mos. $1,221.80."]

*Saturday, April 28.* [Sam] Parker called—told me of the mean action of the Government—they sent for Genl. Adams of Colorado and kept him talking for two hours [and] when he got back to his rooms a P.G. spy was in his room overhauling his carpet bag evidently looking for papers. The spy pretended to be drunk and he [Adams] kicked him out.[37] He [Parker] also told me R[obert] Waipa says he must not give the P.G. cause to suspect him, because being in the Police he [Parker] may be of service when the time came for a change. Eveline told me Charlie [Wilson] had tried to separate two fighters and wanted me to know beforehand for fear that people would stuff me with untrue reports. Admiral Irwin and staff left for San Francisco by the *Australia* today.

*Monday, April 30.* Went to Kealohilani with J. Heleluhe, Wakeke, Keala, Milaina, Aipuuiliili, Kuaiwa, and Paoakalani to drive. Had a nice bath and came home by Kapiolani Park. Stopped [at Ainahau] to inquire after [James] Hay Wodehouse, and Annie said everything seemed encouraging. Loaned $50.00 to Auhea Lokana to pay interest on their place at Kawaiahao (Mortgage is held by Willie Hopper).

**Wednesday, May 2.** Today the voting for a Constitutional election took place and it was a failure all over the islands. It is said they (P.G.s) only got 1,200 votes and there are 9,554 voters all over the islands.[38]

*Friday, May 4.* Poor Dr. Trousseau died this afternoon at 4:00 P.M. It is said he took an overdose of morphine to see if he could get sleep and told Makanoe not to wake him till four P.M. When she went up he was stiff and almost dead. Nothing could restore him. He was a dear friend of John and loved this his adopted country.

*Saturday, May 5.* Dr. Trousseau left all his property to Makanoe.[39] Bruce Cartwright[40] and Hugh McIntyre[41] are executors of his will.

1892 the consul of France. In April 1894, Henry Leon Verleye replaced him as consul, but upon the latter's death in May 1895, Vizzavona assumed the position pro tempore for about a year.

37. This was Captain Charles Adams, U.S. Navy retired, who had just left Honolulu for San Francisco April 28, 1894, on the bark *Albert*. The *Daily Bulletin*, May 1, 1894, reported that just prior to his departure, "He told his friends a story of his having been greatly annoyed by P.G. spies, one of whom capped the climax on the eve of his departure by rifling his trunk.... He said ... it was the third occasion upon which ... his private apartment had been invaded by the same spy." The manager of the Arlington Hotel, where Adams was staying, expressed some doubt about the circumstances, and the matter was then dropped.

38. This was an election to select six delegates to a constitutional convention, for which a total of 8,733 votes were cast.

In the *Daily Hawaii Holomua*, March 21, 1894, in an article titled "They Don't Vote," Edmund Norrie commented: "From Hawaii to Niihau every loyal citizen will stay at home and refuse to recognize a government representing nobody, respected by nobody, and despised by all." *Daily Bulletin*, March 28, 1894. His remarks resulted in charges of sedition from the Provisional Government.

39. Makanoe, "widow of Kaaepa" and Trousseau's long-time lady companion, was left his personal effects; his real estate, including an ostrich farm with 28 ostriches at Kapahulu; and a boathouse housing a steam launch, a catamaran, and several other boats, all heavily mortgaged.

40. Bruce Cartwright (b. 1853–d. 1919) was the son of Honolulu lawyer A. J. Cartwright.

41. Hugh E. McIntyre (b. 1844, Tahiti–d. 1912, Honolulu), the son of grocer Hugh McIntyre, was a Honolulu merchant and the president of Henry May & Co.

*Monday, May 7.* Yesterday the funeral of the late Dr. Geo. Trousseau took place from his residence and had a very large attendance. He was much loved by all his friends, which means all over these islands. Strange to say all the P.G. Ministers went to the funeral and mixed up generally with the Royalists and seemed to court the society of the latter whereas before they would scowl at the royalists and turn their backs, but now are only too eager to mix with them. Heard today Thurston advised the P.G. to ask me to compromise—and they are to restore me and to have two of their party as my Ministers and two of my own choice and let them manage the Gov't and when they are firmly established they are to overturn me again. Hitchcock wrote down they had C. B. Wilson on their side.[42] Bye and bye they will have all their own way.

*Monday, May 21.* Sent Wilcox's Blount report to Kaunamano.

*Tuesday, May 22.* Gave my genealogy to Meekapu for Kanui.

*Thursday, May 24.* Queen Victoria is 75 years today. Saw last eve, Kahakuakoi is suing with Mossman for Kanaina's property.[43] Told Auhea to go to C. W. Ashford to bring her claims on for Kekauluohi's property. He said he would do his best. C. W. thinks she has best claim.

*Friday, May 25.* Had a call from Mr. and Mrs. Twombly, a preacher who was sent for by the P.G., and he spoke as if it was a matter of surprise to him when his dismissal was given him.[44]

*Saturday, May 26.* Auhea came in to say C. W. Ashford has consented to undertake her case. I gave Auhea $50.00 to give to C.W.A. as he had told her his fee was $500.00. I gave her $5.00 for her own.

*Monday, May 28.* Auhea's genealogy was given her this morning... and was presented to C.W.A. at which he seemed so pleased to find she was so closely related to Kamehameha. He actually jumped off his feet and congratulated her. Auhea herself was so pleased that she said when the case is won she would give all to me but that I must give her sufficient to sustain her. I promised I would. [From Liliu's cash accounts for this date: "From J. Heleluhe rent of Spreckels—$500.00."]

42. The document has not been located. Wilson was never on the side of the Provisional Government.

43. In its "Judiciary Jottings" column for May 23, 1894, the *Evening Bulletin* reported: "A replication to defendant's plea in bar has been filed by the plaintiff in the case of *Kahakuakoi alias Kahakuhahoi vs. the Hawaiian Government*. It involves the estate of Kanaina, upon which T. R. Mossman is also prosecuting a claim against the Government, Achi and Kahookano for plaintiff." The history of the Kahakuakoi claim is uncertain, but on September 3, 1898, Kahakuakoi and her husband D. Kealohapauole conveyed to Liliuokalani "all their right, of Dower... and every other right, title, and interest... to the lands, tenements, hereditaments, and estates of the late Charles Kanaina, William C. Lunalilo, Bernice Pauahi Bishop, [and] Queen Hakaleleponi Kalama" stipulating that Liliu "agree... to support and maintain the said parties of the second part in a suitable and proper manner during the term of their natural lives and that of the survivor of them." Bureau of Conveyances, Liber 178, 267.

44. Reverend Dr. A. S. Twombly of Boston arrived in Honolulu on the *Australia* on January 27, 1894, and departed on May 26, 1894, for San Francisco. According to *The Friend*, February 1894, he was here as "temporary supply for Central Union Church for the next few months."

*Tuesday, June 5.* *Gaelic* arrives—no news of great importance. Senator Kyle brought in Congress a resolution that there should be no interference on the P.G. by the U.S. forces—[it] was killed.[45] Frye brought in resolution [for the] same because the Queen had accepted $20,000. When asked his authority—he could not give any—was put down as a liar.[46]

*Wednesday, June 6.* Am not feeling particularly bright today. Laura Kekupoula [?] and Hattie Hiram called and speak of fighting.

*Thursday, June 7.* Dr. T. De Witt Talmage passed through to Australia and called on me with his son at 11:30.[47] Congratulated me on my good health under such trying circumstances. Told him I could not be otherwise seeing I am surrounded by everything that is beautiful, the lovely foliage, the flowers in my flower garden, and the birds that sing so sweetly all tend to make my life one of contentment, and I may add my Maker of all these things watches over me all [and] tends to make my life a happy one.

Mr. and Mrs. J. O. Carter returned from San Francisco today. Rudolph Spreckels called today—he spoke of fights—cautioned him to beware of Sam—said I would study the matter over and let him know.

*Friday, June 8.* Saw Mr. J. O. Carter, he seemed well—he has not given up hopes [of my restoration]—must wait till *Australia* arrives. Mr. Neumann will come back, he advises Arbitration with all the powers. This meets with my views. Asked him if he had seen Spreckels, he said yes. I hold him to say to our friends not to be so anxious to fight. Told Carter about my affairs—he said to wait till Neumann came—how funny. Jennie came and told me of ladies of the P.A.H.A. Aina [the ladies' auxiliary of the Ahahui Hawaii Aloha Aina]. They would send a protest to Minister Willis and all other foreign representatives. I said the latter should be left out—to try also to put the meeting off.

*Monday, June 11.* Seven A.M. yesterday Hannah Evans called and told me Mr. L. had been to see her and told her he had been to take notes at the Constitutional Con[vention] of the P.G.[48] [Mr. L?] Met Mr. S. M. Damon who asked him what he thought of the Con[vention] [and L. said?] that Mr. Dole was trying to get more power than the Queen or any other monarch had ever had. There must be a fight. It has been a very quiet day.

---

45. James Henderson Kyle (b. 1854–d. 1901) was a U.S. senator from South Dakota from 1891. Kyle had revived the Turpie resolution on May 22 "by offering a substitute resolution to the effect that no force would be used to restore the Queen or to destroy the present Hawaiian regime." See William Adam Russ Jr., *The Hawaiian Revolution, 1893–94* (Selinsgrove, Pennsylvania: Susquehanna University Press, 1992), 344–45. For a discussion of the Turpie resolution, see second footnote for July 2, 1894, diary entry (425).

46. William Pierce Frye (b. 1831–d. 1911) was a U.S. senator from Maine who served 1881–1901. The resolution referred to is probably that offered to the U.S. Senate on January 3, 1894. There is no record that Liliu had accepted $20,000 from anyone.

47. Thomas De Witt Talmage (b. 1832, New Jersey–d. 1902) was a clergymen, the head of a large congregation known as the Brooklyn Tabernacle, and an editor of religious newspapers. Various Protestant congregations met Talmage with enthusiasm until he expressed sympathy for the Queen's position.

48. This would have been the Saturday, June 9, 1894, session of the constitutional convention. Mr. L. has not been identified.

*Iolani Palace and grounds viewed from Aliiolani Hale, circa 1889. Hale Akala, the two-story frame-and-lattice building at the left of the palace, was known as the bungalow. In it Kalakaua maintained his private office, which was more congenial and accessible to his subjects than the palace. The bungalow was heavily damaged in the rebellion led by Robert Wilcox on July 30, 1889. At the far right are the towers of Hale Koa, or Iolani Barracks, which housed the Royal Guard. The high wall that surrounds the palace grounds was lowered following the rebellion.*
Hawaii State Archives

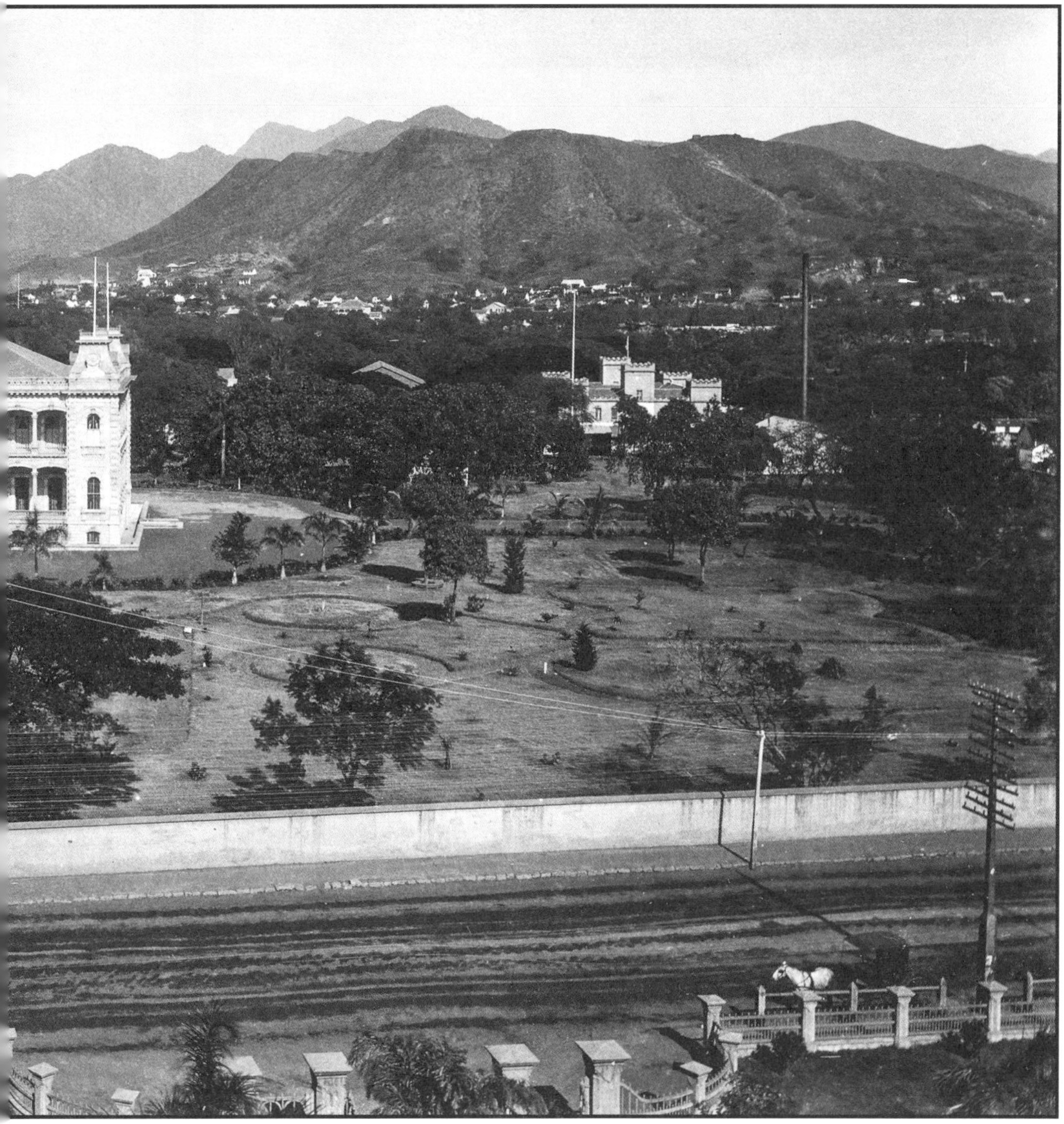

*Tuesday, June 12.* Ten A.M. Had conversation with Rudolph Spreckels. Told him I had had conversation with Mr. Carter and the latter proposed Arbitration, because if this is true the President could not do anything for us—in taking this course it would help President Cleveland. Spreckels shook his head. He thought we ought to make some preparation. I told him to see Mr. Carter first—he said he would, and if he wished to see me [asked] if he might come. I said yes.

I gave to Auhea four copies to give to Mahelona, Okuu, Auhea, Hooponopono, and Luhea of her genealogical tree. On Thursday she will give one to C. W. Ashford. She gave Ashford Lunalilo's photo—and he was immediately struck with the resemblance of Lunalilo to her. Every evidence taken to him will help his case—no doubt she will win above all other claimants. This morning Auhea called. I told her to say to Ashford to try and get her divorce before next court term. She said she would—he [her husband Lokana] had deserted her and did not help her any. Then we should nana aku nana mai [look forward and look back]—and care for each other. I gave her $70.00 Court fees—for three kumuhana [court documents] in her cause, which she gave to C. W. [Ashford] and also his copy of her genealogy—he fairly jumped—everything was so explicit and he had nothing to seek for. Whoever proposed this was a smart person. C.W.A. [Ashford] asked Mahelona if it was correct—M. said it was. C. W. said if he had three witnesses like M. the case would meet with no opposition. C. W. said should anyone come and offer any money not to accept any. Bishop would offer $10–$12,000—then do the next thing.

*Thursday, June 14.* Made a mistake—all that was written on the 13th should have been written for today. Auhea said when that time came she would come here and stay—I said yes—then [said] we would both have to be very careful what we eat. For they would seek to destroy us both—as this case meant ruin to Mr. Bishop and Sam Damon. Next Monday all the witnesses must meet—to see how far they [are] agreed—When Lunalilo's photo was shown to Mahelona he recognized it. August this case will come up.

*Saturday, June 16. Australia* arrived bringing the news that the [U.S.] Senate *have* passed 55 to [zero] that the Hawaiians should choose their own form of government, "that the people of the Hawaiian Is. [Islands] to establish their own form of government and domestic policy and the U.S. in no wise to interfere with their wish[es]—that any interference therewith by any other government will be considered unfriendly act to the U.S." The American Commissioner Willis presented the above to the P.G.s by instructions from Gresham. The P.G. are not happy and our party does not consider it final.[49] They talk of offering me $20,000 and Kaiulani $10,000 a year. Not a cent will I accept and sacrifice the rights of my people.

---

49. The full text of the U.S. Senate Resolution passed on May 31, 1894, establishing a policy of "absolute noninterference" in Hawaiian affairs, was as follows: "Resolved, that of right it belongs wholly to the people of the Hawaiian Islands to establish and maintain their own form of government and domestic policy; that the United States should in nowise interfere therewith, and that any intervention in the political affairs of these islands by any other government will be regarded as an act unfriendly to the United States." The final vote "was 55 yeas, 0 nays, but 30 did not vote." Russ, *Hawaiian Revolution*, 345.

*Monday, June 18.* Wilcox and others called. I had only one answer yesterday, not to be despondent—that the news was good for our side. Bush and Nawahi want my opinion—same as above. They went to the H.H.A.A. [Hui Hawaii Aloha Aina] and mentioned the same.[50] It was left to a committee to draft a protest to foreign powers—another committee was appointed to attend to matters in case extreme measures have to be taken.

Asked N [Nowlein?] to see A.J.C [Alexander J. Cartwright]—met Carter, Cornwell, and Parker—said a protest ought to be presented to foreign representatives—showing after news of Saturday [June 16] my protest to U.S. all connected with our case and also ask them to interfere about the P.G. Republic because it is not of the people. Sent for Widemann, asked him to meet other friends about the above. He [said he] would. Auhea tells me Mrs. Pratt will bring suit for the Kamehameha property.[51]

*Wednesday, June 20.* Sent to C. W. Ashford the $50 that he sent back yesterday, to go to him towards his pay as Attorney for Auhea's case. It is now $150 Auhea has paid to Ashford, leaving him $350.00 yet to be paid.

This has been a day of excitement,[52] and I asked Mr. R. W. [Wilcox] and Mr. W. [Charles Wilson] to put their heads together and think for the good of the people. Sent W. to Mr. F [?] to ask if assistance could be given. Cautious ans[wer] good.

[Captain] Rooke called on Admiral Walker and said are you going to land your men. Walker could not say—Rooke said, if anything takes place on shore I will land my men to protect my nationality. Do you think I will stay on my ship calmly and see [or] have them slaughtered? No. I will [Entry ends thus.]

---

This text was published in the June 18, 1894, *Pacific Commercial Advertiser*, along with accompanying correspondence. The transmittal letter from Secretary of State Walter Q. Gresham to Albert S. Willis in Honolulu, dated June 2, 1894, stated specifically: "This declaration...is entirely satisfactory to the President." The *New York Times* editor remarked: "The...correspondence, which is self-explanatory, disposes of the dream of the royalists that the United States would interfere in their favor." *New York Times*, June 1, 1894.

50. The Hui Hawaii Aloha Aina (Hawaiian Patriotic League) was founded in 1892 chiefly under the auspices of Robert W. Wilcox, and was (as its oath stated) "established to promote justice and equal rights [and] the political government of Hawaii of the people, for the people, and by the people." At a meeting held at Waikiki, April 19, 1892, Wilcox explained to recruits the need for arming themselves: "Let everyone provide himself with a rifle as I believe we will have to resort to bayonets to get that 'pono kaulike' [equal rights and justice]." Hawaii State Archives, Attorney General Files, Series 506, Box 4, Hawaiian Patriotic League.

On July 15, 1893, the league addressed a lengthy statement to President Grover Cleveland on political affairs in the islands. See the transcript in the Morgan Report, vol. 2, 1719–37, which also includes the league's constitution in Hawaiian and English, 1737–39.

51. Liliu here means the Crown lands. Franklin S. Pratt, the husband of chiefess Elizabeth Kekaaniau, had in fact, on February 19, 1893, while serving as Hawaiian consul general in San Francisco, forwarded a letter to U.S. Vice President Levi P. Morton informing the latter of his wife's interest in claiming the Crown lands on the slim basis that she had been one of the alii (chiefly) students at the Chief's Children's School in Honolulu. Mr. Pratt died in February 1894, and nothing came of the matter, although Mrs. Pratt's relatives occasionally raised the claim subsequently. Descendant Matt Mattice of Honolulu made Pratt's file on the matter available to me.

52. Liliu is here referring to public response to the news (received in Honolulu on June 16) that the U.S. Congress had adopted a policy of strict noninterference in Hawaiian affairs.

*Thursday, June 21.* Signed a protest written by Widemann with the approval of Carter and Parker, Cornwell, and others, to foreign representatives here, stating why we have taken this step on account of the Constitution of the P.G.[53]

Parker went on board the USS [*Philadelphia*]—Admiral Walker says noninterference. W. says he was sorry for Queen—[W. G.] Irwin approached him on giving me salary of $25,000. Parker tells him to put it in writing.

*Friday, June 22.* Parker has just been to Minister Willis—[Willis] tells him he recognizes him as Minister [of] Foreign Affairs of H.I. Presented him a copy of the Senate resolution that came Saturday. That he had no official notice from U.S. that the President approved of the resolution. Good—it is not for the Chinese, [or] Portuguese but meant for the Hawaiians—that the President of the U.S. still feels as he W. [Willis] did—that Stevens was wrong. Parker will meet those friends tonight, to consult on our situation. Seward tells me Willis told Wodehouse yesterday he would not recognize the P.G. when they proclaim their Constitution. Signed four more documents of protest for Mr. Widemann. Rickard was sent for by Rooke.

*Monday, July 2.* Grand Mass Meeting of the Hawaiian people at Palace Square at five P.M. Nearly 5,000 were gathered there. The Central Committee of the Ladies' Patriotic Association, Mrs. James Campbell president, and the Central Committee of the Gentlemen's Hawaiian Patriotic Association, were present. Speakers were Bush and Nawahi, Widemann and Carter. Nawahi pointed out to them the fact that when they proclaim the Republic they are not of the same standing as individuals as when recognized by all the powers—they discard their individuality therefore will not be recognized [by?] the P.G.[54]

Wray Taylor yesterday told Auhea that the P.G.s are all aware that they are going to crumble to pieces, but they are planning now to deport me and to be very watchful. Sam Parker said he too had been offered amount of money. It is said the P.G. will proclaim Martial Law today. I don't think they will dare to—also that they are going to steal me away if they can and send me by the *Belgic*. We will see. Cleghorn came in to say from Wodehouse, that I should have no fears. My subjects, being anxious for

---

53. The protest was an attempt to prevent foreign governmental representatives from recognizing the "Republic." In an article on the document, the *Pacific Commercial Advertiser*, June 23, 1894, remarked: "This document was addressed to the diplomatic representatives of all foreign powers, and called attention to the alleged fact that Liliuokalani was still the rightful ruler of Hawaii, while the pretended Republic was declared to be founded upon a usurpation. The protest was the work of a prominent royalist, and was not sent until it had been considered by the leading confidential advisors of Mrs. Dominis." The article continued that it had been sent to U.S. Commissioner Willis, who declined to receive it, "greatly to the consternation of the royalists." The editor thought it probable that the same would happen with other diplomatic representatives, excepting perhaps that of Great Britain. The text of the protest appeared in the *Daily Bulletin*, August 13, 1894.

54. In its coverage of the rally, the *Pacific Commercial Advertiser*, July 3, 1894, reproduced Joseph Nawahi's remarks as follows: "The matter of the 17th of January, 1893, has not been settled yet. The Queen has submitted her grievance to the United States, but the Provisional Government is not satisfied with this, and is trying to establish a Republic. If I was American Minister, I would order them back to their places . . . until the matter was settled. If they declare this Republic and are not recognized by the other Powers it will be their fault, not ours."

my safety, wished me to see if any protection could be given me by Willis—I sent J. W. Robertson to him—he said he could not—from the receipt of the Turpie resolution.[55] I sent Robertson to Wodehouse, he said [he?] would consider. [From Liliu's cash accounts for this date: "From rent, Hamohamo Rec'd $820.75."]

*Wednesday, July 4.* Eight A.M. A salute of 21 guns was fired for the Republic of the P.G. [Republic of Hawaii].[56]

Widemann called to say not to trust Neumann with money matters. Told [him] Carter was mistaken [that] I had asked him (C) to take charge of my affairs. Widemann thinks [we] ought to send someone to Washington. News by *Mariposa*. Carnot, President of France, was stabbed in the abdomen by anarchist.[57]

*Friday, July 6.* Min. Willis and other foreign representatives recognized the P.G. as they did their former government meaning a *de facto* govt. only. No salutes were fired from the ships.[58]

*Saturday, July 7.* The foreign residents think a Commission ought to be sent to Washington.

*Monday, July 9.* Yesterday decided with Widemann and Parker to send a commission to Washington, though much against my wish, but Widemann felt very strongly there ought to be one sent, and I could say nothing because I had said all along there was no necessity but they outvoted me. I felt it was like my working against my own interest since I had placed everything in the hands of the President of the U.S.

Sent for J. A. Cummins, told him they had decided he should go too, so Major Seward is going as Secretary. This must be a secret mission, but Parker went right over to Wodehouse to prepare them and inform their Ambassador in Washington.

---

55. "On January 8, 1894, Senator David Turpie of Indiana laid before the U.S. Senate a resolution which read as follows: 'Resolved that from the facts and papers laid before us by the Executive and other sources, it is unwise, inexpedient, and not in accordance with the character and dignity of the United States to consider further... either the treaty or project of annexation of the Hawaiian territory to this country at this time.' This resolution became the storm center of an orgy of polemics which lasted off and on almost five months before the Senate found it possible to agree on an amended version." Russ, *Hawaiian Revolution*, 317–19.

56. On July 4, 1894, the Republic of Hawaii was proclaimed, and it would remain the form of government in the Hawaiian Islands until annexation on August 12, 1898. In its account of the proclamation day, the *Pacific Commercial Advertiser*, July 5, 1894, noted: "A more glorious sun could not have risen over the Republic of Hawaii than that of yesterday. At eight o'clock, from the front steps of the Executive Building, the new Hawaiian Ship of State was launched on its voyage. The ceremony was essentially a civil one. No attempt at display was made." On the occasion, President Sanford Dole made an address on a platform before the front steps, and then a proclamation was read. Afterward, Judge J. W. Kalua read the same proclamation in Hawaiian, and Chief Justice Albert Francis Judd administered the oath of office. The *Advertiser* commented: "This was all of the ceremony."

57. Marie François Sadi Carnot (b. 1837–d. 1894) served as president of the French Republic starting in 1887. An Italian anarchist named Sante Geronimo Caserio assassinated him in Lyon, France, on June 24, 1894.

58. The *Pacific Commercial Advertiser*, July 7, 1894, published U.S. Minister Willis's letter of recognition, and commented: "The recognition of Japan is expected this morning, as is that of Portugal. The members of the Consular Corps have all recognized the Government."

*Tuesday, July 10.* Signed three Commissions, one for J. A. Cummins, H. A. Widemann, and Sam Parker, as Commissioners to Washington to see President Cleveland and find out if there is any hope for our restoration. If favorable, well and good, if not [A long dash follows.] Sam tried to sell his secret to W. G. Irwin to get money from him but did not succeed. How mean! Rudolph Spreckels told me so, so I advised him to say all plans were given up.

*Friday, July 13.* The *Rio de Janeiro* arrived and the Commissioners will leave in her.

*Saturday, July 14.* Auhea told me [Wray] Taylor told her some of the P.G.s want to return the Government to me but they were ashamed to. Emmeluth says so. They are constantly meeting but no satisfactory results. That Hitchcock[59] was going to hoist the Republican flag on Molokai but Mr. Meyer told him not to and he did not, which was a strong rebuff to the P.G. Hitchcock is very unhappy.

The *Rio* only left at six this morning, and passed the *Australia* off Diamond Head. The only news by the *Australia* is the great strike in the States.[60]

*Monday, July 16.* Jessie says the day the Republic was proclaimed, the P.G.s were not happy. They were [more] despondent than ever, because they'd not been recognized by the powers. Jessie advised me to make a law not permitting any firms to send for guns, only Govt. That isn't bad. Told her to ask A. who would make the best Chief Justice in case of restoration.

*Wednesday, July 18.* Capt. Rooke of the *Champion* called—Rosa and Jimmie Robertson were present. He said he told Admiral Walker if he landed he [Rooke] would land his men too, in case there was a disturbance on shore. He also told a lot of men standing together, "in 20 days from today I land my men." Frank Brown was present—he related this in Eveline 's hearing. Frank also said he always thought a good deal of me—bosh!

*Wednesday, July 25.* Dole and P. C. Jones went on board [the *Philadelphia*] to see Admiral Walker. The former got no salute.[61] While there they asked the Admiral that in case there was a restoration could he give them protection? There was no answer.

*Saturday, July 28.* Heard today [that] Judge Kepoikai had signed to swear to support the Republic and Constitution of the P.G.—with the hopes he would be reappointed—but he and Kalua are both disappointed. Dickey will get the appointment.[62]

---

59. Harvey Rexford Hitchcock was the pound master and chairman of the road board for Molokai.

60. Liliu is referring to a general strike of the American Railway Union against the hauling of Pullman cars, supporting a strike of 2,500 employees of the Pullman Car Company. The movement spread across the country and culminated in the use of federal troops to settle the matter.

61. The *Pacific Commercial Advertiser*, July 26, 1894, noted that it was an "unofficial visit."

62. Lyle A. Dickey was not appointed. The minutes of the Executive Council stated: "It was decided not to appoint A. N. Kepoikai as Circuit Judge of Maui, but to appoint J. W.

*Monday, July 30.* Heard yesterday the Council of the Republic met to consult on restoring me to the throne—they are divided.[63] Gulick tells me he will wait till we hear from U.S. Guard is always sent to Dole's house—but he never sleeps any two nights in one house. That Emmeluth is building a sandbag fortification around his house, as if that would be any safety.

*Tuesday, July 31.* Royal Hawaiian Band serenaded me this morn. Six A.M. [Abraham] Fernandez family [and] C. Clark's family, Nowlein, Robertson, Prince David, T. Evans, wife and sister, and Eveline [Wilson] lunched with me. Kailinaoa and Hopekaa sailed for Kauai. Robertson found $60.00 and Capt. Nowlein $28 in paper money—Saturday Miliaina found $10.

**Wednesday, August 1.** Lilikalani, Anini, [?] and Oneha were dismissed by A. F. Judd.[64] Told Kaipo and Aimoku to stay a week with me at Washington Place.

*Thursday, August 2. Monowai* brought news of the arrival of our Commissioners in San Francisco and [that] they had gone on to Washington where Blount would meet them.

*Friday, August 3.* Received this morning a book with a card from J. T. Gresham and Grover Cleveland—on Public Works in Chicago.[65] Capt. Hawes, Major Wodehouse's successor, arrived by the *Arawa*.[66]

*Saturday, August 4.* Have been feeling poorly all day. Three P.M. sent J. W. Robertson to Major Wodehouse to ask him to detain the *Champion* as she intended to leave Monday—since it would be dangerous to leave our port without a vessel of war. If the P.G. should attempt to seize the occasion to do me harm, there would be a massacre—and a great destruction of property. Wodehouse will detain her.[67]

---

Kalua to that office." Hawaii State Archives, Foreign Office and Executive Files, Series 423, vol. 2, Minutes of the Executive Council, August 8, 1894.

Auwae Noa Kepoikai (b. December 17, 1861, Wailuku–d. May 9, 1911, Wailuku) became police magistrate of Wailuku in 1886. In 1892, Liliu appointed him judge of the Second Circuit Court for Wailuku, Maui, a position he held until 1894. Judge John W. Kalua succeeded him in that position on September 1, 1894, and served until April 7, 1904.

63. The minutes of the Executive Council meetings on July 21, July 23, and August 3, 1894, contain no reference to any such restoration.

64. E. K. Lilikalani was a clerk in the Judiciary Department, Samuel Oneha was a messenger in the government building, and Anini has not been identified.

65. The title of the book has not been confirmed.

66. Albert George Sidney Hawes arrived at Honolulu as the successor to Major James H. Wodehouse, British commissioner and consul general. Prior to his arrival at Honolulu, Hawes had been in the British diplomatic service in central Africa, and then was a naval instructor in Japan (1871–84) and consul general in Tahiti (1889–94). He died in Hilo on August 6, 1897, at age 54.

67. The *Champion* did not depart from Hawaii as scheduled on August 6, 1897, but the delay may not have stemmed from Liliuokalani's request. The newly arrived British commissioner, Captain A.G.S. Hawes, visited the ship that day at ten A.M. and received a 13-gun salute, after which he was rowed to the USS *Philadelphia*, where he again received the regulation salute. Major Wodehouse's term of office ended on August 7, and he paid a courtesy visit to the HBMS *Champion* on August 9.

An event not recorded in the Queen's diary was the subject of a graceful note in the newspaper:

> ¶ Queen Liliuokalani in adversity is as active, proportionately, in works of charity and benevolence as she always was in prosperity. The Queen has had cleared and plowed at Pauoa a large piece of land to be used as a nursery. About one hundred plots will be laid out, and each piece being 10 x 16 feet. About seventy-five pieces are ready for planting, but as everything is not ready the planting has been deferred until September 2. The place has been christened "Uluhaimalama." It is for a charitable object, the flowers being intended for distribution to hospital and sick homes.[68]

A subsequent article said that each parcel was in charge of an individual member of the Women's Patriotic League, and that "every individual is expected to plant flowers and trees different from those of the others."[69]

*Thursday, August 9.* Joe Carter called. Showed him my present from Cleveland. [He] Inquired about Bush, what I thought of him—whether he was sincere. I told him [what] Mr. Blount had said.

*Saturday, August 11. Australia* arrived, bringing news of the 3rd [that] our Commissioners had called on Secretary Gresham and were to call on President Cleveland.[70]

*Monday, August 13.* Heard today that Willie Allen had said that Minister Willis had said the U.S. would have nothing more to do with me—that he had called here and told me so. There is not truth in it. It must be a made up [story] of the P.G. to deceive themselves.

Poor Pamahoa [Napoleon] died Saturday night of La grippe.[71]

Joe for Hookupu [tribute or ceremonial offering of] puaa [pig], poi, etc. To Ninito [Sumner]—$5.50. [From Liliu's cash accounts for this date: "(To) Mrs. Chase for making holokus—$20.00."]

---

68. *Daily Bulletin*, August 8, 1894.
69. *Daily Bulletin*, October 8, 1894.
70. This news, which appeared in the *Daily Bulletin*, August 11, 1894, was taken from an American newspaper interview (in Chicago, July 29) with Herman A. Widemann, Samuel Parker, John Adam Cummins, and Major W. T. Seward. When Widemann was asked about a rumor that the party bore "a petition signed by the Royalists requesting annexation to the United States, Mr. Widemann said 'No!' most emphatically. 'While we all regard annexation as our ultimate destiny, such a thing is impossible under the present form of government.'— Asked as to the prospects for a restoration of the ex-Queen, Mr. Widemann winked significantly, but refused to make further response."
71. Pamahoa (b. 1830, Napoopoo, South Kona, Hawaii–d. August 13, 1894, Honolulu [according to the *Hawaiian Gazette*, Aug. 14, 1893]) was married to Napoleon (a Tahitian) and was the mother of Mrs. Emma Mahelona, Mrs. Eben Low, Mrs. J.H.S. Kaleo, and Mrs. J. U. Kawainui. Pamahoa had been an active member of the Liliuokalani Educational Society.

*Tuesday, August 14.* Sent to C. W. Ashford by Auhea for his fees to her case, $100.00. Planted trees—Navel Oranges. Ashford says this is the best time to plan and make appointments.[72]

*Wednesday, August 15.* Have a touch of La grippe and sent for Dr. McLennan.

*Thursday, August 16.* Poor Malie Kahai has gone to her last rest. Change of life was the cause.[73]

*Friday, August 17.* Ninito [Sumner] sent me a dish of Papaya and banana cooked in their own [Tahitian] style—very nice. Nancy brought it. Rec'd Capt. Rooke at 11 A.M. He told me Mr. Dole had said that when the time came they would have to act quickly.

[There are no entries between August 17 and September 29.]

*Saturday, September 29.* [Hui] Kawaluonalani contributed $4.00.

[There are no diary entries between September 29 and November 10.]

*Saturday, November 10.* Gave my new constitution in the hands of Mr. R. [Rickard] for them to go over.[74]

*Thursday, November 15.* Bought of Dr. McKibbin through C. T. Gulick the lease of the Miller premises at $500.00 a year. Paid $37.00 for taxes and expenses.[75]

72. The implication was that she should make ready her plans for commissions following the restoration of the monarchy.

73. Maria Malie Merseberg Kahai (b. 1851–d. August 15, 1894, Honolulu) was a relative of J. A. Cummins, and her funeral was held at his residence.

74. On the matter of Liliuokalani's proposed constitution, Sam Nowlein made the following sworn statement before the attorney general on January 17, 1895: "Gulick, Rickard, and myself drew the new Constitution, [and] wrote it out at Gulick's place. We took most of it from the '87 Constitution and some from '64. We made some improvements. The three of us made it up together. We had several meetings preparing it. Gulick did the actual writing of it. After we finished it we got Kaiu to copy it. I took it to him at Washington Place for him to copy it and he wrote it there. It was never written in typewriter.... I never knew there was a typewritten copy. The copy we had made by Kaiu was in handwriting. It is at Gulick's. The copy may have come from Reynolds' but I never saw it before.... Reynolds never had anything to do with the Constitution.... The copy of the constitution we submitted to the Queen was the one in pen and ink written by Kaiu. She sent me back to Gulick with it. There was [sic, were] some alterations to make. That was about the 10th of November. I took it to Gulick's, I don't know whether Rickard was there or not. At any rate we all saw it. We all looked it over and her suggestions... but we did not make any changes. I think she wrote her suggestions on the paper itself and not on separate paper. The last time we met at Gulick's we did not agree about the Constitution and we postponed consideration of it. The disagreement, I think, was about the crown lands.... I don't know where the copy of ours is, perhaps it is torn up.... The provision in our constitution in regard to the crown lands was that the Legislature could pass a bill to sell the crown lands and any such money be placed in the public treasury as crown lands revenue and the Sovereign should have the interest on that money." Hawaii State Archives, Attorney General Files, Series 506, Box 1.

75. The Miller premises on the Diamond Head side of Washington Place were so named for their long occupancy by British Consul William Miller. The property was generally known as "Beretania" or "Beretania cottage," and the road in front of the premises shared that name. The transaction was actually an assignment of a 25-year lease (starting on September 30, 1879) from Lady Mary Hammond Graeme of Freshwater, Isle of Wight, the niece of General William

*Saturday, November 17.* Borrowed of H. E. McIntyre through C. T. Gulick at 9% int, the sum of ($500.00) five hundred.

*Tuesday, November 20.* The *Yorktown* left early this morning for Japan. Mr. Dole went on board yesterday, had a salute of 21 guns. He asked the Captain to stay for fear of an uprising but he could not—Mr. N. sent a message to Mr. F. by Mr. N. No. 1 was to propose a contract between So and So about [Entry ends thus.]

[On Friday, November 30, Liliu entered in cash accounts: "From J. Heleluhe of Mrs. Nicols Mortgage, rec'd. $1,000.00."]

**Saturday, December 1.** *Australia* arrived bringing Major [W. T.] Seward. Good old soul in poor health—threatened with apoplexy.[76]

*Monday, December 3.* Heard good news for our side.

*Tuesday, December 4.* The *Yorktown* must have arrived in Japan ere this. [On this date, Liliu entered in cash accounts: "To Mrs. Dowsett for orchids—Pd. $34.00."]

[On Wednesday, December 5, Liliu entered in cash accounts: "To J. Heleluhe for H. McIntyre to Note & Int. $545.00. To same for Groceries—$55.95. To C. W. Ashford through Auhea for Kanaina case. Pd. $163.00."]

*Tuesday, December 25.* Christmas Day. Very quiet—only Jennie Clark and myself and servants.

*Wednesday, December 26.* Drove out with Auhea and Mary in Manuel Reis' carriage—Joe, Charlie, Jennie in Joe's carriage. This is the first time of my going out since September 1893. The drive did me lots of good.

Three P.M. Sam Parker called to say I ought to call Widemann, Campbell, Carter, McIntyre, E. Macfarlane to consult on situation—next day he would call in afternoon to learn results—that he was going to take his daughter to Kohala and on his return would call with the other members of the Cabinet and resign.

*Friday, December 28.* Mr. Parker asked if I had sent for Widemann and others to consult with me on the situation? I said no. He was disappointed—told him it was treason. He went down to J. O. Carter and sent the latter up. Carter said Widemann told him I had better sell my Pahala and other stocks to pay interest of my debt. Said I'd wait. Carter said Irwin told him to tell me to put in my claim for a salary when the P.G. [legislative] Session sits. Told C. to say I will remain poor with my people. C. told me he thought Damon must have put Sam [Parker] up to say what he did. Heard that R [Robert] Parker was going to be dismissed on the last of the month, that John Colburn was told by C. W. Ashford to resign. He said he wouldn't.[77] [Liliu's cash accounts for this date record: "Gave to S. Nowlein with promise of $50—Pd. $100."]

Miller, to Dr. McKibbin Sr. One of the terms of the lease was that the lessee "erect or cause to be erected a good and substantial brick stone or cement building of the value of $5,000."

76. The *Australia* actually arrived at Honolulu on December 3, 1894.

77. Much was made of this latter remark in 1895 after the failed counterrevolution, when

*Saturday, December 29.* Signed my political Will[78] and Auhea signed a Deed to me of all the property she might gain in Kanaina, Akahi, and other estates, and she is to receive a monthly allowance from me is all she asks—witnessed by Sam Nowlein and C. T. Gulick. I promised her I would in case she won the suit. Signed eleven commissions.[79]

the government had seized the Queen's diary and put it under intense scrutiny. In an affidavit, W. A. Kinney said: "Upon finding the aforesaid statement on said diary, I sent for J. F. Colburn, and asked him what it meant. He told me that some two weeks before the 28th of December, he was down calling upon C. W. Ashford. During the visit, Mr. Ashford said to him, 'By the way, Colburn, do you remember I advised you that the Cabinet in office at the time of the overthrow would have to be the Cabinet in case of restoration, on the theory that all that had intervened during the overthrow was illegal and void. I advised you, therefore, not to resign, but to claim your right as "Minister of the Interior."' 'Yes, I remember.' He then said, 'Well, Colburn, I have changed my mind. I think now that you had better resign.' Colburn then said, 'Why, what has made you change your mind.' Ashford smiled, and replied, 'Well, you may wake up some morning and find that Ashford is the Government.' Colburn retorted, 'Well, I think that the advice you first gave me is good enough for me—I certainly shall not resign.' And there the matter ended." Hawaii State Archives, Attorney General Files, Series 506-2-10, "In the Matter of the Claim of C. W. Ashford."

78. William F. Kaae, the Queen's secretary, testified at her trial in February 1895 that he had "drafted a political will for her" and at the same time made up several commissions for her to sign.

79. The Provisional Government used this entry about signing commissions against Liliuokalani at her trial in 1895, to show that she was in fact intent on regaining her throne. In his sworn statement to the government regarding the 1895 insurrection, W. F. Kaae, who was acting as the Queen's secretary, said: "I wrote out the Commissions of the proposed Cabinet—and others, eleven in all: C. W. Ashford—Attorney General; C. T. Gulick, Minister of Finance; Sam Nowlein, Minister of Interior; R. W. Wilcox, Min. Foreign Affairs; W. H. Rickard, Marshall; A. Rosa, 1st Ass. Justice; V. V. Ashford [sic, C. W. Ashford], 2nd Assoc. Justice; A. S. Cleghorn, Gov. Oahu; J. H. Nawahi, Gov. Hawaii; David Kawananakoa, Gov. Maui; Kalanianaole, Gov. Kauai. I don't remember date of signing these (heard Dec. 28), I saw them signed by Mrs. Dominis. It was in the room upstairs—makai end, Waikiki side. I enclosed them in envelopes & turned them over to her. I was acting as her private Secretary." Hawaii State Archives, Attorney General Files, Series 506, "Insurrection of 1895, Statement No. 167."

Queen Liliuokalani and Sam Nowlein in her Washington Place garden. After she was deposed in 1893, the Queen repaired to her home and lived privately here with her household. Sam Nowlein and Robert Wilcox were the prime movers behind the failed January 1895 counterrevolution intended to restore the Queen's government. On January 16, 1895, following the unsuccessful rebellion, Liliu was imprisoned in Iolani Palace. Investigators searched Washington Place to gather quantities of the Queen's documents and personal papers, including several diaries, as evidence of her complicity in the revolution. Nowlein agreed to turn state's evidence, and at the trial held in the palace throne room, government lawyers presented testimony from him that the Queen knew a rebellion was being planned. The Queen and Nowlein never spoke again.

Severin-Bolster, circa 1890s, Hawaii State Archives

# Counterrevolution of 1895

In January 1895, a counterrevolution convulsed the Hawaiian community, the results of which still reverberate through the community today. It was a last-stand attempt by loyalists to reinstate Liliuokalani to the throne, and though it ultimately failed, it resulted in the ex-Queen's arrest on a charge of treason, in her formal and absolute abdication, in her imprisonment in Iolani Palace, and in the extinction of any possible return to the monarchical form of government in Hawaii.

It was an armed rebellion against the Republic of Hawaii, and it began at the Waikiki beach home of Henry Bertelmann on Sunday evening, January 6, 1895. The seeds for this revolutionary action, however, were planted in early October, and the major conspirators were Charles T. Gulick, a cabinet minister under Kalakaua; Samuel Nowlein, formerly captain of the Queen's Guard; William Henry Rickard, an Englishman; and U.S. Civil War veteran Major W. T. Seward, a close friend of John A. Cummins of Waimanalo. They held meetings at Gulick's house and elsewhere. Nowlein was designated the captain of the enterprise, and Gulick the statesman. They drew up a new constitution, along with other papers, including a proclamation restoring the Queen's government and an article establishing martial law.

In San Francisco, Seward secured a shipment of arms, using monies from an unidentified source. The arms were shipped on the *Wahlberg* to Hawaiian waters. Just 30 miles northeast of Oahu, Cummins's steamer, the *Waimanalo*, intercepted them, transported them to Honolulu, unloaded them on the third of January at Waialae (specifically at Kaalawai Beach), and concealed the goods. The shipment included 288 Winchester carbines with belts and some 50,000 cartridges—as well as two cases, each containing 80 pistols and additional ammunition. Nowlein enlisted a considerable number of natives in squads of 38—a total of about 200 individuals, who assembled at Waimanalo on Saturday the fifth and Sunday the sixth.

Robert W. Wilcox had joined the group and was placed under Nowlein. The rebels' intent was to make a rush upon the city late at night, and but for what happened at Waikiki that effort might very well have succeeded. On Sunday night, when the police department learned that a large group of men had massed at Henry Bertelmann's house at Waikiki, it sent out an investigatory squad. Scuffles ensued, the men fired upon the police, and Charles Lunt Carter, in a rush upon Bertelmann's boathouse, took a bullet and died of his wounds at five A.M. the next morning. Rumors had

*Iolani Palace grand hall. The large staircase made of koa wood led to the family suites on the second floor. On January 16, 1895, after her arrest at Washington Place, the Queen was escorted to Iolani Palace. There, Captain Robert Parker and Deputy Marshall Arthur M. Brown handed her over to Colonel Joseph H. Fisher. They entered the building through the rear door to the central hall and proceeded up the carpeted staircase to the bedroom suite at the southeast corner of the second floor, where she was imprisoned. On January 17, a military tribunal commenced in the former throne room, located through the three doorways to the right of the stairs.*
Hawaii State Archives, circa 1886

been circulating that a group of prominent Hawaiians were soon planning to strike a blow, and the *Pacific Commercial Advertiser*, January 7, 1895, commenced its coverage with this remark: "The blow has fallen."

By nine P.M., 200 men of the national guard had reported for duty, and 500 of the citizen guard had been armed and posted. Firing went on that evening at Waikiki and inland along Waialae Road. Robert Wilcox and his rebels first took a position on the rim and summit of Diamond Head, shooting at government forces below, and another party under Nowlein was at Moiliili, where skirmishes (with heavy shelling) commenced and continued near Palolo Valley. On January 14, government forces captured Nowlein and a party of 39 natives at Waialae just below Kanewai Spring, "mauka of Cleghorn's new windmill."[1]

Early on, Wilcox and his group had retreated from Diamond Head to Manoa Valley, where forces pursued them into the north angle of the valley, known as "the pen." There another battle ensued before Wilcox and his men escaped up a steep trail between Manoa and Nuuanu.

Government men spent more than a week guarding the valleys between Nuuanu and Palolo and scouring the mountain ridges for Wilcox. Some days later Wilcox was captured on the reef near the Kalihi leper station.

The government ultimately took about 140 Hawaiians and some three dozen non-Hawaiians as prisoners of war, but released many of them later without charges. On the sixth of January, the government established a military commission, and as of January 7, it suspended the writ of habeas corpus and instituted martial law.

The counterrevolution now having failed, the question was what to do with the Queen. The Executive Council discussed the matter in meetings, and the following summaries and excerpts are taken from its minutes.

On January 12, 1895, at a meeting of the Executive Council, Minister W. O. Smith brought up the matter of arresting the ex-Queen, but not all members of the council were in favor of the idea. P. C. Jones said he understood "that there was no evidence against her [or] of her being implicated." Several members brought up "the strong popular desire for it" among many residents, while others questioned what effect arresting her would have on the Hawaiian population. A. S. Hartwell and W. D. Alexander were in favor of "placing her under arrest and confining her to her present residence." Alexander thought that the arrest "would impress upon them [the natives] with the fact that monarchy is dead." W. C. Wilder "wanted to know what was going to be done with her afterwards. Was it he asked, the idea to turn her adrift?" C. M. Cooke "was in favor of postponing her arrest until after the trials of Nowlein and Wilcox commenced, then if she was arrested she might be willing to give up her rights and abdicate the throne."[2]

1. *Pacific Commercial Advertiser*, January 15, 1895.
2. Hawaii State Archives, Foreign Office and Executive Files, Series 423, vol. 2, Minutes of the Executive Council, January 12, 1895.

January 14: "S. M. Damon, after more mature deliberation believed that the ex-queen should be arrested at once.... Minister King believed in sending Policemen to arrest her.... Mr. Dole said there was no legal evidence of the complicity of the ex-queen to cause her arrest as in the case of the others [the conspirators]. Mr. McCandless thought if she was put in the Executive building the natives would feel that the authorities were afraid to put her in any other place and she rightfully belonged there."[3]

January 16: "Nine A.M.... The matter of the arrest of Liliuokalani was again discussed, the time for arresting her having been set for ten A.M.... Mr. Smith said that the evidence was ready to proceed with the trial of the ringleaders of the rebellion.... At nine A.M. Deputy Marshall Brown and Police Captain R. W. Parker were presented, and an order from the Commander in Chief was given them to arrest Liliuokalani.... At 10:21 A.M. the officers returned to the Executive Building with Liliuokalani and her maid and delivered them to Lieut. Col. Fisher commanding. She was placed in confinement in the room lately occupied as the Auditor General office."[4]

Immediately following Liliuokalani's confinement, investigators searched Washington Place and took in quantities of the Queen's personal papers, including some of the diaries transcribed here, for use as evidence of her complicity in the revolution.

Trials of the conspirators commenced before a military court (as martial law was still in effect) on January 17 in what had been the Iolani Palace throne room. The first to be tried (January 20) was Robert Wilcox, and he was the only one of the major players who proudly announced that he was guilty of the charges.

Next came Samuel Nowlein on January 22. He supplied the court with details on the documents that the group had drawn up at Washington Place, including a draft of the proposed constitution and a document proclaiming the enactment of martial law. Then William Kaae, the Queen's private secretary, came to the stand and testified about the commissions he had drawn up of new cabinet ministers for an anticipated monarchical restoration, a list the ex-Queen's diary specifically mentioned.

### The Queen's Abdication, January 24, 1895

Liliuokalani formally abdicated the throne late on the morning of January 24, 1895, and declared the Hawaiian monarchy to be forever ended. Both the Queen's lawyers and Liliuokalani herself examined and amended the abdication document before she signed it; however, in her memoir[5] she describes doing so under duress. Some years later, Alfred S. Hartwell,

---

3. Hawaii State Archives, Foreign Office and Executive Files, Series 423, vol. 2, Minutes of the Executive Council, January 14, 1895.
4. Hawaii State Archives, Foreign Office and Executive Files, Series 423, vol. 2, Minutes of the Executive Council, January 16, 1895.
5. *Hawaii's Story*, 315–18.

*Iolani Palace throne room. The palace was the grandest structure in the islands when it was completed in 1882 and included the latest technologies and conveniences—telephones, gaslights (which were soon replaced with electric lights), and indoor plumbing. The gas-fueled chandeliers shown here were replaced in 1886 with cut-glass electric chandeliers that are still in the throne room today.*
Hawaii State Archives, circa 1885

chief justice of the Supreme Court, who drew up the instrument, described the circumstances in a meeting of the Hawaiian Historical Society, reported by the *Pacific Commercial Advertiser*:

¶ Judge Hartwell said that in January 1895, the Queen, then being a prisoner in the palace, following her arrest at the time of the 1895 uprising, Paul Neumann, Charles B. Wilson, and Samuel Parker came to his office and asked him to draft an abdication for the Queen. This was the first intimation that had come to him of any such thought or purpose on her part. He asked these men if they had come from the Queen or really represented her, and if she knew of their mission. They replied that she did. He said that if he drafted an abdication it would be a drastic instrument. Paul Neumann [the Queen's attorney] replied that that was why they had come to him.

Mr. Hartwell then drafted the instrument using a lead pencil and yellow paper of legal size, such as is frequently used in lawyers' offices for first drafts of documents. Drafting abdications, the Chief Justice said... was something he had not often been called upon to do.... When he had completed his draft, W. L. Stanley, who was then in his office... made two copies of it.... One of these copies in Stanley's handwriting was then given to Charles B. Wilson to take to the Queen for her perusal and revision. Mr. Hartwell went to President Dole and stated that Wilson wanted to see the Queen on a matter that he thought it was proper he should see her about, and on that representation President Dole issued orders that Wilson should be allowed to see the Queen.[6]

Later Wilson returned with the copy with some changes in it, and Mr. Stanley made a third copy embodying these changes. This was given to Wilson. He went again to the Queen and returned with still other changes, slight ones, in this copy.

These changes were incorporated in a draft made on parchment paper, Mr. Hartwell having some in his office at that time. Mr. Hartwell then suggested to Neumann, Wilson, and Parker that they get Judge Widemann, W. G. Irwin, and Curtis P. Iaukea, and that they go as witnesses to the execution of the paper, and that they take Mr. Stanley along as a notary to take the Queen's acknowledgment. These three men were sent for. They wanted Mr. Hartwell to accompany them. This he demurred to doing, but finally, on their insistence, he assented.

Arriving at the palace, they all went into the part of the palace reserved for the Queen. There Paul Neumann asked the Queen if she had read the instrument and understood it. She replied that she had read it and understood it. Then he read it to her very carefully and very slowly, and she again said she understood it. Parker then took

---

6. Corroborating this statement, the minutes of the Executive Council outlined the procedure: "Mr. Dole stated that last evening Messrs. A. S. Hartwell, Paul Neumann, Sam Parker, and C. B. Wilson called to see him and asked if they could call upon Liliuokalani to present to her for her consideration and signature a communication addressed to the Government. They gave no information as to the contents or purport of the proposed document. It was decided to grant their request." Hawaii State Archives, Foreign Office and Executive Files, Series 423, vol. 2, Minutes of the Executive Council, January 23, 1895.

the pen and gave it to her and she signed it. Mr. Stanley then took her acknowledgment of it in the usual form—that is, she executed the instrument voluntarily and for the purposes therein set forth.

The whole party, except the Queen, then crossed the hall to President Dole's office, now the Governor's office, and presented the abdication to him. This was the first knowledge of the abdication, up to that time, no one except those mentioned having any information concerning it.[7,8]

The following three documents related to Queen Liliuokalani's abdication are in the Hawaii State Archives, Foreign Office and Executive Files: the letter of abdication, a notarial acknowledgment of the same, and the ex-Queen's oath of allegiance to the Republic of Hawaii. The first and third of these are written in a secretarial hand and are duly signed by "Liliuokalani Dominis." Additionally, each sheet of the abdication letter has also been signed "Liliuokalani Dominis" on the blank left margin of each sheet. The three documents have remained riveted together since the day of their execution. On the verso of the last sheet is the following penciled endorsement: "Letter of Liliuokalani to the President. Received at 11:20 A.M. January 24th, 1895."

¶ Island of Oahu, Honolulu
January 24th, 1895
To the Honorable Sanford Ballard Dole,
President of the Republic of Hawaii.

Sir:

After full and free consultation with my personal friends, and with my legal advisors, both before and since my detention by Military order in the Executive Building, and acting in conformity with their advice and also upon my own free volition, and in pursuance of my unalterable belief and understanding of my duty to the people of Hawaii and to their highest and best interests, and also for the sake of those misguided Hawaiians and others who have recently engaged in rebellion against the Republic, and in an attempt to restore me to the position of Queen which I held prior to the 17th day of January 1893, and without any claim that I shall become entitled by reason of anything that I may now say or do, to any other or different treatment or consideration at the hands of the government than I otherwise could and might legally receive, I now desire to express and make known, and do hereby express and make known to yourself, as the only lawful and recognized head of the Government, and to all the people of the Hawaiian Islands, whether or not they have yet become citizens of the Republic, or are

*The Letter of Abdication
January 24, 1895*

---

7. The minutes of the Executive Council stated: "At 11:20 A.M. Messrs. C. B. Wilson and Samuel Parker were introduced and stated that at the request of the ex-Queen they presented a document [of abdication]." A transcription of the document followed. Hawaii State Archives, Foreign Office and Executive Files, Series 423, vol. 2, Minutes of the Executive Council, January 24, 1895.

8. *Pacific Commercial Advertiser*, August 28, 1908.

or have been adherents to the late monarchy, and also to all diplomatic and other foreign representative in the Hawaiian Islands, to all of whom I respectfully request you to take this statement and action of mine to be made known as soon as may be, as follows, namely:

First, In order to avoid any possibility of doubt or misunderstanding on the subject, although I do not think that any doubt or misunderstanding is either proper or possible, I do hereby fully and equivocally admit and declare that the Government of the Republic of Hawaii is the lawful Government of the Hawaiian Islands and that the late Hawaiian Monarchy is finally and forever ended and no longer of any legal or actual validity, force, or effect whatsoever; and I do hereby for ever absolve all persons whomsoever, whether in the Hawaiian Islands or elsewhere, from all and every manner of allegiance, or official obligation, or duty to me and my heirs and successors for ever, and I hereby declare to all and such persons in the Hawaiian Islands, that I consider them as bound in duty and honor henceforth to support and sustain the Government of the Republic of Hawaii.

Second, For myself, my heirs and successors, I do hereby and without any mental reservation or modification, and fully, finally, unequivocally, irrevocably, and forever abdicate, renounce, and release unto the Government of the Republic of Hawaii and to its legitimate successors forever, all claims of pretensions whatsoever to the late throne of Hawaii or to the late monarchy of Hawaii, or to any part, or to the existing, or to any future Government of Hawaii, or under or by reason of any present or formerly existing constitution, statute laws, position, right, or claim of any and every kind, name, and nature whatsoever, and whether the same consist of pecuniary or property considerations of personal status, hereby forever renouncing, disowning, and declining all rights, claims, demands, privileges, honors, emoluments, titles, and prerogatives whatsoever under or by virtue of any former, or the existing Government, constitution, statute, law, or custom of the Hawaiian Islands whatsoever, save and excepting only such rights and privileges as belong to me in common with all private citizens of, or residents in, the Republic of Hawaii.

Third, I do hereby respectfully implore for such misguided Hawaiians and others who have been concerned in the late rebellion against the Republic of Hawaii such degree of executive clemency as the Government may deem to be consistent with its duty to the community, and such as a due regard for its violated laws may permit.

Fourth, It is my sincere desire henceforth to live in absolute privacy and retirement from all publicity or even appearance of being concerned in the public affairs of the Hawaiian Islands, further than to express, as I do now, and shall always continue to do my most sincere hopes for the welfare and prosperity of Hawaii and its people, under and subject to the Government of the Republic of Hawaii.

Fifth, I hereby offer and present my duly certified oath of allegiance to the Republic of Hawaii.

Sixth, I have caused the foregoing statement to be prepared, and drawn, and have signed the same, without having received the slightest suggestion from the President of Hawaii or from any member or official of the Government concerning the same or any part thereof, or concerning any action or course of my own in the premises.

Relying upon the magnanimity of the Government of the Republic, and upon its protection, I have the honor to be Mr. President

very respectfully<br>
your obedient servant<br>
[signed]<br>
Liliuokalani Dominis

On this 24th day of January A.D. 1895, the foregoing was in our presence read over and considered carefully and Deliberately by Liliuokalani Dominis, and she the said Liliuokalani Dominis thereupon in our presence declared that the same was a correct exact and full statement of her wishes and acts in the premises, which statement she declared to us that she desired to sign and acknowledge in our presence as her own free act and deed; and she thereupon signed the same in our presence and declared the same to be her free act and deed. In witness thereof we have at the request of the said Liliuokalani Dominis and in her presence hereunto subscribed our names as attesting witnesses at the Executive Building in Honolulu on the Island of Oahu, this 24th day of January A.D. 1895:

[signed]<br>
Wm. G. Irwin<br>
H. A. Widemann<br>
Samuel Parker<br>
S. Kaluahookano<br>
Charles B. Wilson<br>
Paul Neumann

---

¶ Honolulu,
Island of Oahu.

On this 24th day of January A.D. 1895, personally appeared before me Liliuokalani Dominis known to me to be the person described in and who executed the foregoing instrument who acknowledged to me that she executed the same freely and voluntarily and for the uses and purposes therein set forth.

W. L. Stanley, Notary Public<br>
[seal follows]

*Oath of Allegiance
January 24, 1895*

¶ Honolulu, Island of Oahu
Hawaiian Islands.

I, Liliuokalani Dominis, solemnly swear in the presence of Almighty God that I will support the Constitution, Laws, and Government of the Republic of Hawaii, and will not either directly or indirectly engage or assist in the restoration of establishment of a monarchical form of Government in the Hawaiian Islands.

[*signed*] Liliuokalani Dominis

Subscribed and sworn to before me this 24th day of January A.D. 1895

W. L. Stanley, Notary Public
[*seal follows*]

## *Liliuokalani's Trial*

Liliuokalani's trial began on February 5 and occupied the next three days. The ex-Queen declined to plead regarding the 13 specifications of the charge of misprision of treason, that is, of having "had knowledge of the commission of Treason against the Republic of Hawaii, and the Government thereof, and having such knowledge concealed the same, and did not as soon as might be disclose and make known the same to some member of the Executive Council, or to some Judge of a Court of Record, or to the Marshall, or to some Sheriff or Deputy Sheriff." Liliu's decline to plead was entered into the record as "Not guilty," and Paul Neumann then defended her.

*Attorney Paul Neumann defending the Queen before a military
tribunal in the throne room converted to a courtroom.*
San Francisco Examiner, February 16, 1895, Hawaii State Archives

## Counterrevolution of 1895

Liliuokalani denied any knowledge of preparations for the failed revolution, but witnesses from her inner circle, and entries from her own diaries (taken from those that the government had earlier seized for evidence), were cited as direct evidence that she was in fact familiar with many (if not all) the details of the event, had been involved in the preparations of both a new constitution and a proclamation declaring martial law upon her restoration, and had just before the event signed commissions for proposed new cabinet ministers. Those testifying for the prosecution were Charles Clark, the husband of her companion Jennie Clark; Joseph Kaauwai, a Washington Place retainer; William Kaae, who had been her secretary; and Samuel Nowlein.

Liliuokalani did not testify on her own account, but on February 7, 1895, her carefully prepared response, written in Hawaiian and interpreted by W. L. Wilcox, was read to the court and filed with the proceedings. It is the only contemporary statement about the counterrevolution that the Queen made, and it is as follows:[9]

> ¶ The movement undertaken by the Hawaiians last month was absolutely commenced without my knowledge, sanction, consent, or assistance, directly or indirectly, and this fact is in truth, well known to those who took part in it.
>
> I received no information from anyone in regard to arms which were or which were to be procured, nor of any men who were induced, or to be induced, to join in any such uprising.
>
> I do not know why this information should have been withheld from me, unless it was with a view to my personal safety or as a precautionary measure. It would not have received my sanction and I can assure the gentlemen of this Commission that, had I known of any such intention, I would have dissuaded the promoters from such a venture. But I will add that had I known, their secrets would have been mine and inviolately preserved.
>
> That I intended to change my Cabinet and to appoint certain officers of the kingdom, in the event of my restoration, I will admit; but that I, or anyone known to me, had, in part or in whole, established a new government is not true. Before the 24th day of January, 1895, the day upon which I formally abdicated, and called upon my people to recognize the Republic of Hawaii as the only lawful Government of these Islands, and to support that Government, I claim that I had the right to select a Cabinet in anticipation of a possibility, and [the] history of other governments supports this right. I was not intimidated into abdicating, but followed the counsel of able and generous friends and well-wishers who advised me that such an act would restore peace and good will among my people; vitalize the progress and prosperity

---

9. The record of Liliuokalani's trial is in the Hawaii State Archives, National Guard of Hawaii, Series 148, February 6–8, 1895. The ex-Queen's statement read during the trial, and transcribed here, is part of that file.

of the Islands, and induce the actual Government to deal leniently, mercifully, and charitably, and impassionately with those who resorted to arms for the purpose of displacing a government in the formation of which they had no voice or control; and which they themselves had seen established by force of arms.

I acted of my own free will, and wish the world to know that I have asked no immunity or favor myself nor pleaded my abdication as a petition for mercy. My actions were dictated by the sole aim of doing good to my beloved country and of alleviating the positions and pains of those who unhappily and unwisely resorted to arms to regain an independence, which they thought had been unjustly wrested from them.

As you deal with them, so I pray that the Almighty God may deal with you in your hours of trial.

To my regret, much has been said about the danger which threatened foreign women and children, and about the bloodthirstiness of the Hawaiians and the outrages which would have been perpetuated by them if they had succeeded in their attempt to overthrow the Republican Government.

They who know the Hawaiian temper and disposition understand that there was no foundation for any such fears; the behavior of the rebels to those foreigners whom they captured and held shows that there was no malignancy in the hearts of the Hawaiians at all. It would have been sad indeed if the doctrines of the Christian Missionary Fathers, taught to my people by them and those who succeeded them, should have fallen like the seed in the parable upon barren ground.

I must deny your right to try me in the manner and by the Court which you have called together for this purpose. In your actions you violate your own Constitution and laws which are now the Constitution and laws of the land.

There may be in your consciences, a warrant for your action, in what you may deem a necessity of the times, but you cannot find any such warrant for any such action in any settled, civilized, or Christian land. All who uphold you in this unlawful proceeding may scorn and despise my words, but the offense of breaking and setting aside for a specific purpose the laws of your own making and disregarding all justice and fairness may be to them and to you the source of an unhappy and much to be regretted legacy.

I would ask you to consider that your Government is on trial before the whole civilized world, and that in accordance with your actions and decisions will you yourselves be judged. The happiness and prosperity of Hawaii are henceforth in your hands alone as its rulers.

You are commencing a new era in its history. May the Divine Providence grant you the wisdom to lead the nation into the paths of forbearance, forgiveness and peace, and to create and consolidate a united people ever anxious to advance in the way of civilization outlined by the American fathers of liberty and religion.

In concluding my statement, I thank you for the courtesy you have shown me, not as your former Queen, but as an humble citizen of this land and as a woman. I assure you, who believe you are faithfully fulfilling a public duty, I shall never harbor any resentment or cherish any ill feelings towards you whatever may be your decision.[10]

[*signed*] Liliuokalani Dominis

At a meeting of the Executive Council on February 26, President Dole suggested the following sentence for Liliuokalani Dominis: "Upon the recommendation of the Military Commission that the accused Liliuokalani Dominis be imprisoned for the term of five years and pay a fine of five thousand dollars and be imprisoned until such fine is paid, such imprisonment to be in the Executive Building or elsewhere as the President and Commander in Chief may direct." The proposition met with the approval of the Executive Council.[11]

On February 27, Liliuokalani was informed that she had been found guilty of seven of the 13 specifications under which she had been charged. and received a sentence of a $5,000 fine and five years' imprisonment. Her prison was a former upstairs guestroom in Iolani Palace, and there she would remain for six months. The diary she kept during her imprisonment follows.

10. This statement of February 7, 1895, was written in Hawaiian and English and placed with Liliuokalani's trial documents. The original signed document is in Hawaiian and is accompanied by a contemporary English version on which is noted that it is a careful translation. The text reproduced here is from that English version. Hawaii State Archives, National Guard of Hawaii, Series 148, Proceedings.

11. Hawaii State Archives, Foreign Office and Executive Files, Series 423, vol. 2, February 26, 1895.

*Ahahui Hawaii Aloha Aina o ko Hawaii Paeaina (Hawaiian Patriotic League of the Hawaiian Islands) was formed in 1893 by Joseph Nawahi to protest Hawaii's annexation to the United States and to maintain the autonomy of Hawaii. During the Queen's imprisonment in 1895, Nawahi founded the Hawaiian patriotic newspaper* Ke Aloha Aina. *In 1897, the league sponsored an anti-annexation petition reaching all island districts. The resulting document, titled "Palapala Hoopii Kue Hoohuiaina, Petition Against Annexation," was transported to Washington, DC, in December 1897 with over 21,200 signatures affixed on more than 550 sheets.*

**Front row:** *S. K. Aki and John K. Prendergast.* **Second row:** *J. W. Bipikane, Joseph Nawahi, J. A. Cummins, John E. Bush, J. K. Kaunamano, and John L. Kaulukou.* **Third row:** *Sam M. Kaaukai, H. S. Swinton, L.W.P. Kanealii, John Sam Kekukahiko, D. W. Pua, A. K. Palekaluhi, F. S. Keiki, J. Kekipi, and J. K. Merseburg.* **Back row:** *J. K. Kaulia and John Mahiai Kaneakua.*

J. J. Williams, circa 1893, courtesy of the Library of Congress

# 1895

This diary has been assembled from two fragments, the first being a leaf of diary entries for February 28–May 21, 1895, found on the verso of a letter that Liliuokalani received while a prisoner in Iolani Palace from Lieutenant John Good of the National Guard of Hawaii. To this there have been added several dated remarks found on the calling card of a friend.[1] I have also included a letter from Liliuokalani to Princess Kaiulani, dated July 31, 1895,[2] in which she describes her living conditions while under house arrest.

The text of the letter from Lieutenant John Good, dated February 28, 1895, and addressed to "Mrs. Liliuokalani Dominis," is as follows: "Madam. Until otherwise directed, it will be the duty of the old and the new Officers of the Day to present themselves at your quarters, for the purpose of verifying your presence. This will be at about 7.50 A.M. each day just after Guard Mounting. This verification will commence this morning."[3] The Queen thereafter utilized the blank portion and verso of that letter as a memorandum of the daily drill. The terse and tedious diary entries reflect the situation in which she now found herself. I have expanded the abbreviations in the original document for the ease of the reader.

The military officers mentioned in this brief diary are: Captain John Good (b. 1849, Rochester, New York–d. 1903, San Francisco)—a Hawaii arrival in 1888, he is now remembered only as the man who shot Leialoha on January 17, 1893, the day of the overthrow; Lieutenant Arthur Coyne (b. 1867, London, Ontario, Canada–d. February 28, 1942, Honolulu); Captain Charles W. Ziegler (b. 1859, Germany–d. 1938, Honolulu); and Lieutenant Ludwig (of whom nothing is known).

*Thursday, February 28, 1895.* 7.45 A.M. Capt. Good and a young Lt. called.
*Friday, March 1st.* 7.40 A.M. 1st Lieut. Four [P.M.] next officer.
*Saturday, March 2nd.* 7.50 A.M. Capt. Good and Lieut. Ludwig.
*Sunday, March 3d.* 7.50 A.M. Capt. Good and Lieut. Coyne.
*Monday, March 4th.* 7.50 A.M. Lieut. Coyne and Lieut. Ludwig.
*Tuesday, March 5th.* 7.50 A.M. Capt. Good and Lieut. Ludwig.

THE DIARY FOR 1895
28 FEB–21 MAY
Hawaii State Archives

1. Bishop Museum Archives, Liliuokalani Collection.
2. Hawaii State Archives, Cleghorn Collection.
3. Hawaii State Archives, Liliuokalani Collection, Box 7, Folder 71.

*One of the nine blocks of a patchwork crazy quilt that Liliuokalani, her companion Eveline Townsend Wilson, and others worked on together during the Queen's imprisonment in Iolani Palace, 1895. Describing her confinement to Princess Kaiulani in a letter of July 31, 1895, Liliu wrote, "My life is not a very dreary one after all, considering. I have Eveline Wilson with me constantly" (Hawaii State Archives).*

*This block includes the name John Henry Nalanieha Tuaorai Tamarii Wilson, the child of Eveline and Charles Wilson. John Wilson served as a longtime mayor of Honolulu. Mrs. Wilson's mother, Harriet Blanchard Townsend, was the Queen's seamstress.*
The Friends of Iolani Palace

*Same date.* A Sergeant knocked at the door and said we will be allowed from today to walk the veranda after five P.M. After gates are closed out in the yard.

*Wednesday, March 6th.* 7.50 A.M. Lieut. Coyne.

*Same date.* 1.15 P.M. Lieut. Coyne told Eveline [Wilson] we could go out on either veranda any time of the day. Seven P.M. had our walk on the front veranda.

*Same date.* 5.20 P.M. the Sergeant said there was a wrangle about my being allowed to go out.

*Thursday, March 7th.* 7.50 A.M. Lieuts. Coyne and Ludwig.

*Friday, March 8th.* 7.50 A.M. Capt. Good and Lieut. Ludwig.

*Saturday, March 9th.* 7.50 A.M. Capt. Good and Lieut. Coyne.

*Sunday, March 10.* 7.50 A.M. Lieuts. Coyne and Ludwig.

*Monday, March 11.* 7.50 A.M. Capt. Good and Ludwig.

*Tuesday, March 12.* Capt. Good and Ludwig.

*Wednesday, March 13.* Lieuts. Coyne and Ludwig.

*Thursday, March 14.* Lieut. Coyne and Capt. [Good].

*Friday, March 15.* Capt. [Good] and Ludwig.

*Saturday, March 16.* Lieut. Coyne and Ludwig.

*Sunday, March 17.* Capt. Good and Lieut. Ludwig.

*Monday, March 18.* C. [Captain Good] and Lieut. Coyne.

*Same date.* [Paul Puhiula Kalakua] Kanoa died.

*Tuesday, March 19.* Coyne and "Don't know his name."

*Same date.* 11 A.M. Mr. Damon said Fisher would see what he could do for my going to dine [?] and comfort. Kanoa was buried and Mary P. McGuire dead.[4]

*Same date.* 12.40 P.M. C. W. Ashford called, said he would turn over his cases to W. Foster.[5] G. C. Potter present.

*Wednesday, March 20.* Capt. Good and Capt. Ziegler. Wilson called eight A.M. Said Mr. Damon will call to see me as he will go to San Francisco. He [Damon] sailed [by the *Australia*, March 20, 1895].

*Thursday, March 21.* Capt. Good and Lieut. Coyne.

*Friday, March 22.* Only Capt. Ziegler.

*Saturday, March 23.* Capt. Good and Ziegler.

*Sunday, March 24.* Capt. Good and Lieut. Ludwig and officer of day.

*Monday, March 25.* Capt. Good and Ziegler.

---

4. The latter statement was an error. Mary McGuire (wife of James McGuire of Kona, Hawaii) lived until July 1, 1917.

5. William Foster, attorney at law and notary public, 13 Kaahumanu Street.

*Tuesday, March 26.* [Blank.]

*Wednesday, March 27.* Capt. Good and Ludwig.

*Thursday, March 28.* Capt. Ziegler and Ludwig.

*Friday, March 29.* Capt. Good and Ludwig.

*Saturday, March 30.* Capt. Good and Ziegler.

*Sunday, March 31.* Good and Ziegler.

**Monday, April 1.** Ziegler and Ludwig.

*Tuesday, April 2.* Good and Ludwig.

*Wednesday, April 3.* Good and Ziegler.

[The following entries of May 16–21, 1895, are transcribed from a calling card found in Liliu's 1898 diary at the Bishop Museum Archives. On the recto is "Me ke Aloha o Mrs. J. O. Carter" (with the love of Mrs. J. O. Carter) and the date of May 18. Added in pencil is the note "frosted cakes from Mrs. J. O. Carter."]

***Thursday, May 16.*** Mr. S. M. Damon called on me. I received him in our Boudoir as our bedroom was being painted. He asked if he could do something for me & had told Tax Collector not to press me, that I could pay as I had property enough. Would send some plants to decorate. I said I couldn't do more but was doing my best through correspondence with Joe Heleluhe. He said he would see Mr. Dole about getting permission for Joe [to see me?]—If I would send Mr. Wilson to him.

*Friday, May 17.* Mr. S. M. Damon sent a pot of dwarf palm, two pots of Maidenhair fern.

*Monday, May 20.* Good news. Mr. D. [Damon] told Mr. W. [Wilson] that before the Legislature sits, we are all to be released except a few. Was told it was pressed on them by W. who told them a petition would be sent in to the Legis[lature] which would [illegible] them [illegible] so they yielded.

*Tuesday, May 21.* D [illegible] one chair one rock[er] one table—next day one rug—[Entry ends thus. No further diary fragments for this year have been located.]

---

Liliu wrote a very interesting letter to Princess Kaiulani describing her present mode of living and putting the best face on the situation. It is as follows:

¶ Iolani Hale, July 31, 1895.

My dear Kaiulani . . . I am still in my prison—Archie [Cleghorn, Kaiulani's father] will tell you all about it. He was here one day last week to see me and again this morning to bid me good-bye before leaving. He came with Mr. Potter,[6] a clerk in the Foreign Office. Your father

---

6. George Clinton Potter (b. 1862, Oakland, California–d. January 27, 1942, Maui) was the husband (married in 1886) of Edith Irmgaard Macfarlane. Potter was military aide to President Dole, had been the secretary of both the board of health and the board of education, and was in the foreign office 1893–1900.

tells me he will probably see you in Scotland.... There is no knowing how this unhappy state of affairs will end. I don't think they know themselves. I hear so little what is going on outside, and very seldom see the papers, but nevertheless days go by very quickly and I manage to keep in good spirits. Since my imprisonment, I have been allowed every comfort and my friends send me flowers, fruit, cake, jellies, soups, and all sorts of delicacies. After office hours I am allowed to go on the verandas and permission [is] given to go downstairs around the house, but not to go within a hundred feet of the fence—but I don't like to go down on account of the soldiers [as] there are so many—the whole basement is full of soldiers. Then some of the officers have their lady friends who stare, so that I prefer to remain in my room till evening when we take our walks out on the veranda. Such lovely flowers are sent in pots all in bloom and my room is a perfect bower of ferns and flowers. All these are a source of pleasure to me and I have two cages of canary birds who are just beginning to sing again after moulting. My life is not a very dreary one after all, considering. I have Eveline Wilson with me constantly until Saturday, and Sunday she goes out to see her family, while Milaina Ahia comes in to stay with me in the meantime. Every morning we rise, we arrange our room, then have our devotions. After that we wait for the visit of the Officers or Military Guards whose duty it is to see and report to the Superior Officers or Colonel that I am safe, then after breakfast and for the rest of the day we are occupied in sewing, fancy work, or darning stockings or mending some rent in our garments or reading—or composing music. And so the day goes by quietly enough. My steward Kalehua brings my meals from Washington Place three times a day, and is a good faithful servant.

These are the only ones allowed to see me. I had almost forgotten to mention Mr. Wilson, who comes in once or twice a week when he has anything to communicate to me. I do all my business with my agent Joe Heleluhe by correspondence, and you cannot imagine what amount of paper I use—although it is a little awkward, still he understands my wishes and manages pretty well.

Your Affectionate Aunt,<br>
Liliuokalani[7]

---

7. Hawaii State Archives, Cleghorn Collection, Box 4.

*Waikahalulu Falls, Nuuanu Stream, circa 1890. Liliuokalani donated her land along Nuuanu Stream to the city of Honolulu. It is known today as Liliuokalani Botanical Garden.*
Hawaii State Archives, circa 1890

# Release and Freedom, 1895–96

On September 3, 1895, President Sanford B. Dole and his advisors made the decision to release Liliuokalani from her detention in Iolani Palace. The minutes of the Executive Council for this date state: "Voted. To recommend to the Council of State that Liliuokalani be released from imprisonment subject to remand on the order of the President, and that she be allowed to reside at such place and subject to such regulations during the remainder of the term of her sentence as the President may direct."[1] Three days later President Dole addressed the following letter[2] to Liliuokalani:

> ¶ Executive Chamber
> Honolulu, Sept. 6, 1895
> Mrs. Liliuokalani Dominis
> Executive Building
>
> Madam: By the advice of the Cabinet and Council of State, I have this day signed an order releasing you from confinement in the Executive Building, which order provides that you may be remanded to confinement at any time upon the order of the President, and also that your enlargement is subject to such conditions as the President may from time to time require.
>
> Until further notice, as conditions of your enlargement you will be required to occupy Washington Place in Honolulu as your residence, and will not be allowed to absent yourself therefrom overnight without the written consent of the President or a member of the Cabinet.
>
> During the term of your sentence, or until the same is modified as to time, you are required to live in a quiet, unostentatious manner and to abstain from having political meetings or other gatherings at your residence or attending such meetings elsewhere.
>
> You will not be allowed to have a retinue or guard, and your attendants will be limited to necessary domestics the number of which is hereby fixed at thirteen men and eight women, besides children. Mr. Wilson and family will be allowed to reside at Washington Place if you desire. In regard to receiving calls, I would call your attention to the impropriety of receiving others under the circumstances than personal acquaintances and those coming on business.

1. Hawaii State Archives, Foreign Office and Executive Files, Series 423, vol. 3, Minutes of the Executive Council, September 3, 1895.
2. Hawaii State Archives, Foreign Office and Executive Files, Series 419, vol. 3, Minutes of the Executive Council, September 6, 1895.

*Washington Place. On June 7, 1894, Liliu wrote in her diary, "I am surrounded by everything that is beautiful, the lovely foliage, the flowers in my flower garden, and the birds that sing so sweetly all tend to make my life one of contentment, and I may add my Maker of all these things watches over me all [and] tends to make my life a happy one."*
Alfred Mitchell, circa 1886, Bishop Museum Archives

Trusting to your own judgment and good faith to carry out the spirit of these instructions, I would intimate that your conduct will have influence upon any future consideration of the further modification of your sentence.

Sanford B. Dole

The release took place on September 7, 1895, and was reported in the *Pacific Commercial Advertiser* two days later:

¶ At 3:30 P.M. on Friday, the 7th, an orderly on guard at the Executive Building announced to the ex-queen, the approach of Colonel McLean who carried the parole-pardon signed by the President [Dole]. On entering the room with Major [George] Potter, the ex-queen, clothed in a holoku, was seated by a table with her work basket and a basket of flowers upon it; and on the floor was a glass vase filled with water and holding goldfish. Mr. and Mrs. C. B. Wilson were present. Colonel McLean did not require her to rise but proceeded to read her the contents of the parole pardon instrument. Major Potter followed and read a letter of instructions or regulations, which required her to maintain her residence in Washington Place with freedom of movement over the island, but without privilege of residing in any other place permanently or temporarily, without authority from the Government. Col. McLean then informed her that the guards were removed and she was free. She smiled and thanked him.

At 5:30 the ex-queen, dressed in a black skirt and black hat, descended the steps of the Beretania side of the building without assistance and with ease, and in company with Mr. and Mrs. Wilson entered a carriage and was driven to Washington Place. Later on, several wagons containing her effects used while she was imprisoned were taken to the same place.[3]

The minutes of the Executive Council on February 6, 1896, note:

¶ President Dole brought up the matter of the confinement of Mrs. Dominis under the conditions mentioned in her letter of release and asked for the sense of the Cabinet on the matter. It was decided to write another letter to her impressing the appreciation of the Cabinet for the good faith with which she observed the requirements of the former letter and releasing her from all restrictions save leaving the Island of Oahu without the consent of the Cabinet.[4]

The next day President Dole addressed Liliuokalani as follows:[5]

---

3. *Pacific Commercial Advertiser*, September 9, 1895.
4. Hawaii State Archives, Foreign Office and Executive Files, Series 423, vol. 3, Minutes of the Executive Council, February 6, 1896.
5. Hawaii State Archives, Foreign Office and Executive Files, Series 419, vol. 3, Minutes of the Executive Council, February 7, 1896.

> ¶ Executive Building
> Honolulu, Feb. 7, 1896
> Mrs. Liliuokalani Dominis
> Washington Place
>
> Madame: With the advice of the Cabinet, I take pleasure in modifying the restrictions placed upon your freedom at the time of your release from confinement.
>
> Until further notice, only the observance on your part of the following conditions will be required by the Government.
>
> Not to leave the island of Oahu without the consent of the President or a member of the Cabinet.
>
> I desire to express my appreciation of the good faith with which you have observed the requirements of a former letter.
>
> [*signed*] Sanford B. Dole

Finally, on October 23, 1896, the Council of State met in the former throne room of Iolani Palace, on which occasion the prime object of discussion was Liliuokalani's pardon. Minister S. M. Damon stated: "The past was in history and the unpleasant features would soon be forgotten in the new era which is dawning upon us."[6] The members unanimously agreed to endorse the recommendation of the Executive Council that they grant a full pardon.

At the end of 1896, Liliuokalani determined to make a trip to the United States, an event that surprised everyone in town. On Friday morning, December 4, 1896, she paid a courtesy visit to Sanford and Anna Dole at their Emma Street home, and Dole wrote F. M. Hatch in Washington as follows:

> ¶ Honolulu, December 4, 1896. Liliuokalani called on me this morning to say good-bye, as she intends to go to the United States by the SS *China*, which sails at ten o'clock. Her leaving seems to be very sudden as there have been no rumors of it; we had no information in regard to it until she called this morning. She tells me that she is going through to Boston to visit her husband's friends. I think she said something about seeing her niece but did not say whether she was going across to England for that purpose or whether her niece would visit her in America. She purposes to stay on her way about a week in San Francisco. I do not know that her trip has any political significance whatever; of course it is possible she hopes to make sentiment in America against annexation but it may be that she is simply going on a private trip for a change.... It would seem that if it was a move for political reasons the information in regard to it would have been likely to have got out before this time, but not a soul seemed to have heard of it.... Joe Heleluhe and Mrs. [Kia] Nahaolelua go with her.[7]

---

6. Hawaii State Archives, Foreign Office and Executive Files, Series 419, vol. 3, Minutes of the Executive Council, October 23, 1896.

7. Hawaii State Archives, Hatch Papers.

A brief article on the Queen's departure appeared in the *Advertiser*:

> ¶ Ex-Queen Liliuokalani, attended by her agent, Joseph Heleluhe, and Mrs. Kia Nahaolelua, left for San Francisco on the PMSS *China* yesterday morning much to the surprise of her many friends, a few of whom learned of the projected departure just in time to get down to the wharf and say good-bye.
>
> Liliuokalani arrived on the Pacific Mail Wharf just a few minutes previous to the departure of the *China*, after having called on President Dole and his wife to advise them of her intended departure. She was met at the foot of the gangplank and escorted aboard by J. O. Carter.
>
> As the *China* slowly backed away from the wharf she stood on the deck and waved her adieus to friends on shore.
>
> Liliuokalani goes abroad simply for a change, hoping to better her health thereby. She will spend some time on the Pacific Coast, and then proceed East, perhaps making Europe her final destination.[8]

Interesting editorial remarks on Liliuokalani's departure also appeared in the same issue:

> ¶ Some of the good people of the community have seen fit to become very much excited because ex-Queen Liliuokalani decided to suddenly and quietly depart for the United States on the steamer *China*, Friday morning. In fact the opposition are almost inclined to think that the political world is coming to an end.... We hasten to allay such erroneous opinions.... Liliuokalani, since the full pardon granted her by the Government, has a right to do just as she pleases.[9]

Liliuokalani and party arrived at Boston on Christmas Eve, 1896. They first put up at the Parker House, then sought more private quarters in a boardinghouse in Brookline. They were near the Queen's "cousins" (actually her late husband's cousins), Mr. and Mrs. William Lee. Lee was a partner in the then-famous publishing house of Lee and Shepard in Boston, the firm that Liliuokalani would choose to publish her memoir, *Hawaii's Story by Hawaii's Queen Liliuokalani*, in 1898. Sarah Lee immediately interested herself in promoting the interests of William Lee's distinguished cousin, becoming a principal editor of the Queen's manuscript and a lecturer on Hawaiian affairs.

8. *Pacific Commercial Advertiser*, December 6, 1895.
9. *Pacific Commercial Advertiser*, December 6, 1895.

*On June 16, 1897, President William McKinley sent an annexation treaty to the Senate. In response, Liliuokalani sent a protest to Secretary of State John Sherman the following day. The treaty languished during the congressional summer recess, and on August 10 Liliuokalani wrote a six-page letter (shown here and on p. 460) to J. O. Carter from the Ebbitt House hotel, Washington, DC. The letter addresses both personal business in Hawaii and the treaty situation.*
Hawaii State Archives

# A Year of Letters, 1897

January 1897 found the Queen and party in Boston but preparing to move to Washington, DC, where she would remain for the year. While no diary for 1897 has survived, excerpts taken from her letters to Joseph O. Carter (and one to James W. Robertson), all of which are in the Liliuokalani Collection and Liliuokalani Trust Collection of the Hawaii State Archives, are presented here in the form of diary entries.

Liliuokalani wrote her memoir *Hawaii's Story by Hawaii's Queen Liliuokalani* in the year 1897. A recently released edition of that work includes an extensive essay on the history of its production.[1] A brief summary of that history follows. *Hawaii's Story* did not achieve the Queen's most cherished hope of its being a means to maintain the independence of Hawaii, for the islands were annexed to the United States on August 12, 1898, less than a year after the book's publication in January.

The idea of writing a memoir seems to have originated with the Queen's relative, Mrs. William Lee of Boston, during Liliu's 1896–97 stay in that city. While in Boston, Liliu also engaged the services of Julius A. Palmer, a Boston newspaperman, who would become her collaborator. In a January 2, 1897, letter to Joseph O. Carter, she commented: "I've let Mr. Julius A. Palmer who offered his services do all my correspondence.... In that he has proved of much service." After settling in Washington, DC, she began dictating her story to him. It was essentially an "as told to" memoir.

In an 1897 article, Palmer had this to say about Liliu's literary endeavors: "Her occupation now is primarily that of a literary worker. She has translated from the Hawaiian of King Kalakaua into English, a manuscript which has just left the press, called 'The Hawaiian Tradition of the Creation of the World,'... she is about to publish a book of Hawaiian songs, ... and she has on hand also 'Leaves from My Diary,' which will be an autobiography. In the presentation of these works I was her stenographer and secretary."[2] Gorham D. Gilman, once a close friend of the Queen, annotated his copy of the completed memoir as follows: "Captain Julius A. Palmer... told me that he 'wrote every page' of the book.... Liliuokalani in the morning told him what her story was and he, in the afternoon, put it into shape."

Production of the manuscript continued throughout the year, with

---

1. *Hawaii's Story*, xv–xxxvi.
2. *Pacific Commercial Advertiser*, August 9, 1897.

(3)

that the most important signatures have already been affixed and only remains to be acted upon by the Senate. It is to be hoped that they will not reject it in the House. I am told there will be a strong opposition made by the Democrats at the coming session. The day for the opening will be the 6th of December. People or members will be straggling in and when Christmas arrives will all go home again till after New Years and some time will be occupied in internal affairs. Hatch is an indefatigable worker. I understand that he is going down to the islands to see Pearl Harbor. I suppose the P.G. will seize on him and never let him go out of their clutches until he leaves those shores. But I only wish you could meet him that he might see the honest side of our community. It is reported that Mr. Lewis Chairman of the foreign Committee is going down also. I have written to the two Political Leagues the Ahahui Aloha Aina and the two Hui Kalaiaina to make & send a protest to this nation to the President and to the Congress against the annexation of Hawaii to the United States asking that the Independence of these Islands should

expressly for Adamson, Judd & Castle that would buy it. I am pleased to see what action

last Friday. His business required his presence at home. We are all well. With love to all
I remain Yours sincerely
Kahuakaimi

drafts forwarded to and returned from Lee and Shepard in Boston. The publisher issued advance copies of the book early in January 1898. A review in the *Boston Evening Transcript*, January 15, 1898, referred to the work as "the Hawaiian ex-queen's literary sensation," and on January 22, 1898, the *New York Times* weighed in with an extensive and largely favorable review. Reaction in Hawaii was more mixed. The *Pacific Commercial Advertiser*, a pro-annexation paper, promptly published a long two-part review discussing the book's faults.[3] The Hawaiian-language newspaper *Ke Aloha Aina* announced receipt of a copy in its March 12 issue, and excerpts from the book translated into Hawaiian appeared in its columns starting on April 2. While that paper generally lauded the memoir, it did give voice to some local criticism regarding Liliu's remarks about the late Queen Emma, whom large segments of the Hawaiian population still regarded with the greatest of respect. Nevertheless, *Hawaii's Story* remains the only memoir written by any of the Hawaiian alii.

*January 2, 1897.* Brookline, Boston. My stay here has been very pleasant. I have taken rooms for our party at a very nice and respectable locality, just a little ways from Cousin William Lee's. Our hostess is a very nice little lady (single) and tries to make everything pleasant for us. There are other boarders in the house but we never see anything of them. We have our own private dining room. Everything is just as I want it to be.

I've let Mr. Julius A. Palmer who offered his services to do all my correspondence and answer the many letters and requests pouring in from all parts of the U.S. In that he has proved of much service.

*January 27.* Washington, DC. We arrived here last Saturday [January 23] 11 A.M.[4] It is very cold here—more so than in Boston where we have been staying a whole month. I could scarcely realize it for my visit there has been very pleasant amongst my friends.... Here we are at the Shoreham right opposite the White House. On Monday I asked to meet the President informally and the interview was arranged for three P.M. of the same day. He greeted me cordially—shaking hands all around, then came and sat near me. Fifteen minutes of pleasant conversation ... about the crooked streets of Boston, and cold weather in Washington—and how long I was going to stay. I told him I was uncertain of how long.

*February 17.* [Cairo Hotel.] I am happy to learn of the failure of the Annexationists at the meeting, but I may inform you that the feeling here is very much against it. Whenever it is mentioned it is immediately put aside.[5]

3. *Pacific Commercial Advertiser*, March 9–10, 1898.

4. The *New York Times*, Sunday, January 24, 1897, reported that the Queen had arrived at Washington "unexpectedly" and registered at the Shoreham Hotel as "Queen Liliuokalani of Hawaii." Accompanying her were Mrs. Kia Nahaolelua, Mr. Joseph Heleluhe, Julius A. Palmer (her acting secretary), and Mr. Henry Welcome of England. Welcome, the *Times* noted, "wears a blue uniform and is a sort of Major Domo."

5. Joseph O. Carter had written to Liliu from Honolulu on January 13: "The meeting to consider the annexation question held last evening was not satisfactory to the government of Mr. Dole, as it failed to call out the general public. W. O. Smith was overheard saying that

Gov. Perkins[6]... told Mr. Palmer that he has found out that he is all wrong in his first decision about the Hawaiian question. Senator Kilburn and others say the same, and all those who have met me and called on me with their wives are so pleased for they find me not as represented by the papers of the opposition. I have met 22 Congressmen and their wives.

*February 27.* It is pleasant for me to state that I am gaining more friends every day. The member from Maine[7] called and said it is his wish that the American people do what was right and offered to do what he could for me. How good of him. Mrs. J. F. Stallings[8] called to see me at my reception on Thursday—200 people came, 20 were wives and daughters of Congressmen and the rest Daughters of the Revolution who were here during their Women's Congress.

Through the assistance of Secretary of State Olney[9] and the coming Secretary of State Sherman,[10] and the help of Senators Elkins[11] and G[eorge] C. Perkins [of California]—two seats will be placed for me in the Diplomatic Gallery on the occasion of the coming inauguration. So you see how kind they all feel towards me?

---

In her published memoir, *Hawaii's Story*, Liliu writes of her visit to George Washington's mansion, Mount Vernon, in 1887. In early March 1897, she made a second visit to the mansion, which her Washington, DC, secretary and newspaper publicist, Julius A. Palmer, recorded. In a March letter, he forwarded an account of the same to the Honolulu newspaper *The Independent*, which published his account in its March 31, 1897, issue:

¶ A few days ago, without a day's notice, she decided to visit the home of General Washington at Mount Vernon, so with her party she went on the electric line which runs to that place from the city. No sooner was it known that Her Majesty was present as a visitor when word was sent to her that the apartments of the mansion, all of which are now closed by iron lattices would be opened specially for her party. This mark of attention and distinction was thankfully declined by the Queen, who replied that she preferred to inspect them from the outside with the other visitors. On her way back to the city her presence excited general notice and on leaving the cars, many were the requests for the

Mr. Hatch had said, in a dispatch to Mr. Dole: 'That a great mistake was made in letting the Queen leave the islands.'" Hawaii State Archives, Liliuokalani Collection.

6. George Clement Perkins (b. 1839–d. 1923) was a U.S. senator from California beginning in 1893, and formerly the governor (1879–83) of that state.

7. Seth L. Milliken (b. 1831–d. 1897) was a U.S. representative from Maine, 1883–97.

8. This was the wife of Representative Jesse F. Stallings of Alabama.

9. Richard Olney (b. 1835–d. 1917) was secretary of state (June 10, 1895–March 4, 1897) under President Grover Cleveland.

10. John Sherman (b. 1823–d. 1900) was secretary of state (1897–98) under President William McKinley.

11. Stephen Benton Elkins (b. 1841–d. 1911) was a Republican U.S. senator from West Virginia in 1895.

privilege of shaking her hand; to a few of these she graciously assented, and then to avoid too universal an ovation, she quietly withdrew to her carriage.

---

*March 16.* Smith, Hartwell, and Thurston are all here I see by the papers —working very hard to gain their cause. The P.G.s have given out that I was going to leave Washington to go to England. There is no truth in it.

I created great interest amongst the Washingtonians [at the inauguration of President McKinley on March 4, 1897] by sitting in the Diplomatic gallery, and the two Secretaries of State (the incoming and the outgoing) were the ones who gave me two seats there.... You ought to have seen Hatch when he heard of it. He abused the Secretaries and all who had anything to do with it—much to our amusement—and to those in power here. I wish you would tell Mr. S. C. Allen this. It seems to me I could just see him lean back and laugh with all his might. It was a grand occasion. The ... galleries were filled. The Congress and the Senate [were] on each side of the lower floor and as the two Presidents walked in and took their places everyone arose and remained standing till after the opening prayer, then new members were sworn in.... It was a grand affair.

*March 22.* [To James W. Robertson] ... The first news of an attempt to assassinate me came from Honolulu—That the principal P.G.s were angry that I had been allowed to come away [from Honolulu] for my presence here was damaging to their comfort and that it was best to get me out of the way. The *Independent* [newspaper] taking it up, it was copied in the Washington papers. Each of us had letters written by different parties, but we kept to ourselves—even Mr. Palmer, an American, had received one too, but when the telephone message came from Pennsylvania, then the whole story came out at the same time of the arrival of Mr. Thurston, and to be aware of him. Soon after Mr. Devine, the proprietor of the [Shoreham] hotel, told us that our rooms were wanted ... so we had to move to this hotel [the Cairo], and our stay here has been very pleasant. Our rooms are on the tenth floor ... said to be very healthy....

We are all enjoying good health.... Every morning there are callers and some spend the evening in my parlors singing Hawaiian Airs—ladies as well as gentlemen, and I am always willing to sing when asked. It astonished them to see how well I speak English as well as sing and play on the guitar and autoharp.

*March 30.* ... All the talk about assassinating me has had the result of bringing me more sympathy and friends, although the excitement has blown over somewhat, but if the intention was to intimidate me in the hope that I would leave Washington, they are much mistaken. I have been taking note of the actions of the Opposition and since they have commenced the move by having their bill brought in [to Congress] it is best for me to wait and see the result of their resolution.... I have a friend who has advised me not to act or take any step, but to wait and watch.

Liliu's just-quoted remarks have to do with an alleged assassination attempt on her life. Though this story has persisted ever since, there is no evidence to support it. As Liliu states, the story appears to have originated in Honolulu and arrived in Washington by telegraph and telephone. The Washington, DC, and New York newspapers. A summary of the matter follows:

At 8:30 on the morning of February 13, 1897, Julius Palmer, the Queen's private secretary, received the news by a long-distance telephone call that an elaborate assassination plot was under way, and that the persons "commissioned to commit the bloody crime" were on their way to the capital. It was suggested that Lorrin Thurston or one of his associates was behind the matter, and Palmer stated to the press that he thought the purpose was "to kill Liliuokalani as the surest means to secure annexation." On the same day a telegram was also received at the Shoreham Hotel, having the following message:

> ¶ My Dear Sister—Ua loheia mai nei e holo aku ana o Kakina e powa i ke'lii, nolaila, e hai aku i keia lohe me ka hakalia ole; e hai aku i na Nupepa. He goes by this steamer. [Dated at Honolulu, Hawaii.][This message the *Independent* newspaper translated as: "It has been reported that Thurston will go there to murder the Queen, therefore give this report without fail; report to the newspapers."]

The newspaper account, which had a New York byline (and was reprinted verbatim in the *Independent* in Honolulu), also stated that immediately upon receipt of the messages, Liliuokalani determined to move from the Shoreham Hotel for safety. However, Liliu's just-quoted letter tells a different story both about the move and about her belief in the alleged plot.

That people in Honolulu didn't take the "assassination" matter too seriously at the time is shown by the fact that when the pro-royalist newspaper the *Independent* published two articles on the matter in its March 2, 1897, issue, one of these appeared under the heading "Probably false."

*April 14.* I have decided to send Mrs. [Kia] Nahaolelua back. We have been in this country longer than I thought we would and from appearances may be here many more long months, so to keep her longer from her family would not be right, so I have decided to have her leave here under the care of Mr. Palmer on the 5th of May, arriving in San Francisco on the 12th—in time to meet Wakeke who I am sending for.... I think Joe [Heleluhe] would like to have his wife here.... Will you engage a berth for her in the *Australia* and give her one hundred dollars ($100) that she might get warm underclothing for herself?

On April 24, in anticipation of Queen Victoria's diamond jubilee, Liliuokalani sent a gift, with a graceful letter:

> ¶ Your majesty. I have the pleasure to send by this mail as my offering to you amongst the many which will doubtless welcome your Jubilee, a volume of my own musical compositions. Amongst these, there is one which I have entitled "The Queen's Jubilee" because it was written as a souvenir of the fiftieth anniversary of Your Majesty's long and glorious reign.
>
> Circumstances beyond my control prevented me from offering it to you before, but I trust it will be found just as appropriate in view of the fact that it has pleased the Almighty Ruler of the Universe to favor your subjects by adding ten more years to the duration of your mild and affectionate rule.[12]

*May 1.* Last Monday we went to New York for a few days and returned on Thursday after spending two very pleasant days with Mrs. Sara Lee who was visiting New York. Tuesday the remains of Gen. [Ulysses] Grant were removed to his new tomb. The procession escorted the President and party from the hotel opposite us and we had an opportunity to see them in front of our Hotel the Albemarle. It was fearfully cold that day.... The next day was lovely and we drove all through the city driving out to the Claremont Hotel to lunch and from there drove by Grant's tomb. It seems grand in its loneliness and I could not help thinking of the Father of his Country [George Washington] lying in his humble tomb at Mount Vernon.

*May 20.* Mrs. Heleluhe arrived here last Monday afternoon the 17th inst. [this month] highly pleased with her trip across the country and says America is a great and beautiful country.

*May 29.* I believe that Mr. Damon knew what he was saying to Mr. Norrie [editor of the *Independent*] when he said that they had notified President McKinley that "unless Hawaii was annexed by the United States before the close of this year that negotiations would be opened for a closer alliance with Great Britain." And he meant it. I have no doubt that they have sent such a message to the President, and that it came through Eddie Jones, since it has been reported so. I think they would like to terrify the U.S. President and his advisors into hastening the Annexation but the difficulty is not with them, it is with the Congress.... I don't think they could get any satisfaction from Great Britain—and may come back Hoka [thwarted].

---

12. Hawaii State Archives, Liliuokalani Collection, Box 7, Folder 80, draft.

| PALAPALA HOOPII KUE HOOHUIAINA. | PETITION AGAINST ANNEXATION. |
|---|---|
| I ka Mea Mahaloia WILLIAM McKINLEY, Peresidena, a me ka Aha Senate, o Amerika Huipuia. | To His Excellency WILLIAM McKINLEY, President, and the Senate, of the United States of America. |
| ME KA MAHALO:— | GREETING:— |
| NO KA MEA, ua waihoia aku imua o ka Aha Senate o Amerika Huipuia he Kuikahi no ka Hoohui aku ia Hawaii nei ia Amerika Huipuia i oleloia, no ka noonooia ma kona kau mau iloko o Dekemaba, M. H. 1897; nolaila, | WHEREAS, there has been submitted to the Senate of the United States of America a Treaty for the Annexation of the Hawaiian Islands to the said United States of America, for consideration at its regular session in December, A. D. 1897; therefore, |
| O MAKOU, na poe no lakou na inoa malalo iho, he poe makaainana a poe noho oiwi Hawaii hoi no ka Apana o _Kalawao_, Mokupuni o _Molokai_, he poe lala no ka AHAHUI HAWAII ALOHA AINA O KO HAWAII PAEAINA, a me na poe e ae i like ka manao makee me ko ka Ahahui i oleloia, ke kue aku nei me ka manao ikaika loa i ka hoohuiia aku o ko Hawaii Paeaina i oleloia ia Amerika Huipuia i oleloia ma kekahi ano a loina paha. | WE, the undersigned, native Hawaiian citizens and residents of the District of _Kalawao_, Island of _Molokai_, who are members of the HAWAIIAN PATRIOTIC LEAGUE OF THE HAWAIIAN ISLANDS, and others who are in sympathy with the said League, earnestly protest against the annexation of the said Hawaiian Islands to the said United States of America in any form or shape. |

IKEA—ATTEST: Enoch Johnson, Kakauolelo—Secretary.  Sept. 11, 1897.

James Keauiluna Kaulia, Peresidena—President.

| INOA—NAME. | AGE. | INOA—NAME. | AGE. |
|---|---|---|---|
| John Cullen, H. G. | 27 | Isaac Waiwahi | 20 |
| Kuniki | 27 | J. N. Kahaleanu | 35 |
| Kaupale | 67 | Kuhimana | 33 |
| T. Pahia | 60 | S. Makana | 28 |
| David Lake | 17 | Pinehaka | 26 |
| John Kaai | 23 | Antone A. Kaumi | 39 |
| Kaelepulu | 69 | B. K. Habai | 49 |
| Kamaka Kauluwai | 59 | Kupahu Poloka | 27 |
| P. Kiha | 49 | Kiope | 37 |
| Kululoa | 18 | Kawelolani | 24 |
| Daniel | 16 | Moki Waiuli | 19 |
| Gabriel | 17 | Maki | 16 |
| H. K. Hoopii | 36 | D. W. J. Kaofuiki | 32 |
| G. P. Pelapela | 35 | S. Kamaka | 17 |
| Peciao | 45 | Kiho | 16 |
| Lahaunui | 23 | Olala | 19 |
| Kae Liilii | 24 | Anaole | 30 |
| Kalei | 28 | John Kaiwi | 15 |
| Samuel Iranuoa | 35 | Kealohaaukai | 15 |
| Lani Makia | 21 | Kamiela | 15 |
| Ioane Kawa | 22 | Kaloha | 37 |
| Hezekia | 18 | Kiha Hana | 40 |
| Iokepa Nauwahi | 24 | Makahoa Haloa | 55 |
| John Kalua | 43 | Hakau Niho | 50 |
| Naihe Pukai | 18 | Kaeo Hapuku | 52 |

In 1897, the Ahahui Hawaii Aloha Aina o ko Hawaii Paeaina and the Hui Kalaiaina circulated petitions opposing annexation. Signatures from men of Kalawao on the Kalaupapa Peninsula, Molokai, are shown here.

National Archives and Records Administration

*Women at St. Philomena Church, Kalawao on the Kalaupapa Peninsula, Molokai, 1901. Emalia Kaaepa Prosser Kaiewe Kaiu (left), from Oahu, was sent to Kalaupapa in 1891 at the age of sixteen when she was diagnosed with leprosy. She was one of five hundred men and two hundred women of the settlement who signed their names in 1897 to the petition opposing annexation.*

*Liliuokalani visited the settlement both as princess and as queen to more fully understand the needs of the residents. Upon her arrival in April 1891 residents greeted the Queen at the landing with "an arch, covered with ferns and leaves, bearing the inscription 'Aloha i ka Moi Wahine'" (Pacific Commercial Advertiser, April 27, 1891).*
Father Joseph Julliotte, Congregation of the Sacred Hearts United States Province; identification by Anwei Skinsnes Law

On the morning of June 16, 1897, the representatives of the governments of the United States and the Republic of Hawaii met in the diplomatic room of the State Department in Washington, DC, for the purpose of signing a treaty providing for the annexation of the Hawaiian Islands to the United States. The *New York Times* reported that it is "an unusual thing for a treaty of such importance to be signed early in the morning, but in this case it was desired that the convention be made ready in order that it might be submitted to the Senate on the day of its execution."[13] Representing the United States were Secretary of State John T. Sherman and two assistant secretaries, and representing the Hawaiian side were Minister Francis M. Hatch, Lorrin Thurston, and W. A. Kinney. Secretary Sherman signed the first copy to be retained in Washington, and F. M. Hatch signed the first copy destined for Hawaii. The signing took place at 9:30 A.M. A printed circular containing the treaty, titled "Text of Treaty" in English and Hawaiian, is dated June 16, 1897, and bears the signatures of F. M. Hatch, Lorrin A. Thurston, William A. Kinney, and John T. Sherman.[14]

*June 19.* Wednesday the 16th of June, the Annexation Treaty was signed by President McKinley and John Sherman, and sent that afternoon to the Senate.... Next day I sent a protest [to the U.S. Secretary of State], accompanied with one from J. Heleluhe on the part of the Lahui, by whom he had been commissioned the right to act for them.

*Liliuokalani's Protest Document Regarding the Annexation Treaty, June 1897*

¶ I, Liliuokalani of Hawaii, by the Will of God, named heir apparent on the tenth day of April A.D. 1877, and [by] the Grace of God, Queen of the Hawaiian Islands on the 17th day of January A.D. 1893, do hereby protest against the ratification of a certain treaty which, I am informed, has been signed at Washington by Messrs. Hatch, Thurston, and Kinney, purporting to cede these islands to the territory and dominion of the United States. I declare such treaty to be an act of wrong towards the native and part-native peoples of Hawaii, an invasion of the rights of the ruling chiefs, in violation of the international rights both towards my people and towards friendly nations with whom they have made treaties, the perpetuation of the fraud whereby the constitutional government was overthrown, and finally an act of gross injustice to me.

BECAUSE, The official protest made by me on the 17th day of January, 1893, to the so-called Provisional Government was signed by me and received by such government with the assurance that the case was referred to the United States of America for arbitration.

13. *New York Times*, June 17, 1897.
14. Hawaii State Archives, Hatch Papers, M-58.

BECAUSE, That protest and my communications to the United States Government immediately thereafter expressly declared that I yielded my authority to the forces of the United States in order to avoid bloodshed, and because I recognized the futility of a conflict with so formidable a power.

BECAUSE, The president of the United States, the Secretary of State, and an envoy commissioned by them reported in official documents that my government was unlawfully coerced by forces, diplomatic and naval, of the United States, that I was at the date of their investigations the constitutional ruler of my people.

BECAUSE, Such decision of the recognized magistrates of the United States was communicated to me and to Sanford B. Dole and said Dole's resignation requested by Albert S. Willis the recognized agent and minister of the Government of the United States.

BECAUSE, Neither the above commission nor the government which sends it has ever received any such authority from the registered voters of Hawaii but derives its assumed powers from so-called Committee of Public Safety, organized about the 17th day of January 1893, said committee being composed largely of persons claiming American citizenship and not one single Hawaiian was a member thereof or in any way participated in the demonstration leading to its existence.

BECAUSE, My people, about forty thousand in number, have in no way been consulted by those, three thousand in number who claim the right to destroy the independence of Hawaii. My people constitute four-fifths of the legally qualified voters of Hawaii and, excluding those imported for labor, about the same proportion of the inhabitants.

BECAUSE, Said treaty ignores not only the civic rights of my people but further the hereditary property of the Chieves [chiefs]. Of the four million acres composing the territory, said treaty offers to annex one million, or 915,000 acres, has in no way been heretofore recognized as other than private property of the constitutional monarch, subject to a control in no way differing from other matters of a private estate.

BECAUSE, It is proposed by said treaty to confiscate said property technically called the Crown Lands [from] those legally entitled thereto, with either now or in succession receiving no consideration whatever for estates, the title to which has always been undisputed and which is legitimately in my name at this date.

BECAUSE, Said treaty ignores not only all professions of perpetual amity and good faith made by the United States in former treaties made with the sovereigns representing the Hawaiian people, but all treaties made by those sovereigns with other and friendly powers, and it is thereby in violation of international law.

BECAUSE, By treating with the other parties claiming at this time the right to cede such territory of Hawaii, the government of the United States receives such territory from the hands of those whom its own magistrates legally elected by the people of the United States and in office in 1893 pronounced fraudulently in power and unconstitutionally ruling Hawaii.

THEREFORE, I, Liliuokalani of Hawaii, do hereby call upon the president of that nation to whom I alone yielded my property and my authority, to withdraw said treaty ceding said islands from further consideration, ask the honorable Senate of the United States to decline to ratify said treaty, and I implore the people of this great and good nation, from whom my ancestors learned the Christian religion, to sustain their representatives in such acts of justice and equity as may be in accord with the principles of their fathers and to the Almighty ruler of the universe, to Him who judgeth righteously I commit my cause.

Done at Washington, District of Columbia, United States of America this seventeenth day of June in the year 1897.

[*signed*] Liliuokalani

[*signed*]
Joseph Heleluhe
Wakeke Heleluhe
Julius Palmer
*Witnesses*

[On the verso in Palmer's hand is written the following:[15]]

¶ On this seventeenth day of June A.D. 1897 at about three P.M. on or within twenty-four hours after the sending of the treaty within referred to, to Congress, a protest, which this is a copy of, was by me delivered into the hands of John Sherman, Secretary of State of the United States and read by him in my presence.

Witness to the signature and to above delivery.

[*signed*] Joseph Heleluhe

---

*July 1.* Nothing new has developed about the annexation, but it was decided yesterday to let the Reciprocity [Treaty] remain as it is for the present. But there are many things that have sprung up in conversation amongst politicians about that point given in Mr. Heleluhe's protest where he mentioned that he had been commissioned by the two societies, Aloha Aina and Kalaiaina, who represented 40,000 Hawaiians to act for them and that those who represented the Republic of Hawaii only numbered three thousand altogether. It was a matter of great surprise.... There is a stupid report issued that I have written Hawaii to have a petition sent from all the Hawaiians protesting against the Annexation. What folly! when all can be found in Mr. Heleluhe's protest. Last Tuesday [June 29] I went to the Senate and sat in the gallery to hear the discussions.

15. Hawaii State Archives, Liliuokalani Collection, Box 4, Folder 42, typescript copy. At the head of the first page is the note "Copy from original on file in Bishop Museum. A. P. Taylor, Librarian, Archives of Hawaii, January 31, 1929." The text of this document also appeared in the *New York Times*, June 18, 1897.

*August 2.* [To James W. Robertson from the Ebbitt House:] It is astonishing with what powers of persistency the Missionary P.G. are endowed. They worked very hard and watched every movement made by parties who would cause an injury to their projects and were always on hand to counteract it. I cannot help admiring them for it. If we only had such men on our side. We had no one here to represent our side from the beginning of the overthrow.... I am told I should have come myself but I was surrounded by spies at the time and could not have got away. However, the Annexation treaty has been postponed by the Senate to come up at the next session on December 5th....

You can form no idea of the complete ignorance of the Senators or people here in regard to our situation. They only know of my being dethroned and sympathize with me, but keep away. When mentioned on the subject, you would have to go through the whole story and that is all—and with these people crying annex, they think they ought to. I could not write any articles, for the papers have all been subsidized. They would not print anything from my side, but would publish all the lies issued by the "man and his party who sleeps with the devil."

I think that my presence here has really been the means of preventing a hasty decision on the part of the Senate....

There will be time enough for me by and by to take a rest but at present I am still at Washington enjoying the bustling life of this great city. I called at the White House the other day and was well received by President McKinley.[16]

*August 10.* [From the Ebbitt House:] The action of the President in sending the Treaty to the Senate with his signature and that of the Secretary of State attached shows how they have been blinded and deceived by the misrepresentations of [Francis M.] Hatch and [Lorrin] Thurston and [William] Kinney. The people here are honorable men. They have no idea that there are such people on this world who can stoop to such low, unprincipled acts as those who represent the government of the Republic of Hawaii. I may admit to you (although the P.G.s may not know it themselves) that the Treaty is partly a success for their side seeing that the most important signatures have already been affixed and [it] only remains to be acted upon by the Senate. It is to be hoped that they will not pass it in the House. I am told there will be a strong opposition made at the coming session by the Democrats. The day for the opening will be 5th of December [but] people or Members will be straggling in and when Christmas arrives will all go home again till after New Year's...

*September 1.* The Queen Dowager Kapiolani has written me asking me for the use of one of my boats to take with her to Kailua. I feel loath to send any of my boats. People who borrow are very careless and perhaps her men may not take as good care of it as they ought to. Her nephews, the two Princes [Kuhio and Kawananakoa], have smashed two of their own boats, and I would not like to lend her mine. I have two boats, one

---

16. Hawaii State Archives, Liliuokalani Collection, Box 7.

is a whale boat, the other a common boat called *Hoaai*, and both are at my boathouse in the care of Kaauwai, one of my ohuas [servants]....

I am getting ready to take a trip to San Francisco, leaving here in the sixth of September, probably arriving there on the 11th. Will stay there two weeks, then return here....

There is nothing of any consequence transpiring here these days—I hope the people will be successful in their canvassing all over the islands, that foreigners as well as natives will take a part in a memorial to be sent to Congress against Annexation, and I pray that it may end satisfactorily.

---

On September 13, 1897, J. O. Carter wrote the following to John Richardson of Wailuku:

> ¶ I can now say to you that the petitions against the passing of Annexation will be circulated throughout the islands, and I hope will be very generally signed. The heading of the petitions, as you will see, allows all nationalities to sign, which I think is the better way. The "Woman's Patriotic League" will circulate the same form of petition. The heading is short and very much to the point, i.e. that we do not wish to be annexed. I feel sure that you will do all you can to insure the largest list of signers. It will be in order for your people on Maui to hold meetings and endorse, by resolutions, the action of the meeting of Hawaiians held here.[17]

J. O. Carter informed Liliu on September 14, 1897:

> ¶ The anti-annexation petitions are being generally circulated and signed. The native Hawaiian meeting protesting against the ratification of the annexation treaty by the Hawaiian Senate was a success. There will be a larger meeting in the near future when natives and foreigners will be heard from.[18]

---

***October 6.*** [To James W. Robertson:] I find that those Congressmen who have been to the Islands have returned after having had a good time at the expense of the American Union Party. Is this a new name for the Annexationists? I can tell you this fact that the newspaper came out one day saying that Senator Morgan and daughters have gone down [to Honolulu], that L. A. Thurston had invited him to go on this trip at the expense of the Sugar Planters—that Thurston had asked him to ask Senator Bacon of Macon, Georgia, and the latter had declined because he did not wish to be influenced by any party on his decision. I only think that this question relating to Hawaii will not be brought up in the two Houses but that there will be some opposition made by the Democrats. I do not think

17. Hawaii State Archives, J. O. Carter Letter Book.
18. Hawaii State Archives, J. O. Carter Letter Book.

that those C.M. [congressmen] have any opportunity of observing things and judging for themselves as they were always taken possession of by the P.G.s until they left. The lady correspondent of the *S.F. Call* I daresay will write truthfully her opinions... but I daresay the P.G. must have given her lots of opposite views to the truthful facts. The *Call* is J. D. Spreckels' paper and favorable to our side.... When we were in San Francisco lately, from September 1 [?] till the 25th the S.F. papers came out with an article saying that I had said as soon as my niece the Princess Kaiulani arrived in S.F. we were going to make an agreement that I would sign my right in favor of her. I had never made the remark and as Mr. Heleluhe had only a few days before presented a petition to President McKinley from the people, I had no authority to act or say anything—so he came out with an article contradicting it. No newspaper would print it except the [*San Francisco*] *Call*....

When we were in S.F. we met several Hawaiians, Mr. and Mr. Widemann with three daughters and their grandchildren, Mr. and Mrs. Fred Macfarlane and two sons, Mr. Ned Macfarlane, Mr. Sam Parker, two daughters and son, Mrs. Lydia Davis, Mr. Annie Brenham, Mrs. Kamaka Fairchild, and Mrs. Gerty Lanse—besides George [Macfarlane] and his lovely wife. I did enjoy being with them. Then the Widemanns went home to the Islands and I missed Mrs. W. very much. Sam and two daughters—Lydia, Annie Brenham, and Mr. and Mrs. Heleluhe, Gen. Warfield, and myself all went to Monterey for one night and had a very enjoyable time at the Hotel Del Monte.[19]

*October 11.* I think from what I hear in this house [the Ebbitt House Hotel] where many members [of Congress] congregate, that they will make strong opposition against Annexation, as it was and still now remains, the policy of all Democrats. I hope you will work with all your power amongst your friends against it. Well, let us hope it will not come to pass.

The "Ratifying of the Annexation Treaty" [by the Hawaiian Senate] is one of the stupidest transactions, to my thinking. What more had they to do with the Treaty—It is out of their hands. [It was] Placed on the U.S. Record, signed by Secretary Sherman, and approved according to the Message to the Senate by the President of the U.S. All that remains is to be acted upon by the Senate. It is virtually out of the hands of the Hawaiian Republic in its original form as present—then in their brilliancy [they] must go and ratify something they have no control of.[20]

---

19. Hawaii State Archives, Liliuokalani Collection, Box 7.
20. The whole business of the Hawaiian Senate ratifying the treaty of annexation was little more than a public show, which had little impact on annexation. At noon on Wednesday, September 8, 1897, the Hawaiian Senate convened for a three-day special session "for the purpose of ratifying the Hawaiian treaty of annexation with the United States." The first session included a long address by President W. C. Wilder, summarizing events from January 1893 to that date. On Thursday, the senate read a protest by Native Hawaiians and laid it on the table, and on Friday, the assembly signed a resolution ratifying the treaty and adjourned. The *Pacific Commercial Advertiser*, September 10, 1897, commented: "The Ratification of the

On October 23, J. O. Carter wrote the following to Liliu:

> ¶ The petitions against annexation are being completed; but because of the unfortunate differences between the Aloha Aina and Kalaiaina societies the signatures are not as general and numerous as your friends could wish. The "Women's Patriotic League" has done far better with its petition than the men have with theirs. As soon as the petitions are placed on my hands I will forward them, if permitted, to you in care of the Messrs. Spreckels of San Francisco.[21]

Then on November 17, Carter informed Liliuokalani:

> ¶ The petition of the "Hawaiian Women's Patriotic League" will go forward to Mr. Spreckels by the bearer,[22] to be forwarded to you at once. The other petition will be taken in charge of by Delegates who go to Washington to oppose Annexation. These petitions need some preparation, binding perhaps, before presentation to the Senate. Some person who knows how such papers are generally arranged will advise you. Enclosed are two sheets which have come into my hands this A.M., which you can include with the others. The Island of Maui is sending John Richardson as a delegate to aid you in opposing annexation, and I trust that he will prove useful to you.... The Princess [Kaiulani] arrived in good health and has been well received by all classes. She is a charming girl, of very engaging manners, and rare good judgment, for one so young.... Mr. William Auld has also decided to go to Washington for the purpose of opposing annexation, and should be very helpful, considering his standing in the Masonic fraternity, in disabusing Senators of the idea that Hawaiians favor annexation.[23]

On November 27, 1897, Carter informed Liliuokalani:

> ¶ The [anti-annexation] Commissioners who took passage on the *Gaelic* were Messrs. Kaulia, Kalauokalani, Richardson, and Auld, and they are probably in San Francisco today. It was not possible for lack of funds to send representatives from the Women's Patriotic League. I have been urged by your haole [white] friends to go and remain in Washington during January and February, but my business does not

Treaty of Annexation by the Senate finally completes the formal action of this Republic in forming a union with the United States. The bolt has been driven through on this side. It remains for the Americans to put a lock nut on the other side."

21. Hawaii State Archives, J. O. Carter Letter Book.

22. The "bearer" was Captain Houdlett. On November 16, 1897, Carter addressed John D. Spreckels in San Francisco: "Captain Houdlett is the bearer of a package addressed to Her Majesty Liliuokalani, containing the petition against annexation circulated and signed by the 'Hawaiian Women's Patriotic League,' and I have asked him to hand it to you. Will you kindly see that the package is forwarded to Her Majesty by Express. There are 10,633 signatures of women, and the petition circulated by the Men's Patriotic Societies have a larger number of signatures, how many I am not able to say at this writing." Hawaii State Archives, J. O. Carter Letter Book, M-35.

23. Hawaii State Archives, Liliuokalani Collection; also in J. O. Carter Letter Book, M-35.

seem to warrant my leaving here. As this is the long session of Congress, there is no certainty when I could leave Washington if I went on. I cannot bring myself to believe that the annexation treaty can pass two-thirds of the Senators and a passage by a joint resolution would take the matter over for another year.

I am glad to know that you have completed your book and hope that its publication will reward you abundantly. I note that you will send me two copies, one of which I am to send to the [Polynesian] Society in New Zealand, and the other for my bookcase.[24]

---

*December 11.* The [Hawaiian] Commissioners appointed by the People arrived here on the 6th, all well. Their presence here has had good effect. The letters of introduction given them by Ex. Senator Dubois and Sen. [R. F. Pettigrew of South Dakota] has been of great help beside their personal advices, all has tended to help them in their work. The result has been that Senator Hoar of the Republican Party offered to take the petitions to Congress, which he did on Thursday the ninth and read it in the House. On Monday the question will be discussed. Yesterday the party took the Memorials to Secretary of State John Sherman at the State Department. There they were received very politely and when [the memorials were] placed in his hand said he would send a copy to Congress. So far all has gone on well and nothing more on their part to do until the end, except to go and make an appearance on the House. It is apparent that there will be strong opposition, and [it is] so very necessary for them to remain all through the discussions, but their funds are getting low. I hope you will use your influence amongst the people to try and raise a few more hundreds to help them along. Good appearance will have good effect, and cause people here to take some interest more especially when they converse as they meet in the parlors.

I have written to Mrs. Campbell—perhaps they might give a concert or a fair towards that object.

24. Hawaii State Archives, J. O. Carter Letter Book.

*The executive committee of Ahahui Hawaii Aloha Aina o Na Wahine o ko Hawaii Paeaina (Women's Hawaiian Patriotic League of the Hawaiian Islands), circa 1893. The women's league worked together with the men's league to petition against annexation. A delegation from the Ahahui carried the petition document to Washington, DC, where Liliuokalani received it on December 6, 1897. It was presented to the U.S. Senate on December 9, 1897. On July 6, 1898, the Senate voted to pass the Newlands Joint Resolution of Annexation, and it was signed by President McKinley on July 7, 1898. Hawaii learned of the event when the Pacific Mail SS Coptic arrived from San Francisco on July 13, 1898, and signaled the news from offshore.*

*The women's executive committee included Lilia Aholo, Abigail Kuaihelani Campbell, Rebecca Kahalewai Cummins, Hattie K. Hiram, Jessie Kapaihi Kaae, Laura Kekupuwolui Mahelona, Emma Nawahi, and Mary Ann Kaulalani Parker Stillman. In this photograph, Abigail is seated left, Rebecca is seated right, and Emma is standing second from right.*
J. J. Williams, Hawaiian Collection, University of Hawaii at Manoa Library

# 1898

*Saturday, January 1, 1898.* Hawaiians at the Ebbitt House, Washington, DC, [are:] Liliuokalani, J. Heleluhe K.C.K., H. M. Secretary, Mrs. W. Heleluhe.

Delegates from Hawaii: J. K. Kaulia, Commissioner [and] President Hui Aloha Aina, D. Kalauokalani,[1] Commissioner [and] President Hui Kalaiaina, Col. J. Richardson, Delegate from Maui. W. Auld, Secretary to Pres. [of] Hui Kalaiaina.

*Monday, January 3.* Went for a walk. John Richardson wants to leave this hotel. Says to Kaulia and Kalauokalani they ought not to stay where I am.

*Sunday, January 9.* Loaa pono o J. K. Kaulia me J. Richardson ia J. Heleluhe e ohumu ana i loko o ka lumi o J. R. no ka waiwai ole o koʻu noho ana i anei. Aole mea i hana ia e maua. E ole lakou i hiki mai nei akahi no a hana ia kekahi hana. Pane ia e Joe.

E hoole mai ana oukou aole i hana Ke Alii—Ekolu Komisina a L— i hoouna mai a i ka ha noho maoli kona kino i anei—a loaa maila ia oukou. Ina i makemake ke Alii e hana no kona pono iho ina i keia la aole oukou i hele mai i anei.

[J. Heleluhe found J. K. Kaulia and J. Richardson complaining in J. R.'s room about the uselessness of my staying here. That we had done nothing. Because *they* came, only now has something been done. Joe responded to them.

Will you deny that Her Majesty has not acted. Liliuokalani has sent for three Commissioners, and the fourth is present here in person, and you've found him. If her Majesty had wanted to act for her own benefit, then all of you would not be here today.]

*Monday, January 10.* Kaulia and Kalauokalani went to Capitol tho' Richardson told them not to. After they had been there few minutes when the Senate went into closed session, President McKinley sent for several members of Senate to discuss Annexation and of course insist on their votes. *MEAN.*

J. Heleluhe went to doctor. Told him he couldn't pay—Doctor says alright.

*Tuesday, January 11.* Kaulia, Kalauokalani, Richardson, Auld went with Mrs. Tucker to Corcoran Gallery—Ten A.M. Kaulia and Kalauokalani

THE DIARY FOR 1898

1 JAN–30 DEC

Bishop Museum Archives

---

1. David Keola Kalauokalani (b. 1874?, Honolulu–d. 1936) was the son of Senator David Kalauokalani and Hattie Mahoe and a graduate of Saint Louis College and Oahu College. After annexation, he was a private secretary to Robert W. Wilcox in the 56th and 57th U.S. Congresses and, later, a clerk for the House of Representatives (Hawaii).

*In 1897, the Hui Aloha Aina (as the patriotic league was popularly known) gathered signatures on their anti-annexation petition from Hawaiians throughout the islands. At a public meeting held in Hilo in 1897, Emma Nawahi, representing the women's league, addressed the women attendees, "This land is ours— our Hawaii. Say, shall we lose our nationality? Shall we be annexed to the United States?" To which the women replied, "Aole loa. [Never!]" Notwithstanding opposition from the Hawaiian people, the U.S. annexed Hawaii in 1898.*
*San Francisco Call*, September 30, 1897, p. 2,
California Digital Newspaper Collection

went again to Capitol—Hawaii Annexation again discussed [behind] closed doors. All our party spent evening at Mrs. Reeside except Wm. Auld. Had cold—Lizzie Reeside danced for us.

*Wednesday, January 12.* Wm. Auld high fever 102. Five P.M.

Kaulia and Kalauokalani went again to Capitol. Door closed. Pettigrew assured Kaulia he would watch the case of Annexation. Senator Elkins asked President McKinley to influence members to vote for Annexation—and he did.

*Thursday, January 13.* Wm. Auld slightly better. Symptoms, Pneumonia. Took walk from [here to] Droop & Sons, Inquired about my music. It would cost £80. Too much. It was a long walk. Mrs. Millmore called to invite me to Maria's wedding tomorrow night—but [I] could not go. Engaged to go to Mrs. Mason's tomorrow.

*Friday, January 14.* Pettigrew told Kaulia not to fear Dole's coming. Went for Mrs. Mason and we drove over to Chinese shop. Bought silk handkerchief—amulet. Auld is better—but doctor saw he had been out.

*Saturday, January 15.* Met Mr. and Mrs. Churchill of Samoa.

*Sunday, January 16.* Went to St. Andrew's Church, corner of 14 and Corcoran St., Washington, DC, with Kaulia, Kalauokalani, Mr. and Mrs. Heleluhe. Mrs. T. Y. Tucker took Heleluhe, Kaulia, Kalauokalani to Georgetown University. I went with Wakeke to Doctors and rode to Georgetown.

*Monday, January 17.* Kalauokalani sick with cold. J. Richardson came in and said he was going to write home to have Kaulia and Kalauokalani ordered home, and for John Baker and Noa Kepoikai [to be] sent [here] in their place. He told me S. C. Allen said he would pay Kepoikai's expenses here.

Today I lectured Joe H[eleluhe] and told him if he continued drinking I would not pay his Doctor bill which is very high—$10—one visit.

Today, doctor changed my capsules for Charcoal and Soda pellet—to chew before swallowing.

Today Kaulia had only $19—due him of his $250 allowance. Kalau [Kalauokalani] paid his hotel bill.

*Tuesday, January 18.* Rec'd news of J. O. Carter's arrival [in San Francisco].

*Wednesday, January 19.* Eight P.M. Taken sick very suddenly pain in chest and back. Sent for Dr. English[2] and Hypodermic injected right arm. Pellets [Entry ends thus.]

2. This was Dr. Charles Hamilton English, a medical specialist with offices at 1107 NW G Street, Washington, DC. English first began treating Liliu in 1897.

In a letter of September 29, 1897, he admonishes her for not taking her medicine and says, "You should have carried the entire supply with you.... You must not lose sight of the fact that your very life depends upon your present care and watchfulness.... There is no return from the grave.... I do not charge for the medicines I furnish, their cost is included in the final fee. These medicines are my secret—they are formulae that I prepared as the result of years of observation and experimentation." Hawaii State Archives, Liliuokalani Collection, Box 7. In a later letter, English claimed to know how to cure the leprosy patients of Molokai.

*Friday, January 21.* 11 P.M. John Bowler arrived by way of New Orleans from San Francisco. Says his heart is affected—had hard time to get consent to leave Hawaii. He says J. O. Carter and Wife are in S.F. and J.O.C. was to leave Sunday night for here but [they have] not yet arrived.[3]

*Tuesday, January 25.* J. O. Carter told me the Hawaiian Commissioners ought to go home—there wasn't sufficient money to pay for their stay. That he has not seen the full amount of $1,475—$80 went to pay for expense of luau, $7.00 for Kaulia's wife.

*Wednesday, January 26.* There are in one bundle, my *Tradition of Creation*—48 paper [covered] books and four cloth [covered].[4]

Saida [Sadie] Carter arrived from Boston. Myself—Wakeke, Joe Heleluhe, John Richardson went to see Kaulia at Providence Hospital. Is [a] little better today. No fever. Notified him that they have to go back to Hawaii. He took it good-naturedly.

Gave names to John Richardson's two mahoe [twins].

1. Moliakalanikula (No ka pono o ka lahui). [Given in honor of the people's welfare.]

2. Kuliapapahikalani (no ke aloha i ka Aina). [Given in honor for love of the land.]

*Thursday, January 27.* Received two copies of my book *Hawaii's Story by Hawaii's Queen*. Reception by Mrs. Evans and Mrs. Bonner, Kalauokalani, Auld, Wakeke, Heleluhe, J. Richardson went. Mrs. Senator Thurston invited me to call at her reception next day.

*Friday, January 28.* 4:30 P.M. called on Mrs. Senator Thurston. Met Mrs. Ingols, Mrs. Schmitt.

*Saturday, January 29.* Will spend the evening with Mrs. and Miss Mason, Mr. and Mrs. Heleluhe, John Richardson, C. W. Stoddard, Mr. and Mrs. Johnson. Kalauokalani went on to Hospital to spend the night with Kaulia. Had pleasant time.

**Wednesday, February 2.** J. K. Kaulia came back from the Providence Hospital today.

*Saturday, February 5.* J. Heleluhe was out walking—Piehu [Iaukea] saw him and sent for him. Offered to take home something. Sent my parcel books by him. He said he has to work very hard.

---

3. Mary Carter, in a letter home dated Washington, DC, January 27, 1898, reports their arrival: "We were a day late.... Arrived here at two, thought it strange that no one met us, [but] the reason was in papa's telegram to 'H.M.'—he didn't state which train we were on. 'H.M.' was going to send Joe H. in a carriage for us to the later train. As soon as we were in our rooms, I heard 'Mary.' I opened the door, 'H. M.' came in, & all of the delegation. She said, 'Oh, Mary, I am so glad to see you...' 'H.M.' sits in the larger parlor [of the Cairo Hotel] evenings and receives. She is very popular.... Wakeke keeps in the background, is very quiet. She really does make quite a good appearance... she is quiet & devoted to 'H.M.' They are all good to me." Hawaii State Archives, J. O. Carter Collection.

4. Liliuokalani is referring to her publication *An Account of the Creation of the World According to Hawaiian Tradition* (Boston: Lee and Shepard, 1897). This is the first English-language translation of the famous Hawaiian creation chant, the Kumulipo, which Liliu translated from a family manuscript formerly owned by King Kalakaua. Lee and Shepard of Boston was the same publishing house that would in 1898 publish the Queen's memoir. A letter to Liliu from Lee and Shepard, September 16, 1897, Hawaii State Archives, shows that as ordered, they had printed and made up 80 copies bound in paper and 20 in cloth. The U.S. copyright for the work is dated January 3, 1898.

*Sunday, February 6.* Letters to Aima [Nawahi], Lela, Hattie Hiram, Kuaihelani [Campbell], [Edward K.] Lilikalani. Mr. and Mrs. Dole leave tonight with suite for Hawaii.

Package of my books was sent by Piehu [Iaukea].

Helen Aldrich Dunning arrived with her husband, saw me in parlor below—came in all at once. Glad to see her.

*Monday, February 7.* Had a reception from three to five P.M. and Musicale from eight to ten.

*Tuesday, February 8.* Took Helen and Chief engineer Dunning to drive at Capitol. Mrs. and Miss Hilborn called to sing and it was all over last night. Rec'd note acknowledging for present from Rep. Hilborn for my book. Kaulia took his doctor's bill to J. O. Carter—he did not give him the money but said he would pay the amount. Good.

*Saturday, February 12.* 9:30 P.M. A reception was given by Mr. and Mrs. Schneider of the Cairo [Hotel], to Minister and Madame Wu. I went with all of my party, Kaulia, Kalauokalani, Richardson, Auld, Heleluhe, and Wakeke. It was very cold night and it was a very brilliant party.[5] That night went up to see Mrs. James Knox Taylor.

*Monday, February 14.* Spoke to J. O. Carter about my Claims of Indemnity on American Govt. to employ a lawyer—or to ask Pettigrew about Calderon Carlisle. He came in that afternoon and said—aole pono e hookomo ka hoopii i keia wa aia pau ka Hoohui Aina ma hope ka'u. [He came in that afternoon and said—the claim shouldn't be entered at this time, when Annexation was done with, mine will come later.] That depends.

*Tuesday, February 15.* News of Grand-Mother Carter's death.[6]

*Friday, February 18.* J. H. Wilson and H. C. Carter arrived, the former from different cities, the latter from Boston. Mrs. Beardslee[7] made some poi from her own taro and sent it for Me and Mrs. J. O. Carter. Wilson told me I should not have paid what I did for my book. They should have paid me. That he could get my book published for me for nothing and make them pay me—how nice. Over 200 D.A.R. [members of the Daughters of the American Revolution] are in this house [Ebbitt House].

*Sunday, February 20.* Two P.M. Hou ia kuu Ai—i ke kui a na ke kui omo koko i omo i ka palahehe ua oi ae ka maikai o ka palahehe no ke ano brown—Loaa eha puu—ua mahelehele a o ka puu kokoke i ka collarbone ua nui iki mai. Ao mai ke kauka me ka waimaka. [Two P.M. my neck was injected with a needle and syringe to draw out blood, drew the pus out. The pus was better, being of a brownish nature. Have four lumps—they are separate, and the lump near the collarbone is a bit larger. The doctor advised tearfully.]

---

5. Wu was the Chinese minister resident at Washington, DC. The invitation from the Schneiders (managers of the Cairo Hotel) is in the Hawaii State Archives, Liliuokalani Collection, Box 7.

6. "Grand-Mother Carter" was Hannah Trufant Lord (b. 1809, Hallowell, Maine–d. January 29, 1898, Honolulu), who married Captain Joseph Oliver Carter (b. 1802–d. 1850) at Honolulu, November 24, 1833. She was the mother of the Queen's confidante and business manager, J. O. Carter.

7. Evelyn was the wife of Rear Admiral Albert Lester Anthony Beardslee (b. 1836–d. 1903), who had been commander in chief of naval forces in the Pacific 1894–97.

*Monday, February 21.* No ka lapaau mai Puu ma ka A-i. Kakahiaka hola 6—1 puna nui Saline Hunyadi—hola 7—2 puna nui laau uliuli me 2 puna nui wai—e hui a inu ae. Eha inu ana o ka la. Na apu elua awakea me ahiahi 1 puna nui. pela me ka wai. Ma mua o ka moe ana 2 puna nui. Pela me ka wai a inu ae. E inu i keia laau i ½ hola ma mua o ka ai ana i kekahi mea a i ole, e inu elua hola ma hope o ka o ka [sic] ai maona ana. Ina e malama ole ia keia luna—e loaa ana ia oe he nahu a me ka hi. Ma hope o na aina a pau e ai 2 hua pelletto. E nau a inu wai aku. E holoholo wawae. 1 hola kakahiaka. 1 hola ahiahi. [Medical treatment for lumps on the neck. Six A.M.—1 tbsp. Saline Hunyadi.—seven A.M.—2 tbsp. dark medicine and 2 tbsp. water, mix and drink. Four times a day. Two portions by noon and in evening 1 tbsp. and 1 tbsp. water. Before bedtime 2 tbsp. and 2 tbsp. water and drink. Drink this a half hour before eating or two hours after a full meal. If the above is not followed you will get cramps and diarrhea. After all meals take 2 pelleto pills. Chew on, then take with water. Walk 1 hour in morning, 1 hour in evening.] Gargle 1 to 2 tablespoons full three to four times a day.

*Tuesday, February 22.* Perfectly harmless to swallow or any or all will do no harm. Sore throat. A spot in the root of the tongue as large as a quarter with green discoloration around the edge showing a most malignant state. Douche three or four times a day in each nostril on account of yellow matter from nose showing that part affected also.

*Wednesday, February 23.* 1:30 P.M. Went to doctor [and] reported hemorrhage. Gave me no ka lepo paa [for constipation].

Prescription. Every morning one tablespoon of Saline or Hunyadi [sic] before eating. Two tablespoons of dark medicine half hour before eating or two hours after eating & not less.

Lepo Paa. E hoomakaukau, 1 quart wai mahana—hookomo eha puna nui Glycerine—hahano a pau pono. Elua hahano ana o ka la. Ua lawa no no na la elua ka hahano ana—a noho wale aku a loihi. Aia no a paa hou. Hou ia kuu a-i ke kui aniani aohe nui o ka palahehe he koko ka nui. Ua emi ka puu o kuu a-i. [Constipation. Prepare 1 quart warm water—add 4 tbsp. glycerin—use entirely for enema. Two enemas a day. Two days of enemas are adequate and will last for a while until constipated again. My neck was injected with a shiny needle. There wasn't much pus but a lot of blood. The lump on my neck has receded.]

*Thursday, February 24.* Glycerin [illegible] Sig. 1—use as directed. No ka lepo paa [for constipation]. ma kela aoao [on opposite page]. [Sketch of hand and finger pointing toward facing page.] [On the bottom of this page is written "Feb 25-'98."]

*Friday, February 25.* Loaned my *Hawaii's Story* to Mrs. Burch.

*Sunday, February 27.* Hoi na Komisina Hawaii i keia la. J. K. Kaulia, D. Kalauokalani na Peresidena o ka Hui Aloha Aina me Hui Kalaiaina—William Auld he Elele a Kakauolelo no ka Hui Kalaiaina—Huli nui aku la ke alo no ka aina hanau a hoike aku i na mea i hana ia e lakou ma

Wakinekona nei no ka kue i ka Hoohui Aina—a no ka pono o ka Lahui. 2:30 P.M. Hele i kahi o ke Kauka. Hou hou ia kuu A-i. He koko ka mea i loaa aka, i mai ua pii ae he maikai oiai ua uuku mai na puu. Ao hou mai e malama loa wau i na lula ana.

[The Hawaiian Commissioners left today. J. K. Kaulia, D. Kalauokalani, the Presidents of the Hui Aloha Aina and Hui Kalaiaina. William Auld, a delegate and secretary from the Hui Kalaiaina. They are headed toward the homeland and will report what they had done here in Washington against Annexation and for the welfare of the people. 2:30 P.M. Went to the Doctor's office. My neck injected again. Blood was drawn, but he said it's much better since the lumps are diminishing. He advised that I follow his instructions completely.]

**Wednesday, March 2.** Hele i kahi o kuu Kauka. [Went to my Doctor's.]

*Saturday, March 5.* Madame H. went to have black velvet jacket made by Madame Goode—30—and silk skirt.

*Sunday, March 6.* No church today. Saw my doctor and the lump in my neck opened and it is to be kept open, a running sore. Told him about dull pain in muscle of right arm. Wrote letters to Aima, Kaulia, Henry, Mrs. Lee, Mr. Snelling.[8]

*Wednesday, March 9.* Ma kahi o kuu kauka—Nana i kuu ai. Wili hou ia ka puka a nui. Ua omaomao ia ke kae o ka hoailona ia o ka poison i loko o kuu kino mai kuu mai inoino he Cancer. Olelo mai ke kauka e nana pono i ke ano o ke koko a me ka palahehe e pili ana ka pulupulu i hookomo ia i loko o ka puka. [At my doctor's. Examined my neck. The opening was made larger. The smear was green, which is a sign of poison in my body from this terrible disease Cancer. The doctor said he must carefully examine the blood and pus on the cotton inserted in the opening.]

*Thursday, March 10.* 7:35 J. O. and Mrs. Carter went to Boston to visit their friends and see their son [Cushman] at school at Roxbury, Boston, Mass.

Kapili hou ia i pulupulu a wehe ia ka pulu kahiko. Hemo wale mai ana no ka umoku [sic] pulupulu. Ua ano omaomao ka loko, a o ko waho he ula koko maloo. Aohe maikai ko'u hiamoe ana i keia po. Ekolu o'u ala ana no. Me ka loaa o na moeuhane inoino. [Cotton was applied again and the old cotton taken out. The cotton plug extracted. Inside was greenish and the outside was reddish with dried blood. I didn't sleep well tonight. I awoke three times with terrible nightmares.]

Ua halalo glycerin—oia [illegible] ka paa. [Had Glycerin enema but still constipated.]

Olelo mai o J.O.C. aole make ou awiwi i ka hoopii i ko'u koi poho. I aku wau e waiho no wau a hoi mai laua. [J. O. Carter said he does not want to rush to bring suit for my damage claims. Said I'll let it go until the two of them come back.]

---

8. N. Greenwood Snelling was the manager of the Boston Clearing House at 66 State Street. He was the cousin of Liliu's late husband, J. O. Dominis.

*Friday, March 11.* Mattie Richardson arrived and asked J. Heleluhe to come and see me. Appointed eight P.M. in parlors. Enjoyed the evening singing. Mrs. Evans and her friend and Mrs. Thurley's daughter were present. J. Richardson, Mr. and Mrs. Heleluhe, and I sang.

Mr. and Mrs. Richardson called to speak again on politics. Shows he does not know anything about the situation. Pettigrew and Dubois are working and [he?] tells Carter that I must be patient—everything will come out right. Senator Bacon[9] will bring in an amendment to his resolution.

Wehe ia ka pulupulu kahiko. Aole i hemo ka umoki pulupulu. Aohe koko. Holoholo ahiahi a hiki i M & 14th St. a hiki i 16th St. Hoi ma ka Herdic. [The old cotton was opened. The cotton plug wasn't removed. There wasn't any blood. Walked around in the evening to M and 14th St, and up to 16th St. Returned on a Herdic.][10]

Halalo Glycerin. Aohe nui. [Glycerin enema. Not much.]

*Saturday, March 12.* Had bad dreams. Dead people and live.

Letters arrived for Kaulia, Kalauokalani, and W. Auld. Opened the two Presidents' [letters][11] and found nothing of importance about our situation. Mr. Kemalena told me he heard that the instructions given to Kolea na ka Aeko—ina e nele ana ka Hoohui ia o Hawaii e ka Senate ua kauoha ia o Komisina Sewall a huki i ka hae Amelika. [Mr. Kemalena (Chamberlain?) told me he heard that the instructions given to Kolea (?) from the Aeko (U.S. President?)—if the annexation of Hawaii is denied by the Senate, Commissioner Sewall is ordered to pull the American flag.][12]

*Sunday, March 13.* Murky morning. Two P.M. My doctor examined my neck. Noke ia i ke kope o loko o ka puka a hookomo ia i ka pulupulu hou. Hoike aku wau i ke ano o ka palahehe i luna o ka pulupulu ke omaomao. [He persisted in scraping inside the opening and inserted new cotton. I discovered that the pus on the cotton was greenish.]

Apono mai kela. He hoailona maikai ka kela. Hoouna hou ia mai he laau hou. Hoonui ia elua puna nui i na inu ana eha o ka la—me elua puna nui wai. [He confirmed that was a good sign. New medicine sent for again. Increased to two tablespoons four times a day with two tablespoons water.]

*Monday, March 14.* Loaned my "Faith of the Fathers" to Mrs. Stephen Rand. Letters from home.

*Tuesday, March 15.* Heard of the death of Mrs. Senator J. M. Thurston very sudden.[13]

Rev. Hira Singh Puri called. [I] sang for him and he was pleased. Wakeke went with Mrs. Tucker to the White House. J. O. and Mary Carter came back from Boston. Did not see Mrs. Lee.

---

9. Augustus Octavius Bacon (b. 1839–d. 1924) was a U.S. Senator from Georgia.

10. A herdic was a small horse-drawn omnibus with side seats and an entrance at the back.

11. These were letters from the presidents of the two Hawaiian political groups, not communications from the president of the United States.

12. Harold Marsh Sewall (b. 1860, Maine–d. 1924) was a commissioner general and legislator for the U.S. Consul at Samoa (1887–92) and a U.S. minister in Hawaii (1897–1900).

13. This was the wife of John Mellen Thurston (b. 1847–d. 1916), U.S. Senator from Nebraska, 1895–1901.

*Wednesday, March 16.* I kahi au o kuu kauka. emo ole ia holoi ana mai i ka puu o kuu ai o ka pau no ia. Omaomao ka pulu i umoki ia'i—olioli loa ia—he maikai ka ia hoailona—o ka pau ana ia o ka poison i waho o ke kino. [I was at my doctor's and in no time at all the lump on my neck was cleaned and that was all. The cotton plug was greenish. He's overjoyed as this is a good sign of the end of the poison out of my body.]

Mai laila hele maua e ike ia Mrs. English, aole o ka hale o ka sister kai loaa'ku. Akahi no wau a lohe mai ia J. Richardson e hoomoe ia ana ka pila Hoohui Aina—a e hoihoi ia ana ma ka Joint Resolution. Ke i mai nei o Mary C. e noho ana paha 'uanei laua, olioli loa laua no keia mea hou. [From there went to see Mrs. English. She wasn't at home but met the sister. I've heard from J. Richardson that the annexation bill will be tabled and will be brought back in a joint resolution. Mary C. (Carter) says they might stay here. They were overjoyed with this news.]

*Thursday, March 17.* Nui na leka mai Aima mai, e hoike mai ana i ka nui o na kala i lulu ia e ka lahui no na Elele o ia o Kaulia me Kalauokalani— a ma loko o ka leka a ka Puuku Lucy Peabody la loaa ana ia'u he $900.00 ka nui. Na'u e malama e kaana e like me ka mea pono—no laua a no lakou paha eha. Oiai ua hoi lakou ua ninau aku nei au ia Aima i ka mea pono e hana ai no keia mau dala. Paina me Mrs. Milmore, Wakeke, me J. W. Douglass.[14] [There are many letters from Aima reporting the amount of money donated by the people for the delegates Kaulia and Kalauokalani. Enclosed in a letter from Treasurer Lucy Peabody I received the sum of $900.00. I am to administer and apportion what is necessary for the two of them or maybe the four of them. Since they've left, I asked Aima (Nawahi) what is the best thing to do about these monies. Dined with Mrs. Milmore, Wakeke, and J. W. Douglass.]

*Friday, March 18.* Ten P.M. Kuka me J. O. Carter e pili ana no ko'u nele i ke kala ole. [Ten P.M. Talked with J. O. Carter regarding my lack of funds.]

*Saturday, March 19.* Komo wau o ka lumi o Mr. and Mrs. J. O. Carter. Ma laila laua me J. Richardson e hana ana. Ma hope hele mai o J.O.C. a hoike aku wau i ka Nota i hoouna ia mai e Lucy Peabody he $900.00 no na Elele Hawaii. Nana o J. O. Carter a olelo mai iau e lawe ai au i ia mau dala, a nana no e pani aku ke hoi ia i Hawaii i ke kala a ke "Aloha Aina." [I went to Mr. and Mrs. J. O. Carter's room. The two of them were there with J. Richardson working. Later J.O.C. came and I showed him the note from Lucy Peabody, $900.00 for the Hawaiian delegates. J. O. Carter looked at it and told me to take the money and he'll reimburse the money to the "Aloha Aina" when he returns to Hawaii.]

*Sunday, March 20.* Aie i ka haole Cashier o ka Ebbitt nei $10—i mea e hookaa au i kuu kauka. [Owe the American Cashier of the Ebbitt $10— to pay my doctor.]

*Monday, March 21.* No ke kikoo kala Hale Baneko o Bishop & Co., no $900 ma kuu inoa Queen Liliuokalani countersign ia e J. O. Carter Jr.

---

14. John Watkinson Douglass (b. 1827–d. 1904) was a lawyer practicing in Washington, DC, from 1875.

No. 22408—To Messrs. Laidlaw & Co., 14 Wall Street, New York, a i hoaie ia ma ka inoa o ka Baneko o California, a i kakau ia e Bishop & Co., ma ka la 20 Mar. 1898. [The Bank of Bishop & Co. check for $900 is in my name, Queen Liliuokalani, countersigned by J. O. Carter, Jr. No. 22408. To Messrs. Laidlaw & Co., 14 Wall Street, New York and drawn on the name of the Bank of California and signed by Bishop & Co., on Mar. 20, 1898.]

*Tuesday, March 22.* Hookaa ia na dala $10.00 i aie ia i ke Cashier o ka Ebbitt nei. [Paid the $10.00 owed to the Cashier of the Ebbitt (Hotel) here.]

Five P.M. went for Mrs. Milmore and bade good-bye to Mrs. Harold and Mrs. Swift,[15] then went with [Mrs.] Milmore and Wakeke to dine with Mr. and Mrs. Holt.

Imi mai ana o J. R. me J. H.—i nana 'ku ka hana—ua ona o J. H. a pakike mai ana ia'u i laila. Lapuwale ka hana a ka poe ona. [J. R. and J. H. (John Richardson and Joe Heleluhe) came around to look. J. H. was drunk and was rude to me there. People who are drunk act so foolishly.]

*Wednesday, March 23.* Went to the doctors two P.M. Nana ia kuu Ai a me ke ano o ka palahehe he omaomao a mahalo i ka loaa o ke ano o ka mai ma ka hookahe a hoohamama ana i na puka o kuu A-i. Ua emi mai ka puu nui ma kuu poohiwi. [Went to the doctor's two P.M. My neck was examined and the pus was greenish. I am gratified at finding out about the nature of the disease by draining and opening the holes of my neck. The large lump on my shoulder has receded.]

Makena eha i ka houhou i ke kui me ka pulupulu. No kuu uwe ole manao o Wakeke he lealea wau a nanea i ka o'e a ke kauka. [It hurts terribly to be poked by the needle and then the cotton (inserted). I don't cry (so) Wakeke thinks I enjoy being probed by the doctor.]

Mrs. and Miss Mason called to invite [me] for Saturday at six P.M. Madame Baroness Von Orendorf and son and Mademoiselle des Vinsens called and spent evening. Mrs. and Miss Weaver[16]—Hoi koke no laua Invite mai o Madame e hele i kona wahi. I ka oniki liilii no o J. H. i lalo o ka ona mai ia. Kiekie kuu ukiuki. [They left quickly. Madame invited me to visit her home. J. H. (Joe Heleluhe) was on the small balcony drunk. I was extremely annoyed.]

*Thursday, March 24.* He la ua keia—pii nae maua hola 12 P.M. me Wakeke i kahi o Mrs. Braendle—he lunch me elua wahine a na Senator Jones[17] me Madison—sister in law a Senator Steele[18]—Mrs. Capt. Lamberton[19]— Hola 1—hiki mai ana o Prof. Mori, a Russian Pianist. [Rainy day today. However, at 12 noon Wakeke and I went up to Mrs. Braendle's place—a lunch with the wives of Senators Jones and Madison—the sister-in-law

---

15. Grace Virginia Swift was the wife of U.S, Admiral William B. Swift (b. 1848–d. 1919).

16. Mrs. Mary W. K. Weaver of 1614 Q Street, Washington, DC, in 1905 sent Liliu a gift with this sentiment: "There is no one who admires and loves you more devotedly." Hawaii State Archives, Liliu Collection, Box 7.

17. James Kimbrough Jones (b. 1839–d. 1908) was a U.S. senator from Arkansas 1885–1903.

18. George Washington Steele (b. 1833–d. 1922) was a congressman from Indiana 1881–83 and 1895–1903.

19. Lila Stedman was the wife of Captain (later Rear Admiral) Benjamin P. Lamberton (b. 1844–d. 1912).

of Senator Steele—Mrs. Capt. Lamberton—one P.M. Prof. Mori, a Russian pianist, is coming.] He wanted Mrs. Braendle to write a play for him about me. Now he met me and was pleased in the meeting. Mrs. Jones sent me home in her new carriage.

*Sunday, March 27.* Hele i kuu kauka. Ke nui nei ka puka o ka palahehe a i mai ke maikai loa a ke hoea mai nei na ouli maikai o ka lanakila ma luna o keia mai ai kanaka, a manaolana ae ke ola. Aohe nui o ka eha i keia oʻe ana me ke kui i na puka elua. [Went to my doctor. The opening of pus is getting larger and he said it's very good. Good signs are appearing of overcoming this man-eating disease. There is confidence of recovery. The probing of the two openings with the needle didn't hurt much.]

*Wednesday, March 30.* Hele hou i ke kauka. Nui na poe mai e kali ana. Ua ano ole ka hoʻo ana i ka pulupulu a hookuu mai ana—He mai lohi keia o ke ola. Aia no a emi loa na puu a palupalu na aa a-i o ke ola ia o keia mai. [Went again to the doctor. There are many sick people waiting. The stain on the cotton was colorless. It is clearing up. This disease is slow to heal. When the lumps diminish completely and the neck muscles become flexible, then this disease is cured.]

*Sunday, April 3.* Went to St. Patrick's Church. Father McGee[20] and Father Stafford officiated. Then to the doctors. Okioki ia kuu Ai a kahe a wai ke koko—i nui ka palahehe. Eha loa ia kuu A-i. Palm Sunday—Haawi i ka palms i kiss ia e Father Mcgee a loaa ka makou palm. [My neck was cut into and blood flowed like water—with much pus. My neck hurt terribly. Palm Sunday—The palms were given and kissed by Father McGee and we received our palm.]

J. Richardson, Mr. and Mrs. Heleluhe, and Mrs. Tucker all gave me their share.

*Wednesday, April 6.* Hele i kahi o kuu Kauka me Mrs. Tucker me Wakeke. Ke pii lohi nei ke ola o kuu A-i. He [Went to the doctor with Mrs. Tucker and Wakeke. My neck is getting steadily better. A (Sentence ends thus.)]

*Sunday, April 10.* Went seven A.M. to St. Andrews to Communion. It was a full service. 11 A.M. Mrs. Tucker came over with Mr. and Mrs. Heleluhe [and] we went to St. Patrick's—it was so full. J. H. came home and it rained very heavily. After service Wakeke and I went to my doctor. Okioki hou ia kuu ai. [My neck was opened again.]

*Saturday, April 23.* Wakeke and Mrs. Tucker went to Theatre at Lafayette Square, came home. Five P.M. Hoopunipuni mai akahi no a pau ke keaka, eia ka i kahi o Kann. Hele loa Chevy Chase he loa ia mau wahi. Noho wau hoopaa i kuu palm cross i hana ia me ka loke ma ka centre o ke cross all made of palm. [Five P.M. Lied that the play had just ended, yet are here at Kann's (a department store). Chevy Chase is a long way from this area. I stayed. Affixed my palm cross made with roses in the center of the cross all made of palm.] It is very pretty.

---

20. This was Father Joseph McGee. In Liliu's 1903 diary, she says his church was on 14th Street and Whitney Avenue, Washington, DC.

*Sunday, April 24.* Mrs. Tucker came round and I showed her my cross and asked her to take it to Father McGee with a bow of Hawaiian colors, saying it represented Hawaii at the foot of the Cross—father was much pleased and showed it to his boys, also to Sister Angelica.

*Wednesday, April 27.* Hele i ke kauka. [Went to the doctor.]

*Saturday, April 30.* Last payment of Ebbitt House, Ninety six dollars. J. Heleluhe asked Mr. Burch, Manager, to wait further payment until my money came from Honolulu, in as soon as Mr. J. O. Carter reached Honolulu he will send me money. Mr. Burch said he would.

**Sunday, May 1.** Hele i ke kauka nui ka hauoli no ka emi o na puu Cancer. Hookuu ia kekahi puka e paa hookahi puka ia hoopilapilau ia nei. [Went to the doctor. Am overjoyed the cancerous lumps have gone down. One opening was allowed to close. One opening has become smelly.]

*Wednesday, May 4.* Hele i ke kauka. [Went to the doctor.]

*Sunday, May 8.* Hele i ke kauka. Ke holo pono nei ka emi o na puu o kuu ai. Ua nui keia la. He Crupe ko maua o Wakeke. Hiki ae ana he wahine like kona mai me koʻu. Ma ka waiu nae kona puu. [Went to the doctor. The lumps on my neck are successfully going down. Today it is raining heavily. Wakeke and I have the Croupe. A woman came in with a disease like mine but her lump is located on the breast.]

*Tuesday, May 10.* 11 A.M. Kipa mai o E. E. Settle.[21] M. C. and wife and daughter e ike ia. Maikai ko makou launa ana noi mai iaʻu e command ia ia ma na mea a pau a i na wa a pau. Mahalo! Hele i kahi o Mrs. Mason a makana o Wakeke he mau pine kui papale ia Miss Myrta Mason. [11 A.M. E. E. Settle visited. M. C. and wife and daughter were seen. We had a nice visit. He requested I command him for any matter at any time. Thank you! Went to Mrs. Mason's. Wakeke gifted some hatpins to Miss Myrta Mason.]

*Wednesday, May 11.* Hele i kahi o ke kauka, aohe nui o kana hana ana. [Went to doctor's office, he didn't do much.]

*Thursday, May 12.* Lohe mai la mai ia J. Heleluhe ua halawai mai la me kekahi C. M. a hai mai iaia e lawe ana lakou ia Hawaii a e haawi ana nae lakou iaʻu i uku hoomau no koʻu wa e ola ana. Auwe! kuu aloha i kuu Aina hanau a me kuu lahui aloha. Ka iwi o kuu iwi ke koko o kuu koko. Aloha! Aloha! Aloha! [Heard from J. Heleluhe that he met with a C. M. who said they are going to take Hawaii and they will grant me a pension during my lifetime. Alas! My love for my homeland and my beloved people, the bones of my bones, the blood of my blood. Aloha! Aloha! Aloha!]

*Saturday, May 14.* Loaa mai he omole laau—ua hoololi iki ia ʻe. 2 puna nui me 2 puna nui wai i ke ala ana. 1 Hola 11—1—4 P.M. 2 i ka hoi ana e moe. [Received a bottle of medicine. There was a minor change to 2 Tbsp. with 2 Tbsp. water upon waking. 1 (Tbsp. at) 11, one, and four P.M. 2 (Tbsp.) at bedtime.]

21. Evan E. Settle (b. 1848–d. 1899) was a Kentucky lawyer and congressman (from 1896).

*Sunday, May 15.* Hele i ke kauka. Wehe ia he puka hou a hoomau ia no ka hamama o ka puka kahiko—lohi ke emi ana o na puu e aho nae ia ke ole ka make. E hoomau aku no ka hoomanawanui. Akahi no a i mai ke kauka ua makaukau oia e hele me au i Hawaii a ola kuu mai hoi mai ia. Olelo aku wau ua loli koʻu hoi no ke kali i ka mea e hana ia ana i loko o ka hale Senate a apono mai ana ia. [Went to the doctor. A new opening was made and the old one was kept open. The lumps are going down so slowly, but it's better than dying. Will continue to persevere. The doctor says he is prepared to go with me to Hawaii and when my disease is cured he'll leave. I said my return has been changed to wait out what is being done in the Senate, he consented.]

*Tuesday, May 17.* Hana ano e mai la no hoi o Wakeke i ka maua hele. Four P.M. hele maua ma 14 a ma 15th St., i New York Ave, kau ma ka Herdick pii a 16th ma Corcoran St. lala hele a kahi o Mrs. Milmore aole o laila hele loa maua iho ma New Hampshire Ave ma Q St., hiki i Connecticut or 20th St. kau ma ke kaa Uwila Kau e au mamua koiala hoi aela no ia ma ka noho ma hope a aka mai ana. Komo mai ana he haole ma koʻu noho paa wau no ka mea e holo mai ana he kaa Uwila ma o—Kanalua iho la o Wakeke o ka hele hou o ka noho paha—E ole ke conductor ku ai ke kaa a lele au. He nui ka wa i hana opulepule ai o Wakeke iaʻu. Ninau ae au ia Wakeke eia ka ua hala me Mrs. Tucker i kahi o Ka Presedena. [Wakeke acted strangely on our outing. Four P.M. we went along 14th Street and 15th Street to New York Avenue, then rode on a herdic up to 16th Street along Corcoran Street, got off, went to Mrs. Milmore's. She wasn't there. We went down New Hampshire Avenue, along Q Street, until Connecticut or 20th Street, got on the streetcar, I got on before her. She went to the seat in back and laughed. An American got on by my seat. I sat firm because a streetcar was coming from over yonder. Wakeke was confused whether to continue on or stay seated, if it weren't for the conductor, when the car stopped I would have gotten off. Many a time Wakeke has acted strangely with me. I questioned Wakeke. Come to find out she had gone with Mrs. Tucker to the president's.]

*Wednesday, May 18.* Kauka kai i mai ua makaukau oia, a hakalia iaʻu ke hiki e hoike aku i kona alanui e pono ai ma laila. [Doctor said he is ready, but will wait for me so I can explain the best way for him to get there.]

*Thursday, May 19.* Hookaa no ka Ebbitt 274.00—J. H. 50—Olioli loa wau no ka pau o kuu aie. [Paid the Ebbitt $274.00. J. H. $50. I am very happy my debts are discharged.]

11 A.M. Iho mai o Mrs. Milmore a koi ia maua o Wakeke e hele i ka holo kaa i Chevy Chase—Hola 1—hiki i ka hale nei. [11 A.M. Mrs. Milmore came down and Wakeke and I were asked to go on a carriage ride to Chevy Chase. 1 P.M. came home.]

Omole laau hou keia—hoololi hou. 1 puna nui laau 1 puna nui wai—4 inu ana i ka la. [This is a new bottle of medicine. Changed again to 1 Tbsp. medicine 1 Tbsp. water, four times a day.]

*Friday, May 20.* I anei o Mrs. Weaver, informal call i mai he omaimai ke kaikamahine a e hoouna ana i Cleveland, a o ke keiki hoi e hele ana a hui me ka puali i keia la, apopo 2 P.M. hele nui ae e ike Presidena, 4 P.M. kau ma ka B. & O.R.R. [Mrs. Weaver is here, informal call. Said her daughter is ill and is sending her to Cleveland, and the son is going to meet the soldiers today. Tomorrow two P.M. (the soldiers en masse) go to see the President. Four P.M. Board the B. & O.R.R. (Baltimore & Ohio Railroad)]

Hai mai ia J. R. aohe maka pii i kahi o ka Baroness—ua lilo ka laua. Hoouna wau i kuu *H Story* ia T. B. Reed. [Told J. R. no one was at the Baroness's. The two of them had gone. I sent my *Hawaii's Story* to T. B. Reed.]

*Sunday, May 22.* Hoi mai ke kauka. Aole i nui ka oki ana. [The doctor returned. Not much operating done.]

*Monday, May 23.* 2 P.M. Hele me Wakeke i kahi o Mrs. Mason—ua hele e ike i ka holo o ka nephew i ke kaua. Hoi wawae mai laila a ka hale kuai o Kann. Nui ka ua a ina aole ua ina ua hiki loa i ka hale nei. [Two P.M. Went with Wakeke to Mrs Mason's—went to see the nephew sail off to war. Walked back from there to Kann's store. There was heavy rain. If it hadn't rained we would have reached home.]

*Wednesday, May 25.* Kahi o ke Kauka. Hookahi hola ke hou ana i kuu A-i. Aole eha loa. Huli mai o Mrs. Tucker i laila. Hoi mai i na laau a holo makou i Chevy Chase. [Doctor's office. Probed my neck for one hour. Not much pain. Mrs. Tucker came around there and requested medicines. We went to Chevy Chase.]

Hoike aku wau i ke kauka i ko'u makemake e hoi i Hawaii no ke pohihihi o ko'u mau waiwai o hope. [I expressed to the doctor my desire to return to Hawaii because of the confusion over my properties of late.]

*Thursday, May 26.* 8 P.M. Mrs. Stephen Rand[22] and her sister Mrs. Miller and daughter and friend called to hear me sing. Mrs. English and her sister Miss Chambers called at the same time. After the others went the two latter stayed and we had a very pleasant chat.

Four P.M. Called on the Baroness von Orendorf and Mlle. des Vinsen and Mr. Orendorf with J. Richardson and J. Heleluhe and wife. While there Baron Von Schenargaslarg [visited?].

*Friday, May 27.* ~~Mrs. Rand & her sister.~~ 11½ A.M. I went with Richardson, Heleluhe, and wife to call on Mrs. and Mr. Smallwood.

*Saturday, May 28.* Hiki mai o Mrs. Reeside me elua lady mai Philadelphia—12½ hiki mai 100 poe hui Mason me ka lakou wahine lala mason e ike ia'u. Himeni makou ia Aloha Oe—a hookani au ia Star Spangled Banner a himeni lakou a pau loa a piha ia lakou i ka olioli no'u. [Mrs. Reeside came with two ladies from Philadelphia—12:30 100 Masons and their female Mason members came to see me. We sang "Aloha Oe" and I played "Star Spangled Banner" while they all sang. All of them were filled with good tidings for me.]

---

22. This was the wife of Stephen Rand (b. 1844–d. 1915), a naval officer who retired with the rank of rear admiral.

*Sunday, May 29.* Kahi o ke kauka. Olioli ia i ka emi o ka puu o kuu A-i. Aohe ano maikai loa o kona ola ke ae mai nei nae e hele i Hawaii. [Doctor's office. He's overjoyed the lump on my neck went down. He is not in very good health but has agreed to go to Hawaii.]

**Wednesday, June 1.** Ke Kauka i keia la a hai aku la i ka hoi o makou i Hawaii. I mai naʻu aku no e noonoo i na kala kupono au e uku aku ai iaia o ka mahina. Hou ia i puka hou ma kuu a-i. 5 P.M. Kuka iho la makou e haawi iaia $300—o ka mahina—e ae ana paha? aole paha? [At the doctor's today and mentioned our returning to Hawaii. He said I am to consider a suitable salary I am to pay him per month. A new opening was made in my neck. 5:00 P.M. We discussed giving him $300 per month. Perhaps it's acceptable? Probably not?]

*Thursday, June 2.* Hoi hou e kuka me ke Kauka no ka $300—aohe ae mai aohe hoole mai—no laila manao wau he uuku loa kela $300—i kona manao. [Came back to discuss with the doctor about the $300—he didn't accept or reject it. I think in his opinion the $300 is quite meager.]

*Saturday, June 4.* Kuka iho la me J. R. e hele e kamailio pu me Sen. P.[23] no ka uku au ke koi poho ai. Hala ku no hoi kela i ke Kapitala hoi mai ana o J. H. i mai ana e hoopanee ka hoi o makou i H. Ua loaa mai nei iaia he haole i i mai iaia e hoohui iana o Hawaii a e loaa na naʻu he haawina uku hoomau. Ae aku wau e noho. [Discussed with J. R. about going to talk with Sen. P. about payment I should press in the damage claim. He went to the Capitol. J. H. (Heleluhe) came back saying to postpone our return to Hawaii. He met an American who said "Hawaii is going to be annexed and I will get a pension." I agreed to stay.]

Eight P.M. Hui hou me J. R. i ka parlor Hoike mai oia ua hoike mai o P. oia mau no ke oni paa o ka ninau aole i kuemi ka aoao ona. [Eight P.M. Met again with J. R. in the parlor. He said P. explained the question remains firm. His side hasn't retreated.]

*Sunday, June 5.* Hele i ke Kauka. Ke emi maikai nei na puu a pau a nui ka oli oli o ke Kauka. Hai aku wau ua panee ka hoi o makou i Hawaii—ke kumu no ke ano ikaika o ka Aoao hoohui—ina e Hui pono wau. [Went to the doctor. All the lumps are going down satisfactorily. The doctor is very happy. I said we had postponed our return to Hawaii, the reason being the strength of the annexation party, if I am to prevail successfully.]

Four P.M. Makou e-ha me Mrs. Tucker & [illegible] o Miss Williams. [Four P.M. The four of us and Mrs. Tucker (met?) at Miss Williams's.]

*Monday, June 6.* Hele maua o Wakeke i Hospital Hill—He maimai o Mrs. Mason. [Wakeke and I went to Hospital Hill. Mrs. Mason is ill.]

*Wednesday, June 8.* Mai kahi o ke kauka. Aole o nui loa ka oe ana. Ano omaimai maoli ke kauka. [From the doctors. Not much probing. The doctor is somewhat ill.]

---

23. Richard Franklin Pettigrew (b. 1848–d. 1926) was a U.S. senator from South Dakota (1889–1901). He was strongly opposed to Hawaiian annexation. The "damage claim" Liliu refers to here was connected with her claim to the Crown lands.

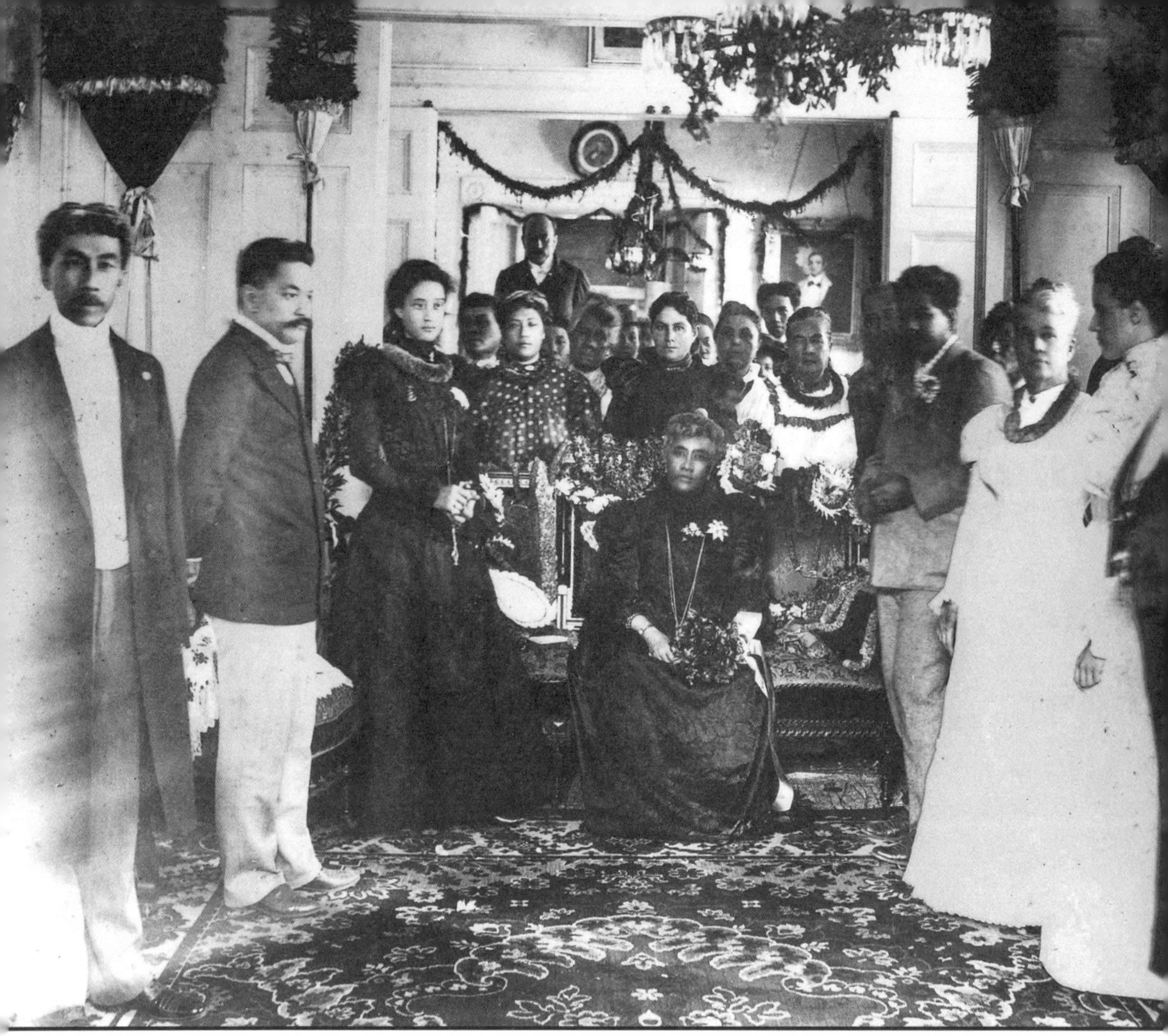

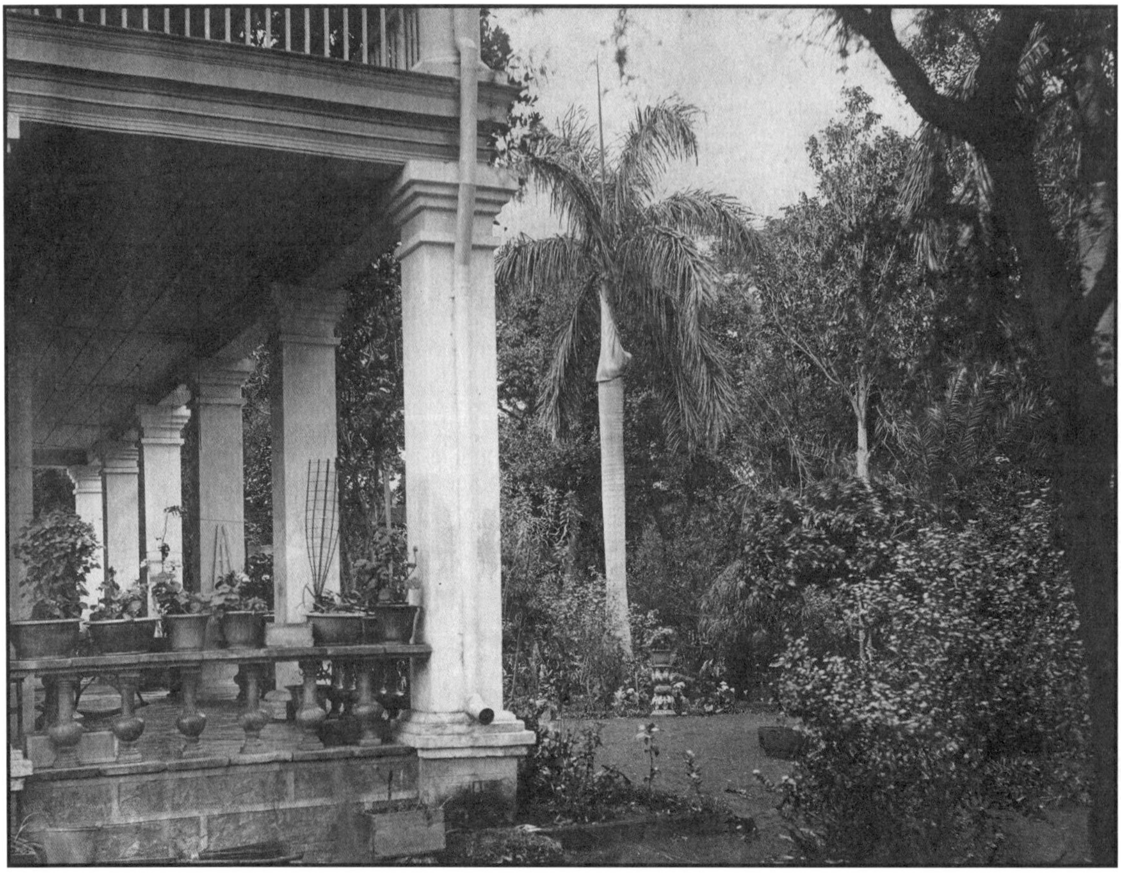

OPPOSITE

*The Queen and her supporters at Washington Place after her return from Washington, DC, August 2, 1898. Front row, left to right: Joseph Heleluhe, David Kawananakoa, Kaiulani, Liliuokalani, Jonah Kuhio Kalanianaole, Mary Carter, and Saide "Liliu" Carter. The youthful portrait of Liliuokalani's husband, John O. Dominis, painted in 1847 by Joel Blakeslee Knapp hangs on the back wall.*
Frank Davey, Bishop Museum Archives

*Washington Place lanai and garden.*
Alfred Mitchell, circa 1886, Bishop Museum Archives

*Lowering the Hawaiian flag, August 12, 1898. On this day, the Republic of Hawaii ceded control to the United States during a ceremony at Iolani Palace. The Queen, her family, and her associates chose not to attend the ceremony and remained at Washington Place.*
F. J. Lowrey, Hawaii State Archives

On June 16, 1897, a treaty of annexation was signed in Washington, DC, by John Sherman, on behalf of the United States, and by F. M. Hatch, Lorrin Thurston, and W. A. Kinney on behalf of the Republic of Hawaii. The Hawaiian Senate promptly ratified the treaty, but it was never submitted to the U. S. Senate for ratification. Instead of following that course, the Joint Resolution (Public Resolution No. 51), introduced by Francis G. Newlands, passed both houses of Congress and was approved by U.S. President William McKinley July 7th, 1898.[24]

In April 1898, President McKinley and Congress declared war against Spain, turning Hawaii into a critically important center of naval operations. In the end, it was the Spanish-American War and the argument for permanent rights to Pearl Harbor that propelled the annexation of Hawaii through Congress. Public Resolution No. 51 of the 55th Congress of the United States of America, headed "Joint Resolution to Provide for Annexing the Hawaiian Islands to the United States," read as follows:

> ¶ *Resolved by the Senate and House of representatives of the United States of America in Congress assembled,* That said cession is accepted, ratified and confirmed, and that the said Hawaiian Islands and their dependencies be, and they are hereby, annexed as a part of the territory of the United States and are subject to the sovereign dominion thereof, and that all and singular the property and rights hereinbefore mentioned are vested on the United States of America.[25]

It was signed by Sereno E. Payne, speaker pro tempore of the House of Representatives, and Garret A. Hobart, vice president of the United States and president of the Senate, and noted as "Approved July 7, 1898, William McKinley."

*Saturday, June 11.* Mrs. Milmore and Mrs. Tucker hele makou me J. Heleluhe i Glen Echo i ka holo kaa hoi mai me ka luhi.[26] [Mrs. Milmore and Mrs. Tucker, we went with J. Heleluhe to Glen Echo on a carriage ride. Returned tired.]

*Sunday, June 12.* Hele hou i ke kauka—ua oluolu iki o ia. Okioki hou ia kuu a-i. Kamailio hou maua no ka hele i Hawaii a aole ae loa mai. [Went again to the doctor's. He was somewhat better. My neck was operated on again. We talked again about going to Hawaii. He didn't completely agree.]

---

24. See Hawaii State Archives, A. S. Hartwell Papers, Folder 8, typescript memorandum.
25. William Adam Russ Jr., *The Hawaiian Republic, 1894–98* (Selinsgrove, Pennsylvania: Susquehanna University Press, 1961), 354. The version actually signed by President McKinley is in the National Archives, Washington, DC. A photostat of the signed original is now with the version sent to the Hawaiian government (and annotated as Public Resolution No. 51) in the Hawaii State Archives, Foreign Office and Executive Files, Box 69.
26. In the 1903 diary, Liliu lists Mrs. Mary L. Milmore as living at 1713 Corcoran St., Washington, DC, and gives the address of Mrs. T. F. Tucker as 52 Broadway, Room 913, New York City.

*Tuesday, June 14.* I kahi o Mrs. Mason. Mr. and Mrs. Hane a'u—I ka hale no laua. Nui na mea hoolana. E hoi ana a hoi hou mai. E loaana no ka mea i makemake ia i loko nae o ka nui o ka lilo. Aole e like me ka mea i makemake ai aka ma lalo mai. Hai mai he mau enemi ko'u, a e kiai ko'u poe ia'u aole ae e hele hookahi noho hookahi. [At Mrs. Mason's. Mr. and Mrs. Hane and I at their home. Much encouraging news, I will make a claim and leave. What is desired will be obtained despite the immense cost. Not exactly as what is wanted, but less. Was told I have enemies and my people will guard me. Am not allowed to travel alone or stay alone.]

*Wednesday, June 15.* Kahi o ke kauka. Ae mai e hele ana oia me a'u. Nui na olelo ana no na mea e pili ana no na mai o-o a me kana mau mea e hana'i. Ua o'e no i kuu a-i. [Doctor's office. Agreed to go with me. He talked a lot about illnesses of old age and his treatments. He probed my neck.]

Hoouna mai ana o Mrs. Mason i kuu pahu Omau Amethyst. [Mrs. Mason is sending my amethyst pin box.]

Kahea mai ana o Miss Mason ma ke telephone ia J. R. e pii aku makou. Haawi au 1 pine ia J. H. pela me Wakeke. [Miss Mason telephoned J. R. that we are coming up. I gave a pin to J. H. and to Wakeke.]

Pii aku makou—i laila o Mrs. Brown.[27] [We went up. Mrs. Brown was there.]

Ka olelo kupanaha ana. [Unusual statements.]

Aole kula he kala nae me kekahi metala e. [illegible] mahina o ka aina a'u e makemake nei e kuai—E kuai au i kekahi apana no $250,000 o kahi i mahiai ia la. E pono na kahi poe e e eli no ka mea he nui ka lilo. E hookoe i kekahi wahi kuleana i loko o ka metala e loaa 'na. [No gold, there's silver with other metals upon the property I wish to buy. I will buy a parcel for $250,000 of the cultivated area. Other people should do the digging because the expenditure is immense. Shall reserve a portion of the interest in the metal found.]

*Thursday, June 16.* 1 P.M. Sent J. Heleluhe with $300 to pay Dr. Charles Hamilton English as agreed by former conversation with him that should he Consent to go with me to Honolulu, I would pay him the amount of $350 every month for three months or five months or as long as I am in Honolulu until released.[28] J. H. gave him the amount and brought home receipt.

I find my error. ~~Should have made papers of agreement first stating for the length of time of stay in Honolulu. That from the moment of 1st payment my usual payment of 2—a week ceases~~.

*Friday, June 17.* Miss Mason called at five P.M. Her mother not so well. Gave her $15—for six Amethyst stones.

*Sunday, June 19.* Hiki hou i kahi o ke kauka. Kamailio no ka hele i Hawaii. Ae mai e hele ana no me a'u. Maikai kela! alaila aole e hopohopo no kuu A-i. A i ko'u manao e ola ana no i loko o ekolu mahina aka, he maikai no e hoomau aku no eono mahina hou a akaka loa ke ola aole e hoi hou mai.

---

27. In the 1903 diary, Liliu lists Mrs. Brown as Marie L. W. Brown, 37 Corcoran Building, Washington, DC.

28. See diary entry for February 1, 1900 (513).

Ua hai mai e hoi mai ana i loko eono mahina, hoi aku no hoi au e hoi hou mai ana no hoi au i loko oia wa. [Went again to the doctor's. Talked about going to Hawaii. (He) Agreed to go with me. That's wonderful! Then I won't worry about my neck and I think it will heal within three months but is best to continue (treatment) for six months until it is clear that it's cured. Said he will come back within six months, but I can come and go during that time.]

*Monday, June 20.* 6:30 A.M. Holoholo a ka Shoreham kau ma ka Herdic hiki i kahi o Mrs. Milmore—noho iki, iho i kai o Dupont Circle kau ke kaa Uila hiki me ka luhi nui o ke kino i ka hale nei Ebbitt House. Hui iho la ma kuu lumi nei me Mrs. Milmore, Mrs. Mason, Mr. Douglas. Ahiahi hai mai o J. Heleluhe aohe moku e hoi ai. Ina ma Vanekouva hiki ma ka *Warrimoo* ia la la 20 o July e haalele ai ia Wakinekona nei. [6:30 A.M. Went about the Shoreham. Rode a Herdic to Mrs. Milmore's. Stayed a while, then went down seaward of Dupont Circle. Rode the streetcar and reached Ebbitt House fatigued. Met in my room with Mrs. Milmore, Mrs. Mason, Mr. Douglas. Evening. J. Heleluhe said no ships are going back. If from Vancouver on the *Warrimoo*, then must leave Washington July 20.]

*Tuesday, June 21.* 7 P.M. Hiki i kahi o Mrs. Mason—nanea loa ia me laua kani ka hola 8—awiwi no ka hala 8 P.M. iho i lalo i ka parlor a hiki mai ana o Mrs. T. Reddington. [7 P.M. Went to Mrs. Mason's. Relaxed with them until 8 o'clock. The hour went by so quickly. 8 P.M. went down to the parlor as Mrs. T. Reddington was arriving.]

*Wednesday, June 22.* La hanau o J. Heleluhe me J. Kaipo Aea. 43 M. H.—16 M. H. Hiki mai o Mrs. Milmore hai aku wau i koʻu makemake ia J. W. Douglas e aie i mau kala naʻu i $2,000.00 Apopo hui makou i kahi o Milmore e noonoo a kuka. ¼ to two P.M. hele i kahi o ke kauka. Hai mai ua inflame ia ka puka o kuu A-i. No ke aha la? Ke ano onahia iki aela ka wai omaomao o luna o ka pulupulu o kuu ai. Aia no a emi loa na puu elima o kuu A-i a laila pau ke omaomao o ka wai. 7 A.M. Hele maua o Wakeke e holoholo ma G St. a waiho i ka omole laau i kahi o ke kauka. Hoi ma 9th St. huli ma F St. 6 blocks a hiki i ka hale. [Birthdays of J. Heleluhe, 43 years old; and J. Kaipo Aea, 16 years. Mrs. Milmore came. I told her of my wish for J. W. Douglas to loan me $2,000. Tomorrow we'll meet at the Milmores' to consider and discuss it. 1:45 P.M. Went to the doctor's. Said the opening on my neck is inflamed. Why? The greenish secretion on the cotton from my neck has diminished a bit. When the five lumps on my neck go down then the greenish fluid will stop. Seven A.M. Wakeke and I went on G St. and left the medicine bottle at the doctor's. Went back along Ninth St., turned on F St., six blocks until home.]

*Thursday, June 23.* Kakau ia J. A. Palmer, e like me kana i i mai ai, "i na wa a pau au e makemake ai i kala hai mai iaʻu a e loaa no ia oe." Aole no i pau loa kaʻu wahi kala aka no ka manao ana e hoi i Hawaii ua kaili ia na moku Hawaii o ia o *Alameda* ma no laila e pono e hoi ma Vanekova, a he ala loihi kela a nui ka lilo. No laila ua noi au e kokua mai. [Write to J. A. Palmer for the reason he had said, "Anytime you want money to tell me and you'll get it." My funds are not completely gone but am intent on returning to Hawaii. The Hawaiian ships *Alameda* and others were seized.[29] Therefore we have to return by Vancouver and that is a longer and more expensive route. So I asked him for help.]

*Friday, June 24.* I anei o Mrs. English 8 P.M. Ui no hoi. Imi mai ana ke kauka ka uhoi no ia. Rheumatism mau wau i keia mau la hookahi ae nei pule. Noi mai o Mrs. E—i hele e paina me lakou ae aku wau. [Mrs. English is here eight P.M. So pretty. The doctor was looking for us, then left. I am constantly rheumatic these days for the past week. Mrs. E—requested I dine with them. I accepted.]

*Saturday, June 25.* 9:30 A.M. Pii maua o Wakeke i 1224 13th St., e ike ia Mrs. English a hai aku ia ia aole au e hiki aku ana i laila e paina me lakou i ka la apopo. Hoi wawae mai laila a G St. 1107 a hiki kahi o Merts F St. & 11th St. [9:30 A.M. Wakeke and I went up to 1224 13th St., to see Mrs. English and tell her I won't be able to dine with them tomorrow. Walked back from there to G St. 1107 to Mertz's place F St. and 11th St.]

*Sunday, June 26.* Hele i kahi o ke kauka. Ke mau la no ke omaomao o ka palahehe aia a pau ia a laila pau na puu liilii elima. Ke emi ihola nae a ua uuku loa. Ninau hou mai no ke kukui—I aku wau e loaa ana no—I mai kela $2.00 no ka mahina no hookahi kukui. [Went to the doctor's. The pus is still greenish. When it stops then the five small lumps will disappear. But they're diminishing, getting smaller. He asked again about the lamp. I said I will get it. He said it's $2.00 per month for one lamp.]

*Tuesday, June 28.* Loaa mai he pane mai ia J.A.P. no ka mea i hoike ia la 23—A oi lewalewa iho Wilimana—Kakau ia J.D.S. no ia mea hookahi a me C.R.B. [Received a reply from J.A.P. (Julius A. Palmer) about the matter made known on the 23rd—Since Wilimana is left dangling. Wrote to J.D.S. (John D. Spreckels) about this same matter and C.R.B. (C. R. Bishop).]

*Wednesday, June 29.* Kahi o ke kauka. [Doctor's office.]

*Sunday, July 3.* Hele i kahi o ke kauka. Kamailio maua no ka hele i Hawaii—hai mai e hele ana i Nu Ioka i chemicals apopo. [Went to doctor's. We talked about going to Hawaii. Said he is going to New York tomorrow for chemicals.]

*Monday, July 4.* Hola 7 A.M. A ike ia Mrs. English lawe pu me ka omole i pau o kuu laau—i hai aku aohe moku. 8 P.M. Hele au me J. Heleluhe i kahi o Mrs. Mason. Paapu o Penn Ave., i na kanaka wahine keiki ua helelei he ua. 9:30 P.M. hoi mai—omaimai Wakeke. Ui ka wahine a ke Kauka. Nine 40 P.M. Loaa mai he telekalapa mai C. R. Bishop ae mai ana e hoouna mai ana i Elua Tausani. [Seven A.M. Went to see Mrs. English,

---

29. The U.S. government had commandeered the two vessels to transport troops to the Philippines at the beginning of the Spanish American war.

took along my empty medicine bottle. There aren't any ships. Eight P.M. Went with J. Heleluhe to Mrs. Mason's. Pennsylvania Avenue was crowded with men, women, and children. It rained. 9:30 P.M. came back. Wakeke ill. The doctor's wife is pretty. 9:40 P.M. Received a telegram from C. R. Bishop confirming he will send $2,000.00.][30]

*Tuesday, July 5.* Hiki hou i 1224—13 St. me ka leka na ke kauka e hai aku ana e hiki aku ana wau e kuka pu me ia no na laau e lawe ai i Hawaii. 2 P.M. Aole i hele i kahi o ke kauka. Loaa kuu omole laau hooikaika kino. [Came again to 1224 13th St. with a letter for the doctor saying that I will come to discuss with him about the medicines to take to Hawaii. 2 P.M. Didn't go to the doctor's. Got my bottle of health tonic.]

Five P.M. Loaa mai he telegram mai J. D. Spreckels e ae mai ana e hoouna mai no ia i Elua Tausani, ka la 10 ae. [Five P.M. Received a telegram from J. D. Spreckels agreeing to send $2,000 on the tenth.]

8 P.M. Owau, J. Heleluhe, J. Rikikini pii i kahi o Mrs. Reedside, hiki ae o Mrs. Potts. 10:30 P.M. hoi mai. [8 P.M. I, J. Heleluhe, (and) J. Richardson went up to Mrs. Reeside's. Mrs. Potts came. 10:30 P.M. We returned.]

Pane ia ka C. R. Bishop telegram 10 A.M. Pane ia ka J. D. Spreckels 10:35 P.M. [10 A.M. Answered C. R. Bishop's telegram. 10:35 P.M. answered J. D. Spreckels.]

*Wednesday, July 6.* Hele i kahi o ke kauka. Ua piha kona lumi i na ukana no ka makaukau i ka hele i Hawaii—Noi mai i mau kala in advance—I aku wau e hele ae ia i ka Ebbitt House hora 11 A.M. la apopo. Ae mai. [Went to the doctor's. His room was filled with baggage preparing for the trip to Hawaii. (He) requested some money on advance. I said to come to the Ebbitt House 11 A.M. tomorrow. He agreed.]

8:30 P.M. Hoi ai o J. R. a hai mai ua holo maila ka Hoohui Aina. Loaa ia Haki. E pau nui ana i ka hoi apopo. [8:30 P.M. J. R. (John Richardson) returned and reported annexation has passed. Hatch has it. It'll all be over at the end of day tomorrow.]

---

On July 6, 1898, the U.S. Senate read for the third time the joint resolution to annex Hawaii: "In answer to the question, 'shall it pass?' the vote stood yeas 42, nays 21, not voting 26. The subject was finally ended. Except for the President's signature, Hawaii was annexed."[31] President William McKinley signed the joint resolution on July 7. Everyone in Hawaii would learn of the event when the Pacific Mail S.S. *Coptic* arrived from San Francisco on July 13, 1898, and at 3:30 P.M. signaled the news from offshore Waikiki. The headline of the following morning in the *Pacific Commercial Advertiser* announced, "Annexation! Here to Stay!"

---

30. Liliu had asked for a loan from Charles R. Bishop to meet expenses in Washington, DC. On July 19, 1898, Joseph O. Carter wrote to Bishop, "The difficulty experienced in keeping the Queen in funds has arisen in my not having timely notice for remittances. I am glad that you have advanced the required sums and have to advise you that I paid the sum advanced with charges to your a/c with Messrs. Bishop & Co. of which payment they will notify you." Hawaii State Archives, J. O. Carter Letter Book.

31. *The Hawaiian Republic*, 353.

*Thursday, July 7.* Waited at 11 A.M. for Kauka [doctor]. He did not come, but some Maryland teachers called—12:30 P.M. J. H. went with me to Mrs. Milmore's—Of course _____ was there. Dined and she came home with me at 3:30 and found Kauka [doctor] had called and gone. So sat down, wrote a note inclosing $300 "pahi" [paid] in advance. Evening Mrs. Braendle and Josephine called.

*Friday, July 8.* 9.4 A.M. received a receipt from Kauka Iniliki [Dr. English] for the amount sent to him of $300.00. Wrote to J. O. Carter and informed him of my having written to C. R. Bishop and J. D. Spreckels for the loan of $2,000—that their answers had been favorable by telegraph.[32]

*Sunday, July 10.* Kahi o ke kauka—i mai aole i lawa loa kona makemake. I aku wau e nana wau a ina e hiki ana haawi hou aku. [Doctor's office—said what he wanted isn't sufficient. I said I'll see and if possible I'll give him more.]

Loaa mai 4 P.M. ka pepa kikoo kala o $2,004.00 mai C. R. Bishop a he Nota kekahi no ia mau heluna kala ia J. O. Carter no ka uku ana i loko o ekolu la ma ka uku panee 6 cts. ma one ct exchange—ma ke kala kula o Amelika. [Four P.M. Received the draft for $2,004.00 from C. R. Bishop. There was also a Note for that amount to J. O. Carter for payment within three days at interest of 6 cts and one cts exchange if in American gold dollars.]

*Monday, July 11.* WEA.[33] Maikai. Pane i ka leka a C. R. Bishop a kakau pu ia J. O. Carter e hai aku. Haawi au ia J. Richardson $100.00 i mea nana e hoi ai i Kapalakiko o i mai e hele mua ana i Bosetona. [Weather fine. Answered C. R. Bishop's letter and also wrote to J. O. Carter to say I gave J. Richardson $100.00 to return to San Francisco. Said he would go to Boston first.]

*Tuesday, July 12.* Loaa mai ka draft a J. D. Spreckels me Nota no $2,002.50—ma ka uku panee o 7 per ct. hoomaka ana mai ka la 5 July. Wire koke ia ka loaa ana mai. Kikoo ia ma ka Baneko Riggs. Uku koke o J. Heleluhe i ko makou kaa e hoi ai. [Received the draft from J. D. Spreckels with Note for $2,002.50 with interest of 7 per ct. commencing July 5. Wired immediately the receipt thereof. Drawn on the Riggs Bank. J. Heleluhe promptly paid for our carriage to return in.]

Haawi au ia J. Heleluhe $100 no kona mau mahina elua a umi kala no kona hoomanawanui ana. [I gave J. Heleluhe $100 for his two months (salary) and ten dollars for his patience.]

---

32. The letter of July 8 has not been located. However, a letter Liliu wrote to Joseph O. Carter, dated "The Ebbitt House, Washington, DC, July 11, 1898," says: "I wrote you on the eighth of this month notifying you of my wish to return and that I had written to Mr. C. R. Bishop and in case he failed, to J. D. Spreckels for a loan of two thousand dollars. They both wired back that they would send me a draft for that amount. Mr. Bishop sent his and it reached me on the tenth and Mr. Spreckels has not, so I wired him this evening of the fact. The interest on [the loan] is six percent per annum and one cent exchange commencing from the fifth of July, but he asks me to pay him in San Francisco. . . . I wired to Mr. Spreckels that we were going home and will be in San Francisco on the 21st as we leave here on the 17th. . . . When this reaches you the *Philadelphia* will have arrived with the three Commissioners Morgan, Hitt, and Cullom are from here and Dole and Frear will be from Hawaii, these [men] to decide what form of government Hawaii is to have." Manuscript collection of Don Medcalf.

33. The pages in this diary are preprinted with the words "Wea." (weather) and "Ther." (indicating temperature) for the convenience of the diarist.

*Wednesday, July 13.* Ebbitt House. I anei ke kauka i hele mai ai e hana i kuu A-i. Nui kana okioki ana aole nae he eha. Akamai launa ole kuu kauka. [The doctor came to treat my neck. Did much cutting but it wasn't painful. This doctor is exceptionally skilled.]

*Thursday, July 14.* Aole hana. [No activity.]

*Sunday, July 17.* Ought to leave here by train [today].

*Monday, July 18.* WEA. Maikai. [Weather fine.]

*Monday, July 25.* WEA. Maikai. [Weather fine.]

*Tuesday, July 26.* Gaelic ka moku. [The ship is the *Gaelic*.]

**Monday, August 1.** WEA. Maikai. [Weather fine.]

*Tuesday, August 2.* Arrived [at Honolulu] four P.M. Was enthusiastically [received] by the people. Prince David came on board with Presidents of Aloha Aina and Kalaiaina.

---

Liliuokalani and party arrived at Honolulu on the *Gaelic* (Captain Finch) seven days out from San Francisco on the morning of August 2, 1898. Under the heading "Home Sweet Home," the *Independent* of that date gave its readers an account of the sad event.

> ¶ At two o'clock this morning, the *Gaelic* steamed to the Pacific Mail dock through the calm sea, on which the rays of the bright moon were playing hide and seek.
>
> On board the fine boat was One passenger who experienced the painful happiness of returning to her home and to her friends, after seeing all that was dear to her and her people fading into the Past.
>
> Queen Liliuokalani was on board the *Gaelic*, and in her insurpassable dignified style she received her friends who sought her presence immediately after the docking of the steamer.
>
> The Princess Kaiulani, Prince David Kawananakoa, Governor Cleghorn, Mr. J. O. Carter, Mrs. Carter and daughters, and many other prominent citizens and many faithful Hawaiians were there to bid a hearty aloha to the Aliiaimoku [referring to the Queen], who returns to her home on the day of sorrow and grief to every patriotic Hawaiian.
>
> The Queen was overcome with emotions, when she met her royal relations and the friends who have assisted her in the noble fight for her beloved country and her people.
>
> After a brief conversation and a handshake with the people who presented their respects to the Alii, she proceeded to her carriage which was waiting on the Pacific dock. Attended by Princess Kaiulani, Prince David, and Governor Cleghorn, Queen Liliuokalani drove to her home among the enthusiastic cheers of the people assembled on the wharf and the weird wailing of a number of ancient Hawaiians.
>
> At Washington Place Queen Liliuokalani was received by her numer-

ous retainers and, after a brief conversation with them, the royal lady, who was greatly fatigued, retired to rest.

Her Majesty looks very well after her nineteen months' absence, but the people are grieved to learn that the health of their beloved alii [chief] is far from good, and that she has considered it advisedly to engage the services of Dr. English, a prominent Washington physician, who accompanies Her Majesty.

The Queen will remain here for a short while and then return to the States, in the care of her physician.

The meeting between Queen Liliuokalani and her royal niece was very affectionate. The distinguished ladies had not met for some time. and the Queen was visibly pleased by finding a niece in the charming and beautiful Kaiulani.

The reports in regard to the Queen's future movements as far as the Crown Lands are concerned are simply the evaporations of "yellow" journalists. No "Program" has been laid out for the future actions of Queen Liliuokalani, who quietly will await here the arrival of the Commissioners entrusted with the formation of a government for Hawaii, the latest territorial acquisition of the United States of America.[34]

---

*Thursday, August 4.* Aole hana. [No activity.]

*Monday, August 8.* WEA. pono. [Weather good.]

---

Ten days after the Queen returned to the islands, the Republic of Hawaii ceded control of the islands to the United States. The Republic also conveyed title to Hawaii's public lands to the United States; the resolution regarding annexation called for the United States to enact special laws for the management and disposition of government and Crown lands. The *Evening Bulletin* reported: "Hawaii is under the Stars and Stripes. The union of the Hawaiian Islands with the United States was consummated. This great event was formally enacted at sharp 12 o'clock, meridian, this the 12th day of August A.D. 1898."[35] The Queen, her family, and her associates chose not to attend the ceremony and remained at Washington Place.

---

*Sunday, August 14.* Aole hana. [No activity.]

*Monday, August 15.* WEA. pono. [Weather good.]

*Monday, August 22.* WEA. laki.[36] [Weather calm.]

---

34. *Independent*, August 2, 1898.
35. *Evening Bulletin*, August 12, 1898.
36. The Queen is possibly using "laki," lucky or fortunate, for "laʻi," calm, with the intent of saying: It is fortunate that the weather is calm.

*Monday, August 29.* WEA. laki. [Weather calm.]

*Sunday, September 4.* Aole hana. [No activity.]

*Monday, September 5.* WEA. pono. [Weather good.]

*Monday, September 12.* WEA. pono [Weather good.]

*Wednesday, September 14.* Aole hana. [No activity.]

*Monday, September 19.* WEA. Maikai. [Weather fine.]

*Monday, September 26.* WEA. Maikai. [Weather fine.]

**Monday, October 3.** WEA. Maikai. [Weather fine.]

*Tuesday, October 4.* Aole hana. [No activity.]

*Monday, October 10.* WEA. pono. [Weather good.]

*Friday, October 14.* Aole hana. [No activity.]

*Saturday, October 15.* Jessie Kaae offered [Sentence ends thus.]

*Sunday, October 16.* 7:30 A.M. Akana came to Washington Place. I was sitting on the veranda near my bedroom. He told me Wong Kwai would pay as high as $2,300—and no higher for Lumahai. I told him Jessie [Kaae] offered me $2,400 so I considered [Entry ends thus.][37]

*Monday, October 17.* WEA. Laki. [Weather calm.] Saw Jessie Kaae at her residence 7:30 A.M. She offered for her pake [Chinese] $2,400 [for the lease of Lumahai] Mr. Fawn [sic, name may be misspelled].

*Tuesday, October 18.* 11 A.M. Told Lot Lane that I would close bid for lease of Lumahai at $3,500. 2:30 P.M. He called again with J. Lane and said Achuck & Co.—would take the unleased portion for term [of] ten years.

Wong Kwai—another Pake [Chinese] and [illegible] Fernandez called on J. Heleluhe [at] seven. Lot Lane said Achuck & Co. will come with him tomorrow at 2:30 and close the bargain and pay the full Amt. of $1,750—half yearly rent for uncultivated portion of Lumahai.

*Wednesday, October 19.* Ten A.M. was served with an injunction by the Court not to sell or lease any portion of Lumahai. Lot [Lane] came in to say he would come at 2:30 P.M. with Pakes [Chinese] and money—J. O. Carter was sent for and came. Said he would give [put the] case in A.G.M. Robertson's hands. Day set by court for hearing is ten days from today.

---

37. Liliuokalani had been bequeathed a life interest in the ahupuaa (land division) of Lumahai on Kauai, by the will of Bernice P. Bishop. A good portion of the land was in rice production, and had been under a ten-year lease (starting January 1, 1883), signed by Bernice Pauahi Bishop and Charles Reed Bishop with Chulan & Co., a Honolulu partnership or hui (consisting of Chulan, Wong Kwai, Alee, and Chan Fook), at a rent of $1,200 per annum. On January 1, 1890, Liliuokalani sublet 94 acres of Lumahai to Wong Kwai for an annual rent of $800 per annum. Hawaii State Archives, Liliuokalani Collection, Box 1, No. 44–45. This lease arrangement would cause her trouble several years later. In 1898, Wong Kwai brought suit against Liliu over an agreement (or a memo dated October 15, 1898) that created an extension of the lease with Joseph Heleluhe, the Queen's agent, for Lumahai, at an annual rent of $2,300 paid semi-annually for a term of ten years, to begin January 1, 1900. On October 17, 1898, Wong Kwai met with Liliu, who accepted and ratified this agreement. But when the lessee attempted to make payment, Liliu refused to accept the same and threatened to lease the land to another party. Wong Kwai took Liliu to court over the matter and in January 1901 won his case. *Pacific Commercial Advertiser*, January 29, 1901.

*Thursday, October 20.* Notified Mr. J. O. Carter to write Mr. C. B. Wilson to vacate my premises as I had received application for rent. He said (Wilson) that he would not leave.[38]

*Monday, October 24.* WEA. laki. [Weather calm.]

*Saturday, October 29.* Nothing heard from Court. Four P.M. Am told the case of Lumahai will be postponed indefinitely. Lunched at Mrs. Mana's— [with] Princess Kaiulani, Prince Kawananakoa.

*Monday, October 31.* WEA. pono. [Weather good.] Akana told me that he would get the Chinese settee for less than $65.00. Dr. English went down and got it for $40.00. Was there fraud?

Two P.M. Went up to Kainana's and lunched with Mrs. Fernandez, Mr. and Mrs. Auld, Aimoku and Mollie, Kealakaihonua.

**Tuesday, November 1.** Wrote to J. O. Carter to notify Wilson again to leave, if not from this date he is to pay rent of $50.00 per month.[39] Sent him (J. O. Carter) a receipt for $250.—100 of H. A. Co's shares.

*Friday, November 4.* Aole hana. [No activity.]

*Monday, November 7.* WEA. pono. [Weather good.]

*Thursday, November 10.* Hai i ke Kauka i koʻu pilikia Ua ano e aela. [Told the doctor about my problem. He was indifferent.]

*Friday, November 11.* Mai aole hiki mai. [Sick. Doctor didn't come.]

*Saturday, November 12.* Mai aole hiki mai. [Sick. Doctor didn't come.]

*Sunday, November 13.* Mai aole hiki mai. [Sick. Doctor didn't come.]

*Monday, November 14.* WEA. laki. Aole hana. [Weather calm. No activity.]

Mr. J. O. Carter gave me a note on Claus Spreckels & Co., Bankers No. 24415—for $10,000—in U.S. Gold to the order of H. M. Liliuokalani.

Boarded the *Coptic* [at] four P.M.

Ke kanaka kai ka hale ia la a po. Ke Alii wahine Kaiulani me Koa. Kahalelaukoa me Kauka. [People at the house all day. Princess Kaiulani with Koa, Kahalelaukoa, and doctor.]

Kaiulani Archie & Koa

---

38. On October 22, 1898, Joseph O. Carter informed Liliu: "Upon receipt of your note I at once called upon Mr. Wilson and gave him the notice you suggested. Mr. Wilson declined to accept the notice and made the following statement, upon which he based his statement: 'The Queen wished to deed the premises I occupy to my wife Evelyn, but as the Queen was imprisoned, and my wife was with her as a companion during the imprisonment, I suggested making the deed to Mr. Cecil Brown, as trustee, and this was done. The understanding was that when I paid the sum the Queen gave for the property, plus interest and taxes, the Queen would give my wife a deed for the premises. I am negotiating a sale of the place for $12,500.' I said to Mr. Wilson that if my recollection of the matter was correct . . . Mr. Cecil Brown had deeded the property to you with his (Wilson's) consent, and in that case I could not see how he (Wilson) could give a title in case he negotiated the sale." Hawaii State Archives, J. O. Carter Letter Book. See also footnote for November 1, 1898, diary entry (this page).

39. Carter wrote Wilson as follows: "November 1st, 1898. Dear Sir. Referring to my verbal notices to you to vacate the premises occupied by you as a residence, the title to which rests in H. M. Liliuokalani, and your refusal to do so, I have now to say that in case you remain on the Premises you will be expected to pay rent for the same at the rate of fifty dollars per month. It is desired that you vacate at once in order that the premises may be placed in good repair." Hawaii State Archives, J. O. Carter Letter Book.

J. O. Carter and family—Victoria's family, Batty Allen, Mrs. Campbell, Aima [Nawahi] came to the *Coptic* to see me off. Did not intend to sail until the 29th, but the story will be unfolded someday and thereby hangs a tale.[40]

[Written upside down at bottom of page is her translation of a name song for Queen Emma, "Na Hala o Naue."]

> NA HALA O NAUE
> Beauteous are the Hala Ah Yes, ah!
> Of Naue by the sea Ah yes, ah!
> See how they're pressing...
> To join Haena...
> Longing eyes brightly gleam...
> As the birds spy the flowers...
> Proclaim her name...
> Kaleleonalani ah yes, ah.

*Tuesday, November 15.* Steamer *Coptic*.

*Wednesday, November 16.* Steamer *Coptic*. Had a conversation with George [Macfarlane] on [the Crown Lands] Claim—U.S.A., Dr. English, on goods and health. Someone on board told me that I forbade the band to come to the steamer. I denied the truthfulness of that report. The *Coptic* was denied that pleasure because I was on board—and for the first time—I didn't miss it at all.[41]

*Thursday, November 17.* Steamer *Coptic*.—Cried—Met Mrs. [A. A.] Sedgewick, mother of Prof. Sedgewick at Kam[ehameha] School. Went on deck three hours. Met Mr. Curtis—talked on several matters, [he] gave me names of men wishing to lay Cable—Scrymoer, Pierpont Morgan, D. O. Mills—Pac. Cable Co. More conversations with George [Macfarlane], on [my] U.S.A. claim. [illegible]

*Friday, November 18.* Steamer *Coptic*. Went with Myra on deck at seven A.M., stayed till 11:30. Went and dined upstairs—was introduced to Mrs. Hitt and her son—Mr. and Mrs. [F. W.] Dohrman, Mrs. [Neville] Castle.

*Monday, November 21.* WEA. laki. [Weather calm.] Arrived San Francisco and stayed at California Hotel.

---

40. According to the *Independent*, November 15, 1898: "There was quite a large gathering at the advertised hour of the departure of the *Coptic* yesterday evening; and Queen Liliuokalani held quite a reception assisted by Princess Kaiulani, Prince David, Mr. Cleghorn, Mr. and Mrs. J. O. Carter, and others." The article said that other passengers included Dr. English and Paul Neumann. The "tale" is nowhere explained.

41. The editor of the *Independent* commented on the Royal Hawaiian Band's absence from the wharf: "Of course, upon such an occasion the courtesy of the Government band was not extended, although when Topeka's Queen left for Hilo a few days ago she was escorted to the steamer by the ex-Minister of Foreign Affairs and feted by the band." *Independent*, November 15, 1898.

*Tuesday, November 22.* Met the Fetii Alii [Prince] Arthur G. Brander of Tahiti. He is so nice.

*Wednesday, November 23.* Brander comes again. It is so good of him. His ways are so like the Hawaiians.

*Thursday, November 24.* This Afternoon signed two instruments—one giving full power of Attorney to G. [George] W. Macfarlane, the other according to him and Mr. Lilienthal one-fourth of the benefits received from my claims of crown lands.

Left San Francisco at 5 P.M. for the east. Doctor [English], Jennie, Myra, and O wau no hoi [myself].

---

The November 24, 1898, diary entry refers to two "instruments," or legal documents signed by the Queen, that would have seriously compromised any revenues to the Queen from the Crown lands had she regained control of them.[42] The first of these documents appointed "George W. Macfarlane, our true and lawful attorney in the matter of the lands called or referred to as the Hawaiian Crown lands and revenues and income thereof already collected, or to be collected, for us and in our name, place, and stead to ask, demand, sue for, recover, collect, and receive all such sums of money, debts, dues, accounts, legacies, devises, interests, dividends, annuities, and demands whatsoever as are now or shall hereafter become due, owing, payable, or belonging to us."[43] The two-page typed document has a cover labeled "Jesse W. Lilienthal, Attorney at Law, 202 Sansome St., San Francisco." With the first document is an indenture of the same date agreeing to convey to Macfarlane "his successors, nominees, or assigns forever" an undivided share "not less than one-third" of the revenues or income of the Hawaiian Crown lands. (Both documents have had their signatures cut away, thus rendering them invalid.)

On December 22, 1898, having seen the document and interviewed Mr. Macfarlane, J. O. Carter wrote an uncharacteristically stern letter to the Queen about the matter:

> ¶ I was amazed and indignant and told him [Macfarlane] very plainly what I thought of it. You may be sure, that I told him that if it becomes known that your claims have been placed in the hands of a syndicate you will lose the sympathy of many friends who will lose all interest in your righteous claims. You say that the syndicate is to have "one-fourth" of any sum raised on your behalf. The document says 33 percent, unless I am mistaken. I am indignant that he should have advised a syndicate and more as that the terms are so extravagant.[44]

---

42. Hawaii State Archives, Liliuokalani Collection, Box 1.
43. Hawaii State Archives, Liliuokalani Collection, Box 1, No. 3.
44. Hawaii State Archives, J. O. Carter Letter Book.

*Saturday, November 26.* Arrived Salt Lake City 8 A.M. Wrote to J. O. Carter from there.[45]

*Monday, November 28.* WEA. Maikai. [Weather fine.]

*Wednesday, November 30.* Arrived at the Ebbitt [House], Washington, DC.[46]

**Sunday, December 4.** Aole hana. [No activity.]

*Monday, December 5.* WEA. pono. [Weather good.]

*Tuesday, December 6.* Four P.M. Arrived here (1418 15th St., Washington, DC) and moved into Mrs. Slosson's house. Went around to Mrs. English and she told me that the Doctor has just left for Cincinnati and would be back in a few days. Arranged [Entry ends thus.]

*Saturday, December 10.* And aole i hoi mai o K. E. [K. E. (Kauka or Dr. English) didn't return.]

*Sunday, December 11.* Mrs. E. writes he will be back tomorrow [and] that she wants to see [me]. I went over with Jennie and Myra. They went out to ride in Cars, I stayed with her and all came home only to find Paul Neumann had been here.

*Monday, December 12.* Weather pono. [Weather good.] Recd letters per Joe H. & Wakeke [illegible].

*Tuesday, December 13.* Nana ke Kauka i kuu Ai. [The doctor examined my neck.]

*Wednesday, December 14.* Aole hana. [No activity.] ~~Must send.~~ I sent Report of Hawaiian Commission—Message from the President of the U.S. to F. Wundenburg.[47]

*Saturday, December 17.* Drove out with Mrs. E. [English.]

*Sunday, December 18.* Did not go to Church.

*Monday, December 19.* WEA. Maikai. [Weather fine.] Ten A.M. Mr. J. W. Douglass called and witnessed my signature of three Protests. Addressed them for me and took them personally to the Senate, House, and to the Secretary [of State]—they were addressed [to]: the President; the Senate of the United States; the Speaker of the House of Representatives of the United States.

Went to the Kauka [doctor]—got large bottle of dark medicine—my umbrella and cloak.

Wrote to Mrs. Gulick—not to let Eccles come—to B. Cook—to Aima and Wakeke. K. asked if I heard from home.

45. Liliu's letter to Carter of this date said: "We arrived here 8:30 at this hotel [the] Knutford—but we leave this evening on another train and will reach Washington on Tuesday. All are well and in good spirits." Hawaii State Archives, J. O. Carter Collection.

46. On the last day of November 1898, "Liliuokalani and servant" returned to Washington, DC, from Honolulu, and she leased Mrs. Slosson's house at 1418 15th Street, which she wrote was "a three-story house just large enough for us three and a servant girl."

47. The report is titled *Message from the President of the United States, Transmitting the Report of the Hawaiian Commission, Appointed in Pursuance of the Joint Commission to Provide for Annexing the Hawaiian Islands to the United States*, 55th Congress, 3d Session, Senate Document No. 16 (Washington, DC: Government Printing Office, 1898).

¶ Washington, DC, December 19, 1898[48]
To the Senate of the United States.

I, Liliuokalani of Hawaii, made heir apparent on the 18th day of April 1877, and proclaimed Queen of the Hawaiian Islands on the 20th day of January 1891, do hereby earnestly and respectfully protest against the assertion of ownership by the United States of America of the so-called Hawaiian crown lands, amounting to about 1,000,000 acres, and which are my property, and I especially protest against such assertion of ownership as a taking of property without due process of law and without just or other compensation.

Further supplementing my protest of June 17, 1897, I call upon the President and the national Legislature and the people of the United States to do justice in this matter and to restore to me this property, the enjoyment of which is being withheld from me by your Government under what must be a misapprehension of my right and title.

Liliuokalani

*Liliuokalani's Protest to the U.S. Senate Regarding Her Claim to the Hawaiian Crown Lands, December 1898*

---

*Thursday, December 22.* Kahi o ke Kauka [doctor's office.]

*Sunday, December 25.* Went to communion 7 A.M. with Myra. 4 P.M. Mrs. English called with her niece.

*Monday, December 26.* WEA. pono. [Weather good.] Went to Doctor's—he was not at office. Forgot that all offices would be closed. Rode in cars all that day and ended at Mrs. Mason's.

*Tuesday, December 27.* 1:30 P.M. found doctor at office. Gave him a sofa pillow made of Hawaiian flag. He said I should only be the one to use it. Came away and forgot to pay.

*Friday, December 30.* Lent Makanoe [Kaaepa] my *Hawaii's Story*.

"How beautiful is that love which only springs from purity."[49]<br>[signed]<br>Liliuokalani<br>With sincere affection<br>Your loving cousin.

[The diary ends thus.]

48. Reprinted in the *Pacific Commercial Advertiser*, December 30, 1898, from a Washington, DC, newspaper of December 20, 1898.

49. The first line of this entry is in ink, then the following sentiment starting with "how beautiful" is in pencil and may well be the reminder of an inscription to be written in a book or even on a photograph. I have not attempted to trace the origin of this sentiment.

*Princess Kaiulani at Ainahau, Waikiki, circa 1897. The Waikiki property that became known as Ainahau was a baptismal gift to Kaiulani from her godmother Princess Ruth. Kaiulani was educated in England for several years before returning to Hawaii in 1897. In anticipation of her return, her father, Archibald Cleghorn, completed the new two-story house. Her childhood home remained on the grounds and is visible in the background.*
Hawaii State Archives

# A Summary of 1899

No diary for 1899 has survived, but here again, as was the case for 1897, extracts from Liliu's letters help fill in the void. The first order of business for Liliu in Washington, DC, was to petition Congress seeking redress for her claim to the crown land revenues (see 507). "Congress opens tomorrow," she noted in a January 3, 1899, letter.[1] As already mentioned, George Macfarlane and others in San Francisco were busy attempting (unsuccessfully) to form a syndicate to press the claim.

In February, she learned of the serious illness of Princess Kaiulani, and then on March 17, 1899, she was informed by a cable from Joseph O. Carter of the princess's death at Ainahau, Waikiki, on March 6. Writing to Sarah Carter on March 23, she commented: "My dear niece was all I had near me in this world—but He who controls our destiny in this life has chosen to call her away to Himself. His will be done."[2]

But life was not always filled with the pain of loss. On April 24, she wrote:[3] "Spring has truly come and in this city the trees are perfectly lovely and the air so soft and pleasant—so like our Hawaiian climate."

Not many of the Queen's personal letters of this period have survived. One of these, a letter to John Dominis Aimoku,[4] is so appealing that I have included it here:

1418 15th St. N.W.
Washington, DC
March 15, 1899

My dear Aimoku,

Your letter of the first of March has been received and I find by yours that you have not received any from me. Why I receive all your letters and answer them as promptly, say, two or three days after the receiving of yours—same as Kaipo, J. Heleluhe, and all the other folks at home. But do not feel discouraged but write often because your letters give me so much pleasure. I am pleased to hear you are well and I may say I am enjoying as good health as can be expected, seeing I am still in the doctor's hands. Myra and I always go to the doctor's office a half mile from here and we have to go partway in the Herdic or omnibus and the rest on electric cars and walk a block to reach the doctor's office. This would be on 16th Street—and on 14th Street we take electric cars, then walk three blocks. The walk is good for me—and when

---

1. Letter to Fred Wundenberg, Hawaii State Archives, Liliuokalani Collection.
2. Hawaii State Archives, Liliuokalani Collection.
3. Letter to Henry C. Carter, Hawaii State Archives, J. O. Carter Collection.
4. Bishop Museum Archives, Liliuokalani Letters.

it is a pleasant day—we go to see Mrs. English, then we walk home—about six blocks, that would be like the distance from the Royal Mausoleum to Washington Place. It is so cool here I do not feel fatigued to walk, but I know I would not be able to do it in Honolulu [where] it is so warm and I've tried it. Today it has rained all day—Last week there have been terrible storms of snow in the west—many lives lost—One man and wife and young were living inside the house. A blizzard blew the man and woman out and the boy was left unharmed. The man was blown 700 feet from his house up against a wire fence with such force his hand was taken off—and the wife 200 feet and she was killed. Oh, so many deaths by this last storm or blizzard. Washington has seen its heaviest storm but I am glad that no bad results have been heard from—only the inconveniences that attended it to us who had to keep up fires in the dining room grate to keep the parlor warm. It was difficult to get coal—and it was a good opportunity for dealers in coal to raise their price—so with firewood, and hacks raised the fares. No [street] cars could run—the snow was too thick. Our pipes were frozen, the gas would not burn, and [we] had to go back to kerosene lamps, but now everything is all right and the young shoots of leaves are coming out on the trees for this is the commencement of spring and the trees will come out in their beauty.

Myra and I went out the other day and when we came home I found two bouquets of Roses—one was La France and the other American Beauties—Oh, they reminded me so much of home for they scented the whole house. These flowers were sent me by a young doctor who called on me and was so pleased with his visit.

I only wish you were nearer to me, but as it is impossible we must be content to write, and I hope in a few months I may be able to come home—so we must practice patience.

From your loving Hanai<br>Liliuokalani

The new year also found Liliuokalani busy paying attention to the management of her landholdings. There was a dispute over a portion of Princess Kaiulani's estate, and difficulties with Charles B. Wilson that culminated in a breach of friendship over the claim to a calabash that had belonged to one of her ancestors.

Liliu celebrated her 61st birthday in Washington, DC, on September 2. The following day, she wrote to Henry Carter (Cushman): "I did not feel a day older than I did 16 years ago when we were in Honolulu—for we had a lovely sunshiny day."[5]

On December 19, she informed her business agent, J. O. Carter: "I have bought me a Locomobile for $650—I anticipate much pleasure from it. Will sell horses and carriages when I get home."[6] Liliuokalani's expected return was then delayed many months, but by May 1900 she was in San Francisco, and en route for home.

5. Hawaii State Archives, J. O. Carter Family Papers.
6. Hawaii State Archives, J. O. Carter Letter Book.

*Princess Kaiulani at seventeen during her visit to New York, Boston, and Washington, DC. On March 1, 1893, Kaiulani, accompanied by her guardian Theophilus H. Davies, arrived in New York from London on her way to Washington, DC, where she hoped to influence public opinion to support restoration of the Hawaiian monarchy. She was received by President Grover Cleveland and his wife, Frances, at the White House. She left Washington on March 18, 1893, and returned to England. She did not return to Hawaii until 1897.*
Elmer Chickering, 1893, courtesy of the Library of Congress

*Queen Liliuokalani. On September 2, 1900, the Queen celebrated her sixty-second birthday with a morning concert at Washington Place performed by Captain Henry Berger and the Royal Hawaiian Band and featuring her compositions. At midday, she attended a luau in Kahala given in her honor.*

Frank Davey, circa 1900, Hawaii State Archives

# 1900

This diary is composed of two fragments, both found in the Hawaii State Archives, Liliuokalani Collection. The first is a long memorandum concerning her relations with Dr. Charles H. English. According to her 1897 diary, Liliuokalani first began seeing Dr. Charles H. English, a physician based in Washington and Cincinnati, Ohio, to cure a persistent infection, which English suggested was cancer. Under his care, Liliu seems to have gradually recovered, and, wanting to retain his services, she arranged for him to accompany her back to the Hawaiian Islands in 1900. The memorandum summarizes her subsequent troubles with the doctor.

The second and concluding text, dated September 2, 1900 (the Queen's birthday), is from an old photostat (the original of which is now unlocated).

*On the first of February 1900,* Dr. English consented to accompany me to Hawaii as my physician and to remain for 18 months or 12 months, as the condition of my health may appear at the end of that time—for the sum of $300 a month and at the end of the term (12 or 18 months) I was to pay him $5,000.00.[1] In the meantime should the Congress accord to

THE DIARY FOR 1900 [FIRST FRAGMENT]
1 FEB–13 SEPT
Hawaii State Archives

---

[1] On August 13, 1900, Dr. Charles H. English commenced a lawsuit for breach of contract against "Lydia Dominis" in the First Circuit Court in Honolulu. He alleged "that the said defendant engaged and hired the plaintiff (English) for the period of eighteen months, to commence on the 14th day of May, A.D. 1900 and to continue until the 16th day of November, A.D. 1901, at the end of which said period . . . the defendant agreed to pay to the plaintiff in addition to the sum of Three hundred dollars per month the sum of Five thousand dollars." English further stated that on the 10th of July 1900, he had been wrongfully "forced and compelled . . . to leave her service to perform his duties . . . without a lawful cause" and therefore he was due compensation of $5,000 "and the cost of this action." The suit was put on the calendar for September 5, 1900, and then was discontinued. Hawaii State Archives, First Circuit Court, Law 4757.

Dr. English's suit was settled in a somewhat oblique manner so as to avoid publicity, as evidenced by this letter to Carter from John F. Colburn, of the Kapiolani Estate, found in the Hawaii State Archives, J. O. Carter Papers. Carter's papers also preserve Liliuokalani's canceled check reimbursing Prince David Kawananakoa for this amount.

Dear Sir.

I find a copy of my letter to you under date of Nov. 9, 1900 as follows:
The amount paid by Prince David Kawananakoa for the settlement of the claims of Dr. English against HM Liliuokalani on Sept. 11, 1900 as $1300. Thirteen hundred dollars distributed as follows: To the Doctor 1000.
       For his passage to S.F. 75.
       To his attorney 225. = 1300.

Yours truly, John F. Colburn

me some recompensation his pay was to be raised higher. That we were to leave here [Washington] in the month of March.... His request was exorbitant—but my anxiety to return to the islands was of such importance that the amount charged seemed secondary to me.

On the fifth of December 1899—Doctor [English] borrowed of me $200.00 to be returned in 90 days. He asked me to wait until he received his salary for attending me to Hawaii.

*Thursday, February 8.* Gave to Doctor English $480.00. He told me the full amount he would like to have would be $1,350.00 that he might buy some Demijohns and other materials necessary to take to Hawaii.

*Friday, February 9.* I gave him $870.00 which made the amount of $1,350.00 complete—and he remarked at the time that he would pay me in installments from time to time from his wages.

*Sunday, March 18.* I reminded Dr. English of the $200.00 borrowed of me last Dec. 5th, 1899—and due this date. He asked me to leave it till he received his pay of $300 a month—This made the amount due me altogether $1,550.00.

*Tuesday, May 1.* Talked over our first agreement with the additional clause that should Congress accord to me some recognition, his salary was to be raised to $400 a month, and when he saw that my health was sufficiently restored he would release me and I was to pay him the $5,000.00. I agreed to this.

*Sunday, May 13.* The Doctor asked if I could give him one month's pay in advance—I told him I would pay him next day.

*Monday, May 14.* The day of our departure from here [Washington, DC], I paid him $300. He then asked me if I would be willing to advance him three months' pay $900, and from this date to July I could keep his monthly allowance until the amount of $1,550 he owed me had been paid.

Strange to say—I find in my memorandum that I consented to advance him the $900 and yet have not recorded whether I did give the amount to him or not. Have I been hypnotized by this man?

*Wednesday, June 13.* Honolulu. He [English] came over to my house and asked for $100.00, which I gave him to send to his wife—this amount to be taken from his salary—and yet on the 15th I find he came and asked me to pay him the remaining Two Hundred dollars—and forgetting entirely the agreement we had made on the 14th of May—I paid to him the amount.

*Sunday, June 17.* He [English] informed me of his intention to leave for this country [to go from Honolulu to Washington, DC].

*Sunday, July 1.* Wrote the Doctor a letter releasing him from further attendance on me.

*Monday, July 2.* Doctor [English] asked if I wasn't going to pay him anything—I told him I would pay him $2,500 (which he did not deserve)—he asked me for $3,000. I gave him no answer.

*Tuesday, July 3.* Doctor came back to my house and asked me if I would pay him the Five thousand dollars. I said I could not as it was impossible for Mr. J. O. Carter to raise the money. When could he have $2,500 the money which you were ready to have[?] He then asked me for $300, which was given him.

*Tuesday, July 10.* Paid into Dr. English's hand $2,200.00.

*Tuesday, August 14.* Dr. English entered suit against me for $5,000.00.

*Thursday, September 13.* J. O. Carter paid [reimbursed] to John Colburn for what he paid to Dr. English [and] to return letters and correspondence between us, $1,500.00. I feel that I have been imposed upon by the Doctor and that ... he has already been paid his full dues and more. The amount of $900, which I dare say [I] must have given him, though I have now inserted it in my figures.

---

President McKinley signed the Hawaiian Organic Act on April 30, 1900. This act defined the political structure and powers of the newly established territorial government, including the establishment of the Hawaii Territorial Legislature, and provided for U.S. congressional representation in the form of a nonvoting delegate.

Liliuokalani returned to Honolulu from Washington, DC, at midnight on June 4, 1900, on the *City of Peking*. With her were Joe Heleluhe, Myra Heleluhe, and Dr. C. H. English. The *Independent* (June 5, 1900) noted that she returned very quietly and was met at the wharf by Prince David Kawananakoa and driven immediately to Washington Place, where Mrs. J. O. Carter met her.

When Robert Wilcox, who had also returned on the same vessel, was interviewed on the ship as to his political future, he answered: "What am I going to do in politics down here? ... I don't see what we have to do with the Republican or Democratic parties in these Islands. We are hardly a territory yet.... I am for home rule, myself.... I think we ought to establish a party to study the interests of the Islands alone.... We can represent ourselves better by a home party than through Mainland politics."[2]

Despite Wilcox's offhand reference to the formation of such a party, the action had been planned for some time. On Thursday June 7, 1900, when the *Pacific Commercial Advertiser* reported the commencement of a convention for that purpose the previous day, it revealed that Native Hawaiian delegates had arrived from the outside islands, and had all stated themselves in favor of an Independent or Home Rule Party, rather than aligning themselves with either the Democratic or Republican Parties. They claimed that they controlled two-thirds of the votes of Hawaii and would use those votes to elect a candidate of their choice both for local offices and for a delegate to Congress.

---

2. *Pacific Commercial Advertiser*, June 5, 1900.

One of the speakers at the convention, David Kalauokalani, the newly elected president of the Independent (or Home Rule) Party, stated: "We have been made a portion of the United States of America, which gives us all citizenship. We have been given the right of balloting without restriction, and can now vote for members of both the Senate and the House of Representatives.... You are assembled here today for the purpose of considering the report of our special delegate Robert W. Wilcox.... You are assembled here today to decide whether we will be Republicans or Democrats."[3]

Mr. Kaulia, another speaker, reminded the audience: "During the last seven years ... here there has been but one party—the Annexation party. At the present day it has split up into the Republican and Democratic parties.... I say let us go on free and independent. During the past seven years we were deprived of our benefits.... You must remember that the Republican party has threatened us; as do the Democrats. They say in their threats that we will be disenfranchised.... I say let us organize an Independent Party."[4]

In his address, Robert Wilcox reminded the delegates: "The question of the restoration of the monarchy is gone from us forever. We are now a people, however, who can vote. You all know we have two-thirds of the votes of this country. I say to you that the people who have been living on your rights and held the reins of government are now without that power. If you want to rule, it is for you to decide. If you don't want to rule you must so decide.... The Queen feels happy because now two-thirds of the voting power rests with you. The monarchy is like a dear person that has died. Let it go. Look to the future."[5]

After the morning session of the convention, the delegates proceeded to Washington Place, where, following a short reception, the ex-Queen addressed the assembly for nearly ten minutes, "speaking slowly and distinctly so that not a word should be lost." She in part said: "It is useless for us to abstain from taking our future stand. Our future prosperity depends on it. As soon as the United States flag was hoisted over these Islands, and our Hawaiian flag was lowered by the authority of the American government, it meant that it had come to stay. It is my wish for your future welfare to stand shoulder to shoulder and seek every means that will conduce to the benefit of the whole nation. When the flag went down, it went down for good. We must now do our duty as American citizens."[6]

On June 14, 1900, in accordance with an act of Congress approved on April 30, 1900, Hawaii became an integrated part of the United States, as a territory. On November 6, 1900, Independent Party candidate Robert Wilcox, whose candidacy the ex-Queen supported, was elected as an independent for both the remainder of the 56th U.S. Congress and for the full session of the 57th U.S. Congress. Independent Party candidates were also elected to legislative positions in the Territorial House of Representatives and as senators for the first Territorial Legislature.

---

3. *Pacific Commercial Advertiser*, June 7, 1900.
4. *Pacific Commercial Advertiser*, June 7, 1900.
5. *Pacific Commercial Advertiser*, June 7, 1900.
6. *Pacific Commercial Advertiser*, June 7, 1900.

*Sunday, September 2, 1900.* How sad! and yet I gave my consent to have the old Royal Hawaiian Band who are now the Government U.S. Band come and serenade me on this the occasion of my 62nd birthday. My consent is the healing over of ill will of all past differences caused by the overthrow of my throne and the deprivation of my people of their rights. Tho' for a moment it cost me a pang of pain for my people—it was only momentary, for the present was a hope for the future for my people.

Ten A.M. Went to Kahala with Mr. and Mrs. Mana and children, Mr. and Mrs. Auld, Kaipo, Myra [Heleluhe], Aimoku [Dominis], Kalahiki, Wakeke, Paoakalani, J. [Joseph] Aea, [Elizabeth] Mahiai Robinson.

THE DIARY FOR 1900 [SECOND FRAGMENT] 2 SEPT

Hawaii State Archives

---

On September 3, 1900, in its report on Liliuokalani's birthday, the *Pacific Commercial Advertiser* noted:

> ¶ Queen Liliuokalani celebrated her sixty-second birthday yesterday in a quiet manner. Bright and early throngs of Hawaiians gathered at Washington Place eager to wish her happy returns of the day. Leis of the hala flowers were brought to her in abundance, filling the reception room where the visitors were gathered.
>
> Liliuokalani attended early communion at St. Andrew's Cathedral accompanied by two or three intimate friends. Shortly after eight o'clock Captain Berger and the Government band filed into the grounds [of Washington Place] and rendered a concert composed of many of the native airs and songs composed by Liliuokalani together with grand selections from operas.
>
> Native singers were present to assist the band. The musicians were cordially greeted by the queen upon the main lanai of the residence. In the forenoon she was driven to Kahala beyond Diamond Head where a luau was given in her honor. The queen looks much improved since coming back to her native land.

*Queen Liliuokalani, eighth monarch of the Hawaiian Islands, January 29, 1891, the day she ascended the throne. As reigning monarch, Liliuokalani held the Crown lands of Hawaii. On August 12, 1898, the Republic of Hawaii ceded all Government and Crown lands of the former Hawaiian Kingdom to the United States. Following annexation, the Queen repeatedly sought compensation from the United States for the Crown lands.*
Hawaii State Archives

# Afterword

Liliuokalani lived as a private citizen from 1900 onward, but she did not retreat into complete seclusion as some accounts have portrayed. In January 1901, when she was in Hilo, she and a convivial party celebrated Abigail Campbell's 18th birthday. She was again in Hilo in June that year, and on the eighth she noted in her diary: "All went to a concert at Haili Church—I played the Organ." In Honolulu on May 4, 1901, she went to the opera with Prince David Kawananakoa and Mrs. J. O. Carter.[1]

More important, Liliu's 1901 diary reveals her gradual reconciliation with the turbulent events of the past decade. On September 2, her 63rd birthday, she noted:

> ¶ Was woke at five o'clock by my faithful people, with mele [songs] of my ancestors on praise of their deeds—seven A.M. the Hui Akala came with contributions & presents of pig and dainty dishes & Hawaiian delicacies. Eight A.M. Berger's Band serenaded me & the Military Co. under Capt. Hopa came to assure me of their loyalty—9:30 A.M. all the members of the Legislature who were friendly came to my breakfast—Mr. S. M. Damon was one—was glad to see him. 12 P.M. Gave a public reception to all. 2.30 P.M. Had a luau for all... my oldest friends—& R. W. Wilcox and wife were there.[2]

She did not neglect observances of past ceremonies and rituals honoring and commemorating departed alii (chiefs). At 5:30 A.M. on May 13, 1901, she went privately with Prince David to the Royal Mausoleum "to deposit Kamehameha into the coffin. Four persons are placed in the same coffin." These were the bones of the great chiefs of Hawaii Island, Liloa, his heir Hakau, Kamehameha, and Umi, which King Kalakaua had retrieved in earlier years from Hawaii Island.

In 1910, when the bodies of the alii, including her husband and her siblings, were transferred from the old mausoleum to their new and final resting places, Liliuokalani and her brother-in-law Archibald Cleghorn were present, and that most final of farewells deeply affected them both.

A continuing focus in Liliuokalani's life was her claim before the U.S. Congress for the Crown lands, which she believed were hers for life and which by her account were estimated to be worth $6 million to $10 million. In March 1901, she wrote to R. W. Wilcox, the Hawaiian congressional delegate, in Washington, DC: "I would like 5 M's for my rights or

---

1. Bishop Museum Archives, Liliuokalani Collection, 1901 Diary.
2. Bishop Museum Archives, Liliuokalani Collection, 1901 Diary.

to have receipts of C.L.s [Crown lands] accorded to me during my lifetime [and] to have my Claims brought before the Court of Claims & afterwards to Congress. Have no doubt by aid of the document the C.C.'s [Court of Claims] will decide for me & Congress will recognize it."[3] The claim was several times brought before Congress and the courts, particularly the U.S. Court of Claims, but she did not prevail. In the last appeal in 1910, the court ruled against her, and there the business ended.

As the new century progressed, she paid serious attention to building up her estate. Following the long custodianship of J. O. Carter, Curtis P. Iaukea now became her general manager, and he served his former monarch long and well. With him, she formed the idea of a charitable trust, and it was Iaukea who proposed to Liliuokalani that in forming such a trust she needed to carefully define the instrument's purposes with the aid of top lawyers. With this in mind, in 1909, she agreed to appoint William O. Smith, considered the best lawyer in town, to the task. This was indeed a courageous act on her part, for Smith had been one of the group that had engineered her overthrow in 1893. Her appointee took on the task with Iaukea, they established a trust, and together they successfully defended her interests in an unseemly family quarrel over assumed inheritances.

From 1910 onward she remained in the islands, where close friends entertained her, and she appeared at selected public functions. Several times, the aging Liliu fell seriously ill and doctors despaired of her life, but each time she rallied. Always, though, her well-guarded privacy gave her an almost mythic presence among her former subjects—so much so that when the funeral of Prince David Kawananakoa took place on June 21, 1908, many Hawaiians flocked to the ceremonies held at the Royal Mausoleum because most of them had never seen the Queen.

Liliuokalani died on November 11, 1917, at Washington Place, Honolulu. She lay in state in Kawaiahao Church and then received a state funeral in the throne room of her former palace. The crown of state she never wore adorned her koa and kou wood coffin. On her head she wore the diamond tiara that she had worn in London in 1887, and on one of her wrists the bracelet the Duke of Edinburgh had given her in 1869. She was buried with full honors in the Royal Mausoleum in Nuuanu Valley. The day after her decease, Riley H. Allen, the editor of the *Honolulu Star Bulletin*, published a touching and prophetic tribute to her:

> ¶ It is not improbable that in generations to come this queen and Kamehameha I will become the two leading figures of Hawaii's monarchical history, though her reign was very short indeed. We can today see how her figure has emerged from the storms of animosities and become surrounded with deference and affection. Future readers will see her not only as a queen in the midst of political combats, but as a

3. Bishop Museum Archives, Liliuokalani Collection, 1901 Diary.

woman who took her place in the society of her time, after the abrogation of her royal regime, and passed through life with an actual strengthening of valid claims to the respect of those around her.

They will see her not only as a ruler...but as a philanthropist, an artist, a musician, affable and accomplished friend, gracious hostess, and devoted champion of her race. Long after her much discussed and much opposed policies have been forgotten as mistakes, her admirable traits will be remembered.

That varied estimates will be made of her is but natural. It seems likely that even those who most bitterly opposed her will find cause to soften their judgements of two decades ago...to accord to Hawaii's dead Queen a tribute of admiration and respect in which the hostilities of the past are forever buried and the many fine qualities of Liliuokalani are forever enshrined.[4]

4. *Honolulu Star Bulletin*, November 12, 1917.

*A child on Kauai, circa 1892. In the early 1900s, Queen Liliuokalani formed the idea of a charitable trust and worked together with Curtis P. Iaukea and W. O. Smith to establish the Queen Liliuokalani Trust in 1909. The Queen designated orphan and destitute Hawaiian children as the primary beneficiaries of her estate. Today, her legacy continues to improve the welfare of her beneficiaries.*
Alfred Mitchell, Bishop Museum Archives

# Bibliography

ADLER 1966
Adler, Jacob. *Claus Spreckels: The Sugar King in Hawaii*. Honolulu: University of Hawaii Press, 1966.

ALEXANDER 1896
Alexander, William D. *History of Later Years of the Hawaiian Monarchy and Revolution of 1893*. Honolulu: Hawaiian Gazette, 1896.

BLOUNT REPORT 1893
[The Blount Report.] U.S. Congress. House of Representatives. *President's Message Relating to the Hawaiian Islands. December 18, 1893.* 53d Cong, 2d Session. Ex. Doc. 47. Washington, DC: Government Printing Office, 1893.

DOLE 1936
Dole, Sanford B. *Memoirs of the Hawaiian Revolution*. Edited by Andrew Farrell. Honolulu: Advertiser, 1936.

GREGG 1982
Gregg, David Lawrence. *The Diaries of David Lawrence Gregg: An American Diplomat in Hawaii 1853–1858*. Edited by Pauline King. Honolulu: Hawaiian Historical Society, 1982.

IAUKEA 1988
Iaukea, Curtis Piehu, and Lorna Kahilipuaokalani Iaukea Watson. *By Royal Command: The Official Life and Personal Reminiscences of Colonel Curtis Piehu Iaukea at the Court of Hawaii's Rulers*. Honolulu: Hui Hanai, 1988. The manuscript of this memoir and several earlier drafts in Iaukea's hand are in the Hawaii State Archives, Iaukea Collection, M-70, and whenever possible I have relied on these archival texts.

KUYKENDALL 1967
Kuykendall, Ralph S. *The Hawaiian Kingdom*. Vol. 3, *The Kalakaua Dynasty, 1874–1893*. Honolulu: University of Hawaii Press, 1967.

LILIUOKALANI 2013
Liliuokalani, *Hawaii's Story by Hawaii's Queen Liliuokalani*. Rev. ed. with annotations by David Forbes. Honolulu: Liliuokalani Trust, 2013. First published 1898 by Lee and Shepard, Boston.

MCGUIRE 1887 [1957]
McGuire, James W. L. *A Short Description of Queen Kapiolani's Voyage to England to Attend the Jubilee Celebration of Queen Victoria of England in the Year 1887*. Typescript, Hawaii State Archives, Library Collection,

1957. Published in Hawaiian as *He Moolelo Pokole no ka Huakai a ka Moiwahine Kapiolani a me ke Kamaliiwahine Liliuokalani a ka Iubile o ka Moiwahine Victoria a Beretania Nui*. Honolulu: Collegiate Press, 1938.

MORGAN REPORT 1894

[The Morgan Report.] U.S. Congress. *Hawaiian Islands. Report of the Committee on Foreign Relations, United States Senate, with Accompanying Testimony, and Executive Documents Transmitted to Congress from January 1, 1893, to March 10, 1894*. 52d Congress, 2d Session, vols. I and II. Washington, DC: Government Printing Office, 1894.

RUSS 1961

Russ, William Adam, Jr. *The Hawaiian Republic (1894–98)*. Selinsgrove, Pennsylvania: Susquehanna University Press, 1961.

RUSS 1992

Russ, William Adam, Jr. *The Hawaiian Revolution (1893–94)*. Selinsgrove, Pennsylvania: Susquehanna University Press, 1992. First published in 1959.

THURSTON 1936

Thurston, Lorrin A. *Memoirs of the Hawaiian Revolution*. Edited by Andrew Farrell. Honolulu: Advertiser, 1936. See also the memoir manuscript in the Hawaii State Archives, Lorrin A. Thurston Papers, M-144, as it differs in some important respects.

YARDLEY 1981

Yardley, Paul T. *Millstones and Milestones: The Career of B. F. Dillingham, 1844–1918*. Honolulu: University of Hawaii Press, 1981.

# Index

*Italicized page numbers refer to captions*

Achi, William Charles, 67, 67n147, 133n27, 247, 315n1
Aea, Joseph Kaiponohea (Kaipo), 6, 6n15–6n16, 38n25, 57, 76n193, 80, 82, 84, 84n236, 85, *88*, 91, 93, 93n270, 141–42, 298
Aea, Joseph Kapeau, 6n15–6n16
Aea, Kahae, 47, 80–81, 84, 84n236, 91, 93, 93n270
Ahahui Hawaii Aloha Aina (Patriotic League), 320n14, 330, 330n54, 331, 331n58, 333–34, 339, 340n88, 342, 361, 361n167, 364, 401n246, 402, 414–15, 423, 423n50, 424, *446*, 470, 474, *478*, 500
Ahahui Hawaii Aloha Aina o na Wahine (Ladies' Patriotic League), 331n58, 332–33, 332n70, 342, 361n167, 419, 428, 472, 474, 476
Ahia, Milaina, 185, 185n66, 451
Aholo, Lilia, 13, 13n60, 226, 226n72
Aholo, Luther, 13n60, 178, 236, 236n107
Aholo, Lydia Kaonohiponipo-niokalani, 6, 6n18
Aikanaka, chief, xxiii, xxvi
Ailau, John Keakaolani, 37n17, 409
Ailau, Mary Pitman, 37, 37n17, 45, 45n56, 46, 47n63, 145n68
Aimoku, John Dominis (hanai child), 10, 10n40, 38n25, 68n150, *88*, 509–10
Ainahau, Waikiki, xxx, xxxi, xxxii, 26, 135, 138; festive poi supper, 26; Likelike at (1855), *128*; party at, *115*
Alapai, John W., 14, 14n64, 215, 215n13
Aldrich, Mary Hale Brown, 23, 23n103–23n104, 45n55, 181
Aldrich, William A., 7n22, 23n103, 236
Aldrich, William H., 23n103, 55, 55n107
Alexander, William D., 278, 278n76, 373, 373n209, 386n228, 413, 435
Aliiolani Villa (Liliu's cottage at Waialua), xxxvi–xxxvii, *254*
Allen, Cordelia Church, 7, 7n23
Allen, Elisha H., 146n74, 224, 224n59

Allen, Riley H., 520–21
Amalu, Robert K. (Lopaka), 51
American flag, 321, 321n18, 334–35, 335n78, 345–46
American League, 387n229, 412n17
amnesty, for P. G. officials, 381–84, 394–98, 401
Ando, Taro, 60, 60n120, 60n123, 109n315, 109n317
annexation, 295n129, 318, 319n12, 322n21, 327, 327n37, 332, 344n103, 346, 347n111, 348, 351, 355, 357, 359n157, 393, 399, 416, 425n56, 428n70, 456, 465, 498
annexation ceremony, *493*, 501
Annexation Club, 286, 286n96, 412n17
annexationists, 286, 292, 334, 350, 350n125, 356, 370, 387n231, 393, 408, 461, 472
annexation resolution, 293, 293n123
annexation treaty (16 June 1897), 201n130, 406, 468, 471, 494
anti-annexation petitions, 466, 472, 474–75
apu popolo (health tonic), 81–82, 81n218
Ariimanihinihi, Alexandra Kealatane, 365, 365n185
Armstrong, Henry R., 102, 102n298, 104, 147n78, 153, 153n89
Arning, Dr. Edward, 22, 22n94–22n95, 84, 84n237
Arnold, Sir Edwin, 279–80
Arthur, President Chester A., 5n10, 14n65
Ashford, Clarence W., 160, 160n109–60n110, 265, 265n30, 286n95, 319n12, 413n21, 416
Ashford, Volney V., 167n134, 282, 285, 285n92, 286, 286n95, 358n154, 358n155
Atherton, Joseph Ballard, 172, 172n8
attorney general appointment, 301–4
Auhea II, chiefess (Kekauluohi), 413n21, 413n24, 418, 422
Auld, William, 63, 63n135, 474
Austin, Jonathan, 171, 171n3, 180n36
Auwaiolimu, Oahu, 52

525

Baker, John T., 40, 40n33, 132n25, 272, 272n56, 320
Baker, Robert H., 36, 36n10, 116, 179n33, 241
Baldwin, Henry Perrine, 288, 288n100
balls, 84, 84n237, 121, 185, 188, 192, 228; children's fancy dress ball, 276–77, 276n70, 277n71; at Lahaina, 245; royal/state, 69, 69n156, 184, 184n62, 206, 206n156, 222, 224, 248, 278–79, 290–91, 291n110, 300, 300n144
baseball, 66, 66n143, 207, 207n160
Bayonet Revolution (1887), 13n61, 154–55, 247
Beckley, Emma Kaili Metcalf, 113, 113n329. *See also* Nakuina, Emma
Beckley, Mary, 17, 180
Berger, Prof. Henri, 9, 9n35
Bernice Pauahi Bishop Museum, xii, xiii, xvii, 7n22, 177–78, 232n98
Bertelmann, Henry C., 204, 204n145, 433
B. F. Ehlers (dry goods importers), 42, 42n42, 43
Bipikane, J. W., 282–83, 330n54
Bishop, Bernice Pauahi, xi, xii, xxiii, xxvii, xxxv n1, 7n22, 7n26, 8, 8n33, 14n62, 43n44, 55, 55n108, 161, 161n115, 164, 225n62, 502n37; anniversary of her death, 118, 120, 203, 205; birthday, 124, 244; death of, 205n147, 315n3; will of, 11, 11n45, 14
Bishop, Charles R., xi, xxvii, 7, 7n22, 23n103, 55, 165, 177, 179n33, 184, 241, 260, 315n3, 322, 498n30, 499
Bishop, Sereno, 30, 202
Bishop, W. Irving, 184, 193
blacks, American, immigration scheme for, 350n125
Blount, James H., xxviii, 11n46, 316, 333–34, 334n73, 335n78, 338, 338n82, 346, 365–66
Bouliech, George, 5n13, 173, 173n16
Bowen, William, 14n67, 340, 341, 341n92, 344, 348
Boyd, Edward S., 257n13
Boyd, Hannah, 257n13
Boyd, Helen, xxxii
Boyd, James H., xxxii, 80n215, 112, 142, 152, 155, 182n49, 223, 223n54
Boyd, Robert Napunako, 157, 173, 173n9, 236, 241n127; and Wilcox Rebellion, 233–38
Boys' Reform School, 93, 93n271–93n272, 103n303
Brickwood, Louisa Brownscombe, 42, 42n37, 103n302, 172, 178
Brigham, William T., 232, 232n98
Bright, John Maipinepine, 27, 27n119
Brodie, Dr. John, 37, 37n15, 57, 63–64, 131n21, 197
Brown, Capt. John H., 23n103, 45, 45n55, 197n115

Brown, Cecil, 29, 29n124, 40, 40n33, 165n129, 308; and 1890 elections, 247
Brown, Godfrey, 156n101, 160n110, 248
Brown, Irene Ii, 113n328, 252
Brown, John E., 179n32, 283–84
Bush, Caroline Paakaiulaula French Poor, 10n40, 38, 38n25, 217n23
Bush, John E., 48, 48n70, 106, 240n122, 247, 332, 332n69

cabinet, 85, 248–49, 256
cabinet crisis, 304–9, 311, 340–41
Campbell, Abigail Kuaihelani Maipinepine, 35n2, 95, 176, 183, 187, 214, 225, 343, 379, 424, 475, 476, 481, 504
Campbell, Charles J., 233, 233n99
Campbell, James, 13n61, 81n221, 95n279
Canavarro, Antonio de Souza, 139, 139n38, 173, 173n15, 271n52
Carter, Capt. Joseph, xxxiii
Carter, Charles L., 350, 350n124–350n125, 433
Carter, George R., xxxiii, 239n115
Carter, Hannah Lord, xxxiii
Carter, Henry Cushman, 73, 73n178, 510
Carter, Henry A. P., xxxiii, 156n101, 238n115
Carter, J. O., xxxi, xxxiii, 60n121, 73n178, 77n201, 163n120, 195n106, 316–17, 382, 393, 395–96, 401n243, 410, 457, 459, 461n5, 472, 474, 499n32, 503, 505, 511, 520
Carter, Liliu (Sarah) Mitchell, 77n201
Carter, Mary Elizabeth Ladd, xxxiii, 60, 73n178, 77n201, 410, 480n3
Cartwright, A. J., 38, 138n37
Castle, William R., 67n147, 168, 168n136, 171, 171n3, 283, 322
C. Brewer & Co., xxxiii, 7n25, 71n165
Central Union Church, 70n158, 286n94, 369, 369n197
chanting, 122, 122n353
Charlton, Richard, xxxvii
Chase, Charles D., 216n20, 380, 414
chiefs, preservation of remains of, 91, 91n261, 519–20. *See also* Royal Mausoleum
Chief's Children's School, xxvii, 423n51
child labor, 93, 93n271–93n272
Chinatown, 40n31; fire (April 18, 1886), 64–66, 70n158 (*See also* fire relief)
Chu Lan & Co., 80, 80n211, 229, 229n85
Clark, Charles H., xv, 94n275, 442
Clark, Jennie, 94, 94n275, 443
Cleghorn, Archibald Scott (husband of Likelike; Liliu's brother-in-law), xxxi, xxxii, 19, 39n27, 85n240, 120n345, 135, 138n37, 142, 155, 171n1, 172, 176n28, 182n49, 259–60, 280, 288, 307–9, 332, 332n67, 519
Cleghorn, Helen, 182, 182n49, 223n54

Cleghorn, Princess Miriam Likelike (Liliu's sister), xxiii, xxvi, xxx, xxxi, xxxii, 33, 52, 67–72, 72n167, 82, 90, 131, 133–34, 203; at Ainahau (1855), *128*; anniversary of her death, 178; with daughter Kaiulani, *126*; death of, 134, 134n32–134n33; funeral of, 134–35; will, 138n37, 139

Cleveland, President Grover, 144, 250, 327–28, 327n37–327n38, 332–33, 381, 423n50

Cogswell, William, 251, 315n2

Colburn, John F., 38, 38n22, 309, 316–17, 389–93, 412n20

colonization land scheme, 81, 81n221, 82–83, 83n232, 84

Commercial Hotel, 80–81, 80n213

Committee of Safety, 289n104, 359

Coney, Eleanor Kaikilani, 257, 257n12, 268, 268n37

Cooke, Amos Star, xii

Cooke, C. M., 435

Cornwell, William H., 3n2, 300, 300n142, 308–9, 311, 316–17, 401n243

counterrevolution (January 1895), xv–xvi, xxxi, 35n6, 239n115, 301n147, 305n166, 333n72, 335n77, 350n124, 372n206, 430n77, 433–35; Liliu's response to, 442–44

Coyne, Arthur, 447–50

Creighton, Robert J., 85, 120, 120n347

crimes: embezzlement (from post office), 287n97; murder, 260, 260n21; robbery of crown jewels, 339, 339n85; shooting incident, 330, 330n57; stabbing incident, 195

Crowningburg, David, 46, 46n62, 48, 48n71, 194

crown lands, 161, 161n111, 163, 257–58, 258n15, 259, 275, 281n79, 318n7, 344n103, 360, 372n207, 423n51, 505, 507; Liliu's claim to, 507, 509, 519–20

crowns, 146n76; vandalized, 339, 339n85

Cummins, John A., 33, 38n21, 38n26, 130n12, 183, 183n52, 225, 225n60, 248, 330n54, 426, 429n73; birthday, *190*; and counterrevolution, 433–35

Daggett, Rollin M., 14, 14n65, 29, 29n128

Damien, Father, 63, 63n136, 215n14

Damon, Rev. Samuel C., 8, 8n30, 57n114, 70n158, 71, 75n189, 315n3

Damon, Samuel M., 163n120, 235, 235n103, 291n112, 315–16, 315n3, 316–17, 321, 321n19, 405–06, 436, 450, 456

Davies, Theophilus H., xxxii, 146, 146n77, 189, 189n90, 380, 380n223

de Fries, Emma Kanoa, 372, 372n207

destruction, of documents, xv

Deverill, W. F. H., 220, 220n39

diaries, Liliu's, xv–xix, 431n77, 436; diary for 1888, *xv*; editing of, xxi–xxii; language of, xxi–xxii; list of, xviii–xix; names in, xxii

diaries, of children of alii, xi–xiii

Dickson, Sarah ("Mother Dickson"), 75–76, 75n190, 192

Dillingham, Benjamin F., 60n122, 81n221, 216n19. *See also* colonization land scheme

disease, 372. *See also* leprosy and lepers

disenfranchisement of Native Hawaiian voters, in Bayonet Constitution, 249

Dole, Anna, *410*

Dole, Sanford B., xvi, 30, 37, 37n20, 160n108, 171, 171n3, 174n21, 260n21, 283–84, 317, 325, 325n29, 373n209, 386n228, *410*, 425n56, 436, 439–41; health of, 368, 368n193; and Liliu's release, 453–56; response to Willis (December 23, 1893), 399–400; and Wilcox Rebellion, 236

Dominis, Capt. John (father of John O. Dominis), xxviii–xxix, xxxvii, 45n55, 179, 297

Dominis, John O. (Liliu's husband), 12, 19–20, 25, 32, 43, 45, 47, 78, 85, 111, 142, 173, 179n33, 201, 232, 293n124; account of his life, 286–88; and Aliiolani Villa, xxxvii; anniversary of his death, 303; becomes "His Royal Highness," 251; and Chinatown fire, 66; death of, 251; and diaries, xv; and drinking, 217; in England, 148, 152, 155; estate of, 275; friends of, 203n137; and government appointments, 62, 64; governorship, 116, 116n332; health of, 3, 30, 36–37, 40, 44, 107–8, 113, 130, 144, 159, 164, 166, 181, 187, 197–98, 207, 213, 218, 224, 228, 238; and Liliu, 79–80, 82, 86 (*See also* marriage, of Liliu and John O. Dominis); made commander in chief, 116; marriage (*See* marriage, of Liliu and John O. Dominis); and mother's fall, 140 (*See also* Dominis, Mary Jones); obituary, xxviii; photographed in 1887, *151*; portrait as a boy, *151*; and Privy Council, 50; relatives of, 55n107; residence of, 118; social life, 90, 183n56; son of, 10n40; summary biography, xxviii–xxix; trip around Oahu, 18, 18n76; trip to England, 140–55

Dominis, Lydia K., xxiii. *See also* Liliuokalani, Queen

Dominis, Mary Jones (mother of John O. Dominis; Liliu's mother-in-law), xxviii–xxix, xxxvii, xxxvii n5, 7, 43, 46, 55, 75, 80, 85, 107, 111, 124, 130, 140, 142, 162, 175n25, 176–78, 182, 197; birthday, 197; death of, 227, 227n75, 409; health of, 197, 200

Dominis family, xvii, 23n103
Dowsett, Annie Kahawalu, 273n63
Dowsett, David Aikanaka, 127, 127n3
Dowsett, Dora, 129, 129n10
Dowsett, James Isaac, 44n51, 127, 167, 167n134, 184, 236
Dowsett, John McKibbin, 76n192, 184, 184n58
Dowsett, Mary, 44n51, 129n10
Dowsett, Ned, 236
Dowsett, Samuel Henry, 129n10
drowning, 352n130

elections, 39–40, 40n32, 42, 42n36, 54; of 1890, 247; of 1892, 270. *See also* Hawaiian legislature
electric light display, 94n274, 96
Ellis, Rev. William, xi
Emma, Queen (Emma Rooke), xi, xii, xxiii n1, xxvii, 28, 41n34, 42, 74n184, 129n4, 161n114, 461; death of, 27, 27n120–27n122, 29, 29n126
Emmeluth, John, 291n112, 369n198
Ena, John, Jr., 15n69, 72n173, 164, 164n123, 227, 227n74, 261, 261n23
Ena, Mary Lane, 17
England, Liliu's visit to: arrival at San Francisco, 143; arrival in Liverpool, 146; departure, 140–42; return to Hawaii, 155; stay in Boston, 144–45; stay in London, 147–54; stay in New York City, 145–46; stay in Washington, DC, 143–44
English, Dr. Charles Hamilton, xix, 479, 479n2, 495, 501, 513–15
E. O. Hall & Son, Ltd., 125, 329n49, 377n214
Evans, Hana Kaniau, 101, 101n294, 291n113
Evans, Thomas E., 101n294, 116, 116n331, 269, 269n43, 291n113, 292
Everett, Thomas W., 62, 62n131, 179n33, 272n61, 282, 282n85

Fayerweather, Mary Kolimoalani Kekahimoku Beckley, 195, 195n107
Feary, Jerome, 351, 351n126
Fernandez, Abraham, 108n312, 265, 265n32, 273, 273n62
Fernandez, Minerva Davis, 108, 108n312, 265n32
Finlay, Mrs. (fortuneteller, card reader), 222n49, 223
fire, 41, 41n35, 64–66, 82, 90, 90n257, 92, 208, 208n164, 217, 223, 223n51; Chinatown (April 18, 1886), 64–66, 70n158 (*See also* fire relief)
fire codes, 65
fire relief (for Chinatown fire victims), 67, 69–72, 74–75, 77–78, 81, 84, 87
Fire Relief Fund, 78, 81, 84, 87
fish and fishing, 18, 20, 23, 23n101, 25, 25n106, 41, 157, 186, 205, 219, 221, 221n44, 223

Fishel's store (Chas. J. Fishel or Fischel), 37, 37n19, 79
Forbes, Anderson O., 51
Forbes, Maria, 5n8
Fornander, Abraham, 62, 62n131
Fort Street Church, 31, 70n158, 164, 164n121
fortunetelling, 37, 43, 216, 222n49, 223, 239, 286–88, 291–306, 342, 345. *See also* Wolf, Gertrude
Foster, Mary Robinson, 15n70, 195, 195n107, 343
Fourth of July holiday, 86–87, 86n242, 192, 192n93
friends: of Kalakaua, 13n59, 14n65, 36, 36n8, 103n304, 127n2, 305n166; of Liliuokalani, 17, 42, 42n37, 44n54, 45n55, 53n100, 63n135, 66n144, 68n150, 72n170, 72n172, 73n175, 94n275, 101n294, 103n302, 105n307, 116n331, 144n63, 170, 181, 184n60, 204n141, 221n44, 271n54, 291n113, 296n131, 297n135, 305n166, 315n3, 321, 459. *See also names of individuals*

garden party: Queen Kapiolani's, 42, 42n43; Queen Victoria's, 153n94, 154
Gardinier, Gertrude, 53, 53n98, 57
Gay, Charles, 42, 42n41
Gay, Francis, 83, 83n227, 328
Gay, James, 182n51, 353, 353n135
genealogical claims, 372n207, 413, 413n24, 418, 422
Gibson, Walter M., 33, 62n131, 85, 103n301, 104–5, 104n305, 116, 132, 132n23–132n24
Giffard, Walter M., 176, 176n28, 203, 315
Gilman, Gorham, 8, 8n33, 144, 144n63, 459
Good, John, 447–50
Goo Kim Fui, 25, 25n108; clothing store, 25, 25n108, 181, 181n40
government archives, preservation of, 278, 278n75–278n76
government buildings, Honolulu (1889), 34
governors' appointments, 272, 276–77, 281–82
Great Mahele, xxvi
Green, William L., 160n110, 186, 186n69
Gregg, David L., xxiii, xxvii
guard, Liliu's, 385, 385n226, 405–6; withdrawal of, 325–26, 325n29, 341
Gulick, Charles T., 54n103, 85, 305, 305n166, 307–8, 381, 433–35

Haaheo, Mary, 73, 73n177
Haalou, chief, 322
habeas corpus, suspension of, 435
Hakau, chief, 519
Haleakala (Bishop residence), xxvii, 7n23
Haleakala Boys' Boarding School, 157
Hale Naua, 161, 164, 164n125, 222, 222n47, 270, 270n48, 329, 331, 331n60

Halualani, Liwai K., 105
Hamakua, Hawaii, xxvii
Hamohamo (Kealohilani; Liliu's residence at Waikiki), xxxvi, 6n15, 123, 162, 182n47, 226n69, 242n128
Hana, Maui, 322
hanai, xxiii
Hanaiakamalama (Queen Emma's house at Nuuanu), 74n184
Hanapi, Edward, 129n11
Harrison, Louisa, 139
Harrison, President Benjamin, 273, 322
Hart, Capt. Isaac, xxxvii
Hartwell, Alfred S., judge, 283, 334, 334n74, 435–39
Hassinger, John A., 44, 44n53, 215, 215n17
Hastings, Alice Makee, 197, 197n117, 220, 220n41
Hastings, Frank P., 269, 269n45, 334, 334n74
Hatch, Francis M., 201, 201n130, 412n17, 456, 468, 471, 494
Hawaii, Republic of, xxxi, xxxii; cedes control to US, 501; proclamation of, 354, 354n140, 425, 425n56, 426; recognition of, 425, 425n58
Hawaiian artifacts, 22n95, 30, 42, 42n38, 67, 80, 91, 95–96, 103, 105, 153, 184, 189, 248, 270, 270n48, 330–31, 331n60, 510; crowns of Kalakaua and Kapiolani, 339n85; feather capes, 248; featherwork, 44–45 (*See also* kahili); "Kihapu," 331, 331n60; lau hala mat, 103; lei, 80, 95, 219, 225n63; lei hala, 265; lei hulu, 96; Makaloa mat (1885), 89; "Makau," 331, 331n60; umeke (calabash), 110, 117, 120, 510. *See also* Hawaiian products, sent to Paris Exhibition
Hawaiian Board of Missions, 68n151, 214n9, 239n118
Hawaiian Colonization Land & Trust Co., 81. *See also* colonization land scheme
Hawaiian constitution: constitutional convention, 311; constitutional crisis, 311–13, 338, 338n82; constitution of 1864, 158; constitution of 1887 (Bayonet Constitution), xxx, 160n108, 160n110, 165n129, 167n131, 174n21, 179n33, 186n70, 199n120, 234, 247, 249, 311; new constitution proposed by Liliu, 296, 296n131, 309, 352–53, 355, 355n144, 360, 363, 383, 388–92, 429, 429n74, 442; of Republic of Hawaii, 444
Hawaiian Evangelical Association, 238n113, 356n146
Hawaiian flag, 316, 320n13, 321, 321n18, 335, 335n78, 338n79, 346
Hawaiian Historical Society, xii, 278n76, 438
Hawaiian independence, 208n166, 238
Hawaiian League, 174, 174n21, 176, 227–28, 358n155

Hawaiian legislature, 118, 118n341, 196n114, 199, 199n120, 223; "Act Relating to Internal Taxes" (1892), 293n122; "Act to Abolish the Office of Governor," 165, 165n128, 167, 167n131, 168; "Act to Convene Delegates to Frame a Constitution…" (1890), 249; "Act to Provide for and Regulate the Internal Police of the Kingdom," 165, 165n128, 168; "Act to Provide for the Organization, Regulation, and Discipline of the Military Forces of the Kingdom," 165, 165n128, 167–68; appropriations bills, 292n119, 293n120–293n121; "Extraordinary Session" (November 3, 1887), 160; "Hawaiian Bank Act" (proposed, 1892), 301n149; lottery bill (1893), 315, 315n1, 345, 355; opening of, 67–68, 67n148, 186, 186n70, 248, 281, 284–85; ratification of annexation treaty, 473, 473n20; territorial legislature, 515
Hawaiian monarchy, overthrow of (1893), 289n104–289n105, 391–93, 408
Hawaiian products, sent to Paris Exhibition, 211, 215, 215n18, 221–22
Hawaiian Supreme Court, 52n92, 251, 260n21; *Everett v. Baker*, 179n33
Hawaiian Tramways Co., 226, 226n71
"Hawaii for the Hawaiians," 158
"Hawaii Ponoi" (Hawaiian anthem), 9n35
Hawaii State Archives, xi, xvi, xvii, xix
Hayashi, T., xxxvi
Hayselden, Frederick, 103n301, 371, 371n203
Healani (Kalakaua's boathouse), 45, 45n59, 49, 77, 107, 210
Heleluhe, Joseph (Joe), xv, 3, 3n1, 6n19, 7n20, 19, 19n84, 268, 367, 450–51, 456–57, 461n4, 464, 470, 515
Heleluhe, Myra, 465, 515
Herbert, Allen (Papa), 42, 42n40, 207, 207n163
Hilo, Hawaii, xxvii, xxix, 32–33, 35n1, 97–102, 202n134, 228, 519
Hilo Boarding School, 51–52, 67n147, 124n362–124n363, 355n142. *See also* Lyman Memorial Fund
Hinano Bower (sleeping place), 41, 46, 104, 112, 117, 135, 162, 174n22, 187, 199
Hind, Robert Robson, 408, 408n10
Hitchcock, Harvey Rexford, 426, 426n59
Hoapili, J. G., 5n12, 37, 37n18
Hobart, Garret A., 494
Hoffnung & Co., 146n76, 153n91, 157
Holt, Hanakaulani, 241, 241n124
Holt, James R., 42, 42n39
Holt, Robert W., 27, 27n114
Holt, William, 109, 109n316
Honohina, Hawaii, xxvi
Honolulu Fire Department, 78, 78n206
Honolulu Iron Works, 189, 189n90
Honolulu street railway scheme, 81, 81n222

Honolulu Water Works Department, 54–55, 54n103, 111n322, 116
Honuakaha, Honolulu, 236, 236n104
Honuaula, Maui, 157
Hookano, 142, 142n51
Hookena, Hawaii, 50, 50n80, 51n87, 188
hookupu, 121, 121n349, 266, 306, 377n215
Hooulu Lahui Society, 40n30, 69, 121, 124–25, 129–30, 133, 140, 176, 179–80, 182, 184, 206, 211, 215, 218, 223–24, 238, 243, 248
Hopkins, Charles L., 46n61, 220, 220n40
horseback riding, 93, 100, 188
Hospital Flower Society, 248
house moving, 109
House of Nobles, 7n22, 14n67, 48n70, 60n118, 103n304, 160n108, 239n118, 270, 272n57–272n58, 277n73, 288n100, 300n142, 355, 355n144, 356n146
Hui Aloha Aina (Patriotic League), 478. See also Ahahui Hawaii Aloha Aina and Ahahui Hawaii Aloha Aina o na Wahine
Hui Hololio (horse-riding association), 253, 273, 327, 358
Hui Imi Pomaikai o Waikiki (Waikiki Improvement Association), 223–24
Hui Nihoa, 105, 105n307, 111, 120–21, 121n349
hula, 106, 122, 122n353, 198, 241, 304; hula Pele, 205
Hulihee Palace, Kailua, Kona, *230*
Hustace, Frank, 8n28, 78n206, 112, 112n326
Hutchinson, Ernest, xxxvi

Iaukea, Charlotte Kahaloipua Hanks, xxxii, *17*, 76n192, 180
Iaukea, Curtis P., xvii, xxix n12, xxx, xxxii–xxxiii, *17*, 19n81, 32–33, 54, 54n102, 72n167, 90, 90n256, 103–5, 116, 142, 148–49, 152, 154–55, 161, 161n112, 163n120, 179n33, 225n62, 289n105, 318n7, 520; as chief of staff, 277; as crown lands commissioner, 258n14; on Wilcox Rebellion, 234–35
Iaukea, J. W., xxxii
ice cream party, 94, 121
Ii, Irene, 113, 113n328
Independent (Home Rule) Party, formation of, 515–16
insane asylum, 63, 63n135
insurrection (July 30, 1889), 158, 292n116
Inter-Island Steam Navigation Co., 164, 164n123, 182n48, 227n74
Iolani Palace, 43, 43n43, 52, 61, 69, 71, 77, 90, 102, 110, 123, 125, 135, 164, 186, 270, *314*, *404*; Grand Hall, *434*; and Hale Naua, 161, 164, 164n125, 222, 222n47, 270, 270n48, 329, 331, 331n60; Liliu's imprisonment in, 445–51; under provisional government, 354–55, 354n139, 355n141; royal guards (1889), *313*; Throne Room, *437*; viewed from Aliiolani Hale (1889), *420–21*; and Wilcox Rebellion, 233–38
Irwin, Robert W., 8, 13n57, 15, 15n73
Irwin, William G., 56, 77, 77n200, 257, 277, 298, 329, 329n50, 343, 343n102, 353, 366, 370, 426, 441
Isenberg, Daniel P. R., 200, 200n128, 372, 372n205
Isenberg, Paul, 272, 272n57

Jackson, George Edward Gresley, 93, 93n271
Jackson, Wallace, 255, 255n5
James (Liliu's brother), xxiii
Japanese, 8, 8n32, 9, 9n39, 13, 13n57, 43, 43n49, 44n52, 60, 60n120
Jones, John C., 23n103, 45n55
Jones, Peter C., 71, 71n165, 171, 171n3, 308, 329, 329n47, 329n51, 435
Judd, Albert F., xvi, xvii, 186, 240, 319, 425n56
Judd, Charles H., 33, 43, 103–5, 103n304, 104, 161n113, 185n64, 203n137
Judd, Dr. Gerrit P., xii, 102n297, 103n304, 238n115

Kaae, Jessie, *17*, 73, 340, 340n88
Kaae, William F., 431, 431n78, 436, 442
Kaai, Samuel W., 3, 3n6, 70, 70n162
Kaai, Simon, xxxv, 13n61, 70n162
Kaai, William F., xv
Kaaipulu, 322
Kaauwai, Joseph, 442
Kaauweloa, 92n264, 257, 257n11
Kaawaloa, Hawaii, xxvi, 52, *190*
Kaehuwahanui, 52n93, 60, 60n118, 277n73
Kahahawai, 283
Kahana, Oahu, xxvi, xxvii
Kahiku-o-ka-Moku (cave), Hawaii, 178
kahili (royal feather standards), 42, 42n38, 44–46, 67, 91, 95, 105, 105n307, 120, 124, 135, 161, 161n114, 162–64, 166, 184, 198, 266, 330, 330n52
Kahoalii, Grace Kamaikui Wahinekaili, 129, 129n4
Kahookano, J. H., 415–16
kahuna, 73, 323, 323n25, 349, 361
kahu, Liliu's, 322
Kaiaiki, Charlie, 141, 141n46, 142
Kaihupaa, xxxii
Kailua, Hawaii, xxvi–xxvii, 32, 45, 52, 188
Kaimimoku, 283
Kaiulani, Princess Victoria, xxxi–xxxii, 135, 138n37, 142, 182, 182n49, 186, 197, 277, 359, 380, 381n223, 447, 450–51; at age 17 on US trip, *511*; at Ainahau, Waikiki (1897), *508*; birthday, 115, 118,

118n342, 203, 203n140, 307, 377, 377n215; death of, 509; estate of, 510; health of, 474; as heir apparent, 251, 259–60, 275, 319, 377, 386n227; with her mother Likelike, *126*; intended trip to US, 328, 328n40; Liliu's advice to, 409, 409n13
Kakaako, Honolulu, 90, 93, 184
Kakaako Church, 93, 96; Sunday School, 84
Kakina, John, 96, 96n280
Kalaiaina society, 470, 474, 500
Kalakaua (king; Liliu's brother), xxix, xxix–xxx, xxxii, 11n49, 31–32, 36n9, 48, 51–52, 54, 60n120, 67, 84, 86, 92, 96, 116, 118, 161, 165, 177, 186, 188, 305n162, 459, 480n4, 519; accession, xxiii, 273; anniversary of his death, 261; and Bayonet Constitution, 154–55, 160n108; birthday, 109–10, 110n319, *115*, 250; birth of, xxvi; and Board of Genealogy of Hawaiian Chiefs, 91, 91n261; and Chief's Children's School, xi; and Claus Spreckels, 56n109, 90; coronation (1883), xxix; coronation day anniversary, 223; death of, *246*, 250, 267; and diaries, xiii; and dismissal of Judd, 104–5; estate of, 275, 275n66, 292n114; financial affairs, 163, 163n120, 164, 258n15, 277n72; and funeral of Queen Emma, 27n121, 29, 29n126; golden jubilee birthday, 121, 121n349, 122, 122n353, 123; and government appointments, 55–56, 85; and Healani (boathouse), 45, 45n59, 46n59, 49, 77, 107, *210*, *212*; and "Hoola Lahui," 40n30, 69, 121; illness of, 127; and inheritance, 138n37; interviewed by Wodehouse, 227–28; landau of, *59*; and landholdings, xxvii, 13, 13n58; letter (February 8, 1888), 177–78; and New Year's reception (1888), 171, 171n2; and Ocean Island, 112; and Order of Kapiolani, 106; and Pearl Harbor, 156, 156n101, 160; proposed abdication of, 167–68, 167n134, 168, 168n136, 174–75, 174n22, 176, 178, 234; and purge list, 62, 62n131; with royal orders and decorations, *137*; search for ancestral remains, 177–78; sleep habits, 274; threats against his life, 358; trip to Kailua, 184–85; trip to San Francisco (1890), 248, 250; views on Austin scheme, 203; visits to/from Liliu, 23, 61–62, 68, 71, 83, 162; and visit to England, 140; visit to Hawaii Island, 45, 45n58, 50, 50n80; and Wilcox Rebellion, 233–38
Kalalau, Kauai, 83n227, 362–65
Kalanianaole, Jonah K., prince, 12, 12n54, 155n97, 159, 177, 276, 316

Kalapaki, Nawiliwili Bay, Kauai, *263*
Kalauokalani, David, 6n15, 477, 477n1, 516
Kalaupapa, Molokai, 7n26, 74n180, 176n26, 184n60, 196n112, 289n106, 362, 467
Kalawao, Molokai, 92n266, 274, 289
Kalehua, 451
Kalua, John W., 3, 3n4, 42n36, 133, 133n29, 425n56, 427n62
Kaluaikoolau (Koolau), 362–64
Kaluaikoolau, Piilani, 362
Kamakau, Elizabeth (Lizzie) Kapoli, 7, 7n26, 124, 124n360, *170*, 176, 176n26, 177, 184, 184n60
Kamalama, Kapalu, 178
Kamamalu, Victoria, xxxi
Kamehameha I, 67n147, 68n150, 208n167, 519; bones of, 177–78
Kamehameha II (Liholiho), 164, 177
Kamehameha III (Kauikeaouli), xi, xxxii, xxxvii, 19n82, 41n34, 52n91, 164, 177
Kamehameha IV (Alexander Liholiho), xi, xii, xxiii n1, xxvii, xxxii, xxxv n1, 27
Kamehameha V (Lot Kapuaiwa), xi, xii, xxxv n1, 27n115, 49n73, 232n97, 260, 274; leprosy policy, 362
Kamehameha Schools, xi, xxxv n1, 6n15, 7n22, 214n9, 261, 288, 288n99, 288n101, 355n142; Founders' Day, 244
Kamoiliili Church, Honolulu, 131n19; Sunday School, 57, 77
Kanoa, Paul Puhiula Kalakua, xxxv, 67, 67n146, 78n204, 85, 85n239, 117, 229n89, 449
Kaohiwaena, H. K., 284
Kapaakea, Caesar (chief; Liliu's father), xxiii, *xxiv*, xxvi–xxvii, xxix
Kapalama (house of Liliu's), 10–11, 15, 18
Kapena, Alexandrina Leihulu, 27, 27n116, 36n11, 75, 75n185, 81, 84, 86, 102, 102n300, 103, 195, 195n107, 253, 253n3–253n4
Kapena, Emma Malo, 64, 64n137, 65, 65n141, 66
Kapena, John M., 27n116, 36, 36n11, 71, 75, 75n185, 85, 102n299, 104, 104n305
Kapiolani (chiefess; grand-aunt of Liliu), 193, 193n100
Kapiolani, Queen (Dowager Queen), xxix, xxx, 13n59, 19n80, 31, 36, 36n9, 39, 40n30, 42, 42n43, 43–45, 47, 49, 52, 55, 61, 67, 69, 71, 103, 106, 117, 117n340, 124, 129–31, 143–44, 147–49, 152, 154, 162, 179, 181, 184n62, 201, 343n98, 359, 361, 413, 471; birthday celebration, 35n1, *125*, 209, 247; dress of, 68n149, *136*, 186, 188; health of, 202, 216, 259; portrait in coronation gown (1883), *58*; residence, 226n69; trip to England, 140–55
Kapiolani Home for Girls, Honolulu, xxix

Kapiolani Maternity Home, Honolulu, xxix, 40n30, 248
Kapiolani Park Association, xxxii
Kapooloku (sister of Kapiolani), 130. *See also* Poomaikelani
Kau, xxvi, 133–34, 134n31
Kauai, L., 85, 85n238, 229
Kauai Industrial School, 262, 284, 284n90
Kauhane, Rev. James, 236, 236n105, 356, 356n146
Kauikeaouli Day, 19n82, 52
Kaukelehua, D., 130
Kaulia, Asa, 13n55, 40, 40n33
Kaulukou, John Lot, 49, 49n74, 62, 91n259
Kaulukou, Lot, 415
Kaumakapili Church, 3n5, 30, 30n129, 40n30, 72n167, 77, 148, 168, 168n135, 174n19, 180, 214, 214n8, 215, 215n13, 218–19, 228, 238–39, 290, 290n107; Sunday School, 125, 169, 229
Kaumualii, king of Kauai, xxix, 19n80
Kaunamano, J. H., 234–35, 305, 305n162, 330n54
Kawaiahao, 78, 110, 138, 292
Kawaiahao Church, 29n126, 53–54, 84n234, 90n251, 171, 204, 298n138, 520; Sunday School, 84
Kawaiahao Seminary, xxxi, 9, 9n36, 10, 14, 22, 55, 69n157, 75n186, 131n20, 140–42, 168, 187, 213n4, 265
Kawainui, Hattie, 127, 127n2
Kawainui, Joseph U., 62, 62n130, 127n2
Kawananakoa, David, prince, 12, 12n54, 124, 155n97, 183n56, 197, 197n118, 251, 275–76, 316, 471, 515; birthday, 224n58; funeral of, 520
Kawao, Emma, 139
Kawehena, xxxvi, 6, 7n19, 77n202
Keala Hale (Poikeala Hale), xxxv–xxxvi, 54, 84, 90, 96, 104, 108, 110, 113, 159
Kealahou, Hawaii, xxvi
Kealakekua, Hawaii, xxvi, xxvii
Keaweaheulu, chief, xxiii
Keelikolani, Ruth Keanolani Kanahoahoa, princess (Princess Ruth), xxxv n1, 7n26, 14, 49n73, 55n108
Kekaulike, princess, 19n80, 155n97
Kekauluohi, chiefess, xi
Keliiahonui, Edward A., prince, 12, 12n54, 124, 155, 155n97, 156
Keliikuewa, P., 283–84
Keohokalole, Ane (chiefess; Liliu's mother), xxiii, *xxiv*, xxvi–xxvii, xxix, 11n49, 25n110
Kepoikai, Auwae Noa, judge, 245, 245n143, 427n62
Kilauea volcano, Hawaii, 12, 12n52
Kinimaka, Hanakeola Leleo, 208, 208n164, 362, 362n170
Kinney, W. A., 199n120, 431n77, 468, 471, 494
Knudsen, Valdemar, 294, 294n128

Kohala, Hawaii, xxvi, 43n46
Koheo, xxvii
Kona, Hawaii, xxvi, xxxi, 177–78, 251
Konia, Laura, chiefess, xxiii, 7n22
Koolaupoko, Oahu, 24
Kuhio, Jonah, prince, 7n19, 124, 226n69, 471
Kuhio Park, Waikiki, xxxvi
Kuihelani, Huaka, chief, 52n93, 60n118, 72n172, 277, 277n73
Kula, Maui, xxvi, xxvii
Kulaokahua, Honolulu, 21n90, 49, 56
kumu (staff of kahili), 91
Kunuiakea, prince, 363

Lahaina, Maui, 30, 32, 36, 75, 97, 116n331, 119, 244–45
Lanai, 42n41, 103n301
land fraud, xxvii
landholdings, of Liliu's family, xxvi–xxvii
Lane, Lot, 283–84
Lane, William C., 27n115, 187, 187n74
Lanihau, Anna, chiefess, 85n239, 92n262
Lee, Sara, 459, 465
Lee, William, 145, 145n64, 457, 461
Leialoha, 316n4, 374, 447
Leleiohoku, William Pitt (Liliu's brother), xxiii, xxvi, xxx, xxxv n1, 14, 14n62, 61, 183, 183n55
leprosy and lepers, 7n26, 22n94, 184n60, 215, 215n15, 224, 274, 289, 362–65, 467
Liberal Party, 264, 264n28, 265, 270
Lilikalani, Annie K., 36n12, 138, 138n36
Lilikalani, Edward, 40, 40n33, 427, 427n64
"Liliu" (Saide, daughter of J. O. Carter), xxxiii
Liliuokalani, Queen (Lydia Kamakaeha; Lydia Kapaakea Paki; Mrs. John O. Dominis), xi, xxvi, 138n37; abdication of, xxxi, 14n67, 158, 344, 344n103, 346, 433, 436–43; accession of, xxx, 247, 250–51, 256, 265–68, *518*; at age 62 (1900), *512*; and alleged assassination attempt, 463–64; appeal to the American people, 364; arrested for treason, 433, 435–36; birthday, 32–33, 105–6, 198, 198n119, 238n114, 306, 510–11, 517, 519; birth of, xxvi; boats belonging to, 471–72; burial of, 520; and cabinet, 256; carriage accident, 195; claim to crown lands, 507, 509, 519–20; and cleaning, 95, 107–8; as commander in chief, 387–88; convicted of "misprision of treason," xxxi; death of, 520; departure for US, 456–57, 504; deposition of, xxx, 316–18; description of (1892), 280; as diarist, xi–xiii; dress of, 186, 193, 229, 303, 364; education, xxvii; excursion to Hawaii Island (October 1885), 32–33; excursion to Nihoa (July 1885), 30–31; fears for her life and safety, 329, 329n43, 340, 347, 354–57,

357n151, 366–67, 369–70, 382, 385, 407, 427, 463–64; finances of, 21, 38n24, 43, 47, 51–52, 123, 200, 203, 377, 377n214, 378–79; fined by Hawaiian Republic, 444–45; founds Uluhaimalama plant nursery, 428; at Hana Plantation (1883), 2; health of, 11–13, 18, 37, 39, 41, 44, 51, 57, 61–62, 64, 69, 78, 80–83, 92, 96, 102, 117–18, 141–42, 145–47, 153, 159, 162, 177, 197, 219, 226, 251, 303, 351, 365–67, 427, 429, 457, 479, 481–506, 509–10, 513–15, 520; as heir apparent, *xxiv*, xxvi, xxx, 119, 167–68, 167n134, 168, 168n136, 247; and her family, xxiii–xxxiii; household of, 3n1, 6n19, 10n40; imprisonment at Iolani Palace, xix, xxxi, 6n19, 94n275, 433, 444–45; and Independent Party, 516; influence of, 39, 43; interception of her letters, 361; interest in dreams, 46, 95, 130, 180, 195, 222, 238, 273–74; jewelry, 148; and Kalakaua, xxix (*See also* Kalakaua); at Kalakaua's 50th birthday, *115*; kicked by a horse, 225; letter of abdication, 439–41; letters, xix, xxxiii, 111n323, 271n54, *458*; love of gardening, 5, 7n19, 10–11, 45, 47–49, 52–56, 60–61, 66, 75, 77n202, 87, 97, 102, 107–8, 116, 159, 161, 183, 364, 372, 407, 412, 429; love of singing, 463, 484, 490; marriage (*See* marriage, of Liliu and John O. Dominis); memoir (*Hawaii's Story by Hawaii's Queen*), ix, 457, 459–61, 480; moods of, 18, 20, 22, 42, 52, 76–77, 82, 104, 108, 113, 116, 118, 154–55, 183, 327, 419; mourning for husband, 253; musical compositions, 176, 213, 223, 300, 300n143, 329, 340, 465, 504; names of, xxiii–xxvi; oath of allegiance to Hawaiian Republic, 442; offered throne, 174–76; at Palolo property (1885), *xxi*; pardon of, xxxi; parents and siblings of, *xxiv*; pension for, 344, 344n103; political views, 39–40, 48, 91, 162; political will, 431, 431n78; portrayed in court dress, *xi*; post-accession tour, 251; power of attorney, 38, 38n24, 319, 319n11, 323, 335n76, 345, 347, 357, 357n152, 505; privacy of, 520; proposed deportation/banishment of, 356, 356n148, 424; protest of annexation treaty, 468–70; protest regarding claim to Hawaiian crown lands, 507; at Queen Victoria's jubilee, *151*; receives Grand Cross Order of Kapiolani, 106; refusal to acknowledge P.G. authority, 317–18; as regent, xxx, 247, 250; relations with family and friends, xxxi–xxxiii; release from imprisonment, 453–56; and religion, 5, 179, 406; request for protection, 385; response to trial, 442–44; retirement, 324–25; return from US, 500–501, 515; with royal siblings, *xxiv*; salary of, 321, 321n20, 324, 326, 329, 335, 378, 430; with Samuel Nowlein, *432*; sends commission to Washington, 425–28; sentencing of, 444–45; and sewing, 61, 83, 109, 129, 167, 182, 199, 217, 225 (*See also* sewing society); signature as "Liliuokalani Dominis," 439; signing of commissions, 431, 431n79; sleep habits, 60, 96, 130, 274; state carriage of, 174, 174n20, 176, 181, 186, *310*; statement to James Blount, 364; stay in Washington, DC, 6n16, 459–75, 506; thoughts on solitude, 77, 102, 104, 113; trial by Republic of Hawaii (1895), 14n67, 256n9, 442–45; trip to England, 6n16, 140–55, 280; trip to Hilo, Hawaii, 97–102; use of code, xvii; visit to San Francisco, xiii; and Wilcox Rebellion, 233–38, 236n110, 241; will, 138, 140; writings, 268n38, 459, 480n4

Liliuokalani Hui Hookuonoono (Liliuokalani Benevolent/Savings Society), 46–47, 47n63, 48, 52n93, 56–57, 57n112, 68–69, 76–79, 85–87, 96, 106, 109–10, 113, 117–18, 120, 122, 122n351, 127, 130, 132, 134–35, 139–40, 155, 165–66, 172, 175, 177–79, 202, 297, 361, 363, 365, 368

Liliuokalani Hui Hoonaauao (Liliuokalani Educational Society), 42, 42n37, 71–72, 72n167, 73, 76–77, 79–80, 87, 91–95, 97, 102–3, 105–11, 113, 116–18, 120–21, 127, 131–32, 139–40, 156–57, 166–67, 169, 171–73, 176–78, 180–87, 189, 192–93, 196–99, 201–2, 206, 208–9, 211, 213, 217–18, 221, 226, 228, 238, 242, 242n129, 256, 259, 269, 271, 297, 371, 377, 406, 414, 428n71

"Liliuokalani of Hawaii," xvii

Liliuokalani Protestant Church, Oahu, 254

Liliuokalani Trust, ix, xxvi, xxxvi, xxxvii

Liloa, chief, 177, 519

Lima Kokua Society, 75, 214n9

literacy, xi

Loe, 6, 7n19

Logan, Daniel, 368, 369n199

Loomens, Albert, 173n9, 233–38, 241n126–241n127, 242

lottery scheme (1892–93), 67n147, 291–92, 291n113, 299–300, 303–8, 311, 346, 364

luau, 14, 14n68, 31, 44, 44n51, 52, 71, 71n163, 72, 75, 75n187, 82, 84, 97, 103n303, 104, 111, 121, 127, 131–32, 133n28, 160, 164, 175, 178, 183, 207n161, 217–18, 221, 221n46, 228n79, 265–68, 267n35, 270–71, 273, 289, 297, 304, 306–7, 340n89, 358, 358n156, 377n215; honoring Abraham Hoffnung (1888), *212*; at Kawaiahao Female Seminary (1885), 4

Lunalilo (William Charles Lunalilo), xi, xxvii–xxviii, xxix, 5n11, 413n21, 413n24; birthday, 220n38

Lunalilo Home, 5, 5n11, 43, 43n45, 220n39
Lyman, Isabella, 5n8–5n9, 47n63, 100n292, 101n296, 102, 202n134, 228n78
Lyman, Rufus A., 49, 49n73, 412n16
Lyman Memorial Fund (of Hilo Boarding School), 51n89, 124, 124n363, 125

Maalaea, Maui, 3, 52, 102
Macfarlane, Edward C., 307, 316–17, 373, 373n209, 382
Macfarlane, Emilie, 117n337, 120, 120n346, 332n70, 339, 339n86
Macfarlane, Frederick W., 204, 204n141, 339n86
Macfarlane, George W., 147n79, 204n141, 509
Macfie, Robert A., 195, 195n110, 229, 229n88
Mackintosh, Rev. Alexander, 135
Mahaulu, Archibald Scott, 233, 233n100
Mahiai, Elizabeth, 44, 44n54
Mahoe, Deborah, xxxv
Mahukona and Kapaau, Hawaii, 52n90, 97, 97n286, 101
Maikai, Samuel I. U., 36, 36n12, 138n36
Mainalulu, 8, 8n34, 25, 25n107
Makaehu, xxvii
Makaiki, Tamar, 77n198
Makee, Alice, 35, 35n3, 269n45
Makee, Capt. James, 35n3, 220n41, 269n45
Makena, Maui, 75n188, 102
Makoleokalani, Kalua, 157
Malaekahana, Oahu, xxvi
Malina, Peter, 263
Malo, David (historian), 27n116, 29n125, 102n299
Malo, David, Jr., 29n125, 30
Malo, Emma, 27n116, 36n11. *See also* Kapena, Emma
Mana, John, 73n175, 221n44, 297, 297n135
Manaku, David, 55, 55n105, 63, 63n133
Markham, George, 283
marriage, of Liliu and John O. Dominis, xxvii–xxix, 12–13, 20, 66, 74, 79–80, 85–86, 90, 130, 132, 164, 294
martial law, 352–53, 362, 424, 435
Martin, Dr. G. H., 11, 11n47, 13, 44, 92, 142, 159
Mary (Liliu's sister), xxiii
Maui, 43, 60n118, 179n33, 251
Maule, W. S., 11, 11n48, 133, 133n30
Mauna Loa, volcanic eruption, 133–34, 134n31
Maxwell, George W., 283
McCully, Lawrence, judge, 281–82, 282n81
McGrew, Dr. John S., 12, 12n51, 334, 334n74

McGuire, James W. L., 142, 142n50, 143, 146, 146n73, 147–48, 152, 153n92–153n93, 154, 331, 331n63
McInerny's (clothing/shoe store), 181, 181n41
McIntyre, Hugh, 139n39, 417, 417n41
McKinley, President William, 463, 471, 494, 515
McWayne, Dr. Albert, 117, 117n336, 298, 298n137
"Mele Aloha Aina" (Patriot's Song), 336
Merrill, George W., 33, 86, 86n244
milkshake stand, 222, 223n55, 239
Miller, William, xxxvii
Millis, Fred W., 53, 53n96, 57n115, 61
Mills, E. G., 377
Mills, Ellis, 368, 393
Mills, Susan L., 55, 55n107, 56, 56n111
missionaries, xi, 6n19, 10n42, 49n73, 66n144, 68n151, 193n100, 214n9, 238n113, 283, 320–21, 327, 349, 354, 356, 415n29, 444, 471. *See also names of individuals*
Miss Ogden's School, xxxi
Mitchell, Alfred, 53, 53n97, 60, 282n83
Moiliili, Honolulu, 435
Mokuaikaua Church, Kailua, Kona, 230
Molokai, 251
Morgan, James F., 131, 131n18, 239, 239n120
Morningstar, Louis, 372, 372n208, 376–77, 376n212
Moses (brother of Kamehameha IV and Kamehameha V), 206n154
Mott Smith, Dr. John, 271, 271n54
Mount Vernon, Liliu's visit to, 462–63
Muolaulani (Palama; residence of Liliu's), xxix, xxxv–xxxvi, 18, 22, 22n99, 27n122, 30, 38, 75, 87n245, 87n249, 106, 117, 140–41, 162–63, 181, 183, 185, 194–95, 240, 273

Naalehu, Hawaii, 256n8
Nahaolelua, Elizabeth Kahele (Kia), 53, 53n100, 456–57, 461n4, 464
Nahinu, D. H., 50n80, 51–52, 305, 305n163
Nakookoo, J. K., 21n91, 219, 219n29
Nakuina, Emma Beckley, 177, 179, 269, 323, 331n60
Nalanipo, Lahapa, xxxii
Namakeha, Bennett, chief, xxix
Naone, David Lima, 22, 22n98, 167, 167n130
National Reform Party, 40n32, 247, 340
Nawahi, Joseph K., 293n123, 296n131, 308, 330n54, 382, 424n54
Neumann, Paul, xvi, 14, 14n67, 85, 301n148, 304, 306–7, 309, 316–17, 319, 319n11, 363, 442, 442–45
Newlands, Francis G., 494

no-confidence resolution, proposed, 290n108
noninterference policy, US, 422, 422n49, 423n52, 424
Nordhoff, Charles, 340n90, 360–61, 361n167
Norrie, Edmund, 324n27, 335n75, 372, 372n206
Nowlein, Samuel, xv, 35n6, 54, 81n223, 272, 272n61, 292, 292n116, 315n1, 381, 429n74, 432, 436, 442; and counter-revolution, 433–35
Nua Ahua i Puna, 46
Nua Lehua, 55, 64–66, 68–69, 72, 75, 77, 82, 86, 103–4, 113, 135
Nuuanu Valley, 139, 155, 185

Oahu College (Punahou School), 67n147, 83, 83n230, 189n88, 226n67, 403n249
Oahu Railway & Land Co., 60n122, 216, 216n19
Ocean Island (Moku Papapa), 112
Oggel, Rev. Engelbert C., 8, 8n31, 70n158
Ohule, Kuiaha, East Maui, xxvi–xxvii
Omaopio, Maui, xxvi
Onomea Bay, Hawaii, 98–99
opium, xxx, 290n109, 295, 300, 300n145, 307, 311
Opposition Party, 171, 171n3, 219
overthrow of monarchy (1893), 289n104–289n105, 391–93, 408

Paauhau, Hawaii, xxvi, xxvii
Pahau, Mary Purdy, 10n40, 68, 68n150
Paki, Abner, chief, xxiii, 7n22
Paki, Lydia Kamakaeha, xxiii. *See also* Liliuokalani, Queen
Palau, Robert, 283–84
Palmer, Julius A., 459, 461, 461n4, 462, 464
Paloka, 283
Palolo, Oahu, 41, 60
Paoakalani, Waikiki, *xxxiv*, 7, 7n20, 55, 96–97, 118, 367
Paris Exposition Universelle, proposed visit to, 215, 215n12, 216, 216n21, 219–20, 220n35
Parker, Capt. Robert W., 233–35
Parker, Harriet Napela, 72, 72n172, 111n325
Parker, John, 35n2, 123n354, 236n108
Parker, John P., xxvii, 35n2, 123, 123n354
Parker, Robert, 236, 236n108, 436
Parker, Samuel, 33, 35, 35n2, 72n172, 111n325, 259–61, 277n73, 280, 288–90, 291n112, 305–7, 309, 311, 316–17, 338, 338n82, 345, 360n161, 370, 388, 426, 439n7
Parker Ranch, Hawaii, xxvii, 35n2, 123n354, 236n108

Payne, Sereno E., 494
Pearl Harbor: L's excursion to (1892), 302; US interest in, 156, 156n101, 160, 194, 194n105, 332n65, 494
Pele, 222; Chiefess Kapiolani's defiance of, 193, 193n100
People's Ice & Refrigeration Co. (PIR), 172–74, 176, 176n27, 179–80, 182–83, 198–200
Peterson, Arthur P., 249, 291n112, 299, 299n140, 301, 301n147, 305, 309, 311, 316–17, 390, 392
Phillips, John, 315n1, 416
photography, 22, 70, 70n59, 148, 269
Pilipo, J. W., 27, 27n117, 100, 100n288
Pinkham, Lucius Eugene, 177
Pitman, Benjamin, 37n17, 145, 145n68
Pohukaina School, 172n5, 188, 188n83, 196
Poomaikelani (Virginia Kalanikuikapooloku Kalaninuiamamao; Kapo; Pooloku), princess, 19, 19n80, 32–33, 51, 121, 131, 140, 142, 236, 236n107, 361; birthday, 414
Poor, Henry Francis, 38n25, 287, 287n97
Porter, Theodore C., 329, 329n51, 331, 331n59
portraits, of Liliu, John Dominis, and the late King Kalakaua, 251, 315n2
Potter, George C., 450, 450n6, 455
Pratt, Elizabeth Kekaaniau, chiefess, 127, 127n1, 343, 407n7, 423n51
Pratt, Frank S., 407, 407n7, 423n51
Privy Council, 7n22, 13n61, 14n67, 20n85, 36n10–36n11, 48n70–48n71, 62n131, 87n248, 94n275, 179n31, 245n142, 260n21, 272n58, 277n73, 305n163, 353n136
protectorate, proposed, 240, 240n122, 402n248
Provisional Government, xvi, xxx, xxxii, 14n67, 160n108, 239n117, 282n85, 289n105, 295n129, 321, 321n18–321n20, 324–25, 325n29, 335, 357, 360, 369n198, 373n209, 377n215, 407–8, 408n8–408n9, 471; "Act concerning Seditious Offenses" (1893), 324n27; Act No. 6, 315n1; amnesty for members, 381–84, 394–98, 401; constitutional convention, 419, 424; declaration of, 313; establishment of, 316–18, 392; and Kauai leprosy incident, 362–65; military, 338, 359, 370
prowler (Washington Place), 187, 402, 405
Pualeilani (estate owned by Kalakaua), Waikiki, xxx, 226, 226n69, 259
public lands, title conveyed to US, 501
Pukalani, Maui, xxvi
Puna, xxvi
Punahou Preparatory School, 83n230, 356, 359n158, 367, 367n190, 369, 403, 408n9

Punahou School, 37n20, 55n107, 56, 56n111, 57, 83, 239n117, 358n154
Punaluu Hotel, Kau, Hawaii, *230*
Puowaina (Punchbowl Crater), xxiii, xxvii
purge, governmental, 62, 62n131
Purvis, Edward W., 65n140, 104–5
Puuloa (Pearl Harbor), Treaty of, 194
Puuohulu, 194

Queen's Hospital, xxiii n1, xxvii
Queen's Medical Center, xxiii, xxiii n1
quilts: flag, *375*; patchwork crazy *448*
quilting, 217

races and racing, 79, 225, 285; Kamehameha Day, 79, 79n209
rally, of Hawaiian people, 424
rebellion of January 1895, 158
Reciprocity Treaty (1875), xxix, 56n109, 160, 194n105, 273n64, 470; supplementary convention to (1887), 156, 156n101
Reform Party, 40n32, 247, 261, 291n111, 340, 408
*Report of Her Majesty Queen Kapiolani's Visit to Molokai*, by H.R.H. Princess Liliuokalani, *July 1884*, 74, 74n180
residences, Liliu's, xxxv–xxxvii. *See also* names of residences
restoration: hopes for, 341–43, 343n97, 346, 347n111, 351–53, 353n134, 354, 360, 364, 366, 369–71, 373, 376, 378, 380, 385, 403, 406, 415, 418–19, 426–27, 428n70, 431n79, 442–43; US and, 381, 383, 386, 386n227–386n228, 387n230–387n231, 395–400, 402, 413. *See also* counter-revolution (January 1895)
revolutionary movement, 282–84
Rice, Mary Waterhouse, 288, 288n98
Rice, William H., 171, 171n3, 239, 239n117, 263, 272, 288n98, 306, 306n167
Richardson, George E., 133n30, 245, 245n142
Richardson, John, 48, 72n172, 272, 272n58, 382, 474
Rickard, William Henry, 353, 353n137, 433–35
Robertson, James W., xxxii, 39, 39n27, 139n41, 182n49, 251, 384–85, 459, 463, 471–72
Robertson, Rose, xxxii, 182, 182n49
Robinson, Aubrey, 31
Robinson, James, 10n41, 65n139, 117n336
Robinson, Lucy, 117n336, 298n137
Robinson, Mark P., 308, 375, 408, 408n11
roller coaster, 12, 12n53, 226, 226n70–226n71
Rooke, Captain, 423
Rooke House (residence of Queen Emma), 27, 45n56

Rose, Antone, 87, 87n248, 416
Ross, Manuel, Jr., 283
Royal Hawaiian Band, 6n16, 9, 9n35, 31, 44n52, 49n78, 131n17, 155, 330, *336*
Royal Mausoleum, Nuuanu, 7n22, 135, 161, 161n115, 164, 177–78, 333n71, 519–20
royal orders, 269, 269n45, 273; Order of Kalakaua, 9, 9n38, 260, 267; Order of Kamehameha I, 259–61; Order of Kapiolani, 193, 260–61; Order of the Burning Torch of Liliuokalani (proposed), 259, 259n20; Star of Oceania, 260
Royal School, Honolulu, xxvii, xxviii–xxix, 74n183, 94–95, 95n277, 196
royal standard, 316, 318. *See also* kahili

Sabbath observance, 68
Saint Andrew's Cathedral, xxvi
Saint Louis College, 96, 96n282–96n283, 173n17, 196
Saint Philomena Church, Kalawao, Molokai, 467
Schaefer, Frederick August, 139, 139n41, 173, 173n14
Schmidt, Heinrich W., 8n27, 168, 168n138
schools, 3, 51, 51n85; country school, Maui (1885), 4. *See also* names of schools
sea bathing, 25, 55, 64, 72, 86, 101, 107, 111, 159, 183, 226, 243, 274, 296, 318, 325
Seamen's Bethel Church, Honolulu, 57n114, 62, 62n132, 70, 70n158
secret ballot, 247, 247n2
"seized papers," xv–xvi
self-determination, Hawaiian, 422
Severance, Mrs. Lucinda, 101n295
Severance, Mrs. Anna, 140n42
Seward, W. T., 333, 333n72, 430, 433–35
sewing society, 226; Hui Limahana, 214, 214n11, 215, 217, 219, 221–22, 224, 238; Stranger's Friend Society, 81, 81n219
Sheldon, Henry L., 7n21, 229, 229n90
Sheldon, John, 324, 324n27, 335n75
Sheldon, Sophie (Sophy), 7, 7n21, 57n21, 79, 82, 173, 195
Sherman, John T., 144, 144n58, 468, 470, 475, 494
Skerrett, Adm. J. S., 366, 366n186, 367–68, 367n192, 370
Smith, Alexander, 283
Smith, Rev. James William, 284n90, 289n105
Smith, William O., 289, 289n105–289n106, 313, 368, 368n196, 391, 435, 520
Smithies, George E., 82n223, 329, 329n48
smuggling, 243, 333n72. *See also* opium
Sons of Hawaii Party, 264, 264n29, 268
Soper, John H., 239, 239n119, 329n46

Spencer, Charles N., 74n181, 248, 256, 256n8
spies and spying, 367, 380, 388, 403, 405, 417
Sprague, Roberta, xvii
Spreckels, Claus, 21, 21n88, 56, 56n109, 90, 90n254, 91, 91n258, 290–91, 291n112, 292, 299, 329n50, 344–45, 347, 360, 364–66, 370
Spreckels, John D., 366, 370, 499, 499n32
Stangenwald, Dr. Hugo, 39, 39n29, 41, 43
Stevens, John L., 265n33, 317, 321n18, 334, 334n74, 341, 341n91
Stevenson, Robert Louis, 38n25, 46n59, 221, 221n46, 226n68
Stoltz, Louis H., 362–65
sugar industry, xxix, 38n21, 188n80
Sumner, John K., 206n154, 208n169
Sumner, Ninito, 206, 206n154, 365
Sunday School Convention (Hawaii Island), 97–102, 97n285, 101n293
Sunday Schools, 51, 51n87, 77, 83, 97n285
Synge, Robert F., 146, 146n77, 148–49, 149n84, 152

Tehuiarii, Rev. Tute (Kuke), xi
temperance, 57, 57n116
Ten Eyck, Anthony, xxxvii
Thrum, Thomas G., 21, 21n93, 281n80
Thurston, Lorrin Andrews, 157–58, 160, 160n108, 160n110, 163n120, 168n136, 171, 171n3, 174, 174n21–174n22, 256n10, 285n92, 286n96, 313, 322, 356n148, 358n155, 359n157, 386n228, 388–93, 464, 468, 471, 494
tramcars, 220, 220n34, 221, 221n43
Trask, Albert, 187
Trask, Sarah Maalea, 187
treason, 158, 282–84, 286n95, 287n97, 290n108, 382, 388, 430; Liliu's trial for, 442–45
trials, of counterrevolutionists, 436
Trousseau, Dr. Georges Philippe, xxviii, 36, 36n8, 251, 366, 417
Turpie resolution, 425, 425n55
Turton, Annie, 159, 161
Turton, Edith, 103, 103n301, 161

Uluhaimalama, Pauoa, Oahu, 428
Ulukou, Annie, 40n30
Ululani, chiefess, 132, 132n25, 272n56
Umi, chief, 177, 519
US Congress: "Hawaiian Organic Act" (1900), 515; "Joint Resolution to Provide for Annexing the Hawaiian Islands to the United States," 494, 498
US congressional representation, for Hawaii Territory, 515

vessels: *Akamai*, 232, 232n95; *Alameda*, 12, 12n54, 22, 22n100, 180, 207, 224n59, 340, 361, 363, 370–71; *Albert*, 417n37; *Alert*, 22n100; *Arawa*, 427; *Aurora*, 36n7; *Australia*, 22n94, 76, 76n194, 76n196, 140–41, 155, 185, 197, 242, 242n130, 268, 274, 288, 298, 321, 331, 343, 348, 359–60, 363–65, 371–72, 380, 406, 413, 422, 426, 428, 430, 430n77, 464; *Birnham Wood*, 112; *China*, 368; *City of Peking*, 43, 43n49, 515; *City of Rome*, 146; *City of Tokio*, 8, 8n32; *Claudine*, 321–22; *Coptic*, 504; *Corwin*, 401; *C. R. Bishop*, 14, 18, 18n78, 19, 31, 182; *Diana*, 11n46; *Discovery*, 243, 243n133; *Dubordieu*, 248, 299–300; *Dunnottar Castle*, 112; *Eleu*, 142, 155; *Gaelic*, 419, 474, 500; *G. W. Elder*, 49; *Halcyon*, 290n109, 300n145; *Hall*, 385; HBMS *Caroline*, 171, 171n1, 174, 184; HBMS *Champion*, 288, 288n102, 427n67; HBMS *Conquest*, 155; HBMS *Cormorant*, 186, 186n68, 193, 228, 228n77; HMS *Heroine*, 67, 70n160; HMS *Satellite*, 67, 70n160; HMS *Triumph*, 67, 70n160, 71, 71n164; *Iwalani*, 30–31, 363; *J. A. Cummins*, 142, 183, 188; *James Makee*, 112; *Jones*, xxviii; *Kaala*, 182, 182n48; *Kaimiloa*, 93n271; *Kerguelen*, 6; *Kinau*, 3, 32, 36n9, 36n13, 42, 51, 61, 97n285, 102, 118–19, 188, 206, 228n78; *Likelike*, 3, 8, 36n13, 61, 92n266, 93, 118, 229; *Mariposa*, 8, 13, 43–44, 44n50, 56n110, 57n116, 82n224, 303, 322, 322n21, 378–79, 425; *Mikahala*, 209, 236n107; *Min*, 174, 174n19; *Miowera*, 371, 371n204; *Monowai*, 327, 427; *Morning Star*, 68n151; *Oceanic*, 377; *Pheasant*, 272, 276, 276n68; PMSS *China*, 457; *Rio de Janeiro*, 426; *Rush*, 334; *San Francisco*, 281, 281n78; *Sisters*, xxxii; SS *Australia*, 49n72; SS *China*, 456; SS *Servia*, 154; SS *Waialeale*, 112; *Swiftsure*, 206; *Thaddeus*, 6n19, 66n144; *Tsukuba*, 109, 109n315, 109n317; USS *Adams*, 155, 183n56; USS *Alert*, 203, 203n137; USS *Boston*, 304, 306, 320, 320n13, 341n91; USS *Charleston*, 248, 250; USS *Mohican*, 171, 189, 189n91, 245, 366n186; USS *Omaha*, 195, 195n109; USS *Pensacola*, 264n27, 278n76; USS *Philadelphia*, 378, 382, 401, 416, 427n67; USS *Vandalia*, 171, 183n56; *Wahlberg*, 433; *Waialeale*, 229, 232, 363; *Waimanalo*, 433; *W. G. Hall* (*Malulani*), 37, 37n14, 45n58, 50, 50n80, 60, 90, 134n31, 178, 188, 236, 244; *William Nelson*, xxxvii; *Yorktown*, 430; *Zealandia*, 61, 78
veto power, king's, 167n131

Victoria, Queen, 148–54, 250; diamond jubilee of, xxxii, 465; golden jubilee of, xxx, xxxii, 6n16; letter to Liliuokalani, 342, 342n93; musical compositions from Liliuokalani, 465
Vida, Daniel, 294n127
Volcano House, Hawaii, 256, 256n10, 261
Von Holt, Bertha, 183
vote of censure, 165, 165n129

Waialua, Oahu, 182, 201, 253–55
Waiamau, Rev. J., 3, 3n5, 54
Waikahalulu Falls, Nuuanu stream, 452
Waikapu sugar plantation, Maui, 3n2, 300n142
Waikiki, *iv (image on xxxviii)*, 53, 55, 74–76, 78–80, 86, 93, 95, 103, 111, 113, 123, 157, 159–62, 181, 183, 189, 195, 223n57, 229, 272, 367, 370
Waikiki Church, 53
Waikiki Kai school, 22
Wailiula o Mana (Mirage of Mana), 232, 232n92
Wailuakio, Palama, Oahu 80, 87, 87n247
Wailuku, Maui, 32, 60n119, 118
Waimanalo, Oahu, 38n21, 183
Waimea, Hawaii, xxxii–xxxiii
Waipio, Oahu, 252
Wakeke, 6, 6n19
Walker, John S., 54n103, 353, 353n136
Walker, Thomas R., xxxi–xxxii, 74n182
Wallace, Rev. George, 135
Ward, Victoria Robinson, 10, 10n41, 15n70, 65n139
Washington Place (residence), ix, xv–xvi, xxviii, xxix, xxxv, xxxvi, xxxvii, 3n1, 6n17, 31, 40–41, 45–46, 48, 53, 53n100, 57, 62–63, 66, 72, 74, 76, 80, 83–87, 91, 95–97, 102–3, 107–11, 113, 116–17, 120, 124, 142, 162, 164, 166, 182, 185, 194, 453, 454, 455, 493
Waterhouse, Henry, 171, 171n3, 236, 239, 239n118
Waterhouse, John T., 181, 288n98
Waterhouse & Co., 10, 10n44, 45
Wayland, Francis, 5, 5n7
Whaley, Capt. William, 290, 290n109, 300, 300n145
White, William, 304, 304n156, 311
Whiting, William A., 256, 256n9, 294, 406, 406n4
Whitney, Henry M., 54–56, 62, 62n131
Widemann, Herman A., 41, 41n35, 76n192, 120n346, 316–17, 339n86, 379n218, 411, 426, 428n70
Widemann, Wilhelmine, 76, 76n192, 184
Wight, Dr. James, 43, 43n46, 195n107
Wilcox, Elizabeth Kahuila, 39, 39n28, 40n30, 45

Wilcox, George N., 308
Wilcox, Gina (Gina Sobrero), 157, 169, 169n139, 172n6
Wilcox, Robert William, xxxv–xxxvi, 35n6, 48n70, 157–59, 172n6, 174n22, 175, 175n24, 176, 178, 180, 227, 227n73, 233, 241, 241n126–241n127, 249–50, 267, 282–84, 287n97, 290n108, 305n162, 319n12, 515, 519; and 1890 elections, 247; annexation resolution, 293, 293n123; attempted assassination of, 307; and counterrevolution, 433, 435–36; and Independent Party, 516; and Patriotic League, 423n50; and Wilcox Rebellion, 233–38
Wilcox, William Luther, 39n28, 174, 415, 415n29, 442
"Wilcox government" (1892), 308, 311
Wilcox rebellion (1889), xxxv–xxxvi, 173n9, 233–38, 241, 241n126–241n127
Wilder, Samuel G., 102n297, 161n110, 196, 196n114, 197, 197n116
Wilder, W. C., 322, 435, 473n20
Wiliokai, Cain David, 205, 205n152
Williams, Florence, 146, 146n71, 255, 255n7
Williams, J. J., photographer, 21n92, 30, 315n1
Willis, Albert S., 368, 380, 380n222, 381–85, 393–401, 422, 424n53; memorandum on "Hawaiian question," 396–99; report to US Secretary of State, 383–84
Wilson, Charles B., 6n19, 11, 11n46, 13, 54–55, 54n103, 78n206, 111n322, 116, 158, 164, 174n22, 236n108, 241, 267, 272n61, 282–83, 304, 304n160, 307, 317, 335n77, 439n7, 451, 453, 455, 510
Wilson, Eveline Malita Townsend (Kitty), 6, 6n19, 66n144, 181, 451
Wilson, W., 174–75
Wiltse, Capt. Gilbert C., 304, 304n157
Wiseman, Mollie Still, 15n72
Wiseman, Sir William, 171, 171n1, 174, 184, 184n62, 240
witchcraft, 73, 323, 323n25, 349, 361
Wodehouse, Annie Pauahi, xxxii
Wodehouse, James Hay, xxxii, 74, 74n179, 160, 165n128, 193n95, 227–28, 305n165, 370, 384–85, 427n66
Wolf, Gertrude (fortuneteller), 216n20, 286–88, 291–306, 342, 380, 414

Ziegler, Charles W., 447–50

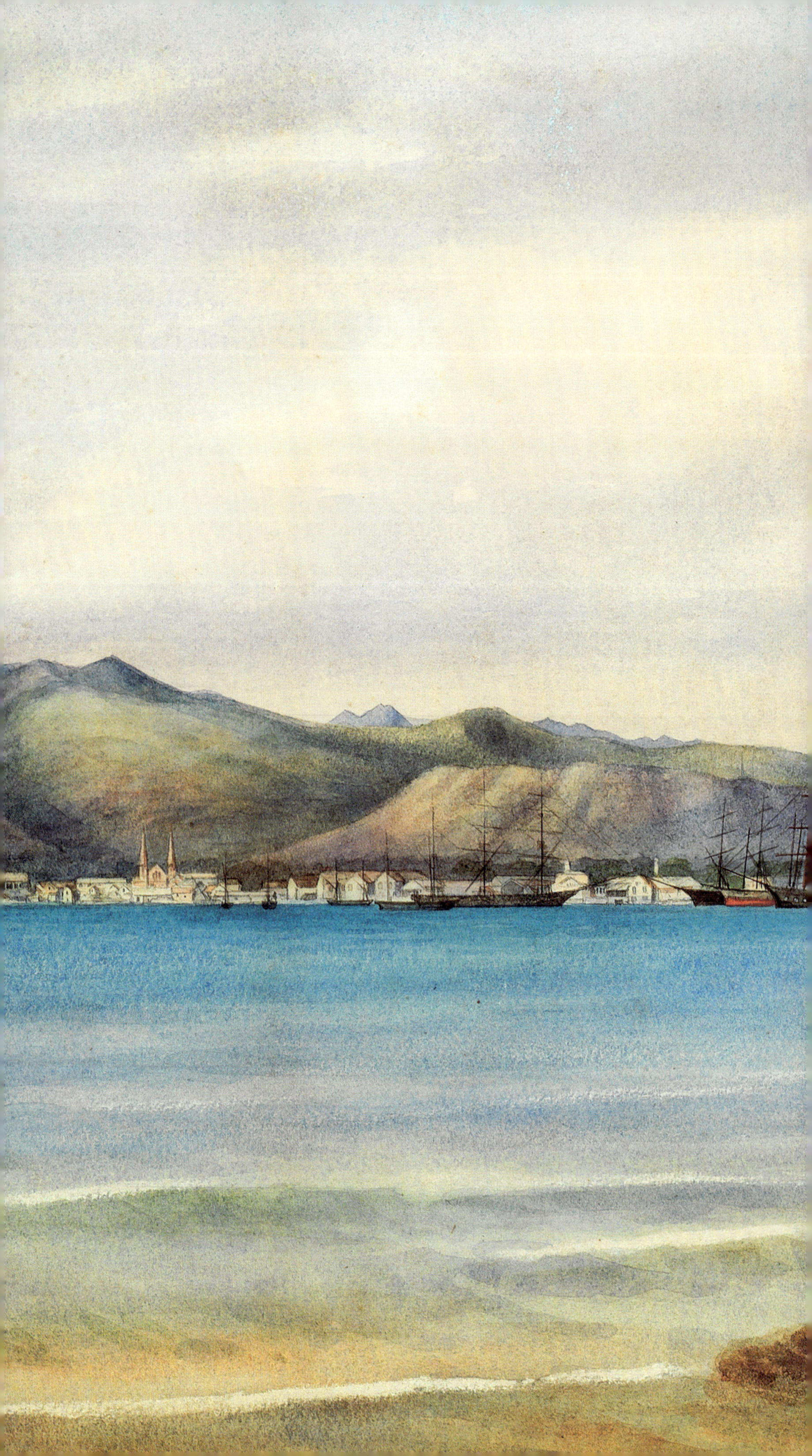